Jack Wylie

ROYAL CANADIAN AIR FORCE
OPERATIONS OVERSEAS
1940 - 1946

D1274435

TOKYO

Karachi

Imphal • Myitkyina

Calcutta • Chittagong

Bombay

Mandalay

Akyab

HONG KONG

Arabian Sea

RANGOON

Bay of Bengal

Bangalore

BANGKOK

Cochin

SAIGON

PACIFIC

OCEAN

Trincomalee

COLOMBO

Kelai

Male

Koggala

South China Sea

Addu Atoll

SINGAPORE

Diego Garcia

INDIAN   OCEAN

Tropic of Capricorn

THE CRUCIBLE OF WAR, 1939–1945

THE OFFICIAL HISTORY OF
THE ROYAL CANADIAN AIR FORCE
VOLUME III

BRERETON GREENHOUS
STEPHEN J. HARRIS
WILLIAM C. JOHNSTON
and
WILLIAM G.P. RAWLING

The Crucible of War, 1939–1945

The Official History of The Royal Canadian Air Force Volume III

Maps and charts by
William R. Constable

Published by University of Toronto Press
in cooperation with the Department of National Defence
and the Canadian Government Publishing Centre,
Supply and Services Canada

© Minister of Supply and Services Canada 1994

Co-published by University of Toronto Press Inc. in cooperation with the Department of National Defence and the Canada Communication Group – Publishing, Supply and Services Canada.

All rights reserved. No part of this publication may be reproduced, stored in a retrieval system, or transmitted in any form or by any means, electronic, mechanical, photocopying, recording, or otherwise without prior written permission of the Minister of Supply and Services Canada.

Printed in Canada
ISBN 0-8020-0574-8
Government catalogue number D2-63/3-1994E

Printed on acid-free paper

Canadian Cataloguing in Publication Data

Main entry under title:

The Official History of the Royal Canadian Air Force

Contents: v. 3. The crucible of war, 1939–1945
Brereton Greenhous ... [et al.]
Includes bibliographical references and index.
ISBN 0-8020-0574-8 (v. 3)

1. Canada.   Royal Canadian Air Force – History.
I. Canada.   Dept. of National Defence.

UG635.C2W57 1980   358.4'00971   C80-094480-1

This volume will also be published in French translation.

Illustrations in this book come from the Department of National Defence, Ottawa, and the Imperial War Museum, London, England; acknowledgment is hereby given for permission to reproduce them. Codes at the end of captions represent negative numbers at the DND (PL, PMR, RE, HC, PT, LMG, MSG, EMR) and the IWM (B, C, CH, CL, H, HV).

Note: In the writing of this volume the authors have been given full access to relevant official documents in possession of the Department of National Defence. The inferences drawn and opinions expressed are those of the authors, and the department is in no way responsible for their reading or presentation of the facts as stated.

Contents

Part IV: The Bomber War

Part V: Air Transport

Appendices

Maps, Figures, and Tables

Figures

Tables

Acknowledgments

The constant support over the years of now-retired Major General C.J. Gauthier has been of inestimable benefit in the preparation of this series of official histories; and the keen interest taken by successive chiefs of the Defence Staff, Generals Ramsey Withers, G.C.E. Theriault, Paul Manson, and John de Chastelain and Admiral John Anderson, has made our task more rewarding. We also wish to acknowledge the more recent encouragement provided by the deputy minister, Department of National Defence, Mr Robert Fowler, and the assistant deputy minister (policy and communications), Dr K.J. Calder.

We must also express out thanks to Dr W.A.B. Douglas, director-general history, Department of National Defence, his successive senior historians, Dr G. Norman Hillmer and Dr Roger Sarty, and his senior archival officer, Owen Cooke. Without their enthusiastic and unstinting support over the past ten years this volume would have taken much longer to write – or perhaps would never have been written at all.

We have also to acknowledge the generous assistance of the Air Historical Branch of the Ministry of Defence and the Public Record Office in London, England; the Militärgeschichliches Forschungsamt in Freiburg, Germany; and – last but not least – our own National Archives of Canada in Ottawa and the Canadian Forces' Mapping and Charting Establishment.

Many individuals (whose names are listed alphabetically, without rank or title, for fear of committing some grave injustice) have also helped us in significant ways. We are grateful to each of them, and only hope that we have not forgotten anyone. Valued benefactors who prepared narratives or draft chapters, provided translations, shared their expertise and the findings of their own work, or conducted large research projects specifically for us were John Armstrong, Tom Belton, Michael Bitten, Andrew Byrne, John Campbell, Rob-Roy Douglas, Hugh Halliday, Norman Hillmer, Bill McAndrew, Brian McCormack, Terry Melnyk, Vincent Rigby, Carl Vincent, Marcus Weinberger, and David Wiens.

Additional assistance, no less appreciated, was provided by Vince Bezeau, Suzanne Bourgeois, David Camfield, Isabel Campbell, Karen Collett, Hélène Desjardins, Lisa Dillon, Greg Donaghy, Bob Garcia, Dan German, David Hall, Fainula Kurji, Réal Laurin, Gloria McKeigan, Marc Milner, Faye Nicholson,

Donna Porter, Ray Proulx, Sylvia Roberts, Christine Rowe, Andrea Schlecht, Herb Sutherland, Bonnie Symons, Lynne Thacker, Walter Wagnleithner, Elizabeth Walker, Michael Whitby, and Loretta Wickens.

At the same time, the principal authors wish to make it clear that they, and they alone, are responsible for all errors and omissions, whether in the body of the book or in this list of acknowledgments.

Abbreviations, Acronyms, and Codenames

AASF	Advanced Air Striking Force
Abigail	bombing campaign against selected German towns (autumn 1940)
a/c	aircraft
AC	Army Co-operation (squadron)
ACAS	Assistant Chief of the Air Staff
A/C/M	Air Chief Marshal
ADGB	Air Defence of Great Britain
ADI (K)	Assistant Directorate of Intelligence (Department K)
AEAF	Allied Expeditionary Air Forces
AFC	Air Force Cross
AFDU	Air Fighting Development Unit
AFHQ	RCAF Headquarters, Ottawa
AFU	Air Fighting Unit
AGLT	Automatic Gun-Laying Turret
AI	airborne interception radar or Air Intelligence
ALO	Air Liaison Officer
A/M	Air Marshal
AMP	Air Member for Personnel
AOC	Air Officer Commanding
AO-in-C	Air Officer-in-Chief
AOC-in-C	Air Officer Commanding-in-Chief
AOP	Air Observation Post
APC	Armament Practice Camp
API	air position indicator
Argument	concentrated attack on German aircraft production (February 1944)
ASR	air-sea rescue
ASSU	Air Support Signals Unit
ASV	Air to Surface Vessel (radar)
A/V/M	Air Vice-Marshal
B-bomb	buoyant bomb
Barbarossa	German attack on Soviet Union (June 1941)

BCATP	British Commonwealth Air Training Plan
BdU	Befehlshaber der U-boote (U-boat Headquarters)
BDU	Bombing Development Unit
Benito	German night-fighter control system
Berlin	German AI radar
Bernhardine	data transmission system used for German night-fighter control
Big Ben	V-2 rocket
Bodenplatte	Luftwaffe attack on Allied airfields in Northwest Europe (1 January 1945)
Bombphoon	Hawker Typhoon modified for employment as a fighter-bomber
Boozer	warning device to bomber crews that Würzburg was in use
BR	Bomber Reconnaissance (squadron)
Briar	device to disrupt Egon
Bugle	Allied air attack against communications in the Ruhr (1944–5)
Bumerang	device which detected (and jammed) Oboe transmissions
Cab rank	Small formation of fighters/fighter-bombers available for immediate close tactical support
CAF	Canadian Air Force (1920–4)
Carpet	device to jam Würzburg GCI radar
CAS	Chief of the Air Staff
CBO	Combined Bomber Offensive (1943–5)
Chastise	air attack on German dams (May 1943)
Cigar/Airborne Cigar	jamming of German VHF fighter radio communications
Circus	fighter-escorted daylight bombing attacks on short-range targets aimed at bringing Luftwaffe to battle
Clarion	American operation to disrupt German communications and morale by widespread bombing and fighter attacks (February 1945)
CMU	Care and Maintenance Unit
CO	commanding officer
Cobra	American breakout near St Lo, France (July 1944)
Cork	Coastal Command anti-U-boat patrols (1944)
Corona	counterfeit orders transmitted by radio to German night-fighters
Crossbow	attack on V-weapon launching sites
DAF	Desert Air Force
DAO-in-C	Deputy Air Officer-in-Chief
DAOC-in-C	Deputy Air Officer Commanding-in-Chief

Dartboard	jamming measure against German fighter communications
DAS	Director of Air Staff
DBOps	Director of Bomber Operations
DCAS	Deputy Chief of the Air Staff
DDBOps	Deputy Director of Bomber Operations
Deadly	anti-E-boat patrol area off Belgian and Dutch coasts
Derange	anti-U-boat patrol area in Bay of Biscay
DFC	Distinguished Flying Cross
DFM	Distinguished Flying Medal
DGO	Director General Organization
DGP	Director General Personnel
Diver (and anti-Diver)	attacks by (and defensive patrols against) V-1
Donnerkell	device to detect Oboe-equipped aircraft
Dracula	plan to capture Rangoon by airborne and amphibious assault (1945)
Drumstick	jamming of German W/T fighter control channels
DSO	Distinguished Service Order
Dudelsack	device that jammed British R/T and W/T
Dunkelnachtjagd	early night air defence system without searchlight assistance
Düppel	German Window
DZ	dropping zone
e/a	enemy aircraft
EATS	Empire Air Training Scheme
Eclipse	plan of action to be taken in event of early German surrender
Egon	radio navigation aid for German night-fighter force
Elefant	early warning radar
Enigma	German encoding machine
Epsom	Second British Army crossing of the Odon and Orne rivers (June–July 1944)
ETA	estimated time of arrival
Exodus	evacuation to UK by air of former Allied prisoners of war
F/(F)	fighter
FAA	Fleet Air Arm (Royal Navy)
FCP	Forward Control Post
FEM/AG	flight engineer mechanic (air gunner)
Fidget	jamming measures against German night-fighter control channels
FIDO	Fog Investigation Dispersal Organization: system for clearing fog from runways

Fishpond	radar device warning of presence of other aircraft
F/L	Flight Lieutenant
Flak	Flugabwehrkanon: anti-aircraft artillery
Flamme	device that homed on IFF and Mandrel transmissions
Flensburg	device allowing night-fighters to detect, and home on, Monica, Mandrel, and Piperack
Flower	offensive patrols over German night-fighter airfields
F/O	Flying Officer
Fortitude	cover and deception plan for Overlord
FR	fighter reconnaissance
Freya	early warning radar
Freya-Halbe	countermeasure used against Mandrel
F/Sgt	Flight Sergeant
Fuller	plan implemented in February 1942 to attack major German fleet units in the English Channel
G-H	radar blind-bombing device
GAF	German Air Force
Gardening	aerial minelaying
G/C	Group Captain
GCI	Ground Controlled Interception
Gee	radio aid to navigation
Gerhard	device that detected Monica transmissions
Geschwader	Luftwaffe formation, generally of three Gruppen
GHQ	General Headquarters
Gilbey	anti-shipping patrols off Dutch coast
Gisela	German attack on Bomber Command airfields (March 1945)
GOC	General Officer Commanding
Gomorrah	concentrated incendiary attacks on Hamburg (July–August 1943)
Goodwood	Second British Army attack southeast of Caen (July 1944)
GP	general purpose (bomb)
GPI	ground position indicator
GR	General Reconnaissance (squadron)
Grocer/Airborne Grocer	device to jam German AI radar
Gruppe	Luftwaffe formation, generally of three Staffeln
GSU	Group Support Unit
H2S	radar aid to navigation and target identification
H2X	American version of H2S
HC	high capacity (bomb)
HCU	Heavy Conversion Unit
HE	high explosive

Heinrich	device that jammed Gee transmissions
Helle Nachtjagd	air defence system that depended on searchlights
HF	high frequency
Himmelbett	air defence system based on strict radar ground control
Hoden	anti-E-boat patrols
Horchdienst	German signals intelligence service
Hurricane	plans for concentrated air attacks on Ruhr (spring 1945)
Husky	Allied invasion of Sicily (July 1943)
HWE	Home War Establishment (RCAF)
Hydra	German naval cypher
Hydra	Bomber Command attack on Peenemünde (August 1943)
IE	initial equipment
IFF	Identification Friend or Foe: electronic means of identifying aircraft at a distance
Intruder	RAF/RCAF night-fighter employed to disrupt enemy's communications and use of airfields
Jadgschloss	early warning radar
JATP	Joint Air Training Plan
Jim Crow	fighter anti-shipping reconnaissance
Jostle	measures to jam German R/T fighter transmissions
Jubilee	amphibious assault on Dieppe (19 August 1942)
Kiel	infra-red detection device
Korfu	radar homing device used against H2S
LAC	Leading Aircraftsman
Lagoon	long-range anti-shipping reconnaissance
Laubfrosch	device to detect H2S transmissions
Laus	anti-jamming device used to limit Window's effects on Freya and Würzburg radars
Lichtenstein	airborne interception radar
L/L	Leigh Light
LMF	lack of moral fibre
LZ	landing zone
Mammut	early warning radar
Mandrel	electronic jamming of German early warning radars
Manna	air operation to feed Dutch (April–May 1945)
MAP	Ministry of Aircraft Production
Market Garden	Allied operation to establish a bridgehead across the lower Rhine (September 1944)
MB	'long' Window to jam German SN2 radar
Metox	device to warn U-boats of approaching aircraft using radar
MEW	Ministry of Economic Warfare
Millennium	'thousand-bomber' raid on Cologne (May 1942)

Monica	radar device to warn bomber crews of the approach of enemy fighters
Moorings	anti-U-boat patrol area off Iceland
MT	motor transport
MTB	motor torpedo boat
Musketry	anti-U-boat patrol area in the Bay of Biscay
MV	merchant vessel
Naxburg	ground-based radar to track H2S transmissions
Naxos	airborne variant of Naxburg
NCO/nco	non-commissioned officer
Neptun	AI radar
(Musical) Newhaven	(Oboe-assisted) method of blind H2S ground-marking followed, if possible, by visual identification
NJG	(Nachtjagdgeschwader) Luftwaffe night-fighter formation
Noball	V-I launch site and storage facilities
Nomad	anti-shipping patrol
NPAAF	Non-Permanent Active Air Force (RCAF)
OBE	Order of the British Empire
Oboe	radar blind-bombing device
OC	officer commanding
OKL	Oberkommando der Luftwaffe: Luftwaffe headquarters
OKW	Oberkommando der Wehrmacht: Armed Forces headquarters
ORB	Operations Record Book
Orgelpfeife	German countermeasure enabling a single night-fighter to simulate a larger force
ORS	Operational Research Section
OSHQ	RCAF Overseas Headquarters, London
OTS	Operational Training Squadron
OTU	Operational Training Unit
Overlord	Allied invasion of France (June 1944)
(Musical) Paramatta	(Oboe-assisted) blind ground-marking
Percussion	anti-U-boat patrol area in the Bay of Biscay
Perfectos	British device that triggered German IFF
PFF	Pathfinder Force (No 8 Group, Bomber Command) specially trained for target-finding and -marking
Pickwick	daylight bombing method
Piperack	jamming device used against German AI radar
Plunder	21 Army Group crossing of the Rhine (March 1945)
P/O	Pilot Officer
Pointblank	directive establishing priorities for the Allied Combined Bomber Offensive (June 1943)

Popular	photo-reconnissance mission
Postklystron	device to jam H2S
PRC	Personnel Reception Centre
PRU	Photographic Reconnaissance Unit
Pruning	large-scale Gardening operation (March 1943)
PSP	perforated steel planking
RAAF	Royal Australian Air Force
RAF	Royal Air Force
Ramrod	Fighter Command effort to bring Luftwaffe to battle by selective bombing of ground targets with a few heavily escorted bombers
Ranger	daylight incursion to disrupt enemy's use of airfields
RDF	radio direction-finding (first British term for what became generally known as radar)
RFC	Royal Flying Corps
Rhubarb	freelance fighter sortie over France and the Low Countries
RN	Royal Navy
RNZAF	Royal New Zealand Air Force
Rodeo	offensive fighter sweeps (without bombers) over enemy territory
Rooster	Coastal Command tactical control system employing ASV and airborne homing beacons
Rosendaal	device allowing night-fighters to home on Monica
Rover	armed reconnaissance sortie or forward ground control for same; in Coastal Command, an anti-shipping patrol
RP/rp	rocket projectile
R/T	radio telephone
Sägebock	device to detect Allied IFF
SAP	semi-armour-piercing
SASO	Senior Air Staff officer
Scarecrow	alleged (but non-existent) German pyrotechnic device simulating the destruction of a bomber in the air
Schräge Musik	slanted or jazz music: upward-firing cannon mounted in German night-fighters
SEAC	Southeast Asia Command
Seaslug	anti-submarine patrol area in the Bay of Biscay
Seelöwe	plan for the invasion of Great Britain in 1940 (Sealion)
Serrate	device enabling British night-fighters to home on radar transmissions of enemy aircraft
SFTS	Service Flying Training School
Sgt	Sergeant

SHAEF   Supreme Headquarters Allied Expeditionary Force
Shaker   1942 target-identification technique employing
                      incendiary bombs dropped by Gee-equipped
                      aircraft
Shiver   jamming device used against Würzburg GCI radars
S/L and S/Ldr   Squadron Leader
Sledgehammer   plan for limited invasion of France (1942)
SN2   German AI radar
Spanner   infra-red detection device
Sprat   Bomber Command attack on Dortmund
                      (6/7 October 1944)
Spring   II Canadian Corps attack on Verrières Ridge
                      (July 1944)
SS   Schutzstaffel: Nazi paramilitary and security force
Staffel   Luftwaffe formation, generally of nine aircraft
Starkey   deception operation simulating invasion of
                      France (1943)
Steinflug   proposed intruder operation against Bomber
                      Command airfields (winter 1943–4)
Steinbock   air attacks on London (1940)
TAF   Tactical Air Force
Thunderclap   proposal for massive air attack on Berlin
                      (August 1944, spring 1945)
TI   target indicator
Tiger Force   RAF/RCAF contribution to air war against Japan
Timothy   strafing sortie under Rover control
Tinsel   jamming of German R/T fighter communications
                      and control channels
Torch   Allied invasion of northwest Africa
                      (November 1942)
Totalize   First Canadian Army attack towards Falaise
                      (August 1944)
Tractable   First Canadian Army attack to close Falaise gap
                      (August 1944)
TRE   Telecommunications Research Establishment
Triton   German naval cypher
UHF   ultra high frequency
Uhu   data transmission device used in German
                      night-fighter control system
Ultra   signals intelligence derived from penetration of
                      German Enigma cyphers
UP   unrotated projectile (rocket)
USAAF   United States Army Air Forces
USAFE   United States Air Forces in Europe
USSBS   United States Strategic Bombing Survey
USStAF   United States Strategic Air Forces

V-1	unmanned German 'flying bomb'
V-2	long-range German rocket
Varsity	airborne operation to establish bridgehead on east bank of the Rhine (March 1945)
VC	Victoria Cross
VCAS	Vice Chief of the Air Staff
VCP	Visual Control Post
Vegetable	sea mine dropped by aircraft
Veritable	First Canadian Army attack on the Rhineland (February–March 1945)
VHF	very high frequency
Village Inn	see AGLT
VLR	very long range (as applied to aircraft)
Wacht am Rhein	German Ardennes offensive (December 1944)
(Musical) Wanganui	(Oboe-assisted) sky-marking with coloured flares and markers
Wassermann	early warning radar
W/C	Wing Commander
Weeding	large-scale Gardening operation (March 1943)
Wilde Sau	freelance night-fighter (Wild Boar)
Window (Chaff)	strips of metallic foil dropped from aircraft to confuse German radar
W/O	Warrant Officer
WOAG	wireless operator (air gunner)
WOM/AG	wireless operator mechanic (air gunner)
W/T	wireless telegraphy
Würzburg	ground-controlled interception radar
Ypsilon	radio navigation aid
Zahme Sau	ground-controlled pursuit night-fighter (Tame Boar)

General Introduction

This is the third of a projected four-volume series outlining the history of the Royal Canadian Air Force, which was promulgated (by administrative fiat) on 1 April 1924 and absorbed into the tri-service Canadian Armed Forces (via the Canadian Forces Reorganization Act) on 1 February 1968.

The first volume in the series, S.F. Wise's *Canadian Airmen and the First World War* (1980), essentially concerned itself with the aviation backgrounds of Canadians who participated in the creation of military airpower while serving in the British flying services. Their wartime experiences provided the foundation on which the ethos and character of the RCAF was built and provided the next generation of airmen with an 'instant tradition.'

The second volume, W.A.B. Douglas's *Creation of a National Air Force* (1986), recounted the vicissitudes of the new service until the outbreak of the Second World War and dealt with that part of its history during the Second World War which occurred in the Western Hemisphere – the operations of the Home War Establishment, including the Aleutian campaign and the Battle of the Atlantic, and the creation and concerns of the British Commonwealth Air Training Plan that made Canada, in President Franklin Roosevelt's words, 'the airdrome of democracy.'

This volume traces the activities of the RCAF Overseas – those parts of the service which were based (at various times and in widely differing quantities) in Northwest Europe, the Mediterranean, and the Far Eastern theatres of war. In one major respect it differs from the earlier volumes, and (almost certainly) from the volume yet to come, which will follow the fortunes of the post-Second World War RCAF. For reasons explained in Part One, Air Policy, a substantial majority of the 93,844 RCAF personnel who served overseas between 1940 and 1945 did not serve in Canadian squadrons: and probably every one of the five hundred-odd squadrons (and a large proportion of the innumerable ancilliary units) that fell under the worldwide operational control of the Royal Air Force included RCAF men at one time or another. Their stories will not be found here.

To write them would be to write the entire history of the air war, a multi-volume task quite beyond the financial and human resources of this directorate. Rather, our mandate was to prepare an institutional history of the RCAF; that has meant ignoring the vast contribution of all those Canadians who served outside its organizational structure except in those rare cases where the circumstances of an individual impinged directly upon it.

Non-flying personnel have also been lightly treated in these pages, except, perhaps, in regard to the creation and implementation of policy. The *raison d'être* of an air force – any air force – is to fight, and it is, by and large, the fighters who determine its nature, provide the measure of its success, and set its future course. Moreover, non-fighting activities – maintenance, administration, training, radar monitoring, flying control, flying support, for example, – although vital to success, tended to be routine and repetitive, and are therefore relatively poorly recorded. Within the limitations imposed on us by length we feel we have done what we can to pay tribute to the part that non-flying personnel played in the ultimate successes of the RCAF.

One notable exception to that rule of thumb is to be found in the later stages of the Northwest Europe campaign when airfields of the Second Tactical Air Force were not only subject to sporadic attacks by enemy fighter-bombers, which led to a number of battle casualties among groundcrews and administrative personnel, but also faced the occasional threat of German counter-attacks on the ground. We should like to take this opportunity to record that, overall, 337 non-flying personnel lost their lives in the line of duty, sixty-two of them directly to enemy action.

We have mentioned the role of women in the context of Overseas Headquarters and No 6 (RCAF) Group headquarters, but gone little further because, in our opinion, though their contributions as individuals were as great as those of men doing identical or similar work, their numbers were relatively small and their overall impact on the service not great. Similar constraints apply to visible minorities, although students of social history will be aware that there is a credible and growing body of scholarship that specializes in the history of these groups in the wartime services.

To all those who, on reading this work, feel themselves, their relatives, or their friends slighted we offer our apologies and the poor excuse that perfection is harder to achieve in history than in most disciplines.

As with the earlier volumes, this book is divided into parts, dealing in turn with Air Policy, the Fighter War, the Maritime Air War, the Bomber Air War, and the Air Transport War. Each part opens with a brief introductory summary of its contents and is written to stand alone, so that those readers whose interest is restricted to one functional aspect of Canada's air war may happily limit themselves to reading this general introduction, the key Air Policy section (which we believe will prove unusually interesting and instructive to Canadians), that other section which particularly concerns them, and the introductions to the remaining sections.

However, we like to think that most readers will eventually find the story sufficiently absorbing to cover it all. *Per Ardua ad Astra* – Through Adversity to the Stars – is as true of reading history as it is of learning to fly.

PART ONE

Air Policy

Prime Minister Mackenzie King (centre) and the RCAF's chief of the air staff, Air Vice-Marshal G.M. Croil (right centre), bid farewell to No 110 Squadron, prior to that unit's departure for the United Kingdom on 31 January 1940. (HC 9284)

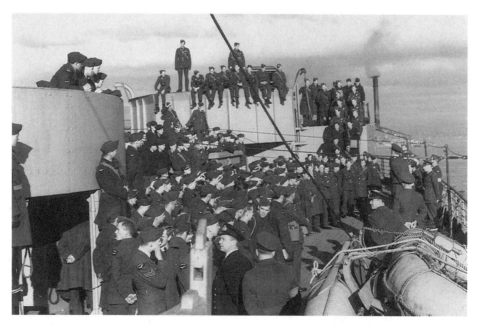

Another shipload of BCATP graduates arrive in the United Kingdom, where the majority of Canadian aircrew were posted to RAF rather than RCAF units. (PL 4881)

Air Commodore G.V. Walsh, air officer commanding, RCAF in Great Britain, 7 March to 15 October 1940. (PL 2344)

Air Commodore L.F. Stevenson, who replaced Walsh as air officer commanding, RCAF in Great Britain, believed that Canadian airmen could best serve the war effort as members of RAF units and formations. (PL 4311)

Group Captain A.P. Campbell, the senior air staff officer at Overseas Headquarters during 1940–1, who could not accept the RCAF's Canadianization policies and was therefore posted back to Canada, chats with the Duke of Windsor. (PMR 24-244)

Minister of National Defence for Air C.G. Power, whose concerns were always more political than aeronautical, enjoys a conversation with his Air Ministry hosts during his July 1941 visit to the United Kingdom while the Canadian AOC, Air Commodore Leigh Stevenson, looks on. (PL 4406)

Prime Minister Mackenzie King meets the pilots of a newly formed Canadian fighter squadron, No 412, in August 1941. (PL 4585)

'Chubby' Power with British prime minister Winston Churchill during his 1941 visit to the United Kingdom. On the left is Canadian high commissioner Vincent Massey. (PL 4395)

Air Marshal Harold Edwards, air officer commanding-in-chief, RCAF Overseas, 24 November 1941 to 31 December 1943, spent two difficult years attempting to reassert a measure of national control over Canada's overseas airmen. (PL 10133)

Aircrew assemble at No 3 Personnel Reception Centre in Bournemouth, England, prior to an inspection by King George VI. Posting of Canadian personnel throughout the training chain, from Bournemouth to operational squadrons, was controlled by the RAF for most of the war. (PL 4753)

Air Vice-Marshal W.A. Curtis, deputy AOC-in-C, RCAF Overseas, and Group Captain H.L. Campbell (right), director of air staff at Overseas Headquarters, on a tour of North Africa in April – May 1943. Both men would later serve as postwar chiefs of the air staff. (PL 10290)

Winston Churchill, accompanied by the RAF's chief of the air staff, Air Chief Marshal Sir Charles Portal, returns to the United Kingdom after the Casablanca Conference, 1943. (CH 8550)

Sir Charles Portal visits the Canadian pilots of No 417 Squadron in Italy, December 1943. Squadron Leader A.U. Houle stands facing the camera. (PMR 77-524)

The RCAF's portly chief of the air staff, Air Marshal Lloyd Breadner, shakes hands with the air member for training, Air Vice-Marshal Robert Leckie. The British-born Leckie had originally been loaned to Canada by the RAF to help run the BCATP. He transferred to the RCAF in April 1942 and was selected to replace Breadner as CAS when the latter left Ottawa in December 1943 to become AOC-in-C, RCAF Overseas. (PL 21717)

Avro Lancaster Xs of 428 Squadron prepare to depart Middleton St George on 31 May 1945 for the return flight to Canada, where they were scheduled to become a part of Tiger Force. (PL 44319)

Squadron and station personnel watch a Lancaster X of 420 Squadron take off from Tholthorpe in June 1945 on its return flight to Canada to join Tiger Force. (PL 44840)

Introduction

In late August 1939 the RCAF comprised twenty squadrons, eight regular and twelve auxiliary (or reserve), of which all were understrength and all but one equipped with aging aircraft that in no way could be considered first-line machines. Even so, the air staff was in the process of drawing up ambitious contingency plans aimed at producing twenty-four squadrons for service overseas within about two years of the outbreak of war. (Army cooperation squadrons would be the first to proceed abroad, to support Canadian formations in the field.) The twenty-four squadrons of this expeditionary air force were in addition to whatever units would have to remain at home for local defence – seventeen according to the August calculations – and such expansion would clearly require the creation of a large domestic air training scheme.

These plans were drafted before the government had decided its war policy, but by and large they reflected what was known or assumed about its preferences in organizing the country's military effort for another world war. Legislation passed in the 1930s (the Visiting Forces Act) laid down and reinforced the principle that, wherever and whenever possible, Canadians should serve in distinctly Canadian units and formations under Canadian commanders. At the same time, it seemed likely that the government would give priority to the RCAF in the belief that the casualty rate in the air war would be much less than that on the ground.

Events soon overtook these plans. When the British government made known the emphasis that it, too, intended to place upon air power, and the difficulties it anticipated in bringing the Royal Air Force up to its desired strength, the Canadian government agreed to participate in, and help finance, a mammoth, Commonwealth-wide, air training scheme that would see the majority of graduates initially placed at the disposal of the Air Ministry, for service with the RAF, irrespective of their nationality. But not all; and not forever. Although the language of the December 1939 British Commonwealth Air Training Plan agreement was imprecise, Ottawa believed that it had arranged for all Canadian graduates of the BCATP to serve eventually in RCAF squadrons overseas. London, however, preferred to think that only some of them would be posted to a limited number of Canadian squadrons – which might be either RCAF or 'Canadian RAF' and which need not be fully manned by Canadians.

The crisis caused by the successful German Blitzkrieg on France and the subsequent Battle of Britain delayed further discussion of this issue until the winter of 1940–1, when the Ralston-Sinclair Agreement established that twenty-five RCAF squadrons would be formed overseas. That would still leave thousands of Canadian airmen to serve in RAF and other Commonwealth units, but so long as these twenty-five squadrons were formed quickly – and Canadianized quickly – Ottawa seemed content with the degree of recognition Canada's contribution to the air war would receive. By September 1941, however, some 4500 Canadian aircrew had proceeded overseas, but fewer than 500 were serving in RCAF squadrons. The rest were scattered throughout the RAF, often beyond the reach of Canadian authorities enquiring after their welfare, a development which caused the government in Ottawa not inconsiderable embarrassment. The national air force created in the 1930s had taken on a decidedly neo-colonial flavour.

Much of the political and administrative history of the RCAF during the Second World War consequently involved finding ways and means of working out the language of the 1939 air training agreement to meet Canadian demands to form RCAF squadrons overseas as quickly as possible and to fill them with Canadians – a process that came to be called 'Canadianization.' Ottawa also endeavoured to ensure that Canadian airmen, wherever they might serve, would be governed by RCAF policies and regulations regarding pay, promotion, commissioning, and repatriation, all of which were more generous than the corresponding RAF policies. As the number of RCAF squadrons overseas grew, it was also important that they be organized into higher formations – a Canadian bomber group and, since a Canadian fighter group proved impossible, Canadian fighter wings.

For a myriad of reasons, some more justifiable than others but none entirely compelling, progress on all these fronts was very slow – indeed, painfully so. When not being prodded, the Air Ministry and the RAF's operational commands rarely bothered to post Canadian aircrew to RCAF squadrons on a priority basis, or to see to it that Canadian personnel policies were adhered to. At times, their lack of compliance seemed nothing less than obstruction. But it must also be said that Canada's prodding and complaining about the slow pace was neither continuous nor consistent, and this lack of consistency made life difficult for Air Marshal H. Edwards, the one RCAF Overseas Air Officer Commanding-in-Chief to have taken up the Canadianization question with vigour.

Looking ahead, however, and following a second major air training conference in 1942 and further negotiations in February 1944, Canada was eventually able to organize thirty-eight RCAF squadrons overseas – including the fourteen of No 6 (RCAF) Bomber Group – while transferring a further nine directly from the Home War Establishment.[*] While that total went far beyond the air staff's August 1939 plan, it should be pointed out that on a squadron basis the RCAF's

---

[*] This total does not include Eastern Air Command's No 162 Squadron, which was loaned to Coastal Command from January 1944.

contribution to the air war grossly underrepresented its commitment in air and groundcrew. In the summer of 1944, as the overseas service neared its peak wartime strength, there were 10,200 aircrew and 25,300 groundcrew overseas in RCAF squadrons, headquarters, training units, and personnel depots, and an additional 16,000 aircrew and 6500 groundcrew in comparable RAF billets. In terms of aircrew alone, the RCAF contributed about 19 per cent of the total aircrew establishment of the five hundred squadrons at the disposal of Sir Charles Portal worldwide, while claiming only just under 9 per cent of the squadrons. Moreover, even then, the overall Canadianization rate in RCAF squadrons was less than 80 per cent.

The sense of disappointment with the RCAF's institutional experience in the war against Germany fundamentally influenced the plans made for its contribution to the war against Japan. Although these plans never had to be fully implemented after the Americans used the atomic bomb against Hiroshima and Nagasaki, senior politicians and airmen alike had decided that the RCAF must stand on its own as the embryonic national air force it had been before war broke out.

1

The Re-creation of a Colonial Air Force, September 1939–May 1941

As readers of volume II of this series will know, the Royal Canadian Air Force became an essentially military service only in 1938, having spent much of the previous fourteen years engaged in such activities as forest patrolling, aerial photography, and police liaison in the service of other government departments. The prewar RCAF was very small. Its total strength on 31 August 1939 was 4061, all ranks, of whom 3048 were regulars. There were 298 Permanent Force officers (235 of them pilots), of whom one-fifth had been appointed since the turn of the year. Well educated for the time, practically all of those commissioned since 1924 had graduated (usually in engineering or applied science) from a civilian university or the Royal Military College of Canada. So small was the officer corps, and so slow the rate of promotion, however, that at the outbreak of war the most senior of those who had joined since 1 April 1924, C.R. Slemon, was still only a squadron leader, serving as senior staff officer at Western Air Command headquarters.[1]

Policy and direction, therefore, were in the hands of veterans of the First World War who had joined the fledgling Canadian Air Force between 1919 and 1923, when the only criterion for selection was a solid record (or better) as a wartime flyer. While most of them had finished high school, only four had university degrees, and they all filled technical appointments. Four officers – J.L. Gordon, G.M. Croil, L.S. Breadner, and G.O. Johnson – had attended the Imperial Defence College in London, while another twenty had been to the Royal Air Force Staff College at Andover. Although they had surely benefited from these courses, what they had been taught – geopolitics and principles of imperial defence at IDC; the theory of air power at Andover, with heavy emphasis on strategic bombing – had little relevance to the problems they faced after 10 September 1939 in how to mobilize, organize, equip, and train squadrons for overseas service. Furthermore, two dozen trained staff officers and 235 pilots represented a miniscule talent pool from which to find good senior commanders, their staffs, or even squadron commanders for the twenty-three squadrons (and associated training establishments) which were to be mobilized at the outbreak of war – much less the additional eighteen it was hoped would be dispatched overseas within the next two years.[2]

Typical of the RCAF's older breed was Air Vice-Marshal G.M. Croil. After serving in the RFC and RAF during the First World War, he had joined the CAF as one of its charter members and earned a reputation as an honest and sincere 'straight-shooter' in a career which combined staff service at headquarters and seven years (1927–34) as the commanding officer at Camp Borden. Appointed senior air officer in 1934, when the air staff still reported to the army's chief of the general staff, he became the first chief of the air staff (CAS) when the RCAF became completely independent in 1938. It was under Croil's steward-ship that the RCAF entered the war; and it was Croil who, in the beginning, worked hard to ensure that Canada's national air force was not left out of the fighting overseas.[3]

That task had begun in late August 1939, when the three service chiefs had outlined to defence minister Ian Mackenzie their thinking on what Canada should do in the early stages of a war that now seemed inevitable. Government policy since 1923 (but particularly since 1936) had required Canadian military planners to focus on home defence, and that was taken into account in Croil's submission: of the twenty-three RCAF squadrons to be mobilized immediately, seventeen would remain at home for direct defence or to safeguard 'trade routes adjacent to our territory.' In line with long-standing assumptions, how-ever, the CAS recommended that an army cooperation wing of three squadrons (which could be equipped with Canadian-built Westland Lysanders and serve with a Canadian Expeditionary Force) should be provided 'from the outset,' adding that the RCAF could also dispatch the personnel for a bomber wing of three squadrons (but with no aircraft or equipment).[4]

Having proved acceptable to Mackenzie, these proposals were laid before the Cabinet's defence committee on 5 September. Knowing his audience, Croil carefully explained that 'expenditures and enlistments to date bore no relation' to the dispatch of an expeditionary force overseas, but he also observed that 'so far as the air was concerned, the only likelihood of any attack on Canada would be an odd bomb here or there for moral effect and to discourage Canada from sending her forces outside the country.' If, as he suspected, Canadians made 'an immediate and overwhelming demand for active intervention with armed forces in direct aid of Great Britain' once the decision to go to war had been taken, that contribution to be worthwhile would have to be made abroad. What he could not yet say, with any certainty, was how soon the six squadrons might proceed overseas, or where and when the bomber squadrons would be furnished with aircraft and conduct their operational training. Since they would probably be equipped with aircraft purchased in Britain, the United Kingdom was the likeliest venue.[5]

For the longer term, the air staff was also working on a scheme to form an additional eighteen squadrons – personnel, less all equipment – for dispatch overseas 'at the rate of six per month from the date of departure of the original six.' Although nothing indicated what type of aircraft they would use – bomber, fighter, or some other – the air staff calculated, in some arcane fashion quite incomprehensible to a mere historian, that twenty-four overseas squadrons would require 3000 aircrew (including 1200 pilots) and 8200 groundcrew a year to keep them up to establishment. That would entail setting up a new training organization; and to that end, the CAS seemed prepared to delay the dispatch overseas of at least the bomber wing. 'From the point of view of efficiency,' he explained later, 'it would be much better to retain all personnel here for the proper conduct and expansion of the training scheme.'[6]

On 6 September, before this idea had been put forward, a telegram arrived from London announcing the British government's doubts about the RAF's ability to meet its own manpower requirements 'if, as seems likely, intensive air operations develop in Western Europe.' Asking Ottawa not to form and train complete units for dispatch to Europe, except for those which would support an expeditionary force, Whitehall suggested 'that the best way in which Canada could assist would be to concentrate first on the individual training of pilots, observers, and particularly air gunners and W/T operators' for service in RAF units; but 'when sufficient officers and personnel were available in England and France the aim would be to form a Royal Canadian Air Force contingent' by recalling them from their British squadrons. To begin with, it was hoped, Canada might train as many as 120 pilots a year, and through 'the rapid expansion of present training facilities using civilian aerodromes,' the goal was to increase that number to 2000. In addition, London asked for 'the immediate enlistment of skilled mechanics both for Canadian expansion and for Royal Air Force.'[7]

There were obvious differences between the Canadian and British proposals in terms of where and when, and under whose direction, RCAF squadrons would be formed. However, they were not necessarily irreconcilable, as it seemed that both would eventually produce RCAF squadrons abroad. The question was whether Ottawa was willing to see Canadian airmen spend some time in RAF squadrons until the RCAF was ready to form its own – and that both the air staff and the Cabinet were prepared to accept. To meet Britain's immediate requirements, they were also prepared to dispatch, within six weeks, 'a number of Canadian Officer pilots with considerable flying experience on civil types but untrained in service duties, plus a number of newly enlisted airmen of various trades.' Quoting the CAS verbatim, however, Prime Minister Mackenzie King reiterated: 'It is the desire of this Government that Canadian Air Force units be formed as soon as sufficient trained personnel are available overseas for this purpose, such squadrons to be manned by and maintained with Canadian personnel at the expense of the Canadian Government. Owing to the shortage of service equipment in Canada, Canadian squadrons overseas would require to be completely equipped by the United Kingdom authorities, at Canada's expense.'[8]

The chiefs of staff met with the government's senior ministers again on 15 September, by which time Croil had heard that the British were likely to ask for a four-fold increase in the number of pilots to be trained. Fearing that his political masters might react positively to such a request, the CAS explained what a mammoth undertaking that would be – he had estimated the cost of the smaller Canadian plan at over $100 million – and cautioned that the impact of adopting the British proposal 'immediately would be so staggering as to baffle the best efforts of those responsible.' Better, he advised, to proceed with the air staff's original concept aimed at providing the manpower for twenty-four RCAF squadrons by the end of 1941; and once that had given evidence of success, to expand the training system 'to meet the United Kingdom's request in full.'[9]

Whatever the case, Croil now doubted whether, apart from the army cooperation wing, it was wise to send any RCAF personnel overseas on loan in the short term, their talents being of more immediate use at home in setting up the training scheme. With the RAF facing the possibility of 'extremely heavy … wastage' and serious disruption to its own training facilities:

… we can best help … by concentrating our entire efforts, after securing our home defence upon the production of the greatest number of trained personnel in all categories. Our own Royal Canadian Air Force, now at slightly over half the required strength, designed for and employed for home defence, will be able to contribute little to this problem. I recommend therefore that we should not consider the despatch of any personnel at present to the Royal Air Force, but rather that we should absorb all resources of trained airmen available in Canada with the object of securing as many instructors as possible … as it is only by so doing that we can exert our fullest effort to the task of providing an adequate supply of trained personnel in the shortest possible time.[10]

Yet within the week, 'in accordance with verbal instructions' (probably from Norman Rogers, who had replaced Mackenzie as minister of national defence on 19 September 1939), Croil advised London that twenty-five RCAF pilots and eighty former civil pilots would soon be dispatched 'for service with the Royal Air Force on loan.'[11] Even though the pace of mobilization and the number of squadrons to be sent overseas were being cut back in order to concentrate on training, for which these pilots would have been useful, the government wished for political reasons to see Canadian airmen overseas in the very near future. 'The present policy of the Government,' the CAS explained to his colleagues on 25 September, 'is to retain an Air Force in Canada for home defence and to despatch overseas trained personnel (both officer and airmen) to serve with the Royal Air Force (on loan).'

Later it is anticipated that it will be possible to organize the overseas personnel (supplemented by transfers from home establishments) into squadrons of the Royal Canadian Air Force.

The peacetime policy for the organization of the RCAF was the ultimate development of 23 squadrons … At the moment it is impossible to organize, train and bring a force of 23 squadrons and their necessary training, administrative and maintenance units to full War Establishment and at the same time be prepared to despatch drafts of personnel overseas to serve with the Royal Air Force (on loan).

From a review of the situation it has been determined that the maximum number of squadrons that we can, at the moment, bring up to establishment and equip and maintain is 15 (12 for home defence and 3 for attachment to the C[anadian] A[ctive]

S[ervice] F[orce]), the completion of the remaining 8 to be held in abeyance for the time being. This reduction in the number of squadrons will make it possible to meet the desires of the Government to have the Royal Canadian Air Force represented overseas as soon as possible by drafts of personnel.[12]

The next day, however, the Air Ministry asked Ottawa not to send either military or civilian pilots, 'pending important new proposals from London for Canadian air contribution.' Arriving on the 27th, these proposals raised the total aircrew training requirement to a staggering 20,000 a year, with pupils coming from all over the Commonwealth. While elementary training 'would be established in each Dominion according to its capacity,' it was suggested that advanced training 'should be centred in Canada.' The Air Ministry, however, still 'contemplated that the first call on Dominion personnel who had received their training in schools under the scheme would be for such air force units of Dominions as the participating Dominion Governments might be prepared to provide and maintain.'[13]

At this stage, although Canada's initial overseas commitment had been halved from six to three squadrons (all of them dedicated to army cooperation duties), and even more resources would have to be devoted to training, nothing had happened on either side of the Atlantic to confound the air staff's plan for raising a major RCAF presence overseas within two years. If, indeed, the formation of twenty-four squadrons was taken for granted, it might explain why, in Ottawa's reply, the focus was on the myriad of technical and financial details which would so dominate the Empire Air Training Scheme (EATS) and its Canadian component, the British Commonwealth Air Training Plan (BCATP). Croil's confidence about the ultimate nature and status of Canada's contribution to the air war may also explain why, on 4 October, the day after defence minister Rogers complained that the dispatch of just three squadrons would not 'satisfy public sentiment,' the CAS was reluctant to form what would amount to a fourth RCAF squadron overseas from Canadians already in the RAF. The infrastructure that would entail, including 'a RCAF headquarters, a pool of officers and a pool of airmen to replace wastage' as well as 'a constant flow of ... replacements,' would be too great a drain on efforts to develop the training system.[14]

Lord Riverdale, a prominent industrialist with extensive experience of business negotiations in Canada, arrived in Ottawa later in the month to begin conversations relating to the empire air training proposal. By then, the British apparently wanted an RAF-controlled scheme, paid for by Ottawa, that would enlist trainees directly into the RAF, much as the RFC/RAF had drawn upon Canadian manpower during the First World War, and there was no longer any mention of forming an RCAF contingent from Canadian graduates. Indeed, in Whitehall's eyes, RCAF units were unnecessary for the successful prosecution of the war. Irritated by the 'sort of railroading, taking-for-granted style which Riverdale adopted,' however, Mackenzie King left no doubt that he wanted Canadians to join the RCAF, not the RAF, forcing the British negotiators to concede, privately, that the training scheme would have to maintain a 'Canadian façade.'[15]

Nevertheless, as negotiations proceeded and the nature of British thinking became clearer, Croil saw the prospect of a distinct RCAF presence overseas receding into a very distant future – if, indeed, it remained an objective at all. On 23 November he sought to remind the government how important the matter was. 'It would be detrimental to Canadian prestige as a nation,' he told Rogers, 'to restrict its official air effort to Home Defence and Training.' The Training Scheme will prepare Canadians for combatant duties in the air but if Canada has no squadrons overseas, the work of the individuals will be merged in the RAF. We have every reason to expect that Canadians will do well in the air. If they can serve in Canadian squadrons they will bring credit to Canada as a nation, and build up traditions for the RCAF and their squadrons.' According to his calculations, 'the proposed RCAF effort in the Training Scheme is equivalent to the maintenance of at least 50 squadrons in the field,' and on those grounds alone it was not 'unreasonable to ask the RAF to co-operate in arranging and financing a token RCAF Overseas Force' of fifteen squadrons controlled by 'an Overseas Headquarters, RCAF, to operate under RAF Headquarters in the field.'[16]

Once the thorny question of financial responsibility had been laid to rest, Canada's negotiators turned their attention to the question of RCAF representation in active theatres of war – and they wanted much more than Croil's modest proposal for fifteen squadrons. Their view of Article XV of the proposed agreement (which dealt with the question of national identification and affiliation) was simple, open-ended, and, Mackenzie King insisted, 'a prerequisite to signature' by his government: 'Canadian personnel from the training plan will, on request from the Canadian government, be organized in Royal Canadian Air Force units and formations in the field.' King was asking for much more than either the Australians or New Zealanders, who seemed satisfied with vague language which would leave it to Whitehall to initiate discussion on recognizing their contributions either through the formation of dominion units 'or in some other way.'[17]

Though still audible in King's words, the faint echoes of Croil's original twenty-four squadron plan would soon fade away entirely. That plan, it will be recalled, had looked to the dispatch of RCAF units complete in both air- and groundcrew; but with the enormous task of training now ahead, it was assumed (by Canada) that Canadian groundcrew would stay at home to service BCATP machines while RAF technicians remained in England and France to service RCAF squadrons. That made good, plain sense, for a number of reasons, yet it was the lack of an RCAF groundcrew component on which London's resistance to the formation of Canadian squadrons overseas now began to be centred. 'More than 50% of the squadrons of the Royal Air Force would be called Dominion squadrons,' the British War Cabinet objected, 'because their pilots were of Dominion origin, although by far the greater part of their personnel [ie, groundcrew] would be from the United Kingdom.'[18] London also preferred that dominions pay for the upkeep of their own squadrons, but because of Canada's three-year $350 million undertaking to finance the BCATP, the British agreed to pick up the cost of maintaining fifteen RCAF squadrons overseas. For those dominion aircrew surplus to their own establishments and flying with the RAF, it was also proposed that they should wear 'on their uniforms ... such distinguishing emblem as each Dominion may select.'[19]

In Ottawa, meanwhile, and entirely on their own, the Canadian CAS and Air Chief Marshal Sir Robert Brooke-Popham, the senior RAF representative with the Riverdale mission, had arrived at a solution which, at the symbolic level, would have offered Canada even less than the British appeared willing to give. 'For a squadron to be called a Royal Canadian Air Force squadron,' they agreed, 'it must consist wholly or predominantly of Canadian personnel both air and ground.' With almost no Canadian groundcrew proceeding overseas, the number of such squadrons would necessarily be very limited, but 'in order to accelerate Canadian representation at the front' Brooke-Popham was willing to ask the Air Ministry 'to form as a temporary measure a limited number of squadrons composed of RCAF flying personnel and Royal Air Force mechanics. These squadrons to be known as Royal Air Force (Canadian) Squadrons, and will be transformed into RCAF squadrons as and when Canadian ground personnel becomes available.' As Croil had agreed in September, the Canadian aircrew would 'remain RCAF and be counted as loaned to the Royal Air Force.'[20]*

Ottawa flatly rejected the Croil/Brooke-Popham concept, insisting instead that 'the Canadian pupils, when passing out from the training scheme, will be incorporated in or organized as units and formations of the Royal Canadian Air Force,' with groundcrews furnished by the RAF substituting for their Canadian counterparts needed for the training scheme. On 16 December, therefore, Riverdale phoned his secretary of state for air, Sir Kingsley Wood, asking that Article XV be interpreted so that 'all Canadian trainees would go into RCAF units if the Canadian Government so requested'; but since this was precisely the case that King had made and London had rejected only a few days before, it should come as no surprise that Riverdale was instructed to 'stand fast.'[21]

Meanwhile, the Canadians were urging Riverdale to 'exercise his own authority' in settling the Article XV question, so that air training could proceed. Their pressure was effective. Riverdale yielded and, although 'the numbers [of squadrons] to be incorporated or organized at any time' remained to be worked out by the two governments, he accepted in principle 'that on the request of the Canadian Government ... the Canadian pupils, when passing out from the Training Scheme, would be incorporated in or organized as units and formations of the Royal Canadian Air Force in the field. The detailed methods by which this can be done would be arranged by an Inter-Governmental Committee for this purpose under Paragraph 15.' Once Ottawa dropped the word 'the' before 'Canadian pupils' (offering the British delegation hope that not all of

---

* O.D. Skelton, undersecretary of state for external affairs and King's chief adviser, was also becoming concerned about Canada's commitments if it was anticipated that all Canadian graduates of the BCATP were to serve in RCAF squadrons. The British government could not be expected to bear the entire cost, he argued, but if Ottawa had to 'pay the Piper' the bill might exceed $750 million a year.

them had to be posted to RCAF squadrons), the agreement was signed by Riverdale and King shortly after midnight on 17 December.[22]

There was no rejoicing in London. The chancellor of the Exchequer, for one, protested that 'he had not agreed that Canada could insist on unlimited units of the RCAF being provided at the expense of the United Kingdom tax payer,' while a surprised and angry Sir Kingsley Wood urged Riverdale to write a further letter to Mackenzie King asking that questions regarding 'the number, composition and organisation of the RCAF units to be eventually formed having regard to all the circumstances' be left to subsequent government-to-government discussion.[23]

Having just concluded a difficult round of talks in which Ottawa had made the organization of RCAF squadrons the *sine qua non,* Riverdale warned his masters that reopening the issue 'might even put the agreement itself in peril.' The British Cabinet had to rest content with his assurance that the outcome of any discussions would be 'satisfactory,' given 'the greatly improved atmosphere of the past few days.' It could also draw some consolation from the fact that the RAF remained responsible for the formation of RCAF squadrons overseas, for, as Wood told his colleagues, 'it should be noted that practical difficulties would in all probability prevent the formation of a larger number of units of the RCAF than we in fact contemplated.'[24]

With the BCATP agreement signed, Ottawa turned its attention to the many problems involved in setting up a vast training organization, and (as Riverdale may have foreseen) the eventual disposition of RCAF graduates does not appear to have been given much further thought either by the overworked staff at Air Force Headquarters (AFHQ) or the government. Such was not the case in London, however, where both the Air Ministry and the Treasury Office were determined to circumvent Riverdale's agreement to form Canadian aircrew into RCAF squadrons. After a brief delay 'to assess the requirements, as regards composition and organisation, of the enlarged Air Forces at which we are collectively aiming,' the officials planned to have their negotiating position 'definitely ready in two months' time.'[25]

Whitehall hoped that further discussions on Article XV could be held in London, where 'these questions can be more expeditiously and satisfactorily dealt with in immediate contact with the Departments of the Air Ministry, who alone have a central view and detailed knowledge of all the requirements.' The Air Ministry and the Dominions Office also banked on involving representatives from Australia and New Zealand, who had been far less demanding over the formation of dominion squadrons overseas. Indeed, they anticipated that being forced 'to explain in the presence of their somewhat incredulous Australian and New Zealand colleagues the vital political importance which Canada attaches to their men not being placed at the unfettered disposal of the United Kingdom Command ... would strain even the resources which Canadian Ministers possess.'

For once, the Canadians were a match for their crafty allies. Australia and New Zealand readily agreed to meet in London, but the Canadians would not be drawn, Croil observing that Canada was 'not interested in, nor should we risk being influenced by, the actions of the Australian and New Zealand Governments.' Moreover, since the discussion would focus principally on the formation of Canadian squadrons, about which the opinion of the Canadian government was critical, Ottawa was as logical a site as London.[26]

Determined not to hold talks in Canada, and hoping that Ottawa's attitude might yet soften, the British government chose to delay taking up the issue while continuing to develop a more detailed position on Article XV. Their revised terms, limiting RCAF representation to those squadrons completely manned by both Canadian air- and groundcrew, were finally relayed to the British high commissioner in mid-April. Before he could sound out the government, however, the Germans had launched their Blitzkrieg in the west, and there were more pressing matters to worry about than the organization of the RCAF overseas.[27]

The widening war, and Canada's expanding commitments, had already produced a reorganization of the Cabinet which, in turn, quickly led to personnel changes at Air Force Headquarters. C.G. Power, former postmaster-general, had been appointed minister of national defence for air (and associate minister of national defence) on 23 May. Norman Rogers, killed in an air crash on 10 June 1940, had been replaced on 5 July by J.L. Ralston, who continued to be regarded as the senior defence minister even while having primary responsibility for the army.

A jovial, chain-smoking, hard-drinking Quebecker, Power did not believe he could work effectively with the earnest, somewhat puritanical Croil. 'To my civilian mind he was altogether too regimental. I got the impression, rightly or wrongly, that friendly, sympathetic co-operation with him would, owing to our fundamental differences of temperament, be difficult if not impossible. I wanted friendship and co-operation; he, I imagine, expected me to give little more than routine supervision, leaving to him the unquestioned authority over the members of the service, and possibly over the purely civilian functions of the department ... I requested him to hand in his resignation as Chief of Staff, and to accept a position as Inspector General of the Royal Canadian Air Force.'[28]

As a replacement, the minister found a kindred spirit in Croil's deputy, Air Commodore L.S. Breadner. 'Big, bluff, hearty, and congenial,' Power later wrote, Breadner 'almost at once became a close friend as well as a valued associate. We worked together in closest companionship ... and [I] could not wish for any happier time than the time I spent in toil and play with him.'

Personal charm was one of the new CAS's more notable characteristics. A native of Carleton Place, Ontario, Breadner had completed only three years of high school before joining the family's jewellery business in Ottawa. In 1915 he had enlisted in the Royal Naval Air Service and spent most of the First World War as a fighter pilot in France. After the war, as a skilful pilot, he found employment as a certificate examiner with the Canadian Air Board before joining the RCAF in 1922.[29] He rose rapidly within the air force's ranks, being selected to serve as acting director under Lindsay Gordon from 1928 to

1932. Gordon found him to possess 'a highly developed sense of humour and although not of a placid disposition, he is generally reasonable, good natured, tolerant and cheery.' His personal qualities were equally evident to the staff of the Imperial Defence College which Breadner attended in 1936, the commandant describing him as 'an officer with a cheerful and likeable disposition, and a sense of humour, who, in consequence, is very popular with the other students of all services.' His abilities, however, were considered to be 'of a practical sort' and he was seen as 'pre-eminently a man of action.'[30]

When Breadner assumed the post of chief of the air staff on 29 May 1940, only one of the three army cooperation squadrons originally intended for overseas had been dispatched, No 110 Squadron having arrived at Old Sarum, in Wiltshire, to support the 1st Canadian Division, on 26 February. In anticipation of its arrival, on 1 January the RCAF's Air Liaison Office (which had been operating in London since 1919 to keep Canadian air officials informed on the latest aviation developments in the United Kingdom) had been upgraded to the status of an RCAF headquarters. The first air officer commanding, RCAF, in Great Britain, Group Captain G.V. Walsh, had arrived on 3 March.

With only one squadron to administer, the new headquarters was, for the moment, primarily concerned with establishing its own organization and creating a Records Office to keep track of RCAF personnel overseas. However, its intended relationship to the Air Ministry, as set out by Canadian high commissioner Vincent Massey in a letter to the dominions secretary in April, was clearly 'not [one] of subordination.' 'Details will be taken up between the two,' he explained, 'but if questions of policy arise, the channels of communication will be through the High Commissioner for Canada to or from the Department of National Defence in Ottawa.'[31]

Massey's pronouncement was based on instructions he had received from Ottawa on the interpretation to be placed on the Visiting Forces Act of 1933, the statutory basis governing the application of military law when troops from one Commonwealth country were stationed in another. When Canada had become a legally sovereign country on the passing of the Statute of Westminster in 1931, Canada's armed forces 'became with relation to the Forces of the United Kingdom, to all intents and purposes, foreign Forces in the same sense as those of the United States or any other foreign Power.' In order to place the administration of military discipline on a legal basis (since British military law no longer applied to the forces of the dominions), corresponding Visiting Forces acts were passed by the United Kingdom and Canada in 1933. Under their terms, organized national forces 'serving together' (that is, co-located but not under unified command) were each responsible for their own discipline according to their own military law. Once these forces were placed 'in combination' (that is, under unified command, usually for operations), their own military law would continue to apply but the combined force commander had the authority to convene and confirm the findings and sentences of courts martial. Canadian servicemen attached to British forces, including RCAF personnel in RAF squadrons, were subject to the military law of the force to which they were attached – and vice versa, although it was eventually decided that for serious offences the sentence of the guilty party would be referred to his own government for confirmation.[32]

The act did not specify the relationship that would normally exist during training, nor did it address questions of organization or the military chain of command. Ottawa had clear ideas on both matters and, as Massey explained to the dominions secretary, 'the control of the organization and administration of the Royal Canadian Air Force serving overseas will be exercised by the Minister of National Defence of Canada ... through the Chief of the Air Staff [of] (Canada).' RCAF squadrons 'serving together' with the RAF were to be commanded by Overseas Headquarters (although the British would provide training facilities and instructors), but once OSHQ placed them 'in combination' the RAF would exercise operational control and be responsible for training. And, since these discussions took place before the fall of France, at a time when it was still anticipated that the war would be fought on the Continent, Ottawa agreed that the RAF should take over responsibility for administration and discipline of RCAF squadrons after they had moved to Europe.[33]

Air Ministry officials tended not to differentiate between 'serving together' and 'acting in combination,' and were inclined to interpret the Visiting Forces Act as placing dominion units under RAF command immediately on their arrival at an RAF base; but 'in all these matters,' an Air Ministry minute explained, 'it is necessary to proceed with tact and discretion in view of Canadian sensibilities and susceptibilities.' The Canadians are afraid, we imagine, that, if we insist that the Visiting Forces Act gives our C[ommanding] O[fficer]s full powers of command, the RCAF HQ here would become insulated and relatively meaningless. At the same time we feel that their insistence on their "rights" is theoretical rather than practical in the sense that if our COs exercise their powers unobtrusively no complaints will be made.'[34]

To many Canadians, however, their country's sovereignty was more than a matter of mere theory. The senior soldier overseas from 1939 to 1943, General A.G.L. McNaughton (who, as chief of the general staff in the early 1930s, had been a key player in drafting the Visiting Forces acts), believed that maintaining control of its armed forces was, in fact, the 'acid test' of Canadian sovereignty; but that task, as Lester Pearson (secretary at Canada House in 1940) has pointed out, 'was not made easier ... by the feeling sometimes encountered on the highest political and military levels [in Whitehall] that Canadian formations overseas were really an integral part of the British imperial forces and, as such, subject to the direction and control of London. This was not at all the position of the Canadian government who were determined to keep control of their own overseas forces and maintain their separate Canadian identity.'[35]

The German attack on France and the Low Countries in May 1940 hastened the need to define Overseas Headquarters' role more precisely. Nine days after the Blitzkrieg began, the British government asked Canada to dispatch a second army cooperation squadron as well as a fighter unit to bolster Britain's air defences. Within the month Nos 112 and 1 Squadrons had arrived in the United Kingdom and for the moment (and in line with Massey's instructions in April) everyone agreed that, since the two units were based in England, personnel administration, including such matters as courts martial, 'pay, promotions, posting, records, etc,' would 'still remain the responsibility of the RCAF' even after they had been placed 'in combination with' the RAF. All casualties to RCAF personnel were also to be reported directly to OSHQ.[36]

Overseas Headquarters, in short, was laying an effective base for its authority over Canadian squadrons overseas; but its effort was soon eroded and undermined by the actions of senior officers in Ottawa who, Power recalled, evinced a cavalier attitude to the niceties of constitutional processes.

When I came into the department, I found that, in the view of the service personnel (particularly in the higher brackets), there was an idea that the minister was little more than a mouthpiece to express in Parliament the views and opinions of the members of Air Council. Indeed Air Council had assumed to itself powers of administration and direction far beyond that which I, as a parliamentarian, thought it should.

One of my first tasks was to make it clear that the service members of Air Council ... had no authority to give directions, and must confine themselves to the duty of making recommendations to the minister. It took some time before they fully accepted this idea.[37]

In fact, Power did not rein in his advisers nearly as quickly as his memoirs suggest, so that during his first five months in office, for example, he was not even aware of the nature of the bargaining that had taken place during the 1939 negotiations and was totally in the dark as to the agreement that had been reached with Lord Riverdale in regard to Article XV. Indeed, Breadner attempted to exploit this situation at the end of August 1940 in order to gain the minister's support for a course of action that was diametrically opposed to the Cabinet's own plans for Canada's overseas air force. The status of OSHQ – and the relationship of RCAF units overseas to the Air Ministry – were directly involved.[38]

Following the collapse of France – an armistice with Germany was signed on 25 June – the British government asked Ottawa's permission to transfer four of its service flying training schools from the increasingly crowded and dangerous skies over Britain to the relative safety of North American air space. While the Cabinet had no objections to the transfer, it was not willing to see an RAF headquarters established in Canada, however, and required the schools to be placed under RCAF administrative control. Manufacturing an analogy, Breadner informed Air Commodore Walsh that it was, 'under [the] circumstances, not consistent for us to maintain RCAF Headquarters overseas,' and he therefore proposed reducing it once again to the status of a liaison office and 'handing over responsibility [for] war records, training and care of replacements personnel to RAF.'[39]

Although the recommendation to close down OSHQ did not reflect his government's current policy, Breadner may have been thinking about administrative economies. Since the overseas air force would have to come under RAF operational control in any case, an argument could be made (as it was at the Air

Ministry) that a Canadian administrative headquarters was superfluous. At Overseas Headquarters, however, Breadner's telegram caused considerable consternation. In the absence of Air Commodore Walsh (confined to hospital since 9 August with a bad heart and suffering from chronic fatigue), a response was prepared by his senior air staff officer, Wing Commander A.P. Campbell, in consultation with officials in the High Commissioner's office. Together, they raised a number of questions about maintaining the Canadian identity of RCAF squadrons and the welfare of their men which should have been obvious to the air staff in Ottawa but, given its preoccupation with the BCATP, apparently were not.[40]

Breadner quickly reversed himself, telling Campbell to cancel his instructions of 31 August because 'other considerations render untenable the proposal we suggested.'[41] However, that was not the end of his meddling. In late September, when the fragile nature of Walsh's health compelled him to leave London, his successor, Air Commodore L.F. Stevenson, was told by Breadner and Power, in a pre-departure briefing, that apart from the three Canadian squadrons already committed, it had been decided 'as a matter of national policy to integrate all RCAF personnel into the Royal Air Force' and that Overseas Headquarters would function as a liaison office.[42]

In fact, this so-called national policy was entirely the creation of AFHQ, there having been no reference to, or approval from, the Cabinet, and approval was not sought until two weeks later when the unwitting Power finally submitted the air staff's views to the Cabinet War Committee, explaining that they 'had been going on the assumption that Canadian pilots and air crews would be incorporated into the RAF, and that RCAF squadrons, overseas, would be limited probably to the three squadrons now in the United Kingdom. This question related directly to a recommendation of the Air Staff that the RCAF headquarters in the United Kingdom be abolished and a simple liaison office be substituted. This was proposed by the Air Staff on the understanding that Canadians from the Plan would be absorbed into the RAF, and that administration, Command and promotions would be matters solely for the RAF.'[43]

Having negotiated hard the previous autumn in trying to ensure that Canadian airmen would be assigned to Canadian squadrons, the prime minister was stunned to discover the extent to which Power did not know the government's policy; and, in what could only have been an embarrassing moment, Mackenzie King forcefully outlined his position, paying particular attention to the fact 'that the question of identification of Canadians graduating from the Plan had been regarded as of the highest importance from the Canadian point of view.' Not only had the issue been 'fully discussed' in the 1939 negotiations, but an understanding of the proper interpretation to be placed on Article XV had been confirmed in an exchange of letters between Norman Rogers and Riverdale. 'Canadian pupils would be incorporated in or organized as units and formations of the RCAF in the field,' Ralston observed, leaving little doubt that 'the view apparently taken ... by the Air Staff was quite inconsistent with the understanding which had been reached with the UK representatives.'[44]

With the first BCATP graduates soon scheduled to go overseas, it was time
for someone to take up the detailed methods by which they would be formed
into RCAF squadrons; but, in light of what had happened, the Cabinet decided
that Ralston, not Power, was the man for the job, and it was added to the
itinerary planned for his forthcoming visit to London. It was not only Power
whose competence was being questioned, however, for King's opinion of
Breadner had also diminished, and not just because of the bad advice he had
given his minister. During the presentation of air force estimates to the War
Committee of the Cabinet 'there was an error of fifty millions' which was
'explained away as a sort of joke by Breadner who was representing the air
officials. The Minister of the Department himself had known nothing of it.'[45]

Only the CAS was laughing. For his part, Power was busy reviewing the
BCATP files, and within three days a chastened Breadner was instructed to
produce a much-revamped paper outlining how Article XV could be implemented to reflect Cabinet policy and ensure that the overseas air force was not
cast adrift.[46] Turning his back on the argument that the provision of Canadian
groundcrew was a prerequisite to the formation of RCAF squadrons, the CAS
now proposed that 'the number of squadrons to be designated RCAF or
Canadian RAF should be in proportion to the Canadian output of the J[oint]
A[ir] T[raining] P[lan], and its capacity for producing not only the initial
strength of aircrews of such squadrons, but maintaining their total requirements
in reinforcements.' After subtracting the aircrew graduates required in Canada
as instructors or for the Home War Establishment, Breadner calculated that
thirty-three RCAF squadrons could be formed overseas by October 1941, and
seventy-two squadrons by April 1942, with a maximum of seventy-seven
squadrons once the BCATP reached maturity.[47]

Ironically, it was now the turn of Overseas Headquarters to have second
thoughts about the status of Canadian airmen in England. 'In order to secure
equality of treatment, ensure smooth administration and for benefit of common
cause,' Wing Commander A.P. Campbell explained, 'all RCAF personnel in UK
should be under one control.'* To that end, there was no need for an Overseas
Headquarters, and Breadner's earlier suggestion to reduce it to a liaison office
seemed sensible. While the position of liaison officer should remain a senior
appointment, Campbell added, he would need 'no executive authority except
over own staff.'[48]

As we have seen, Air Vice-Marshal L.F. Stevenson, who arrived in London
as air officer commanding in mid-October, had been apprised of the alleged
goals of Canadian air policy before the embarrassing Cabinet meeting of 9
October (and before Breadner had revised his interpretation of Article XV).
Consequently, he was being true to his original brief when, on 16 October, he

---

* Although his mother was Canadian and he had been born in Hamilton, Ontario, Campbell
had spent his formative years in Scotland, where his father was an officer in the Black
Watch and a member of parliament for North Ayrshire; as he would later acknowledge, his
'early associations were all a mixture of British Army and Scottish politics' - Canada was
known 'only by hearsay.' As a result, it might be said that he came by his view of the RCAF
as an appendage to the RAF honestly enough.

opened discussions with the Air Ministry in order to work out how the three existing RCAF overseas squadrons could be brought under RAF control, and to reduce the role of Overseas Headquarters to that of a liaison office. He also approached the director-general of organization, Air Vice-Marshal L.N. Hollinghurst, with a proposal apparently put forward by Campbell for the disposition of graduates of the air training plan, suggesting that a block of RAF squadron numbers be set aside for those units to which Canadian aircrew would be posted – a step that would not only recognize Canada's contribution but also might simplify the formation of RCAF squadrons once they could be provided with Canadian groundcrew. 'We agreed,' Hollinghurst confirmed two days later, 'that apart from any possible legal objections, there were moral objections to a Squadron being called RCAF squadron if the flying personnel only was Canadian, i.e. your chaps would feel that they were sailing under false colours.' At the same time, Hollinghurst was confident that the 'man in the street in Canada' would consider the RAF (Canada) units 'Canadian Squadrons from the word "go."'[49]

Both Stevenson and Hollinghurst felt that 'practical difficulties' of the sort adumbrated by Sir Kingsley Wood almost a year before would not only limit the number of RCAF squadrons to be formed, but also decree that none of them would be entirely Canadian and that not all Canadians would be posted to them.

To ensure a degree of flexibility from the posting point of view, it would of course be necessary to limit the number of Squadrons so designated – this would mean that some of the RCAF trainees would serve in (British) RAF Squadrons until vacancies occurred in the RCAF or (Canadian) RAF Squadrons. In practice, however, I do not think it would be difficult to strike the happy mean – particularly as to start with the senior post in the Squadrons would have to be filled – in so far as they could not be filled by skimming the cream of the existing RCAF Squadrons – by loaned RAF personnel, Canadian or British, until the fledglings have worked their way up.[50]

Stevenson's short message to Ottawa describing his talks explained only his proposal for establishing a 'block of numbers for squadrons to be officered by Canadians,' adding that 'during initial stages RAF officers will predominate but gradually Canadians would take over.'[51]

Two days later he addressed the question of No 112 Squadron, which was currently 'serving together' as a non-operational, composite squadron providing reinforcements to both Nos 1 and 110 Squadrons, and so came under his jurisdiction. Since no RAF formation was willing to assume responsibility for such a mongrel unit, Stevenson recommended converting it either to a fighter or a bomber squadron, so that it could be turned over to RAF control and 'placed in combination,' thereby hastening the process by which he could turn his headquarters into a liaison office. And that, he believed, might also hasten the process by which RCAF officers were prepared for 'higher executive appointments overseas'; for 'if RAF given free hand in promotion personnel and administrative control of squadrons, and if this headquarters relinquishes participation in these matters, consider RAF will take more interest in RCAF squadrons and personnel who may be attached.'[52]

Despite the arrival, on 26 October, of a warning not to open discussions with the Air Ministry on reducing the status of overseas headquarters, neither Stevenson nor Campbell had any inkling that almost everything they had done that month ran counter to their government's policy. Indeed, it was only on 31 October that Breadner informed them of some of the changes that had taken place almost three weeks before and what impact they would have both on their own status and the immediate future of the three RCAF squadrons already in England.[53]

Nothing, however, was said about the long-term possibility of organizing as many as seventy-seven squadrons from air training plan graduates. Stevenson's reply was limited to what he had been told and it may be that, in his emphasis on incorporating Canadian squadrons into RAF groups, he was labouring under the mistaken impression that, so far as Ottawa was concerned, the three squadrons already in England represented the total to be organized.

Cabinet's desire to retain RCAF Headquarters in name at least was realized. Name comparatively unimportant but clarification [of] functions imperative. Unless Canada prepared to establish and operate a group, any lesser number of squadrons must be incorporated in RAF groups, and unless AOC Group has absolute administrative and operational control of his squadrons confusion, lack of interest and inefficiency must result … Therefore see no alternative but closer attachment RCAF squadrons acting in combination with RAF and withdrawal this Headquarters from active participation in squadrons affairs. Partial control RCAF squadrons this Headquarters tends [to] tie hands [the] RAF and threatens operational and administrative efficiency.[54]

Given what AFHQ knew about recent Cabinet decisions relating to Article XV and the government's interpretation of the Visiting Forces Act, Stevenson's insistence on granting the RAF 'absolute administrative and operational control' over Canadian airmen should have set off alarm bells in Ottawa. Why it failed to do so cannot be explained by the documents but, as we shall see, time and again senior air officers in Canada evinced little interest in maintaining a distinct RCAF organization overseas. Perhaps their minds were fully occupied with the immense problems of the BCATP. As for Stevenson, living in London under the ever-present threat of Luftwaffe bombing, his affinity for 'operational and administrative efficiency' in order to guarantee Britain's survival, no matter what their effect on Canada's contribution to the air war, was perhaps understandable.

All the to-ing and fro-ing between December 1939 and October 1940 about where Canadian aircrew would serve happened because, as we have seen earlier, the discussions to hammer out just what Article XV meant had not yet taken place. Ottawa's interest in re-opening these discussions – and the importance of giving the RCAF due recognition – was made clear to the British high commissioner in Ottawa, Sir Gerald Campbell, on 17 October. BCATP graduates would soon be crossing the Atlantic in large numbers, necessitating some decision, but 'the underlying reason at this juncture,' Sir Gerald recorded, was that air minister Power saw 'the day coming when Australian squadrons, fighting under their own name, will achieve fame in the Near East and his political position will become extremely delicate if he is unable to point to RCAF squadrons formed in the United Kingdom out of airmen trained under the Joint Air Training Plan [JATP]* ready for similar feats should the occasion arise. When I asked him about ground crews, he said that the provision of ground crews from Canada would be absolutely impossible in view of the large number of training fields and aerodromes being established here, not only for the Joint Air Training Plan but for our own schools which are being sent over, and he did not think that we could hold Canada responsible for not supplying ground crews. He did not like the idea of all Canadian squadrons being RAF (Canada).'[55]

Power's opinions counted for little in London. Ignoring what he had said about not providing Canadian groundcrew and RAF (Canada) squadrons, the EATS committee advised Campbell to pass on the gist of the Hollinghurst/ Stevenson discussions about allocating blocks of numbers to the various dominions 'without of course disclosing the origin of the proposals so as not to compromise Air Commodore Stevenson in any way.'[56]

When he raised the subject with Power and Ralston on 16 November, Sir Gerald concluded that, while they might be moved, King would not. 'The impasse holds,' he informed the Dominions Office, 'and although the Chief of the Air Staff of the Royal Canadian Air Force has had some success in convincing his Minister of the difficulties inherent in a demand for more than a token number of RCAF Squadrons, and although Colonel Ralston appeared to have an open mind, I understand that the Prime Minister, supported by some of his colleagues, is still insisting on the establishment of RCAF squadrons to the full extent which he now calculates at 77 squadrons. It is still argued that this is Canada's chief war effort, [and] that the Canadian people must be allowed to know and share the achievements of their airmen.'[57] Based on his conversation with the two ministers, Sir Gerald anticipated that Ralston would 'endeavour to get the maximum number of squadrons possible designated RCAF' in his upcoming negotiations in London, 'though he may limit his demand to a figure proportionate to Canada's contribution to the JATP.'[58]

Taking somewhat better notice of Canadian concerns (but no less determined to maintain control over postings and to resist forming 'a disproportionately high number of RCAF squadrons,' particularly if RAF groundcrew were to be involved), the EATS Committee used a new set of calculations – the so-called 'manpower basis' – to arrive at a new size for the RCAF overseas.

This basis would give Canada an ultimate total of 27 squadrons which would be built up to gradually and would, it is hoped, be reached by February, 1942.

---

* Alternate term occasionally used in place of Empire Air Training Scheme.

These 27 squadrons, together with the 3 RCAF squadrons already in England, would give Canada a total of 30 RCAF squadrons in the theatre of war, and it is suggested that an endeavour should be made to settle the question on the basis of allowing Canada that number of RCAF squadrons.[59]

Under the impression that all Canadian aircrew would serve in RCAF squadrons with RAF groundcrew, however, the Cabinet War Committee in Ottawa had begun to focus on Breadner's calulation of seventy-seven squadrons as the ultimate size of the RCAF overseas. It was that number which Ralston mentioned when he spoke to the British high commissioner on 16 November, and that seems to have been the number in his mind when he took off for England a few days later.[60]

Flying the Atlantic at the end of November in the unheated fuselage of a bomber, the sixty-year-old Ralston suffered a severe chill which brought on a crippling case of sciatica that forced him to conduct most of his business while in pain and confined to a wheelchair. His illness also forced the Air Ministry to alter its strategy in dealing with him. Officials had originally hoped to take him on a tour of RAF headquarters and stations in advance of opening talks on Article XV, in the belief that it would 'broaden his outlook' if he were 'allowed to absorb some of the spirit of Britain and particularly obtain an insight into the actual work of the RAF' before speaking for the RCAF. Yet Ralston's initial confinement to a London hospital, where he experienced the German 'Blitz' first hand, and his later forays into the East End, where 'entire blocks of flats and other dwellings had been smashed to rubble, and the air-raid wardens helped the homeless hundreds in trying to salvage a few pitiful remains or recover the bodies of their loved ones,' may have achieved the same purpose. Although he would not admit to having been anglicized by his experience, Ralston told Mackenzie King on his return that 'he felt the situation for Britain was much more terrible than people realized' and 'that everything possible should be done to help win.'[61] His outlook may also have been influenced after meeting the pilots of No 1 Squadron, RCAF, shortly after landing in the United Kingdom. 'They felt that all RCAF pilots coming from Canada who were not needed for RCAF reinforcements, should be pooled with the RAF, with the understanding that the RAF, in posting these Canadians to RAF units would keep them together as much as possible ... I got a distinct impression that there was no desire on the part of these pilots, for distinctive Canadian formation, over and above such units as would be self-contained, ie., complete both in Canadian aircrews and Canadian groundcrews.'[62]

Since Breadner would not arrive in London until after the Article XV negotiations had been largely concluded, Ralston had to rely primarily on Stevenson for assistance, with help from Lester Pearson at the Canadian High Commission. Although everyone agreed that Canadian graduates could not be simply enrolled in the RAF, 'with individual identification only,' Stevenson and Canada House were poles apart in the advice they tendered. The former was still enamoured of the scheme he and Hollinghurst had concocted to create a block of 'Canadian' squadrons in the RAF, primarily because it would enhance 'operational efficiency.' Stevenson tried to convince the minister that Canadian supervision of RCAF personnel could adequately be handled 'by having senior officers come from Canada to get experience and be in a postion to take posts such as Group, Station and Sector Commanders, in RAF'; but Ralston insisted that 'there should be a Canadian Headquarters, with which RAF using these squadrons made up largely of Canadian pilots from the Plan, would clear.' Canada House also objected to the surrender of administrative authority and control that Stevenson's plan entailed, arguing that the Canadian RAF squadrons would, in fact, 'not be any different from ordinary RAF squadrons.' 'For the JATP graduates the Canadian Government would have no responsibility and squadrons formed from them would not be any different from an ordinary RAF squadron. Canadian graduates of the plan would, therefore, in one sense, be divorced from their own country's war effort; nor would this be a voluntary choice on their part, as is the case of Canadians who come to this country from Canada to join the RAF. Furthermore, few of the squadrons in question, even with 100% Canadian flying personnel would have Canadian commanders.'[63] The diplomats similarly rejected Stevenson's contention that promotion opportunities would be limited if Canadians were confined only to RCAF squadrons because the current situation (on which he based his argument) was due 'to the fact that there are so few Canadian squadrons here; a difficulty which would not exist if the number of such squadrons increased.'[64]

Sensing that it would not win British support, Pearson discounted the possibility of embodying 'all the Canadian graduates in RCAF squadrons with United Kingdom ground crews,' suggesting instead 'the embodiment of a certain number of Canadian graduates in RCAF squadrons; the others to be RCAF officers attached to the RAF but to be grouped, where possible, in the same squadron.' The issue to settle, therefore, was the extent of Canada's initial entitlement; and on that score it was Stevenson who submitted a plan based on an Air Ministry formula that would 'allow for about 25 RCAF squadrons.' By assuming that there were five 'training, supply, and operational personnel' for every member of an operational air crew and using manpower figures provided by Ottawa, Stevenson managed to produce a final total of twenty-six RCAF squadrons – a figure close to the Air Ministry's own calculation of twenty-seven. In order to reach that total, however, the AOC's figures went up only to January 1942, while the BCATP was not expected to reach its peak until January 1943, and he had to use an actual tail-to-tooth ratio of four to one, not five to one, in his calculations.[65]

Aware that Stevenson's proposal was based on an Air Ministry formula, the diplomats at Canada House endorsed his advice as 'a compromise solution which ... should be acceptable to all concerned.'

We can, I think, fairly ask for 25 RCAF squadrons equipped by the RAF, who will also supply the ground crews; other Canadian pilots to be identified with Canada and, where possible, enrolled in RAF (Canadian) squadrons ...

The 25 RCAF squadrons will be serving in combination with the RAF under the Overseas Visiting Forces Act, but it should be made clear that on any *major question of policy* concerning their use the Canadian government would be consulted through RCAF HQ or Canada House. In respect of operational and administrative matters not involving questions of policy, no such consultation would be necessary. The RCAF squadrons would be under the immediate control of the higher RAF formations just as a Canadian division in a UK Corps or a Canadian corps in a British army is under control of the GOC.[66]

Ralston, whether influenced by the pro-RAF attitude of No 1 Squadron's pilots or by a new-found sympathy for Britain's plight, decided to accept this recommendation completely rather than carry on with the demand for seventy-seven squadrons. When the two sides finally sat down to discuss Article XV at the Air Ministry on 13 December, therefore, Ralston announced to his hosts that 'there were two principles which the Canadian Government desired should govern the settlement of this question. a) When there was Canadian participation in active operations, the Canadian people should be in a position readily to realise that Canadian personnel were taking part. b) There should be some arrangement whereby, in connection with major operations, there was supervision by Canadian officers in regard to the employment of Canadians in those operations.' He concluded by suggesting that 'if the number of air crews greatly exceeded the requirements of the twenty-five squadrons ... the balance should be utilised to form Royal Air Force (Canada) squadrons.'[67]

For the British negotiators, who had spent the past year worrying that Ottawa might insist upon posting all Canadian BCATP graduates to RCAF squadrons, having their own proposal represented as the Canadian bargaining position must have been very satisfying indeed. Sir Archibald Sinclair's understated reply was 'that we had been approaching the problem on much the same lines.' While willing to form twenty-five squadrons, however, the Air Ministry was not prepared to contemplate the formation of RAF (Canada) squadrons to handle 'surplus' RCAF aircrew despite Ralston's suggestion 'that the segregation of Canadians in squadrons of one type or another would be beneficial from the United Kingdom point of view, in that it would tend to promote *esprit de corps*.' Conceding that Canada's air effort 'clearly justified some representation in the field' but citing 'posting difficulties' and the 'probable canalization of opportunities for promotion amongst Canadians,' Sinclair advised against keeping Canadians together. However, all proposals were left to be examined over the weekend until negotiations were resumed on Monday.[68]

When Ralston telegraphed the results of his meeting to Ottawa the following day he still hoped that Canadian RAF units might yet be formed, although he admitted that 'squadron identification of Canadians outside ... RCAF squadrons seemed to give more trouble.' What he demonstrably did not understand was that the BCATP would shortly be producing thousands more Canadian aircrew than would be required by the twenty-five RCAF squadrons he had settled for. Indeed, as things turned out, he rather naïvely told Ottawa that 'as a matter of fact the question of these twilight formations will not presumably arise until the 25 squadrons are filled up, which may be a year.' Mackenzie King and Power were also looking forward to the creation of these RAF (Canada) squadrons but, reflecting his immense confidence in Ralston's abilities – a confidence he did not extend to Power – the prime minister was 'satisfied to follow your judgement' in reaching an agreement.[69]

While Ralston was conferring with Ottawa, Air Ministry staff were reviewing the response to be made to the questions raised in the Friday session, including the Canadian request to have some means of 'supervision by Canadian officers in regard to the employment of Canadians' in major operations. By Monday morning they had agreed that 'a senior officer of the RCAF' should be permitted access to senior RAF officers, including the CAS, and that 'any representations which [Canada] desire[s] to make in regard to the employment of RCAF units or personnel will be welcomed.' They also felt that the transfer of RCAF groundcrew from Canada (with their necessary replacement by Britons) should be encouraged 'with the object of forming homogenous RCAF squadrons,' even though they were aware of 'the general view of the [British] Cabinet against sending trained personnel from the United Kingdom.'

As for the number of RCAF squadrons to be offered, it was agreed that it 'should be 25, and that the numbers should not be increased … except as a bargaining matter if difficulty were experienced in persuading Mr. Ralston to abandon RAF (Canada) squadrons.' Surplus Canadians 'should be posted to the Royal Air Force,' but RCAF officers would be considered for senior appointments in the RAF command structure when qualified. Perhaps most damaging to Canadian aspirations, however, the Air Ministry opposed the formation of RCAF stations or groups since 'such an arrangement … would tend to destroy the essential mobility and elasticity in the Royal Air Force.'[70]

If the Air Ministry's officials were still expecting a tough negotiation, they had entirely underestimated the degree to which their position was being advanced as his own by Air Vice-Marshal Stevenson. Prior to the Monday afternoon session, he had prepared his own memorandum for Ralston, questioning the wisdom of forming RCAF-designated squadrons with British groundcrews and, echoing Hollinghurst's argument of two months earlier, suggesting that such squadrons 'would be sailing under artificial identification,' a situation that could be corrected by interchanging RCAF and RAF ground personnel. He also embraced the Air Ministry's view on the question of forming Canadian stations and groups. 'In order that operations and rest may be spread fairly throughout all squadrons of the Air Force, complete flexibility with regards to movements should be permitted. The Air Officer Commanding-in-Chief should therefore have the utmost freedom with respect to the movements and employment of RCAF units within the limits of the safeguards [for consultation] … It therefore would be most difficult to create purely RCAF sectors and groups, although this might be found more feasible as time goes on. It therefore appears that purely RCAF establishments will stop at squadrons.'[71]

For the most part, Ralston was persuaded, his misgivings centring on the number of RCAF squadrons to be formed. Declaring that 'Canada was providing in air-crews a better type of personnel,' the minister 'enquired whether the formation of additional squadrons could not be carried out without any substantial increase in the existing rearward organisation.' His worry 'was that the number of squadrons arrived at was purely approximate,' and he did not want to see 'a rigid acceptance of whatever arithmetical results might accrue from the application of a formula.' Twenty-five might be acceptable as an initial target but, as Ralston sensed, there was a risk that a 'purely approximate' figure might become a firm upper limit.[72]

Continuing to labour under the illusion that the problem of surplus aircrew would not arise for some time to come – a misconception encouraged by his hosts – the Canadian minister was ready to leave that question to a later date. The meeting's British secretary was uneasy, however, and on his return to the Air Ministry 'asked [an official] to work out the figures using the programme for formation of squadrons and showing in respect of pilots only, what Canadian personnel would become available after the requirements of the 25 squadrons had been met ... Between now and December next some 2300 Canadian pilots will have become available beyond those required for the 25 squadrons programme.' When the numbers were extended to March, the discrepancy was even greater, as 3800 of the 5000 pilots expected in the United Kingdom would be posted to RAF units. Apparently, no one in Ottawa – and certainly no one advising Ralston – had done the same calculation.[73]

A draft agreement was produced the following week, initialled by Ralston, and, together with the minister's comments, transmitted to Ottawa for War Cabinet consideration by the 24th. Beginning with the formation of the first three units in March 1941, twenty-five RCAF squadrons were to be formed by April or May 1942, with all RCAF postings being centrally controlled by the Air Ministry – a point, Ralston told Ottawa, on which 'Stevenson feels strongly.' So far as surplus aircrew were concerned, the practicality of forming RAF (Canada) squadrons would be reviewed in September, but the minister repeated the Air Ministry's doubts about being able to work out an effective solution.[74] At Canada's suggestion, the question of exchanging senior officers had been deleted from the draft and was dealt with in separate correspondence between Sinclair and Ralston. After confirming that the intent behind paragraph six was to send RAF groundcrew to Canada to replace RCAF groundcrew sent overseas, the Cabinet approved the agreement on 2 January 1941 and the Ralston-Sinclair Agreement was signed by both parties on the 7th.[75]

In commenting on these negotiations in his official history of Canadian war policy, *Arms, Men and Governments*, C.P. Stacey contends that 'it is amply clear ... that the Canadians in these discussions felt themselves hamstrung by one awkward fact – that Canada was allowing Great Britain to pay the Canadian airmen whose status was in question.' He goes on to argue that 'Ralston himself must have been the more aware of this aspect since as Minister of Finance in 1939 he had had a primary responsibility for the arrangements.'[76]

There is no denying the fact that by the time Ralston arrived in London, Britain was in desperate financial straits as it tried to pay for its war effort. A huge debt had piled up because of purchases in Canada, and to reduce it steps had been taken to repatriate Canadian government and railway bonds, liquidate British holdings in Canada, and transfer gold. These measures were not enough, however, and in November 1940, finding the financial cupboard bare,

London had gone 'hat in hand to Canada' for additional help. Ottawa had obliged, but was far too gentlemanly to bring that obligation into the current negotiations, and, indeed, Ralston only raised the financial aspect once – in his 14 December telegram to Ottawa in which he reminded his Cabinet colleagues that 'the United Kingdom was providing ground crews, pay and allowances and initial and maintenance equipment.'[77]

In that context, it must be remembered that Canada's desire to form RCAF squadrons overseas would not have increased the financial encumbrance on the British Treasury, but sought only to ensure that its air arm was organized in such a way as to give due recognition to Canada's contribution. As Riverdale himself had observed in March 1940, it would have made 'small difference to us financially whether the ground crews are British or Canadian, or half one and half the other, as there is no question at all that we have undertaken to fight the 43 Canadian Squadrons* at the front and look after them completely after they are in our hands.'[78]

Furthermore, although the full extent of Canadian generosity to the United Kingdom could not be known – by war's end, in outright gifts alone, it was estimated by the British Treasury at $3 billion – an initial and helpful response had been made to the British request of November 1940, so that there was no cause for embarrassment on that score either. But perhaps the most telling argument is that even in their own preparations for the Ralston-Sinclair meetings, British officials did not raise the issue of money as a possible negotiating point.[79]

If the financial aspects are to be discounted, then, it remains to explain why Canada's politicians, after enunciating the principle that Canadian airmen should serve together in RCAF squadrons, accepted twenty-five as an initial figure while allowing, as King himself acknowledged, that 'a very large number' of Canadian graduates 'will be utilised by reinforcement to Royal Air Force Squadrons.' On this point it is difficult to argue with Stacey's observation that 'it seems fully apparent that the Canadian negotiators leaned over backwards to avoid embarrassing the Royal Air Force or ... presenting unreasonable demands.' That attitude clearly motivated Ralston and was reinforced by the advice he received from both Overseas Headquarters and Canada House. That Mackenzie King also readily accepted the results of Ralston's negotiations perhaps only serves to demonstrate the confidence the prime minister placed in his minister's judgment.[80] It is also likely that the twenty-five squadron total, which was to be reviewed in September in any event, seemed a sizeable commitment to a government whose air force at that time consisted of only twelve operational squadrons in Canada and three overseas.

Nevertheless, the implications of the Ralston-Sinclair Agreement represented an enormous compromise by Canada. For by settling on just twenty-five squadrons in the first place and then failing to gain any sort of assurance that Canadian aircrew outside them would serve together in the same units, Ralston

---

* The total number of squadrons that the Air Ministry calculated could be formed if all Canadian aircrew were posted to RCAF units.

did not achieve even the compromise solution recommended by Canada House. As a result, the implementation of the agreement came to resemble a combination of its rejected first and second options, with a minority of RCAF aircrew being 'kept together in squadrons ... given a special Canadian identification' and the majority simply being 'enrolled in the RAF with individual identifaction only' and 'divorced from their own country's war effort.'[81]

While settling the initial number of squadrons to be formed overseas, the Ralston-Sinclair Agreement still left the status of Overseas Headquarters and its role in the administration of those squadrons up in the air. For his part, Stevenson's view that complete responsibility for all Canadian units in the United Kingdom should be handed over to the RAF, and that Overseas Headquarters should be converted into a liaison office, had not changed.[82] Meanwhile, little in the way of policy direction emanated from Ottawa as Power, by and large, continued to acquiesce in the management of programs reflecting the air staff's preferences while offering little in the way of political input. Such was the case at an expanded meeting of the Air Council, held on 21 February 1941, to brief the AOCs of the various home commands on 'general policy matters.' According to the CAS, 'the dual role of the RCAF in the war effort' was 'to get as many trained personnel as possible in the front line overseas' and 'to provide the air defence of Canada.' As for Overseas Headquarters, the government's decision (as expressed on 9 October) not to allow it to be reduced to the status of a liaison office seemed to matter hardly at all.[83]

This confusing situation had still not been corrected by early April when the Australian air liaison officer in London sought advice from Stevenson on the best way to arrange the administration of RAAF squadrons. While reiterating his opinion that responsibility for operational control, discipline, and administration of all dominion units should be given over entirely to the RAF, the Canadian also observed that his views had not, as yet, been accepted by his government.

No arrangements have been made with respect to the administration of the 25 squadrons being formed under a recent agreement ... I assumed that these squadrons would be administered entirely by the RAF, assisted by RCAF officers who would be filling positions in various stations and formation Headquarters ...

I have discussed, informally, with Canada House officials the administration of the 25 squadrons, and I believe they take the view that the RAF ground crews should be attached to the 25 RCAF squadrons and be administered by this Headquarters. I feel that this is a step in absolutely the wrong direction.

Therefore, in respect of [administration] this question has not been decided, but it has been recommended that both the 3 present squadrons and the 25 new squadrons be attached to the RAF for all purposes, and that Canadian control be exercised only by the RCAF officers posted to positions in RAF stations, groups and commands within which RCAF squadrons are operating.[84]

Stevenson submitted his recommendations to Canada House on 3 April and to AFHQ the following day. Although quite happy to look after the personnel

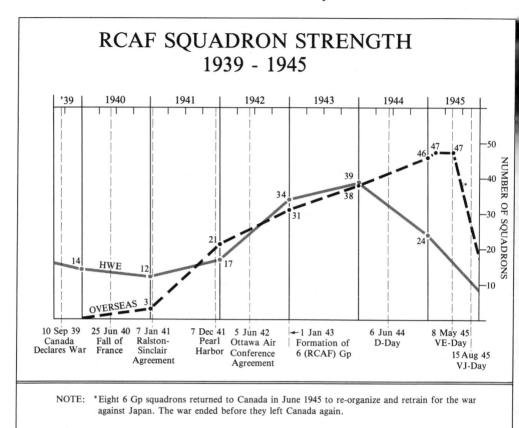

RCAF SQUADRON STRENGTH
1939 - 1945

NOTE: *Eight 6 Gp squadrons returned to Canada in June 1945 to re-organize and retrain for the war against Japan. The war ended before they left Canada again.

Reproduced by Mapping and Charting Establishment.   ©Compiled and drawn by the Directorate of History.

of Overseas Headquarters, he observed that 'the present system of dual control of RCAF Squadrons by Air Ministry and RCAF Overseas headquarters is definitely wrong.'

This Headquarters, in point of fact, is not a Headquarters at all as it commands no units but endeavours only to undertake certain administrative tasks, jumping a wide gap between this Headquarters and Squadrons, which could be done better by the RAF in the normal channel of Station, Group and Command Headquarters.

The 'long distance' administration by RCAF Overseas Headquarters of RCAF Squadrons, working intimately under the Headquarters of other formations should have been recognized as impracticable before it was adopted and it is high time the system be changed ...

I am, however, convinced of the desirability of retaining some measure of supervision of medical and dental treatment for Canadians and of their personal comfort, and therefore this Headquarters should retain responsibility for medical, dental and auxiliary services, as well as maintaining watch on their method of employment.[85]

While his remarks referred specifically to the three existing overseas squadrons, Stevenson believed that 'the same factors apply to the 25 Squadrons being formed,'[*86] and he requested that the deputy chief of the air staff (DCAS), Air Commodore G.O. Johnson, who was shortly to proceed overseas for a period of duty with the RAF, 'be given direction on this subject and authorized [to] turn over sqns on his arrival after satisfying himself as to desirability.'[87] As Stevenson had anticipated, his proposals were endorsed by Breadner and recommended to the Air Council. It was left to Power 'to determine the policy to be submitted to the War Committee [of Cabinet].' One month later, however, the minister still had not seen fit to present Stevenson's proposal to Cabinet, even though Johnson had already departed for London with instructions to hand over total responsibility for the administration of RCAF squadrons to the RAF.[88]

In the absence of any clear understanding of their responsibility for Canada's airmen on the part of the air force's senior officers, it was left to Canada House in London to protect legitimate national interests. As a contemporary critique of air force practice, Lester Pearson's views deserve to be·quoted at length:

I am impressed with the importance of the administrative difficulties referred to in the memorandum which arise out of divided control. It is, for instance, obvious that promotions and discipline are inter-related aspects of control. To leave the former with RCAF Headquarters and the latter with the RAF seems illogical. But the question is not, of course, merely one of logic. It is how to combine operational efficiency with the recognition of the fact that the squadrons in question are Canadian and that those in command of them are ultimately responsible to the Canadian Government, via RCAF Headquarters.

I do not myself think that the Canadian Government would wish to turn over to Air Ministry control all the matters recommended by Air Commodore Stevenson, unless there were arrangements to ensure that the specific Canadian interest in these matters was safeguarded. Take repatriation, for instance. It may be, as Air Commodore Stevenson says, a routine matter. But if the repatriation of Canadians were left entirely to the RAF, individual cases might not be approached in the same way as they would be by a Canadian Headquarters. Air Commodore Stevenson admits that himself, when he states that whereas RCAF Headquarters would, in the normal course, send home Canadians unfit for operational work, the RAF might keep them in this country for a

---

[*] It does not appear that Overseas Headquarters felt any responsibility for BCATP graduates attached to the RAF at this time. As far as Stevenson's SASO was concerned, Overseas Headquarters was only responsible for permanent members of the RCAF. In discussing the length of time that RCAF personnel should serve overseas, A.P. Campbell 'felt that personnel trained under the BCATP and attached to the RAF need not be considered' since 'it may be assumed that BCATP graduates will serve overseas for as long as the RAF require them, which presumably means for the duration of the war … We must not forget that it is highly unlikely that BCATP graduates will be granted any Canadian leave and this will lead to unfavourable comparisons. It may be difficult enough to reconcile the return of many Permanent Force personnel to Canada after one year's service overseas with the fact that BCATP graduates serve overseas for the duration.'

thousand and one jobs. That course would have certain advantages, but it might also have disadvantages and result in the retention in this country of persons who, for one reason or another, should be returned to Canada ...

Air Commodore Stevenson's solution is that practically all control and administration should be turned over to the RAF, with RCAF officers attached to the various Departments of the Air Ministry which would exercise such control. This might be satisfactory if those Canadian officers remained as members of RCAF Headquarters, posted to these various Air Ministry divisions, and if they had the right of access to and direct communication with RCAF Headquarters. It seems to me that there must be a line of responsibility direct from the attached officers to RCAF Headquarters, just as there should be some parallel line of responsibility from RCAF officers in the field to RCAF Headquarters; even when the squadrons are under RAF control.

Without knowledge of the administrative and technical questions involved, it is not easy to make useful observations on a matter of this kind. At the same time, technical and operational considerations cannot be allowed to obscure the fundamental fact that, by some means, the responsibility for all RCAF squadrons in the field to the Canadian Government through an RCAF Headquarters overseas must be admitted in principle and worked out in practice.[89]

Pearson sent Stevenson a copy of his views in mid-April together with the suggestion that 'Mr. Massey thinks it might be a good idea if the three of us had a talk about this matter.' There is no evidence that such a meeting took place or that Pearson's memorandum was ever transmitted to AFHQ in Ottawa. Indeed, that it had entered a void – and that declared Cabinet policy continued to be given short shrift – was plainly demonstrated by Air Commodore Johnson after he arrived in the United Kingdom on 20 April. Having first repeated the air staff's desire to turn over the administration of overseas squadrons to the RAF in return for Canadian administration of British schools in Canada, he not only echoed Stevenson's views on administration and the status of Overseas Headquarters at a meeting of the EATS Committee, but also volunteered, in response to questions, that AFHQ had no right to recall BCATP graduates to Canada. They were, he said, 'at the disposal of the UK Government.' On further prompting, he also agreed that the existence of an RCAF liaison organization in Britain should not, under any circumstances, 'be used as a channel in any matter in which the proper official channels were appropriate and had not already been used.' It was left to Percivale Liesching, representing the Dominions Office, to remind everyone that paragraph nine of the Ralston-Sinclair Agreement safeguarded Canadian access to Canadian airmen and that its terms should not be departed from.[90]

By 12 June the DCAS was able to send Breadner a draft memorandum of agreement incorporating most of the points discussed with the EATS Committee. Under its terms, the Air Ministry was to post all overseas members of the RCAF, except those serving at Overseas Headquarters, which was itself to be 're-organized as a Canadian Air Liaison Mission.' (Johnson's covering letter noted that the high commissioner had objected to the use of the word 'liaison' as involving a 'loss of prestige'; but the DCAS did not recommend any alterations.) Moreover, all 'RCAF squadrons and units in the United Kingdom, or other threatre of war, to which they have been moved with the concurrence of the Canadian Government, including Nos 400, 401 and 402 Squadrons which are financed by Canada, and the 25 squadrons to be organized and financed by the United Kingdom ... shall be administered by the Air Ministry of the United Kingdom through the appropriate RAF formations, without prejudice to the terms of the said Memorandum of Agreement.'[91]

Johnson's draft agreement was never brought before Cabinet, for by the time Power finally raised the question of overseas policy on 24 June, his outlook had changed dramatically. As though suddenly awakened to the consequences of policy made by the air staff, he no longer wished to see responsibility for the administration of the RCAF Overseas delegated wholesale to the Air Ministry or any change in the status of Overseas Headquarters. His deeds fell short of his words, however, so that, as Breadner pointed out the following October, 'the reciprocal terms in respect of the administration of RCAF Squadrons in [the] United Kingdom [embodied in Johnson's agreement] have, in all essential respects, already been put into effect.' Indeed, its terms would continue to determine how RCAF squadrons overseas were administered until a revised arrangement was formally concluded at the Ottawa Air Training Conference in June 1942.[92]

By then significant damage had already been done. As of June 1941, 2900 Canadian BCATP graduates had been sent to the United Kingdom, of whom only some 700 would have been required to fill the thirteen RCAF squadrons, formed or forming, overseas. Yet these units were by no means fully manned by Canadians. Three more squadrons had been added to the order of battle by the end of September, but the size of the manpower pool in England was growing at an even faster pace. Of some 4500 RCAF aircrew overseas on 30 September, fewer than 500 were serving in Canadian units. For the other 4000, it was quickly apparent that Overseas Headquarters was unable even to keep track of them, let alone maintain any sort of watch over their welfare.[93]

Ironically, one of the first Canadian airmen to experience the impotence of Overseas Headquarters was A.P. Campbell, who had left his position as Stevenson's right-hand man in May 1941 to take over command of RAF Station Digby. Under RCAF regulations, commanding officers were entitled to special duty pay, a bonus that was not advanced by the RAF. Campbell wrote to Overseas Headquarters in September seeking the extra money, but was told by the accounts officer 'that it is very unlikely that it will be possible to grant this extra pay to RCAF officers, for it would, *ipso facto,* entitle all graduates of the BCATP to the same privilege; and, as you know, we have enough difficulty even trying to locate their whereabouts without having to establish what specific positions they were filling at any one period.'[94] Such an admission only underlined the fact that the Canadian air staff had failed the 'acid test' and that Ottawa could not be said to have control over its own airmen. As a result, the RCAF Overseas now had to be 'Canadianized,' a process that would prove to be a long-drawn-out and frustrating experience.

2

The Foundations of Canadianization,
June 1941–June 1942

On 23 June 1941, thirteen months to the day after assuming his appointment as minister of national defence for air, C.G. Power finally wrote to Prime Minister Mackenzie King and admitted that all was not right with Canada's overseas air force.

No *mea culpa,* Power's letter merely expressed a desire to draw King's 'urgent attention to certain matters which have been causing me grave concern for some time past.' According to the minister, it was only 'the rapidly increased output of the JATP' that had now 'brought home to us some of the difficulties regarding Canadian Air Force personnel serving with United Kingdom forces, which though they were to some extent visualized at the time of the signing of the JATP agreement did not assume great significance until we were face to face with the actual facts of the situation.' That was putting the best possible light on his stewardship to date: belatedly, Power had apparently begun to realize the nature of his responsibilities as minister.

There are today in Great Britain, and probably spread elsewhere throughout the war zone, well over five thousand of our young Canadian men, members of the RCAF, who are the moral, if not the legal responsibility of the Canadian Government ...

At the time of the signing of the Agreement you, more than anyone else, had a full appreciation of the difficulties which this aspect of the scheme would eventually entail. Fortunately, your insistence on a saving clause, whereby some identification of our people became possible has permitted us to keep the status of young Canadians to something other than that of hirelings or mercenaries in the service of another State, which however closely we may be associated with it by ties of blood, interest or sympathy, is not the homeland of these young men ...

... we cannot ... completely divest ourselves of the duty which we owe to the Canadian people and to the parents of these boys in keeping in the closest possible touch and exercising the utmost supervision as to their care, comfort, protection and identification, which supervision appears to be impossible under the present system.[1]

That the position of Canada's airmen as 'hirelings or mercenaries' of the RAF should suddenly have concerned Power after a year-long period of indifference as to their fate may be wondered at; but it would seem that the politician in him had come to realize the degree to which the government's fortunes might suffer as a result of its imperfect supervision of Canadian airmen. To illustrate the problem, the minister cited several examples of RCAF airmen who had recently been reported missing on operations about which the government could not provide relatives with any details. One case involved an airman whose family were personal acquaintances. 'Fortunately they made no enquiries of me,' Power admitted, for 'had they done so, I could give them no information because the Canadian Government had none to give.' Moreover, the situation – and the embarrassment – would only get worse as even more BCATP graduates became casualties. It was therefore time to act, and Power proposed not only the strengthening of Overseas Headquarters, 'particularly in records offices ... even at the risk of somewhat expensive duplication,' but also that he go to London in order to clarify and find a solution to the problem.[2]

Power's request placed his colleagues in a quandary when it was presented to Cabinet the next day. While recognizing the need to send someone to London, they were leery of selecting Power for fear that his intemperance might embarrass them. Only two weeks earlier, he had been found, thoroughly inebriated, wandering the corridors of Parliament Hill by Cabinet colleague Ian Mackenzie, who had quietly steered him into an office and summoned the prime minister. King was not surprised to learn 'that Power was again on one of his sprees' and 'talked with him quite seriously though quietly'; but the latest binge had convinced King that it was 'a serious thing to have the Air Force controlled by a man as weak as he has become of late and I feel the responsibility that rests upon myself in relation to it.' For partisan political reasons, however – Power was the Liberal party's main anglophone Quebec organizer – he would not replace him.[3]

In the end, the Cabinet agreed that Power should go, provided he was supervised by a colleague. With that less than ringing endorsement, the minister of national defence for air and his chaperone (ironically, fellow-drinker Ian Mackenzie) departed for Britain at the end of the month. The party also included Breadner and the air member for personnel (AMP), Air Commodore Harold Edwards – the latter apparently as a result of a memorandum he had submitted in early June outlining many of the problems developing overseas. Besides the well-known difficulties associated with administration, personnel requirements, and the records office, Edwards was concerned about the commissioning of BCATP graduates, 'which seems to have bogged down,' and the 'interpretation of the Visiting Forces Act which, from the queries received from overseas, seems to be a very obscure subject there.' His misgivings had not been shared by his colleagues in June, and at that time the CAS had rejected his request to visit England; but now that Power himself had concluded that action of some kind was required, Edwards could go.[4]

The Canadians arrived in London on 1 July 1941 and spent their first week touring various RAF establishments. Once discussions began, however, Power wasted little time in outlining Ottawa's concerns.

At the present time there were in the United Kingdom some 5000 aircrew personnel and 1000 radio [radar] personnel. He estimated that in total there would be 16,000 RCAF personnel serving with the Royal Air Force in January 1942, and about 40,000–45,000 in January 1943. He went on to point out that all these members of the RCAF were well-educated citizens of the Dominion, and that the Canadian Government had a moral responsibility in regard to their general conditions and welfare while serving with the RAF. They remained members of the Royal Canadian Air Force, and the connection between them and their Home Government must be more than a gesture, particularly in regard to ranks below commissioned rank ... It was necessary ... to provide closer access to individuals, for steps to be taken in regard to their general welfare and for the RCAF authorities to have some voice in the promotion of RCAF personnel.

To accomplish these goals, Power explained, would require a personnel directorate at Overseas Headquarters as well as guarantees of greater access to RAF posting, records, and pay offices. In addition, more information must be made available to Canadian authorities in regard to the disposition of individuals.[5] The British were troubled by Power's message. While acknowledging the 'national demand in Canada for the close affiliation of RCAF personnel,' parliamentary undersecretary of state for air Harold Balfour wondered how it could be accommodated in a single 'channel of direct command.' Postings and promotions, for example, had to 'treated as a whole throughout the personnel serving with the Royal Air Force,' the RAF's air member for personnel, Air Vice-Marshal P. Babington, observed, 'otherwise it was impossible to have absolute fairness.' It was simply 'undesirable that there should be watertight compartments dealing with postings of personnel for a particular Dominion or Allied country.' There being little the Air Ministry could do to prevent Ottawa from increasing the size of Overseas Headquarters, however, it was accepted that action should proceed on the lines indicated by the Canadian minister.[6]

In some areas, such as the mechanics of providing Canadian groundcrew for the Article XV squadrons, the exchange of senior officers, and improving the procedures for notifying next-of-kin of RCAF casualties, there was relatively easy agreement. On the question of publicity for Canada's participation in the air war, however, the Air Ministry was loathe to break the rule of anonymity by which all air operations were referred to simply as RAF actions. Commissioning policy also proved contentious, as the Canadians expressed their dissatisfaction with a quota system that allowed only 20 per cent of wireless operators and air gunners eventually to reach commissioned rank. Moreover, Power wanted to increase the percentage of commissions automatically granted to pilots and observers on graduation from service flying training schools to 50 per cent, while Babington would only accept that 'if personnel suitable for commissions were being kept in the ranks because of the quota, the numbers would be increased.' 'Suitable' was left undefined, and commissioning policy would continue to provoke disagreement throughout the war.[7]

Having deprecated the idea of creating RCAF stations and groups during

Ralston's January visit, the British now conceded that 'it would be quite feasible to form RCAF bomber groups when the bomber squadrons became available,' but cautioned that additional units could not be formed quickly. Power was nevertheless quick to emphasize 'that the principle of a Canadian bomber group was accepted and would be a definite objective although delayed.' A Canadian fighter group, however, was rejected by the British unless '40 to 50 RCAF fighter squadrons were available for the purpose,' a possibility that the limits imposed by the Ralston-Sinclair Agreement precluded. Undaunted, Power 'agreed that if 40 to 50 RCAF fighter squadrons were available no difficulty would arise' and then, as the meeting was drawing to a close, suggested 'that the limit of 25 to the number of RCAF squadrons to be formed should now be removed.' Taken aback, Balfour responded evasively, claiming that the question 'would require consideration by the United Kingdom authorities and consultation with other Dominions concerned'; and Power chose not to press the matter. Although fewer than half the twenty-five squadrons had as yet been formed, the minister's proposal was a clear indication of Canada's future intentions.[8]

As an attempt to correct the problems confronting the RCAF Overseas, Power's trip to London was a moderate first step. Although the Air Ministry now understood that Ottawa was to be kept better informed as to the whereabouts of Canadians serving in the RAF and would maintain a greater supervision over their welfare, Power had not attempted to reassert Overseas Headquarters' responsibility for administering RCAF units and controlling postings and promotions, authority only recently ceded to the RAF by the DCAS, G.O. Johnson. Had he done so, many of the delays and frustrations of the next two years might have been circumvented in one stroke. Moreover, despite Power's insistence that Overseas Headquarters keep in closer touch with Canadian airmen, both Breadner and Stevenson continued to distance themselves from the RCAF Overseas. Following the minister's return to Canada, their plans to disband the overseas record office and merge its personnel into the RAF Record Office went ahead even over the objections of the RCAF's own records officer.[9]

Unable to track the exact whereabouts of individual airmen, Overseas Headquarters was nevertheless gaining a reasonable impression of their concerns from British censorship reports on outgoing Canadian mail. Passed on by the Air Ministry, these letters indicated that most Canadians had to make an adjustment to English food and living standards. More disturbing, however, was the evidence of persistent and pronounced hostility between Canadian airmen and RAF non-commissioned officers (NCOs), a sentiment exemplified by one warrant officer at Cranwell who had 'greatly antagonized the Canadians in the past by calling them a "bunch of rotten colonials" in his first lecture.' More generally, 'complaints of English inhospitality continue to appear in this correspondence in considerable volume.'

The feeling of being unwanted and the antagonism towards the RAF, though by no means universal, are as strong as ever among many Canadian personnel.

TABLE 1
RCAF Personnel Overseas, 1941–5

Date	Aircrew	Groundcrew	Women's Division	Total Strength
30 Sept. 41	4,500[a]	2,300	0	6,829
31 Dec. 41	6,721	4,987	0	11,708
31 March 42	8,867[b]	7,482	0	16,623
26 June 42	10,305[c]	8,940	0	19,636
25 Sept. 42	10,360[c]	10,038	42	20,440
25 Dec. 42	12,197	11,420	41	23,658
26 March 43	14,977	16,699	123	31,799
25 June 43	16,366	20,847	251	37,464
30 Sept. 43	19,646	22,508	546	42,700
31 Dec. 43	21,916	23,459	895	46,270
31 March 44	22,728	26,054	1,040	49,822
25 June 44	25,671	29,438	1,112	56,221
25 Sept. 44	28,215	31,510	1,364	61,089
31 Dec. 44	25,678	34,825	1,470	61,973
31 March 45	22,246	34,256	1,365	57,867

Sources: AMP Progress Reports, DHist 73/1174; 'Strength Return by Units,' DHist 181.005 (D850)

[a] approximate

[b] Not including prewar regulars and reservists mobilized following the outbreak of war.

[c] At the Air Ministry's request, Canada suspended drafts of pilots and WOAGs during June and July 1942. When drafts were scheduled to resume, shipping delays continued to restrict the flow of aircrew from August to October and only 1100 RCAF aircrew reached Bournemouth during these three months, two-thirds of Article XV requirements. This was the only occasion during the war, however, when the overall supply of Canadian aircrew did not meet the RCAF needs.

[A] preference for Scotland ... is still most marked. Scottish hospitality is referred to repeatedly, and Canadians stationed in England frequently go to Scotland for their leave. The Canadian seems to find an immediate affinity with the Scot ...

Not all Canadians are discontented; many are happy and full of enthusiasm, and many speak most warmly of English hospitality. In the balance against the disgruntled ... must be set the good morale of [the others]. But the scales still tilt towards the disgruntled side ...

Canadian airmen attached to the RAF complain that they are 'forgotten men.' Many feel that the Canadian authorities take no interest in them, and do not pass to them their fair share of comforts from Canada.[10]

With considerable justification, Stevenson dismissed much of this grumbling as a reaction to wartime conditions in Britain.

Whereas RAF personnel are used to rather indifferent accommodation, messing and treatment and accept it as inevitable, members of the RCAF have probably been used to better accommodation, messing and recreational facilities and therefore complain. There is unquestionably much room for improvement in messing and in accommodation, particularly with respect to heating, but under present conditions it would be impossible to bring these deficiencies up to a state which would satisfy the average Canadian.

The complaints are, however, giving the RAF considerable concern, and I am sure that some improvement will result.[11]

What could not be so easily dismissed were the differing British and Canadian attitudes towards authority. It was clear from the censors' findings that RCAF other ranks experienced difficulty adjusting to the RAF's formality and reserve.

... class distinctions in the RAF strike Canadians as undemocratic. Canadians have little sympathy for the 'old school tie' ...

The other side of the picture is the Englishman's view of the Canadian. Quoting from an RAF report: 'The New World – American and Canadian alike – is impetuous, enthusiastic, sometimes childish, often self-assured and usually not a little boastful. It likes to seem tough and it likes to show off.' One RAF officer, the CO of an RCAF squadron, told us that Canadians are erratic: they want quick excitement, but cannot settle down to a hard grind. Another RAF officer, the CO of an OTU, said that the Canadians are a pretty unsophisticated lot, who come over with a chip on their shoulder, and put on a tough exterior to cover up a sense of inferiority. A number of RAF officers told us that the Canadians don't know how to hold their drinks. On the other hand, many RAF officers in Canadian squadrons spoke in glowing terms of the fine qualities of the Canadians, especially their friendliness, and resented the possibility of being posted out of the RCAF squadron. An RAF flight-sergeant who had many years in the service expressed his liking for the RCAF squadron because relations with Canadian officers were on a more satisfactory human basis.[12]

Differences between class-conscious Britons and more egalitarian Canadians also influenced the approach the RAF and RCAF adopted to questions of command. To the traditional English mind, leadership was more a function of style than competence, and men had to be the 'right type' in order to be commissioned. Canadians preferred the more functional approach of the Americans, who related rank to the job done and commissioned all pilots, navigators, and bomb-aimers. Commissioning aside, the English view of Canada as a classless society also influenced the RAF's perception of Canadians as suitable commanders. Its bias against RCAF officers was typified by the commanding officer of RAF Digby (which had housed an RCAF fighter wing since April 1941) in a letter to No 12 Group Headquarters in July 1941.

I am of the opinion that the present system of forming Canadian stations manned entirely by RCAF personnel is a mistake, and I am not even convinced that it is a good thing to retain RCAF squadrons as such. My reasons are as follows:

The influence of Canadians in an English Squadron is excellent and I cannot help feeling that the converse is also true. Because of characteristic differences of expression in English and Canadian pilots – an English squadron having a number of Canadian pilots in it is ensured of a vivid display of guts in a tight corner – which is of great benefit to the squadron as a whole. On the other hand, the presence of RAF pilots in a squadron which has a number of Canadians, tends to sober them down a bit, and improve their discipline.

It is probably not generally appreciated that discipline in a RCAF squadron is usually of a type quite different from that of an English squadron. The following conversation recently overheard between a RCAF squadron commander and a RCAF M[otor] T[ransport] driver, driving a lorry, will best explain what is meant:

The squadron commander: 'Hey Bill, where are you going?'

MT driver: 'Lincoln.'

Squadron commander: 'Can you give me a lift?'

MT driver: 'Sure, hop in.'

The possibility is that the MT driver employs the squadron commander in peace time in his work in Canada and therefore, nothing is thought by the Canadians themselves of such conversations; but it is a state of affairs which has definitely to be reckoned with on a station.

I have the greatest admiration for the Canadians who were in the Air Force in the last war, and the RCAF who are on this station now; but I cannot help feeling that Canadians and Englishmen would benefit by serving in the same units.

Although it is possible to train pilots, flight commanders, and even squadron commanders in a comparatively short time, it takes a lot of experience over a period of years to become acquainted with all the administrative paraphanalia connected with the successful running of a station. It is, therefore, impossible for Canadian officers with only a few years service to have absorbed sufficient knowledge to be able to run the administrative side of a station satisfactorily.

To refer to a particular instance, I am sure it is not in the interests of the war effort as a whole that this station should be run entirely by Canadians, and I give the experiment eight or nine months as a maximum before it will fail.[13]

Ironically, the English mindset indirectly cost the anglophile Stevenson his job, albeit through a case of his own making. In late September he visited Fighter Command Headquarters to investigate complaints that No 402 Squadron was being assigned Hurri-bombers – fighter-bomber Hurricanes – rather than the Spitfire Vs in service with the other Canadian fighter squadrons. The man with whom he had to deal, Sir Sholto Douglas, was noted for his condescending attitude towards 'colonials' – a trait that later on proved especially galling to his American allies[14] – and, as Stevenson later explained to Breadner, he had taken: 'rather a strong stand, stating that he had no intention of changing his plan for equipping 402 with Bomber Hurricanes and inferred it was none of my business. I feel that his attitude was one of a very senior officer dealing with a subordinate and that he did not take into account the fact that I was representing yourself in presenting the matter.'[15] Pointing to the recent appointment of an air marshal to fill the senior RAAF post in London, Stevenson believed that 'on many occasions my rank, as compared with those with whom I was dealing, was a handicap which could not help but be reflected in the consideration given by senior [RAF] officers to RCAF affairs.'

You may consider that, as the Senior RCAF Officer Overseas, I must maintain RCAF interests – on the other hand, if one is required to 'dig in one's heels,' so to speak, discussions become complicated as between senior officers and junior officers, in the course of which some unfriendliness may creep in, which would be entirely absent when all concerned are on an equal footing.

Therefore, I recommend to you that a Senior Officer be granted the rank of Air Marshal and posted to the appointment of Air Officer Commanding, RCAF in Great Britain, to supersede myself.[16]

This recommendation, perhaps the wisest advice he was to give in his thirteen months overseas, was quickly acted upon by Ottawa. On 24 October Overseas Headquarters was informed that Air Vice-Marshal H. Edwards, the former air member for personnel (AMP), would be sent to London to replace Stevenson as air officer-in-chief, RCAF Overseas (AO-in-C.)[*][17]

While this move was, in great part, a direct result of Stevenson's own recommendation, it was also evidence that Power did not consider him the man to carry out the Canadianization of the RCAF Overseas. Indeed, Stevenson's continuing opposition to the minister's new course was made abundantly clear soon after his return to Canada. Taking a highly unusual step for a serving officer, Stevenson denounced the government's air policy at a press conference, telling his audience that Canadianization would reduce the efficiency of the British air effort. 'Personally I don't approve. The best squadrons are the mixed squadrons. Every man has something to give, if you put them together they pull. Much better results are achieved by mixing the men ... Canadian aircrews in England are operating under very highly skilled staffs. Any weaklings are tossed out. There is absolutely no mercy about it. The Canadians are well looked after by RAF men with two years war experience ... They are working hard, fighting hard and doing a great job.'[18]

The Cabinet minutes reviewing Stevenson's press conference recorded 'that expressions of personal opinion of this kind by Service officers, contrary to Regulations, were not to be tolerated,' but his promotion to air vice-marshal and appointment as AOC, Western Air Command – a position that had assumed great importance in Canada following the Japanese attack on Pearl Harbor two weeks earlier – went ahead as planned.[19]

The new air officer-in-chief was, like his Air Council peers, a veteran of the First World War. As AMP since February 1940, Edwards had an intimate knowledge of the RCAF's organization and manpower resources – a valuable asset in any discussion with the Air Ministry on the disposition of Canadian aircrew. Described as 'the most forceful man in the RCAF,' Edwards 'was the logical choice [as AO-in-C] because he ... had a good overall view of the RCAF,' even though Breadner had initially 'wanted to go overseas himself' as Stevenson's replacement. Edwards's recognized proficiency 'in administration, Air Force Law, [and] Departmental procedure' and his 'keen interest in the

---

[*] Stevenson's title had been air officer commanding, RCAF in Great Britain, until 6 November 1941, when it was changed to air officer-in-chief (AO-in-C), RCAF Overseas. The appointment became air officer commanding-in-chief (AOC-in-C), RCAF Overseas, between 16 July 1942 and 4 February 1943, when it was changed again to air officer commanding-in-chief, Headquarters, Royal Canadian Air Force Overseas.

discipline and welfare of both officers and airmen' were decided advantages;
but there was also a combative side to his character that would not easily
accept the condescending attitude British airmen still frequently adopted
towards their dominion colleagues. Edwards was not afraid to use plain language if he thought it likely to produce results.[20]

Air Commodore W.A. Curtis was appointed his deputy. Like Breadner and
Edwards, Curtis was a veteran of the Royal Naval Air Service during the First
World War, but unlike them he had gone into private business after the war,
becoming founder and president of a prosperous insurance firm. His astute
business skills translated well to air force administration, and his sound reasoning and considered approach to Air Ministry liaison would prove a restraining
influence on the more emotional Edwards. With his chief frequently rendered
hors de combat by ill-health throughout their two years in London, Curtis's
role at Overseas Headquarters was destined to be a large one.[21]

Before proceeding to the United Kingdom, both officers met with Power to
discuss overseas policy. While Edwards's claims that '"Chubby" gave me
damn little lead' other than a mandate 'to put the RCAF on the map' were
undoubtedly true in terms of the specific direction he received, the minister did
not mince words in indicating what he had in mind. According to Curtis, they
were 'instructed to make the Canadians known' and 'to get as many of the
squadrons as possible complete with Canadian aircrew and Canadian commanding officers.' These instructions harmonized with Power's desire to lift
the twenty-five squadron limit, for if the Article XV squadrons were completely
filled with Canadians while thousands of others were being posted to RAF
units, Ottawa would be in a stronger position to request a further allocation of
squadrons. Until the existing RCAF squadrons were fully Canadianized, however, the Air Ministry could deny the need for more Canadian units, no matter
how many thousands of RCAF aircrew were serving in RAF squadrons. Already,
following the September 1941 review required by the Ralston-Sinclair Agreement, the Air Ministry had indicated that it was 'unlikely that it would be
possible to form, by the 30th June, 1942, any more Dominion squadrons than
those already agreed to.'[22]

As if to demonstrate the impracticalities of forming RCAF squadrons, the Air
Ministry had organized only twenty-two before the June deadline – asserting
that it was impossible to do more – while forming thirty-nine RAF squadrons.
Yet the latter included some 2000–3000 Canadian airmen, about three times
the number serving in RCAF squadrons, suggesting that these impracticalities
had little to do with the gross supply of Canadian BCATP graduates. Indeed,
10,000 of them had arrived in the United Kingdom by the end of June.[23]

AFHQ knew what was happening and, prompted by the Air Ministry's warning that changes in Bomber Command establishments would delay the creation
of new units – squadrons would expand from sixteen to twenty-four crews –
Ottawa decided on 17 October to alter the form of its Article XV contribution.
Instead of five new bomber squadrons, it asked the Air Ministry to form five
new RCAF fighter squadrons. Although it was explained that to do so would re-

duce the number of Canadians able to be posted to RCAF squadrons by more than 1000 (single-seater fighters required no navigators, bomb-aimers, air gunners, or radio operators), Ottawa was not dissuaded, AFHQ shrewdly calculating that it was better to form the fighter squadrons immediately, while 'the additional RCAF personnel that will be serving in RAF squadrons will provide a basis for claim for additional RCAF squadrons.' It was that policy – to form the twenty-five Article XV squadrons as quickly as possible and then press the Air Ministry for more – which Power communicated to Edwards and Curtis before they left for London.[24]

There was nevertheless much to do before they could begin, if only to remind the overseas staff that Stevenson's era was over. 'I found the place, to be quite honest with you, as dead as a door-nail,' Edwards informed AFHQ, 'everyone complaining that they had nothing to do, but nobody doing anything about it.'

In fact, I am pretty disgusted with the whole thing ...

The discipline of the place is lousy. The men are turned out in a frightful manner. Nobody seems to give a goddam whether the ship sinks or swims, but above all, I found that everybody was diametrically opposed to all the policies emanating from Canada.

I got all the officers together the moment that I appeared in the office, and for the first time in my life I felt I was in a hostile atmosphere, but I do think that when I had finished with them, they were more friendly disposed, and could see the light as I wished them to see it.

As far as our troops in the RAF are concerned, I find that they are being dispersed all over Hell's half acre, without restraint. The officers that we have put in the posting departments have apparently, due to poor direction, just let the thing slide, and have done little towards concentrating our troops into Canadian Squadrons ...

Stevenson's declaration to the Press in Canada, on his arrival, will give you a clearer picture of exactly what I mean.[25]

Edwards soon fell ill, however, so that Curtis had to inform the Air Ministry of the new attitude.

Definite instruction have been received at this Headquarters from RCAF Headquarters, Ottawa, to the effect that action is to be taken to ensure that the personnel comprising the aircrews of all RCAF squadrons, is to be made completely Canadian as rapidly as possible.

In spite of the very evident desire to co-operate toward achieving this end on the part of both Air Ministry and this Headquarters, there have been many recent examples of postings which have had the effect of postponing, rather than advancing, the date of arriving at a condition under which all aircrew positions in RCAF squadrons would be filled by RCAF personnel ...

There are RCAF officers with considerable operational experience who are considered competent to fill the squadron and flight command vacancies in the newly forming

RCAF squadrons, yet apparently due to the fact that recommendations for postings are frequently made at the Group level, RAF personnel are posted to positions in RCAF Squadrons at considerable inconvenience to the RAF, when, in actual fact, eligible RCAF personnel are available in other Groups.

As a temporary remedy to this indesirable situation, it is requested that, before postings are made which affect the positions of squadrons and flight commands in RCAF squadrons, the proposed postings be referred to this Headquarters, and that before vacancies in RCAF squadrons are filled by RAF personnel, this Headquarters be asked for recommendations of RCAF personnel, it being understood that, subject to RAF concurrence, the vacancy be filled from RCAF personnel.

Curtis went on to give examples of RCAF officers whom he had considered capable of filling the vacant commands of Nos 416 and 417 Squadrons, but who had been posted to RAF units while RAF COs (one of them a New Zealander) were sent to the Canadian squadrons. To avoid any repetition, Curtis recommended posting RCAF officers to the staff of each command and group to advise them on Canadian personnel matters 'and maintain contact with this Headquarters in all cases of postings affecting RCAF aircrew personnel.'[26]

It was about time. Not only was the process of forming RCAF squadrons in arrears, but they were (in some cases) only nominally Canadian. Although the aircrew component of the nine single-seat fighter squadrons was 94 per cent RCAF, in the others the figure stood at just 43 per cent at a time when Canadians were still being posted to RAF squadrons in large numbers (see table 2). Determining who was responsible for this unsatisfactory state of affairs was difficult, however. Under the RAF's decentralized system, the Air Ministry played only a very general coordinating role, while Flying Training Command screened and posted aircrew to Advanced Flying Units (AFUs) and the operational commands controlled the OTUs, where crewing-up took place and whence crews were posted to their squadrons. The OTU was the crucial focus. It was there that RCAF crews would, or would not, be formed; and it was there where decisions were taken to post them to RAF or RCAF squadrons: but it was easy for one element in the chain to pass the blame elsewhere whenever Overseas Headquarters enquired about the lack of progress, and it did not take long for the forthright Edwards to become exasperated with the entire process. As he confided to Ottawa in early January, 'I find myself in the state that I want to get at somebody's liver, fry it and jam it down his neck, but for the moment I cannot get my hands on the proper person.'[27]

The AO-in-C vented some of his frustrations at a press conference in January when he revealed that during a recent visit to eight Article XV units he had found a 'disappointingly low' number of RCAF aircrew in the 'so-called Canadian Squadrons.' Although concerned about how Edwards's outburst might affect his own reputation, Power nevertheless accepted its essential truth and, with Breadner, reaffirmed their earlier instructions to the AO-in-C to Canadianize the RCAF Overseas as quickly as possible. An overall Canadianization

TABLE 2
Canadianization Rates, 1941–5

Date	RCAF Aircrew in RCAF Squadrons	RCAF Aircrew in Non-RCAF Squadrons	Other Aircrew in RCAF Squadrons	Total Aircrew in RCAF Squadrons	RCAF in RCAF Squadrons (Canadianization rate, %)	RCAF in Single-seat Squadrons (%)	RCAF in Crewed Squadrons (%)
31 Dec. 41	597	—[a]	532	1,129	52.9	94.0	43.0
26 March 42	878	—[a]	421	1,355	64.8	95.5	58.7
26 June 42	928	—[a]	384	1,312	70.7	96.3	64.8
26 Sept. 42	1,261	—[a]	494	1,755	71.8	97.1	67.1
26 Dec. 42	1,656		776	2,432	68.1	97.6	64.6
26 March 43	2,032	2,155[b]	1,073	3,105	65.4	99.4	61.6
26 June 43	1,900	2,213[c]	952	2,852	66.6	98.7	62.7
26 Sept. 43	2,441	2,534	1,326	3,767	64.8	98.6	61.2
26 Dec. 43	2,689	2,787	1,335	4,024	66.8	98.4	63.6
26 March 44	3,320	3,409	1,288	4,608	72.2	99.6	68.9
26 June 44	4,024	4,272	1,198	5,222	77.2	99.8	75.0
30 Sept. 44	4,855	4,566	1,167	6,022	80.6	99.6	79.1
31 Dec. 44	5,433	4,753	941	6,374	85.2	99.5	84.2
31 March 45	5,160	4,524	691	5,851	88.2	100.0	87.2

Sources: RCAF Squadron ORBs, DHist; RCAF Squadron Progress Reports, DHist; AMP Progress Reports, DHist 73/1174; 'Statistical Return on Canadianization,' DHist 181.003 (D3596); 'Strength Return by Units,' DHist 181.005 (D850)

[a] figures unavailable
[b] as of 30 April 1943
[c] as of 31 July 1943

rate hovering below 50 per cent was unacceptable in itself, but also weakened Canada's claim for additional squadrons. 'If Air Ministry is responsible,' the CAS told Edwards, 'please convey to it in strongest possible terms Canadian Government's desire to use Canadians in Canadian Squadrons and keep continued pressure to this end. Our policy must be to build up Canadian Squadrons as quickly as circumstances permit.'[28]

With thousands of RCAF aircrew already overseas and so few in Canadian squadrons, Power concluded that the Air Ministry must have obstructed Canadianization in some way, and he told the CAS that if the situation did not improve dramatically in the near future, he would attempt to embarrass the British into action by revealing the lack of progress to the House of Commons and the Canadian press. The CAS relayed the minister's views to Edwards in early February, asking whether 'early and effective remedial action' could be taken.[29]

Edwards himself moved quickly and boldly. Although cautioning Ottawa that the process was not as simple as everyone seemed to think (in part because of the restrictions against breaking up formed crews), he was prepared to block all postings to RAF squadrons 'until this demand has been met.'

I am putting officers in each command to watch postings ...

I cannot get to the root of the trouble. The Air Ministry is most co-operative but people in the field do not or will not realise the importance of this matter. The Air Ministry has sent and continues to send strong letters to commands. If I cannot make a more satisfactory report by March 1st I shall be prepared to recommend that the RCAF be withdrawn from Air Ministry control and that we organize our own air force, the Joint Air Training Plan Agreement notwithstanding.[30]

Two weeks later, the air minister signalled to 'approve your action in notifying Air Ministry that serious situation might ensue if proper action not, repeat not, taken in immediate future.' In the meantime, Edwards had reminded Babington of Ottawa's concerns and that 'everything possible must be done to bring about the Canadianization of RCAF Squadrons in this country immediately.'[31]

The new Canadian attitude did not go unnoticed – or unchallenged – by the Air Ministry. Babington was quick to point out, in the case of a recently formed bomber squadron, No 420, for example, that his branch 'did not get sufficient warning from D[irector] of O[perations] of the type [of aircraft] selected when this Article XV Squadron was being formed and we were, therefore, unable to get the RCAF personnel into the Hampden OTU in sufficient time for them to be trained when the Squadron was formed.'[32] The AMP went on to assure Edwards that commands would make 'adjustments as far as they can,' but stressed that the RAF 'cannot now break up these crews in order to rectify matters without imperilling their safety and general operational efficiency.' Nonetheless, he had 'again written to Commanders-in-Chief personally ... and impressed upon them the need for Canadianising and maintaining the Canadianisation of the Article XV units.'[33]

Certainly his letter to the AOC-in-C of Coastal Command, Air Marshal Sir Philip Joubert de la Ferté, had not minced words.

I am bound to say that, as regards your Command, the position is not satisfactory and indeed it looks as if very little effort has been made at the OTU's when crewing up personnel to ensure that the crews are all Canadian or Australian or whatever the case may be. Indeed, it almost looks as if somebody had taken the trouble to thoroughly mix up the crews so as to ensure that they are *not* 100% Canadian, Australian, or whatever is required.

I must appeal for your personal help in getting the position right as soon as possible. The Dominions, particularly Canada and Australia, are complaining in no uncertain voice that their Article XV Squadrons are not being Canadianised or Australianised as the case may be, and that they are full of other nationalities whilst at the same time their own nationals are scattered about the RAF in more than adequate numbers to man their own squadrons if they had been put into the right place. With the Canadians and Australians this complaint has become a first class political issue, and the Canadians have gone so far as to forbid us to post any Canadians overseas until their squadrons are Canadianised. I am doubtful whether they would attempt to uphold that veto if it was challenged, but you will recognise that feelings are a little strained, and that it is essential for us to remove the cause of this feeling as soon as it possibly can be done.

… I think you should tell your OTU commanders that they have definitely got to crew up Canadians together, and Australians together, and so on, and that they are not to make up mixed crews until they have made up the maximum number possible from each Dominion's personnel.[34]

These instructions were taken to heart by at least one of Joubert's sub-ordinates. Group Captain I.T. Lloyd's No 16 Group quickly achieved a vast improvement in No 407 Squadron when the replacement of second pilots by observers in Hudson crews allowed for the exchange of RAF for RCAF aircrew with RAF Hudson squadrons in the group. By the end of March, both of No 16 Group's RCAF squadrons, Nos 407 and 415, were 96.9 per cent Canadian – a sharp contrast with No 18 Group's lone RCAF unit, No 404, which remained at a disappointingly low 43.5 per cent even though its three-man Blenheim crews should have been easier to fill with RCAF aircrew than the four-man crews in No 16 Group's two squadrons. As a result of No 16 Group's efforts, the Canadianization ratio in Coastal Command as a whole improved from 45 per cent in January 1942 to 79 per cent six months later.[35]

There were positive signs in Bomber Command as well, where the acting AOC-in-C, Air Vice-Marshal J.E.A. Baldwin, filling in at High Wycombe prior to the arrival of Sir Arthur Harris, clearly accepted 'the necessity for ensuring that Dominion personnel go to appropriate Squadrons.' Writing to the AOC of Bomber Command's operational training group at the end of January, Baldwin explained that 'if you will let the Operational Groups know when you have Dominion crews available for disposal, I will take the necessary steps to see that the Operational Groups do post them to the right Squadron, anyhow until such time as these Squadrons are complete and up to establishment with Dominion crews.'[36]

The AOC concerned, Air Commodore F. MacNeece-Foster, shared Baldwin's belief that Canadianization should (and could) be achieved quickly. While some planning would be required, particularly in view of 'the rival calls of type of aircraft and nationality,' he nevertheless did not see 'that there should be any real difficulty.'

My rough estimates of my present pupil population indicate that there are about 1,500 Dominion personnel to 2,700 English personnel. While it may have resulted in Dominion personnel going to English squadrons I cannot see why, if the matter is handled carefully, the Dominion Squadrons should not be full of their own personnel.

This is particularly the case in view of the relatively few Squadrons which are as yet allotted to the Dominions. My 'P[ersonnel]' Staff are going into this matter very carefully and I would indeed ask you as Commander-in-Chief to send an instruction to the Operational Groups so that the question of the suitable allocation of Dominion personnel from the OTUs may be constantly in their minds.

It is really our duty to allot Dominion personnel to a particular Group and we await the instruction of the Group as to what Squadrons they go to; so, au fond, the ultimate responsibility must inevitably be on the Operational Group – always provided that we in the OTUs split up our personnel as far as possible into Dominion crews in the first instance.[37]

Neither Baldwin nor MacNeece-Foster remained in their appointments for long, however. With Harris's arrival at High Wycombe, the former returned to No 3 Group (where he proceeded to Canadianize No 419 Squadron fully within three months) while MacNeece-Foster was retired from the RAF (on the grounds of age) a month later. Meanwhile, their positive attitude to Canadianization was not shared by many of their colleagues. As Curtis later recalled, 'most of the British officers were very unco-operative – unwilling ... [The AMP] said he would do his best to further Canadianization but go down to another level and they didn't give a damn what he said.'[38]

The views of Air Vice-Marshal Slessor, AOC of No 5 Group, were typical.

Under the Empire Air Training Scheme the policy was to form what became known as 'Article XVI [sic] Squadrons,' composed exclusively of nationals of the various Commonwealth countries contributing to the Scheme ... I felt that in deciding on the Article XVI system we were missing an invaluable opportunity of cementing the Commonwealth by mixing up the best youth of its many constituent countries side by side in the same squadrons, living and fighting together and thus getting to know each other and forming lasting friendships. I discussed this view with Air Vice-Marshal McKean, the able head of the RAF Mission in Ottawa, and urged it on Mr. Power, the Canadian Air Minister, and his deputy Mr. Duncan. But I was on a bad wicket; the political factor was too strong and Canadian public opinion would not have been satisfied with anything less than their own Canadian squadrons fighting in the forefront of the battle. That is a very understandable attitude, and anyway the Article XVI system was retained and ultimately produced scores of excellent Commonwealth squadrons within the framework of the RAF – the Canadians had a whole Group, No 6, in Bomber Command later in the war. It was inevitable, but I still think it was a pity from the broad point of view of Commonwealth unity.[39]

Slessor's attitude was reflected in his record of postings to the two RCAF squadrons in his group; but when Curtis complained to the Air Ministry about the lack of cooperation from 'some OTUs and Groups in Bomber Command,' No 5 Group quickly absolved itself of any responsibility for the fact that only thirty-nine of 172 aircrew in Nos 408 and 420 Squadrons were RCAF. Rather, London was to blame. 'This business of Article 15 Squadrons is awfully difficult,' Slessor explained, 'particularly until we can persuade the Air Ministry to post Dominion crews to the right OTUs serving the proper Dominion Squadrons.' We have had an awful lot of trouble with the Australian Squadrons from this cause. What happens at the moment of course is that we get driblets of crews at odd times and they have to go anywhere where there is a vacancy; subsequently it is very difficult to move them because it means breaking up crews and usually they are extremely averse to leaving the Squadron with which they have begun their operations.'[40]

To demonstrate that he was not opposed to Canadians per se, Slessor went on to point out the large numbers of RCAF crews serving in his other squadrons – refuting his 'driblets' allegation in the process – but would not allow that they could be moved to his two Canadian units. 'I have one Squadron, No. 61 (Manchester), which has a Canadian Wing Commander commanding it[*] and quite a lot of Canadian crews, and when the question of the formation of 420 was in the wind I wanted to turn over 61 to be an Article 15 Canadian Squadron and form 420 as an ordinary RAF Squadron. They would not do that without changing the number of 61, and the Squadron were very averse to just that, as, of course, they would be very opposed to having their Canadian crews posted away to other Squadrons.'[41]

In No 3 Group, meanwhile, Baldwin continued to crew up Canadians and post them to No 419 Squadron with relative ease, casting some doubt on the validity of Slessor's arguments. While the latter's two Canadian squadrons were only 22.6 per cent RCAF at the end of January and 33.8 per cent one month later, No 419 was 58.2 per cent Canadian at the end of January and 83.7 per cent by 28 February. The figures for the end of June presented an even sharper contrast. While the RCAF squadrons in Coastal Command's No 16 Group and Bomber Command's No 3 Group were a combined 94 per cent Canadian at the end of June 1942, those in Nos 4 and 5 Groups (Bomber Command) and No 18 Group (Coastal) were only 54, 52, and 41 per cent Canadian, respectively; none of them had any special aircrew requirements other than the standard numbers of pilots, observers, wireless operators, and air gunners – of whom there were more than 10,000 overseas at the end of June but only 928 in RCAF squadrons.[42]

---

[*] This was, of course, a Canadian in the RAF.

In Fighter Command, where single-seat squadrons did not pose the same obstacle to Canadianization, the difficulties centred around the three night-fighter squadrons and the appointment of RAF squadron and flight commanders to RCAF units. Explaining why, in mid-February 1942, seven of the eleven squadrons under his command should still have British commanding officers, Sholto Douglas maintained (perhaps rightly) that the Canadians had 'so far produced very few officers fit to lead squadrons in battle. We shall have to wait, until some of the Canadian officers in the Canadian squadrons qualify for command. It is no use, however, the Canadian authorities trying to wish on to me middle-aged RCAF Squadron Leaders to command Canadian day squadrons. In fact it would be sheer murder to put this type of officer to lead a fighter squadron on an offensive "sweep."' As for the night-fighter units, Douglas promised that 'every Canadian pilot and Radio Observer who goes through my Night Fighter OTUs will be posted to a Canadian squadron so long as there is a vacancy. This process, however, is bound to take time.'[43]

Fighter Command's comments did not ring true to Edwards's director of air staff, Wing Commander G.R. MacGregor, himself a veteran of the Battle of Britain with No 1 (now No 401) Squadron – and only, at best, a lukewarm supporter of Canadianization. MacGregor pointed out that nine Canadian officers had 'been promoted to squadron command while serving in the RAF' (although primarily in RCAF squadrons) while four promising RCAF flight lieutenants had recently been posted from Canadian units to command flights in RAF squadrons. 'Nothing is further from [OSHQ's] intention than that Canadian squadrons should be led by officers of limited experience or ability for no better reason than that they are Canadian, but the present policy of posting away from Canadian squadrons officer pilots acting as flight commanders … can never produce the desired Canadianization.' Douglas's promise to Canadianize his night-fighter squadrons as vacancies occurred, meanwhile, 'will undoubtedly take an infinite amount of time since the C-in-C has stated in a letter that vacancies in Canadian Night Fighter Squadrons will not be created except through normal wastage which at the present rate of casualties means approximately never.'[44]

Tempers flared when, a short time later, Edwards met with Douglas, to discuss some of the difficulties. 'My biggest opponents were Sholto Douglas of Fighter Command and Leigh-Mallory of No 11 Group – it didn't take long to find that out … I felt that it was a great moment, Sholto, standing high and clear by his successes of the Battle of Britain, was hostile. I told him our problem and he almost laughed. We came to severe grips and I am afraid the language was not as diplomatic as it might have been but I do think that he might turn around to our side.'[45] Even the good-natured Curtis found the behaviour and attitude of certain British officers difficult to swallow. As he later recalled, 'Leigh-Mallory was one of those who was opposed [to Canadianization]. He was a big fellow and full of hot air. You couldn't talk to him. He was a puffed-up, chest-out, big fellow but prick him and he would collapse.'[46]

Curtis and Edwards nevertheless remained optimistic that progress was possible. When they repeated to Babington their own view that 'crews must be made up all-Canadian in OTUS' in order to 'keep pals together,' the AMP responded positively enough. 'Most OTU Groups now realise the necessity for taking every step to see that Dominion personnel go to the correct Dominion Squadrons, and I have rubbed this point in to all operational Group Commanders. By the end of the month I feel certain we shall see a real improvement.'[47]

Indeed, after three months of impressing upon the Air Ministry the importance of Canadianizing RCAF squadrons, Overseas Headquarters had reason to be optimistic. The overall percentage of RCAF aircrew in Canadian squadrons had increased from 53 per cent at the end of December to 65 per cent by the end of March 1942, and in those squadrons with two or more per crew the numbers had improved from 43 per cent to 59 per cent. However, most of the improvement was still accounted for by the impressive results achieved by Nos 3 and 16 Groups, whose three Canadian squadrons were now 93 per cent RCAF. The rest in Coastal and Bomber Commands were only 45 per cent Canadian, a scant 10 per cent increase over the December figure. Canadianizing the single-seat squadrons remained a straightforward task, with 95.5 per cent of the fighter pilots being RCAF, but five of the eleven Canadian fighter units continued to have RAF commanding officers even though Overseas Headquarters had convinced Fighter Command to cancel Squadron Leader L.V. Chadburn's posting to the Middle East and appoint him CO of 416 Squadron.[48]

Despite Edwards's cautious optimism, he remained acutely aware that as air officer-in-chief he could only plead his case to the Air Ministry and had no power to implement changes himself. 'My position is ridiculous,' he wrote Power at the end of March,' I have a high-sounding title with no authority.' Undaunted, however, he assured Ottawa that 'whatever difficulties may be presented, or whatever opposition, personal or otherwise, I shall inevitably meet with, you may rest assured that I will go ahead even if it brings about my social, if not my official, utter damnation.'[49]

Edwards's mandate went well beyond Canadianizing RCAF squadrons, and to increase his influence over the lives of RCAF airmen he wanted to have some input into those Air Ministry processes that affected Canadians in them.[50] 'I dropped a hint in a devious way,' he had told AFHQ in early January, 'that I would not be satisfied, as far as Canadian representation and control is concerned, with less than membership on the British Air Council.' Apparently it is shaking them to the core, realizing as they do, the justice of the request and yet the extraordinary situation that it would create. Harold Balfour, I am told through my moccasin telegraph, spilt the thing in Council the other day, and was pounced upon by the rest of the Council. I can only wait for a week or two to see which way the cat jumps, before tearing off the silk gloves and going into battle.'[51] To strengthen his hand, Edwards had recruited the Canadian high commissioner in the United Kingdom, Vincent Massey, to press his suggestion, but Massey made no better progress than Edwards and the proposal was flatly rejected, not least because it would 'open the door to similar requests' from Australia and New Zealand. The most that the Air Ministry was willing to offer was an invitation for Edwards 'to attend a meeting of the Council when some predominantly Canadian matter of sufficient importance is under discussion. This, however, will be a rare occurrence.'[52]

In Ottawa, meanwhile, the AO-in-C's initiative was also deemed 'neither necessary nor desirable' by both Power and Breadner, perhaps because they did not want to create a similar opening for an RAF representative on Canada's Air Council (Robert Leckie, an RAF officer on loan,[*] sat on council as the air member for training and did not represent British interests).[53] A frustrated Edwards could only lament his continuing lack of power. 'As far as my own position is concerned, in spots it is ludicrous, for although we are breaking in everywhere we can and taking control wherever we can, I have no command whatsoever except the handful of men at Headquarters. It just means this, that I, or the man who may replace me, will get tired of breaking his way in, with the consequent nuisance and unpopularity.'[54]

In the one area where Edwards did exercise control – Overseas Headquarters – he had long since taken practical steps to increase its effectiveness. The first problem to be addressed had been to develop a means of tracing the whereabouts of RCAF airmen in RAF units, a point that was driven home to Edwards when he attempted to locate his own nephew. 'No one could tell me and it struck me that if I, as an Air Vice-Marshal, could not find my nephew, what hope was there for the ones who did not have an uncle as an Air Vice-Marshal ... The Air Ministry has decentralized postings (God forbid that we should ever do the same!) and consequently the only way to find out where a man is, is by first knowing where he was last (and few people know) and start on the way from there.'[55] Accordingly, a Records and Statistics Directorate was established in London with a card index system to keep track of Canadians from posting lists, Post Office reporting cards, and pay ledgers. Although 'only as accurate as available sources permit,' it was 'the first even approximate picture of the situation ever compiled' and enabled headquarters to answer 'an ever growing stream of inquiries, including some which emanate from the Air Ministry itself.'[56] He also increased the Canadian medical staff at RAF hospitals, set up leave facilities for RCAF airmen, improved the haphazard postal services available at RAF stations, and began a newsletter called *Wings Abroad* with items of specific Canadian interest. In making these moves, Edwards was simply recognizing that the needs of Canadian and British airmen were not identical. 'If an English boy does not get his mail it is unimportant, in that within a short space of time he can get leave to go and see his family or he can send a telegram for nothing. To a Canadian boy, who has no similar privilege, a letter or a parcel is of much greater significance and importance. It boils down to this, that to a Canadian lad, a letter is as equal in importance as four days leave.'[57]

There were changes, too, in the overseas staff. While holding himself, as former AMP, 'entirely blameworthy' for earlier appointments, 'when anyone [who] fell short of requirements in was posted to England for duty,' he now

---

[*] The British-born Leckie had spent ten years of his youth in Canada.

asked for good men.[58] His pleading did not go unheeded, and Wing Commander H.A. Campbell – not to be confused with the anglophile A.P. Campbell – was posted to Overseas Headquarters the following month. Hugh Campbell had previously worked for the air member for training in Ottawa, Air Commodore Leckie, who had found him to be 'an exceptional officer both in his service knowledge and capacity for hard work. I have a very high opinion of his capabilities.'[59] That opinion was soon endorsed by Curtis, and in July Campbell replaced MacGregor as director of air staff (DAS) in London because of the latter's attitude to Canadianization. (It was, he had said, 'all right in due course, but in the meantime it was necessary to to get on [with the] war and Canadians could do that much better by being mixed with the RAF and other Dominion Air Forces than they could as a separate entity.'[60]) Together, Curtis and Campbell were two of the RCAF's most capable staff officers,* and both strongly supported Edwards's efforts to re-establish a measure of national control over Canada's overseas airmen.

Part of that process involved strengthening the ties between Overseas Headquarters and individual squadrons. To that end, a conference of commanding officers was convened on 6 March 1942, at which Edwards and Curtis acquainted everyone with the new direction in Canadian air policy and impressed upon them the importance that Ottawa now attached to filling the existing Article XV units with RCAF aircrew as quickly as possible.

The Canadian Government has now decided that definite steps must be taken immediately to carry out the original intention and to have implemented the policy for Canadianization of the RCAF Squadrons. The problem at hand now is to effect as nearly complete 100% Canadianization of Article 15 Squadrons as is possible, consistent with efficient operation, within the next two to three months. It is understood, of course, that this cannot be accomplished without some inconvenience and disruption of the even tenure of squadron operation, but as the job must be done, the sooner serious concerted action is taken the more likelihood there is of accomplishing our purpose in the time allotted.[61]

In view of the Air Ministry's haphazard approach to the probem, Curtis suggested that the COs take a more active role and proposed that 'where other Empire personnel are mixed with Canadians on RCAF formations, immediate steps should be taken to divorce these men and crew up completely with Canadians.' Although this ran counter to the general policy of avoiding the breaking-up of formed crews, changes in crew composition in multi-engine squadrons (as second pilots were replaced) and the current decrease in operational activity meant that some moves might be possible. 'It is appreciated,' he explained, 'that 100 per cent Canadianization of RCAF Squadrons and Stations is a large order for Commanding Officers. It is not intended that it be pushed to the extent of requiring a squadron to be pulled out of operations, or cause too much confusion. It must be kept within bounds so that operations are

---

* Both would serve as CAS after the war.

efficient. While no actual dead-line has been set as to when this must be effected, every effort is to be made to accomplish our goal within the next two or three months. Now is believed to be the best time because of the present lull in operations.'[62]

Whether or not it was his intention, Curtis's remarks left the distinct impression that mixed crews were to be broken up and re-formed with RCAF personnel, a misunderstanding that Edwards soon had to clarify. For if there was one way to guarantee British opposition to Canadianization, it was to attack the sanctity of the formed crew.[63] 'The policy,' the AO-in-C repeated, 'is to post on arrival from the OTUs only, and Dominion aircrews in non-Dominion Squadrons are to remain in those Squadrons at any rate for their first tour of operations.'

The suggestion that crews were to be broken up because of political pressure is quite unfounded.

It is requested that you will pass this information to all Dominion personnel, and reassure them that they will not be posted from their crews until the completion of their present tour.[64]

While Canadianization lay at the centre of Ottawa's air policy, the 6 March meeting had also allowed Overseas Headquarters to explain the services it provided – medical, chaplaincy, and the like – and to discuss uniquely Canadian approaches to trade-testing for groundcrew, remustering to aircrew, and promotion and commissioning policy. In addition, the COs were informed that liaison officers would be sent into the field to 'cover the Article 15 Squadrons, and afterwards as many other Units where there are RCAF personnel as possible, for the purpose of helping Commanding Officers to deal with problems which arise in the treatment of RCAF personnel ... It was stressed that these officers will not act in the capacity of "inspecting officers," but are provided for the purpose of co-operating with Commanding Officers in dealing as far as possible with problems found, and reporting to this Headquarters any difficulties that cannot be settled during their visit.'[65]

The sensitive question of 'waiverers' – aircrew who suddenly refused to fly – was discussed by the overseas director of personnel, Wing Commander J.L. Jackson, who announced that any recommendation to deprive a man of his flying badge 'must eventually find its way to this Headquarters for submission to the Minister.' 'This subject has been clearly defined by the Minister of National Defence for Air, who has ruled that no personnel shall be deprived of their flying brevet without his approval.' It was clearly Ottawa's intention to handle these cases in as humane a way as possible, without making 'what is already unpleasant any more grim than can possibly be helped' or 'make the man feel that the removal of the badge is the end of the road.' However, he '...stressed that there should be no thought that this Headquarters was trying to handle waiverers with padded gloves, and that if a man was not suitable for flying duties the intention was to remove him from such work as quickly as possible but to do it without breaking him. If the Station Commander approves, the man will and must fly. There are borderline cases of men who might be made good flyers with proper handling.'[66]

On the question of discipline and morale, subjects dear to Edwards's heart, the COs were told that the AO-in-C was 'of the opinion that it is not all it should be at many units throughout the UK.' Part of the problem lay in the fact that 'aircrew, both junior officers and NCOs, had the mistaken impression that once they left their aircraft their responsibilities and duties ceased.' By far the greatest difficulty seemed to be experienced with aircrew NCOs. 'These person-nel do not appear to be NCOs in the normal sense of the term and apparently do not consider themselves to be. Many do not assume the responsibilities of the rank nor set the example expected of them. Matters were made somewhat worse through their apparent automatic promotion to Flight Sergeants, which had the effect of making the groundcrew NCO feel that his rank was not worth working for; that his authority had slipped and that his position had been emasculated, all of which is having a bad effect on the general discipline and morale.'[67]

Explaining Canadian policy to RCAF COs was a relatively easy task compared with convincing British officers of its necessity. Even when corresponding with Overseas Headquarters on their efforts to 'Canadianize' the RCAF units under their command, many senior RAF officers attempted to persuade the Canadians that the policy was ill-advised. The AOC of No 4 Group, for one, Air Vice-Marshal C.R. Carr, himself a New Zealander in the RAF, claimed to 'have noticed a decided disinclination on the part of some Canadians in the Group to be posted from the Squadrons where they have been operating and have made friends.'

They must leave the crews they have been working with and start afresh with stran-gers ...

I feel that your Canadians miss a lot by being posted direct to RCAF Squadrons. In RAF Squadrons they mix and operate with English personnel and personnel from the other Dominions, and all get to know and respect each other. The various personnel gain a great deal from this association and assimilate fresh ideas from many parts of the world, which broadens their outlook.[68]

Not surprisingly, Carr's tepid reaction to Canadianization was reflected in his feeble attempts to place RCAF aircrew in his lone Article XV squadron, No 405. While that unit's ratio of Canadian aircrew improved from 49.3 per cent in February 1942 to 56.6 per cent in March, it declined to 50.3 per cent by July.[69] If, as Carr had claimed in his letter, he was breaking up crews containing RCAF members, he was clearly not posting the latter to No 405 Squadron.

There was evidence that some Canadians were 'not at all anxious to be put into Article XV units' and that a few of them 'had put in applications to remain with RAF units.' Babington reassured Edwards that the Air Ministry would take no account of these exceptions and that its primary goal was 'to get RCAF personnel into the RCAF squadrons.' There were, however, 'two reasons which RCAF personnel adduce which have considerable force.'

The first one is that if a Canadian is crewed-up with one or more British personnel or is serving in a RAF unit they more frequently go to RAF homes when on leave or go on leave anyhow with RAF personnel who know the way about this country better than they do. This will not be so easy for them when they are in RCAF units because they will not have the same guidance by RAF people.

The other point is an old one, and that is that they are very happy where they are and they don't want to be moved, having presumably got the squadron spirit.

I do not suppose that the first of these reasons had ever been realised by any of the political people, even if the latter may have been, and you may like to draw their attention to it.[70]

Despite Babington's contention 'that a real effort is being made' to post Canadian aircrew to RCAF squadrons, by applying a very broad interpretation to 'operational efficiency' he could, at the same time, justify posting more highly skilled RCAF aircrew to RAF squadrons even when vacancies existed for all-Canadian crews in Article XV units. Quoting a note from Bomber Command, on 23 February the AMP had reported that 'the big snag is that we have to select more promising pupils for training and transfer ... to the Middle East. Many of the more promising candidates are those from the Dominions and we cannot send poor material to fly these machines out. Another limiting factor is that the next best brand of pupil is selected for training as a pilot for heavy bombers and here, again, a certain number of Dominion personnel are concerned.'[71]

There was a logic to this, despite the fact that no RCAF squadron had yet switched to four-engine machines, and Edwards did not contest the procedure. Moreover, given the surplus of Canadian aircrew available in the United Kingdom, the practice of selecting higher-rated pilots for heavy bombers or the Middle East need not have retarded the pace of Canadianization, although it did have an indirect impact in terms of determining who would be available to become flight and squadron commanders. Nonetheless, by June 1942 it was becoming still more evident to Overseas Headquarters that 'to achieve Canadianization, it will be necessary for planning to take place in the OTUs' where crews were initially formed, and where unhelpful AOCs, like No 5 Group's Slessor, could still post RAF crews to RCAF squadrons, and vice versa.[72]

This time Babington's reply focused on an alleged shortage of Canadian aircrew in the United Kingdom (which meant that 'the necessary quantity of all categories of RCAF aircrew were not always available at the appropriate moment') and on imbalances in output from OTUs which meant that when Canadian crews did graduate there were sometimes no vacancies in RCAF squadrons 'whereas there are vacancies in other units.'[73] However, as recently as 15 April the Air Ministry had informed Overseas Headquarters that 'due to congestion in the various stages of training, they will be unable to accept any further RCAF personnel for training' for a two-month period in either the wireless operator (air gunner) or pilot categories.[74] 'It is of utmost importance that sending of pilots to this country from SFTSs in Canada should be held up temporarily in view of alarming way in which they are accumulating at Bournemouth. Unless it is held up at once, period of waiting for OTU training, which is already too long, will have to be progressively lengthened.[75] Under the circumstances, Babington's explanation had a decidedly hollow ring.

Still, opposition to Canadianization was not confined to the RAF, as Edwards discovered during a meeting at No 12 Group Headquarters in April where, much to his chagrin, the greatest hostility came from A.P. Campbell, Stevenson's former SASO and the current commander of RAF Station Digby in Fighter Command. After the meeting, Edwards took Campbell aside and 'pointed out to him that whatever his opinion might be our policy should be furthered by everyone in a position to do so.'

Campbell could not change his opinion. I have given him several days to reconsider his stand and had him come to London on Wednesday. He still holds that our policy is wrong and he cannot change. I pointed out that whatever a man's opinion might be it must be submerged if it conflicts with the policy which has been laid down by those in authority. I have told him that he cannot remain in England under these circumstances and that I am recommending his return to Canada at an early date ... I regret that this action is necessary and would impress that Campbell otherwise is doing a good job and that personal relations previously existing between us have not been disturbed by this. Nevertheless I feel that if Canadianization is to be pursued with any speed whatever such obstructing influences must be removed.[76]

At Edwards's request, Campbell was removed from command of Digby and repatriated to Canada. Posted to Eastern Air Command in October 1942, he resigned from the RCAF in May 1944 on receiving a permanent commission in the British service.[77]

Although the improved Canadianization percentages at the end of March 1942 led Edwards to report that 'considerable progress' was being made, he was convinced that any attempt to establish a national identity for the RCAF Overseas was doomed to failure so long as Canada's air force continued to be administered by Whitehall. Furthermore, even if he had enjoyed some success in improving Canadianization rates, making himself unpopular in the process, there was still the problem of RCAF personnel serving in RAF squadrons. What was required, Edwards told Ottawa at the end of March, was a new approach.

Whether we get the Article 15 Squadrons Canadianized or not is not, to my mind, the proper answer. Under the existing conditions we shall never be able to have a truly Canadian Air Force overseas. I think that in time the only way to do it is to follow roughly the processes that the Americans are proposing. They admit that there must be unified direction, and, as far as Fighter Command is concerned, Chaney, the American Chief here, is recommending ... that their Fighter units and formations should take their instructions from Fighter Command. As far as Bomber Command is concerned, they are all out to have a Bomber Command of their own which will operate independently but get direction as to objectives from the Air Ministry, where they would have representation, in order not to have the RAF and themselves doing the same job.[*]

Whether the British Authorities would agree to such a change or not, bearing in mind the Joint Air Training Plan Agreement, I do not know, but I do think that sometime in the future the people of Canada will make the discovery that they have not got an Air Force at all, with consequent complaint. It would, of course, run into more money. Whether Canada would be prepared to meet it or not, or whether we could do it through Lease Lend or not, I do not know, but I do feel that more and more developments will be unsatisfactory ...

To have a unified Canadian Air Force overseas, with Canadian control and, of course, complete co-operation, is, to my mind, our only and final objective, if for no other reason than to meet the demand of national pride.[78]

It was just this policy that Edwards hoped to impress on the Canadian government if he was granted permission to attend the May 1942 Ottawa Air Training Conference that was being organized to extend the BCATP agreement for a further three years.[79]

He was not alone. The air member for organization at AFHQ, Air Commodore A.T.N. Cowley, had arrived at remarkably similar views and presented them to the CAS in April. 'The greatest contribution Canada can make towards ultimate victory,' he told Breadner, 'is to develop overwhelming air strength.'

In the BCATP Canada has demonstrated her ability to organize, build and operate a machine to produce pilots, air observers and wireless operator air gunners in numbers heretofore thought fantastic.

But the role of schoolmaster and supplier of fighting men is not enough. Canada should fight – not as a part (however vital that part may be) of the great RAF, but as a self-trained, self-equipped, self-controlled RCAF ... We must completely equip and train fighter, bomber, reconnaissance and army co-operation squadrons, wings, groups and commands so that as soon as is humanly possible Canada will have a powerful striking force which may be used either for the defence of Canada at home, or in any theatre of war as may be decided by the Supreme Council of the United Nations.[80]

The government, too, was unhappy with the status quo, having informed London in early May that Canada's overseas 'organization should be such as will permit the RCAF to exercise maximum control of RCAF squadrons overseas that is consistent with the maximum efficiency of our united efforts.' The Cabinet also wanted to have the 'Canadian quota of squadrons ... increased in keeping with the increased effort and finance that Canada is putting into training in Canada,' the additional units to 'include the squadrons necessary for close co-operation with the Canadian army ... Most of these ... would be employed operationally in other commands ... until such time as the Canadian army becomes actively engaged in operations.'[81]

---

[*] A degree of British control that the Americans rejected when they finally arrived in force.

The British representatives arrived in Ottawa with the sure knowledge that 'the main snags are going to be Power's strong desire for 100% commissions amongst aircrews ... and his anxiety to press ahead faster with Canadianisation in Britain,' but they were probably quite unprepared for the extent to which Edwards's recommendations had been adopted as Canadian government policy.[82] In Cabinet on 22 May, for example, Power had bluntly acknowledged that although 'the United Kingdom were strongly opposed to a policy of Canadianization' and 'many senior RCAF officers agreed with this view,' the tremendous build-up of Canadian aircrew in England was reason enough for proceeding with 'the agreed government policy of providing, so far as possible, for incorporation of Canadian personnel in all-Canadian squadrons.' To absorb the surplus Canadian aircrew, he proposed seeking a specific commitment from the British 'as to a definite number of all-Canadian squadrons' and then, to ensure that they were Canadianized, to give Overseas Headquarters 'control over postings of Canadian personnel.' Similarly, 'Canadian records should be under Canadian control so that the government would have full and up-to-date knowledge of the movements of all Canadian aircrew, whether serving in RCAF or RAF squadrons.' While agreeing that 'it was not practicable to go the length of asking for an independent Canadian Air Force,' the Cabinet concluded that 'Canada should contend for as much autonomy as was possible.'[83]

Mackenzie King explained the broader motives underlying his government's policy in a subsequent conversation with the governor general, Lord Athlone, to whom he described 'how difficult it was to get the British to allow us to have Canadian squadrons in England. When we wanted to get a thing done we did it through the Americans. We had had, for example, with the Munitions Board, more trouble with the British than we had had with the Americans ... Power was fighting for the right to have Canadian squadrons instead of having Canadians mixed up with Australians, New Zealanders, etc., simply [as] ... part of the Royal Air Force. I spoke of Churchill making no mention whatever of the Dominions and ... asked how he could expect us to get French Canadians to enlist on the score that it was Canada's battle that was being fought and not some Empire affair.'[84]

When the British and Canadian delegates finally sat down to begin their private negotiations on 23 May, Power immediately raised the issue of an independent RCAF overseas. 'The going today has been fairly sticky,' Harold Balfour reported to London later that night, 'and there is a big drive for general Canadianization.' Three days later, Power handed him 'an amazing document' – Edwards's memorandum – 'setting out the ultimate Canadian objective which is really an independent air force in the same way as the USA have, and with no closer relationship than that of the USA. However, Power asked me to hold this document as he had not shown it to Mackenzie King.'[85]

Why Power should have kept Edwards's memorandum from the prime minister, and told Balfour as much, is difficult to understand unless it was a negotiating tactic aimed at displaying his essential reasonableness. The message it contained was not new, Balfour having already been told much the same story by Ralston and Massey, and it did not conflict in any way with what

Mackenzie King was saying. Indeed, for the longer term Balfour was convinced that 'our Government is going to have to face an independent Canadian movement so far as the RCAF is concerned.' In the meantime, however, he was confident that 'we shall be able to surmount Canadianization difficulties, meeting them on many minor points, but giving away nothing in principle if we act swiftly.'[86]

The concessions the British delegates were willing to grant in order to delay that eventuality for as long as possible were outlined to the Air Ministry by Hollinghurst.

We are being pressed very strongly by Canadian Government to implement understanding that eventually there would be Canadian bomber group ... Compromise suggested after tiring discussion is: 405, 408, 419 and 420 Squadrons to be concentrated in a single group and to be located in proximity to each other. Stations at which squadrons are located to be commanded by RCAF officers provided suitable officers available. Station headquarters personnel to be replaced gradually by RCAF personnel when available. Selected posts at Group Headquarters to be double-banked by RCAF personnel so as to provide nucleus Canadian group staff. Any additional RCAF bomber squadrons formed to be placed initially in the selected group. Canadian bomber group to be formed as soon as it is an economic formation. This group will of course be within Bomber Command.

We appreciate fully practical advantages of this compromise including different aircraft equipment of existing RCAF bomber squadrons. Nevertheless with precedent of United States bomber force in mind, Canadians are firm that there must be a Canadian group ...

We have agreed as aim, repeat aim, only that an additional ten, repeat ten, RCAF Article XV squadrons should be formed within normal expansion during 1942. These will include any additional RCAF army co-operation squadrons decided upon. Balance bomber squadrons. Progress to be reviewed in August.

As regards fighter squadrons, Canadians appreciate difficulty of Canadian fighter group but request that two fighter stations additional to Digby be converted gradually to Canadian stations.[87]

By and large, these were not difficult concessions for the Air Ministry to make. The principle of forming a bomber group had already been conceded during Power's trip to London the previous July, and the formation of up to ten additional Article XV squadrons and two fighter stations was not particularly problematic given the 9000 RCAF aircrew now serving in RAF units. Yet Whitehall was not happy, especially with the bomber group proposal. Insisting that 'we must preserve homogenity of aircraft equipment in each Group,' the Air Ministry nevertheless wanted to retain the freedom to equip Canadian units with any type of aircraft, even if this meant that some of the RCAF's bomber squadrons would have to serve in other groups.[88]

As the man on the spot, Balfour sensed what could be pushed and what was best left alone, and he chose not to pass on London's counter-proposal in the hope that the Canadians would be satisfied with what they had gained and thus be readier to make concessions in other areas. And, indeed, they were. Having initially asked that '100% commissions should be given to the 3 major members of aircrew [ie, pilot, navigator, and air bomber], irrespective of personnel being of commissioning quality and standard,' after 'long arguments' they had 'abandoned this principle and we have reached an agreement ... by which, in return for some complication of the machinery, present standards of commissioning of United Kingdom, New Zealand and Australia will be maintained with result that Canadians are generally likely to conform. Power definitely stated today that he did not wish to lower the officer class or have lower standards than other partners in the plan but we feel it probable that political considerations may to some extent whittle down this intention.'[89] Nonetheless, the British minister was confident that he had 'arrived at a formula which, I think, gives us 95 percent of what we want. Australia and New Zealand are standing by us as regards retaining standards, and I believe Canada will, in practice, broadly do the same.'[90]

Ottawa had at least been granted the power to decide for itself the extent to which its airmen would be granted commissions. In future, 'all pilots, observers, navigators and air bombers who are considered suitable according to the standards of the Government of Canada and who are recommended for commissions will be commissioned.' The quota system of the 1939 agreement would still be applied to both wireless operators and air gunners, but 'some flexibility will ... be permitted to ensure that airmen in these categories who have the necessary qualifications are not excuded from commissions on account of the quota.'* As part of this concession, however, the British also insisted that 'individuals who are to be commissioned at the sole instance of the RCAF authorities will be transferred to an RCAF squadron or be repatriated before such commissioning will be put into effect,'[91] even if it meant breaking up crews in the midst of their operational tour – a practice that, until now, had been entirely deprecated. Clearly, where British interests were at stake, more flexibility than usual was possible.

When on 24 May the two delegations met privately for the second time, the Canadian quest to gain 'as much autonomy as was possible' centred around the question of 'the status and function of the Air Officer in Chief of the RCAF Overseas.' As Balfour had expected, this part of the negotiation proved to be the most contentious. In a general discussion of the control exercised by Overseas Headquarters over RCAF personnel in the United Kingdom, Power accepted the fact 'that this control should not be permitted to interfere with operational efficiency,' but he felt that a greater measure of control should be possessed by RCAF Overseas Headquarters.' It was left to Edwards 'to outline his proposals in detail.'[92]

Balfour described the negotiations to the Air Ministry the following day.

---

* This policy would result in (among others) at least one air gunner who had previously been convicted of murder, had his death sentence commuted to life imprisonment, and then been pardoned gaining a commission. See Brereton Greenhous, '"You Can't Hang a Million Dollars": The Life and Times of George Rutherford Harsh,' *Canadian Defence Quarterly* 19 (June 1990): 56–60.

... we have virtually reached agreements on all Canadianisation points except that of status and functions of Canadian Headquarters overseas referred to in following paragraphs. This measure of agreement is subject, however, to your concurring in proposals [for a Canadian bomber group] ...

Apart from this the main outstanding issue is control of RCAF squadrons and RCAF personnel attached to RAF through increased status and responsibilities of Canadian Overseas Headquarters.

We told Power that the questions raised were fundamental in relationships of force of one country in Commonwealth operating on territory of another. Relations are in the main governed by the Visiting Forces Act but Power maintained that Canada's ready co-operation in JATP effort has prejudiced her opportunity of having an air force operating in Britain under self-contained conditions as McNaughton's Canadian army, and is anxious for political reactions [and insists therefore] that a great measure of control of RCAF units by Canadian Overseas Headquarters should immediately be agreed to. We replied that although these questions were doubtless ones which warrant early exploration, nevertheless a Training Conference of Air Ministry delegates in Ottawa was not the appropriate body to do this work and, amongst other considerations, many of the proposals put forward in [the Canadian] memorandum lie in the field of operations.[93]

Power, however, was not easily deflected. The Visiting Forces Act applied only to the legal relationship between the RCAF and the RAF in terms of the application of military law, and did not address the central issues of control and administration so important to the Canadian government. As a result, Balfour had little choice but to discuss the six measures Power had placed on the table.

1. Canadian Headquarters Overseas shall have the control over discipline and postings and internal administration of all Canadian squadrons overseas.
2. Canadian Headquarters Overseas shall be consulted on matters of strategy and tactics in which Canadian squadrons are concerned.
3. Canadian Headquarters Overseas shall have the full responsibility for discipline and administration of Canadians in reception depots and postings therefrom.
4. Canadian Headquarters Overseas shall have a general supervision over RCAF personnel attached to RAF [and] shall be entitled to enquire into and make direct representations to the Air Ministry regarding the well-being and interests either individual or collective of such personnel.
5. Canadian Headquarters [Ottawa] will be entitled to recall to RCAF overseas or to Canada any individual provided there are no objections on the ground of immediate operational expediency.
6. In order that Canadian Headquarters Overseas shall be fully informed as to proposed utilisation of Canadian personnel and as to changes of Air Ministry policy which marks Canadian personnel, Air Officer Commanding Overseas shall be made an ad hoc member of Air Council to be consulted when matters affecting Canadians are to be discussed.[94]

As might have been expected, these proposals were hotly debated over the next several days – and at a pace set by Balfour. 'Our JATP work has been constant day and night ... We [the British delegation] all agreed that the best policy was to push on and give our Canadian friends not a moment's peace or rest. We have found the atmosphere surprisingly good. We have big differences but there have been no frayed tempers except very occasionally, and [United Kingdom high commissioner] Malcolm [MacDonald] and I have found Power in a cheerful – in fact jovial – and not unhelpful attitude of mind. I hope he lasts the pace which has been and is swift!'[95]

Balfour's confidence was not misplaced. For all of Power's tough talk and posturing, and despite the backing he had from his Cabinet colleagues and Edwards, the British delegation would give up very little. Nowhere was this more clearly demonstrated than over the question of the control of postings to RCAF units. As Edwards had consistently explained (and as a report on Canadianization the following year would confirm), Canadian control throughout the chain from Bournemouth to Article XV squadrons was 'tantamount to the success of Canadianization.' Yet this key recommendation was 'abandoned' by Power, albeit 'after much argument,' during the first day's discussion of the six points. Similarly, although the Canadians continued to seek control over discipline and internal administration, the British stood fast, and 'Power was persuaded to withdraw' these claims a few days later. In a last-ditch effort to gain at least some measure of influence over postings, however, Power asked that 'a separate Canadian P[ersonnel] R[ecption] C[entre] at Bournemouth' be established 'with some control of postings.' It was eventually agreed that 'the O[fficer] C[ommanding] RCAF Personnel Reception Centre will be responsible for the selection of RCAF personnel for postings from the PRC to training and other units.' However, this limited extension of Canadian authority still did not address the RAF's failure to post sufficient RCAF aircrew to the OTUs backing Article XV squadrons in order to form all-Canadian crews. To that end, Power was able to add a provision to the agreement calling for the establishment of 'a central postings organization and a central record office, the staff of which will include RCAF personnel' to facilitate arrangements for posting RCAF aircrew to Canadian squadrons.[96]

Two of the other six points in the Canadian memorandum were settled without much debate. The second proposal for consultation 'on matters of strategy and tactics in which Canadian squadrons are concerned' was also withdrawn by Power, while the responsibility for maintaining a general supervision over RCAF personnel contained in the fourth paragraph merely restated provisions already made in the Ralston-Sinclair Agreement. The sixth paragraph proved somewhat more contentious, but Balfour was once again able to report that 'in face of arguments Power abandoned proposal that Edwards should be ad hoc member of Air Council.' In doing so, however, the Canadian minister had 'stressed that Ralston-Sinclair Agreement had not worked out in practice and that Edwards did not get information he felt Canada should have.' To address these concerns, the British delegates agreed that 'there shall be consultation before decision on administrative matters ...' but not on 'day-to-day routine operations.' The Air Ministry agreed that the Canadian AO-in-C would 'be furnished with advance information about any major questions which arise from time to time affecting the employment of RCAF personnel and squadrons.'[97]

With these issues settled, the point that provoked the greatest discussion was Power's request that Ottawa should 'be entitled to recall to RCAF overseas or to Canada' any RCAF personnel serving in RAF units. Balfour believed that the British delegation had to 'resist this entirely for obvious reasons and also on grounds that it is outside Conference scope. We feel we must stand fast on this.' Having given way on most of the original six points, Power was equally determined to reassert Ottawa's sovereignty over its own citizens, but when faced with Balfour's resolute resistance the Canadian minister asked that the question be referred to the Air Ministry. Balfour agreed, carefully prompting London that 'it would be most helpful if you could reply supporting our arguments against Canada's proposals on merits of case, and our contention that these matters are of a scope much wider than we here can deal with.' As instructed, Sir Archibald Sinclair told Power that the Air Ministry was 'sorry that we have not felt able to accept' his recall proposal 'for the cogent reasons which Balfour will have explained to you.'[98]

When handed the reply, Power 'accepted it courteously' though Balfour felt that 'it achieved no concrete alteration of view.'

Tacked on to this question of administration and powers of RCAF Headquarters overseas in regard to RCAF personnel is the whole issue of Canada's control of her own forces overseas and Power's keen desire for an ultimate position for the RCAF parallel with that the McNaughton and the Army. He and his colleagues are in fact trying to guard the theory of their constitutional positions in a form of words, and will not make a new agreement with anything like Article 14 of the old one which lays down that the output of the JATP other than that required for home purposes shall be at the disposal of the United Kingdom Government.

In face of our continued resistance Power took the issue to his War Council today although Prime Minister was absent. He tells me they were in full support and High Commissioner and I both feel Prime Minister will undoubtedly back his Ministers, especially in light of present difficulties with Nationalist Quebec. Amongst other things we stressed that if we give a right to Canada other Dominions will require the same and allied countries may also press for concessions. We must at all costs preserve our ability to conduct operations and though we are very sure that a conflict is, in practice, never likely to arise between the RCAF and RAF or between the two Governments we must eliminate risks of operational effect on any such conflict.[99]

As Power had informed his British counterpart in the negotiations, the Canadian Cabinet had indeed 'approved the principle of control of RCAF personnel by Canadian Headquarters Overseas, subject to considerations of operational expediency.'[100] Yet, when Balfour insisted 'on the final decision resting with those responsible for the conduct of operations,' Power relented, and a new clause was drafted for the Air Ministry's approval.[101] 'RCAF personnel placed at the disposal of the United Kingdom Government will be attached to the RAF. The RCAF reserve the right to recall any officer or airman so attached to service with the RCAF, subject to operational expediency. The final decision as to operational expediency rests with those responsible for the conduct of operations.'[102]

Even this paragraph did not go far enough in London's eyes, the Air Ministry insisting that '"operational expediency" is interpreted in a wide sense and covers operational training requirements, for example, A[dvanced] F[lying] U[nit]s and OTUs. We would like acceptance of this broad interpretation recorded in some way in the records of the Conference.'[103] After confronting Power with this latest demand, Balfour realized he had pushed the Canadians about as far as he could and informed London that 'short of provoking a major Conference crisis,' he could 'do no more than provide [the] safeguards' contained in the original draft. 'Power declines to put on paper confirmation of a broad interpretation of "operational expediency." Alternatively I tried to extract a confidential note from him to myself. His reply to both proposals is that we must have some trust and politically he cannot "water down" any further the general provisions and he already regrets having conceded the final decision to ourselves but will stand by what he agreed with me. He gave me full verbal assurance that if we trust the RCAF we shall not in any way be disappointed.'[104]

By the time the British delegates left Ottawa in early June, they had neatly deflected Canada's drive for greater autonomy by adhering to Balfour's original strategy of 'meeting them on many minor points, but giving away nothing in principle.' Not only had the British been able to circumvent Canada's insistence on its right to recall RCAF airmen serving in RAF units, but they were obligated to form only ten additional Article XV squadrons – a number well short of that required to absorb even half the RCAF aircrew being sent overseas – and with no deadline as to their formation. In the event, the last three Article XV squadrons would not be organized until late 1944; yet in December 1943 less than a third of the 9118 RCAF aircrew in operational employment overseas were in RCAF units.[105]

Nonetheless, the Canadians did not walk away from the conference empty-handed. Their gains included the formation of a Canadian Personnel Reception Centre at Bournemouth, with some influence over postings of personnel to the RAF's training organization, and the creation of a central postings organization to facilitate the posting of aircrew to RCAF squadrons. In addition to reaffirming Canada's right to be consulted on 'major operational questions,' they had also agreed that 'any army co-operation squadrons allotted to Canadian Army formations will be RCAF squadrons,' and that Overseas Headquarters would be consulted before posting RCAF squadron COs and all 'RCAF officers of the rank of wing commander and above.'[106]

The key British concession, however, had been the agreement to form a Canadian bomber group. Even though the principle of forming such a group had already been conceded during Power's trip to the United Kingdom the previous year, concrete action was now proposed, including the formation of a Canadian Bomber Group Progress Committee 'to keep the carrying out of this policy ... under constant review.' By conceding these points, Balfour had achieved his main objective of keeping Canadian airmen generally under the RAF's control. The extent to which Ottawa's objectives had been met, however, would only become evident following Edwards's return to Overseas Headquarters.[107]

3
Struggle and Dissent,
June 1942–May 1945

It was an optimistic Edwards who returned to Overseas Headquarters from the Ottawa Air Training Conference at the end of June 1942. Back in London, the AO-in-C told his staff that negotiations had been 'most amicable and that the requests of the RCAF were acceded to almost without exception.' Canadianization was now 'to proceed as rapidly as possible,' with the number of RCAF squadrons being increased from twenty-eight to thirty-eight, and its progress 'reviewed in September 1942 to ascertain if a further increase is advisable.' The belief that Overseas Headquarters' status had been enhanced by the Ottawa agreement was also reflected in Edwards's promotion to Air Marshal and the adoption of the new title of air officer commanding-in-chief.[1]

That optimism carried over to the successful first meeting of the Canadian Bomber Group Progress Committee on 3 July, which held out the promise of a speedy and relatively straightforward formation of an RCAF group.[2] The new, more assertive Canadian attitude was again in evidence the following month when Power arrived in the United Kingdom to discuss the overseas air force with the Air Ministry. Informed by Balfour that he might 'anticipate trouble' from the AOC-in-C of Bomber Command, Sir Arthur Harris, over formation of the Canadian bomber group, Power, according to his own account, did not mince words.

To Bomber Command, travelled down with Balfour. He made some reference to Canadianization. I told him I was fed up with going around asking favours and would ask no more. I realized that there was so much antagonism that from now on I would run my own show.

He talked of Bomber Group and intimated that Harris was sticky on it. I said that if Harris mentions it to me I would most impolitely tell him to go to hell and that it was none of his business but a matter of Government policy. Balfour agreed.[3]

Balfour's apprehension was undoubtedly fueled by Harris's recent fulminations against nationally distinct units and formations. The AOC-in-C was already 'most perturbed' at the idea of forming an RCAF group and found it 'quite unacceptable' to have 'almost the entire expansion going into Canadians for the rest of the year.' 'What with Canadians, Poles, Rhodesians and Australians

we shall ... very soon arrive at the stage where most of the operational squadrons are manned by coloured troops.' That would be unfortunate because, from
his perspective, 'the British, being in general better educated and more amenable to discipline, are apt to be quicker in the uptake during the complicated
training which has to be given.'[4]

Happily – and usefully – Harris kept his opinions to himself when he met
with the Canadian air minister at High Wycombe on 19 August. Hosting a
Canadian delegation that also included Breadner, Edwards, and the recently
appointed AOC of the Canadian group, Air Vice-Marshal G.E. Brookes, Sir
Arthur presented himself as one of the RCAF's greatest supporters, even
agreeing 'to the principle of withdrawing complete RCAF crews from RAF
squadrons or to assist existing units which had suffered abnormal losses. He
also promised full support in forming complete RCAF crews at OTU's'[5] and went
on to assure his guests 'that he believed the details could be worked out most
effectively.' Power was clearly impressed with Harris's remarkable, if not
altogether genuine, performance. 'As a matter of fact, when we did see Harris,
he was most co-operative and expressed the willingness to help us in every
way, and, of all the senior Officers we have met overseas on our two trips,
Harris has put himself out more than anyone else, thus belieing [sic] the reputation which has been built up for him both by our people and by the UK authorities.'[6]

Other RAF senior officers appeared equally cooperative. Fighter Command
agreed to convert Redhill, Digby, and Fairwood Common into completely
Canadianized RCAF stations and suggested that 'at a later date, it may be
possible to allocate a sector in No 11 Group area to the RCAF.' On the surface,
at least, Power's trip seemed to reaffirm the positive atmosphere that had
emerged from the Ottawa conference, and he assured Mackenzie King that the
contacts he had 'renewed with the many senior officials of the United Kingdom Government will have done much to improve relations of the RCAF in the
United Kingdom.'[7] Nevertheless, a cautionary note had already been sounded
at the end of June by Overseas Headquarters' war diarist, who noted the continuing strained relationship between Overseas Headquarters and the Air
Ministry. 'A factor which should be recorded is that of a sense of frustration
which dogs our efforts here. While it may be unfair to say that Air Ministry
personnel are not fully co-operative with this office, a distinct impression is
conveyed that we have a nuisance purpose only. Thus it is difficult to develop
a real effort for mutual helpfulness and assistance with the Air Ministry. This
attitude does nothing to increase the effectiveness of our work.'[8]

Over the course of the next six months, the Air Ministry's failure to meet
all its Ottawa obligations – and the perception that it often considered Overseas
Headquarters irrelevant – turned Edwards's initial optimism to disappointment
and despair. The first indication that his status was not all he had hoped came
in August, when the Air Ministry did not inform him in advance that RCAF
squadrons would take part in the raid on Dieppe, for consultation of that kind,
he believed, was 'within the spirit' of the Ottawa agreement. In fact, the
unorthodox process by which Operation Jubilee came to be launched and the

need to limit knowledge of the raid to those directly in the chain of command were, perhaps, reason enough for him not to have been forewarned; but from an air force perspective there was an even more compelling excuse for the Air Ministry's failure to contact the Canadian AOC-in-C. Unique an event as the raid was in its scale for the navy and army, for Fighter Command it was little more than another in a long series of fighter-sweeps over France and not notably larger than a number of earlier ones (see chapters 5 and 6).[9]

Justified or not, the unhelpful impression left by Dieppe was not improved when Edwards contacted the Air Ministry in September to implement Ottawa's instructions 'to make the necessary arrangements … for the establishment by the RAF of a central posting organization and record office' as provided for in the Ottawa agreement. To help overcome the impediments to Canadianization presented by the British system of decentralized postings, the AOC-in-C also proposed setting up a board, 'with myself as president and with a limited number of members of senior rank from the Air Ministry and this Headquarters,' to 'deal with the broader policy of posting affecting RCAF personnel.'[10]

That did not sit well with the new RAF air member for personnel (AMP), Air Marshal Sir Bertine Sutton, who, while acknowledging that there had been some difficulties, nevertheless observed (somewhat less than honestly) that the terms of the Ottawa agreement were 'in fact implemented by there being a central posting organization, namely the Air Ministry, in the posting branch of which there is RCAF representation.' Trying to bypass Sutton, Edwards pressed ahead with the establishment of a Personnel Reception Centre (PRC) at Bournemouth 'controlled functionally by RCAF Overseas Headquarters.' Of course, neither the PRC nor Overseas Headquarters would have any influence over postings from the AFUs – that remained Flying Training Command's responsibility – but Edwards apparently hoped that if all-Canadian crews were assembled by the RCAF staff at Bournemouth, RAF authorities would subsequently keep them together throughout their operational training.[11]

Unfortunately, No 3 (RCAF) PRC was failing to meet its objectives soon after opening on 1 November 1942. 'The intention of the Ottawa agreement was to create a Canadian Personnel Reception Centre and thereby place control of postings [from the PRC] under this Headquarters,' Curtis explained only three weeks later, but 'this has not worked out in practice. At present PRC is responsible to 54 Group and in turn to [Flying Training] Command and Air Ministry in all matters and not this Headquarters. RAF Station Headquarters was superimposed on the Canadian PRC recently, and although commanded by a Canadian, the purpose is defeated.' As a result, postings from Bournemouth continued to be handled by 'a small selection and posting organization' run by two RAF officers that was 'independent of the station and reports direct to Training Command.' It was not until the following summer that an agreement was reached that would allow the RCAF to staff the aircrew selection boards at 3 PRC.[12]

At the same time, however, Edwards was making considerable gains in establishing an RCAF presence throughout Great Britain. Beginning in September he had divided the United Kingdom into seven geographical districts 'to facilitate the work of his field personnel' – including chaplains, public relations officers, doctors, and supervisors of auxiliary services – and to provide a 'channel of communication for RCAF personnel on matters concerning their RCAF career, pay, allowances, promotion, remusterings, etc.' As a result, district headquarters were established (in numerical order) in London, Exeter, Huntingdon, Birmingham, York, Edinburgh and Inverness. Similarly, the ever-increasing number of Canadian aircrew serving in the Mediterranean and the Far East led to the opening of a District Headquarters, Middle East, in Cairo on 25 September 1942 and another in Delhi, India, the following summer.[13]

Edwards enjoyed less success when it came to creating a 'War Room' at his headquarters. Since returning from Ottawa, Edwards had 'been endeavouring to have established in this Headquarters a War Room which will accumulate information from the Air Ministry and the War Office, so that I may have a complete picture at all times of the war situation at any given moment. Air Ministry are offering a certain amount of resistance to the idea and are loath to release to me the information which I would require.' Power had taken the matter up during his August visit but had wisely – and more accurately – referred to it as an 'RCAF Intelligence Room.' He tied the question to his own desire 'to issue *communiqués* covering RCAF operations in this country and also to have more information of an operational nature on hand than was at present made available.' As he explained to wary Air Ministry officials, 'he felt that the RCAF should issue its own *communiqués* just as he understood the US Air Forces were doing. He wanted the Canadian people to feel they were in the war and to stimulate recruiting.' Despite Sir Archibald Sinclair's suggestion that 'the Canadian public could ... be kept fully informed by other means,' the RCAF was granted the right to release its own communiqués to the Canadian press.[14]

While Edwards's War Room did not begin functioning until the new year – the Air Ministry remained 'a little loath to allow us to attach an officer to their war room for experience, and to supply us with all the up-to-date "gen"' – the RCAF released its first communiqué on 9 September stating that 'members of an RCAF bomber squadron took part in the raid on Frankfurt last night and returned without losing a crew.'[15] Intended for North American release only, it nonetheless appeared in London's evening papers – to the chagrin of the Air Ministry but much to the satisfaction of Overseas Headquarters.

The first RCAF Overseas *Communiqué* was issued this date in the form of a flash. It was passed by AI 6, Air Ministry, approved by the DAOC-in-C and released by the Ministry of Information at 1240 hours ... Repercussions from this publication were widespread. G[roup] C[aptain] Heald, in charge of AI 6, was sent for by the Secretary of State, the Vice Chief of the Air Staff and the Permanent Under Secretary also being present. G/C Heald was instructed to take all possible steps to prevent any further RCAF announcements being issued in the UK. It was considered that other Allied Nations would request the same privilege which would seriously interfere with the RAF *Communiqué*. A ridiculous note was sounded when the *Times* enquired if this was the first occasion that a Canadian squadron had operated over Germany.* If this enquiry is indicative of the English papers' knowledge of the activities of Canadian squadrons, it would appear that the issuance of such *communiqués* has been too long delayed and that efforts should be made to have them continue. This appearance of an RCAF *communiqué* in the British Press was welcomed by RCAF personnel who have always felt that Canadians did not receive enough mention in the RAF *communiqués*.[16]

Even as Overseas Headquarters was savouring its public-relations triumph, a storm of controversy was breaking in the Canadian press. On 5 September, in a candid but 'off the record' discussion with a group of visiting Canadian journalists about the problems of Canadianization, Edwards had imprudently criticized the editorial policy of several Canadian newspapers, observing that 'some people are talking a lot of bloody nonsense about splitting the Empire. If Canadians who see it from that point of view want to be mugs all their lives, that's their business. I can see no reason against Canadianization.'[17]

When asked which papers he was referring to, Edwards replied, '[John] Bassett's paper in Montreal [the *Gazette*] and George McCullagh's in Toronto [the *Globe and Mail*].'[18] According to the *Gazette* reporter present, Edwards 'threw in the remark ... more by way of carrying on the discussion than by making any deliberate attack on the newspapers in question,'[19] but the leaked comments provided those papers opposed to Canadianization with fresh ammunition. Breadner quickly cabled Edwards to inform him that 'your statement to Canadian editors as reported on this side ... is causing very considerable furore here.'

Bassett talked half hour with Minister and dealt at length on your lack of diplomacy. *Gazette* in editorial headed 'Air Marshal Edwards is Wrong' categorically denied your charge and stated you must have been misinformed. This morning's [Ottawa] *Journal* carries full column editorial generally upbraiding you. Have not yet seen *Globe and Mail* reaction. Minister feels however that whole of Press in Canada will take up cudgels and that members during next session will make strong attacks on the Government. Discussed this question at length with Minister this morning who requests I wire you and ask that you give serious consideration to an immediate statement notifying all concerned that you had been misinformed as to the attitude of the papers concerned. I feel certain that only by such action can you save the government, this department and yourself any unnecessary headache and that present snowball of criticism levelled at yourself will become an avalanche directed at you for the sole purpose of causing your removal.[20]

---

* The first RCAF participation in a raid on Germany had come fifteen months earlier and, by this time, four squadrons were involved in the strategic bombing campaign on a more or less regular basis.

Based on the editorial opinion of the Ottawa *Journal*, Edwards appeared to be in trouble. 'Apart altogether from his bad language it looks to us as though Air Officer-in-Chief Edwards should keep his mouth shut about government policy or any public discussion of government policy ... It is to be hoped that Air Minister Power will not make a fool of this country and do an evil in the war by any interference with the complete control of the Royal Air Force over the direction of the Canadian air help. Any Canadianization which may mean any divisibility of air command or even merely multiplying jobs or increase the personal importance of officers like AOC Edwards seems to us, if we may be pardoned for quoting the gentleman's own phrase, to be "bloody nonsense."'[21]

Reiterating its view that Canadianization posed a threat to a united British Empire, the *Globe and Mail* was also critical of Power.[22] However, the *Gazette* not only made it clear that it did not oppose the government's policy, but Bassett also insisted that Edwards 'retract [the] allegation his paper is anti-Canadianization.'[23] The worst of the storm had been weathered but, in response to a strong appeal from Breadner, Edwards released a statement that he was 'very pleased to learn that the information I had received that the Montreal *Gazette* and *The Globe and Mail* of Toronto were opposed to the concentration of Canadian flyers in Canadian organizations, is not true.' He also suggested that the entire controversy 'might be a good thing if it were made clear once again to the people of Canada that so called Canadianization of the RCAF has nothing to do with combat control, which must obviously be exercised by a single operational agency, but is designed solely to advance the efficiency and well-being of our lads for the benefit of the common cause.'[24]

Edwards' retraction safeguarded his appointment as AOC-in-C, but the 'Battle of the Bloody Nonsense,' as he called it, had produced an interesting and valuable insight into the state of Canadian public opinion. Although a June 1942 public-opinion survey had found 51 per cent of Canadians opposed to the idea of a 'separate' air force overseas and only 31 per cent in favour,[25] the Gallup organization had not extended its questioning to examine attitudes to the issue of grouping Canadian airmen into RCAF squadrons – which was, after all, the essential substance of Canadianization. Had they done so, if editorial opinion in the wake of Edwards's remarks is any indication, the pollsters would have received a quite different response. For contrary to Power's initial fears that 'the whole of Press in Canada will take up cudgels,' only the *Globe and Mail*, the Ottawa *Journal*, and the *Toronto Telegram* were unalterably opposed to Canadianization. The Kitchener *Daily Record*, for example, observed that 'grouped solidly together, our boys will be happier and will fight with that team spirit that is so necessary in winning victories,' while the *Winnipeg Free Press* ridiculed the *Globe and Mail*'s 'absurd hullabuloo,' particularly in light of the demands it was making to commission all RCAF air-crew.[26] To the *Vancouver Daily Province*, 'the storm was largely synthetic, with the air marshal an innocent victim.'

The RAF and the RCAF are fighting the same battle in the same spirit and with the same determination. There is no suggestion anywhere that the RCAF should operate indepen-

dently or under its own command ... Men from Canada are more at home in their
daily lives, with other men from Canada. To overcome discrimination in rates of pay
and other difficulties it is well that, so far as possible without weakening the joint
effort, Canadian airmen should serve in Canadian squadrons. For that purpose, as more
men come from the training centres, additional Canadian squadrons should be organized, and men already serving in the RAF should have the opportunity, as conditions
make it possible, of becoming attached to them.'*27

The attitude of airmen overseas to Canadianization was a topic in a 'Morale
Survey' conducted in the fall of 1942. Beginning in September, and for the
next three months, two RCAF officers, Squadron Leaders J.D. Parks and G.
Vlastos, visited some 'thirty RAF and RCAF stations.' Meeting 'several hundred
officers and airmen of the RCAF not only on the stations visited but also, more
casually, on trains, in hotels, clubs, restaurants, etc,' they concluded that
'morale is fundamentally sound'; and where there was friction between British
and Canadian personnel (and the greatest desire on the part of the latter to
serve in Canadian units), it was found predominantly among RCAF other ranks.
Parks and Vlastos confirmed that there was 'a certain degree of truth in allegations made by RAF and RCAF officers that Canadian airmen are harder to
discipline than other airmen in the RAF,' but attributed much of the difference
to their North American outlook.

Canadians have no veneration for spit-and-polish. And they dislike discipline when it
appears as the arbitrary will of a person in a superior rank. They must feel that discipline makes sense before they accept it whole-heartedly. When it goes flatly against
common sense they despise it. On one station in the Shetlands where the weather is
often foul, we found Canadians very bitter over orders which forbad them to wear
their:
(i) crewneck sweaters to and from work;
(ii) rain-coats unless it was actually raining (though the rain might start at any
moment);
(iii) socks rolled over the tops of their rubber-boots (according to common Canadian
practice.)28

Other rank morale also suffered from the two services' differing attitudes
towards promotion.

The Canadian airman expects to get ahead fast. If he enlisted during the first year
of the war, he is apt to think of himself as an old-timer, and regard two or three
stripes as his due. The RAF flight-sergeant who took five years or more to get his
third stripe may look askance at such exalted aspirations in a mere novice. In
seniority and experience the Canadian is at a heavy disadvantage when assimilated
to a longer-established organization like the RAF. If he is promoted in spite of this

---

* Support was also expressed in the *Toronto Star*, the *London Free Press*, the *Financial
Post*, the *Ottawa Citizen*, the *Edmonton Journal*, and Quebec's *L'Action Catholique*.

disadvantage, there will be jealousy and bad feeling among the RAF men; if not, he will compare his status with that of his friends who are getting better advancement at home, and he will complain bitterly that he is being penalized because of his overseas service.

'Shadow-roster' promotions have eased this situation. But the Canadian airman who is an LAC in Britain and a Corporal in Canada feels something strange about this double life. He is apt to say to himself that, since he belongs to the RCAF, not the RAF, he is *really* a Corporal; and he will then blame the RAF for keeping his stripes off his sleeve in Britain.[29]

If nothing else, the Parks-Vlastos survey indicated that, as with the public at home, there was genuine support for the government's air policy among servicemen in the United Kingdom. 'Canadianization is being welcomed by most of the officers and practically all of the airmen with whom we discussed it.'

The predominant feeling seemed to be that:
(a) Canadian airmen are best disciplined by Canadian officers and NCOs;
(b) Canadian procedure with respect to promotions, remusterings, etc. is best administered by Canadian officers and NCOs;
(c) Canadians make the best COs of RCAF squadrons (we met two RAF COs of RCAF squadrons, and neither seemed a great success as a leader, though they were both experienced flyers and fighters);
(d) Nevertheless, Canadianization should not break up operational crews. And it should not pull a Canadian out of an RAF squadron unless he himself desires the change.[30]

These findings were supported by evidence from the operational training units, where it was apparent that 'Canadian trainees, particularly NCOs ... favour all-Canadian or substantially Canadian crews.'[31] Whitehall, however, continued to be uncooperative. Only a week after rejecting Edwards's request to establish a central postings organization to oversee Canadianization, Sir Bertine Sutton wrote to the Canadian AOC-in-C to assert 'that complete Canadianization is an impossibility.' Using Ottawa's figures for the projected four-weekly output of RCAF personnel from the BCATP, he claimed that the training scheme in Canada was responsible for all the difficulties.

If the Bomber intakes were limited to the [RCAF] aircrew in smallest supply, we could form 101 complete [heavy bomber] crews per 4 weeks (excluding Flight Engineers) [which were remustered from groundcrew and posted to the Heavy Conversion Units], and would then have rather over 200 Navigators and 200 Air Bombers surplus, who would have to team up in RAF, RAAF or RNZAF squadrons; we would also have 468 pilots (not all of whom could go to fighters as there wouldn't be the vacancies), and 30 spare [air gunners].

You will see therefore, that complete Canadianisation is an impossibility, short of tearing up the whole established training organisation in Canada and remodelling it to match the present requirements of aircrew by categories. Even supposing this were possible, proportionate requirements of the different aircrew categories change from month to month as the expansion proceeds, and, of course, change even more violently if the crew composition of aircraft is altered to meet new operational policies ...

The best we can ever do is to say that *as far as possible* we will endeavour to match RCAF crews in Article XV squadrons although there will always be instances when odd crews must be made up by RAF, RNZAF and RAAF personnel. As far as matching crews in other squadrons is concerned, this is, and always will be a physical impossibility.[32]

Sutton's argument ignored the fact that Edwards's immediate goal was to fill the existing RCAF squadrons with Canadian aircrew, not to form all-RCAF crews for RAF squadrons. While the AMP's letter implied that 101 all-Canadian crews fell short of Canada's Article XV requirements, the actual needs of the five existing RCAF bomber squadrons was only thirty crews every four weeks, even when allowing a generous supply of six crews per squadron per four-week period. Taking into account the six new squadrons to be formed in October and November, the RCAF still required only sixty-six crews per month, of which eighteen would need a flight engineer and an extra air gunner. Far from demonstrating the impossibility of complete Canadianization, Sutton's totals would, in theory, have allowed the RCAF to man seventeen bomber, fifty twin-engined fighter, and sixty-seven single-seat fighter or army cooperation squadrons with all-Canadian crews.[33]

Edwards passed the AMP's comments on to Ottawa, emphasizing 'the necessity for matching [aircrew] before embarkation wherever practical.'[34] He clearly believed, however, that RAF antipathy to Canadianization was on the increase.

It has been felt that for some time there has been a strong anti-Canadianization feeling existing in certain circles of the RAF but it is one of those intangible things which is sensed rather than seen. The general impression is that pressure is quietly being brought to bear by deed and word of mouth with a view to impressing on RCAF personnel the benefit of remaining with RAF units. This is particularly noticeable where there are small numbers of Canadian personnel at RAF units and by suggestion every inducement is held out to Canadians to retain an RAF attachment rather than a straight RCAF membership. Much stress is laid upon the Empire idea of mixed crews but the opponents of Canadianization naturally omit the fact that posting to a straight RCAF squadron has many additional benefits which are well known to members of the Article XV squadrons.

Since the anti-Canadianization feeling appears to be increasing, I can see no other alternative but to take the whole question up on a Government to Government basis. This seems to be the only solution to a vexacious problem. While I am loth to recommend this action, Canadianization has been accepted as a policy but, to some extent, has been accepted in certain quarters of the RAF in the nature of a challenge. It is essential, therefore, that the question be settled once and for all.[35]

At the end of October Edwards left on a two-month tour of the Mediterranean, India, and Ceylon. By the time he returned to London, the most encouraging development was the progress made in creating a Canadian bomber group. Six new squadrons had been formed in No 4 Group during October and November, bringing the RCAF total to eleven, and a good beginning had been made in placing Canadian aircrew in the first two of them. By year's end, Nos 424 and 426 squadrons were 79 and 73 per cent RCAF in aircrew, respectively. Less satisfactory results were achieved with the other four, Nos 427, 428, 429, and 431, when they were formed in early November: despite receiving a nucleus of ten crews from 419 Squadron, No 427 was only 54 per cent Canadian, while No 428 was slightly better at 57 per cent. Nos 429 and 431, meanwhile, were only 33.6 and 16.7 per cent Canadian by the end of December.[36]

Refusing to accept any responsibility, and suggesting that a decision taken in March 1941 was 'fairly recent,' Bomber Command's senior training officer, Air Vice-Marshal A.J. Capel, explained the poor results in early January 1943.

It must be remembered, however, that the decision to have all Canadian and Australian squadrons has been a fairly recent decision and consequently it will take some time before the designated OTUs turn out a sufficient number of Dominion crews to fill and to replace wastage in the Dominion Squadrons. It is perhaps not realised that, for example, a crew which reached a heavy Operational Squadron on November 7th was posted into an OTU on July 15th, and it will further be realised that on July 15th no rapid expansion of Bomber Command was in view, the Canadian Group and the large number of Canadian Squadrons had not been even discussed* and the fact that 3 more Australian Squadrons would be formed was not known. For this reason, no pre-arranged plan could be made to produce the correct number of Dominion crews between October 1st and November 7th when the majority of these new Dominion Squadrons formed.[37]

Capel's recollection of events ignored the large numbers of RCAF aircrew, of all categories, that had been fed into the OTUs the previous spring, totals that vastly exceeded the needs of Canada's Article XV squadrons. In the two-month period from mid-May to mid-July 1942, for example, No 3 PRC had posted a total of 2281 Canadian aircrew – 921 pilots, 537 observers, 374 wireless operators, and 449 air gunners – to Flying Training Command. These men, who still had to complete their AFU and OTU training, did not emerge from the operational training pipeline until October and November. Since the four-weekly aircrew requirements for all squadrons overseas, even after the formation of the six new bomber squadrons, amounted to only 498 aircrew (consisting of 139 pilots, 93 navigators, 66 air bombers, 84 wireless operators, 89 air gunners, 21 flight engineers, 3 FME/AGs, and 3 WOM/AGs), there would still have been more than 1200 aircrew available to fill the new squadrons – provided the RAF posted them to the OTUs backing the Canadian squadrons.[38]

---

* In fact, the Canadian Bomber Group Progress Committee had met for the first time on 3 July with Bomber Command representation.

Since that did not happen, the Canadianization figures that confronted Edwards on his return to London were bitterly disappointing. After a full year of cajoling, pleading, and badgering the Air Ministry, the number of Canadian aircrew in RCAF squadrons at the end of December 1942 stood at only 68.1 per cent, a decline of 2.6 per cent from the previous June. Given the steady flow of over 5000 RCAF aircrew that had arrived in the United Kingdom in the first six months of the year – two to three times as many as were required by RCAF squadrons – Air Ministry protests that Canadianization presented insurmountable difficulties appear hollow, particularly when those same officials did not experience similar problems posting far more limited selections of Polish, Czech, Norwegian, or Free French aircrew to their respective national squadrons.[39]

The simplest solution would have been to allow Canada to control RCAF postings and remove the burden of Canadianization entirely from the hands of reluctant RAF officers, but since that option had been fiercely resisted by the Air Ministry at the Ottawa conference, Edwards's ability to influence the situation had remained as ethereal as ever. That did not stop Ottawa from continuing to press Overseas Headquarters for some improvement in the situation, however, and on 9 January 1943 Breadner cabled Edwards 'that the total Canadian aircrew in each of the following squadrons is less than 60 per cent: Squadrons 418, 422 and 423. Why?'[40] Eleven days later, the CAS questioned why the '4 most recently formed bomber squadrons, Nos 427, 428, 429, and 431 are commanded by RAF personnel. Also that percentage of Canadian aircrew Nos 429 and 431 only 33.61 and 16.67 respectively.'[41]

Breadner's prodding evidently convinced Edwards that it was time for a showdown with the Air Ministry over its apparent inability to convert policy into practice. The AOC-in-C went straight to the heart of the matter and, in his signal to Ottawa, laid the blame where it clearly belonged.

I could not agree more with your query. The answer is simply for reasons that I have given you many times during the past year. The question of manning RCAF Squadrons with one hundred per cent Canadian aircrew has been continually referred to Air Ministry authorities ever since my arrival overseas. We all appreciate that certain difficulties were apparent but as over a year has now elapsed since the problems were realized I can see no reason why our objective should not have been reached by now and can only conclude that for some reason unknown to us an attempt is being made to frustrate the implementation of this policy. I have today sent an official letter to the Air Ministry pointing out that sufficient time has now elapsed to put into effect any necessary corrective measures and bearing in mind the large number of RCAF Aircrew arriving in this country and the small proportion required by our Canadian units, there is no reason why the Canadianization of our squadrons should not have been completed long ago. I have requested that instructions be issued that no RCAF aircrew are to be posted from the United Kingdom except to Canadian units until the RCAF squadrons have one hundred per cent RCAF aircrew and that I am recommending to you that this Headquarters take over the postings and records of all RCAF personnel. This I do hereby recommend most strongly. The numbers required to completely Canadianize our squadrons are so small as compared with the numbers arriving in this country that this whole question is ridiculous ... The fault lies with the provisions of the JATP Agreement whereby our personnel are turned over to the RAF for disposal and while we can recall any officer or airman it is subject to operational expediency, the final decision on which rests with the RAF. The expression 'operational expediency' is used greatly, almost to the same extent that many shortcomings are hidden behind the expression 'there is a war on' ... To give you some idea of the atmosphere, one member of the Air Council advised me that if my Headquarters had never been formed it would have made no difference to the war. It is easy to be wise after the event but we should never have participated in the JATP but should instead have built up an Air Force of our own. I have sent a copy of this signal to the Air Ministry. Only 585 aircrew required to complete Canadianization our squadrons and yet there are approximately 8518 RCAF aircrew in the UK excluding Bournemouth where there are 4000 aircrew, the majority being RCAF.[42]

As his deputy, Curtis, later recalled, the direct approach was in keeping with Edwards's character.

He was having a lot of trouble with the Air Ministry on Canadianization and he wrote a letter – or signal – to the effect that the RAF was not co-operating and that we would be better off by ourselves. He sent this over to Power. When I came into his office at nine o'clock he showed me the signal. I said, 'You didn't send that?' He said, 'Oh yes I did – four hours ago.' I asked him why he didn't let me see it so that we could talk it over. He replied, 'If I did that you would have talked me out of it and I didn't want that to happen' ...

I don't know just what set him off. It may have been something he thought of in the night because he sent the message to Canada in the morning – a few hours before the sun was up. But he was under quite a bit of pressure from Canada and had to report every month on Canadianization.[43]

Edwards's letter to the Air Ministry, which charged that British officials were always well prepared with excuses but were never ready to take corrective action, was equally blunt.

I am at a loss to know why the implementation of the Canadianization policy is proceeding so slowly and can only assume that it is being unfavourably received in certain quarters of the RAF to such an extent that progress is being retarded.

Canadian aircrew have been proceeding, in very large numbers, to the United Kingdom for almost three years and it is difficult to understand why the small proportion required to fill the Canadian squadrons could not be provided. This is particularly disturbing as it could so easily have been arranged, without disrupting other units, if it had been implemented through initial postings ...

I regret very much that it is necessary to write a letter of this nature, but I do think that the co-operation which we anticipated has not been given. We, on our part, have done everything possible to carry out the provisions of the JATP Agreement. You will note ... that thousands of groundcrew personnel are being posted overseas. This, as you know, is not part of the agreement and is being done in order that the RCAF may provide greater assistance. It seems rather futile, however, to send such large numbers of groundcrew, which involves the taking up of valuable shipping space, when the simple matter of posting aircrew, in small numbers from the thousands available, cannot be arranged without ill feeling.[44]

As Edwards had expected, his letter did not go unchallenged, the task of responding falling to Sir Bertine Sutton and the director-general of postings, Air Vice-Marshal J.J. Breen. Using a carefully woven combination of irrelevant, misleading, and false information, the latter immediately prepared a memorandum concluding that posting Canadian aircrew to RCAF squadrons was too difficult an undertaking ever to prove successful. Breen claimed that 'arrivals of air crew personnel have always been irregular' and pointed to the low number of pilots that had arrived in June and July 1942 even though Canadian pilots, at the Air Ministry's request, had not been sent overseas in those months because of the huge build-up of aircrew at Bournemouth. He also claimed that only eight Canadian pilots were available for posting from AFUs in January 1942 when, in fact, more than 1200 had arrived during the last three months of 1941. He then went on to state that this had delayed Canadianization because the intake into 'No 22 OTU, which is a Canadian OTU in Bomber Command,' had to be postponed, a deliberate misrepresentation since, as Breen was aware, the RCAF's bomber squadrons were spread over three groups in January 1942 and 22 OTU was not designated a Canadian OTU until the following September.[45]

Subsequently, Breen's misrepresentation of the problems served as the basis for discussion at an emergency meeting of the Empire Air Training Scheme (EATS) Committee the following day, which ended with Balfour's declaration 'that in view of the cogent reasons which had been advanced in explanation of our inability to proceed more rapidly with Canadianisation and the numerous explanations which had been given to RCAF Overseas Headquarters, he was at a loss to understand the statements in the letter and signal under discussion.' Perhaps sensing that the weakest link in the RCAF chain was at the top, the committee decided that the wisest course would be to have Sir Charles Portal invite his Canadian opposite number to London, to 'satisfy himself as to the steps taken by the Air Ministry to implement the policy of Canadianisation.'[46]

As it was, the Air Ministry seemed to have a keener appreciation of what drove Power and Breadner than did Edwards. Having been constantly urged to Canadianize the RCAF Overseas as quickly as possible, the latter clearly expected Ottawa to support the position he had taken and to 'hear quite heavy [Air Ministry] reverberations.' 'You may expect an approach to the Canadian government through a different channel complaining of inaccuracy of my statements and protesting my lack of diplomacy,' he cabled on the 27th. 'As far as inaccuracy is concerned you have the answers. As far as diplomacy is concerned I have tried that for fourteen months.'[47] Breadner promptly cautioned Edwards that 'our signals were not intended to start you on the warpath,'[48] but the AOC-in-C remained convinced that 'this matter had to come to a head sooner or later. It is either that my interpretation of what we want and what we are entitled to is wrong or else the Air Ministry is wrong. The only way to find out is to come out into the open. An understanding must be reached if I and my successors are to live a life that more nearly approaches one that is fit to live.'[49]

After discussing the situation with Power, Breadner sent Edwards a curiously tremulous response. 'Strongly urge you do not take up an uncompromising position. You did go off the deep end and apparently have stirred up much more hard feeling than subject warranted. Minister feels you should have made sure of his backing before going to bat. Possible therefore he may not be in position to support you in your action. You should do all in your power to pour oil on troubled waters and not under any circumstances go gunning. Would it help your position any if you returned here immediately to get things straight this end? If so let us know and come ahead. Nothing reported here yet and if you can stop it you should do so. Good luck.'[50]

The last comment was particularly appropriate as Edwards could now feel the rug being pulled out from under him. 'Your cable strikes strange notes. You demand vigorous action and protest the slothful inactivity in pursuit of your declared policy. I fight for this and now must struggle both ways without aid. To compromise now would determine the end of the RCAF as an entity overseas. To pour oil on troubled waters would avail nothing. Coming home would bespeak weakness which I cannot accept. I have done all with firmness, candour and truth conscientiously believing that I was right. I stand or fall on that come what may.'[51]

The possibility of ending 'the RCAF as an entity overseas' might not have been particularly disturbing to Breadner, who had spent his first year as CAS trying to eliminate the RCAF Overseas anyway. Power's concerns were more political. Sensitive to the lack of trust that Mackenzie King placed in him, Power preferred to keep air force problems as far from the Cabinet table as possible.[52] Despite his August boast to Balfour that he was 'fed up with going around asking favours' and was quite prepared to tell the RAF 'to go to hell'[53] if he encountered any opposition to Canadianization, that resolve now took a back seat to his overwhelming desire to have the entire matter kept quiet. In an effort to prevent the disagreement from reaching his colleagues, Power turned to the United Kingdom's high commissioner in Canada, Malcolm MacDonald, who promptly reported his conversation to London.

I had [a] conversation with Power yesterday evening about Edwards' letter to the Air Ministry ... He was extremely upset when he received Edwards' actual reply. He feared a first class row which would have been extremely embarrassing to all concerned including himself and the Canadian Government. It would have been very difficult for him to recall Edwards from his post on an issue connected with Canadianization in which Edwards would appear as the most eager champion of the policy. At the same time, he felt strongly that although he is himself, like Edwards, a keen supporter of Canadianization, Edwards' way of going about this business was seriously wrong. He felt extremely troubled as to what practical steps could be taken to avoid a serious crisis when Portal's message to Breadner arrived. Power is deeply grateful to Portal both for his intervention and for its form. He feels that discussions between Portal and Breadner have a chance of clearing the whole matter up reasonably satisfactorily ...

He was most anxious to know whether I agreed that this was likely. I said that he could accept it as an unqualified fact that you and the Air Council wished to implement as quickly as was practicable the Canadianization policy as agreed between the two Governments and that he felt sure that Breadner's talks in the Air Ministry would lead to the re-establishment of a close understanding on that matter. I did not feel so confident that Edwards' personality was the right one for carrying out the Canadian part of co-operation in Britain. I much liked some of Edwards' qualities including his frankness and I also felt it was possible that this incident would leave consequences on the personal side which made the future difficult. I was sure however that our people in the Air Ministry and elsewhere in the RAF who were working with Edwards would not allow this incident to increase difficulties either personal or administrative in any way.

Power said that it would be difficult to bring Edwards back to Canada for the present at any rate. He clearly distrusts Edwards' inclination to make indiscreet statements to the press. But he said that if the present difficulty did not smooth out on the personal as well as other sides, he might have to consider bringing Edwards away from Britain for some other duty a little later on. He is however, hopeful that this will not be necessary. He told me that he would keep me fully informed of any matters arising out of all this and that if he wanted my informal help in any way would like to avail himself of it.

I do not think he intended me to telegraph to you as fully as this though he did not say that I should not do so. But what he was very anxious that I should convey to you and Portal is his very real gratitude to Portal for having saved an extremely awkward situation ...

It is no business of ours of course to influence the appointments of high officers in the RCAF. That is entirely the reponsibility of the Minister and his advisers here. You would deplore and Power would resent any other situation. But he is the sort of man with whom I can discuss such matters on my own responsibility as a personal friend quite frankly and informally and without giving offence.[54]

Not surprisingly, Power's renunciation of his AOC-in-C severely undermined the latter's position, while Breadner's hurried trip to London in early February only reinforced British intransigence. According to Vincent Massey, the Canadian CAS 'very nearly had to disown' Edwards in making his peace and, drawing the appropriate conclusions, the Air Ministry would continue to make little progress in Canadianizing the RCAF Overseas until 1944.[55]

Whitehall's ruffled feathers having been smoothed, Breadner cabled Power that he was 'satisfied that Portal is out to ensure that when I return I will be able to report to you that under the difficult circumstances confronting them, Air Ministry are doing all that is possible and practicable.'[56] Other RCAF officers were less easily reassured, however. On 4 February Curtis and Air Commodore E.E. Middleton, the deputy air member for personnel at AFHQ, pointed out to Breen the extent to which the Air Ministry had failed to imple-

ment the Canadianization policy, and only after 'considerable discussion' was
it finally 'agreed that the most serious difficulty in achieving 100% Canadianisation was the unpredictable output from the AFUs.' Even then, it was up to
one of the RCAF representatives to make the elementary suggestion 'that each
input to AFUs contain a due proportion of RCAF personnel.' Such a common-
sense approach had not previously been followed since 'as far as was possible
those who had been at the PRC longest were posted to AFUs irrespective of
nationality.'[57]

The chief result of Breadner's pacifying mission came in the form of a letter
from Sir Bertine Sutton to all AOsC-in-C and AOsC on the subject of Canadianization. According to the AMP, 'it was felt that all concerned should be
reminded once again of the views of both Services which are in complete
agreement on this subject.'

Canada is a Dominion and as such is no less entitled to a separate and autonomous Air
Force than is the United Kingdom. This right she has temporarily surrendered in the
interests of war efficiency, accepting the fact that unity of organization and of operational command is essential in the prosecution of total war.

The recognition by Canada of this need for unity has, however, placed upon us
the responsibility of maintaining and encouraging the esprit de corps of that part
of the RCAF which became part of the Imperial Air Forces in the United Kingdom ...

The object of this letter is, therefore, to urge upon you once again the importance
of sparing no effort to implement the formation of the Canadian Squadrons and the
crewing together of RCAF personnel, and to ask you to encourage in any way you can
the sense of esprit de corps in the Royal Canadian Air Force. It will make for greater
efficiency amongst its members during the war and will help Canada in the post-war
period to form as a separate Service, the forces which have done so well in the present
war.[58]

As C.P. Stacey observed in *Arms, Men and Governments, The War Policies
of Canada, 1939-1945*, Sutton's missive amounted to a 'frank and rather hard-
favoured statement of what the Royal Canadian Air Force had lost by the
British Commonwealth Air Training Plan ... A situation where the Air Ministry was calling upon RAF Commands to foster the *esprit de corps* of the RCAF,
and was indulgently acknowledging "the right of the RCAF to some form of
self-expression" was not a satisfactory one from a national point of view.' He
also suggested, however, that Sutton's recognition of Canada's fundamental
entitlements represented a 'considerable and one might say final success for ...
Canadianization ... which from this time onward met few of the obstacles that
had hindered its progress hitherto.' The more accommodating British attitude,
he added, was materially influenced by Ottawa's decision, on 22 January 1943,
to pay the full cost of the RCAF Overseas – a step which solved 'the contradiction between the manly policy of independence which Canada was trying to
follow in respect of the RCAF Overseas and the idea of allowing Great Britain
to pay most of the bill.' Now, however, with Ottawa responsible for financing,

'the whole Canadian position of Canadianization – both moral and practical –
was ... vastly strengthened.'[59]

In fact, it would take a full year before the obstacles began to fall. Despite
a near doubling of the number of RCAF aircrew serving overseas in 1943 from
11,790 to 21,540, that year the overall Canadianization rate actually decreased
from 68.1 per cent in January to 66.8 per cent in December; as can be seen
from table 2, it was only in 1944 that great strides were made and the figure
reached 85.2 per cent.[60]

Furthermore, the links between the Air Ministry's more open attitude and
Canada's assumption of financial responsibility for the RCAF Overseas appear
tenuous at best – if, indeed, they existed at all. The Canadian government had
taken that decision not to gain leverage over the Air Ministry, but as a book-
keeping exercise designed to 'have the effect of increasing our expenditure in
sterling in the United Kingdom, thereby providing indirectly additional Canadian dollars to Britain to assist her in purchasing supplies required from
Canada.' And when Edwards was informed of the fact, several days after he
had sent his harshly critical letter to the Air Ministry, he was warned not to
draw inappropriate conclusions. We feel 'Air Ministry may mistrust our reasons for suddenly wanting to pay our share,' Breadner explained, 'and therefore consider that any pressure for control other than is necessary for effective
working of pay arrangements may be viewed with suspicion and for that
reason be ill-timed.' Edwards agreed, replying that he 'would certainly have
avoided this angle if I had known that you were pursuing the suggestion I put
forward months ago.'[61]

It was nevertheless tempting for the staff at Overseas Headquarters to read
between the lines, and, anticipating that the new financial arrangements would
necessitate the drafting of a revised text governing the status of the RCAF
Overseas, the directors of air staff and personnel, Group Captains H.A.
Campbell and F.G. Wait, hoped, among other things, that Edwards would
'have more say in the operational equipment to be used by our Squadrons. The
present provision of obsolescent equipment for RCAF Squadrons is beginning
to have an adverse effect on the morale of the RCAF, and to produce a lack of
desire on the part of RCAF personnel to serve in Canadian units.'[62]

Any perception that RCAF squadrons did not 'get the good aircraft'
threatened Canadianization, and Edwards turned to the Air Ministry for help
in squelching the rumour. But because seniority played a part in determining
when squadrons would receive new equipment, and since there were differences between types (that the Halifax loss rate was higher than the Lancaster's
in 1943 could not be hidden), invidious comparisons based on the experience
of just a few squadrons could always be drawn and then generalized upon.
Power himself told Edwards in April 1943 that he would soon embark on a
drive to secure better aircraft for Canadian squadrons – a drive which, in fact,
never materialized.[63]

As we shall see later in this volume, allegations of widespread discrimination against RCAF squadrons in the matter of equipment do not stand close
scrutiny. But perceptions can be as important as reality in shaping attitudes,

and there is no denying the fact that many Canadian aircrew believed that their squadrons had been unfairly treated and that ill-feeling developed as a result. Thirty years later, in a statement reflecting his general frustration with the RAF's treatment of the RCAF, Curtis (who had left London in December 1943) still recalled that 'the thing that constantly amazed me was the manner in which the British would allocate new aircraft to all of their squadrons first before Canada could receive any' – a recollection which was at best an imperfect rendering of reality.[64]

If the issue of aircraft allocations was a complex one, commissioning should have been very straightforward. The 1942 Ottawa agreement had stipulated unequivocally that all RCAF pilots, navigators, and air bombers who met the appropriate Canadian standards would be commissioned, regardless of the 50 per cent limit imposed in 1939. Yet, in November 1942, Power was surprised to learn that only 28.7 per cent of RCAF pilots and observers overseas were, in fact, commissioned. With commissions in the field still subject to Air Ministry approval* and the RCAF automatically promoting 25 per cent of its pilots and observers on graduation from the BCATP, those figures meant that the RAF was commissioning fewer than 4 per cent of Canadians. That reluctance did not extend to its own aircrew, however, as on 1 September 1942 57 per cent of RAF pilots and observers were officers. The discrepancy was even greater in the case of pilots, as 67 per cent of those wearing RAF uniforms held commissions compared with only 29 per cent in the RCAF.[65]

According to the Air Ministry, part of the problem was 'that Commanding Officers of some Royal Air Force units may be reluctant to recommend a Royal Canadian Air Force airman for a commission, though considered suitable, because he is junior to a Royal Air Force airman who is not considered suitable and therefore not recommended.'[66] However, it was Overseas Headquarters' belief that the impression among RAF officers 'that politics played an important part' in Canada's desire for more commissions had 'created a mild antagonism amongst CO's and, in some cases, resulted in adverse recommendations insofar as our personnel were concerned.'[67]

While these difficulties did not trouble Whitehall, Power was anxious to accelerate the Air Ministry's commissioning process which, given the 2059 Canadian aircrew officers overseas in August 1942, was 1978 commissions short of even the old 50 per cent standard. Aware that the Canadian press fully supported commissioning all aircrew, he advised the British high commissioner in early January 1943 that, if the Air Ministry did not take action to grant commissions to the percentages agreed upon in 1939, 'the RCAF would commission the shortage themselves using as recommendations for commissioning those ... that had been made when these airmen graduated from training schools in Canada.'[68]

---

* Not until February 1944 did the RCAF win the right to commission any and all aircrew serving overseas without reference to the Air Ministry; but the latter required that for Canadians in RAF squadrons this could occur only on completion of their operational tour and that they must then be transferred to RCAF squadrons or repatriated to Canada.

His warning had little effect. On 12 February 1943 the EATS Committee (which included Balfour, Sutton, and Sir Christopher Courtney, the RAF's air member for supply and organization) decided to tell Power, 'more in sorrow than in anger, that while we accepted the right of the Canadian authorities to set their own commissioning standards, we proposed to maintain our existing standards' for fear of the adverse effect 'a general lowering of the standards of leadership and other officer-like qualities' would have on operational efficiency. The committee's position reflected the strong opposition of both Sutton and Courtney to any wider granting of commissions, and was taken in spite of Bomber Command's desire, as a minimum, to commission all pilots and navigators of heavy-bomber crews. It also flew in the face of the committee's previous insistence that operational efficiency could only be determined by the commander on the spot, for in this instance it was decided that operational efficiency was best defined by Whitehall.[69]

In the end, Ottawa and London simply agreed to disagree, Canada circumventing the RAF's reluctance to commission Canadians in the field by the simple expedient of commissioning a larger number of BCATP graduates.[70] By these methods the percentage of commissioned RCAF pilots, navigators, and bomb-aimers serving overseas increased from 28.7 per cent in August 1942 to 52.2 per cent a year later (compared with 54.3 per cent of RAF aircrew in the same categories) and to 74.3 per cent by August 1944 (63.4 per cent in the RAF). Among RCAF wireless operators and air gunners, the percentage of officers increased from 8.6 per cent in August 1942 (11.1 per cent in the RAF) to 15.5 per cent in August 1943 (14.8 per cent in the RAF) and to 25.7 per cent by August 1944 (25.8 per cent in the RAF).[71]

The RAF's reluctance to commission RCAF aircrew may well have reflected wider British doubts about the leadership qualities of Canadian airmen – an attitude Curtis encountered in May 1943 while on tour in the Middle East. During a stopover in Gibraltar, Curtis 'struck up with the Under Secretary for Air. We discussed Canadians and he told me that Broadhurst [commander of the Desert Air Force] said Canadians make good flyers but they're not good leaders. I disagreed and said that Canadians were on par with the RAF but Balfour merely repeated Broadhurst's observation. We left it at that but I was annoyed as hell about it' – and he was certain 'that an RCAF officer will have little opportunity to command.'[72]

Similar attitudes also hampered Overseas Headquarters' efforts to place senior RCAF officers in RAF units and formations to gain operational and staff experience. Curtis later recalled a British 'refusal to post a Canadian group captain to an anti-submarine formation on the grounds that such appointments were reserved for wing commanders who had finished a tour of duty and were due for promotion; not even one exception could be made.'[*] And when H.A.

---

[*] Group Captain Martin Costello was eventually posted to command Castle Archdale in October 1943. Only one RCAF officer, Group Captain C.R. Dunlop who had commanded No 331 (RCAF) Wing in North Africa during the summer and fall of 1943, was ever appointed to command an RAF Wing – No 139 Wing of 2 Group, Second Tactical Air Force, from November 1943 until January 1945.

Campbell left Overseas Headquarters for the Middle East in the summer of 1943, to gain operational experience with a British formation, he was 'kept supernumerary for months with no duties or responsibilities' until injured when his jeep struck a mine and he had to be repatriated to Canada.[73]

Following the formation of No 6 Group in January 1943, the RCAF's main concerns over Canadianization were focused on meeting the large aircrew intake of its bomber squadrons. Initially requiring 366 aircrew every four weeks, the formation's expansion to thirteen heavy-bomber squadrons by year's end increased that figure to 588 every four weeks (as compared with only sixty-four for RCAF coastal and seventy-three for RCAF fighter squadrons). As might be expected, Canadianization ratios sometimes fluctuated significantly as No 6 Group squadrons converted to four-engined machines and when casualties were abnormally heavy, but some of the difficulties experienced (particularly in Coastal and Bomber Commands) were directly attributable to the fact that not all aircrew trades were trained in Canada. The specialist navigators required by the RCAF's five Beaufighter and Mosquito squadrons, for example, had to be selected at Bournemouth and sent on a wireless or radar course in the United Kingdom before being posted to OTUs in Fighter and Coastal Commands, while No 6 Group's RCAF flight engineers (largely remustered groundcrew from overseas squadrons) also received their training in the United Kingdom.[74]

The supply of flight engineers had not been a problem when No 6 Group was formed as, with only three heavy-bomber squadrons on strength, the number of volunteers for training easily met RCAF requirments. Indeed, at that time the flight engineer trade was the most Canadianized of the lot – 74.7 per cent – followed closely by air gunners (70.7 per cent) and well ahead of pilots, navigators, bomb-aimers, and radio operators, none of which had reached 60 per cent. When the remaining squadrons began converting to Halifaxes and Lancasters over the summer and fall of 1943, however, the number of groundcrew volunteering to remuster did not keep pace, and the trade's Canadianization rate fell to 23.4 per cent. To alleviate the situation, the Air Ministry asked Canada to follow the recent RAF example and train sufficient flight engineers to match the BCATP's output in the other bomber trades. Although Canadian-trained flight engineers began to arrive at Bournemouth in increasing numbers by the summer of 1944, the supply never met more than a third of No 6 Group's requirements.[75]

One other aircrew category that presented problems during 1943 was the number of Canadian wireless operators/air gunner (WOAGs) being posted to No 6 Group. While the supply of WOAGs had been well in excess of RCAF requirements throughout most of 1942 (as fewer than 400 of the 2700 WOAGs overseas were needed for RCAF squadrons), by year's end an increasing number of those arriving at Bournemouth had completed an operational training course at one of the four RAF OTUs located in Canada and, as such, were already part of a four-man crew. At the RAF's request, the initial arrangements for these transferred OTUs – three of which trained Hudson or Hampden crew for Coastal Command and the fourth Ventura crews for No 2 Group in Bomber

Command – called for 45 per cent of their pupils to be RAF graduates of the BCATP. Since very few British wireless operators were trained in Canada, only RAF pilots and navigators were fed into the OTU courses and their crews had to be filled by adding two dominion – usually RCAF – wireless operators. Much as the RCAF wanted an OTU capacity established in Canada, at least in part to meet the needs of the Home War Establishment, the prospect of training large numbers of mixed RAF/RCAF crews did not meet Ottawa's overseas objectives even when the agreement was revised, so that 85 per cent of the trainees for the three coastal OTUs would be RCAF.[76]

By agreeing to post greater numbers of RCAF aircrew to the Canadian-based OTUs, Air Force Headquarters had overlooked the fact that these were coastal units whose graduates would be posted to Coastal Command where the RCAF had few squadrons. It was left to Edwards to point out the illogic of the new arrangement.

An agreement was made with the Air Ministry that the two Hudson OTU's located in Canada are to be populated by 85% RCAF, 10% RAAF and 5% RNZAF. Although I fully agree that we should train as many RCAF personnel as possible in the OTU's in Canada, I cannot, for the life of me, see what we are going to do with 85% of the people graduating from the Hudson OTU's. As you know, we have only one Hudson squadron over here, and obviously the majority of the people coming from the Hudson OTU's in Canada will have to be dispersed in Coastal Command amongst RAF squadrons, which is exactly what we are trying to avoid. I appreciate that you will need a few for your own Hudson squadrons, but I don't imagine that the wastage in them is very high.

Our main interest, now, is in the Bomber field, and I think you will agree that we should concentrate on this. Perhaps, if we had been consulted on this point, we could have come to a more sensible arrangment.[77]

Given that the RCAF's predominant need for wireless operators was in Bomber Command, it made sense to divert Canadian WOAGs in the mixed RAF/RCAF crews to No 6 Group. Moreover, that solution would have had little effect on operational efficiency since the obsolescent radio equipment available in the Canadian-based OTUs so reduced the value of the instruction given there that all graduates had to take a second OTU course in the United Kingdom where, in the event, most of the four-man crews were broken up for training on larger aircraft. At Overseas Headquarters' urging, the Air Ministry eventually agreed to divert 'some Hudson and Ventura crews to Bomber Command OTUs feeding Article XV squadrons,' but for most of 1943 over half the RCAF wireless operators arriving at Bournemouth, whether in all-Canadian crews or not, were posted to Coastal Command for service in RAF squadrons.[78]

However, these very specific anomalies do not explain why Canadianization rates for the other bomber trades – pilot, navigator, bomb-aimer, and air gunner – remained so low throughout 1943. At the end of July, for example, only 68 per cent of pilots, navigators, and air bombers and 72 per cent of air gunners in Canadian bomber squadrons were members of the RCAF. Moreover, while No 6 Group received 1211 pilots, navigators, air bombers and air gun-

ners from July to September, only 890 of them, or 73.5 per cent, were RCAF.
Yet over the same period, 1044 Canadian aircrew in those categories were
posted to RAF squadrons in Bomber Command – clear evidence of an abundant
surplus. Even among RCAF wireless operators, only forty-seven of the sixty-six
posted to Bomber Command went to RCAF squadrons.[*79]

The effects of Bomber Command's relative indifference to Canadianization
were most clearly demonstrated in mid-June 1943, when it designated a third
OTU to back No 6 Group. Since no plans had been made to feed RCAF aircrew
into No 24 OTU before it was switched to support the Canadians, throughout
July and August its predominantly RAF graduates were posted to No 6 Group's
squadrons. In response to Edwards's complaints, the AMP explained that his
staff had been 'willing to withdraw this non-Canadian element from No 6
Group and put it into No 4 Group but Bomber Command and the Air Ministry
Organisation and Planning authorities protested so violently that the proposal
had to be dropped and it was ultimately agreed with your Headquarters that
since these crews were required in No 6 Group to complete ... their expansion
they should not be withdrawn.' The lesson having been learned, that mistake
was not repeated when No 82 OTU was designated to support the Canadian
group in September. Although RCAF aircrew were immediately posted into it,
its output did not go to No 6 Group until predominantly Canadian crews began
graduating in December.[80]

The demonstrable lack of progress in Canadianizing RCAF squadrons despite
an equally obvious surplus of RCAF aircrew convinced Edwards to approach
the Air Ministry once again about the situation, but the reply he received
differed little from those which Overseas Headquarters had been receiving
since early 1942.[81] 'I am sorry to see that you are not satisfied with the progress of Canadianization,' Sutton observed. 'I can only assure you that we are
straining every nerve to get the policy implemented in the shortest possible
time without adversely effecting the operational effort. I did hope that I had
made it clear that it was not a process which would show rapid results and that
the progress would be gradual. In the circumstances I do not think that the
results are unsatisfactory in view of the many circumstances operating against
it.'[82]

Nonetheless, the formation of a Canadian bomber group, with its supporting
array of OTUs and Heavy Conversion Units (HCUs), had finally created a
structure that could simplify the Canadianization process – provided Flying
Training Command posted RCAF aircrew to No 6 Group's OTUs. And by
September 1943 there were signs that that was beginning to happen, as 93 per
cent of the pilots, navigators, and air bombers graduating from No 6 Group's
three OTUs were RCAF. Less satisfactory progress was made for air gunners and

---

[*] Although a report on Canadianization prepared in the fall of 1943 by Group Captain Denton Massey indicated a slight deficiency in air gunners, his calculations were based on supplying eighteen heavy bomber squadrons from 1 January 1943 when the RCAF had only three
heavy- and eight medium-bomber squadrons. During the first twenty weeks of 1943, for
instance, Massey set the No 6 Group requirements at 1088 air gunners, whereas they actually
totalled only 420.

wireless operators; and even though there was an abundant supply of aircrew in all trades except flight engineers during the last three months of 1943, the Canadianization rate in RCAF bomber squadrons improved by a meagre 3 per cent, to 62.6 per cent, by year's end.[83]

There was still room for improvement; and how things could be improved was pointed out by Group Captain Denton Massey, who (in July) had been assigned by Edwards 'to investigate and report on the present state of Canadianization.' Completing his work in November, Massey identified a single, over-arching complication. '*Postings* of aircrew from No 3 (RCAF) PRC right through to HCUs for Bomber Command, or Squadrons for Coastal and Fighter Commands, *are completely in the hands of the RAF*, the RCAF Posting authorities have officially no authority whatsoever in these movements under the authority given to them and conduct only a "watching brief." Any influence which the RCAF posting people exert is merely through the courtesy of those who are in actual authority under the RAF.' The solution, therefore, was to establish a wholly Canadian training chain in the United Kingdom – including four all-important AFUs – with postings 'entirely in the hands of an RCAF Aircrew Posting Branch' so that only Canadian aircrew went to Canadian OTUs. That, he concluded, would ensure 'the success of Canadianization.'[84]

Edwards had appointed Massey to his task and could be expected to support his conclusions. But ill-health ended Edwards's career, and on 1 January 1944 Air Marshal L.S. Breadner, who had long wanted a posting to London, became AOC-in-C Overseas.[85] The former CAS who, at Power's prompting, had routinely prodded Edwards about the slow pace of Canadianization would, however, quickly revert to the form he had displayed four years before, when strengthening the national identity of the RCAF Overseas had been an incidental concern at best. Massey's eminently sensible conclusion that RCAF control of postings was the best guarantee of Canadianization, for example, he dismissed off-handedly, telling Ottawa on 5 February that the proposal was 'uneconomical due to the fact that they were already being done by the Air Ministry.'* Similarly, when Power asked him to comment on 'suggested amendments to JATP agreement' before his meeting with Balfour to work out how far to reduce the size of the BCATP, Breadner replied that he did 'not recommend discussions on any items therein with Balfour at present time' – confirming his contentment with the Air Ministry's handling of RCAF airmen.[86]

---

* On page 299 of *Arms, Men and Governments,* C.P. Stacey quotes the 'Comments of the AOC-in-C' interleafed at the end of the full Massey report as belonging to Edwards. Since these comments disagree with a number of Massey's suggestions and are contrary to both Edwards's repeated statements and the recommendations of his own headquarters staff in December 1943, it seems most unlikely that they were written by the out-going AOC-in-C. Breadner also concluded his 5 February letter to Power with the statement that 'particular comment on the recommendations are interleafed in the full report' as, indeed, they are. There is no similar indication that Edwards ever commented on the report. In fact, the Overseas Headquarters' war diary states that the Massey report was not submitted until 24 January 1944, long after Edwards had returned to Canada. It would appear, therefore, that the comments Stacey attributes to Edwards were almost certainly those of Breadner.

For whatever reason, Power did not seek to gain Canadian control over postings when he sat down with Balfour; but the atmosphere of their talks, the latter reported, 'though charming personally,' was nevertheless 'grim and extremely nationalistic officially.' The 'trend of Canadian thought ... is hardening towards much greater control of personnel during remainder of war with Germany, and undoubtedly leading up to demand for operational responsibility for all Canadian units in second phase of policing of Europe and Japanese conflict ... Most serious claim is firm request to wash out safeguarding words negotiated with difficulty last conference that operational expediency should limit RCAF HQ London's possible activities.'[87]

Power took the position that 'these terms are too indefinite to be workable. They are capable of being put up on any occasion to block the granting of our requests. As the final decision as to operational expediency rests with the RAF, we have not a chance, the shoe should be on the other foot. We should decide the terms and conditions of service of our personnel and have the final say as to where they will serve.'[88] Although he had 'wished operational expediency decision definitely to be in Canadian hands,' Power finally agreed, 'after long – sometimes heated – discussion,' that 'the final decision as to operational expediency will be a matter for discussion between RCAF and RAF.' Even so, Canada had extended its control over RCAF airmen to the extent that such matters as repatriation, tour lengths, and commissioning were now firmly within Ottawa's purview, and the amended agreement stipulated that RCAF airmen in RAF units were only attached to that service and could be recalled, upon notification, within a two month period – the RAF reserving a similar right for British airmen attached to RCAF units. The length of operational and non-operational tours was also specified, together with a new provision that 'on completion of an operational tour, all RCAF personnel will be placed at the disposal of the AOC-in-C, RCAF Overseas' who would, in consultation with the commander-in-chief concerned, 'place at the disposal of the RAF such personnel as are required for instructional duties' in the same proportion as the ninety-odd squadrons worth of RCAF aircrew 'in front-line squadrons.' Finally, the agreement also set up a Joint Demobilization Committee to oversee the prompt demobilization of RCAF personnel serving in RAF units.[89]

As important as these developments were for the overseas air force, the Canadianization process received its biggest boost – and the British attitude towards the Canadian service its greatest shock – as discussion turned to the RCAF's role in the war's 'second phase,' following the defeat of Germany, when a few Canadian squadrons would be part of the occupying force in Europe, but most would be formed into 'a fully integrated Canadian Air Force available for service wherever the Canadian government may decide.' To carry out that policy, 'RCAF personnel, who are presently attached to the RAF, will at once become effectively and unconditionally at the disposal of the Canadian government.'[90] With that statement, presented to Harold Balfour in an aide-memoire dated 10 February, Ottawa made it clear that the lingering effects of Article XIV of the original 1939 BCATP agreement, which had placed Canadian aircrew 'at the disposal of the Government of the United Kingdom,' would end with the defeat of Germany and that the RCAF would once again become an autonomous air force – albeit with a surplus of personnel and a shortage of formed units.

Having hoped to use Canadian aircrew to flesh out the RAF's own 'stage two' commitment, the Air Ministry was perturbed by Canada's determination to field an 'independent ... force' in the war against Japan, in part because 'it went considerably beyond what the Air Staff had hitherto had in mind.' But it was recognized that 'in principle RCAF autonomy in the second phase was difficult to resist,' and in the end Whitehall had to accept that Air Ministry control of Canadian airmen – even those in RAF squadrons – was coming to an end.[91] Each command was duly informed that 'for the Japanese war there would be "a fully integrated Canadian Air Force available for service wherever the Canadian Government may decide,"' and for that reason, 'after the conclusion of hostilities with Germany, all Royal Canadian Air Force personnel shall be unconditionally at their disposal.'

The present requests of the Canadian Government represent one more step in a logical progress towards the formation of a fully integrated Canadian Air Force. The number of Royal Canadian Air Force units is now such that the United Kingdom Government cannot but recognise – and has recognised – the soundness of the Canadian case, made as it is by a self-governing Dominion on behalf of its own nationals ...

The [Air] Council appreciate that there may be administrative difficulties in putting the revised arrangements into practice, but they are confident of your full support in overcoming the difficulties and implementing the inter-Governmental agreements. Every effort must be made by all concerned to give prompt and careful attention to the instructions which will be issued and to observe them both in the letter and in the spirit. This is all the more important since the Canadian Government have represented that, in their view, there have been instances in the past of unreasonable delay in the application of agreed arrangements. No doubt there have been genuine misunderstandings, but no shadow of misunderstanding must be allowed to occur in the future which could possibly impair the excellent relations which have been established between the two Forces or the close ties subsisting between the two Governments and peoples.[92]

The new attitude gave a final impetus to the Canadianization of the Article XV squadrons and a new term for the process – 'unscrambling.' Since RCAF aircrew would not be available to reinforce the RAF during the Japanese war, at long last the British had a positive incentive to Canadianize RCAF units if for no other reason than to reduce the number of Canadian airmen that would have to be 'unscrambled' from RAF units at the end of the war in Europe.[93] After making little or no progress for nearly two years, Canadianization now flourished. From a mere 66.8 per cent in December 1943, the Canadian aircrew content of RCAF squadrons jumped to 77.1 per cent by June 1944 and to 85.2 per cent by year's end. On 31 March 1945, as the war in Europe was rapidly drawing to a close, the Canadianization ratio reached 88.2 per cent.

By early 1944, however, the RCAF was looking well beyond the question of Canadianizing its forty-four Article XV squadrons and, with an eye on Pacific commitments, sought to concentrate Canadian aircrew surplus to their requirements in a relatively small number of 'nominated' RAF units. Having first been raised by J.L. Ralston as far back as 1940 and reaffirmed, albeit vaguely, by the 1942 Ottawa air training agreement, this was not a new idea; but it was not until the summer of 1943 that arrangements had been made to select ninety-three RAF squadrons for the surplus Canadian aircrew, and only after Power and Balfour sat down in February 1944 that specific posting instructions were issued to most RAF commands.[94]

The idea was never popular in London, the Air Ministry's director general of organization (DGO) having told Fighter Command at the end of August 1943 that 'this is a political move which has been forced on us by the Dominion governments. We realize how irksome it will be from everyone's point of view, but it will have to be faced. These "nominated" squadrons will be ordinary RAF squadrons in every sense of the word and there will be no difference between them and any other RAF squadrons in any way whatsoever ... DG of P's immediate aim will be to have prepared 30 to 40 per cent Canadian crews in each "nominated" squadron.'[95]

The proposal also lacked a certain precision. Aware, perhaps, that the RCAF could fill about ninety squadrons in total with Canadian aircrew – including the forty-four Article XV squadrons – Edwards had wondered whether 'we have taken on too many' when ninety-three were chosen for nomination. For the result, if Canadian aircrew were distributed equally among them, would be precisely as the DGO forecast – each would be somewhat less than half RCAF. Indeed, when Power and Balfour met in Feburary 1944 the lack of clarity resulted in considerable confusion. Having just worked out a scaling-down of the BCATP to the point where it would support a total of ninety-three RCAF squadrons – and declaring, at the same time, that ninety-three squadrons would likely represent Canada's air force commitment to the war's second phase – for some time the Canadian minister could not decide whether the ninety-three 'nominated' squadrons actually included the forty-four RCAF units already overseas, or whether the ninety-three were entirely in addition to the Canada's Article XV establishment, giving a grand total of 137. On the other hand, he was not at all confused about the ultimate goal of nomination – that the squadrons should be as Canadianized as possible and ideally '100 per cent RCAF.' Although that was clearly impossible if 137 squadrons had to be considered, at the end of the day it was decided that there would be ninety-three nominated squadrons after all, but forty-nine would have first call on Canadian surplus aircrew and Power hoped that they, at least, would be 100 per cent Canadian.[96]

The Air Ministry would not make any such promise, and contrary to an initial undertaking by Balfour allowed only that '100 per cent, or as near as possible, of the output of RCAF aircrews should go to Article XV and RAF nominated squadrons.' Moreover, there is clear evidence that key players in the Air Ministry wanted to a avoid a situation in which nominated RAF squadrons became so Canadianized that, for example, they could lay claim to an RCAF commanding officer.[97]

In Coastal Command, where the process of Canadianization had often been lethargic, the fact that Whitehall was now the problem was obvious to the RCAF staff officer.

Advice with respect to this policy was received by Coastal Command from Air Ministry in the first instance in November 1943. The Command promptly submitted recommendations for nominated squadrons ... No one at the Command protested the policy in any way. It was accepted calmly.

In May 1944, the Command was asked by Air Ministry to select among the list of nominated squadrons, three squadrons for priority nomination. This was promptly done and again without advancing any protest.

Now it appears that someone at Air Ministry (probably Air Council level) has 'invited' this Command to send in an objection to the policy and to urge that RCAF aircrew personnel be not allowed to infiltrate any particular RAF squadron beyond 50% of its strength.

Air Ministry officials advised senior officers of Coastal Command that although as a result of Captain Balfour's talks in Canada, it was the intention to man these nominated squadrons to 100% RCAF aircrew, after Captain Balfour's return it was pointed out to him by the RAF that it was not considered desirable from the disciplinary and other points of view that aircrew should be 100% Canadian and the remaining personnel Royal Air Force. In other words, these RAF folk are attempting to block a policy that would result in some RAF ground personnel in these units coming under the command of general list officers of the RCAF. On the other hand, they find it difficult to understand the dissatisfaction of the RCAF with the present situation and the alternative which spreads such large numbers of RCAF aircrew surplus to the requirements of RCAF units into so many units that these aircrew must always be in a minority and under the command of RAF officers.[98]

Here was reason for Breadner to protest, but under his leadership Overseas Headquarters rarely stirred in order to defend Canadian policy. No complaint appears to have been made.

It is not surprising, then, that the degree of concentration of Canadians in nominated squadrons was far less than that which Power had in mind. By 31 March 1945, when the effects of the policy should have been most pronounced, only 2001 of 4524 RCAF aircrew still serving in RAF squadrons had been posted to nominated units, and the Canadian aircrew component approached 45 per cent in only a handful of them. In single-seat squadrons, where concentration should have been easiest, the policy was almost completely ignored, so that three-quarters of the Canadians were actually serving in other than nominated squadrons and only one or two in each of the designated units. Coastal Command's record was also poor, there being little difference between the number of Canadians in nominated and un-nominated units even in Liberator and Halifax squadrons, for which there were sufficient RCAF aircrew to have fully Canadianized all three that had been nominated. Bomber Command did better in Nos 3 and 4 Groups; but No 1 Group, which had the highest proportion of Canadians outside of No 6 Group, had distributed them evenly, while No 5 Group appears to have been entirely unaware of the policy.[99]

Still, even such an imperfectly implemented policy paid some dividends, at least in theory, when in May 1944 the Air Ministry proposed converting a number of nominated squadrons into RCAF units as a means of persuading Canada to post additional RCAF groundcrew to the United Kingdom. (There was, by now, a serious shortage of manpower in all the British services.) Non-committal at first, Power eventually authorized Breadner to negotiate the transfer of fourteen squadrons in order to meet the RCAF's recently revised 'second phase' contribution of fifty-eight squadrons. Talks were still in their preliminary stage, however, when Canada's second-phase commitments were further curtailed in September.[100] Repatriation fast became Overseas Headquarters' main preoccupation, and by December all personnel not immediately required for further duties overseas were being returned to Canada. As a result, the size of the RCAF Overseas, which had reached a peak strength of 64,382 in October 1944, began a gradual decline even though the number of aircrew in operational squadrons held steady.[101]

Although still undertaking some 'second-phase' planning in February 1945, Overseas Headquarters became involved in a final Anglo-Canadian policy dispute when the AOC-in-C of Bomber Command moved unilaterally to extend the length of the first operational tour of his bomber crews from thirty to thirty-six sorties. Although Sir Arthur Harris was responding to a looming manpower shortage (caused by cuts in OTU capacity to permit the transfer of RAF ground personnel to the army), his action violated the terms of the Balfour-Power agreement, which required government-to-government consultation before conditions of service could be changed. Typically, however, Breadner said nothing, and it was left to the new minister of national defence for air, Colin Gibson,* to put forward objections which, from Ottawa's perspective, were entirely sensible. How could the public be expected to understand the need to lengthen Bomber Command's operational tour when there was a surplus of trained aircrew in Canada who had been refused operational postings to the United Kingdom?[102]

Aware that they 'had no right to continue to apply the extended tour to RCAF personnel' after Ottawa had refused its permission, the British Air Council issued instructions 'to postpone the introduction of the extended tour of 36 sorties for all RCAF aircrew in Bomber Command;' but Harris failed to do so, arguing the 'we now have the tail wagging the dog' as a 'result of the whole-sale "alienisation" of the Royal Air Force.' The matter 'should be brought to a showdown in the highest quarters,' and if the Canadians refused to fall into line their wishes should be ignored. Sir Charles Portal agreed, asking that it be 'made clear to the Canadians that their refusal to come into line with us would

---

* C.G. Power had resigned from the cabinet in November 1944 over the conscription issue.

mean the reduction of the bomber effort. Their refusal would stand on record for all time.'[103]

The question was finally resolved at a meeting between Portal, Harris, and Breadner on 14 March, when the latter explained that he had been authorized by Gibson to agree to a 'points' system similar to the one that had been in effect during the previous summer. This compromise was acceptable to the British officers provided 'the [points] rate would be worked out so as to require crews to do, on an average, about 35 actual sorties' and also allowed Breadner 'to explain to his Government that the adjustments in 'points' were made to accord with the changed situation and that although the risk for the crews would be somewhat increased, it would be nothing like what it had been in the worst days when the tour had been fixed at its present level on a sortie basis.' With the fighting on the Continent rapidly drawing to a close, however, the agreed 'points' system was rendered unnecessary before it could be put into effect and, on 15 April, High Wycombe issued instructions reducing first-tour length to thirty sorties by month's end. Even so, Bomber Command calculated that twenty-nine RCAF aircrew had been killed or captured while flying first-tour sorties beyond the thirty limit.[104]

The dispute was one of Breadner's last acts as AOC-in-C before being replaced at Overseas Headquarters by Air Marshal G.O. Johnson on 1 April 1945. With the surrender of Germany in May, Johnson's main task was to oversee the repatriation of RCAF personnel and to administer the RCAF's thirteen-squadron contribution to the British Air Forces of Occupation (Germany). Following the disbandment of the last RCAF squadron serving with that force, Overseas Headquarters was itself disbanded on 22 July 1946.[105]

4

Cutting Out a Paper Tiger, 1943–5

'Canada had not an acre of land or property in the Orient,' Prime Minister Mackenzie King told the Cabinet War Committee in October 1944; and apart from the citizens of British Columbia – and perhaps the families of the soldiers lost at Hong Kong nearly three years before – Canadians thought not one whit about the Pacific and the war against Japan.[1]

That was not the case in the Department of National Defence, and more particularly in Air Force Headquarters, where the question of what Canada should do in the second phase of the war – the occupation of Germany and carrying the fight to Japan – was widely regarded as an opportunity to right the wrongs of Article XV and the disappointing process of Canadianizing the overseas air force. As far back as November 1943 Power had explained that in the campaign against Japan, Ottawa would have the chance to 'bring our own men into our own squadrons under our own direction' for the final phase of the war.[2]

And it was to be on a large scale. When King discussed the matter further with his air minister in January 1944, Power had expressed the desire to field sixty or seventy squadrons. The navy, too, might play 'a prominent part,' but the two agreed 'that there was really no place for sending any army over the Pacific.' Even so, the prime minister had doubts about the country's enthusiasm 'about going on with the war with Japan,' and he was surer still that 'we will get little credit for anything we do, either on the part of the US or Great Britain.' Canada would contribute – it always had, and King acknowledged the 'obligation to share with ... the British, Americans and Australians' – but in January 1944 his preference was to do so modestly. For the moment, then, the size and nature of Canada's commitment was less important than letting the British know of Ottawa's determination to decide where, and under whom, Canadians would serve. 'We could not,' Power observed later, 'await the decision of the Air Ministry on whether a given [RAF] squadron containing a number of ... RCAF personnel and stationed in, let us say, Egypt or Burma, would remain there. The future of Canadian boys, I said, must not be dependent on the convenience or interest of the government of any other country.'[3]

That was the message Power delivered, with the prime minister's approval, to his British counterpart, still Sir Archibald Sinclair, on 18 January 1944.

Besides seeking timely unscrambling and repatriation of Canadian airmen from RAF squadrons – to afford 'early demobilization' to those who desired it and to guard against their serving in British units in the second phase – Power addressed the limits of Canada's commitment to the war in the Far East. Not only would it be measured against 'our position as a Pacific power,' membership in the Commonwealth, and proximity to the United States, but, to ensure that it was determined 'by her desired foreign policy,' there would be no premature undertaking to place Canadian forces under British control or send them to a theatre of operations (South-east Asia, for example) where British interests prevailed.[4]

Harold Balfour, British parliamentary undersecretary of state for air, encountered the same attitude when he arrived in Ottawa in February to discuss the scaling down of the BCATP. From his perspective, the Canadian minister was 'grim and extremely nationalistic officially,' and the talks revealed that Ottawa was 'hardening towards much greater general control of personnel during remainder of war with Germany, and undoubtedly leading up to demand for operational responsibility for all Canadian Units in second phase of policing of Europe and Japanese conflict.' Under the circumstances, meeting with Power had been 'about as much fun as being on the end of a pin.'[5]

Although reductions in the BCATP were geared to meet diminished second-phase requirements, Balfour had never meant to take up the issue of Pacific War commitments with the Canadians. He had little option, however, when Power handed him an aide-memoire outlining the Canadian government's intentions. Revised by the prime minister and approved by Cabinet, it made abundantly clear that any forces Canada might send to the Pacific would be organized on a strictly national basis, with Canada's membership in the British Commonwealth being only one of a number of factors which would determine the country's participation in phase two. There were, indeed, a number of considerations, such as defence of the Pacific Coast and questions of supply and equipment, which 'may render it advisable for Canada to play her part in the Japanese war in very close co-operation with the United States, at any rate in certain operational areas.' It was to be understood, therefore, that 'after the German war is over, RCAF personnel who are presently attached to the RAF will at once become effectively and unconditionally at the disposal of the Canadian Government [and] all RCAF personnel will be regrouped into national units or formations.'[6]

In negotiating the Balfour-Power Agreement, therefore, Ottawa made it clear that air training would be structured in such a way that the country would 'have at her disposal, after the period of deployment on the termination of the German war, a fully integrated Canadian Air Force available for service wherever the Canadian Government may decide that it can be most usefully employed in the interests of Canada, of the Commonwealth and of the United Nations.' For King, this was 'the strongest assertion made thus far of Canada's position as a nation, demanding an equal voice on matters which pertained to her own forces.'[7]

Inevitably, the Canadian plan was not welcomed in London. The process of unscrambling the RCAF from the RAF would 'take some time and involve a certain degree of disorganization in the post-German war period and according-ly ... affect Air Staff decisions and plans which are being made at the present time.' In particular, it would disrupt plans for '... Canadian participation in all theatres during the Japanese phase in domestic, European and South East Asian areas. They had allowed for a considerable strength of 100% Canadian Squad-rons which could no doubt, in certain instances, be grouped into small Cana-dian formations with the RAF organisation; but also, outside these formations, substantial quotas of RCAF personnel in our own squadrons on whom the RAF would be relying to a substantial extent to maintain its strength.'[8]

The air staff realized, however, that they 'were bound to recognise the Cana-dian Government's right in principle to set up such an objective.' Although accepting that the RCAF would field a 'self-contained and self-supporting' force against Japan, Whitehall nonetheless hoped 'that in the event we shall find that they are prepared to be reasonable in the exercise of the control which they are claiming after the defeat of Germany.' Moreover, Power had assured Balfour 'that there was no question of Canada's not being willing in the post-German phase to place her Air Force under the strategical direction of the Royal Air Force.' Similar assurances were given to Malcolm MacDonald, the British high commissioner in Ottawa: Power preferred to continue on at Britain's side after the defeat of Germany because it was 'in the family. The devil you know rather than the devil you do not.'[9]

What, then, had been the meaning of the aide-memoire handed to Balfour on 10 February? Arnold Heeney, the influential Cabinet secretary, feared that it might be taken as merely another, pro-forma, demand for status 'rather than a warning that the Canadian government intend to have and exercise a real freedom of choice' in deciding both the size of their forces and the theatre in which they would be employed. When the Cabinet met on 22 February to approve the Balfour-Power agreement, Heeney made this case, pointing to the contradiction between the independence demanded on 10 February and the fact that the forty-seven RCAF squadrons allocated to the Pacific were all destined for Air Command, South East Asia. (Out of the phase two total of ninety-three, forty-six would remain in Europe.) The Cabinet secretary got the desired reaction. King said 'forcibly' that ninety-three squadrons were too many, and objected to the very idea of a Southeast Asia commitment – even though 413 Squadron and over 1300 men were already serving in that theatre – when Can-ada's interests lay in the Pacific, closer to home.[10]

The British were subsequently told that Ottawa did not feel committed to the figure of ninety-three raised during the Balfour-Power talks and, for the moment, there would be no commitments on the nature or extent of Canadian participation, either for the war on Japan or for the policing of Europe after Germany's defeat. This was a standard line for a government which, for two decades, had been arguing that hypothetical commitments to future British courses were dangerous and impolitic. Indeed, fearing the thin edge of the wedge in such matters, it was also entirely characteristic of the prime minister to turn down Power's request in March 1944 to allow a surplus Catalina squadron to be sent to Australia – on the grounds that it was a British effort to get a commitment in that area 'and to follow on with others later.'[11] While a prime-ministerial initiative for an independent RCAF force in the Pacific fitted the nationalist pattern King had demonstrated since the original BCATP negotiations in 1939, he was always assiduous in avoiding creeping entanglements.

Not in the least dissuaded by Ottawa's most recent pronouncements, the Air Ministry pressed for more information on Canada's phase two plans and asked Air Marshal L.S. Breadner, recently installed as AOC-in-C, RCAF Overseas, to provide details; but Mackenzie King was reluctant to say anything until the forthcoming prime ministers' conference in London. Nor did the British have, as yet, a strong sense of their own commitment to the Pacific, although the Air Ministry was at least hoping that target establishments would be based 'on the assumption that each participant will be responsible for its own organization and backing of administrative, training and ancillary services.'[12]

As it happened, little was achieved at the political level during the April conference. King played his usual cautious game in the British capital, simply stating that the Canadian parliament must have the final say on any new commitments, and endeavouring to ensure that the meeting's final communiqué conveyed no impression that there was a clear Commonwealth policy on the Japanese war. 'What our plans would be,' said King, 'would depend on how the war developed.'[13]

More definite figures were produced at the service end, even though there was as yet 'no background of agreed higher strategy or of political authority.' The RCAF, for instance, proposed a self-contained force of seventy-two squadrons under the 'direct control of the supreme commander.' There were more than enough aircrew then serving overseas to fill that number. Sixty squadrons – forty-five combat and fifteen transport – would be designated for Southeast Asia or, if it was to become a theatre of operations, to the north Pacific, because it 'would be intolerable to see thousands of US aircraft going through Canada and on to Japan without Canada taking an active part in the air war in this theatre.'[14]

Indeed, in negotiations with the RAF during the conference, Breadner suggested that it was 'in the minds of the Canadian Government' to make 'a strong Canadian contribution to south-east Asia organised in RCAF formations with a small contribution of mainly tactical types to the policing of Europe.' He also agreed on a planning figure of fifty-eight Canadian squadrons for phase two, forty-seven of which would go to Southeast Asia (made up of fourteen heavy-bomber, eighteen day-fighter, one night-fighter, one fighter-bomber, one light-bomber, two air/sea rescue, and ten transport squadrons) and eleven to the occupying forces in Europe. Neither Breadner nor the RAF seemed to notice – or know – that the Canadian prime minister had very clearly told his Cabinet in February that he did not want a big commitment to Southeast Asia. They did, however, canvass the possibility of a Canadian contribution to a strategic bomber force against the home islands of Japan. That at least was closer to Canada, and closer to where Mackenzie King wanted the RCAF to operate.[15]

The Breadner planning document returned to Ottawa with King, where it was eventually considered by the Cabinet. While the British were concentrating their efforts in Southeast Asia (Burma, Malaya, Singapore, and the Dutch East Indies), the Canadian politicians felt that 'Canadian and indeed Commonwealth interests might be better served if the Canadian contribution to the war against Japan were made in an "American" theatre, namely the North or West Pacific.' On 14 June the Cabinet tentatively accepted the figure of fifty-eight RCAF squadrons as a basis for planning phase two commitments, but made it clear that the government must have the freedom to choose the operational theatre it thought best. Obviously, the matter had to be discussed at the highest level with their allies.[16]

The government immediately contacted, however, was in London, not in Washington. Mackenzie King got in touch with Churchill on 27 June and reiterated his desire for the north Pacific. 'It would clearly be very difficult,' he said, 'to have the major Canadian air effort based, say, on south-east Asia if large United States forces were to operate from Northwest America.' His air minister, meanwhile, instructed Breadner to open discussions with the Air Ministry about a proposal to convert fourteen nominated RAF squadrons (the difference between the fifty-eight squadron figure and the forty-four Article XV squadrons) into complete RCAF units. Power thought the squadrons selected for transfer ought to be overwhelmingly made up of bomber, transport, and fighter types, with the emphasis on the latter. Lone or 'orphan' squadrons – those units that could not easily be grouped into an RCAF formation – were to be eschewed, 'owing to difficulties in administration and supply of aircrew.'[17]

Such specific demands – and Canada's preference to serve in the north Pacific – disturbed the British. 'Each dominion,' an Air Ministry official wrote, 'had concentrated on the more attractive roles, and acceptance of their pro-posals would have left the RAF with a hopelessly unbalanced force.' London therefore asked that the RCAF increase the number of squadron types it was willing to take on and accept some orphans as well. Typically, Breadner pronounced this reasonable, 'not more than our share,' and suggested to Ottawa that Canada had 'no alternative but to accept.' More than that, if the government was going to dispatch the RCAF to act with US forces in the north Pacific, the Air Ministry ought to be informed. The British were planning 265 squadrons for the Japanese war, and were counting Canada's forty-seven among that number.[18]

Breadner was no longer in a position to influence policy as easily as he had when CAS. Moreover, Air Vice-Marshal W.A. Curtis was now the air member for air staff at Air Force Headquarters and he effectively argued against the Breadner plan because it did 'not appear to indicate any intention on the part of Air Ministry to form integral RCAF Groups or Formations.' Curtis was prepared to up the ante by only two air/sea rescue squadrons, should there be over-water operations, and one air observation squadron, if the army needed that capability. Power agreed. The RCAF could find forty-seven squadrons of three types, although the three additional squadrons suggested by Curtis might also be supplied. But forty-seven squadrons of too many types would mean that they would be 'scattered throughout the RAF organization ... We would place ourselves in the unenviable position of having to accede to the requests of the RAF.' If the Air Ministry did not 'see fit to accept this proposal,' the RCAF would send even fewer – thirty-eight squadrons – but again solely of three types: fourteen each of heavy bomber and long-range fighter and ten transport.[19]

The aim, as Power put it to Breadner on 25 July, was to have Canada 'provide two or three RCAF Groups under the command of an RCAF Headquarters which, in turn, would function under the operational direction of a supreme commander,' either British or American. Having already recommended the organization of two airfield construction units of about 5000 men each, complete with the requisite engineers and machinery, Breadner hoped that the RCAF would be providing its own maintenance and supply organization as well, which 'would immeasurably increase our independence of the RAF.' Such units were indeed necessary if the RCAF were to field a completely autonomous force in the Pacific, but the Canadian CAS, now Air Marshal Robert Leckie, was uncertain of the air force's ability – or perhaps the government's willingness – to do so. In his opinion, RCAF independence might well be limited, at least initially, to operational units and formation headquarters. 'We cannot expect to achieve the status of a completely independent Air Force quickly,' he explained, 'but rather by a process of growth. If, after we have our headquarters, groups and squadrons formed, we find we still have the energy, money and men to spare, we can take up these other commitments gradually, relieving the RAF as we do so.'[20]

In August Balfour again met with Power in Ottawa. Not yet having completed their own planning, the British were not keen to have the matter of squadron types to be organized for the Far East discussed at all, but the Canadian minister took the initiative, reiterating his offer of up to forty-seven squadrons of three basic types (unless the RAF would prefer only thirty-eight instead), although he also indicated his willingness to consider forming a wing of three general reconnaissance (GR) squadrons for service against enemy submarines and shipping in the north Pacific. However, if operations from 'North-western America' were prosecuted against Japan, he explained that the bulk of the RCAF would have to operate in this theatre 'for political and other reasons.'[21]

Although Balfour and the vice chief of the air staff, Sir Douglas Evill, were confident that they would eventually 'reach a reasonable arrangement with Breadner over the Canadian contribution,' Power's position was worrying. The RAF had always counted on a significant contribution of RCAF squadrons for a strategic bomber force against Japan, and the withdrawal of a large number for service in the north Pacific would have serious consequences and call for a much increased RAF commitment. The RAF had also tried to allocate a share of the principal strategic roles to each dominion participating in the proposed Far Eastern force, but the RCAF's unwillingness to commit to more than three basic squadron types would 'react on the pattern of the RAF in that theatre and tend to increase the lack of balance already very noticeable in its projected make up.' The Air Ministry not only wanted additional squadron types, but also more second- and third-line servicing and administrative units behind the RCAF's own squadrons. By the end of August, however, London had conceded the Canadian case on squadron types: the RCAF's contribution would be made up of transport, heavy-bomber, and fighter squadrons only.[22]

That still left the question of geography to be resolved. In an aide-memoire prepared for the Canadian government in late July, the British War Cabinet planning staff, while not ruling out service in the north Pacific, had set out their hopes that the RCAF would support the British Army in Southeast Asia and that the heavy bomber squadrons would join the strategic bomber force 'wherever it may be deployed.' Power retorted, through Breadner, that 'the Canadian Government has not changed its attitude and still persists that if hostilities take place in the North Pacific, Canada's principal effort should be in that theatre.' The air minister had his leader's support in this regard, although Mackenzie King was determined not to have as large a force as he was sure Power wanted. King told Cabinet on 31 August that 'Canada's contribution should be one made north of the Equator, as had been the case with our contribution to Europe,' while Power chimed in that this Canadian effort ought to be alongside US forces.[23]

On 6 September 1944 Cabinet met for the entire afternoon. Members had before them a chiefs of staff recommendation that Canada ought to be represented in the final assault on Japan as a means of 'avenging Hong Kong, saving face in the East, and restoring Canadian military prestige.' No one disagreed, nor was there apparently any demur from the chiefs' assertion that the north Pacific was of 'particular importance to Canada both geographically and politically.' There was also a consensus that the contribution of the air force ought to be smaller than contemplated, although there would be more questions and inevitable pressure from the defence ministers for larger commitments.[24]

King returned to the attack a week later. The Cabinet had assembled in Quebec City, where the prime minister was scheduled to host US president Franklin D. Roosevelt and British prime minister Winston Churchill as they and their chiefs of staff met to discuss the higher direction of the war. The prime minister recorded in his diary that the Cabinet was badly divided. Two Nova Scotia ministers, J.L. Ilsley and Angus L. Macdonald, were strong advocates of 'fighting anywhere and making no distinction between the north Pacific and the South Pacific.' Naval minister Macdonald, a resolute opponent of his leader on a broad range of issues, underlined the navy's wish to serve with the British. Ilsley, the minister of finance, added that service in the north Pacific would mean service with the Americans, and that in turn meant costly new equipment and weapons acquisitions. There is no record of other opposition, but clearly the prime minister believed himself under siege. 'I had to do most of the fighting myself to maintain what I would call the only tenable position which means keeping our forces for North and Central Pacific areas.'[25]

The prime minister also thought that he would have to confront the British directly – Winston Churchill first and then his chiefs of staff – 'in order that I could explain the political situation and what would be involved in raising an issue in Canada on the question of fighting what would be termed Imperial wars.' As it turned out, however, Churchill assiduously cultivated King, giving him precisely what was needed to fight the doubters in his own government. The 'Octagon' Conference was a thoroughly Anglo-American affair – King having no part in the strategic discussions that focused on the Pacific war – but the gathering provided a forum for Canadian discussions with British and American leaders and in particular for a special meeting of the Canadian Cabinet at the Citadel on 14 September. Churchill was present, and the Canadian and British chiefs of staff joined in later.[26]

Not yet aware that Churchill would be helpful, King warned his British counterpart that he must keep the political imperative very much to the fore: 'we were contemplating a general election ... he would understand that our policies would have to be considered in light of the issues that might be fought out on the platform and we wanted to be perfectly sure of our position.' Churchill understood completely. According to the prime minister, he did not expect Canadians 'to fight in any tropical region.' The 'real position was that the Americans wanted to control the whole war in the Pacific themselves. That the British felt that they must go in and recover possessions in Burma, Singapore etc. That this would be done by the British themselves. That he would not expect us to participate in that area.' When the chiefs of staff joined in the discussion, Churchill turned dramatically to his chief of the air staff and asked, 'Why do you put such a heavy burden on the Canadians?'[27]

For King this was complete vindication. Every argument he had put forward in Cabinet had been sustained. There was no need for service in the south, no need for an air force as large as the RCAF and the RAF were contemplating, and probably no need for a military commitment at all until the last phase of the war against Japan itself, a phase that might be many, many months in the future. 'Churchill indicated he thought we were generous in our readiness to participate in the Pacific. He made mention of Hong Kong and our feeling perhaps that we would wish to be represented on that account.' And Roosevelt, with whom King discussed the matter on 14 September, agreed that Canada's contribution need not be large and need not come 'for some time.'[28]

The Quebec Conference accepted in principle that Canadian forces would participate in phase two of the war. The Americans agreed that a Commonwealth fleet should contribute as soon as possible to the US effort in the main theatre of operations against Japan, and that a self-contained Commonwealth force of long-range bombers would be formed to take part in the assault against the Japanese home islands. The British specifically offered forty long-range bomber squadrons, twenty of which would act as aerial tankers, but serious questions remained about the feasibility of refuelling Lancasters and the locations of suitable bases and facilities. Final arrangements were left for the most senior military planners to discuss after Quebec. With the Lancaster's design a full generation behind that of the Boeing B-29 Superfortress currently in service with the USAAF in the Pacific theatre – carrying three tons of bombs, the latter had an operational range of 3000 miles, twice that of the Lancaster – it was apparent that the impact of such a Commonwealth force, 'whose presence in the main theatre was judged not to be strategically essential,' would be limited. Nevertheless, a provisional plan was accepted by the joint chiefs of staff on 27 October (subject to suitable bases becoming available) for an Anglo-Canadian bombing force of three groups to participate in the final attack against Japan.[29]

At the Canadian Cabinet meeting of 14 September, the chief of the British air staff, Sir Charles Portal, indicated that he expected the RCAF contribution to the war against Japan to be eighteen heavy-bomber and fourteen fighter squadrons. Later that day, however, in talks with the Canadian chiefs, Portal added ten transport squadrons, one air/sea rescue and one AOP squadron, making a total of forty-four for the Pacific, while fourteen more would be used in the policing of Europe. Curtis commented that the RAF had accepted 'our ultimatum' and 'decreased the numbers of types as we requested.' Portal, however, had made the fatal tactical error of minimizing his requirements when presenting them to his political audience earlier in the day, giving King ammunition in his effort to reduce the number of RCAF squadrons below the fifty-eight that had been agreed upon that spring. Although Curtis still favoured a major commitment, Leckie explained that he had already been instructed to submit a proposal substantially paring down the earlier demands.[30]

Less than a week after the Quebec Conference, the CAS submitted a new plan for phase two, and it is perhaps no coincidence that it set forth a new total of thirty-two squadrons, seven for Europe and twenty-five for Japan.[31] Air Force Headquarters argued that 'the minimum number of heavy bomber squadrons that could be formed into an integral self-contained strategic air force to have reasonable effect on the enemy is considered ... to be ten squadrons ... Therefore, it is proposed that for participation in the war against Japan, the basic RCAF contingent should be ten heavy bombers, eight long-range fighters and seven long-range transport.' It was convenient, even desirable, to continue service alongside the British, the memorandum continued, but experience had shown that the RCAF must never again allow its contribution to be subsumed by a military ally.

From the experience gained in the United Kingdom, it is apparent that, unless the RCAF component is organized as an integral formation, the effort of the Canadians becomes clouded by the activities of the air forces of our larger allies, such as the USAAF and the RAF. This is apparent by the fact that Canadian participation in the air war over Germany never received due recognition until such time as No 6 RCAF Bomber Group was formed and commenced operations as a wholly Canadian component. Therefore, it is considered necessary that our air force, which will operate against Japan, should be organized into a Canadian formation, and it is proposed that the forces detailed above be formed into an RCAF composite group, commanded by a Canadian Air Officer Commanding ...

Therefore, it is proposed that the RCAF composite group come under the operational control of the RAF commander in the field in a similar way that No 6 Group comes under the operational control of Bomber Command. However, the administrative control should be purely Canadian and therefore the RCAF composite group should be directly under a RCAF Headquarters for administration.[32]

Leckie also scaled-back Canada's groundcrew requirements and rejected a British request for 25,000 personnel to serve behind RCAF squadrons in the Pacific theatre. 'I have given this most careful thought and consider it out of line. You will appreciate,' he told the minister, 'that these personnel will not be under our immediate command but will be working with similar RAF units and, therefore, we lose all the benefits that we hope to gain from an integrated Air Force.' Instead, the CAS suggested an 'Aerodrome Construction, Maintenance and Defence Unit of 6000, all ranks, complete with aerodrome construction equipment ... self-contained under the direction of a Canadian AOC-in-C.' These 6000 would be part of a group of approximately 15,000, all ranks, who would be used as replacements or in support of combat units to handle matters such as base hospitals and supply depots. This would bring the entire phase two force to just under 33,000 men, costing $160,591,000 to start and $331,165,000 annually.[33]

The latest proposal was taken to Cabinet on 20 September. It remained on the table, Mackenzie King again making it clear that he wanted token forces only in the Pacific. The government's business, he insisted, was to save the lives of young men. The prime minister then stated that he wanted every member of the Cabinet to express his views, a manoeuvre that had the effect of isolating the service ministers. 'There were only the three defence ministers,' King recalled, 'who said nothing but realized that they were put on the spot.'[34]

A hard decision on the commitment for phase two was not taken until the end of 1944. On 11 December the Cabinet, with the chiefs of staff present, approved a commitment of eleven squadrons for the occupation of Europe and twenty-two for operations against Japan, and it was now agreed that the RCAF would be employed with the RAF in the Pacific theatre, eliminating the necessity of unwanted expenditures on American equipment. The establishment was set at 23,000, not the 33,000 desired by the air staff.[35]

The Minister, in his anxiety to obtain War Cabinet approval for the 33 Squadron proposal, agreed to delete the personnel requirements for ancillaries and CMU [Construction and Maintenance Unit] and gave the figure 23,000 as the complement necessary. In addition to this 10,000 reduction to the original estimate, squadron types were changed and our participation altered from 25 and 7 to 22 and 11. I did not agree to the 23,000 figure as representing the bare squadron requirements for the 33 squadrons in the final proposal which was approved by War Cabinet Committee.

I am afraid the 23,000 figure will have to stand for the time being, at least until the Minister for Air is appointed and the opportunity for re-opening with War Cabinet presents itself.[36]

The new limit on establishment had serious implications. Leckie pointed out that 23,000 were not enough to meet even the bare squadron requirements. Certainly there could be no contribution beyond the designated squadrons themselves – nothing, therefore, in the way of ancillary units, which were so essential to the operation of a group, not even enough for a group headquarters, unless reductions were made elsewhere. Air Vice-Marshal J.A. Sully wrote to Colin Gibson* in January 1945 that such units directly supported the group's activities, and 'since they will come under the RCAF Group Headquarters, it is most desirable that they be Canadian rather than RAF.'[37]

The government also opted for a different number of squadrons and a different balance in the force for Japan than Leckie had recommended. This was the direct consequence of representations made by the Air Ministry after it received notification of Leckie's thirty-two squadron proposal. 'While we must naturally conform to your Government's decision in these matters,' Air Marshal Evill wrote on 6 October, 'I must frankly admit that it confronts us with certain difficulties in keeping up the necessary front line strength.'

As regards the Far East theatre, I think you are aware that we are planning to deploy a force of about 36 Lancaster Squadrons capable of operating at increased normal range by means of the flight refuelling technique. We have planned that the fighter support for this force shall be long range fighters to act as escorts or support for the strike element of the bombers. It would, therefore, produce a better balance in your force if we retained this same proportion in the RCAF Squadrons. I should like to suggest, therefore, that the RCAF contribution in the Eastern Theatre should consist of 12 HB (potentially 6 Strike and 6 Tanker Squadrons) and 6 Fighter Squadrons, and I see no difficulty in organizing these 18 squadrons as an RCAF formation.[38]

Evill's reconfiguration won the day. There would be twelve heavy-bomber squadrons, six long-range day-fighters, three transport squadrons, and one air/sea rescue squadron. The Air Ministry accepted the concept of an RCAF formation headquarters to administer Canadian units and hoped that Ottawa would see 'that throughout we have done our best to provide for self-contained Canadian formations. In the active theatre our proposals constitute the RCAF units as a single Canadian task force. In the European theatre they will be Canadian Wings under the appropriate functional Command though with an RCAF HQ on present lines.'[39]

The twelve bomber and six fighter squadrons would form one of Tiger Force's three groups. It was not expected that these units would be needed for at least three months after the war in Europe had ended, an event projected to take place at the end of June 1945. All the overseas heavy-bomber squadrons were to remain operational. Five fighter squadrons – Nos 401, 402, 403, 438, and 440, in addition to 400 Squadron, then an army cooperation unit – would

---

* C.G. Power had resigned from Cabinet on 23 November to protest the imposition of conscription for overseas service. Naval minister Macdonald took on the air portfolio until Colin Gibson was appointed acting minister for air on 10 January 1945.

form the fighter element. Transport squadrons would be derived by converting 422 and 423 squadrons (flying boats) and 407 Squadron (general reconnaissance), while 404 Squadron would become the air/sea rescue unit. In making these selections, Breadner attempted to give the oldest squadrons the 'place of honour' for the war that was to come.[40]

Planning for 'Tiger Force,' the name which the RAF had given to the very-long range (VLR) Pacific bomber force, was beginning to take shape by year's end. The first administrative outline for 'Operation Mould' (later changed to 'Operation Tiger') was completed on 23 November 1944, setting out the composition of the force, types of aircraft, training, maintenance organization, lines of communication, planning and intergroup coordination, and manpower requirements. A commander-designate of the force, Air Vice-Marshal Hugh Lloyd, was appointed the same month. The RAF intended to deploy thirty-six heavy-bomber squadrons equipped with Lancasters (and later re-equipped with Avro Lincolns) and would use air refuelling to bomb Japan from as yet undetermined locations in the Pacific. Eighteen fighter squadrons, initially Mustangs, eventually to be de Havilland Hornets, would escort the bombers, and the force would include four long-range transport, one air/sea rescue, and one photo-reconnaissance squadron.[41]

The problem of providing ground support for such a force remained unresolved, but Ottawa was not alone in its desire to shift some of that burden onto an ally. The British hoped that much of the infrastructure and logistical support for Tiger Force would be provided by the Americans, although it was a source of concern that so little concrete discussion had taken place with Washington. As Portal wrote on 27 January 1945, 'It is becoming increasingly important to start planning with the Americans for the participation of our VLR Bombing Force in the Pacific war ... We know very little about American plans for the establishment of VLR bases and are conscious of the difficulties ... It is highly desirable that the American agreement in principle to our participation should be translated into firm arrangements for the division of responsibility for the provision of facilities.'[42]

At the Yalta Conference in February 1945, however, the British learned the full extent of Washington's indifference to supporting a token British contribution to the final attack on Japan. According to the Americans, their resources were fully stretched and Tiger Force would have to be self-supporting 'from tide-water to aircraft.' 'This placed the project on a completely different footing. It meant mounting a large force on a base or bases, whose precise nature was still unknown but which must be built and equipped entirely with British resources over British lines of supply, at a distance of over 14,000 miles from England.' Compounding the problem, it would be a long time before there was an American decision about just where Tiger Force might be based.[43]

The Canadian government naturally wanted a volunteer force. Yet by early 1945 Overseas Headquarters was arguing the case for simply posting all personnel for phase two. It made sense for some categories – command positions, certain aircrew, and specialist trades such as Lancaster radar mechanics – to be assigned, and the policy would be equitable only if it was applied to all personnel. In addition, it would 'simplify enormously the work of repatriation and manning.' Air Force Headquarters agreed, although individual needs and aspirations would be taken into account whenever practicable, and there would be the right to appeal any decision. There would also be an emphasis on men who had not served overseas or not completed a tour of duty. The Cabinet wisely decided, however, that the force to be employed against Japan would be chosen only from those who elected to serve. The prime minister announced the decision to Parliament on 4 April 1945. Any whiff of conscription, he thought, 'would be just suicidal and absolutely wrong.'[44]

It was also agreed that squadrons ought to be returned to Canada for re-forming and re-equipping. Leckie was originally of the view that Canadians ought to remain in Britain for reasons of convenience and continuity, but by January 1945 he was arguing that there were 'strong reasons from the point of view of morale why the formation and training of the RCAF VLR group should be carried out in Canada.' By then Overseas Headquarters had surveyed 'many of our personnel,' and warned that 'they all affirm that they will not volunteer unless first given leave in Canada.' King's 4 April announcement to parliament regarding conscription confirmed that no one serving in Europe would proceed to the Pacific without volunteering, getting the opportunity to come home, and having thirty days disembarkation leave. This arrangement had the added advantage that the Pacific route could be used for shipping the Canadian component of Tiger Force to the Far East, relieving pressure on the much-used Middle East route. 'If one of the objects of mounting the VLR force is that it should be a self-sufficient RCAF Task Force,' Overseas Headquarters affirmed, 'then it must obtain this self-sufficiency during the build-up and this can only be done in Canada.'[45]

The availability of personnel for airfield construction was rapidly moving towards the centre of the Air Ministry's preoccupations. The RCAF's construction and maintenance unit, however, had been one of the cuts made to the thirty-three squadron proposal before it had been taken to Cabinet at the end of 1944. A month later the Air Ministry, casting around for 15,000 men to build aerodromes, approached the RCAF to enquire if the Canadians 'could not go even further' than the promised squadrons. Leckie replied that the decision was the government's, but a construction and maintenance unit would have to be 'in lieu of, and not in addition to, some portion of the Force already agreed upon.' In short, the 23,000 ceiling would stand.[46]

Other RCAF officers remained wary of the ceiling's effect, however. In the opinion of Sully, it was 'considered most important that the RCAF Group have two labour constructional units which will be large enough to ensure that the Canadian force may be as self-sufficient as possible.' The view of the RAF that was conveyed to Canada, indeed, was that the whole question of US acceptance of Tiger Force 'would stand or fall by whether we showed ourselves genuinely willing to provide all we could by way of supporting, ie., constructional, manpower.' The British calculated in mid-February 1945 that they would need 30,000 of these workers and they looked to Canada to supply a significant proportion.[47]

The RCAF could therefore be expected to return to the charge. When the United States Army Air Force requested information on 7 February about the provision of works construction units, they were told that Leckie was making 'tentative enquiries to reactions in Canada' to the provision of one or two Construction Wings that would have to be formed as units. On 28 February the RCAF was once again before Cabinet asking for 6000 construction personnel and other additions to the force. At the time of the 'Octagon' Conference at Quebec, it was explained, planning had been based on the understanding that the US would make available operational airfields in the Pacific. The Americans, however, were not in a position to do this, and the Anglo-Canadians would have to provide services for themselves. This raised the question whether the number of RCAF squadrons ought to be reduced to allow for the necessary support personnel within the agreed limit of 23,000, or whether the Canadian commitment should be expanded to 40,000 in order to include supply, construction, and ancillary units 'which would permit of their organization as a fully integrated and independent group within the British force.' The politicians did not budge: 23,000 it would have to be, although the air staff was instructed to examine carefully the 'new circumstances' and what they meant for 'an appropriate Canadian contingent to the Pacific.'[48]

The commander of Tiger Force was in Ottawa at the time pressing the case for construction personnel. Lloyd let it be known that he needed 10,000 Canadian engineers, even if that meant fewer squadrons. The Americans had made it clear to him that the British 'would have to pay our full "entrance fee" in the construction of airfields. There was no question of doing it "on the cheap."' Nor was there any question of assistance from the USAAF. The British would have to think in terms of a location, perhaps in the Philippines, 'where we could go in and support ourselves in every respect.' Leckie was again sympathetic, telling Lloyd that 'Canada should make a handsome effort in constructing airfields on the basis that it would be far better to deploy six Squadrons by the end of this year than to deploy none this year but ten Squadrons midway through next year.'[49]

Despite the Cabinet's decision to maintain the 23,000 ceiling, air force planners continued to favour a more substantial contingent. With an increase in phase two personnel, they argued, it would be possible to concoct a force of twelve bomber and six fighter squadrons, along with one air/sea rescue squadron, supported by administrative, medical, signals, logistics, and aerodrome defence personnel as well as a 6000-strong construction unit. These 32,709 men comprised 'the smallest unit which the RCAF might reasonably expect to man and still be given control as a purely RCAF force.' The alternative was to place the Canadian contingent at the disposal of the Air Ministry for use in whatever capacity would best assist the RAF, and thus to concede that RCAF independence was lost – exactly the situation that had beset the service through four years of European war and caused such endless hassling between Ottawa and Whitehall. After considering these options, the chiefs of staff decided to seek an expanded commitment from Cabinet one more time.[50]

Facing a groundcrew shortage themselves, the British CAS also approached his prime minister to ask that pressure be put on Ottawa for a promise of specialized construction men. After all, this was a field in which the Canadians were admitted to excel. A provisional offer of works engineers had already been made, but Portal wanted a concrete commitment of 'help in this form.' The result was a vaguely worded communication from Churchill to King on 20 March asking for his 'blessing to the efforts we are making to ensure that our contribution should be prompt and effective.' The RAF was negotiating for a base area in the Calgayan valley in northern Luzon, and it was 'most desirable ... that the British and Canadian Bomber Force should be self-contained and not dependent on the Americans for the construction of airfields and the provision of other facilities.'[51]

What Churchill did not say was that the whole question of RAF involvement in the Far East was at issue. The Air Ministry's own plans for Tiger Force were being drastically scaled down, evidently because it was not judged possible to supply and maintain the large contingent which had originally been contemplated. And further reductions, Breadner reported home on the same day Churchill sent his message to King, might be in the offing. The force might even be squeezed down to only a handful of squadrons. The AOC-in-C intended 'to take the stand that this proposed alteration in the size and nature of the total commitment would require Canada to examine once again what proportion she is prepared to undertake and that negotiations to determine this must be government to government.' Leckie agreed that the new information changed everything. Previous calculations had been thrown into the 'melting pot.' King's reply was accordingly cautious and non-committal 'We have been concerned to ensure that we do not find ourselves involved, on somewhat scanty premises, in a disproportionate commitment. Particularly is this so since the practical utility of certain of the proposals which have been made seems open to question as respects considerations of both time and space. We have as yet seen no statement of the latest proposals. When they have been received they will be given immediate consideration.'[52]

Churchill, receiving this communication, wondered what all the fuss was about. 'Shall we not have,' he minuted to his air planners, 'far more British aircraft than can be provided with jumping off points?' But Canada was needed. His air staff pointed out that the British prime minister was overlooking the requirement for construction personnel. Portal now wanted 10,000 Canadian engineers, as well as ten RCAF bomber and three VLR transport units. That was about half of all the squadrons that were now projected for a greatly reduced Tiger Force, and he concluded that 'if the Canadians do not come in with us our impact on the enemy is likely to be on a very small scale.' Whitehall had serious doubts about Britain's capacity to mount a major offensive against Japan without a drastic reduction in the operational commitments planned for other theatres, even after embracing an American assurance to provide air defence for Tiger Force that had allowed the fighter element to be dropped from their requirements. The idea was even in the air that the RAF's next step would be 'to take the resources which are available without affecting other plans, offer them to the United States for pooled action in the theatre, and request that a token force be sent to operate on bases built by the Americans.' In view of the British mood, Overseas Headquarters went so far as to advise Ottawa that the RCAF might not be required in Tiger Force at all.[53]

Nevertheless, that time was not yet. The RCAF understood that the British would soon be asking for a commitment of thirteen VLR squadrons and 18,400 men. They were also hoping for the 10,000 engineers and a further 8000 men for the eleven squadrons engaged in the occupation of Germany. Even though there was no official request, this proposal was put before Cabinet on 19 April, but the answer was the same as it had been each time an attempt had been made to break away from the 23,000 limit. No sufficient reason, in the view of the politicians, had been advanced for an increase in the agreed commitment for participation in the Pacific War.[54]

Perhaps reflecting the view of British authorities, the new AOC-in-C at Overseas Headquarters, Air Marshal G.O. Johnson, was immediately critical of Ottawa's 'indecision' over Tiger Force. He suggested that RAF planning had been 'seriously' hampered, and that 'an early and firm decision concerning our participation is urgently required.' Ottawa had been crystal clear in its policy, however – there was a 23,000 ceiling, and there would be no construction unit in addition to that total – although the government held open the possibility of changes once the British made known the 'actual need' and the 'probable effectiveness' of the force.

Johnson's concerns that the RCAF might not be pulling its weight did not receive a very sympathetic hearing from Curtis, who was temporarily filling in as CAS. In sending news of the Cabinet's decision of 11 April, Curtis told Johnson that the British would certainly be disappointed by the decision not to send engineers, but it might assist him in his discussions if he pointed out that 'since the RCAF has devoted the major portion of its war effort to a secondary role in Phase I in the form of the BCATP we might expect to devote our major effort in Phase II directly against the enemy.' Johnson should also know that, whatever private complaints Whitehall might have about the Canadians, recent British actions had given rise to doubts in Canada about whether any kind of bomber force at all was necessary.[55]

Certainly there were doubts in Washington about the need for Tiger Force, and the British were finding the United States a difficult and sceptical ally as they attempted to negotiate their way into the air war against Japan. Air Vice-Marshal Lloyd, back in Washington at the end of April 1945, found himself forced to make an 'off the record' promise of 20,000 engineers by 1 October and eight Lincoln squadrons by 1 November simply to get a hearing from the Americans. 'I knew the bid would be entertained only if the Engineer force was really big, as only a big force could do the job in the time and so play a part in the landing on Japan.' Lloyd returned home warning that speed combined with a willingness to take on a major construction project was 'the essence of this proposal and if we cannot meet the time programme as suggested, or meet the Engineer requirement, we should abandon the Tiger Force operation.' He also 'wheeled and dealed' with the Americans for a base. This time they discussed the possibility of using the tiny island of Miyako in the Ryukus chain near Formosa and adjacent to Okinawa, just 990 miles from Japan. Okinawa had been attacked by the Americans on 2 April and Miyako was slated for similar attention in due course. As the fighting on Okinawa raged on, however, plans for a move against Miyako were set aside. Tiger Force had yet to find a home.[56]

Without a base it was difficult to make specific decisions, and in London Johnson's frustration now shifted from Ottawa to Whitehall. He was discovering that the changing situation was so nebulous that he could report no definite plans about the size, nature, and timing of the RCAF's contribution. The British could provide no satisfactory information about the 'practical military utility and necessity' of the operation against Japan, and he was becoming convinced that 'the US will have forces more than sufficient for the task and bases available, and therefore a British or Canadian VLR force is not militarily essential but is solely a political British prestige consideration.' Britain had committed itself publicly to a major role against the Japan home islands in its efforts to restore imperial prestige in the Far East, and it would not be easy to back down from such pronouncements.[57]

It now seemed likely that the British would be seeking eight heavy-bomber and three transport squadrons, and some 2000 engineers from the RCAF. To prepare the ground for the bomber component, Johnson asked that Nos 419, 428, 431, and 434 Squadrons stand down from operations as soon as possible so they could return to Canada for training. Nos 408, 420, and 425 were to be next, and, along with 405 Squadron, would complete the bomber force. These squadrons would not be ready before 1 October, and they would not be among the first units deployed to the Far East. After taking leave, personnel were slated to report to their squadrons for training, which would be carried out on Canadian-made Lancaster Xs at Eastern Air Command bases over a six-week period. This would be followed by a transfer to Britain for another six weeks of conversion training to Lancaster VII's or Lincolns, if available. As for the prospective transport squadrons, No 426 Squadron was transferred to Transport Command on 25 May, but Nos 422 and 423 were still on coastal operations. The Liberators planned for these squadrons would not be available until at least September. Johnson wanted permission to begin assigning Canadians to staging posts in Southeast Asia and to detail groundcrew for service in England. Leckie, while sanctioning the formation of a transport wing, stepped firmly on both of these suggestions.[58]

On 30 May an American offer of a base finally came. Okinawa had fallen, and it had more numerous facilities for aerodromes than previously thought: Washington said that they could provide room on the island for ten squadrons immediately; the other ten squadrons might come later depending on developments. But there were limits and conditions. The United States wanted firm evidence of a British intention to take on their own logistics and construction work. In fact, 15,000 engineers would have to be quickly on the ground if ten squadrons were to be operational by 1 March 1946. If only half that number of engineers were available, Lloyd was told that 'all we could expect' was four squadrons by early 1946. The Tiger Force commander was left 'in no doubt that if we wanted to improve on our rate of deployment we must give more engineers.' He stressed to Whitehall 'that the Americans distrust us. They think we are trying to deploy our Force on the cheap.' Although realizing that they could not provide a full complement of construction personnel or logistics support – and counting on Canadian engineers to help offset the deficit – the British chiefs of staff nonetheless accepted the American offer on 4 June. The first cargo ships for Tiger Force sailed from Liverpool on the 20th.[59]

Whitehall now approached Canada with a firm request for assistance. Churchill sent King a message on 16 June, underlining the need for construction engineers, 2500 of whom it was earnestly desired would be Canadian, asking for two bomber squadrons for Tiger Force's first deployment, and holding out the hope that 'another six Canadian heavy bomber squadrons will be available for the second contingent of 10 squadrons if and when this is approved.' Having had an intimation that this communication was coming, the Canadian Cabinet had already authorized a construction contingent, as well as two bomber and three transport squadrons, all of which could be provided within the 23,000 ceiling, but King and his ministers deferred consideration of six additional bomber squadrons for the next deployment.[60]

By the time that King replied to Churchill, however, it had undoubtedly been brought to his attention that only 335 volunteer construction personnel had yet been found among 6600 who had been approached. His telegram of 19 June, therefore, committed only two bomber and three transport squadrons. The question of construction personnel was being 'actively explored,' but no specific number could be promised.[61]

Having accepted the American offer in the hope that both the United States and Canada would make good the RAF's own manpower shortages, the British chiefs of staff were disappointed with Ottawa's response. They vented their frustrations at a meeting on 22 June, accusing Canada – rather unfairly, given that they were attempting to play the same game themselves – of being 'up to their old tricks of trying to get out of their proper share in providing the unspectacular but necessary support for their operational units.' Portal followed up this discussion with a message to Leckie suggesting that 'at no time have we received any warning that you might not be able to participate on the agreed basis.' The Canadian CAS disagreed and reminded Portal that he had never given definite support to an engineering contribution. Nevertheless, he understood and shared his British counterpart's embarrassment at the turn of events: 'the difficulty in which you now find yourself and which from a planning angle is similar to my own is thoroughly appreciated.'[62]

The RCAF also asked Cabinet to make a decision about the six additional bomber squadrons for the second echelon. On 28 June the air minister, Colin Gibson, told his colleagues that definite plans were proceeding for a reinforcement of ten Tiger Force squadrons. The prime minister remained wary of a major commitment, but Leckie was told to return with the fullest possible details about the financial and personnel requirements of the force for Japan. This he did on 12 July. He needed 15,000 men, he said, and the cost, including training in Canada, was estimated to be $143.5 million right away and $192.1 million annually after that. These projections included the six extra squadrons, equipment, maintenance, medical and other essential services, but not construction engineers, few of whom were willing to volunteer. Cabinet gave its approval and London was informed, 'You can make it clear to Air Ministry that the provision of these 6 additional bomber squadrons for the Pacific was authorized on the condition that the occupational force be reduced by two bomber squadrons [from eleven to nine] thus keeping the total manpower allotment within the 23,000 approved limit.'[63]

The advanced element of Tiger Force was to consist of one RAF Mosquito and nine Lancaster squadrons, five from the RAF, two from the RCAF, and one each from Australia and New Zealand. The follow-up element would be made up of one Lancaster-Catalina air/sea rescue squadron and eleven Lincoln squadrons. Two RCAF squadrons, numbers 419 and 428, were to be at their base and ready to operate by 1 January 1946. The force would ultimately consist of two operational groups, one Canadian and one British, and, when the second contingent arrived in theatre, a Canadian group headquarters was planned. Tiger Force Headquarters itself would be integrated and 50 per cent Canadian. The RCAF was making an effort, wherever possible, to have fully Canadian units in support of squadrons 'on a basis commensurate with our front line effort.' Consistent with the prime minister's policy announced on 4 April 1945, the RCAF was canvassed for volunteers – 21.5 per cent of the 103,402 men and women interviewed by 15 June had volunteered for service in the Pacific. The Tiger Force commander agreed to the participation of women, members of the Women's Division having volunteered at a much higher rate than men.[64]

The British chiefs of staff assembled on 6 August to discuss the latest developments with Lloyd, freshly returned from the United States, where he was still complaining about the uncertainty of a Canadian engineering contribution. On the same day, an American B-29 dropped the atomic bomb on the Japanese city of Hiroshima. This was followed by a second atomic attack on the 9th, this time on Nagasaki, and Japan surrendered unconditionally on 14 August.[65] Tiger Force, it turned out, was never more than a paper tiger.

PART TWO

The Fighter War

No 110 Squadron groundcrew in the machine shop at Odiham, mid-1940. (PMR 93-297)

Among the officers of No 1(F) Squadron, RCAF (later No 401), photographed at Croydon in July 1940, were a number who would play prominent roles in the history of the RCAF Overseas. Back row, l to r: R. Smither, T.B. Little, A.M. Yuile, E.W. Beardmore, B.D. Russel, E.C. Briese. Middle row: B.E. Christmas, Capt W.D. Rankin (medical officer), O.J. Peterson, G.R. McGregor, A.D. Nesbitt, S.T. Blaiklock, H.de M. Molson, E.M. Reyno, J.P.J. Desloges, E.A. McNab, P.B. Pitcher. Front row: G.G. Hyde, W.P. Sprenger, J.W. Kerwin. (PMR 80-620)

Wing Commander R.W. McNair, DFC and two Bars, of Springhill, Nova Scotia, was a highly successful fighter pilot who became a respected wing leader. The photo shows him early in his career as a pilot officer with No 411 Squadron. (PL 4988)

An Me 109E brought down in the Battle of Britain. (PL 3054)

Prime Minister Winston Churchill inspects bomb damage after the Luftwaffe's first major raid on London, 7 September 1940. (H 3976)

A No 1 Squadron Hurricane is refuelled in October 1940. (PMR 93-295)

Pilot Officer John Gillespie Magee, the author of 'High Flight,' in the cockpit of his No 412 Squadron Spitfire. (PMR 76-245)

Fitters work on the engine of a Lysander of No 110 Squadron, RCAF (later No 400), in a hangar at Odiham in the autumn of 1940. The objects in the stub wing protruding from the undercarriage are light bomb racks. (PMR 93-296)

Navigator's view of the cockpit of a No 406 Squadron Beaufighter. (CH 4893)

Pilots and observers of No 110 Squadron run to their Lysanders during an exercise. The two men in the foreground are an army liaison officer and his wireless operator. (CH 2414)

A No 410 Squadron gunner enters the turret of a Defiant night-fighter in late 1941. (PL 4799)

The undercarriage of a No 401 Squadron Hurricane II undergoing maintenance in the summer of 1941. (PL 4471)

A Beaufighter II of No 406 Squadron being refuelled. (CH 4895)

Bombing-up a No 402 Squadron Hurricane in early 1942. (PL 7122)

No 402 Squadron groundcrew inspect the carburettor air scoop of a Hurricane IIB. (PL 7121)

Air Marshal Sir Trafford Leigh-Mallory, AOC-in-C Fighter Command (here bearing a curious likeness to Adolf Hitler), speaks to an army liaison officer during Exercise Spartan. (H 27941)

One of the RCAF's top fighter leaders was Wing Commander L.V. Chadburn, DSO and Bar, DFC, who commanded the RCAF's Digby Wing and No 127 Wing of Second Tactical Air Force before his death in a flying accident on 13 June 1944. He is seen here when he commanded No 416 Squadron in late 1942. His Spitfire carries the squadron's distinctive lynx and maple leaf emblem. (PL 15079)

Spitfire Vs of No 421 taxi out in March 1943 bearing the temporary white markings applied to some aircraft participating in Exercise Spartan. (PL 15556)

Skeet shooting was considered a useful exercise for hand/eye coordination and provided practice in deflection shooting. (PL 7755)

The threat did not always come from the air or anti-aircraft guns. While reconnoitring a new airfield in Sicily, Squadron Leader P.S. Turner, DSO, DFC and Bar, and Flight Lieutenant A.U. Houle, DFC, of No 417 Squadron had their truck strike a Teller mine. Turner was trapped in the cab, 'badly lacerated and suffering from shock.' Houle was blown out of the door and 'had both eardrums punctured & was off flying 5 weeks.' His hat can be seen lying on the ground. (PMR 529)

A Spitfire V of No 417 Squadron in front of the Italian farmhouse that served as squadron headquarters at Lentini West, Sicily, during the autumn of 1943. (PL 18285)

With Marshal of the Royal Air Force Lord Trenchard are (l to r) Group Captain D.M. Smith, commanding No 39 (Reconnaissance) Wing, Squadron Leader R.A. Ellis, commanding No 400 Squadron, Wing Commander E.H. Moncrieff, commanding No 128 Airfield, Air Vice-Marshal W.F. Dickson (RAF), AOC No 83 Group, and Squadron Leader H.P Peters, commanding No 414 Squadron. Peters was to be killed in action on 4 November 1943. (PL 19596)

Pilots and ground personnel of No 430 Squadron with a Mustang I, in September 1943. (PL 22792)

Pilots of No 401 Squadron in the autumn of 1943. Flying Officer William T. Klersy, destined to become one of the RCAF's most successful pilots, is second from the right. (PL 22010)

Flight Lieutenant George Beurling, DSO, DFC, DFM and Bar, touches up the victory markings on his Spitfire, in late 1943, when he was flying with No 403 Squadron. (PL 22170)

Flight Lieutenant M.A. Cybulski (right) and his RAF navigator, Flight Lieutenant H.H. Sadbroke, stand by the badly burned tail of the No 410 Squadron Mosquito in which they shot down an enemy aircraft over the Netherlands on 25 September 1943. Their Mosquito was spattered with burning fuel and had one engine knocked out, but it reached the United Kingdom safely. (PL 19740)

The mainstay of the three RCAF army cooperation squadrons overseas during most of 1942 and 1943 was the Mustang I, seen here at dispersal in late 1943 while a captured Focke Wulf 190 flies low over the field. (PL 26337)

Fighter pilots of No 416 Squadron and a unit Spitfire in late 1943. (PL 15081)

A Messerschmitt BF 109 under attack by Squadron Leader A.U. Houle of No 417
Squadron over Anzio on 7 February 1944. Houle eventually shot the tail of the enemy
fighter off, some of the pieces damaging his Spitfire. (PMR 77-520)

With levelling jacks supporting the wings and rear fuselage and a plumb bob hanging
from the machine's nose, the guns of a Spitfire are harmonized. (PL 18516)

Briefing No 417 Squadron pilots before an operation, Marcionise, Italy, 22 January 1944. (PMR 77-528)

Arming the 20-millimetre Hispano cannon of a Spitfire. (PL 27501)

Wing commanders (Flying) carried their initials as code letters on their aircraft rather than using the codes of any of the squadrons making up the wing. Wing Commander H.C. Godefroy, DSO, DFC and Bar, held that appointment in No. 127 Wing from 19 September 1943 to 15 April 1944 and is seen here standing by his Spitfire IX at the end of that tour of duty. (PL 29352)

A recently delivered Mosquito is readied for operations by groundcrew of No 418 Squadron in the spring of 1944. (PL 29463)

Prior to the invasion of Europe, the Supreme Allied Commander, US General D.D. Eisenhower, inspects the Second Tactical Air Force station commanded by Group Captain C.R. Dunlap, RCAF. On Eisenhower's right is Air Marshal Sir Arthur Coningham, AOC-in-C Second TAF, and on his right, Air Chief Marshal Sir Trafford Leigh-Mallory, commander-in-chief of the Allied Expeditionary Air Forces. Dunlap, on Eisenhower's left, would subsequently become the last Canadian chief of the air staff, 1962–4. (PL 28711)

No 411 Squadron groundcrew apply white identification stripes in preparation for. D-Day. (PL 30827)

Air Marshal Sir Arthur Coningham addresses personnel of No 143 (RCAF) Wing of Second TAF on the eve of Operation Overlord. (PL 30188)

A Spitfire IX undergoes an engine change shortly before the Normandy invasion. (PL 29564)

Air Marshal Sir Arthur Coningham, commanding Second TAF, Air Vice-Marshal Harry Broadhurst, AOC No 83 Group (which contained the RCAF squadrons of 2nd TAF), and Air Chief Marshal Sir Arthur Tedder, deputy supreme commander of the Allied Expeditionary Forces, confer in Normandy. (CL 285)

No 417 Squadron 'erks' erect a mess tent in 1944. (PL 27748)

No 412 Squadron Spitfires at their new base of Beny-sur-Mer (B 4) soon after the Normandy landings. (PL 30268)

Groundcrew dig slit trenches in the early days of the Normandy campaign. Enemy activity was largely confined to sporadic bombing by night. (PL 30059)

A Repair and Salvage crew recovers a No 403 Squadron Spitfire in the field. (PL 31115)

Repacking a parachute in Normandy. (PL 31784)

A No 440 Squadron Typhoon serves as backdrop while part of a French field is cleared of its wheat crop. (PL 31378)

For a period in 1944, No 418's Mosquitos carried nose art representing characters from Al Capp's 'Li'l Abner' comic strip. This aircraft was normally flown by the squadron commander, Wing Commander R. Bannock, DSO, DFC and Bar, and shows his personal score of both enemy aircraft (swastikas) and V-1's. (PL 33521)

Typhoons of No 143 Wing in a maintenance area during the Normandy campaign. (PL 30262)

No 409 Squadron armourers work on the cannons of a Mosquito in the summer of 1944. (PL 31818)

A No 442 Squadron Spitfire undergoes an engine change in August 1944. (PL 31363)

Groundcrew load an oblique camera into a Spitfire XI of No 400 Squadron in the autumn of 1944. (PL 40301)

A Typhoon gets reammunitioned at Eindhoven, Holland, in the autumn of 1944. (PL 33858)

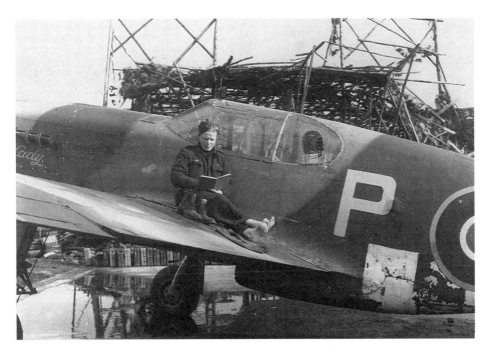

Reading and drying-out! No 430 Squadron operated the venerable but effective Mustang I on fighter reconnaissance operations with Second TAF until the end of 1944. (PL 3336)

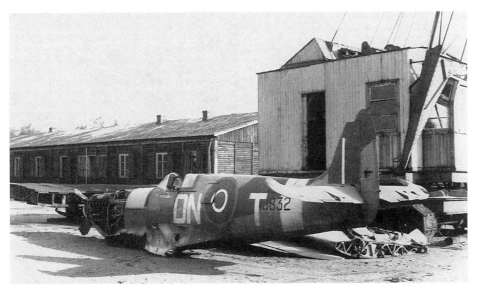

This aircraft (or what was left of it) was discovered in a German salvage yard in November 1944. Its previous owner had been a pilot of No 416 Squadron, a prisoner of war since May. (PL 33706)

A Typhoon of No 438 Squadron taxis through a flooded area at Eindhoven, Holland, in the late winter of 1944–5 (one of the wettest on record), while a pilot practises his dinghy drill watched by an airman trying to keep his feet dry by squatting on jerricans. (PL 42099)

In order to cope with crowded tarmacs and poor forward visibility (and a certain amount of surplus rainwater), this No 400 Squadron Spitfire is guided towards a dispersal area at Evère by two groundcrew in December 1944. (PL 40401)

Flak damage sustained by a No 416 Squadron Spitfire on Christmas Eve, 1944.
(PL 41349)

Aftermath of the Luftwaffe's New Year's Day strike against Eindhoven. (PMR 74-318)

With Spitfires of No 412 Squadron in the background, groundcrew clear away snow at Heesch. (PL 41492)

Spitfire XVIs of No 403 Squadron at Evère, in early 1945. (PL 41857)

De-icing a Mosquito XIII of No 409 Squadron at Vendeville, France, in early 1945.
(PL 41735)

Water-soaked accommodation area of No 39 (Reconnaissance) Wing at Eindhoven in
March 1945. (PL 42674)

Typhoons of No 143 Wing take off from Eindhoven in March 1945. (PL 42816)

No 443 Squadron Spitfire XIVs buzz the mobile flying control installation at Petit-Brogel, Belgium, in March 1945. (PL 43236)

No 412 Squadron Spitfire IXs undergoing maintenance at Heesch in March 1945.
(PL 42422)

A No 143 Wing convoy crosses the Rhine on a Class 80 Double-Single Pontoon Bailey
Bridge in April 1945. (PL 44575)

The Typhoon squadrons of No 143 Wing became the first RCAF air units to operate from German soil when they moved into Goch in the last days of March 1945. They were close to the front, and armed groundcrew are seen in the back of a truck moving up to their new station. (PL 42792)

Members of a Canadian Mobile Photographic section listen to British prime minister Winston Churchill announcing the end of the war in Europe. (PL 44125)

Introduction

Captivated by the strategic bombing doctrine enshrined in the concept of an 'independent' air force, the Royal Air Force paid scant attention to the question of air defence for the first fifteen years following the end of the First World War. That situation changed in the summer of 1934 when British politicians, frightened by the prospect of German rearmament, compelled the air staff to reconsider the balance to be maintained between bomber and fighter. A separate Fighter Command was established in 1936, and by 1938 government policy was clear. In the event of war with Germany, the RAF's first responsibility was to defend Britain from attack: and the fighter aircraft then entering service, the Hawker Hurricane and Supermarine Spitfire, were perfectly suited to this defensive role. Only later would the Air Ministry launch a bombing offensive against the Fatherland – an offensive which, according to the thinking of the time, would not require fighter escorts.

Supported by Chain Home radar stations and a complex network of ground observers and controllers, Fighter Command won the Battle of Britain in the summer of 1940. At that juncture, the strategic rationale for maintaining a large force of short-range day interceptors based in the United Kingdom all but disappeared. However, since it was impolitic for psychological reasons to dispatch many of them to other theatres, some new employment had to be found. Hence the offensive fighter sweeps conducted over northeastern France and Holland in 1941, whose main object, beyond keeping Fighter Command staff and pilots busy, seems to have been to establish a vague, uncertain air superiority over the enemy and thus further secure British air space.

Once Germany attacked Russia, a strategic rationale was found for the fighter offensive – to compel the Luftwaffe to move forces from the Eastern Front to the west. 'Leaning forward into France,' however, was something of a failure: the RAF/RCAF lost far more pilots and machines than the enemy, and significant attrition of the German fighter force in the west had to wait on the evolution of the American long-range fighter and its conjunction with the USAAF daylight bombing campaign over Germany itself – aided and abetted by the inept planning of the Luftwaffe's leadership.

Meanwhile, with the evolution of fighter-bombers and the development of new fighter weapons systems (particularly the rocket projectile), Fighter Command found a new lease on life in supporting ground operations. That role had been inherent in the formation of the short-lived (and largely neglected) Army Co-operation Command, and was demonstrated more concretely in the operations conducted by the Desert Air Force in the Mediterranean theatre. It would reach its zenith with the creation of Second Tactical Air Force, which supported the Anglo-Canadian 21st Army Group throughout the Northwest Europe campaign.

As part of Canada's modest rearmament program, in February 1939 the RCAF's Calgary-based No 1 (Fighter) Squadron began to exchange its Armstrong-Whitworth biplanes for more modern Hawker Hurricane Mk Is. Sent to England in June 1940 to bolster the depleted strength of RAF Fighter Command, No 1 (which became No 401) was the only RCAF unit to fly in the Battle of Britain and claimed its first victories on 26 August 1940.

No 1 Squadron was not the first RCAF unit to arrive in England, however. No 110 (Army Co-operation) Squadron – later No 400 – equipped with Westland Lysanders, had been dispatched overseas in February 1940 to work with Canada's one-division expeditionary force. No 112 (Army Co-operation) Squadron joined it in June 1940, but in December was redesignated No 2 (Fighter) Squadron – later No 402 – and re-equipped with Hawker Hurricanes. All the RCAF fighter squadrons eventually flew variants of the Spitfire, while fighter-bomber squadrons flew either Spitfire variants or the Hawker Typhoon.

The renumbering scheme noted above, which saw the RCAF allocated the block of RAF squadron numbers falling between 400 and 449 (450–499 were assigned to other Commonwealth Air Forces), was implemented to avoid the confusion that would result if, for example, two No 1 (Fighter) Squadrons, one RAF, the other RCAF, happened to be serving in close proximity to each other and messages were misdirected. Symbolically, allocating these blocks of numbers to the dominion air forces recognized national contributions to the air war while, at the same time, proclaiming and confirming the extremely close relationship that existed between them and the RAF.

No 414 Squadron joined No 400 Squadron in Army Co-operation Command in August 1941, both units then being equipped with Curtiss Tomahawks and later with North American Mustang Is. Brought together into No 39 (Army Co-operation) Wing, RCAF, they were joined by No 430 Squadron in January 1943. Following brief stints with Fighter Command, and subsequently assigned to the fighter-reconnaissance role, the three squadrons again served together as No 39 Wing in No 83 Group of the Second Tactical Air Force.

Most Canadian fighter squadrons were either formed in, or assigned to, Fighter Command – redesignated as the Air Defence of Great Britain between November 1943 and October 1944. Although Ottawa's hopes that an RCAF fighter group paralleling the Canadian bomber group might be formed were not realized, two Canadian fighter wings were established in England, the first at Digby, the other at Kenley, until their squadrons were transferred to Second

Tactical Air Force (TAF). Formed in the summer of 1943, Second TAF would eventually comprise No 2 (Bomber) Group, and Nos 83 and 84 Composite Groups, the former being about half Canadian. Ottawa had hoped that No 83 would be associated with First Canadian Army; however, a complex series of strategic and political decisions in air and ground policies led to the group's serving primarily with Second British Army. More and more, fighter forces, including the Canadians, were used for air support of ground forces, their ranges increased with the introduction of jettisonable auxiliary fuel tanks.

As Canadian fighter squadrons moved to the Continent after the invasion of Normandy, at one time or another all of them would serve in Second TAF, including the six squadrons from the Home War Establishment transferred overseas between November 1943 and February 1944. Eventually, ten Canadian squadrons would see service in the day-fighter role, three as night-fighters, three as fighter-bombers, and one in the Intruder role. Two RCAF fighter wings (Nos 126 and 127) and one fighter bomber-wing (No 143) operated throughout the campaign in Northwest Europe. They provided a small part of an overwhelming Allied air superiority.

The Luftwaffe was not a major factor during the Overlord campaign, but as Allied armies approached the Rhine it began to play a greater part in defending the Fatherland. German fighters (including the jet-powered Me 262) endeavoured to frustrate Allied air interdiction and support of ground forces. By that time, however, German technology was more than matched by Allied numbers and training.

The RCAF night-fighter squadrons had joined the order of battle in the late summer of 1941 to help deal with the Luftwaffe's bombing raids against Britain and then to support Bomber Command's night offensive against Germany. By mid-1944 the Canadian night-fighter squadrons were equipped with de Havilland Mosquitoes and had moved to the Continent as part of Second TAF.

No 418 Squadron operated as Canada's only Intruder unit, ranging far and wide by day and night against German fighter bases and lines of communication and, in 1944, taking on the V-1 rockets. In August 1944 it, too, was transferred to Second TAF for close support work, and it moved to Belgium in March 1945.

No 417 Squadron, meanwhile, was the only RCAF fighter unit to serve beyond the bounds of the Home War Establishment and Northwest Europe. It left Britain for Egypt in April 1942 and served in the Desert Air Force and in Italy until the end of the war.

5

Establishing a Presence, 1940

At the end of the First World War contemporary air-power theory, based on the limited precedents of 1917 and 1918, held that future wars could be settled quickly, cheaply, and relatively painlessly through the 'knock-out blow' – an unstoppable and devastating bomber attack on an enemy's commercial and industrial centres. Bombers were everything and fighters a distracting and wasteful nothing. Political realities nevertheless dictated that some lip service be paid to assuaging civilian anxieties, and in 1922 Air Commodore J.M. Steel of the Air Ministry and Colonel H.J. Bartholomew of the War Office were instructed by the chiefs of staff to create an air defence plan for Britain based on a proposed fourteen bomber and nine fighter squadrons. When, in 1924, this force was increased (on paper) to thirty-five bomber and seventeen fighter squadrons, the proportion of squadrons changed slightly in still further favour of the bomber.[1]

Adolf Hitler's accession to power in January 1933, together with Germany's withdrawal from the League of Nations in October and the 1935 recreation of a German air force in brazen defiance of the Treaty of Versailles, led the British government to re-examine its defence requirements. There then appeared a series of expansion schemes, each intended to counter, as cheaply as possible, the threat posed by a proliferating Luftwaffe. Still, assigning priority to bombers as it did, the Metropolitan Air Force (the operational part of the RAF based in Great Britain) of Schemes A through H was meant to intimidate rather than defend; and only with Scheme J of October 1937 did the government's attitude begin to change and planning turn towards putting the air force on a more balanced war footing. Sir John (later Lord) Slessor, then the RAF's deputy director of plans, has described Scheme J, calling for some thirty-three fighter squadrons (with immediate reserves) by June 1941, as 'the first scheme based on estimates of minimum overall strategic requirements.'[2]

The shift in emphasis towards fighters seems to have been largely driven by the need for politicians to be able to talk in terms of 'parity' with the Luftwaffe, whatever that might mean, and by the economic reality that fighters were cheaper and quicker to build than bombers. A more significant change in the relationship between fighter and bomber, brought about by the invention

of 'radar' (radio-direction-finding, or RDF as it was initially called), was completely ignored by the politicians.

What the evidence suggests ... is that the debate about air programmes between the
Air Ministry on the one hand and the Cabinet on the other, in the period 1936-39, was
largely unaffected by technical developments, radar among them ... The views of most
Ministers, and the decisions of the Cabinet, were based upon financial and political
arguments, hardly ever on strictly military ones. If Ministers wanted more fighter
aircraft, and we have seen that they did, they could have greatly strengthened their
arguments by reference to improved machines, Hurricanes and Spitfires, as well as
radar. Ministers as a whole did not do this and nor, at any rate in the Cabinet debate,
did either Secretary of State for Air for the period. These were years in which, in the
RAF, the balance was tipping temporarily in favour of defence. Major strategic decisions were not ostensibly made for that reason.[3]

Nevertheless, by the end of 1935 five 'detection stations' had been authorized for the shores of the Thames estuary and the coastlines abutting on them,
the first instalment of a chain of twenty such posts stretching from the Tyne
to the Solent. The evolution of radar in the hands of Robert Alexander Watt,[*]
one of those rare people whose administrative skills matched his abilities as a
scientist, was extraordinarily swift. By July 1937 the secretary of state for air,
Lord Swinton, was able to tell the Defence Plans (Policy) subcommittee of the
Committee of Imperial Defence that these 'Chain Home' stations 'gave an indication of approaching aircraft at distances of about 100 miles, and thus
enabled very early warning to be given to all parts of the defensive system,'
while 'the technique of the co-operation of fighter squadrons with this method
of detection was being actively developed.' During the 1937 exercises, however, Fighter Command's old-fashioned, twin-gun biplanes were quite unable
to match the speeds of the latest monoplane bombers; Flight Lieutenant E.A.
McNab, an RCAF exchange officer flying with the RAF that summer, reported
that his formation of Gloster Gauntlets could only watch Bristol Blenheim
bombers 'disappearing in the distance.'[4]

Before the war began, work had already started on a supplementary system
of thirty 'Chain Home Low' stations which could detect low-flying aircraft
sneaking in at altitudes below 3000 feet, the minimum height covered by the
original system. That addition was completed just before the main phase of the
Battle of Britain began in August 1940, enabling the RAF to fight with every
possible advantage that radar offered. With the introduction of radar it was no
longer necessary to maintain standing patrols in order to intercept enemy
bombers. Defences could now hope to thwart the enemy with far fewer
machines and with much less wear and tear on them and their pilots, thus
multiplying their effectiveness by a factor of at least three or four – and
possibly as much as five or six.

---

[*] He was knighted in 1942 and then hyphenated his name to Watson-Watt.

Easier to put through, because it initially involved little or no capital expenditure, was the decision in 1936 to abolish the homogeneous Metropolitan Air Force in favour of separate functional commands for fighter, bomber, and maritime (or coastal) operations. Adhering to the principles of 1918, the new Fighter Command included in its span of operational control anti-aircraft artillery and searchlight units which were formally part of the British Army rather than the RAF. Its first air officer commanding-in-chief (AOC-in-C), appointed on 14 July 1936, was Air Marshal Sir Hugh Dowding.

Dowding was quick to test a new control system during the summer defence exercises of 1937, in which British air space was divided up between a number of fighter 'groups,' with each group further subdivided into 'sectors.' A main airfield within each sector was designated as the 'sector station,' where representations of the current situation could be plotted when warning of an attack came through the Chain Home system, supplemented by the eyeballs and binoculars of the volunteer Observer Corps posts sprinkled about the countryside. Both transmitted the enemy's height, speed, and direction by landline to Fighter Command headquarters at Bentley Priory (near Stanmore, Middlesex), and from there both information and orders were issued to the appropriate group and sector operations rooms where plots were constantly updated and monitored.

The task of directing, or 'vectoring,' the fighters on to enemy formations over high-frequency (HF) radio channels was the responsibility of the sector 'controller,' usually a former fighter pilot himself. Of course, once they had been vectored into visual contact there remained the twin problems of first catching up with the enemy aircraft and then shooting it down. To that end, much faster, multi-gun, monoplane fighters were beginning to join the RAF's order of battle. The Hawker Hurricane, with a top speed of 335 miles per hour (compared with the 274 miles per hour of the Heinkel 111, Germany's standard bomber of the day), began to come into service at the end of 1937, while the Supermarine Spitfire, with a maximum speed of 360 miles per hour, would follow in June 1938. Both were armed with eight wing-mounted .303 machine-guns, capable between them of firing 146 rounds per second for a theoretical fifteen seconds.[5]

Another method of concentrating firepower, thought the air staff, was to direct several fighters in such a way that each got a clear field of fire upon a single bomber from the rear or side, either simultaneously or in very quick succession – a process that the RAF tried to achieve through carefully regulated, close-formation attacks. These rigid systems minimized the fighters' other great asset, manoeuvrability, but that hardly mattered. 'Manoeuvre at high speeds in air fighting is not now practicable,' proclaimed the 1938 *Manual of Air Tactics*, 'because the effect of gravity on the human body during rapid changes of direction at high speed causes a temporary loss of consciousness.'[6]

Since twisting and turning at Hurricane and Spitfire speeds was not practicable, the air staff gave virtually no thought to the possibility of fighter versus fighter combat. The new fighters' only conceivable mission was to shoot down bombers, a process best achieved through tightly controlled attack formations and tactics based on a section of three aircraft, either in close echelon or – most commonly – a tight vee, or 'vic.' Unfortunately, such formations also ensured that two out of every three pilots spent more time vigilantly watching their leader, in order to avoid collisions, than they did searching the sky for enemies. They were thus more likely to become victims than victors, surprise being the very essence of successful air fighting.

In contrast, the basic German formation (a result of Luftwaffe experience in the Spanish Civil War) was the Rotte, two aircraft in near line-abreast, about 250 yards apart. Each pilot searched inward, as well as to his front, scanning the hemisphere of sky beyond and behind his partner for any sign of the enemy. Two Rotten formed a Schwarm, in which the lateral relationship of each machine corresponded roughly to the relationship of the finger tips on an outspread hand – therefore to be known in English as a 'finger four' – although there might well be a slight difference in height between each pair, an arrangement which gave the Schwarm even more flexibility in changing direction. It was a much looser arrangement than the vic, enhancing the concept of mutual support while minimizing the danger of collision. Should the Rotte or Schwarm be approached from behind by enemy fighters, a hard 360° turn away from the angle of attack by the leading machine or pair, while the one closer to the enemy turned tightly in the opposite direction, into the attack, would usually result in the attackers being sandwiched between them.[7]

Whatever the relative weakness of its tactical doctrines, however, in the three years between 1936 and 1939 Fighter Command had undergone a dramatic transformation for the better. A memorandum prepared in early 1938 by Air Vice-Marshal Sholto Douglas, assistant chief of the air staff, illustrates the change. 'I think that within the last few months, what with the advent of the eight-gun fighter, RDF, and the Biggin Hill Interception scheme [sector controller system], the pendulum has swung the other way and that at the moment – or at any rate as soon as all our Fighter Squadrons are equipped with Hurricanes and Spitfires – the fighter is on top of contemporary bombers.'[8]

None of this had much immediate relevance in Ottawa, although the government was firmly convinced 'that the first line of defence for the Dominion of Canada must be the air force.' One third – $11.5 million – of a vastly increased defence budget was assigned to military aviation in 1937–8. It was badly needed, for only two years earlier 'it was reported to the minister [of National Defence] that there were only twenty-three aircraft of service type in Canada. All were obsolescent except for training, and none were suitable for active service under present day conditions. There were no air bombs in Canada for immediate use.'[9]

The prospect of attacks on Canada from the air appeared remote even in 1939, since the country was separated from every likely adversary by great expanses of water. 'The only air menace that North America has to fear for the present, is that of planes launched from ships,' wrote C.P. Stacey in *The Military Problems of Canada*. Such a threat could best be countered, according to contemporary theory, by using naval forces or land-based torpedo-bomber and bomber aircraft to sink those ships. There was a requirement, also, to provide specialized (and relatively cheap) army cooperation machines to work with any militia expeditionary force which might be mounted. Thus the provision of fighter aircraft had had a lower priority than that of other types in the eyes of the general staff (to which the air force was subordinate until November 1938) and the Cabinet. In 1938 the RCAF's only regular fighter squadron was flying nothing more modern than five Armstrong-Whitworth Siskin IIIA biplanes (the survivors of eight purchased between 1928 and 1931), each armed with only two .303 machine-guns and incapable of more than 150 miles per hour. But fighters were cheaper to buy than bombers: the first eight Hurricanes would arrive at Halifax in February 1939.[10]

Nor did the growing European crisis have much immediate effect on the RCAF's flying training program. Despite the spectacular rise in funding and the doubling of its meagre strength between 1936 and 1939, Air Vice-Marshal G.M. Croil pointed out in December 1938, with commendable honesty, that the prolonged parsimony of the interwar years meant that 'it is not possible to take full advantage of a sudden and relatively large increase in appropriations.' Furthermore, 'where time permits, increases should not be too sudden nor, in comparison to the previous year, too large,' if standards were to be maintained.[11] This was particularly true in the realm of pilot training, which was necessarily a sluggish process at first, requiring the training and certification of additional instructors by those few already qualified before any large-scale expansion could even commence.

RCAF recruitment standards were extraordinarily high. There was no dearth of young Canadians eager to become fighter pilots (many of them had obtained civil flying licences at their own expense), but until 1939, when a four-year 'short-service' scheme was introduced, a permament commission required either graduation from the Royal Military College of Canada or an engineering degree, as well as the appropriate level of physical fitness. Moreover, a reserve commission in one of the Non-Permanent Active Air Force (NPAAF) squadrons was all too often dependent upon living in, or close to, a major centre of population and moving in the right social circles. The RAF, in contrast, had offered short-service commissions from 1934, and 'colonials' were welcomed. Consequently, while the RCAF recruited only fifty-four general list (ie, aircrew) candidates to permanent commissions in 1938 and 1939, it recommended triple that number for short-service commissions in the RAF. Many more went to Britain at their own expense and applied directly to the Air Ministry. By 1940 there were at least 441 Canadians commissioned in the RAF, and probably a majority, inspired by the records of such First World War Canadian aces as Bishop, Barker, Collishaw, and MacLaren, were either fighter pilots or yearning to become such. Nearly all held short-service commissions, but a few held permanent appointments. There were also a hundred or so non-commissioned Canadian aircrew in the RAF's ranks.[12]

The German annexation of Austria in March 1938 and of Czechoslovakia's Sudetenland in October increased European tensions and furthered the likelihood of war. The subsequent occupations of Bohemia and Moravia in March

1939, in blatant violation of the Munich Agreement, confirmed the need for Britain to strengthen its defences; and, that spring, the air staff argued that fifty-two fighter squadrons were the minimum necessary to defend the British Isles.[13] When Great Britain declared war on 3 September 1939, Fighter Command had only thirty-nine squadrons in hand, however, and four of those, equipped with Hurricanes, were promptly dispatched to France as part of the Advanced Air Striking Force (AASF). Two more would be added later. Meanwhile, the Air Ministry took advantage of the 'phoney war' to set about organizing eighteen additional squadrons.

One of the eighteen was No 242 (Canadian) Squadron, RAF. Formed at Church Fenton in Yorkshire, it was the result of a public-relations exercise benefiting both the Canadian and British governments. On 12 September 1939, six days after British prime minister Neville Chamberlain made the initial proposals for what would eventually become the British Commonwealth Air Training Plan (BCATP) and just two days after the Canadian declaration of war, Prime Minister Mackenzie King, anxious for a significant Canadian presence overseas and believing that an air force contingent would probably prove most economical in human terms (thus reducing the likelihood of conscription, which had wrenched the nation apart in 1917), declared, 'It is the desire of this Government that Canadian Air Force units be formed as soon as sufficient trained personnel are available overseas for this purpose.'[14]

The British, lusting to display the solidarity of empire and commonwealth, were equally keen to see an RCAF unit in the field. They first suggested that an RCAF maritime reconnaissance squadron be based in the Caribbean, but a lack of suitable aircraft thwarted that proposal.[15] Moreover, with the opening of negotiations for what would become the politically preferable BCATP, the Canadian government was already having second thoughts about overseas commitments. O.D. Skelton, undersecretary of state for external affairs and one of King's closest associates, explained to the British high commissioner in Ottawa: 'Whilst it is for many reasons desirable that Canada's contribution to the air war should be recognized and confirmed by the early participation of Royal Canadian Air Force units overseas, it must be borne in mind that the immediate despatch of even one unit would seriously detract from the inception and development of the scheme for training in Canada.' Sending an RCAF squadron overseas, therefore, 'should not now be contemplated.'[16]

The Air Ministry put forward an alternate idea: something might be done with Canadian airmen already in the RAF or serving with it as RCAF exchange officers. By the end of October 1939 arrangements were complete for the formation of a fighter squadron with Canadian aircrew, providing Mackenzie King with a 'much to be desired recognition of Canadian participation'[17] at virtually no cost to his government in people, machines, or dollars. An RCAF officer already in England, Squadron Leader F.M. Gobeil, a highly-anglicized, French-Canadian graduate of the Royal Military College, was placed in command.

Since all – or nearly all – of the squadron's non-flying personnel was British, and only the commanding officer was RCAF, the record of its training in England and its misfortunes during the Battle of France (10 May–18 June 1940) lie outside the bounds of this volume.[18] Casualties were heavy. Of the twenty-two pilots on strength on 10 May, seven were killed in action, three captured, and three wounded. Replacements, for the most part British, had begun arriving in late May and early June, and when the legendary Squadron Leader Douglas Bader took over command from Gobeil on 24 June 1940, No 242's last link with anything formally Canadian was cut. Sent to the Far East in December 1941 (to be annihilated in the Dutch East Indies by early March 1942), it was then just another RAF unit with perhaps rather less than the usual proportion of Canadians to be found in British squadrons.

Meanwhile, in the eyes of the air staff, there were other threats to be faced and conquered besides those posed by the Luftwaffe. Much of the German success on the ground, in Poland, Norway, and France, had been due to the tactical and operational integration practised by their air and ground forces. The whole concept of integrated ground/air operations was anathema to the RAF, however. Its existence as a separate, independent service was predicated on the argument that strategic bombing was *the* war-winning weapon, and only reluctantly had senior officers even come to admit that there was a role for the air superiority fighter. With no little regret they had always accepted that the army was entitled to a minimal degree of what was known as army co-operation (ie, the use of limited air resources for reconnaissance and artillery-spotting duties that had been the primary function of the air arm during the First World War), but it was the least of their priorities. Prewar doctrine, such as it was, had called for one army cooperation squadron to be assigned to each infantry corps, and – as they were incorporated into the order of battle – one to each armoured division. To divert more valuable and limited resources to ground operations, a procedure which conceivably might also give the army some say in their handling, was unthinkable.[19]

It was, of course, true that the War Office had an obsolete understanding of how air power should be applied. The army sought nothing less than self-contained air forces under military control – an air 'brigade' for each field army, similar to the arrangements that had prevailed in 1917 and 1918 – while the Air Ministry insisted on the benefits of centralized control, citing enhanced flexibility and economy of force when employing finite air resources and arguing that the air arm should not be subordinate to ground commanders.[*20]

Canadian airmen, in contrast, were more amenable to army cooperation, possibly because Canadian airmen had been largely 'bush pilots in uniform' during the interwar years; perhaps because the RCAF had only become an independent service in 1938; and certainly because Canada's dominant military mind between the wars was that of soldier-scientist A.G.L. McNaughton, a dedicated advocate of air power in the land battle. In fact, while prewar British

---

[*] The controversy may be followed in A.W. Tedder's *With Prejudice* (London 1966), B.L. Montgomery's *Memoirs* (London 1958), J.C. Slessor's *The Central Blue* (London 1956), Henry Pownall's *Chief of Staff* (London 1972), and C.E. Carrington's *A Soldier at Bomber Command* (London 1985). Carrington's is the only published account by anyone intimately involved in the issue.

establishments called for one army co-operation squadron per infantry corps (and one per armoured division), the RCAF was thinking in terms of a three-squadron army cooperation wing 'for despatch overseas if required.'[21] When the first squadron went to Britain in early 1940, however, it inevitably became embroiled in all the troubles which frustrated its RAF peers, in addition to those problems inherent in the broader picture of Anglo-Canadian cooperation.

On 24 November 1939, in London, Air Commodore L.S. Breadner had met with Sir Kingsley Wood, the British secretary of state for air, Canadian high commissioner Vincent Massey, and Wing Commander Vernon Heakes, the RCAF's liaison officer with the RAF, to consider what air units the RCAF should provide in support of a Canadian component of the British Expeditionary Force, either of one division, or, later perhaps, a two-division corps. Wood told the Canadians that the Air Ministry would be pleased if an army cooperation squadron arrived in the United Kingdom with the 1st Canadian Division that was expected at the turn of the year. Both division and squadron would subsequently be sent to France as part of the BEF; the soldiers would join IV British Corps and the airmen could then become the corps squadron.[22]

No 110 Squadron, RCAF, flying Westland Lysanders, was selected and placed under the command of Squadron Leader W.D. Van Vliet, who was a graduate of both the RAF Staff College and the RAF's School of Army Co-operation, where he had passed out first in his course. His Staff College instructors had found him 'an honest, great-hearted and cheerful personality ... His sincerity and honesty of purpose are marked.' He was 'a hardworking, sound and practical officer with definite tenacity of purpose,' and the commandant was 'impressed with his mental honesty.'[23] His unit was an amalgam of Permanent Force and Auxiliary airmen. Its core was No 110 (City of Toronto) Squadron, reinforced by Permanent Force personnel from No 2 (Army Co-operation) Squadron and supplemented by Auxiliaries from Winnipeg, Calgary, and Regina. The squadron arrived in England in late February 1940, still largely untrained, ostensibly to work with the 1st Division until both reached expeditionary force standards. It was, however, condemned to thrash about in a political and bureaucratic maelstrom for many months to come, a struggle that would frequently frustrate everyone concerned, most of all Van Vliet. At the vortex of events, he was compelled to juggle demands, requests, and suggestions from a quite unreasonable number of superiors while trying to maintain the morale of his subordinates in an extraordinarily difficult environment.

As an RCAF unit, No 110 Squadron was subject to the newly-formed Overseas Headquarters in London, while as an army cooperation squadron it was part of the RAF's No 22 Group, responsible for army cooperation training. Major-General McNaughton, the general officer comanding (GOC) of the 1st Division and also the senior Canadian military officer overseas, considered that it came under his operational command, even if its administration and supply were RAF/RCAF responsibilities – while he himself was functionally subordinate to the War Office in London, but, at the same time, had an overriding political tie to the Canadian government in Ottawa.

To make an awkward situation worse, there was no provision in British (or Canadian) war establishments for an army cooperation squadron to be allocated to a single infantry division. As we have noted, British doctrine called for one squadron per infantry corps, of two or three divisions; but McNaughton crustily proclaimed his 'understanding that 110 (AC) Squadron, RCAF, has been provided primarily for the purpose of working with the Canadian forces in the field, and I hope that there will be no doubt that our requirements in this connection will have priority.'[24] Thus, at least until the 2nd Division arrived and a Canadian corps organization could be established, the squadron found itself adrift between the rock of McNaughton and the hard place of air force insularity.

For example, on 6 May 1940 Norman Rogers, minister of national defence, met with Sir Samuel Hoare (who had succeeded Kingsley Wood as secretary of state for air) to try to clarify financial relationships created by wartime circumstances. To Rogers, financing the BCATP and whatever units the RCAF sent overseas were both part of one overall arrangement. Indeed, in accepting a larger share of BCATP costs the government had reduced the number of army cooperation squadrons it had been planning to send overseas from three to one, Ottawa providing only the pay and allowances of its personnel while Whitehall supplied equipment and maintenance. That, of course, fitted in very poorly with McNaughton's insistence that the squadron be, in effect, an integral part of the Canadian Army Overseas, which was completely financed from Canadian resources. Hoare pointed out the anomaly, suggesting that once a Canadian corps had been formed and the squadron was working exclusively with it, 'it might be reasonable to suggest that it should be equipped and maintained in the same way that Canadian Troops were.'[25] The meeting then turned to the more immediate problem of No 110's affiliations when the 1st Division went to France, no one foreseeing the imminent Blitzkrieg that would make such discussion totally irrelevant.

On their arrival in England, the squadron's pilots and air gunners had initially been kept busy with individual and specialist training at the School of Army Co-operation near Salisbury. By June their basic training was complete and they were moved to Odiham, in Hampshire, for operational training, still flying the twelve Lysanders they had brought from Canada. 'Its concept and design made it a very versatile aircraft, on top of which it had excellent short take-off and landing capabilities ... Unfortunately the designers were still thinking in World War I terms when they put it on the drawing board. German *Blitzkrieg* and the Junkers 87 '*Stuka*' made the Lysander obsolescent when they invaded Poland and they really made it obsolete after Dunkirk. It was a flying coffin after that disaster, although we, fortunately, didn't have to prove the point.'[26]

Whatever the dangers inherent in flying Lysanders in a combat environment – and they would have been immense – because the squadron was still comfortably ensconced in England, aircrew morale did not suffer much until the onset of the Battle of Britain, when they became mere bystanders, grounded for the most part in order to keep the skies clear for Fighter Command.[27]

Inactivity did not sit well with a squadron that had been the first RCAF unit overseas and expected to be the first to see action. Nor did it please Van Vliet (now promoted to the rank of wing commander), who 'began to show the effects of his mounting concern over the predicament we found ourselves in,' according to Flight Lieutenant C. Carling-Kelly, who commanded 'C' Flight. 'Young healthy pilots, rarin' to go, eating their hearts out as we watched the daily air battles from the safety of our shelters around the station. It was a bad situation and Van [Vliet] kept more and more to himself, confiding in no one … We all had our dreams, it was the futility of them that was beginning to erode our morale, including [that of] the CO.'[28]

In due course, the departure of six pilots for fighter training prior to posting as replacements to No 1 (Fighter) Squadron RCAF – which was, by August, critically involved in the Battle of Britain – only made matters worse for those who remained. In Overseas Headquarters the problem was seen and understood, and the first step in solving it seemed to be a change of command. 'W/C Van Vliet had trained the squadron from the beginning and had a wide margin of age and experience over most of his officers, thus creating a relationship between them more like that of an instructor to his pupils. This relationship was ideal during the period of training but was … less desirable now. The opinion of this HQ was that the stage had now been reached where the handing over to a younger Commanding Officer was essential.'[29] Van Vliet was repatriated to Canada (where he died of a heart attack two years later). He was first succeeded by his second-in-command, Squadron Leader E.H. Evans, who was promoted to wing commander's rank (but then posted back to Ottawa after only a few weeks), and subsequently by R.M. McKay, another graduate of the RAF Staff College, similarly promoted, both of whom had been with the squadron since it left Canada.

There was every prospect that, even though most of the bureaucratic issues that had beset No 110 Squadron had been ironed out by the early fall of 1940, the morale problem would recur with the dispatch in June of No 112, the second element of the RCAF's proposed three-squadron army cooperation wing. It had been offered by Ottawa on 11 May – the day after Hitler's offensive in the west began – 'if its presence in the United Kingdom would be regarded as a more useful contribution at an earlier [rather] than at a later stage.' By the 19th the Blitzkrieg threat had become critical, and Viscount Caldecote, Britain's assistant secretary of state for the dominions, was telling the Canadian high commissioner in London that his government 'would welcome' the arrival of No 112, together with 'as many fully equipped Lysander aircraft as possible.'[30]

Apparently Ottawa had waited upon a formal acceptance of its offer, for No 112 Squadron's advance party embarked at Halifax the next day and the balance of the squadron sailed on 11 June, exactly a month after the offer had been made. In their response, the British had asked that Ottawa 'might consider the possibility of sending as many field-equipped Lysander aircraft as possible for use by No 112 Squadron.' This would have required an initial strength of twelve machines, plus four in immediate reserve, but so tightly were the Canadians stretched that even to provide the initial twelve would have necessitated the temporary closure of the Army Co-operation School at Camp Borden. Five were all that could be spared and the RAF had to find the others. Arriving at High Post, near Old Sarum and the RAF's School of Army Co-operation, No 112 Squadron set about mastering the same obsolete equipment and tactics that No 110 had been practising for the past six months – until, in March 1941, it was redesignated as a fighter unit and re-equipped with Hurricanes.[31]

Meanwhile, the radical transformation of the strategic situation following the fall of France led to a fundamental overhaul of Britain's defences, and Lieutenant-General McNaughton found himself commanding VII (British) Corps, the ultimate reserve south of the Thames, consisting of his own infantry division together with a British armoured brigade and two brigades of New Zealand infantry which he quickly amalgamated into an ad hoc armoured division. His assigned corps squadron was No 110 and, for the moment, no one fussed over its technical status or its financing, all emphasis being on its tactical and technological shortcomings. Had the air battle been lost and Hitler actually committed himself to the invasion of Britain, no doubt VII Corps would have soon found itself leading a desperate fight and its squadrons of Lysanders would have been 'sitting ducks' in a relentlessly hostile environment. Happily, Fall Seelöwe (Operation Sealion), the proposed amphibious assault on Britain, was cancelled on 12 October: there would be no landing on British shores in 1940, or (at least until the equinoctal gales were over) in the spring of 1941. On the basis of signals and photographic intelligence, Prime Minister Churchill and his key advisers knew by the end of that month that the residual risk of invasion would be 'relatively remote,' although they were not so reckless as to broadcast their conclusions. On Christmas Day 1940 VII Corps was dissolved and the newly arrived 2nd Canadian Division joined with the 1st to form I (Canadian) Corps. No 110 Squadron – in March 1941 it became No 400 – finally fitted into the regulation Anglo-Canadian military mould.[32]

The Battle of Britain would be half over before an RCAF contingent was ready to enter it, but it is necessary to review its progress to that point if only to correct some common misconceptions. The shortage of fighters and experienced pilots alleged by so many historians to have plagued Air Chief Marshal Dowding throughout the battle is one of those enduring myths which cluster about legendary events. True, the battle of France had left Fighter Command in poor shape – it had lost some nine hundred aircraft in six weeks, and half as many pilots – but the factories and the flying training schools had responded promptly to the crisis. As the British official historian of war production has pointed out, 'Fighter Command emerged from the Battle in the autumn with more aircraft than it possessed in the beginning,' and the number of fighters available for operations rose day by day, from 565 on 22 June to 666 on 13 July, then to 749 on 10 August, and 764 on 31 August. Thereafter, it declined slightly, but never dropped below 715 during the rest of the battle.* Moreover, pilot strength also rose, from 1396 on 10 August to 1492 on 14 September – an increase of nearly a hundred as the battle peaked – and to 1752 by 12 October, though such figures were achieved only through a combination of drastic cuts in training time and transfers from other commands, neither of which did much to guarantee a large force of experienced fighter pilots.[33]

However, Dowding did have to face and master a whole new series of operational problems presented by the German occupation of France and the Low Countries. The prewar plan for the air defence of Britain had been predicated on the assumption that German bombers would be flying, unescorted, from bases in Germany. Now, with the enemy occupying the Channel coast, most of the United Kingdom lay within easy reach of their bombers, and the southeastern part of the country was even within the range of the waspish, pugnacious Messerschmitt Me 109s, thus enabling the Luftwaffe to bomb a variety of targets – from radar stations to the Houses of Parliament – under the protection of fighter escorts.

From Berlin's perspective the situation was not nearly so bleak, but it was still curiously unnerving. Hitler had never wanted to fight the British in 1939 and was hoping that the collapse of France would persuade them to sue for peace, or at least accept an offer to negotiate.[34] When Churchill declined to do either, the Germans faced the formidable problem of what to do next. On 30 June 1940, at Hitler's behest, Reichsmarschall Hermann Göring laid down the first clear statement on how his air force intended to deal with a still-belligerent United Kingdom. First it would drive the RAF out of the air, destroy its ground organization, and disrupt the British aircraft industry. Then it would 'dislocate Britain's supplies by attacking ports and harbour installations, ships bringing supplies into the country, and warships escorting them. These two tasks are to be carried out in concert and not treated separately. Meanwhile, as long as the enemy air force remains in being, the supreme principle of air warfare must be to attack it at every possible opportunity by day and by night, in the air and on the ground, with priority over other tasks.'[35] The main weight of the offensive would be borne by Luftflotte 2, headquartered in Brussels, and Luftflotte 3, with its headquarters in Paris. They could muster, between them, some one thousand serviceable twin-engined bombers, three hundred single-engined dive bombers, two hundred and sixty twin-engined fighters, and seven hundred single-engined fighters.[36]

It was plain that Fighter Command was facing a formidable adversary. British fighters may have enjoyed a superior dog-fighting capability through being able to out-turn the enemy, but that failed to compensate for the Germans' greater speed, rate of climb, and diving performance, factors which usually enabled them to exercise the initiative. 'During the final phase [of the

---

* Luftwaffe intelligence assessed Fighter Command strength at only 400 to 500 machines on 1 August, with monthly production limited to 200 – 'comparable to German production figures and, in fact, less than half Britain's true monthly production.' M. Probert and S. Cox, eds., *The Battle Re-thought: A Symposium on the Battle of Britain* (Shrewsbury, England, 1991), 21

Battle of France] Me 109s avoided dogfights whenever possible and frequently carried out one assault in a steep dive, and then broke away by continuing the dive far below the British fighters. This form of attack from cloud cover or the direction of the sun was frequently successful in picking off the rear members of our fighter formations.'[37]

RAF pilots were still far from appreciating the marvellous degree of mutual cover and support provided by the Schwarm, but their vics were not quite as tight as they had once been and they had now added a 'tail-end charlie' – one or more pilots detailed to fly above and behind the main formation, weaving to and fro in order to keep watch astern. 'It should be a fundamental principle,' proclaimed a Bentley Priory memorandum issued in mid-June, 'that the rear units of any formation should be employed solely on look-out duties to avoid any possibility of surprise from astern or above.' However, 'having frequently flown in that tail-end position,' one veteran pilot has recorded, I 'knew full well the difficulty and hazards involved. If you weaved too much, you got left behind. If you did not weave enough, you got picked off.'[38] He might have added that, even if your weaving was just right, either the formation had to slow down slightly to allow you to keep up or your fuel consumption would be significantly higher than that of your comrades, perhaps compelling an early – and solitary – return to base.

Flight analysis showed that an Me 109 which had fallen into British hands in May enjoyed two distinct technical advantages over the Spitfire and the Hurricane. The Rolls-Royce Merlin engine that powered both British types relied on a float carburettor that starved the engine of fuel when negative gravity was induced as an aircraft was bunted sharply over from level flight into a steep dive. The 109 had fuel injection which kept its engine functioning properly regardless of the aircraft's attitude. The Messerschmitt also had a variable-pitch, constant-speed propeller rather than the two-pitch version – coarse and fine – of the Spitfire and Hurricane, a refinement that contributed substantially to its superior speed and rate of climb, especially at heights above 20,000 feet.

The first problem could not be dealt with immediately; until the introduction of a diaphragm-type carburettor for the Mark V Spitfire in late 1941, British pilots would have to be content with flipping into a half-roll and then entering the dive from an inverted position if they sought to follow an enemy down while staying reasonably close to him. Plans to introduce constant-speed propellers were already in hand, however, and between 22 June and 15 August more than a thousand Spitfires and Hurricanes were modified. Their engines had already been adapted to use 100-octane fuel imported from the United States (the Luftwaffe used 87-octane throughout the war), and the combination of constant-speed airscrews and a higher octane rating put the climb, ceiling, and speed of the Spitfire on a par with that of the Me 109.[39] The Hurricane, however, would never do quite so well.

The most important technological factors working in Dowding's favour were the combination of radar with sophisticated communication and control networks. The Germans were well aware of the Chain Home system – its towering masts dotted the English coast and were impossible to disguise – but they drastically underestimated its effectiveness while miscalculating its application.

As the British fighters are controlled from the ground by R[adio]/T[elephony] their forces are tied to their respective ground stations and are thereby restricted in mobility, even taking into consideration the probability that the ground stations are partly mobile. Consequently the assembly of strong fighter forces at determined points and at short notice is not to be expected. A massed German attack on a target area can therefore count on the same conditions of light fighter opposition as in attacks on widely scattered targets. It can, indeed, be assumed that considerable confusion in the defensive networks will be unavoidable during mass attacks and that the effectiveness of the defences may thereby be reduced.[40]

There was a crucial flaw in this assessment. Thinking, perhaps, in terms of their own predilections in organizing air defence, they were assuming that the British control system was equally as inflexible as the Luftwaffe's, with individual machines under the direction of a specified controller unable to move easily from one area to another. It followed logically that a mass attack launched on a narrow front should overwhelm local defences; but, in fact, as outlined earlier, British radar stations fed information through Fighter Command's filter room to group operations rooms, and then to the sector controllers who directed as many aircraft as seemed necessary (or were available) to deal with an attack. Isolated mass raids only made it easier for the controllers to concentrate a large number of fighters in the appropriate sector.

Oberfeldwebel Gottfried Leske, the pilot of a Heinkel 111 who flew throughout the Battle of Britain (but was shot down and captured in early 1941), recorded in his diary the Luftwaffe's forming-up procedure, which British radar could usually 'see' and promptly report to Bentley Priory.

As always, we assembled shortly before we came to the Channel. The way we get into formation is technically very interesting. The best way to describe it is to think of the start of a trotting race. Circling all the time, the ships gradually get into formation, until all are placed, or rather moving, in the appointed battle order. And then slowly the whole formation begins to move across the Channel. In the meantime the destroyers [Me 110s] and fighters [Me 109s] have come up ... And now all the pilots open up on the throttle and begin to pick up speed ...

Once we are across the Channel anything can happen. But strangely, as a pilot I'm not so much worried about running into the enemy as I am about keeping my ship in the formation ...

And then those Spitfires and Hurricanes are there ... Bursts of machine-gun fire from all sides. Sometimes when the English have good luck, they catch one of us bombers, and then we see our comrades dangling from parachutes, trying to make the land, lost to our cause – at least until we free them from their prison camp.[41]

In accordance with Göring's directive, the Luftwaffe attacked the Chain Home system as well as airfields in its attempt at 'destroying his ground organi-

RCAF OVERSEAS
ORDER OF BATTLE

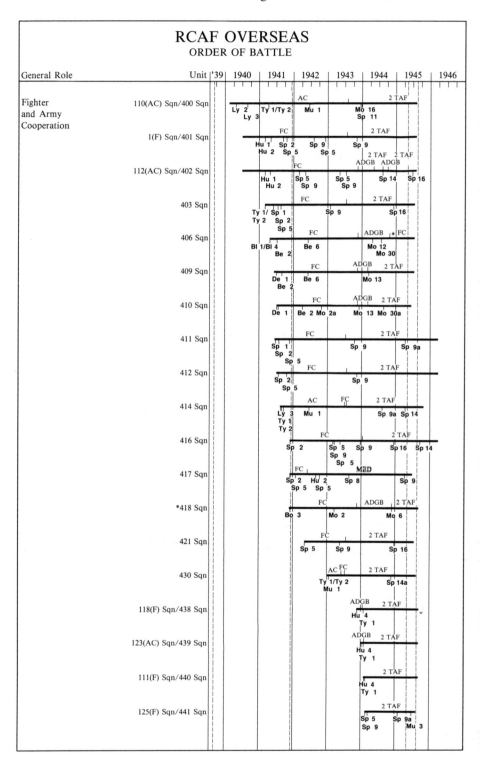

General Role	Unit	'39	1940	1941	1942	1943	1944	1945	1946

Fighter and Army Cooperation

- 110(AC) Sqn/400 Sqn — AC; 2 TAF; Ly 2, Ly 3; Ty 1/Ty 2; Mu 1; Mo 16, Sp 11
- 1(F) Sqn/401 Sqn — FC; 2 TAF; Hu 1, Hu 2; Sp 2, Sp 5; Sp 9, Sp 5; Sp 9; 2 TAF, 2 TAF
- 112(AC) Sqn/402 Sqn — FC; ADGB, ADGB; Hu 1, Hu 2; Sp 5, Sp 9; Sp 5, Sp 9; Sp 14; Sp 16
- 403 Sqn — FC; 2 TAF; Ty 1/Sp 1, Ty 2, Sp 2, Sp 5; Sp 9; Sp 16
- 406 Sqn — FC; ADGB, *FC; Bl 1/Bl 4, Be 2; Be 6; Mo 12, Mo 30
- 409 Sqn — FC; ADGB, 2 TAF; De 1, Be 2; Be 6; Mo 13
- 410 Sqn — FC; ADGB, 2 TAF; De 1; Be 2 Mo 2a; Mo 13 Mo 30a
- 411 Sqn — FC; 2 TAF; Sp 1, Sp 2, Sp 5; Sp 9; Sp 9a
- 412 Sqn — FC; 2 TAF; Sp 2, Sp 5; Sp 9
- 414 Sqn — AC, FC; 2 TAF; Ly 3, Ty 1, Ty 2; Mu 1; Sp 9a Sp 14
- 416 Sqn — FC; 2 TAF; Sp 2; Sp 5, Sp 9, Sp 5; Sp 9; Sp 16 Sp 14
- 417 Sqn — FC; MED; Sp 2, Sp 5; Hu 2, Sp 5; Sp 8; Sp 9
- *418 Sqn — FC; ADGB, 2 TAF; Bo 3; Mo 2; Mo 6
- 421 Sqn — FC; 2 TAF; Sp 5; Sp 9; Sp 16
- 430 Sqn — AC FC; 2 TAF; Ty 1/Ty 2, Mu 1; Sp 14a
- 118(F) Sqn/438 Sqn — ADGB, 2 TAF; Hu 4, Ty 1
- 123(AC) Sqn/439 Sqn — ADGB, 2 TAF; Hu 4, Ty 1
- 111(F) Sqn/440 Sqn — 2 TAF; Hu 4, Ty 1
- 125(F) Sqn/441 Sqn — 2 TAF; Sp 5, Sp 9; Sp 9a, Mu 3

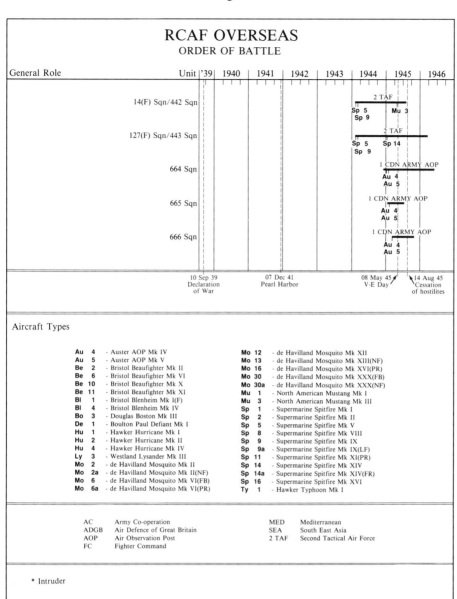

RCAF OVERSEAS
ORDER OF BATTLE

General Role	Unit	'39	1940	1941	1942	1943	1944	1945	1946
	14(F) Sqn/442 Sqn						Sp 5 / Sp 9	2 TAF — Mu 3	
	127(F) Sqn/443 Sqn						Sp 5 / Sp 9	2 TAF — Sp 14	
	664 Sqn						Au 4 / Au 5	1 CDN ARMY AOP	
	665 Sqn						Au 4 / Au 5	1 CDN ARMY AOP	
	666 Sqn						Au 4 / Au 5	1 CDN ARMY AOP	

10 Sep 39
Declaration
of War

07 Dec 41
Pearl Harbor

08 May 45
V-E Day

14 Aug 45
Cessation
of hostilites

Aircraft Types

Au 4	- Auster AOP Mk IV	
Au 5	- Auster AOP Mk V	
Be 2	- Bristol Beaufighter Mk II	
Be 6	- Bristol Beaufighter Mk VI	
Be 10	- Bristol Beaufighter Mk X	
Be 11	- Bristol Beaufighter Mk XI	
Bl 1	- Bristol Blenheim Mk I(F)	
Bl 4	- Bristol Blenheim Mk IV	
Bo 3	- Douglas Boston Mk III	
De 1	- Boulton Paul Defiant Mk I	
Hu 1	- Hawker Hurricane Mk I	
Hu 2	- Hawker Hurricane Mk II	
Hu 4	- Hawker Hurricane Mk IV	
Ly 3	- Westland Lysander Mk III	
Mo 2	- de Havilland Mosquito Mk II	
Mo 2a	- de Havilland Mosquito Mk II(NF)	
Mo 6	- de Havilland Mosquito Mk VI(FB)	
Mo 6a	- de Havilland Mosquito Mk VI(PR)	
Mo 12	- de Havilland Mosquito Mk XII	
Mo 13	- de Havilland Mosquito Mk XIII(NF)	
Mo 16	- de Havilland Mosquito Mk XVI(PR)	
Mo 30	- de Havilland Mosquito Mk XXX(FB)	
Mo 30a	- de Havilland Mosquito Mk XXX(NF)	
Mu 1	- North American Mustang Mk I	
Mu 3	- North American Mustang Mk III	
Sp 1	- Supermarine Spitfire Mk I	
Sp 2	- Supermarine Spitfire Mk II	
Sp 5	- Supermarine Spitfire Mk V	
Sp 8	- Supermarine Spitfire Mk VIII	
Sp 9	- Supermarine Spitfire Mk IX	
Sp 9a	- Supermarine Spitfire Mk IX(LF)	
Sp 11	- Supermarine Spitfire Mk XI(PR)	
Sp 14	- Supermarine Spitfire Mk XIV	
Sp 14a	- Supermarine Spitfire Mk XIV(FR)	
Sp 16	- Supermarine Spitfire Mk XVI	
Ty 1	- Hawker Typhoon Mk I	

AC	Army Co-operation	MED	Mediterranean
ADGB	Air Defence of Great Britain	SEA	South East Asia
AOP	Air Observation Post	2 TAF	Second Tactical Air Force
FC	Fighter Command		

* Intruder

zation.' Heavy attacks were made on six stations in the southeast on 12 August, with considerable damage done; one, Ventnor, was knocked out for eleven days, but an ordinary radio transmitter was soon putting out pulses on the same frequency and 'though these produced no echo, the enemy, hearing them, could only suppose that the station had been repaired.' Meanwhile, the Reichsmarschall cancelled any further attacks on radar targets, arguing, 'It is doubtful whether there is any point in continuing the attacks on radar sites, in view of the fact that not one of those attacked has so far been put out of action.'[42]

Two days earlier, his pilots had turned their attention to airfields. The primary targets, of course, were Fighter Command bases, but poor intelligence (or faulty navigation) meant that many sorties were misdirected. Of the three airfields which received the worst damage in the initial raids, Andover, Detling, and Eastchurch, none belonged to Fighter Command, but German intelligence officers seemed unaware of this mistake and thought that British defences had been struck a heavy blow. Over the next three weeks, however, the Luftwaffe did find and bomb a number of fighter fields, concentrating its attention on the sector stations of Tangmere, Kenley, Biggin Hill, and Hornchurch. Damage on the ground was mostly confined to buildings, and non-flying personnel suffered the bulk of the casualties, although opposing these raids cost Dowding a great deal in the air. Nearly a hundred of his pilots were killed between the 8th and the 18th, and sixty others were wounded, representing about 15 per cent of those he had in hand.[43] The supply of new pilots and replacement aircraft was adequate, but the strain of operations upon both pilots and groundcrew was a continuing concern.

When bad weather compelled some reduction in their scale of attack between the 19th and the 23rd, German commanders also took stock. Between 13 and 19 August they had lost, one way or another, nearly three hundred aircraft, or more than 10 per cent of the combined strength of Luftflotten 2 and 3. More to the point, such losses were indicative of a major effort which had, nonetheless, failed to diminish the RAF's considerable and effective opposition. For Dowding, there were some welcome reinforcements at hand. Several of the squadrons mangled in France had now been reformed, and the Fleet Air Arm had contributed another two squadrons to the relatively low-key operations of No 13 Group in the north, enabling him to move two of his own squadrons further south, into the heart of battle. Pilots who had escaped from countries occupied by the Germans were now training on British machines and would very shortly add three more squadrons (two Polish and one Czech) to his strength.[44] And, on 17 August 1940, No 1 Squadron, RCAF, became operational.

On 11 May 1940, a day after the initial German thrust into France, Holland, and Belgium, the Canadian high commissioner in London, Vincent Massey, had told Anthony Eden, British secretary of state for dominion affairs, that 'in the light of yesterday's critical developments ... the Canadian government would be glad to give immediate consideration to any suggestions which the Government of the United Kingdom may wish to make.' The British responded with several, among them 'the possibility of making available a Royal Canadian Air Force squadron, both aircraft and personnel, at an establishment, if possible, of sixteen initial equipment [aircraft].'[45]

On 21 May Ottawa signalled back that 'we are sending at earliest possible moment No 1 Fighter Squadron RCAF, together with all available Hurricanes, fourteen in number, it being understood [that the] United Kingdom will provide reinforcements as required, there being no facilities for [operational] training here.' The squadron, then stationed at Dartmouth, Nova Scotia, was ordered to pack its Hurricanes into crates and prepare to move overseas. Eight officers and eighty-six other ranks from No 115 Squadron were promptly posted in to bring the unit up to strength and, less than three weeks after the warning order had been issued, the crated Hurricanes were being loaded aboard ship and twenty-one pilots, seven other officers, and 314 airmen were filing aboard the *Duchess of Atholl*, bound for the United Kingdom.[46]

The additional officers and men from 115 Squadron were something of a mixed blessing for the commanding officer, Squadron Leader E.A. McNab, who has already appeared in this narrative as an exchange officer serving with the RAF. No 115 was an Auxiliary squadron from Montreal, its personnel relatively unskilled and inexperienced by the standards of the regular air force. One of the new officers, nevertheless, was considered qualified to assume the role of senior flight commander and McNab's second-in-command despite his hoary years by fighter pilot standards. Thirty-eight-year-old Flight Lieutenant G.R. McGregor, a telephone company executive and three-time winner of the Webster Trophy, awarded annually to Canada's top amateur pilot,[47] had joined the Auxiliary Air Force in October 1938 with the rank of flying officer. Both he and McNab were to prove excellent leaders, ensuring that No 1 Squadron would have a more distinguished early combat record than some of the RCAF units that would form overseas later.

The Canadians arrived in England on 20 June and were promptly plunged into the rustic splendours of RAF Station Middle Wallop, in deepest Hampshire. A few days later there was a visit from the AOC-in-C, who, as Lieutenant-Colonel H.C.T. Dowding of the Royal Flying Corps, had had a great many Canadian airmen under his command on the Western Front during the First World War. Now, 'the pilots were introduced to him. He also inquired as to what degree of training the Squadron had reached. When the Air Chief Marshal was told that the Squadron's Hurricanes were not of the latest type, he immediately made arrangements to replace these A[ir]/C[raft] with new Hurricanes.'[48]

Three new machines were delivered the same day and practice flying began on the 26th. Both pilots and groundcrew still needed a great deal of training – most particularly those who had come from No 115 Squadron and had flown in, or worked on, nothing more sophisticated than the Fairey Battle. For the pilots, flying regulations in Britain's crowded airspace were much more rigorous than those promulgated in Canada. There were new radio procedures to learn, medical aspects of high altitude flying to understand, more navigation and armament topics to master. In line with RAF practice and the demands of the abominable vic, much attention was paid to formation flying, especially in climbing and diving turns. 'The important thing is to teach the pilot to stick to his leader at all times.'[49]

As the Canadians worked their way closer to the RAF's understanding of operational competence, it was perhaps inevitable that questions should arise regarding the relationship between the squadron and superior RAF formations on the one hand and RCAF Overseas Headquarters on the other. When Group Captain G.V. Walsh, the RCAF's senior officer in the United Kingdom, visited Croydon on 11 July, McNab told him that, in an emergency, the air officer commanding No 11 Group planned to use the squadron on operations. Walsh was concerned for two reasons, as he subsequently explained to Air Vice-Marshal Keith Park, the AOC in question. First was the issue of operational readiness; he thought the squadron was not yet sufficiently trained, for, in his mind, only nine of the twenty-one pilots were marginally competent. 'Except under extreme emergency, I would not care to authorize its operational employment. In fact, I am not prepared to authorize the employment even of the pilots whose training approaches the operational standard unless the RAF themselves [sic] give a considered opinion that they are fit for the role to be given to them.' His second reservation concerned the maintenance of the squadron's Canadian identity; Ottawa had, as yet, made no arrangements to replace the casualties bound to occur once the unit went into action and, 'it might very well happen that if the unit was used prematurely replacements of casualties could not be made from RCAF personnel, and therefore the Unit, as an RCAF unit, might cease to exist.'[50]

Park, a New Zealander, and perhaps therefore able to appreciate Canadian concerns more readily than a British-born officer, adopted a placatory tone. He was surprised that someone, unidentified, had misinformed McNab – his practice was not to deploy a squadron on operations until it had at least fourteen pilots fully qualified. He went on to express his gratitude for the offer of the squadron in an emergency. Such an emergency, he added, 'I interpret to mean a "blitzkrieg" against the country, and not the present half-hearted scale of attack of merely a hundred aircraft at a time, as has recently occurred on the Kentish coast.'[51]

Walsh was equally conciliatory in his response, assuring Park that he wished no special treatment for his men. Once the squadron had the requisite fourteen trained pilots, he was prepared to alter the squadron's status from serving 'together with,' to acting 'in combination with,' the RAF (see Chapter 1), and he outlined the bureaucratic channel for formally implementing the change. That procedure was not immutable, however, as far as he was concerned. 'Should a grave emergency arise where the services of every available pilot might be required and the Squadron has not been trained to full capacity, I will, on notification from either Fighter Command or yourself by signal, telephone or dispatch rider, place the Squadron as acting "in combination" at once, leaving you free to employ qualified personnel immediately on operations. Legal confirming action can then be taken in due course.'[52]

Unlike some other occasions later in the war, there seems to have been a genuine mutual willingness to cooperate. Park would have liked the Canadians to fill a gap left when one of his squadrons was withdrawn to Scotland for rest and recuperation, but, he explained to Walsh, he had not told McNab, 'because I do not wish them unduly to press onwards or in any way skimp their operational training.'[53]

Nevertheless, this exchange of letters probably led to an increase in the tempo of practice flights. By 23 July all pilots had logged sixteen hours or more on Hurricanes and were averaging three hours flying a day while rehearsing squadron-strength interceptions. As they became more confident they apparently also became more adventurous, for a patronizing staff officer found it necessary to remind McNab that 'any breach of Air Regulations or any foolhardy flying would be severely dealt with.' Other Britons were less hidebound and more cooperative. McNab had informally arranged for some advanced training with the commanding officer of the RAF's Air Fighting Development Unit at ADFU Northolt, Wing Commander G.H. Vasse, 'who would act in the capacity of instructor-umpire-critic, taking sections, flights, and the squadron in succession into the air, and criticising and directing them in the proper methods of attack.' Hearing about that, Park thought that the Canadians might even be relocated to the same airfield with the ADFU, but the move proved impracticable for administrative reasons.[54] However, they flew from Croydon to Northolt every day to train under Vasse.

On 8 August Walsh visited the squadron to see for himself how their training was proceeding.

Special instructions were given to Wing Commander Vasse not to favour the Canadians in any way and to be sure that every possible angle of their training should be covered and criticized by outsiders, that is RAF Officers, in order to make the individuals and the unit as a whole realize the importance of what they might consider minor details. Wing Commander Vasse stressed the point that the Squadron had no idea of how to carry out attacks when they arrived but the last few attacks they had undertaken were beginning to show a decided improvement. He said that the Officers were all seemingly quite capable and very enthusiastic. He regretted that the training had to be interrupted for half a day to allow for the inspection at Croydon by the Rt. Hon. Vincent Massey, High Commissioner for Canada. It was explained, however, that this was unavoidable and it was hoped that the interruption would not prove too serious.[55]

Early in the month, in final preparation for the shift to operational status, McNab was attached to No 111 Squadron RAF and – on 11 August – was credited with shooting down a Dornier 17. By the 15th, McGregor was also acquiring a taste of operational experience with the same British squadron as his compatriots took off from Croydon for a last day's training at Northolt. Appropriately, perhaps, as they returned in the evening the reality of war was brought home when they 'found the Station had been bombed, the armament and Orderly rooms being completely demolished.'[56]

Although his diary entry has been misdated to the 18th by his editor (it was acquired in partly undated, loose-leaf form), apparently Gottfried Leske was one of those who attacked Croydon.

This time we were to bomb the aerodromes that ring London ... There were twenty of us, including ourselves. Before and behind us were many tight sections of pursuit planes.

The air was soupy at 3,000 meters, but it improved as we approached the Channel ... High above us our tough little Me[sserschmitt]s are flying. Already we are over Croydon, then over our target. It is shaped like a heart and lies close to a big highway. The Ju[nker]s in front of us have already laid their eggs. One of the hangars seems to have been hit, but otherwise they haven't done much damage ...

We finally managed to get rid of our packages. But Zoellner says he didn't think they did much good. Probably just made a few big holes in the field. Well, that's better than nothing.[57]

With Croydon temporarily unusable, No 1 Squadron RCAF was moved to Northolt, finally assessed as operationally ready for action.

McNab later described his squadron's battle innoculation, on 24 August 1940, as 'the lowest point in my life.'[58] Twelve keen Canadians were patrolling over the Tangmere field at 10,000 feet, assigned to cover Spitfires landing and taking off, when he spotted three twin-engined aircraft in line astern, 4000 feet below and flying towards Portsmouth where a major raid was just taking place. He led his men towards them and ordered an attack, but then recognized them as Blenheims and broke away, followed by his own 'Blue Section,' before anyone had opened fire. However, his instructions to the other two sections, transmitted by HF radio, were either not heard by them or not understood.[*] The Blenheims fired off recognition flares, but the keyed-up Canadians mistook them for incoming tracer rounds. One section attacked and damaged a Blenheim; the other first shot down a second Blenheim, then finished off the one already damaged.

A Coastal Command report of the incident, attached to the Canadians' Operations Record Book, told the tale from the victims' perspective.

Three Blenheims (long nosed) of 235 Squadron letters F, AI, and E were circling Thorney Island at 8,000 feet during the air raid.

At 1640 [hours] E was approached by Hurricanes and all the Blenheims fired the recognition signal (Yellow Red). A Hurricane then attacked E and shot the Blenheim down in flames into the sea off Wittering. One body picked up out the sea by boat and it is believed that the other member of the crew may have bailed out.

---

[*] VHF was still coming into service and generally only Spitfires were fitted with it, while HF – widely used by military and civilians alike – was not always reliable at such close ranges.

At 1640 AI was attacked by 6 Hurricanes, the first attack damaged the wings, fuselage and starboard engine and holed the perspex at the front of the aircraft. The Blenheim took avoiding action and fired another cartridge. A second attack was made by a Hurricane without results. The Blenheim crash-landed at Thorney Island aerodrome with wheels and flaps out of action. The crew escaped with cuts and bruises.[59]

The whole incident was remarkably similar to the notorious 'Battle of Barking Creek' on the third day of the war, when a gaggle of Spitfires had attacked two Hurricanes under the impression that they were Me 109s. Then, one Hurricane had been shot down and its pilot killed; now, two Blenheims had been destroyed and at least one crewman killed. No official recriminations seem to have followed either mishap, however, senior officers apparently understanding that the fog of war falls particularly heavily upon newcomers to battle. Indeed, such errors were not uncommon, and throughout the war a considerable number of aircraft fell to friendly fire. More than once, Canadians would be the victims.

Two days after their ill-judged attack on the Blenheims the Canadians were sent to North Weald, substituting for a front-line squadron which desperately needed rest. From there, in the company of Spitfires, the Canadians intercepted two dozen or more Dornier 215s, escorted by fighters. While the Spitfires engaged the escort, McNab ordered an echelon starboard attack on the bombers, and in the confused combat that followed the squadron was credited with three Dorniers destroyed and three damaged, though return fire took its toll. Three Canadians, including McNab, were shot down and one of them was killed. The survivors were, however, airborne the next day.[60]

Their next encounter came on 31 August. While patrolling the English coast near Dover, they were bounced by a formation of Me 109s which, coming out of the sun, quickly shot three of them down; all three pilots survived, but two were badly burned about the hands and legs. In the late afternoon of the same day, the eleven Hurricanes still fit to fly intercepted a formation of fifty bombers escorted by a 'large group' of Me 109s. They claimed two of the German fighters and one bomber destroyed, and one of each damaged, while losing just one machine of their own whose pilot suffered 'quite severe burns' before baling out.[61]

The following morning brought more of the same when they met 'twenty to thirty' enemy bombers, this time with a screen of Me 110 fighters (not the most effective escorts) at 18,000 feet over Biggin Hill. The Canadians were still using the standard attack formations which they had been so carefully taught, but which were not always appropriate, even against bombers flying in formation. 'Flight Lieutenant McGregor after two vectors [given by an air controller] sighted about twenty enemy bombers with escort above ... [He] gave orders for a head-on attack. After forming line astern by sections, he led his section echeloned to port, delivering his attack about ten degrees off enemy port bow and below ... Attack did not develop quite as expected as squadron was climbing to the bombers height at close range.' The diary records that a Do 215 and an Me 110 were shot down and four other enemy aircraft damaged. The Canadian squadron lost two machines and one pilot, who was badly burned.[62]

Fighting intensified through the first week of September as the Germans pressed their attacks against Fighter Command bases. On the 3rd the Canadians were ordered to patrol the south coast of England, where they found Me 109s flying far above them, at 30,000 feet, a height at which 'it was impossible for us to engage them.'[63] The next day, however, they were more successful. Eleven Hurricanes were 'vectored onto a formation of about twelve or fifteen Me 110s at 15,000 feet near East Grinstead,' which had formed a defensive circle in order to protect themselves against an attack by faster and far more manoeuvrable Spitfires. The latter were running low on fuel and had to leave the scene, but McNab positioned one section to attack from the side and, while the Germans concentrated on that threat, McGregor's section was able to get above them. 'We saw them below us and just dived down into them for all we were worth to try and break up the circle. I got inside their circle going in the opposite direction, and plastered them as I went by. As they broke up, I got on the tail of one of them and gave him a long burst and saw him catch on fire and dive down to earth. Then I went back to look for others.'[64] The station intelligence officer believed that two Me 110s were destroyed in this action, one probably destroyed, and five more damaged.[65]

The last ten days of August had cost Fighter Command 231 pilots, or almost one-quarter of Dowding's initial strength, and 60 per cent of those casualties were experienced flyers who could only be replaced by inexperienced graduates of Operational Training Units (OTUs). The first week of September saw no let-up in the pressure, and maintaining a unit's morale and combat effectiveness in the course of this intensive fighting involved an impossibly delicate balancing act – as pilots gained practical experience they were likely to be killed, wounded, or mentally exhausted by the strain, or else promoted into other squadrons to take the place of flight commanders who had become physical or psychological casualties. The desperate need for replacements forced Dowding to alter his training and posting procedures, and some pilots were switched directly from Bomber Command to Hurricane and Spitfire squadrons, while the length of OTU courses was cut in half.[66]

On the Canadian side, the problem of replacing casualties had been concerning Group Captain Walsh for some time. It will be remembered that when Ottawa had assigned No 1 Squadron to the defence of Britain, the British had agreed that the RAF would provide any reinforcements needed, 'there being no facilities for [operational] training' in Canada. Back then, the Air Ministry had estimated fighter wastage rates during 'intense' fighting – such as that which was now prevailing – at eight aircraft and four pilots each month. In the event, however, that had proved to be a gross underestimate, and if RAF pilots were to be posted in as replacements, the squadron would soon lose its Canadian character and become a British unit in fact if not in name. A pipeline was needed to feed in a continuing supply of RCAF aircrew, as and when required; the lack of Hurricanes in Canada meant that such reinforcements would have to be trained in RAF OTUs in the United Kingdom. When Walsh pointed this out to Ottawa, he was told that twelve Harvard-trained pilots would be sent, 'but none came. He cabled again, asking for only six, and was told that they would be sent, but again none came, [since] pilots had to be "ploughed back" into the BCATP.'[67]

While No 1 faced reinforcement problems, the two other RCAF squadrons already in the United Kingdom were essentially unemployed. Despite having been in England longer than No 1 Squadron, Walsh pointed out, 110 Squadron was unlikely to see any action unless Britain was actually invaded, when desperation might bring almost anything to pass. No 112 had reached Britain in late June, but its operational debut would also be some time in coming unless the Germans actually put troops ashore in the United Kingdom. 'It must be admitted that Army Co-operation Squadrons, even in a restricted role, are still necessary,' Walsh argued, 'but it will undoubtedly be very galling for the pilots of the Squadrons to be kept continuously in practice for an occasion which may never arise, while later arrivals from Canada are making their presence felt against the enemy.'[68]

Noting that several No 110 Squadron pilots had already begged informally for an operational posting – but not telling Ottawa that he had, in fact, asked for volunteers! – Walsh was 'certain that once No 1 Canadian (F) Squadron becomes engaged [in the battle], I will receive numerous applications for transfer to the Fighter Squadron as soon as vacancies become available.' He therefore requested authority 'to train a number of our A[rmy] C[o-operation] pilots in Fighter pilot roles, provided they are, of course, suitable.' According to his own account of this bureaucratic coup, permission was denied, but he then cabled back that Ottawa's response had arrived too late and the deed was already done. Six volunteers were hurriedly dispatched to an OTU, given the shortened course, and posted to No 1 Squadron at the end of the month.[69]

July and August had cost the Luftwaffe nearly three hundred Me 109 pilots (some 26 per cent of those available) and about four hundred bombers and their crews. Although the effectiveness of attacks on their air defences were worrisome to the British, Fighter Command seemed, from a German perspective, to be as strong in early September as it had been when the battle had begun a month earlier. That was not the story Göring was spreading, however. He was busy overestimating RAF losses and (deliberately) under-reporting his own – a political tactic that could only rebound upon him in the event that Adlergriffe (Eagle Attack) should fail.[70]

Meanwhile, the problem remained of how to go about completing the destruction of Fighter Command, a process that was going rather too slowly to meet the requirements of Fall Seelöwe. Perhaps Dowding could be tempted to fight en masse by an attack on London? Hitler's mind had been firmly set against targeting residential areas, but, on the night of 24/25 August, some bombers had 'overshot their targets, the oil installations at Rochester and Thameshaven, east of London, and dropped their loads over the centre of the capital.' Churchill had responded by ordering attacks on Berlin, a reprisal –

three reprisals, in fact – which outraged Hitler. On 31 August he authorized the Luftwaffe to retaliate in kind, and gave Göring the opportunity he sought.[71]

The commander of Luftflotte 2, General Albert Kesselring, also favoured switching the objective from Fighter Command itself to the immoveable hub of empire. Should damage to No 11 Group's southern airfields become unbearable, he argued, Dowding could simply move his squadrons north and west, to bases just out of range of German fighters but from which they could still defend southeastern England. Unescorted attacks on more distant airfields, beyond the range of fighter cover, meant that his bombers would simply be shot out of the sky. 'We have no chance of destroying the English fighters on the ground. We must force their last reserves of Spitfires and Hurricanes into combat in the air,' and attacking London was the way to do it. Hugo Sperrle, of Luftflotte 3, was in fundamental disagreement. He thought that there was little prospect of driving the British fighters from the skies, particularly since the need to provide close escorts for the bombers put his own fighters at a tactical disadvantage. The better strategy was to continue applying pressure upon Fighter Command airfields for the present. (He does not seem to have argued for a return to attacking radar stations in conjunction with airfields, the original German strategy which probably still offered the best chance of success.)[72]

Meeting with the two on 3 September, Göring, no doubt heavily influenced by Hitler's change of mind and the damage to his own prestige associated with British attacks on Berlin, ruled in favour of Kesselring. The Luftwaffe had been attacking airfields for a month now, without any apparent decision, and any alternative looked good to a man as intellectually shallow and publicity-conscious as the Reichsmarschall.[73]

During the first day of the mass raids on London, No 1 Squadron was scrambled three times, but only its commanding officer saw any combat. Since the British did not yet know about Göring's new strategy, the Canadians' job on 7 September was to protect Northolt while the two RAF squadrons based there flew interception missions. Their Operations Record Book noted that 'a 200 plus raid penetrated to London where heavy bombing occurred but although we sighted part of this raid we were not allowed to engage as Control insisted on maintaining Station defence.'[74] The only hint of action came in the last patrol of the day. Whether Squadron Leader McNab was with his squadron during the first two scrambles is not clear, but during the third, when one flight took off at 1708 hours and the other thirty minutes later, he appears to have been away on his own, 'on an independent flight in the general direction of Beacon Hill.' His combat report stated that he was 'flying easterly towards a position over Maidstone [on the Channel coast] at 21,000 feet, in company with a Spitfire about 500 yards to my starboard, when approximately five Me 109s ... crossed in front of me ... I attacked the rear one with a deflection shot and followed into line astern using my excess speed due to height to follow. The Me 109 climbed and I fired 150 rounds from each gun dead astern from about 150 yards. The E/A suddenly climbed vertically and fell straight down. I got a glimpse of white vapour from below his fuselage before breaking off [my attack].'[75] His victim was assessed as 'probably destroyed.'

Those pilots who were assigned to intercept enemy formations now discovered that the escorting fighters had adopted a different tactic to complement the bombers' altered strategic purpose. During previous attacks on radar stations and airfields the Me 109s had (quite properly) ranged freely in the general vicinity of the bomber phalanx, seeking to engage the British fighters long before they could attack the vulnerable Heinkels, Dorniers, and Junkers. Now they clung to their charges like sheepdogs to their flock. One group would fly in close contact with the bombers and another immediately above and behind, even though this restriction robbed the Messerschmitts of their greatest assets, speed and performance at altitude, and deprived them of their most successful tactic, the quick dive through an enemy formation followed by a climb back to altitude before their prey could react.[76] Many years later, one-time fighter pilot Johannes Steinhoff* recalled belonging 'to a wing whose express task was to escort the bombers to London and southern England.'

I can think of no more idiotic occupation for a fighter pilot than this shuttle service to London and back. 'Stay with the bombers at all costs,' we were strictly ordered. 'Don't engage in combat with the Spitfires. Don't let them lure you into attacking them even when they are in an ideal position. Remain with the bombers.' That was hammered into us *ad nauseum*. And if a man had done that sixty times, as I did, if he had bumbled rather than flown alongside the Heinkels or Dorniers ... as they crawled along ... if he had seen, time and again, the gleaming contrails high overhead as the Spits' reception committee, forewarned by their long-range direction finders on the ground, waited for this procession above Dover ... if a man had experienced all that, how could he possibly fail to have doubts about the sagacity of the high command?[77]

On 9 September the Canadians had their first experience with close escorts, as twelve of them, together with the Poles of No 303 Squadron, spotted a large formation of bombers in the Guildford area. Working with ground control, McNab tried to manoeuvre his pilots into a position above and behind the enemy, but, while doing so, they were attacked by the covering Me 109s. The combat that followed was even-handed. The squadron claimed one German fighter destroyed and three others damaged, while one Canadian (one of those transferred from No 110 Squadron) flying as 'tail-end charlie' was shot down and wounded. McNab might be justly criticized for putting an inexperienced newcomer in the most isolated – and therefore most dangerous – position in the formation, but the veterans of No 1 were now his friends, a friendship tempered in battle. Like many another commander through the ages, he perhaps found it easier to hazard the life of a comparative stranger rather than that of a cherished comrade.

---

* Steinhoff rose to become chief of staff in the postwar German air force, and ended his career chairing NATO's Military Committee.

The intelligence report on this engagement illustrates the gravest tactical weakness which still beset Fighter Command.

The Squadron was in line astern when the engagement started and when attacked by e[nemy]/a[ircraft] most pilots found e/a on their tails and broke away before being able to fire …

Some of the pilots were able to fire at the enemy, but with no conclusive results, while others were unable to find a target due to the suddenness of the attack and having to break away on finding themselves the object of attack.[78]

The enemy pilots, in their Schwärme, rarely had such problems, but although their tactics were better, the intelligence assessments presented to their leaders were as weak as the strategies laid down by Berlin. In the course of the now discontinued airfield raids, 'runways and buildings were usually only slightly damaged and could be repaired overnight,' recalled then Oberstleutnant Adolf Galland, 'At Luftwaffe HQ, however, somebody took the reports of the bomber or Stuka squadrons in one hand and a thick blue pencil in the other and crossed the squadron or base in question off the tactical map. It did not exist any more – in any case, not on paper.' As for the shift to bombing economic objectives, 'failure to achieve any noticeable success, constantly changing orders betraying lack of purpose and obvious misjudgment of the situation by the Command, and unjustified accusations had a most demoralising effect on us fighter pilots, who were already overtaxed by physical and mental strain.'[79]

Meanwhile, Gottfried Leske complained that the 'English' (Germans rarely distinguished between the various Commonwealth contingents in the RAF's ranks) '[are] always there when we come, and they send up hordes of fighters. Not that it will help them,' he added optimistically. 'They can't keep it up much longer.'

Sometimes when we come, in many layers and one formation closely following another, it's hard to imagine how a single English fighter will manage to get between us. It's as though we formed a wall. It really takes nerve to dive in between us the way they do. It's practically suicide. Because even if the Tommy is lucky enough to get one of our ships, he can't count on coming out alive.

Sometimes I get annoyed when the Hurricanes squeeze themselves in between us like that. I mean annoyed, nothing else. It's how you'd feel if you were on parade and some damned civilian suddenly got into the parade and upset the whole marching order. It doesn't even occur to me then that these Tommies are trying to do more than just disturb our marching order. I just feel that they don't belong and that they really ought to know better.

It's funny the ideas you get. Maybe it's because you can't hate your opponent every day and every minute. We know the English are our enemies and that we must beat them and that we will beat them, but we can't keep hating every damned pilot of every damned Hurricane.[80]

No 1 Squadron's next engagement was on 11 September when an afternoon patrol near Gatwick sighted about twenty Heinkel 111s, with a fighter escort 3000 feet *below* the bombers. The Canadians dived into the bomber formation, broke it up, and pursued the Heinkels individually. The enemy fighters failed to intervene and, when the claims had been tallied, the Canadians were credited with two He 111s destroyed and two more damaged. Flying Officer A.M. Yuile also claimed a Ju 52, although it is hard to imagine what that slow and unwieldy three-engined transport was doing in the midst of a formation of higher-speed Heinkel bombers. Two of the Canadians were shot down, one of them with wounds.[81]

On Sunday, 15 September – the high point of the battle by most accounts, now celebrated as 'Battle of Britain Sunday' – the Germans launched an attack on London by 123 bombers, escorted by over 650 fighters. At 1100 hours radar picked up enemy formations gathering over Boulogne and Calais, and the bombers were under constant attack from the time they crossed the English coast. Of the twenty-four squadrons scrambled to counter this raid, all but two managed to engage the raiders. The Canadians left Northolt at 1140 hours, 'with orders to patrol at 15,000 feet,' according to the squadron intelligence officer. 'Not long after they were attacked from above by Me 109s out of the sun, who made the attack and then sheered off before most of the squadron were able to fire.' Two Canadians were shot down, one of whom died, while the other, Flying Officer A.D. Nesbitt (who would subsequently command the squadron and was destined to finish the war as a group captain commanding No 143 (RCAF) Wing of the Second Tactical Air Force) claimed one Me 109. On a second sally, flying in conjunction with two other squadrons which tackled the covering fighters, the Canadians were able to close with a formation of Heinkel 111s and shoot down two, claim two more and an Me 109 as 'probably destroyed,' and damage several others, with only one of their own slightly wounded.[82]

At the end of the day Fighter Command was credited with 185 German aircraft destroyed while losing twenty-five of its own (a total which included the RCAF losses), but postwar analysis has revealed that the enemy loss was actually only sixty-one (of which twenty-six were fighters) while Dowding's casualties numbered thirty-one.[83] There were always great difficulties in establishing an accurate count since no pilot, having fired on an enemy machine, could afford to follow its subsequent gyrations for more than a few seconds if he hoped to avoid being shot down himself. Thus an enemy who dived away, accelerating and trailing exhaust smoke, could easily leave his attacker with the impression that he was going down on fire and out of control. There were, as always, exceptions, in which the outcome was irrefutable. No 1's Flying Officer P.W. Lochnan shot down a Heinkel 111 with the help of 'three Spitfires and two other Hurricanes,' then, in a scene reminiscent of popular war films, landed his machine in a field beside the downed bomber and personally captured the crew.[84] One is left to wonder, however, how many of the other five pilots involved also claimed that particular victory.

The Germans were back in force on the 16th and McNab took his squadron into the air in mid-afternoon.

As we climbed through the cumulus [clouds] we could see the first wave coming in. There must have been a hundred bombers in stepped-up formation with easily as many fighters surrounding them. British squadrons of Hurricanes and Spitfires were about to engage. Our Wing continued climbing and then we saw our target – the same size following the first wave. Just before we went in to the attack I looked over the channel to see the same number approaching, and our squadrons climbing [at] full throttle to intercept. It was a terrific battle. There must have been nearly a thousand aeroplanes milling in a small area just south of London. It was a quick shot and away for someone was sure to be on your own tail.[85]

On 18 September the Canadians were in action again.

The Squadron led by Flight Lieutenant McGregor joined up with 229 Squadron with orders to patrol Biggin Hill-Kenley, and were then vectored to the area North of Dungeness.
    Flying at 20,000 feet they were suddenly attacked by Me 109s and broke away, not being able to reform after. They patrolled individually but without contact except in the case of Flying Officer [O.J] Peterson who had climbed up to 27,000 feet where he sighted 3 Me 109s below. He attacked the No. 3 which went into a flat dive with smoke coming from the belly.[86]

Peterson, who would be killed in action on 27 September, claimed this 109 as probably destroyed and a second as damaged. He was lucky this time, since the Me 109E could outperform the Hurricane at any height but its advantage increased dramatically above 20,000 feet.[*] The experience of Flying Officer F.W. Beardmore, who also 'patrolled individually,' could be regarded as more typical – he was shot down, but was able to parachute to safety.[87]
    The next ten days were relatively quiet as the squadron experimented with Air Vice-Marshal Trafford Leigh-Mallory's controversial 'big wing.' To this point in the battle No 11 Group, covering London and the southeast, closest to the enemy, had committed its squadrons independently, even though several might eventually be engaged at once – a tactic which ensured that they would get into action as quickly as possible. Even with radar, there was little time to spare if the enemy was to be intercepted before he reached his objectives and, in Air Vice-Marshal Park's opinion, massing several squadrons under one commander and then launching them all at the enemy at one time would take too long. The Germans were likely to have concluded their bombing and be well on their way back to the Continent before contact could be made.[88]
    Leigh-Mallory, the frustrated AOC of No 12 Group (he was senior to Park, but commanding a group that was only on the fringes of the battle), prodded

---

[*] Several observations in the squadron diary make it clear that the Canadians were well aware of that.

by his protégé, Douglas Bader, argued that some delay would be justified if the Germans could be hit harder – and the best way to do that was to strike with larger formations even if the enemy could only be caught on his way home. His was a view shared by the assistant chief of the air staff, Air Vice-Marshal Sholto Douglas, who would become the next AOC-in-C of Fighter Command.[89]

No 1 Squadron's first experience with the recommended 'big wing,' however, was less than satisfying. 'Heavy fog impeded enemy operations during the early part of the day but by noon the weather had cleared and at 1800 hours a wing formation took off to intercept. There was some doubt amongst the three Squadrons as to which squadron was to lead and all took off together, fortunately without accident. The matter straightened itself out in the air ... but no interception was made, although enemy aircraft were seen a long way off the coast. This was the first Wing Formation operational flight from Northolt.'[90]

Even when procedures had been properly established, attempts to employ any kind of coordinated 'big wing' concept were doomed to failure when battle was finally joined. 'Situational awareness' – a term that had not yet been coined – was a key factor in aerial combat, but mentally it was impossible for even the most experienced pilot to hold in his mind the relative geometry of half a dozen shifting, jinking, machines – of which his was one – for more than a few frantic seconds at most. 'Command' in the usual sense of the word was out of the question once contact was established and the shooting began. Squadrons immediately broke down into smaller units, usually pairs or individual aircraft, Schwärme or 'finger fours' at most, each skirmishing in its own isolated battle over many cubic miles of airspace.

In hindsight, then, training time might have been better spent experimenting with different formations within the squadron. Curiously, however, given the hierarchical nature of military institutions and Fighter Command's prewar doctrinal rigidity, decisions of that kind were now left to the men who actually flew, so that there was no coherence in tactical doctrine. As the Commonwealth's premier ace of that war, Air Vice-Marshal J.E. Johnson, has noted, tactics had become 'the opinion of the senior officer present';[91] but when squadron formations broke up into the inevitable, kaleidoscopic confusion of small-scale engagements, the 'senior officer present' might well be a twenty-two-year-old from Moreton-in-the-Marsh, or Moose Jaw, Saskatchewan. Generally speaking, military intellectuals they were not; consequently, there was much warmth but little analytical thought put into the tactical debate, leading, in the absence of higher direction, to a growing lack of uniformity.

Some ideas caught on, often apparently among more than one squadron at a time. One notable innovator was an older South African, Squadron Leader A.A.N. Malan, who adopted a formation of three sections of four aircraft instead of four sections of three. 'When the melee began and the formation broke up, the four aircraft sections split easily into two ... Malan's theory was that a three-aircraft fighting unit contained one too many; and a lone fighter in the combat area was a sitting duck.'[92] So far, so good. He placed the four aircraft of his sections in line astern, however, the last one still being 'tail-end Charlie.'

Malan's approach was taken up in Tactical Memorandum No. 9, distributed in December 1940, the tone of the memorandum being merely advisory, not mandatory. 'Many squadrons now favour working in Sections of four aircraft with the object of being able to operate in pairs if the Squadron breaks up and dogfighting develops.' Further, 'it has been found that pairs of aircraft can keep together much better than Sections of three aircraft, and that they can afford better mutual support to each other in a dogfight.'[93] Bentley Priory was not yet ready to abandon the idea of weavers, despite being aware of some of its disadvantages. 'The method generally adopted of guarding against surprise is to provide "weaving" aircraft ... These aircraft turn continuously from one flank to the other so that they can keep a constant look-out behind ... There is a tendency for the "weaving" aircraft to lag behind the main formation and it is particularly important that the Formation Leader flies at a speed which will enable them to keep in very close contact with the Squadron formation.'[94]

No 1 Squadron was now down to fourteen pilots, and 27 September brought more losses as the Luftwaffe made its last major effort to bomb London by day. Shortly after 0900 hours, and in the company of No 303 (Polish) Squadron, the Canadians sighted a group of thirty Ju 88s heading for London with an escort of single- and twin-engined fighters. Polish-Canadian efforts led to claims of one Ju 88, four Me 110s, and one Me 109 destroyed, one Ju 88 probably destroyed, and one Me 110 damaged. Two Canadians 'had their aircraft shot up and made safe forced landings,' at Gatwick and Kenley, respectively, while a third was shot down and killed.[95]

These misfortunes were reflected in the second patrol of the day when the squadron could only muster eight machines. This time they flew in the company of No 229 Squadron, but it should be borne in mind that these were not 'big wing' formations; even if the squadrons chose to link up in the air, each still operated independently under the exclusive command of its 'senior officer present.' Near Gatwick about twenty Me 109s were sighted, 2000 feet above the Hurricanes. 'Keeping watch on the enemy, the Squadron did an irregular patrol until three of the enemy made a diving attack, fired a short burst and climbed again. As they went by, Red 1, Flight Lieutenant McGregor, got in two good bursts on one of the e/a which started smoking and spun down towards the ground. No other pilots were able to fire.'[96]

In mid-afternoon the Canadians, now reduced to six serviceable aircraft, scrambled for a third time, again in the company of No 229, the two units successfully attacking a group of Dorniers and claiming five destroyed and one damaged. This success, mirrored by those of other squadrons from No 11 Group, ended (for the most part) the appearance of obsolescent Dornier 17s and Heinkel 111s in the daytime skies, leaving the Luftwaffe to rely on the faster Ju 88 and a fighter-bomber variant of the Me 110 for what day-bombing there was. Future raids generally came in high and fast, making it extremely difficult, if not impossible, for the Hurricanes to reach the enemy. Even Spitfires had trouble unless they were already aloft when the incoming raiders were plotted.

The Canadians flew two patrols in company with Nos 229 and 303 squadrons on 28 September, when 'large numbers' of Me 109s were seen far above them. The enemy fighters were probably covering Ju 88s or Me 110s which the Canadians did not see, for they chose to leave the Hurricanes alone and the latter simply could not climb high enough to get within range. This frustrating experience occurred with increasing frequency through the last week of September and into the following month. On 1 October the squadron diarist noted that 'long patrols were carried out and visual contact was made with large numbers of Me 109s on each occasion but they stayed about 5,000 feet above and we were unable to engage them.' The next day, 'several patrols were carried out but although Me 109's were seen we were unable to engage them as they had their usual height advantage and refused to come down.'[97]

Blows were still given and taken, but those inflicted on the Canadians, combined with the introduction of a cold or influenza virus into the squadron's ranks, were taking their toll, making the shortage of pilots within the unit most noticeable and affecting morale among those still fit to fight. The return of three who had been wounded raised the number available to twelve; five others, including the commanding officer, were sick or in hospital, although morale rose on 4 October when the squadron learned that McNab had been awarded a Distinguished Flying Cross (DFC), the first member of the RCAF to be so decorated.

In early October the Battle of Britain was winding down, but it was not quite over. On the 5th the Canadians contacted approximately sixty Me 109s escorting fifteen Me 110s. 'Considerable milling about' resulted and one Hurricane, flown by Flying Officer H. de M. Molson (scion of the famous brewing family and later to be a long-time member of the Senate), went down; though wounded, Molson managed to bale out of his aircraft. 'He was amply revenged,' at least as far as the unit diarist was concerned, 'as the squadron bag for the fight was three Me 109s destroyed, one Me 109 damaged and two Me 110s damaged.'[98]

By now the squadron had been in almost constant action for nearly two months, and losses had been heavy – three killed and eight wounded out of the twenty-one original pilots and six reinforcements from Nos 110 and 112 squadrons. The squadron medical officer, Captain R.J. Nodwell of the Royal Canadian Army Medical Corps (doctors, never mind flight surgeons, had not yet entered the ranks of the RCAF overseas), who had been hospitalized with pneumonia early in September, was shocked by the changes he found on his return.

On [re]joining the Squadron 30/9/40 it was noted that there was a marked change in the general reactions of the pilots as compared to three weeks previously.

There is a definite air of constant tension and they are unable to relax as they are on constant call. The pilots go to work with forced enthusiasm and appear to be suffering from strain and general tiredness ...

This constant strain and overwork is showing its effects on most of the pilots, and in some it is marked. They tire very easily, and recovery is slower. Acute reactions in the air are thereby affected. There is now a general tendency to eat irregularly or to have a sandwich in place of a hot meal. The pilots are becoming run-down and infections which would otherwise be minimal are becoming more severe. There is a general state of becoming stale. Needless casualties are bound to occur as a result of these conditions if continued.

It is considered that personnel engaged in active flying should have at least 24 hours off once a week, in which to get a good sleep, a 48 hour leave regularly every two weeks, and a two week leave every three months.

It is recommended that the Squadron as a whole, be given respite from their strenuous duties to allow for recuperation, and that definite leave periods be enforced to provide proper relaxation and rest.[99]

Unknown to the good doctor, however, the Battle of Britain was ending. Fighting continued through October, but as the autumn weather deteriorated German attacks gradually petered out. On the 8th the squadron was ordered out of No 11 Group to one of the quiet backwaters of No 13 Group; its new base, where it would spend the next two months in rest and recovery, was Prestwick, on the west coast of Scotland, 'where the quarters were found to be comfortable and the food excellent.' There was a change of command as McNab was promoted to wing commander and attached once more to the RAF. Flight Lieutenant McGregor, also awarded a DFC (together with Flying Officer B.D. Russel), was promoted to fill the vacancy created by McNab's departure. The most dangerous opponent his squadron would face during its stay at Prestwick was a barrage balloon which broke free of its mooring. One pilot was dispatched to shoot it down into the sea.[100]

In December the squadron moved further north, to Castletown, near Thurso on the northeastern tip of Scotland, where it became part of the defences of the Home Fleet, stationed in the Orkney Islands' Scapa Flow. An important target for the Germans in the event of invasion, but beyond the range of their fighter aircraft, its aerial tranquility was disturbed only by high-flying photo-reconnaissance machines that were quite out of the Canadians' reach. 'All accommodation is very cold and not good. Thurso is a very small village with little entertainment, few women and the coldest hotel rooms ever experienced. Dispersal is in an old dilapidated farmhouse. It is dark until 0915 hours, and the sun goes down about 1530 hours and never gets very high up in the sky.'[101]

A week later McGregor was posted out, to take command of No 2 Squadron RCAF, and Flight Lieutenant Paul B. Pitcher found himself commanding a unit in desperate administrative straits. The other ranks were housed in a camp which lacked piped water, where there were no tables in their mess halls, there was no fuel for the stoves, and there were eight miles of blizzard-wracked 'highway' between airfield and living quarters. The only bright spot in a dismal picture was the relative abundance of good Scotch whisky.[102] Squadron Leader Pitcher (apparently doomed to inherit difficult commands, a fate that will lead him to appear in this story more than once) was perhaps fortunate at this point to undergo, in quick succession, a bout of measles, 'near pneumonia,' and scarlet fever – a sequence of events which led to a prolonged stay in hospital, followed by sick leave and a staff posting.

In mid-February the squadron, led by the senior flight commander, Flight Lieutenant Nesbitt, started south to Driffield in Yorkshire. No sooner had it arrived there than orders came to continue south at the end of the month, to Digby, in Lincolnshire. There it would re-equip with Hurricane IIs and turn to convoy protection duties over the North Sea and the English Channel and – eventually – to offensive operations over the French coast and the Low Countries.[103] The Germans having given up on invading Britain, any serious aerial fighting to be done during daylight hours would have to take place over occupied Europe. Fighter operations were about to enter a new phase, one in which the RAF and the RCAF would – for good or ill – take the war to the enemy.

6

Turning to the Offensive, 1941–2

For Fighter Command the campaigns of 1939 and 1940 had been strategically defensive enterprises, but in the early spring of 1941 it began, more and more, to take the offensive. At first, the commitment was minimal. Typically, with cloud forecast over the Continent and authorization from group headquarters, two or three pilots would plan their own operation, code-named a Rhubarb, selecting a course which they hoped would lead them to surprise some insouciant enemy airman en route to pay a social call at another base, or perhaps startle a pair of novices simply putting in essential flying hours. Using cloud cover they would stalk their foe, pounce when the opportunity arose, then re-enter the cloud before they could be attacked themselves by a stronger force. If they encountered no unsuspecting victims, they might attack targets of opportunity on the ground before recrossing the Channel.

The main motive for these early intrusions seems to have been to provide excitement and just a whiff of danger for aspiring young fighter pilots. They were not universally popular. 'I loathed those Rhubarbs with a deep, dark hatred,' wrote J.E. Johnson, the Englishman destined to become the Commonwealth's highest scoring ace and to command a Canadian fighter wing for many months later in the war. 'Apart from the *Flak*, the hazards of making a let-down over unknown territory and with no accurate knowledge of the cloud base seemed far too great a risk for the damage we inflicted.'[1] Fighter pilots being what they were, many more were happy to jink their way across the English Channel on what were virtually independent missions. After the war, however, the Air Ministry had to admit that it was 'difficult to believe that Rhubarb operations interfered with the working of the enemy war machine to any great extent.'[2]

A more formal and slightly more effective use of air resources involved the dispatch of larger formations on 'fighter sweeps over enemy territory without bombers,' sometimes referred to as Rodeos. Operations on that scale had to be authorized by Bentley Priory and planned and coordinated by group headquarters. They were seen to be 'useful as a means of training pilots, and of exercising them on occasions when bombers were not available.'[3] Five squadrons of Spitfires flew the first Rodeo on 9 January 1941, but such undertakings were still not an effective way of bringing the enemy to battle when he willingly paid the insignificant price of ignoring them. A bomber force – with the consequent threat, however remote, of substantial damage to such strategically important targets as factories or power stations – was needed to persuade the Luftwaffe to come up and fight on the RAF's terms.

On 10 January 1941 several fighter squadrons accompanied a flight of medium bombers bent on attacking airfields on the edge of the Forêt de Guines, south of Calais, in the first of what were subsequently labelled Circuses. It was still not possible, however, to exercise any real compulsion upon the enemy, since none of the targets within the range of fighter cover were really critical. The enemy might choose to fight, but could not be compelled to do so. Moreover, while the concept of Circuses was happily embraced by Fighter Command's current AOC-in-C, Air Marshal Sholto Douglas, it was not nearly as well received by Bomber Command's Sir Richard Peirse, who questioned his Blenheim bombers being used as 'bait.' Doubtfully, Peirse told the new CAS, Sir Charles Portal, that 'if we do (and we do) want engagements, then they must be profitable to us either because we shoot down more fighters than we ourselves lose, or because we inflict material bombing damage on the enemy. Preferably a combination of both.' Portal, however, promptly responded that he regarded 'the exercise of the initiative as in itself an extremely important factor in morale, and [he] would willingly accept equal loss or even more in order to throw the enemy on the defensive, and give ... [their] units the moral superiority gained by doing most of the fighting on the other side [of the English Channel].' He, too, disliked the term 'bait,' however, and told Peirse that 'it need not be mentioned to the Blenheims.'[4]

While they usually enjoyed an overall numerical superiority – often, indeed, a very substantial one – in their Circus operations, Fighter Command pilots were always at a tactical disadvantage. In what was almost a mirror image of the frustrations Jagdflieger had incurred in escorting bombers over England during the previous autumn, the British and their Allies were constrained by the requirement to remain in the immediate vicinity of the bombers when providing close cover – a commitment which both slowed them down and left them subject to German tactical initiatives. Even when flying as high cover, with more freedom to manoeuvre, they were condemned to fly well below the effective ceiling of the Messerschmitt 109E, since the Spitfire VB which had begun to enter service in February 1941 was still inferior to its German counterpart at heights over 30,000 feet. 'When it comes to fighter v. fighter and the struggle for the altitude gauge,' a senior staff officer told Douglas, 'we must expect for the time being to be at a disadvantage as compared with the improved Me 109 that we are now meeting.'[5] Moreover, were they so unfortunate as to be shot down, the likelihood of German airmen surviving to fight another day was good. Fighter Command's pilots, in contrast, were now almost always lost, since a parachute descent onto French or Belgian soil usually led to a prison camp.

Tactically, however, Fighter Command was making some progress. The new AOC-in-C had established a new appointment – wing commander (flying) – to lead each fighter wing in the air. The Tangmere wing was given to Douglas

Bader, who took on Flying Officer Hugh Dundas as his wingman and doctrinal acolyte. As Dundas later related: 'I was in favour of trying line-abreast formation, already extensively used by the Germans. I argued that four aircraft, flying side by side, each one about fifty yards from his neighbour, could never be surprised from behind. The two on the left would cover the tails of the two on the right, and vice-versa ... If attacked, you would break outwards, one pair to port, the other to starboard.'[6]

One morning Bader decided to experiment along those lines, and four pilots took off for the Pas de Calais. When 'half a dozen' 109s attacked them, they broke outwards in typical German fashion and, although they mistimed the break on this first attempt, they shot down at least one Messerschmitt. 'That afternoon we had a post-mortem. We all agreed that the main advantage of the new formation had been proved. It was practically impossible to be taken by surprise from behind.' Indeed, 'the tactical superiority of the section of two or four was so clear,' reported Douglas, that 'it was decided that the section of two aircraft should be adopted, and in the spring of 1941 a new sub-division of the [fighter] Squadron into two Flights each comprising three sections of two aircraft was standardized throughout the Command.'[7]

In May the first Me 109F appeared, giving the enemy a renewed technological advantage. 'At all heights a Spitfire can turn inside a Bf 109,[*] but the 109 appears to have quicker initial acceleration in a dive and also in climbing.'[8] This ability to out-turn an enemy was a definite defensive asset, but of very little value when attacking. The 109F had a better ceiling than any RAF fighter and a better overall performance. Whenever they chose to fight, the 109s simply dived through the stacked British formations, then zoomed off to regain the height advantage and dive again, if and when the situation warranted another attempt.

With the Germans holding a technological edge even over the Spitfire, the air environment over France was certainly not one in which the Hawker Hurricane could flourish. The two Canadian fighter squadrons that were operational in the spring of 1941, Nos 401 and 402 (formerly Nos 1 and 2), were both equipped with Hurricane IIAs and consequently spent much of their time flying defensive patrols over southern England and coastal convoys. On 15 April, together with two RAF Spitfire squadrons, No 402 participated in an uneventful Rodeo which took its pilots over Boulogne, that being the RCAF's first offensive fighter mission.[9] Most Rodeos (and Circuses) were equally tranquil, the Germans choosing to fight only when they were quite sure of their tactical advantage, with radar helping them come to such a determination.

Although these various fighter offensives were often led by distinguished veterans of the Battle of Britain, they also involved many inexperienced pilots, a good proportion of them coming directly from OTUs. A rough estimate of wastage, including postings to other theatres and to staff appointments,

---

[*] German airmen, and Allied ones as well, often referred to the Me 109 as the Bf 109, *Bf* standing for Bayrische Flugzeugwerke A.G., the company which had designed and built the first 109s and 110s before being reorganized as Messerschmitt A.G. in July 1938. The Me designation is employed throughout this volume, except when engaging in direct quotations, as in this case, since it was the most commonly used abbreviation among Allied airmen.

between August 1940 and April 1941 showed a turnover of 1300 pilots, 115 per cent of the effective August strength.[10] In March, the wing commander (tactics) at Bentley Priory complained that 'the average number of experienced war pilots in squadrons I have visited lately is five, and I don't think Squadrons are being allowed to do nearly enough training of their inexperienced pilots. Squadrons ought to go up and carry out surprise attacks on each other, and especially practise regaining formation after being split up. I think perhaps fighter pilots are so busy keeping formation that they are not able to keep a good enough look-out.'[11]

Under the guise of maintaining morale, Fighter Command nevertheless pressed on with its Circuses. Mid-June brought the largest yet, with more than 250 fighters escorting eighteen Blenheims of Bomber Command's No 2 Group to attack a chemical plant and power station near Bethune. As usual, no damage was done by the bombing, but this time the Luftwaffe reacted strenuously, shooting down nine of the intruders. Douglas was, however, able to take a positive view of the affair. He reported that 'although we lost nine pilots, those who returned reported a very favourable outcome of their combats,' and 'it seemed that the long-expected "fighter battle on terms tactically favourable to ourselves" had come at last.'[12]

Coincidentally, two days later policy-makers reviewed the ultimate purpose of these offensive operations, subsequently ordering a major modification which may have been necessary for political and grand strategic reasons but which did nothing to ease the strain on squadron pilots. For some time intelligence sources had been identifying German movements towards, and concentrations along, the Russian border, all pointing to an imminent attack on the Soviet Union. During the first week of June, decrypts of Luftwaffe Enigma cyphers – the special intelligence which the British code-named Ultra – established that the transfer of Luftflotte 2 from France to the east was substantially completed. Another Blitzkrieg was clearly in the making and there was little confidence in London that the Russians could resist it. On 17 June the CAS asked Douglas, in consultation with his colleagues at Bomber and Coastal Commands, to devise 'the most effective means possible of checking the withdrawal of Luftwaffe Units to the East – where the German attack on Russia was imminent – and, if possible, forcing the enemy to return some of the Units already withdrawn.'[13]

Douglas met with his fellow commanders-in-chief on 19 June (just three days before the Germans invaded the Soviet Union) to consider how that might be done. They agreed it was unlikely they could mount direct attacks in sufficient strength to bring back significant numbers of enemy fighters from the east, but they concluded that the violent reaction which had distinguished the Bethune raid might mean that the enemy was sensitive to attacks there – apparently dismissing out of hand the possibility that the Luftwaffe was simply taking advantage of a fleeting tactical opportunity rather than deliberately defending some key interest.

Since the enemy had reacted most energetically so far to the CIRCUS against a target near Bethune on 17th June and another against a target in that area on 21st May, we concluded that the industrial area which included Bethune, Lens and Lille was probably his most sensitive spot [within range of fighter escort]. By attacking this area it was hoped to induce him to concentrate in North-East France such fighter units as he still had in the West. Bombers without escort might then hope to reach West and North-West Germany in daylight round the flank of the defences, and this in turn might force the enemy to bring back fighters from the Eastern Front in order to defend the Fatherland.[14]

The rate and weight of Circuses was increased and, on 8 July 1941, an RAF squadron of Boeing B-17 Flying Fortresses made its first appearance over enemy-held territory. With an operational ceiling of 30,000 feet, eleven 50-calibre machine-guns, and the acclaimed Norden bombsight, it was thought that these early 'Forts' would be able to fly successful missions unescorted. But, in the course of twenty-six such raids (mostly in the form of individual sorties, a technique rightly criticized by the Americans), 'they were far from successful,' four Fortresses being lost before the end of September for no observable gain. 'In 51 sorties by individual aircraft, 26 were abortive and no bombs were dropped. There were difficulties with the Norden bombsight, numerous mechanical failures and a tendency for the guns to freeze up at altitude. Most serious of all was the inadequate defensive armament. All guns were manually operated and there was a blind spot at the tail. It was decided to abandon operations over Europe.'[15] An attempt to bomb the nearest German targets with smaller, lighter, British-built aircraft led to an attack on two power stations, near Cologne, on 12 August. Fifty-four Blenheims were used, together with 'an extensive series of diversions and fighter-escort flights ... but the limit of the fighters' range was reached well short of Cologne ... Most crews reached the targets and reported accurate bombing but ten aircraft were shot down by *Flak* or fighters – 18.5 per cent of the attacking force.' On the 28th, eighteen Blenheims attempted another low-level attack on Rotterdam docks, only to lose seven out of seventeen.[16] The influential AOC of No 5 Group, Air Vice-Marshal J.C. Slessor, was soon noting that 'this day bomber business ... is terribly uneconomical,' and that approach, too, was tacitly abandoned.

Fighter Command had already accepted that its own offensive would have to be restricted to French and Belgian air space and limited to 'the destruction of certain important targets by day bombing, and incidentally the destruction of enemy fighter aircraft.'[17] This variation, emphasizing the destruction of ground targets and focusing around the protection of a few heavy bombers, would subsequently be called a Ramrod; and it committed the machines involved to relatively deep penetrations of French airspace in pursuit of 'sensitive' targets.

In these upcoming operations a few RCAF officers would find themselves assigned greater responsibilities than fell to squadron commanders despite the absence, as yet, of any Canadian fighter formation.* The first of them was

---

* In air force terminology, a squadron was a unit, while any grouping of squadrons was a formation.

Gordon McGregor, DFC, whom we have already met as a thirty-eight-year-old Battle of Britain pilot.[18] In mid-April 1941 he became wing commander (flying) for RAF Station Digby, in Lincolnshire, where the wing included No 401 Squadron. On 3 July 1941, flying its Hurricane IIs as one of the Digby squadrons, and so far employed only on defensive operations, it staged south to West Malling. From there, forming a wing with two British squadrons, the Canadians took off to participate in their first offensive sweep.

Apparently they were intended to act as a diversion for an early Ramrod although, with two out of three squadrons flying Hurricanes, they were probably more temptation than distraction from an enemy perspective. Fortunately, the Germans were not to be tempted or distracted on this particular occasion, and according to the somewhat cynical squadron diarist 'with some sort of cohesion the two Hurricane squadrons made a tour of France and returning to the coast again, saw the bombers go out, some AA fire, a red blob suspended in the sky, and some say thousands of unidentified aircraft some distance away.' Two days later, after a second uneventful sweep – 'It was a pleasant outing, no Jerries being seen, no AA fire just nothing' – Pilot Officer Hugh Godefroy, flying his first Circus, 'was startled at the number of aircraft in the formation. Above us were the Spitfires, a squadron at every thousand feet up to twenty-seven thousand ... Below us, like a mother hen with its brood, was a single four-engined [Short] Stirling bomber surrounded by squadrons of Hurricanes.'[19]

After these operations, none of which had incited a German response, No 401 Squadron joined No 402 on the sidelines to await the day when they would be re-equipped with machines more appropriate for the work in hand. The timing was fortuitous and fortunate: enemy opposition increased or declined in apparently random sequences, but Fighter Command had now lost 121 pilots while claiming – undoubtedly with wild exaggeration – to have 'destroyed 321 German fighters.'[20] On the Allied side, at least one Canadian in the RAF with first-hand involvement in the fighting clearly distrusted those figures. At a No 11 Group conference, Winnipegger John Kent, DFC, leader of the Polish wing at Northolt, audaciously 'raised the question of just what our purpose was in carrying out these operations.'

If it was to destroy the industrial potential of the various targets and so reduce the contribution of industry in the Occupied Countries to Germany's war effort I maintained that it would require a far greater bomber force than we had so far escorted.

If, I continued, the bombers were merely there as bait to bring up the fighters ... we should restrict our radius of activity to that which would permit us to fight without the nagging fear of running out of fuel. This mental obstacle seriously interfered with a pilot's fighting spirit and it was my opinion that we had already lost far too many first class men because these factors were not receiving sufficient consideration.

But the AOC declined to recommend or support any shift in strategy 'and we continued to go to Lille and lose good men, all to little purpose.'[21]

At Bentley Priory, however, the AOC-in-C was himself becoming a doubter. He pointed out to Sir Wilfred Freeman, the vice chief of the air staff (VCAS), that

taught by experience, the enemy has vastly improved his RDF warning system and his system of reporting our fighters after they come within visual contact of his Observer Corps. We hear the German fighters receiving their instructions in the air about the approach of our main force when the latter are still over British territory. In the course of the battle over occupied territory we frequently hear the enemy giving accurate information to his fighters about the whereabouts and direction of flight of our patrols. (Sometimes on the other hand his information is wide of the mark.) The consequence of this improvement in the enemy's defence organization is that a larger proportion of his fighters are brought into the battle from the right direction and at the right height to give him the greatest possible tactical advantage. This does not happen of course on every occasion, but it does quite frequently.

Douglas therefore proposed reducing the scale of his offensive once the Russian front had stabilized. Instead of frequent, almost regular, raids at times which the Germans could readily predict from their weather charts, he suggested it would be enough to indulge in 'periodical offensive sweeps to give the fighter boys a "jolly" and some practical training, and to keep up their spirits and morale. It will also annoy the Hun and keep him on his toes if he never knows when we are going to put over another fighter sweep.'[22] That, surely, was as far as a commander could go (if he wished to retain his appointment) towards suggesting that his pilots were being squandered on fruitless, ill-considered missions.

There were, nevertheless, more than enough pilots graduating through the training system to make up losses. Indeed, RCAF graduates of the BCATP were now appearing in such numbers that it was possible to begin implementing Article XV of the BCATP Agreement and form Canadian squadrons in the United Kingdom. The first such unit was No 403 which, authorized on 1 March 1941, became operational on Spitfire Is in May under a British commanding officer, Squadron Leader B.G. Morris. It converted to Spitfire VBs in August, flying its first offensive mission on the 5th, losing Morris (who became a prisoner of war) on the 21st. He was succeeded by Squadron Leader R.A. Lee-Knight, who was killed in action only five weeks later. Four more British officers would command the squadron before it was finally turned over to a Canadian, Squadron Leader L.S. Ford, DFC, on 13 August 1942.

In September 1941 two more RCAF Spitfire squadrons, Nos 411 and 412, both formed in June, joined the battle. Making them fully Canadian in fact as well as in name was not an easy task, however, given the enormous demands for skilled tradesmen in the BCATP and, especially, the difficulty of providing newly trained groundcrew and administrative staff in the right proportions and numbers. By far the greater part of a fighter squadron consisted of non-flying personnel, and No 411 could only report itself 70 per cent Canadian by July 1942, while the other two squadrons, Nos 403 and 412, were no better off.

There were brief moments in 1942 when the Canadian composition of their non-flying elements exceeded 80 per cent (apparently as new drafts from Canada destined for currently forming squadrons were temporarily posted in), but it would be mid-1943 before all three could consistently report they were 100 per cent Canadianized.[23]

It should be pointed out, perhaps, that the measure of Canadianization was one of service affiliation rather than nationality, and that some members of the RCAF were not Canadians. One of No 412 Squadron's pilots, for example, was a British-educated Anglo-American, twenty-year-old Pilot Officer J.G. Magee, who had enlisted in the RCAF in September 1940. A year later, in the weeks before joining his squadron, Magee had learned to fly a Spitfire at an OTU in South Wales, an experience he found so exhilarating that he was driven to compose a sonnet about it. Less than three months after penning 'High Flight,' perhaps the best-known and celebrated poem of the Second World War, John Gillespie Magee died when his Spitfire collided with another aircraft while on a training exercise.

Even if it was possible to have all the pilots Canadian, it was not always practicable to do so, for qualified commanding officers and flight commanders were essential. There was good reason for the succession of British COs in No 403 Squadron, since Canadians of the right calibre were hard to find at this early stage of the war and the demand for them was outstripping the supply.

One of the few who had shown the requisite abilities in the eyes of Overseas Headquarters was No 411's Squadron Leader Paul Pitcher, whose unit flew its first offensive sorties on 20 September. No 412, under Squadron Leader C.W. Trevena (also RCAF), was only a day behind. Pitcher, a lawyer and prewar auxiliary airman from Montreal who had flown with No 401 Squadron in the Battle of Britain (and very briefly commanded it in the spring of 1941, before he fell sick), found that establishing a sound ethos and maintaining morale in his new appointment was no easy task. No 411's early experiences were a litany of mishaps, with the first crash occurring on 3 July, followed by ground collisions, heavy landings, raising the undercarriage too soon, landing with the wheels retracted, trying to take off with the brakes on, and even crashing into a totem pole at the end of the runway! When Pilot Officer W.F. Ash took up Pilot Officer R.W. McNair in an open cockpit, two-seater trainer and indulged in some unpremeditated aerobatics, he lost McNair, who drifted earthwards by parachute after 'accidently loosening his harness pin.'[24]

These various and apparently unending misadventures were the visible signs of a disciplinary malaise that took its toll on morale. After a spell of bad weather and of operations being cancelled for various reasons, the squadron diarist reported, in an unusually candid entry, 'Two squadron formations were carried out, and after each one there was such a lot of harsh criticism and "bitter recriminations" that about one more Balbo* ought, just about, to split

---

* A 'Balbo' was a massed formation of aircraft, so called after the Italian air marshal of that name who promoted mass flights during the 1930s in order to publicize Italy's growing air force. Balbo was shot down and killed by 'friendly fire' in 1940, while flying to Tripoli to take over the Italian air command in Libya.

up 411.' A few days later, in a squadron which had now been categorized as 'day operational' for better than two weeks, 'Two pilots scrambled to convoy a destroyer (though they didn't know it was a destroyer since they had not learned the code-words for various naval craft). They did not find the destroyer though, and patrolled the sunken vessel again.'[25] Earlier entries in the diary make no mention of any 'sunken vessel,' but use of the word 'again' suggests that No 411 had unwittingly patrolled over a wreck more than once.

The one bright spot was McNair, who registered the squadron's first victory, over an Me 109F, on 10 October.

The Wing Commander gave the signal to return to base and then the squadron turned to proceed towards the English coast.

I heard someone over the R/T saying 'There were scattered forces of Me 109s over Boulogne.' I went over at about 18,000 ft and saw numerous a/c below me at quite a low altitude. I dived on them and while still at about 5,000 ft above them I pulled up over the sea and came back on them again in a slow dive. I saw a group of seven E[nemy]/A[ircraft] circling a pilot in the sea, I picked out one, opened fire at him at about 250 yds, a quarter astern; he went into a sharp left-hand diving turn. I got on his tail and gave him a 3-second burst closing to 60 yds. I overshot him, pulled away to the right, and in going down I saw him go straight into the sea.

That ingenuous account depicts very well the bold but thoughtful novice taking a good look before committing himself, and then relying on surprise – but not excessive speed – to dive through six opponents while shooting down a seventh.

McNair would eventually be credited with fourteen enemy aircraft destroyed, three probably destroyed and thirteen damaged, but his first victory was very nearly his last. He broke clear and set a course for home but, his vigilance perhaps impaired by the euphoria of victory, he did not see the machine that shot *him* down until it was too late. Fortunately, the German who ambushed him in mid-Channel was no virtuoso of air fighting, either.

I continued on towards home when an E[nemy] A[ircraft] dived on me from port side out of the sun, his burst hitting my engine. I took violent evasive action, by skidding and slipping turns. The E a/c was now on my tail, putting in a continuous burst, scoring a number of hits. The cockpit became full of smoke, and the E a/c overshot me, coming directly in front of me at about 50 yards and about 10 ft above. I pulled up and gave him a burst, saw hits registering and his hood came off. Only my starboard guns were firing. Flames were now coming out of my cockpit, so I put my nose down. Finding that my engine was cutting out, I pulled up to 400 feet, and baled out into the sea. I was picked up about 15 minutes later.

This second Messerschmitt was originally assessed as 'damaged' in McNair's combat report, a claim subsequently changed to 'probably destroyed' (which seems more likely) and then back to 'damaged.'[26]

By 7 November the pilots of No 411 had claimed only two enemy machines destroyed, one probably destroyed and one damaged, while losing two of their own to the enemy and two more destroyed and ten damaged through their own ineptitude. A squadron history prepared in 1957 notes that the 'talk around the barracks and the messes was all of volunteering for overseas'; and in mid-December, given the opportunity to volunteer for service in the 'Near, Middle and Far East, all pilots submitted their names.'[27] Four days later, exactly six months after the squadron had been formed, two more pilots were lost when '... an error in navigation on the part of the leader took the section over Calais instead of Dover, when returning from a Convoy Patrol near the French coast. The section was pounced on by five Me 109s and the two pilots concerned 'bought it' ... It has been a tough month for this unit. Four pilots killed, at any rate missing, and some five flying accidents. Our motto 'Inimicus Inimico' – 'Hostile to an enemy' – should more aptly be read 'Hostile to Ourselves.'[28]

The unfortunate Pitcher was replaced by another Canadian of much greater combat experience, Squadron Leader P.S. Turner, RAF. Turner, a Torontonian, well knew the dangers of complaisant or unassertive management from his unhappy experiences as a pilot officer with 242 Squadron during the Battle of France; and he had learned much of the art of leadership from a subsequent commanding officer, the already legendary Douglas Bader. At the same time, he understood – and could sympathize with – the foibles and idiosyncrasies of his fellow-countrymen. As the year turned, the squadron diary detailed fewer mishaps and recorded more and more successful sorties.

Squadron Leader C.W. Trevena, the initial commander of No 412, had begun his service career in the ranks of the Non-Permanent Auxiliaries before being commissioned in July 1937. He had gone overseas with No 110 Squadron, and been one of Group Captain Walsh's volunteers posted (after an abbreviated OTU fighter course) to No 1 Squadron as a replacement pilot in the later stages of the Battle of Britain. Three months as a flight commander with No 403 in the spring of 1941 had led to his appointment as commanding officer of No 412 at the end of June. By the time his command became operational, however, at the end of August, it was rivalling No 411 at accidentally destroying its own aircraft.

Its first offensive sorties were flown on 21 September but were not marked with any great success. That may have been, in part, because the Germans still had a technological edge with their fuel injected engines. At the end of October, however, 'Sgt. Pickell returned from the Rolls Royce works at Hucknall with a new Spitfire VB which had been fitted with a new negative 'G' carburettor which now prevents the engine cutting when the control column is pushed sharply forward. Previously RAF fighter aircraft were at a disadvantage in carrying out this manoeuvre when in combat with German fighters which are fitted with the fuel injection system. Incidentally, 412 Squadron is the first Unit in the RAF [sic] to be fitted with this new gadget.'[29] Unfortunately, the 'gadget' proved to be no more than that, and of no help to No 412 Squadron. In July 1942 the AOC-in-C Fighter Command was telling the secretary of state for air: 'Our engines are still liable to temporary failure in flight under negative 'G' conditions. Although many attempts have been made to eradicate this defect from the standard type of carburettor and to develop and produce injection type carburettors which function perfectly at all altitudes, our latest type, the Spitfire IX, is still affected by this serious drawback. This defect is in fact the practical fighter pilot's chief bugbear at the present time.'[30]

After only two months on operations Trevena was posted out and shortly afterwards returned to Canada, where he would be discharged on medical grounds in October 1943. He was replaced by Squadron Leader J.D. Morrison, who was 'well qualified to command a squadron both from the point of view of flying and administration.' Morrison, who had been granted one of the RAF's first short-service commissions in 1939, had also gone overseas with No 110 Squadron in February 1940, then served briefly with 85 Squadron, RAF, and had been promoted to flight lieutenant, joining No 1 (subsequently 401) Squadron, RCAF, in November, just after the Battle of Britain. He would retain command of No 412 until killed in action on 24 March 1942.[31] His death merely re-emphasized the difficulty of establishing effective squadron and wing leadership in the early and middle years of the war – all too often, leaders and prospective leaders, fighting under grave disadvantages of one form or another, were killed before they could realize their full potential.

To complicate the lives of those who organized training and developed tactics (not to mention the pilots trying to master their dangerous trade), the Luftwaffe began introducing a radial-engined fighter, the Focke-Wulf 190, towards the end of September 1941, as 401 Squadron was converting to Spitfire Vs. This new machine demonstrated all the advantages of the 109F as well as a phenomenally rapid rate of roll – perhaps the most useful of all combat manoeuvres. 'When the FW 190 was in a turn and was attacked by the Spitfire, the superior rate of roll enabled it to flick into a diving turn in the opposite direction. The pilot of the Spitfire found great difficulty in following ... A dive from this manoeuvre enabled the FW 190 to draw away from the Spitfire which was then forced to break off the attack.'[32]

By mid-October No 401 Squadron was operational on its Spitfires and was promptly shifted south again, to join two RAF squadrons in the Biggin Hill wing of No 11 Group. Those pilots who had flown with the squadron in the Battle of Britain had, however, moved on or become casualties, and now their successors had a rude introduction to offensive operations when the wing set out on a Rodeo over the Pas de Calais on 26 October 1941. Approaching the French coast, one of the other squadrons peeled off to investigate four aircraft flying below them which turned out to be Spitfires. Unfortunately, 'the manoeuvre tended to disorganise the wing formation which also had to contend with a strong following wind which blew them inland.' Trying to re-establish some sort of cohesion, the Canadians then 'orbitted with the Wing south west of Nieuport, the formation becoming loose and the sections far apart,' which only made matters worse.

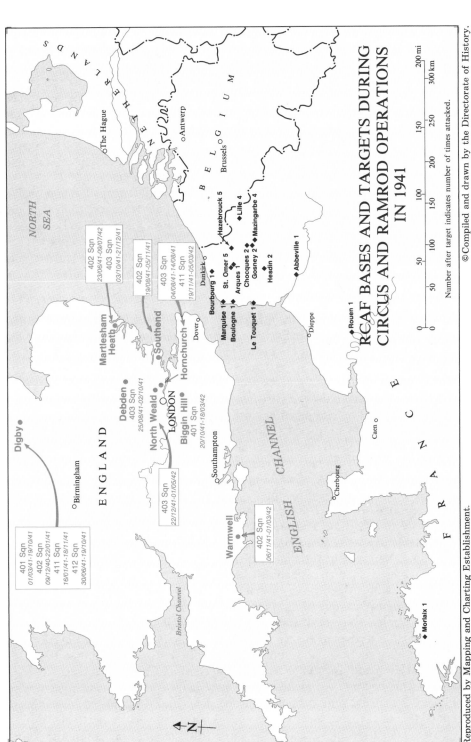

RCAF BASES AND TARGETS DURING CIRCUS AND RAMROD OPERATIONS IN 1941

Number after target indicates number of times attacked.

©Compiled and drawn by the Directorate of History.

401 Sqn
01/03/41-19/10/41
402 Sqn
09/12/40-22/01/41
411 Sqn
16/01/41-18/11/41
412 Sqn
30/06/41-19/10/41

402 Sqn
23/06/41-09/07/42
403 Sqn
03/10/41-21/12/41

402 Sqn
19/08/41-05/11/41

403 Sqn
04/08/41-14/08/41
411 Sqn
19/11/41-05/03/42

403 Sqn
22/12/41-01/05/42

401 Sqn
20/10/41-18/03/42

403 Sqn
25/08/41-02/10/41

402 Sqn
06/11/41-01/03/42

ENGLAND

NORTH SEA

NETHERLANDS

BELGIUM

FRANCE

ENGLISH CHANNEL

CHANNEL

Bristol Channel

Digby

Birmingham

Martlesham Heath

Southend

Hornchurch

Dover

Debden

North Weald

LONDON

Biggin Hill

Southampton

Warmwell

Caen

Cherbourg

Dieppe

Rouen 1

Morlaix 1

The Hague

Antwerp

Brussels

Dunkirk

Bourbourg 1

St. Omer 5

Arques 1

Chocques 2

Gosney 2

Hesdin 2

Marquise 1

Boulogne 1

Le Touquet 1

Hazebrouck 5

Lille 4

Mazingarbe 4

Abbeville 1

0   50   100   150   200   250   300 km

0   50   100   150   200 mi

N

Reproduced by Mapping and Charting Establishment.

As they turned for home, 'very considerable numbers' of enemy aircraft attacked the now widely scattered formations. 'The greatest losses were suffered by 401 Squadron who, probably through inexperience, may not have been keeping a look-out as strict as would have been kept by more experienced pilots,' adduced the wing intelligence officer, a conjecture readily reinforced by the report of one pilot who only became aware of the enemy as the machines on each side of him fell out of the sky. Five Canadians were killed or captured – one of them, Pilot Officer Wallace Floody, to distinguish himself subsequently in the 'Great Escape' from Stalag Luft III (see chapter 21) – and another parachuted to safety after reaching the English coast.

The squadron was credited with one Messerschmitt destroyed, one probably destroyed, and two others damaged. A few weeks later two more Spitfires were lost, but the Canadians gained a measure of revenge on 22 November as Nos 401 and 72 squadrons encountered 'considerable numbers' of enemy aircraft and the former claimed four of them destroyed, one probably destroyed and four damaged. Two of those shot down were the new Focke-Wulfs, Sergeant J.A.O. Lévesque being credited with the first such machine to fall to the RCAF.[33]

Meanwhile, doubts about the offensive's effectiveness, deteriorating weather, demands from the Middle East for more fighters, and stabilization of the Eastern front combined to effect further policy changes before winter set in. The AOC-in-C's proposal of 29 August 1941 was adopted and Circuses and Ramrods, which tied the fighters to relatively slow-moving bombers, were now only to be undertaken in 'specially favourable circumstances,' while 'a rigorous offensive should be continued against shipping and "fringe targets."'[34]

It is difficult to draft an accurate balance sheet measuring the degree of success or failure in all these operations. The only acceptable numbers concern the five-and-a-half months between 14 June and 31 December 1941, when Bentley Priory lost 395 of its pilots killed, taken prisoner, or missing (with another sixteen lost on anti-shipping strikes). In exchange, 731 enemy aircraft were reported to have been destroyed, but actual Luftwaffe losses from all causes were (we now know) only 154, of which fifty-one were not even attributable to RAF/RCAF action;[35] probably at least half the Germans who were shot down survived to fight another day.

The five Canadian squadrons claimed twenty-two enemy machines destroyed, with fifteen more probably destroyed and twenty-eight damaged, while losing twenty-one of their own pilots – No 412 claimed only *one* enemy aircraft, but lost three of its own – but it is impossible to determine the number they actually accounted for.[36] As the RCAF claimed a lower ratio of victories to losses than the RAF, its figures are probably less inaccurate than those for Fighter Command as a whole, and it may be that Canadian losses exceeded those of the enemy by a factor of only two or three to one, as compared with Fighter Command's ratio of four to one. But failure cannot be measured in numbers alone: it also has to be gauged against aims and objectives.

Air Marshal Douglas, despite his earlier reservations concerning the nature and style of the offensive, had by now adopted a more positive stance in this regard. In taking the initiative the RAF had gained a moral ascendancy over the Luftwaffe, he argued, a conclusion remarkably similar to (and just as mistaken as) that reached by Sir Hugh Trenchard to justify his heavy casualties when he was commanding the Royal Flying Corps on the Western Front in 1916 and 1917.[37] As for the efforts to limit German reinforcement of the Eastern front, and even to draw some formations back from the east, the AOC-in-C claimed partial success. While he admitted that the Luftwaffe had not been pressured to withdraw any air units from Russia, his pilots, he suggested, had kept significant numbers – two top-quality Geschwader amounting to some 260 fighters – in northern France.

With fifty years of hindsight, however, it seems reasonable to assume that the retention of so few fighters and rather more pilots to oppose the approximately 1200 machines and many more pilots then available in the United Kingdom was a minimal precaution on the enemy's part. Douglas acknowledged that it was 'most unlikely that, even without the offensive, the Germans would altogether have denuded the Western Front of fighters,' noting that 'so long as even the threat of an offensive was present, a substantial defensive force would doubtless have been retained in the West in any case.' He concluded, rather lamely, that: 'One of the clearest lessons which was later seen to emerge from this experience was that fighters operating from this country over Northern France could, at sufficient cost, inflict such losses on the opposing fighter force as would bring about a local and temporary air superiority. But this achievement could, of itself, have no decisive military value: the ability to create this situation was valuable only if means were at hand of exploiting it by some further move capable of producing a decision.'[38]

On the far side of the world another powder keg had exploded, and shock waves struck the RCAF Overseas as well as Canada's Home War Establishment and Western Air Command. The Japanese invasion of Malaya, paralleling attacks on Pearl Harbor and the Philippines from 7 to 10 December 1941, led the British chiefs of staff to call for fighters from the Mediterreanean theatre to be sent to India, in order to bolster British defences there. At the same time, Middle East Command needed all the fighters it could muster to restrain the Luftwaffe which, despite its lesser numbers, was currently maintaining air parity – and sometimes air superiority – over the RAF in the Western Desert, largely by virtue of its tactical edge. The CAS 'made promises of large reinforcements which should arrive in the Middle East by the end of April.'[39]

That commitment was made just as Air Vice-Marshal Harold Edwards – who had replaced L.F. Stevenson in London with orders from Ottawa to 'put the RCAF on the map' – was proposing that, if the RAF should decide to transfer any more squadrons to the desert, it might consider an RCAF Squadron 'so that it may form a focal point for the many RCAF crews now serving in the Middle East.' There had been some talk of sending an RCAF Spitfire squadron to the desert in mid-1941, but nothing had come of it. Now, however, the Air Ministry was quick to accede to a request which fitted in so conveniently with its needs; and on 26 March 1942 C.G. Power told his Cabinet colleagues that the selected squadron would be No 417,[40] formed four months earlier at the

alluringly named Charmy Down, in Somersetshire, under the command of an
RAF New Zealander. If the squadron was to become the 'focal point' that
Edwards sought, however, it would need a Canadian commanding officer with
substantial diplomatic and administrative skills. On 23 March, the same day the
squadron was officially assigned to the Middle East theatre, Squadron Leader
Paul Pitcher, was posted to command it.

There were many RAF men in the squadron's ranks, while many of those
who were Canadian were not particularly well qualified. Pitcher made attempts
over the weeks before embarkation to bring in seasoned RCAF tradesmen, but
they were hard to find and even harder to pry loose from their current appointments, even though Overseas Headquarters was demanding the maximum
possible level of Canadianization. By 13 April, when No 417 Squadron sailed
for Egypt, the overall figure was 72 per cent, with all the pilots and 70 per
cent of the non-flying staff in the squadron being Canadian.[41]

As we shall see in subsequent chapters, the squadron's operational experiences over the next three years were not much different from those of other
Canadian fighter squadrons. Because of its prolonged isolation in the Mediterreanean theatre, however, the application and maintainence of Canadianization
policies took on peculiar overtones for No 417. Replacements, especially in the
form of experienced pilots to serve as flight commanders and their deputies,
were sometimes hard to acquire. Paradoxically, at other times the problem was
reversed as staff officers had to deal with overqualified Canadians for whom
there were no further promotion possibilities in-theatre, short of posting them
to RAF squadrons or formations. An experienced flight commander with No
401, for example, might be promoted to command another RCAF fighter squadron in the United Kingdom easily enough, but his counterpart in No 417 had
only one possibility open to him if he was to remain with an RCAF unit; he
would have to wait for his own squadron commander either to be posted
elsewhere or to become a casualty.

No 417 was still in England and still working up to operational standards
when, in mid-February 1942, the Luftwaffe combined with the Kriegsmarine
to effect the 'Channel dash' of the battlecruisers *Scharnhorst* and *Gneisenau*
and the heavy cruiser *Prinz Eugen* from the Atlantic port of Brest into the
North Sea. The RAF's failure to respond promptly and adequately, despite the
existence of a detailed contingency plan for Operation Fuller, meant an opportunity wasted for Bentley Priory, which must bear a substantial part of the
blame.

Some 280 aircraft, Me 109s, 110s, and FW 190s working in shifts, served as
guardian angels for the German flotilla. Coastal Command and Fighter Command reconnaissance failures allowed the enemy to enter the Strait of Dover
– halfway home – before the British were able to launch their first strike,
undertaken by six obsolete torpedo-armed Fairey Swordfish biplanes of the
Fleet Air Arm with five fighter squadrons detailed to protect them. The Hornchurch wing, consisting of Nos 64 and 411 squadrons, was to fly as close
escort and try to suppress anti-aircraft fire, while the three-squadron Biggin
Hill wing, which included No 401, was to act as top cover. Only one of these

five squadrons succeeded in rendezvousing with the Swordfish, however, and an excessive emphasis on security ensured that none of them really understood the importance of the task at hand and only a few even knew what the task was.[42]

No 411 Squadron, led by Squadron Leader R.B. Newton, RAF (on his first day in command), was late getting into the air owing to 'difficult weather conditions.' Perhaps there seemed to be no great urgency, since the Canadians were only ordered to do an 'E-boat search.' Their subsequent patrol did not 'bring the Squadron into contact with the main enemy convoy,' although they 'received the attention of flak ships with no damage to ourselves.' A second mission, in mid-afternoon, found them covering the withdrawal of bombers which had vainly sought the enemy through heavy cloud cover.[43]

No 401 Squadron also failed to make the rendezvous on time, delayed by a security muddle which would have been comic if it had not been for its tragic consequences. The battle plan for Fuller was locked in a safe at Biggin Hill, but the station intelligence officer had taken a day's leave, neglecting to leave the key in his deputy's charge. It was not until Group Headquarters impatiently queried the wing's failure to respond that the pilots were ordered to take off 'to intervene in a battle between German E-boats and British MTBs.' Low cloud and mist mixed with driving rain ensured they would not make visual contact with the Swordfish, while the fact that the Fleet Air Arm and Fighter Command used different radio frequencies prevented air-to-air communication. Leaving the Swordfish to their fate (they were all shot down by Flak and fighters and only five of eighteen crewmen survived), Nos 401 and 128 squadrons carried out a patrol north of Calais and 'numerous dogfights ensued when considerable numbers of Me 109Es and Fs and FW 190s were engaged in combat.'[44]

No 403 Squadron, as part of the North Weald wing, was ordered 'to maintain air superiority between 1430 and 1500 hrs whilst the main attack by Coastal and Bomber aircraft was taking place.'[45] The wing took off at 1410 hours, expecting to link up with the Debden wing over Manston, but layered clouds apparently thwarted the process. Indeed, the Canadians now found themselves proceeding independently, in three sections of three machines each – shades of the now discredited vic! – led by their British commanding officer, Squadron Leader C.N.S. Campbell. Campbell became separated from the others off the French coast but, after jousting briefly with three Messerschmitts attacking two Hudson bombers, he was re-united with the two Spitfires of his own Red section and three from another squadron. '109s kept breaking cloud base but upon [the Spitfires] turning towards them, took cover.' Yellow and Blue sections, meanwhile, were claiming one enemy aircraft destroyed and another damaged in the tangle of small-scale engagements brought about by poor coordination of effort in cloud-riven skies.

Several other pilots had brief combats with Messerschmitts as they darted in and out of low clouds, but made no claims. By the end of the day Fighter Command had lost twelve pilots and seventeen machines while shooting down seventeen enemy fighters and accounting for eleven German airmen. But if the

tactical battle ended in a draw, there could be no doubt which side had won
the strategic, operational, and public relations battles. The 'Channel block' had
failed ignominiously.[46]

With the Fuller fiasco behind them and the Wehrmacht turning to the offensive again in the east, the British chiefs of staff once more considered the
question of how their various forces might best help the Soviet Union in 1942.
The Royal Navy was doing all it could to ensure that North American supplies
reached Murmansk; in North Africa, an out-generalled and ill-led Eighth Army,
pursued by the Afrika Korps, was in retreat towards El Alamein and the Nile
delta; Malta was fighting for its life and absorbing fighter resources; and
Bomber Command was now endeavouring (with very limited success) to
destroy Germany's industrial base and the morale of its people. The air staff's
proposal for Fighter Command was an enhanced offensive, its intelligence
branch estimating that 'a total of 200 [enemy] day fighter casualties per month
from all causes on the Western Front would result in a [long-term] decline of
the enemy's strength, and that a total of 250 would necessitate reinforcement
in the West at the expense of the German single-engined fighter force in
Russia.'[47]

Of the 250 hoped-for casualties, half would have to be inflicted in combat,
while the other half could be expected in the form of accidents incurred in the
course of operations and training. Bringing the enemy to battle posed a most
difficult problem, however – what would compel the Jagdflieger to come up
and fight? With the new auxiliary fuel tanks just coming into use, the radius
of effective fighter operations had risen to about 190 miles from No 11 Group
airfields, and within that range priority was assigned to potential Circus targets
based on their economic importance and the degree of damage which might
be inflicted by quite small bomber forces. Power stations came first and six
major factories second: there were fifty-eight targets altogether, forty-one in
France, twelve in Belgium, and five in the Netherlands.[48] Whether any of
these were of sufficient importance to lure the Luftwaffe into the air remained
to be seen.

A comparison of opposing capabilities seemed to favour the Germans. 'This
year we are worse off for formation leaders and experienced pilots than we
were in 1941,' declared Bentley Priory analysts. They went on to speculate that
'owing to so many having been sent overseas ... it seems reasonable to suppose that Fighter Command has been more drained of experienced pilots than
the opposing fighter forces on the Western Front' – a supposition that took
little or no account of German wastage in the east. Additionally, 'we start this
year's operations at a technical disadvantage greater than that prevailing at the
end of last year. Fighter Command is still equipped with the Spitfire VB, while
the enemy has the Me 109F and is getting FW 190s in increasing numbers.'
Both the Me 109F and FW 190 could fly faster (by about twenty miles per
hour) and higher (by more than 2000 feet) than the Spitfire VB. Moreover, RAF/
RCAF sallies were as predictable as Luftwaffe reactions were not. 'The restricted area of enemy territory within the radius of action of our fighters limits
the variations which can be made in the tactical conduct of our offensive

operations. Such operations are therefore bound to have a certain similarity, and it will be difficult to achieve surprise.'[49]

Nevertheless, staff officers calculated (wrongly, as we have seen) that since Fighter Command had inflicted 120 losses per month on Luftflotte 3 in 1941 while using twenty squadrons, 'if our effort this year were half as great again as it was last year, this would not only allow for the increased disadvantage under which our fighters would operate, but would give a margin to ensure that last year's enemy casualties were exceeded.' In other words, in order to achieve the required battle attrition of 125 enemy aircraft per month, Douglas would need an additional ten squadrons. That number would permit the offensive to proceed despite its own wastage, predicted (wrongly again – the RAF/RCAF would lose fewer aircraft and more pilots than expected) at 112 pilots and 330 aircraft monthly. Thus, 'the aim may be attained by continuous intensified CIRCUS and other offensive operations on the lines of those carried out last year. An average of six bomber sorties a day, with a maximum of 30/36 sorties on any given day, should be allocated to CIRCUS operations.'[50]

The Germans were not expected to open a major campaign in Russia before the conclusion of the spring thaw and No 11 Group was to be reinforced by the required ten squadrons before then. Current operations would continue on a modest scale until the enemy had resumed ground offensives in the east, at which time they would be expanded by half. 'You are terribly short of fighter aircraft,' noted the prime minister, early in March, 'but it pays to lose plane for plane. If you consider CIRCUS losses will come within that statement, it w[oul]d be worthwhile. But beware of the future.' In the event, the pace quickened earlier than expected, with an average of 826 sorties a day between 13 and 17 April 1942 and over a thousand on the 16th. (Coincidentally, a month later Bomber Command would launch its first thousand-bomber raid.) The Germans responded selectively, as they had in 1941, intervening only when they felt circumstances favoured them. Fighter Command lost thirty-four aircraft in March and ninety-three in April, while claiming a total of 114 enemy machines destroyed. In fact, between the beginning of March and the end of June the Luftwaffe lost only fifty-eight machines in combat, while Bentley Priory, claiming 197 victories, lost 259. As for the five RCAF squadrons, they lost twenty pilots while claiming to have shot down nine enemy machines.[51]

Once again it is impossible to determine the number of enemy aircraft they actually destroyed, but this time the Canadian proportion was probably close to the overall Fighter Command ratio of over four lost for every one actually shot down. Nevertheless, since no one at Bentley Priory – or, indeed, in the Air Ministry or the War Cabinet – knew at the time how bad that ratio was, morale did not suffer unduly. Individual pilots who lost friends and colleagues were usually consoled by the belief that their squadron or wing was giving as good as it got.

That was not the case on 2 June 1942, however, as No 403 Squadron lost six pilots in the course of a single disastrous sweep. At the time the squadron was under the command of a New Zealander, Alan Deere, DFC and Bar, the unit's sixth non-Canadian commanding officer in the thirteen months since its formation. Early that morning the squadron flew a sweep along the French coast notable only for the complete absence of either Flak or enemy aircraft. Back for breakfast at North Weald by 0730 hours, the pilots then prepared, together with the Hornchurch wing, to trail their coats in the vicinity of St Omer where the Luftwaffe maintained a major fighter base. The Canadians were assigned to serve as top cover, above and behind the two Hornchurch squadrons, at 27,000 feet.

A ground controller in England, relying on radar, informed them as they crossed the French coast that Germans were already in the air, but No 403 saw none of them on its outward leg. When the first enemy machines appeared, they were closing on the Canadians from the rear; then more were seen, above and to the left, and yet more on the right. The Luftwaffe had waited until the wing was most vulnerable – on its way home, with fuel supplies dwindling, having lost several thousand feet of valuable height. Deere, highly experienced pilot that he was, found himself 'engulfed in enemy fighters – above, below, and on both sides, they crowded in on my section.'

Ahead and above I caught a glimpse of a FW 190 as it poured cannon shells into the belly of an unsuspecting Spitfire. For a brief second the Spitfire seemed to stop in mid-air, and the next instant it folded inwards and broke in two, the two pieces plummeting earthwards; a terrifying demonstration of the punch of the FW 190's four cannons and two machine-guns ...

There was no lack of targets, but precious few Spitfires to take them on. I could see my number two, Sergeant [H.] Murphy, still hanging grimly to my tail but it was impossible to tell how many Spitfires were in the area, or how many had survived the unexpected onslaught which had developed from both sides as the squadron turned to meet the threat from the rear. Break followed attack, attack followed break, and all the time the determined Murphy clung to my tail until, finally, when I was just about short of ammunition and pumping what was left at a FW 190, I heard him call.

'Break right, Red One; I'll get him.'

As I broke, I saw Murphy pull up after a FW 190 as it veered away from me, thwarted in its attack by his prompt action. My ammunition expended, I sought a means of retreat from a sky still generously sprinkled with hostile enemy fighters, but no Spitfires that I could see. In a series of turns and dives I made my way out until I was clear of the coast, and diving full throttle I headed for home.[52]

Murphy also got back to North Weald, but six of the Canadians did not, one being killed and five spending the rest of the war in prison camps. Moreover, three of the aircraft that returned had to be written off. The squadron engineering officer obtained nine replacements that same afternoon, and groundcrews working through the night had thirteen machines serviceable by next morning. All their efforts went for naught, however, for no sooner were they ready than the squadron was declared non-operational and sent first to Martlesham Heath, a quiet backwater in No 12 Group, and then on to Catterick in Yorkshire, to recoup. Deere protested personally to his group commander, Air Vice-Marshal

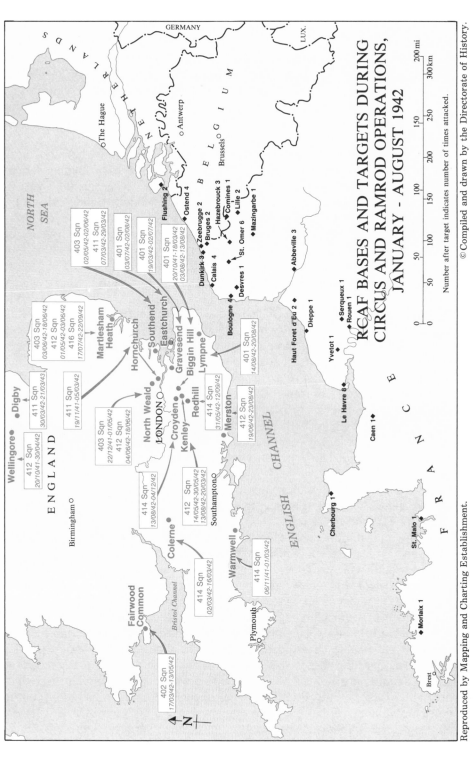

RCAF BASES AND TARGETS DURING
CIRCUS AND RAMROD OPERATIONS,
JANUARY - AUGUST 1942

Number after target indicates number of times attacked.

© Compiled and drawn by the Directorate of History.

Reproduced by Mapping and Charting Establishment.

Trafford Leigh-Mallory, insisting that squadron morale had not been affected by its misfortune and that his pilots wanted to remain active. Leigh-Mallory (a notably pessimistic and unsympathetic character) was not to be moved, alleging that, somehow, Deere had not been 'entirely blameless' in what had happened because he was 'rather too fond of a fight' and took 'unnecessary risks.'[53] Even today, it seems a peculiar charge. It was not Deere's policy that had led to the wing sweeping over France, and he had hardly chosen to be ambushed.

By mid-June the assistant chief of the air staff (operations) had concluded that while 'day offensive operations have succeeded in inflicting serious losses and in holding a considerable enemy fighter force on the Western Front which has absorbed the output of his most modern fighter types,' the FW 190 was so technologically superior that Fighter Command's offensive must be modified. The Mark V Spitfire was simply inadequate, and therefore 'Typhoons should be employed in day offensive operations as soon as they are available in sufficient numbers and trained operationally, with a view to determining the extent to which they will assist in restoring the technical balance.'[54]

Unfortunately, the Hawker Typhoon would never be effective in an air superiority role. It had initially been put into service in September 1941 and, with a maximum speed of more than 400 miles per hour and an armament of twelve .303 machine-guns, the Air Ministry had expected it to match or surpass the Me 109 and FW 190. But it quickly proved a great disappointment. The original 24-cylinder Napier Sabre engine was unreliable and major modifications were required; there were problems with the tail structure; and its great weight left the 'Tiffie' with an inferior rate of climb and a disappointing performance at altitudes over 20,000 feet, a handicap that made it virtually useless in its intended air superiority role. The engine reliability problem would be solved by the fall of 1942 and a variant mounting four 20-millimetre cannon would then be employed in intercepting low-level 'hit and run' raiders over England. Its weakness at height, however, made it quite unsuitable for Circus or Ramrod operations.

Meanwhile, the air staff advised, 'deep penetration in CIRCUS operations should be avoided except in respect of bombing targets, the damage or destruction of which will justify an adverse casualty balance in the fighter forces involved,' while 'fighter sweeps designed to bring the enemy fighters into the air should be planned and conducted with restraint, and should aim at meeting the enemy in combat under favourable conditions.' Indeed, 'if the tactical conditions are likely to become adverse in any particular operation, combat should if practicable be avoided.' At the same time, the AOC-in-C at Bentley Priory was insisting that it was 'of vital importance that our pressure on the enemy should not be weakened to an extent which will enable him to reduce his fighter forces on this Front'; and intelligence information had to be continually monitored, 'so that our operations may again be intensified if there are any signs of withdrawal or weakening of the German fighter forces in France.'[55]

At the Air Ministry, the director of intelligence was vaguely optimistic in early July, estimating that German fighter reserves were down to about two hundred first-line aircraft, half of them less than fully effective. 'There is no doubt that Fighter Command's offensive during the past few months has contributed substantially to the present satisfactory situation, and further intensive operations would be likely to cause the Germans most serious embarrassment.' Such optimism in the Air Ministry was harshly contradicted by operational reality. The intelligence assessment was based on an Enigma decrypt which revealed that the Luftwaffe had imposed flying restrictions on its formations in Russia and was experiencing difficulties in supplying aircraft to North Africa, problems that were more a matter of operational logistics than German manufacturing capacity at this stage of the war. Meanwhile, attrition continued. In June Fighter Command lost fifty-nine aircraft against thirty-two enemy claimed and twelve actually destroyed; in July the figures were sixty-two admitted losses against twenty-nine claimed and sixteen actually shot down. When the AOC-in-C passed his operational summary on to Leigh-Mallory at No 11 Group, he tried to make the best of a bad job, remarking, 'It does show that our fighter offensive is having an appreciable effect and that the losses we have sustained have not been fruitless.'[56]

If the day-fighter war was not going exactly as Bentley Priory might have hoped, after dark the clash between the RAF/RCAF and the Luftwaffe brought forth a whole different category of challenges. Having learned in the Battle of Britain that daylight attacks were more dangerous to the attacker than to the target, German bombers now flew mostly at night. That strategy had initiated a war of electronic measures and counter-measures relying, in the British camp, on newly evolved and developing technology and an enormous degree of concentration, patience, and stamina in radar operators and pilots. The problem was that of placing night-fighters in the right place at the right time, for while the original technology of the early radar stations could provide information about direction and numbers of hostile aircraft it could not quite pinpoint their location. By day, that hardly mattered; it was enough for the ground controllers to place their pilots within two or three miles of the enemy in order to ensure visual contact. But at night, when visibility was only a few hundred yards at most, more precision was needed.

From 1938 work had been progressing in the electronic realm of airborne interception (AI) radar, incorporating a detection device small enough to be installed in a night-fighter and sufficiently unerring to lead the pilot into visual range of his target at night. The need for an AI operator, however, as well as a pilot, brought up the question of a suitable airframe. It was not so much a matter of picking the best aircraft but of determining which of those available was the least ill-suited to the role, and experimental sets were fitted initially in Fairey Battles, then in Blenheims and Defiants. All were disappointing, with neither the AI set nor the aircraft performing to the required standard. There would not be a confirmed AI destruction of an enemy machine until the night of 22 July 1940, eight months after the first installations.

A year later three technical innovations, working in combination, dramatically improved the performance of night-fighters. The first was better control,
which came in late 1940 in the form of ground control interception (GCI) radar,
whereby a controller on the ground could vector the night-fighter into the
general vicinity of a bomber. Fighter Command figures on night interceptions
indicate that, in November 1940, AI-equipped fighters flying without GCI
control flew nearly ten sorties for each contact made, while, in May 1941, AI
interceptors supported by GCI required only three sorties for each contact. Then
came the twin-engined Bristol Beaufighter, which was more than 40 miles per
hour faster than the contemporary Junkers Ju 88, while its armament of four
20 millimetre nose-mounted cannon and six .303-inch machine guns lodged in
the wing-roots gave it impressive firepower. Finally, the introduction of AI
Mark IV, able to maintain contact until the target was less than two hundred
yards away, though still not guaranteeing a visual sighting, improved the odds
tremendously.[57]

When three RCAF night-fighter squadrons, Nos 406, 409, and 410, were
formed in the spring and summer of 1941, the first two had the good fortune
to be equipped with Beaufighters almost immediately, but No 410 was condemned to languish on Defiants until the following summer and would not be
completely re-equipped with Beaufighters until January 1943. Initially, No 406
– based at Acklington, in Northumberland – was favoured with a number of
pilots who had received some night-flying training on their Hurricanes posted
in from 401 Squadron; five months later, however, only 29 per cent of the
aircrew and 8 per cent of the groundcrew were Canadians. The percentage of
RCAF groundcrew would climb steadily until July 1943, when all three squadrons could report a level of 90 per cent, but acquiring Canadian AI operators
was a struggle. As there were no facilities for training them in the BCATP
schools 'because the radar air interception (AI) equipment was on the secret list
and available only in Britain,' most of the operators had to come from the RAF.
Thus, through the greater part of the war, many of the aircraft in Nos 406, 409,
and 410 squadrons were flown by RCAF pilots, while the AI equipment was
operated by RAF radio/navigators, and none of the three squadrons achieved
even 90 per cent Canadianization among aircrew until late in 1944.[58]

The first Canadian success came on 1 September 1941 when, on a moonlit
night, Flying Officer R.C. Fumerton and Sergeant L.P. Bing (one of the rare
RCAF radio/navigators) of 406 Squadron shot down a Ju 88 over northeastern
England. It was the first of many claims for Fumerton, who was to become
one of the RCAF's most successful night-fighter pilots and, in August 1943, the
squadron's first Canadian commanding officer. The engagement was also fairly
typical of the slow, deliberate procedure involved in aerial interception at night
– a process that contrasted dramatically with the lightning-quick, almost reflex-
ive, nature of day-fighting. The Canadians were initially vectored towards the
raider by a ground controller until, at a range of about a mile, the unfortunate
bomber appeared as a blip on Bing's radar screen. Closing the range, Fumerton
visually identified the Ju 88 as it passed in front of him, slightly above and
travelling from right to left. He briefly lost sight of it in a cloudbank, but

following Bing's instructions he regained visual contact in clear air and pulled into a position behind and below the Junkers. When he opened fire at pointblank range, the bomber's starboard engine immediately caught fire. Fumerton gave it one more burst and his target 'fell in flaming pieces.'[59]

No 406, perfectly situated at Acklington to intercept raids on the industrial northeast of England, claimed four more victories before Christmas (two in one night during a German attack on Tynemouth). No 409 Squadron was stationed at Digby, in Lincolnshire, and No 410 was split between Ouston, north of Durham, and Dyce, northeast of Aberdeen, all three bases well away from the Luftwaffe's favourite targets. Inevitably, they saw less action. No 409 shot down one bomber on the night of 1/2 November, but No 410, flying its Defiants without AI radar and even further away from the action, made no contact with the enemy at all.[60]

'Blind,' undergunned German bombers posed little threat, but operating high-performance aircraft in darkness, often during poor weather and before the development of blind landing systems, was dangerous enough. Before the turn of the year the three squadrons had suffered a total of eight aircrew killed in various mishaps, including Wing Commander N.B. Petersen, who had taken command of 409 Squadron on its formation in June. He was succeeded by Wing Commander P.Y. Davoud, transferred from No 410 Squadron the day after Peterson's death. Davoud was an RMC graduate who had held a short service commission in the RAF from 1933 to 1935 and had then taken a civilian job as a bush pilot for three years before becoming head of the Hudson's Bay Company air transport division until the outbreak of war. Not even his wide experience and considerable leadership talents could prevent the accidental loss of six more aircrew over the next half year.[61]

In March 1942 Bomber Command attacked the German city of Lübeck, a Hanseatic port of more historic than military significance, chosen primarily because it was easy to find and was expected to burn well. In response, Hitler ordered a series of retaliatory raids on equally inappropriate British targets that were slyly dubbed (by British propagandists) 'Baedeker raids,' a reference to the classic prewar tour guides which emphasized their historic significance. The first was launched against Exeter in southwest England, on the overcast night of 23/24 April. The heaviest attacks, killing more than four hundred people, were against Bath on 25/26 and 26/27 April, and on the next night the enemy switched his attention to eastern England, dispatching forty-five bombers against Norwich. On the night of 28/29 April, when York was the target, some of No 406 Squadron's Beaufighters were in a position to strike; the squadron was now based at Ayr, in Scotland, but a detached flight operating from Scorton, some thirty miles northwest of York, was credited with a Dornier 217 that crashed near Malton. Two nights later, during a scattered German attack of some twenty-five aircraft upon the Tyneside area, the Canadians claimed one Ju 88 destroyed and several more damaged.[62]

The last effective attack of the campaign was again against Exeter on 3/4 May and the RCAF units, flying from stations remote from routes to and from that city, played no part. Altogether, the enemy flew 716 sorties in the course of the Baedeker raids, and the British claimed forty-five aircraft destroyed or probably destroyed, while German records list thirty-four bombers missing, with another four lost in flying accidents, or a loss rate of 5.4 per cent of the attacking force – for the Luftwaffe, a costly piece of retaliation, for the night-fighter force of Fighter Command a vast improvement over its performance of the previous winter.[63] There would be long periods of the war when Bomber Command loss rates would hover around 5 per cent, but while British production (of aircrew and aircraft) could deal with such depletion, German production, given the demands of the Eastern Front, could not.

By early 1942, with fighting taking place in Europe, Africa, and Asia, the Canadian government had recognized the consequences of its participation in a global conflict, and two more divisions, the 3rd and 4th, were preparing to go overseas while the creation of the 5th – like the 4th, ultimately to be an armoured formation – had been authorized. All that raised questions of air support. Doctrine, it will be remembered, had called for one army cooperation squadron to work with each infantry corps and every armoured division; and in the spring of 1940 there had been a second RCAF army cooperation squadron in England which might well have been assigned to that role. But in December of that year No 112 (AC) Squadron had been redesignated No 2 Squadron, re-equipped with Hawker Hurricanes, and turned into a fighter unit (it became No 402 in March 1941). Looking ahead, in May 1941 General McNaughton had called for another army cooperation squadron to be formed so that armour and air 'could grow up side by side.'[64] No 414 Squadron was established at Croydon, south of London, on 13 August, to await the arrival of the 5th Canadian Armoured Division at the end of the year.

Since they were still flying Lysanders, it was perhaps fortunate for both Nos 400 and 414 squadrons that McNaughton's forces were retained in the United Kingdom for the time being and not sent to some more active theatre of war. Over the summer of 1941, however, both re-equipped with the Curtiss Tomahawk. Although the four-gun Tomahawk was certainly no Spitfire – 'the P-40 design was obsolete by European standards before the prototype ever flew'[65] – it was a fighter, with a maximum speed of 350 miles per hour compared with the Lysander's meagre 230. The Lysander had been crewed by a pilot and air-gunner, but the latter was now superfluous since the Tomahawk was a single-seater, and at least one of them was known to complain.

I wish Headquarters in London would make up their minds [as] to what they are going to do with us. Most of us wish that they [would] send us back to Canada as instructors. I think for sure that every one of the Air Gunners is fed up with this country ...

Here is my routine for the past week here. Up at 7 and go to breakfast because we have eggs ... on parade at 8.15 which lasts till 8.30 then to the Gunner's rooms till 9, then back to the Sergeant's Mess and play pool till dinner time, then after dinner I usually go to bed until 3, or go and play a couple of sets of tennis.[66]

In a military environment idleness quickly leads to discontent. Even the groundcrews, whose duties were essentially the same whether the squadrons were engaged in training or operations, found that a service life focused entirely around maintenance and training soon became excessively tedious, inevitably with an adverse effect on morale. Field exercises, carried out in conjunction with both British and Canadian ground formations, did little to lift dejected spirits, and it would be November 1941 before any aircraft were authorized to fly over enemy territory. Understandably, things were worst in the unit which had been committed longest. 'Morale and *esprit de corps* among the personnel of No 400 Squadron RCAF is at a very low point,' the personnel officer at Overseas Headquarters informed Air Commodore Stevenson in July 1941. 'Conditions existing in that Unit at the present time are such that, unless immediate corrective action is taken, there is liable to be a serious internal "split-up."' Squadron and station medical officers were concerned about the 'ill-feeling and unrest' prevailing, he added. 'Several of the junior officers who are full of initiative and ambition have, in an informal way, asked to be posted to a more active branch of the Service and this, I am sure, is not due to a lack of moral fibre but an honest desire to do a worthwhile job of work in the war effort.'[67]

So delicate was the situation that the censors singled out No 400 Squadron for special attention in a report which described morale as 'undoubtedly low,' and they added that the outlook at Odiham was 'one of unruly discontent.' But, while they argued that living conditions were at the root of the problem and explained how 'boredom and inactivity greatly aggravate the situation,' it may well have been the other way around. One writer lamented that 'here we are 21 months over here and no scrap yet. It sure gets you down. Having to waste our time here when we could sit down back home and do the same. Russia is doing the work and all we have been doing [are the] preliminaries and taking the bows. It can't last forever and soon we will be caught short and [have] nowhere to turn ... Has it got me down. I'll say so. I'm bored stiff. The longer I stay here, the more I hate this place.'[68]

Pilots relieved their feelings to some extent by taking deliberate – and illegal – risks, some of them quite spectacular.

Three of our fellows were playing around one day, when one of them takes a notion to fly under a bridge. He came out Okay. Bridges aren't what they are at home ... I imagine they couldn't have had more than 10 ft. clearing [sic]. The second guy thought that was nothing, so he looped around it, under, then over, then under again. He came out Okay. The third guy thinks that's nothing. He shows them both up by doing a slow roll under the bridge – only he didn't quite make it. He lost about $3^1/_2$ ft of his port wing ... He crippled [sic] back to the field though, and found out that his flaps weren't working ... He done the cutest summersault you ever heard of ... We had another chap clip the bottom off his wing on a German gun post one day, scraping all the paint off and putting a couple of guns out of action. He wasn't supposed to be over there. Another guy was flying a Lizzie [Lysander] along one day when he decided to see who was in the train down below. He flew alongside it for a while, looking in at the window, and slapped down a signal post with his wing ... Another guy took down a hotel sign with the bomb ring on a Lizzie and came back with it dragging behind him.[69]

The bridge referred to was one over the Winchester bypass; the aircraft in question were Tomahawks; and the feat is well authenticated.

The squadron's rank and file lacked such outlets for their frustrations and perhaps that magnified their day-to-day problems. In the fall of 1941 Army Co-operation Command decided that all airmen at Odiham, British and Canadian, should be fed through a single kitchen and mess hall, and the specifically Canadian facilities of No 400 Squadron were closed down. Not surprisingly, the men took great exception to the new system.

We now eat with the RAF. The technical name for the unseasoned pig swill we're fed is 'plain wholesome food.' The lunches are edible but uninteresting. The other three meals aren't big enough to keep a canary in good voice. And the mess stinks to high heaven, a greasy lavatory smell that is enough to kill the finest appetite, mother. You may think I'm joking, still, this is the plain, simple truth – *we're hungry all the time.* I'm speaking for myself and Rusty and every other Canadian on this accursed station.[70]

If the writer was not, in fact, speaking for all his comrades, he certainly represented a large sample judging by the number of basically similar complaints cited by the censors. A Canadian soldier, however, an anti-aircraft gunner, saw Odiham from a very different perspective.

My detachment is finally attached to the 400th Air Squadron. The airmen here are very good to us but are a spoiled and pampered lot. That's all I can say for them. They should be sent to the Army for a few months or a year and they might realize how comfortably off they are now. They have warm rooms, fireplaces in each room, linoleum on the floor, beds and mattresses, canteens and about five meals a day, yet they think the world is against them and [that they] are badly abused.[71]

Sinking morale at squadron and station was aggravated by more 'ill-feeling and unrest' generated at higher levels by the on-going doctrinal disputes and bureaucratic squabbles between army and air force over the army cooperation function. Colonel Charles Carrington, the British Army's liaison officer at Bomber Command, found that, even in April 1942, 'there has been a change for the worse in the past year ... the prospect is terrifying.' A month later Air Vice-Marshal Edwards apparently intervened to put forward a Canadian view. He sent the Air Ministry's director of military co-operation a paper condemning the current RAF approach to integrated air/ground operations. Unfortunately the paper itself is not on file, but there is what appears to be an earlier draft of it in General McNaughton's papers, which suggests that he approved of it and that the critique may even have originated with him. The argument was brutally frank, claiming that cooperation between the army and air force 'still hardly exists' because of the 'strong bias of senior Air Force officers' in favour of strategic bombing.[72]

On 11 June Sir Henry Pownall, vice-chief of the imperial general staff, noted in his diary that 'we have launched our paper on air support for the Army, saying that we need 109 squadrons, roughly half of the fighter-reconnaissance and half of bomber-reconnaissance types ... Our difficulties are going to be great, in that provision for our air needs is bound to cut across and interfere with production of heavy bombers and fighters for the RAF, and of course the Air Ministry is going to sing that tune loudly. Army Co-operation has been the Cinderella branch of the RAF, and the Army's efforts to get proper air support in reconnaissance, bombing and fighter cover has never had a fair deal ...'[73] In the event, it would take a combination of hard-won North African battle experience in the form of 'lessons learned,' bitter in-fighting on an interservice bureaucratic level, and the unbridled ambition of Air Marshal Sir Trafford Leigh-Mallory, who was promoted to the post of AOC-in-C Fighter Command at the end of 1942 and 'who saw in Army/Air Co-operation a new field for the Fighters to conquer,'[*74] to bring about the demise of Army Co-operation Command and the formation of a Second Tactical Air Force in June 1943.

Meanwhile, when McNaughton (under whose operational authority No 400 Squadron still came) authorized the squadron's first Rhubarbs, or freelance offensive sorties over enemy territory, the opportunity was welcomed. Several such missions were flown in November and December 1941 when weather conditions favoured the Tomahawks by providing adequate cloud cover. They encountered no opposition until 13 December, when two of them were trapped by half a dozen German fighters and both were lost in the Channel. Those were the squadron's only operational losses in six months, in part, perhaps, because the Tomahawks required intensive maintenance and the daily availability varied between nil and six. Moreover, Populars (photo-reconnaissance missions, another army cooperation responsibility) were only flown when the weather was just right, so that by May 1942 'both for training and operations they [Canadians of 400 Squadron] have been practically impotent for months.' Nevertheless, Stevenson told the AOC-in-C Army Co-operation Command 'that since these operations have commenced there has been a tremendous improvement in the outlook of 400 Squadron and I think that the initiation of these offensive sorties will have done much to relieve the tedium for Army Co-operation Squadrons.'[75]

First Canadian Army had come into existence on Easter Monday 1942. Its commander, who appreciated the potential of tactical airpower, at least on a theoretical level, better than most general officers, visualized an RCAF army cooperation wing of six squadrons to go with it, or double what the air staff now thought appropriate. The CAS, Sir Charles Portal, explained that one limiting factor was the provision of a suitable airfield, but McNaughton had

_____

* Was this 'vision' affected by his experience as air commander for the Dieppe raid and the critical analyses that followed it? See chapter 7.

a ready solution to that difficulty – his army engineers would build one! Work on Dunsfold, in Surrey and in the heart of the Canadian Army's overseas garrisons, began on 4 May. It usually took the British, even in the urgency of war, about a year to build an airfield similar to that planned for Dunsfold and to make it operational. McNaughton's sappers and airmen did it in six months.[76]

In both Canadian squadrons the Tomahawks were replaced by North American Mustangs in June 1942, at least in part because of McNaughton's badgering of the Air Ministry and War Office. The Mustangs, early models powered by Allison engines and armed with .30 and .50 calibre machine-guns, were not as potent as the later, Merlin-engined versions, but they could outrun FW 190s and the Me 109F at low level and were able to evade the enemy on occasion, or even fight him when they must, with some faint prospect of success.[77] With these relatively high-performance aircraft it was practicable to insert both squadrons gradually into the overall fighter war, a process made easier – and, to some extent, inevitable – by the need for flights over France and Belgium to be directed by Fighter Command's sector control systems. For the moment, technology, more than doctrine, was bringing Fighter Command and Army Co-operation Command closer together.

Bentley Priory faced the inevitable with a stiff upper lip. 'As time goes on in this war we have been finding that fighter aircraft have been subjected to all sorts of queer roles,' announced a memorandum of March 1943. 'The old idea of the fighter being the destroyer of enemy bombers alone has changed, and we now find that we have to cope with anything from the heavily defended bomber down to the lightly motorized [army] column.'[78] But although acquiring the capability to engage the enemy on more or less equal terms did great things for the morale of army cooperation squadrons, the assignment of fighter units to a fighter-bomber role struck a heavy blow to the self-esteem of those pilots first assigned to such duties. No 402 Squadron, for example, a recent foster-child of the fighter clique, had been horrified by a decision in the fall of 1941 to re-equip it with Hurribombers – Hurricane IIs equipped to carry 250 lb bombs. The argument put forward to meet their plaintive yelps by Air Commodore L.N. Hollinghurst, director-general of organization in the Air Ministry, was less than honest. 'Far from being armed with an obsolescent type of aircraft, they [402 Squadron] are armed with one of the newest types, and employed on a novel, and, at the present time, vitally important tactical task; that of sinking enemy small ships with bombs carried in fighters, and also attacking small, vital ground objectives from a low height in enemy occupied territory.'[79] The task may have been novel, but the Hurricane IIB could not be fairly described as 'one of the newest types,' and No 402's most notable attempt at 'sinking enemy small ships' was far less successful than they believed at the time.

A reconnaissance report had alerted them to the presence of four German minesweepers operating off the Ile de Batz, near Brest, on 16 February 1942. Squadron Leader R.E.E. Morrow (who had joined the unit as a pilot officer when it was still No 112 Squadron) led six Hurribombers from Perranporth, in Cornwall. They flew at sea level until, forty minutes out, they climbed to 2000 feet and spotted five enemy 'destroyers,' steaming in line, directly ahead. The Canadians broke into three pairs and attacked. 'Diving from 2000 feet in a beam attack firing a 14 second burst with his machine guns and releasing his bombs at a height of 100 feet, Red 1 observed strikes from his machine guns on the superstructure; Red 2, P/O Ford followed his leader in his dive and released his bombs at a height of 800 to 500 feet on the same target. Red 2 also attacked with his machine guns, giving a 10 second burst.'[80] Flak 'was very intense ... the heaviest and most intense AA barrage [the pilots] have ever seen.' The pilots of escorting Spitfires reported direct bomb hits on two vessels, as well as machine-gun strikes, and the Canadians claimed to have sunk one destroyer and damaged a second. German records, however, only list two minesweepers suffering 'light damage, and ... a few casualties.'[81]

Even the success which they thought they had achieved did nothing to reconcile the pilots to this new role. Morrow reported that 'considerable dissatisfaction is felt by the pilots of this Squadron with their present equipment,' and Air Vice-Marshal Edwards took up the cudgels again, this time with the Air Ministry. Within weeks of its attack on the minesweepers, No 402 took delivery of Spitfire VBs and the commanding officer was writing to Edwards 'to extend to you the most sincere thanks of myself and the other Officers and Pilots of 402 Squadron for the efforts you have made on our behalf in the matter of Squadron equipment.'[82] The squadron was back to what all true fighter pilots considered their only proper function – shooting at other pilots – only in time to discover that more and more of Fighter Command's resources were being diverted towards the ground war.

In March 1942 Air Marshal Sir Arthur Barratt, the AOC-in-C Army Co-operation Command, testily remarked that while, finally, he had a system in place to coordinate Bomber Command's No 2 Group aircraft with his own, Bentley Priory's burgeoning interest in attacking ground targets had inserted a new factor. 'The picture becomes a little complicated,' Barratt noted, because Fighter Command 'are all out to play in this business, as are their Group Commanders, and I rather fear that there is a danger of a series of different regional arrangements being made by each Army Commander with his adjacent Group.' A few months later the Army's liaison officer at Bentley Priory had also commented on the crossing of functional lines. 'Two Commands are at present studying Army Air Support – Fighter Command and Army Co-operation Command. Both are carrying out research almost independently with resultant waste of effort and confusion.'[83]

Sir Sholto Douglas had informed his groups in January 1942 that in future they would be playing a more active role in army support. If effective cooperation was to be established, he instructed, 'it is essential that a much closer liaison should be established between the two services than generally exists at present. In bringing about this liaison it should be borne in mind that although 15 Squadrons have been earmarked for Army support duties, such duties are not outside the scope of any Fighter Squadron and training should therefore not be confined to these Squadrons, but should be extended as far as possible to all Day Fighter Squadrons in the Commands.'[84] He went on to suggest a number of minimum steps that groups might take. They should liaise directly with the army and corps headquarters in their areas, while group and sector controllers should familiarize themselves with the signals systems which had been developed for providing close support. Local joint exercises should be organized, officer exchanges should be arranged, and 'fighter pilots should practise map reading and memorizing.'[85]

Meanwhile, the Army Co-operation School at Old Sarum conducted courses for air and ground formation commanders and senior and junior staff officers without reference to Fighter Command's army support training. The school arranged joint exercises and, in April 1942, GHQ Home Forces issued general instructions for their conduct, the principal objects being: 'To train Army and RAF formations to work together in battle with the fullest knowledge of each other's possibilities, limitations and procedures ... To train RAF squadrons in the problems of rapid briefing, navigation, recognition and tactics peculiar to Army Air Support,' and, 'to train army units in the rapid and effective defence against enemy air attack.'[86] Field manoeuvres were complemented by command, staff, and signals exercises to develop joint procedures and coordinate the delivery of their firepower to the right target at the right time.

One of the more important exercises was Dryshod, held just two weeks before the disastrous Dieppe landings in August 1942, during which each of the exercise armies deployed an air staff working with an Air Support Signals Unit, or ASSU, which communicated front-line requests to supporting air formations. Commanders and staffs learned much about wireless and equipment faults, target indication and recognition, the need to place air liaison officers (who were, in fact, soldiers) with squadrons, ways to improve both preliminary ground and air briefings, passing information, and establishing clear lines of responsibility between the services. Exercises necessarily lack the harsh reality of actual operations but they are the means of developing and learning principles and procedures on which operations can subsequently be based. Of the value of Dryshod in identifying the fundamentals of joint army-air force action, for example, Colonel Carrington has remarked that 'there was everything to be learned from the lessons of Dryshod, nothing to be learned from Dieppe, except how not to do it, a little late in the War to learn that lesson.'[87]

7

The Turn of the Tide, 1942–3

'The weight of the war is very heavy now,' reflected Winston Churchill on 7 March 1942, 'and I must expect it to get steadily worse for some time to come.'[1] The turn of the year would see the turn of the tide, but the spring, summer, and early fall of 1942 were not happy times for the Allies. Much of the Far East had been lost to the Japanese, and by mid-summer the Germans were in Egypt, two misfortunes which exposed the beleaguered – and once more, retreating – Russians to new potential threats. At the end of June the Germans launched a new offensive in the Caucasus that raised the possibility (which the Allies had to consider, though the Germans were not thinking along such lines) of a gigantic pincer movement, starting from Ukraine on one side and North Africa on the other, and meeting somewhere in Syria, Iran, or Iraq.

The situation at sea was, if possible, even more worrisome, for during the previous six months more than four million tons of Allied shipping had been lost to enemy action. In the air, on 31 May, Bomber Command managed the world's first thousand-bomber raid and the scale of its air offensive was growing month by month; but in a broad strategic context the activities of the Western Allies were still doing little to distract the Wehrmacht from its major campaigns against the Soviet Union. Understandably, then, throughout the spring and early summer Josef Stalin was harshly demanding a 'Second Front Now' to take some of the weight off his hard-pressed armies.

The Americans toyed with the idea of invading the Brittany peninsula (though only if the Russians appeared to be in imminent danger of collapse), but the British chiefs of staff were determined to reject Operation Sledgehammer out of hand. Each of them had his own good reasons for disapproval, but those of the CAS, Sir Charles Portal, centred on the question of fighter support, which he saw as an essential element in establishing a major bridgehead on the Continent. 'We could not afford more casualties than might result from one or two months' fighting,' he told his peers. Among many Western leaders, however, and not least among the chiefs of staff, there was a not-quite-muted suspicion, which Stalin was doing nothing to nullify, that if the Allies did not put in a major effort soon he just might sign a separate peace with Hitler.[2] For the British, the *pis aller* was a major seaborne raid on a scale they hoped would lead Hitler to reinforce his defences in the west at the expense of his armies and air fleets in the east.

The vicissitudes of planning and mounting the disastrous Dieppe raid of 19 August 1942 – Operation Jubilee – are recounted in C.P. Stacey's official history, *Six Years Of War,* and in Brian Villa's revisionist work, *Unauthorized Action: Mountbatten and the Dieppe Raid.*[3] An initial plan, differing in its tactical details – Operation Rutter – was cancelled at the last moment because of bad weather. Final plans required that the 6000-odd Anglo-Canadian troops involved in the operation set sail from five different Channel ports, shuffle themselves into battle order in the course of a night-time crossing averaging one hundred miles, and then make five closely coordinated landings along an eleven-mile stretch of rockbound coast. The objective selected (which had, of necessity, to be one within range of fighter cover projected from England) would test the prospects of capturing a small port without irrevocably damaging it. It was an overly complex and inflexible plan in which delay or failure at any point must endanger the whole operation; nor did it commit sufficient firepower, by air, land, or sea, to offer a reasonable prospect of success.

In the course of those inconclusive battles of attrition that had frustrated his squadrons while 'leaning forward into France' over the past eighteen months, Sir Sholto Douglas, the AOC-in-C of Fighter Command, had now succeeded in establishing a vague and uncertain air superiority over all the airspace within reach of Fighter Command. The closer to home, of course, the more certain that superiority, and it was a bold and relatively rare German airman who ventured over English soil by daylight in 1942. Once in a while, a Rotte of fighter-bombers might wing in at low level, drop their bombs, and race back across the Channel,* but it was far more difficult for German photo-reconnaissance pilots to carry out their assignments. Profitable intelligence-gathering required that the aircraft maintain a steady course at a selected altitude (depending on the tactical purpose of the sortie) and that such sorties be made frequently, since much of the art of photo-interpretation lay in comparing photographs of the same area taken at relatively short intervals. Ideally, such sorties should be flown whenever the weather was suitable – perhaps once or twice a week – but only rare combinations of weather and circumstance made that possible for the Luftwaffe. One set of photographs a month, which was all that the enemy could manage in the late spring and early summer of 1942, permitted little comparative analysis and ensured that only an uncommon combination of pure chance and intuitive interpretation was likely to reveal anything of significance.[4]

There were no such revelations concerning Jubilee. One incomplete reconnaissance was carried out between 28 and 31 July, after Rutter had been abandoned, but the next – flown for the first time by a pressurized Ju 86P, with

---

* As they did at 0615 hours on 7 July 1942, hitting two ships anchored in the Solent and already loaded with Canadian troops destined for Dieppe in the course of Operation Rutter, the first (and subsequently abandoned) version of Jubilee. Their bombs failed to explode, passing right through the hulls of the ships and causing only four minor casualties.

an operational ceiling in excess of 41,000 feet* – was not until 24 August, five days after the raid.[5] Thus their most reliable form of intelligence, photo-recon-naissance, gave the Germans no forewarning of the biggest raid yet mounted against Hitler's Festung Europa.

The aim, from an air perspective, was identical to that long – and so far, vainly – embraced by Bentley Priory: to create conditions that would compel the Luftwaffe to come up and fight on British terms. RAF intelligence estimated that approximately 260 German fighters were based within range of Dieppe, and in addition the enemy had about 120 bombers within easy reach which could threaten both troopships and naval escorts. The Fighter Command order of battle for Dieppe included forty-eight Spitfire squadrons – four of the new Spitfire IXs, forty-two of Vs, one of VBs, and one in the process of converting from VBs to VIs.[6] Altogether, in Spitfires alone, the RAF had more than triple the German fighter strength, and finally, after almost three years of war and a decade of technological development, a few British fighters would match the Germans in quality as well as quantity. The Spitfire IX was 'outstandingly better than the Spitfire V, especially at heights above 20,000 feet,' according to the RAF's Air Fighting Development Unit. 'On the level the Spitfire IX is considerably faster and its climb is exceptionally good ... Its manoeuvrability is as good as the Spitfire V up to 30,000 feet, and above that is very much better. At 38,000 feet it is capable of a true speed of 368 mph, and is still able to manoeuvre well for air fighting.' It could thus match the Focke Wulf 190 and Me 109F.[7]

As well as the Spitfires, eight Hurricane squadrons (two carrying bombs, the rest armed with four 20-millimetre cannon) were available for close support, while three of the new Hawker Typhoon squadrons were assigned to diver-sionary tasks. Four Mustang squadrons of Army Co-operation Command (including the two Canadian units, Nos 400 and 414) were assigned to provide continuous reconnaissance of the approaches to the Dieppe area. Five light bomber squadrons – three of Douglas Boston IIIs from Bomber Command's No 2 Group and two of Blenheims from Army Co-operation Command – were on hand for tactical bombing and smoke-laying. Completing the air order of battle were a few 'Intruder' versions of the Boston III (two of these from No 418 Squadron), carrying a smaller bombload and four 20 millimetre cannon as well as the standard four machine-guns, together with two squadrons of B-17 heavy bombers from the United States Army Air Forces which were assigned to attack the nearest German fighter airfield, at Abbeville. All, except for the B-17s, would operate under the control of Air Vice-Marshal Trafford Leigh-Mallory, sitting in No 11 Group's operations room at Uxbridge, just west of London.[8]

---

* No current Spitfire could match that, but in September a high-altitude version of the De Havilland Mosquito, capable of reaching 42,000 feet, was waiting for the next incursion by a Ju 86P. The Junkers was beset by technical problems, however, and its sorties met 'with very little success.' It never reappeared in the west.

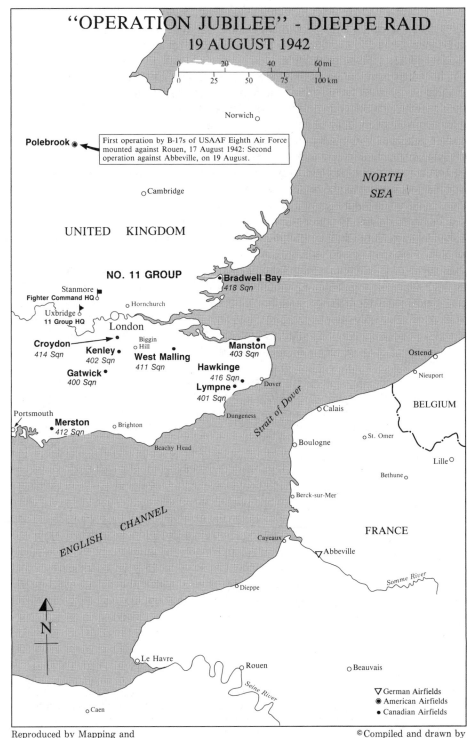

"OPERATION JUBILEE" - DIEPPE RAID
19 AUGUST 1942

First operation by B-17s of USAAF Eighth Air Force mounted against Rouen, 17 August 1942: Second operation against Abbeville, on 19 August.

NORTH SEA

UNITED KINGDOM

NO. 11 GROUP

Stanmore
Fighter Command HQ

Uxbridge
11 Group HQ

London

Croydon
414 Sqn

Kenley
402 Sqn

West Malling
411 Sqn

Gatwick
400 Sqn

Merston
412 Sqn

Biggin Hill

Bradwell Bay
418 Sqn

Manston
403 Sqn

Hawkinge
416 Sqn

Lympne
401 Sqn

Ostend

Nieuport

BELGIUM

Calais

St. Omer

Lille

Boulogne

Bethune

Berck-sur-Mer

FRANCE

Cayeaux

Abbeville

Somme River

Dieppe

Beachy Head

ENGLISH CHANNEL

Strait of Dover

Dover

Dungeness

Brighton

Portsmouth

Hornchurch

Cambridge

Norwich

Polebrook

N

Le Havre

Rouen

Beauvais

Seine River

Caen

▽ German Airfields
◉ American Airfields
● Canadian Airfields

Reproduced by Mapping and
Charting Establishment.

©Compiled and drawn by
the Directorate of History.

Leigh-Mallory had designated Air Commodore A.T. Cole as his personal representative aboard the raid headquarters ship, HMS *Calpe*, which also carried the ground-force commander, Major-General J.H. Roberts of the Canadian Army. With Cole was an air controller and a signals officer, while another air controller was in HMS *Fernie*, the alternate command ship. Pre-planned air operations were closely coordinated with proposed sea and ground movements, but the two controllers supposedly had the necessary command and signals capabilities to exercise a measure of independent, 'on-scene' authority over aircraft in their vicinity. Appropriately enough, the controller on *Fernie* was responsible for coordinating air cover, while close support was to be fine-tuned by the controller on *Calpe*.

The first aircraft left the ground at 0422 hours, when two Bostons from each of Nos 107, 418, and 605 squadrons set out across the Channel to bomb the key coastal defence batteries at Berneval and Varengeville at 0445. One of the two machines from No 418 returned to base after developing engine trouble on the outbound flight, while the other was shot down. Nor does it seem that any of the four RAF Bostons succeeded in hitting – or even threatening – their targets, since both were still intact when British commandos arrived on the scene some thirty to ninety minutes later. Just as No 418's Boston went down, and about the time the first Canadian soldiers struggled ashore at Pourville, the first Spitfires appeared, two of them attacking a lighthouse west of Dieppe which was thought to be an observation post for the coastal battery at Varengeville. Fifteen minutes later more Bostons and Hurricane fighter-bombers attacked the coastal batteries again, and this time major damage was inflicted on the Varengeville site, currently under attack by commandos, when charges stacked beside the guns were blown up by some projectile. (The commandos attributed the explosion to a bomb from their mortar, but German accounts blame fire from low-flying aircraft.)[9]

Forty-five minutes before that, at 0520 hours, Bostons and Blenheims had laid a smoke screen over the headlands overlooking the Dieppe foreshore and along the waterfront in order to shroud the approaching landing craft from view, while cannon-firing Hurricanes swept in across the esplanade. 'The main targets consisted of guns hidden in caves in the actual headlands and also a row of houses along the front which contained guns and were strengthened with concrete,' although later reflection led to the belief that 'we might have achieved more by using the *Cannon fighters and Hurri-bombers* against the *6" [coastal defence] Batteries* and the *Bostons* for the *attack of houses* on the front at low level.'[10]

For those air-support demands which could not be pre-planned, lessons laboriously learned through trial and error over the past two years were simply not applied. Army Co-operation Command had developed a system of Air Support Signals Units (ASSUs) who should have been able to use their own radio nets – called tentacles – to transmit requests for support directly to an Army Air Control Centre aboard *Calpe*. The latter, jointly manned by army and air force officers, would evaluate requests and establish priorities, issuing the appropriate orders directly to squadrons, where air liaison officers

(ALOs) would brief pilots, giving them a soldier's perspective of their goals and tasks.

This system, which deliberately bypassed an assortment of specialized army and air force headquarters, had been designed to respond more quickly to the often unpredictable realities of ground combat. Fighter Command, however, not Army Co-operation Command, was running the ground-support aspect of Jubilee, and there had been little coordination and cooperation between them. Requests for support originating with brigade headquarters on the beaches – consisting of the brigadier, his brigade major, and three or four signallers – were passed through the army command radio net to Roberts's staff (Cole and his controller) aboard *Calpe* and then retransmitted to No 11 Group HQ at Uxbridge. Uxbridge, after due consideration, then issued instructions by telephone to an appropriate sector station which, in turn, ordered off aircraft to fulfil them.[11] The procedure was clumsy and slow; worse, it failed to discriminate in any realistic way between suitable or unsuitable targets, nor did it provide any knowledgeable advice on how targets might be identified and attacked. Especially frustrating to those who had worked at developing the new system was the way in which the expertise of ALOs at the airfields was jettisoned by both ground and air commanders. 'At Fighter Command [Lieutenant-Colonel] Ralph Stockley had not even been let into the secret [of the raid], and his assistant at 11 Group, where Leigh-Mallory fought the air battle, had been "frozen out." There were no ALOs with the Fighter Squadrons who carried out low-level attacks and therefore no adequate briefing, no ASSU tentacles forward to the beaches and backward to the airfields.'[12]

The air superiority battle, understandably, went much better. For the first hour after the initial landings, while six fighter squadrons orbited overhead, the Luftwaffe hardly challenged, but 'enemy fighter opposition, which had been only moderate in the earlier period of the operation, began to increase appreciably about the time [0715 hours] No 403 arrived to give low cover for the ships lying off the beaches.' Flying Spitfire VBs, three pilots of No 403 claimed to have destroyed six enemy fighters, while the squadron lost three of its own. Between 0730 and 1050 hours both sides intensified their effort, air activity eventually peaking during and after re-embarkation, when nine RAF and RCAF squadrons were engaged. During this later phase, two pre-planned diversionary air raids vainly attempted to distract and disrupt enemy fighter control systems. In one, four Spitfire IX squadrons (including Nos 401 and 402) escorted twenty-four B-17s of the United States Army Air Forces on their first operational mission to bomb the German fighter base at Abbeville-Trucat, while in the other a Typhoon wing protected nine Boulton-Paul Defiants which attacked shipping in Ostend harbour.[13]

The intensity of opposition over Dieppe seems to have varied considerably and bore little relation to the number of Allied aircraft actually present. No 411 Squadron flew 'four operational sweeps during the day, the first being the only one that provided much activity.' It, like Nos 403 and 416, was flying Spitfire VBs and, after its first mission in which two pilots were lost and another slightly wounded, 'the pilots reported that they seemed outnumbered 3 to 1, that the top cover squadron was too high to provide protection, and our aircraft too slow to compete with FW 190s.' Nevertheless, they claimed a half-share in one FW 190 destroyed, and another probably destroyed. On their second and third patrols they encountered no enemy aircraft, and, on the last, 'one Do 217 was seen and attacked ... It dropped its bombs about one mile from the [returning] convoy and travelled too fast for our aircraft to get within 300 yards.'[14]

While each fight was special and unique to the pilot involved, one man's experience may be taken as typical. Older than most of his peers, with a background in law, thirty-one-year-old Flight Lieutenant J.M. Godfrey's Dieppe battle actually began the day before the assault, when No 412 Squadron flew two defensive patrols intended to ensure that no enemy reconnaissance aircraft would find the assembling convoy. That night: 'I was in bed by 11 and was awakened rudely at 3.'

I jumped into my clothes and went downstairs for breakfast. We had an egg, which was a great treat, and by 4 a.m. we were all in the flight [room] waiting for instructions. We were told that it was to be a Canadian Army landing at Dieppe and that we were to stand by for further instructions. At 4:45 the phone rang from 'ops' and instructions were given that we were to take off with the rest of the Wing at 6 and go over to Dieppe, and stay over the town for half an hour to protect our boats from dive bombing etc. The names went up on the board and I was not down, so I sat back and relaxed.

The squadron took off at 6, and about an hour later the boys started to straggle back. Over Dieppe it had been impossible to keep the squadron together and everybody split up into twos. The sky was evidently filled with a swirling mass of Spitfires and FW 190s milling around ... Everybody had a squirt at about 3 Jerrys but it was impossible to see the results, because as soon as a pilot squirted he could be sure a Jerry was on his tail and had immediately to take evasive action. We were much encouraged when all our boys returned safely. The names went up for the second show and I was down to fly as No 2 to a lad who had had about 30 sweeps under his belt and was a very cool and cagey pilot.[15]

No 412 was detailed to escort Hurricane fighter-bombers on a low-level attack against artillery firing from behind the eastern headland. 'Of all the jobs that could have been assigned to us,' Godfrey thought, 'this undoubtedly was the worst.'[16] As a neophyte operational pilot (he had left Canada only in April, after two years as an instructor), he kept his reservations to himself, but learned later that his distaste for low-level work was common. Pilots preferred to fight enemy aircraft, where skill and experience were the distinctive characteristics of combat, rather than face the chancy, indiscriminate, German Flak.

Rendezvousing with the Hurricanes, both squadrons flew across the Channel at sea level. Godfrey followed his leader, Pilot Officer J.N. Brookhouse, inland for about three miles, being shot at all the while by scattered Germans on the ground.

After about 3 miles, we swung to the left. I was following J[ohn], slightly to the right
and about 75 yards behind ... After we had made our turn to the left we were in a bit
of a gully with trees on either side and no trees ahead. The ground started to rise and
there, at the top of the rise, was a big *Flak* position. We were going so fast that we
were on it before we realized it. All hell was breaking loose. There were heavy ack-
ack guns and I don't know how many machine guns, etc. blazing away at us from
point blank range. We had come right up a funnel completely exposed. The next thing
I saw was the tail of John's kite just blow away, and the fuselage break in two right
behind the cockpit. His kite seemed to go slowly over on its nose. I didn't see it hit
the ground as I was past [it], but one of the other lads saw it and it really spread itself
all over the ground. I don't suppose poor John ever knew he was hit before it was all
over.[17]

Godfrey found himself in the midst of the Hurricanes, which had now finished
their bombing runs. Terse comments and instructions on his VHF radio told him
that two more machines had been hit by Flak, and that their pilots were baling
out. The survivors, including Godfrey, made their way over the coast through
a curtain of ground-based fire, and a few minutes later another pilot reported
that he was baling out over the Channel. The remainder made their way back
to England.[18]

At 1340 hours orders came to escort more Hurricanes attacking the same
troublesome guns. This time, however, No 412 was to stay offshore, ready to
provide the return escort, rather than go right in with the attackers.

There were FW 190s all over the place around 2,000 feet, and we were the only Spits
at our height. Some 190s started to dive down on the Hurries. We tore after them and
they, seeing us coming, started to break away. Just then, someone yelled, 'Red Section,
break.' There were some 190s on our tail. We went into a steep turn to the right and
shook them off. I lost the others for a few seconds. The *Flak* started to come up at us
in great volume. Red balls were shooting past my nose, uncomfortably close. I spotted
my No 1 and joined him. Just then the CO yelled, 'Let's get out of here'. We dove
down onto the sea, going all out and weaving as hard as we could. The Hurries were
about two miles out to sea on the way home. We managed to keep the Jerrys busy so
that none of them had been attacked. We stayed with them on the way home, weaving
around them with our heads turning about 120 to the minute, looking for Huns.
However, none chased us back and we landed with the whole squadron intact.[19]

The squadron was released at 1800 hours, then alerted for a defensive patrol
an hour or so later, and finally stood down for the day at 2100 hours, without
claiming any victories and having lost one pilot and two aircraft.[20]

The newest RCAF fighter squadron, No 416, had been formed at Peterhead
in Scotland on 22 November 1941, and became operational on 1 February
1942 under the command of Flight Lieutenant (very shortly afterwards, Squadron Leader) Lloyd Chadburn. Chadburn, who had tried unsuccessfully to enter
the prewar RCAF, was finally accepted in 1940, but not before being turned
down by both the Royal Canadian Navy and the Royal Air Force for reasons

now unfathomable. He had gone overseas with No 112 (Army Co-operation) Squadron at the end of that year, transferred to No 412 Squadron in June 1941, and to No 19 Squadron, RAF, as a flight commander in September, before being posted to command No 416. His forte was leadership and, as of the eve of Dieppe, he had still not claimed any air-to-air successes although, in November 1941, he had been credited with a relatively rare air-to-sea victory when his cannon fire was wrongly believed to have sunk an E-boat off the Dutch coast.[21] On 19 August his squadron's first two patrols over Dieppe were uneventful, but in the course of the third it tangled with about fifteen FW 190s escorting Ju 88 bombers and claimed to have shot down three of the enemy without loss, Chadburn 'probably destroying' a Ju 88. Next day, the squadron diarist reported that '22 pilots were on one or more sorties and everyone had gained a tremendous amount of confidence from this first engagement with the enemy as a squadron.'[22]

The four army cooperation squadrons had a different task, flying their Mustangs on tactical reconnaissance missions 'to discover movements of enemy reinforcements towards the area in which our Army is operating.' The most likely reinforcement routes were the roads from Rouen, Le Havre, and Amiens – there was a Panzer division based at Amiens – and each approach was covered hourly. In this case, pilots were briefed by ALOs on their missions, routes, and procedures, and pairs were dispatched in turn, the lead pilot to observe ground activities, and his wingman or weaver to watch the sky for enemy fighters. Results were disappointing, for 'although much negative information was received, the only positive information was a report of three to five light tanks 10 miles south of Dieppe. The results of this reconnaissance did not appear to justify the scale of effort or the casualties' – particularly, a cynic might think, since the report of tanks was certainly in error. The Germans were able to deal with the Dieppe raid from local resources, so, although the Panzers at Amiens had been put on alert, there were no approaching mechanized columns for the Mustang pilots to find and report. Searching for them was, however, fraught with danger.

Most sorties were flown in the immediate vicinity of the port, where roads were regularly patrolled at half-hourly intervals, but after-action analysis suggested that this 'should be discouraged. Every half hour a pilot would fly up or down the same road so that the [anti-aircraft] gun crews were ready for him. Although it is difficult to vary such tasks, irregular timing would help,'[23] a blindingly obvious conclusion, but one only achieved at a cost of ten aircraft missing. Many of the strands woven into the hazardous trade of tactical reconnaissance – aircraft performance, tactical deployment, low-level flying, luck, skill, and guts – came together during one No 414 Squadron sortie, Flying Officer H.H. Hills reporting that:

Flight Lieutenant Clarke and myself were to do a Tac/R in the Dieppe-Abbeville area. I was flying weaver. We made landfall approximately 7 miles west of Dieppe, turned east towards Dieppe. At this time I observed two Focke-Wulfe 190s at 1,000 feet; we were at nought feet at all times, travelling the opposite direction. I warned my Flight

Lieutenant of Bandits but received no answer. The enemy aircraft turned and followed us, holding his [sic] height, and made a diving attack on us as we turned south at Dieppe. Flight Lieutenant Clarke was watching his road and did not hear my repeated warnings or see the enemy aircraft himself and was weaving very slightly.

I had swung out on my leader's port [side] before the attack and both enemy aircraft were diving on him in line astern about 200 yards apart. I turned in between the two Focke-Wulfes and gave the leader a short burst from which I observed no results, other than making him stop firing at Flight Lieutenant Clarke and begin jinking. By this time the Focke Wulfe behind me had opened fire on me but his fire was passing on the port side. I was [turning] at 100 [degrees] port at the time, so I slipped violently to starboard, towards the ground. The Focke-Wulfe passed me and started a steep turn to starboard. I followed and gave him a 2 second burst from a quarter astern at 150 yards range. I observed parts flying off, and an explosion about one foot behind the engine cowling on the starboard side of his fuselage, and black smoke began pouring out of his engine. He immediately slowed down and flew straight and level. I gave him another 2 second burst from dead astern at 50 yards range. More parts came off and his cockpit cover came off. His engine was stopped by then.

I figured he was done, so turned away to go back and help Flight Lieutenant Clarke. I looked back at the Focke-Wulfe I had hit, and it went into a grove of trees with dense black smoke coming out of the aircraft. There was no explosion when he hit.

Flight Lieutenant Clarke was circling about 2 miles south of Dieppe with white smoke coming out of his aircraft, and the [other] Focke-Wulfe was about 100 yards behind him flying at the same speed. The Focke-Wulfe turned and dove south. He was at 800 feet and went down to nought feet. I followed but was unable to catch him. After about a minute chase, I saw another Focke-Wulfe at 100 feet diving on me from the starboard beam. I turned sharply into him and got on his tail but was unable to get in firing range as he ran west. I then saw the other Focke-Wulfe coming back at me from the south, so I turned north and headed for the cliffs. On reaching them I turned on the one chasing me, trying to surprise him by coming up from behind the cliff. He had climbed to about 600 feet though, so he saw my turn and tried a full deflection shot at me ... I dove down to water level and headed towards a Destroyer with the Focke-Wulfe a half mile behind me. He followed me about two miles out, gaining slowly, and then turned away south-west. I returned to base. All the fighting and manoeuvering was done between 250 and 300 mph indicated air speed.[24]

Enemy fire had damaged Clarke's lubrication and cooling systems. He ditched his Mustang alongside a British destroyer and, according to war correspondent Wallace Reyburn, an eye-witness to the event, was picked up without getting his feet wet.[25]

In the days that followed, it became obvious to even the most obtuse that the Dieppe raid had been a technical as well as an operational failure. Colonel C.E. Carrington, the army's liaison officer at Bomber Command and a concerned observer of army/air relationships, recorded that 'September was a flurry of post-mortem examinations at various levels ... Whitewashing apologies were issued by the top people and anguished discussions followed between the staff officers who studied technical failures.'[26] Carrington himself prepared and forwarded a paper on 'the misuse of 2 Group in Jubilee, the only corner of the muddle that I was entitled to speak upon with authority.'

I examined the close-support attacks made by 2 Group bombers: the first attack missed a pre-arranged target by about two thousand yards; the second was indiscriminate bombing of a large area in which there might or might not have been Canadian troops; the third was not a suitable target. 'If they could have found it, they could not have hit it and, if they had hit it, the battle would not have been affected.' The only useful thing 2 Group did that day was to lay smokescreens, and even these prevented the Headquarters ship from seeing what happened on the beach.[27]

The army's liaison officer at Army Co-operation Command and his counterpart in the combined operations room of GHQ Home Forces were equally depressed. They spoke gloomily of 'an Army/Co-op defeat' and complained that 'no use was made of the organization they had been patiently building up for years ... Woodall and Oxborrow said it all resolved itself to forming a mobile advanced HQ under a senior RAF officer directly linked with the military headquarters and with the airfields ... Army Co-op Command ... put out seventy-two low-level reconnaissances, and lost ten of them ... to no purpose, since they had no direct links with the forward troops.'[28]

There had been 'a senior officer directly linked with the military headquarters' – in this case Air Commodore Cole aboard HMS *Calpe* – 'and with the airfield,' but his was not an advanced headquarters, nor was Leigh-Mallory much concerned with forward ground/air co-ordination, as yet. Flight Lieutenant C.A. Kidd, RAF, the controller on board *Calpe*, would have been happier with at least two more squadrons available for ground support, one of them under his direct control, and he complained of the lack of information reaching him. 'No signals were received by me from Uxbridge,' he reported, 'so that it was not known what targets had been accepted and what squadrons were on their way.' Nor was he able to obtain current information from the troops on shore, recording that, in his opinion, forward controllers needed to be close to the leading troops, where they could actually observe the flow of battle and talk directly to pilots over VHF radio.[29]

Even the Germans thought that 'the employment of the enemy air force and the tactics were extraordinary.' Generalfeldmarschall Gerd von Rundstedt, commander-in-chief in the west, found it 'incomprehensible why, at the beginning of the enemy landings, the Dieppe bridgehead* and other landing places were not isolated by a continuous curtain of bombs so as to prevent, or at least delay, the employment of local reserves.'[30]

From the Olympian perspective of No 11 Group's operations room, however, Leigh-Mallory felt that 'the excellent communications and flexible control facilities of the normal fighter organization at home proved most efficient for such combined operations,' and concluded that it 'would be most undesirable,

---

* The scale of the raid led von Rundstedt to view it (wrongly, of course) as a tentative invasion, to be reinforced if successful.

if not dangerous, to vest more control in the ship than is absolutely necessary.'
In his view control was best exercised through the existing Group-Sector
system – one which could readily be adapted from defensive to offensive
purposes.[31]

Squadron Leader J.H. Sprott, RAF, *Fernie*'s fighter controller, could not have
disagreed more, arguing that authority should be vested further forward.

Being in control of only the lowest Squadron of Fighters was a disadvantage, and I
could never be quite sure which was the lowest Squadron ... In any future operation
of this nature the Fighter Controller should have at least four Squadrons under his
control during the [period of] greatest activity, and two at least under decreased
activities ... He should then be able to detach, or request the Squadron Commander
to detach, the appropriate number of aircraft to deal with any hostile aircraft ... This
suggestion is, I am certain, sound, as on numerous occasions during the operation
when enemy aircraft were seen approaching, more than sufficient Fighters attacked,
and in some cases one or other side approaches to the Convoy were left open.[32]

In other words, forward air control faced a problem analogous to fire control
in army units; without proper direction and supervision, soldiers might concentrate all their fire on one small group of the enemy, allowing others to escape
unscathed or even overrun their position.

From an air-to-air perspective, Jubilee could well be categorized as a
super-Circus in which Dieppe was the target and the bomber element had
been replaced by troops of the 2nd Canadian Infantry Division. Viewed in
that light, it was certainly not the disaster for the RAF/RCAF that it was for
the Canadian Army. Indeed, it marked a significant turning point in the
progress of the fighter offensive, a point from which the RAF and RCAF really
began winning the battle of attrition, though their losses would be more than
twice as great as those of the Luftwaffe for some months to come. Although
the earlier Circuses and Ramrods had produced a *perceived* loss rate (by the
British) of approximately two of their own machines for each German, the
true ratio had been better than four to one. Jubilee, in which the RAF/RCAF
had lost ninety-nine of its own machines while claiming ninety-one enemy
aircraft destroyed, with thirty-eight 'probables' and 140 damaged, seemed
eminently satisfactory in comparison; and although the correct figure had
been only forty-eight German losses (with no more than twenty-four damaged),[33] the actual ratio was similar to the perceived – and acceptable – one
of the preceding campaigns.

Nine RCAF squadrons – six fighter, two fighter-reconnaissance, and one
Intruder – had been committed, losing fourteen aircraft and nine pilots, with
another ten machines damaged and three pilots slightly wounded. They
claimed, in return, to have destroyed ten enemy aircraft, with two more probably destroyed and fourteen damaged – the squadron counts ranging from No
412's loss of two machines and one pilot without causing any injury to the
enemy to 416's claims of three destroyed, one probable, and seven damaged
with only two of its own machines requiring repairs.[34] In evaluating such

claims, however, the excitement and confusion of battle and the natural tendency among pilots fighting for their lives to declare an enemy aircraft destroyed even if they did not actually see it hit the ground must be taken into account. It seems likely that the RCAF balance sheet on this occasion was very similar to that of the RAF – two or two-and-a-half losses for each victory.

No German bombers had been involved in the air battles that accompanied the Circus and Ramrod operations of the past eighteen months; but at Dieppe enemy bombers had been brought into play, and better than half of the Luftwaffe's losses consisted of light and medium bombers, while the RAF lost only six of those types. The totals of fighters and fighter-bombers lost were eighty-nine RAF/RCAF to twenty-three Luftwaffe, or a ratio of roughly four to one – only fractionally better than that incurred in earlier Circuses and Ramrods. The RAF/RCAF lost sixty-eight pilots, fifty-one killed and seventeen taken prisoner, all but four of them from single-engined machines. German aircrew losses are not known, but were probably not more than thirty pilots. On the evening of 19 August only seventy of the 230 German fighters that had been serviceable that morning were still combat-ready, but hasty repairs and immediate deployment of reserves brought the number up to 194 before dawn on the 20th, although one after-action report recorded that 'there were no further reserves available.'[35]

Strategically, the Luftwaffe's predicament was growing worse as the Germans were now beginning to pay the price for thinking only in terms of a short war and for the overconfidence inculcated by the relatively easy successes of 1939 and 1940. Winston Churchill's prewar propaganda strategy of maximizing the Luftwaffe's strength and exaggerating its potential had terrified Britain and the Soviet Union (and worried the United States), and all three powers set high targets for aircraft manufacture even before the outbreak of war. Production rose steadily thereafter. In January 1940 the number of British aircraft coming off the assembly line was already better than 50 per cent higher than that in Germany, and a year later the British doubled their monthly output while the enemy only increased his production by half. The Germans began closing the gap early in 1942 as the so-called Göring expansion program went into effect,[36] but, by then, the Luftwaffe was fighting the Russians as well as the British and Americans, and was losing most of the increase to the apparently insatiable appetites of the Eastern front. Meanwhile, American production was gearing up to previously unimaginable heights.

What was Bentley Priory going to do with all these aircraft? For the time being pilots would continue to defend the British Isles while preparing for the cross-Channel amphibious assault on Festung Europa that American entry into the war made both possible and inevitable. Until the Allies actually invaded Northwest Europe, however, Douglas's March 1942 directive – to bring the Luftwaffe into the air, where 'we shall inflict casualties in the fighting whilst the additional flying which is forced upon the enemy will increase his normal wastage' – continued to determine operational goals.[37]

In the aftermath of Jubilee there was still little enthusiasm among the fighter staff for the idea of committing fighter aircraft to the ground battle. Moreover, with no immediate prospect of a campaign in Northwest Europe – and little likelihood of another major raid on the Dieppe scale – there was no apparent incentive to train squadrons in such tasks, while occasions to challenge the Luftwaffe for air superiority in more glamorous air-to-air combat were relatively plentiful in the skies of northern France, Belgium, and the Netherlands.

Perhaps equally influential in limiting the fighter to its traditional role, however, was the lack of any weapon-system both powerful and precise enough to be useful on the battlefield that could be carried into combat by fighters or fighter-bombers. Bombs, effective enough when they hit the target or only narrowly missed it, could still be aimed at low level only by 'guesstimate,' while machine-gun or cannon fire lacked the requisite hitting power to destroy hardened targets or the sustainability to neutralize them for any significant length of time. Rocket projectiles, in the form of a 3-inch rocket with alternative warheads – high-explosive or armour-piercing – which to some extent combined the advantages of bombs and cannon shells, were in the experimental pipeline but would not reach squadron service until mid-1943.[38]

In the Middle East, however, the potential significance of tactical air power was becoming clearer every day, whatever its shortcomings. The ground and air commanders there, General Sir Bernard Montgomery and Air Marshal Sir Arthur Tedder, were both quick to appreciate the possibilities opened up by air support of ground forces, once air superiority had been achieved. That had come about with the arrival of the first Spitfires in the Western Desert, in the summer of 1942, and more and more the DAF was committing light bombers and fighters to the land battle. When Feldmarschall Albert Kesselring, the Luftwaffe officer who had just been appointed Oberbefehlshaber Sud (C-in-C South) visited the Afrika Korps after El Alamein, he was soon reporting to Hitler that, 'for the first time the RAF has appeared in sufficient strength to be a decisive factor in the [ground] battle.' From his perspective worse was to come, as he rightly predicted that 'this is probably only the initial phase of the stepping-up of Allied air activity which we must expect.'[39]

In the United Kingdom, General McNaughton had a similar faith in the potential of airpower to influence the land battle directly. Working from the perspective of army cooperation, his ideas (and demands) went deeper than those of any British general except, perhaps, Montgomery. He had been pushing hard for the creation of army co-operation wings since March 1942, envisaging a tactical air force that might eventually provide 'not less than five squadrons for each division.'[40] At the time, that ratio must have seemed ludicrous to most air and ground commanders and their staff officers – although by the end of the war there would be better than four squadrons of Second Tactical Air Force to each division, or equivalent, of 21st Army Group.

With the upcoming conversion of the 4th Canadian Infantry Division into an armoured formation, a third army cooperation squadron would be required but there had, as yet, been no decision as to whether the new unit would come from Canada or be formed in the United Kingdom. Meanwhile, McNaughton continued to pursue his policy of constituting a full, three-squadron wing under the command of First Canadian Army, finding an ally in Air Marshal Harold Edwards, who, on 5 September, approved the organization of such a formation by 15 November 1942.[41]

In the early part of that month, McNaughton and staff officers at Fighter and Army Co-operation Commands ironed out the final details for the formation of 39 (RCAF) Reconnaissance Wing headquarters. Only one of its two squadrons – Nos 400 and 414 – would train with the army at a time, though they would both retain close personal liaison with 1 Canadian Corps and the 5th Canadian Armoured Division – each of which, according to plan, would be allocated one of the squadrons when operations began. In November, No 414 was still listed on the 5th Division's order of battle but, effective 4 December, both squadrons would come under command of 39 Wing, itself attached to First Canadian Army, and 'sq[uadro]ns which are released from their Army commitments will undertake active operations in affiliation with Fighter Com[man]d, under the control of 39 Wing.'[42]

Associating squadrons of Army Co-operation Command with Fighter Command in this manner was evidence of the former's difficult position in the airpower hierarchy. It was, in effect, only an air force in theory, for no one yet knew when or how it would make its contribution towards fighting the Germans on the ground. As one staff officer pointed out, 'During the present defensive period of the war the Corps and Divisions of the Army have not sufficient use for Army Co-operation Squadrons to keep them fully employed.' Even so, another RCAF army cooperation unit would be mobilized at the end of the year, with the formation of No 430 Squadron.[43]

The idea of concentrating Canadian squadrons to create larger formations was not limited to army cooperation units. In the summer and fall of 1942 there were seven RCAF day-fighter squadrons in Fighter Command, and during a summer visit to Britain Air Minister Power, in discussions with Sholto Douglas, broached the possibility of creating Canadian stations. Douglas promptly agreed that Redhill (Biggin Hill sector), Digby (Digby sector), and Fairwood Common (Fairwood Common sector) could be completely Canadianized. An RCAF wing would also be established in the Kenley sector (and hence be informally known as the Kenley wing). Indeed, at a later date it might be possible to allocate an entire sector in No 11 Group to the RCAF.[*] Meanwhile, on 16 September, RAF Digby became RCAF Digby under the command of Group Captain A.E. McNab, DFC.[44]

In September, as the Allies probed the possibilities of an invasion of Northwest Africa (Operation Torch), fighter operations over Northwest Europe decreased in intensity. Through the last four months of 1942 the RAF/RCAF flew less than half the number of offensive sorties than in the period from

---

[*]As will be seen, the formation of No 83 Group a year later forestalled any plans to create a Canadian sector.

March to June.[45] When Spitfire squadrons operated on offensive missions, they were likely to support the USAAF which, since August, had been testing its doctrine of formation precision bombing by daylight in attacking targets in France. The tendency towards ever-larger escort formations protecting 'boxes' of bombers meant that leadership was more important than ever if missions were not to fall apart through a missed rendezvous or poor flying discipline. J.E. Johnson's description of his duties gives some indication of a wing leader's burden in the autumn of 1942.

My job would be to lead and to fight. To bring the greatest number of guns to bear against the enemy in the shortest possible time. To cut down losses to a minimum and to avoid the bad bounce. To control the progress of the engagement and to keep the whole wing together as a fighting force and not get split up into isolated, ineffective packets – by far the most difficult task. These goals could only be achieved through a high standard of flying, perfect discipline and strict radio drill.[46]

That, of course, was the principle; in practice, any significant opposition could, and did, break up and disperse fighter formations. A typical example can be found in a 6 September mission involving Nos 401 and 402 Squadrons. They were escorting B-17s on a strike against the Avion Potez aircraft factory at Meaulte, used extensively as a repair facility. Despite attempts at suppressing fighter opposition by diversionary bomber strikes against the fighter fields at St Omer/Longuenesse and Abbeville/Drucat, the bombers were harassed continually while in French airspace.[47]

The 26 Fortresses arrived at the rendezvous five minutes early and did not wait for the four Spitfire squadrons of the escort to form up; as a result the whole formation was badly dispersed and some 30 enemy fighters, attacking in small groups, were able to harass both the bombers and the Spitfires. Heavy *Flak* was again encountered and several of the bombers were hit, one being lost. The results of the bombing could not be observed. On their way in to the target, Blue section of No 401 became detached during a skirmish and was heavily engaged throughout the remainder of the operation. The only claim made however was by F/Sgt E. Gimbel who inflicted damage on one FW. No losses were suffered by this section or squadron but Sgt G.J. Roan of No 402 had to bale out over France and was taken prisoner.[48]

Circus 224 on 9 October (the largest to that time) saw more than one hundred Fortresses and Liberators, with Nos 401, 402, and seven other fighter squadrons as escorts, strike at the Fives-Lille locomotive works – a far cry from the days, only eighteen months earlier, when a *single* Stirling bomber had served as bait. Several diversionary sweeps involving Nos 412, 416, and 403 Squadrons were supposed to distract the enemy, but the Luftwaffe was not fooled. The main attack 'encountered intense heavy *Flak* along the route and one bomber was seen to crash and three more did not return ... Several engagements occurred in which F/Lt G.B. Murray and F/Sgt E.L. Gimbel shot down an FW which was seen to crash. F/Lt Murray also damaged a second fighter of the same type.'[49]

No pilots were lost on that occasion. Already the Germans were pulling their fighters back, deeper into France, to avoid having them destroyed on the ground, and were relying more and more on anti-aircraft artillery to defend targets in northern France and the Netherlands. There were over 5500 heavy, and 15,000 medium and light, Flak guns deployed in the west* by the end of 1942, representing a heavier investment in anti-aircraft artillery (and gun crews) than on all other fronts combined. This growing emphasis on Flak was an unmistakeable indicator of the Luftwaffe's decline, marked by inadequate training due to fuel rationing and the unending need for reinforcement pilots. Already the fourth Gruppe of each Geschwader, which had acted as a reserve training squadron, had been disbanded, its pilots needed in Russia and North Africa. German trainees now flew no more than 160 training hours on machines that bore little resemblance to the fighters they would finally be assigned to, while Commonwealth pilots were receiving as much as 360 hours of advanced training on fighter-type aircraft.[50]

For the RCAF, the year 1943 started as 1942 had ended. January activities for Nos 401 (switching from Spitfire IXs to VBs as it moved to a quieter sector), 402 (IXs), 412 (VBs), and 416 (VBs) included nine Circuses, which generally met with little opposition, while Nos 403 (VBs to IXs), 411 (VBs), and 421 (VBs) concentrated on defensive patrols and scrambles. Perhaps the most exciting operation of the winter was part of a series of Ramrods on 17 January involving Nos 401, 402, and 412 squadrons. Their first sorties, at 1105 that morning, were routine, but 'less than two hours after their return the three squadrons took off again to repeat the operation.'

The ground strafers were most successful, No 412 attacking six locomotives in the area around Yvetot, while No 401 shot up three trains near Fontaine, Cany-Barville and Bolbec. The first, a coal train, was badly damaged and forced to stop by the pilots of Blue section, who also shot up a factory or distillery southwest of Fontaine. While the Spitfires were engaged on this ground-strafe about a score of FW 190s began bouncing them in diving attacks from the sun ... Many individual dogfights resulted as the fighters swirled about over Bolbec. W/Cdr J.C. Fee, DFC, who had led both the day's operations, took the brunt of the attack and both he and his number two Flying Officer M.J. Sunstrum, were lost.'[51]

A posthumous Bar would be added to Fee's DFC a month later, the citation noting that he was 'a brilliant leader who has set a splendid example of courage and determination.'[52]

In the first twelve days of March 1943 Exercise Spartan provided pilots and groundcrew with an opportunity to experience life in the field, as it rehearsed air and ground forces in the expansion of a bridgehead which planners saw as

---

* This total includes those protecting the German fatherland.

the third phase of invasion operations, after the assault and the establishment of a lodgement. From an air perspective, it was 'a full scale try out of the use of a Composite Group, consisting of light and medium bombers, day and night fighter and fighter reconnaissance [army cooperation] squadrons working through a common operations room in direct contact with the army commander.' Taking the role of invader was First Canadian Army, supported by six army co-operation squadrons, including Nos 400 and 414, seven fighter squadrons, including No 412, four army support squadrons (destined to become Typhoon units), and two light-bomber squadrons. The British defenders had similar air resources which included Nos 411 and 421 squadrons. Within each 'army,' air action was co-ordinated with the land battle through a composite air group organization which could mount a variety of missions, with the group's commander operating from army headquarters, thus guaranteeing close liaison.[53]

The concept of the composite group proved so sound that the Air Ministry's director of organization decided to retain z Group headquarters, which had been formed to support First Canadian Army on the exercise, as a permanent component of the RAF's order of battle. Effective 1 April 1943, staff were posted to it and the new organization was designated No 83 Group, with headquarters at Redhill. In the next few months this staff would oversee the development of subsidiary headquarters and administrative units, including supply and transport, repair and salvage, and a mobile field hospital. One or two at a time, several squadrons joined the group to familiarize themselves with the new organization, and headquarters organized short training exercises for their benefit. The first RCAF units to arrive, Nos 400 and 414, began setting up their tents on 4 July.[54]

In March 1943, at the end of winter, the operational tempo for Fighter Command squadrons had reached a five-month low, but thereafter it increased steadily until September. In mid-April Air Marshal Sir Trafford Leigh-Mallory, who had succeeded Douglas as AOC-in-C, reassessed some of Bentley Priory's objectives. Though 'the destruction of enemy aircraft and the pinning down in North-Western Europe of the maximum enemy air forces remain our primary aims ... the enemy cannot effectively be brought to battle in the air unless worth-while targets in enemy occupied territory are attacked.' Therefore, 'our major fighter offensive operations must be in co-operation with bombers of the British and United States Bomber Commands, and with our own fighter/bombers.' In other words, more Ramrods; and as these became progressively larger – posing a greater threat to the enemy, at least in theory – protecting the bombers would become a more complex business. Since, generally speaking, British fighters were best able to combat their German counterparts at medium altitudes, bombers – the Luftwaffe's target – would fly at ten thousand feet in order to bring about medium-altitude battles. Some fighters, however, were better fitted to provide high cover while others were more suited to medium-level work, requiring a division of labour between Spitfire IXs, which would fly well above the bomber formation, and Spitfire Vs, which would provide close escorts below 15,000 feet.[55]

Tactics, too, became ever more sophisticated as more bombers were incorporated into Ramrods and staff officers brought ever more covering fighters to bear. In mid-1943 Bentley Priory, following the advice of No 11 Group, increased the number of fighter wings escorting bomber formations. To what was already an impressive conglomeration of aircraft, organized into escort wing, escort cover wing, high cover wing, target support wing, forward support wing, and rear support wing, tacticians added a 'bouncing' wing, whose role was to range far afield from the bombers and surprise enemy fighters as they took off or climbed to engage the main formation, together with a 'rover' wing that flew virtually independently in the general area of the Ramrod target and routes, with the simple objective of destroying any enemy aircraft which crossed its path. Not all these wings would be necessary all the time; for example, a forward support wing might be dispensed with for attacks on targets close to the coast.[56]

A continent away from Bentley Priory, on the grossly overcrowded outpost of Malta, some sixty miles off the southern tip of Sicily, Canada's representative fighter squadron in the Mediterranean theatre was one of the Desert Air Force units participating in the pre-invasion phase of Operation Husky – the combined assault on Sicily that, just one week later, would make the first permanent breach in the coastal defences of Festung Europa. 'One of the disadvantages of Malta is that the squadron is so scattered,' moaned the squadron diarist. 'Officers living in the Modern Imperial Hotel in Sliema, NCO pilots in the Balluto Hotel on St. Julian's Bay … the ground NCOs in the Malta Poorhouse, near Luqa village, and the airmen in tents in fields and quarries in the valley below the aerodrome.'[57] Rank clearly had its privileges in No 417 Squadron.

Despite being 'so scattered,' the Canadians were much better off on Malta than they had been at Port Tewfik, in the Gulf of Suez, when they had first arrived in the Middle East thirteen months earlier. Then No 417 had been a fighter squadron without fighters; and even when aircraft did appear, the squadron's lot had not been a happy one during the intervening year. Its frustrations had been many and its gratifications few throughout the North African campaign.

The airmen had been told that Spitfires would be awaiting them at Tewfik, but Luftwaffe successes in the desert, its pressure on Malta, and the unexpected demands of the Far East had turned British logistical planning on its head and the supply pipeline into a shambles. Because of the compelling needs of Malta, only enough Spitfires had been available in Egypt to equip one of six newly arrived squadrons – an experienced RAF unit – which was soon in action.[*] Another squadron was sent to Cyprus, and three more were broken up to reinforce other units in the Western Desert which were being badly battered by the Luftwaffe. But, for political reasons, there could be no question of breaking up the RCAF squadron, even though not every Canadian was in favour

---

[*] The DAF's standard fighter in mid-1942 was still the Hurricane II, no match for the Messerschmitt 109E, never mind the 109F.

of Canadianization if it interfered with the prospect of seeing action. Forty-five years later the officer who took No 417 to the Middle East, ex-Squadron Leader Pitcher, recalled 'most emphatically' that 'at no time was the suggestion made to me that the squadron should be split up to reinforce other squadrons already in action. If it had, I and all the other pilots would have jumped at it as we were thoroughly fed up with the existing state of inactivity ... maintaining the separate identity of Canadian units often took precedence over the expeditious prosecution of the war.'[58]

Although there was much frustration and dissatisfaction at the time, perhaps the pilots of No 417 were lucky that their squadron was neither broken up to provide reinforcements, nor issued with obsolescent aircraft and sent forward into battle. Nevertheless, their misfortunes during the ensuing six months were subsequently outlined in High Commissioner Vincent Massey's December complaint to the Dominions Office (at the behest of the War Cabinet in Ottawa), in partial response to a British desire to transfer two RCAF bomber squadrons to the Middle East.

A Canadian Fighter Squadron was sent to the Middle East the first week in June, 1942, but did not receive its aircraft until the first week in September and it was then supplied with aircraft 'rejects' from the Fighting French which had to be replaced by other Hurricanes. This squadron had been an efficient Spitfire Squadron in England but was assigned to air patrols over the Nile Delta, well behind the front line. It has not been able to get into action ... although less experienced squadrons similarly equipped have been given the opportunity to engage in active operations in the Western Desert.[59]

As has been explained, there were some good reasons why the Canadians were not yet flying Spitfires, and it was simply not true that 'less experienced squadrons similarly equipped' had received better opportunities. Nevertheless, Massey's intervention may well have proved fruitful as, by the end of the year, Tedder would decide 'that I can start at once to rearm fully No 417 Squadron with Spitfires and will transfer it to the Western Desert for operations in the near future.'[60]

Even for those who do the fighting, war can be a tedious exercise, with long periods of inactivity preying on morale; and No 417 had faced more than its fair share of boredom. After months of ferrying aircraft (across Africa from Takoradi, on the west coast, to Egyptian bases), servicing B-25s, and otherwise doing all manner of things but make war, the squadron had become operational, on obsolescent cannon-armed Hurricane IICs, on 13 September 1942.[61] The Canadians were, however, kept largely out of harm's way on anti-reconnaissance patrols over the Suez Canal. Encounters with the enemy were rare, and usually marred by the failure of the Hurricanes' cannon, so the unit managed only a single victory, a Ju 88, on 26 September. Two pilots were killed in operational accidents. The only other event of note during this period was the replacement of Pitcher (whose health had been a source of some concern since a bout of pneumonia in 1941) by one of his flight commanders, newly promoted Squadron Leader F.B. Foster, on 16 November.[62]

The Canadians acquired their first Spitfire VBs and VCs in October 1942, and carried out their last operation with Hurricanes on 13 January 1943.[63] Finally able to fight on technologically near equal terms, but not tactically – the DAF still employed the abominable vic – the squadron was ordered to Tripoli, the recently captured Libyan capital, in mid-February, where it became part of No 244 Wing. For the moment, however, duties were still similar to those performed in Egypt, as its pilots flew defensive patrols over the ships bringing supplies into Tripoli along the Libyan coast. It was not stimulating work; in nearly five hundred sorties flown between 27 February and 11 April 1943, pilots saw the enemy only twice, and even then could not get close enough to engage.

In mid-March the commanding officer led half the squadron further forward, to Ben Gardane, across the Tunisian border. There, they flew one convoy escort, on the 22nd, and shot down a Heinkel 111 in a one-sided combat – six Spitfires against the lone bomber – before being assigned to protect Allied light bombers harrying German forces retreating from the Mareth Line. Six uneventful days passed before they rejoined the rest of the squadron at Mellaha,[64] and the whole unit finally caught up with No 244 Wing at Goulvine, a hundred miles south of Tunis, on 11 April 1943.

The enemy was now squeezed into a Tunisian enclave nowhere more than fifty miles deep, and the air battle began to increase in intensity as the Luftwaffe struggled to protect the tenuous German supply line – by air and sea – from Sicily and to frustrate Allied air support of ground forces. On 19 April twelve of No 417's pilots were covering Kittyhawk fighter-bombers attacking ground targets at low level when they were surprised by more than twenty Me 109s, probably flying out of Sicilian bases. In the mêlée over the Gulf of Tunis that followed, the Germans shot down four of the Spitfires,[65] and survivors' reports make it clear that the Canadians still had much to learn. They were caught completely unawares by aircraft attacking out of the sun in pairs and 'finger-fours.' One of the Canadians, a very lucky Flying Officer E.W. Mitchell, 'immediately did a steep turn to port and on completing the turn found one Me-109 in my sights.'

I opened fire at extreme range and closed to about 200 yards, using up all my ammunition in the process. Just before my ammunition was exhausted the Me-109's belly tank dropped off together with pieces from [its wing] root and large quantities of black smoke poured [sic]. Toward the end of my attack I noticed tracer near my port wing. As soon as my ammunition was exhaused I took violent evasive action and discovered four 109s on my tail. After doing a steep spiral down to sea level I headed for the coast with two 109's on my tail ... Halfway across the peninsula one aircraft left me and I continued to the east coast with one 109 after me ... I shook [off] the last enemy aircraft and continued to base.[66]

The enemy held his shrinking Tunisian perimeter for another three weeks (Bizerta and Tunis both fell on 7 May, the former to the Americans, the latter to the British), finally surrendering the Cape Bon redoubt on 13 May. During

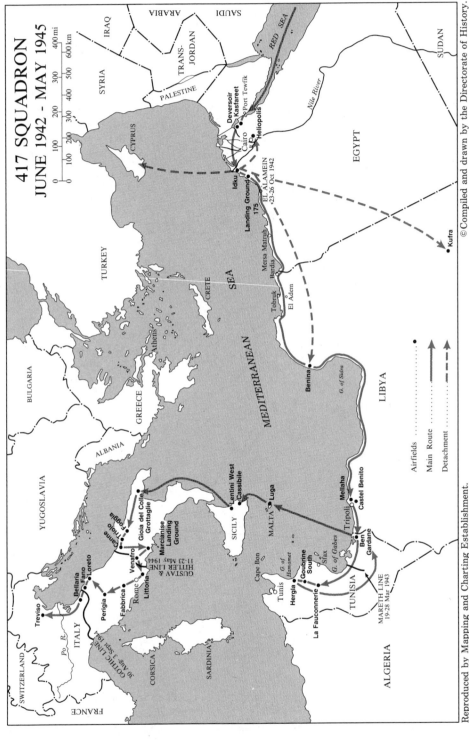

417 SQUADRON
JUNE 1942 - MAY 1945

Reproduced by Mapping and Charting Establishment.

© Compiled and drawn by the Directorate of History.

that time the air fighting was often as intense as that on the ground, but No 417 Squadron played little part in the battle, most of its effort being expended on uneventful anti-shipping patrols; one pilot did succeed in shooting down an Italian fighter, a Macchi 202, on 28 April. The most exciting event recorded by the squadron diarist during the final week of fighting was on 6 May, when the officers' mess tent burned down.[67]

Meanwhile, the spectre of Canadianization haunted the new commanding officer. On St Patrick's Day, 1943, Foster had found time to draft a long letter to Wing Commander D.S. Patterson at District Headquarters in Cairo.

As the only Canadian Unit in the Middle East this squadron operates under difficulties which do not confront squadrons in the UK and stations in Canada. The rapid expansion of the number of Squadrons in the UK and Stations in Canada have provided opportunities for rapid promotion for deserving airmen. Their contemporaries in this Squadron however, have no such opportunities no matter how skilled and how deserving. It is scarcely exaggeration to say that some of our better men would have already received accelerated promotion to fill establishment vacancies if they had been with RAF Squadrons. This is true not only with ground crew but also with aircrew. It is noted, for example, in the most recent RCAF list of Squadrons, that two pilots of 416 Squadron, our contemporary Fighter Squadron, have been promoted to Flight Commanders in other Canadian Squadrons, an opportunity not available to our equally senior and experienced officers.[68]

The comparison with 416 Squadron was ill-judged. No 417 may have had 'equally senior and experienced officers,' but they were not nearly as skilled and combat-experienced as their colleagues of 416. Initially flying convoy protection patrols off Scotland, just as 417 Squadron had done off the Egyptian and Libyan coasts, 416 had been posted to Fighter Command's No 11 Group in time to participate in the Dieppe raid, in which (as we have seen) it had claimed three enemy machines destroyed, one 'probable' and seven damaged, without loss to itself. Since then the squadron had been busy with sweeps, Rhubarbs, Circuses, and Ramrods over the English Channel and northern France, where the Luftwaffe sent the cream of its pilots and the latest models of Messerschmitt and Focke-Wulf. The squadron as a whole was a good deal more experienced than No 417, and its stars shone much more brightly. One of its flight commanders, Flight Lieutenant P.L.I. Archer, DFC, already had four victories to his credit.[69]

Foster, however, recommended several of his pilots for promotion and posting 'to any vacancy which may exist,' and shortly afterwards ten pilots (only one of them non-commissioned) were posted, with at least two of them going to RAF squadrons in the theatre. Foster himself, and both his flight commanders, left the squadron in June and were eventually repatriated to Canada. Flying Officer R.L. Patterson was promoted to command one flight, and Flight Lieutenant A.U. Houle was posted in to take over the other.[70]

Finding a replacement for the squadron commander sparked a flurry of signals between RAF Middle East, RCAF District HQ in Cairo, and RCAF Overseas Headquarters. Consistent with the policy of Canadianization, Overseas Head-quarters wanted the appointment filled with one of its own, but there was no RCAF officer in the theatre whom the RAF considered qualified. Air Vice-Marshal Broadhurst, the DAF's commander, felt that 'owing to the lack of operational experience of the Squadron as a whole, that strong leadership and an officer of outstanding operational experience should be posted' to No 417. He and Wing Commander Patterson finally reached a compromise which Edwards, in London, accepted somewhat reluctantly, in the appointment of Squadron Leader P.S. Turner, DFC and Bar, who had 'turned around' No 411 Squadron in 1942. Turner had since served in Malta and, more recently, as a senior controller in the Sector Operations Room in Heliopolis, Egypt. Other than his failure to be in the RCAF, the twenty-nine-year-old Turner's qualifi-cations were near perfect. With at least ten enemy aircraft destroyed and four or more 'probables,' two DFCs, and more than seven hundred hours of combat flying to his credit, he had a reputation as a disciplinarian where business was concerned, 'deadly serious' in the air but 'one of the boys' in the mess;[71] and he was a Canadian, who understood and appreciated the foibles of his fellow countrymen, whatever badges he might wear.

Army Co-operation Command had played an important role in developing and propagating the concept of air support of ground forces, but, as a training and experimental formation, it still lacked the communications and command structure to operate in the field; and since it was 'now necessary to pass from the phase of development to the phase of action,' it could be dispensed with. On 1 June 1943 the command was disbanded and its component parts merged into a tactical air force within Fighter Command – though 'in order to ensure that full use is made of the large store of knowledge and experience possessed by Headquarters Army Co-operation Command, the staff of the Headquarters will be largely used to form Headquarters Tactical Air Force.' On 28 June the change in designation from Army Co-operation (AC) squadrons to Fighter Reconnaissance (FR) squadrons became official for Nos 400, 414, and 430, as well as the appropriate RAF units.[72]

At the time of the changeover from Army Co-operation Command to Fighter Command, the air force and its ground-bound brethren were still working out the details of air-support operations. One important area in which army and air staffs had to coordinate their activities was in landing facilities. If they were to provide adequate support for armies in the field, squadrons would need refuelling and ammunition facilities close to the front, and there was much animated discussion over how these were to be provided since the Germans would doubtless do everything possible to destroy existing facilities before they fell into Allied hands. In the first few days or weeks of a continental cam-paign, immediately after the amphibious assault, construction equipment and materials for airstrips would have to compete for shipping space with other priority items like ammunition and rations. Assuming that an army of two or three corps (which is what each composite air group would be supporting) advanced eight miles each day, the group would probably need six to eight

landing strips the first week and perhaps a further five or six in each subsequent week in order to keep up with the soldiers.[73]

That required the services of Airfield Construction Groups relying on such
prefabricated materials as perforated steel planking (PSP) or rolls of tarred
hessian to set up runways in days rather than weeks. Technically an army
group resource, these units would fall under the command of corps commanders for the first five days after an assault, during which time they would
operate according to a prearranged plan on sites selected off the map (though
the army group engineer and his colleagues were allowed to choose alternates
should circumstances warrant).[74]

In the early months of 1943 Army Co-operation Command had continued
to develop tactics and doctrine, though it was becoming increasingly evident
that its success in doing so would lead to its own demise. By this time there
was general agreement on the basic tenets of aiding ground formations.

That full air support is an essential requirement in all land operations undertaken
against an enemy possessing air power ...

That the paramount factor in providing such support must be the attainment and
retention of mastery in the air ...

That such mastery is attained primarily by the Fighter which by day is superior to
all other types of lesser performance and armament ...

That, accordingly, all air action must be related to fighter action, and that, therefore,
centralised control must be exercised by the Royal Air Force over Fighter Bombers
and specialised types for ground attack and reconnaissance.[75]

Air superiority – a term not yet in general or common use in 1943[*] – could
well have been defined, then as now, as 'that degree of dominance ... which
permits the conduct of [air] operations ... without prohibitive interference' by
the enemy.[76] Traditionally, attaining that objective (or, at least, preventing the
enemy from doing so) had been the business of rival fighter arms, as in the
Battle of Britain. Fighter Command had won that battle, if only by the narrowest of margins, and since then had easily maintained its dominance in
British skies; but its inability to reach out into German air space had compelled
Bomber Command to seek another kind of air superiority, by evasion and
deception, rather than by fighting.[†] Closer to home, having secured British
airspace, Fighter Command had found itself in a kind of operational limbo,
reduced to exercising an uncertain and essentially fruitless version of air
superiority over northern France and the Low Countries. The general progress
of the war was now bringing the prospect of an invasion of Northwest Europe

---

[*] Although Sir Hugh Trenchard had used it as early as 1919.
[†] The USAAF, with its much more heavily armed 'Flying Fortresses,' was still unsuccessfully
endeavouring to achieve the conventional kind of air superiority in its daylight bombing
operations. It would eventually succeed, in the winter of 1943–4, not through the firepower
of its bombers but through the serendipitous development of North American's Rolls Royce-
engined long-range fighter, the Mustang.

into focus, however; and when that prospect matured it would obviously be necessary for Bentley Priory to establish an unyielding superiority in the air space over the beachhead and its environs. Air participation in the ground battle would also be important, and fighter-bombers might have significant parts to play, providing ground support under the umbrella coverage of the air superiority fighters.

The RCAF had its own perspective on all this, shared in principle – but not necessarily in practice – by the Cabinet in Ottawa. The endeavour to implement Canadianization at a moderately high organizational level in the interests of developing a balanced air force (just as First Canadian Army was a balanced land formation, incorporating all the appropriate arms and services) had already led to the formation of No 6 (RCAF) Bomber Group (see chapter 17) and a smaller army cooperation wing. What was required now, in the light of this new emphasis on tactical air power, was the expansion of the latter into a tactical group – a composite formation of fighters and fighter-bombers, and perhaps light bombers, as well as reconnaissance units. The attempt to establish it set in motion a byzantine struggle involving Bentley Priory, the Air Ministry, Air Force Headquarters in Ottawa, RCAF Overseas Headquarters, and First Canadian Army, as every Canadian concerned began to explore the possibility of forming a tactical group to operate with the latter.

In mid-February, a month before Spartan, Air Marshal Harold Edwards had already asked Air Minister Power to consider forming a composite group so that 'RCAF Units could retain their identity.' In a visit to First Canadian Army Headquarters just after Spartan, Group Captain D.M. Smith, commanding No 39 (Reconnaissance) Wing, informed General McNaughton that Edwards was studying the problem and had asked Ottawa for the necessary authority to form a group. Such a formation, requiring some eleven thousand groundcrew and hundreds of aircraft and aircrew for its several dozen squadrons, was not a commitment to be undertaken lightly. Nevertheless, Smith was anxious that Ottawa act quickly, as it was 'now or never' if the RCAF wanted to consolidate its strength in the United Kingdom.[77]

Staff officers and politicians in Canada in no way shared his sense of urgency, however, and signs that the RCAF was becoming troublesome again on the Canadianization issue caused some consternation within the Air Ministry. The director of policy there told his superior, Air Vice-Marshal C.E.H. Medhurst:

As regards the Canadian Composite Group, I think we should discourage this proposal since the segregation of Dominion Air forces into such a Group would inevitably destroy some of its flexibility for employment. We have in the past experienced so much trouble in this respect that I feel it would be a mistake to ask for more ... There would also be the natural tendency to demand that a Canadian Composite Group, if formed, should be employed in the same operational area in which Canadian land troops are located. This might prove a further embarrassment.[78]

Medhurst repeated that opinion to Sir Christopher Courtney, the Air Council's member for supply and organization, suggesting, ominously, 'that we rid them [the RCAF] of any idea of forming a Canadian Composite Group in the near future.'[79]

Sir Douglas Evill, vice chief of the air staff, was willing to be flexible, but only to a point. Policy governing the re-organization of the RAF for continental operations called for the formation of a second composite group (to be identified as No 84) which might train for operations in support of First Canadian Army. The VCAS thought it appropriate to include in it as many Canadian squadrons as might be available, and Courtney agreed, noting that the use of more RCAF squadrons would take some pressure off the British. Evill also suggested the new group's headquarters be established at Gatton Park, where First Canadian Army Headquarters was located. No 83 Group, already resident in the area, might move to Oxford, preparatory to affiliating with Second British Army.[80]

On the surface, the first British moves in this Canadianization chess game were reasonable. It made sense to allocate the experienced formation – No 83 Group – to the army which would, most likely, make the initial landings in Northwest Europe; and, with the 1st Canadian Division on its way to the Mediterranean, the prospect of a weakened and unbalanced Canadian army leading the assault was quickly dimming. However, as Air Vice-Marshal W.A. Curtis, Edwards's deputy at Overseas Headquarters, pointed out, Second British Army was still forming and No 83 Group had no one but First Canadian Army to train with. There was also some doubt as to whether Second British Army, once it was formed, would be more capable or better prepared for the assault than the Canadians.[*] Air Marshal Sir Trafford Leigh-Mallory agreed with his RCAF colleague, though his reasons for doing so are unknown and it is doubtful whether they had anything to do with Canadianization. McNaughton apparently cared little which group trained with his army, as long as it incorporated those Canadian squadrons trained in tactical support.[81]

For the time being No 83 Group continued to work with First Canadian Army, McNaughton accepting the affiliation in principle but hesitating to commit himself fully until Ottawa decided whether or not to form an RCAF composite group. He was well advised not to hold his breath, for Mackenzie King's cabinet was dealing with more important issues such as the defence of the St Lawrence and an acute labour shortage that had already affected production of coal, nickel, and lumber. Thus when, at the end of April, Air Commodore W.M. Yool, the Air Ministry's director of organization, asked if the RCAF was willing to form 'airfields' (the confusing nomenclature bestowed upon the logistical and administrative organizations that supported wings) in the new No 84 Group, Edwards was forced to answer, in the most diplomatic terms, that 'the whole question of Composite Groups is being discussed in Canada at the

___

[*] At this time First Canadian Army still comprised an army headquarters, two corps headquarters, two armoured divisions, two infantry divisions, and an armoured brigade. The decision to sent 1st Canadian Corps Headquarters and the 5th Armoured Division to Italy did not come until October.

present time and while I am hopeful that we will receive a favourable reply I would like to defer giving a definite decision until a little later on.'[82]

On 19 May the Overseas Headquarters diary recorded that 'the DAOC-in-C [Curtis] advised that the policy to have the balance of RCAF Squadrons all Bombers might have to be altered in view of the possible changes now under consideration and it may be necessary to make some of them Fighter Squadrons.' A few days later, Air Vice-Marshal W.F. Dickson, No 83 Group's RAF commander, proposed that his reconnaissance wing be formed from the three RCAF fighter-reconnaissance squadrons. One of its three fighter wings could also come from RCAF resources, namely the four Spitfire squadrons based on Kenley-Redhill. The other two fighter wings would be provided by the RAF.[83]

In early June the affiliation issue began to sort itself out. Leigh-Mallory and General Sir Bernard Paget, the commander of British Home Forces, agreed that No 83 Group would be affiliated with First Canadian Army, and No 84 Group, when formed, with Second British Army. On the 16th, however, Breadner reported to his minister that, 'in this connection, Air Ministry have approached the AOC-in-C Overseas in an unofficial way, for the views of the RCAF in regard to assuming responsibility for one of the groups as a Canadian Composite Group to operate with the Canadian Army' – but to do so would require an additional 12,500 personnel. At a subsequent meeting of the War Cabinet Committee, however, Mackenzie King pointed out that 'there had been general agreement that the Canadian war effort had reached its maximum.' The best that could be done was to authorize exploratory discussions with authorities in the United Kingdom so long as they would not involve further expenditures or demands for personnel.[84]

Leigh-Mallory had not waited for Canadian authorities to make up their minds on the matter, but had moved quickly to organize No 83 Group, filling the seventeen positions in each of the advanced and rear headquarters with RAF officers. Edwards found such haste disturbing and complained angrily to McNaughton in a telephone conversation of 19 June. A memorandum by the latter records that

he had been very disappointed ... to find that 83 Gp had been completed by Air Marshal Leigh-Mallory – there were two suitable Cdn Air Vice Marshals available to Com[man]d, one here and one in Canada – these and other Cdn officers had been shut out by the action taken – he had a talk with Leigh-Mallory this morning and had expressed his dissatisfaction, and that he could do nothing under the circumstances about setting up the Cdn part in the G[rou]p until the matter had been approved by the Cdn War Cabinet – he had said, however, if Leigh-Mallory felt it necessary as a matter of urgency for the prosecution of the war, he [Edwards] could, on his own responsibility, proceed.[85]

McNaughton had complaints of his own, similar to those of Edwards, for 'without any written instruction we had found ourselves associated with 83 Gp and it had been necessary to proceed with arrangements for training and organization provisionally.' When, on 24 June, Ottawa finally authorized Canadian participation in No 83 Group (but not an exclusively Canadian group), some of the pieces fell into place; Leigh-Mallory confirmed that about half the squadrons and personnel in the new group would be Canadian and that he would welcome more, as well as additional staff officers.[86]

In July the RCAF squadrons were organized around 'airfields,' with Nos 401, 411, and 412 forming 126 Airfield while 403 and 421 went to 127 Airfield, the two being grouped together in 17 (RCAF) Fighter Wing. The three fighter-reconnaissance units made up 39 (RCAF) Reconnaissance Wing. The eight airfields in No 83 Group were its logistical and support organizations, each responsible for three squadrons, the latter being thus stripped of much of their groundcrew. By the end of July, within the Second Tactical Air Force (Second TAF), 376 officers, 133 NCO aircrew, and 1,678 groundcrew were RCAF, but only six of thirty-four staff positions at group headquarters were Canadian. Though the RCAF was certainly underrepresented on the staff side, it should be remembered that Ottawa had only given permission for a Canadian contribution to the new formation a month before.[87]

The airfield organization was designed to allow squadrons to move from station to station without the long logistical 'tail' that had been associated with such moves in the past, permitting commanders to concentrate air units wherever they were needed with less delay. Of course, frequent moves were nothing new. No 401, though the least transient RCAF squadron to date, had moved sixteen times in thirty months, while No 421 had moved most often – fifteen times in thirteen months. When the latter celebrated its first anniversary in April 1943, it had already been based at Digby, Fairwood Common, Warmwell, Exeter, Ibsley, Angle, Zeals, Charmy Down, and Kenley.[88]

Throughout the summer, while the three fighter-reconnaissance squadrons concentrated on training, the pace of operations for the seven day-fighter squadrons picked up dramatically. In the latter part of July and all through August Ramrods made up the great bulk of missions, with each squadron flying more escort sorties than all other operations combined. Most were uneventful – in aircrew slang, 'a piece of cake' – though mechanical breakdown could add excitement to an otherwise routine flight.

At about 1226 [hours, 28 July 1943] S/Ldr McNair developed engine trouble when just off the coast ... left wing with P/O Parks escorting him. S/Ldr McNair lost height from about 20,000 ft to 10,000 ft and when about 12 miles off French coast at Dunkirk his engine caught fire and he lost control of his aircraft and dived for the sea. He was able to get out of his kite at about 5000 ft and parachute opened at about 2000 ft. P/O Parks gave a Mayday for him and Orbited him for approx 1:30 hours until relieved by 411 Squadron. Real good show by Parks. When the Squadron heard of S/Ldr McNair's difficulty they immediately pancaked [landed] at Manston and refueled and took part in the A[ir] S[ea] R[escue] and saw a Walrus pick up the Chief and they escorted him to Hawkinge. The Chief was burned about the face and had a real close call, but is resting satisfactorily in hospital and should be back in a few days.[89]

McNair would demonstrate his full recovery by shooting down an Me 109 south of Ghent at the end of August, his eleventh of sixteen victories.[90]

Standard procedures had not changed, and those squadrons equipped with Spitfire IXs (at this time Nos 403 and 421) flew top cover while the other RCAF squadrons in their VBs or VCs stayed close to the bombers. The Spitfire IX pilots had more opportunity to engage the enemy, and in July and August they claimed twenty-two aircraft destroyed compared with six for the five other squadrons. Flying VBs could thus be rather dull work, and No 411's narrative history relates that 'the pilots' only victories were on the ground – at volley-ball.'[91]

By the end of the summer of 1943 the Luftwaffe was in desperate straits, and the German training programme was in ever-growing disarray. Total losses in the first six months of 1943 had been high (almost nineteen hundred aircraft in each of the Eastern and Mediterranean theatres, and almost fifteen hundred in the west), and although industry was gearing up to replace these losses, aircrew were a different matter entirely. The equivalent of two-thirds of the fighter pilots available at the beginning of the year had been shot down by late June, and July and August proved even worse as the Americans sent their aerial armadas ever deeper into German territory. On each of the three fronts – Northwest Europe, Mediterranean, and Eastern – the Luftwaffe lost more than a thousand aircraft in those two summer months. In July it lost 335 fighters in the west, in August another 248; and over the next three months, losses averaged 280 a month. Even though losses in the east and south were dropping dramatically – less flying was being done – these were, in the long run, intolerable rates. To Hans Jeschonnek, the Luftwaffe's chief of staff, the situation was hopeless, and on 18 August he committed suicide.[92]

While in Northwest Europe the Allies built up their forces and otherwise prepared for an invasion to be carried out sometime in the indeterminate future, in the Mediterranean theatre operations against one of the Axis homelands were an imminent fact. On 20 June 1943 No 417's war diary recorded two noteworthy events: the first was a visit to Luqa by the king; the second was an operational entry: 'A sweep carried out over Sicily.'

No 244 Wing, of which 417 Squadron was a part, was one of the Spitfire formations that had been transferred to Malta in order to support the invasion of the Italian island. Though its first mission was a fighter sweep, No 417's operations in preparation for the assault consisted primarily of escorting Mitchell, Marauder, and Liberator bombers as they bombed Sicilian defences. The Luftwaffe was a prime target, so German airfields were harassed day and night, aeroplanes being destroyed on the ground, while many air- and ground-crew were killed or wounded, and those who survived were soon exhausted through lack of sleep.[93] Johannes Steinhoff, a fighter pilot writing years later, recalled the effects of one such attack.

Then it was quiet. Dust came drifting in through the two entrances of our dungeon and only an occasional explosion could now be heard. Circumspectly we climbed up the steps into the open where the scene of destruction brought us up short. Near the entrance, the patch of withered grass which extended up to the ramparts of the aircraft pens had been churned into a hideous landscape of craters, while above the spot where we had parked the 109s two columns of oily black smoke rose high into the air. Fragmentation bombs had perforated their fuel tanks and ignited the petrol. Above the burning aircraft the air shimmered with heat. An enormous dust cloud hung over the rest of the airfield like a white blanket, veiling it from sight. But we could see all too clearly what was left of our two burning aeroplanes, now beyond anyone's power to save.[94]

On 9 July 1943 the Canadians received their final briefing before the invasion, code-named Operation Husky. 'Pilots ... learned to their surprise that in the vast armada they have been protecting is the 1st Canadian Division. We had all been so sure that we would be the first Canadian unit ashore in the invasion of Europe, but we are glad to hear that the Canadian Army was getting a chance at action.'[95] The next day, as American, British, and Canadian troops waded through the surf to establish themselves on Sicilian soil, the squadron launched thirty-four sorties, either patrolling the area around Cape Passero, in the vicinity of the Canadian landings, or escorting Marauders in a bombing raid on Caltagerone. The Luftwaffe failed to make an appearance,[96] so those on patrol could afford to take in the scale and strength of the Allied forces moving onto the island. Pilot Officer Hedley Everard was one who was deeply impressed:

It was a perfect summer day and as dawn illuminated the scene below, I was astounded to see more than a thousand ships of all sizes floating on the azure sea. Brilliant flashes from the muzzles of battleships and cruisers identified the positions of the capital ships and their targets ashore were marked by smoke and dust. Radar scanners operating from Malta and on special sentinel ships told us that the hordes of aircraft below were all friendly. The waves of Dakotas carrying supplies inland for forward airdrops were clearly visible and unmolested, except by desultory ack-ack fire from scattered gun emplacements. Lines of barges carrying men, equipment and tanks etched the waters between anchored supply ships and the smoke-screened beaches. The military might displayed below was evident from horizon to horizon.[97]

The British landed on the southeastern shore of the island, the Canadians on the southern tip, and the Americans along the southern coast, altogether a front of some seventy miles. On 16 July, while Eighth Army engineers put the finishing touches to the airfield at Cassabile, some ten miles south of Syracuse, No 417 began flying from that installation. Missions were routine; top cover for Kittyhawk fighter-bombers, air-sea rescue, and fighter sweeps. Although there was no air-to-air combat the Canadians did come uncomfortably close to action on the ground, for the new airfield was still within range of German artillery, while the Luftwaffe attacked it sporadically by night, though without inflicting casualties.[98]

A week later the Canadians shifted to Agnone, but they soon left when shellfire and mines made the site too dangerous for efficient operations. Their next home was Lentini West, 'a newly made aerodrome in the heart of a great field of wheat,' where the squadron, no longer considered 244 Wing's junior unit, obtained the lone farmhouse as a pilot's dispersal and the only shaded area for its tent lines.[99] Only two short weeks were spent in these pleasant surroundings, however, the unit then moving to Gerbini, another target for Luftwaffe night bombing. On 11 August:

At about 2015 hours enemy aircraft began to bomb Augusta to the east of us, an almost nightly performance. Bombers however began to work westward, bombing Agnone, Lentini East and then our airdrome Lentini West. Our runway was located with flares and a considerable number of bombs were dropped. Although casualties of killed and wounded in the Wing were quite severe, no casualties were sustained by our Squadron because our well-dispersed living site is some distance from the runway and because the CO insisted every man have an adequate slit trench by his tent. Three bombs fell near the Squadron living site. Immediately the raid ended Squadron personnel proceeded to the airdrome to put out fires in our petrol dump and ammunition dump and to taxi our aircraft away from fires. Seven of our aircraft were hit, two being write-offs, and our Macchi 202 had a wing blown off. Operations reported raid as 50 plus. A number of delayed action bombs were dropped, one near our operations room, which was vacated until the bomb exploded on August 13.[100]

The next day the squadron sent out a detachment to attend the funeral of fifteen members of the wing killed in the raid.

Towards the end of the Sicilian campaign (which concluded on 17 August) No 417 concentrated on escorting fighter-bombers and light bombers on interdiction missions, mainly against the ports Axis forces were using to evacuate the island. Usually Flak was of much greater concern than enemy aircraft, but on Friday the 13th Italian fighters mounted the only deliberate air-to-air attack on the Canadians of the campaign. Four Spitfires were searching the seas north of Messina for a downed pilot from another squadron when they were surprised by several Macchi 202s. The engagement ended without loss to either side. Flak, however, took a toll, with one Canadian pilot (who had only joined the squadron the previous day) becoming a prisoner of war and another collecting shrapnel in his leg but managing to return to Lentini.[101]

Regrettably – and somewhat inexplicably – Allied air power failed to prevent the Germans from evacuating the bulk of their forces across the Strait of Messina, so that by the morning of 16 August only a small rearguard remained on the island. Thus, for the Germans, 'what was originally thought to have been an undertaking that would likely end in disaster had turned into a stunning success.'[102]

Even as the enemy successfully withdrew, No 417 was re-equipping with new aircraft. Seven Spitfire VIIIs arrived with promises of more to follow, and, as the first few were delivered to the Canadians within a month of the new model's first appearance in the Mediterranean theatre, it suggested, more clearly than any memorandum could, that the AOC-in-C now viewed the squadron as a first-line unit. The Mark VIII was an improvement over the Mark V in key respects. Armed with two cannon and four machine-guns, and retaining the ability of the latter to turn tightly, it was faster (408 miles per hour compared with 369), and able to climb higher (43,000 feet compared with 37,000). These characteristics enabled it to match the best German fighters available in Italy (the Me 109G and FW 190A) until the introduction of the FW 190D later in the year.[103]

On 21 August the pilots resumed operations with their new machines and, patrolling over the toe of Italy between Melito and Bagnara, they covered Kittyhawk fighter-bombers harassing enemy transport and communications. There was still no significant opposition from Axis fighters, but one Spitfire was hit by Flak over Bagnara, its pilot managing to bring his machine close to the Sicilian coast before baling out, where he was rescued unhurt by an army motor launch and its Sicilian crew.[104]

On 2 September the 1st Canadian Division led the British Eighth Army in a virtually unopposed landing on the tip of the Italian peninsula, at Reggio di Calabria; and the next day a month of cloak-and-dagger negotiations concluded with signatures on articles of Italian surrender, to come into effect on the 8th. Hitler had foreseen that likelihood, and German forces in Italy were poised to strike. Rome was occupied, and all nearby airfields secured, while the disarming of Italian troops proceeded apace. In twenty-four hours the Germans were in control of northern and central Italy, despite another major Allied landing in the Gulf of Salerno, which lay close to the limit of the range of land-based fighter air cover and hence air superiority.

In Northwest Europe the events that unfolded in August and September 1943 were tinted with routine rather than drama, though beginning on 25 August the pace of Fighter Command's air effort quickened in the opening phases of Operation Starkey. The latter, which was to last until 9 September, ambitiously attempted to achieve two main goals: to make the enemy believe an invasion of the Pas-de-Calais was imminent, and so draw the German fighter force into the air at times and places advantageous to the Allies; and to rehearse some aspects of a genuine invasion, including air operations, ground logistics, and communications.[105]

To this end, fighters, bombers, and coastal aircraft from British and American air forces would operate, once again, under the immediate direction of No 11 Group, at Uxbridge. Unlike Jubilee, however, Starkey would be controlled out of a combined Army/Air Operations Room under the ultimate authority of Lieutenant-General Sir Frederick Morgan, chief of staff to the Supreme Allied Commander[106] (and whose peculiar status revolved around the fact that there was, as yet, no Supreme Allied Commander), even though any air activity that developed would be exclusively of the air-to-air variety.

In the event, the Germans were not fooled for a moment, as Morgan related with admirable honesty and no little embarrassment.

Out to sea we could see the Navy as usual delivering the goods. There were the minesweepers having swept channels right up practically to the muzzles of the German coast defence batteries which had displayed little interest beyond a few fortunately badly-laid rounds. Up Channel, in full view from both coasts came an impressive convoy of merchantmen that might well have been carrying the infantry of our invasion force instead of merely anti-aircraft armaments, as was actually the case in view of the possibility of hostile air attack. Down to the hards all along the coast marched streams of troops of which the main bodies turned about on arrival at the beach while their anti-aircraft armament embarked in the waiting landing craft and put to sea for a nice voyage in the *Skylark*. The sky reverberated with the roar of great formations of American and British fighters racing for the battle that they failed to find. We were told that a German coast artillery subaltern on the far shore had been overheard calling his captain on the radio to ask if anybody knew what all this fuss was about. Were our faces red?[107]

Starkey was the first large-scale operation – it might better have been labelled an exercise – involving No 83 Group and the eight RCAF fighter and fighter-reconnaissance squadrons that made up half its strength. Though it did not persuade the Luftwaffe to risk its fighters in aerial combat, it did demonstrate that 'the flexibility of our present organisation allowed very large numbers of Squadrons to be transferred to and operated by No 11 Group with ease, rapidity and smoothness and with a minimum of paper work.'[108]

As a training exercise, then, it was a success. But what of all the smaller versions of Starkey that had been the backbone of operations since Dieppe? Were they also no more than realistic training exercises? The Luftwaffe in Northwest Europe was weak by September 1943, and the Circuses, Ramrods, Rangers, and other air operations may have been partly responsible; but if one compares the Luftwaffe's sporadic reaction to Fighter Command's earnest endeavours over France with its desperate (and costly) efforts to bring down American bombers over Germany it becomes obvious that the latter was deemed the greater threat and combatting it worth the greater price.

Meanwhile, for the Germans, the general situation was more than worrisome. In the east the outcome of the disastrous Kursk offensive had allowed Russian armies to take the initiative they would retain until they reached Berlin; and over Germany itself the Combined Bombing Offensive was placing an increasing strain on Luftwaffe fighter strength. Though, as yet, the only place where the Americans and British were fighting on the ground was in Italy, their main blow, whose preparation was progressing apace, would inevitably fall on Northwest Europe, just as the Americans had always insisted. In striking that blow, air power would play a vital role.

8

Preparing for D-Day, 1943-4

At the Quebec Conference of August 1943, in often spirited discussions concerning the feasibility and timing of a cross-Channel attack, negotiators accommodated both British caution and American zeal to set a tentative date – the early summer of 1944 – for the invasion of Northwest Europe.[1] Staff officers now knew when land, air, and naval forces had to be ready to strike, and fighter pilots saw a shift in emphasis from a war of attrition to more prosaic preparations for invading the Continent. To that end, between November 1943 and February 1944 the RCAF day-fighter force would expand from ten to sixteen squadrons and diversify to include not only fighter and fighter-reconnaissance units, but also a Typhoon fighter-bomber wing as well as a high-altitude photo-reconnaissance squadron.

Allied planners were confident, and with good reason, for the air power they wielded was awesome, with about four thousand bombers and five thousand fighters available by D-Day. One component of this vast air armada, under Air Marshal Sir Arthur Coningham, was the Second Tactical Air Force, eventually composed of four groups: No 2 Group (previously part of Bomber Command) was made up of light bomber and Intruder forces, No 85 Group was composed of night-fighter and other miscellaneous units, while Nos 83 and 84 groups initially incorporated fighter and fighter-bomber squadrons from Fighter Command (soon to be renamed the Air Defence of Great Britain, or ADGB) and reconnaissance squadrons from the soon-to-be disbanded Army Co-operation Command. The RCAF fighter squadrons (except for No 402) and the three fighter-bomber units that had arrived in the United Kingdom between November 1943 and February 1944 – Nos 438, 439, and 440 Squadrons – all moved to No 83 Group,[2] making up about half its strength.

Also available for Operation Overlord would be the American Ninth Tactical Air Force, together with Coastal Command squadrons and heavy bombers from Bomber Command, and the bombers and escort fighters of the US Eighth Army Air Force. All of this might be seen as something of a sledgehammer to crack a nut, for the Luftwaffe was in no condition to put up much of a fight. By the autumn of 1943 'every fighter that the factories could produce [was] needed for the defence of the *Reich*,' while in October Ultra (decrypts of highly-sensitive German communications) revealed that the Oberkommando der Luftwaffe had ordered replacement aircraft to be shipped directly from factories to the fronts – a sure sign that reserves were dangerously low. The much-battered enemy was now operating in the certain knowledge that he was greatly outnumbered on all fronts, a state of affairs aggravated by bizarre decision-making on the part of his high command. In August 1943, for example, General Dietrich Peltz and some of his bomber units were brought back from Italy, to IX Fliegerkorps, not to prepare to meet the inevitable invasion but for an ill-advised and inevitably ineffective aerial offensive against Britain.[3]

Meanwhile, German production between July 1943 and June 1944 could do no more than replace wastage, total strength remaining static at between 5000 and 5500 aircraft. Of those, 1500 to 2000 were deployed on the Eastern Front, some 750 on the Mediterranean and Balkan fronts, with a variable number undergoing repair or refit. That left a force of around 2000 aircraft to cover Northwest Europe and defend Germany proper. If replacing aircraft was a major challenge, replacing pilots bordered on the impossible.[4]

By the beginning of 1944 long-range, Merlin-engined North American P-51 Mustangs were escorting bombers of the US Eighth Air Force on daylight raids against targets which, in accordance with the Pointblank directive (see chapter 19), included aircraft factories and hydrogenation plants producing aircraft fuel. In March 1944, their range further boosted by jettisonable external fuel tanks and their numbers increasing month by month, the Mustangs were reaching Berlin and taking a heavy toll of German fighter pilots who were joining their operational units with far too little training to match the Americans in combat. The Luftwaffe was caught in a vicious and apparently irrevocable cycle of losses and shortages, requiring a reduction in training and reduced competence leading to ever more losses and even greater shortages. 'During the late spring [of 1944] standards fell still further when the B flying schools [roughly equivalent to the BCATP's Service Flying Training Schools] were disbanded. Fighter pilots went into action with only about 112 hours flying [experience].' Their Canadian counterparts would have accumulated three times that.[5]

Even if the Luftwaffe stayed on the ground, Flak provided its own hazards to Allied flyers. Rhubarbs, as always, were especially dangerous, and a memorandum prepared by Bentley Priory's senior air staff officer finally suggested that such operations tilted the attrition scale unduly in favour of the Luftwaffe. Losses to Flak were heavy when crossing the coast, in making a second pass at a target, or in attacking trains in stations and marshalling yards. Avoiding heavily defended areas and maintaining the element of surprise were thus critically important in ensuring a pilot's survival. The memorandum also complained that pilots were wasting their efforts on 'not worth while' targets like gun posts, ... signal boxes, railway wagons, and brick buildings, thus risking – and sometimes losing – their lives to no purpose.[6]

In early October staff officers calculated that, in 630 Rhubarb sorties, 9 per cent of committed aircraft had been destroyed or written off and another 5 per cent damaged; and though various ground targets had been attacked successfully there was no definition by which the campaign as a whole could be termed 'successful'.[7] In the end, however, the belief that a war of attrition was bringing the Luftwaffe to its knees predominated, so that Rhubarbs continued for the moment, despite casualties.

The three RCAF fighter-reconnaissance squadrons flew low-level photo-reconnaissance missions which, in many respects, were just as dangerous as Rhubarbs, though perhaps with more valuable results when things went right. No 430's experiences in November were typical; it flew six photo-reconaissance missions, each with one aircraft carrying the cameras and another as escort. The first was an attempt to photograph four bridges over the Seine, which was only partially successful. Three missions that followed were total failures, the first because of oil on the camera lens (a common problem), the second because of cloud over the target area, the third when the camera-carrying machine, after having successfully photographed coastal batteries along the Dutch coast, developed engine trouble and crashed into the sea. The last two missions, to Caen-Carpiquet aerodrome (a place that was destined to play a significant part in First Canadian Army's Normandy campaign eight months later) and the Dutch coast, met with little Flak and no hostile aircraft, and returned to England with the required photographs.[8]

Escorting bombers, now the day-fighters' main role, was a different kind of war altogether. While Rhubarbs allowed fighter pilots to get into as much trouble as they chose, Ramrods compelled them to adhere to pre-flight briefings and keep to their assigned roles within increasingly complex fighter formations. Since Spitfire VBs could not compete with Me 109s and FW 190s above 19,000 feet, they were relegated to close escort work. Squadrons were thus always happy to shift to Spitfire IXs, which offered them a wider variety of roles, including free-wheeling diversionary sweeps which, had they been flown in another context, would have been classified as Circuses in their own right.[9]

Wisely, the Luftwaffe still only fought at times and places of its own choosing, preferring larger formations to deal with the aerial armadas the Allies were sending over occupied Europe. Even so, the Germans, showing tactical common sense, only carried out attacks if they thought they had the advantages of height and sun, as on Ramrod 237 on 22 September (an attack on Evreux aerodrome). No 416 Squadron was flying to starboard and slightly behind the bombers.

As the bombers approached the target Wing Commander Chadburn flying Black 1 saw 30 plus FW 190s and Me 109s ahead and on the same level as the bombers. The apparent intention of the E[nemy] A[ircraft] was a head-on attack on the bombers.

The Wing Commander took the Squadron in front of the bombers in order to break up this E/A formation. As they approached 12 of the E/A turned into them, the remainder turning off. Four or five of the E/A were firing head on into the Squadron.

Black 1 did a head on attack on the nearest a/c from about 400 yds. He saw strikes and explosions in the engine. As he broke off two other E/A following their No 1 fired

at the Wing Commander while the Wing Commander returned the fire of the leading
aircraft of these two with a 2 second burst from 20 mm and m[achine] g[uns] and saw
hits on the starboard wing.

Six E/A then came in from the starboard and the Wing Commander broke the
Squadron into them. As they did so the Wing Commander saw one FW 190 streaming
white smoke heading down towards Bernay. The six E/A then broke straight down and
away from the squadron, the rest of the E/A were not seen.[10]

In spite of the above, there was little enough to shoot at; and, until the
RAF/RCAF began to support Anglo-Canadian armies in Northwest Europe, much
time would be spent in training. When the highest-scoring Canadian of them
all, ex-RAF ace Flying Officer George Beurling, DSO, DFC, DFM and Bar, who
had been credited with twenty-eight victories while flying in the defence of
Malta during 1942,[*] joined 403 Squadron in September 1943, Wing Commander Hugh Godefroy suggested the best contribution he could make in his
new unit would be to sharpen the marksmanship skills of the greener pilots.
Beurling arranged a deflection shooting device with a model of an Me 109
mounted on a swivel post as it would appear at three hundred yards from the
cockpit of a Spitfire. Andy Mackenzie (whose BCATP training was detailed in
volume II of this series), one of the newly arrived pilots with no 421 Squadron, later recalled his lessons. 'He'd adjust the model and ask me to call off
the angles. He'd say that the fleeing airplane is going such and such a speed
and he'd move the model around to different positions, each time asking me
to guess the angle. I made up a chart on a Sweet Caporal cigarette package
and actually stuck it in the cockpit of my Spitfire. I studied it religiously.'[11]
Mackenzie's education was to some purpose, as he was credited with three
victories in his next thirty sorties, compared with his squadron's wartime
average of one victory for every 138 sorties.[12]

At the level of operational planning, the change in strategy from defending
the British Isles to using them as a base from which to invade the Continent
was reflected in the RAF's reorganization of its fighter force. On 13 November
the Allied Expeditionary Air Force (AEAF) was officially formed under Air
Chief Marshal Sir Trafford Leigh-Mallory and, two days later, Fighter Command was dissolved, its tactical elements being apportioned between the
Second Tactical Air Force (with its headquarters initially at Bracknell, in
Berkshire, some thirty miles due west of London, and subsequently at Uxbridge) and the newly created Air Defence of Great Britain command. Among
the Canadians, all but No 402 Squadron joined No 83 Group of Second TAF.
(Why No 402 should have remained with the ADGB is a mystery, but even
when it was rotated to the Continent some months later it was replaced by
another RCAF squadron.) No 438 Squadron, recently arrived from Canada,[13]

---

[*] Beurling, from Verdun, Quebec, had joined the RAF in 1940 after being rejected for aircrew training by the RCAF because of his lack of education. He transferred to the RCAF on 1
September 1943, subsequently served with Nos 403 and 412 Squadrons, resigned his commission 16 September 1944, and was killed in a flying accident on 20 May 1948, while on
his way to join the nascent Israeli Air Force.

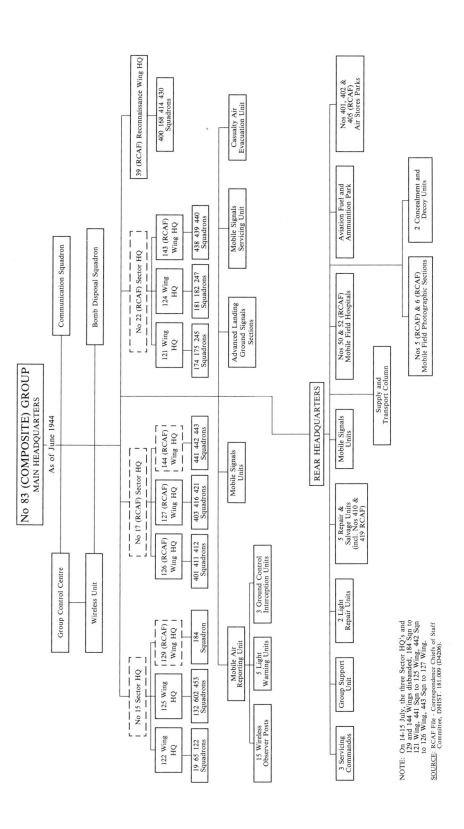

No 83 (COMPOSITE) GROUP
MAIN HEADQUARTERS

As of June 1944

Communication Squadron

Bomb Disposal Squadron

Group Control Centre

Wireless Unit

39 (RCAF) Reconnaissance Wing HQ

400 168 414 430 Squadrons

Casualty Air Evacuation Unit

No 22 (RCAF) Sector HQ

121 Wing HQ — 174 175 245 Squadrons

124 Wing HQ — 181 182 247 Squadrons

143 (RCAF) Wing HQ — 438 439 440 Squadrons

Mobile Signals Servicing Unit

Advanced Landing Ground Signals Sections

No 17 (RCAF) Sector HQ

126 (RCAF) Wing HQ — 401 411 412 Squadrons

127 (RCAF) Wing HQ — 403 416 421 Squadrons

144 (RCAF) Wing HQ — 441 442 443 Squadrons

Mobile Signals Units

No 15 Sector HQ

122 Wing HQ — 19 65 122 Squadrons

125 Wing HQ — 132 602 453 Squadrons

129 (RCAF) Wing HQ — 184 Squadron

Mobile Air Reporting Unit

5 Light Warning Units

3 Ground Control Interception Units

15 Wireless Observer Posts

REAR HEADQUARTERS

3 Servicing Commandos

Group Support Unit

2 Light Repair Units

5 Repair & Salvage Units (incl. Nos 410 & 419 RCAF)

Mobile Signals Units

Nos 50 & 52 (RCAF) Mobile Field Hospitals

Supply and Transport Column

Nos 5 (RCAF) & 6 (RCAF) Mobile Field Photographic Sections

Aviation Fuel and Ammunition Park

2 Concealment and Decoy Units

Nos 401, 402 & 405 (RCAF) Air Stores Parks

NOTE: On 14-15 July, the three Sector HQ's and 129 and 144 Wings disbanded, 184 Sqn to 121 Wing, 441 Sqn to 125 Wing, 442 Sqn to 126 Wing, 443 Sqn to 127 Wing.

SOURCE: RCAF File - Correspondence Chiefs of Staff Committee, DHIST. 181.009 (D4206).

was also assigned to No 83 Group; it was one of six squadrons transferred from home defence in Canada to the fighting front as the threat to North America faded from exiguous to non-existent.

The possibility of sending more fighter squadrons to the European theatre had been discussed at the Quebec Conference in August 1943, when Sir Charles Portal and his Canadian counterpart, Air Marshal Lloyd Breadner, had considered a recommendation to disband four fighter and two army cooperation squadrons, equally divided between Canada's Atlantic and Pacific coasts, and to reform them overseas. Breadner was keen on increasing the Canadian contribution to No 83 Group which, at the time, he thought would be supporting First Canadian Army. Portal, for his part, gave assurances that the squadrons would remain intact and that the Air Ministry would keep their personnel 'as near one hundred per cent Canadian as possible.'[14] 'They [the air staff] suggest that the squadrons, if sent, might be equipped and trained for the Fighter/Bomber role, and every effort would be made to associate them with the operations of the Canadian Army insofar as this can be achieved without prejudice to maintaining the flexibility of organization, between Fighter Command and the Composite Groups and between one Composite Group and another, which is essential to operational efficiency.'[15]

To the three squadrons in eastern Canada slated to go overseas the new policy was 'welcome news in units for which there had been little excitement in the way of enemy air attacks or landings, and whose only opportunity for action had been inshore anti-submarine patrols, a task for which the aircraft [Hurricanes] were ill-suited.' Thus No 123 (Army Co-operation Training) Squadron went overseas before Christmas 1943 to become 439 (Fighter-Bomber) Squadron, while Nos 125 and 127 (Fighter) squadrons became 441 and 443 respectively. The other three squadrons came from Annette Island, just north of Prince Rupert, where they had been guarding Canada's west coast from the threat of Japanese attack. With the Aleutian islands of Attu and Kiska once more in American hands, 'the role of the Annette squadrons had become increasingly inconsequential' and Nos 14, 111, and 118 squadrons therefore became Nos 442, 440, and 438, respectively.[16]

In late October, before any of the new squadrons had arrived, Fighter Command (which was still exercising a supervisory role over the embryonic ADGB and Second TAF) moved to ensure that the additional units would operate with Canadian staff officers and would form wings and airfields designated as RCAF. Deciding what role they would play proved far more difficult. In the August discussions, all six squadrons had been allocated to ground attack duties but on 11 November Leigh-Mallory, having been warned by the Air Ministry that Typhoons could not be produced at anticipated levels, decided that all six would be equipped with air-superiority fighters. Less than two weeks later, having received information that, in fact, enough Typhoons were available to equip three new squadrons, he rescinded that decision. Three units would be equipped with Typhoons, three with Spitfires.[17]

Maintenance, supply, and ancillary units were also tossed into the Canadianization cauldron. After further discussion concerning the Canadian contribution to No 83 Group, the RAF agreed that three repair and salvage units, three air-stores parks, a mobile field hospital, and a casualty air evacuation unit would be formed from RCAF personnel. The people needed to fill these posts were to begin arriving in January 1944, and authority was later given for the formation of three mobile field photo sections of which two, Nos 5 and 6, would be RCAF units.[18]

Unfortunately, these British attempts to accommodate the wishes of their junior partner were based on shadows, for Second TAF's order of battle had not yet been established. Canadianization within No 83 Group soon reached the heights of complexity as many of the units the RCAF was planning to create turned into phantoms. The new organization, it turned out, would not have three repair and salvage units, but only two. Air-stores parks were also reduced, but No 406 would become RCAF while No 404's deficiencies would be made up from RCAF resources. Finally, Second TAF staff officers suggested that twelve mobile signals units become RCAF, two each in 17 Wing, 126 Airfield, 127 Airfield, 39 Wing, 128 Airfield, and 129 Airfield.[19]

At first those in No 83 Group who wore RCAF flashes on their shoulders could take pride in their relationship with First Canadian Army, for in June 1943 Sir Bernard Paget, C-in-C Home Forces, had informed General McNaughton that 'the plan now contemplated was that the Cdn Army would have its own assault divs under com[man]d, and would follow them in to enlarge the bridgehead.' No 83 Group, having been the first of its kind to form and consequently having the most experience, fully expected to support the assault forces in the forthcoming invasion, and that those forces would be Canadian. But there were clouds on the horizon. The dispatch of the 1st Canadian Infantry Division to invade Sicily that same month, and the decision to send the 5th Armoured Division to the Mediterranean in due course, threatened First Canadian Army's role as the assault formation for the landings in France, for Canadian components would be in short supply. In early September, however, Lieutenant-General Sir Archibald Nye, vice-chief of the imperial general staff, laid McNaughton's fears to rest. 'Gen Nye stated most emphatically that [the move of 5th Canadian Armoured Division] would not affect the Canadian Army, as it was very probable that Brit [formations] would be placed under [McNaughton's] com[man]d.'[20]

There was much discussion in the months to follow about the part Canadians would play on D-Day, but there could be no final decision until a supreme commander arrived on the scene. McNaughton was unhappy with the aura of indecision, complaining that 'the whole set up was like mercury, very shifting and difficult to grasp.' Paget did nothing to clarify matters. On 19 October he stated that McNaughton's men would be part of a build-up and break-out force, but the following month he insisted that he was only presenting one possible course of action, as 'First Cdn Army might lead the assault in which conditions I [British] Corps might be placed under com[man]d First Cdn Army.' If so, it would not be commanded by McNaughton, who had resigned on 13 November, having lost the confidence of his superiors, British and Canadian alike. Finally, General Sir Bernard Montgomery, on his appointment as overall ground commander for Overlord, put an end to all speculation in January 1944 by choosing Second British Army for the assault role.[21]

That decision had far-reaching implications for airmen as well as for soldiers, for the former now had to decide whether they wished to put national interests first and join their ground-bound brethren in a secondary role, or whether the RCAF should pursue its own interests as an institution and continue to support the assault formation as it had been (and still was) training to do. At a meeting on 30 January, Group Captain G.G. Truscott, the director of air staff at RCAF Overseas Headquarters, Air Vice-Marshal W.F. Dickson, RAF, commanding No 83 Group, and Group Captain D.M. Smith, RCAF, commanding No 39 Reconnaissance Wing, 'strongly recommended' that 'the RCAF participation in 83 Group should remain unaltered and that the Canadian Army should use 84 Group' in the forthcoming campaign. They reasoned that '83 Group has been developed as the initial striking force on behalf of the RAF.'

It has been in existence for eight months and during that time has been carefully developed and groomed for its role. With this in mind it has been given priority [in training and equipment] over 84 Group and is the only one that can be ready to do the job in the time available ...

The Units and Staff of 83 Group have been functioning together as a team for several months now and the splitting of that team by transfer of Canadian units to 84 Group would jeopardize the success of the operation ...

With reference to the agreement that Canadian Squadrons shall be used in co-operation with Canadian Army Forces it is pointed out that [the latter] will be part of the Second [British] Army in the initial assault. The First Canadian Army will exist principally only in name as a large portion of its force will be British.[22]

'It is felt that the fact that the Canadian Army has not been picked to launch the first assault is no good reason why the RCAF should relinquish its honoured position,' concluded Truscott, 'and actually, adds another reason why we should retain it.'[23] Air Marshal Breadner (who had been the RCAF's chief of air staff in Ottawa for the past three-and-a-half years but had just relinquished that appointment in order to take over as AOC-in-C, RCAF Overseas) accepted those judgements without demur, and the deed was done, without any reference to Ottawa. The tactical group which included all the appropriate RCAF units would work with Second British Army; the other, which included 'a large proportion of Polish, Czech, etc. Units' as well as RAF squadrons, would work with First Canadian Army.

Until they moved to the Continent, the squadrons of Second TAF were the administrative responsibility of the ADGB, so that by the end of February the RCAF fighter force was organized as follows: Nos 402, 441, 442, and 443 were based on 144 (RCAF) Airfield, though, for the moment, No 402 was Canada's sole representative with the ADGB while the other three were 'lodger' units with No 12 Group; Nos 438, 439, and 440 were based on 143 (RCAF) Airfield and were officially part of No 22 Wing, but lodging with No 13 Group. Nos 401, 411, and 412 were with 126 Airfield and Nos 403, 416, and 421 with 127

Airfield, all part of No 17 Wing; while, since October, Nos 400, 414, and 430 (with No 231 Squadron, RAF) had formed 39 (RCAF) Reconnaissance Wing, based at Redhill.[24] These sixteen squadrons represented the pinnacle of Canada's contribution to the fighter war.

Good communications were vital if Bracknell was to co-ordinate successfully the activities of such disparate squadrons fulfilling such varied roles. Air Marshal Sir Arthur Coningham, the AOC-in-C, concluded that No 83 Group carried too large a communications load, and his solution was to reduce the number of subordinate headquarters that would have to be involved in operational decisions. Airfields were paired so that, instead of having two airfield headquarters and a wing headquarters, the wing commander would control both airfields in operational matters through the senior airfield headquarters while the individual airfield organizations would continue to deal directly with group headquarters on administrative issues.[25]

AIRFIELD ORGANIZATION, 83 GROUP

Lines of Command ————————

Lines of Administration ════════════

For example, 126 and 127 airfields would often be paired in the several campaigns to come, occupying the same areas as they made their way across Northwest Europe. Operationally, the headquarters of the senior airfield commander controlled both units.

While the organization of Allied tactical air forces was being revised to meet the requirements of Overlord, so was their list of targets. The Air Ministry still emphasized that rolling stock and locomotives were of primary importance, but the assistant chief of air staff for operations proclaimed on 26 November that, in future, attacks on them must fit into the larger plan. 'The policy of fighter attacks on the railway transportation system particularly locomotives, trains, and signal boxes in enemy occupied North-West Europe, has again been under consideration with all interested departments, and it has been decided that attacks on these targets shall be discontinued forthwith. Attacks of this nature will in the future only be authorized when it is desired to immobilise communications in a definite area in support of a special operation, e.g. 'Overlord.' Your plans for this operation may, therefore, include provision for this form of attack if it is so desired.'[26] Thus even Rhubarbs lost their free-wheeling flavour.

Indeed, they were soon almost extinct. To no small extent, policy-makers sought to maintain French goodwill in the lead-up to Overlord, and, at the end of November, Second TAF announced that 'attacks on the electric power systems of the leading industrial areas of France or the other occupied countries in NW Europe are not likely to produce any large or immediate effect on the enemy's war effort. Attacks will, on the other hand, create much distress among the civilian population and may prejudice the success of future military operations in those countries.' Rangers were increasingly substituted for Rhubarbs, with no more than four aircraft per mission in deep penetration raids to shoot down German fighters; not by enticing them to combat, but through aerial ambush as they taxied, took off, or landed in the course of training or routine flights.[27] Results were not encouraging.

If attacks on power stations were no longer acceptable, there was soon a new set of targets to take their place, which would have little or no adverse impact on the French. On 21 September 1943 Winston Churchill, in a speech to the House of Commons, had alluded to 'new methods and new weapons' that the enemy was developing. In early November photo-reconnaissance of the Pas de Calais revealed a number of suspicious sites whose most intriguing features were ramps that looked vaguely like ski-jumps, engendering animated debate as to their purpose. An answer came on the 28th, when a Mosquito pilot photographed similar sites at Peenemünde, the German rocket development centre, showing a diminutive airplane – too small to accommodate a pilot – apparently ready for launching.[28] On 2 December a panel of experts concluded that 'the enemy is experimenting with an expendable pilotless aircraft. If this is the aircraft which has been detected by reconnaissance at Peenemunde, which has a wing span of approximately 20 feet, it could carry an explosive charge of up to 1 ton of HE and reach the London area from the French coast ... [and] it seems highly probable that the "ski" sites in Northern France can be identified with pilotless aircraft and an attack early in the new year can be contemplated ... Until further evidence is available, the most practical counter measure is to bomb the sites'[29]

This was Operation Crossbow, the air assault on V-1 sites which were codenamed Noballs. Hitler had specifically commanded that the launch sites have maximum protection, for he was relying on the V-weapons to save his tottering empire, and emplaced to protect them were, quite literally, thousands of anti-aircraft guns. Reconnoitering and attacking such targets was hazardous at best and suicidal at worst, although providing high cover for bombers was rather less dangerous than doing the actual bombing. Reconnaissance was made doubly perilous by the need to photograph targets from no great height both before and after bombing, in order to assess damage. On the latter occasions, at least, there would be little chance of catching the Germans by surprise.[30]

One of the first Crossbow attacks involving the RCAF was on 20 December, when Nos 403 and 421 squadrons (127 Airfield), with Nos 401, 411, and 412 (126 Airfield), provided fighter sweeps to support attacks by more than a hundred Marauder light bombers in the morning and a similar group of Mitchells and Bostons in the afternoon. The Luftwaffe rose to meet them in some force; engaging 'eighteen Me 109s and twenty-plus FW 190s' over Merville, the squadrons of 127 Airfield claimed six aircraft destroyed, one probably destroyed, and three damaged in the morning sweep. Tragically, they also lost Squadron Leader J.F. Lambert, leading No 421 for the first time, who destroyed one of the Messerschmitts before being killed himself.[31]

Although his tenure in command proved brief, Lambert was typical of Canadian operational leadership at this time. The war was now in its fifth year and the problems that had once beset the RCAF in finding qualified and competent commanding officers for a quickly expanding force were things of the past. They had been largely solved by the harrowing processes of natural selection, and though many promising leaders had not survived the hazards of battle, and others had been trapped by the pitfalls of an impersonal and unfeeling administration, enough of their colleagues had remained operational to ensure that Canadian fighter squadrons were, on the whole, now very well led. Of the sixteen fighter units, nine would have the same squadron commander from the formation of Second TAF until D-Day. Of the others, No 411 had the highest turnover, with one killed in action, one injured in a flying accident, one – an American – transferred to the USAAF, and two coming to the end of their tours.[*] In all, twenty-six men served as Canadian squadron leaders during this time, of whom only two were repatriated owing to a perceived inability to lead their units – one, obviously unsuitable, having slipped through the selection net, and the other apparently the unfortunate victim of a hasty and arbitrary decision.[32] In both cases the ready availability of other experienced leaders made them easy to replace.

Like so many of his colleagues, Lambert had been promoted and appointed on his proven operational merits rather than on background, training records, or paper qualifications for command. Raised in Winnipeg, he had been an audit clerk with a firm of chartered accountants when the war began. He enlisted in August 1940, passing through the BCATP pilot mill without distinguishing himself in any way. Indeed, on graduation he had been rated as 'unsuitable' for commissioning, and, after attending a fighter OTU in England, he had been posted to an RAF Spitfire squadron in July 1941, where he learned the fundamentals of his trade as a non-commissioned officer. In December he had been 'attached' to 402 Squadron (still flying Hurricanes, and out of the mainstream of the fighter war), and was commissioned in February 1942. Shortly there-

---

[*] Personnel officers, unaware of the exact date set for the landings (security surrounding Overlord was very tight) continued to post men out when they had completed two hundred hours, even if their experience would have been of great value during the intial stages of Overlord and they themselves had elected to stay on.

after, he was posted to another RAF Spitfire squadron, No 185 in Malta, when the siege of that island was approaching its climax.[33]

In his brief sojourn there, Lambert only claimed one-and-a-half victories, but he served as a flight commander for a short time and his wing commander reported, 'he has shown great keenness and the ability to lead.' Shot down on 30 July 1942, he parachuted into the sea with 'slight' wounds to his right hand, arm, and shoulder, and when he came out of hospital it was time to return to the United Kingdom. There were no gallantry awards to accompany his departure, but he was assessed as 'a good fighter pilot'[34] by that eminently well-qualified judge, Air Vice-Marshal Keith Park, who had been one himself in the First World War, had commanded No 11 Group throughout the Battle of Britain, and was now AOC-in-C, RAF Mediterranean.

Back in England, Lambert became an instructor, where 'on arrival [he] was inclined to look on OTU as rest both physically and mentally. Worked hard latterly ... Rather untidy officer.' The last sentence of that assessment was shared by his next squadron, No 403, where the unofficial diarist reported that it was hard to recognize him when he appeared (for his wedding) with his hair combed and his buttons shone.[35] By that time Lambert had been commanding a flight for six weeks – there were no intimations he had but a fortnight to live.

He was succeeded by Squadron Leader W.G. Conrad, who had served in the Middle East with Nos 274 and 145 squadrons, being credited with three-and-a-half destroyed and receiving the DFC; Conrad had been shot down once, in the Western Desert in June 1942, but managed to rejoin his unit. In May 1943 he had been posted to No 403 Squadron, adding two more to his score, though almost falling into enemy hands after a collision with another Spitfire over France. Evading capture, he returned to Britain courtesy of the French 'underground,' taking command of No 421 in January 1944.[36]

In the latter months of 1943 No 400 Squadron was more concerned with alterations in equipment than changes in command, spending far more time in training than on operations as it converted from fighter-reconnaissance work, in which it had used Mustangs for low- and medium-altitude missions, to becoming No 83 Group's photo-reconnaissance unit (PRU) on high-altitude Spitfire XIs and Mosquito XVIs. Two pilots arrived on 7 December to give instruction (on the ground, since the aircraft were single-seaters) for the Spitfire XIs, two of which appeared on the 22nd. The Mosquito flight began to take shape as the first navigators showed up on the 14th, and when Mosquito deliveries actually started on the 27th instruction could begin immediately. Meanwhile, the squadron continued to fly its operations in Mustangs, with ten Populars – twenty sorties – in December and twenty-six in January 1944. The flying-bomb sites may have been objects of great concern, but there were many other targets as well, and the first Crossbow photo-reconnaissance flight (by a Mustang) specifically labelled as a Noball was not until 2 February. The first Spitfire took off to photograph a Noball site on the 13th.[37]

The turn of the year had brought No 430 Squadron to its first anniversary – with nearly double its establishment of sixteen aircrew on strength to celebrate the occasion, for trained fighter pilots were becoming as plentiful in the RCAF as they were scarce in the Luftwaffe. Two days later the squadron was taken off operations and sent north, to Peterhead in Scotland, to spend two weeks at an armament practice camp (APC) honing its shooting skills, as did all single-engined squadrons in preparation for D-Day. Quarters at Peterhead were 'pretty grim and cold,' and the mess was 'not too comfortable,'[38] so pilots were happy to get back to Gatwick and reconnaissance operations. Most were directed against airfields and bridges in that part of France embracing the Baie de la Seine where Overlord would be launched in mid-summer – although, of course, that was still the most secret of secrets, known only to the highest commanders and certain members of their planning staffs.

Between such missions there was unending participation in air/ground exercises. Exercise Eagle, in Yorkshire, meant that 'the cameras were "clicking merrily" from first light to dusk.'

'Enemy' concentrations were uncovered and reported for bombing attention, and information gathered on the movement and disposition of the 'hostile' forces …
… One major lesson learned was the importance of having all the components of the fighter/recce organization close together. At Clifton the headquarters, photo section, Army photo-interpretation section and R[oyal] A[rtillery] counter-battery officer were all housed in the same block of buildings, with the result that the time spent in dealing with messages was reduced to a minimum. On the other hand, landline communications with the Army control were poor, so that much time was lost in getting information to where it was required.[39]

Back in the real world, on 8 February 1944, things did not go too well, either.

[Flight Lieutenants J.H.] Taylor and [R.F.] Gill and [Flying Officers R.G.] Belli-Bivar and [C.E.] Butchart, carrying oblique cameras, were detailed for the bridge popular. After crossing the French coast at 6000 feet near Trouville, the section separated and, diving to the deck, headed for the targets. Taylor and Gill completed their assignment, the bridges over the Orne river south of Caen, and Belli-Bivar and Butchart photographed all but one of the bridges on the river north of Caen. Later in the day Butchart went out again with Taylor to take shots of the one bridge that had been missed. While Taylor was making his run light *Flak* opened up at him; Butchart spotted the gun position and 'pranged' it successfully. The two pilots then completed the mission and made their exit on the deck. On return to base, however, they found that by some strange gremlin interference no magazines had been inserted in the cameras and their sortie was in vain! The next morning Taylor and Gill tried again and this time the cameras were loaded and all went well.[40]

Thankfully, such frustrating oversights on the part of groundcrew were rare; Flak, however, was not.

The long run-up to Overlord brought little excitement for day-fighter units. In the last few weeks of February most of the sorties to escort bombers were simply '"long stooge jobs" – ask anyone who has sat for two hours in the restricted cockpit of a Spitfire how long 120 minutes can be and how cramped or weary muscles can get.' Combats were rare, with Canadian pilots claiming only a single victory in February and averaging only five per month from January to March.[41]

Typhoon squadrons, whose main role was ground attack work, would eventually gain some proficiency in what was, to airmen in the United Kingdom, still something of an arcane specialty. In March 1944 there were questions as to how to train them, for it had been found impracticable to teach pilots the wide variety of roles assigned to the Typhoon (including rocket attacks, bombing, strafing, and smoke-laying). Coningham decided that squadrons must specialize, some as fighter-bombers, others as rocket-projectile (RP) fighters; though versatility was preferable in principle, a five-hour changeover time from rocket rails to bomb-racks (more than six hours to switch the other way) effectively excluded multi-purpose work.[42]

By the time Nos 438, 439, and 440 squadrons arrived in Britain, RP Typhoons had already been allocated, so, by default, and together with four RAF squadrons from 84 Group, they were selected for the fighter-bomber role. As Typhoons were still in short supply and it was important to conserve them for the upcoming invasion, they were not to be used in bomber escort work. Nor were they to carry out indiscriminate offensive operations in small numbers; indeed, as far as possible Typhoons would be limited to one sortie a day, and would carry out Ranger operations only if they were carefully planned in advance and had No 11 Group's approval. On such missions, they would only be allowed to attack the enemy in the air and were not to attempt strafing airfields. All operations had to be planned with an exceptionally close eye on the weather in order to reduce the number of aborted missions, which inflicted unnecessary wear on the aircraft. In mid-March, and in such circumstances, the newly arrived Canadian Typhoon wing joined the air offensive.[43]

Two of the new Spitfire Squadrons, Nos 441 and 442, carried out their first offensive sorties at the end of the month. The wing was under the leadership of Wing Commander J.E. Johnson, RAF – already one of the Commonwealth's top scoring aces and destined to accumulate thirty-eight victories – but on this occasion radio trouble forced him to hand over to a deputy.

Shortly afterwards the aerodrome at Dreux was sighted and as the Wing flew by on the west side many twin-engined aircraft could be seen in the dispersals. W/C Wells instructed No 442 Squadron, the top squadron, to remain at altitude as a decoy and as top cover, and himself led No 441 Squadron from up sun in to attack. The Squadron dived very rapidly to ground level on the south side of the airfield and made an extremely fast run across it at about 400 miles per hour, each pilot selecting his target on the run in. The Spitfires continued low down and fast for a couple of miles after the attack, then pulled up fast and reformed without any difficulty.[44]

Johnson attributed the success of this first operation to the aerodrome's location, which was far inland and thus less likely to expect attack, and to the fact that three wings of Fortresses had already gone by, returning from more distant targets, leading German anti-aircraft gunners to relax (they may also have been watching the decoy squadron). Further, the attacking aircraft were difficult targets, coming in out of the sun at high speed.[45]

Such operations were still very much ad hoc affairs, for doctrine guiding the use of day-fighter and fighter-bomber squadrons in Overlord was not hammered out until March 1944. 'The primary role of Typhoon fighter/bomber squadrons will be attacks in close support of our ground forces using bombs or RP and cannon,' while 'the primary role of Spitfire and Mustang III Squadrons will be that of day fighting ... Their secondary role will be ground attacks using bombs and/or guns; bombing attacks are to be carried out by dive-bombing.'[46] Second TAF thus tried to strike a balance between the essential task of maintaining air supremacy and secondary responsibilities of interdiction and close support. Conspicuous in its absence was the matter of escort work, of the kind still practiced on Ramrods and Noballs, perhaps because the bomber's role in the upcoming offensive was still in question. Until 6 June, however, Ramrods continued to account for the bulk of RCAF day-fighter missions.

If fighters were to join the land battle by actually dropping bombs, then they would have to learn a new trade – dive bombing. Spitfires, designed for air fighting and with pilots trained in that task, could not do it well, as Hugh Godefroy's recollections make clear.

The target was to be approached at eight thousand feet. When it was opposite the wing tip, the aircraft was to be turned and dived at an angle of sixty degrees holding the bead of the gun-sight on the target. At three thousand feet a gradual pull-out was to be executed and on the count of three, the bomb was dropped ...

It wasn't long before we discovered that this technique of dive-bombing was extremely inaccurate. One could only take a guess at what was a 60° dive. Without dive brakes, Spitfires dived so fast that the hands of the altimeter went around in a blur. Pulling out at exactly three thousand feet with the use of an instrument that lagged was impossible.[47]

Misses of from seventy to almost three hundred yards, depending on the angle of the dive, were the norm.[48] Unless bombing accuracy could be improved through relentless practice, any effect that dive-bombing would have was likely to be more of a nuisance than a serious ordeal for the Wehrmacht.

The first Canadian dive-bombing operation, against a bridge in northern France, was carried out on 8 June by No 440 Squadron's Typhoons, but results were poor, the bombs overshooting the target. The next day No 438 claimed to have done better; though one aircraft was unable to release its bombs, the others managed to attack with two each, the mission being 'carried out very successfully' with 'all the bombs being seen to burst in the target area.'[49] On 22 April No 416 pilots attacked Noball sites at Bonnières, in the Pas de Calais, and were 'amazed at their accuracy on this their first attempt.' That was an expression that might be interpreted in other than the obvious way, however, and the alternative meaning was probably the correct one. The AEAF's Operational Research Section, after examining photographs, interpreters' reports, and pilots' claims, concluded that Spitfires required 90 to 180 sorties to lay a single bomb on a bridge (the figures for Typhoons were exactly half that), while RP-equipped aircraft, able to use their gunsights to aim their rockets, needed less than four.[50]

At least the Luftwaffe could offer little opposition, lacking time, fuel, and skilled pilots as it attempted to gather strength to meet the invasion which now seemed certain in the summer of 1944. II Fliegerkorps, one of the Luftwaffe's most experienced close-support formations, moved up from Italy, while IX Fliegerkorps received reinforcements. X Fliegerkorps, an anti-shipping forma-tion, was brought in from the Balkans and absorbed the units of Fliegerführer Atlantik, which ceased to exist. At the same time the torpedo-bomber units based in the south of France came under Fliegerdivision 2, which was also joined to X Fliegerkorps. Units that had been withdrawn from operations after being badly mauled in battles with American long-range fighters trained their replacement pilots in anti-invasion operations, veteran Heinz Knoke recalling that, in his squadron, 'every pilot has received extensive theoretical training in preparation for operations against landing-craft and transports.'[51]

The Oberkommando der Luftwaffe recognized that its forces would be outnumbered, regardless of what units it sent to the West, but pilots would be operating near their own bases and it was hoped that shorter distances-to-target would, in part, offset the Allies' numerical advantage. Formations-in-training prepared to operate in an emergency, while all fighters were equipped to act as fighter-bombers. It was all far too little and much too late to make up for years of bad planning and, according to one senior German commander writing after the war, 'the deployment of the Luftwaffe to defend against the invasion was a complete failure.'[52]

The Germans were in no position to threaten Britain through aerial assault, and in the closing months of 1943, RAF/RCAF night-fighter crews could consider themselves fortunate if they made any contacts at all. A remarkable exception was a sortie by No 410 Squadron's Flying Officers R.D. Shultz and V.A. Williams (who had first flown together on 23 June 1943 and been credited with a Do 217 in their eleven sorties to date).[53] They took off on 10 December for a routine patrol over the North Sea.

After receiving the normal help from ground control, a visual [sighting] of a Do 217 was obtained at a range of 7000 feet and the Mosquito closed in rapidly to 150 feet, when the e[nemy] a[ircraft] fired a long burst and peeled off to port. The Mosquito was not hit and following the Jerry down got in a short burst which set the starboard engine on fire. The e/a continued evasive action losing height rapidly and at 9000 feet our pilot fired a long burst which resulted in a large flash and explosion on the star-board side. All return fire had ceased by now, but the Hun kept up evasion, trying to gain cloud cover at 7000 feet, however he went straight through it. The Mosquito followed and at 1500 feet the e/a steadied up, opened his bomb doors and tried to jettison bombs which were not seen to fall. Our pilot fired another long burst from quarter astern and the Do 217 was seen to hit the sea burning furiously. After climbing as fast as possible to 15000 feet another visual of a Do 217 was obtained at 7000 feet range. F/O Schultz opened fire from dead astern at 900 feet and closed in. The e/a blew up when the Mosquito was 50 feet behind and our aircraft flew through the debris. There was no evasive action or return fire on the part of the e/a and our crew thinks the bombs must have blown up as a considerable jar was felt when the Dornier exploded. Immediately after this second combat our crew obtained a visual of a third Do 217 at a height of 12000 feet, range 7000 feet, 10 degrees to starboard. A long combat then ensued during which the enemy pilot showed a high degree of airmanship and F/O Schultz had to make every use of the manoeuvrability of his aircraft in order to follow him. The Mosquito fired a number of short bursts at the Dornier but even though both its engines were on fire the enemy pilot still took violent evasive action right down to sea level, while every available gun put out a defensive barrage. The Mosquito was hit in the nose while a cannon shell smashed the instrument panel just missing the pilot by three inches. The final burst caused the e/a's port engine to blaze and the Jerry eventually hit the sea going straight in. The Mosquito's starboard engine started to splutter and the pilot was about to feather it when the port engine picked up and after the port had been feathered the fire went out. The pilot managed to get his aircraft to Bradwell Bay on one engine despite the fact that his temperature gauges had been shot away.[54]

Three victories in the course of a single sortie brought Shultz and Williams a DFC each. They would fly another thirty sorties together before completing their tours in late May 1944, claiming their fifth and last enemy aircraft on 13 February.[55]

Meanwhile, those few bombers operating against the United Kingdom were mostly Me 410s and Ju 188s, faster than their predecessors and, to avoid detection, timing their raids to coincide with the return of British bombers from Germany. Intruders, which the Allies found so useful, went against Hitler's philosophy that 'terror is broken with terror, and by no other means,' so that, after a few operations in mid-to-late 1943, German aircraft and crews trained for intruder work were assigned to other duties.[56]

On the night of 21/22 January 1944, in the midst of Bomber Command's assault against Berlin, the Germans launched their bombers on the first major attack of a new campaign – Fall Steinbock – 'when virtually every serviceable aircraft [462] in the west was ordered to bomb London.' The British capital continued to be a target through February, but in the three months that followed the Luftwaffe shifted its effort to ports and shipping, where it was far more likely to hinder Allied preparations for Overlord. Most of these attacks were pathetic failures, however, and the enemy's air resources proved incapable of forcing any significant delay on the Allied invasion build-up, achieving little more than the loss of 329 bombers.[57]

For those whose task it was to oppose these attacks, the rules of night fighting had not changed – location and equipment largely determined success. No 406 was one of the units contributing to the German casualty rate, claiming its first victory on the night of 19/20 March when one Beaufighter was sent off to investigate a radar contact over the Channel which turned out to be a Heinkel 177 fleeing to the south. The Beaufighter made a classic radar interception from the rear, closed to 'approximately 25 feet' before obtaining positive identification, and literally blew the bomber out of the sky, returning to Exeter with a windscreen covered in oil and the starboard aileron warped by the heat of the Heinkel's explosion. Eight nights later, during a major attack against Bristol, the Canadians managed to intercept and destroy two more. The diary noted that three victories in one week 'have caused great jubilation' among the air- and groundcrew, but at the same time the diarist complained that 'the inferior speed of the Beaufighter prevented several more kills.'[58]

Lack of speed was certainly not a problem with the Mosquitoes of No 410 Squadron operating from Castle Camps, some fifty miles north of London. On the night of 3/4 February, Flying Officer E.S.P. Fox and his navigator, Flying Officer C.D. Sibbert, scored the squadron's first success of the campaign, the interception serving as an excellent example of the complexities new technologies, developed by both sides, had introduced to night air combat.

We were scrambled at 0400 hours under G[round] C[ontrol] I[nterception] Trimely ... Vectored 140° then over to [VHF radio] Channel 'G'; vectored 120°, then 100°. Given a 'bandit' crossing starboard to port. Contact obtained at 0430 hours, range 3 1/2 miles at 18,000'. Turning port we closed to 2,000'. The Hun was dropping window.* We lost contact temporarily and asked Control for help. Contact regained before a vector could come through. Range was closed to 200' with enemy aircraft doing very violent evasive action. I gave him a 1 sec burst, but missed as the Hun peeled off to starboard. The enemy aircraft was identified as a Do 217. We turned starboard, then port and contact was regained. The enemy aircraft was followed for 10 mins through very violent evasive action. Visual obtained. Range 1,000' at 13,000'. Closed to 200' and gave him a 2-second burst ... The Hun exploded and immediately went straight down in flames.[59]

No 410 Squadron Mosquitoes were credited with the destruction of nine enemy aircraft during the four months of Steinbock, or one success for every thirty-eight sorties.[60]

In March 1944, while still in the midst of fending off the bombers, night-fighter preparations for the invasion of France began, with 409 and 410 squadrons joining No 85 Group of Second TAF. For the time being, however, they remained under the operational control of the ADGB,[61] to which No 406 was still permanently assigned. Early in May they were advised that their centimetric AI radar was now cleared for use over the Continent, and on the night of 28/29 May a Mosquito of 410 Squadron chased a Junkers 88 as far as Lille, where it shot the bomber down in flames.

For Typhoon squadrons, preparations for Overlord involved moves to advanced landing grounds.

---

* Radar-jamming chaff, known to the Germans as *Düppel*.

The camp at Funtington ... consists of two grass runways, an old farmhouse, taken over as [No 143] A[ir]F[ield] Headquarters, three blister hangars and some small shelter blisters which are being utilized for tools and ammunition. With the rain falling everything is a sea of mud in which personnel wallow as they put up tents, dig slit trenches and get settled down. Most of the tents, which were packed while still wet, leak profusely and the men are covering their blankets with raincoats. The airmen's mess is set up in a blister hangar and for the day many of the men are sitting on the floor. But all personnel are digging to make life as comfortable as possible, designing stoves from old petrol cans, setting up wash basins and stands for shaving. The nearest 'pub,' just 50 yards from the 438 Squadron Dispersal, is unable to cope with the Airfield demand and is already dry until Tuesday.[62]

The fighter-reconnaissance squadrons endured similar hardships – though many a Canadian infantryman who had just spent an Italian winter alternating between soggy trenches and unheated farm outbuildings north of Ortona would have considered Funtington to be the lap of luxury.

What the Spitfire squadrons would do in the forthcoming offensive was not entirely certain, for the bomber's role was still in doubt and how bombers were used would determine whether the fighters would be needed for escort duties. The Allies were having difficulty in reaching a consensus on how to apply their abundant resources and, in early 1944, there was much debate as to which direction the air war should take. A meeting on 25 March, presided over by Portal and attended by Eisenhower, Leigh-Mallory, and the commanders-in-chief of the strategic bombing forces, settled the issue. Heavy bombers would continue to strike at German industry and morale, but would also assist the cross-Channel attack by destroying the railway system of Northwest Europe, in what was termed the 'Transportation Plan.'[63] The medium bombers of No 2 Group (now part of Second TAF) would also strike at transportation targets. Escort work would thus be the Tactical Air Force's main task until the troops set out across the beaches, the variety and intensity of such operations being demonstrated on the 27th, when RCAF fighters participated in four different Ramrods.

The first sent Bostons to attack Monceau-sur-Sambre in Belgium, Mitchells and Bostons to bomb a gun position near Cap D'Antifer, and Marauders to pound other coastal batteries in France, all with Spitfires to shepherd them. The second dispatched Mosquitoes against a Noball site, Mitchells to a railway junction at Serqueux (the Spitfires escorting the Mitchells were to dive-bomb the target afterwards), and more Mosquitoes in a low-level attack on another Noball. The third had Bostons and Mitchells (which No 443 Squadron described as Marauders) attacking the Bethune marshalling yards. Finally, Ramrod 803 sent Marauders and Bostons to hammer coastal batteries at Barfleur and Crisebeca, and the escorting Spitfires dive-bombed there as well.[64] Of course, had the Luftwaffe come up to fight before the Ramrods approached their targets, then the Spitfires would have had to jettison their bombs and turn to the work they had been designed for. It was a measure of the Luftwaffe's desperate straits that they did not.

Ramrod 804 the next day was a particularly complex affair, with Mitchells and Bostons of No 2 Group, along with Marauders, bombing the Nantes/Gassicourt railway, other Marauders attacking the Creil marshalling yards with Spitfire escort, Typhoons pounding Noball targets, more Typhoons sweeping through the Caen area, and two Mustang squadrons seeking out the enemy around Nantes/Gassicourt, though without seeing any combat. In May another dimension was added to the Transportation Plan when fighters were dispatched to attack trains in occupied territory; following medium or heavy bomber attacks on railway centres, some routes would become congested and fighters could increase pressure on the railway network by cutting up trains stranded on blocked lines. Attacks on locomotives, which in 1943 had done little but add to the fighters' casualty rolls, were slightly more effective in conjunction with the Transportation Plan although, in fact, heavy bombers attacking marshalling yards would account for 98 per cent of all trains destroyed.[65]

Amphibious forces were training hard, and in early May they carried out the only full-dress rehearsal for Operation Overlord in Exercise Fabius. (There were actually six parts to Fabius, with the 3rd Canadian Infantry Division participating in Fabius III.) Nos 401, 411, 412, and 402 Squadrons provided low beach cover in Fabius I, while Nos 403, 416, and 421 Squadrons did the same in Fabius II, III, and IV. Nos 438 and 439 Squadrons participated in Fabius II and III, each providing twelve fighter-bombers to make dummy attacks on targets of opportunity. After the squadrons had completed their prearranged tasks on D-Day they would be available for close support, and on Exercise Fabius air staffs also rehearsed the procedures for allocating aircraft at short notice in order to meet army and navy requests for help.[66]

From 1 April to 5 June the AEAF flew more than 3200 reconnaissance sorties, the RCAF fighter-reconnaissance squadrons contributing over 700 of them. The failure rate diminished, but only slightly; in May No 414 flew 142 Populars, of which ninety were fully successful and eight partially so. Of the forty-four failures, thirty were due to unfavourable weather and fourteen were blamed on technical problems, mainly engine trouble. Targets, such as railways, radar sites, communications centres, Noballs, and gun positions, reflected the variety of tasks allocated to the air forces as a whole in the month before the landings, while it was important to fly over all possible beaches along the coasts of France and Belgium in order to keep the enemy unsure of the Allies' actual plans. Oblique photographs of beach areas helped determine tactics and objectives for the troops going ashore, though they also revealed how difficult the task might be. Eisenhower, for one, found cause for reflection, as 'Pictures were studied and one of the disturbing things these continued to show was the growing profusion of beach obstacles, most of them under water at high tide.'[67]

No 400 Squadron's tasks showed as much variety as in previous months, though its Mosquito XVIs were withdrawn and replaced with Spitfires in May, taking advantage of the increased supply of Spitfire XIs while the Mosquitoes could be used to form a reserve for No 34 Wing. In May No 400's reconnaissances included the areas around Caen and Bayeux, near the actual invasion beaches, but the squadron was also an integral part of the deception plan, which called for twice as many operations in the Pas-de-Calais area as in the Baie de la Seine.[68] Deceiving the Germans was, however, only part of the reasoning behind attacking these targets, for they also included airfields and railway marshalling yards – the former accommodating aircraft the Allies would like to see destroyed, the latter able to funnel reinforcements west if they were still in good order when D-Day came.

Even before the lead-up to Operation Overlord, the Axis domain had been shrinking noticeably. In the Mediterranean, on 3 September 1943, elements of the 1st Canadian Infantry Division had led the Eighth Army's assault on the toe of the Italian 'boot' at Reggio di Calabria. The German High Command had decided the area was expendable, so the Canadians met with no opposition, the 3rd Brigade occupying Reggio before noon. The stiffest resistance of the day came from a puma, recently escaped from the bombed zoological gardens, which showed a carnivorous interest in the brigade commander. Within a week Canadian ground forces had advanced a hundred miles.[69]

No 417 Squadron met with no greater resistance in the air as it protected Supermarine Walrus flying-boats on air/sea rescue work, escorted Curtis Kittyhawk fighter-bombers and Martin Baltimore bombers, and, through a series of standing patrols, sought to deny the enemy use of the air. Enemy fighters and fighter-bombers were spotted several times, at least once while dropping bombs on ground forces, but the Canadians were not able to bring them to action in the first days of the campaign.[70] It was not until 4 October that they met the Luftwaffe, Flight Lieutenant Albert Houle, DFC, later recalling the event.

We saw ten or twelve FW 190s bombing the harbour [in the Termoli area]. I was the only one successful in dropping my long-range tank. The others did not have enough speed, with their tanks on, to get into the fight. My goggles were sucked off my forehead when I opened the coop-top to clear condensation and they got caught in the slipstream. My head was bouncing like a Yo-Yo so I tore them off and from that time onwards flew without them ... I found out for certain that the Spit VIII could catch a 190 but in the dogfight the airscoop on my aircraft had closed and the resulting loss in ram pressure cut down my power and speed. Although I could still hold my own I couldn't close the distance to deadly range. The engine started to run rough due to too rich a mixture and lack of air. As I was deep into enemy territory and completely on my own I pulled back on the stick and climbed until the reduced pressure on the scoop enabled me to again open it, then turned for home with the trusty old Merlin engine once more running velvety smooth. I rejoined the remainder of the section over Termoli, finished the patrol and returned to base with them. When we got back the 190 was confirmed by the other boys who saw it go into the water off Vasto point. That was the first squadron victory since the Sicilian campaign had started, and the first time the Jerries had shown up with any consistency.[71]

There were often complications with jettisonable fuel tanks, the most common problem being the locking mechanism, which sometimes released the tank prematurely and sometimes clung to it when the pilot desperately sought to rid himself of what was, in combat, an unwanted burden. Bert Houle again:

The failure of the other three pilots to get rid of their long-range tank was disappointing and could have been dangerous. We had been thoroughly briefed on how to get rid of them. They were hung below the cockpit by sliding a rear flange into two forward-facing hooks. The front flange fitted into two rear-facing hooks which could be tripped from the cockpit by pulling a lever. The only problem was that the air pressure sometimes held the tank in place even though the hooks were tripped. When the lever was released the hooks went back into place and again secured the tank. Our orders were to pull back on the stick slightly, thus pulling extra gravity so that the front of the tank dropped and the air pressure swept it away. In their excitement the other three pilots must have forgotten this manoeuvre and I was in the fight all by myself.[72]

The weather deteriorated in November, forcing a significant reduction in operations. On the 25th, the Canadians moved to Canne, on the Adriatic coast, putting them within thirty miles of German positions along the Sangro River. 'The field here was a very small, rather hazardous strip running at right angles to the beach; high winds frequently swept down the coast, making cross wind landings on the single metal runway a difficult and tricky operation.'[73]

The Eighth Army, including 1st Canadian Division, opened a rain-drenched offensive along the Sangro in late November. The attack was intended to draw German resources from the American Fifth Army front and thus ease the latter's advance up the Tyrrhenian shore. It failed, however, to reach its objective – the lateral road from Pescara to Rome – as tenacious German defenders gave ground slowly and grudgingly, the whole slogging match eventually climaxed by a bloody and bitter Christmas battle in the streets of Ortona.[74] During the offensive, No 417 and the other three squadrons of No 244 Wing patrolled the battle zone, hunting for German fighter-bombers. On 30 November a rare appearance by the enemy enabled the Canadians to claim two destroyed and one probably destroyed.

After a few minutes patrol ground control sent through two plots of eight and twelve e/a respectively and gave instructions to top cover to climb to 26,000 ft ... F/O 'Doug' Eastman's target disintegrated after he had fired twenty rounds from each cannon. W/O Johnny Johnson gave a FW 190 a short burst with his cannon. He closed in and gave it another burst. There didn't seem to be any reaction so he pulled up alongside it and saw that the cockpit was a mass of flames ... The FW turned over and dived into the deck. F/O O'Brian ... got in a burst at a FW 190 and started to follow it. With clouds of glycol streaming from its engine, it headed for the ground. However, he lost it in cloud and when he emerged, could only see a large puff of smoke on the ground in the general line of the e/a's flight. The rest of the Jerries jettisoned bombs and went nose down for home.[75]

As 1943 drew to a close, the Canadians, now commanded by Houle, concentrated on four- and eight-aircraft patrols over the lines near Orsogna and Ortona. During late December they expanded their repertoire to include two-aircraft Jim Crows – weather and so-called shipping reconnaissance missions (actually speculative anti-shipping strikes) – over the Adriatic, which led to the beginnings of a ground attack role for the squadron. On 8 January 1944 two pilots on a Jim Crow blew up a locomotive on the Dalmatian coast and four other pilots strafed a power station north of the German lines in Italy, and over the next few days the squadron completed a series of strafing attacks on trains, trucks, buses, and other targets of opportunity. Pilots had mixed feelings about such operations, Houle later reflecting: 'We expected to lose men. You must get down within reach of their guns in order to shoot, and it is always dangerous.'[76]

On 22 January Anglo-American troops landed near Anzio, on Italy's west coast, behind Kesselring's main defences south of Rome. The Allies hoped to force a German evacuation of the Monte Cassino stronghold by this direct threat to his lines of communication, but excessive caution combined with quick and fierce German counter-attacks pinned the landing force into a tenuous lodgement. 'I had thought that we were hurling a wild cat on to the shore,' wrote Winston Churchill, 'but all we had got was a stranded whale.'[77]

The landings at Anzio posed the kind of strategic threat that, from Kesselring's perspective, justified risking his meagre air strength as part of a coordinated effort to throw the Allies back into the sea. No 417, along with the other squadrons of No 244 Wing, was detached from the Desert Air Force – abandoning its role in support of Eighth Army – and moved to an airfield near Naples, where it was placed under the US XIIth Air Support Command specifically to support the bridgehead at Anzio. It remained there for the next three months, almost all its work being standing patrols intended to frustrate fighter-bomber attacks against Allied ground forces and shipping in and around the beachhead.[78]

No 417's performance over that time demonstrated the importance of leadership, proper training, and experience in creating an effective air weapon. Between 22 January and 29 March its pilots met the enemy in twenty-four engagements; they were never surprised, as they had been in North Africa, and generally they managed to achieve the advantages of height and speed. They were credited with nineteen German aircraft destroyed, while losing six Spitfires; and only one Canadian was killed, though several others were wounded.[79]

A scheme developed early in April brought pilots and groundcrew much closer to the land battle as, in turn, each of the wing's four squadrons flew the final patrol of the day over the Anzio beaches and then, instead of returning to airfields near Naples, landed at the Nettuno strip, inside the bridgehead. The next morning that squadron flew the dawn patrol. In due course No 417 pilots returned to Marcianise with 'livid descriptions of guns thundering all night and spoiling their sleep'; and twelve ground crew got to share the experience when they volunteered for a two-week detail servicing the machines at Nettuno.[80]

Air fighting began to peter out. German aircraft stopped their direct support of the Wehrmacht as the battle approached a stalemate – losses had become too prohibitive – and the Canadians encountered the enemy only twice during

April. This may have been fortunate, for the intense pace of operations at Anzio was taking its toll. There were plenty of replacement pilots available but the right kind of Spitfire was in short supply, and by early April losses had combined with normal operational wear to reduce the squadron's complement of aircraft from eighteen to twelve. Spitfire VIIIs, with their superior combat range and better handling at low altitudes, were unavailable and one flight was re-equipped for a short time with Spitfire IXs.[81]

Having done their share at Anzio, the squadron transferred in late April to the forward air strip at Venafro, near Monte Cassino – a move that encouraged both air- and groundcrew to make slit trenches their first priority. They were soon put to use, for on 19 May ten Focke-Wulfe 190s dive-bombed the town and the airfield, causing 'some amusing scenes on the Squadron as everyone dove for shelter when the bombs began dropping.' There was no lasting damage, and Spitfires of 145 Squadron caught the raiders, destroying one and damaging others.[82]

Operations then settled into a routine until 12 May, when the US Fifth and British Eighth Armies – the latter now incorporating I Canadian Corps* – launched their spring offensive against the Winter Line. Two days later six Spitfires intercepted eighteen-plus Me 109s and FW 190s over Cassino, and in the confused mêlée that followed two of the German fighters were destroyed and three were damaged. One of the Spitfires was also shot down, but the pilot parachuted to safety.[83] Again, the squadron's success, while outnumbered three to one, was an indication not only of the Luftwaffe's growing weakness in pilot training but the greatly improved combat skills of the Canadians. By the end of the month (and into the first weeks of June) No 417's reconnaissance patrols were ranging north of Rome, in the vicinity of Lake Bracciano, though it encountered German fighters only once – as mentioned above – during the entire offensive.

Coordinated attacks from the Anzio bridgehead (after 125 days of isolation) and up the Liri valley, on the Cassino front, now convinced Hitler that a defence south of Rome could not be continued and he authorized a withdrawal to the north so that German forces could regroup.[84] Generalfeldmarschall Albert Kesselring, the German commander-in-chief, proclaimed Rome an 'open city'; Fifth Army units entered on 4 June 1944, but their accomplishment was quickly overshadowed by events eight hundred miles to the northwest – on the beaches of Normandy.

The launching of Operation Overlord was preceded by a month of highly intensive air operations. On 8 May one of the top priority items was the Douai marshalling yards, which were allocated to the RCAF's Typhoons, and leading the operation was Wing Commander R.T.P. Davidson, DFC, a Vancouverite who had joined the RAF in 1937 and served in every major theatre of war except the Pacific. Credited with five victories, Davidson had participated in

---

* Composed of the 1st Infantry and 5th Armoured Divisions, as well as the independent 1st Canadian Armoured Brigade.

the successful campaign to eject the Italians from Greece in late 1940, fought against the subsequent German invasion of the Greek mainland in April 1941, flown a Hurricane against the Japanese from Ceylon (now Sri Lanka) in the spring of 1942, begun flying Typhoons in April 1943, and taken command of 143 (RCAF) Airfield that autumn.[85] His DFC citation noted that he 'has displayed extreme keenness for ops.' This particular day 'dawned bright and clear though there was a heavy white frost. Nine aircraft from the Squadron, plus the Wing Commander, Flying, in another aircraft, departed for Manston at 0850 hours. At the last minute, W/Cdr Davidson's own aircraft became unserviceable [and had to be replaced]. Eight of these aircraft, having gassed up and bombed up at Manston, participated in an "ops" wing sortie against the marshalling yards at Douai, France. This is the farthest point that aircraft from this Squadron [No 438] have bombed. The results were very good, but the Airfield received a sad blow when W/Cmdr Davidson's engine cut out over France and he, presumably, made a forced landing.'[86] Davidson, having experienced mechanical breakdown twice in one day, was the only pilot not to return. There had been no Flak. He survived the landing, was rescued by the French 'underground,' and would emerge from hiding in September as the Allies moved through France, to add a Croix de Guerre to his DFC.[87]

On 21 May Allied air forces intensified their attacks on the railway network in Northwest Europe, launching a total of almost seventeen hundred sorties. Second TAF and ADGB made their contribution, of almost four hundred sorties, through Ramrod 905. RCAF participation consisted of Nos 402, 403, 416, 421, and 441 squadrons. But fighters strafing moving trains were less effective than bombers attacking marshalling yards: of 159 locomotives claimed destroyed, the fighters of all air forces accounted for only three; at the same time, they suffered the highest casualties – including twenty-one RAF/RCAF aircraft and twenty pilots – representing 5.4 per cent of those committed. The Canadians lost four pilots, a slightly lower loss rate than ADGB/Second TAF as a whole. The next day, 'at long, long last,' the Luftwaffe came out to fight. No 416 dispatched its aircraft in sections of six (three pairs) instead of four, and reported: 'Things are really shaping up for the boys. The score for today was 4 more trains and (5) Hun aircraft, which were destroyed by F/Ls Forbes-Roberts, Mason, Patterson, F/O McFadden and P/O Palmer.'[88]

The way in which the squadron diarist brusquely related five victories to five pilots makes air-to-air combat seem much simpler than it really was. In this case, three of the five actually saw their victims crash, but the other two claims were far more complex. Flight Lieutenant Mason managed a short burst at one aircraft but then came under attack from a second. All he could say about his victim was that he 'began to level out at tree-top level and went down into a large field at over 250 mph. I was right on the deck behind him and he did not come up from the field. I was unable to see him crash as the other aircraft was breaking in to me.' He claimed one success, however, because Pilot Officer Palmer had 'observed an aircraft crashed in a field, with a little smoke or dust rising from it but not being on fire.' Forbes-Roberts presented a similar problem, reporting that 'I saw one aircraft below me, apparently taking off [from] a landing strip. I opened up and broke right and down on him, getting in two short bursts, first with machine gun only and then with machine gun and a few rounds of cannon. I saw two small strikes. He broke away from me due to my excess speed.' Forbes-Roberts claimed this aircraft as destroyed because Patterson had reported, 'During my attack I saw a single engined aircraft spinning about 500 yards away to my left about 500 feet,' and Palmer had 'sighted a parachute near the landing strip.' According to Forbes-Roberts 'this parachute could not have come from any of the other four aircraft which were destroyed, I [therefore] claim this one as destroyed,' ignoring the possibility that the pilot floating earthward had baled out of the same aircraft Mason had claimed.[89] Intelligence officers sifting through the information available could arrive at several possible conclusions. At worst, either the aircraft Palmer saw in the field had landed rather than crashed, in which case Mason's claim was void; or the aircraft had indeed crashed but the parachutist that led Forbes-Roberts to claim a victory had, in fact, baled out of it, in which case Forbes-Roberts's claim was void. In either case one would conclude that four German aircraft had been destroyed. Intelligence officers, however, were convinced by Forbes-Roberts's statement that 'this parachute could not have come from any of the other four aircraft,'[90] and credited all five pilots with kills.

As far as aerial gunnery was concerned, a new gyroscopic sight made it much easier for the average pilot to calculate the correct deflection angle in air-to-air fighting. Preliminary combat analysis in the early part of 1944 showed that the new sight had doubled a pilot's chances of bringing down an enemy; Spitfire IXs with the old reflector sight shot down thirty-four aircraft in 130 engagements, while those equipped with the gyroscopic sight destroyed nineteen of thirty-eight. However, many experienced pilots, Hugh Godefroy among them, who had spent years learning and developing their deflection shooting, preferred the old method. As Godefroy related after the war, 'I was too long in the tooth and set in my ways to change. I kept the gunsight shut off where the bead would stay in the middle and shot just the same as I always had.'[91]

'Train-busting' was now a daily occupation. On 23 May No 144 Wing (on 12 May 'Wing' was officially substituted for 'Airfield,' thus returning to a more familiar terminology)[92] took off on a sweep to support a Fortress and Liberator attack on airfields, marshalling yards, railway stations, and an aircraft factory. Rodeo 295 involved twelve Spitfires from each of 441, 442, and 443 squadrons. The first two found little to do, but No 443 accounted for two trains.

When the Squadron was in the area west of Chartres a goods train was sighted and F/L I.R. MacLennan DFM shot it up. A few minutes later a passenger train was spotted and an attack was made but the first attempt was unsuccessful. Finally two aircraft from Blue Section led by F/L D.M. Walz dived from 13,000 feet and destroyed the engine and, in addition, what appeared to be a signal house or a blockhouse beside the railroad track was damaged. No enemy aircraft were sighted and the only Flak encountered was some light Flak in the Chartres area.[93]

Spitfires were being called upon to carry out an ever-wider variety of tasks, and one could find no better example than Ramrod 942 of 29 May. The operation involved seven RCAF squadrons: No 402 escorted Bostons as they attacked the marshalling yards at Monceau-sur-Sambre; Nos 441, 442, and 443 (along with Typhoons of Nos 439 and 440) carried out dive-bombing operations against Noball sites; and Nos 401, 411, and 412 set their sights on various transportation targets, including three trains and a barge.[94] Thus the Spitfire, originally designed as a short-range interceptor, was being called upon by 1944 to work as an escort fighter, ground attack aircraft, photo-reconnaissance platform, and dive-bomber.

As May gave way to June, the first day of the month offered few opportunities to prepare for invasion since the weather (now of much concern to Eisenhower and his staff) allowed only eight sorties by RCAF fighter squadrons: two on weather reconnaissance, four on a defensive patrol, and two on escort duties, all uneventful. The following day was far better, No 143 Wing's Typhoons flying thirty-four sorties against targets around Le Havre. Of the reconnaissance squadrons, No 400 continued to fly exclusively on photographic sorties, while tactical reconnaissance (relying on the human eye and brain) made up the bulk of Nos 414's and 430's missions.[95]

Meanwhile, the destruction of the Luftwaffe as a fighting force continued apace, not because of Circuses, Ramrods, Rodeos, or any of the other sweeps designed to entice its fighters into the air, but rather thanks to Operation Argument. Refining the policies arrived at during the Casablanca conference of January 1943, the Pointblank directive issued the following summer had established a combined bomber offensive aimed at the destruction of Germany's war potential through 'round-the-clock' bombing, with the US Eighth Air Force applying its doctrine of precision daylight bombing while Bomber Command concentrated on night-time area raids. Unknown and unconsidered at the time was the critical importance of Pointblank's intermediate objective, the attainment of air superiority.[96]

The Luftwaffe, however, would not be destroyed in a knock-out blow inflicted by aerial bombing but in a desperate war of attrition of which the main instrument on the American side was the P-51 Mustang. This superb long-range fighter was not the result of any careful and considered prescription on the part of British or American air forces and designers, but the product of serendipity pure and simple. Originally developed for the Royal Air Force, its first generations were underpowered and hence, as we have seen, banished to the operationally less relevant Army Co-operation Command. The problem was the Allison engine, which produced less than 1100 horse-power; the solution was the dual-supercharged 1520 horse-power Merlin engine developed by Britain's Rolls Royce, in conjunction with the jettisonable long-range fuel tank. The result was an aircraft that could escort bombers on deep, daylight penetration raids, meet the enemy in his own airspace, and defeat him there.[97]

Technology determines nothing in and of itself and is useless unless applied with intelligence and forethought. Though it had taken the US Army Air Forces something on the order of three decades to realize the vulnerability of unescorted bombers, they now seized the opportunities the Mustang offered. In January 1944 General James H. Doolittle, commanding the Eighth Air Force, had changed the doctrine which guided American use of the fighter arm. No longer would the escorts' main task be to 'bring the bombers back alive,' but 'to destroy German fighters.'[98] The Mustangs were released from the invisible harnesses that had tied them to the bombers and they proceeded to engage their Luftwaffe counterparts wherever they could be found, often strafing them on their own airfields. 'Wherever our fighters appeared, the Americans hurled themselves at them. They went over to low-level attacks on our airfields. Nowhere were we safe from them; we had to skulk on our own bases. During takeoff, assembling, climbing, approaching the bombers, once in contact with the bombers, on our way back, during landing, and ever after that the American fighters attacked with an overwhelming superiority.'[99]

The Germans also faced commitments elsewhere. The defence of the Reich came first but aircraft were badly needed on the Eastern front, where the Luftwaffe was still heavily involved in the first half of 1944 trying to stem a Russian advance into the Balkans. Casualties there were less severe, however, so 'the Luftwaffe used Russia as a school for inexperienced pilots.' (The situation would get far worse when the Russians launched their major offensive against Germany proper, exactly three years after Barbarossa.) By the end of May the Germans had 891 aircraft in France, of which 497 were serviceable, to face the nine thousand the Allies could muster against them, five thousand of them fighters. Additionally, a coded order was supposed to throw almost all units defending the Reich into the anti-invasion battle, thus giving the Luftwaffe another six hundred aircraft – still a pitiful force – to fight off the Allies.[100]

Anti-aircraft deployment was more promising, as many an RCAF pilot could testify. On their western front (including Germany) the Germans had available over 22,000 light and medium and almost 11,000 heavy guns, as opposed to some 8000 and 4000 respectively, in Italy, the Balkans, and the East. Maintaining and operating them and their radar systems required the services of over a million men, women, and boys, who had to be housed, fed, and munitioned. Moreover, anti-aircraft artillery was defensive in nature, and the Luftwaffe needed fighters, fighter-bombers, and ground attack aircraft if it was to thwart Allied ground and naval forces. Unfortunately for the Germans, 'when June, 1944, eventually arrived, the Allies possessed so great a preponderance of strength in the air that nothing but a major blunder or deliberate treachery could have prevented success.'[101]

9

The Normandy Campaign,
June–August 1944

'One evening ... the sky over our house [at Taunton, in south-western England's Somersetshire] began to fill with the sound of aircraft, which swelled until it overflowed the darkness from edge to edge,' wrote British historian John Keegan, recollecting from his childhood the eve of Operation Overlord. 'Its first tremors had taken my parents into the garden, and as the roar grew I followed and stood between them to gaze awestruck at the constellation of red, green and yellow lights which rode across the heavens and streamed southwards towards the sea.'

It seemed as if every aircraft in the world was in flight, as wave followed wave without intermission ... The element of noise in which they swam became solid, blocking our ears, entering our lungs and beating the ground beneath our feet with the relentless surge of an ocean swell. Long after the last had passed from view and the thunder of their passage had died into the silence of the night, restoring to our consciousness the familiar and timeless elements of our surroundings, elms, hedges, rooftops, clouds and stars, we remained transfixed and wordless on the spot where we stood, gripped by a wild surmise at what the power, majesty and menace of the great migratory flight could portend.

Next day we knew. The Americans had gone. The camps they had built had emptied overnight. The roads were deserted. No doubt, had we been keeping check, we would have noticed a gradual efflux of their numbers. But it had been disguised until the last moment and the outrush had been sudden. The BBC news bulletin told us why. 'Early this morning units of the Allied armies began landing on the coasts of France.'[1]

As the Keegans bore witness to the opening stages of Overlord, Spitfires of Nos 401, 416, 441, and 443 Squadrons shepherded convoys setting out from southern English ports towards the Norman shore. Their patrols were uneventful, and only No 418 (Intruder) Squadron, which spent some hours of the night attacking German airfields and Flak posts in northwestern France, could report any excitement; of its nineteen crews, eighteen flew on missions in 'the greatest single-night's work ever performed by the squadron,' and though one Mosquito, hit by Flak, was forced to crash-land, its crew walked away from the wreck.[2]

The Allied air forces met with no opposition in the air, for the Luftwaffe had become a mere shadow of its former self, with no hope of stemming the Allied tide. Stationed within range of the Baie de la Seine and the Cotentin peninsula were the formations of Luftflotte 3, with a theoretical fighting strength of 481 aircraft, of which sixty-four were for reconnaissance and only a hundred were fighters; but on D-Day 'not more than 319 aircraft could meet the enemy,' compared with the eleven thousand that the Allies had allocated to Overlord – an overwhelming ratio of about thirty-five to one in favour of the latter. Moreover, orders for the transfer of formations from other areas to help deal with the immediate threat (an operation that had been planned in some detail months before) were not even issued until the following day, such was the uncertainty and disquiet in German headquarters.[3]

Canadian fighter pilots were thus witnesses to the epic events unfolding on the beaches, but they had little else to do but watch.

At 2330 hours on the night of the 5th the pilots had been called together for a short address by Group Captain W.R. MacBrien, which was followed by an intensive briefing lasting until 0130 hours. Two hours later the pilots were roused and the Squadrons put in a state of readiness. At 0620 hours No 127 and No 144 Wings took off, with both Group Captain MacBrien and W/C L.V. Chadburn flying with 403 Squadron, a total of seventy-four aircraft, No 127 Wing to patrol the western and No 144 Wing to patrol the eastern section of the landing area ... but there was no sign of the enemy aircraft and relatively little Flak, except from Le Havre at the eastern end of the patrol. The wings returned to land at base at approximately 0820 hours, shortly after No 126 Wing with thirty-seven aircraft had taken off for the second stage of the beachhead patrol.[4]

In the course of the day only two RCAF squadrons reported contact with the enemy: No 442 sighted, but was unable to attack, two FW 190s, while No 401 climbed to intercept a formation of over twenty aircraft which also turned away before the Canadians could engage them. 'While the Squadron was climbing to ward off this danger, a lone enemy aircraft sneaked through the hole in the "umbrella," dropped a single bomb on the beach and made good its escape,' in one of only two instances where German fighter-bombers succeeded in attacking the bridgehead.[5]

The Allies had expected to launch an average of four sorties per day per aircraft in the initial stages of the invasion, but Luftwaffe inactivity diminished the need for intercepts and patrols and, in the event, only 1.28 sorties per aircraft were carried out on D-Day. That average rose to 2.28 on D+1, the nine RCAF day-fighter units with No 83 Group spending many a tedious hour patrolling over the crowded (and scrap-strewn) beaches, where they were joined by No 402, still with the ADGB. For most units, the daily program called for four patrols over the beaches, each of two hours' duration.[6]

On D-Day the three Canadian Typhoon squadrons – bomb-carrying Typhoons were colloquially known as Bombphoons – had been among the busiest units in the AEAF, each flying three ground attack missions. First, with twelve aircraft each, they had attacked beach defences in conjunction with the initial assault. From left to right, as one looked across the Channel towards the French coast, landing areas had been divided into five beaches: Sword (British), Juno (Canadian), Gold (British), Omaha (American), and Utah (also American). No 438's task was to hammer two concrete blockhouses overlooking Gold beach, near Le Hamel, where the British 50th Division led the assault. Just after the landing ramps were lowered, No 439 attacked two strong points on Juno beach, moments ahead of 3rd Canadian Division's assault brigades, while No 440 bombed Sword beach and swept inland to strafe a suspected 88 millimetre gun position. A second operation that afternoon found the Typhoons bombing targets of opportunity around Caen, but the few they found were of little significance. Eight aircraft from No 440 directed their attention and their bombs on one of the roads, wrecking one truck and damaging another; eight from No 439 simply jettisoned their bombs; and nine from No 438 attacked three armoured cars, registering near misses while suffering damage to one aircraft from Flak.[7]

So far they had operated without serious casualties, but their luck would run out on the final flight of the day, an early evening armed reconnaissance of the Caen area. No 440 dispatched eight Typhoons which located some enemy transport and destroyed two trucks with bombs and strafed two others, but one aircraft was badly hit by Flak and had to crash-land back at base while another was holed in its fuel tanks and was forced to land at an alternate field; a third pilot failed to return – his grave would be found on 29 June. No 439 had the good fortune to find an armoured column, either of the 12th SS or 21st Panzer Division, which it attacked with bombs, while eight aircraft from No 438 attacked four trucks and strafed a column of troop carriers. Several machines were slightly damaged, but all returned safely. No 440 Squadron was the hardest hit of the RCAF units on D-Day, losing three aircraft and one pilot (No 430 was the only other Canadian squadron to lose a pilot, also in the early evening).[8]

Trying to impose order on the natural chaos characteristic of such activities were Fighter Direction Tenders and Headquarters ships. The former directed day-fighters onto Luftwaffe formations whenever these units made their rare forays over the invasion areas, while the latter gave instructions to the fighter-bombers and aircraft engaged in tactical reconnaissance. Unlike the catastrophe at Dieppe, two years earlier, these controllers had direct communication with the pilots overhead at all times. Tenders and ships were moored in the roadstead in the centre of the British and American beach areas and, as there was too much beach (about eighty miles' worth in total) for a single controller to cover, the British and Americans each had their own network.[9]

Late that night, Prime Minister Winston Churchill telegraphed his contentious ally, Josef Stalin, to report that 'everything has started well. The mines, obstacles, and land [coastal defence] batteries have been largely overcome. The air landings were very successful, and on a large scale. Infantry landings are proceeding rapidly and many tanks and self-propelled guns are already ashore.' As for Second British Army, it had suffered over four thousand casualties (about a thousand of them Canadians) while landing more than 74,000 troops in two bridgeheads, one fifteen miles wide and five miles deep and the other five miles wide and four miles deep.[10]

From the German point of view, 'first developments were unpromising' in the opinion of General Walter Warlimont, then Hitler's deputy chief of operations staff.

The OKW Operations Staff had been allowed to know little of the conduct of the war in the air; we were therefore unpleasantly surprised to find that the Gruppen, the standard unit used by us to order and by OKL [Oberkommando de Luftwaffe] to report reinforcements, when they actually appeared on 6–7 June were at only a third of their planned strength, in other words consisted only of ten instead of thirty serviceable aircraft ... The first few 'jet fighters,' 'miracle weapons' like the rockets upon which Hitler had counted so much, made little difference; the enemy's air superiority was even greater than had been expected and from the first day of the invasion the Luft-waffe's inferiority was so great that it became the prime factor in making any com-mand action or movement well nigh impossible.[11]

Warlimont's report was heavily tainted by interservice rivalry, and German soldiers would continue to blame the Luftwaffe for many of their troubles in the months to come, but it was the air arm's inherent weakness, vis-à-vis Allied air forces, that made it such a convenient scapegoat.

Luftwaffe reinforcements, however, began to arrive at the front starting on D+1, so that the odds of Canadian pilots engaging the enemy in the air increased slightly and defensive operations quickly settled into a routine punctuated by brief but turbulent skirmishes. The monotony of its first shift on 7 June ended in spectacular fashion for No 401 Squadron. At about 1030 hours the Canadians were flying through cloud at 2000 feet when they narrowly avoided entangling themselves in the cables of barrage balloons flown by some of the ships below. Just as they banked and turned, one of them saw a Junkers 88 collide with a balloon cable and crash to the beach. The German was not alone. 'Suddenly the air seemed full of Ju 88s,' and soon twenty-four machines were involved in aerial combat, flying in and out of cloud, and trying to dodge the balloons as well as the anti-aircraft fire thrown up by hundreds of ships anchored off-shore. It was, of course, a one-sided combat. When the mêlée was over, eight Canadians between them claimed six enemy machines destroyed, and one probable. On its second patrol, the squadron claimed two more destroyed, for a total loss of one.[12]

Actively engaged in avoiding the Luftwaffe were the pilots of No 400 Squadron as, in the days following the landings, they carried out frequent reconnaissance flights over enemy territory to monitor Wehrmacht activity. Although enjoying considerable independence once they were in the air, the photo-reconnaissance pilots were given detailed guidance before takeoff by an army liaison officer and his RCAF counterpart, who plotted the positions of the objectives for the pilots' map traces and arranged them in order of priority. Pilots were also briefed concerning the coverage required and the altitude at which pictures should be taken, while the wing intelligence officer provided information about Flak concentrations and enemy air units. Upon returning to base, the pilot made out a report to accompany his pictures while the photography section removed the camera magazines from the aircraft and developed the film, running off three prints of each negative for the Army Photo Interpretation Section, where they were carefully examined and the information obtained forwarded to corps or army headquarters. Throughout the Northwest Europe campaign, two RCAF Mobile Field Photographic Sections based at the group's rear headquarters would each reproduce hundreds of thousands of aerial photographs every month.[13]

Once troops were ashore, the two RCAF Mustang squadrons began to apply the training that had been part of their syllabus since the days of Army Co-operation Command. For No 414, the hours spent practising its army support role had always exceeded operational flying time except for the last two months of 1942 and, of course, May 1944. Until the eve of D-Day, after almost two years as an operational unit, the squadron had flown some 1400 sorties; in the three months following D-Day it would equal that number, and the nine hundred hours flown operationally in the invasion month would remain a unit record until the end of the war.[14]

With the exception of some unsatisfactory artillery spotting (for which the Mustang was a thoroughly unsuitable aircraft) and a few photo-reconnaissance sorties, both fighter-reconnaissance squadrons concentrated their efforts on tactical patrols. These patrols combined routine sorties, as teams searched the roads leading to the beachheads at first and last light, with impromptu ones during the day as they flew tactical reconnaissances in accordance with army requests. German dispositions were well known, and the Mustangs could warn of any developing counter-attack on the part of 21st, 12th SS, or Panzer Lehr divisions. In doing so pilots were briefed before taking to the air, but they transmitted vital information, such as the location of troop concentrations or Panzers, directly to Kenway, the Group Control Centre, which in turn relayed the information to the army or other air force units. Despite new tactics, which saw the Mustangs operate in fours, with two aircraft for observation and two as escort, these patrols were costly.[15]

Flak was everywhere; the German front-line bristled with concentrations of small calibre (20- and 30-millimetre) anti-aircraft artillery made invisible (until they opened fire) by the arts of camouflage; and, though flying above three thousand feet put pilots out of range of light Flak, they were still within the range of heavier guns, so that maintaining a straight course was hazardous, if not suicidal. Thus a typical flight pattern involved a weaving dive from twelve to ten thousand feet, then climbing back to eleven thousand after thirty seconds or so. No 440 Squadron lost three machines to Flak on 7 June, although one pilot managed to make his way back to Allied territory three days later.[16] On the 8th, No 416 suffered its first casualty of the campaign when Warrant Officer J.C.R. Maranda, patrolling Utah beach and the Cotentin area, was hit by anti-aircraft fire and tried to make for an emergency landing strip in the British sector.

He jumped over the beach, but wind drifted him about a quarter of a mile off-shore and some two miles from the ships and tenders lining the assault beach. s/L Green called 'Research' (the Controller on the Battleships) and asked for a tender, which apparently set out before w/o Maranda reached the water. Apparently he was unable to release his parachute, and the remaining three pilots of Red Section, who circled the spot to direct the tenders, saw him struggling with it. After about five minutes the parachute sank, dragging w/o Maranda under the surface.[17]

The toll continued to mount in the days that followed, No 414 Squadron having six pilots killed or wounded between 9 and 23 June, while on the last day of the month three machines from No 421 were holed in an action that destroyed one truck and damaged another, hardly a fair exchange.[18]

Flak alone, however, was no deterrent, and the Allied bombing and interdiction effort was delaying the approach of I SS Panzerkorps, III Flakkorps, and the paratroopers of II Fallschirmjägerkorps into the Normandy battle area. 'Our operations ... are rendered exceptionally difficult, and in part impossible, by the strong and often overwhelming superiority of the enemy Air Force,' Generalfeldmarschall Erwin Rommel complained.

The enemy has complete control of the air over the battle area up to a distance of about 100 km behind the front, and with powerful fighter-bomber and bomber formations, immobilises almost all traffic by day on roads or in open country ... Movements of our troops on the battlefield by day are thus almost entirely impossible, while the enemy can operate without hindrance. In the country behind, all roads are exposed to continual attack, and it is therefore very difficult to bring up the necessary supplies of fuel and munitions ... Neither our flak nor our Air Force seems able to put an end to these crippling and destructive air attacks. Our troops are fighting as well as they can with the means available, but ammunition is scarce, and can be supplied only under the most difficult conditions.[19]

Unable to compete by day, the Germans threw what aircraft they could into the struggle after dark. Flying from English airfields, but under the control of mobile GCI sets which went ashore with Allied ground forces, the Mosquito night-fighters of No 410 Squadron flew over 650 beachhead patrols and were credited with destroying twenty-eight enemy aircraft for the loss of only two crews (compared with No 421, the highest-scoring Spitfire squadron, which claimed twenty and lost seven). Over the same period No 409 flew a similar number of patrols, and received credit for twenty-two victims at a cost of seven men – two of them when their Mosquito struck debris from a Ju 88 they had just destroyed over Caen. The Luftwaffe, meanwhile, manged to sink only the destroyer *Boadicea* and sink or damage seven smaller craft by direct attack, although sixteen other Allied vessels were lost when they struck mines, most of which had been laid by air.[20]

Still smarting from having to fly obsolescent Beaufighters, No 406 Squadron saw rather less action. It had been assigned to Channel patrols far removed from the activity on shore, and these were, without exception, completely uneventful. To relieve the tedium, crews were assigned a few night Rangers over northern France, but, as the moon was in its dark phase, little could be seen on the ground and map-reading was 'impossible.' 'It is now evident,' the squadron diarist asserted, 'that these [night Rangers] are more or less useless.'[21] The mood in the squadron worsened as June progressed. 'A very serious shortage of aircraft exists at present,' the ORB explained on the 16th, 'due to losses by damage and a high percentage of others requiring parts. Most of the aircraft on hand and serviceable have only a few hours to go before major overhauls are necessary, some being already due, and flying has had to be curtailed to the bare minimum in order to conserve aircraft for scrambles and necessary operational sorties.'[22]

By mid-July only nine machines, a mixture of worn-out Beaufighters and Mosquitoes, could be considered airworthy, and Wing Commander R.C. Fumerton penned a brutally frank letter to ADGB headquarters. The first RCAF pilot to destroy a German aircraft at night, Fumerton had served in North Africa and Malta, brought his score up to fourteen, been awarded the DFC, and risen to the rank of wing commander. Blunt and direct, fiercely loyal to his subordinates, he was not one to mince words.[23]

Since coming to Exeter and thence to Winkleigh, Mosquitoes still hanging at the end of the rainbow, the hours on our Beaufighters gradually expired, some of them being replaced by old aircraft from 409 Squadron, 410 Squadron and various other squadrons ... We now find ourselves with more time expired aircraft about to be replaced by near time expired aircraft – still Beaufighters.

... Such a record would make even a Japanese diplomat red with rage. If it were only a case of swallowing pride the solution would be simple, but as Commanding Officer of this Squadron, I must flatly refuse to have the aircrew jeopardizing their lives by continually flying the 'clapped out' aircraft of other squadrons.[24]

Fumerton's exasperation apparently shocked the hierarchy into action, and on 20 July the 'clapped out' machines were supplemented by ten Mosquito XXXs fitted with the latest Mark X AI. The next day at least one of the new Mosquitoes, along with a Beaufighter, was in the air, guarding shipping off the Brittany peninsula, and, when a formation of seven Do 217s approached a flotilla of destroyers, the two aircraft accounted for three of them. 'This,' commented the ORB, 'coupled with the arrival of the new equipment, has raised morale and keenness to a high pitch.'[25]

But it was not to last. On 25 July three crews disappeared on a day Ranger over northern France. Also, Fumerton had obviously gone too far with his blast to ADGB, for the AOC of No 10 Group, Air Vice-Marshal Charles Steele, was soon asking that he be posted. On 26 July the squadron commander was unceremoniously transferred to Canada, ostensibly for having reached his physical 'limit,' and replaced by one of his flight commanders, Flight Lieutenant D.J. Williams. The squadron diary declared that the men were 'shocked and stunned' at the move.[26]

With their greater range, Mosquito squadrons based in England could still carry out lengthy patrols over the beachhead. Spitfires and Typhoons, in contrast, wasted precious and limited endurance flying across the Channel and back with each sortie, so the construction of airfields in France became a priority. Two servicing commandos and construction wings moved to the Continent on D+2 and began work on the first of the Normandy airfields near Ste-Croix-sur-Mer, which had fallen to Canadian troops on the first day of invasion. Their initial task was to establish emergency landing strips, where aircraft in trouble could avoid the hazards of crash landing or baling-out over the Channel and which, once completed, could be developed into refuelling and rearming strips for British-based units. Later still, they could be improved and graded to the status of landing grounds which would serve as permanent wing facilities incorporating twelve-hundred-yard long, hard-surfaced runways.[27]

Work progressed despite enemy shelling, and at noon on D+4 Nos 303 (Polish) and 130 Squadrons flew in to a strip near Gold beach, the first RAF units since 1940 to land in France. Later, 144 (RCAF) Wing refuelled and rearmed at B-3, near Banville, and its squadrons became the first in four years to operate, at wing strength, from French soil.[28] A few days later the wing moved its base to B-3, much sooner than had been anticipated.

No 144 Wing with a strength of 39 officers and 743 other ranks at the end of May, was apparently originally scheduled to cross the Channel somewhat later than the other Spitfire Wings. 'A' Echelon received its initial warning only on June 1st. The following day instructions were received that the Advance Party was to move on June 5th, while the Main Party was to be in readiness from 0600 hours on June 4th. Great consternation ensued when instructions were received on June 3rd that the Main Party was to move to the Concentration Area at 0700 hours on June 4th, a full day before the Advance Party was scheduled to leave. There were violent protests that 'someone had boobed,' and appeals to higher authority for delay, but there was no postponement of effort. By working virtually all night, Wing personnel completed preparations on time. The Main Party moved off at exactly 0700 hours, and arrived at Old Sarum precisely on scheduled time. Here they remained until the move to the marshalling area, which began shortly after reveille at 0330 hours on June 9th.[29]

Pilots and groundcrew left the comforts of Britain behind in moving to the Continent. For a time, at least, sleep became a rare and well-appreciated luxury, home was often a slit trench, and dust saturated clothes, bodies, and food. By mid-June such moves were routine and avoided the kind of panic that had accompanied No 144 Wing's relocation. They were also quick. When one No 403 Squadron pilot took to his parachute after his engine failed over France, he landed unhurt within friendly lines and, as a downed flyer, had little

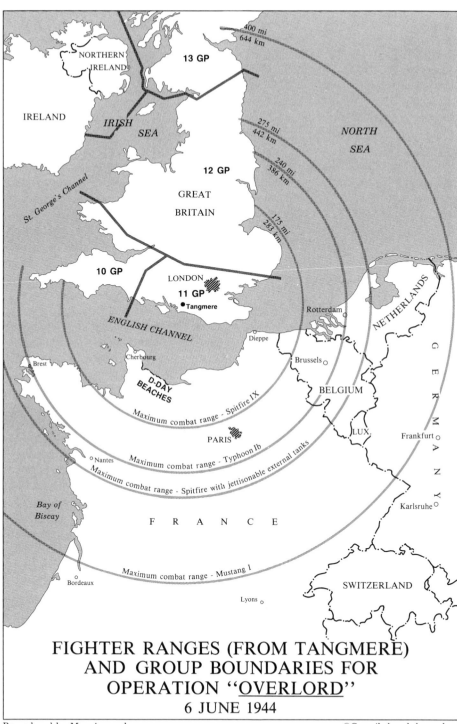

400 mi
644 km

275 mi
442 km

240 mi
386 km

175 mi
283 km

NORTHERN
IRELAND

13 GP

IRELAND

IRISH
SEA

St. George's Channel

12 GP

GREAT
BRITAIN

NORTH
SEA

10 GP

LONDON

11 GP

Tangmere

ENGLISH CHANNEL

Rotterdam

Dieppe

NETHERLANDS

Cherbourg

Brest

D-DAY
BEACHES

Brussels

BELGIUM

GERMANY

Maximum combat range - Spitfire IX

PARIS

Maximum combat range - Typhoon Ib

LUX.

Frankfurt

Nantes

Maximum combat range - Spitfire with jettisonable external tanks

Bay of
Biscay

F   R   A   N   C   E

Karlsruhe

Maximum combat range - Mustang I

Bordeaux

Lyons

SWITZERLAND

FIGHTER RANGES (FROM TANGMERE)
AND GROUP BOUNDARIES FOR
OPERATION "OVERLORD"
6 JUNE 1944

Reproduced by Mapping and
Charting Establishment.

©Compiled and drawn by
the Directorate of History.

difficulty hitching a ride on a destroyer back to England; but when he arrived at Tangmere he found his unit had left for Normandy.[30]

Luftflotte 3, meanwhile, was also reinforcing, and one hundred more German fighters arrived in France by 10 June. The aerial component of Hitler's response to the invasion nevertheless involved not so much piloted aircraft as his weapons of revenge, the totally indiscriminate V-1 'flying-bombs,' the first of which were launched at London on the night of 12/13 June. By 0600 hours on the 16th about 120 missiles had left the ground, of which about 30 per cent reached Greater London; and at a commanders' conference that morning Leigh-Mallory, now AOC-in-C of the AEAF, reluctantly accepted that Second TAF and the Allied bomber forces would have to help in the Crossbow campaign by attacking launching sites.[31]

Coningham allocated seven squadrons to the task, including the Canadian Bombphoons. An attack by No 438, conveniently still based at Hurn, close to England's south coast and northeast of Bournemouth, exemplified the difficulties posed by such bombing operations.

This Squadron was responsible for the standby of two pilots at the end of the runway from 0430 hours to 2315 hours but, regardless of that, squadron made three separate 'ops' sorties against a NOBALL target, landing at Manston to refuel and re-bomb for the second two. On the first there were eight a/c, on the second six and on the third five. On the first sortie the target couldn't be found but a successful attack was made on a 10 vehicle convoy. On the second the target was bombed with only five aircraft. Two aircraft were abortive due to engine trouble. Although there were no direct hits on this trip, there were very near misses. On the third trip, five aircraft found the target again obscured by clouds and the bombs were dropped on the West wall of France as they returned to Base.[32]

The squadron diary did not define just how close a 'very near miss' was, but on the whole such bombing was ineffective. Thanks to large concentrations of light multiple Flak it was also so costly that, after 20 June, fighter-bomber attacks on V-1 sites all but ceased, the task being left to medium and heavy bombers that attacked – often fruitlessly – from heights above the range of light anti-aircraft guns. Such was the threat of the V-1, however, that fighter-bombers still had a role to play – mounting anti-Diver patrols on the English coast, searching for flying-bombs in flight primarily to give the ADGB and British anti-aircraft batteries advance warning.[33]

One of the squadrons receiving such warnings was No 418, whose activities saw an abrupt change from supporting Bomber Command's interdiction campaign over France to dealing with the hundred or so V-1s the Germans were now launching every day. ADGB assigned twelve units to the task of intercepting these flying-bombs: eight single-engined squadrons (equipped with Tempest Vs, Typhoons, and Spitfire IXs and XIVs) and four twin-engined Mosquito squadrons. The Mosquitoes were intended for night interceptions, and because the V-1's bright exhaust made it visible for miles, the Intruder squadrons which had not yet been equipped with AI were among those recruited. No 418 flew its first anti-Diver patrol on the night of 16/17 June.[34]

Searching for flying-bombs dominated the squadron's activities for the next ten weeks and by the end of August crews had flown nearly four hundred sorties, but their efforts were not well-rewarded – at low altitudes Mark II Mosquitoes were barely fast enough for the work (it was usually necessary to attack from a dive) and a crew had to be either very skilled or very lucky to bring down a bomb. Flying Officer D.N. McIntosh, a navigator/radar operator, later described one chase:

I looked down. Sure enough, there was a red glow, the exhaust of a V-1. It seemed to be moving fairly slowly, poor judgement on my part. We went into a dive to get more speed. The V-1 was ahead of us. In the blackness, of course, all we could see was that small burning sun in front of us. Because the V-1 was smaller than a plane, you had to get fairly close to get in a telling shot.

We were doing more than 350 mph by this time but we weren't gaining. In fact, we were dropping back a bit. In a minute or so, we had to face the truth that the damn thing was running away from us.[35]

No 402 Squadron's experiences were somewhat different. In early August it began to switch over from the Spitfire IX to the Spitfire XIV which, with its Griffon 65 engine, could overtake flying-bombs. Moving to Hawkinge on the 9th to begin V-1 patrols, pilots declared themselves happy with their new aircraft and their new role. 'The view of the Channel from Hawkinge is excellent and we can watch these bombs coming in from the other side very easily. Sometimes four or five come over almost together and all personnel are becoming extremely "sound" conscious.' Seeing and hearing the missiles was not enough, however, and for the first few days No 402's pilots experienced considerable frustration, mounting a hundred sorties without success, while the anti-aircraft gunners in the vicinity averaged at least 60 per cent hits. Two days later the squadron scored for the first time, downing three, and its eventual tally would rise to five.[36]

By mid-June Spitfire squadrons were thus allocated tasks depending on which formation they belonged to, those of ADGB concentrating on defensive duties, either searching for flying bombs or patrolling over the Normandy beachhead, while their colleagues in No 83 Group, along with the rest of the AEAF, turned to the offensive. Once this change had occurred, 'there was not a single sortie which did not result in some kind of action.' On 14 June, for example, Nos 126 and 144 Wings escorted bombers to the E-boat pens at Le Havre, the raid being something of an experiment – though a highly successful one – as Bomber Command's first attempt at daylight operations since No 2 Group's move to the tactical air force in May 1943. Only one Lancaster was lost, and No 127 Wing 'covered itself with glory' when eight pilots of No 421 attacked a formation of about twenty FW 190s and Me 109s and came out of the mêlée claiming eight victories, two probables, and two damaged, for the loss of one pilot and three aircraft (two of the latter in crash landings).[37]

Fighter squadrons now employed a number of different tactical formations depending on role and circumstance. Perhaps the most useful, especially when the enemy came up in strength, was the 'fluid-six,' developed in North Africa and offering flight commanders both additional flexibility and greater fire-power. Such developments, however, could not mitigate against simple rotten luck, one section of four from No 443 Squadron disappearing on 16 June when it ran into a large number of Focke-Wulf 190s.[38]

At the time we knew nothing of the circumstances, only the bare fact that a complete section of four aircraft had failed to return from a scramble. The four aircraft had taken off late in the evening and eventually located a force of Focke-Wulfs, which they attacked. In the fading light they were not aware that they had engaged a far superior force. The Germans, realizing their advantageous position, stayed to fight, and all four Spitfires were shot down. [Flight Lieutenant D.M.] Walz's own aircraft was hit in the engine and the petrol tanks exploded. He lost little time in baling out and landed safely in a field. After some adventures on the ground he was eventually assisted by the local peasants and returned with the tragic story.[39]

The three others had been killed in their aircraft.

Flying the widest variety of missions was the Spitfire IX. Aside from protective patrols and sweeps in search of the Luftwaffe, Spitfire IXs also began to attack targets allocated to them by the army or to patrol designated areas searching for enemy transport. They continued to dive-bomb some of their objectives, with the usual mixed results. On 17 June twelve machines of No 443 Squadron set out to bomb four bridges east of the Caen canal but managed only two hits (while having two bombs hang up). Five days later, despite plastering a suspected ammunition dump near Caumont, there were no spectacular secondary explosions – possibly an indication that no dump existed. That same day 126 Wing sent Nos 411 and 401 squadrons on dive-bombing missions, but these proved somewhat embarrassing as both units entirely missed their targets.[40]

The more specialized Bombphoons generally enjoyed greater success. On 24 June No 143 Wing, with twenty-four aircraft, attacked the village of Cheux, an objective for 15th (Scottish) Division in Montgomery's Operation Epsom, due to open the following day; and although four of the forty-eight bombs missed, the others were accurate, both AEAF and Second Army commending the three squadrons on their work. The need for ground troops to follow up immediately was, however, driven home by the 2nd Gordon Highlanders, who reported on the 26th that 'A very heavy storm broke just as the Coys started and it was obvious that there would be no opportunity for the promised air support,' resulting in some very bloody fighting. The 46th (Highland) Brigade, of which the Gordons were a part, echoed that view, stating that 'weather was bad and no air s[up]p[ort] was possible; the speed of the advance was in consequence slower than was hoped.' Rain was not, thankfully, a factor everywhere that day, and in an attempt to interdict possible German counter-attacks the wing's No 439 Squadron flew against bridges, experiencing extremes of failure and success. Of the three missions, the first, against the highway bridge across the Orne at Amaye, was completely off the mark; a second attack on the same target scored two direct hits and four near-misses, though the bridge still stood; and the third, against a structure at Thury-Harcourt, was a total success, ten direct hits completely destroying the target.[41]

Near the end of June, Operation Epsom, which was supposed to bring Caen within the grasp of Second British Army, ground to a halt despite support from Bomber Command and the fighter-bombers of Second TAF. What Epsom managed to do, however, was to bring out the Luftwaffe, as did the American capture of Cherbourg. 'They are putting more fighters up now,' Leigh-Mallory observed, 'in order to defend some of their more important rail movements.'[42] No 411 Squadron encountered fifteen FW 190s on the 27th, claiming to have destroyed one and damaged three, but losing one pilot captured. The following day the three Spitfire wings flew 314 sorties, 'and took an amazing toll of enemy aircraft,' according to the AFHQ narrative, 'twenty-six destroyed, one probably destroyed and twelve damaged,' though losing five pilots to Flak. On the last day of June Normandy-based Spitfires claimed a further eighteen destroyed and three damaged in 323 sorties, 144 Wing getting credit for an incredible (even given the usual inaccuracies of such claims) ten destroyed and one damaged in 112 sorties.[43]

Above the land battle, then, the tactical air forces had by and large achieved their primary objective of securing air supremacy over Normandy, an easier task than anticipated given the state of the German air force in mid-1944. Forced off their bases close to the front and operating from facilities around Paris, enemy fighters could spend little more time over the battlefield than their enemies, losing an advantage the Luftwaffe leadership had counted on to help make up for deficiencies in numbers and quality. Losses of up to 10 per cent on one operation were not unusual, and in June RCAF pilots alone claimed a hundred German aircraft destroyed, two probably destroyed, and thirty-five damaged. No 421 Squadron led the way, claiming twenty destroyed; No 442 followed with fifteen, and No 401 with fourteen-and-a-half. No 411's claim of twelve-and-a-half destroyed in June matched the total achieved in its entire history before D-Day.[44] No doubt these claims were reported with the usual exaggeration, but the totals were still significant. Although German fighter production would rebound, the loss of so many pilots could not be made good.

The German army, too, was bleeding in France, 'losing an average of 2,500 and 3,000 men a day, yet reinforcements were crawling across France with fatal sluggishness, lapsing into confusion after they crossed the Loire and entered the most deadly fighter-bomber target zone.'[45] Prisoners of war captured in the course of the campaign served as expert witnesses to the effects of allied air power. 'A *Gefreiter* of the 2nd Panzer Division was a gunner in a Mark IV on the move (date and place unknown), when they were attacked from the air by fighter bombers. The bombs all missed narrowly, but several cannon shells pierced the armour in front of the turret, killing the W/T operator and one other. The engine caught fire, so the crew abandoned the tank and watched it burn out.'[46] They were not alone, as an Obergefreiter from the same division 'observed a Tiger tank brought to a standstill by cannon fire from the air, which ripped off the tracks.'[47] The commander of Panzer Lehr, General-leutnant Fritz Bayerlein, later argued that his formation, 'worth four armoured divisions of the kind used in the East ... should not have been sent into action in the West, because even this highly-trained and heavily-equipped Division had no chance under the conditions of air superiority which it was bound to meet in the West.'[48]

To maintain pressure against the Wehrmacht required Herculean efforts on the part of maintenance personnel. On 1 April the aircraft serviceability rate had been 74 per cent; this rose, in spite of the heightened tempo of operations, to 88 per cent on 5 June and dropped only marginally, to 85 per cent, as the number of sorties and hours flown began to peak. The Germans would have been envious, had they known; according to intelligence reports only about half their single-engined fighters were serviceable in mid-June.[49]

With Second TAF seemingly doing well, Air Marshal Coningham (who had fallen out with Montgomery, his fellow-egotist, near the end of the desert campaign) was energetically complaining about the latter's slow rate of advance. In his initial planning, Montgomery had hoped to take Caen on D-Day and the open country to the south of the city – ideal for airfields – in the days that followed. Indeed, Coningham had hoped to have a good number of his Spitfire and Typhoon squadrons established in France by the end of June, and all of them within seven weeks. Without French bases he did not feel he could launch operations at a rate sufficient 'to maintain air superiority ... [nor] harass enemy communications and delay the build-up of enemy ground forces which could ... concentrate in superior numbers against the bridgehead.'[50]

Sir Arthur Tedder, another critic of Montgomery's, was also concerned with the lack of elbow room for the tactical air forces. Tedder, as Eisenhower's deputy, was worried that, despite what airmen had achieved in slowing the movement of German forces to the battlefront, the Wehrmacht might yet 'assemble a reserve ... overcome the good effects of the Transportation Plan and drive the Allies back to the water's edge.' Broadhurst, more closely involved in day-to-day operations, was less worried[51] and, in any case, the front did begin to move in July as Second British Army, assisted by the heavy bombers of the US Eighth Air Force and Bomber Command as well as the mediums and fighter-bombers of Second TAF, moved on Caen, taking most of the city on the 9th. For the tactical airmen, the most immediate benefit from the liberation of the city was the removal of 'a strong enemy Flak point from the pilot's consideration.'[52]

In the Typhoon squadrons, ground support operations were the order of the day as Second Army tried to hammer its way down the road towards Falaise. Aircraft waited at readiness until called upon, but many missions ended in failure and frustration, No 438's attempts on 9 July being typical: 'It was an Army Co-op effort and was not successful. The Squadron failed to find the target at the proper time and as it was a bombing show very close to our own line only one pilot recognized the target well enough to drop his bombs.' No 439 was more fortunate, sending nine aircraft against vehicles in a small wood southwest of Tilly, all of which managed to drop their bombs in a tight group and follow up with strafing attacks. Directly in front of 50th British Division (which Canadian Typhoons had supported on D-Day), the copse may have contained elements of the redoubtable Panzer Lehr, and the attack thus earned a congratulatory message from XXX Corps which concluded that, 'It was indeed an exhilarating sight for our forward troops.'[53]

One squadron diarist noted that pilots 'realize to a greater extent what full support means to the Army after having had numerous conversations with troops in the front line.' Yet there was little they could do to make the average soldier more directly aware of their efforts. Always poised to take cover from the ubiquitous German mortars, constantly aware of the possibility of being sniped at, and most secure at the bottom of his slit trench, the infantryman rarely saw the fighter-bombers upon which his commanders relied so heavily. As one reconnaissance regiment observed, 'Visible air support is a great morale raiser for troops who do not understand what air support is when they can't see it.' A regimental war diary might mention a Typhoon attack once or twice in the eleven-month campaign in Northwest Europe, but no more.[54]

The average soldier was probably even less aware of the activities of the Spitfire squadrons which, while preferring to take on the Luftwaffe in dogfighting, did not hesitate to attack ground targets and often served as fighter-bombers. Jacks-of-all-trades like their RAF counterparts, the Canadian Spitfire squadrons were heavily involved in the July offensive, and even No 402 (still part of ADGB) began to escort bombers to France. As usual, weather often interrupted operations, but pilots had to be prepared to carry on as soon as conditions improved, and also had to be ready to change from one role to another.[55]

On 2 July, for example, No 401 Squadron waited until mid-afternoon to take off on a dive-bombing operation, but then had its target changed from a small town and crossroads to a couple of bridges eight miles south of Caen, where I SS Panzerkorps was headquartered. Its primary mission completed, the squadron then swept the area looking for Wehrmacht transport but sighted two dozen enemy aircraft instead. In the dogfight that followed Flight Lieutenant I.F. Kennedy shot down an Me 109 and Flying Officer W.T. Klersy destroyed another. 'F/L Kennedy's guns jammed after he had hit the Hun badly but he flew alongside the Jerry as he went in to crash. The enemy pilot waved frantically that he was through and had to crash land. He evidently thought he was going to receive the finishing touch. On crashing into a field the enemy kite was smashed completely.'[56]

Other successes followed. On 13 July No 441 Squadron, while on a reconnaissance in the Argentan area, southeast of Falaise, spotted a dozen FW 190s and claimed to have shot down ten without loss. The next day No 416 (which had been formed, it will be remembered, in November 1941) was engaged in a routine defensive patrol when it ran into a formation of Me 109s and experienced its most successful day to date, claiming seven destroyed and three damaged in three combats, while suffering only one Spitfire damaged.[57] Under such mounting pressure, and suffering irreplaceable losses in pilots, German aircrew now looked on bad weather as a godsend; and the breather provided by summer storms was critically important to the German groundcrews, who could use the time to improve on the generally abysmal serviceability rates in their front-line units. After a bout of rain in July, for example, the technicians managed to get 65 per cent of the Luftwaffe's 450 aircraft in hand ready for operations – but it did them little good. No sooner were their machines flying again than the wastage rate began to climb.[58]

While usually engaged in protecting their own forward lines of communications, German fighter-bombers sometimes attacked the Allies' airstrips in the beachhead – against very long odds. 'Bags of excitement this afternoon when several Jerry Aircraft flew over our dispersal,' reported No 439 Squadron on 14 July. 'They were entertained with a great reception of Flak to the accompaniment of Spitfires. Our guests retired rather rapidly, leaving some of their numbers behind. After supper enemy aircraft again came over our dispersal probably much to their regret as they were just greeted by Ack-Ack, and chased about by Spitfires. One was seen coming down, hell bent for election. It hit the ground a few miles away and exploded.'[59]

At headquarters commanders worked to alter the organization within Spitfire wings in order to render them – so it was hoped – more efficient. Effective air support leans heavily on the smooth flow of information, where the delay between transmission and reception of a message is dependent, in no small part, on the number of hands it must pass through. On 14 July, in order to streamline communications, the Spitfire wings were reorganized and expanded from three-squadron to four-squadron formations and sectors were eliminated from the chain of command, for early experience in the bridgehead had demonstrated that No 83 Group's signals units were not up to the task of maintaining an uninterrupted flow of information between wings, sectors, and higher formations. The decision led to the disbandment of No 144 Wing – it being the most recently formed – with its squadrons transferred to 125 (RAF) Wing, 126 Wing, and 127 Wing.[60]

In the Mediterranean theatre, the experiences of No 417 Squadron mirrored those of its Spitfire brethren in Northwest Europe. The Luftwaffe in Italy was so weak that there could be no justification for keeping fighter squadrons employed exclusively on air superiority duties. Therefore, soon after Squadron Leader O.C. Kallio replaced a tour-expired W.B. Hay, three of the Royal Navy's Fleet Air Arm pilots were attached to the Canadians for three weeks to teach ground attack tactics. Racks for 500-lb bombs were fitted under the wings of the Spitfire VIIIs, and pilots began to practise bombing runs over nearby Lake Vico, with results similar to those in Northwest Europe – that is to say, mixed at best. Their first sorties as fighter-bombers occurred on 26 June with an uneventful attack on a crossroads near Aqualagna in which two of twelve bombs may have hit close to the target.[61]

As in France, such low-level attacks against ground targets were significantly more dangerous than combatting German fighters. Between the creation of the squadron in November 1941 and the end of May 1944, eight pilots had been killed, gone missing, or been captured as a result of enemy action; four of them in one day, on 19 April 1943, during the Canadians' first real introduction to air combat. In contrast, from June 1944 until hostilities ceased eleven months later, the squadron lost nineteen pilots, mostly to Flak, and at least ten more were forced down during this period, parachuting to safety behind Allied lines. Grim reality was foreshadowed in the death of one pilot in June and reinforced on 3 July when another pilot was killed by Flak; two more died within a week, one while attempting to strafe a truck.[62] In all, the shift to a ground attack role contributed to a six-fold increase in the squadron's monthly casualty rate.

As Allied armies pushed north, beyond Rome, No 417 first moved from Venafro to Littorio (just outside the Eternal City) on 10 June, then to Fabrica on 17 June, where operations were washed out by rain for three days. (It was here that the unit formally converted to a fighter-bomber role.) On 3 July the Canadians reached Perugia, about eighty miles north of Rome, where they remained until late August. The new field had a good runway, and the men were able to pitch their tents in an orchard near the landing strip. The weather, however, was hot, dry, and oppressive, suitable for operations but not for comfortable living, and the only bathing facility was a small muddy stream. Flies and dust led to an outbreak of gastro-enteritis, though the use of flytraps and the new insecticide, DDT, eventually brought it under control. (There was also an outbreak of venereal disease, the squadron medical officer detecting eight cases during July and August.)[63]

During the summer Allied troops slowly drove the enemy back, with the southern half of Florence – that part of it south of the Arno River – falling on 13 August. The advance forced No 417 to shift bases again, and often; on 23–26 August it moved to Loreto airfield, twelve miles south of Ancona and within one mile of the Adriatic coast, the move leading the squadron diarist to reflect upon the importance of air power in the Italian campaign: 'First light this morning beheld a dusty caravan proceeding bumper-to-bumper through the treacherous, winding roads of the Appenines. It is very gratifying to know that our convoys of 100 or more vehicles can proceed, bumper-to-bumper, from one place to another with little fear of bombing or straffing [sic] from the enemy.'[64]

The writer had hit upon one of the most marked characteristics of the war in Europe at this time – the completeness of Allied air superiority and the freedom of movement it allowed. On 15 August I Canadian Corps, which had been in reserve in the vicinity of Foligno, on the western slopes of the Appenines, began to move across the mountains, preparatory to the assault on the Gothic Line which (it was hoped) would carry the Eighth Army into the Lombardy plain. 'A million shells were transported and 12 million gallons of petrol. The Canadian Corps alone moved some 280 carriers, about 650 tanks and some 10,700 wheeled vehicles during the ensuing week.' The Germans knew about this move from their Italian agents on the ground, but the Luftwaffe was incapable of informing or interfering. During the summer of 1944 the Desert Air Force had twenty-three squadrons of fighters while the US Fifteenth Air Force added another twenty-four, for a total Allied force of not less than 650 fighters; in contrast, on 20 July there were just sixty-one available to the Germans in Italy.[65] As in Northwest Europe, the Luftwaffe in the Mediterranean could do little more than bewail its fate.

Between 26 June and 5 September the Mediterranean weather was perfect for flying, and pilots were up almost every day, sometimes on escort missions for medium bombers, but mostly on Rovers or armed reconnaissance sorties. Rovers began in mid-August, the name referring to forward observation posts, each with an air force officer and an air liaison officer who would select targets and then transmit their locations directly to the fighter-bombers.

A fundamental part of the organization was the provision of a 'Cab-rank' of aircraft timed to arrive in that area at regular intervals of about 30 minutes. These aircraft would be briefed at their airfields to attack pre-selected targets but, for a period of about 20 minutes before the attack, they would be required to orbit close to the forward line in order to give Rover an opportunity to call and brief them for the attack of priority 'fleeting' targets. If no call was received the aircraft would attack their original targets and return to base.[66]

Facing a similarly devastated Luftwaffe, airmen in France were also able to experiment with their tactics and organization, exploring ways to provide close air support to the army with as few delays as possible. The key, of course, was to get controllers close to the front, and to this end 'visual control posts' – armoured cars or tanks, in, or close to, the front line and fitted with radios to connect them with brigade HQs, the 83 Group control centre, and any aircraft under their direction – were organized and sent well forward. There they would either instruct aircraft already in 'cab rank' – on station, waiting for assignment – to a specific objective, or they could call for support from group and take over direction of the aircraft the latter scrambled. The similarity with Italian Rovers is obvious.[67]

After several years of development, trial, and error, it was now possible for hard-pressed regiments and battalions to call for quick (or 'impromptu') air support; and the time between request and response was reduced from an hour or so to a matter of minutes. At least that was so in theory: but army and group headquarters were not always co-located, and the army and air staffs sometimes spent considerable time in discussion 'before orders were issued for the engagement of the target.'[68]

It should also be noted, moreover, that impromptu tactical support figured fourth on the air force's list of priorities, behind the maintenance of air superiority (or, preferably, air supremacy), interdiction missions aimed at limiting the enemy's ability to maintain large forces in the field, and pre-planned close support. Though Pointblank and the ineptitude of the German high command had allowed the achievement of the first some time before Allied armies stormed the beaches of Normandy, nagging doubts remained in the minds of British and American planners as to the kind of resistance their enemy would put up in the air. It was not until 14 June, as we have seen, that they felt sufficiently confident to allow tactical formations to take the offensive; and not until July that they seriously considered releasing substantial forces for close support work. Even so, the airmen involved learned the intricacies of their new role more or less on the job, for training in the necessary techniques before the campaign had been rudimentary, emphasis being given instead on the combat skills needed to fight off the Luftwaffe.

One of the first tests of the new close support technique was Second British Army's next attempt to bludgeon its way through the copse-dotted farmlands to the east of Caen – Operation Goodwood. As with previous attacks, this one, when it opened on 18 July, was preceded by a massive bombardment, 'one of the most awesome air attacks ever launched on ground troops,' which saw over 15,000 bombs falling on German positions on and near the Orne. Less typical was the reliance on tanks, especially those of the 7th, 11th, and Guards Armoured Divisions, in order to limit the mounting casualties to infantry formations. The mailed fist, however, was not up to such an ambitious undertaking and, after some initial success, the assault bogged down and came to a halt in bad weather on the 20th (the same day German officers attempted – unsuccessfully – to assassinate Hitler).[69]

Air officers blamed the loss of momentum on the army, the AOC of No 83 Group observing 'that if the armour had gone on, accepting more casualties, it could have reached Falaise that evening but this was an appreciation for the Army to make and he could therefore not table any official pronouncement on this aspect of the battle.' He had based his criticism on his understanding that Montgomery was prepared to lose four hundred tanks in the battle, but stopped instead after half that number became casualties.[70]

Broadhurst also criticized the army for its use, or misuse, of heavy bombers. Before the attack, he had produced a map of known enemy anti-tank positions behind the front line and had offered to have the bombers pummel them in a second pass – the first would concentrate on the German defensive crust – but Second Army refused on the grounds that its own tanks would be deep within German defences, among the anti-tank weapons, before that bombing could begin. The air forces did their job in the first phase, giving the 'outer edge of the enemy defensive area a terrific crack,' but, in the event, that was insufficient to guarantee success on the ground.[71]

The sad fact of the matter was, that despite years of training, Anglo-Canadian ground formations were not up to the task of breaking through well-prepared German defences. Inadequate cooperation between infantry and armour was a major weakness, compounded by an excessive reliance upon ponderous, set-piece, frontal assaults that wore the defenders down through attrition but cost the attackers dearly. The generals, having miscalculated the number of infantrymen needed for this kind of fighting, now found it next to impossible to make up the shortage. Even when commanders recognized these problems, the middle of an offensive was no time to reinvent doctrine or retrain an army group, so the air forces were called upon to increase firepower to the point where German defences – it was hoped – would crack.[72]

Once the initial heavy air bombardment had ended, air support in Goodwood was the task of Second TAF alone. Rocket Typhoons and Bombphoons were on call throughout the attack to take out anti-tank guns or armour impeding the British advance, and one visual control post (commanded by Second Lieutenant P.M. Roberts of the 29th Armoured Brigade, the lead formation of the 11th Armoured Division) proved the potential of 'cab rank.' Operating from a Sherman tank, just as the offensive was losing momentum, this young officer directed fighter-bombers onto several targets, including a concentration of tanks in Bourguébus Wood, and Panthers and Tigers dug into houses in Bourguébus village, which elements of 7th Armoured Division were subsequently able to occupy as the limit of their advance. He also called on cab rank aircraft to destroy enemy tanks moving towards Bourguébus and a bridge near Soliers, but when another bridge came up as a target he had run out of the red indicator smoke shells he was using as target markers.[73]

Roberts's exploit was an exception to the general rule, however, the experiences of his divisional headquarters being more typical as its Visual Control Post (VCP) was put out of action in the first hours of battle. Later, 21st Army Group reported some dissatisfaction with the new procedures in its report on the Normandy Campaign: 'The Visual Control Post, as its name implies, was intended for visual control of aircraft. Experience has shown that in average country the number of occasions on which the apparatus can be sited on a feature sufficiently commanding to obtain a visual look-out over the target area, is too few to be of practical value.' Instead, the VCP, now referred to as a Forward Control Post (FCP) and with an airman added to its strength, stayed close to divisional or corps headquarters and briefed aircraft on the way to their targets. According to 21st Army Group, this system was the 'quickest and most effective form of intimate air support.' No 83 Group agreed, adding that the FCPs proved capable of maintaining contact with aircraft at twenty to twenty-five miles range thanks in great part to the heroics of maintenance staff, who managed to keep equipment functioning under very trying conditions and through intensive (and exhausting) operations. They could call on aircraft already in the air in their cab rank or at readiness on the ground, and then brief them on the way to the objective, with local artillery marking the target with coloured smoke.[74]

With the failure of Goodwood, Second British Army receded into the background of the battle for Normandy. The Americans began their massive right hook, Operation Cobra, on 25 July, while First Canadian Army undertook Operation Spring – the first phase of an intended advance from Caen to Falaise. As we have noted, First Canadian Army was formally associated with No 84 Group; but because the latter's headquarters and control centre would not arrive in France until 6 August, the job of organizing close support for the Canadians fell to No 83 Group on this occasion. Unhappily, that resulted in a jury-rigged communications system between No 83 Group, First Canadian Army, and Second British Army.[75] Spring was an unmitigated disaster. Lieutenant-General Guy Simonds's II Canadian Corps failed to take any of its objectives, and though close air support might have been extremely useful, there is no evidence that any was requested. Total casualties were about 1500, of whom 450 died. 'Except for ... Dieppe,' the Canadian Army's official history observes, 'there is no other instance in the Second World War where a Canadian battalion had so many casualties in a single day ... The 2nd Canadian Corps had struck a stone wall.'[76]

The 'stone wall' made Typhoon operations significantly more complex. Intent on denying the approaches of Falaise to Montgomery for as long as possible, soldiers of what was left of the I and II SS Panzerkorps had prepared deep, thick-roofed dugouts all through the area of Verrières Ridge; and although these could still be bombed, the fuse settings required to penetrate them rendered the bombs much less effective against 'soft' targets of opportunity like transport or airfields. For a time, then, No 83 Group had lost some of its flexibility.[77]

As it was, the nearly static front in the Anglo-Canadian sector opened up when, having punched through the enemy's defences on 25 July, the Americans poured into his rear areas. By early August the German Seventh and Fifteenth Armies had been almost completely enveloped, so that, as Generalleutnant Hans Speidel later remembered, 'Two army commands, four corps commands, nine infantry divisions, and about five Panzer divisions were being pressed together in a square about six to ten miles in size between Falaise and Argentan, under converging artillery fire of all calibers and exposed day and night to continuous bombing.' Those who could were struggling through the escape route to the east, which the Allies eventually called the Falaise Gap. After flirting with the possibility of launching an airborne operation to close the corridor, and deciding that it was too risky, Montgomery chose instead to use the tactical air forces to block the enemy's escape. From 4 August pilots were kept on thirty or sixty minutes readiness, and when they did fly targets were plentiful.[78] But with the front now increasingly fluid, mistakes were also common.

Wing Commander Judd led our squadron this afternoon in a Wing Show against an organized enemy defensive locality at Canteloup ... just East of Aunay-sur-Odon. The target was very near our bomb line and the weather was sunny but very hazy. Our own artillery was to lay Red Smoke as a signal to attack the target but no Red Smoke was seen. Wing Commander Judd then split the wing up into squadrons and led 439 Squadron down on some transport he had seen on the road just north of Aunay-sur-Odon. As the third man down released his 1000-lb bombs, he realized that the vehicles were our own. All our remaining aircraft held their bombs and released them safe at various other points ... Unfortunately, the six bombs released on the convoy were quite accurate and five or more MT were knocked out ... The entire incident was extremely unfortunate and it is hoped that none of our Army lost their lives as a result of this error.[79]

Such incidents did not diminish the Typhoon pilots' zeal in seeking out German transport; 'but the dry weather and the lack of defiles enabled the enemy to carry out diversions of traffic across country when the main roads and railways were obstructed by bombing. In spite of the special effort of the Tactical Air Forces in trying to seal the gap ... it was not possible in practice to make such interdiction of this gap entirely effective.'[80] Closing it could not be achieved by the relatively painless application of air power, but would require hard fighting on the ground.

Aspiring, above all, to come to grips with their German counterparts, the now-fluid front offered Spitfire pilots more opportunities to practise the less romantic aspects of their trade as the Luftwaffe worked ever harder to defend its airfields and the army's lines of communication. After an armed reconnaissance on 27 July, for example, No 442 reported that its pilots 'damaged more MT and gun sites. They sighted two enemy aircraft south of Liseux, gave chase to the Dreux area aerodrome where they were bounced by 40 Me 109s and FW 190s. The squadron was split and had the hottest time so far, the Huns showing plenty of offensive spirit.' No claims were made. That day No 401 met the enemy on more even terms, its twelve aircraft encountering fifteen, and had better luck, as 'a real dog-fight followed and the Squadron did itself proud,'[81] claiming eight destroyed.

There was also some excitement within the reconnaissance squadrons, in their case over technical changes, as policy-makers suggested in late July that they convert to the state-of-the-art Spitfire XIV or XXI. No 400, already equipped with unarmed photo-reconnaissance Spitfire XIs, pined for the excitement of the occasional dogfight; so much so that the arrival of an RAF armourer was interpreted as a sign that the squadron would convert to Spitfire IXs, 'and the approach of the day when the Squadron pilots would have a more positive reply to enemy aircraft than the usual "evasive action."' Two squadrons did in fact switch to new machines, with one flight from No 400 converting to Spitfire XIVs equipped with both oblique and vertical cameras (which became known as the Spitfire XIX), and No 414 re-equipping with Spitfire IXLFs with oblique cameras only. No 430 was supposed to get modified Spitfire XIVs when they became available, but those pilots in No 400 hoping for a more exciting combat role were disappointed as the Spitfire XIX, like its predecessor the Mark XI, was unarmed.[82]

To the Germans, fighter-reconnaissance units were an obvious danger regardless of how they were equipped. On 28 July, a typical day, weather forced the cancellation of several missions; but those pilots who managed to complete their tasks discovered the locations of over twenty tanks and even more transport, and No 430 managed to get excellent photographs of gun positions (for which it received a letter of congratulations from XII Corps) while the latter prepared to move against elements of II SS Panzerkorps as part of the general advance.[83] More complimentary messages came in on 2 August.

In addition to the photographs taken on the Photo/R missions, which were of predetermined targets, pilots also photographed targets of opportunity encountered during tactical reconnaissance sorties ... The photographs were processed and interpreted immediately after their return, and some sixty tanks and twenty other vehicles were recognized in the pictures. These were subsequently attacked by Typhoons with the result that thirty-seven tanks were destroyed and most of the mechanized transport.

The prompt detection of the arrival of such reinforcements, and the swift reorganization of air attack, was undoubtedly of the greatest value to the Army. That this value was recognized is indicated by a message received at 83 Group Headquarters, from 2nd Army on the morning of August 3rd: 'Forward troops signal, Great show put up yesterday. Very useful Tac/R and splendid work on Tank Concentrations. Thank You!'[84]

Most sorties were still in support of Anglo-Canadian formations grinding their way forward, especially VIII and XXX British Corps from 30 July to 6 August as they advanced through Caumont and Mont Pinçon respectively; but in the early days of August First Canadian Army began planning a breakthrough battle from the left of the Allied line, called Operation Totalize, in which Second British Army would play a supporting role. The Canadians had Falaise as their objective, a daunting task that would prove a severe test for commanders, staff officers, and soldiers alike.[85]

Available information indicates that the forward positions are supported by the bulk of the enemy's tanks and self propelled guns (many of which are dug in) whilst a proportion of the enemy infantry are employed on the improvement of the rearward position. They are accordingly available in this rearward position to form the nucleus of defence in the event of a break in by our forces. The enemy apparently relies on being able to get tanks and self propelled guns back to support the infantry available in the rearward position in the event of the forward position being penetrated and overrun. Thus, in effect, two operations are required to break in, break through, and penetrate fully the enemy defensive system in this area.[86]

Massive air support, including the aircraft of No 83 Group, was part of the solution, but only an intelligent and imaginative application of such resources would lead to success.

If all available air support is used for the break in on the enemy's forward defensive position, there will be no fire support available for the break through on the rearward defensive position except diminished gun support, unless a substantial pause is introduced, with resultant loss of momentum. If, on the other hand, the break in is supported by heavy night bombers operating at night, and all available gun support, the heavy day bombers and medium bombers together with such heavy night bombers as may be made available on the turn around will be available for the break through, at a time when gun support begins to decrease. In this manner it should be possible to maintain a high tempo in the operation through to its final objectives.[87]

On 8 August over a thousand heavy bombers pounded their targets until midnight, II Canadian Corps moving forward just before the last bombs fell, guided by artillery markers and artificial moonlight created with searchlight beams reflecting off clouds. The tactical air forces prepared to harass the enemy at daylight, should he attempt to retreat, and hoped to rout him, but the ground attack did not move forward as quickly as planned. Typically, the Canadians were met by successive lines of infantry and anti-tank guns braced by dug-in Panther and Tiger tanks, which soon brought both armour and infantry to a halt.[88]

Results were disappointing from the army's point of view, but the air force judged its own success or failure according to different criteria, and on 9 August No 439 reported one of the most spectacular engagements of the battle as it supported Second Army's operations to the right of the Canadian offensive.

This job turned out to be the Christmas package of the day. The enemy were reported to have dug in at Jean Blanc, and created what promised to be a very troublesome foremost defended locality. Our squadron, led by F/L Scharff, took off at 19:15 hours carrying 500lb bombs to blast this foremost defended locality into submission. The heavy haze had dissipated somewhat by this time and the target was quite easily approached from the northwest at 6,000 feet. An almost vertical dive attack was carried out from the southeast and the entire west half of the village seemed to rise into the air. F/L Scharff led the boys back in a beautiful straffing [sic] attack from the southwest at 1,000 feet right down to the tree tops. All fields, bushes, and roads leading into the village of Jean Blanc from this direction were viciously sprayed by cannon fire. At this point our own artillery dropped more red smoke-shells on the northwest corner of the target so we roared in again with cannon talking! This time the attack was pressed home until some of the aircraft were in danger of being hit by ricochets as they zoomed over the town. A small orchard in the northwest corner of the town was sprayed unmercifully in this attack and the Jerries glimpsed in there, had to be a long, long way down into their slit trenches to escape it. A large wooden house was burning furiously and the entire village was choked in a mantle of smoke and dust. On the last attack the pilots turned away in a steep turn between the central church and the adjacent buildings. In this case to say that the mission was successful is a gross understatement even if written with a capital 's.' All aircraft and all jubilant pilots returned safely to base, feeling that close support was rendered to our armies.[89]

The offensive, however, came up short of the mark. From 7 to 11 August the Canadians and British advanced nine miles, but the front stabilized before they could penetrate to Falaise, forcing them to prepare for yet another attack.[90]

While the Canadians planned the successor to Totalize, code-named Tractable, Typhoons continued to strike at German positions, but such intense effort led to strained conditions on the airfields, where the very dirt seemed to have allied itself with the enemy. 'Speaking of dust, we plow through about four inches of it whenever we come to Dispersal,' reported No 438's diarist. 'To help matters along, the road for tracked vehicles goes all along our dispersal tent and Orderly Room truck. When the wind blows in the wrong direction, we and all the equipment are caked with it. It's a peculiar dust, light as a feather and when one steps in it or a wheel plows through it, it mushrooms up just like smoke.' The solution was straightforward. 'For the first time in France, the runway was sprayed with water to reduce the hazard of take-off and landing, due to heavy billows of dust. This should promote speedier take-offs and landings as considerable time is wasted waiting for dust to clear. A pipe line had been installed on both sides of the runway for this purpose and will prove invaluable once the system is organized.'[91]

Just in time, as Allied land and air forces combined to destroy the German Seventh Army. Operation Tractable saw First Canadian Army fighting its way towards Falaise, which troops entered on the 18th, while Second British Army advanced on the Canadians' flank and American forces swept around the far right and encircled the bulk of the enemy's forces. The latter thus found themselves in a pocket whose only opening – to the east – was slowly being closed by Canadian forces moving southward and Americans advancing north to meet them. The ever-narrowing gap forced the Germans to move by day as well as by night in a desperate attempt to get their soldiers and equipment out of the pocket before it closed, thus offering the tactical air forces perfect targets of opportunity. Except for Nos 400 and 402 (engaged in reconnaissance and V-1 hunting, respectively), all RCAF fighter squadrons, including the Spitfires, entered the fray without regard to aircraft types or designated roles. From D-Day to the end of July No 416 had left seventy-five vehicles destroyed, smoking, or damaged, but in the first fortnight of August it accounted for 117. Attacks were not only aimed at transport, but at communications in general. Beginning in August, No 403, when on armed reconnaissance, equipped six of twelve Spitfires with bombs to attack road and rail junctions as well as bridges, the other six acting as escorts; but the Germans were not about to allow themselves to be slaughtered, and anti-aircraft artillery was very much in evidence.[92]

On the 13th, No 442 posted the highest (and hence grisliest) score in 83 Group, with sixty vehicles and ten tanks accounted for in thirty-five sorties as pilots flew as low as possible – debris from an exploding truck damaging the wing of one Spitfire. The next day No 126 Wing set an all-time record, to date, with 211 vehicles claimed destroyed, smoking, or damaged, with No 442 again leading with seventy-seven vehicles, five tanks, and six armoured fighting vehicles. On the 15th, some Typhoons began to operate without bombs, relying on their four 20 millimetre cannon to destroy vehicles, thereby eliminating the time spent in bombing-up to increase the number of missions they could carry out in a day. At Broadhurst's orders, following the Luftwaffe's redeployment to airfields around Paris, some squadrons gave up finger-four and fluid-six formations and operated in pairs, cutting down on turn-around time by eliminating the need to form up, and increasing the number of missions a pilot could fly in a day from the usual three or four to as many as six.[93]

The Allies dominated the skies over the Falaise pocket, with collision a far greater hazard than the Luftwaffe. When on the 15th No 414 left Odiham for B-21 and began tactical reconnaissance missions, its pilots having completed their conversion training to Spitfires, it found more and more aircraft operating over an ever-diminishing territory. In mid-month, crews had even more trouble than usual differentiating between friend and foe on the ground and in the air, so higher headquarters decided to allocate zones between the tactical air forces to allow each formation to familiarize itself with a given area. The American US Ninth Air Force was given the main task of attacking enemy forces within the pocket while Second TAF tried to prevent movement through the gap, attacked convoys making for the Seine crossings, and intercepted supply echelons trying to bring up fuel and ammunition to the beleaguered Seventh Army.[94]

No 441, with 125 (RAF) Wing, recorded that 'the slaughter was at its height when No 441 Squadron entered the arena on the afternoon of 18 August,' as it attacked with 500-lb bombs, 20-millimetre cannon, and machine guns. No 126 Wing declared that 'today was the biggest day for Allied aircraft since "D" Day,' and 'the entire Wing had the best day in its history insofar as enemy transport was concerned,' claiming over seven hundred vehicles destroyed or damaged, while pilots often ran out of ammunition or were low on fuel before running out of targets. Casualties among the Spitfires were light. No 442 had four aircraft hit by Flak but lost no pilots, while No 411 had one pilot bale out. No 401 was the hardest hit that day, losing two pilots missing in fifty-one sorties (six operations) while accounting for 167 vehicles.[95]

No 127 Wing listed the 18th as 'the busiest day in [its] history,' claiming to have destroyed or damaged almost five hundred vehicles in 290 hours of flying time, expending about thirty thousand rounds of 20 millimetre ammunition in the process.[96]

At 18.00 hours all patrols and readiness were cancelled and a concerted effort from the entire Wing was requested to attack transport in the Vimoutiers area. From then onwards until dusk every available aircraft, including the Group Captain's Spitfire V, was put into the air. They took off in two's and flew until they ran out of ammunition. They returned to base, were refuelled and rearmed, and were off again. When operations finished 486 vehicles of one kind or other had been destroyed or damaged, making an average of 2$^1/_2$ vehicles per sortie flown. A number of our aircraft were hit by *Flak* and several crash landed away from base but only one pilot, F/O Leyland of 421 Squadron, went missing.[97]

The Typhoon squadrons had been developed and trained especially for this kind of work, and on the 18th they inflicted severe punishment. All of No 438's fifty-seven sorties were strafing operations, on which it lost two aircraft with their pilots, while No 440's experiences were similar. 'The Squadron was called upon to make an all-out effort strafing the retreating Germans and MT convoys in the Falaise sector. This was a record-breaking day for the Squadron and surpassed the previous record day of one month previous, July 18 [Operation Goodwood]. In all a total of 54 sorties were flown for a total of 52 operational hours.' Like their colleagues on Spitfires, Typhoon pilots often ran out of ammunition before they ran out of targets, though of No 440's seven missions on the 18th the last two uncovered no enemy. 'Everywhere was strewn smoking vehicles and wreckage ... Everyone did their utmost to keep our aircraft up in the air and the co-operation of the groundcrew was magnificent,' while 'one outstanding feature was the fact that not one bomb was dropped and for the first time Typhoons played the role of fighters to a greater extent than ever before.'[98]

The slaughter continued for days, though Second TAF's claim of over three thousand vehicles destroyed on 18 August would not be surpassed.[*] On the evening of the 19th the pocket was finally closed when Poles fighting as part of First Canadian Army met with Americans at Chambois, but the bloodletting continued through the 20th, when a final German attempt to break out of the trap failed and more precious tanks, trying to open the pocket from the outside, were destroyed. With weather closing in, the 21st proved to be a bad day for flying, but pilots and ground crew who had been pushing themselves to exhaustion did not complain. 'At the risk of being considered unpatriotic, we record with some personal satisfaction that weather prevented any flying today.'[99]

More than ten thousand German troops died in the Falaise pocket and a further fifty thousand were taken prisoner, while about twenty thousand escaped, fortunate to leave behind an area that was both junkyard and slaughterhouse. Sir Arthur Coningham later reported 'a scene of major destruction and carnage,'[100] while the supreme allied commander, General Dwight D. Eisenhower, rarely given to hyperbole, could not forget what he saw there, two days after the battle was over.

The battlefield at Falaise was unquestionably one of the greatest 'killing grounds' of any of the war areas. Roads, highways, and fields were so choked with destroyed equipment and with dead men and animals that passage through the area was extremely difficult. Forty-eight hours after the closing of the gap I was conducted through it on foot, to encounter scenes that could be described only by Dante. It was literally possible to walk for hundreds of yards at time, stepping on nothing but dead and decaying flesh.[101]

The Allies needed the road network around Falaise to continue their advance, so infantry and armoured units saw for themselves the destructiveness of air power. As the 2nd Argyll and Sutherland Highlanders of Dempsey's Second British Army moved forward, 'The route took the Bn through a road 7 miles long where the most appalling destruction had been caused on enemy transport by the RAF. Dead Germans, dead horses and mangled transport were heaped up on the verges of the road.'[102] If the sights of butchery were enough to suppress appetites, the odour was worse.

The acrid smell of burning and burnt-out vehicles was bad but the stomach was turned by the stench of the dead men and horses – and there were thousands of dead horses.

---

[*] It should be noted that claims of vehicles destroyed, like air victories, were usually greatly exaggerated, not only because of the normal confusion arising from dozens of aircraft operating in the same area but also because many destroyed vehicles still looked sound from the air and would thus be targets for several attacks. Operational Research Sections found only three thousand vehicles of various types in the Falaise Pocket after the battle - the result of ten days' fighting by air and ground forces.

The smell was all-pervading and overpowering. So strong in fact that pilots of light artillery observation aircraft flying over the area reported that the stench affected them even hundreds of feet in the air.

Above the battlefield shimmered a miasma of decay and putrefaction; everything was covered with flies and blue-bottles. In the hot August sun the cattle which had been killed only days before were masses of crawling maggots, and the unburied Germans, swollen to elephantine grossness by the hot sun inflating the gases in the stomach, lay with blackened faces in grotesque positions. Here there was no dignity of death.[103]

In the midst of the carnage, pilots who had been shot down during the fighting attempted to make their way back to friendly lines. One of these was Flight Lieutenant A.F. Halcrow of 411 Squadron. He had just finished strafing a convoy in the early afternoon of 18 August when he committed a classic error, coming around for another run against the trucks. A burst of 20 mm Flak struck his glycol and oil lines, 'the engine about leaped out of its mountings,' and Halcrow baled out. Captured almost immediately following his landing, his captors helped themselves to the food and cigarettes in his escape kit. Halcrow was now in the situation about which pilots often speculated: What would happen if they fell into the hands of enemy troops they had just been strafing? In this case, the Germans behaved correctly. Hauled into the presence of the local commander, he was questioned briefly and then placed with seven other prisoners, mostly Americans. Having surmised that the guards were a mixed lot of Romanians, Greeks, Italians, Poles, and Russians, the Canadian and a few other prisoners tried to talk their way to freedom, but the Germans were not so naïve as to leave prisoners in the hands of unreliable troops, and there was always a 'pure' German nearby to supervise the guards.

After spending the night in a barn, 'along with seven cows,' the prisoners were loaded into a truck, but the convoy came under severe shelling, forcing guards and prisoners alike to scatter for shelter. Halcrow and an American found themselves in a German dressing station, which was dive-bombed by Republic Thunderbolts of the American tactical air force, and in the ensuing disorganization the Canadian, along with a German stretcher-bearer, decided to make their way to British lines, which they did with the help of a 'large' Red Cross flag and directions from the local parish priest. Three days after being shot down, the pilot joined the ranks of the tiny minority who managed to avoid a prisoner-of-war camp after baling-out over enemy territory.[104]

In the larger scheme of things, the American break-out spread to other parts of the front in late August and Allied forces soon overran France and Belgium. The front line crept further away from bases in the British Isles, forcing those night-fighter squadrons guarding the troops from the air to move to the Continent to hunt bombers operating almost exclusively after dark. Already scheduled to join Second TAF, No 409 began to operate from Carpiquet aerodrome (near Caen) on 24 August, covering the advance into Belgium.[105] No 410 moved to Glissy, near Amiens, on 22 September, and by the end of the month its aircrew had flown a series of defensive missions over Belgium and Holland, penetrating as far as Aachen in Germany. Both squadrons found their sorties to be generally quiet, although several crews reported – with considerable interest and some awe – the spectacular night-time launchings of V-2 rockets (see chapter 10).[106]

The main effort, of course, still took place during the day, and near the end of August the fighter-reconnaissance squadrons were introduced to innovative operational procedures as pilots assumed short-term duties with the army in the front line. On the 20th one of them was attached to an armoured reconnaissance regiment, and two days later, from a scout car near the front, he directed 430 Squadron on three tactical reconnaissance missions, sending pilots to check out areas along the army's axis of advance, which took it through Amiens and Arras, while the Canadians cleared the Channel ports on the left and the Americans (with French divisions) liberated Paris on the right. No 414 began similar operations, by now labelled contact reconnaissance patrols, in mid-September, and they proved most useful in a mobile battle or during a pursuit, when Army Headquarters was not up-to-the-minute on events at the front and hence incapable of properly briefing reconnaissance pilots. Furthermore, the system allowed information to reach – quickly – those units that most needed it, namely, those leading the advance.[107]

For RCAF fighter pilots, the Normandy campaign ended when the front line moved to the Seine, outside their operational range. As they prepared to move on and ready themselves for the next battle it was time to take stock – which, for Spitfire pilots, meant counting up hours flown, aircraft shot down, and vehicles shot up. All nine squadrons with No 83 Group were satisfied with their performance, with the three least successful each claiming nineteen enemy aircraft destroyed, and the three most successful claiming over thirty (401 claimed forty-three and a half), for a grand total of 239. In all, fifty-eight RCAF Spitfire pilots were killed or captured in the course of the campaign, with twenty-one brought down by Flak, seventeen shot down by enemy aircraft, twelve crashing due to mechanical failure or similar problems, and eight lost to undetermined causes.[108]

The three RCAF Typhoon squadrons lost twenty-five pilots, seven from each of Nos 438 and 439, and eleven from No 440, while casualties among the reconnaissance squadrons were less evenly divided. No 400, concentrating on taking high-altitude photographs, lost no pilots on operations, but Nos 414 and 430, flying at low altitudes to get a close look at the enemy and sometimes strafe his transport, lost four and six, respectively.[109]

Air power had proven crucial in the Normandy campaign, as 21st Army Group was quick to acknowledge. German commanders could well have echoed that view. In a postwar interrogation, Göring unwittingly admitted his own weaknesses as a commander when he suggested that 'the Allies owe the success of the invasion to their Air Forces. They prepared the invasion, they made it possible, and they carried it through,' while without such air power, Göring claimed, it would have been possible to bring up German reinforcements and make full use of armoured units. General Jodl, Hitler's chief of staff, agreed: 'I am of the opinion that had we been able to oppose the Allies in the air in equal strength the Anglo-American invasion would have been repulsed. Success was due solely to unquestioned Allied air supremacy.'[110]

Yet the story of Second TAF during the battle for France was not one of perfect success. Although the Spitfire IX was one of the best close-in fighters of its time, like all Spitfire variants it had evolved from a design specification dating from the mid-1930s and aimed at securing British air space from attack. As a result, its maximum practical range of 430 miles, which translated into a radius of action of about 170, rendered it useless after the break-out. Montgomery's 21st Army Group had been forced to rely on American aircraft 'at a time when air support was most needed to support the advance and to take advantage of the favourable targets which a forced retreat presents to air attack.'[111]

War is a complicated business, and though the British and Americans (especially the latter) commanded immense resources, there was nothing to guarantee this materiel would be well applied in every case. Neither of the two major national air forces involved in the Normandy campaign had seen fit to equip itself with long-range fighters until the autumn of 1943. Thus in the summer of 1944, even as air forces were learning more about the tricky business of supporting ground troops, a task which, ideally, required a capability for prolonged loitering over the battlefield, there were not enough Mustangs to go around. The Spitfire could not be replaced, and RCAF pilots would have to do their best with the tools available.

10
Final Battles, 1944–5

The summer of 1944 saw Allied forces break out of their crowded beachhead in Normandy and overrun large areas of France and Belgium, their advances closely followed and supported by the tactical air forces.

One evening following a hurried departure by German garrison troops, we landed our Spitfires on Brussels main aerodrome at Evère. The British troops had not paused here during their hot pursuit of fleeing Germans. Consequently, when we airmen entered Brussels main square at dusk, on September 6th, we were soon mobbed by thousands of cheering civilians. I have never before or since heard such spontaneous roars of welcome. Crowded sidewalk restaurants were serving heaping plates of rabbit and venison stews, and every table was adorned with long loaves of fresh, French bread. Huge jugs of red wine from seemingly inexhaustible cellars were replenished at every table by laughing, drinking, shouting waiters. Street musicians entertained the passing parade of singing, well-dressed civilians, surging along the avenues to the next square. It was Mardi-Gras and every other fete that had been suppressed for five years. Groups of roistering citizens, would capture a prize pilot for their celebrations and carry him with them as they progressed from one bistro to the next. The beaming landlords proclaimed free drinks for their regular patrons and for the conquering heroes. Late in the night I was carried by my jubilant liberators to one of the best rooms in the central Majestic Hotel. Mercifully sleep terminated the lengthy patriotic speeches of my benefactors. Before dawn I was awakened by a waiter with a huge pot of coffee and a large omelette made with fresh mushrooms. The thoughtful, kind celebrants had re-assembled all the missing pilots at my hotel, and a convoy drove us back to Evère. Hang-overs were forgotten or disregarded, overwhelmed by the enormity of that previous night's welcome.[1]

For fighter units it was time to relocate forward, closer to the new front, and 'the ground crew enjoyed themselves immensely during these moves.'

They have been seeing a great deal of France and its inhabitants. The road has led through many blasted towns and villages and it seemed rather strange that the people of these towns will still smile and wave at us even though their homes have been demolished. We have also seen the results of our strafing of enemy transport, German

MT vehicles by the score litter the fields along the highway. Knocked out enemy tanks and armoured vehicles as well as some of our own were also seen.[2]

The obvious success of the Normandy campaign was, to some extent, deceptive, however, having done little to sort out all the difficulties of army/air force cooperation. The soldiers were particularly impressed by close support work – and the closer the better – while Air Marshal Sir Arthur Coningham, Second TAF's commander, perceived more important tasks for his pilots. 'It is doubtful,' he observed after the war, 'whether the Army appreciate that the best application of our tactical bombing effort is often well ahead of the advance,' on interdiction missions. Moreover, in spite of doctrine stressing unity of effort in the air, 'boundaries between army formations were applied to supporting squadrons and groups as well, with the consequence that German forces unwittingly crossing these imaginary lines were suddenly immune to air attack.'[3]

Experience gained in the desert campaigns of North Africa and through the experiments and exercises of Army Co-operation Command had demonstrated the need for close liaison between ground and air forces. Air conferences, or army/air staff meetings, were supposed to convene every day (though in reality it was every other day), and on these occasions staff officers in blue and khaki discussed intelligence reports, the army's air requirements, priorities, airfields, and future moves. Each meeting was, in theory, followed by directives from the group headquarters to its constituent formations stating in general terms what air operations were to be carried out next day, while, if further resources were required, the necessary requests were submitted to Second TAF and 21st Army Group.[4] Calls for quick, or 'impromptu,' support would, of course, be dealt with on their merits as they arose.

Doctrine and theory quickly broke down under the pressure of operations, however.

Throughout the campaign considerable difficulties were experienced between Army HQ and Tac Group HQ staffs over the manner in which the available air resources were being employed, and particularly in regard to the engagement of targets nominated by the Army. It was considered that these difficulties were due to personalities and consequently were at their worst when the HQs were separated.

An analysis of the periods when relationships were at their best and when the results achieved reached the highest levels, shows that the variations were closely related to the personality aspect. When there was a clash of personalities, both staffs were affected at all levels and the RAF attitude tended to become one in which an Army requirement was regarded with suspicion, and as something to be treated as an opportunity for destructive criticism rather than a matter of joint interest and importance.

Under the circumstances requirements for air action other than those of direct military interest, were frequently used as a reason for refusing Army requests, although the facts did not always support the contention.

These remarks refer to the higher level of Army/Tac Gp HQ and are not applicable to the lower levels of GCC, Wings, and Squadrons, or to the pilots themselves.

In all these cases the whole approach to the support of the Army was different and was marked by enthusiasm and a readiness to do the job which was wholly admirable.

It was felt that the origin of these difficulties had its root in Air Force anxiety to preserve the autonomy and separate entity of their service, an anxiety emphasised in their view by the fact that the main function of the Tactical Air Force is to provide air support for the Army. In fact, the principle regarded as being at stake was never questioned by the Army at any time whatsoever, and any fears which may have been entertained in Air Force circles cannot be considered as having the smallest foundation.[5]

As Major General C.C. Mann (once chief staff officer of First Canadian Army) explained in 1946, everyone had ignored the 'human factors,' and for that reason 'this conception – that war-like operations can be conducted with maximum efficiency under a system of Joint Command at this level [army/group]' – was 'unsound.'[6]

If staff officers at the army/group level had trouble getting along, it may have been a result of the poor example being set by their superiors. After four months of operating on the Continent, Coningham and Montgomery continued to bicker over the use of air resources. Taking up his cause with Harold Balfour, the undersecretary of state for air, Coningham hoped 'that Balfour now realised why he was so averse to bombing Allied villages just because the Army thought that as road centres their destruction would hinder the enemy; a view that was making him unpopular "in high places."'[7]

Even though the commander of 21st Army Group and his counterpart at Second TAF were responsible for planning and executing all ground and air operations in the British area, the former 'spent most of his time at a forward Tactical Headquarters whereas Coningham remained at his Main Headquarters in Brussels ... However, what Coningham called the "deliberate disassociation" of Montgomery from his Main Headquarters caused problems. "He and I used to meet at his Tac HQ at intervals to discuss and to decide upon our joint plan for the conduct of the battle by the Army and Air Forces in the British sector," but the absence of Montgomery from daily meetings meant that the "responsible Soldier" was not in touch with the "responsible Airman." This method of doing business, thought Coningham, was wrong.'[8]

Personality clashes within the high command were certainly not smoothed over by Operation Market Garden, an attempt to seize a corridor to the Rhine and a bridgehead over the river which the Allies could use to outflank the Siegfried Line and end the war by Christmas. In planning it, the lessons of North Africa – especially the need for unity of command in the air – had been jettisoned. Second TAF was not allowed to enter the area while troops and supplies were being dropped and was banned from attacking targets of opportunity on the ground unless the enemy fired first – no doubt a precaution to avoid firing on friendly troops but, at the same time, a notable loss of firepower. As a result the only Canadian fighter unit to be directly involved in the Arnhem operation was No 402, which as an ADGB squadron escorted some of the air-transport missions.[9] Complications did not end there, however, for the entire operation was controlled from London by US General Lewis H. Brereton's First Allied Airborne Army headquarters, so that the airmen of No 83 Group had no means of contacting the soldiers except through the latter's commanders in England. Thus the inevitable problems associated with air/ground operations were vastly compounded by the Allies' own organization.

Market Garden, though ultimately unsuccessful, posed a serious threat to the German position on the Western Front and the enemy reacted according-ly. In the words of No 83 Group's ungrammatical diarist, 'in this latter half of the month, the German Air Forces, which had by now come to rest in German bases and which had time to collect itself after its rout from France, re-appeared and threw themselves in great strength into opposing the push into Holland.' The first intimation of this came on 25 September, while the British were admitting failure in the Arnhem sector and ordering the battered remnants of the 1st Airborne Division to withdraw. No 441 Squadron was patrolling the Nijmegen area when it encountered twenty or more Me 109 fighter-bombers, ostensibly on their way to destroy the bridges upon which army units, thrusting towards Arnhem, relied for resupply. The Germans jettisoned their bombs, and another force of Me 109s, acting as high cover, then pounced; by the time the turbulent mêlée ended, No 441 claimed three enemy machines destroyed while losing two pilots of its own, both of whom were killed. No 416's experiences were almost identical. 'At last the Hun is starting to come up and fight and the boys chalked up three 190s to their credit, however all was not milk and honey because we lost F/L Errol H. Treleaven and F/L "Dyke" England got pretty badly shot up, and was taken to the hospital.' In all, RCAF squadrons claimed thirteen victories while losing three pilots killed.[10]

Though postwar commentaries have claimed that, 'by early September the air situation in the west could scarcely have deteriorated further, and to all intents and purposes the Luftwaffe was a spent and exhausted force with seemingly little future prospect of recovery,' the performance of German pilots over the Arnhem corridor 'was the first sign of the very remarkable recovery which was to make itself obvious over the next few months.' The 27th was a record day as No 83 Group's wings claimed forty-six enemy aircraft shot down, two probables, and twenty damaged in the Luftwaffe's continuing and determined effort against the bridges at Eindhoven and Nijmegen. Among the RCAF formations, No 126 Wing claimed twenty-two destroyed and ten dam-aged. Of its four squadrons, No 412 had the best reason to be satisfied, as 'today was the biggest scoring day in the squadron's history with 14 enemy aircraft destroyed and 7 damaged.'[11] Even the Typhoons had opportunities to fight their enemy in the air, an excellent boost to morale after months of being shot at, often accurately, by multi-barrelled anti-aircraft artillery. No 438 was carrying out its usual rail interdiction missions when four of its aircraft were jumped by about twenty Me 109s and FW 190s; and in the ensuing dogfight Flight Lieutenant H.G. Upham shot one of them down for the squadron's first kill of the war.[12]

All in all, No 83 Group lost fifty-nine pilots in the month of September, or one for every 155 sorties flown, a casualty rate it could well bear indefinitely, while the Typhoon pilots, who had seen so many of their friends fall to enemy Flak during the Normandy campaign, lost only two or three aircraft per squadron in the course of the month.[13]

Calm followed the storm, and units took advantage of a diminished intensity in operations after Market Garden to take turns on two-week refresher training at one of the many armament practice camps in England, relearning both air-to-air fighting and bombing skills, though some pilots 'felt the expenditure of ordnance was a total waste of time and money. Hell!, we had been doing nothing else for months and we were considered pretty good.' In fact, the opposite was probably true. Postwar analysis indicated that to obtain a hit on a pinpoint target required, statistically, an average of 463 bombs; at armament practice camps, however, where there was no Flak, 'only' 110 bombs were needed to achieve the same results. The wings also carried out training at their own airfields – a high priority given the number of replacement pilots coming on strength every month – and in 127 Wing all incoming pilots had to complete a five-hour operational training course before flying any missions. Interestingly, this rule applied to second-tour men as well as pilots fresh from Operational Training Units, an indication of how rapidly tactics and techniques were changing.[14]

With few German aircraft operating during daylight hours and the army's need to clear the Scheldt estuary and open the port of Antwerp before it could advance into Germany, both defensive patrols and close support receded into the operational background. Second TAF concentrated on bombing and armed reconnaissance missions usually aimed at road, rail, and canal traffic, and railway interdiction increased in sophistication, bomb-carrying fighters now endeavouring to make three cuts on each line so that repair crews could not work on all of them simultaneously. Normally, after-action reports were tinged with ambiguity, but sometimes results could be spectacular, as in No 438's 16 September attack in which it claimed the utter destruction of an ammunition train. If sufficient fuel remained after the main task had been carried out, the flight was then free to seek out and strafe secondary targets, usually along roads or railways,[15] though strafing and bombing required different tactics. With the latter, 'one dives directly on the target at a 50° angle or more, releases the [bombs] and hopes that good ol' Isaac Newton will carry them the rest of the way, in the proper manner, while one politely and post haste got the hell away. With guns, it's different: one dives about half a mile from the target, levels out on the deck, centers the ol' needle and ball, steadies the luminous bead on the target and blasts away. One is then pretty sure of creating quite a mess at the receiving end.'[16]

For the three RCAF reconnaissance squadrons, operations were less varied, and their pace was set more by the vagaries of weather than the activities of friendly or enemy forces. Thus in October, even though Anglo-Canadian armies were no longer engaged in a major offensive, 5 (RCAF) Mobile Field Photographic Section (one of two in 83 Group) processed some 469,000 photographs; in its busiest twenty-four hours it produced 26,400, while on only four days that month did Second Army request fewer than 10,000 prints. For those taking the pictures the job was exacting, especially for No 400 Squadron, whose missions – many against targets in Germany – were true tests of endurance. On 4 September one pilot landed after dark with only fifteen gallons of fuel in his tanks – enough for fifty miles – after more than four hours in the cramped cockpit of his Spitfire.[17]

Because of where they were now flying, encounters with P-51s (American Mustangs) escorting B-17 Fortresses would become a common occurrence for daylight reconnaissance operations, and not all American pilots were grade A in aircraft recognition. On 5 October, 400 Squadron's 'F/L P.G. Wigle was bounced by 4 American Mustangs Mk. III at 17000' near Deurne. Two Mustangs fired at 600 yards range. Pilot evaded first two a/c which fired and noted battle letters of other two aircraft which were PZ-W and PZ-V. F/L G.S. Brown was continually bounced by Mustangs escorting Bombers in Almelo Area.'[18]

All pilots faced a variety of hazards, hence the Allied policy of giving aircrew a break from the dangers of operations. RCAF Spitfire squadrons rotated pilots after each had flown two hundred hours, but Typhoon pilots, carrying out a higher percentage of dangerous low-flying missions in more temperamental aircraft, were posted to instructional or other duties after a hundred sorties. Squadron Leader H.H. Norsworthy, DFC, for example, completed his tour after 102 hours in the air. In order to minimize the stress that inevitably accompanied the end of their tours, pilots were commonly 'screened' before reaching the hundred-sortie mark. In No 438 a pilot could be taken off operations anytime after his ninetieth,[19] with Flying Officer I.W. Smith, the last of No 439's originals (who had been with the unit when it was No 123 in Canada) being screened out after ninety-five. 'He has had a rough time, and met with three accidents during his tour. The first when he ran into a bomb dropped by his Wing Leader on landing; the second on landing from operations with a flat tire that almost caused his Typhie to overturn; the third was the worst, he was making a forced landing on returning from operations and his aircraft slid into a forest knocking off both wings.'[20]

The policy of replacing pilots before they self-destructed or became a burden on their comrades led to a heavy turnover within units. Five new pilots arrived on No 401 Squadron at the end of September 1944, when 'many of the original D-Day Squadron are already back in England or on the last few hours of their tour.' Similarly, in mid-December, No 411 reported that none of its airmen had seen action with the unit before its move to France in June. On occasion, however, the number of available pilots slowed to a trickle. 'Replacements have been badly needed but we have been advised that at present the supply at 83 G[roup] S[upport] U[nit] is exhausted,' reported 440 Squadron in late November, and the problem was still acute a month later. 'Considerable difficulty has been experienced in obtaining replacements. 83 GSU at times have none available for posting and during heavy operational periods, a great strain is thrown on the remaining pilots.'[21] (The Germans faced far worse problems, one of which was the lack of any system of operational tours. Their pilots flew until they were killed or permanently disabled, or carried over the edge of mental breakdown.)

Leadership was important at such times, and some squadron commanders stayed on longer than the two hundred hours or hundred sorties dictated by policy, Squadron Leader W.G. Dodd, DFC, accumulating three hundred hours (in eighteen months) on No 402 before he departed.[22] When a CO did leave, however, it often meant promotions for some of those remaining. 'Late in the day word was received that the OC [of 411 Squadron], Squadron leader R.K. Hayward's tour was finished. F/L E.G. Lapp ... was appointed to command the Squadron in his place and was promoted to the rank of Squadron Leader. F/O G.F. Mercer ... was appointed as Commander of "B" Flight and was promoted to Flight Lieutenant. The promotion of these officers was well received by all. S/Ldr Hayward DFC brought the Squadron through a most difficult period due to an almost complete turnover of pilots. The state of morale is very high which augurs for continued good results in future.'[23]

For those who were screened the separation could be bitter-sweet, as Bill Olmstead remembered, decades after giving up command of No 442 Squadron.

Experience had proven that it was difficult to obtain a posting to an operational squadron. Now I was to learn that it was also difficult to leave. Records had to be completed, which would take a week or so. All my flying clothes had to be returned to stores with explanations of why I had so few remaining of the many signed for over the years. 'Lost due to enemy action' satisfied the stores officer as he signed off my equipment, including 'Pistol, revolver,' 'Jacket, Irvine' and 'Mae West.' The finality of the procedure seemed prophetic in a way, for I realized that I was through with operational flying forever, that an important stage in my life was complete ...

My last few days of waiting seemed interminable. It was difficult to accept that I no longer had a position of command, with duties to perform that required concentration and action. By December 22 I had received all of my clearance documents, said final goodbyes, and trudged out to the waiting Anson aircraft for the trip to England. Within minutes the lumbering Anson circled the 'drome and then set course due west for the three-and-a-half-hour flight to Tangmere. Much further west lay Canada and home, but strangely that knowledge did not prove very comforting. I knew that I was leaving a way of life that I would never know again, the struggle for survival that few would understand except those who had lived it, and it was tearing me apart.[24]

The need to administer such changes meant that, regardless of what happened at the front, the paper war continued unabated, oblivious to any so-called quiet period in the campaign. An air force built on the concept of permanent bases and entrenched administrations at every level found it difficult, at the higher levels, where such circumstances still prevailed, to understand the problems that beset the administrative echelons of the Tactical Air Force. A squadron's administrative burden was sufficient to cloud the distinction between the important and the mundane and at times administrators' frustrations were reflected in Operations Record Books as they were asked to carry out near-impossible tasks.

Why are we continually hounded for routine returns when mail to the UK takes up to ten days to arrive? The desk division should also take into account that our working conditions are far from the best and that also we move around a great deal and this makes it very difficult to time our returns right. Trying to run an orderly room out of a couple of tin boxes isn't the easiest job in the world.[25]

The frequent moves posed other challenges: many maps that squadron head-quarters held were never issued, for example, but there was, initially, no procedure for disposing of them and storing the surplus became something of a burden. It was not until the end of December, six months into the campaign, that procedures were inaugurated by which such useless materials could be disposed of.[26]

Administrative challenges were numerous, arising from all aspects of oper-ations – including obvious material needs. At times just trying to keep a squadron supplied for routine flying was a logistical nightmare, and the com-plaint that 'we haven't got enough gasoline to do local flying' kept unit quar-termasters on their toes trying to locate supplies of fuel. Even clothing could pose a problem. In Normandy, to take one case, dusty RAF/RCAF blues had quickly come to resemble the blue-gray of the Wehrmacht. The simple solution was to have all personnel wear the army's khaki dress, but as late as Novem-ber some had not made the switch, and headquarters at No 83 Group thus felt the need to order all aircrew to wear khaki when on flying operations.[27]

Lack of, or delayed, mail is a universal complaint among service people, and the wartime RCAF was no exception, though there were occasions to take advantage of misdirected missives. 'Life in the Squadron is pretty much the same, except for the fact that mail and parcels arrived some of which belong (or did belong) to pilots whose tour had expired and, as everybody claims, willed their parcels to the active pilots – so now everybody has that satisfied feeling of eating someone else's food and wearing other people's clothes – which are clean.'[28]

Discipline was another matter to be addressed, though most of the time what few disciplinary problems there were could be dealt with summarily, such as the two pilots in No 421 who were given orderly room duty, confined to barracks, and grounded for 'breakage after a small party.'[29] At other times stronger measures had to be taken.

An unfortunate incident occurred in the Mess last night when F/Lt. F.X.J. Regan ... having had a few drinks took it upon himself to criticize vehemently the morale of the Squadron and the efficiency of its pilots. This has happened before and F/Lt Regan had been warned, however, last night was the last straw and the Wing CO is posting him today. F/Lt Regan is our only second tour pilot and a good one – but we cannot afford to have men of his temperament wrecking the morale of the Unit.[30]

The squadron concerned – No 438 – had just lost its newly-promoted Com-manding officer, Squadron Leader P. Wilson, who had been killed in action on New Year's Day, 1945, after only one day in command. For the moment, the squadron was without a CO and, when he did arrive, Squadron Leader J.E. Hogg, DFC, would be killed after a tenure of only two months. It is, perhaps, worth noting that the squadron diarist made no attempt to refute Regan's allegations – indeed, the ORB for the next day observes that a party held at the 'Officer's Club' was 'a huge success' and 'the "get together" afterwards did a lot towards improving the Squadron spirit.'

The post–Market Garden lull allowed a reorganization within the RAF, in which Nos 402 and 441 replaced each other in No 83 Group and Fighter Command, respectively. Accordingly No 441 found itself escorting bombers flying daylight missions from the United Kingdom, while No 402 engaged in potentially more exciting fighter sweeps and armed reconnaissance sorties (without, however, a concommitant rise in its loss rate), its diarist noting that 'the new operational status of the Squadron has much increased the keenness of the pilots.' The most important change was not in the nature of operations but in living conditions, with No 441 gleefully recording that 'the squadron personnel are getting settled into a life of luxury on a permanent station [Hawkinge, Kent] again,' while No 402 stoically related that 'the change to living under field conditions [at Grave, in the Netherlands, with 125 (RAF) Wing] was made without too much difficulty – everyone buckled down and made the best of it.'[31]

That testimony is further evidence that, though pilots and groundcrew were willing to do their duty and preferred to be in the thick of things, rather than back in England, they were not anxious to live uncomfortably while doing it. Units invariably did their best to alter their environment. No 440, for example, went to some trouble in October installing a wooden floor, wooden doorway, and stove in its dispersal tent. 'The dispersal is now very comfortable and is being visited by pilots of other Squadrons in order to get ideas for their own.' All the items of a normal life had to be attended to, No 403 bragging that 'the squadron is now the possessor of four German cars three of which were brought back from Gladbach yesterday, and more furniture for the dispersal and billets.' In other matters, however, and particularly food, a distant and seemingly sadistic administration was in charge, and one diarist noted that he 'never knew that there was so much corned beef in the world. It's all we get three meals a day.'[32]

Nor were No 83 Group pilots and groundcrew targets for V-2 rockets, which on 8 September added yet another challenge to the fighter-bombers' repertoire when the first of over five hundred of them exploded on London.[33] Like the V-1 flying-bomb, the V-2 carried a one-ton warhead, but because it was a supersonic missile, falling to earth from the stratosphere, it gave no warning of its arrival and was entirely immune to direct attack. It was also a totally indiscriminate weapon, not even capable of hitting London with any consistency. Unlike the V-1, it was 'fired from a base only a few yards square, which could be set up rapidly on any small open space,' wrote Coningham.

Furthermore, the enemy appreciated our unwillingness to carry out attacks against sites which were concealed in built-up areas [of Holland], which would entail casualties to the friendly inhabitants, and he deliberately made more and more use of such sites to deter our counter-measures from the air ... The best method available to me for dealing with these harassing weapons was to try and reduce their rate of fire by disrupting the communications to the sites, while the strategic air forces played their part in destroying the manufacture and storage installations further back.[34]

A few weeks after the first V-2 – code-named Big Ben – landed in London, however, pilots began picking up signs – 'contrails,' or condensation trails from the heat of the rocket exhaust – that might help locate launch areas. Some of the first reports came from pilots in 400 Squadron, which on one occasion spotted no fewer than five contrails exiting from the same area. Other units began to report sightings soon thereafter, while at night No 418 added its eyes to the search for Big Bens, looking for the flame of rocket exhausts.[35] As locations were established, possibilities arose of interdicting the supply of rockets to the launch areas.

Whether to isolate V-2 sites or as part of the general offensive against the German communications system, railways always figured prominently on the list of priorities for fighter-bomber operations. While heavy bombers attacked rail centres and marshalling yards and certain major bridges, mediums attacked other bridges and railheads, and fighter-bombers concentrated on rail-cutting and patrolling railway lines to attack rolling stock.[36] No 438 struck hard on 2 October.

Today was the best day we have had at Eindhoven. The sun shone brightly all day and visibility was unlimited. Results also were almost unlimited. Four dive bombing shows were done, three of them with 500 lb bombs, the other using 1,000 lb bombs. The score for the three using 500 lb bombs plus strafing was 6 trains attacked, with 5 of them damaged, the sixth, an ammunition and petrol train of 30 cars believed totally destroyed. It was very spectacular with the smoke rising to a thousand feet. Four tracks were cut as well and a barracks and store room set on fire. On the 1,000 lb raid the Squadron, in conjunction with 440 Squadron attacked the Marshalling Yards at Geldern. All bombs fell on target and results were excellent with all ten tracks cut, double tracks into the yards cut, 20 goods trucks destroyed and the station and town damaged by strafing.[37]

Attacks with bomb and bullet against railways and locomotives were now routine, but some operations – against special targets – required much more planning and preparation. Lock gates on Germany's Dortmund-Ems Canal (which both 143 and 124 wings were to attack on 29 October) were just such an objective, described in 438's diary as 'probably the most important target we have had for ages.' The operation, which aimed at lowering water levels in a section of the canal and hence impeding barge traffic, was a complex affair; while three squadrons (including Nos 438 and 440) prepared to dive-bomb the lock gates with their 'Bombphoons,' a squadron equipped with rocket-firing Typhoons would try to suppress the Flak positions that guarded the locks, a process requiring intimate coordination and precise timing. 'Attack made according to plan,' reported No 438's diarist, 'but lock gates up [ie, open]. Wing dropped 32 × 1000 lb bombs at target point. ... Lock machinery believed surely out of commission.'[38]

More and more, Spitfires also played a role in the offensive against communications, and in the last days of September No 126 Wing replaced its Spitfire IXBs with IXEs, which carried more powerful armament – two .50-calibre machine guns instead of the four .303s that supplemented the two 20 millimetre cannon – and wing racks for two extra 250-lb bombs. A thousand pounds of ordnance (a 500-lb bomb under the fuselage and a 250-lb bomb under each wing) was a heavy burden for a Spitfire, and when, on 18 October, No 412 completed its first sorties with such loads, four aircraft were found to have 'wrinkled' wings on their return. No 442 carried similar bomb loads the following day, however, and Spitfires would continue to haul thousand-pound burdens in spite of possible structural stress; replacement wings were easily obtained. With new aircraft or old, Spitfire squadrons took to their rail-cutting tasks with gusto, and No 442 spoke for many of them: 'After nearly a week of no operational sorties, the Wing started off hammer-and-tongs on its rail interdiction program,' though, admittedly, 'not having bombed in three months the pilots were [either] rusty or completely inexperienced.'[39]

In carrying out such missions little was seen of the Luftwaffe's conventional aircraft, though its phenomenally fast jet fighters were appearing more frequently and 'the miserable tale that the enemy aircraft pulled away became all too frequent.' One pilot in No 441 saw his bullets strike home, but 'no appreciable difference in speed was observed,' and a colleague in No 442 could do no more than damage one a few days later. On 5 October, however, No 401 scored a confirmed kill in air-to-air fighting against a jet when five pilots ganged up on an Me 262.[40]

Conditioned by years of searching empty skies, I became aware of a moving speck ahead and below my flight path. It was approaching rapidly and as I radioed this information to my comrades, the wary bandit half rolled into a vertical dive. A similar manoeuvre and my Spit was screaming for the deck about 800 yards behind the unrecognizable aircraft. A glance at the airspeed indicator confirmed that I had exceeded the maximum safe flying speeds for Spitfires. Although the flight controls stiffened up alarmingly, I pursued my prey whose German markings were now visible. When it appeared that the target and I would become two smoking craters in the blurred countryside, the invader commenced his pull-out. It became evident that I must pull-out of the dive more sharply to get within firing range. I 'blacked-out' as the excessive gravity forces buffeted my aircraft. As vision returned my aircraft gave a sudden lurch. Ahead the strange twin engined fighter filled my gunsight. Soon cannon strikes were seen in the right engine which immediately streaked dense white smoke. A barely controllable skid in my aircraft eased as I decelerated rapidly. A horizontal distance of some 100 yards separated our two aircraft when I glimpsed another Spitfire 200 yards astern pouring cannon fire into the crippled Hun. In rapid succession three other Spits made high speed passes, all registering strikes on the now flame streaked fighter. As the last Spitfire began its attack the German pilot tumbled out of his cockpit ... At a long hectic debriefing it was recorded that we had shot down the first jet-propelled aircraft by British Forces.[41]

An important task for German jets (and piston-engined aircraft) was the harassment of Allied airfields, which, like Grave, were obviously more susceptible to hit-and-run attacks the closer they were to the front – and to Luftwaffe bases in Germany. Suddenly, groundcrew found themselves in the heat and chaos of battle, though squadron diarists often described such attacks light-heartedly. '"Jerry" started to work on us today, dropping anti-personnel bombs around the drome. Several of the boys picked up minor *Flak* wounds as souvenirs, and our Orderly Room looks like a Sieve.' Casualties and the frequency of such attacks could be worrisome, however; four days later, still at Grave, No 421 Squadron reported that 'Jerry came over several times today and dropped 25 pound demolition bombs around the dispersal area. Several ground crew types were seriously wounded and one died as a result of his wounds. The lads are all a bit twitchy because the attacks happen very suddenly and with no warning.' On 12 October 'we had a visit from the jet jobs again today and they dropped two 250 pound HE bombs and killed five men and wounded many more. He [sic] also wrote off one A/C and severely damaged several others. Later two more were dropped but they missed the drome by quite a margin.'[42]

With Second TAF trying to get its units as close to the front as possible, on a few rare occasions even the German army could pose a threat. On 8 October B-78, at Eindhoven, was put on alert as a small pocket of German troops on the other side of the Wilhelmina Canal threatened the base and the infantry units holding the line of the canal were not sure they could contain them. No 400 Squadron and No 143 Typhoon Wing spent the rest of the day preparing to fight, not in the air as they had been trained, but on the ground; and just before midnight No 400 issued rifles to all its personnel, who made their way to shelters to await further instructions. After four hours they were allowed to return to bed, albeit fully dressed with rifles handy, and it was later revealed that enemy patrols had been seen one to two thousand yards from the officers' quarters.[43]

The Typhoon wing's experiences were similar. 'Early in the morning the tannoy aroused all personnel from their slumbers with the news that a pocket of Jerries were close to our field and that an attack was imminent. Officers and Airmen reported to action stations as instructed and awaited further orders. No offensive was made but although we returned to continue our broken slumbers somewhat after, we had to keep our small arms at hand for any eventuality. It is understood that Jerries had been engaged by the RAF Regiment' whose duty it was to guard airfields.[44]

With the front now semi-static, the Germans found time to position anti-aircraft batteries in greater numbers. Second TAF noted on 29 November that 'an interesting feature of the rail cutting in Germany itself was the Ack Ack defences found to be located at vulnerable points. In some spots, especially on Tuesday, this was quite intense, suggesting that the enemy had moved up batteries from deeper in the Reich, to make a 20-mile protective belt between the Rhine and the Ruhr rivers.' Much of the anti-railroad work fell to the RCAF who, representing about a quarter of Second TAF's fighters and fighter-bombers, accounted for over half the rail cuts and a third of the locomotives claimed as destroyed (though less than a fifth of the rolling stock).[45]

Since low cloud and rain or snow often masked ground targets, squadrons began experimenting with a 'blind bombing' technique. Ground Control Interception radar (GCI), with its ability to determine range and direction of aircraft, could guide pilots to the vicinity of a target while the fighter-bombers, flying at eight to ten thousand feet, were beyond the range of light anti-aircraft fire. An Operational Research Section would later report that the technique was as effective as visual level bombing methods – meaning it was not sufficiently accurate for targets like railway lines, bridges, or enemy artillery batteries, but might succeed in hitting a large or dispersed factory or vehicle park. On 30 November No 438 managed to complete such a mission, and though good results were claimed, pilots were more impressed by the fact that the new technique would 'mean much more flying for the Squadron.'[46]

After dark, 409 and 410 squadrons continued with the same familiar work that had engaged their attention since August and September – protecting ground forces from predacious night-bombers and fighter-bombers. Though these nocturnal operations, relying on mottled green electronic displays and the unemotional voice of a controller on the ground, might seem particularly unexciting, statistically each time they went up night-fighter crews had a better chance of shooting down an enemy aircraft than the pilots of the more glamorous Spitfire squadrons. The night-flyers averaged thirty-four sorties per victory, while the day-fighters needed 119. On 23 April 1945 409 Squadron shot down six machines in the same night, though only one of the victims, a Focke Wulf 190, could have been considered a modern operational aircraft; the rest were a mixed bag of obsolete Ju 87 Stukas and Ju 52 transports. Over the whole course of the campaign, the two Canadian night-fighter squadrons flying from continental airfields claimed a total of fifty-three enemy aircraft destroyed, while their own casualties amounted to twenty-one aircrew – with over half the latter dying in flying accidents.[47]*

Also operating at night (and sometimes during the day), though exclusively against ground targets, were the Intruders of 418 Squadron, which, in November, had gone to Hampshire to join their brethren in Second TAF as the sole RCAF unit in No 2 Group. After six weeks of training in ground attack techniques and procedures, they became operational and, in the war's remaining months, would support 21st Army Group – never again claiming an enemy

---

* Two 409 Squadron aircraft were lost on 29 September and others on 29 November 1944 and 12 January 1945. No 410 Squadron losses were on 20/21 October, 29 November, and 21 December 1944, and on 6/7 March and 9/10 March 1945. A tenth aircraft (with its crew) was lost in a flying accident after the end of the war, on 11 May 1945.

aircraft destroyed in the air. Routine on any given night called for the squadron to dispatch ten to twelve Mosquitoes on individual patrols over the battle lines to attack, with bomb, cannon, and machine-gun, prearranged objectives or targets of opportunity; when weather conditions made it difficult to see targets, the squadron would attempt blind bombing.[48]

Wing Commander Fumerton having sacrificed his career to get No 406 re-equipped and reassigned, the squadron's pilots were learning to fly Mosquitoes in early November while navigators trained in a whole new array of electronic aids, including AI Mark X, Monica, and Gee. The RCAF wanted them to replace No 418 in the Intruder role, but whether a replacement was necessary was very much in doubt, for by December 1944 the German night-fighter force, like its daytime counterpart, was in serious disarray: the Allied liberation of France and the Low Countries had deprived its crews of their early warning system, while limitations in fuel and training forced an inexorable decline in skills. Needed or not, after six weeks of intensive training 406 Squadron replaced No 418, undertaking its first sorties on the night of 5/6 December 1944. Penetration patrols became the unit's stock-in-trade until the end of the war as it ran up its score largely at the expense of the Luftwaffe's novice pilots, claiming twenty-three aircraft in the air and ten on the ground while losing eleven men killed.[49]

In the Mediterranean, No 417 Squadron was now operating from Fano, on the Adriatic coast about fifty-five miles southeast of Ravenna. Its Spitfire VIIIs – good judges thought this the best of all the Spitfire variants 'from the pure flying point of view' – flew ground attack missions, bombing enemy-occupied houses, gun positions, and the odd bridge. In November, Timothy sorties were introduced, though each was 'no more than a strafing mission without bombs carried out under Rover control.' Weather ruled, and the fall rains seriously hindered operations; over the ninety-two days the squadron flew from Fano, weather scrubbed out flying on thirty-six, and the previous average of twenty-one sorties per day dropped to twelve. But bad weather benefited the squadron in one way – the high casualty rate of the summer ended, and only four Spitfires and one pilot were lost during the fall.[50] Winter would bring a change for the worse, again.

By early December the Eighth Army had battered its way northwards as far as Ravenna, making it necessary for the squadron to move again. On the 4th the airmen left their comfortable billets at Fano and erected tents – in the rain – at a landing strip at Bellaria, just north of Rimini, where they would experience two of the costliest months in the squadron's history. The string of losses began on 10 December, when two Spitfires collided during a Rover mission, neither pilot surviving, and it continued the next day when a pilot was shot down by Flak and captured. Then, on 31 December, the first of a rash of mechanical failures forced one pilot to crash in the sea, his body washing ashore several months later. This was followed within a few days by a pilot having to make a wheels-up landing when his engine cut out over the aerodrome, while another had to jettison his bomb for the same reason, the projectile striking a building about a mile from the airfield and killing several soldiers.[51]

Encounters with the Luftwaffe were rare, however, and when, on 22 December, three Me 109s intervened during a four-Spitfire patrol in the Verona area and badly shot up one aircraft, it was the squadron's first sight of an enemy fighter in six months. The 109s reappeared in the new year, when eleven of them attacked five of the Canadians, who reported a short dogfight which the enemy quickly broke off.[52]

In Northwest Europe Hitler staked his last significant reserves of men and materiel on the outcome of his Wacht am Rhein offensive in the Ardennes. On 16 December 1944 seven Panzer and thirteen infantry divisions crashed through VIII US Corps lines and headed for the Meuse, intending to cut the Allied front in two, seize Antwerp (which was rapidly becoming Eisenhower's main port), and isolate Allied armies in the north. Despite the assistance afforded by abominable flying weather, which gravely handicapped the Allies in the early days, the offensive was stopped in its tracks ten days later, just short of the Meuse. During the battle, and once the weather improved, German air activity in the area increased noticeably, including Me 262s on ground-support missions.[53]

On the 17th – the day after the Ardennes offensive began – Second TAF had agreed to support the Ninth US Air Force, leaving only a few units to protect the Anglo-Canadian front. Patrols were flown largely behind German lines opposite First US Army, serving as an advanced protective screen against Luftwaffe fighters and fighter-bombers while also providing intelligence about enemy movements – information Allied commanders badly needed to get themselves out of the predicament that weak intelligence work had put them in. When the skies finally cleared on 23 December, five days of intense aerial activity followed. On Christmas Eve, as airfields instructed their personnel to carry weapons, the tactical air forces launched so many sorties that air-traffic controllers were almost overwhelmed, and a few Allied pilots were shot down by American anti-aircraft artillery. On Christmas Day, fighters of No 83 Group sighted no fewer than thirty-one Me 262s,[54] German air activity being the heaviest since Market Garden, and the not-so-surprising result was an increase in aerial combats. Squadron Leader J.E. Collier, commanding No 403, shot down an Me 262 single-handedly, the first RCAF pilot to do so.

I was flying KAPOK leader on a patrol in the Malmedy area. I was flying on a westerly course about 15 miles SW of Aachen at 14,000' [feet] when 3 a/c were observed at 3 o'clock 1,000' above and flying in formation on a westerly course toward Liege. I identified the a/c as Me 262s and I set my gyro sight at 50' span. I ordered the Squadron to drop tanks and open up. I was unable to drop my own jet tank. The enemy aircraft continued to do a slow orbit to port gradually going into echelon starboard. They slowly turned across in front of us at about 1000 yds range and 2 of the enemy a/c sighted us and dived away to the east but the leading enemy a/c continued his turn. I [closed to] about 50 yds range in a steep turn to port and the enemy a/c straightened out in front of me and opened up. At 150 yds I fired a 4–6 second burst and observed numerous strikes on the fuselage and port wing. The port nacelle began to throw considerable white smoke. The enemy a/c was increasing the range fairly rapidly. I continued firing long bursts and obtained more strikes at 5–600 yds. When my gyro sight was at maximum range I aimed above the e/a and although the e/a was at approximately 1000 yds believe I obtained 1 or 2 more strikes. At this time the e/a was diving on a course of approximately 70°. At about 10,000' I ran out of ammunition but continued to follow using cine gun. At about 8,000' the port nacelle of a/c was throwing considerable white smoke and I observed the e/a do a slow half roll to starboard and a parachute open. The e/a crashed approximately 6-8 miles E. of Aachen.[55]

Slower than the German jets in any case, Collier's Spitfire was further handicapped by his inability to jettison his external fuel tank and, since jets were normally reserved for the most experienced German pilots, one can only speculate what had so distracted the enemy as to enable Collier to get so close in the first place. An hour or so later 'the long queue of airmen waiting for Xmas dinner [on B 88, at Heesch, in Holland] bit the dust as one man when an Me 262 was clobbered by the cannon fire of F/L Jack Boyle of 411 Squadron right over base.' In his case, Boyle was just pulling out of a steep dive, in which he had built up 'excessive speed,' allowing him to keep up with the marauding Me 262 long enough to shoot it down. The jet crashed about five miles from the strip.[56]

Piston-engined aircraft were also in evidence and, in all, RCAF fighter pilots claimed eighteen destroyed that Christmas weekend, while losing eleven of their own. With the Ardennes offensive in full swing, the Luftwaffe was trying to protect the railways that German ground commanders needed to resupply their spearheads; and even the Typhoons of 439 Squadron, which so far had only one enemy aircraft to their credit, shot down two more on 29 December. For 126 Wing, the 29th proved 'a day of many highlights,' with eleven enemy shot down, five of them credited to a single pilot, Flight Lieutenant Richard Audet.[57]

I was leading Yellow section of 411 Squadron in the Rheine/Osnabruck area when Control reported Huns at Rheine and the Squadron turned in that direction. An Me 262 was sighted and just at that time I spotted 12 e/a on our starboard side at 2 o'clock. These turned out to be mixture of approximately 4 Me 109s and 8 FW 190s.

1st Combat

I attacked an Me 109 which was the last a/c in the formation of about 12 all flying line astern. At approximately 200 yards and 30° to starboard at 10,000 feet I opened fire and saw strikes all over the fuselage and wing roots. The 109 burst into flames on the starboard side of the fuselage only, and trailed intense black smoke. I then broke off my attack …

2nd Combat

After the first attack I went around in a defensive circle at about 8400 feet until I spotted an FW 190 which I immediately attacked from 250 yards down to 100 yards and from 30° to line astern I saw strikes over cockpit and to the rear of the fuselage, it burst into flames from the engine back and as I passed very close over top of it I saw the pilot slumped over in his cockpit, which was also in flames ...

3rd Combat

My third attack followed immediately on the 2nd. I followed what I believe was an Me 109 in a slight dive. He then climbed sharply and his coupe top flew off about 3 to 4,000 feet. I then gave a very short burst from about 300 yards and line astern and his aircraft whipped downwards in a dive. The pilot attempted or did bale out. I saw a black object on the edge of the cockpit but his chute ripped to shreds. I then took cine shots of his a/c going to the ground and the bits of parachute floating around. I saw this aircraft hit and smash into many flaming pieces on the ground. I do not remember any strikes on this aircraft. The Browning [machine-gun] button only may have been pressed.

4th Combat

I spotted an FW 190 being pursued at about 5,000' by a Spitfire which was in turn pursued by an FW 190. I called this yellow section pilot to break, and attacked the 190 up his rear. The fight went downward in a steep dive. When I was about 250 yards and line astern of this 190 I opened fire, there were many strikes on the length of the fuselage and it immediately burst into flames. I saw this FW 190 go straight into the ground and burn.

5th Combat

Several minutes later while attempting to form my section up again I spotted an FW 190 from 4,000', he was at about 2,000'. I dived down on him and attempted a head-on attack. I slowed down to wait for the 190 to fly in range. At about 200 yards and 20° I gave a very short burst, but couldn't see any strikes. This a/c flicked violently, and continued to do so until he crashed into the ground.[58]

No other RCAF pilot, nor any other pilot of Second TAF, ever shot down five aircraft in a single sortie – but many of the circumstances surrounding Audet's victories were typical of aerial combat in the last year of the war. In fifty-two missions after his arrival on the Continent in mid-September he had engaged the enemy only three times, and those without success. As with most other Spitfire pilots, his days had been spent on uneventful patrols and interdiction missions – some of the latter on dive-bombing runs against railway lines; but by 22 January, less than a month after his first victory, Audet had accumulated a total of ten-and-a-half enemy aircraft destroyed in the air, all of them fighters, one of them a jet. Then, with the Luftwaffe entering another recovery stage in its operational cycle, Audet's opportunities, like those of the RCAF as a whole, dried up. Tragically – but also all too typically – he was killed by Flak on 3 March while attacking a railway siding.[59]

Those who became prisoners of war were more fortunate, but gliding to earth under a parachute was no guarantee of safety, as Hedley Everard, shot down on Christmas Eve, could well attest. After capture and interrogation, he was moved to more permanent facilities, but the journey held dangers of its own.

It was very dark by now as the vehicle lumbered down some secondary tree lined roads. In the distance ahead, I saw the glow of fires, and as we approached and stopped, I realized that it was the burning remains of a military convoy. My spirits sank as I heard from the shouts of the surviving truck drivers that they had been hit by rocket-firing Typhoon fighter bombers just before dusk.

The anger of my guards was evident, as I was made to dismount and marched into the midst of the dirty, disheveled survivors. Even without being told by my armed escort, these people recognized me as one of the airborne destroyers of their friends searing in their vehicles. And to me, this carnage, now seen at close range, was what I had seen many times through my gunsights during repeated straffing attacks. These German convoys, like their trains, were heavily defended with anti-aircraft guns and we also suffered heavy casualties and damage in our interdiction sorties ...

For reasons I will never know, the angry murmurs from this rag-tag group slowly subsided. They stared at me, some with scowls, some with quiet hatred, others looked away. I can only guess that my burned face, which had recently begun to drip, must have conveyed, that I too, had been punished by fire, and that we were all living in hell.[60]

Everard eventually wound up joining nine other aircrew, who had baled out of heavy bombers.

Soon we were led out, arranged in pairs then marched up the street with two guards forward and two to the rear. From whispered conversation I knew we were in Dusseldorf. As we neared the main railway station the pedestrian traffic increased since no vehicles could manoeuver in the rubble-strewn streets. This situation became extremely dangerous when the taunts and jeers of the citizens turned into a barrage of stones. One Canadian informed me that the city had been his bombing target the previous night, and hence the angry crowd. When the guards were struck by the thrown debris, they levelled their automatics at the people and we were hustled off into a room in the relatively warm station cellar. It is a wonder that we were not abandoned by the guards to the angry mob, some of whom may have lost loved ones in the previous night's bombardment.[61]

Meanwhile, the Luftwaffe was accumulating as many fighter aircraft as it could for one last, desperate, ill-considered, gamble. At first light on 1 January 1945 a fighter force of some thousand machines (and pilots) set out to attack eleven major Allied airfields in an attempt to restore some kind of balance to the aerial battlefields of the Western Front. A high proportion of the pilots were novices, fresh from underfuelled flying training schools, but if they could catch enough of the Allied tactical air forces on the ground, and not lose too many machines in doing so, then they might yet achieve a notable victory. The airfields in question were excellent targets, for atrocious weather and transportation difficulties had forced British and American air formations to concentrate their resources on facilities that had permanent runways, while the fields themselves were familiar to many German leaders who had been flying out of them themselves only a little time before.[62] Three of these targets, Eindhoven, Heesch, and Evère, were homes to RCAF wings.

Two of the latter, Nos 39 and 143, were based at Eindhoven, which was to suffer severely in Fall Bodenplatte. Targeted by 3 (Udet) Jagdgeschwader, Canadian Spitfire and Typhoon pilots found themselves the objects of massed and determined ground attacks for the first – and last – time in the war. They were taken completely by surprise, with eight Typhoons from each of Nos 438 and 440 Squadrons lined up for takeoff. Two that managed to get into the air were shot down by the swarming German fighters; the other fourteen were shot to pieces on the ground, one pilot managing to escape from his aircraft and take shelter in the dispersal building, though injured by flying glass. Three pilots from the Typhoon wing were killed. Having disposed of all the machines on the runway, the attackers circled and strafed the base for over twenty minutes, their main opposition coming from three squadrons of RAF regiment anti-aircraft gunners.[63]

Groundcrew also fought back, one of them Sergeant W.L. Large, of 438 Squadron.

I was down the road from dispersal waiting to see the Sqn take off when I saw a number of e[nemy]/a[ircraft] making an attack on the airfield. I first thought this was a hit and run raid, but after the second and third wave had passed over and I saw e[nemy]/a[ircraft] circle the field and continue their attacks from out of the sun, I figured they were playing for keeps and therefore hurried back to dispersal where our Bren guns were kept. There I saw F/Sgt McGee and we decided to take a whack at anything flying over the dispersal. We each took a Bren gun and two boxes of clips and stood outside the dispersal door and waited for any Jerry who came within range ... One aircraft coming from the south turned off the runway and made a steep climbing turn about 120 yards away from us at a height of not more than forty feet. We both fired, each emptying a full magazine at him. We saw strikes down the engine cowling in the direction of the cockpit and saw small pieces fall off.[64]

Three days after the attack a burnt-out FW 190 was discovered near the airfield, sufficient evidence to give Large and McGee credit for one enemy machine destroyed. The attackers lost ten pilots killed or missing and six captured, but left Eindhoven a shambles; thirteen were dead and dozens wounded, thirty-one aircraft were left burning or shot-up and many buildings

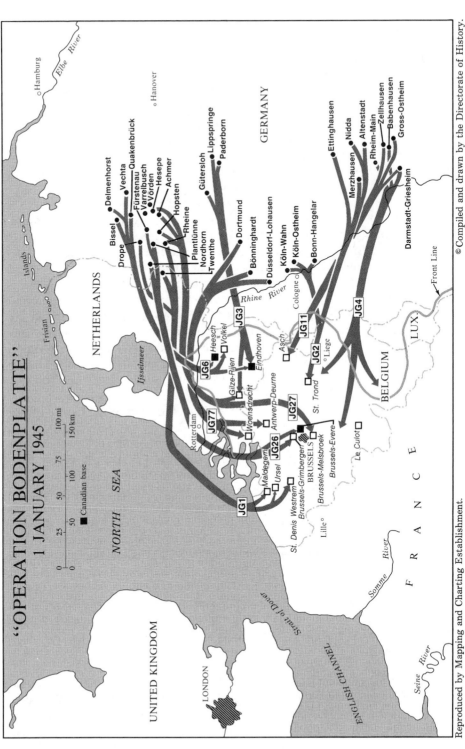

"OPERATION BODENPLATTE"
1 JANUARY 1945

UNITED KINGDOM

LONDON

NORTH SEA

Strait of Dover

ENGLISH CHANNEL

F R A N C E

Somme River

Seine River

NETHERLANDS

Frisian

Islands

Ijsselmeer

Rotterdam

Rhine River

GERMANY

Hamburg

Elbe River

Hanover

○ Delmenhorst
● Bissel
● Drope
● Vechta
● Fürstenau
● Varrelbusch
● Vörden
● Quakenbrück
● Hesepe
● Achmer
● Hopsten
● Rheine
● Plantlünne
● Nordhorn
● Twenthe

● Gütersloh
● Lippspringe
● Paderborn

● Dortmund

● Bönninghardt

● Düsseldorf-Lohausen
● Köln-Wahn
● Köln-Ostheim
● Bonn-Hangelar

Cologne ○

● Ettinghausen
● Merzhausen
● Nidda
● Rheim-Main
● Altenstadt
● Zellhausen
● Babenhausen
● Gross-Ostheim

● Darmstadt-Griesheim

Heesch ■ Volkel
Glize-Rijen
Eindhoven ■
Woensdrecht
Antwerp-Deurne
Asch □

JG3
JG6
JG77
JG26
JG11
JG2
JG27
JG4
JG1

St. Trond □
○ Liege

Maldegem □
Ursel □
Brussels-Grimbergen □
BRUSSELS ■
Brussels-Melsbroek □
Brussels-Evere □

St. Denis Westrem □
Lille ○

Le Culot □

BELGIUM

LUX.

Front Line

© Compiled and drawn by the Directorate of History.

■ Canadian base

0   25   50   75   100 mi
0 50 100 150 km

Reproduced by Mapping and Charting Establishment.

damaged, while several bomb and petrol dumps added flames and explosions to the general confusion.[65]

At Heesch, from which 126 Wing was operating, German fighters caught ten Spitfires of No 401 Squadron lining up for takeoff; but they all managed to get into the air and force their opponents into confused dogfighting in which the Canadians claimed six enemy aircraft destroyed without loss. Other squadrons, which had taken off some minutes before the attack and been recalled by radio, accounted for many more. In all, 126 Wing claimed nineteen German pilots brought down for the loss of one of their own killed and another wounded, while damage was limited to a hole in the 411 Squadron dispersal tent.[66]

At Evère, home to 127 Wing, local conditions favoured the Germans as a combination of rain and frost had turned the runways into skating rinks, keeping early morning patrols on the ground. The attack that followed was fierce but short, lasting some twelve minutes and accounting for twenty-four of the approximately sixty Spitfires on the field. Wing Commander J.E. Johnson, RAF, who led the Canadian wing, thought 'we had escaped lightly,' however, 'not one Spitfire should have remained undamaged at Evère.' I and III Gruppen of 26 Jagdgeschwader lost eleven pilots killed, missing, or captured – some brought down by their own Flak on their way to the objective – while casualties among RCAF air- and groundcrew amounted to two killed and twelve wounded.[67]

In all, material losses were 'by no means negligible,' Second TAF having lost 127 aircraft destroyed and 133 damaged. (American forces lost 36.) It was not, however, the kind of devastating blow the Luftwaffe had hoped to strike, and its own loss of three hundred machines with 214 pilots (a third of them to 'friendly' anti-aircraft fire) was nothing if not catastrophic. Following on the heels of two disastrous months in which almost eight hundred pilots had been killed or fallen into Allied hands, Bodenplatte, according to Werner Girbig, 'amounted to total defeat. The home-defence formations equipped with the standard types of fighters never recovered from the blow. Their subsequent operations were insignificant seen against the situation as a whole and offered no further threat to the domination of the enemy air forces.'[68]

In the aftermath of Bodenplatte the Luftwaffe could do nothing but concentrate its ever more meagre efforts on defensive patrols. Intelligence summaries had little doubt as to what German fighters were trying to protect. 'The obvious interpretation of this concern is that our attacks on railways in this area are becoming more than a nuisance, bearing in mind that the railways must be carrying a considerable amount of supplies for the present German offensive, to say nothing of the probability that the divisions being moved down from Norway are using these routes.'[69]

Once again the front stabilized and Second TAF found itself supporting a less active 21st Army Group, ground operations being largely curtailed by inclement winter weather. Under such circumstances the air force's role was to prevent enemy air attacks on friendly troops or reconnaissance over friendly territory, to meet the army's needs for information, and to support whatever minor operations ground commanders might decide upon in order to improve their positions. Air operations thus became less intense, No 83 Group continuing to carry out interdiction sorties beyond the Rhine while No 84 prepared to support First Canadian Army's forthcoming offensive – Operation Veritable – to close on that waterway.[70]

For some larger operations, however, composite groups were no longer tied to a particular land formation and were instead given a specific role to play in support of the army group as a whole. Thus Veritable, which began on 8 February, saw No 83 Group Spitfires assigned to provide fighter cover while its Typhoons joined No 84 Group on close support missions.[71] There was little for the Spitfires to defend against, and the five obsolete Ju 87s that No 442 Squadron shot down on the first day of the offensive could not have been much of a challenge.[72] The Typhoons were far more active, No 439's diarist unable to contain his glee. 'The air activity today was a treat for sore eyes, the pilots claimed that there was 10/10ths aircraft [ie, maximum coverage] over the early morning target area.' Of the squadron's six operations, most were four-aircraft patrols, for a total of thirty-two sorties, but keeping the machines flying in abominable weather was no easy task. 'Great credit is due to the ground crew for their part in today's attack as working conditions are far from ideal with water and mud everywhere. Some of the aircraft are parked in pools of water – bombing up and servicing of the kites is no picnic under such conditions. Out of 17 aircraft, 15 were on ops at one time today, which speaks well for the serviceability state.'[73]

When the weather cleared a little on 14 February, the Allied air forces prepared for a massive effort, flying some nine thousand sorties – more than at any time since the Normandy campaign. No 83 Group claimed its thousandth enemy aircraft that day, destroyed or damaged a record number of jets and locomotives, and made more rail cuts than in any previous twenty-four-hour period. No 126 Wing's Spitfires flew their greatest number of sorties to date – 237 – with the two busiest squadrons managing fifty-four and fifty-three, respectively, while among the Typhoons, No 440 established a new squadron record with fifty-five sorties. 'This close co-ordination for the first time on such a scale between Canada's air and ground forces is historically significant,'[74] wrote an anonymous staff officer at Overseas Headquarters, noting that RCAF squadrons had now flown almost fifteen hundred sorties in support of First Canadian Army. It would never happen again.

One area where co-ordination was critical was on the ground, between the various maintenance services, and Operations Record Books leave little doubt that servicing echelons put a tremendous effort into maintaining high serviceability rates of 75 per cent or more. At times, and inevitably, ground crew could rightfully complain of being taken for granted by an impersonal system that was interested in operational effectiveness but not necessarily in how it was achieved. 'Moving day meant much work to most sections of the Wing, but the armourers felt they had been particularly hard done by. After yesterday's record breaking day of rails cut and bombs dropped, the armourers fitted three bombs per kite through the whole Wing – in the dark. And today, weather cancelling ops, these bombs were gently dropped before take off to the new site, and again going late into the night, the armourers diligently bombed up every kite.'[75]

Working conditions were perhaps the technician's main challenge as he battled with Northwest Europe's winter climate, and one fighter-bomber squadron suggested in October that 'on looking around the dispersal, it appears that it may be easier to use floats on the Typhies instead of wheels.' When serviceability rates did, on occasion, fall below optimum levels, there was a marked hesitancy to blame groundcrew. On one occasion 'every one blamed 150 grade [fuel] for all engine failures,' while on another 'problems with flats [were] due perhaps to using brakes on long taxy before take-off.'[76]

Nevertheless, with groundcrew ensuring enough aircraft were always available for major operations, on 21 February the various Allied air forces launched their own air offensive, Operation Clarion, designed to strangle communications to the Ruhr. Heavy and medium bombers were given the task of cutting bridges and viaducts while fighter-bombers continued to harass railway traffic, a role they had fulfilled (with some interruptions) since the fall. On the 22nd, No 439 announced 'enormous operational activity' with its greatest number of sorties ever, resulting in twenty-eight railway cuts, one road bombed, the destruction of three flat cars, one armoured vehicle, and two tanks. Such attacks were, of course, hazardous, and due not only to Flak, weather, or mechanical failure. As No 442 reported, 'on one of the afternoon shows, S/L [M.E.] Jowsey had to bale out over Germany. It is believed that he was the victim of a freak accident, being hit by his own bullets ricocheting while strafing some M[echanized] E[nemy] T[ransport]. He was seen to land and the Squadron feel he is OK.'[77] The hunch was accurate, for Jowsey evaded capture and was back in England by 5 April, though he would see no more combat.

Except for the curious circumstances of his loss, twenty-three-year-old Squadron Leader Milton Jowsey, DFC, was an excellent example of the kind of leader that the RCAF now had in abundance after four years of war. Joining the RCAF in 1940, after graduating from Ottawa's Glebe Collegiate, he had earned his 'wings' and a commission in July 1941 and been posted overseas (via Iceland) the following month. After attending a fighter OTU in England – there were none in Canada until July 1942 – he had been sent to the Middle East. Serving in RAF squadrons, he was promoted to flying officer in July 1942 and flight lieutenant a year later, helping to 'finish off the Luftwaffe in Tunisia' and sharing in the first victory credited to the Desert Air Force 'operating from captured airfields in Sicily.' Given credit for shooting down four enemy machines, his DFC citation proclaimed him 'a cool and capable leader,' noting that 'his courage and determination to engage the enemy have set a fine example to his fellow pilots.' Repatriated to Canada in November 1943, he was back to Europe a year later, posted in to No 442 Squadron as a flight commander and as successor to Squadron Leader W.A. Olmstead, DSO, DFC and Bar, when the latter's tour expired on 13 December 1944. By that time he had added one FW 190 destroyed and another probably destroyed to his record of successes.[78]

Jowsey had shot himself down while strafing targets of opportunity, but the effectiveness of such attacks on the enemy – now standard procedure for those who had completed their pre-arranged tasks – had never been fully evaluated. To shine some light on the subject, Second TAF's Operational Research Section examined cine-gun film of strafing runs that had taken place from December 1944 to March 1945 and concluded that, in general, they brought good results. At least 40 per cent of those against locomotives and 30 per cent of those against road vehicles were well executed, accurate, and effective, while most of the rest caused some damage. The best tactic, it seemed, was to open fire from six to eight hundred yards range against locomotives or five to seven hundred yards against road vehicles, closing to about three hundred yards in a gradual dive while firing a single long burst.[79]

Target policy was similar to that of a year before, with aircraft allowed to attack only purely military targets on German-occupied territory, while Germany itself was to be treated unmercifully. 'Freedom to roam over Germany with a squadron or flight of eager pilots was like the gathering of vultures at a carcass. Everything below was a war-legitimate target. Hitler's War Machine, that I had vowed to help destroy years ago in Canada, had shrunk to its original German borders. There were no Burmese coolies below my wings now; no desert Arabs; no Italian peasants; no French farmers, no Dutch civilians – all were enemy.'[80]

In carrying out such attacks in late February and early March, Typhoon squadrons found the enemy air arm to be a limiting factor for the first time in months. 'The Luftwaffe in the past week has become particularly aggressive in attacks on small groups of aircraft,' Wing Commander Dean Nesbitt, DFC, a Battle of Britain veteran now commanding 143 Wing, explained. 'Our splurge of record breaking rail cuts and sorties was made possible by flying in small units of four and sometimes two aircraft. Luckily, the Hun was too slow in taking advantage of this and Intelligence reports indicate that our rail cutting has had the desired effect on front line problems of supply for the enemy. Therefore, there is no longer any need to expose the pilots to unfair disadvantage. All missions now are carried out by large formations.'[81]

From the end of February to mid-March, encounters with enemy fighters were more common as the Germans put up large forces by 1944 standards, sometimes numbering a hundred or more, in an attempt to mitigate poor pilot quality through quantity. As a result, in the week leading up to 21 March, about half the 1650 sorties carried out by RCAF units in Second TAF were fighter operations such as sweeps, patrols, and escort work, and only a fifth dedicated to rail interdiction.[82]

With the Allies in full possession of the west bank of the Rhine by 10 March, it was time to start detailed planning for an assault crossing and a ground campaign that would take the war to the heart of Germany. Strategic bomber forces, meanwhile, were attacking jet bases, and roughly half the bomber effort for the month was directed against airfields, so that the Luftwaffe, already suffering severely, would be less likely to put in an appearance over the bridgeheads. On 7 March the First US Army had captured intact the Ludendorff railway bridge at Remagen and by the 10th a substantial lodgement had been established on the far bank; and on the 22nd – one day before Montgomery's offensive was due to start – the Third US Army captured a bridge at Oppenheim, south of Mainz. By mid-March the Luftwaffe was in dire straits, as casualties and emergency withdrawals to the east (where Soviet armies were no more than forty miles from Berlin in the north and pressing through western Hungary in the south) left it with less than 1100 aircraft on the Western Front. A further series of attacks on German airfields, commencing the 21st, rendered most bases unserviceable.[83]

Operations to form bridgeheads over the Rhine would involve airborne landings (Operation Varsity) as well as assault water crossings (Operation Plunder) and – staffs having learned from the Arnhem catastrophe – this time air support was closely integrated and planned at Second TAF. No 83 Group was given responsibility for maintaining air supremacy over the battlefield and for fifty miles beyond, while also attacking Flak positions and answering requests for close support. The latter operations would rely on a sophisticated system of communications between ground and air forces as forward control posts, each made up of an air liaison officer and an RAF controller, linked aircraft in flight with ground formations down to brigade level, while each armoured brigade maintained a Sherman tank as contact car to keep in touch with air and ground reconnaissance units. Final preparations took place during the evening of the 22nd, and, in 126 Wing, 'everybody left the briefing room with a clear idea of the importance of the part that this Wing was to play in keeping the Luftwaffe off the backs of our advancing ground forces.'[84]

The artillery barrage that accompanied the assault crossing of the Rhine on the night of 23/24 March was one of the heaviest of the war: bombers attacked communications, airfields, and batteries within range of the bridgehead; and when the sun rose No 83 Group aircraft attacked every enemy gun position that opened fire and attempted to keep the skies clear of German aircraft.[85] Air/ground cooperation was excellent, as the usually critical Coningham reported after the war.

During the hours of daylight on D-day, 83 and 84 Groups RAF and XXIXth US Tactical Air Command flew strong defensive fighter patrols over the assault areas, and offensive sweeps over the enemy day fighter bases in the Twente-Enschede, Rheine and Paderborn areas to prevent the German Air Force interfering with the elements of the Second British and IXth US Armies engaged in expanding the bridgeheads established on the east bank of the Rhine during the preceding night ... 83 Group maintained one 'cab rank' of four aircraft over its advanced Group Control Centre on the west bank of the Rhine, with two squadrons at readiness on the ground. There was one contact car with each of the two assaulting British divisions, and a further two contact cars were safely flown in with the airborne divisions. Immediate support requests from the four divisions were filtered at the advanced G[roup] C[ontrol] C[entre], and those that were accepted were passed to the aircraft, which were handed over to the control of the Forward Control Post (contact car) concerned.[86]

The extent of the air support provided for the airborne divisions was in marked contrast to the experience at Arnhem, the air forces answering thirty calls for impromptu missions during the day, while two wings of Typhoons were permanently employed in suppressing any Flak that might threaten troop-carriers. Operational researchers noted that the effect of the Typhoons' new cluster bombs was similar to that of rockets, managing few direct hits but discouraging anti-aircraft gunners from using their weapons.[87]

Already before 2nd Army's operation began 8th [US] Air Force had rendered unserviceable all airfields hitherto associated with the enemy's jet aircraft. In addition to further bombing attacks today, their fighters were ranging over most of NW Germany in order to intercept at the earliest moment, any aircraft that took off from the area or were called into it from outside. Further to this, the three fighter Groups comprising 2nd Tactical Air Force maintained strong fighter patrols over the battle area, and for some distance beyond it. Accordingly it is hardly surprising that not a single case of interference from the air with either the ground or the airborne forces has so far been reported today.[88]

The same was true of the days that followed, and the Rhine crossing was a complete success.

Anglo-Canadian and American forces thus advanced out of the Rhine bridge-head and towards the Elbe as the war moved into its final fifty days. The offensive soon outranged No 83 Group's bases, and in early April No 400 Squadron – flying Spitfire PR XIs, with substantially greater endurance than the Spitfire IX – complained that 'the progress of the forward troops makes the duties of the other Squadrons in the Wing difficult to carry out due to lack of range.' Indeed, 'several tasks for this Squadron have been cancelled by Army because of the swift movement of armour, etc.'[89]

With Allied forces advancing into Germany, the Italian campaign looked – to participants as well as observers – to have become nothing more than a sideshow, though no less brutal for that. In early 1945 No 417 switched from close support to interdiction duties, attacking observation posts, rail lines, bridges, and transport, and with better weather (starting in the last week of February) the squadron flew far more often. Of note at Overseas Headquarters were the nominal rolls for March 1945, which revealed that the squadron had finally achieved the goal of 100 per cent Canadianization; it had always been close to this figure in aircrew and the last RAF pilot to fly with the squadron had departed the previous September, but a hundred RAF technicians had accompanied the squadron to Egypt in 1942, and some of them represented skilled trades difficult to fill. Their number only gradually shrank as Canadian replacements became available, and it was not until 31 March 1945 that the squadron diary reported 'nil' RAF officers or airmen on strength;[90] No 417, in all its glorious isolation from the rest of the Canadian war effort, would fight the last full month of the war as an all-RCAF unit. (Isolation, because, in that same month, I Canadian Corps left Italy, moving to Northwest Europe for the last weeks of the war.)

German defences in Italy finally cracked in April, with Anglo-American armies launching a long-awaited spring offensive on the 8th. No 417 supported the attack as Allied formations broke through German positions on the Senio River, crossed the Po, and advanced into the Venetian plains; one city after another fell and by 30 April Venice itself was in Allied hands.[91]

During the last week of April, operations diminished in intensity as resistance crumbled and bad weather grounded the Spitfires for several days. German forces in Italy surrendered on 2 May, and the following day the squadron moved to Treviso, the unit diarist commenting on the difference between territory that had been fought over and the area it was moving into, which had not.

It was interesting to note a considerable improvement in the people and the countryside as we advanced north of the Po River. South of the river are the heaps of rubble left by our bombers and the cheerless people who continue to exist in the shattered villages. At the great river, which seems to be the dividing line, this desolation reaches its peak. Skeletons of guns and motor transport line the banks and the bloated bodies of horses and oxen lie here and there in the stream.

Travelling north from the Po, these evidences of war gradually lessen. Fewer buildings bear the tell-tale pock marks of house-to-house fighting; there are no signs of shelling, and only the obviously military target has been reduced to a pile of brick, dust, and twisted metal girders.[92]

In Northwest Europe, the success of Plunder and Varsity had left RCAF squadrons anxious to cross the Rhine, leading many of them to claim 'firsts.' 'The advance party of 414 Squadron proceeded to B-104 Airfield, Wesel Area, in conjunction with 'A' Echelon of 39 Wing. This territory was quite recently captured by the Army and it is believed that this detachment is one of the first, if not the first group of RCAF personnel to cross the Rhine.' No 439 claimed to be the first RCAF squadron to land its aicraft in Germany on 30 March and, being on German territory, armed everyone in the unit to guard against saboteurs. No 406 Air Service Park took similar precautions. 'Immediate steps are being taken to ensure that all personnel are familiar with, and know how to fire and dismantle all types of weapons used for defence. The precaution is being taken with an eye to future moves which will no doubt take us into German territory, and also the fact that this Unit might not be under the protection of an airfield which have [sic] RAF Regiment personnel for this purpose.'[93]

In the first fortnight of April, Second British Army drove forward two hundred miles from the Rhine to the Elbe, the rate of advance leading some pilots to complain that their orders were out of date. 'Stories or briefings change a bit each time they pass from mouth to mouth and they sure do pass through a lot of mouths before they get to us.' Exceptions to the rule were the Air Observation Post (AOP) squadrons – recent additions to the RCAF, though the Royal Air Force had seen fit to introduce them in late 1942.

AOPs were the ultimate example of air/ground cooperation, ironically with army officers as pilots while maintenance and administrative staff wore air force uniforms. Their early days in the RAF had been rocky, the air staff fearful of the resurrection of an army air arm; so the first to enter operations, No 651, did not reach Tunisia until November 1942, where it was engaged in its primary role of spotting for artillery batteries with unarmed, American-designed, Taylorcraft Austers. The RCAF's AOPs were even longer in entering operations, for though the first army officers to train in such duties had completed their courses in late 1941, General McNaughton had decided, for reasons unknown (but probably connected with their apparent inability to survive in anything less than a totally permissive environment), that there would be no Canadian observation squadrons.[94]

Not until September 1944 did his successor, General Crerar, revise that edict. The first such unit, No 664, was formed on 1 December and equipped with the Auster IV – a three-seater, high-wing monoplane with a maximum speed of 130 miles per hour and a cruising speed of 112 miles per hour – but it could fly as slowly as 40 miles per hour and needed only seventy-five yards of grass runway to take off and even less to land. Two more squadrons, Nos 665 and 666, were formed in the months to come but, appearing so late in the war, only the first two would actually serve on operations, which, with the Luftwaffe no longer a threat, included front-line reconnaissance as well as artillery spotting; No 664's first operation, on 29 March, was a reconnaissance mission, as was No 665's last on 7 May. In all, Nos 664 and 665 flew 619 and 58 sorties, respectively, the former losing one aircraft and two aircrew killed.[95]

For Spitfire and Typhoon pilots, armed reconnaissance missions, greatly aided by the clear spring weather, continued as they swept ahead of quickly advancing columns to hinder any German attempts either to recuperate or retreat. On 16 April No 403 proclaimed, 'A beautiful flying day, and one of the best kills the Squadron has had for many a month, many M[echanized] E[nemy] T[ransport] destroyed in the five armed recce operations carried out, and the pilots are in very high spirits having so much action in one day.' Sometimes the opportunity for air-to-air action presented itself, only for the squadron to find that it could not take advantage of it. On the 17th No 411 reported: 'Again today enemy motorized and railway equipment score mounted but after expending all ammo on ground targets on one mission the Squadron sighted 15 Me 109s but nothing could be done.'[96] Nevertheless, 'the week ending Wednesday April 18 has been one of noteworthy achievement for RCAF squadrons based on the Continent. All our Spitfire and Typhoon squadrons operating with 83 Group have now moved forward to airfields in Germany, bases formerly occupied by units of the German air force. From these newly acquired airfields our fighter bombers have carried out the most intensive programme of armed reconnaissances since D Day, aimed at the fleeing German transport in the path of the advancing allied armies.'[97] Indeed, No 402 found that the last half of April 'proved to be the most active and profitable two weeks yet recorded,' and 'the fact that the aircraft were now based within easy striking range of the fleeing foe had a telling effect on all types of the enemy's transport.'[98]

Air operations became more hazardous again as Allied troops crossed the Elbe on 29 April, for 'in contrast to the ground, opposition in the air was relatively heavy over the Lauenburg bridgehead. Both jets and normal fighters were involved,' and 'it may be the case that the G[erman] A[ir] F[orce] is thoroughly disorganised and working under extreme difficulty, but the scale of effort put up today once more shows clearly how the GAF is able to improvise in difficult circumstances.' Indeed, the Luftwaffe reacted sharply to the Elbe crossings, sending more aircraft against the bridges than No 83 Group had seen in weeks, with the rather bizarre result that spirits *rose* within RCAF units. No 402 claimed eight destroyed and four damaged on the 30th alone, though No 443 reported that 'the month ended with another batch of uneventful patrols. We are hoping for more action or peace, the sooner the better.'[99]

One who had much to give thanks for in the last days of the war was a pilot in No 412 Squadron.

Thanks to accurate pin-pointing of F/O G.M. Horter's ... aircraft which had crashed on the 28th April, the squadron Medical Officer, F/L J.E. McAllister ... was able to locate the crash and found F/O Horter still strapped into the cockpit and alive, although in a semi-conscious state, after having spent forty hours in that position. An Army Unit near by, had seen the aircraft crash and the explosion and flames. Having already lost a Lieutenant and a Sergeant in that vicinity recently, they were not anxious to investigate the crash, presuming that the pilot would have been killed on landing. He is now in hospital, on the S[eriously] I[njured] list, suffering from exposure, immersion feet [sic], fractured left humerus and lacerations of the face, left wrist and thigh. It is thought that he will recover. It is virtually a miracle that he is alive, as the a/c was completely broken up. The only factor that probably saved his life, was being strapped into the cockpit, as otherwise he would have been thrown into a deep ditch of water, which was certainly too deep for him to get out of in his injured condition.[100]

No 52 Mobile Field Hospital (RCAF) was certainly well able to receive him, having, on average, filled only thirteen of its seventy-one beds daily in the last full month of the war.[101]

Air Vice-Marshal Broadhurst later observed that some of the most intense aerial operations of the campaign were in its final days, though experiences varied widely as squadrons changed roles every day or even from one mission to another. On 1 May No 416 reported that 'pilots are getting bags of Jerry transport now, but no aircraft,' while No 414 declared the 2nd 'a red letter day for the Squadron' when it claimed six aircraft destroyed and two damaged. No 400 also had cause for celebration on the 2nd, for not only did a reconnaissance sortie locate advancing Russian troops, but 'in mid-afternoon a German training aircraft landed at B 154 with two [members] of the Luftwaffe flying from an airfield being overrun by Russians.'[102]

Such incidents were far from isolated as Germans in and out of uniform attempted to avoid capture by vengeful Soviet armies. One major escape route was through the Baltic, which naturally attracted the attention of tactical air forces always on the lookout for bottlenecks.

Today's picture with M[echanized] e[nemy] t[ransport] fleeing bumper to bumper was very similar to the Falaise Gap last summer when we scored such a huge success. The last mission of the day was the best. It was directed against a large troop ship and out of 22 × 1,000 lb bombs dropped, direct hits were scored with four, and many were near misses. One bomb hit on the bow, one at the stern and 2 near the bridge amidships. Great numbers of smaller ships were seen as well as quite a number of subs. This Squadron came in for some glory today when ... F/O W.F. Birch dropped the 10,000th bomb dropped by 143 (RCAF) Wing.[103]

Crowded shipping was sufficiently tempting to distract Typhoons from some of the best targets they had seen in months. 'A report came back flashing the news that Jerries retreating east of Lübeck met those retreating west from the Russian front, making a lovely mess of men and vehicles but this was not for us, instead we commenced chasing German shipping which is escaping with troops presumably to Norway ... The Flak boats threw up a mass of metal at the Typhies and all in all it was a dicey do.'[104] Anti-shipping strikes continued on the 3rd and 4th, and only the surrender of German forces in the area put an end to them.

In Northwest Europe some squadrons had already started celebrating when German forces in the Netherlands surrendered on 4 May, though No 438 had warned, 'we shall see what tomorrow will bring.' Others were less cautious, No 403 among them. 'What an evening of celebration with the news of the Canadian armies in the north being victorious and the surrender of the enemy. Just Norway and southern Germany to clean up now. The bar was thrown wide open, and guns of every description firing away in the small hours in celebration.' On the 5th No 412 reported that 'there was no Operational flying today. Possibly it was just as well, as it will give everyone an opportunity to recuperate from yesterday's spontaneous outlet of pent-up feelings.'[105]

When Admiral Dönitz surrendered all German forces on the 7th, there was no longer any doubt. 'This is it, the Nazis have surrendered. Official VE Day will be tomorrow but nobody waited till then to start celebrating. The bar was the scene of a well organized assault, and the fun was still going strong in the early hours of the morning.' No 441's Operations Record Book entry for the 8th was the shortest of the war: 'VE-Day'[106] was all it said.

Taking stock of the Northwest Europe campaign, from 6 June 1944 to 7 May 1945, 196 Canadian pilots and groundcrew died serving with the fighter and fighter-bomber squadrons of the RCAF Overseas. The three hardest hit were the Typhoon squadrons, with thirty-one pilots and groundcrew of No 440 losing their lives, thirty in No 439, and twenty-six in No 438. No 439 Squadron calculated that over 60 per cent of Typhoon pilots became casualties before completing their tours. In contrast, 400 Squadron, concentrating on photo-reconnaissance, usually above the Flak and rarely engaging the Luftwaffe, lost only a single pilot.

As for the damage inflicted on the enemy, No 126 (RCAF) Wing was the top-scoring formation in Second TAF, credited with 361 confirmed victories in the air and on the ground, while its 401 Squadron was the most successful single unit, with 112 aircraft destroyed in the air and fifteen on the ground. The two highest scoring pilots in the campaign were Flight Lieutenant D.C. Laubmann, DFC and Bar, of 412 Squadron, and Squadron Leader W.T. Klersy, DFC and Bar, of 401 Squadron, credited with fourteen-and-a-half and thirteen-and-a-half victories, respectively.[107] (Klersy was killed in a flying accident two weeks after the fighting ended.)

With the war over, flying went on but perspectives quickly changed. On 7 May No 438 Squadron announced that 'a meeting of the Squadron pilots was held today with the object of getting sports under way.'[108]

PART THREE

The Maritime Air War

One of No 407 Squadron's Lockheed Hudsons. Originally designed as a civil aircraft, the slow, underarmed Hudson was ill-suited to the anti-shipping operations on which it was employed. (PL 4622)

Pilot Officer W.B. Cooper and crew inspect the Flak damage done to their Hudson on 10 October 1941. (PL 4729)

No 407 Squadron's first commanding officer, Wing Commander H.M. Styles (left), and 'A' Flight commander, Squadron Leader P.E. Lewis, both RAF, pose in front of a Canadian Hudson. Styles, 'the Hollywood director's idea of an RAF operational wing commander,' proved to be a popular leader among his Canadian aircrew. (PL 4610)

No 413 Squadron formed at Stranraer, Scotland, in July 1941 and operated Consolidated Catalina flying boats, such as the one pictured above, over the Indian Ocean from April 1942 to December 1944. (PL 4634)

Officers of No 404 Squadron in front of one of the unit's Bristol Blenheim IV fighters in 1941. Seated in centre, with the dog between his feet, is the squadron's commanding officer, Squadron Leader P.H. Woodruff, RAF, of Edmonton, Alberta. (PMR 72-35)

Wing Commander R.G. Briese, seen looking through the roof hatch of a Catalina, was a prewar RCAF officer and the first commanding officer of No 413 Squadron. He went missing on an operational flight over Norway on 22 October 1941. (PL 4630)

Squadron Leader L.J. Birchall at the controls of a 413 Squadron Catalina. Birchall located the Japanese carrier force that was preparing to attack Ceylon on 4 April 1942 and transmitted a warning before being shot down. Together with the survivors of his crew, he spent the rest of the war as a prisoner of the Japanese. (PL 7405)

Silhouetted against the tropical sun, RCAF fitters work on a Catalina of No 413 Squadron at Koggala, Ceylon, in the summer of 1942. (PL 10008)

A ground collision involving a Handley-Page Hampden torpedo-bomber of No 415 Squadron and a Boeing 'Flying Fortress,' also of Coastal Command, 1943. (PMR 82-007)

In order to work in the frigid waters of Lough Erne at Castle Archdale, Northern Ireland, mechanics had to put on rubberized wading suits before making their repairs. (PL 40986)

Short Sunderland U of No 422 Squadron at the instant of touchdown. This particular aircraft sank U-625 on 10 March 1944. (PL 40996)

The interior of a Nissen hut, common to most wartime RAF stations, usually accommodated fourteen men. In the centre is the sole (and inadequate) source of heat, a small coal-burning stove. (PL 45598)

Working from a floating platform, mechanics examine one of the four Bristol Pegasus engines of an RCAF Sunderland flying-boat. (PL 31437)

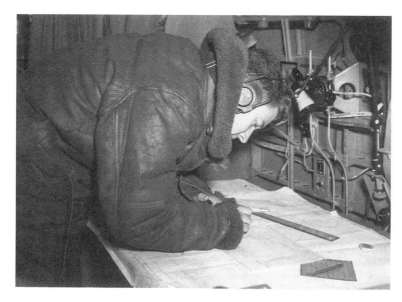

Accurate navigation was vital to Coastal Command operations. Flying Officer Jack Ritchie works at the navigator's desk of an RCAF Sunderland. (PL 22077)

The maintenance area for the Sunderlands of No 422 Squadron at Castle Archdale, Northern Ireland, in mid-1944. (PL 33252)

A Sunderland is beached for maintenance. Hauling these 26-ton aircraft ashore could be a ticklish business. (PL 15751)

The Blohm and Voss BV 138 flying-boat attacked by Flying Officer S.S. Shulemson of No 404 Squadron goes down in flames on 28 July 1943. (PL 19522)

The downed boat on the surface. Both photographs were taken by Shulemson's navigator, Sergeant A.D. Glasgow. (PL 19523)

A Leigh Light-equipped Vickers Wellington Mark XII similar to those used by No 407 Squadron. The retracted Leigh Light is visible on the underside of the fuselage just behind the wing, while the ASV III radar is located in the dome under the nose. (RE 19876-11)

A Fairey Albacore similar to those used by No 415 Squadron to chase German E-boats in the English Channel. With a cruising speed of only 115 miles per hour, the Fleet Air Arm biplane was not what Overseas Headquarters had in mind when they sought to replace obsolescent Hampden torpedo-bombers in the Canadian unit. (PL 130488)

No 404 Squadron personnel line up for tea and buns at a Church of Scotland van in the summer of 1943. (PL 19439)

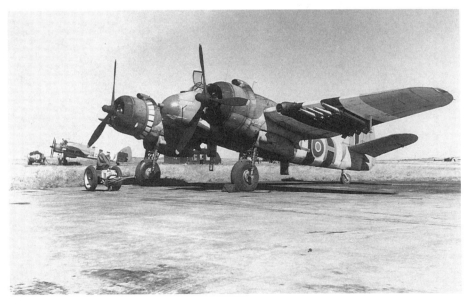

A Bristol Beaufighter Mark X of 404 Squadron with freshly painted invasion stripes in June 1944. The primary anti-ship weapon used by the Canadians was the 3-inch rocket with a 25-lb armour-piercing warhead launched from underwing rails. (PL 41049)

Four German M-class minesweepers on fire and sinking in Bourgeneuf harbour on the Biscay coast after a 404 and 236 Squadron strike on 8 August 1944. (PMR 93-071)

One of two Sperrbrechers – small, heavily armed merchant vessels used as Flak ships - sunk off Royon, Brittany, by a combined 404 and 236 Squadron strike on 13 August 1944. (PMR 93-080)

Splashes from both machine-gun fire and depth charges entering the water mark the start of the successful attack on U-625 by Sunderland U of 422 Squadron on 10 March 1944. (C 4287)

The crew of U-625 take to their life rafts after the successful attack. Escaping the U-boat did not ensure survival, however, as none of the submariners photographed by the circling Canadians were ever seen again. (RE 68-586)

Servicing a Leigh Light Wellington. The beam gun position clearly shows the aircraft's geodetic lattice-work construction that made it such a rugged machine, capable of withstanding great punishment. (PL 40927)

The German torpedo boat *T.24* (foreground) and the destroyer *Z.24* under attack by Beaufighters of 236 and 404 Squadrons off Le Verdon, France, on 24 August 1944. (PMR 93077)

An armourer slides a 3-inch rocket onto the underwing rails of a Canadian Beaufighter. (PL 41007)

A Beaufighter Mark X of 404 Squadron fires off its rocket projectiles. (PMR 92-580)

The German merchant vessels *Aquila* and *Helga Ferdinand* under attack by Beaufighters of 144, 455, and 404 Squadrons in Midgulen Fjord, 8 November 1944. The photograph was taken from the No 404 Beaufighter piloted by Flying Officer L.C. Boileau. Both ships were sunk. (PMR 93-079)

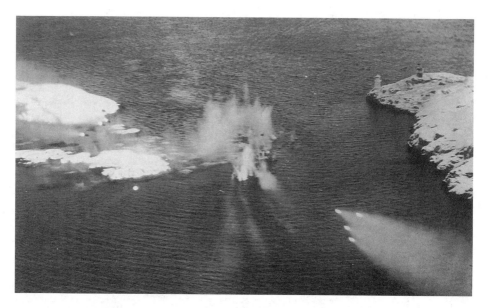

Eight rockets from Beaufighter H of 404 Squadron head for the Norwegian salvage tug *Blaaveis* in Sognefjord, Norway, on 9 January 1945. The tug was destroyed in the attack. (PMR 92-586)

The 9 February 1945 attack on the German destroyer *Z.33* in Forde Fjord as seen from Beaufighter T of 404 Squadron piloted by Flying Officer H.P. Flynn. Anti-aircraft fire from Flak batteries located on the fjord's cliffs took a heavy toll from the attacking aircraft. (PMR 93-087)

Introduction

Ottawa's decision (in line with British priorities) to place the greatest emphasis on strategic bombing and to assign second place to fighter and fighter-bomber operations meant that the RCAF contribution to Coastal Command was limited to eight squadrons. Even so, one of them, No 162, was really part of the Home War Establishment, being loaned to Coastal Command and operating out of Reykjavik, Iceland, and Wick, Scotland, after January 1944. Since it was never formally a part of the RCAF Overseas, its story was told in the second volume of this series. A Canadian bomber squadron, No 405, served briefly in the command for four months during the winter of 1942/3.

Three more squadrons, Nos 413, 422, and 423, were formed in the United Kingdom, to be employed against the German U-boat menace in European and North Atlantic waters. However, the transfer of the first-formed, No 413, to Ceylon (now Sri Lanka) in the spring of 1942 delayed full participation in the North Atlantic anti-submarine campaign by RCAF Overseas squadrons until the following year. At that time the two remaining flying-boat squadrons, together with the Leigh Light-equipped Vickers Wellingtons of 407 Squadron and the Handley-Page Halifaxes of No 405, were able to take part in a fruitful offensive in the Bay of Biscay.

The success that aircraft enjoyed against surfaced U-boats over the summer and fall of 1943 led to the introduction of vessels fitted with Schnorkel tubes. By permitting submarines to remain submerged throughout their cruise, these devices encouraged the enemy to embark on the cautious inshore campaign in British waters that characterized the last eleven months of the war. It also reduced the value of aircraft as U-boat killers. While the RCAF squadrons in Coastal Command sank, or shared in the sinking of, nine submarines (not including the six destroyed by 162 Squadron), only two such successes were achieved after the D-Day landings.

Although the strategically defensive task of anti-submarine operations dominated the maritime air war, both in terms of the resources employed and its importance to the overall Allied war effort, a small proportion of Coastal Command strength was used to conduct an anti-shipping offensive along the coasts of Northwest Europe. As a secondary campaign fought by one of the RAF's less glamorous commands, the direct attack on German shipping has not received as much attention from historians as have the air aspects of the anti-submarine war or the numerically larger battles waged by Fighter and Bomber commands. Thus the hazardous nature of many of the attacks, as well as the significant effects they eventually had on the German economy, have largely escaped public notice.

The three RCAF squadrons that took part in the anti-shipping war made a significant contribution to the success that Coastal Command eventually achieved. As exemplified by the experience of 407 Squadron during the first year of its existence, however, that success was delayed by the obsolete and inappropriate aircraft with which the strike squadrons were initially equipped – another indication of the low priorities usually accorded to Coastal Command and of the Royal Navy's view that anti-shipping operations were of less than overwhelming significance. For the first three years of the campaign, most attacks would prove to be deadly exercises in futility while the goal of creating a successful strike force remained but a distant objective.

Equally frustrating, if less dangerous, were the organizational misfortunes of No 415 Squadron. Formed as a torpedo-bomber unit in August 1941, it was initially equipped with obsolescent aircraft – first Bristol Beauforts, then Handley-Page Hampdens – and assigned to a series of marginal, ineffective roles. It was moved nine times in the first fifteen months of its existence, before being divided into two flights (one equipped with Wellingtons, the other with Fairey Albacore biplanes) and scattered in detachments around the British coast. Discipline and morale suffered accordingly, until salvation came (after many complaints) with its transfer to Bomber Command in July 1944.

No 404 Squadron initially flew the long-range fighter variant of the Bristol Blenheim light bomber and embraced more fulfilling roles, but it was not until the spring of 1943 that Coastal Command was finally provided with the aircraft it needed to create a successful strike force. The Bristol Beaufighter, with some machines modified to carry torpedoes, combined sufficient firepower to suppress shipborne Flak with the speed and manoeuvrability that previous torpedo-bombers had lacked.

Better, more sophisticated tactics helped, too, and when the strike-wing technique was extended to the Norwegian coast later that summer, 404 Squadron added a refinement of its own by adopting the 3-inch rocket projectile (RP) with a 25-lb armour-piercing warhead as its main anti-shipping weapon. Other squadrons followed suit, and the RP-equipped Beaufighters proved their worth the following year when the Canadians helped to shield the western flank of the Operation Overlord invasion area from interference by German naval forces.

There was yet another aspect to the maritime air war in which Coastal Command might have been expected to play a major role. Throughout the war, air-dropped mines were sown by night in the approaches to German ports (and those of occupied countries) and at 'choke points' along the coastal waterways of Northwest Europe. These minefields required the enemy to expend considerable efforts in sweeping operations, yet still left much uncertainty and nervousness in the minds of merchant seamen since those not swept accounted for significant amounts of shipping.

Some mines were dropped by Coastal Command aircraft, but from the outset of the mining campaign, in April 1940, by far the greatest number were laid by Bomber Command. Not only was the Wellington – which Bomber Command had in relative abundance – a better machine for the purpose than Coastal Command's Beauforts and Hampdens, but, as the former's four-engined Short Stirlings and Handley-Page Halifax IIs and Vs became obsolescent in terms of deep strikes into Germany, they were increasingly used on Gardening operations. Thus the story of aerial mining has been left to the section of this volume devoted to the bomber war.

Throughout the final two years of the war the number of Canadians serving in Coastal Command averaged between two and three thousand. As Canadian strength reached its peak in June 1944, there were 2065 Canadians serving in RCAF squadrons and a further 919, mostly aircrew, serving in RAF units.

The small number of RCAF maritime squadrons and the variety of aircrew required meant that there were great difficulties in 'Canadianizing' the RCAF squadrons. At various times, eight squadrons flew ten different types of aircraft operationally, each with its unique crew composition, and not all aircrew categories were provided for in the RCAF training pipeline. No 404 Squadron, for example, had a high proportion of RAF navigators (W) – navigators who were also trained as wireless (radio) operators – in its two-man Beaufighter crews because there was no appropriate training provided in Canada. Similarly, a shortage of flight engineers and wireless operators (mechanics) hampered the Canadianization of the two Sunderland squadrons until experienced flying-boat crews were posted from the Home War Establishment to Coastal Command beginning in February 1944.

Morale was something of a problem throughout the command. At various times, low priorities in equipment, inadequate accommodation, and a lack of public recognition, compounded by the inevitable tedium of anti-submarine patrolling on the one hand, or the sometimes desperate nature of anti-shipping strikes on the other, did little for the spirits of maritime airmen. In addition, to a greater extent than in other commands, interservice relationships with the RAF seem to have added to the frustrations that beset Canadian flyers.

11

The Anti-Submarine War
in European and Far Eastern Waters,
1941-5

In the later stages of the First World War, anti-submarine patrols of the Royal Naval Air Service and (after 1 April 1918) the Royal Air Force had enjoyed considerable success in countering the German U-boat threat – though not always, or even largely, by sinking them. Submarines, which normally attacked on the surface, nevertheless depended on concealment to survive, and the proximity of patrolling aircraft usually persuaded their captains to submerge, protecting their boats but also spoiling their attacks. Of course, whenever a submarine was sighted on the surface (or, as was more likely, in the process of submerging), the airmen made every effort to destroy them; but successes were rare, in large part because they had to rely on bombs which had been designed to damage or destroy land targets. The Royal Navy's principal anti-submarine weapon, the depth charge, was too awkward and heavy for the aircraft of the time to carry, and contact-fused bombs had to register either a direct hit or a very near miss to sink or damage a submarine.[1]

Aircraft were greatly improved during the interwar years, but anti-submarine weaponry changed not at all. The first depth charge issued to operational squadrons of Coastal Command in July 1940, the 450-lb Mark VII, was still one designed exclusively to naval specifications and therefore too bulky to be carried by any Coastal Command aircraft of the time other than flying-boats, of which there were only a limited number. Although the lighter, more compact 250-lb Mark VIII was introduced in the spring of 1941 (shortly before No 413, the RCAF's first overseas anti-submarine squadron, began forming), its Amatol filling had only 30 to 50 per cent of the explosive force of the Torpex-filled Mark XI that would succeed it in 1942.

Moreover, a U-boat of Second World War vintage was only likely to be destroyed, even by a Torpex depth charge, if the explosion occurred within nineteen or twenty feet of the hull, and the pressure-sensitive detonator in use until mid-1942 had a minimum setting of fifty feet, too deep to destroy submarines close to the surface. It would not be until July 1942 that the Mark XIII Star 'pistol,' capable of detonating a depth charge in fifteen feet of water, would come into service. Until that time a submarine on the surface was safe from anything but a severe shaking. Thus the early history of anti-submarine operations in the Second World War was very similar to that of the First, with the greatest success being suppression, rather than destruction, of U-boats. Indeed, despite having made 245 attacks since the beginning of the war, by September 1941 Coastal Command's score stood at only 'three sinkings shared with surface escorts, one boat that had surrendered to aircraft, and a handful of boats damaged.'[2]

However, the inability of aircraft to destroy submarines scarcely diminished Coastal Command's usefulness in the defence of shipping, upon which Britain's survival depended. For a main purpose of maritime forces was to ensure the 'safe and timely arrival' of merchant vessels, and to that end the near-perfect security of shipping under adequate air protection was a vital contribution. This was especially so because the Royal Navy was desperately short of ocean-going anti-submarine escort vessels.[3]

Air power effectively supplemented the overworked naval escorts because the arrangements for command and control, developed in the last years of peace, fully integrated the maritime air force into the navy's system of operational control. The boundaries of Coastal Command air groups coincided with those of the navy's home commands, and air and naval commanders shared 'area combined headquarters' where they worked together in the same room, over a common plot on which was displayed information fed directly from the Admiralty's operational intelligence centre. The senior naval officer gave general direction, for he was best equipped to comprehend the situation at sea, while the air group commander was free to carry out his mission in accordance with his professional judgment and his detailed knowledge of the air resources to hand. It was a marvellously flexible way to overcome the gulf of incomprehension between officers of two services whose experience was in vastly different environments.[4]

Expansion of Coastal Command had a central place in the urgent efforts to strengthen Britain's maritime forces during the dark year following the fall of France. At this time the United Kingdom was utterly dependent on long overseas trade routes that were made even more vulnerable by German possession of bases extending from the northern tip of Norway to the Franco-Spanish frontier. The number of merchant ships lost to U-boats soared to five hundred in the nine months between June 1940 and March 1941, as compared with only two hundred during the first nine months of the war. There was also a need to deploy aircraft and ships for anti-invasion duties on the east and south coasts of the United Kingdom.[5]

Growth was substantial, although it by no means met the extreme demands of these circumstances. Of the ten squadrons added to the twenty-nine of November 1940, two were flying-boat squadrons and four consisted of land-based anti-submarine machines (usually referred to in service terminology as general reconnaissance, or GR, squadrons). Average strength grew from 201 aircraft in November to 298 in June 1941, with the greatest improvement coming in the realm of long-range GR squadrons available for convoy escort. Those increased from one Armstrong-Whitworth Whitley squadron to one Vickers Wellington and two Whitley squadrons. There was also one squadron of Consolidated B24 Liberators in the process of forming. Modified to extend

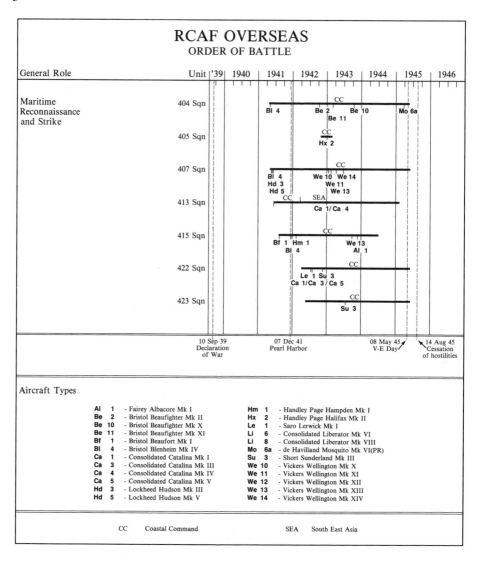

their range by removing equipment not strictly necessary for anti-submarine work and replacing it with additional fuel tanks, these first very-long-range (VLR) Liberators, armed with eight depth charges, could provide protection from seven hundred to one thousand miles out from base and still spend at least one-third of their time in the vicinity of a convoy, on a sortie that might last as long as fourteen hours.[6]

The flying-boat squadrons were due to be upgraded when deliveries of Consolidated Catalinas, expected in early 1941, would permit the replacement of obsolete Supermarine Stranraers and Saro Lerwicks. The Catalina's twenty-five-hour endurance allowed it to provide convoy escort up to six hundred miles from base, although its slow cruising speed of only 115 miles per hour was a disadvantage. Of the remaining aircraft in the command, the Short Sunderland flying-boats had an effective radius of 440 miles, the Wellingtons and Whitleys 340 miles, while the Lockheed Hudsons could manage no more than 250 miles.[7]

In the spring of 1941 German tactics in the North Atlantic revolved about single U-boats shadowing convoys during daylight hours – always on the surface, since their underwater cruising speeds were insufficient to keep up with even the slowest convoys – and then, through Admiral Karl Dönitz's headquarters (Befehlshaber der Unterseeboote, or BdU), calling in other boats to attack at night. 'The large number of convoys attacked at night after air cover was supplied the preceding day demonstrated that the existing policy of providing as many convoys as possible with at least a few hours' escort by a single aircraft was failing to drive off shadowing submarines,' explained the author of volume II of this series, *The Creation of a National Air Force*. If the shadower could be suppressed, however, so that he could not report on the convoy's location and progress, the whole pack could be thrown off the scent. And if the longer-range aircraft slowly becoming available were used to sweep areas beyond normal U-boat shadowing range, on the convoy's axis of advance, 'studies of past operations suggested that aircraft with this roving commission were three times as likely to find U-boats as aircraft closely circling a particular convoy. Nevertheless, constant close escort remained essential for convoys being shadowed, especially in the hours before sunset when the U-boats were closing to their attack positions.'[8]

The Germans were in the process of expanding their submarine fleet from a mere thirty operational boats in April 1941 to sixty by August, of which thirty-nine were in the Atlantic. Coastal Command therefore needed more than just better operational procedures to keep up. By the end of April 1941 the delivery of Catalinas from the United States had enabled the Air Ministry to re-equip five anti-submarine flying-boat squadrons (increasing their initial establishments from six to nine machines at the same time), and to form another flying-boat squadron at the end of June. The new squadron, No 413, was the third RCAF unit to be formed in Coastal Command since the Ralston-Sinclair Agreement had been signed in January[*] but, as had been the case with previous RCAF accretions, its aircrew would initially 'be found from the RAF except in so far as RCAF personnel [are] immediately available.' They would be replaced, however, 'as pilots, etc. of the RCAF of requisite experience become available.'[9]

In anticipation of its formation, Air Commodore L.F. Stevenson, the RCAF's air officer commanding (AOC) overseas, had telegraphed Ottawa on 28 June, 'asking whether Canada could supply a Commanding Officer, one or two Flight Commanders or other experienced pilots' for the new unit. He found it 'regrettable that an RCAF Flying Boat Squadron should form in the UK and the

---

[*] The first RCAF units formed in Coastal Command were, as we shall see, Nos 404 and 407 squadrons, which spent their first eighteen months of operations engaged in anti-shipping and long-range fighter duties.

RCAF not be in a position to supply a large percentage of the Flight Commanders and Crews. Flying boat operations is one [sic] in which the RCAF is particularly well experienced, and even though coastal operations in Canada are important, it is felt that provision of RCAF crews for No 413 Squadron should be given every consideration.' Although Ottawa was able to find a commanding officer and two flight commanders for him, 'all qualified on Catalinas,' Stevenson was told that 'no further trained pilots can be spared at present.'[10]

In part, at least, that was because Ottawa, which often had trouble looking beyond the immediate needs of the BCATP and Home War Establishment, was busy forming a Catalina squadron of its own in Eastern Air Command. It would seem, nevertheless, that enough graduates of GR schools – the primary training grounds for anti-submarine flying – were being posted overseas to provide No 413 Squadron with a reasonable percentage of Canadian aircrew. Knowing that fifteen were due to arrive in the United Kingdom in June, forty in July, and a further twenty-four in August, Stevenson suggested to the Air Ministry that they be posted directly to the Canadian squadron.[11] But, in a strange piece of bureaucratic logic, the Air Ministry argued that it was more important to keep Coastal Command's OTUs filled with GR-trained pilots than it was to provide qualified Canadian aircrew for a soon-to-be-operational RCAF squadron. The diversion of pilots 'directly to squadrons,' Stevenson was told, 'would almost certainly lead to OTU capacity being left unfilled.'

There is not, of course, the same objection to sending E[mpire] A[ir] T[raining] S[cheme] produce which has not been through the GR Schools in Canada direct to 407 and 413 Squadrons because the majority of pilots required for filling the OTUs must be GR trained. I think, however, we can compromise over this question. Of the arrivals you refer to ... 8 (but only 8) are now in this country. There will be no OTU vacancies to absorb them before 26/7/41. I therefore suggest that these pilots should be posted into 407 Squadron now, with the proviso that if, on the 26th, we cannot meet the Coastal OTU requirements from subsequent GR trained EATS arrivals together with the output of the home schools, we will temporarily transfer these 8 pilots to a[n] OTU to finish their operational training. Similarly, if in the future the GR trained material available for OTUs should be in excess of OTU requirements the surplus should be posted direct into 407 and 413 Squadrons.[12]

Although this bizarre arrangement clearly placed the needs of the RAF's training organization ahead of those of RCAF operational squadrons, Stevenson accepted it; and when 413 Squadron began forming in July 1941, at Stranraer in southwest Scotland, many of its aircrew came from RAF Blenheim squadrons. The most notable influx of Canadians came in mid-August, when the three officers promised by Ottawa arrived on the scene. Wing Commander R.G. Briese, who had joined the RCAF in 1932 and was regarded as a 'highly capable officer in all respects,' had already commanded an operational training squadron at Patricia Bay, BC. His two flight commanders, Flight Lieutenants L.H. Randall and J.C. Scott, were posted from No 5 (BR) Squadron in Dartmouth, NS. More Canadians arrived in September to take over the non-flying duties of medical officer, squadron adjutant, and engineer officer. Still, when the squadron completed its training at the end of September, only 10 per cent of its complement was RCAF.[13]

Briese was already hard at work trying to replace his RAF aircrew with Canadians, telling Stevenson that 'pilots trained on boats in No 13 OTS (RCAF) will not require to be sent to an OTU here. They should, however, have a period of about one month to qualify as second pilot before assuming crew duties.' Although he was personally familiar with seven pilot officers from his former command whom he would have welcomed on his new one, and had passed on their names to Stevenson (who had raised the matter with the Air Ministry), no one on his list was posted to No 413.[14]

The squadron began the move to its first operational base at Sullom Voe, in the Shetland Islands off the north coast of Scotland, on 3 October 1941. It arrived there 'with high morale and great expectations' despite the bleak surroundings and poor weather that plagued a station which was 'a mixture of peacetime Camp Borden (without Wasaga Beach), Sable Island and Alliford Bay.' Flying conditions were often abysmal. Although the islands were 'quite low, the highest point being under 1500 feet ... low [cloud] ceilings prevail, and it is often necessary to approach base at 100 feet or less.'[15]

After two days of familiarization flying, No 413 undertook its first operation, escorting a convoy east of the Orkney Islands on 5 October, and it mounted fourteen more convoy patrols over the next two weeks, all of which were uneventful. On 22 October, however, a photo-reconnaissance of the Norwegian coast was ordered by Group HQ, a mission which, of necessity, involved flying well within range of enemy fighters and far beyond the protection of friendly ones. The slow, cumbersome Catalina had never been designed, or armed, to survive air-to-air combat, and, in the absence of cloud cover, the sortie was something of a suicide mission. Indeed, as one of the flight commanders reported, it was later learned that the mission 'had been refused for this reason by another squadron.' The obvious degree of risk involved may explain why Briese chose to fly on this operation himself, as a supernumerary pilot. Catalina G took off in the dark hours of 22 October and was never seen or heard from again.[16]

The loss of Briese was a blow, and others would follow. Gale-force winds and frequent snow, sleet, and hail severely limited operational flying and reduced the effectiveness of the few patrols that could be carried out over the next few weeks. During one particularly bad storm, on 11 November, four machines were sunk at their moorings and the loss did not please Coastal Command Headquarters at Northwood. Within a week, the acting squadron commander, a Canadian in the RAF, had been replaced by Wing Commander J.D. Twigg, 'a clever, hard working officer who has personality [and] set a fine example by his flying leadership.' The RAF station commander was also transferred to other duties the following month.[17]

Under Twigg's hard-driving command, No 413 Squadron's record of aircraft serviceability improved steadily, despite the difficulty of working on unprotected boats that were often coated with ice in the early mornings. But groundcrews were rewarded with time off during slow periods, 'a procedure that was not common before,'[18] and, with so many machines fit for operations, the squadron flew 330 hours during February 1942, primarily on night reconnaissances off the Norwegian coast. At the end of the month, however, Twigg was told that his unit would be moving to Ceylon almost at once. The shift was part of a larger transfer of Catalina squadrons to the Far East, where the enemy's many successes (including the sinking of the British capital ships *Prince of Wales* and *Repulse* by air attack) had given Japan maritime supremacy in the Indian Ocean and now threatened Britain's communications with India.[19]

This unexpected move was complicated by the fact that the RAF did not want Twigg to retain command of the squadron. A personality clash with the new RAF station commander at Sullum Voe had led that officer to recommend that 'Twigg be found employment more suited to his abilities.' Overseas Headquarters quickly discovered that the fault lay more with the station commander than Twigg – who had simply refused a late-night summons from bed to join in a juvenile 'pants pulling-off' contest in the mess – but Stevenson was apparently unwilling to go head-to-head with Northwood. Twigg was sent to a bomber OTU (for familiarization on type prior to being posted to 408 Squadron), where his assessment recorded that he 'was one of the best officers ever to have gone through that OTU, is an excellent pilot, efficient officer and likeable personality.' In his new command, furthermore, he would be described by another RAF station commander as 'a courageous and able operational pilot... the all-round performance of this [408] Squadron from the point of view of discipline, flying, esprit-de-corps and operational successes has improved very noticeably and continues so to do.'[20]

Combined with the futile loss of Wing Commander Briese and his crew, this posting-out of another popular and efficient commanding officer built resentment of the RAF among the Canadians in the squadron. 'When 413 Squadron, after so short a period at Sullom Voe, was peremptorily transferred to Ceylon with the stipulation that Wing Commander Twigg was not to retain command,' one veteran recalled, 'the feeling grew ... that there was undue interference on the part of the RAF and the suspicion that they wished to be rid of us.' However, the next commanding officer, Wing Commander J.L. Plant, a prewar RCAF regular, quickly proved to be 'an outstanding personality both in his Squadron and on the Station ... His discipline and power of command of his men were above the average' – skills and talents desperately required to hold the squadron together and to restore morale.[21]

While approving the squadron's move to Ceylon, Ottawa deplored the fact that it included so few Canadians. Overseas Headquarters was instructed to 'make every effort [to] increase numbers [of] RCAF personnel with this unit,' since once it reached south-east Asia the prospects of maintaining, never mind reinforcing, a Canadian identity would inevitably fade. A large influx of RCAF groundcrew increased their proportion to 70 per cent by the time they sailed from Britain on 18 March, but the aircrew component could only

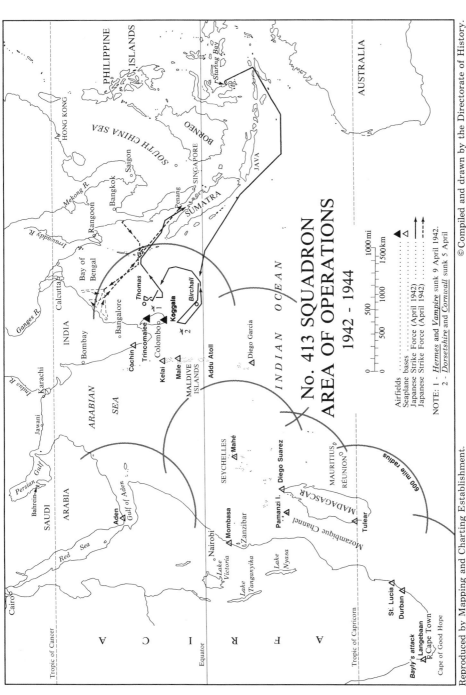

No. 413 SQUADRON
AREA OF OPERATIONS
1942 - 1944

NOTE: 1 - *Hermes* and *Vampire* sunk 9 April 1942.
2 - *Dorsetshire* and *Cornwall* sunk 5 April

Airfields ....
Seaplane bases ....
Japanese Strike Force (April 1942) ....
Japanese Strike Force (April 1942) ....

0   500   1000   1500 km
0   500   1000 mi

Reproduced by Mapping and Charting Establishment.

© Compiled and drawn by the Directorate of History.

be boosted to 48 per cent. The squadron's four remaining Catalinas were flown to Ceylon by its most experienced crews.[22]

The first reached Koggala, Ceylon, on 28 March 1942, fully a month ahead of the squadron's shipborne groundcrews, but just in time to meet a crisis. Rangoon had fallen on 7 March and, with British forces in full retreat towards Mandalay, the British chiefs of staff feared on 2 April that 'an invasion of Bengal, an assault on Ceylon, or an attack on our Eastern Fleet* would each if successful prove a devastating blow ...'[23]

In order to secure the sea route from Singapore to Rangoon, the Japanese had dispatched a large fleet including five carriers and four battleships to strike at British naval bases in Ceylon, while a second, smaller fleet raided shipping in the Bay of Bengal. The Royal Navy's commander-in-chief, Sir James Somerville, wisely decided to keep his much weaker force well to the south-west of Ceylon, beyond the range of the enemy's carrier aircraft, leaving the responsibilities of reconnaissance and warning to one RAF Catalina squadron and the newly arrived boats of No 413.[24]

The first two Canadian Catalinas began patrolling soon after their arrival and, in the early morning hours of 4 April, Squadron Leader L.J. Birchall and his crew (composed of one other Canadian, Warrant Officer G.C. Onyette, and seven RAF men) took off for a patrol area 350 miles south of Ceylon. After twelve hours of fruitless searching Birchall was about to return to base when one of his crew spotted ships on the southern horizon. 'We were at about 2,000 feet altitude at the time and hence we slipped in underneath the Japanese outer air patrol,' Birchall later recalled. 'As we got close enough to identify the lead ships we knew at once what we were into, but the closer we got the more ships appeared and so it was necessary to keep going until we could count and identify them all. By the time we did this there was little chance left ... All we could do was put the nose down and go full out, about 150 knots.'[25] Without cloud cover, the Catalina was easy prey for carrier-borne Japanese fighters: 'We immediately coded a message and started transmission... We were halfway through our required third transmission when a shell destroyed our wireless equipment ... We were now under constant attack. Shells set fire to our internal tanks. We managed to get the fire out, and then another started, and the aircraft began to break up. Due to our low altitude it was impossible to bail out but I got the aircraft down on the water before the tail fell off.'[26]

Eight of the nine crewmen managed to get out of the Catalina before it sank, but two of them – badly wounded, unconscious, and in life jackets – were unable to dive and thus avoid the fighters that continued to strafe the survivors. The other six, including the two Canadians, were eventually picked up by a Japanese destroyer and spent the rest of the war in prison camps. Birchall, subsequently labelled by the Canadian press as the 'Savior of Ceylon,'†

---

* Consisting of four old and slow R-class battleships, the more modern *Warspite*, two large and one small aircraft carriers with seven cruisers, sixteen destroyers, and seven submarines.
† In fact, the Japanese were only concerned with destroying the remnants of Somerville's fleet and had never intended to invade Ceylon.

received a DFC for his actions that day and an OBE for his exemplary conduct while a prisoner.

Alerted by Birchall's message, Ceylonese ports were quickly cleared of shipping while forty-two fighters, mostly Hurricanes (of which at least eight were flown by Canadians in the RAF), scrambled to intercept the enemy as they struck Colombo on the morning of 5 April. The Japanese lost only seven aircraft to the RAF's nineteen, but, distracted from their bombing, they did little damage to the port. (The cruisers HMS *Dorsetshire* and *Cornwall,* which had put out to sea, were later sunk by a second strike force.)

Four days later, Flight Lieutenant R. Thomas, flying No 413's only operational aircraft (the other two were being serviced after reaching Koggala on 6 April), reported the Japanese fleet two hundred miles east of Trincomalee – just minutes after an incoming Japanese air strike had been identified by shore-based radar. His machine was also shot down, with no survivors. Although greater damage was inflicted on Trincomalee than on Colombo, the heaviest blow fell when a second strike force sank the carrier *Hermes,* a destroyer, a corvette, and two tankers which were imprudently returning to port after the first attack. Its mission accomplished, the enemy fleet then sailed back to its Japanese bases.[27]

No 413 Squadron continued to operate from Koggala with only two aircraft until late May, when four more Catalinas and the squadron's groundcrew arrived. Their appearance caused some crowding and the Canadians had to share the two landing runs on Koggala Lake with an RAF unit, while most of the groundcrew had to be quartered twenty miles away.[28] Many of them

were disgruntled to find themselves shunted to the Far East, to a very alien environment and a base with largely non-existent barracks, messes and work-shops ...

... perhaps most significant was the frustration felt by all of us at being transferred from the UK just when the real Battle of the Atlantic was to start, with the opportunity for action which this offered, to the Indian Ocean backwater where we continued to play only a defensive role.[29]

In the absence of the Japanese, woefully indiscriminate pilots of the Royal Navy's Fleet Air Arm proved to be almost as dangerous. On 3 August 1942 Squadron Leader L.H. Randall and his crew were engaged in an exercise to locate, shadow, and report on a maritime task force. Sighting it, the Catalina crew began to signal their report when the 'blister watch reported two aircraft thought to be [Fairey] Fulmars on starboard quarter.'

Catalina turned towards sun to make the expected dummy attacks more difficult. Catalina was flying at about 50' in excellent visibility. The two aircraft made a quarter attack and opened fire shooting away the rudder and aileron controls. The two aircraft then did a climbing turn to the rear. Catalina fired the correct recognition signals (Red Red) from starboard pilot's window. The two aircraft again attacked from above and astern killing the flight engineer, Sgt Meiklejohn [RAF], wounding the wireless operator, Sgt Palmer [RAF] and grazing the navigator P/O Williams and also the electrician

LAC R.L. Craggs. The two aircraft turned away and were not seen again. S/L Randall then climbed the Catalina to 1500 feet and with great difficulty managed to control the aircraft with the engines. Petrol and oil were pouring from the tank. On the approach, it was discovered that the wing floats could not be lowered. Under these conditions the aircraft was waterborne at 20.13 hrs. There is no question that the exceptional ability and the cool and level headed manner in which S/L Randall handled his aircraft saved it and the lives of the members of his crew. It was later confirmed that the two attacking aircraft were Fulmars from the Fleet Air Arm.[30]

Although the twin-engined Catalina bore a very faint resemblance to the Japanese four-engined Navy Type 97 flying-boat, the fact that the nearest Japanese base was more than a thousand miles away, together with the firing of appropriate recognition flares, should have encouraged the fighter pilots to investigate their target more closely before opening fire. A conference was convened at No 222 Group headquarters to discuss the navy's 'shoot first, ask questions later' approach, but, other than an apology, there was little that could be done. However, the 'tragic and unfortunate accident' does not appear to have had an adverse effect on squadron morale. As their living quarters at Koggala were completed, the squadron's 'generally low' morale began to show a significant improvement, although the lack of serviceable aircraft – only three out of the seven on strength – remained a major concern for several months.[31]

As fears of a Japanese invasion receded, the Catalina squadrons turned their attention to the matter of suppressing enemy submarines, a business for which they were much better fitted. But Japanese doctrine called for submarines to operate in conjunction with surface forces rather than prey on merchant shipping, and, once the fleet that had raided Ceylon returned to Singapore, they directed only a few of their smallest and oldest boats to a *guerre de course* in the Indian Ocean. The Germans, in contrast, made a determined effort to operate U-boats in the Indian Ocean throughout 1942 and 1943, despite the often dangerous voyage around the Cape of Good Hope and the logistical difficulties inherent in operating more than 10,000 miles from their Biscay bases.[32]

Given the vast extent of the Indian Ocean and the small numbers of enemy submarines there at any one time, it is not surprising that sightings were a rare occurrence. From September 1942 until November 1943, the Canadians routinely flew two Catalinas from detachments in the Persian Gulf and Gulf of Aden without ever sighting a Japanese submarine. They also maintained detachments along the African coast to counter German activity in those waters, which often worked at distances from their Ceylon base quite inconceivable to GR crews who flew in the North Atlantic and Northwest Europe theatres. One aircraft, captained by Flight Lieutenant G.H. Bayly, flew fifteen operational sorties from Langebaan, on the west coast of South Africa, over 5000 miles from Koggala. While engaged on convoy escort, on 5 June 1943, Bayly attacked U-177 with three depth charges, forcing the submarine to break contact with the convoy but not inflicting any physical damage. That was one of only four attacks – all unsuccessful – made by 413 Squadron in the Far

East. The majority of flights were, 'like those in any other coastal general reconnaissance squadron, long and monotonous. Whether a crew was tasked to patrol shipping lanes, do a sweep or search a specific area, the problems were much the same. Excitement was the exception and yet maximum effort and attention were vital.'[33]

The transfer of three Catalina squadrons to the Far East in the spring of 1942 had left Northwood with only six flying-boat squadrons in home waters. As compensation for the lost units, it was authorized to form three new units and to re-equip a fourth. Two of the new squadrons, Nos 422 and 423, were the fifth and sixth Canadian units to be established in Coastal Command, but the process of becoming both Canadian and operational was strewn with obstacles. Although No 422 was officially formed on 2 April 1942, it was not until June that its first airmen were posted to Lough Erne in Northern Ireland. The commanding officer, Wing Commander L.W. Skey, a Torontonian who had joined the prewar RAF, did not arrive until 9 July and the first boats, obsolete Saro Lerwicks allotted for training purposes only, were not received until two weeks later. The first Catalina was received on 31 July, when the squadron had attained a total aircrew strength of seventy-three, of whom nineteen, or 26 per cent, were members of the RCAF.[34]

While the majority trained on the Lerwicks, three of the most experienced crews and the only three Catalinas on strength were detached to an RAF unit in late August, in order to provide escorts on the southern portion of the convoy route between the Shetland Islands and Murmansk. A shortage of Catalinas caused by increased American requirements in the Pacific theatre – the RAF/RCAF received only what the Americans were willing to give them – meant that no more were available; and when the three on detachment returned at the end of September, the Canadians were ordered to pass them on to an OTU pending their own re-equipment with Sunderlands. The Lerwicks, meanwhile, were sent to the scrap-heap. Left without aircraft, the bulk of the squadron's aircrews were employed ferrying Catalinas from Boucherville, Quebec, to the United Kingdom, and it was not until the ferrying operation was completed in mid-November 1942 and the squadron moved to a new base at Oban, Scotland, that it received its first Sunderlands.[35]

Although the RCAF objected to the RAF's 'uneconomical as well as disconcerting' decision to re-equip the squadron with Sunderlands, Stevenson's successor, Air Marshal H. Edwards, AOC-in-C of the RCAF Overseas, was assured that it was in keeping with the 'present policy ... to restrict the employment of the Catalina in home waters.' And since many of its experienced crews had been posted out to other Catalina squadrons, No 422 required a further three months of retraining before it finally became operational on 1 March 1943, eleven months after its formation.[36]

Categorized by one impressed passenger as 'definitely a boat,' the massive Sunderland, with four engines to the Catalina's two, could not compare with the latter in terms of range and endurance, although it did have a slight advantage in cruising speed.* A modification of the prewar Empire-class civil fly-ing-boats, the Sunderland boasted 'a hull, a bilge, port holes, two decks and a galley, complete with stove.'

The bomb bay is located on the lower deck approximately midway between the leading edge and the trailing edge of the wing [depth charges were mounted on a rack in the bomb room and slide out under the wing through a panel in the side of the hull]. Forward of the bomb bay is the galley, and next is a cabin with two bunks and a table where the crew may rest or eat. In the nose is the mooring gear, washroom and front turret. On the upper deck is the first and second pilots' cockpit and tables and instrument panels for the navigator, wireless operator, radar operator and flight engineer. Aft of the bomb bay, the combined hull and fuselage taper off unobstructed to the rear turret in the tail. The Sunderland, with its four fixed [.303] guns in the nose and also a nose turret, mid-upper turret, tail turret and [.5] galley guns is a formidable bat-tleship.[37]

The other Canadian squadron, No 423, also got off to a slow start but gen-erally had a less disruptive training experience than No 422. Formed at Oban on 18 May 1942, the squadron did not receive its first Sunderlands until 17 July. By the time it became operational at the end of October, aircrew strength had reached ninety-three, forty-nine of whom were RCAF, including nineteen of the twenty-five officers, although the commanding officer was English. Within days of becoming operational, No 423 was transferred to Castle Arch-dale on Lough Erne in Northern Ireland, its home for the remainder of the war.[38]

Throughout the fall of 1942, the RCAF took an active interest in manning both squadrons with Canadians. In September, Group Captain F.G. Wait, the director of personnel at Overseas Headquarters, had pointed out to the Air Ministry that No 422 had only '9 RCAF officer aircrew and 11 RCAF NCO air-crew on strength,' while an RAF squadron which also flew Catalinas 'had 14 RCAF officers and an unknown number of Canadian non-commissioned air-crew.' Since this appeared 'to be a little one-sided,' Wait wanted to know 'whether it would be possible to completely Canadianize No 422 as far as flying personnel is concerned,' presumably by a simple switch of aircrew between the two units. Apparently it was not possible, for nothing was done. In a similar vein, he had tried to arrange the exchange of two RAF flying-boat captains in 423 Squadron for two RCAF captains serving at Gibraltar. Despite the approval of both commanding officers, Northwood 'regretted that it is impossible, at the present time, to effect the exchange suggested owing to operational requirements.'[39]

Nor did Wait's efforts have much effect on 423 Squadron, whose Canadian aircrew component improved from 51.5 per cent to just 57 per cent between September 1942 and January 1943. Proportionally better results were achieved

---

* Neither boat could match the speed of a Liberator, and thus the area of ocean covered during a set period of time.

in No 422, the turnover in aircrew following its re-equipment with Sunderlands bringing an improvement from 20.8 per cent to 53.7 per cent during the same period. The lack of more substantial progress, however, was of concern in Ottawa, and in a blunt telegram to Edwards on 9 January 1943 the chief of the air staff, Air Marshal Lloyd Breadner, wanted to know why the aircrew total in both squadrons was less than 60 per cent RCAF. His query led directly to Edwards's decision to confront Air Ministry officials about the lack of progress in Canadianizing RCAF squadrons later in the month (see chapter 3 above).[40]

Meanwhile, the disagreement between the Air Ministry and the Admiralty (and within the RAF as well) over the allocation of aircraft to Coastal Coastal remained unresolved. Although Air Chief Marshal Philip Joubert de la Ferté had successfully rebutted a proposal put by Prime Minister Churchill to transfer all his land-based squadrons to Bomber Command, he was less effective in arguing for more VLR aircraft. His appeals were rejected out of hand by Sir Charles Portal, who wanted to reserve all Liberators and Lancasters – for they, too, could be modified – for other commands or theatres. The Lancaster was the best of the heavy bombers, Portal told the prime minister, and giving up as few as thirty of them would 'most seriously affect our hitting power,' since no other machine could carry large bombs to Berlin. All twenty-two Liberators, meanwhile, were earmarked for the Middle East, where they alone could be used for strikes against Tripoli or the Romanian oil fields at Ploesti.[41]

The contretemps was not finally resolved until November 1942, when Churchill was persuaded to convene a Cabinet-level committee, chaired by himself and including the chiefs of the naval and air staffs, to examine the issue. There was, by then, good reason to reconsider the security of Britain's Atlantic lifeline. In late summer, Dönitz had shifted his offensive into the mid-Atlantic air gap, that expanse of ocean between the limits of patrols from Iceland and Newfoundland. In those waters U-boats could move rapidly on the surface to concentrate against convoys, while the Allies' inability to read U-boat radio traffic (following the introduction of the new Triton cipher by BdU earlier in the year) had greatly reduced the likelihood of routeing convoys clear of the submarines' patrol lines. If losses like those between August and November – eighty ships totalling 490,511 tons – continued, both British war production and the build-up for the eventual cross-Channel invasion would suffer. Under the circumstances, the Anti-U-boat Warfare Committee's decision was inevitable. On 13 November it concluded that the minimum requirement for VLR aircraft based on the eastern side of the Atlantic was forty machines, and a reluctant Portal agreed to have thirty-three Liberators (which the Air Ministry, after much prodding, had recently allocated to Coastal Command) modified into a VLR configuration.[42]

While this decision was a vindication of Joubert's thinking throughout 1942, he had little time to savour the moment. His relations with Portal had soured since the summer, particularly during November when Joubert took the opportunity of a visit to Northwood by the deputy chairman of the Anti-U-boat Warfare Committee, Sir Stafford Cripps, to circumvent the usual chain of command and press his personal views on the organizational changes needed to improve the coordination of the anti-submarine campaign. He advocated the creation of a specific anti-submarine command – a matter that was essentially the Admiralty's business – which 'would have under its control all the British and Canadian anti-submarine aircraft operating in the Atlantic,' and he backed his oral argument with a letter that went to both Cripps and Portal. The latter, who always feared the consequences of treading on the navy's sensitive toes, immediately wrote to the First Sea Lord disassociating himself from the proposals.[43] He also objected to Joubert's attempt to bypass him.

I very much doubt whether it is wise or proper for us to suggest to a member of the War Cabinet how the Admiralty are to improve their organisation. I suggest that on this we should do better to mind our own business ...

... I am very sorry that you should have sent this document to the Lord Privy Seal without obtaining my approval or that of the Secretary of State. This would have been incorrect even if the document had described a thoroughly worked-out scheme affecting only Royal Air Force responsibilities. It is even more regrettable inasmuch as your proposals are really very much in embryo and are not confined to Air Force matters.[44]

Within a week of receiving that letter, Joubert was informed that he would be replaced by Air Marshal Sir John Slessor.[45]

During his term as AOC-in-C, Joubert had overseen the transformation of Coastal Command from an instrument capable only of frightening U-boat commanders into submerging to one which, with the help of radar, better depth charges, and operational research, was rapidly becoming the most effective submarine killer in the Allied arsenal. More importantly, it was supplying regular, effective protection to convoys up to four hundred miles from shore and, on occasion, to much greater distances, with the precious few VLR aircraft available. It is, nevertheless, questionable whether Joubert had been a good choice to lead Coastal Command during the difficult period of 1941–2. Despite his dedication, enthusiasm, and technical expertise, he was possessed of 'a somewhat acrimonious temperament' and prone to a degree of 'outspokenness [that] did not please the politicians he had to deal with.' His determination in pressing a case, by any means at hand, was interpreted by some as disloyalty. His lobbying of Cripps was certainly seen in that light by Portal, who had undoubtedly come to the conlusion that he needed an AOC-in-C whose loyalty, both to himself and the bomber offensive, was beyond question.[46]

Slessor, a former bomber group commander and senior staff officer at the Air Ministry, combined in his person both the political sensitivity and strategic viewpoint that Portal was looking for. He was also fortunate enough to assume command at Northwood just as the balance of the Battle of the Atlantic was about to shift. The assignment of sufficient VLR Liberators to close the mid-ocean air gap, the advent of naval support groups and escort aircraft carriers, together with the repenetration of BdU's ciphers in late March 1943, would provide the Allies with the means necessary to defeat Dönitz's 'wolf packs.'[47]

Slessor's first test came quickly, when he had to deal with a very strong joint United States/Royal Navy demand to increase the number of long-range patrols in the Bay of Biscay. He rejected the plan, arguing that it would not be in the best interests of either Coastal or Bomber Command.

In spite of my bomber background I should not have hestitated to support a claim for 190 additional first-line heavies in Coastal Command if I had believed that the result would be to tip the scales of the Battle of the Atlantic in our favour. But I was convinced it would not. What I wanted was aircraft of the right type, with the right sort of radar equipment and with crews trained in the right way – and I wanted them quickly. *Now* was the time when we wanted to kill U-boats, while we had the bulge over them with the ten-centimetre ASV, and I was relatively uninterested in what would be happening in six months time ...

I did not believe that nearly so many aircraft were really necessary to achieve decisive results, and anyway thought that to loot Bomber Command was the wrong way to set about getting them.[48]

Unless there were drastic changes in the close but favourable balance of the air/sea war, any further expansion under Slessor was likely to be limited to occasional slight increases in squadron establishments and the re-equipping of existing squadrons with more up-to-date aircraft.[49]

Operations in the Bay of Biscay, which would eventually involve all the RCAF's maritime squadrons in the United Kingdom, occupied an increasing proportion of the anti-submarine effort during the spring and summer of 1943. Attacks on U-boats in transit to and from the Biscay ports had begun in the spring of 1941, following the formation of No 19 Group in the southwestern approaches. The effectiveness of daylight patrols was soon nullified, however, when Dönitz ordered his submarines to proceed on the surface only at night. While ASV II radar, which operated on a wavelength of 1.5 metres, could locate surfaced U-boats at distances of six miles or more, it was blinded by sea returns during the critical last mile of the approach. In moonlight the submarine might occasionally be 'eyeballed' at that range, but more often than not it was indistinguishable in the dark or masked by the electronic clutter that filled the radar screen, so that attacks simply petered out. One successful experiment, however, had involved illuminating the submarine in the beam of a powerful 24-inch naval searchlight fitted in a retractable under-turret on a Vickers Wellington. Having previously backed the disappointing Turbinlite, in November 1941 Joubert had urged the installation of these Leigh Lights in thirty Wellingtons, but the Air Ministry had ruled that the equipping of further aircraft 'must await operational results obtained by the initial six aircraft already ordered.' As a result, the first Leigh Light squadron, No 172, did not commence operations until June 1942, and then with only four aircraft.[50]

During their first two months of night operations, the four Leigh Light machines sank one submarine and damaged two others; but by September outward-bound U-boats were being fitted with the Metox search receiver, capable of detecting metric-band radar transmissions in time for the submarine to dive before an aircraft got close enough to use its Leigh Light. Despite their growing ineffectiveness, night patrols nevertheless took on a greater significance during November and December 1942, as No 19 Group assumed responsibility for protecting the convoys supporting the Anglo-American invasion of northwest Africa. Fifteen Handley-Page Halifaxes from Nos 158 and 405 Squadrons were loaned to Northwood by Bomber Command to meet these responsibilities, as were sixteen Liberator bombers from the US Eighth Air Force. Despite the increased emphasis on the Biscay area, however, Coastal Command still had 'ample medium range squadrons,' including Nos 422 and 423, 'to afford consistent air cover to both Torch and trade convoys out to 400 miles from British bases.'[*51]

The selection of No 405 as one of the two squadrons to be transferred may well have been made in order to provide it with a respite from the heavy losses it was incurring on bomber operations. After losing fifteen crews in June and July 1942, the squadron had participated in only six missions during August, with two losses, but on resuming a heavier schedule in September and October it had lost a further ten aircraft. Unfortunately, the change of scenery, from Topcliffe in Yorkshire to Beaulieu, Hampshire, did not end the squadron's difficulties. During November one Halifax failed to return from a sortie over the bay, while the mid-upper gunner of another shot down his own machine when he accidentally fired a burst into the port inner engine. Only the bomb-aimer, who managed to bail out, and the flight engineer survived the crash.[52]

Over the course of the next month, four more aircraft went down after experiencing engine failures. One crash, which killed fifteen air- and ground-crew transferring from their old base to the new one, came as a 'severe shock': the entire squadron was grounded for a week in early January while the aircraft were inspected and the problem – 'serious "engine breathing" difficulty' due to 'ring gumming' – was corrected. Wing Commander A.C.P. Clayton, a Canadian in the RAF, recalled that 'gradually, we re-built morale, and solved the aircraft serviceability shortcomings. We ended one month [February] flying more sorties than any other squadron in the group.'[53]

Frustrating all Coastal Command's efforts, a total of 286 U-boats passed through the Bay of Biscay during the November 1942 to January 1943 period, with only twenty-two being attacked by aircraft. None was sunk and only two were damaged, one of which, U-263, was heading back to port on the surface

---

[*] Contrary to the statements made on pages 537–8 of *The Creation of a National Air Force*, the delay in providing VLR Liberators for the mid-ocean air gap, once the Anti-U-boat Warfare Committee had convinced Portal to agree to the conversion in November 1942, was due to the time needed to modify the aircraft rather than an unwarranted commitment to the bay offensive. In urging the speedy delivery of further Liberators to the United Kingdom at the end of November 1942, the Air Ministry explicitly told Washington that it had been 'decided to convert to very long range ... and concentrate in two squadrons all Liberators in Coastal Command. To do this means withdrawing Liberators at present employed on anti-submarine work in the outer reaches of the Bay of Biscay.' By 1 March 1943 there were thirty-eight VLR Liberators with Nos 120 and 86 squadrons and only six LR Liberators operating in the bay with No 224 Squadron.

on 27 November when it was attacked again and further damaged by a No 405 Halifax. Despite tactical innovations such as the intermittent use of ASV, or the flooding of certain areas with radar transmissions in attempts to convince the U-boats to submerge at night (compelling them to surface during the day in order to recharge their batteries), poor results plagued No 19 Group's operations until new ASV III radar sets, whose 10-centimetre wavelength could not be detected by Metox, were introduced in the spring of 1943.[54]

The next Canadian squadron to join in the bay offensive, No 407, had spent the first eighteen months of its existence flying Lockheed Hudsons on hazardous anti-shipping strikes off the Dutch coast (see chapter 12). In October 1942, prior to the Operation Torch landings, it had been transferred to St. Eval, in Cornwall, to reinforce No 19 Group's anti-submarine patrols in the bay; after a month of uneventful daylight sorties, Northwood had decided that the Hudson did not have sufficient range and the squadron returned to Norfolk and No 16 Group. Its future appeared uncertain in early November, when instructions were received to transfer ten aircraft to other units and, with only four machines remaining on strength, the squadron was left virtually non-operational for the next two months. This lack of direction, together with the loss of two crews in training accidents (including that of its British commanding officer), did little to improve the squadron's plummeting morale. The future finally seemed resolved, however, when the Air Ministry asked Overseas Headquarters for permission to post it to the Mediterranean during November.[55]

Squadron personnel were innoculated against a range of likely African diseases and sent on embarkation leave, only to have the proposed move cancelled two weeks later, once again leaving the unit in limbo. Air Marshal Edwards considered that the time was opportune to convert it to bombers, for employment in the soon-to-be-formed Canadian bomber group; Ottawa, however, did not think he should 'press for conversion if Air Ministry hold views that such action will minimize [the] war effort.' Finally, in mid-January 1943 the Air Ministry decided that the squadron should remain in Coastal Command, to 'be re-equipped very soon,' and following a month of anti-submarine training on Wellington XIs in northern Scotland it moved to Chivenor, in Devon, on 31 March 1943. The new base, which featured 'extensive hutted accommodation,' would be No 407's home for twenty of the next twenty-six months. The squadron received new Wellington Mark XIIs equipped with Leigh Lights and the latest centimetric ASV III radar.[56]

When they began operations on the night of 19/20 April, these Canadians represented a major reinforcement to No 19 Group's night offensive in the bay, joining No 172 Squadron, the only other Leigh Light unit equipped with centimetric radar, in the latest patrol scheme. Operation Derange had commenced at dawn on 13 April and covered a large strip of ocean two hundred miles wide, extending from Cape Finisterre to the southwestern tip of Ireland. With the U-boats unable to pick up centimetric radar transmissions, the Wellingtons achieved seventeen sightings in less than five hundred hours of flying. Twelve of them resulted in attacks, and two outward-bound U-boats were seriously damaged (both by 172 Squadron) and forced to return to port. Despite a shortage of trained crews that limited No 407 to no more than three sorties per night instead of the normal five or six, and the Canadians' relative inexperience on Leigh Light operations, the squadron managed three of the seventeen sightings and two of the attacks.[57]

To counter this renewed threat by night, U-boats in transit were ordered to submerge during darkness and to surface by day only long enough to recharge their batteries. This brought an immediate increase in the number of daylight sightings during the first week of May, and a marked increase in the lethality of attacks as four U-boats were sunk and three were damaged. However, since the only Canadian squadron operating in the area, No 407, was flying at night it did not share in these successes. Dönitz – who still directly controlled BdU despite having been promoted to be commander-in-chief of the Kriegsmarine in February – had instructed his commanders to remain on the surface and fight it out if they were caught by surprise and lacked the time to dive to safe depths. Nevertheless, most of them chose to dive whatever the circumstances. Of the forty-three U-boats attacked during the last three weeks of May, only seventeen remained on the surface to fight back; two of the three sunk were among the latter.[58]

In the absence of night-time contacts, the three Leigh Light squadrons, Nos 172 and 407 on Wellingtons and No 210 on Catalinas, turned to day patrols after 20 May, although the Canadians also continued their routine night operations. One No 407 aircraft accounted for both of the squadron's sightings and its lone attack during a daylight patrol on 24 May. In both instances the U-boats chose to submerge immediately on spotting the aircraft and were safely below the surface before the Wellington could cross their tracks. Although depth charging was not recommended if a submarine had disappeared from view for more than thirty seconds, Flight Sergeant N.C.C. Luther hopefully (but vainly) dropped his charges ahead of the swirl left by the first U-boat sighted, forty-five seconds after it had submerged.[59]

At the end of the month, Dönitz introduced yet another tactical innovation, instructing his U-boats to make the Biscay passage by daylight, in groups of up to six in order to maximize their anti-aircraft fire. Although initially successful, that tactic, too, soon proved costly. From 12 June until 2 August, when BdU finally returned to the old practice of submerging by day and running on the surface at night, twenty U-boats were sunk and twelve were damaged. Three of the boats were destroyed by ships of the 2nd Escort Group, while the remaining twenty-nine were sunk or damaged in air attacks by No 19 Group.[60]

Having withdrawn from the North Atlantic convoy routes after the catastrophic losses to U-boats there in May, Dönitz was now dispatching most of his submarines to the Brazilian and West African coasts where there were fewer air escorts. The shift had enabled Slessor to redistribute his forces in turn, moving several squadrons no longer required for Atlantic convoy escort to two new patrol areas in the bay, where the enemy's tactics were providing plenty of daylight targets. Beginning on 15 June, Nos 422 and 423 Squadrons both began patrols in the Seaslug area of the outer bay, in addition to occasional convoy escorts northwest of Ireland. A further reinforcement was provided by the torpedo-bomber Hampdens of No 415 Squadron, temporarily transferred from their anti-shipping role to fly patrols in the Musketry area, east of Seaslug and northwest of Cape Finisterre. No 407 Squadron, meanwhile, continued to fly a full schedule of night Musketry patrols, missing most of the daylight action.[61]

While the decision to remain on the surface and fight it out was proving costly, a group of two or three U-boats provided a formidable target for any aircraft. The most commonly encountered boats, the Type VIIc, had a standard anti-aircraft armament of one 20-millimetre cannon and several machine guns, while the larger Type IX carried an additional 37-millimetre gun behind the conning tower; a second 20-millimetre cannon had already been mounted on some boats. Previously encouraged to attack surfaced U-boats because they presented 'a much better chance of a kill than one submerged,' pilots who sighted two or more boats obviously willing to 'fight it out' were now instructed 'to shadow and start the homing procedure until more aircraft appeared on the scene.'[62]

These instructions were acted upon on 14 June when an RAF Whitley sighted the in-bound U-564 and U-185 in the Musketry area. After being fired at, the Whitley circled just out of range and called up additional aircraft until a No 415 Hampden joined it two hours later. After receiving permission from base, the Whitley then attacked U-564, sinking her outright, but was heavily damaged by Flak and crashed into the sea during the flight home. The Hampden, regrettably, continued to shadow U-185 and did not attack even when the submarine stopped to pick up the survivors of U-564. Indeed, the Canadians were still earnestly shadowing their enemy when a flight of Junkers 88s, sent out to escort the U-boats, shot them down.[63]

The same procedure was attempted by a No 422 Sunderland when it spotted three U-boats at the southern edge of the Seaslug area three days later. The Canadians circled and exchanged gunfire with the enemy flotilla, unable to home-in other aircraft because of a transmitter failure, and they eventually lost sight of the boats in the haze. A No 423 Squadron flying-boat also began circling the three submarines it found on 3 July, while calling for back-up, but after initially holding it off with Flak the Germans chose to submerge while the Sunderland was not in position to depth charge them.[64]

Such incidents were not unique to Canadians squadrons. Other U-boat groups frequently evaded attack because of delays in homing in aircraft or a failure to coordinate the actions of those present. To increase the effectiveness of patrols, therefore, Slessor amended his orders on 22 July, directing crews 'to attack at once from low level making the fullest use of front guns to smother the U-boat flak.' The new instructions improved results immediately. Nine submarines were sunk in the two-week period following their promulgation, as opposed to the eight that had been destroyed during the previous five weeks.[65]

The RCAF squadrons were not well placed operationally to share directly in these attacks, however. The Sunderland crews responsible for sinking five of the U-boats were all based in No 19 Group, which patrolled in the Musketry area; No 15 Group's squadrons (including Nos 422 and 423) not only covered the more distant Seaslug area but also had to provide a significant number of convoy escorts. Of the other two Canadian squadrons, No 407 worked mostly at night, when the U-boats were submerged, and No 415, inexperienced in anti-submarine operations, was unable to make more than two fruitless sightings. Despite flying over seven hundred sorties and accumulating just under seven thousand operational hours during June, July, and August, only two Canadian aircraft contributed to the destruction of any U-boats, and both of those actions occurred on 2 August, the same day that Dönitz finally acknowledged that his policy of group sailings was not paying off.[66]

Hampden A of No 415 Squadron, flown by Squadron Leader C.G. Ruttan, caught U-706 on the surface in the Musketry patrol area in mid-morning.

Pilot immediately went in to attack, but crew of U-Boat began firing as S/Ldr Ruttan broke away to come in for attack from starboard quarter. Front gunner fired 10 rounds from A/C but guns then jammed. Attack continued and A/C A/415 dropped 6 × 250 D[epth] C[harges]s across course of U-Boat from 100 feet. Immediate results could not be seen as tail of A/C obstructed view. U-Boat did not submerge but appeared to be a little lower in the water and speed reduced to 9 knots, thus apparently being disabled. At 0917 a [USAAF] Liberator was sighted and went in for direct attack on U-Boat and dropped its [twelve] DCs. After Liberator's attack U-Boat not seen again. Three minutes later a number of bodies, about 15, were seen to come to the surface, surrounded by large quantities of wreckage and diesel oil.[67]

According to the four survivors, the bridge watch was concentrating its attention on the circling Hampden and did not see the approaching Liberator until it was too late.[68] Meanwhile, No 407 Squadron's commanding officer, Wing Commander J.C. Archer, RAF, was flying one of the unit's first daylight patrols in almost seven weeks when he attacked and damaged U-106, 250 miles northwest of Finisterre, less than an hour later. Unable to submerge, the submarine was sunk later that day by aircraft of 228 and 461 Squadrons.[69]

Having lost four submarines in the first two days of August, Dönitz signalled his captains to abandon group passages until the end of the month, when a new radar search receiver should become generally available, and to try instead to enter the bay by sailing close to the Spanish coast, surfacing only at night. An immediate decline in the number of sightings led Northwood to conclude correctly that the enemy had once again altered its tactics and, after 11 August, both Leigh Light Wellington squadrons were assigned a full schedule of night patrols. The Seaslug and Musketry schemes were cancelled and replaced by a less intensive but more widespread system of patrols known as Percussion. No 415 Squadron returned to the more hazardous task of anti-shipping strikes, and both of the Canadian Sunderland squadrons were withdrawn from the bay the following month.[70]

However, No 407 Squadron continued to operate there for the remainder of the year. Of the thirteen U-boats sighted in September, eleven were encountered at night by Leigh Light squadrons; three of them were sighted by No 407, which also recorded the only U-boat destroyed by No 19 Group. On the night of 6/7 September, Pilot Officer E.M. O'Donnell and his all-Canadian crew were some two hundred miles off Cape Finisterre when the radar operator obtained a contact at eight-miles distance. At a height of six hundred feet and less than a mile range, the Leigh Light was switched on to reveal a U-boat 'low in the water but not submerging.' Unfortunately, the Wellington's 'position was unfavourable for attack,' and the light was switched off as the pilot circled for another run. When the U-boat was illuminated a second time it had begun a crash dive, but five depth charges were dropped across its track 'from starboard bow to port quarter,' about twenty-five yards ahead of the swirl. Although assessed at the time as 'probably sunk,' O'Donnell and his crew had actually destroyed U-669.[71]

While Leigh Light operations were not particularly hazardous, especially when compared with anti-shipping strikes, No 407 Squadron's morale began to deteriorate in the fall of 1943 as a result of the inadequate living conditions encountered at Chivenor. Among the Canadians' complaints was the RAF's failure to issue airmen with sheets, which, coupled with 'the RAF standard of infrequent washing of blankets,' led to outbreaks of impetigo. Food was also poor, meals being 'unappetizing, badly cooked and sloppily served' on dishes that were 'consistently dirty,' but efforts to improve the situation, especially in the airmen's messes, proved futile. Although an RCAF squadron leader from District Headquarters in Exeter visited the squadron to try to get something done at the end of September he was unable, singlehandedly, to raise British culinary standards.[72]

The poor fare served at Chivenor was in sharp contrast with that found on a neighbouring American base, where those invited 'had a meal that reminded you of home. Everything was clean and well cooked and all food served was rationed food. Why we can't have the same in the Officer's Mess here is beyond us.' A mess meeting held at Chivenor 'turned out to be a joke as far as the officers of this Squadron were concerned,' complained the squadron diarist. 'There was definitely nothing gained by this meeting as any suggestions by 407 Squadron officers were laughed at. It was just a waste of 225 man-hours and nothing worth while gained.'[73]

Morale was not helped by the transfer of more than a hundred groundcrew to a common servicing echelon under the control of the RAF. This change was part of the increasingly centralized 'planned flying and maintenance' concept intended to maximize the use of aircraft, but it 'did not please the airmen as they regretted and resented loss of direct contact with ... their own squadron and their own aircraft.'[74] They thought that it 'tends to defeat its own purpose in some degree because the groundcrew, as well as aircrew, lose personal interest in an individual aircraft. Where one aircraft is assigned to one crew and the same groundcrew services it constantly, the groundcrew becomes as much interested in the joint effort as though they were in the flying section of the team. When they no longer have constant, personal contact with one aircrew, they are apt to become indifferent and, on occasions, even slipshod. They become merely routine mechanics.'[75]

An influx of RAF aircrew in September reduced the Canadian content of the squadron – which had stood at over 90 per cent for the past eighteen months – to 86.6 per cent.[76] The difference in numbers was small, but aircrew were the acknowledged 'cutting edge' of a unit, who supplied what prestige and glory there might be, and groundcrew – Canadian groundcrew, at least – generally preferred to work for aircrew of their own kind.

The cumulative effect of life at Chivenor became apparent at the end of September, with 'an appreciable drop in morale among aircrew over the past few months and this is reflected throughout all personnel of this squadron. There is not the former keenness to fly either on operations or on exercises and tests and this would appear to be due to a loss of confidence in the aircraft both as to its initial worth and the maintenance of it. Crews requiring two operational meals in connection with a single trip are still being asked to pay for their second meal despite the fact that they miss one and frequently two meals in the mess.'[77]

The Canadians' sagging spirits were not improved by the decreasing number of U-boat sightings being made. The squadron continued to fly night patrols until the end of January 1944, but after O'Donnell's successful attack in early September there were few sightings and only three attacks, none of which achieved success. Three aircraft were lost on operations, including that of Wing Commander Archer. Two probably fell victim to German long-range fighters patrolling the bay, while the third may have been shot down while attacking U-966 on the night of 9/10 November. When the new commanding officer, Wing Commander R.A. Ashman (a prewar regular who had entered the RCAF in January 1939 after acquiring a degree in electrical engineering), joined the squadron in early November he became the first RCAF officer to command it – and would retain his command for the next year. He already had more than a thousand hours of operational flying to his credit, in both Eastern and Western Air commands of the Home War Establishment, including a stint with 115 (F) Squadron in the Aleutians.[78]

Squadron morale improved briefly during a month-long transfer to St Eval, a move made necessary while the deteriorating runways at Chivenor were being repaired. The Canadians 'noticed the striking difference in [the] standard of messing' at their temporary station, an improvement that partially compensated for the fact that St Eval was infested with rats. On returning to Chivenor, however, the poor living conditions once again 'contributed to the general lowering of the morale of the Squadron.' Not until February 1944, when it was transferred to Limavady in Northern Ireland, did the diarist find that 'both officers and other ranks are benefiting from the improved diet and are more contented. Hence the morale of the Squadron has risen noticeably,' a state that was 'undoubtedly … contributed to by good weather and good food, ample billet space and agreeable working conditions.'[79]

Given the difficulties that Canadians were experiencing in adjusting to British standards of diet and sanitation, both Ottawa and Overseas Headquarters in London were anxious to group RCAF squadrons together, perhaps on a Canadian-administered base, with an eye to developing an environment that would improve morale and unit efficiency. Air Marshal Edwards had approached the Air Ministry at the end of June 1943 to suggest that his three flying-boat squadrons, Nos 413, 422, and 423, 'be formed into an RCAF Flying Boat Wing and stationed at Castle Archdale or alternatively some other Flying Boat Station mutually acceptable.' While recognizing the difficulties of bringing 413 Squadron back from the Indian Ocean, Edwards was hopeful that No 422, then stationed at Bowmore, on Scotland's Isle of Islay, might be transferred more quickly, noting that it had 'had a particularly strenuous time, having been stationed since becoming operational in unpalatable surroundings and operating under tiring and trying conditions.' Bowmore was considered 'most unsuitable both from an operational point of view and also from the point of view of morale,' since many of the unit's maintenance and administrative tasks had to be conducted from other stations. Edwards also hoped to provide a more Canadian atmosphere by posting RCAF personnel 'to fill certain key positions in the establishment of a[ny] station' from which the Canadian squadrons would be operating.[80]

In discussing the matter with Northwood, Edwards learned that Slessor was not anxious either to move the RAF squadron at Castle Archdale or to replace the station commander. He was, however, prepared to consider transferring No 422 Squadron to the Irish base 'in a few months time.'[81] His reluctance to alter the situation at Castle Archdale was understandable given that the RAF's inspector general had already found it to be 'an excellent station. For an operational station, quite exceptional. The administration, organization and discipline of the station appeared to be on a high level and everything was found in good order … There is a tradition growing up in too many operational stations that because the units are operational, therefore all standards of upkeep, cleanliness, tidiness and deportment may be relaxed … Castle Archdale is a good example of the high standards that can be maintained.'[82] Even on a well-run base, however, the general cleanliness of the Canadians stood out. 'I wish in particular, to commend No. 423 (Canadian) Squadron. All their quarters, including those of the aircrew, were exceptionally well kept, and the way the quarters had been furnished by the men themselves indicated the interest that they took in making them comfortable, clean and pleasant to live in. The same applied to their workshops, hangars, technical accommodation and to the flying boats themselves.'[83]

Slessor's desire to retain the current RAF station commander until his tour expired was tempered by his view that 'one never knows with the Canadians, they are a bit liable to get on their high horse'; but when the British incumbent was posted in October 1943, he was replaced by Group Captain Martin Costello, RCAF. Costello had previously served in Eastern Air Command in Halifax as senior air staff officer and in Ottawa as deputy air member for air staff. Although he was later joined by a half-dozen more Canadian officers, station headquarters and base administration remained, at best, Anglo-Canadian organizations.[84]

When No 422 Squadron finally joined No 423 at Lough Erne, in November 1943, the Canadian content among groundcrew of the two units stood at 72.5 and 85.6 per cent, respectively, while the continuing shortage of RCAF flight engineers and wireless operator/mechanics (who had to be trained in the United Kingdom) contributed to the relatively low figures of 52.5 and 46.5 per cent, respectively, among aircrew. Although operating out of Castle Archdale, No 422's headquarters and accommodation were located at St Angelo, several miles to the south. The separation of aircraft from living quarters 'was naturally not convenient to those who had to travel back and forth and, after many complaints, the whole squadron was finally moved to Castle Archdale in April 1944.'[85]

Although Coastal Command's primary effort during the spring of 1943 had been in the Bay of Biscay, No 15 Group had continued to provide escorts for North Atlantic convoys. It was during one of these patrols that a No 423 Sunderland spotted U-456 – already damaged following an attack by a No 86 Squadron Liberator – in the vicinity of a convoy. When it appeared that the U-boat was going to stay on the surface and fight it out, Flight Lieutenant John Musgrave decided to call in nearby naval escorts; only when the submarine began to dive in order to escape the approaching vessels did he deliver an attack. The U-boat was subsequently destroyed by depth charges from HMS *Lagan* and HMCS *Drumheller*.[86]

Responding to the build-up of submarines using Norwegian bases, in July 1943 Northwood established a new patrol scheme (codenamed Moorings) between the Faröe Islands and Iceland, to be flown daily by those aircraft not detailed for bay patrols or convoy escorts. Flying Officer A.A. Bishop[*] and his crew were engaged in a Moorings patrol on 4 August 1943 when they spotted the 1688-ton re-supply submarine, U-489. The U-boat remained on the surface, where its 20-millimetre and 37-millimetre cannon provided a formidable defence, and began weaving in an attempt to keep the Sunderland on its stern.[87]

Because of this the [tactic] skipper did not go straight in but circled about a mile away at a height of 600 feet trying to find some way of getting Jerry at a disadvantage. During this time the boys in the galley were busy shooting pictures ...

We turned in towards the U-boat at around 1200 yards and opened fire with our .5-inch [machine] gun ... then we opened fire with our .303 Vickers [machine gun].

At this point the Jerries who, as far as we could tell, hadn't hit us yet, started to register a few. From there on in it was a steady rain of lead, wounding the second pilot and the second wireless operator who was down in the nose on the [.303 machine] gun ...

___

[*] Wrongly identified in volume II of this history as the son of W.A. Bishop, the First World War flying ace; he was no relation.

We managed to hang on and dropped our six depth charges right up the track of the U-boat from dead astern... By the time we had released the depth charges the aircraft had a terrific fire in the port wing, the aileron controls and elevator trimming tabs were shot away and things didn't look so good ...

We bounced on the swell twice and the third time the port wing dropped ... the float broke off, the wing tip caught in the water, and the aircraft cartwheeled straight into the sea ... The starboard wing, now also on fire, and the fuselage from it back to the tail was still afloat. One of the boys sat on the tail plane for a few minutes, but soon had to jump into the water as the kite sank in four or five minutes. The skipper came up on the port side, swam back [to] where he found the second wireless operator struggling in the water, badly wounded. They stuck together until rescued.[88]

Bishop and five of the eleven crewmen managed to scramble into an inflatable dingy and were soon joined in the water by the submariners as they abandoned their sinking U-boat. 'The Jerries sat quite comfortably on their rafts 100 yards or more away, and made no attempt to come and pick us up. The first wireless operator saw smoke on the horizon, but none of the rest of us knew anything about a Destroyer coming until it was right beside us and had launched a whaler to pick us up. They had seen us go down to attack, and followed the smoke from our burning fuel to our position.'[89] Both Bishop and Musgrave were awarded Distinguished Flying Crosses.

Most patrols were less eventful. Following their withdrawal from the Bay offensive in mid-September, both 422 and 423 Squadrons were kept busy in the Moorings area.

Having reached their area they will take up a course directly east and west and continue on it for 100 or 150 miles, turn north or south 20 miles or so and return the same distance. For the duration of their patrol they continue covering that same area. They keep constant watch but that does not mean the gunners in their turrets and the two functioning pilots sit or stand there with binoculars glued to their eyes. The signals officer does the watching in his curtained-off dark room where he watches his radar equipment for any variation in landscape or seascape.

Flying evenly and uneventfully over the barren ocean at 2,000 feet rapidly becomes monotonous and surprisingly tiring. To minimize the monotony and especially give those in cramped, cold or confined positions a change, most crews normally change around every hour ...

The patrol continues, eventlessly. The navigator periodically climbs up and peers out the astrodome. Just as regularly he checks on the wind-drift, with the assistance of a spare gunner who takes the reading on the drift indicator in the tail. In between times, he continues to pore over his charts, making calculations, checking time and position, keeping his log up to date. He is the one member of the crew who works continuously throughout the trip, even eating at his little table.

The crew take turns being cooks for the day. The meal is staggered, of necessity, two or three eating at a time in the wardroom. The rest have to be on duty and, anyway, the stove is only large enough to prepare for about three at once.

The day drags on. Periodically, the radar operator picks up something which turns out to be a surface vessel. Or two or three grey corvettes, which from 2,500 feet and six or seven miles could be mistaken for submarines. The skipper has the flare pistol ready to fire off a cartridge with the colour of the day in case of doubtful identification. Perhaps a Liberator or Fort[ress] in transit crosses the patrol area.

Since a submarine-sighting is something merely hoped for and rarely attained (a large proportion of aircrew complete a whole tour of 800 hours without seeing a submarine), the biggest thrill most crews get is to come upon a big convoy spread out on the mid-Atlantic for miles, slowly crawling towards the British Isles.

To vary the long day, there's dinner. A couple of hours later there's another cup of steaming tea. Two or three hours after that, more tea with biscuits or sandwiches. Finally, tired and bored and probably cold, they leave their patrol and head for base, so as to arrive back on scheduled time.[90]

For most crews, the greatest threat they had to face was that posed by the weather, 'more dangerous and incalculable than any human enemy. And there is nothing a crew can do about it, once caught.' Weather also governed the rhythm of operations and was responsible for cancelling or curtailing about one-fifth of all sorties. Most of the time this was due to the weather at base, either at the time of takeoff or that forecast for the time of return, but unfavourable conditions in the patrol area accounted for two-thirds of weather-related cancellations of Moorings flights.[91]

By routeing his submarines independently and keeping them submerged as much as possible, Dönitz was able to pass nine boats through the Moorings area in September 1943 with only one being attacked, and that unsuccessfully, while a further twenty-six made the passage in October without being sighted.[92] The Canadians' last victory of 1943 was scored by a No 423 Sunderland, piloted by Flying Officer A.H. Russell, while escorting a convoy west of Ireland on 8 October. Dropping out of low cloud, he caught U-610 on the surface and, in an exceptionally precise attack, sank it with three well-placed depth charges.[93] Nine days later, in the same area, Flight Lieutenant P.T. Sargent of 422 Squadron attacked one of two surfaced U-boats observed while patrolling in the area of convoy ONS 20. His first run was met by a heavy Flak barrage from the two boats. What happened next was recorded by his second pilot, the senior survivor among his crew.

As the first attack resulted in an undershoot with a hang-up [of one depth charge which failed to release], the skipper pulled around sharply going into a second attack immediately. This time no evasive action was taken, the skipper apparently determined that the attack be successful and only two depth charges being left with which to attack.

On the run-in, Ack Ack hits were numerous, both front gunners and the navigator being hit, as well as some damage being caused to the engine controls in the cockpit. In spite of this, Flight Lieutenant Sargent continued his attack and, on the report of the rear gunner, obtained a perfect straddle with the two depth charges ...

Exceptional courage and gallantry was shown by Flying Officer Chesley Steeves, the navigator. F/O Steeves, standing at the navigator's table on the second attack, had his left leg completely blown away by an explosive shell. In spite of this he refused to lie down ... and succeeded in giving the writer [Flying Officer A.R.B. Bellis] the D[ead] R[eckoning] position of the attack and a course to steer to the nearest convoy before collapsing and dying within a few minutes.[94]

Its controls shot away, the Sunderland crash-landed within sight of a British destroyer, with three of the crew – including the group gunnery officer who had been manning one of the .5-inch galley guns – already dead. Two others were seriously wounded. Sargent himself was either killed in the crash or knocked unconscious and sank with his boat; and Bellis would have suffered a similar fate if a seaman from the destroyer had not dived overboard to pull him from the wreckage. It took 'almost two hours' of artificial respiration to revive him. Meanwhile, a 'seriously damaged' submarine fled the scene. Bellis and the radio operator who had signalled the destroyer, Warrant Officer W.F. Beals, were each awarded the DFC.[95] Neither Sargent nor Steeves were decorated, however, since only the Victoria Cross, among Commonwealth awards for gallantry, could be awarded posthumously at that time.[*]

Although BdU attempted to improve its fortunes in 1944 by establishing submerged patrol lines within 250 miles of the Irish coast, the continued inability of submarines to operate on the surface under the threat of Allied air power thwarted Dönitz's every effort. Underwater, the U-boats were too slow and their endurance too limited to be successful. Of the 3360 merchant ships that crossed the patrol lines, only three were sunk. German losses, however, totalled twenty-nine submarines, of which eighteen were accounted for by surface escorts and six by Coastal Command, two of them by RCAF aircraft. The first Canadian success came on the night of 10/11 February when a No 407 Squadron Wellington flown by Flying Officer P.W. Heron swept in on a radar contact and, illuminating U-283 with its Leigh Light, sank it with a stick of six depth charges.[96]

A month later a Sunderland of No 422 Squadron flown by an RAF pilot accounted for U-625. The submarine took two-and-a-half hours to sink and, during that time, bereft of more depth charges, the Sunderland circled it. Before taking to their liferafts, the Germans flashed the signal 'Fine Bombish' to the airmen. Nothing further was ever heard of the more than twenty submariners photographed in the water. BdU had received U-625's distress signals and dispatched two U-boats to attempt a rescue, but by 12 March they concluded that 'U-625 must be considered a total loss.'[97]

---

[*] When a Liberator of No 200 Squadron engaged in a similar attack was shot down on 11 August 1943 with the loss of all on board, its RNZAF captain was awarded the Victoria Cross on the evidence of German survivors. But the Liberator was a much faster machine than the Sunderland - which meant that the apparent risk was predictably less - and it had come under the fire of only one U-boat.

Planning for Operation Overlord had begun in early 1943, but those plans drawn up prior to January 1944 were primarily concerned with the forces directly involved. Coastal Command's role in protecting the flanks of the invasion corridor and its sea communications across the Atlantic had not been considered in any detail until late January, while the development of an operational plan was complicated by concurrent proposals to reduce its size and strength substantially. Seizing an opportunity presented when the prime minister suggested that some anti-submarine squadrons might be able to reinforce Transport Command during the critical initial phases of the invasion, the CAS asked for further cuts (despite warnings from his staff that any reduction in the anti-U-boat effort 'would probably lose more than it would gain')[98] on the grounds that an 'absolute minimum of resources should be devoted to the defensive and the maximum to the offensive.'

Bearing in mind the over-riding importance of Overlord, a suitable way to tackle this problem would be, I think, something on the following lines.

First of all, estimate what rate of sinkings our present strategy could stand. (It might possibly be about the 300,000 tons per month which during a period of heavy sinkings was thought to be an average loss which we could stand.)[*]

Then estimate the minimum anti-submarine resources in aircraft, escort carriers etc. required to limit the rate of loss to this figure ...

We could then consider how to effect cuts in Coastal Command and overseas anti-submarine and anti-shipping forces ... In the result it should be possible to throw up large man-power resources for strengthening Bomber Command, AEAF and Maintenance Command and possibly to make available a number of squadrons equipped with aircraft suitable for taking a direct part in Overlord.[99]

At Portal's behest, then, and ignoring its own previous advice, the air staff drafted a proposal recommending that Northwood give up seventeen of its thirty-four squadrons at home and an additional twenty-four overseas. The attempted finesse was foiled, however, when the director of operations (maritime) and the vice-chief of the air staff obtained a copy of the proposal before it reached Portal and amended it to take into account the Admiralty's more significant objections – much to the dissatisfaction of the CAS. Refusing to accept their greater estimate of the U-boat threat, either to Overlord or the North Atlantic convoys, and convinced that the anti-shipping strike wings would have few useful targets, Portal now instructed his personal staff officer to produce yet another draft which, as before, argued for deep cuts in Northwood's order of battle.[100]

However, at a full Air Ministry meeting held on 22 March 1944, Portal found himself virtually alone in his desire to carry these reductions through. Opposed by the VCAS, DCAS, the air member for supply and organization, and

---

[*] Actually, during the first five months of 1944 the Allies averaged only 100,000 tons of shipping lost per month worldwide.

the new AOC-in-C at Northwood, the CAS was finally persuaded that the proposed cuts would not result in any appreciable increase in Bomber Command's strength and might even make that command's future expansion more difficult to justify. After further consultation with Douglas, Portal decided that it would be wiser to 'defer the review on the needs of the Air War at sea until after Operation Overlord when there might well be grounds for a much more drastic reduction.'[101]

With the question of its future establishment settled for the moment, the staff at Northwood was able to draw up a more precise 'Directive on the Role of Coastal Command in Overlord.' The seven anti-submarine squadrons in Nos 15 and 18 Groups formerly assigned to the Northern Transit Area and Atlantic convoys were reduced to four, with most of their aircraft deployed for anti-submarine operations in the southwestern approaches to the English Channel. Although 422 and 423 Squadrons would both stay in No 15 Group at Castle Archdale, they, too, were to operate in the southwest approaches under No 19 Group's control, as was 407 Squadron at Chivenor. In all, No 19 Group would have eight Liberator, five Wellington, two Halifax, and six Sunderland squadrons available for anti-submarine operations. These aircraft were to be employed in a series of 'box' patrols, flexible enough that they could be shifted, either individually or as a whole, up-Channel towards the invasion area much as a cork might be pushed into a bottle. Those Cork patrols that abutted on the French coast would be protected by fighters of the Allied Expeditionary Air Force and were among the most important since 'the enemy will almost certainly move his U/Boats [towards the invasion corridors] under the cover of his fighters and shore defences.'[102]

No 407 Squadron returned to Chivenor in late April, in preparation for D-Day, and the airmen were pleased to find that conditions there had improved significantly during their three-month absence. The food was noticeably better, even though the medical officer reported 'mild outbreaks of stomach upsets, which may or may not be attributable to the present messing facilities.' Steps 'taken with a view to improving the washing of dishes and silverware' subsequently solved the hygiene problem, and the men's health remained 'quite good' throughout the summer.[103]

Once settled, the squadron quickly resumed its anti-submarine sweeps in the Channel and Bay of Biscay. Success came within a matter of days, during the early hours of 4 May. Flying Officer L.J. Bateman and the crew of Wellington M were about two hundred miles north of Cape Finisterre, when they obtained a radar echo which proved to be a surfaced U-846. Bright moonlight made the Leigh Light superfluous.

M tracked dead over U-Boat and, aiming at the bow as centre of stick, released six × 250 Torpex D[epth] C[harges] from height 150 feet. Points of entry were not observed owing to glare of tracer from M's rear guns, and flak and tracer from U-Boat, while the depth charge plumes obscured any evidence of the explosions with relation [to] the U-Boat. Immediately after the DC explosions all flak from the U-Boat ceased. M continued on course and then did climbing turn to port obtaining height of 1500 feet and circled position of attack at range two miles... When a complete circuit had been made, contact was lost.[104]

U-846 sank with the loss of all hands.

As the hours of darkness diminished with the approach of summer – a decided disadvantage for the enemy – No 18 Group launched a new offensive off the Norwegian coast following BdU's decision to reinforce its Arctic flotillas (in anticipation of an Allied invasion of Norway, part of the Overlord deception plan) and pass U-boats into the Atlantic via the northern route. Nos 422 and 423 Squadrons sent detachments to Sullom Voe from 18 May until 6 June. At 0719 hours on 24 May an RAF Catalina attacked U-476 northeast of the Faröe Islands, causing serious damage which left it dead in the water.[105] The attack began a confusing series of encounters between submarines and flying-boats that continued throughout the day as both sides searched for the disabled U-boat within a relatively small piece of the Atlantic Ocean.

Later that morning, Flight Lieutenant R.H. Nesbitt, flying a Sunderland of No 423 Squadron, made contact with the Catalina and took over the search for U-476. At 1419 hours the radio operator overheard a distress call from an unidentified source just as the second pilot glimpsed 'what appeared to be a large puff of smoke or splash 10/15 miles north.' Turning to investigate, they sighted U-921, which was searching for the crippled U-467. Heavy but inaccurate Flak and skilful manoeuvring on the part of the enemy caused the inexperienced Canadians to drop their depth charges wide of the mark, but their machine-gun fire inflicted casualties and forced U-921 to make for port.[106]

While making their approach, Nesbitt's crew had reported the wreckage of what appeared to be an aircraft in the water, 'whitish grey in colour – wing-like in shape and was amid oil or fuel slick.' Both the distress call and the wreckage may have come from Sunderland R of 422 Squadron, flown by Flying Officer G.E. Holley, which went missing during the day. U-921's log records being attacked by a Catalina at 1415 hours followed by a Sunderland at 1434 hours, but Coastal Command reports indicate that the only Catalina attack made on 24 May was the early morning encounter of the 'Cat from 210 Squadron with U-476.' Did the crew of U-921 misreport Holley's Sunderland as a Catalina? Perhaps they hit it but were unaware of its fate as it disappeared from view, desperately transmitting distress signals before crashing into the sea.

A more precise determination of what happened is complicated by the fact that a third German submarine, U-990, came across the wreckage of an aircraft's tail unit afloat in the water, five hours prior to locating the damaged U-476 at 0015 hours on 25 May. The crippled U-boat was scuttled and, after transferring to U-990, the survivors of U-476 were informed of the aircraft wreckage, which they assumed was the remains of the Catalina that had attacked them the previous morning. Based on their claim, the RAF's Air Historical Branch later credited U-476 with the destruction of the Sunderland; but since the survivors of U-476 also stated that their 'boat was not troubled for 17 hours after the attack' by 210 Squadron's Catalina at 0719 hours, and

Holley did not depart Sullom Voe until forty minutes later, it was not possible for U-476 to have shot down the missing Canadians. Sunderland R is more likely to have been the so-called Catalina that initially attacked U-921 at 1415 hours. What is certain is that the Kriegsmarine lost one submarine and the RCAF one flying-boat.[107]

Anticipating a major landing somewhere along the French coast in the summer of 1944, BdU had been holding some seventy submarines in readiness to meet the invasion fleet, half of them (including nine of the new Schnorkel boats) stationed in the Biscay ports and the other half in more distant Norwegian waters. (The adoption of Schnorkel, an air induction trunk and exhaust pipe that enabled U-boats to use their diesel engines while submerged at periscope depth, meant that submariners could now remain under water for days at a time, and by the end of May the Germans had fitted some thirty operational boats with the device.)[108] By noon on D-Day – 6 June 1944 – all the Schnorkel boats were at sea with orders to attack shipping making for the Normandy beaches. At the same time, the conventional boats from Lorient, St Nazaire, and La Pallice were dispatched to form a patrol line stretching from the Isles of Scilly to the Franco-Spanish border, in order to block the Atlantic approaches to the cross-Channel invasion corridor and screen the Biscay coast against any secondary landing there. Those at Brest were ordered to the south coast of England, between The Lizard and Hartland Point.[109]

Instructed to reach their stations quickly, most boats, including those with Schnorkel, surfaced after dark on the 6th in an effort to make a faster passage. That was a mistake. Eleven air attacks were made during the night, two submarines were sunk, and six were damaged and driven back to base. Dönitz then recommended that the others travel submerged as much as possible, but, in a region of strong, often adverse, currents and rip-tides, that could be a slow and laborious business. By the evening of 10 June, none of the Schnorkel boats had reached their assigned patrol areas, one having been sunk and two others damaged enough to compel their return to Brest; and all eight of the conventional boats sent to patrol south of the Scillies had either been sunk or damaged by air attack. On 12 June, satisfied that a landing on the Biscay coast was not going to be attempted, BdU recalled all the non-Schnorkel boats to port.[110]

The RCAF components of Coastal Command played no direct part in any of those successes. After flying convoy escorts early in the month, Nos 422 and 423 Squadrons both began a heavy schedule of Cork patrols on the 9th, but as their patrol areas, in 'choke points' off Land's End and in the approaches to the St George's and Bristol channels, were north of the region in which the U-boats were deployed, no sightings were made.

No 407 Squadron's night-time Cork patrols in the Bay of Biscay and the approaches to the English Channel were of an entirely different character. Two crews flew on D-Day and one, led by Squadron Leader D.W. Farrell, never returned, possibly having been shot down by U-621 during the early hours of 7 June. More positive results were achieved late on the 20th. Southwest of the

Isles of Scilly, Flying Officer F.H. Foster and crew located U-971, a Schnorkel boat based in Norway and ordered to the Channel area on 9 June.[111]

The submarine had had a complicated passage. Attacked by a four-engined aircraft while on the surface just north of the Faröes on 15 June, 'U-971 opened fire with all her armament and the aircraft [probably from an OTU] turned away.' When attacked by Foster's crew just before midnight, U-971 suffered severe damage and was forced to submerge. Engaged repeatedly over the next few days, the U-boat was eventually finished off by HMCS *Haida* and HMS *Eskimo*. The captain and fifty-one of his fifty-three man crew were rescued.[112]

Their movements inhibited by day and night, few of the Schnorkel boats ever reached the invasion corridor. By daylight, Schnorkels left a small but visible wake and an exhaust trace, while at night the 3-centimetre ASV sets now coming into use could detect a Schnorkel head in seas less turbulent than those produced by winds of Force 3 on the Beaufort scale. If they chose to run submerged without their Schnorkels, however, the drain on their batteries whenever the tidal stream was adverse often prevented U-boat commanders from using their electric motors. They were also unwilling to use their transmitters, thereby leaving BdU unaware of their progress and unable to coordinate operations.[113]

Indeed, only U-621 reached the invasion area by 15 June and that to little effect. Three more boats arrived during the last week of June, but only U-984 was able to achieve significant results, sinking three large cargo ships. Meanwhile, a combination of dense air cover and roving groups of escort vessels accounted for seven of the Schnorkel boats in transit, three sunk by surface vessels, two by aircraft, and two shared. Again, the three RCAF squadrons, continuing their uneventful Cork patrols and until now equipped with the old metric radar, had no part in these successes. In late July, however, Nos 422 and 423 Squadrons were both withdrawn from operations for two weeks in order to train on the 10-centimetre ASV III radar with which they were finally being supplied.[114]

Operation Cobra, the American breakout from the Normandy beachhead, began on 25 July; and by the first week of August, with the US Third Army racing into Brittany, the German submariners were forced to abandon their northern Biscay ports. Dönitz sent sixteen boats to La Pallice and Bordeaux, but (proving beyond doubt how dangerous these waters now were) only nine arrived. Many were sent to Norway and it was in the north, therefore, that Coastal Command gathered its strength to destroy those making that passage. Nos 422 and 423 Squadrons flew an increasing number of sorties after returning to operations on 6 and 7 August, and they were soon joined by 407 Squadron when that unit moved from Chivenor to Wick on the 24th.[115] Successful or not, these patrols, lasting up to fourteen hours, could be gruelling.

The engines were started at 1330 hours, moorings were slipped and we taxied on to the Lough [Erne]. By that time the engines were warmed up and ... the Sunderland with its 11 tons of petrol and depth charges became airborne and we set course for St.

Johns Point in Donegal Bay. The radar was checked as we were approaching Church Hill, and then picked up St. Johns Point, bang on. The guns and camera mechanisms were then checked, bomb doors opened and the trolleys were run out with the depth charges. The depth charges were then brought back into the bomb bay and the doors closed. Having cleared the coast line, we set course for the patrol area and arrived there at approximately 1600 hours.

... it was estimated that we would be able to make two complete sweeps of the patrol area during our allotted time. St. Kilda, which is a dot on the map, appeared out of the mist as an immense barren rock rising sheer from the sea and was apparently a valuable aid to the navigator in an otherwise empty expanse of water.

Hot tea, prepared by one of the crew, was passed around with sandwiches at approximately 1700 hours and was a welcome break. Flying at 800 ft. we continually ran into wisps of cloud below the cloud base and visibility was not good. During the patrol we made five radar contacts which were investigated and found to be small surface craft. We could imagine the feeling of the crews of these ships at seeing an aircraft without warning appear from the clouds and flying straight for it. Fortunately, they have probably reached the stage in this war that all aircraft which they encounter over this stretch of water are friendly. We had a hot meal in considerable comfort at about 1900 hours. It was prepared on the galley stove and consisted of potatoes, beans, canned beef and an egg, and was delicious.

... We had to drop down to 600 feet to get under the cloud base. The skipper took a turn at navigating while the navigator had his meal. Periodically during the trip the gunners and wireless operators changed watches as the first gunner detailed each person over the intercom to his position. From time to time came a voice on the intercom checking the D[ead] R[eckoning] compass, which is located in the tail, against the reading of the repeater on the bridge. Between times the binoculars were in constant use, scanning the horizon, and a radar operator was perpetually watching the radar screen in the darkroom and reporting the blips to the skipper. The navigator was busy at all times at his table, plotting courses, getting drifts, fixes, three-course winds with flame floats, and altering courses.

On leaving the patrol area at approximately 0100 hours we set course for base and got into clearer weather where the beacons along the coast were visible for miles. We soon picked up the ... lights at Castle Archdale and became waterborne without incident at approximately 0300 hours in a downfall of rain ... No incidents to report.[116]

Despite the hazards, Dönitz kept some boats in the English Channel to continue the attack on Allied supply lines and, perhaps, to tie down some aircraft that might otherwise have been seeking U-boats making for Norway. He also moved some Schnorkel boats to inshore positions along the convoy routes south and northwest of Ireland and off the north coast of Scotland, thus forcing Northwood to give priority to its inshore patrols over ocean convoy support and to curtail operations against the escaping Biscay boats in the Northern Transit Area. No 407 Squadron continued to fly in the Transit Area, but both of the Canadian Sunderland squadrons flew an increasing number of their patrols in inshore waters, either southwest of England or northwest of Scotland.[117]

Dönitz's move of his most modern boats to coastal waters marked the beginning of the final phase of the submarine war. By the fall of 1944 U-boat commanders were using their Schnorkel only at night for a short time to recharge their batteries and were remaining submerged for their whole patrol. As a result, contacts became relatively rare events, and the meagre results reflected this new reality. In September 1944 nearly 14,000 flying hours resulted in only five sightings and no actual attacks, although a promising contact by a No 423 Squadron Sunderland on U-482's Schnorkel, which was 'about 2 ft out of the water,' was wasted. 'Unfortunately the D/Cs failed to release as A/C tracked directly over submarine, and before another attack could be made the Schnorkel had disappeared.' October, which saw the number of U-boats on patrol reduced to a mere five as BdU reorganized its submarine fleet and expanded its Norwegian port facilities, was similarly frustrating. Despite a further 5445 hours on inshore patrols, there were no U-boat sightings to report.[118]

The monotony of fruitless patrolling, compounded by the relative remoteness of Castle Archdale from any major town (the gloriously green, notoriously quiet, Irish countryside held little appeal for young men who dreamed of bright lights, dances, and noisy 'pubs'), no doubt exacerbated the tensions which continued to plague RCAF/RAF relations. In October, a visiting RCAF historian commented on the problem.

Because of the comparative isolation of 'C.A.,' much more than average of the off-duty time of the staff is spent around the messes. Where messes in bomber stations in Yorkshire, for example, are almost completely deserted early in the evening, there is always a fair crowd in the messes at 'C.A..'

Despite that added use, little apparent effort was made to bring the appearance and comfort of Castle Archdale messes even up to average. That fact, combined with almost maximum monthly [financial] assessments on the officers, caused constant irritation. If they could see a good part of the money being spent, instead of merely building up mess reserves, Canadian officers said they would be glad to pay in any reasonable amount.

This whole question adds to the ill-disguised feeling between the RAF and the RCAF groups on the station. Normally there seems to be a degree of cleavage between S[tation] HQ and the squadrons on any station but when SHQ is RAF and the squadrons are RCAF, the situation calls for unusual diplomacy. And the Canadian officers consider it inappropriate to have a somewhat arbitrary RAF officer, who reputedly openly professes his dislike of Canadians, as P[resident of the] M[ess] C[ommittee] of a mess in which a substantial majority are Canadians. The sergeants' mess similarly has an RAF PMC.

The cleavage is furthered by the fact that the SHQ staff in general is older than the aircrew officers and, as a whole, by age and custom, is not given to as boisterous goings-on in the mess. There is difference of opinion over the almost-constant playing of 'hot' popular orchestral recordings on the record-player attached to the radio. Aircrew suggest those who don't like it could use the other, quieter lounge, where bridge is played almost day and night. They take a 'dim view' when the radio is sent

out to be overhauled and comes back fixed so that the radio receiver works but the
record-player won't.

These undercurrents, of course, are rarely obvious in the mess and do not seem to
interfere with amiable relations between individuals. However, there is a natural
tendency for anyone to mingle more readily with those he already knows or with
whom he has common work interests.[119]

Notwithstanding the undertone of danger implicit in mounting long, maritime patrols, the lack of operational excitement had its own distinct impact –
or, rather, lack of impact.

There seems a great lack of tension and little 'shop talk' ... They grouse about the
almost constant cloudiness, which is depressing; about the rain which falls several
times a day for eleven months a year; about the monotony of their patrols which are
exhausting without resulting in a sense of something specific accomplished (like dropping a bomb on a target). Many claim they would prefer to be flying bombers, despite
the much higher loss ratio, because they would be 'doing something.' In a second tour
in Bomber [Command], too, they would have a definite number of trips to do. 'When
you get them in, you pick up your bets and you're through,' as one navigator put it ...
Navigators especially complain that they were put into Coastal involuntarily; that when
they did well at Observers' School, they were then sent on a GR course, which permanently earmarked them for Coastal Command.

Despite all that and perhaps because of the difference in tempo on a flying boat
station, life seems to move along in an easy, regular way. The age-range of the aircrew
is approximately the same as on any bomber station. If there is any difference in
temperament and attitude, it is probably the result of environment rather than original
selection.

A fundamental variation which doubtless has much to do with shaping mental
attitudes is that the 'boatmen' feel they can look ahead; in short, that they have a much
better than even chance of surviving a tour. So they become interested in saving pay,
in taking classes or courses in their spare time. They take a more responsible attitude
about their diversions, with V[eneral] D[isease] no problem on the station. Because
they are under less constant worry, they can sit and play bridge or sit around the mess
sipping a Guinness without continually talking 'shop.'[120]

After moving to Wick in August, 407 Squadron spent two-and-a-half months
flying over the Northern Transit Area, recording three U-boat sightings and
two well-executed attacks in October, although only that of Flying Officer J.E.
Neelin on the 30th did any damage. Neelin's depth-charging of the torpedo
transport submarine U-106I off the coast of southern Norway left the U-boat
unable to dive. Although subsequently attacked by an RAF Liberator while on
the surface, it reached Maalöy Sound, where BdU hoped 'to repair her as she
is particularly valuable.'[121]

October's 17,800 hours of inshore and transit-area flying produced only
eleven actual sightings – ten of which occurred off the Norwegian coast – and
led to an understandable feeling of frustration throughout the command. Unfor-

tunately, it also led Northwood to accept as authentic a number of reported Schnorkel sightings that were, in fact, naturally occurring disturbances on the ocean's surface, such as spray-filled whirlwinds or innocent spouting whales. Prior to the advent of Schnorkel, Coastal Command had correctly identified aircrew reports of slow-moving waterspouts as a small surface whirlwind, colloquially known as a 'willywaw.' These natural phenomena were soon forgotten, however, when the desire to find U-boats began to exceed the ability to do so. Indeed, these false sightings were given added credence when the December issue of *Coastal Command Review* published a picture of a willywaw described as 'the "smoke and wake" type of target' that 'confirm[s] the presence of a *SCHNORKELLING* U-boat.'[122]

For the remainder of the war, aircraft routinely attacked any willywaw, whale, oil slick, or piece of flotsam that an active imagination could possibly construe as evidence of a submarine. During the last four months of 1944, for example, No 423 Squadron made seven sightings of the 'smoke and wake' type that were undoubtedly whirlwinds or spouting whales, and four of them were attacked. On 11 September a Sunderland on an inshore patrol southwest of the Hebrides spotted 'whitish vapour or steam on the surface about 9 mi[les] distant' that 'dispersed freely as it was blown away.' On the aircraft's approach, 'the vapour disappeared, as if cut off and a slight wake was seen extending some 100 ft. from the apex.' Although the aircrews' description is of a willywaw rather than a Schnorkel head, the phenomenon was depth-charged; the original postwar analysis credited the Sunderland's attack with the probable sinking of U-484. In retrospect, it seems far more likely that the German submarine was sunk by HMCS *Dunver* and HMCS *Hespeler*.[123]

By early November BdU had routed a dozen of its Norwegian-based boats back to the English Channel in a vain attempt to reopen the attack on cross-Channel shipping. Informed by special intelligence – Ultra – of the move, Northwood redeployed squadrons to patrol the threatened area. No 407 was transferred back to the familiar surroundings of Chivenor on 11 November and began patrolling the English Channel two nights later, while the small Canadian enclave at Castle Archdale was broken up when 422 Squadron was dispatched to Pembroke Dock, in south Wales, on 4 November. This move does not appear to have been made for operational reasons, however, since the Canadian squadron simply exchanged bases with an identical RAF unit. No explanation was provided to Overseas Headquarters and, reflecting the indifference of Air Marshal Breadner, the AOC-in-C Overseas, none was asked for – a somewhat disappointing ending, given the great difficulty his predecessor had originally experienced in persuading the British to co-locate the two squadrons.[124]

The new dispositions did little to alter the previous pattern of inshore operations. Only three U-boats achieved any success during November and December (sinking seven merchant ships and one frigate and damaging two other vessels), while six were lost. Four of the six were sunk by warships, one by air attack, and one foundered after running aground.[125] On the night of 29/30

December a Leigh Light Wellington, flown by Squadron Leader C.W. Taylor of 407 Squadron, was on patrol when it homed onto the Schnorkel of U-772.

There was full moonlight at the time 2/10 cloud and [the sea was] smooth. Weather was fair but visibility impaired by haze. Captain immediately altered course to 151° and at 0211 in Pos. 50.05N – 02.31W Captain and second pilot sighted, up-moon, dead-ahead, one half mile away, a very pronounced wake and then a schnorkel on Course 300° Speed 6 knots. A/C was too high to attack during first run and Captain turned to port and made 2nd run on course 270°. During this time contact was maintained on Radar at 3/4 mile. L/L was switched on at 250' but illumination was affected by haze although target was picked up by it. Target was also clearly visible by moonlight. At 0213 6 D[epth] C[harge]s were dropped from 125' ... and all were seen to explode by rear gunner. The first thirty yards on starboard quarter. No's 2 and 3 straddling schnorkel about 10 to 15 yds astern of it ... Schnorkel disappeared immediately after the attack and radar contact was lost and not picked up again.[126]

The sinking of U-772 was the sole victory that Coastal Command aircraft could claim exclusively during the last three months of 1944. It marked the end of a year in which considerable improvements were made in the number of Canadian aircrew serving in both 422 and 423 Squadrons, much of the progress resulting from a Canadian proposal made in January 1944 to transfer up to 150 flying-boat crews a year from the Home War Establishment to Coastal Command. After undergoing an OTU course in the United Kingdom, the first four such crews were posted, two to each squadron, in May 1944. Two more arrived at 422 Squadron in June, and with these additions both units could finally claim two-thirds of their aircrew to be Canadian. Although more crews continued to arrive during the remainder of the year, the posting out of tour-expired airmen meant that the net increase in Canadians was relatively small. Only in March and April 1945 were sufficiently large numbers of Canadians posted to 422 and 423 Squadrons to bring their strengths to 84.5 and 82.8 per cent, respectively.[127]

In the Indian Ocean, meanwhile, No 413 Squadron had spent most of 1944 flying uneventful convoy escorts, offensive sweeps, and search and rescue missions. The squadron's employment and its 'consistently small percentage of Canadian aircrew' – less than 50 per cent since April 1943 – led the minister of national defence for air, C.G. Power, to recommend converting it to an RAF squadron in June 1944 and reforming a new 413 Squadron in No 6 Group in an attempt to 'do away with as many orphan squadrons as possible.' While Breadner initially (and typically) recommended against taking action, arguing that No 413's 'operational employment now appears satisfactory,' by October he was willing to agree to its withdrawal from the Far East and its conversion to a bomber unit. On 8 December the squadron became non-operational pending its return to the United Kingdom. A few crews with less than two years service in Ceylon were transferred to RAF squadrons – a most unusual procedure at this stage of the war – while the remainder embarked for England on 21 January 1945.[128]

The new year brought little change in the monotonous but effective patrols being flown by most of Coastal Command. While No 423 Squadron continued to range over the northwest approaches from its Castle Archdale base, both 407 and 422 Squadrons, as part of No 19 Group, provided air cover in the St George's, Bristol, and English channels. Willywaws and oil slicks continued to be the most common targets attacked. In the inshore and transit areas surrounding the United Kingdom, aircraft reported 149 sightings during the 1 January–8 May period. In only fifty-two instances, however, was a German submarine present in the vicinity of the sighting. Of the thirty-four attacks made on genuine targets in these waters, twelve were successful, with eight U-boats being sunk in the transit areas and four inshore. Two other sinkings were shared by both air and naval forces. None of these successes involved RCAF anti-submarine aircraft in Coastal Command, which, by the end of the war, had accounted for eight U-boats.[129]

12

In Search of a Strike Force, 1940–2

Although the Kriegsmarine and the facilities in German harbours had featured prominently in the RAF's prewar plans, the Air Ministry had not made any specific preparations to attack enemy merchant shipping at sea. Rather, Coastal Command's principal duties were seen as 'trade protection, reconnaissance and co-operation with the Royal Navy' – of which reconnaissance was considered to be the most important. On the outbreak of war in September 1939, the British government implemented a general air policy (discussed in more detail in chapter 14) aimed at limiting civilian casualties. Initially, operations were to be directed against only the most unambiguous military targets: 'enemy warships, troopships and auxiliaries in direct attendance on the enemy fleet, provided that these targets had been previously identified beyond doubt.' Merchant vessels were simply to be identified and shadowed, their movements being reported to the Royal Navy, and for a time crews were even prohibited from retaliating against ships that opened fire on them.[1]

These restraints on offensive action were largely irrelevant, however, since Coastal Command's only strike capability in September 1939 consisted of two squadrons of obsolete Vickers Vildebeest torpedo-bombers. As a temporary measure, Bomber Command loaned it two squadrons of Handley-Page Hampdens, equipped and trained exclusively for bombing operations, to act as a strike force should air reconnaissance discover suitable targets of the battleship or cruiser class.[2]

The German invasions of Denmark and Norway in April 1940 forced White-hall's hand, however, and as the campaign in Norway developed the Air Ministry gradually relaxed its restrictions on what could be attacked. In July a 'sink at sight' policy was adopted for the North Sea, from just south of Tromso almost to the Hook of Holland, while the English Channel and Bay of Biscay were added in September. But the mere declaration of such zones did not mean that Northwood's ability to conduct an effective anti-shipping campaign had in any way increased. Although the two Vildebeest squadrons had been re-equipped with Bristol Beaufort torpedo-bombers by early 1940, one of them had been assigned to minelaying activities before it could be trained in anti-shipping strikes, while the other had such difficulty converting to its new type (and the engines on its Beauforts were so unreliable) that it was not permitted to fly out to sea.[3]

For anti-shipping operations, then, Air Chief Marshal Sir Frederick Bowhill was left with five squadrons of less-than-satisfactory Lockheed Hudsons, two of Bristol Bleinheims – not much better – and one of Avro Ansons, much worse. These were supplemented during the summer of 1940 by two more Blenheim squadrons from Bomber Command and a mixed and doubtful bag of three of the Royal Navy's Fleet Air Arm (FAA) squadrons: one of Fairey Swordfish, one of Blackburn Skuas, and one of Fairey Albacores.[4] Crews on reconnaissance flights were now permitted to initiate attacks on shipping as opportunities arose, although results were understandably meagre. Between April and September 1940 Coastal Command sank only two small vessels in direct attacks at sea, while Bomber Command and the FAA added another ten. Aerial mining, carried out by both Bomber and Coastal commands but largely by the former, accounted for fifty-six enemy ships, totalling over 58,000 tons.[5]

Such sluggishness in anti-shipping policy and operations did not fit with the priority that the British government attached to the economic blockade of Germany. Of particular importance were German iron-ore imports – ten million metric tons in 1938, half of it from Sweden – but the significance of the Swedish supply went beyond quantity alone. Production of high-grade steel suitable for armour plate and gun barrels depended largely on the Bessemer process which, in turn, required ores of high phosphorus content. This Swedish iron had in plenty, and German foundries relied especially on supplies mined from the Kiruna and Gällivare districts of northern Sweden. Swedish ore was so essential to the German armaments industry, in fact, that as late as 1944, when the Reich's inland transportation network was under considerable strain, Germany went to great lengths to sustain its coal exports to Sweden in order to complete the exchange for ore.[6]

In summer, the iron was usually shipped from the Swedish port of Lulea on the Gulf of Bothnia, through the Baltic to Kiel, from where it went by canal to Rotterdam and thence up the Rhine to the Ruhr. In winter, when the gulf froze over, it went by rail from Sweden to the ice-free port of Narvik in northern Norway. From Narvik, freighters followed the Inner Leads between the mainland and the numerous offshore islands which sheltered the convoys from both Atlantic weather and surface attack. Ships were not forced into the open sea until they reached the southern coast of Norway, and once they entered the Skaggerak, en route to Kiel, they were again safe from most threats.

In addition to Swedish ores, the Narvik convoys also carried copper, pyrites, fertilizers, fish products, and pulp and paper. At Kiel the southbound convoys were joined by grain and timber shipments from the Baltic, and all these goods were then moved through the Kiel Canal into the Heligoland Bight and along the North German and Dutch coasts to Rotterdam. 'Of that part of the traffic that penetrates to the West, a very important part is destined for Rotterdam. It is estimated that some 3,000,000 tons of Swedish iron ore reaches this port each year, for unloading into barges for onward transmission to the Ruhr. Other cargoes reaching Rotterdam consist of some 100,000 tons of fertilisers,

150,000 tons of pulp and paper, 100,000 tons of pyrites and copper ore, 400,000 tons of grain and 100,000 tons of timber ... Returning vessels carry coal, coke and general cargoes, and the route followed is again outside the [Frisian] Islands, through the Kiel canal, where part disperses into the Baltic, and the remainder goes through the Great Belt, to re-appear later off the Norwegian Coast.'[7] Shipments of coal and coke paid for the iron ore, while up to half of northbound traffic carried military supplies for the German occupation forces in Norway. Although the importance of these cargoes could be – and was – overestimated by the Ministry of Economic Warfare (MEW), they were, nevertheless, significant components of Germany's industrial system and the Wehrmacht's logistics, and the vessels that carried them were the prime objectives of anti-shipping operations in the North Sea.[8]

As in the case of the U-boat war, anti-shipping operations were coordinated by Coastal Command and the appropriate Royal Navy headquarters. Once the threat of invasion had receded and there was less need for defensive reconnaissance, Northwood was able to transfer more resources to anti-shipping activities. By the turn of the year, four patrols along the Danish and Norwegian coasts, between the Horn Reefs and Stadtlandet, were being flown three times a week by aircraft of No 18 Group – always provided there was sufficient cloud cover for them to evade enemy fighters. When weather conditions were suitable, sorties were occasionally carried out to the north, between Stadtlandet and Trondheim, or further east into the Skagerrak. No 16 Group was responsible for the area between the Horn Reefs and Cherbourg, and No 15 covered the Brest and Lorient shipping routes. Patrols were normally carried out by single aircraft, usually Blenheims or Hudsons armed with 250-lb general purpose (GP) bombs. Of the sixty-three attacks made by Coastal Command aircraft between June and December 1940, forty-one were made from heights between 500 and 2000 feet and only seven were delivered from below 500 feet.[9]

Without an effective bombsight, low-level approaches seemed to be the only tactic that offered a reasonable chance of success. The Hudsons were equipped with the Mark IX sight, but since it required accurate data on the aircraft's ground speed, wind speed, and direction and the ballistic characteristics of the bomb being dropped, it was seldom used. In fact, even when fed the correct information, the Mark IX still lacked that degree of accuracy required to hit a target as small as a coastal freighter. Accordingly, low-level attacks in which the pilot 'eyeballed' the target and released his bombs when it seemed to him the correct time to do so – usually just as the target disappeared from sight beneath the nose of his aircraft – were the preferred technique and, understandably, the number of enemy merchantmen sunk continued to be disappointing. The Germans lost only nine vessels totalling 15,468 tons throughout the April 1940–March 1941 period. A further sixteen, totalling nearly 50,000 tons, were damaged, for the loss of fifty-one aircraft.[10]

The aerial minelaying campaign (code-named Gardening) begun in April 1940 achieved better results. By the end of March 1941 nearly 1500 mines had been laid in 'gardens' from the Bay of Biscay to the western Baltic, one-third of them by Coastal Command and two-thirds by Bomber Command. They accounted for ninety-nine ships averaging a thousand tons each, and damaged another thirteen, for the loss of only thirty-nine aircraft.[11]

Canadian participation in the early stages of the anti-shipping offensive was limited to an uncertain number who were already serving in the RAF. Of the six Canadian maritime squadrons eventually formed, only three, Nos 404, 407, and 415, would take part in Coastal Command's anti-shipping campaign. Moreover, even their story was not a cohesive one. Flying different types of aircraft, in different roles, from different stations, they seldom saw each other and, for most of the war, all they had in common was their link to RCAF Overseas Headquarters in London.

The first squadron, No 404, was formed on 15 April 1941 at Thorney Island, just east of Portsmouth, as a coastal fighter unit in No 16 Group. April was a cruel month for the Allies, one which saw shipping losses reach the highest tonnage yet as Admiral Dönitz's U-boats began to develop 'wolf-pack' tactics in the North Atlantic. The RAF's search for air superiority over France was costing Fighter Command dearly (see chapter 6) and its strategic bomber offensive was making minimal impact on the German economy while incurring persistent casualties. The Soviet Union was still linked to Germany, and the United States, though generally sympathetic to the allied cause, still showed no signs of formally entering the fight.[12]

It was during these grim times that No 404 Squadron would, 'to commence with, be found from the RAF except in so far as RCAF personnel [are] immediately available. It is the intention, however, that the RAF personnel will be gradually replaced by RCAF personnel as pilots ... of requisite experience become available either from the Empire Training Scheme [BCATP] outputs or from existing RCAF Units.' The first to join the squadron was its commanding officer, Squadron Leader P.H. Woodruff, a native of Edmonton, Alberta, who had joined the RAF in 1937 on a short service commission. Although one complete crew was posted in from an RAF squadron, there was some difficulty in obtaining any more 'due to the Coastal Command OTUs being filled and Fighter and Bomber Commands being unwilling to part with their OTU graduates.'[13]

As an interim measure, and as a means of providing Canadian aircrew immediately, the air officer commanding, RCAF, in Great Britain, Air Commodore L.F. Stevenson, suggested 'that as the Commanding Officer, No 404 Squadron, is a fully qualified Coastal Command twin-engined Fighter instructor and that as the Squadron is starting from scratch, it might be reasonable in this instance to post aircrew straight from P[ersonnel] R[eception] C[entres] to the Squadron.' On this occasion the Air Ministry concurred and eight pilots and five wireless operators/air gunner (WOAG), all RCAF, arrived at Thorney Island on 10 and 11 May – prompting Stevenson to predict that the squadron would be '50 per cent Canadian in one month 75 per cent Canadian in three months and 100 per cent Canadian in five months.' He was quite wrong. The squadron was still only 45 per cent Canadian in aircrew, and 4.3 per cent in groundcrew, when it became operational four months later.[14]

To carry out its coastal fighter role, the squadron was equipped with the same variant of the Blenheim IV used by three of Coastal Command's four other long-range fighter units. The Blenheim had been designed as a light bomber (a role which it was still fulfilling with No 2 Group in Bomber Command) and modified for use as a fighter by adding a pack of four fixed, forward-firing .303 machine-guns beneath the fuselage. Although its top speed of 260 miles per hour was quite fast by prewar standards, the Blenheim fighter variant could 'no longer be regarded as a match for enemy fighters or more recent long-range bombers.' The Blenheims IV have neither the armament nor the speed to give combat on anything like even terms to the Focke Wulf [200] or the He 111, and they cannot therefore be expected to give adequate protection to our shipping in the local areas and convoy routes where enemy long-range bombers are operating with such success against our shipping.'[15] Moreover, the machines allocated to No 404 Squadron had been transferred from an RAF unit, which was re-equipping with Beaufighters, and five of the fifteen were in such poor condition that they could not be restored to operational standards.[16]

The second squadron, No 407, was formed at Thorney Island on 8 May as a general reconnaissance unit under an English commanding officer, Wing Commander H.M. Styles, who had been a flying training instructor since the outbreak of war. Described by one of his Canadian pilots as 'good-looking, blond, blue-eyed, the Hollywood director's idea of an RAF operational wing commander,' Styles was handed the difficult task – on his first operational assignment – of turning untrained crews into an operational squadron in just three months; but 'God was with us,' one pilot recalled, 'and our successes were due in large measure to his leadership.' Once again, since there were no RCAF aircrew immediately available with GR training, No 407 received RAF aircrew posted from other squadrons. Canadian pilots did not begin to arrive until mid-June, following completion of their course at the GR school at Squires Gate, and a few more were found by posting in men who had already been GR-trained in Canada before they were transferred overseas. By the time the squadron became operational in early September, fourteen of the eighteen crews were captained by RCAF pilots. Since twenty-eight of the thirty-eight WOAGs were RAF, however, only 45 per cent of the total aircrew component was Canadian, and a shortage of Canadian groundcrew meant that the squadron commenced operations with only fourteen of its more than two hundred tradesmen being members of the RCAF. It was not until March 1942 that training establishments in Canada could produce sufficient graduates for the groundcrew to become 50 per cent Canadian.[17]

Although No 407 had initially been designated to fly Blenheim IVs, it was informed at the end of May that it would be equipped instead with Lockheed Hudsons, ordered in 1938 as a navigation trainer but pressed into an operational role because of the woeful inadequacy of the Avro Anson as anything else. The Hudson's bomb-carrying capacity of 1000 pounds was barely adequate for anti-shipping operations, and the two fixed .303 machine-guns firing forward, together with two more in a rear-upper turret, were certainly not enough for the crew of four – pilot, second pilot or observer, and two WOAGs – to hold their own in air combat, never mind to suppress enemy Flak. Indeed, before No 407 began to receive its Hudsons, other anti-shipping squadrons had already concluded that they 'do not appear to be suitable for operations.'[18]

The various shortcomings of his aircraft were well known to Sir Frederick Bowhill, and he put his concerns in writing shortly before relinquishing command to Sir Philip Joubert de la Ferté on 14 June 1941. Not only had Northwood 'not been consulted as to what types of aircraft we require and what are necessary,' Bowhill complained, but there seemed a strong possibility that in the future Coastal Command would be 'saddled with any cast-off aircraft that [the Air Ministry] do not know what to do with.' What he wanted was the de Havilland Mosquito 'or some American aircraft with sufficient speed and endurance and ... adequate defensive armament' for reconnaissance work and 'the [Douglas A-20] Havoc or some suitable fighter-bomber' for anti-shipping operations, since 'the attack on shipping can only continue to be carried out by Hudsons at great hazard and with heavy losses.'[19]

Submitted just two days before he left Northwood, Bowhill's proposals gathered dust in London while his successor took some time to confer with his staff and think things through for himself before recording his opinion. Eventually, however, Joubert came to the same conclusion as his predecessor, telling the Air Ministry on 14 September that there was a need 'for faster and better armed aircraft to carry out visual reconnaissance of the enemy coast-line where fighter opposition may be expected. At the present moment such reconnaissances are being carried out by Hudson and Blenheim fighters. The casualties suffered by these aircraft are becoming serious and it is considered that something of the nature of a Mosquito, i.e., a fast two-seater with good armament and fair navigational facilities and with long endurance, will be required in the very near future if this work is to continue effectively.'[20]

Through no fault of his own, Joubert's timing could scarcely have been worse. Sir Charles Portal, the chief of the air staff, was preoccupied with protecting Bomber Command and saving the bombing offensive – and, indeed, with persuading Winston Churchill that the strategic bomber force be increased to four thousand front-line machines – and the question of improving Coastal Command's anti-shipping capabilities was very low on his list of priorities. It was only on 1 December 1941, for example, that the CAS promised Joubert that he would 'receive an official reply in the near future.'[21]

Six days later Japan attacked Pearl Harbor, Germany declared war on the United States, and the nature of the war changed fundamentally. Although the United States was now an ally rather than a cooperative neutral (and so perhaps better able to simplify the rules regarding British procurement of American-built machines like the Havoc), the matter of actual supply became more complicated, as the Americans began to build up their own forces more rapidly. With most of the early Mosquitoes reserved for Bomber Command or night-fighter duties, and with Beaufighters being used as night-fighters, Intruders, and in the Middle East (Northwood would not have enough of them to form an effective strike force until the fall of 1942), Joubert would have to make do for the time being with obsolescent Hudsons and Blenheims for reconnaissance and bombing; while the only torpedo-bombers available were four squadrons of Beauforts, severely limited by their operational radius of 420 nautical miles. Since Hampdens, with their greater range, could be used as torpedo-bombers against targets as far away as Kiel and to lay mines in the Kattegat, Joubert hoped to have three squadrons equipped with that type.[22]

While Coastal Command's immediate strengthening was not one of Portal's top priorities, it did not stagnate altogether in 1941. Two new squadrons were formed in August, both on Beauforts. No 489 was designated as a Royal New Zealand Air Force unit, while No 415 became the RCAF's thirteenth Article XV squadron when it came into existence at Thorney Island on 20 August. Its commanding officer was Squadron Leader E.L. Wurtele, a Montrealer who had joined the RAF in 1935, spent most of his prewar career in the Fleet Air Arm, and more recently had flown Blenheims on convoy escort duties and Beauforts on minelaying sorties. This experience counted for little during Wurtele's first five-and-a-half months on the squadron, however, because a lack of equipment severely limited the amount of flying training that could be conducted. With just six Beauforts on hand, the squadron managed an average of only eighty-six flying hours per month and, since it was acting as a temporary OTU and had more than twenty pilots under training, each of them averaged fewer than five hours per month.[23]

Nos 404 and 407 Squadrons were more fortunate in acquiring aircraft and managed to complete their training by late August. No 404, flying out of Skitten, a satellite station of Wick in northern Scotland, was part of No 18 Group and flew its first operational sorties on 22 September 1941, supplying four Blenheims for convoy escort in the North Sea. To the south, No 16 Group, in which 407 Squadron became operational on 1 September, covered the English Channel as well as the North Sea from the Channel Islands to the Horn Reefs. It was engaged in anti-invasion searches at dawn and dusk (although there was little prospect of an invasion of England once Hitler began preparing for his attack on Russia), protection of convoys, and night-time anti-shipping patrols and strikes. Daytime responsibility for the 'Channel Stop' in the Strait of Dover, meanwhile, was turned over to the Hurricane fighter-bombers of Fighter Command's No 11 Group in early October.[24]

Lacking the fast, cannon-armed torpedo-bombers that would later encourage the development of 'strike-wing' tactics, No 16 Group tried to use the cover of darkness or foul weather along with a low-level approach to elude enemy fighters and provide a measure of surprise. Even when operating at night, however, these tactics proved too costly to be effective – Coastal Command lost fifty-three crews on anti-shipping strikes from January to June 1942, twenty-five of them in May alone – and such attacks were finally abandoned in June 1942.[25]

Nowhere was the deadly combination of inadequate aircraft and low-level tactics more clearly demonstrated than by the experience of No 407 Squadron during its first ten months of operations. Flying out of North Coates, on the east coast of England, the Canadians were one of seven squadrons available to

No 16 Group for its night offensive. Since its Hudsons were equipped with air-to-surface vessel (ASV) radar, one of the squadron's main tasks was to carry out Rovers off the Dutch coast between Borkum and the Hook of Holland. Rovers were free-ranging patrols 'by varying numbers of aircraft according to ... availability. On some occasions aircraft would carry out individual reconnaissances and strikes; at other times a combined operation in force would be the order of the day. Variety in the place, time and numbers of aircraft taking part were the keynotes.'[26]

Northwood took little interest in establishing tactical doctrines for anti-shipping operations, beyond prescribing low-level night attacks in principle, and much was left to individual units. The tactics employed by No 407 Squadron were developed by Wing Commander Styles and seem to have been better than most. 'Hit and run with the emphasis on the unexpected ... was an approach well suited to the temperaments of the individualistic Canadians. Mass attacks were out, and individual attacks would take place during twilight hours, at night, or during bad weather in daylight, and the dirtier the day or night the better. Long run-ins that gave the defenders a chance to get set were a no-no. You took one pass and got out. Radar would lead us to the convoys, and German fighters were to be avoided.'[27]

Logic would seem to dictate that a Hudson crew, catching sight of enemy shipping, should have transmitted its location back to base before launching an attack and running the risk of being shot down. That way, others could then respond even if the first crew on the scene was lost, but most Rovers attacked first and reported later, either by radio on their way home or sometimes not until they had actually reached base and could make a verbal report. There were good reasons for delaying the report: although 'Special Intelligence' – decrypts of high-grade German cyphers – was not often 'of direct importance in guiding the RAF's bombing attacks on coastal shipping to their targets' at this time, the combination of that intelligence, coastal radar reports, and increasingly useful interpretations of reconnaissance photographs provided 'a virtually complete knowledge of the enemy's coastal shipping routines in the entire area from the North Cape to the Spanish frontier which in turn determined the RAF's reconnaissance programme.' Sometimes, then, the existence, general whereabouts, and movements of German convoys were well known to the Admiralty. In addition, the German radio intelligence service (Horchdienst) was so efficient and the Luftwaffe's fighters so responsive that an immediate reaction to an intercepted sighting report risked being met by fighters scrambled specifically to meet just such a blow. Better, perhaps, to let the enemy wonder whether the initial contact would be followed up or not?[28]

In addition to its attacks on merchant shipping off the Dutch coast, No 407 was also responsible for conducting Hoden patrols against light naval forces. With the approach of winter came an increase in the activity of German light surface forces, and the squadron's task was to locate and shadow these E-boats, using ASV radar, until surface craft or heavily armed Beaufighters could reach the scene. Once either arrived, the Hudsons would illuminate the E-boats with parachute flares.[29] This proceedure, however, held little attraction for the Cana-

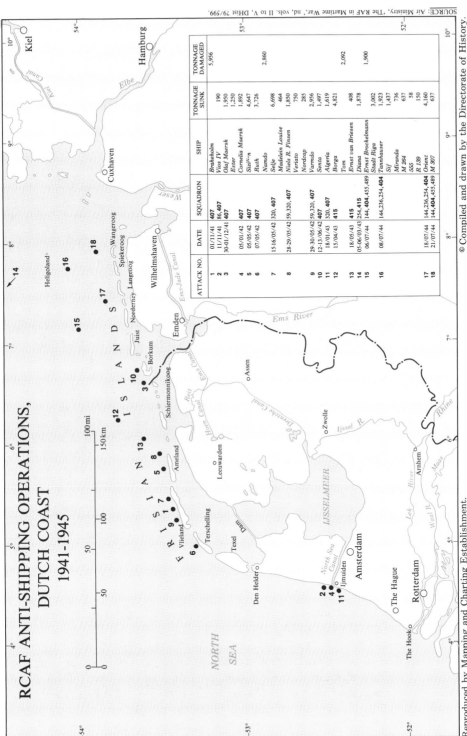

RCAF ANTI-SHIPPING OPERATIONS, DUTCH COAST 1941-1945

ATTACK NO.	DATE	SQUADRON	SHIP	TONNAGE SUNK	TONNAGE DAMAGED
1	01/11/41	407	Braheholm	190	5,956
2	11/11/41	86,407	Vios IV	1,950	
3	30-01/12/41	407	Olaf Maersk	1,250	
			Ester	1,892	
4	05/01/42	407	Cornelia Maersk	4,647	
5	05/05/42	407	Statirn	3,726	2,860
6	07/05/42	407	Ruth		
7	15-16/05/42	320, 407	Namdo	6,698	
			Selje	464	
8	28-29/05/42	59,320, 407	Madelein Louise	1,850	
			Niels R. Finsen	750	
			Veriato	285	
9	29-30/05/42	59,320, 407	Nordeop	2,956	
10	12-13/06/42	407	Varmdo	1,497	
11	18/01/43	320, 407	Senta	1,619	
12	15/04/43	415	Algeria	4,821	2,092
			Borga		
13	18/05/43	415	Tom	408	
14	05-06/03/43	254, 415	Ernst van Briesen	1,878	1,900
			Diana		
15	06/07/44	144, 404, 455, 489	Ernst Brockelmann	3,002	
			Stadt Riga	1,923	
16	08/07/44	144, 236, 254, 404	Tannhauser	1,437	
			Sif	736	
			Miranda	637	
			M 264	58	
17	18/07/44	144, 236, 254, 404	R 139	150	
18	21/07/44	144, 404, 455, 489	Orient	4,160	
			M 307	637	

© Compiled and drawn by the Directorate of History.

Reproduced by Mapping and Charting Establishment.

SOURCE: Air Ministry, 'The RAF in Maritime War', nd, vols. II to V, DHist 79/599.

dians. 'To get good coverage you had to stay on a steady course dropping flares at fairly short intervals, so you flew across the sky telling every German night fighter in the vicinity precisely where you were and the course you were flying. In a shipping attack you could sneak in and get out quickly, but with the Hodens you flew along counting the flares and praying. The moment the last flare was gone you went into a great slipping turn to get to sea level, and thanked your lucky stars you had made it once again.'[30]

During No 407's first month of operations, September 1941, fourteen Hoden sorties failed to find a single E-boat, while twenty-three Rovers led to nine attacks on merchant vessels, with the squadron claiming three direct hits. Although postwar research revealed that no German ships were, in fact, damaged by air attack off the Dutch coast during September, the safe return of all the attacking aircraft bolstered the squadron's confidence in its hit-and-run night-time tactics.[31]

The increasing amount of shipping to be found in the hours of darkness off the Dutch coast – a result of daylight attacks by No 2 Group of Bomber Command – led Joubert to intensify his night Rover effort in October. During the final quarter of 1941, No 407 made fifty-two attacks on enemy ships, sinking only three and damaging one other, while in No 16 Group as a whole, ninety-eight were attacked, of which seven (totalling 23,558 tons) were assessed at the time as sunk and twenty-two as damaged. The true figures were six (12,698 tons) sunk, three of them by 407 Squadron, and only two damaged; but the perceived results were enough for Northwood to declare that 'the quarter has been unquestionably the most successful since the start of attacks on enemy shipping.'[32]

Despite the emphasis that Styles had initially placed on individual attacks, sighting reports now often resulted in the dispatch of a multi-aircraft strike force to engage a convoy. A Hudson piloted by Sergeant D.A. Ross was flying a Rover along the Dutch coast just after dusk on 31 October when its radar indicated a convoy of ten to fifteen ships off Terschelling. Selecting a merchantman of about 4000 tons, Ross attacked from a height of fifty feet, subsequently claiming that one of the bombs was believed to have hit at the foot of a mast.[33] After landing back at North Coates some two hours later, Ross's report was forwarded to Group Headquarters at Chatham, and a strike force of eight more Hudsons from No 407 and three Blenheims from an RAF squadron was dispatched between 2252 hours (a lapse of one hour and ten minutes) and 0039 hours (just under three hours after Ross's return) on 1 November. One machine came back early, but seven of the Hudsons located the convoy and carried out low-level attacks.

P[ilot] O[fficer] Cowperthwaite attacked a vessel of 5,000 tons N. of Terschelling from 50 ft. As a result of the attack a large dull red flash was seen from the vessel. P/O McCulloch attacked an M[erchant] V[essel] of 3–4,000 tons off Vlieland the results of the attack were unobserved. Considerable flak was forthcoming and the aircraft received two hits in the port wing. There were no casualties. P/O Codville attacked an 800 ton MV north of Terschelling. No results were seen. P/O Shankland saw a large explosion as a result of his attack on a 6,000 ton M.V. off Terschelling. His port engine was put out of action by enemy fire however he returned and made a successful landing on one engine. P/O Cooper attacked a 3,000 ton vessel off Vlieland. The rear gunner saw two explosions after the attack. P/O Dann returned with nothing to report. Sgt. Moss scored a direct hit on a 7,000 ton tanker North of Terschelling. A large flash was seen from the centre of the target. As a result of anti-aircraft fire the undercarriage was rendered U[n]/S[ervicable] but the pilot made a successful belly-landing on his return without suffering any casualties. S[quadron] L[eader] Lewis [the A flight commander and only non-Canadian pilot involved in the operation] attacked an M.V. of 3–4,000 tons North of Terschelling [and] a large flash was observed followed by sparks and smoke issuing from the vessel.[34]

The squadron was credited with three ships 'damaged,' but post-war research revealed that only the *Braheholm* of 5676 tons was hit off the Dutch coast on 1 November.[35]

The fact that so many ships merely sustained damage, despite the claimed accuracy of the bombing, reinforced growing suspicions within the squadron that their 250-lb Semi-Armour Piercing (SAP) bombs might be defective. It was not so much the defectiveness, however, as the ineffectiveness of their ordnance that was the cause of their frustration. Originally designed for use against warships with protective plating, the SAP series included only a small proportion of actual explosive in comparison with the weight of metal casing required to penetrate armour plate, and its blast effect was therefore diminished. Some, dropped from masthead height, did not explode at all, because they were not in the air long enough for the wind-driven vane which activated the fuse to arm the bomb fully. Instead, they simply penetrated the deck, sometimes exiting through the hull and leaving behind an easily plugged hole.[36]

No 407 Squadron was condemned to use SAP bombs until late May 1942, when they were finally replaced by 100-lb anti-submarine bombs and 250-lb general purpose bombs. The problem with fusing, however, was not discovered until September 1942, and then only through reports from Swedish sailors on the Rotterdam route. 'A very great number of our bombs fail to explode. One ship arriving in Cuxhaven had a dud bomb sticking out of its side and its presence was unknown to the crew until shoremen pointed it out to them. On many occasions duds are picked up by members of ship's crews and thrown overboard. German sailors have been heard repeatedly to say that the cause of so many of our bombs not exploding is the low height at which they are dropped, and probably bad setting of the fuses.'[37]

The threat posed by air strikes and offensive forays by the Royal Navy's motor torpedo boats (MTBs) had forced the enemy to adopt a convoy system by January 1941, particularly in those areas vulnerable to air attack. These convoys were initially guarded by armed trawlers, but as shipping losses mounted over the summer of 1941 the number of Flak ships assigned to them had to be increased until, by the end of winter, they often outnumbered the vessels being escorted. The most common escorts carried three or four batteries of quadruple 20-millimetre cannon, while larger ones mounted up to ten batteries, some composed of 37-millimetre guns. The merchant ships themselves were also armed, usually with a 20-millimetre cannon forward and one on each wing of the bridge, and attackers often had to contend as well with the land-based Flak found along the Dutch coast and in the Frisian Islands. By September 1942 Northwood estimated that there were eighty-four heavy and 139 light batteries between Borkum and the Hook of Holland.[38]

Twenty-eight attacks by 407 Squadron during September and October resulted in the loss of one machine, which failed to return from a Hoden patrol on 10 October. November, which saw the squadron involved in twenty-four of the thirty-six attacks recorded by No 16 Group, also brought the loss of only one aircraft. However, the increasing weight and effectiveness of the enemy's Flak became apparent the following month when, despite bad weather that limited the squadron to only seven attacks, four machines were lost. Flying at night, often in miserable weather conditions, station-keeping within a formation of aircraft could be extraordinarily difficult, even when the pilots resorted to the dangerous practice of switching on their navigation lights (thus increasing the risk of enemy fighter interception). A coordinated night attack by several aircraft, therefore, was virtually impossible.[39]

While night attacks undoubtedly improved the immediate prospects of survival for strike squadrons, the policy also created problems of its own. Winter weather in the North Sea was only predictable to the extent that it was rarely good for flying, and often only marginally so. Moreover, it could change from bad to worse with a frightening rapidity quite beyond the capacity of meteorologists to predict, putting crews under considerable stress just by being in the air. 'Night after night we took off into the pitch black and, buffeted by rain, sleet and turbulence, flew along the German and Dutch coasts, groping through the murk for ships that became scarcer and more difficult to locate as the weather deteriorated... You got off on your own, flew to the enemy coast using elementary navigation and primitive radar to locate targets and determine landfalls. When you returned to base it was up to you to get down, and on misty mornings with limited visibility it could be challenging.'[40]

Since most aircraft patrolled alone, it was not always possible to determine the circumstances in which those that did not return met their fate. While the machines lost on 5 November and 1 December were certainly brought down by shipborne fire, one that failed to return from a Rover on 22 December was most likely shot down by coastal batteries. The fate of the other two crews missing in December is uncertain; they could just as easily have fallen victims to weather or accident as have been intercepted by enemy fighters or shot down by anti-aircraft fire.[41]

The strain of operations was reflected by an increase in the incidence of flying accidents unconnected with the weather. On 11 December a Hudson returning from a Rover patrol with a faulty radio mistook a guide beacon for a flare path light and made a crash landing in a nearby beet field. In his squadron commander's view: 'this pilot, who has carried out a fair number of night operational trips, has flown through some very dirty weather and carried out his attacks on shipping with marked success ... Recently he has shown signs of strain, marked by lack of confidence in his blind flying ability. This caused him to hurry onto the ground as soon as he saw a flare path. He is being sent on a Blind Landing Course, it is hoped that this will enable him to regain confidence in himself on instruments.'[42] The individual concerned subsequently completed a second operational tour before being repatriated to Canada in September 1944.

Another Hudson was damaged in early January when an undercarriage leg snapped after a heavy landing in a cross wind. Two weeks later the same pilot, returning from an operation, stalled his aircraft while attempting to abort a landing. The crash killed all five airmen aboard while thirteen groundcrew, attempting to rescue them, died when the bombload exploded. Bad landings during the next four weeks seriously damaged two more machines, and another fatal accident occurred on 17 February when an aircraft crashed on takeoff, killing all on board. Although the crash was attributed to mechanical failure, the loss of two crews in flying accidents within a month could be ill-afforded by a squadron which was already suffering heavy casualties on operations.[43]

During the war, service mail was routinely censored, not only for breaches of security, but also for assessments of morale on stations and within units. Such a report on North Coates, in late January 1942, singled out No 407 Squadron, whose personnel appeared 'to be suffering from strain and exhaustion after a long period of continuous operational flying.' An unattributable hand minuted that there 'was no foundation for the assertion,' pointing out that the 'average monthly flying time for aircrew [was] 15 [hours].' Although that was true, such statistical averages did not allow for the fact that bad weather could wash-out flying for days at a time and thus confine a month's operational flying to the space of a week or ten days, or that some crews might fly more often than others. 'So far this month it's been sleep all day and get up in time to fly all night again,' wrote Pilot Officer C.F. Race on 8 January, after having flown operationally on seven of the previous nine nights and eleven of the previous seventeen. 'I really think we must be the only squadron in England that flies every night without rest.' A sergeant in his crew noted, 'I have just heard that we are going out again tonight.' 'They must think we are a lot of machines,' he went on, showing more than a trace of paranoia, 'or maybe it is because we are Canadians. They certainly don't send the English squadrons out every night. I know that from talking to the boys of the other squadrons.' Another sergeant, D.A. Ross of Sherbrooke, Quebec, reported that 'we [407 Squadron] have been out 9 successive nights [2 to 10 January, during which Ross flew on five successive nights, the 4th to the 8th] ... I was so tired I didn't know what I was doing.'[44]

The anxious hours aircrew spent in the dispersal hut waiting for a Rover patrol to return, with the possibility of being dispatched to attack a reported convoy looming in their minds, also played a stressful part in their lives. 'For every operation we undertook,' one No 407 veteran recalled, 'it seemed that we stood by a dozen times, and the uncertainty of waiting was often far worse than the real thing.' 'We were always waiting to go out,' observed another, 'and it didn't pay to have too much imagination while you were sitting in a hut, nerves tightening and just waiting for orders to attack a well defended convoy. It was the most difficult part of shipping strikes.'[45]

An actual attack may well have been less stressful than the long wait that preceded it. On the night of 28 December, Styles led ten Hudsons on an anti-shipping strike. Three located the convoy and made attacks.[46]

When finally we were ordered to attack, it was a different story. After the engines fired and jumped into life, all the uncertainties disappeared. Suddenly, we were part of the action and absorbed in preparation and flying. The hundred and one little things that had to be done blotted out those tormenting uncertainties.

It turned out to be a difficult trip. About an hour and a half after taking off, blips of the ships appeared on the radar screen. They were strung out at about three miles distance and there were a lot of them. Then we could see the convoy, steaming line astern in … two [columns] with flakships interspersed under a clear, but dark evening sky.

Almost before we had time to consider its composition or pin-point the location of the escort vessels, very heavy flak opened up at the front of the convoy, followed by the bright red flash of a bomb exploding.

'Christ! We're not the first in.' All my plans were out the window.

We turned and for a moment flew parallel to the line of ships, still hugging the water. Then we saw a large vessel near the rear which was not flying a balloon and appeared to be guarded by a single flakship. It was a good target and the light was right. 'Perhaps these buggers are preoccupied with the action up front.'

At maximum speed, with bombs readied and doors open, we skidded into position. The approach seemed to take forever and we sweated and waited. The first little indications of flak were the little coloured blobs of light that seemed to hang motion-less in front of you before flashing past. It was a powerful wall of fire and we were not going to sneak in.

Then we were firing back and the smoke from the front Brownings filled the com-partment – the designers had forgotten about ventilation – but we didn't give a damn; better to gag on the smoke and have them keep their heads down. We went in very low and released our bombs just before pulling up over the stern of the vessel. Then back down on the water, skidding from side to side to avoid the flak.

The machine-gun and cannon fire intensified as we flew out, and Ken Wallis fired back at everything that came into his sights, but an explosion was not observed on the ship and we couldn't believe it. It is not easy to miss from fifty feet under what had to be ideal conditions, and she was a big one too, about 7,000 tons.

After it was over, I experienced the usual excitement and relief, and then settled down for the flight home. It was a pleasant night, no night fighters, and everything seemed to be in order. After landing and debriefing, I didn't give it another thought until the next time. The real stress had been the waiting, not the operation.[47]

There is good evidence that more rest was needed, not only from operations but also from the living conditions at North Coates. 'Oh, what a desolate, miserable spot it is,' wrote one flying officer, 'no township within 14 miles.

Our sleeping quarters are 4 or 500 yards from the mess and it's most unpleasant facing the elements about 11 p.m. ... There is no fire in the room [and, of course, no central heating], so I flop into bed and shiver myself to sleep.' A new arrival reported that he was 'on the worst and dirtiest camp in England but on one of the best squadrons in England, 407 ... The grub is poor, quarters worse, and [I have] never been in so much dirt and filth in all my life.' It was not only Canadian aircrew who complained. The station 'was built during the last [1914-18] war as a summer training camp and is in a very dilapidated condition,' wrote a British aircraftsman employed on general duties. 'In fact, a farmer couldn't keep cows in these huts, water pours in the roofs and we have to bore holes in the floor to let the water out.'[48]

No 407 Squadron's losses continued to mount in January and early February. An all-RAF crew failed to return from a Rover patrol on 31 January. Eight days later another Hudson was lost on a similar mission. However, the greatest single blow to morale occurred on 12 February in operations against the German battlecruisers *Scharnhorst* and *Gneisenau* and the heavy cruiser *Prinz Eugen* during their breakout from Brest and passage through the English Channel.[49]

The background to Operation Fuller has already been described in chapter 6 of this volume and need not be recounted again. Suffice it to say that inadequate reconnaissance arrangements went awry, a senior officer of Fighter Command failed to exercise his initiative, and the enemy warships, having left Brest shortly after nightfall on 11 February 1942, were north of Le Havre and closing quickly on the Strait of Dover before they were reported, only an hour before noon on the 12th.

The tardiness of this recognition forced a hurried reaction that seriously compromised the entire operation. Joubert urged the AOC of No 16 Group to launch a delaying attack with RAF Beauforts from Thorney Island 'even if only a portion of the forces were available and if necessary without fighter escort.' In the rush to attack the German ships while they were still within range, however, coordination between the various commands degenerated into chaos. An attack by the Beauforts was ordered shortly after noon. Incredibly, the first four to arrive over Manston (at 1400 hours) were left circling the airfield, waiting for a fighter escort that had already been dispatched to the scene of action because No 16 Group headquarters had relayed the change of plans to the Beauforts by Morse radio message, forgetting that the torpedo-bombers had had their W/T continuous wave radios removed two weeks earlier in order to install new R/T voice communications. Only after landing at Manston were the Beaufort crews informed of their target and sent off to make their attacks individually and without escort, as best they could. The main Coastal Command effort, meanwhile, was to be delivered by nine more Beauforts, with Hudsons from 407 and 500 Squadrons making diversionary bombing runs at 5000 feet in order to draw the Flak away from the much lower-flying torpedo-bombers.[50]

No 407, having received a 'report of 25 to 30 ships ... including 3 battleships' at noon, was ordered to launch every available aircraft. Eight crews took off, to meet with the Beauforts and three RAF Hudsons over Manston. Although the rendezvous was successful, they had been informed that a fighter escort would join up with them over Manston. When no fighters appeared the Beauforts attempted to lead the strike force out to sea, but the Hudsons, unable to communicate with them directly, failed to follow; Beauforts and Hudsons then aimlessly circled the airfield until, at 1530 hours, the Beaufort leader 'decided to go alone and set course for an estimated interception point based on his 1330 hour position for the enemy.' This time Squadron Leader W.A. Anderson, with four other No 407 crews and one of the RAF Hudsons, followed the torpedo-bombers, only to lose contact with them in the rain and low cloud. The remaining Hudsons returned to base.[51]

On reaching the target area two of the Canadian crews decided to drop their bombs without breaking through the cloud base, a wholly counter-productive exercise given the purpose of their mission (an unseen and unheard diversion was no diversion at all), while a third vainly attacked a German destroyer discovered entirely by chance. Anderson and Flying Officer L. Cowperthwaite were last seen launching an attack against one of the battlecruisers. Seven of the nine Beauforts launched their torpedoes, all to no effect; and all of them returned safely to base.[52]

The final effort to sink or damage the enemy ships came at last light as the flotilla was north of The Hague, off the Dutch coast. Twelve Beauforts, dispatched from Thorney Island, reached the vicinity of the German ships but were unable either to maintain formation or to locate their targets in a heavy rainstorm that had reduced visibility to half a mile. Two of them failed to return, 'but whether from Flak or flying into the sea in the prevailing conditions was never established.' The Germans reached safety in the Heligoland Bight by dawn on 13 February.[53]

Coming only two months after the British battleships *Prince of Wales* and *Repulse* had been sunk by Japanese air attack off Malaya, the successful passage of three major enemy warships through the Strait of Dover was a terrible affront to British pride. A parliamentary furore led the Cabinet to establish a board of enquiry which concluded that, 'apart from the weakness of our forces, the main reason for our failure to do more damage to the enemy was the fact that his presence was not detected earlier and this was due to a breakdown of night patrols and the omission to send out strong morning reconnaissance. All operational orders said they [the German ships] would pass through [the Strait of Dover] in darkness.'[54] Flight Lieutenant Gerald Kidd, in peacetime a London lawyer but now an air controller who had been intimately involved in some of the blunders that beset Fuller, was more specific. 'The fact remains,' he observed in a report submitted to Fighter Command, 'that upon them [Coastal Command] greatly depended the chance of obtaining early warning of the departure of the ships and also of an early attack upon them being executed ... Coastal Command, charged with the responsibility of keeping guard, let the Germans go and bungled the subsequent attack.'[55]

For his part, Joubert preferred to lay the blame on the 'inadequate resources' allocated to his anti-shipping forces, asserting angrily that 'if the Air Ministry in its wisdom deprives this Command of the tools necessary to its work, that work will be badly done.' The AOC-in-C could, with considerable justification, point to the fact that he had had only three understrength Beaufort squadrons available for use against the German ships, and that they were serving more as OTUs for Mediterranean torpedo squadrons than as anti-shipping units with operational responsibilities in home waters. Indeed, one of them, after spending the month of October 1941 on torpedo training, had been forced to revert to minelaying at the end of November, after eleven of its most experienced crews were posted to the Middle East, while the other two had been unable to practise with any regularity because of a chronic shortage of torpedoes. (Fewer than thirty were allocated to Coastal Command each month, for both operational and training needs.) Nevertheless, Joubert could not dodge his command's responsibility for having failed to report the enemy movement earlier; nor had it made the best possible use of its resources.[56]

The loss of nine crews in only two-and-a-half months of operations had left No 407 with a grave shortage of experienced flyers, and on 14 February 'No 16 Group ordered the squadron to be taken off operations for a period in order to reform and for training purposes.' Two weeks later a scarcity of replacement aircraft led Northwood to prohibit all offensive operations against merchant shipping. Although the order was rescinded six weeks later, after Joubert had received Air Ministry assurances that twenty-six more Hudsons would be available by the end of April, the importance of giving 'due consideration ... to the necessity for conserving aircraft' continued to be emphasized.[57]

This brief suspension of operations allowed the squadron to complete the changeover in crew composition begun the previous November. As second pilots qualified to become captains of their own crews they were replaced by observers, so that by the end of March all crews consisted of a pilot, an observer, and two WOAGs. The restructuring of crews happened to coincide with a request that the squadron post all pilots in excess of establishment to other Hudson-equipped squadrons – thereby providing No 407 with an excellent opportunity to further the goal of Canadianization. The units concerned were instructed by Northwood to 'agree [on] the names of the pilots to be posted, bearing in mind that 407 Squadron is primarily to retain its strongest pilots, but at the same time releasing as many non-Canadian pilots as possible.' As part of the process, the training group was to post twenty-one observers from GR schools to No 407, 'selecting Canadians so far as resources permit.'[58]

In practice, the posting scheme soon grew to include all aircrew trades as the Canadian squadron's RAF aircrew were simply exchanged for RCAF aircrew from the other squadrons in the group. On 9 February, for example, No 407 received four Canadian WOAGs from one RAF squadron while posting three non-Canadian observers to another. Six days later, 'six RAF and Newfoundland WOAGs were posted to No 59 Squadron in exchange for six Canadian WOAGs from the same squadron.' By 18 March No 407 had taken in eleven RCAF pilots, sixteen observers, and forty-four WOAGs while posting out all but two of its RAF aircrew. (Of the remaining RAF officers, one was the commanding officer, Wing Commander A.C. Brown, DFC, who hailed from Winnipeg.) By these means the Canadian content of the squadron's aircrew improved from 51 per cent in mid-January to 98 per cent by the time the squadron had completed its retraining period at the end of March. Among groundcrew, who were not involved in the posting scheme, the improvement over the same period was less dramatic, the figures being 32 per cent in January and 63 per cent by early April. This degree of Canadianization was only made possible because Joubert chose to ignore the standard Air Ministry argument against breaking up crews – namely, that such a course would imperil their safety and general operational efficiency. His actions may have been influenced by a letter from the air member for personnel, Air Marshal Sir Philip Babington. Pointing to growing pressure from the RCAF, the AMP had urged Joubert to pursue 'dominionization' with greater vigour.[59]

In his reply, Joubert had lamely maintained that 'so far as resources permitted, Dominion personnel were selected' in the formation of dominion squadrons, the fact that RAF aircrew had been posted in being taken as prima facie evidence 'that at the time Dominion personnel were not available.' Ignoring the shortage of serviceable aircraft and the inability of Northwood's inadequate training organization to provide sufficient aircrew for newly formed squadrons, he asserted that 'the formation of th[ese] Squadron[s] was considerably delayed in waiting for the [dominion] personnel to be posted.' He then pointed to 407 Squadron as an example of 'transferring Canadian personnel ... from Command resources,' but wrongly declared that it was 'almost completely Canadianised' in mid-February 1942. Finally, he attempted to deflect further criticism by suggesting that Canadianization was lagging simply because of a shortage of Canadian OTU graduates, but this argument also had a hollow ring, given the fact that Canadian aircrew had been kept waiting at No 3 Personnel Reception Centre for as long as fourteen weeks before commencing OTU training. Perhaps it was his own recognition of the weakness of this argument that led him to encourage the exchange of personnel in order to strengthen No 407's Canadian content.[60]

Ironically, at the same time that 407 Squadron was smoothly exchanging aircrew with its RAF counterparts, Babington was informing the new AO-in-C Overseas, Air Vice-Marshal Harold Edwards, that the Canadianization of RCAF Coastal squadrons was 'reasonably good with the exception of No 407 (Hudson) Squadron. There are 21 RCAF Hudson pilots in RAF squadrons, but without considerable breaking up of crews nothing further can be done at the moment.' In regard to observers, Edwards was assured that 'there is sufficient material in Coastal Command to rectify the position numerically, but as in the case of Bomber Command, it would mean the general breaking up of crews and this is even more undesirable within Coastal Command because, quite apart from the imperilling of operational efficiency and safety of crews which would be entailed by breaking up, certain squadrons have definite operational areas to cover and it would be quite futile to take crews who have the experience of the Norwegian Coast and transfer them, for example, to English Channel work as that would be wasteful of a great deal of most valuable local

knowledge. Similar consideration applies for other localities.'[61] Babington
either had deplorably little knowledge of Coastal Command deployments or
was deliberately trying to deceive Edwards, since squadrons were frequently
moved about to meet operational demands. And, given the relative ease with
which No 407 Squadron 'Canadianized' its aircrew, Edwards's subsequent exasperation with Air Ministry fears of 'imperilling operational efficiency' may
be viewed with some sympathy.

In contrast to the night operations being conducted by No 16 Group, the sorties
flown off the Norwegian coast by No 18 Group were usually carried out in
daylight, a circumstance imposed to some extent by the combination of longer
distances from base and fewer hours of darkness during the northern summer.
With Coastal Command's own Blenheim fighters easily outclassed by the
enemy, however, an essential requirement for daylight operations was a sufficient degree of cloud cover to enable aircraft to elude the Me 109s and 110s
which patrolled the Norwegian coastline. It was Northwood's policy, therefore,
'for the GR aircraft to fly at a low altitude over the North Sea to the Norwegian coast, and then, by taking full advantage of cloud cover, make a quick
sweep into the fjords and if a target was found to carry out an attack.'[62]

    Such sorties were conducted by two squadrons of Hudsons, one of Blenheim
bombers, and one of Beaufort torpedo-bombers. No 404 Squadron's Blenheims
became operational at the end of September 1941, flying out of Dyce, near
Aberdeen, on the Scottish coast. Their duties were largely confined to convoy
escort and reconnaissance patrols, but unlike 407 Squadron's operations off the
Dutch coast they only reported shipping and were not required to make any attacks; that lack of direct contact with the enemy was reflected in the loss of
only one crew as a result of enemy action during 1941. In fact, No 404's total
of seventy-nine operational casualties during the entire war was seventeen
fewer than the number incurred by 407 Squadron up to the end of May 1942.[63]

    Nevertheless, life was not easy. Plagued by quickly-moving fronts, the Cana-
dians often found inclement weather to be as great a danger as the enemy.

When the clouds were low and rain and sleet reduced visibility to only hundreds of
yards you had to balance the importance of the job against the fact that it was now
getting dangerous to fly; and you went deeper and deeper into the murk hoping that
it *might* get better if you carried on just that little bit further. You often ended up
squeezed into a couple of hundred feet of airspace between the grey wispiness of the
lowest part of the cloudbase and the heaving desolation of the North Sea below, which
would smash you into scrap metal if you hit it. At this stage you usually took out the
automatic pilot and flew manually, and then the strain started in earnest. If you once
lost sight of the sea in a wisp of cloud then you had immediately to pull up into the
overcast with no hope of getting down through it again, and you climbed, hoping to
break out of it in due course and that it would eventually clear enough to give you a
safe landing back home. The belt of Scottish hills that lay inland at varying distances
from the coast made flying low when lost in cloud a dodgy business ... We had no
instrument landing system for the all-important final approach and touchdown, and it

was at this stage of the flight, when so near home, that many aircraft and crews met their end.[64]

One such accident occurred on 19 October 1941 when a Blenheim returning from a convoy escort failed to locate the airfield at Dyce, even though people on the ground could clearly see the aircraft's navigational lights through the mist. After flying to and fro for two hours looking for a break in the weather, it eventually crashed into the sea, killing all on board.[65]

These adverse flying conditions were particularly prevalent in the Shetland Islands, to which the squadron moved in late October. It was not unusual during the winter months for 'high winds, rain, snow and poor visibility' to restrict 'flying to a minimum.' Despite these handicaps, the Canadians were credited with their first enemy aircraft destroyed on 18 December when a Junkers 88 on a weather reconnaissance was successfully intercepted fifty miles east of the Shetlands by the squadron commander, an Edmontonian in the RAF, Wing Commander P.H. Woodruff. This initial success was followed by claims of one Me 109 'probable' and one 'possible' during No 404's participation in the commando raid on Vaagso, Norway, on 27 December, the largest and most successful such operation to date; one Heinkel 111 'probable' and one He 115 'possible' when they were intercepted off the Norwegian coast on 15 January; and one Ju 88 and one He 111 'damaged' on 7 and 9 February, respectively.[66]

As we have already noted, however, the vastly superior performance of German fighters generally placed the Blenheims at a severe disadvantage whenever they came into contact with such machines. No 404's increasing discontent was brought to the attention of Overseas Headquarters in April 1942 when Woodruff wrote directly to Air Commodore W.A. Curtis, Edwards's deputy:

Our Blenheims are getting rather old and, as you will realise, rather out of date. I am told that there are no Beaufighters to spare but have been given to believe that Mosquitoes are coming out fairly quickly now, and I feel that the Mosquito Fighter would be considerably better for our job than the Beaufighter because of its superior manoeuverability. My boys have done their best with the Blenheims and I feel that they are reaching the stage where they feel they should be supplied with more modern tools, i.e. Mosquitoes. If you could possibly do anything to hurry up our re-equipping I would indeed be very grateful.[67]

Woodruff then turned to the issue of Canadianization, which:

seems to have created a small amount of prejudicial feeling in some quarters and while we have released all our English crews, we have had no replacements. We are now in a very good position at the moment to get new crews right up to scratch for operations as we have plenty of time for training flying. We had three Canadian crews posted to us but unfortunately they were posted away as soon as they got here. While I realize the fact that Squadrons who are doing more work than we are probably require crews more urgently, my aim is to get the Squadron up to strength while we have this chance and then when we are called on for strenuous operations again we will be in a good position. We are at the moment seven crews under strength.[68]

De Havilland Mosquitoes – the 'wooden wonders' that could outpace Me 109s and carried four 20-millimetre cannon – were, of course, out of the question for Coastal Command in 1942; and Curtis's staff could only recommend that Northwood be asked to re-equip the unit with Beaufighters, 'pointing out the squadron's record, and requesting that they be considered for re-equipping, if they have not already been considered.' In the end, however, Curtis repeated to Woodruff Air Ministry declarations that the matter was under review and 'that a high priority rating has been given to your Squadron for its conversion to Beaufighters.' 'High priority' turned out to entail a four-month wait.[69]

As for his concern over Canadianization, Woodruff was assured that 'this situation will be remedied very shortly,' but here, too, progress was slow. The proportion of Canadian aircrew had remained at about 45 per cent since the squadron had commenced operations in September, and it did not rise consistently above 50 per cent for another year. Given the fact that the proportion in the other RCAF strike squadrons exceeded 90 per cent by April 1942, there may have been some truth in Woodruff's contention of 'prejudicial feeling,' though the cause of such feeling and the quarters in which it existed remain obscure.[70]

Meanwhile, No 407 Squadron had resumed operations from Bircham Newton, on the English east coast just south of The Wash, at the beginning of April 1942. Of the squadron's ninety-seven aircrew, sixty-four were recent additions, although many had previous experience with RAF Hudsons. They flew daylight reconnaissance patrols off the Danish coast and night-time Nomads (essentially Rovers under a different name) along the Dutch coast. With the prohibition on anti-shipping strikes still in effect, any vessels that were sighted could only be reported, not attacked, but even so two aircraft failed to return on 5 and 6 April, possibly having fallen victim to the Junkers 88 long-range fighters that guarded the Danish coast. The loss of two crews in two days once again demonstrated the vulnerability of the Hudson, and daylight sorties were quickly cancelled; operations were then confined to carrying out Nomad and anti-E-boat Hoden patrols. Although Nomads were meant to be flown simultaneously by three to four aircraft, each with its own section of the Dutch coast to cover, there was little difference between Nomad patrols and the irregular Rovers the squadron had conducted from its old base at North Coates.[71]

Operations were further curtailed by a shortage of serviceable aircraft. After the loss on 6 April, only two machines were available until replacements could be gleaned from other squadrons. Four arrived by 12 April, but 'all [had] seen considerable service' and were in such poor condition that 'the maintenance section had to work overtime to bring them up to operational standard.'[72] One squadron veteran recalled looking 'over a couple of replacement aircraft that had been flown in ... There was none of that exhilaration and good feeling that had been there months, or was it years, before, when D.A. [Ross] and I had examined our first Hudson. The aircraft I climbed into was old and at the end of its service life. It flashed through my mind that someone was unloading these old crates on 407 because they wouldn't last long anyway.'[73]

The lifting of the prohibition on anti-shipping strikes, together with a resumption of the normal convoy cycle off the Dutch coast with the coming of spring, allowed a greater number of attacks to be made during April. The Canadians managed only four of them, three with unobserved results, and lost two more crews. However, the increasing amount of traffic between the Elbe and Rotterdam convinced Northwood to initiate an all-out effort in early May and No 407 made fourteen attacks during the first week of that month, with only one pilot being wounded by Flak. The strikes were made either in moonlight or at twilight, using the same low-level tactics adopted the previous summer. On the night of 3/4 May, Flight Sergeant E.L. Howey's crew sank the 4647-ton *Sizilien* and four nights later eight machines attacked a convoy off Vlieland, sinking the *Ruth* (3726 tons) and damaging the 2860-ton *Namdo*. A week of bad weather prevented any further sorties until mid-month.[74]

In the early evening of 15 May, reports of a convoy off the Frisian Islands prompted group headquarters to launch two strike forces. One, led by Pilot Officer F.A. Kay of 407 Squadron, consisted of three RCAF Hudsons and eight from No 320 Squadron. They attacked through intense Flak, losing two Hudsons, one from each squadron, while a severely wounded Kay eventually crash-landed his damaged machine at Bircham Newton, killing his observer and injuring the two gunners. The second formation of nine machines, all from 407 Squadron and led by Flight Lieutenant R.M. Christie, launched its follow-up attack on a fully alerted enemy. Three were shot down in the vicinity of the convoy, while a badly damaged fourth crashed at Coningsby, a bomber base nearly fifty miles from Bircham Newton, killing all on board. In Christie's case, all his instruments 'were entirely shot away and his undercarriage failed to function,' compelling him to crash-land, though successfully, at Bircham Newton. In all, the strike cost the squadron twenty-two aircrew killed or missing, and four wounded or injured. Two ships were sunk, the Norwegian *Selje* of 6698 tons and the 464-ton *Madelein Louise;* for his part in the action, Christie was awarded a Distinguished Service Order, a decoration normally reserved for more senior officers and, when given to a junior one, considered second only to the VC.[75]

Once more No 407 was left with only two serviceable aircraft and had to be taken off operations for two weeks until replacement aircraft could be flown in from other units. Operations resumed on 28/29 May when eight machines participated in a strike that resulted in two claims. One of them 'came across an enemy ship on fire ... in tow by another MV' which was in the process of picking up survivors. 'Without more ado P/O [L.J.] O'Connell made an attack dropping his bombs over the two ships and causing large explosions. His rear gunner ... machine-gunned the ships and caused considerable damage and consternation among the enemy.' Meanwhile, Sergeant M.A. Tisdale's attack produced 'a bright yellow flash' and 'dense smoke.'

Another major strike the following night, which included eight aircraft from the Canadian squadron, sank the Swedish ship *Varmdo* of 2956 tons. Flight Sergeant Howey and Pilot Officer O'Connell both claimed hits, the latter going in so low 'that he struck a mast,' and both Hudsons were damaged. Six crews failed to return, one of them from No 407, flown by Flying Officer C.F. Race, whose views on the squadron's workload have been quoted earlier in this chapter. His Hudson was disabled by Flak while diving on the convoy and crashed nearby, the aircraft exploding on impact with the sea. Two of the crew, Flight Sergeant J.F. Clarke and Sergeant W.P. McCarthy, were picked out of the water by the enemy, but the latter died of his injuries before the convoy reached Borkum. Clarke survived, becoming a prisoner of war in Stalag VIII B.[76]

These losses prompted the squadron diarist to observe that 'during the past month six crews have either been designated missing or killed on operations with a loss of twenty-seven lives. This does not take into consideration the fact that after every major operation of this nature at least two or three aircraft are so very badly damaged they are of no use to this or any other squadron.' The casualty rate was not unique. Altogether, Northwood lost forty-seven aircraft on anti-shipping operations in April and May, as the overall loss rate during the latter month rose to 23 per cent of attacking aircraft, a figure approaching that which had forced Bomber Command's No 2 Group to abandon its anti-shipping activities the previous November.[77]

Even when conducted under cover of darkness, low-level attacks were costing almost 20 per cent of the aircraft involved. At a meeting of squadron, group, and command representatives held on 21 May 1942, 'the operational squadrons felt that the casualties recently incurred were due as much to tactics as to shortcomings in the aircraft engaged in the operations. The two weaknesses were that the enemy [presumably through their radar coverage] ... were able to warn the convoys, and that the defences had become accustomed to low level attacks and shaped their action accordingly.' The AOC-in-C, who chaired the meeting, agreed 'that tactics must be varied even at the expense of accuracy' but seemed in no hurry to investigate alternatives. In early June No 16 Group applied for permission to withdraw the Hudson squadrons from anti-shipping operations in order to train them in medium-level attacks from 4000 feet. Joubert agreed to the proposal as an interim measure, pending further consideration of the problem, but not until 1 July did he finally rule 'that mast height attacks against escorted convoys, by day or by night, were at present out of the question.'[78]

The enemy was suffering, too, from air, surface, and submarine attacks, as the total amount of German-controlled tonnage available for commerce declined by 10 per cent, from 1,050,000 tons in July 1941 to 946,000 tons in June 1942. Imports of Swedish iron ore were only 8.6 million tons, or 14 per cent behind schedule. With steel production already stretched to meet the expanding needs of the Wehrmacht, a large-scale shipbuilding program in Germany to replace lost tonnage was not feasible, and any improvement in the situation would require a drastic rationalization of existing resources. In May 1942, therefore, Hitler appointed the Gauleiter of Hamburg, Karl Kaufmann, as Reichskommissar für Schiffahrt with wide administrative powers over merchant shipping and shipbuilding. He moved immediately to raise freight rates, improve the pay and conditions of service of the merchant seamen, and return 300,000 tons of shipping specifically allocated to the Wehrmacht to the commercial pool. Then he attempted to ensure the 'complete utilisation of space in each ship; shorter turn around times by quicker dispatch from individual ports; expansion or rationalization of port facilities including transport services; provision of more port labour and the speeding up of voyage times by reducing the number of ports of call.' A modest construction scheme was also introduced, and 750,000 tons of standard design were scheduled to be delivered by the end of 1945.[79]

The anti-shipping campaign was clearly having some effect, but it had yet to realize its potential. The torpedo was by far the most effective weapon against ships at sea, but torpedoes were in short supply; and while the formation of Nos 415 and 489 (RNZAF) Squadrons in August 1941 had enabled Northwood to maintain six torpedo-bomber units in home waters, until December 1941 they were still flying obsolescent Bristol Beauforts. Moreover, they had not yet been brought up to operational standards when four older, more experienced squadrons were dispatched to the Mediterranean and Ceylon (where the Beaufort might still hold its own) to help combat the German intervention in North Africa and the Japanese threat in the Indian Ocean. In January 1942, however, the Air Ministry had finally allocated twenty-four Hampdens to Coastal Command, enough to re-equip No 415 Squadron and increase its establishment to twenty-two machines. Another unit was similarly re-equipped the following month, while a further two Hampden squadrons were transferred from Bomber Command in April 1942 as it converted to four-engined heavy bombers.[80] Joubert's torpedo-bomber strike force now had the range to reach Denmark. Yet it was not greater range that he needed as much as fast, well-armed, and agile torpedo carriers; in these respects the Hampden was no better than the Beaufort. An infusion of Beaufighters would have been far more useful.

The Hampden's deficiencies notwithstanding, No 415 Squadron's much-increased establishment permitted its crews to spend many more hours of flying training around their base at Thorney Island, but that may still not have been enough. Not entirely satisfied with what he saw on a visit made just before the unit was to move to St Eval in Cornwall, the RAF's inspector general concluded that the squadron would 'require to do a period of thoroughly intensive training when it gets to its new station' before it could be considered 'operationally efficient.' Nevertheless, over the next two months its torpedo-bombing training schedule was continually interrupted by a series of essentially unrelated operational tasks and yet another move. Anti-submarine patrols with depth charges were conducted over the Bay of Biscay to no avail; Rover patrols with torpedoes were flown over the southern reaches of the North Sea after the squadron's return to Thorney Island in May; and crews were introduced to anti-shipping strikes employing the new B (for Buoyant) bomb.[81] As useful as each of these kinds of attack may have been, however, they all demanded different skills in the handling of aircraft and weapons-systems; regrettably, No 415 was given no opportunity to master even one of them.

The B-bomb represented another technological advance. Really more of a mine than anything else, and designed to be dropped in the immediate path of a convoy, it would float up and detonate on contact with a ship's hull. As a result, B-bombs did not have to be dropped as accurately as conventional bombs, but to be effective they had to be planted in quantity, and virtually simultaneously, from a tight formation of aircraft.[82]

In early June 1942, in yet another attempt to develop new tactical procedures, a number of strike squadrons were grouped together on the east coast for joint exercises. A portion of No 415's training was carried out in conjunction with 59 Squadron, which flew Hudsons equipped with ASV radar and a stock of parachute flares, and combined patrols were generally flown in formations of three aircraft, consisting of one radar- and flare-equipped Hudson to locate and illuminate the target and two torpedo-carrying Hampdens to attack it. Despite the fact that torpedo training could only be carried out by small detachments sent in turn to the Torpedo Training Unit at Abbotsinch, the squadron pronounced itself 'one hundred per cent torpedo trained' by the beginning of July. Formation flying and 'high-level' (4000 feet) bombing were also practised, and once again the commanding officer reported that 'high level bombing training by day and by night has … been very satisfactory and above average,' even while the squadron diarist admitted that 'to date crews have not been making good scores.'[83]

Another tactic was added to the squadron's repertoire on the night of 1/2 July, when a formation of four Hampdens armed with B-bombs took off from North Coates to attack a reported convoy, followed thirty minutes later by four torpedo-carrying Hampdens. If the bombers could disrupt the convoy's orderly progression, either by damaging or sinking ships or simply by compelling them to take evasive action and thus weaken the intensity of Flak patterns, then the torpedo-bombers should have a better chance of success – at least in theory. In practice, things were less certain, for although the strike force arrived in the vicinity of the target just after midnight, only one of four low-flying bombers was able to find the convoy and make an attack, while only two torpedo-bombers were able to launch their ordnance, one of them then falling to Flak. No ships were sunk or damaged.[84]

No 415 Squadron's experiments with B-bombs would continue, but only seven of the thirty B-bomb sorties flown during July resulted in 'attacks' – if that is the right word – and not one enjoyed any success. B-bombing required sufficient cloud cover for the Hampdens to evade night-fighters, but it was extremely difficult to maintain the requisite close formation while flying at night in cloud; moreover, cloud often obscured both the flares dropped by the Hudsons and the convoys themselves.[85]

A further tactical refinement was added on the night of 30/31 July for a strike flown by aircraft from Nos 59, 407, and 415 Squadrons. Rather than using a single radar-equipped Hudson to search for the enemy, several were sent out ahead of the bombers, the idea being that the successful crew, or

Rooster, would shadow the convoy while sending out a signal on which the strike force could home. When the others arrived, the Rooster would then illuminate the target and thus initiate an attack.[86] As described in the No 407 Squadron diary, the first use of these tactics, at the end of July, achieved a coordinated, multi-squadron – but still unsuccessful – strike.

It would appear that the scheme was most satisfactory and nearly all aircraft found the target and attacks were carried out on a large enemy convoy off Terschelling. The Wing Commander, when he was satisfied that the Squadrons had homed on his aircraft, climbed from deck level to 4000 feet, dropped a flare to light up the target and circling, dropped his bombs on an enemy ship causing at least two definite hits. The Wing Commander then headed for base. Arriving over the convoy shortly afterwards the remainder of our crews proceeded to drop flares and by the light of these dropped their bombs. Owing to the height which they were flying, 4000 feet, definite hits were not observed. Observation was further complicated by the fact that there was some smattering of clouds in the vicinity which partially obscured the ships. However, taking into consideration [that] nine of our aircraft dropped their bombs over the ships themselves it is pretty conclusive even that if direct hits were not made there were many near misses and the effect of bombing at such close range has proved to be extremely satisfactory. Unfortunately, it is not known what damage was caused, but there is little doubt that it must have been extensive. As this Squadron left the target area, No. 59 Squadron arrived and proceeded to adopt similar tactics. By the light of their flares No 415 Squadron appeared on the scene and dropped their torpedoes. It is evident that several more ships were hit.[87]

What was 'evident' to the squadron diarist (and to the squadron commander who signed the entries) was far from evident to the enemy. In fact, Coastal Command was unable to sink or damage a single enemy vessel in either July or August.[88]

While 407 Squadron continued to use the Rooster technique on anti-shipping strikes until transferred to St Eval (No 19 Group) in October 1942, 415 Squadron moved to Scotland in early August for two months of rest and training. The move was instigated by Joubert in a belated effort to concentrate his four torpedo-bomber units, 'with the object of permitting Squadron training and the studying of torpedo and "B" bomb tactics.' Stating the obvious, the AOC-in-C felt that there was 'much to be done in developing the ability of torpedo squadrons to reach their target and deliver an effective attack.' He went on to suggest fitting 'formation flying lights' on the Hampdens to aid in night flying, a recommendation that ignored the experience of his Hudson captains, who had already tried it and found it wanting. He understood the tactical difficulties sufficiently, however, to recognize that the necessity of operating at night made coordination with the Hudsons difficult and thought it 'doubtful whether long-distance combined attack would be successful but the problem should be examined to see if a solution is possible.'[89]

What was needed, if Coastal Command was to take on heavily defended convoys successfully in daylight, were composite strike wings of fast, manoeuvrable torpedo-bombers escorted by equally fast and manoeuvrable machines able to suppress the enemy's Flak with bombs and air-to-surface fire and at least challenge the enemy's fighters. Given the unlikelihood that Mosquitoes would be made available, Beaufighters were the answer, and Joubert already had the conventional long-range fighter version. At the end of July the Air Ministry allocated the first Beaufighters modified to carry torpedoes (known colloquially as Torbeaus) to No 254 Squadron, and in September it indicated that Joubert might have as many as five Torbeau and five Beaufighter squadrons by the spring of 1943.

The seeds of an effective composite wing had been planted. Both the Torbeau and Beaufighter were heavily armed (each carried four 20-millimetre cannon in the nose and six .303-machine guns in the wings); both had cruising speeds in the 200-240 miles per hour range, making it practicable for them to work with single-seat fighters, if necessary; they were relatively manoeuvrable and their maximum speed of 315 miles per hour afforded their crews some chance against enemy fighters. Not wanting to wait until the spring, Joubert decided in October to withdraw No 143 Squadron from its escort and reconnaissance duties and, co-locating it with No 254 at North Coates, in November formed an experimental composite strike wing of Beaufighters and Torbeaus.[90]

13

A Force to Be Reckoned With, 1943–5

Believing that the interdiction of enemy convoys along the Dutch coast was of such importance that his composite wing of Torbeaus and Beaufighters should become operational as soon as possible, Air Chief Marshal Philip Joubert de la Ferté decided to commit his meagre force to an early operation there even though it had had only a short two weeks of joint preparation. With the torpedo squadron neither fully equipped nor trained, however, and only one squadron of Beaufighters being available for the anti-Flak role, the first strike flown by the North Coates wing, on 20 November 1942, was a disappointing affair marked by a number of tactical blunders. Sinking the Dutch tug *Indus*, of 449 tons, was small compensation for the loss of five aircraft.[1]

Bruised by the experience, the prototype composite wing went back into training while the group staff set about analysing what had gone wrong. They concluded, perhaps obviously enough, 'that co-ordination in attack had to be considered in terms of seconds ... Careful briefing, good leadership, a very high standard of air discipline and skill in attack, [and] close liaison with the fighter escort, were all essential qualities to be acquired before the composite force could hope for success.' Accordingly, No 16 Group added, it was 'essential that a Striking force of this nature should be located at one Aerodrome and trained as a team. The team to consist not only of Torpedo aircraft and [anti-Flak Beau]Fighter Bombers, but also of fighter escort, reconnaissance aircraft and photographic aircraft.'[2]

Still stationed in Scotland – once again at Dyce, on the east coast near Aberdeen – No 404 Squadron had begun to replace its Blenheims with Beaufighter IIFs in September 1942. Powered by Rolls Royce Merlin XX engines, adopted because of a shortage of the Bristol Hercules VI radials used on the Mark VI, the IIF was generally regarded as too slow to be a superior coastal fighter. Yet such was the requirement for long-range machines that at the end of January 1943 the squadron was transferred to Chivenor in southwest England, to provide fighter cover for No 19 Group's anti-submarine operations in the Bay of Biscay. Although the Luftwaffe's attacks on these patrols had diminished in number since autumn, Fliegerführer Atlantik maintained a limited number of Ju 88 long-range fighters on the French coast and there was a resurgence of activity in March when 19 Group lost three crews while accounting for four of the enemy fighters.[3]

No 404 was responsible for two of the four victories when six of its Beaufighters intercepted seven Ju 88s. Three of the enemy 'started a steep climb, taking no other evasive action.'

A[ir]/C[raft] R [Flight Sergeant V.F. McCallan] maintaining an average climbing speed of 160 mph to 4,000 ft had closed within a range of 700 to 800 yards of one Ju 88 which had fallen behind the other two E[nemy]/A[ircraft]. The pilot of A/C R opened fire with cannon at this point from dead astern firing two 3 second bursts and two 4 second bursts at this E/A. From the last two bursts fired both pilot and navigator observed strikes on the port engine and port wing of the E/A. A shower of pieces were seen to be knocked off the port wing, also one portion about one foot square. A heavy cloud of black smoke poured from the port engine continuing until E/A was lost from view. At the time hits were observed the enemy A/C made a violent turn to port, losing altitude on the turn. A/C R attempted to turn inside the E/A and stalled. A/C T [Flight Sergeant H.R. Browne] then made an attack firing two one-second bursts with cannon from astern the Ju 88 at 500 and 300 yards. No hits were observed. The three E/A then gained cloud cover and were not again seen.[4]

The other four German machines were pursued by the remaining Beaufighters, but they were unable to overtake their adversaries. Just before the enemy escaped into cloud cover, Flying Officer R.A. Schoales fired four long bursts from a thousand yards at the Junkers furthest to port. Given the long ranges at which the Canadians had fired, the commanding officer, Wing Commander G.G. Truscott, assessed the engagement as 'inconclusive ... due to inability of Beaufighter Mk. IIF to overtake Ju 88's.' In fact, however, McCallan and Browne in the one case, and Schoales in the other, had managed to shoot down both of the Ju 88s they had fired upon.[5]

With No 404 Squadron still involved in escort work and No 407 transferred to anti-submarine duties in early 1943, the RCAF's only other anti-shipping unit was No 415 Squadron. After returning to No 16 Group in November 1942 it had resumed flying Rover patrols, although since its Hampdens needed favourable conditions of cloud and darkness to survive off the enemy coast, sorties were flown just two or three nights each month. From early November to the end of May 1943, its crews made only twenty attacks against enemy shipping while losing eleven aircraft.[6] The greatest danger remained the intense anti-aircraft fire, as the crew of Hampden F/415 discovered in the early morning hours of 23 December 1942.

Point of strike off the Dutch Coast was reached at 0005 hrs and two flares and flak from unseen ships were observed. At 0020 hrs several ships were seen and F/415 went in for an attack releasing torpedo from 30 to 40 feet at 800 yards. Results not observed due to violent evasive action. Intense and accurate light flak was experienced, three shells bursting within the interior of the fuselage rendering all of the pilot[']s flying instruments unserviceable except the directional gyro, the altimeter and the compass.

The elevator trim control was completely shot away and the aircraft zoomed up to 800 ft with the cockpit full of blinding smoke. Sgt Ellergodt successfully managed to bring [the] aircraft under control and flew it in its disabled condition back to base landing safely at 0324 hrs on 23/12/42. Sgt. Johnson received a small shell splinter in one thumb but the remainder of the crew were uninjured.[7]

Not surprisingly, perhaps, the torpedo missed its target on that occasion. It was not until almost four months later, on the night of 14/15 April 1943, that two crews were able to make a successful attack on a convoy north of Schiermonnikoog, in the Frisian Islands. Both scored hits, the first of which sank the Norwegian vessel *Borga* of 4821 tons while the second, failing to explode, only damaged the Swedish *Tom* of 2092 tons. One month later, a strike by eight machines on a convoy northwest of Borkum sank the German escort trawler *Ernst von Briesen* of 408 tons for the loss of two aircraft. Following a two-week training period in early June, the squadron spent the next two-and-a-half months flying Musketry patrols in the Bay of Biscay as part of Coastal Command's latest anti-submarine offensive.[8]

While Coastal Command headquarters, at Northwood, was preoccupied with the climactic phase of the Battle of the Atlantic in the spring of 1943, the anti-shipping campaign resumed in April with the return to operations of the Beaufighter strike wing at North Coates. The lessons learned from the disappointing attack of 20 November 1942 had been absorbed, and it was agreed that the cannon-armed fighters must take on the escorts to suppress Flak while 'the task of sinking the target ship was that of the torpedo bombers. If experience showed that target ships carried considerable Flak, a proportion of the fighter and UP diversion force would attack her.' 'UP' meant 'unrotated (or rocket) projectile,' and its consideration by the staffs at Northwood and in the groups early in 1943 reflected their eagerness to employ this new, experimental, weapon in the anti-shipping war. Just three months would elapse before they would be used operationally for the first time.[9]

The successful operation of the strike wing also required effective cooperation between Coastal and Fighter commands. The North Coates wing found it difficult to fly the frequent reconnaissances required as well as to carry out its training and strike functions, while a reconnoitering Beaufighter 'had little chance of survival if engaged by Me 109s or FW 190s which were at this time operating off this coastline.' An intercommand agreement was concluded whereby Fighter Command's No 12 Group (initially using Mustang fighters from Army Co-operation Command) would conduct reconnaissance flights, known as Lagoons, along the Dutch coast as far east as Wangerooge in the German Frisian Islands. Northwood would be responsible for its own reconnaissances east of that point.[10]

Increasingly, special intelligence – 'references in Enigma to navigational and other arrangements for convoy movements' – was revealing the enemy's routine, and from it and other sources (including aerial reconnaissance) Northwood knew which swept channels the convoys used, where they spent the night, when they entered and left harbour, and when and where they met their escorts. It was therefore possible to discern when the Germans altered or abandoned their routine, and to deduce, often quite accurately, when especially important convoys were sailing. Intercepted Enigma signals also confirmed actual, rather than claimed, damage done and, more generally, the extent to which the anti-shipping campaign was having an impact on the enemy's ability to move essential supplies by sea.[11]

An opportunity to test the strike-wing tactics again came on 18 April when a convoy was reported off The Hague consisting of one large merchantman and seven smaller vessels escorted by four Flak-ships and four minesweepers. The strike force consisted of nine Torbeaus, twelve anti-Flak Beaufighters armed with cannon and two 250-lb general-purpose bombs, and a high cover of twenty-two long-range Spitfires and eight Mustangs from Fighter Command. Shortly before reaching the Dutch coast, the strike formation began to climb to the designated attack altitude. Locating the convoy, the twenty-one Beaufighters turned in unison. The anti-Flak sections, concentrating on the escort ships, made diving attacks from 1500 feet while the Torbeaus flew in steadily at 150 feet. The entire action lasted only four minutes and left four escorts damaged and the 5000-ton target, *Hoegh Carrier*, sinking. Only two of the attacking Beaufighters sustained light damage, indicating that the Flak defences had been overwhelmed and demonstrating the success that could be achieved by a well coordinated attack. The next two operations, on 29 April and 17 May, confirmed the value of the new tactics as six ships totalling 13,803 tons were sunk for the loss of only one Beaufighter.[12]

These losses – and those attributed to mines and light naval forces – had an immediate impact on Swedish willingness to trade at Rotterdam. During the summer of 1942, the average amount of active shipping tonnage there (excluding tankers and vessels under 1000 tons) had been 100,000 tons, while the comparable figure for the German port of Emden, beyond the range of the strike wing's fighter cover, was 39,000 tons. By May 1943, however, activity at Rotterdam had declined to the lowest levels yet observed, with only 37,000 tons of shipping in the port. Emden, in contrast, had witnessed an increase to a total of 90,000 tons at the end of May.[13]

Despite the strike wing's success – ten ships, totalling 24,222 tons, sank between 18 April and 31 July – the fact that attacks were carried out against only nine of fifty-five convoys sighted between the Elbe and the Hook of Holland during that period led the new AOC-in-C at Northwood to question whether the Beaufighters would not be better employed providing long-range fighter cover in the Bay of Biscay. Already short of fighter escorts for anti-submarine work in the bay and told 'there was likely to be increasing difficulty in finding sufficient fighter escorts for shipping strikes,' the AOC-in-C decided to ignore what had been achieved so far and asked that his Beaufighters be permitted to move south to cover the Biscay anti-U-boat patrols.[14]

Slessor's proposal to reinforce the bay offensive at the expense of the anti-shipping campaign was opposed by both the Admiralty and the Ministry of Economic Warfare – and in strong language. 'The attacks by Coastal Command's Strike Wing and the Nore Flotilla upon enemy shipping, the American daylight bombing, the night bombing and mine-laying of Bomber Command, and the action of the fighter escorts, were all complimentary and cumulative in their results. The effects of each one aggravated and increased those of the others; the cessation of any one might well go far to stultify the activities of the others by creating a loop-hole for escape.'[15] These arguments were persuasive, and it was finally agreed that the North Coates wing would continue to operate on its present scale. For its part, Fighter Command guaranteed to provide three squadrons of escort fighters on all occasions except those when a major daylight bombing raid was scheduled.[16]

Although the Air Ministry had formerly proposed equipping ten Coastal squadrons with Beaufighters by the spring of 1943, there were still only seven in May and, of the four Hampden torpedo-bomber squadrons in the command, only No 144 was re-equipped with Torbeaus. The rest, all dominion squadrons, retained their Hampdens. Conducting operations with aircraft that were quite unsuitable for their role had an understandably debilitating effect on morale, a fact that had been obvious to Air Marshal H. Edwards during a visit to No 415 Squadron in September 1942. However, when he had asked that it be re-equipped with better aircraft, he had been informed that 'questions of this nature must ... be decided from the broad aspect and not with particular application.' The Air Ministry had promised only that the squadron would receive improved Hampdens and for the moment that seems to have satisfied Edwards, who was otherwise distracted by the pressures of forming a Canadian bomber group. The matter was not raised again until July 1943.[17]

Equipment was not the AOC-in-C's only concern. Prior to his visit to No 415, a large number of non-RCAF aircrew (in fact thirty-five of forty-two recent arrivals) had been posted in to the squadron, with the predictable result that its Canadianization rate, which had long stood at 90 per cent or better (and reached 95.6 per cent as recently as 26 August) fell to 65.7 per cent. That, Edwards complained, was 'not in accordance with the spirit of our agreement to post Canadian crews to Canadian squadrons.' A subsequent investigation undertaken by the AOC of No 17 Group confirmed his allegation, adding for good measure that the postings had been 'in direct contravention of both Command instructions and my own.' The group promised to do better in the future – and did so, if only slightly. In November the Air Ministry was able to report that 'a considerable improvement has been effected and today out of a total of 22 crews, 17 are Canadian. Every effort is being made to Canadianize the remaining 5 crews at the earliest opportunity.' However, a year later the percentage had not changed.[18]

Moreover, when a new commanding officer had to be found to replace Wing Commander W.W. Bean upon his repatriation to Canada, the officer proposed by Overseas Headquarters, an experienced Catalina pilot, was not considered suitable by Sir John Slessor because he had no torpedo-bomber experience. The AOC-in-C wanted, instead, 'to post Squadron Leader G.H.D. Evans [RAF] from No 489 Squadron to command No 415 Squadron. This officer has had considerable experience as a Flight Commander in No 489 Squadron, which is a Hampden Torpedo Bomber Squadron.' As there were no equally qualified Canadian candidates immediately available, Edwards had to accept Slessor's man; but he took steps to insure that the situation would not be repeated. On 17 March he informed the Air Ministry that 'a signal has been sent to Air Force Headquarters in Ottawa to post Overseas a squadron leader or wing commander with the necessary background and on arrival he will be posted to Coastal Command for necessary OTU training, at the completion of which he will double bank Squadron Leader Evans and subsequently command No 415 Squadron.'[19]

Questions of national significance concerning No 415 Squadron would not go away, largely because of the perceived adverse effects of its odd-job employment and lack of satisfactory aircraft. In June 1943 Ottawa recommended that an RCAF composite group be formed to support the Canadian Army (see chapter 7); since No 415 seemed to be under-utilized in its present role, Overseas Headquarters raised the possibility of transferring the squadron to the proposed new composite formation. Responding to Edwards's calls to either re-equip or reassign the squadron, the Air Ministry's director general of organization assured him that, although it was to be 'regretted that, for operational reasons, the withdrawal of this efficient squadron from a most important and vital role cannot be contemplated at the present time and it is hoped you will not press us over this as the re-equipment of the Squadron is almost in sight and it would be both unsound and uneconomical to waste all the experience gained by the squadron in torpedo operations with the Metropolitan Air Force.'[20] Having received similarly fulsome assurances in the past, Edwards was not to be placated so easily this time. In a meeting with the air member for supply and organization, Sir Christopher Courtney, on 24 August, he presented his view that 415 Squadron 'should have first class Torpedo aircraft and not Hampdens or Wellingtons or any other kind of Bomber Command obsolete discards.'[21] This time the response came from Slessor.

It has been decided that 415 is to be re-equipped and employed on a new and much more active role. We have just had a thorough review of our commitments and resources, and amongst other things it became plain that we are over-insured in torpedo squadrons, of which we have 5 in Home Waters for which there really is not sufficient employment. On the other hand we have nothing to deal with the E and R boats [German MTBs and small escort vessels, respectively], which are a real menace to the increasingly important Channel and North Sea Convoys. We used to use Whitleys for reconnaissance and close co-operation with our own light coastal craft in the Nore area, and the Fleet Air Arm have been helping us out with Albacores for the strike action against the E and R boats in the Channel – in which, as you may have noticed, they have had some useful success. The Whitleys, of course, are dead and the FAA units are being withdrawn to work at sea.

It has, therefore, been decided to re-equip one squadron as a composite unit with one Flight of Wellington XIII with VHF and ASV III for work with light coastal forces, and one Flight of Albacores ... to beat up the E boat[s]. 415 was selected as it is the only torpedo squadron not included in a Strike Wing, and it knows the Channel and the Dutch Coast well. Incidentally one of the other torpedo squadrons is probably being converted to a long-range fighter for anti-flak escort to Torpedo and R[ocket] P[rojectile] Strikes; that will be one in the North.

I think 415 have rather felt in the past that they were rather nobody's baby – they could not be taken seriously as a Torpedo Squadron with the old Hampden, and they had to be used for all sorts of odd jobs like, recently, helping out with the A/S offensive in the Bay. Their new job will be really interesting and valuable – and may become particularly so next Spring. It will afford a good opportunity for varied experience to the C[ommanding] O[fficer], and as it involves a number of detachments at places like Manston and Exeter, will also give good experience to other more junior officers.

They will come out of the line in the next few days to re-equip.[22]

Replacing obsolescent Hampdens with Fairey Albacore biplanes was not exactly what Edwards had in mind, especially when he knew that the other Hampden units in Coastal Command would soon be re-equipping with Beaufighters for anti-Flak escort work. Citing (in a draft letter that was not sent) his 'responsibilities to the Canadian Government to ensure that Canadian Funds being expended on the RCAF Overseas are productive of maximum results,' he could 'hardly sanction replacement of obsolete aircraft with even more obsolete types which will result in the Canadian effort being still less productive than heretofore.' Furthermore, he added, moving to the kind of operational considerations the Air Ministry so often advanced to support its position, 'the prospect of a Squadron with two types of aircraft will inevitably result in countless maintenance problems coming to the fore and in a very short time will lead to very many difficulties in trying to maintain serviceability.'[23]

Indeed, it appears that Edwards was prepared to go so far as to 'deCanadianize' No 415 Squadron and to use its personnel to better advantage elsewhere but, after meeting with Courtney, he swallowed Slessor's proposals and agreed that it could be equipped 'with Wellington XIII's and Albacores of great and honourable antiquity.' Even so, the Canadian AOC-in-C did not disguise his underlying belief that dominion units were receiving second-class treatment.

415 was specifically mentioned as being one of three (all Dominion) squadrons to be the last on Hampdens. It caused sharp words from Canada and I had hoped that this squadron would have special future treatment. It has got it in a different way ... Jack Slessor explains that they are in the proper group and *the only other Hampden squadrons* are RAAF and the New Zealand squadrons. I could not see the force of this. Nor could I see why this, of all squadrons, should be selected. You explained, and so did Jack, that there was no other way out and that operational expediency demanded this, no matter how objectionable, change. In the face of it there was scant choice. I concurred. I promised to do so in good heart, which I do – but I wonder where 415 will go next.[24]

From a Canadian standpoint, it is unfortunate that Edwards did not press the Air Ministry to team No 415 Squadron with No 404 in an all-RCAF strike wing.

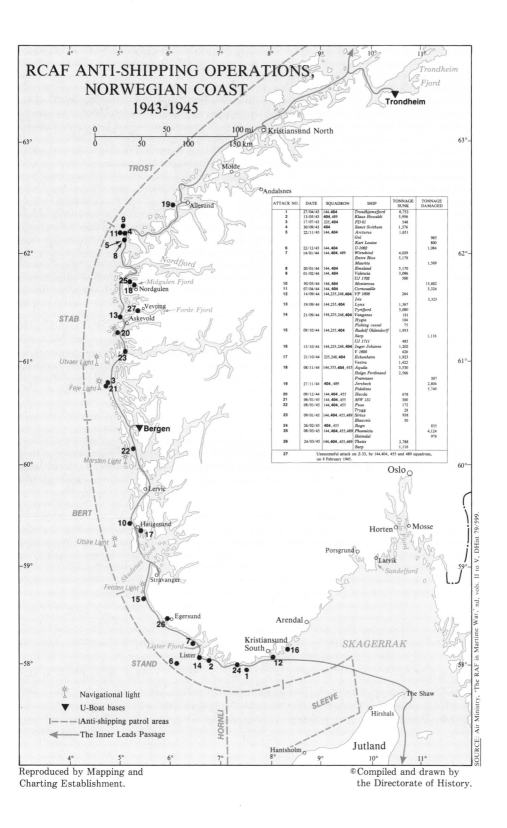

RCAF ANTI-SHIPPING OPERATIONS, NORWEGIAN COAST 1943-1945

ATTACK NO.	DATE	SQUADRON	SHIP	TONNAGE SUNK	TONNAGE DAMAGED
1	27/04/43	144,404	Trondhjemsfjord	6,753	
2	13/05/43	404,489	Klaus Howaldt	5,956	
3	17/07/43	235,404	FD 61	548	
4	30/09/43	404	Sanct Svithun	1,376	
5	22/11/43	144,404	Arcturus	1,651	
			Gol		985
			Kari Louise		800
6	22/12/43	144,404	U-1062		1,084
7	14/01/44	144,404,489	Wittekind	4,029	
			Entre Rios	5,179	
			Maurita		1,569
8	20/01/44	144,404	Emsland	5,170	
9	01/02/44	144,404	Valencia	3,096	
			UJ 1702	500	
10	30/03/44	144,404	Monterosa		13,882
11	07/04/44	144,404	Cornouaille		3,324
12	14/09/44	144,235,248,404	VP 1608	264	
			Iris		3,323
13	19/09/44	144,404	Lynx	1,367	
			Tyrifjord	3,080	
14	21/09/44	144,235,248,404	Vangsnes	191	
			Hygia	104	
			Fishing vessel	75	
15	09/10/44	144,235,404	Rudolf Oldendorff	1,953	
			Sarp		1,116
			UJ 1711	485	
16	15/10/44	144,235,248,404	Inger Johanne	1,202	
			V 1605	426	
17	21/10/44	235,248,404	Eckenheim	1,923	
			Vestra	1,422	
18	08/11/44	144,333,404,455	Aquila	3,530	
			Helga Ferdinand	2,566	
			Framnaes		307
19	27/11/44	404,489	Jersbeck		2,804
			Fidelitas		5,740
20	09/12/44	144,404,455	Havda	678	
21	06/01/45	144,404,455	MW 151	300	
22	08/01/45	144,404,455	Fusa	172	
			Tryg	28	
23	09/01/45	144,404,455,489	Sirius	938	
			Blaaveis	50	
24	26/02/45	404,455	Rogn		835
25	08/03/45	144,404,455,489	Phoenicia		4,124
			Heimdal		978
26	24/03/45	144,404,455,489	Thetis	2,788	
			Sarp	1,116	
27			Unsuccessful attack on Z-33, by 144,404, 455 and 489 squadrons, on 9 February 1945.		

Navigational light

▼ U-Boat bases

Anti-shipping patrol areas

The Inner Leads Passage

Reproduced by Mapping and
Charting Establishment.

©Compiled and drawn by
the Directorate of History.

SOURCE: Air Ministry, 'The RAF in Maritime War', nd, vols. II to V, DHist 79/599.

That would have simplified the flow of Canadian aircrew to both squadrons and provided the RCAF with a higher profile in the anti-shipping war. But pre-occupied now with the teething troubles of the RCAF's showcase formation, Bomber Command's No 6 Group, and already struggling with Northwood to co-locate two Canadian Sunderland squadrons at the same station, the overseas AOC-in-C seems not to have considered the possibility. In the event, Slessor had already decided to pair No 404 with No 144 Squadron after it had converted from Hampdens to Beaufighters – leaving No 415 to chase after E-boats in the English Channel.

While No 415 remained in No 16 Group, the other two squadrons of Hampden torpedo-bombers, Nos 455 (RAAF) and 489 (RNZAF), represented the only force available for No 18 Group's anti-shipping strikes off the Norwegian coast. An RAF squadron, equipped with Beaufighter VICs, performed the group's reconnaissance and long-range fighter escort duties while No 144 was completing its conversion to Torbeaus at Leuchars. In early April these units were reinforced by the return of No 404 Squadron from Chivenor. Having re-equipped with Beaufighter XICs while in No 19 Group, the squadron briefly operated from Tain, before transferring to Wick, on the northeast corner of the Scottish mainland, on 20 April. During their twelve-and-a-half month stay at the new station, No 404 would assume a leading role in the development of No 18 Group's strike-wing tactics, particularly in the use of rocket projectiles as the main anti-ship weapon.

Prior to the Canadians' arrival, the group's operations had consisted primarily of Rover patrols and fleet reconnaissances. Indeed, lacking striking power, it made only four attacks on Norwegian coastal shipping during March, none of which inflicted any damage. The situation improved when No 144 Squadron became operational with its Torbeaus and then again with the arrival of No 404, and one of their earliest joint operations came on 27 April. Following a sighting report of a convoy off Lister Fjord, on the southern tip of Norway, six Beaufighters from No 404 and four Torbeaus were detailed for the attack, refuelling en route at Sumburgh in the Shetland Islands. Flying only fifty feet above the sea in order to avoid enemy radar, the strike force made its landfall near Lister. Five minutes later three ships were sighted and, while the Canadians strafed the two escort vessels with cannon and machine-gun fire, the Torbeaus sank the merchant vessel steaming between them, the Norwegian-owned *Trondhjemsfjord* of 6753 tons. This was the third success registered by No 18 Group during April and the second by 144 Squadron, the other victims being German ships totalling 10,645 tons.[25]

Similar tactics were attempted four days later, on 1 May, when two strike forces, one each from Nos 16 and 18 Groups, were dispatched to intercept the German cruiser *Nürnberg* off the south coast of Norway – very likely as a result of information provided by special intelligence. The Germans rarely allowed their larger ships to sail without air cover, however, and both strike forces were intercepted by a large force of Me 109s and FW 190s (of which an average of fifty were based in Norway throughout the summer of 1943) and one 404 Squadron crew was among the seven lost. Neither force made contact with the German cruiser and their failure to do so reinforced the lesson, already learned on the Dutch coast, that Beaufighter strikes required fighter cover. Unfortunately it would take a further fifteen months before the Air Ministry was willing to apply the lesson to the Norwegian coast and release long-range fighter squadrons to No 18 Group; in the meantime, cloud, not fighters, would remain the prerequisite for success.[26]

Following the 1 May reversal, No 144 Squadron was withdrawn from operations for further training before being posted to North Africa, where the Allies were preparing to invade Sicily on 10 July. Weather conditions, fog and low cloud in Scotland and a lack of cloud cover on the coast of Norway, together with the withdrawal of No 235 Squadron for training with the new 3-inch rocket projectiles in June, further reduced No 18 Group's opportunities for anti-shipping strikes. Consequently, most operations were Rovers by the Hampdens of 489 and 455 Squadrons, escorted by No 404's Beaufighters. One ship was sunk in May and another in June for the loss of six aircraft, none from the Canadian ranks. Meanwhile, the group received a valuable reinforcement with the formation of No 333 (Norwegian) Squadron, a Mosquito reconnaissance unit, which began flying a limited number of missions from Wick and Leuchars.[27]

In the three months since its return to No 18 Group, 404 Squadron had lost only one aircraft on operations. This fact, together with a steady influx of RCAF aircrew, allowed for a substantial increase in its Canadian content from 36.4 per cent in September 1942 to 70.1 per cent in July 1943. Particularly helpful, in this regard, was the fact that the squadron's first RCAF navigators (W) – navigators who doubled as radio operators, for whom there was no training in Canada – had begun to arrive in April. The ratio of Canadian groundcrew during the same ten-month period improved from 65.7 to 82.7 per cent.[28]

Meanwhile, command had passed, for the first time, to an RCAF officer when Wing Commander Gordon Truscott took over in October 1942, replacing Wing Commander E.H. McHardy, a New Zealander in the RAF. Truscott, who had joined the RCAF in 1932, came to the squadron direct from Canada where his last appointment had been as senior air staff officer (SASO) at Eastern Air Command. When he moved on, to Overseas Headquarters as director of air staff in September 1943, he was replaced by another officer from Canada, Wing Commander C.A. Willis, who had led No 8 (BR) Squadron through the abominable weather and logistics problems of the Aleutian campaign for nearly a year without incurring a fatal accident, and who would retain command of No 404 until he was shot down in March 1944.[29]

It was under Truscott that No 404 Squadron began to contribute to the special anti-shipping formation created at Sumburgh in July 1943. Supported by the reconnaissance Mosquitoes of No 333 Squadron, the Canadians would provide anti-Flak escorts for the rocket-equipped (RP) Beaufighters of No 235. Hindered by the poor weather, however, the Sumburgh detachments had to make the most of their limited opportunities (only four strikes were made between 2 July and 4 August). A gallant effort went unrewarded on 4 July when three of the 404 Squadron crews escorted RP Beaufighters on a shipping strike at Kristiansund, in southern Norway.

Take-off was done in bad visibility and heavy rain, but the weather cleared on the Norge coast. There was no cloud covering ... Our a/c circled the Fjord, drawing the fire, while a/c of No 235 Squadron attacked the target. Two (2) a/c of No 235 Squadron made dummy runs up [to] the target, while the rest weaved around the target in Fjord. The area is well defended and heavy flak was experienced from the shore and also from a small convoy outside the Fiord ... Two (2) Me 109s joined as a/c started to leave target ... The E/A attacked the hindmost a/c, which corkscrewed off in different directions. All but K of No 404 Squadron re-formed to head for base ... When last seen K was covering an a/c of No 235 Squadron ... P/O Rumbel and Sgt. Lalonde have been reported missing.[30]

In these sorties, the 60-lb high-explosive warhead used on 235 Squadron's rockets was unable to inflict mortal damage on any of the merchant ships attacked. The only vessel sunk was the escort trawler, *FD 61* of 548 tons, after it was strafed by cannon fire from a No 404 Beaufighter flown by Pilot Officer A. McDonald.[31]

In addition to anti-shipping strikes, the 404 Squadron detachment at Sumburgh escorted 489 Squadron Hampdens on Rovers, flew a limited number of anti-submarine patrols, and sometimes provided cover for naval forces operating in the North Sea. Normally a routine assignment, the naval cover flown on 28 July resulted in one of the squadron's most remarkable successes. Escorting a task force comprising the aircraft carrier *Illustrious*, the cruiser *Belfast,* and a destroyer flotilla as it made a sortie towards the coast of Norway, the Canadians intercepted and shot down four Blohm and Voss 138 flying-boats from Seeaufklärungsgruppe 130, a long-range maritime reconnaissance group based at Trondheim. Two of these unwieldy, ill-armed machines fell to Flying Officer E.J. Keefe, who was making his first operational flight. One of Keefe's own engines was 'put out of action,' his braking was affected, and he had to retract the undercarriage to avoid running off the end of the runway when he came in to land at Wick. 'Complete write-off of a/c but no serious injury to crew.' The other two enemy machines were credited to Squadron Leader A.L. De La Haye and Flying Officer Sydney Shulemson.[32]*

Three of the airmen shot down by Keefe were subsequently rescued by the Atlantic-bound submarine U-489, which was attacked and sunk by a Sunderland of 423 Squadron a week later. The three airmen survived their second ordeal as well, and were among the submariners picked up by a prowling British destroyer. In the long run, Keefe himself was not so lucky. His good fortune – and good shooting – on that occasion had taken him halfway to a

---

* A fifth BV 138 was shot down in the vicinity of the task force by a flight of Grumman Martlets from HMS *Illustrious* led by Lieutenant D.R.B. Cosh, a Royal Canadian Navy officer serving with the RN's Fleet Air Arm.

DFC, which was eventually recommended for that feat and for an attack on a 'large enemy vessel strongly escorted by a/a [Flak] ships' in March 1944. But before the award was promulgated, on 7 July, he would be killed in a flying accident on 28 June.[33]

Following a final Rover patrol on 6 August, the 404 Squadron detachment was recalled from Sumburgh. The entire squadron was then withdrawn from operations to re-equip with Beaufighter Xs and conduct RP training. Although the results achieved at Sumburgh had been disappointing, the idea of using rockets as anti-shipping weapons had impressed the squadron's lone RAF pilot, Squadron Leader A.K. Gatward.[*] Accordingly, when the squadron began RP training at Tain, Gatward 'set about learning all there was to know regarding this new weapon ... He became the outstanding exponent of this weapon and as his confidence and successes grew, so did the Sqdn become the leading specialist in this type of armament.'

Although Northwood provided some initial guidance, the Canadians were left to develop the tactics for RP attacks on their own. As it gained experience, No 404 chose to organize its formations into two sections of seven Beaufighters each. Each section was composed of four anti-Flak aircraft, of which one, the section leader, was armed with both high-explosive rockets and the normal 20-millimetre cannon and the other three with cannon alone, while the three strike aircraft each carried eight rockets with solid 25-lb armour-piercing (AP) heads. The 60-lb HE warhead was preferred for the anti-Flak role because its 'fragmentation properties and accompanying explosion' was 'bound to play havoc with the morale of the escort vessel gunners,' while a near miss could 'produce a column of water approximately 150 feet high which will obscure the view of the escort vessel gunners at a critical moment.'[34]

Sorties were flown 'at a height varying from 100 feet in good visibility to 500 feet in poor visibility.' Upon sighting the target, the section leader climbed to a height of one thousand feet, with the three strike aircraft a hundred feet above him and the other three anti-Flak machines a hundred feet below. Then 'the cannon aircraft break off into a shallow dive opening fire at 1,500 yards,' while accelerating to over 300 miles per hour and pressing home their attacks to within 500 yards of the escort vessels. The anti-Flak leader added his 60-lb HE rockets to the cannon fire, after which it was the turn of the strike crews, who

open fire with cannon in a 10 degree plus dive from 1,100 feet and when they have closed range to 800 yards or less and cannon hits on the merchant vessels are obtained, a salvo of eight 25 lb RP is fired.

The aircraft carrying the 25 lb AP heads have their sights harmonised for both cannon and RP [by aligning the rocket rails at different angles] ... Tests have shown that when cannon hits are registered on the target and the range is closed to 800 yards

---

[*] Gatward had previously made a name for himself by making a solo Beaufighter flight to Paris in June 1942 to drop a French flag on the Arc de Triomphe and strafe the headquarters of the Kriegsmarine.

or less and a salvo of 25 lb RP is fired, two hits will be obtained 15 to 20 feet below the cannon cone, two 20 feet short, two 40 feet short and two 60 feet short of the target. Thus in the case of a merchant vessel two hits would be in the proximity of the water line and the remaining six will be under water hits.[35]

Northwood had originally anticipated using the high-explosive rocket as an anti-shipping weapon, but soon discovered that the alternative armour-piercing head had 'remarkably good under-water ballistics' that allowed it to 'travel nearly 100 ft. just below the surface with sufficient velocity to penetrate the pressure hull of a submarine.' It 'remained intact on hitting the water and had a long, upward curving trajectory which was ideal for offsetting range aiming errors.' Since the HE head broke away from the rocket on impact with the water, it was only effective in the event of a dry hit, and for that reason alone No 16 Group advised that 'cannon fire is very, very much more effective to silence *Flak* than using RP.' The North Coates wing, however, had never used the more effective 25-lb head in its strikes, leading No 16 Group to conclude prematurely that 'in a large Wing melee with some 30 aircraft and pretty intense *Flak*, crews just are not steady enough in their aim, or good enough at range estimation, to secure any reasonable results with their RP.'[36]

The decrease in No 18 Group sorties after August because of the transfer and re-equipping of Beaufighter squadrons came just as Stockholm announced it would no longer allow Germany to use Swedish facilities or territory (including a small stretch of the Trondheim-Narvik railway) for the transport of war materiel and military personnel to and from Norway and Finland. All German traffic would now have to move by sea; but so long as No 18 Group had to restrict its sorties to periods of cloudy weather in order to avoid clashes with German fighters, the opportunities to take advantage of the enemy's increased vulnerability to anti-shipping strikes would be limited.

Accordingly, on 21 September 1943 Northwood asked the Air Ministry to assign two or three long-range fighter squadrons to Fighter Command's No 13 Group in order to provide escorts for the two strike wings No 18 Group expected to have operational by the end of the year. Although both Mustangs and Spitfire Vs and IXs equipped with 90-gallon drop tanks had sufficient range to do the job, Fighter Command declined the request on the grounds that they might run dangerously short of fuel if there were any delays in assembling the strike formations – and, as Air Marshal Sir Trafford Leigh-Mallory put it, because 'fighter escort [was] a very difficult and fatiguing task in the weather conditions prevalent on the Norwegian coast.'[37]

Some reinforcement was received in mid-October when No 144 Squadron returned from the Mediterranean and re-equipped with Torbeau Xs. Until they were transferred to No 19 Group in early May 1944, in preparation for Operation Overlord, Nos 404 and 144 Squadrons operating from Wick became No 18 Group's main strike force. The Canadians' role in these operations was varied; at times flying anti-Flak escort to No 144's Torbeaus and on other occasions providing the main punch themselves with their 25-lb rockets. The first operation by this Wick wing took place on 22 November, when eight

Beaufighters from No 404 and six Torbeaus from 144 Squadron attacked two merchant vessels and two escorts off Stadtlandet: with the Canadians using only their cannon, the Norwegian *Arcturus* of 1651 tons was sunk. Once again, however, the initial success could not be followed up. No substantial damage was inflicted on the enemy over the next month, while No 404 Squadron lost four crews, including two shot down by Flak during an attack on a U-boat and its destroyer escort on 22 December. That was double the number of casualties suffered in the preceding four months.[38]

Bolstered by the addition of No 489 Squadron's Torbeaus in January 1944, No 18 Group made sixty-five attacks – fifteen more than in December – and sank 15,659 tons of shipping. The Wick squadrons had also refined their tactics, relying increasingly on armour-piercing warheads as the main anti-ship weapon, and they enjoyed better results.[39] On 14 January, for example, a combined force of eight Torbeaus from No 144 Squadron and ten RP Beaufighters from No 404, supported by seven other Beaufighters from No 144 in the anti-Flak role, mounted a Rover off southern Norway in an operation managed largely by the Canadian unit. Wing Commander C.A. Willis led the anti-Flak section from No 144, while Squadron Leader Gatward commanded No 404's strike force until he was forced to return to base when his hatch blew open and could not be closed. Flying Officer W.D. Thomsett immediately took over and 'led the formation northward up the coast.'

Off List[er Fjord] a C[on]V[oy] of three M[erchant] V[essel]'s and two E[scort] V[essel]'s was sighted with a second CV some miles astern. At 1153 all a/c attacked, 'O,' 'G' and 'F' obtaining RP and cannon hits on leading EV. 'M' and 'H' carried out RP attacks from either bow on 4,000 ton MV, 'M' scoring two hits and 'H' four. Explosions were seen by 144 Sqdn Torbeaus who also attacked this vessel. 'H' followed up with a cannon attack on the EV astern. 'U' made RP and cannon attack on EV ahead of second CV. Cannon hits were observed but RP's undershot. 'J' was seen diving to attack but suddenly began to emit black smoke and was lost to sight. 'W' turned in to attack but was hit before it could release RP's. Formation broke off to seaward and s[et]/c[ourse for] base without 'J.' About 120 miles from base 'W' was seen to suddenly lose height rapidly and finally ditch. 'F' circled it but no survivors seen in dinghy. Six a/c landed safely at base, five undamaged, 'O' with damage to starboard mainplane. Crews uninjured. This is the biggest operation by the Wick Beaufighter wing since its formation, 24 a/c taking part. In addition to 404 Sqdn's two a/c, one of 144 also failed to return.[40]

A second strike force of eight aircraft from No 489 Squadron attacked the further convoy. Between them, the three squadrons sank the *Wittekind*, a freighter of 4029 tons, and the *Entre Rios*, of 5179, both iron ore carriers, and damaged the Norwegian *Maurita* of 1569 tons. Six days later, five No 404 Beaufighters and an anti-flak escort from No 144 Squadron attacked a northbound convoy off Stadtlandet, sinking the German merchant vessel *Emsland*, of 5170 tons.[41] However, other operations mounted that month proved more dangerous to the Beaufighters than to the enemy. On the 16th a mixed force was patrolling off Stadtlandet when 'two armed trawlers were sighted ... They opened fire and N/404 was apparently hit. Formation s[et]c[ourse for] base at 1426 from Gtterone Light and shortly afterward two explosions were seen from starboard engine of 'N.' It carried on for three minutes, maintaining level course. The pilot was then heard on VHF to say 'This is it, chaps,' the a/c touched down in ditching position, navigator fired a red Very light and the a/c hit the water and broke up. P/144 circled the area but no survivors, wreckage or dinghy seen. All other a/c returned safely to base.'[42] No 404 lost one more machine on 26 January, perhaps because of an unfortunate mistake. Led by Flying Officer Sydney Shulemson, in Beaufighter U, six strike crews from No 404 and six escorts from No 144 were about halfway to Stadtlandet when one of the Canadian Beaufighters developed engine trouble and had to turn back. As it did so, the inexperienced navigator signalled its problem to the remaining aircraft by Morse code, a dangerous break in radio silence that probably alerted the German listening posts along the Norwegian coast. Although the formation arrived off Stadtlandet and attacked three merchant ships and three escorts without interference, they, in turn, were attacked by four Me 109s shortly after turning back out to sea. One Canadian machine crashed in flames and one from No 144 was in danger of suffering a similar fate when Shulemson turned back to engage its pursuer. His fire was 'ineffective,' but the German pilot immediately switched his attack and followed his assailant out to sea. Shulemson 'took violent evasive action, the Navigator opening fire with his B[rowning] M[achine] G[un], and eventually gained cloud cover. Emerging 4 minutes later, the E/A was seen 800 yards astern and continued the pursuit for another 10 minutes until 'U' once again gained cloud cover.'[43] Shulemson was awarded the DSO, an exceptional honour for a junior officer.

The Wick wing struck again on 1 February. Fourteen aircraft, including nine from 404 Squadron, made landfall at Utvaer, with the overcast too low to allow for a coordinated attack even if shipping should be sighted through the mist. Squadron Leader Gatward led the formation north in search of better weather and was rewarded when, seventy-five miles up the coast, he found a five-ship convoy off Stadtlandet. Despite heavy Flak, from both the escorts and the shore batteries, the wing's attack was so effective that only two of the Canadian aircraft were slightly damaged while the enemy lost the *Valencia*, a merchantman of 3000 tons as well as the escort trawler *UJ.1702*.[44]

The Germans now began sailing only on days that were too fine and clear for daylight Rovers without fighter escort; and although No 18 Group mounted a further 171 sorties in February they resulted in just six attacks. The number of sorties rose to a peak of 308 in March, but results were similarly disappointing, only three small vessels being sunk. Perhaps the most daring attempt was made at the end of the month, as the strike wings attempted to locate and attack the southbound German troopship *Monterosa* of 13,882 tons, whose sailing had been reported by special intelligence. The five Torbeaus and four cannon-armed Beaufighters from No 144 Squadron and nine 404 Squadron Beaufighters armed with armour-piercing RP found their prey and her escort – three ships, including a destroyer, and a large number of fighters – near Utsire, north of Stavanger. The Torbeaus attacked with torpedoes and claimed two hits. Meanwhile, led by their commanding officer, the Canadians launched their cannon and RP attack despite heavy enemy fire and succeeded in damaging the *Monterosa*, which limped into Aarhus, Denmark, on 3 April. Two aircraft were shot down, including that of Wing Commander C.A. Willis and his crewmate, who survived their ditching to become prisoners of war.[45]

The wing managed only fourteen attacks in early April, all of them coming on the 7th, when the 3324-ton German freighter *Cornouaille* was damaged. Then, in preparation for Operation Overlord, the squadrons were informed that they would be transferred to Davidstow Moor, under command of No 19 Group, to operate against enemy surface craft on the right flank of the invasion.[46]

Although by far the majority (4097 of 5062) of Coastal Command's anti-shipping sorties between April 1943 and May 1944 did not result in attacks – and the effort cost ninety-six crews, 1.8 per cent of those dispatched – North-wood's campaign became increasingly effective following the reintroduction of the composite strike wing at North Coates in April and the subsequent refining of its tactics. This was the case both in absolute terms and in comparison with other arms and services, and especially in the relationship between tonnage sunk per aircraft lost. From March 1940 to March 1943, for example, aerial minelaying (by both Bomber and Coastal commands) had accounted for the sinking of 369 ships totalling 362,000 tons at a cost of 329 crews (1100 tons per loss), while 447 anti-shipping sorties failed to return from operations which sank sixty-one ships totalling 118,000 tons (263 tons per loss). From April 1943 to May 1944, however, mines laid by Bomber Command sank 182 ships of 138,000 tons at a cost of 142 aircraft (972 tons per loss), while Nos 16 and 18 Groups between them sank 49 ships of 112,000 tons for the loss of 96 crews (1166 tons per loss).

For all of 1943 and 1944, aircraft in direct attack at sea accounted for 31 per cent, mines (the majority of which were laid by Bomber Command) and air raids for 25 per cent each, and the various forms of naval attack for 19 per cent of merchant tonnage sunk in these waters – but for most of that period major naval forces were only sporadically involved in the anti-shipping campaign. When a greater effort was made, off Norway between January and May 1944, submarines sank fifteen ships, carrier-based aircraft eight, and Coastal Command's No 18 Group, nine. No 16 Group added another fifteen off Holland, where the water was too shallow for submarines, and surface ships larger than MTBs rarely ventured.[47]

The proportions and relationships given above are not unimportant. Since major Allied warships and submarines were often doing other things, by mid-1943 the responsibility for destroying, damaging, delaying, and diverting German merchant shipping had fallen mainly on Bomber Command's Gardening campaign and Coastal Command's strike wings, and in this respect it is clear that aerial minelaying, while sinking a larger number of ships, tended to sink smaller ones, averaging about 757 tons, while the strike wings' victims were larger, averaging 2088 tons, and more likely to include the valuable ore carriers. All attacks on shipping, whatever form they took, forced the enemy to change schedules and routeing.

Through special intelligence, the Admiralty (and Northwood) were kept aware of the general impact of the anti-shipping campaign. It had been mitigated to some extent in 1943 by Reichkommissar Kaufmann's program to rationalize Germany's use of maritime resources, but by the spring of 1944 sailings were fully a fifth below his projections. A quarter of all tonnage plying between Norway and Germany's northern ports had been sunk and in May 1944 deliveries of iron ore had fallen to 420,000 tons, just one-third of the May 1943 figure. About one-half of all German naval personnel were engaged in escorting convoys or clearing mines. In June 1944, however, the attack on enemy merchant shipping would all but cease as the Allies turned their attention to Operation Overlord.[48]

Having been chasing E-boats in the English Channel since the fall of 1943, No 415 Squadron was already familiar with the Overlord invasion area. Hunting down these fast motor boats was not an easy task, and it was one which other branches of the service had gratefully abandoned when given the chance to do so. Despite making 187 direct attacks, for example, Fighter Command had not produced 'a single confirmed sinking' before it gave up the job in late 1942 – although it had forced the Germans to limit their E-boat operations to the hours of darkness. The Fleet Air Arm came next, enjoying some success, but it, too, was glad to be out of the business in September 1943, when Coastal Command had taken on the job.[49]

In fact, for all Edwards's doubts, the slow and manoeuvrable Albacores were as well-suited as anything for low-altitude precision bombing attacks against E-boats, and their three-man crews could at least look forward to the possibility of actually inflicting harm on the enemy. Using techniques pioneered by the Fleet Air Arm, the Albacore crews relied on coastal radars to vector them near to their target, at which point they employed their own ASV sets to pick it up. After establishing visual contact, they attacked the E-boat from astern, releasing up to twelve 100-lb anti-submarine bombs. In practice, however, the Albacores had little to do with the E-boats and never did sink one. Employed primarily against the enemy's Channel shipping, the majority of the eleven attacks carried out during their first four months of operations, all without result, were against small merchant vessels, a task for which their old Hampdens would have been better suited.[50]

The Wellington crews, in contrast, while flying only anti-E-boat patrols, never had the satisfaction of making attacks themselves at this time. Carrying no air-to-surface weapons, their business was to locate, report on, and shadow E-boats working farther from shore until Royal Navy gunboats arrived in the vicinity – at which time the Wellingtons were to drop flares to illuminate the enemy so that the gunboats could make their attacks.[*] Codenamed Deadly, Wellington patrols were just that – deadly boring – so that when a delegation arrived at the squadron from Overseas Headquarters on 1 November to 'discuss personnel problems' they concluded that its 'morale is rapidly going.' Over a forty-day period there had been no more than ten of operational flying, and the Wellington flight, lacking 'armament and ... bombs ... feel they are merely stooges.' As for the Albacore crews, the visitors from Overseas Headquarters noted that they 'hate their aircraft and the type of work upon which they are employed.'[51]

There is no doubt that the Wellington flight was dissatisfied and that it would remain so: no targets were sighted in November, December, or January; its ASV radars and VHF radios were frequently unserviceable; and flares remained its only offensive weapon. Their poor morale may not have been shared by the Albacore crews, however. When he visited Manston on 6 November, Sir John Slessor 'found no trace of dissatisfaction – rather the reverse,' and his findings were confirmed by a subsequent Canadian investigation. 'Although their aircraft are old,' the overseas AOC-in-C was told in February, and they too moved between Manston and Thorney Island, 'at least they have the opportunity of hitting the Hun.'[52]

The squadron was nevertheless suffering as a unit. The squadron was divided into two quite separate entities: the Albacore flight at Manston, and the Wellingtons and squadron headquarters at Bircham Newton and Docking, in Norfolk, a hundred miles away by air and twice that by road.[53] With so many of his crews on detachment – Wellingtons were frequently sent to stations as far afield as Wick in northern Scotland while the Albacore flight routinely maintained a four-aircraft detachment at Thorney Island – the commanding officer, Wing Commander C.G. Ruttan, was able to exercise only 'a bare minimum of operational control,' and servicing had become complex. 'Maintenance work of major importance for the Wellingtons and Albacores is carried out at Bircham Newton. Albacore minor repairs and daily inspections are carried out at Manston and Thorney Island. Wellington minor repairs and daily inspections are carried out at Docking and elsewhere as detachments require. These arrangements can hardly be viewed as an asset to good maintenance.'[54]

Ruttan soon made his displeasure known. Speaking primarily for his Wellington crews, and observing that 'squadrons in Canada get more action than this,' he asked that No 415 be equipped 'with modern aircraft' and be given 'a good role.'[55] Air Marshal L.S. Breadner, who succeeded Edwards as overseas AOC-in-C on 1 January 1944, was equally dissatisfied with No 415 Squadron's fate and the state of its morale, and by mid-February he sought Ottawa's help in securing its transfer to another command. 'The situation with respect to this squadron is not happy,' he told Air Minister C.G. Power.

[*] Beginning in January, similar procedures were adopted for use against merchant shipping off the Dutch coast in Gilbey operations, with No 415 Squadron again selected to do reconnaissance and drop flares (but carry no bombs) for No 16 Group Torbeaus.

C-in-C Coastal Command maintains that the role of the squadron is vital at the present time and as only squadron properly trained and equipped it must continue until situation changes. There is no indication that this unit will be re-equipped and I do not see the situation changing until we occupy most of the coast of north west Europe. It would help our situation here if you would make known to Balfour your dissatisfaction with respect to assignment given this squadron. I suggest you demand its withdrawal from Coastal Command where it has never had a decent role. It could be allocated to either Bomber Command or Tactical Air Force. Such a move would require some shift of aircrew personnel, re-equipment and training for new role before becoming operative. For this reason it is bound to be resisted on operational grounds.[56]

Power agreed, and taking advantage of the presence in Ottawa of the British parliamentary under-secretary of state for air to negotiate a major reduction in the size of the BCATP, he asked for the transfer, observing that he was 'not ... very happy about the government of Canada paying for and maintaining a squadron operating on obsolescent aircraft.' Breadner made the same case to Air Marshal Sir Sholto Douglas, the new AOC-in-C at Northwood.[57]

Recognizing that the experiment of a split squadron had not worked, Northwood was ready in mid-February to form two squadrons, one on Wellingtons, the other on Albacores, 'regardless of RCAF participation,' and from 1 March the Wellingtons began to carry bombs on their Gilbey missions off the Dutch coast. By now, however, making either of the two squadrons Canadian would not have addressed Ottawa's other concerns. It wanted fewer coastal squadrons, but if it insisted on transferring No 415 to Bomber Command, there would be a problem of what to do with its existing crews, who had been trained for, and were experienced in, very specific and limited maritime roles.[58]

Matters came to a head in early March, when the Air Ministry offered to transfer No 415 to No 6 Group as soon as a replacement squadron had been formed in Coastal Command. Overseas Headquarters welcomed the proposal even while acknowledging that it would do little to address the immediate morale problem.

While the original intention was to help the personnel in 415 Squadron as well as RCAF efficiency generally, it now appears that the two objects cannot be accomplished by moving the Squadron to Bomber Command.

As the crew composition is so different and the work of the Squadron bears little, if any, similarity to Bomber Command, it is suggested that if 415 moves to Bomber Command, only the HQ should go and new personnel make up the establishment. The present Squadron crews could finish their tour with the RAF Squadron taking 415's place or be used to staff a 'nominated' GR Squadron. This situation would not appeal to the present personnel of 415 in every way, but at least in the future we would have one less Coastal Command Squadron to worry over.[59]

The proposal to, in effect, disband No 415 in Coastal Command and create a new 415 Squadron in Bomber Command won quick approval, although implementation would have to be delayed until after Overlord had taken place.

However, in a sad but somehow fitting dénouement, the squadron itself was not fully apprised of the intended move until Wing Commander C.G. Ruttan innocently asked London to explain why so many RAF air- and groundcrew were being posted to a supposedly Canadian unit.[60]

The armed reconnaissance missions flown by No 415 Squadron's Wellington flight in the three months before D-Day were only marginally more successful than its unarmoured Deadly and Gilbey patrols. Their only success came on 5/6 March when Flying Officer R.H. Watt located a convoy northwest of Borkum. After homing four Torbeaus onto the contact, Watt dropped his bombs and illuminated the ship with flares, allowing the Torbeaus to sink the Swedish *Diana*, of 1878 tons.

Success did not always require that the Canadians make an attack.[61] On 30/31 March, for example, Flying Officer J.A. Enns made contact with a group of E-boats that stopped 'several times ... to try and put A/C off trail,' but Enns's crew: 'illuminated vessels and kept transmitting position to base. Base sent out 2 M[otor] T[orpedo] B[oats] to engage enemy, but after being illuminated and unable to cross patrol [path] of A/C [unobserved], vessels gave up and turned for home at high speed, before our naval forces were able to arrive and engage. High compliments have been paid to crew for their very efficient work during contact with enemy forces on this patrol. Encountered flak from E/boats several times during shadowing, but no damage to A/C or crew resulted.'[62]

Albacore operations from March to May led to a slight increase in the number of attacks and eventually produced the flight's first confirmed successes. On the night of 23/24 March five crews were dispatched to intercept the escorted Italian vessel *Atlanta*, of 4401 tons, on passage through the Channel to Germany. Two of the crews dropped their bombs on the convoy and damaged the target despite fierce return fire that mortally wounded Flying Officer A.F. Hughes, one of the navigators. (*Atlanta* nevertheless managed to complete her voyage.) The most spectacular action, however, came two months later, in the early morning hours of 24 May, against *Greif*, a large torpedo boat-destroyer of the Möwe class, boasting three 127-millimetre main guns and four 37-millimetre anti-aircraft guns. Part of a flotilla of five similar boats and a number of minesweepers moving from Cherbourg to Le Havre, *Greif* was attacked by a single Albacore. Flying Officer W.G. Brasnett (who had claimed a minesweeper the day before) pressed home his strike from 2000 feet and observed one clear hit, a 'large glow' from the target still visible several minutes later. In fact *Greif* had been struck twice, the forward boiler-room caught fire, water poured in, and the boat sank during a futile effort to tow her to shore. Brasnet's accomplishments in these few days earned him the DFC.[63]

In the four months prior to Overlord the Allied air forces had established overwhelming daylight superiority over the French, Dutch, and Belgian coasts – in fact, wherever air superiority fighters could reach. After losing two crews in early February 1944, one definitely and one probably to enemy fighters, the Canadians were not intercepted again until 24 June, and then only at night when a Wellington was attacked by a Ju 88 off the Dutch coast. Indeed, enemy aircraft were reported as being in the vicinity on only ten occasions during this period. Forced to concentrate its fighters against the bombing raids on Germany and on the Wehrmacht's lines of communications between France and the Reich – and never particularly strong in night-fighters – Luftflotte 3 was a greatly diminished opponent.[64]

As we have seen, Northwood's planning for Overlord had been complicated by Sir Charles Portal's proposal to eliminate thirty-two maritime squadrons from Coastal Command's order of battle, including all its Beaufighter strike squadrons,[*] and it was only after the VCAS and DCAS had stepped in to oppose the proposed cuts that Sir Sholto Douglas had a clear idea of what resources he would have on hand to defend the flanks of the invasion against interference by enemy surface craft. When Coastal Command's Overlord directive finally appeared in April, No 16 Group was to deploy five of the seven Beaufighter strike squadrons in the invasion area, three at North Coates and two at Langham. The group also had No 415's Albacore flight and an FAA Swordfish squadron at Manston available for anti-E-boat patrols in the Channel, while No 415's Wellington flight was assigned to anti-shipping reconnaissances on the eastern flank. The remaining Beaufighter strike squadrons, Nos 144 and 404, were to be stationed at Davidstow Moor, in Cornwall, in No 19 Group, while a detachment from No 415's Albacore flight was to operate out of Bolthead.[65]

The directive also laid down a number of tactical changes. Given 'the shallow draught of destroyers and the small target presented by E and W-Boats' [fast midget submarines which the Allies thought were being developed], torpedoes would not be carried by the Beaufighter squadrons during Overlord. Instead, they were to rely on 'RP and bombs as primary weapons against destroyers, with cannon as the anti-flak weapon; on cannon against E and R-Boats, with bombs as a secondary weapon; and on bombs against W-Boats, with cannon as a secondary weapon.' As far as rocket projectiles were concerned, only two Beaufighter squadrons, one of them No 404, were to retain them as anti-ship weapons; and although Northwood had initially decided that only the 60-lb HE head was to be used, after being reminded of the success No 404 had enjoyed with the 25-lb AP head, it was agreed that both squadrons would employ the tactics and RP harmonization developed by the Canadians. The remaining Beaufighter strike squadrons were to carry two 250-lb wing bombs and two 500-lb bombs under the fuselage.[66]

According to Allied estimates, the Germans had deployed 'some 460 miscellaneous surface craft' along the French and Belgian coasts, the most important being 'five "Z" class destroyers, five Möwe class and one "T" class torpedo boats, and 34 E-boats.' (Based on special intelligence, these figures were extremely accurate, exaggerating the enemy's strength by just two torpedo boats and missing the presence of a captured Dutch destroyer.) To counter this threat, particularly that posed by the five destroyers, Nos 144 and 404 Squad-

---

[*] Coastal Command also had one Beaufighter and one Mosquito long-range fighter squadron protecting the Biscay anti-submarine aircraft.

rons began an intensive training program in mid-May, with the technique of night attacks receiving special attention.[67]

On D-Day itself, No 404 Squadron flew its first sorties at 1820 hours when fourteen aircraft were dispatched on an anti-shipping sweep along the Biscay coast, together with seventeen Beaufighters and eight Mosquitoes of RAF squadrons. This strike force intercepted three destroyers off St Nazaire and, with the British Beaufighters providing anti-Flak protection, the Canadians attacked with their 25-lb RP, hitting two and leaving one on fire amidship. A follow-up strike located the damaged destroyers still sailing north in the early morning hours of 7 June, off Penmarch Point, south of Brest.

Five aircraft ['made up of practically new crews'] on individual take off to attack the target damaged earlier in the evening. Airborne 0027/7. They proceeded singly on the same track ... The target of what appeared to be three Narvik destroyers was sighted and the center ship was smoking at the time of sighting. A/C K attacked the center ship, releasing his RP in pairs. The last pair were released from a distance of 200 yards. A/C K claims two direct hits and at least two underwater hits. On pulling away the tail wing received a bullet hole and the navigator's cupola was shattered ... A/C G attacked the first ship going in to 400 yards [before] firing a salvo. Hits by all of them are claimed. A/C Q attacked the rear destroyer and four direct and four underwater hits are claimed. As a/c Q pulled away an explosion was observed from either the 2nd or 3rd ship that lit up the ship ahead. A/C Z and J became separated from the main force and were too far away to attack, but bear out the report of the explosion. They claim that there was a red glow which increased to explosion with a burst of flame 200 ft. high. The ship was seen by all crews to be afire from stem to stern in the interior.[68]

Despite these dramatic accounts of success, the destroyers were not seriously damaged. Z.32 was taking on water from several hits just above the waterline. Rockets had also holed her port side oil bunkers and flooded her rudder compartment, her forward W/T office was destroyed, and one rocket had passed clear through her forward magazine without causing an explosion. (Her crew later found the solid-shot warhead in the hydrophone office and assumed it was a dud.) Z.24 also had her oil bunkers holed and several large fires started. ZH-1 had meanwhile escaped attack by sailing close in to starboard of Z.24.[69]

Thirty-six hours after putting in to Brest to land their dead and wounded, weld plates over the rocket holes, mount more powerful anti-aircraft guns, and replace damaged equipment, the destroyers sailed for Cherbourg, together with the torpedo boat T.24. At 0120 hours on 9 June they were intercepted and brought to action by the 10th Destroyer Flotilla (which included HMCS Haida and Huron) thirty miles northwest of the Ile de Batz. One was sunk, and a second set on fire and driven ashore by the Canadian destroyers. The third destroyer and the torpedo boat escaped and returned to Brest. After making further repairs they returned to the Gironde, where they would eventually be sunk by a 404 and 236 Squadron strike on 24 August.[70]

For the remainder of June, No 404 Squadron flew regular Rover and anti-submarine patrols between the Gironde estuary and Cherbourg. What little shipping that was sighted, mainly minesweepers and escort craft, kept too close to the coastal Flak batteries to be attacked. The Canadians' only success came during the early morning hours of 30 June when ten aircraft, escorted by RAF Mosquitoes, attacked a small convoy west of Lorient, using 25-lb and 60-lb RP to sink the escort vessel *UJ.1408*. Then, with allied armies firmly established in Normandy and only the one destroyer, *Z.24*, and one torpedo boat remaining operational on the Biscay coast, the squadron was transferred to Strubby, on the east coast of England, in No 16 Group, to attack enemy shipping plying between Rotterdam and the Kiel Canal.[71]

No 415 Squadron spent its last two months in Coastal Command flying night patrols against E-boats. Overlord only increased the pace of the squadron's operations, however, and not their effectiveness. The Canadians' main encounters were those of the Wellington flight during attacks on the nights of 6/7, 7/8, 9/10, and 12/13 June and none of the E-boats engaged were hit, although the crews claimed nine sunk and three damaged. One of the Wellingtons was shot down and its crew lost during the last of these attacks. The Albacore flight operated detachments from Manston, Thorney Island, and Winkleigh, on the Channel coast, but had no success despite numerous interceptions and frequent claims of direct hits. The majority of Albacore sorties during the last half of June and early July were smoke-laying missions over the Channel to provide naval cover.[72]

On 12 July No 415 Squadron was officially transferred to No 6 Group, Bomber Command, although maritime patrol sorties continued to be flown until 20 July and the squadron's headquarters staff did not move to RCAF Station Eastmoor, in Yorkshire, until 26 July. The Wellington crews that had not already been posted to other units were absorbed into No 524 Squadron, while the few remaining Albacore crews reformed as No 119 Squadron. Both Nos 119 and 524 therefore had relatively large Canadian contingents, nineteen aircrew serving with the former and seventy-four on the latter. The aircrew strength of the new 415 Squadron was built up by posting an operational crew from each of twelve squadrons in No 6 Group, plus five new crews from 432 Squadron, the other RCAF bomber unit at Eastmoor.[73]

The weakness of the German navy's response to Overlord soon enabled Northwood to reassign six of its Beaufighter squadrons to anti-shipping operations along the Dutch and German coasts, leaving only a squadron at Manston, and the Wellington, Albacore, and FAA Swordfish squadrons near Dover, to cover the eastern flank of the invasion area. The RCAF's lone remaining anti-shipping unit, No 404, continued to use its proven mix of cannon fire and 25-lb AP rockets, as did No 236, which had recently trained using the Canadian technique. Three of the other Beaufighter strike squadrons reverted to the torpedo as their principal weapon.[74]

Daily patrols were made of the Dutch and German coasts by low-flying Beaufighters and, if suitable targets were located – often ones predicted by

Enigma intercepts – wing strikes of thirty to forty machines were then dispatched. On 6 July a strike by the Strubby and Langham wings on a convoy north of Norderney Island sank the German ship *Stadt Riga* of 3002 tons and badly damaged the *Ernst Brockelmann* of 1900 tons. The ten 404 Squadron aircraft taking part in the strike all claimed 'underwater and direct hits with RP on several of the M[erchant]/V[essels].' Two days later a dawn sweep by forty-one Beaufighters of the Strubby and North Coates wings, including ten from 404 Squadron, attacked a convoy of six merchantmen and ten escorts off the mouth of the Weser River, sinking three of the freighters and two escorts. The results left the Canadians 'very enthused about working with these other squadrons,' with 'much comment [being] made on the accuracy of the North Coates and Langham' torpedo squadrons.[75]

Forty-six Beaufighters made a night strike against a well-escorted, five-ship convoy north of Nordeney Island on 18 July, but sank only one of the escorts despite losing three aircraft. The ten Canadian machines all returned safely, although two were damaged by Flak. A forty-five aircraft attack, including twelve 404 Squadron machines, against nine merchant ships and twenty-one escort vessels north of Nordeney, sank the Finnish merchantman *Orient* of 4160 tons and one escort, without loss, at last light on 21 July. The Germans, by using motor minesweepers commonly referred to as R-boats, each of which mounted two 37-millimetre anti-aircraft guns, were able to increase the number of escorts for their coastal convoys. Although the more numerous escorts accounted for eight strike aircraft during July – none from 404 – the Beaufighters sank sixteen vessels, including five merchantmen, totalling 14,437 tons. Their success was aided by the complete absence of the Luftwaffe, but Northwood was convinced that the enemy would soon return to providing fighter cover for its convoys. At the end of July, therefore, the Air Ministry agreed to direct No 12 Group to supply Mustang escorts for all strikes on the Norwegian coast and either Mustangs or long-range Spitfires for those going to the North German coast.[76]

By the beginning of August, Operation Cobra, the First US Army's beachhead breakout launched on 25 July, had isolated Brittany and forced the Germans to transfer their surface forces – such as they were – to the southern Biscay ports while redirecting their Atlantic U-boats to Norwegian bases. Realizing that 'every available ship in Western France from Brest to Bordeaux was pressed into service to keep the beleaguered garrisons supplied,' Douglas quickly redeployed his two RP Beaufighter squadrons to No 19 Group to make 'the best of this opportunity,' No 404 moving all its available aircraft to Davidstow Moor on 5 August and commencing operations along the Biscay coast the next day. On 8 August a wing strike by Nos 404 and 236 squadrons sank four M-class minesweepers south of St Nazaire for the loss of one Canadian crew; on 12 and 13 August they accounted for three Sperrbrechers (merchant ships heavily loaded with anti-aircraft artillery), a minesweeper, and a harbour defence vessel; and a week later sank yet another minesweeper, as well as an escort vessel, thirty-five miles northwest of La Rochelle. The next day it was the turn of the destroyer *Z.24* and torpedo boat *T.24* in the mouth of the Gironde. At that point, with elements of General George Patton's Third US Army driving hard towards the Biscay coast, German maritime operations in the bay were clearly at an end.[77]

As early as 13 June 1944 Northwood had prepared an assessment of the importance of Norwegian coastal shipping in view of the altered strategic situation resulting from Overlord. Planning was based 'on the assumption that … at least 150 U-boats would be based on Norway, of which about 30 would operate against Russian convoys from bases in the extreme north.'

Facilities are available from which this total could be operated, but the geography of the country, and above all its communications would make maintenance and supply a considerable undertaking …

If this new phase of the U-Boat war develops as suggested, the task of the strike squadrons of No 18 Group would be more clearly defined and urgent than ever before, and on their ability to interfere – presumably in cooperation with carrier borne aircraft, and our submarines – will depend the extent of which the enemy will be able to send serviceable U-Boats to sea. In this connection it is perhaps noteworthy that the two 18 Group Strike Wings, operating without fighter cover, our own submarines, and latterly a limited number of strikes by carrier-borne aircraft, were able in the first months of 1944 to sink or seriously damage rather more than one ship out of every five sailing along the Norwegian coast. Such a soft spot, in the enemy's organisation, as envisaged above, has never been accessible to us before, and should be productive of greatly enhanced results if properly exploited.[78]

In an effort to restrict German shipping even further, the Allies asked Stockholm to stop all trading with Germany. The Swedes, however, were as yet unwilling to initiate a complete break and would only agree to withdraw marine insurance from ships sailing to Dutch and German ports lying west of Kiel. Within days the Allies issued a reminder of the hazards Swedish ships would face, timing their words to coincide with the reopening of the mining campaign in the Baltic and Kattegat and an air raid on Stettin that added three more vessels to the Swedes' mounting losses. On 18 August the Swedish government withdrew marine insurance for all ships sailing to Axis ports;[*] and on 19 September the Germans were also denied the use of Finnish shipping when that nation signed an armistice with the Soviet Union.[79]

Two Mosquito and two Beaufighter squadrons, including No 404, were moved to Banff, Scotland, in early September in order to re-open No 18 Group's offensive against Norwegian coastal traffic. Prior to the shift, Wing Commander A.K. Gatward was replaced as squadron CO by Wing Commander E.W. Pierce, who had been one of the unit's first RCAF aircrew in May 1941. Although born and raised in England, Pierce had emigrated to Canada three years prior to joining the RCAF in July 1940. During a two-year tour with the squadron he had developed a reputation as 'a very good officer and operational

---

[*] Sweden reluctantly closed its Baltic ports to German shipping on 27 September and finally placed a total embargo on exports to Germany on 1 January 1945.

pilot' and he now returned after spending a year as a flying instructor at a
Coastal OTU. With his arrival the RCAF content of No 404 Squadron included
thirty-four of the thirty-six pilots and all but three of the 131 groundcrew.
Even the squadron's previous shortage of Canadian navigators (W) was
reduced, with twenty-two of the thirty-six on strength now being members of
the RCAF.[80]

The four-squadron Banff wing commenced operations off the Norwegian
coast on 6 September and by the end of the month had flown eleven strikes or
sweeps. Only two, on 14 and 19 September, led to attacks on convoys, accounting for two merchantmen and one escort vessel for the loss of two aircraft,
while a wing sweep on the 21st sank three small vessels.[81] These operations
also re-acquainted the strike squadrons with the difficulties in attacking shipping along the coast of Norway.

Our knowledge of enemy movements on the Norwegian Coast south of KRISTIANSUND
NORTH has always been very much less complete than in other areas. This, combined
with the greater distance from our bases and the topographical difficulties, has resulted,
according to recent statistics, in less than half the interceptions per sortie which we
have been accustomed to obtain on the Dutch Coast ...

In spite of these difficulties our operations against Norway have not been without
their effect. Already the enemy sails south of STAVANGER by night only, lying up in
narrow fiords like FARSUND and EGERSUND most of the day. However, because it is
difficult for him to get in and out of these places in the darkness, it has been his habit
to sail before night fall and to wait until after dawn before entering these anchorages.

North of STAVANGER the position is reversed. The channels through the Leads are
so narrow that night sailings are avoided and shipping is found moving in small
convoys of usually not more than three or four merchant ships with three or four escort
vessels. Here the enemy has a good warning system and it is his practice, as soon as
the presence of our aircraft is detected, to move into the nearest anchorage where the
steepness of the coast or the land defences make attacks unprofitable. Because of this
large strikes, preceded by reconnaissance aircraft, in this area have been largely
unsuccessful.[82]

To meet the problems presented by these tactics, No 18 Group adopted a
technique known as the Drem system (after the Scottish base where it originated), which was aimed at positioning a strike wing off the enemy coast
at first light in order to catch convoys before they turned into a defended
anchorage. Since 'the technique of wing operations demanded accurate and
compact formation flying' that could not be done in darkness, 'experiments
and trials in August had resulted in a scheme to provide an illuminated
rendezvous at sea. A single night flying aircraft was to lay flame markers in
a pre-arranged position off the enemy coast near to the datum of a planned
dawn strike. The wing was to take off singly in the dark, fly out to the
enemy coast in loose order and on picking up the flame marked rendezvous
was to circle it, form into close battle formation in the faint pre-dawn light
and be on the enemy convoy route at the desired spot during the twilight

before sunrise so catching the enemy ships as they turned into the approaches to the anchorage.'[83]

Drem was most appropriate for the open stretch of water between Stavanger and Kristiansund South, and was first used on 9 October 1944. Eight Beaufighters from No 404 armed with armour-piercing rockets, ten No 144 Squadron Beaufighters, six armed with cannon and four with torpedoes, and eight Mosquitoes armed with cannon flew in the predawn darkness and 'in loose order' to the Norwegian coast. At 0610 hours a Vickers Warwick that had left Banff forty minutes before the first of the strike aircraft began dropping a pattern of marine markers, flame floats, and drift lights in a circle about six miles in diameter, some twenty miles off Skudenes Fjord. Assembling over it and forming into battle order, the wing then set course southeast, until a convoy of five merchant ships and six escorts was sighted in the faint dawn light twenty miles ahead, just off Egersund.

With three Mosquitoes providing fighter cover, the attack began with cannon fire from six No 144 Beaufighters and the other five Mosquitoes, closely followed by the eight Beaufighter crews of 404 Squadron, who released their rockets at ranges varying from 700 to 450 yards and heights between 400 and 500 feet. The Canadians claimed thirty-four 'dry' and sixteen 'wet' hits, on both escorts and merchant ships. Then came the four Torbeaus, which managed at least two hits. Five minutes after engaging the enemy the entire wing was on its way back to Banff with only three aircraft damaged by Flak, leaving behind it two sinking ships, the German merchantman *Rudolf Oldendorff*, of 1953 tons, and the escort *UJ 1711*, and a seriously damaged Norwegian *Sarp*, of 1116 tons.[84]

Since the weather throughout October was generally poor for flying, both in Scotland and off the Norwegian coast, operations on this scale could not be undertaken consistently. On five occasions, however, the wing managed to attack single escorted freighters with some success, No 404 Squadron sinking a merchantman and escort off Kristiansand South on 15 October and two more freighters on the 21st in Haugesund harbour.[85] 'From 3000 to 100 feet, range 400 to 1500 yards, our a/c attacked with cannon, and from 500 to 900 yds with RP. 'H' and 'J' attacked the smaller M[erchant]/V[essel] and claimed 4 dry and 4 underwater hits with RP and concentrated cannon strikes. 'E,' 'M,' 'A,' 'Z' attacked large M/V and claimed 18 dry and 4 underwater hits. Concentrated cannon hits were also effected around bridge and amidships. These attacks together with those of other squadrons, set the 2 M/V well on fire. Considerable Flak ... experienced by our a/c, M/404 (S/L [W.R.] Christison & F/L [W.U.] Toon) returning with a large hole in the port tail plane.'[86] Both the German *Eckenheim*, of 1923 tons, and the Norwegian *Vestra*, of 1432 tons, were sunk.[87]

A decrease in shipping activity in the southern North Sea led to a further reorganization of No 18 Group's strike forces at the end of the month. A four-squadron Beaufighter wing was assembled by transferring two squadrons from Langham in No 16 Group, together with the two Beaufighter units from Banff, to Dallachy; but only four small convoys were attacked in daylight operations during November, resulting in five vessels sunk and five more damaged for the loss of three aircraft. The Canadians participated in two of the attacks without loss.[88]

One feature of the December operations was the reappearance of German fighters off the Norwegian coast, estimated to number sixty-five single-engined and forty-five twin-engined aircraft.[89] A sweep by the combined Banff and Dallachy wings, escorted by twelve long-range Mustangs, was intercepted by enemy fighters north of Aalesund on 7 December. 'Due to an error, presumably in navigation, Banff [wing] leader led the formation over Gossen A[ir]/ F[ield] and approximately 25 S[ingle] E[ngined] F[ighters], Me 109 and FW190s, came up to intercept. Mustang fighters intercepted and prevented serious damage to our a/c. 6 E[nemy]/A[ircraft] and 2 possibles was the Mustang score for the loss of one Mustang. 2 Mosquitoes, and 1 Beau[fighter] of 489 Sqdn. are also missing. S/404 was attacked by a single Me 109; P/O H.F. Flynn was uninjured but W/O M.H. Michael received minor wounds when a cannon shell exploded in the Navigator's cupola. No shipping was attacked and our formation s[et]/c[ourse] for base.'[90]

The group's only success that month came two days later, when the Dallachy wing came across the unescorted Norwegian coaster *Havda*, of 678 tons. Without opposition, the Beaufighters launched a rocket and cannon attack, with several aircraft circling to make a second strafing run. 'The ship was last seen ablaze from bridge to stern and two explosions were also observed. A reconnaissance a/c some 30 minutes later reported the vessel as beached and still burning fiercely.' But having miscalculated badly, Flying Officer A.K. Cooper of No 404 Squadron 'struck the ship's mast during the attack. The port wing fell off, the a/c turned over on its back, fell into the water and exploded.'[91]

The number of sorties flown, however, rose from 544 in October to 677 in November and 823 in December. Since resuming anti-shipping operations, No 18 Group aircraft had sunk thirty-six ships totalling 48,606 tons. Those results were achieved at the cost of twenty-eight aircraft, or an average of 1736 tons sunk per aircraft lost, a better ratio than that established between April 1943 and May 1944 and one that was comparable with the greatly improved results achieved by aerial mining since the beginning of Overlord. From June to December 1944 mines accounted for 124 ships, totalling 74,545 tons, and five U-boats at a cost of 31 aircraft, for a ratio of 2405 tons sunk per aircraft lost. The average size of ship sunk by mines, about 600 tons, was still only half that of No 18 Group's victims; but minefields had the added benefit of interfering with U-boat acceptance trials and training cruises in the Gulf of Danzig.[92]

The Germans' greatest shipping losses between June and December 1944 resulted from bombing raids against their ports, which accounted for 217 enemy vessels (totalling 252,536 tons) and twelve U-boats. Although that was more than five times the amount of tonnage sunk by No 18 Group during its shorter, four-month period of anti-shipping operations – and bombing also destroyed harbour facilities and shipyards – Coastal Command obtained its results with just 608 sorties while Bomber Command and the US Eighth Air Force mounted 15,716. On the basis of tonnage sunk per aircraft lost, No 18 Group accounted for 1736 tons of shipping for each crew, while the comparable figure for the combined bombing forces was 1006 tons for each of the 251 bombers lost. It must be pointed out, however, that the odds of surviving an attack were much better in bombers than they were in Coastal strike squadrons, one in twenty-two strike aircraft being shot down as opposed to one in sixty-two bombers.[93]

The strike wings' contribution would increase in 1945, when direct attacks at sea accounted for 37 per cent of German merchantmen lost to enemy action in Northwest Europe, despite the fact that their Beaufighters and (until March) RP-equipped Mosquitoes lacked the range to interfere with shipping bound for Oslo – through which the Wehrmacht was moving a larger proportion of its Norwegian-bound troops and supplies in order to reduce their exposure to air attack. Along the Norwegian coast, moreover, enemy convoys now moved almost exclusively at night, even in the narrow Inner Leads, sheltering during the short daylight hours under the steep cliff faces lining the fjords. Although that determined both the number of aircraft able to attack simultaneously and, often, the direction of their attacks, daylight operations continued and the risks involved were clearly demonstrated on 9 February when Beaufighters of the Dallachy wing struck a naval force in Forde Fjord composed of one Narvik class destroyer (*Z.33*), two M-class minesweepers, a Sperrbrecher, and at least two other Flak-ships.[94]

By 1400 hours thirty-two Beaufighters, including eleven from No 404 Squadron led by Squadron Leader W.R. Christison, were airborne for Peterhead where they rendezvoused with twelve long-range Mustangs and two air/sea rescue Vickers Warwicks. On reaching the target, the formation leader 'orbitted the force twice to get into a suitable position to attack and then ordered the attack up fjord.' As the Beaufighters made their way in, they met 'an intense crossfire in the form of a box barrage' from the 'naval vessels and from some gun positions on the hill.' And, to compound the problem, no sooner had they completed their attack runs than 'ten to twelve' FW 190s suddenly attacked them.

[Beaufighter] T/404 [Squadron], F/O H.P. Flynn, had an inconclusive combat with 2 FW 190s when he attacked them as they were in pursuit of another Beau. G/404 was chased for some distance by 2 FW 190s and while the crew were uninjured, the a/c suffered considerable damage. S/404, F/O Nelson and W/O Gracie, saw 2 FW 190s on the tail of another Beau and F/O Nelson attacked one and destroyed it. The 2nd FW 190 then turned its attention to 'S' but W/O Gracie with his machine gun[s] got strikes on the enemy a/c and forced it to break off the combat. U/404 was at one time pursued by 3 FW 190s but managed to get away safely. Mustang escort destroyed 2 FW 190s and damaged 2 additional to our claim. In the attack, due to so many of our a/c being missing, it is difficult to assess the damage to the enemy naval force, but the destroyer did suffer some damage, a patrol vessel was set on fire and 2 other ships were smoking when last seen. Most of our missing a/c were seen to crash in the mountains but one, although on fire, made a belly landing on the ice and another was seen to ditch.[95]

According to German records, seven Beaufighters were shot down by Flak while the FW 190s destroyed two other Beaufighters and one of the Mustang escorts. Five of their own fighters were also shot down. The Canadians 'claimed 2 possible RP hits on the destroyer' and '5 dry and 2 possible wets on the E/V.' They had, indeed, damaged *Z-33,* which had to be towed into harbour, but their losses were severe: six of eleven crews failed to return, by far their blackest day of the war, and of the twelve airmen missing only Flying Officer R.J. Savard survived a crash landing to become a prisoner of war.[96]

Operations on 11 and 15 January had cost other squadrons six Mosquitoes and one Beaufighter, but it was the setback on 9 February that lent particular weight to Northwood's pleas for at least one additional Mustang squadron. Clearly, if German fighters, including many of the latest type of FW 190, were stationed in Norway at a time when they were also desperately needed over the Reich, the enemy was placing considerable importance on the protection of his shipping routes and further air battles were likely. Whitehall agreed, and a second Mustang squadron began flying escort duties from Peterhead in early March.[97]

Poor weather and lack of suitable targets reduced the number of sorties in January and February, No 18 Group mounting just 209 and sinking sixteen ships of 27,376 tons for the loss of twenty-six strike crews and three escorts. Improved weather in March brought a record 847 sorties, which accounted for another sixteen ships (23,315 tons) and damaged fourteen more (41,800 tons) for the loss of nineteen strike aircraft, three from No 404, and two escorts. The Canadians had particular success on the 24th, when a strike led by six crews from No 404 claimed two merchantmen sunk.[98]

In January Northwood had suggested that the 'obliteration of the light[houses] on selected stretches of the Inner Leads route might well interdict night sailings completely, or ... force them out to the open sea.'[99] After some opposition by the Norwegian government-in-exile in the United Kingdom, a policy of attacking these lighthouses was approved on 9 March. Three days later, six No 404 aircraft were detailed to destroy three lighthouses on Vaagso using rockets and cannon fire. The commanding officer, Wing Commander Pierce, and a second Beaufighter took out the light at the northeastern tip of Skongsnaes island. 'Light was located and both aircraft attacked with cannon and RP, concentrated cannon hits and 6 RP hits being claimed. Lighthouse was left smoking and much flying debris was seen. One RP from 'E' hit a ridge of rock in front of the light and resulting debris caused considerable damage to this aircraft. 'Z' also suffered some damage.'[100] By the end of the month up to fifteen lights had been put out of action, but the effect on the enemy movements was difficult to discern. With the approach of summer and short, northern nights, the policy was cancelled on 3 April.[101]

March was also the last month during which No 404 Squadron would fly Beaufighters on operations. Transferred to Banff at the beginning of April, the unit began converting to the longer-range Mosquito Mark VI, which was capable of operating in the Skagerrak and Kattegat, but by the time they resumed operations, on 22 April, the fighting was rapidly drawing to a close.

The total dislocation of the German war organization had brought a virtual halt to activity along the Norwegian coast and the southern North Sea, and the only shipping targets left were in the western Baltic and the Kattegat as the Germans evacuated ports threatened by the advancing Soviet armies.

At 0630 hours on 2 May 1945, thirty-five Banff wing Mosquitoes, including four from No 404 Squadron acting as fighter cover together with twenty-four Mustang fighters, left their Scottish bases and headed across the North Sea. The formation swept up the Skagerrak and into the Kattegat before sighting a flotilla of escorted U-boats northeast of Laeso Island. It sank U-2359, one of the dangerous new Type XXI boats, and a minesweeper for the loss of one RAF Mosquito. The following afternoon another strike force of forty-eight Mosquitos was forced to turn back after encountering poor visibility over Jutland.[102] The wing's final operation came on 4 May, when forty-one Mosquitoes, seven from No 404 Squadron, and eighteen Mustangs attacked a small convoy of two freighters and five escorts to the east of Aarhus Bay (500 miles from their base), sinking one merchantman and seriously damaging the other. Despite Germany's imminent collapse, the Flak defences in the Baltic remained strong, and the strike force lost three Mosquitoes and three Mustangs.[103]

The operations of Coastal Command's strike wings were only a minor part of the air war against Germany. Even in March 1945, when the number of squadrons had increased to nine, their total strength amounted to 176 aircraft compared with the 2145 available to Bomber Command. In only two years of operation, however, the strike wings sank about 300,000 tons of enemy shipping – or approximately 7 per cent of all German shipping lost from all causes in northern Europe over the course of the whole war – much of it in waters where mining (itself responsible for 20 per cent of losses) was impractical. The RCAF's contribution of three squadrons to this effort was an important one. Only with the unfortunate No 415 Squadron were Canadian expectations of a useful role denied. During the dark days of 1941–2, 407 Squadron was the most successful of the anti-shipping units, attacking and sinking more enemy vessels than any other squadron in No 16 Group, and its aggressive approach was maintained despite the extremely high casualties incurred. No 404 Squadron, which was fortunate enough to enter the campaign after Beaufighters had become the standard strike aircraft, was instrumental in developing the rocket projectile as a successful anti-ship weapon. The tactics worked out by the Canadians for its use were eventually adopted by all the other strike squadrons.[104]

PART FOUR

The Bomber War

Until the very end of the war the main rear defence provided for heavy bombers was a tail turret mounting four .303-inch machine guns. Although the installation was reliable and the guns could maintain a very high rate and volume of fire, they lacked range and destructive power. (PL 22001)

Preparing for minelaying operations on a Hampden squadron.

A typical bomber squadron operations room in 1941. (RE 74385)

Access to the rear turret was limited and difficult. (PL 4972)

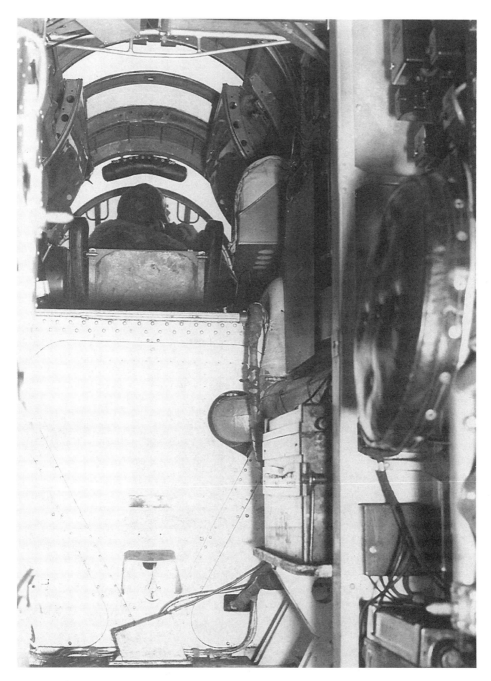

Unquestionably the bomber with the most cramped crew accommodation employed by the RCAF Overseas was the Handley-Page Hampden which, at one time or another, was flown by Nos 408, 415, and 420 Squadrons. This interior view looks forward from the centre of the very narrow fuselage towards the pilot and shows, on the right, the folding seat in the wireless operator's position. (PL 4709)

Until the separate trade of bomb-aimer was introduced, it was the task of the observer to ensure accurate bombing. This is the bomb-aiming position in a No 408 Squadron Hampden. (PL 4708)

Aircrew of No 425 Squadron board the truck that will take them out to their dispersed Wellingtons. (PL 10811)

Air Vice-Marshal G.E. Brookes commanded No 6 (RCAF) Group from its formation in Bomber Command until February 1944. (PL 142657)

Air Chief Marshal Sir Arthur Harris (second from left, front row) and senior staff officers of Bomber Command examine bomb damage photos in the Conference Room at High Wycombe. (HU 43479)

A bomb-aimer at a Heavy Conversion Unit holds a Mark IX Course Setting Bombsight used by Bomber Command in the early years of the war. (PL 19336)

Examining the damage to the wing of a No 408 Squadron Hampden received during an attack on German ships, including the *Scharnhorst* and *Gneisenau*, in the English Channel on 12 February 1942. (PL 7166)

Using the flare chute in a Wellington. The distinctive fabric-covered, geodetic construction of the Wellington's fuselage is prominent. (PL 4661)

Group Captain R. Slemon, senior air staff office, No 6 (RCAF) Group, Bomber Command. (PL 15130)

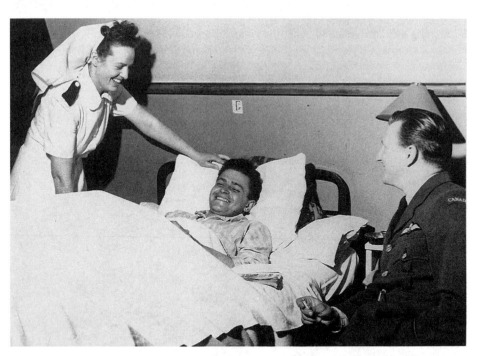

A nursing sister speaks to two crew members of a No 434 Squadron Halifax rescued from their dinghy after ditching following a raid on Germany. (PL 31799)

Group Captain C.R. Dunlap, commanding No 331 (RCAF) Wing in Tunisia. (PL 18186)

The crew of a No 425 Squadron Wellington in North Africa who have just completed a tour of operations in the summer of 1943. For each operation, a musical note was added to the 'Blues in the Nite' on the aircraft's nose. (PL 1803)

A particularly busy part of any bomber station before an operation was the bomb dump. The first tractor is towing two 4000-lb high-capacity bombs, while the second pulls a train loaded with incendiary containers. (PL 26964)

Oxygen was vitally important to Bomber Command aircrew. Here, groundcrew from No 434 Squadron are about to instal fresh oxygen cylinders in a Halifax in the fall of 1943. (PL 22425)

Groundcrew of No 426 Squadron engaged in changing the propellers on the Hercules engines of a Lancaster II. (PL 26008)

Leaning over the tracks supplying ammunition to the guns in the rear turret, a technician adjusts the elevator balance bars of a Halifax. (PL 22921)

Three aircrew from No 426 Squadron examine the damage done to their Lancaster II during a raid on Leipzig on 25 October 1943. (PL 22172)

The burial of three members of No 424 Squadron – Sergeant R.M. Buie, Flight Sergeant L.R. Taylor, and Sergeant A.W. Kennedy – who died in the crash of their Wellington on 11 April 1943. (PMR 93-293)

Part of a typical wartime bomber station, Skipton-on-Swale, Yorkshire, showing the ubiquitous rounded Nissen huts used as living quarters, the ablution huts, and, in the foreground, a 'Static Water Supply,' intended to combat fires, being used as a swimming hole. (PL 45597)

A 331 Wing Wellington taxis through a cloud of North African dust and sand in the late summer of 1943. (PL 18308)

While the dinghy drill to which bomber aircrew were subjected might be viewed as annoying or amusing, on occasion its lessons could be a matter of life and death. This photo shows aircrew from No 425 Squadron undergoing dinghy training. (PL 42464)

Groundcrew swarm over a Halifax II of No 408 Squadron at Leeming, Yorkshire, in August 1943. (PL 19509)

These RCAF men, about to pass under the wing of a Halifax, are employing a common means of transportation for both air- and groundcrew in fuel-starved Britain. (PL 20000)

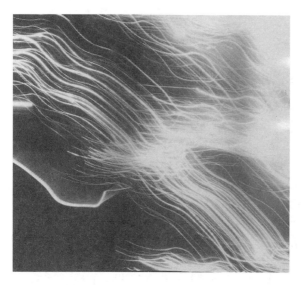

A crew from No 429 Squadron photographed these markers, searchlights, and Flak over Kassel on 22/23 October 1943. It was after this raid that Sir Arthur Harris asked the Air Ministry to state unambiguously that Bomber Command's objective was to attack the German civilian population 'as such.' (LMG 1051)

Cardinal Villeneuve talks with groundcrew of No 425 Squadron during his overseas tour in October 1944. Note the preponderance of day (20) over night (9) operations flown by this Halifax III at this stage of the war. (PL 33476)

Pilot Officer A.C. Mynarski of No 419 Squadron was awarded a posthumous Victoria Cross for his heroism during a raid on Cambrai, France, on 12 June 1944. (PL 38261)

Members of a No 433 Squadron Halifax crew at Skipton-on-Swale are debriefed after an attack on V-1 installations. The two crew members seated on the right are Flight Sergeant N.D. Dixon and Flying Officer T.J. Kelly. At top centre, with his left hand on his cheek, is Group Captain F.R. Miller, the station commander, who would become Canada's first chief of the defence staff, 1964–6. (PL 32767)

Nos 431 and 434 Squadrons are briefed before one of the two very heavy and effective raids mounted by Bomber Command against Essen in October 1944. (PL 33941)

Group Captain J.E. Fauquier, DSO and Bar, DFC, who commanded No 405 Squadron in 1942 and then again in 1944, when it was part of No 8 (Pathfinder) Group, was also the last wartime commander of the RAF's famous No 617 Squadron – the Dambusters. He is standing by one of the 22,000-lb 'Grand Slam' bombs employed by this unit in the last months of the war. (PL 44700)

The pilot and bomb-aimer of a No 428 Squadron Lancaster x stand beneath the open
bomb bay of their aircraft prior to an attack on an oil refinery in the Ruhr late in 1944.
The comparatively short range to the target allowed a full load to be carried, in this case
500-lb general purpose high-explosive bombs. The dome of the H2S radar installation is
visible immediately behind the bomb bay. (PL 40683)

As the war progressed, firefighting equipment at the RCAF's bases in Yorkshire became increasingly efficient. Canadians man a monitor firetender at Linton-on-Ouse in late 1944. (PL 40571)

Fitters of No 420 Squadron work on the Hercules engine of a Halifax in the summer of 1944. (PL 30746)

The rear turret of a No 408 Squadron Lancaster II, badly damaged in a duel with a German night-fighter. (PL 26856)

In March 1944 No 419 Squadron, based at Middleton St George, became the first to be equipped with the Canadian-built Lancaster X. This lineup shows the enlarged bomb-bay doors designed to allow these machines to carry an 8000-lb bomb. KB 711, whose tail can be seen in the foreground, was the first Lancaster X to be lost on operations, going down on the night of 1/2 May 1944 during a raid on the railway yards at St Ghislain, France. (PL 29474)

One of the first Canadian-built Lancaster Xs of No 419 Squadron lands at Middleton St George in April 1944. On the ground is a Halifax II, which No 419 had flown previously and which was still on strength of No 428 Squadron. (PL 29083)

A bombing photo taken during a No 6 Group attack on V-1 launching sites in France in July 1944, showing a Halifax over the craters from previous raids. Flying bomb sites were extremely difficult to destroy. (PL 30780)

General Sir Bernard Montgomery examines the damage to a village caused by a Bomber Command raid mounted to support his army's advance in Normandy. (B 6932)

Damage to Frankfurt caused by Allied raids conducted on the city between 18 and 24 March 1944. (CL 4276)

No 5 Group destroyed the rail yards at Juvisy, France, on 19 April 1944, one of the most successful transportation raids attempted before D-Day. (C4297)

A parachute rigger with an RCAF squadron in the delicate task of straightening the cords of the parachute before repacking. (PL 4915)

A member of the RCAF's Women's Division in the control tower of an airfield in the United Kingdom, maintaining communications with both aircraft and ground control. (PL 22891)

The smoke and fireball caused by the explosion of a Lancaster loaded with a 4000-lb bomb and incendiaries after it crashed while taking off from the RCAF base at Croft, Yorkshire, in early 1944. The crew were fortunate enough to get clear before the aircraft exploded. (PL 44939)

A No 6 Group Halifax photographed during a raid on the French city of Le Havre, which was occupied by the Germans until 11 September 1944. (PL 32846)

Halifax IIIs of No 425 Squadron at Tholthorpe, Yorkshire, late in 1944. (PL 40185)

A direct hit on a bridge with a 22,000-lb bomb – part of the Transportation Plan. The Lancaster is from No 617 Squadron. (PL 144260)

A concentrated mass of Window falls over Münster on 12 September 1944 to confuse the German Flak-control radars. The smoke prevented accurate damage assessments, but the fires burned for several hours. (PL 144263)

The German night-fighter base at Deelen, in Holland, was attacked by day on 15 August 1944. When weather conditions like this prevailed, daylight bombing could be extremely accurate. (PL 144254)

Vokel airfield after an attack by No 6 Group on 3 September 1944. Bomber Command made a number of successful raids against Luftwaffe bases in France and the Low Countries in August and September 1944. (PL 32218)

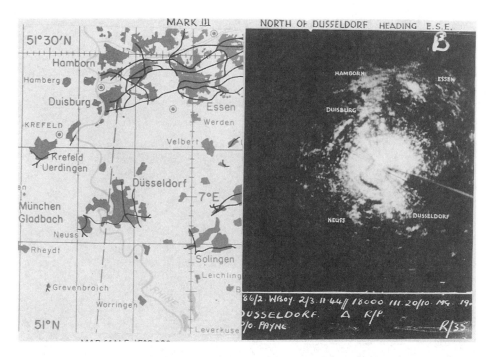

A map and H2S image of Düsseldorf, 2/3 November 1944. All too often, the H2S return over the Ruhr was little more than an unhelpful blob. (PT 302550)

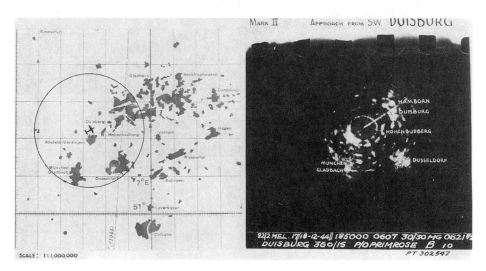

On the night of 17/18 December 1944 the towns of the Ruhr stood out well on the H2S cathode ray screen. (PT 302547)

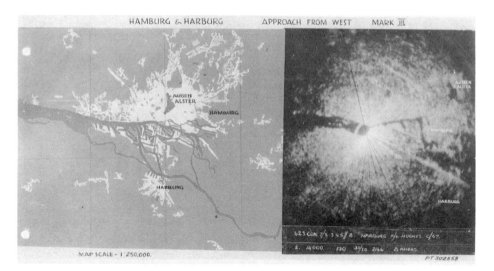

Near the coast, and with the Elbe River, Aussen Alster, and docklands giving a distinctive return, Hamburg was a good H2S target. (PT 302558)

Emden, photographed by a No 419 Squadron crew on the daylight raid of 6 September 1944 – an attack which bothered more than a few crews because, for the first time, they could see the destruction they were causing. (MSG 3996)

Bomber Command lost 95 of the 795 crews dispatched to Nuremburg on 30/31 March 1944, primarily because of the wonderfully clear skies illustrated here in the bombing photo taken by Flight Sergeant H. Menzies of No 432 Squadron. (EMR 843)

Wing Commander R.J. Gray of No 420 Squadron (centre) with Air Commodore J.L. Hurley, Group Captain P.Y. Davoud, Air Vice-Marshal C.M. McEwen, and Group Captain J. Lecomte on the occasion of the squadron's departure for Canada, June 1945. (PL 44838)

Some of the bomb damage in Munchen-Gladbach, early 1945. (PL 42341)

Bomb damage to the south of Cologne cathedral. (PL 42536)

Destruction, mainly by aerial bombing, in the German city of Cologne. (PL 42542)

Groundcrew clear snow from the wing of a Lancaster during the winter of 1944–5 at Middleton St George. (PL 41650)

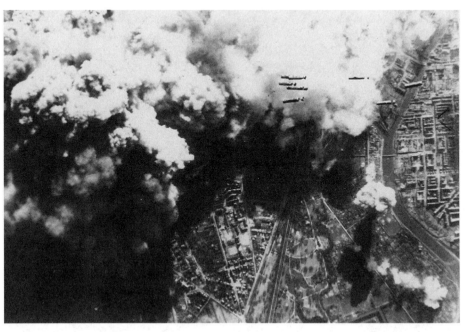

No 6 Group participated in the heavy attack made on Hannover on 25 March 1945 in order to cut the rail lines and roads running through the city and so slow German reinforcement of the Rhine battle area. (PL 144266)

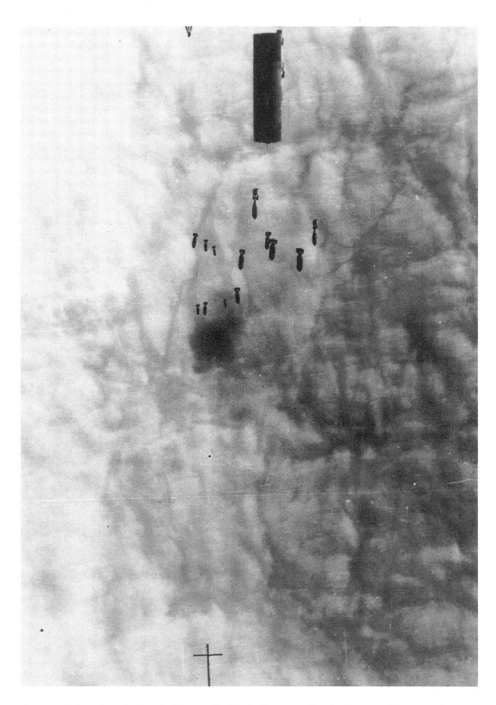

A 4000-lb bomb and a load of incendiaries in the very cloudy sky over Dortmund on 12 March 1945. A total of 1108 aircraft were dispatched to the target (a record), 192 of them from No 6 Group. The 'cookie's' lack of aerodynamic form (and therefore inherent inaccuracy) is obvious. (PL 144267)

An anti-shipping mine, parachuting through heavy cloud, near the mouth of the Elbe River, 22/23 March 1945. (PL 144275)

Nos 4, 6, and 8 Groups attacked Gladbach on 24 March 1945 in support of 21st Army Group's crossing of the Rhine. This No 4 Group Halifax, with fuel tanks ablaze, was the only machine lost. (PL 144284)

Not a 'Scarecrow,' but a No 3 Group Lancaster blowing up in mid-air over Wesel on 19 February 1945. (PL 144292)

No 8 (Pathfinder) Group markers cascade over Nuremburg, 27/28 August 1943. (PL 144305)

Wangerooge, 25 April 1945, where six of the seven crews who failed to return were lost because of collisions. (PL 144281)

Bomber Command attacked Wangerooge, in the Frisians, twice during the war: on 18 December 1939, when twelve of twenty-two machines were shot down, and again on 25 April 1945, two weeks before the war's end. That day seven of 482 crews were lost, six because of collisions, including two from No 431 Squadron and one each from Nos 408 and 426. All told, twenty-eight Canadian and thirteen British airmen were killed. This photograph shows a bomber falling to the ground, broken in half. (PL 144290A)

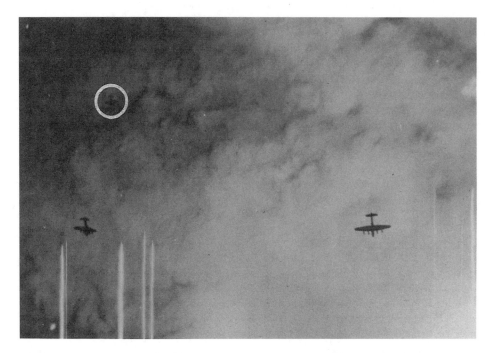

This is one of a very few bombing photos that illustrates a night-fighter (a Ju-88, inside the small circle) in pursuit of a bomber. It was taken over Hamburg on 8/9 April 1945. (PL 144293)

Introduction

At the outbreak of the Second World War, the Royal Canadian Air Force had only one bomber squadron on its Home War Establishment. Formed at Halifax on 5 September 1939, No 10 Squadron was equipped with two-seater Westland Wapiti Mark IIA biplanes, with open cockpits, a maximum speed of 135 miles per hour, and the ability to carry no more than a trivial 580 pounds of bombs. These obsolete machines were intended to suppress enemy submarines in coastal waters (and possibly protect Canada's shores from the remote prospect of seaborne attack) rather than carry out strikes against an enemy's military or industrial centres. Indeed, given the unlikelihood of war between Canada and the United States, there were no such targets within range of Canadian-based bombers, even if they had been of the most modern design. Perspectives were different in Europe, where ranges were shorter and bombers took a prominent place in the arsenal of offensive weapons, either to be used against enemy armies (the Luftwaffe's primary concern) or to deliver 'knock-out' blows against enemy war industries and/or civilian population (the doctrinal underpinning of RAF Bomber Command).

Although the Royal Air Force had more appropriate equipment – and more of it – than the RCAF, experience soon taught its commanders that their prewar doctrines were quite impractical. Unescorted bombers, it was discovered, could not fight through to their targets by day without suffering unacceptable losses. Instead, they must rely on evasion and hide from the enemy; in the autumn of 1940, therefore, Bomber Command turned to night bombing in the hope that certain classes of industrial targets – and certainly the largest cities – could be found in the dark.

Bomber crews had trouble navigating accurately at night, and even greater difficulty locating the precise targets they were ordered to attack. Since the strategic bomber offensive was, by 1941, the only way to strike directly at Germany, regardless of its shortcomings the build-up of Bomber Command won broad – though not universal – support. Canada was quick to join in, and the RCAF eventually mustered fifteen bomber squadrons overseas. All of them were formed in the United Kingdom, largely from BCATP graduates, with the first, No 405, being formed in April 1941.

Initially equipped with Vickers Wellingtons, No 405 Squadron flew its first four bombing sorties on the night of 12/13 June 1941 against the railway marshalling yards at Schwerte in Germany. A second squadron, No 408, formed on Handley-Page Hampdens over the early summer and undertook its first mission on 11/12 August, when it attacked the docks at Rotterdam in Holland. Two more squadrons were formed before the end of the year – one on Wellingtons, one on Hampdens – and they both began flying operational missions a month later. Since the RCAF had no pool of qualified and experienced bomber leaders to draw upon, the commanding officers of all these units (and most of their flight commanders) were usually Canadians serving in the RAF or, when there was no alternative, other RAF officers.

By 1942 the nature of the strategic bombing offensive was changing radically. The Butt Report of August 1941 had revealed that on most nights only a minority of crews bombed within three miles of their aiming point – five miles over the smog-ridden Ruhr – an effort that was demonstrably of little use if their goal was the destruction of specific objectives. Since the British War Cabinet considered it to be of the utmost importance to continue carrying the war directly to Germany, however, over the next nine months Bomber Command was projected into an 'area' offensive – what Adolf Hitler (quickly) and Winston Churchill (eventually) dubbed 'terror' bombing. Sir Arthur Harris, who was appointed air officer commanding-in-chief of Bomber Command in February 1942, became the premier advocate and exponent of that approach, sarcastically labelling those who still thought in terms of precision attacks, 'panacea-mongers.'

What Bomber Command lacked in precision it would now make up with numbers. If one hundred machines could not shut down a particular factory in Essen, perhaps five hundred (or a thousand) could destroy the whole city – if not in one raid, then in ten. Yet accuracy could not be entirely dispensed with, even if it was measured in terms of thousands (rather than hundreds) of yards from the aiming point. In an attempt to improve the record, work on a number of electronic navigation aids was accelerated; a specialist target-marking force (the Pathfinders of No 8 Group) was created; and renewed emphasis was placed on the production of more and better bombers able to carry bigger loads of high explosive and incendiary bombs. Accuracy might be slow in developing, but in the meantime more damage would be done.

The next RCAF bomber squadron to be formed overseas – No 425 in June 1942 – was designated a francophone unit, and every effort was made to post francophones to it so as to encourage French-Canadian enlistment in the RCAF. It was the first squadron to form around an RCAF commanding officer (although No 405 had then been commanded by Wing Commander J.E. Fauquier, DFC, for four months, and two of the other three squadrons already in existence also had RCAF officers in command by the time No 425 was formed).

The first four-engined British bomber, the Short Stirling, had entered RAF service as early as August 1940, but was bedeviled with problems throughout its short operational life. The first four-engined machine to attack Germany, in March 1941, was the Handley-Page Halifax, but it, too, had its teething troubles and initially production was very slow. The first Avro Lancasters were delivered to No 44 (Rhodesian) Squadron, RAF, in December 1941.

All five Canadian squadrons were still flying twin-engined aircraft – Hampdens and Wellingtons – until April 1942, when No 405 Squadron was re-equipped with the unsatisfactory Halifax II. However, allegations that Harris favoured RAF units in the process of re-equipping his squadrons are unfounded. Subject to rational restrictions imposed by the exigencies of maintenance, seniority was the principle on which conversion to newer – and theoretically better – aircraft was based. Old-established front-line squadrons were the first to get them, irrespective of nationality or Commonwealth origin.

Two more Canadian squadrons were formed in October 1942 (both with RCAF commanding officers), bringing the total up to seven, although No 405 was temporarily serving outside Bomber Command. The possibility then arose of creating a Canadian bomber group – the air formation roughly equivalent to an army corps – which was desirable for symbolic reasons and to give more RCAF officers higher command and staff experience. To that end, another four squadrons were hurriedly cobbled together in November.

On 1 January 1943 No 6 (RCAF) Group came into being, commanded by Air Vice-Marshal G.E. Brookes, who was brought over from a training command in Canada to set up his headquarters at Allerton Hall in Yorkshire. Three more squadrons were formed in the summer of 1943, raising the group strength to thirteen. No 405 Squadron had returned from Coastal Command on 1 March, only to be selected to provide the Canadian component of No 8 (Pathfinder) Group in mid-April. It would remain a Pathfinder unit until the end of the war.

The early months of the new group were not entirely happy. Expansion had been too rapid, in air- and groundcrew and in administrative personnel, and the lack of experience soon began to tell. Canadian loss, early return, and serviceability rates were the worst in Bomber Command. Matters were not helped when Overseas Headquarters – with the concurrence of Ottawa, of course – obliged the Air Ministry by detaching three squadrons (Nos 420, 424, and 425) to form No 331 Wing, which was sent to North Africa in May 1943 to support the forthcoming Allied invasion of Sicily and Italy. It remained in Tunisia for six arduous months, twice as long as originally intended, engaged primarily in interdiction bombing of Italian railway junctions and ports. Though their living conditions were harsh, those aircrews were fortunate to have missed the heavy casualties suffered during the later stages of Bomber Command's battle of the Ruhr (March to July 1943) and the initial phase of the battle of Berlin (November 1943).

When No 331 Wing returned to England in November 1943 the three squadrons began converting to the Halifax III – a much superior machine to either the II or V in service with six RCAF squadrons. The Lancaster was generally considered to be the best British-designed heavy bomber of the war in terms of surviveability as well as bombload. Three RCAF squadrons were flying Lancaster IIs, probably the weakest of the Lancaster variants, and would eventually convert to Halifax IIIs. By war's end, however, ten squadrons of No 6 Group would be equipped with Lancasters, six of them with

Canadian-built xs and four with the Merlin-powered is and iiis, both better than the ii.

More and more, the air war over Germany revolved about electronics, as counter-measure was met by counter-counter-measure, ad infinitum. Tactical innovations accompanied the technological breakthroughs, and the advantage swayed back and forth as bomber, night-fighter, and Flak struggled to find and maintain an edge in what was certainly the most sophisticated campaign of the Second World War.

An average casualty rate of 5 per cent per mission was considered to be the most that bomber crews could bear without faltering over any prolonged length of time. Losses on that scale occurred between 1 January and 31 March 1944 when, on twenty large raids to Germany, 754 of 13,259 sorties failed to return – a missing rate of 5.6 per cent. Over the same period No 6 Group's loss rate was higher still, standing at 7 per cent. If morale within Bomber Command should ever have cracked, it was in the first few months of 1944. It did not; and the number of airmen who became neuro-psychiatric casualties was infinitesimal.

In the five RCAF squadrons flying Halifax iis and vs, 10 per cent of sorties failed to return from just six major raids between 14 January and 20 February 1944. Withdrawn immediately from operations over Germany, they were employed for the next two months on minelaying duties. Their transfer to Gardening operations in order to save them from intolerable losses was not a new policy. Harris had done the same thing with his last Wellington squadrons when, also because of the performance of their aircraft, they could no longer survive over the Reich. The significance of Gardening went far beyond the number of enemy ships sunk or damaged: it not only interfered with German coastal shipping, but also impeded U-boat training in the Baltic.

If their shift to minelaying 'saved' the Halifax ii and v squadrons, the rest of Bomber Command was similarly saved in April 1944 when Harris brought the assault on Berlin to a halt. His bombers were needed to prepare the way for the invasion of Europe – Operation Overlord. Placed under the ultimate control of Supreme Headquarters, Allied Expeditionary Forces, in mid-April, Bomber Command's effort was split for the next six months between transportation targets in France and the Low Countries – intended to isolate the Normandy battlefield – and the continuing attempt to destroy the industrial centres of northern and western Germany, especially the Ruhr heartland.

No 6 Group could, and did, participate fully in both these campaigns. In July 1944 No 415 Squadron (which so far had had a most unhappy war in Coastal Command) was transferred to Bomber Command, bringing the group strength to fourteen squadrons.

In February 1944 Brookes had been replaced by Air Vice-Marshal C.M. McEwen, MC, DFC, a demon for training and standards, whose heavier hand soon made an impact on the group. Together with the reduction in loss rates that marked the end of the battle of Berlin, the temporary switch to easier targets, and the acquisition of better aircraft, McEwen's leadership enabled No 6 Group to exceed the performance of comparable bomber groups in the air and on the ground. In fact, from the time that Bomber Command was returned to Air Ministry control in September 1944 until the end of the fighting in Europe, the Canadian group could claim as good an operational record as any.

It is difficult to document the precise extent of the damage inflicted on the German war effort by Bomber Command. It was certainly substantial, particularly in the degree to which the strategic bomber offensive became a virtual second front before D-Day and before the Americans were heavily involved. However, in a pre-nuclear era, airpower alone could not strike a decisive blow, and postwar analysis showed clearly that the damage inflicted on the German war economy was never as great as hoped (and believed) at the time.

14

The Genesis of a Bombing Offensive, 1933–41

In November 1932, three months before Adolf Hitler rose to power in Germany, four years before the creation of the RAF's Bomber Command, and almost a decade before the first thousand-bomber raid, British Prime Minister Stanley Baldwin rose in the House of Commons and disclosed his fears about what might lie ahead. 'I think it is well,' he said, 'for the man in the street to realise that ... whatever people may tell him ... there is no power on earth that can protect him' from high-explosive, incendiary, and poison-gas bombs. A country's only hope, since there was no effective air defence, lay in offence; 'which means that you have to kill more women and children more quickly than the enemy if you want to save yourselves.'[1]

Baldwin's message, or at least his claim that 'the bomber will always get through,' made a profound impact on his audience. The main image of the speech, that of a single, cataclysmic attack capable of knocking out a city in one powerful blow, seemed realistic enough to those who had experienced bombing in the First World War (albeit on a small scale) and understood how greatly aircraft technology had advanced since then. It also reflected conventional wisdom within the Royal Air Force which, shaped by Sir Hugh Trenchard, maintained that a powerful air attack launched against the enemy's war economy would produce such crushing damage to both material resources and civilian morale that the opponent would have to sue for peace.

The doctrinal legacy of this 'knock-out blow' was reiterated in more practical terms by Trenchard's successor as chief of the air staff (CAS), Sir Edward Ellington, when he examined the threat posed by the rise to power of Adolf Hitler and the establishment of a National Socialist regime in Germany. Concerned about the vulnerability of the United Kingdom to air attack, should the Germans ever gain airfields in Holland and Belgium, the CAS urged the creation of a strong force of bombers as the best guarantee of Britain's security; and, for the moment, the government agreed. A separate Bomber Command was formed in July 1936, with its headquarters at High Wycombe, some thirty miles west of London.[2]

A series of revisions to the July 1934 expansion scheme came and went as the air staff and the Cabinet struggled to arrive at a bomber strength able to deliver a 'knock-out blow' without bankrupting the Treasury – the staff basing their calculations on purely military requirements while the statesmen (who, of course, had the final say) tried to balance political, economic, and military factors, usually to the detriment of the latter. Following the Munich Crisis of September 1938, Scheme M, calling for an all-heavy-bomber force of 1360 machines by 1941/2, became the final formal pre-war plan, but it soon had to be revised because of production and development problems involving almost every aircraft type. On 31 August 1939 the total striking force available for strategic operations was about five hundred machines; by mid-September, allowing for the formation of training groups and the dispatch of No 1 Group to France – where it would be primarily engaged in interdiction duties – it was only 349.[3]

Britain had gone to war on 3 September, a fact broadcast to the British public in the sad, flat, disillusioned voice of Prime Minister Neville Chamberlain. Within the half-hour, air-raid sirens sounded over London, prompting Lord Chatfield, minister for coordination of defence, to remark, 'My word, these chaps don't waste much time,' but no bombs fell. 'These chaps,' it turned out, were not bomber pilots of the Luftwaffe but rather Capitaine de Brantes, the assistant French military attaché, returning to London from Paris in his own aeroplane. The sirens sounded in Berlin as well, but there, too, it was a false alarm. Neither capital would be bombed until August 1940.[4]

That was certainly not the kind of air war envisioned by Lord Trenchard, Stanley Baldwin, or Sir Edward Ellington. So far as the German failure to bomb London is concerned, it is clear now, with historical hindsight, that it was contrary to German interests and intentions to conduct an *offensive à outrance* by air against any British city in September 1939. Hoping to fight a series of short, sharp, limited wars against each of his neighbours in turn, Hitler was eager to avoid a general European conflict. He did not regard Britain as a natural or necessary enemy, and the Luftwaffe, in any event, had evolved primarily to cooperate with the army. There was, of course, no good reason why British officials should have known the innermost secrets of German foreign and defence policy. It is evident, however, that they were predisposed to believe that Germany would launch a bombing offensive on London as soon as war was declared, largely because this was the mirror image of what the Air Ministry understood to be the proper application of air power. Furthermore, in October 1936 a joint planning committee had reported that the Germans would have much to gain by launching such an offensive. If poison gas were used along with high-explosive bombs, it was estimated that civilian casualties could reach 150,000 in the first week of war alone.[5]

The possibility that Baldwin's broken city might well be London, coupled with the delays in bomber production, produced a fundamental shift in British thinking in 1937 and 1938 which did much to ensure that Berliners, too, heard only false alarms on 3 September. Not only was Fighter Command to be built up as a shield, to ensure that the United Kingdom survived the first months of war, but, as a hedge against the failure of active air defence, Chamberlain sought an arrangement with Hitler to refrain from attacks against each other's civilian populations; when the prime minister met with the German dictator in

September 1938, at the height of the Czechoslovak crisis, he had already instructed the RAF not to bomb targets likely to put civilians at risk if appeasement failed and war broke out.[6]

Many in the RAF chafed at the prospect of conducting military operations with their 'gloves on,' as they liked to put it, but by November 1938 even diehard advocates of strategic bombing could see the merit of expanding Fighter Command at Bomber Command's expense now that Britain's defences were being bolstered by an early warning radar chain. Accordingly, the constraints on High Wycombe grew stronger. 'I feel I should make it quite clear,' an Air Ministry staff officer replied to a request for information on which German cities were most likely to suffer morale problems in the event of bombing, 'that there is no intention of bombing the civil population as such. Not only has it been definitely forbidden by the Government for political & humane reasons, but also from an operational point of view, which may conceivably carry more weight in war, indiscriminate bombing is a waste of effort.'[7]

It was in this context of limited war, conducted with limited means against limited objectives, that the air staff worked on specific operational plans, and when, on 3 and 4 September 1939, Bomber Command undertook to do what government policy allowed, the results were not particularly satisfying. Seven hours after Britain's declaration of war, twenty-seven Vickers Wellingtons and Handley-Page Hampdens were sent to search for German shipping off the Danish coast. None was found. The next day, fifteen Bristol Blenheims and fourteen Wellingtons were sent to attack German warships in and around Wilhelmshaven and Brunsbüttel. Ten crews failed to find the target, seven were shot down, and the damage done by the rest was negligible. The pocket battleship *Admiral Scheer* was hit by three or four bombs, all of which failed to explode, while the cruiser *Emden* was struck only because a Blenheim crashed into it. Not much to show for an operation which cost 37 per cent of the attacking force,[*] nor for an organization that, only three years before, had been formed with the idea of being able to destroy virtually an entire city in one day.[8]

The ineffectiveness of these operations might have been more excusable if the poor results could be attributed entirely to the technical limitations of bombsights then in use, but bombsights had nothing to do with bombs that did not explode or the ten crews that failed even to find Wilhelmshaven and Brunsbüttel. Their navigation errors reflected a lackadaisical approach to this subject that had plagued the Royal Air Force for many years. It was well known, for example, that most pilots found their way around England 'by map reading or following the proverbial railway line.' Yet despite flying in familiar and friendly skies by day, at least 478 forced landings had been made in 1937–8 simply because pilots had lost their way.[9]

---

[*] In accordance with Air Ministry reporting practices, unless otherwise stated (as is the case here, with the qualifying adjective 'attacking'), Bomber Command loss rates are calculated on the number of aircraft *dispatched* to the target, irrespective of whether they reached their objective or returned to base early for any reason whatsoever.

Air Chief Marshal Sir Edgar Ludlow-Hewitt, concerned that Bomber Command was prepared to operate only in fair weather, when it was most vulnerable, had complained bitterly about such low standards shortly after taking it over in 1937. He wanted his aircraft to be equipped with the radio-navigation aids and direction-finding devices commonly and routinely available to civilian flyers. He also demanded that his crews learn astro-navigation so that – somewhat optimistically – they could fly accurately by night; otherwise, he concluded, his command would remain 'relatively useless.'[10] Dr R.V. Jones, then assistant director of instrument research at the Air Ministry, agreed. He was 'astonished by the complacency that existed regarding our ability to navigate at long range by night. The whole of our bombing policy depended on this assumption, but I was assured that by general instrument flying, coupled with navigation by the stars, Bomber Command ... could find pinpoint targets in Germany at night, and that there was therefore no need for any such [radio navigation] aids ... I was not popular for asking why, if this were true, so many of our bombers on practice flights in Britain flew into hills.'[11] But despite the strong support of Sir Henry Tizard, the Air Ministry's scientific adviser, no progress was made on the provision of navigation aids, while the sextants required for astro-navigation (and designed to Air Ministry specifications) were only just coming into service in September 1939. Bomber crews were thus in no position to do any better than a year before, when Tizard had predicted that the best would be 'pretty certain' only 'of being within ... ten to fifteen miles ... of one's objective' on all but the brightest nights.[12]

Doctrine throughout the 1930s had anticipated that most bombing would be undertaken by day from about 10,000 feet. All bombsights then in service relied on bomb-aimers' (still officially 'observers') being able to see the target clearly enough to direct their pilots to the bomb-dropping point – that notional place in the sky which, when aircraft speed, attitude and altitude, wind velocity and direction, and the ballistic characteristics of the bomb were taken into account, promised a satisfactory hit. The technology required to solve this equation (any error in calculating just one value could produce spectacularly inaccurate results) was several years away, however, and even then it would offer only a partial solution. With the Mark IX bombsight, used by all but No 5 Group in 1939, a miscalculation of wind speed by a mere five miles per hour caused a bombing error of about one hundred yards. The alternative tachometric sight provided to No 5 Group did not require such exact calculations of wind speed,* but demanded dangerously straight and level flight (given the likelihood of opposition) and so was seen to offer little advantage over the Mark IX.[13]

Lack of appropriate gadgetry was not the only problem within Bomber Command. It was only in May 1939 that observers (usually groundcrew whose

---

* The average miscalculation of wind speed on operations, it turned out, would be about twenty miles per hour. The Mark XIV bomb sight used by most of Bomber Command after 1943 still had a bombing error of 330 yards for a fifteen-mile-per-hour windfinding error.

flying duties had been treated as subsidiary and secondary to their normal responsibilities) were accorded the status of specialists and began to receive advanced training, but war had broken out before many of them graduated.[14] Moreover, the absence of any effective opposition during interwar exercises meant that the survivability of a bomber force on operations had come almost to be taken for granted. The potentially devastating effect of anti-aircraft fire (or Flak) on aircraft flying in daylight at the preferred bombing altitude of 10,000 feet was more or less ignored, and it was assumed that speed would allow the new generation of fast bombers to pass through enemy defensive zones quickly enough to make it difficult, if not impossible, for pursuing fighters to catch up.

The Air Ministry had nevertheless concluded that bombers must have some defensive capability, and in 1933 it had pioneered the development of hydraulically operated turrets mounting multiple machine guns. The calibre of these guns had been selected five years before, after much deliberation. Having rejected very light machine-guns (.28-inch) because of their lack of punch, and cannon (20-millimetre and larger) because of their slow rate of fire and small beaten zone, the air staff ultimately chose the familiar .303-inch calibre weapon of First World War vintage rather than the new .5-inch. That was probably a mistake, and one that should have been recognised at the time. That an error might have been made was acknowledged in 1938, after it was learned that the Luftwaffe was adding armour to its fighters, but attempts to fit larger, heavier turrets, housing larger, heavier weapons, to aircraft designed to carry .303 calibre guns were unsatisfactory.[15]

Although Bomber Command was prohibited from attacking the interior of Germany, the first night operation over the Reich also occurred on 4 September, when ten Whitleys carried five million propaganda leaflets (code-named Nickels) to Hamburg, Bremen, and nine cities in the Ruhr – areas known to have had strong socialist or communist sympathies before Hitler came to power.[16] The lessons this operation taught about the physical rigours of long-distance night flights were valid for the whole war. Even without an enemy present, night-bomber sorties (which could not, in the 1940s, be flown at altitudes high enough to avoid bad weather) would be uncomfortable at best and dangerous at worst. On 27 October, for example, one crew reported that they 'experienced icing conditions at 1,000 feet, and ten-tenths cloud with sleet at 2,000 feet. Crystalline ice formed over the turrets, leading edges and cabin windows. At 10,000 feet the temperature was −22°C, the front turret was frozen and the trimming tabs jammed by ice … The cockpit heating system was useless, and everyone was frozen with no means of alleviating their distress. Some members of the crew butted their heads on the floor and navigation table in an endeavour to feel some other form of pain as a relief from the awful feeling of frost-bite …'[17] As a result, they 'felt incapable of cohesion of thought or action, and the rear gunner could not have resisted fighter attack. In any case his vision was totally obscured by ice on the turret.' Rather less was learned about the enemy's defences. Fighters attacked only twice, on 7/8 and 8/9

September, and the attacks were not pressed home, while Flak, considered 'heavy' at times, was not particularly effective, either. Only fourteen aircraft were lost at night between 3 September 1939 and 8/9 April 1940 – the start of the Norwegian campaign – and not all of those were due to enemy action.[18]

While crew comfort and the enemy's state of preparedness were obviously important factors in planning for future operations, the 'Nickelling' lesson that should have counted for most was that navigation by night was considerably more difficult than by day. Indeed, during the first weeks of the war navigation errors were to cause the British government considerable embarrassment as Bomber Command aircraft flew over, or crashed on, neutral Belgian, Dutch, and Danish territory and, on one regrettable occasion, shot down a Belgian fighter. These incidents led initially to an outright ban on further night-time leaflet operations and then, when this was lifted, to a carefully selected 'south-about' route into Germany which decreased the likelihood of British aircraft overflying neutral territory, but which also increased the time spent over the enemy's defences. Although the Air Ministry soon withdrew these restrictions, it continued to prohibit Nickelling west of Saarbrucken, Frankfurt, Paderborn, and Bremen in order to avoid accidental incursions into France and the Low Countries. Accidents still happened, however, and as late as 27 March 1940 an Armstrong-Whitworth Whitley of No 77 Squadron was shot down over Rotterdam by a Dutch fighter. One of the crew was killed and the remainder (including Flying Officer W.P. Coppinger, from Cadomin, Alberta) were interned until the German assault on Holland six weeks later brought about their release.[19]

Lack of basic navigation skills was only part of the problem. Before the war, the air staff had been confident that not only whole cities, but also specific objectives within them could be seen by night from safe bombing altitudes. In particular, the planners assumed that crews should have little difficulty identifying so-called self-illuminating targets like steel mills and oil refineries, or those that lay near prominent geographical features such as rivers and lakes. The experience gained from Nickelling proved otherwise. On clear nights, from 12,000 feet and above, they could barely discern relatively large towns or bodies of water, while roads and small villages could be distinguished only below 6000 feet. Large factory-type buildings (which would be the targets of precision attacks) stood out only below 4000 feet, a suicidal height at which to fly in the face of Flak.

Target-finding at night might yet be practicable, it was suggested, if crews made a timed run to the aiming point from a known landmark, but for the moment that remained an unrealistic proposition. For one thing, the air staff still doubted whether the requisite degree of bombing accuracy could be achieved in cloud (the characteristic winter weather pattern) or when there was no moon. For another, although German air raids on Warsaw and other Polish cities had arguably freed Britain from its promise to US President Roosevelt to refrain from 'the ruthless bombing ... of civilians in unfortified centres,' because of the threat of retaliation the British government was not about to authorize attacks likely to cause non-military casualties even if they were unintentional. Daylight operations, meanwhile, continued sporadically (and largely ineffectively) against German naval forces.[20]

The muted response to Nickelling was appropriate to the threat, but it also reflected the fact that the Luftwaffe, like the RAF, had anticipated that strategic bombing would be carried out by day and had set its priorities accordingly. Thus, while its prewar doctrine had at least addressed the problem of night defence – the intention being to rely principally on Flak, supplemented by searchlights and fighters in a number of well-defined zones – the concept could not be implemented effectively.[*] Priority had been given instead to the expansion of the day-fighter arm, so that of the eleven specialist night-fighting Geschwader authorized on 24 June 1939, only seven had been formed before the outbreak of war and all of them were subsequently assigned to daylight operations. The need for a night-fighter arm was reconsidered in October, but when it was re-established only three Staffeln were formed, on Me 109s and Me 110s. There seemed little point in committing more men and machines to the task when the enemy was only dropping paper.[21]

The Air Ministry accepted this 'phoney war' in the air because it allowed the further strengthening of Fighter Command while High Wycombe was not forced to 'lead trumps from a short suit.' On 22 November, however, under pressure from the Cabinet, the air staff told Ludlow-Hewitt to give priority to the German fleet and to attack it in strength, by day. The first such raid was launched on 3 December, when twenty-four Wellingtons were sent in clear weather to the Heligoland Bight, where they attacked two German cruisers, eight merchant ships, and a number of smaller vessels. One cruiser and one merchantman were reported hit, and a minesweeper sunk, with no loss to the bomber force despite the appearance of several enemy fighters. Indeed, one Me 109 was believed to have been shot down. A second raid was launched on 14 December, when twelve Wellingtons discovered a battleship and a cruiser near the mouth of the Elbe. The cloud base at 800 feet precluded any bombing but did not hinder the efforts of German fighters, which accounted for five of the Wellingtons.[22]

The results obtained four days later were even more discouraging because of the restrictions that still limited what could be bombed, despite Whitehall's insistence that the German fleet be attacked in strength. In perfectly clear skies, twenty-four Wellingtons sent to patrol the German coast found three large warships and four destroyers at Wilhelmshaven and made a good pass over the target. The ships were too close to shore and potential civilian casualties for the attack to proceed, however, and no bombs were dropped. The nearly one hundred enemy fighters in the area, well positioned to intercept because of the warning provided by Freya radar stations on the Frisian Islands, faced no such constraints and, in an entirely unequal contest, they shot down twelve of the Wellingtons. Anti-shipping searches continued into the spring of 1940 but,

[*] In September 1939 the Flak service accounted for about one-third (107,000 officers and men) of total Luftwaffe strength, and was equipped with 2600 heavy anti-aircraft guns (88 mm) as well as 6700 light and medium guns (20- and 37 millimetre). The lethal range of an 88 millimetre shell burst was about thirty feet, for about 1/50th of a second.

unless there was good cloud cover, crews were told to stay away from the German mainland. Losses were negligible, just ten of some 650 sorties (about 1.5 per cent), but so were the results. Few ships were sighted and only one, U-31 (a type VII-A ocean-going submarine), was sunk.[23]

By early 1940, then, British planners were in an understandable quandary. Maritime patrols were producing very little result, while daytime operations near German ports involved unacceptably high casualties. The loss rates likely on raids further inland could only be imagined. Meanwhile, even the most enthusiastic proponents of precision night attacks were beginning to admit that their bomber crews could not win the 'never-ending struggle to circumvent the law that we cannot see in the dark.' As a result, the chief navigation officer at High Wycombe concluded, the most that could be expected of astro-navigation (and even the radio aids then under investigation) was to give pilots a general idea of where their targets were.[*] Neither would direct a bombing force to a specific aiming point.[24]

Looking to the future, but persuaded that Bomber Command required additional time to build up its strength, the air staff now began to argue that the focus of bombing should shift from producing physical damage, which required sustained and intensive operations and demanded more accuracy than Ludlow-Hewitt could guarantee, to lowering enemy morale, which it wishfully thought could be accomplished by as few as two hundred sorties a week. The idea was to dispatch small numbers of aircraft (perhaps no more than thirty) to Germany each night, dispersing them in time and space through as many air-defence zones as possible and setting off almost continuous alarms over the whole Reich. This would upset the 'nerves and digestion' of the German population and might eventually make living conditions so unpleasant that those employed in the war industries would be 'loth to continue at work.'[25]

Momentous results were not anticipated from such an approach in anything but the long term. If real, rather than psychological, damage was to be done, and done quickly, target intelligence suggested that oil was the weak link in the German economy, Russian and Romanian supplies notwithstanding. The destruction of just one major refinery would have a direct impact on the German war effort, while neutralizing the twenty-two largest facilities (of which fifteen were less than 150 miles from the North Sea coast) 'might well prove decisive.'[26]

Hoping for the best, and anticipating that the gloves would eventually come off, the then CAS, Air Chief Marshal Sir Cyril Newall, approved the oil plan in principle on 22 February 1940, and Bomber Command began the slow process of converting to a night-bomber force. After 6 March, crews from Nos 3 and 5 Groups joined those of No 4 Group on Nickel and reconnaissance flights and their training in night operations was accelerated. As this happened, Ludlow-Hewitt became increasingly optimistic about what they might achieve and on 25 March reported that, with experience and practice, his force should

---

[*] In late September 1942 it was estimated that astro-navigation would, at best, bring crews within twelve miles of the target.

be able to fulfil 'the major destructive part of our plan by precision bombing at night,' while targets in the Ruhr could be dealt with 'if necessary in quite a leisurely manner by night, taking advantage of suitable weather conditions.'[27]

It all seemed so easy, but beneath the surface there was reason for concern. When Ludlow-Hewitt left High Wycombe in April 1940 his replacement, Air Marshal C.F.A. Portal (who would be knighted in July), was far from convinced he could accomplish the task. Speaking for his new staff, 'our general opinion,' he told the CAS, 'is that under war conditions the average crew of a night bomber could not be relied on to identify and attack targets at night except under the very best conditions of visibility, even when the target is on the coast or on a large river like the Rhine. Under the latter conditions about 50% of the average crews might be expected to find and bomb the right target in good visibility; if the target has no conspicuous aids to its location, very few inexperienced crews would be likely to find it under any condition.'[28] Furthermore, it was not certain that the introduction of navigation aids would markedly improve the situation because of the 'poor type' of individuals selected to be observers over the previous few years.[29]

A reason to lift the restrictions on bombing came on 8–9 April 1940, when Germany invaded Norway and Denmark. Indeed, the day before Hitler moved, Sir Richard Peirse, deputy chief of the air staff (DCAS), had urged the opening of an air offensive to prevent what he regarded as Germany's next gambit – securing bases in the Low Countries in order to move the Luftwaffe closer to its targets in England and to provide air defence in depth for the Ruhr. The deputy director of plans also urged action. 'We know the brittleness of German morale,' he pointed out with quite unjustified optimism, and so should begin night operations 'directed towards the moral and psychological factor.' The three service chiefs also agreed with Peirse but cautioned that the government might yet be reluctant to unleash an air offensive while Britain had not been bombed.[30] They were right: the political restrictions remained in force throughout the Norwegian campaign.

Nor did the Blitzkrieg against France and the Low Countries, long regarded as the likely signal for expanding the air war, bring about an immediate change. Again concerned that Britain was throwing away an important advantage, the DCAS implored his superior, Newall, to find a way to free High Wycombe's hand. Even if Holland were lost, he explained, the Allied armies might yet 'stabilise a line in Belgium,' and an attack on the Ruhr before the Luftwaffe had built up its defences in the Netherlands might yield significant moral and physical results. The War Cabinet took up the issue the next day, but thought it was not yet propitious to begin bombing German targets. Chamberlain and Lord Halifax continued to worry about the German threat to Britain's aircraft factories and aerodromes, and on this issue they were supported by the new secretary of state for air, Sir Archibald Sinclair, and the CAS, both of whom emphasized the weakness of Fighter Command in the face of German forces operating from Dutch airfields. The new prime minister, Winston Churchill – he had succeeded Chamberlain on 10 May – was also persuaded. 'We should not allow our heavy bomber force to be frittered away and thus deprive ourselves of its principal deterrent effect, and of the ability to deliver its heavy blow.'[31]

The perfect irony of the situation, and of these remarks, was apparently lost on everyone concerned. That the Germans were in Holland, and held Dutch bases, clearly demonstrated that they had not been deterred by the threat of aerial attack. Indeed, the only people who had been deterred – from carrying out their own air plan – were the British themselves. On 15 May, however, with the Germans pouring west from Sedan (and following the Luftwaffe's bombing of Rotterdam the day before), the gloves finally came off and High Wycombe was authorized to attack oil refineries and railroad targets east of the Rhine. The first raid occurred that night, when nearly a hundred bombers were sent to sixteen different targets in the Ruhr. Only one aircraft was lost, but the bombing was quite futile – one dairyman killed in Cologne, and two people wounded in Münster.[32]

Two nights later, forty-eight Hampdens bombed Hamburg and twenty-four Whitleys attacked Bremen, looking for oil refineries, while six Wellingtons bombed Cologne's railway yards. Fires were started in Hamburg and Bremen, and forty-seven people were killed; but in Cologne, as elsewhere in the Ruhr, damage was inconsequential. 'We drove through many of the Ruhr centres ... the Allies were supposed to have bombed ... the last few nights,' an American radio correspondent observed on his way from Berlin to the Western Front on 19 May. 'We naturally couldn't see all the factories and bridges and railroad junctions ... but we saw several, and nothing had happened to them. The great networks of railroad tracks and bridges around Essen and Duisburg ... were intact. The Rhine bridges at Cologne were up. The factories throughout the Ruhr were smoking away as usual ... The British have failed not only to put the Ruhr out of commission, but even to damage the German flying fields.'[33]

Oil refineries and factories, even if they could be hit, were objectives unlikely to have any immediate effect in stemming the German Blitzkrieg and, after a quick visit to France, when he saw at first hand the look of defeat, Winston Churchill ordered the Air Ministry to shift its attack to the Wehrmacht's lines of communication. The density of Western Europe's sophisticated transportation networks meant, however, that unless a dozen or more key nodal points could be destroyed simultaneously – something High Wycombe could hardly hope to do – alternative routes would always be available to the enemy. Knowing this, Portal argued that the bulk of his force should continue its longer-term campaign against the Ruhr, but the directive he received from the Air Ministry on 19 May was unequivocal. Although oil remained on the target list, the railway marshalling yards supporting the German advance were the first priority during this 'critical week.'[34]

Once the last remnants of the British Expeditionary Force had left Dunkirk and the Germans had turned towards Paris and the southwest, Portal was directed to 'give priority to operations in support of the French land forces.' Oil remained the main strategic objective, with aircraft factories in major cities as the recommended alternative on dark nights, but he was warned that these raids were not to 'degenerate into mere indiscriminate action.' They did, although not by design. Industrial haze over the Ruhr and poor navigation by many crews (who, in a continuing effort to spread the alarm, made their own way to the objective by whatever route they preferred) meant that many targets were never identified. German records reveal that 70 per cent of the bombs dropped fell on open countryside.[35]

The fall of France simplified High Wycombe's war, for there was no longer any need to support the army in the field. There were also complications, however, since no one was quite sure how to employ Bomber Command in a defensive struggle for survival. What were the best targets? The Luftwaffe and its bases? Maritime invasion preparations – a target that, in the event, cost Bomber Command some fifty aircraft between June and October? The German aircraft industry? Oil? Or, given doubts about the willingness of British workers to 'carry on in the face of wholesale havoc and destruction,' enemy morale? Moreover, against which of these targets could it operate most effectively? And if Britain was *in extremis*, battling to survive, should the whole strength of the command be thrown into the fray now, against uncertain results, or should it be conserved for better days to come?

At the end of June the Foreign Office was uncritically quoting 'reliable sources' to the effect that the British air raids launched so far against Germany were 'creating havoc and causing panic among the civil population.' People were living in a state of 'acute nervous tension,' it was said, and 'sleepless nights' were having the desired effect on industrial production. Nerves were so frayed that workers had 'begun to imagine and take refuge from non-existent aircraft during the day, as well as at night.' Perhaps, then, an all-out campaign against German industrial centres, putting aside the question of civilian casualties, might have a significant impact on morale and save Britain from invasion.[36]

From 19 June to 13 October High Wycombe received six directives from the Air Ministry (four arrived before 24 July), each of which set down new priorities and methods of attack. These directives reflected changing appreciations of the greatest threat facing Britain, the choices alternating between air raids and invasion, and they established the target lists accordingly: aircraft assembly plants; aircraft storage facilities; airfields in Holland, Belgium, and northwest France; oil; and barges and troopships in the German-held Channel, North Sea, and Baltic ports. Despite their differences, however, these directives had one thing in common: they all provided lists of specific objectives. That issued on 13 July, for example, limited the main effort to fifteen factories and plants, ten of which were related to the aircraft industry and five to oil.[37]

High Wycombe was not happy with any of the new directives. Convinced, still, that his crews could not find and destroy precise targets, Portal asked permission in mid-July to make for the larger industrial towns instead in order to 'undermine morale.'[38] His request was denied, the Air Ministry insisting that material destruction had to be the 'primary object,' but when the Luftwaffe accidentally bombed central London on 24/25 August, Prime Minister Churchill demanded immediate retaliation. About fifty crews were sent to Berlin the next night; six were lost and the bombing, carried out through fog, was as inaccurate as ever, with most damage occurring to farmland south of the capital. Within the city itself, they managed to destroy one wooden summer house and to injure two people. The Germans bombed London again the following day, deliberately this time, but the air staff, trying to avoid a tit-for-tat campaign, selected industrial targets in Leipzig as Bomber Command's next objective. That was not good enough for the prime minister, however, who believed that since the Germans had begun to 'molest' London, it was time to 'hit them hard, and Berlin is the place to hit them.'[39]

Inch by painful inch, both British and German bombing policies were slipping from ones aimed at precise objectives to ones of area bombing with psychological overtones. On 2 September, for example, Portal observed that although he was not yet involved in attempts to burn down whole towns, 'that stage would come.' The next day Churchill asked that Bomber Command 'pulverise the entire industry and scientific structure' of the German war economy; and, three days later, he called for a series of 'minor' but 'widespread' attacks on smaller German towns intended to destroy the civilian population's faith in their air defences. Portal responded with a list of twenty such places and urged that it be made public in order to provide a clear statement that, 'as a reprisal for each night of indiscriminate bombing by the enemy, one of these towns would be selected for indiscriminate bombing by the RAF.'[40]

For the moment, Newall was neither persuaded by Portal nor cajoled by Churchill. But when the Germans dropped thirty-six large and powerful mines on London by parachute, a method of delivery which obviously precluded any attempt at aiming, the prime minister again demanded retaliation. Although he made it clear that he understood it was better to 'concentrate upon limited high-class military objectives,' he asked that Berlin also be attacked with aerial mines. Recoiling at the prospect of engaging in 'indiscriminate frightfulness,' the air staff pleaded that Berlin should be attacked with bombs, not mines, and that High Wycombe should be directed to aim for useful targets like 'the few great power stations' situated in the German capital. The bombing directive issued on 21 September reflected this advice and, when Berlin was attacked, two nights later, the 129 aircraft dispatched were sent to eighteen specific objectives. On 30 September the discontented Portal again made the point that since his crews could not reduce the enemy's means to fight, their efforts should be focused 'primarily against the will of the German people to continue the war' and should thereby meet what his biographer has called both the 'tactical' and the 'emotional' need of the hour. The air staff, however, still did not agree that the German people should become the primary target. Nor did the secretary of state for air, who argued that nothing would be achieved through what he called 'promiscuous bombing';[41] but Sinclair was never a man to press unpopular views in the corridors of power.

As AOC-in-C, Portal had a perfect right to be heard on matters affecting the employment of his command, but he had no reason to assume that the CAS would accept and follow his advice, particularly where it strayed into the realm of high policy. He was not without influence, however, of a powerful, if unofficial, kind. Churchill cultivated an informal process of seeking and expressing opinion outside the formal chain of command, and Chequers, the prime ministerial country home, lay only a few miles from High Wycombe. At least once, in mid-July, Churchill took advantage of a visit by Portal to broach the subject of bombing Berlin, an idea that the latter enthusiastically endorsed.[42]

The extent to which Portal's opinions had weight through this process depended, nevertheless, on Churchill's willingness to dictate to the Air Ministry and the air staff; and that, for all his dabbling in target selection, the prime minister did only rarely. On 4 October, however, having properly impressed his truculent master, Portal was appointed chief of the air staff, *vice* Newall; and the next day Sir Richard Peirse, who had sided with Portal and Churchill on the question of attacking cities during the winter, moved to High Wycombe as AOC-in-C Bomber Command. There were now two officers in key appointments who favoured the idea of carrying the war directly to the German civilian population, with the senior of them, at least, in intimate contact with the prime minister. When Portal now made more widely known his desire to attack industrial areas as often as possible and (following the example of the Luftwaffe's attack on Rotterdam) to make 'the maximum use of fire' during these raids, no one objected. Oil would be the top priority on moonlit nights, but on darker nights Bomber Command was to 'make a definite attempt ... to affect the morale of the German people.'[43]

The new offensive, which began immediately, was soon under fire from Churchill for its lack of intensity. It was a 'scandal,' the prime minister complained, 'that the discharge of bombs on Germany is so pitifully small ... even on good nights' because so few bombers were available. It was also beyond comprehension, he added, that suggestions he had made to improve the situation were being ignored. 'If, instead of simply turning all these down, you and the Secretary of State recognised the need of increasing the bomb delivery and set to work to contrive the means of doing so, it would be a very great help.' Portal lost little time passing on this complaint to High Wycombe. For his part, Peirse reassured the CAS on 13 November that he would not only try to send a large number of bombers to Berlin carrying the largest available bombs, but also that he would 'pick out targets well and evenly spaced ... in an attempt to ensure that the whole city receives some weight of attack.'[44] Clearly, if the spread of attack was so significant, non-industrial damage and civilian casualties were being seen as the direct objectives of Bomber Command's operations, and not merely as by-products of raids on military targets and war industries.

At this stage of the war, the adoption of a bombing policy aimed at German morale through attacks on built-up areas reflected, by and large, an assessment of what Bomber Command could do best, precision bombing being clearly beyond its competence. But there was also an emotional element to policy-making, tied to public demands and fed by the media, that the RAF must respond in kind to the bombing of British cities. If any excuse were needed on this score, it was provided by the German attack on Coventry on 14/15 November and by subsequent raids on Bristol and Southampton. Planning for the retaliatory Operation Abigail, designed to cause maximum damage to a selected German town, began almost immediately, but because of poor weather it did not take place until 16/17 December. One hundred and thirty-four aircraft were sent to bomb the centre of Mannheim – the first occasion when a raid was designed to open with an incendiary attack and follow-on crews were told to bomb whatever fires they saw – and results seemed to be good. About three-quarters of the crews reported having found the city, and 'dense black smoke' was everywhere.[45]

The first campaign against German cities was over almost as soon as it began, however, despite Ministry of Information assurances that the enemy would 'not stand a quarter of the bombing' endured by the residents of British cities. Because of operational and training losses – mainly the latter – the front-line strength of Bomber Command had fallen by a quarter in September and October and it now needed some nursing. Moreover, most operational losses had occurred in the bad weather usually reserved for morale attacks on non-specific objectives, and it seemed sensible, therefore, to restrict operations to clear nights, when precise targets might be bombed successfully. Photographic evidence from Mannheim reinforced this view, proving that the damage to the city was much less than claimed by the crews involved and calling into question the utility of area raids. The most compelling argument for switching objectives came from a special committee struck to analyse the enemy's fuel situation, which, that same 16 December, issued a grossly optimistic report suggesting that the meagre effort (6.7 per cent of sorties to date) made by Bomber Command against Germany's synthetic oil plants had actually done significant damage.[46]

Although photographic evidence available a week later showed that recent attacks on refineries at Gelsenkirchen had, in fact, failed, the special intelligence committee was inclined to believe what it wanted to believe and to ignore any contrary indications. Germany was not only facing a fuel crisis, it said, but her oil industry was extremely vulnerable to attack. Momentarily persuaded that something useful could be achieved, Portal bent with the wind and outlined a bombing program aimed at knocking out Germany's seventeen largest synthetic oil plants and restricting attacks on area targets to those nights when the weather was bad. Notwithstanding its own reservations about the importance of synthetic oil to the German economy and doubts about the vulnerability of refineries (and despite continuing and legitimate concern over German naval strength), the War Cabinet gave its approval to the new program. On 15 January 1941 Sir Richard Peirse was informed that oil was 'the sole primary aim' of his offensive.[47] Even aerial mining, a subsidiary task for Bomber Command since the war began, was removed from the bombing directive.*

---

* It was reintroduced, at the Royal Navy's insistence, ten days later, but only for inexperienced crews or to test out new bomber types before they became fully operational.

Try as he might, the AOC-in-C had difficulty complying with the new policy. Bad weather in January and February restricted operations against oil targets to three nights, while industrial targets were bombed six times, ports five, and miscellaneous naval objectives nineteen times. Never a genuine or a strong proponent of an oil offensive in the first place, and satisfied it was not a practicable objective, Portal now cast about for an alternative, telling Peirse not only that he preferred to return to mass attacks on industrial areas, but also that if the attack on oil was suspended 'we have the consolation of not having wasted much on it since the Cabinet decision.' The CAS then informed his fellow service chiefs that while it was 'virtually impossible for a pilot to select and bomb a particular object on a dark night or in bad weather,' it had 'been proved that even under adverse conditions of weather and enemy activity an *area* can be attacked with success.' By now Peirse did not agree, arguing still that oil targets should and could be destroyed, but at least one of his group commanders was not so sure. Only 'the most obvious targets' had been hit hard, Air Vice-Marshal J.C. Slessor recalled, and then only 'on the clearest moonlight nights.'[48]

In early March, however, with an alarming increase in Allied shipping losses, the prime minister directed that air attacks concentrate on U-boat bases and construction yards. Portal did not like being told to pull the Admiralty 'out of the mess they have gotten into,' but the directive he issued on 9 March complied fully with Churchill's instructions. Coastal cities like Hamburg, Kiel, and Bremen, as well as several French ports, would bear the brunt of bombing until mid-summer, and Bomber Command's contribution to the aerial mining campaign, abandoned just a few months before, would be intensified. Steps being taken to improve performance now assumed a new importance. Instead of allowing crews to make their own way to the target, for example, group staffs were beginning to lay down set courses and timings aimed at increasing the number of bombers over the objective at any one time. (No 4 Group tried for a hundred bombers an hour, No 3 Group for two to three dozen.) There was also a push to accelerate development of radio and radar aids to navigation, although for the moment this met with apathy on the part of the Air Ministry and 'the union of navigators,' which High Wycombe's radar officer found 'remarkably conservative about adopting new ideas.'[49]

At the same time, bomber protection and the German air-defence system were finally being accepted as important and worthwhile areas of investigation. Until the end of 1940 recommendations to improve armament and add armour plating had been dismissed out of hand, the planners at the Air Ministry declaring that bombloads could not be sacrificed and that it was not the business of bombers to engage fighters in combat because the contest could never be made equal. Indeed, they went so far as to argue that crews caught by fighters (and, of course, surviving the encounter) should be told that 'their tactics were faulty.'[50] As the number of bombers being shot down increased, however, British intelligence intensified its effort to unravel the mystery of the air-defence organization established by General Josef Kammhuber, then commanding the Luftwaffe's sole Nachtjagddivision but soon (in August) to become

GERMAN NIGHT FIGHTER DEFENCES
AND BOMBER COMMAND

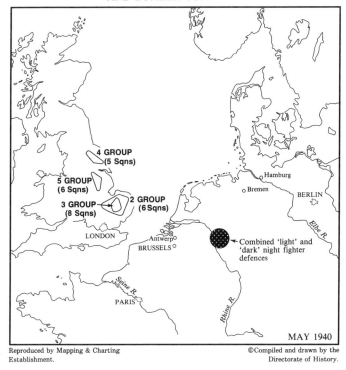

Reproduced by Mapping & Charting
Establishment.

©Compiled and drawn by the
Directorate of History.

General der Nachtjagd and commander of an expanded, all-night-fighter XII
Fliegerkorps.

Much was known already. A network of Freya radar stations on the North
Sea coast provided early warning of the approach direction (but not height) of
aircraft out to a distance of one hundred miles and passed this information on
to a series of combined night-fighter/searchlight 'boxes,' ranging between
twenty and forty miles wide and sixty miles deep, established behind the
Zuider Zee and along the Rhine. On receipt of a Freya warning, the fighter assigned to each box was scrambled to patrol its allocated air space until the
searchlights illuminated a bomber, when interception could begin – a technique
Kammhuber called Helle Nachtjagd, or 'illuminated night-fighting.' Behind
these boxes lay a Flak zone which, early in 1941, was just beginning to be
assisted by Würzburg gun-laying radars.[51]

Once this essential structure was analysed, patterns could be discerned:
losses to fighters were highest on clear nights; lowest on cloudy nights and
outside the searchlight zone; and unaccountably rare above 14,000 feet, even
though this was well within the range of grouped searchlights. As a result,
High Wycombe began to introduce counter-measures. Routes were planned,
when practicable, to skirt Kammhuber's line or to take advantage of gaps
identified in it; and pilots were told to bomb from 16,000 feet, a height from

GERMAN NIGHT FIGHTER DEFENCES
AND BOMBER COMMAND

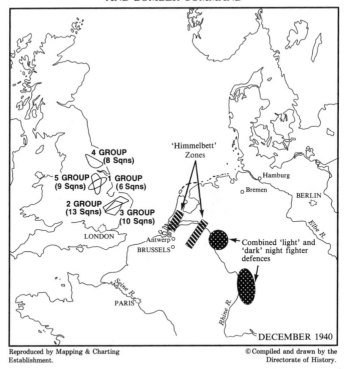

Reproduced by Mapping & Charting
Establishment.

© Compiled and drawn by the
Directorate of History.

which it was felt – optimistically, it turned out – they could still see specific objectives on the ground. When deep penetrations were required, it was also recommended that pilots make maximum altitude over the North Sea, dive through the defensive Flak and fighter belt at best possible speed, and then regain height in the German interior, where defences were weaker.[52]

Unhappy with the futile effort to destroy specific objectives, the air staff and the secretary of state for air began in April 1941 to exert subtle but continuous pressure on the prime minister to resume area raids and to enlarge Bomber Command, so as to 'raise the intensity of our bomber offensive ... to an intolerable pitch.' It was not until 9 July 1941, however, that a new bombing directive was issued which, following 'a comprehensive review of the enemy's ... political, economic, and military situation,' disclosed that 'the weakest points in his armour lie in the morale of the civilian population and in his inland transportation system.' From that date, Germany would be attacked more often and with greater intensity. The number of medium and heavy bombers in squadron service would rise from 388 in March 1941 to 449 in July and 549 in December, and consideration was being given to expanding Bomber Command to 168 heavy, six medium, and twenty light bomber squadrons.[53]

Canada's part in this growth was considerable. In the beginning, the Canadian contribution had been limited to the efforts of the relatively small number of individuals who had joined the RAF in the 1930s, some of whom had been involved in the earliest raids. On 1 March 1941 the first RCAF pilot graduates of the British Commonwealth Air Training Plan (BCATP) arrived overseas, joining thirty-seven observers who had come at the end of November 1940. By mid-April 1680 Canadian graduates were in England, the vanguard of many thousands who would serve with Bomber Command and, in fact, account for at least a quarter of its aircrew strength.[54]

The initial RCAF overseas bomber squadron, No 405, was formed at Driffield, Yorkshire, on 23 April 1941. Allocated Wellington Mark IIs powered by Rolls Royce Merlin Xs, the squadron was assigned to No 4 Group, whose Whitleys were fitted with the same engine. The second squadron, No 408, was formed two months later, on 24 June. Equipped with Hampdens, it was assigned to No 5 Group, which also flew Hampdens, and based at Lindholme, also in Yorkshire. The creation of these two squadrons within six months of the Ralston-Sinclair Agreement (see chapter 1) gave relatively quick recognition to Canada's role in the bomber offensive, but it also required certain concessions. While Ralston had accepted that squadron and flight commanders would probably have to come from the RAF, the orders authorizing the formation of Nos 405 and 408 stated that a majority of the aircrew would be British as well, at least at the outset.

Squadron records confirm that situation. On 18 June 1941 only 16.5 per cent of the pilots in No 405 were Canadian, and of these more than half were Canadians in the RAF. One reason for this composition was that No 405 Squadron was the only Wellington unit in an otherwise Whitley group, and it took some effort (and intergroup cooperation) to winkle RCAF trainees out of No 3 Group's Wellington Operational Training Units (OTUs). Once advised of the problem, however, High Wycombe promised to intervene and apparently did, for in August 45 per cent of the aircrew were identified as Canadian (either Can/RAF or RCAF) and by late fall the RCAF content had risen to 53 per cent. In No 408 the earliest Canadianization figures available show 25 per cent of aircrew positions held by RCAF personnel. Groundcrew and tradesmen figures were considerably lower, and in their first few months the overall RCAF component on both squadrons rarely exceeded 5 per cent.[55]

Flying was the most important element in preparing a squadron for operations: local flying to familiarize pilots and navigators with the regional geography so they could return to base with confidence after long, arduous night operations; cross-country flying to improve navigation and crew cooperation in general; and fighter affiliation exercises – simulated combat manoeuvres – to increase the chances of surviving Flak and night-fighters. The hours available to achieve this practice depended, of course, on the weather, about which nothing could be done, and also on the supply and serviceability of aircraft, both of which could be managed.

It took almost a month before No 405 had twelve Wellingtons, all apparently new machines, but by the end of May none was fit to fly 'owing to nacelle bearing weakness.' The necessary repairs had been made by 3 June, but the next day two other machines undergoing modification were lost, one being burnt out completely following a Luftwaffe raid on Driffield. Replacements arrived the next day, but then all twelve machines were again declared unserviceable, this time because of additional defects in the engine mountings. It took five days before the first four could be modified and repaired, and only seven had been fixed by 11 June. As a result, from 6 May to 11 June, the day before the squadron's first operations, flying had occurred on only seven days. In No 408, in contrast, where Hampdens began to arrive on 10 July, there were few interruptions in flying training due to unserviceability.[56]

Serviceability also depended on the expertise, experience, and efficiency of the groundcrews. At this early stage of the war there was no great pool of experienced servicing personnel in either the RAF or the RCAF, so although new squadrons were provided with a nucleus of trained mechanics and technicians, many were posted in directly from training schools. These men could not be expected to cope effectively with all the problems likely to be encountered in maintaining complex and sophisticated systems under operational conditions. Initially, at least, their presence could be cause for some misgivings. The commanding officer of No 408 Squadron was horrified when he learned he would lose a number of RAF tradesmen as soon as their RCAF replacements arrived, and he protested immediately. In all their training the in-coming Canadians had never worked on Hampdens, he explained, and they were therefore totally unfitted to assume immediate responsibility for maintenance. In the event, the British tradesmen remained with No 408 for two more months, combining their normal duties with the on-the-job training of their RCAF colleagues.[57]

The process of working a new squadron into shape would have been easier if it had remained in one spot. Both Canadian squadrons had to move a month or so after their birth, however, which meant changing over workshops and food services, shifting records, and reorganizing quarters. The moves also interrupted flying training. Of the two, No 405 probably suffered most because, when it left Driffield, it was quitting a permanent, prewar station with all the amenities and comforts provided for the peacetime RAF, while Pocklington, the squadron's new home, had only been opened in June 1941 and the Canadians were its first operational tenants. Nissen huts, built of prefabricated corrugated iron on a concrete base, were the order of the day, and they were cold and damp for much of the year. The 'dreary camp,' John Searby recalled, was 'not a comfortable billet.' Lindholme, No 408's first station, had opened in June 1940, a year before the Canadians arrived. Syerston, in Nottinghamshire, their next billet, was 'wedged between the main A 46 road and the River Trent,' and dated from December 1940.[58]

The crucial factor in operational training, particularly in light of the inconveniences and difficulties noted above, was that the squadrons have experienced senior officers. No 405's first commanding officer was Wing Commander P.A. Gilchrist, who had joined the RAF in 1935. A veteran of No 4 Group's night operations in Whitleys, he had already been awarded the Distinguished Flying Cross 'for gallantry and devotion to duty.' Wing Commander N.W. Timmerman, DFC, who had enlisted a year later and was already a veteran of fifty bombing operations, went to No 408. Each understood the importance of having experienced flight commanders. Timmerman recalls that he spent some time 'persuading 5 Group Headquarters to pry loose two flight commanders, RAF-Canadians like myself, from their units.' Gilchrist was also successful in acquiring experienced Can/RAF flight commanders.[59]

No 405 Squadron's first operation came on the night of 12/13 June 1941, when five aircraft were detailed to bomb the railway yards at Schwerte, a small industrial town in the southeast corner of the Ruhr.[*] As was common in new squadrons, servicing and maintenance problems reduced the scheduled scale of effort. One crew did not take off owing to radio failure and blown fuses, while another, encountering engine problems en route, turned back, jettisoning its bombs east of Groningen in Holland. This was contrary to rules – except in the direst of circumstances, bombs were not to be dumped on occupied Europe – and may have reflected nervousness and uncertainty when confronted with the ordeal of flying over enemy territory for the first time. The three crews who reached Schwerte did so at altitudes between 7500 and 10,000 feet and reported they had bombed the target area, 'bursts being seen and fires observed.' However, they also admitted that 'results were difficult to assess owing to ground haze.' The thirty-eight crews sent from other squadrons (there were also raids on Soest, Hamm, Osnabrück, and Hüls) reported much the same. Some, having difficulty even finding the target area, resorted to bombing on their estimated time of arrival (ETA) – that is, when the navigator thought they should be over the target, based on his calculated course and estimated ground speed – a dubious approximation in most cases.[60]

The squadron's next operation came three nights later when, with ninety-eight aircraft from other squadrons, seven crews were ordered to bomb the main railway station at Cologne, just west of the landmark Hohenzollern bridge over the Rhine – a clear target indicator if ever there was one. One machine failed to take off, the crew reporting gun trouble, and one failed to return. Five crews claimed to have bombed the target, one from as low as 1200 feet. This machine, flown by a British sergeant pilot, was also attacked several times by an Me 110 from 'all directions except frontal' and suffered severe damage. Both engines were hit, and the main plane, rudder, rear turret, and fin were all holed.[61]

Had High Wycombe known the actual results of this raid, it would have taken little comfort from them. The Germans recorded only fifty-five high-explosive bombs falling on the city – the load carried by about a dozen aircraft – and material damage was negligible. Results were even worse the next night, when six Wellingtons from No 405 were among a hundred bombers raiding Bremen. Only two Canadian crews claimed to have found the target through

---

[*] Transportation targets enjoyed a new strategic significance after the Germans attacked the Soviet Union on 22 June, the air staff hoping not only that their destruction would slow the delivery of men and materiel to the Eastern Front but also that the Luftwaffe would be compelled to retain fighters in the west. .

low cloud and haze, and both did so by dropping down to the potentially fatal altitude of 1200 feet. On 22/23 June three of the eight 405 Squadron Wellingtons sent to Wilhelmshaven reported having been 'on target' and another claimed to have been in the vicinity (three others returned early, and one sortie was cancelled), but the bombing again left much to be desired. The only victims were the inhabitants of a small village four kilometres south of Wilhelmshaven, where one house was hit. There was little improvement the night of 4/5 July when the objective was German warships in the French port of Brest. The weather was good, with excellent visibility, and all the crews 'clearly identified the target and ... claimed to have straddled the dock and the cruiser.' But the ship was not damaged.[62]

By now, No 405's effort on most raids had risen to nine or ten machines, and the number of non-starters and early returns was falling as groundcrews learned to cope with the pace of maintenance and repair work in an operational setting. Aircrews were also gaining confidence, and that was just as well, for on 24 July the squadron faced a stern test of an entirely new kind. For some time – and despite heavy losses on earlier such raids – the Air Ministry had been eager to undertake a daylight attack against German warships in French ports, both to destroy these enduring threats to Atlantic convoys and to entice the Luftwaffe's day-fighters into the air. *Gneisenau* and *Prinz Eugen*, then at Brest, were selected, and just before noon on the 24th one hundred bombers were sent out, in perfectly clear skies. Nine came from 405 Squadron. 'All our a[ir]/craft, in face of intense *Flak* and fighter opposition, are known to have been over the target at an average height of about 12,000 ft. Owing to an error in the setting of the distributor arm, one a/craft failed to release its bombs. One a/craft definitely straddled the cruiser, and all the a/craft bombed the target with success, some direct hits being certain ... The docks and surrounding districts were severely pasted. The *Gneisenau* was enveloped in smoke from fires, both on the target and on the quays.' Enemy fighter activity was heavy, but some successes were reported. One crew was 'attacked in successive air - battles by four enemy a/craft ... Fine evasive action and return fire from the rear gunner and the front gunner accounted for two Me's.' With their Wellington extensively damaged, all the crew except the two pilots moved on the flight home to the tail 'in order to weight it down.' The machine crashed three hundred yards from the English coast and everyone was rescued.[63]

There is an unmistakable sense of exhilaration, excitement, and accomplishment in the squadron's record of this raid. Bombing appeared to have been accurate (*Gneisenau* and *Prinz Eugen* were not hit hard, but the dock complex was damaged); moreover, there had been no flinching in the face of strong opposition, although losses amounted to one-third of the squadron's effort. Wing Commander Gilchrist was shot down, but although he evaded capture and eventually made his way to England, he did not return to the squadron (or Bomber Command) again. Squadron Leader R.C. Bissett, DFC, took over temporarily until Wing Commander R.M. Fenwick-Wilson, another Canadian in the RAF (who had been awarded an Air Force Cross in April for bravery in non-combat flying), arrived. One other aircraft was lost, while another, badly damaged, crashed in England. Fortunately, casualty rates so high were not the norm – the loss rate for the entire Schwerte force was just 3.6 per cent, and for all five raids only 1.8 per cent – but single squadrons could suffer severely on any given night.[64] The disruptive effect of such disproportionately high casualties was never easy to undo but was hardest on new squadrons still coming to grips with operations, especially when senior leaders were lost.

After a brief rest, six crews set out for Cologne on 30/31 July, bombing on ETA and reporting only that 'some part' of the city had been attacked. Through 'momentary breaks' in the cloud cover German searchlights had been effective, and for the first time crews complained about searchlight dazzle, the blinding effect of intense light reflecting off smears, scratches, and scrapes on their Perspex (acrylic resin) windscreens. They were not exaggerating. A British artillery officer who flew on a raid at this time commented that searchlights were perhaps the enemy's 'most effective defensive weapon' because they successfully 'prevented us from seeing where we were.'[65] With armoured glass ruled out because of its weight, some squadrons cut out 'clear vision panels' (holes), an unpleasant alternative, even in summer, because of the cold; in others, groundcrews were admonished to take extraordinary care in polishing the Perspex.

On 11 August No 408 Squadron was declared operational and four Hampdens were dispatched to bomb the dock area of Rotterdam in company with thirty other aircraft. The weather was poor, however, with cloud above 7000 feet and mist or haze below, and two crews returned to base with their bombs; the other two, believing they were over the docks, dropped their bombs but could not see any results. Weather was also bad the next night when three aircraft were sent to attack the railway marshalling yards at Hanover. One crew 'had engine trouble and returned to base, dropping bomb load on Lingen.' The others flew through (they could not get above) 10/10ths cloud and an electrical storm en route to the target – which was clear – but no measurable results were observed. Indeed, if the example of one crew from a British squadron at about this time is any indication, the Canadians were probably nowhere near Hanover. Sent to Mannheim through 10/10ths cloud, the RAF crew navigated by dead reckoning to their ETA, broke cloud, followed a river, found a town, and bombed it. When they returned to base, looked at a map, and checked their calculations, they discovered they had bombed Epinal, on the Moselle in France, 150 miles away. They also learned that the Flak which fired on them while they believed they were over the North Sea had come from the Birmingham defences in central England.[66]

Flying conditions remained bad for the rest of the month, and both Canadian squadrons spent an extremely frustrating time flying through the murk to an educated guess at where they should be. In the last week of August, however, No 408 was withdrawn from the night order of battle. It had been decided that Fighter Command's daytime Circus operations (see chapter 6) needed additional bait to draw German fighters into battle. Hampdens were manoeuvrable (although desperately undergunned), and No 408 was among the squadrons High Wycombe selected for the task. After spending a few weeks practising formation flying (and painting the bellies of their aircraft blue), the Canadian crews tackled their first Ramrod on 17 September, six aircraft going to Marquise, near Lille, to bomb a munitions factory. All returned safely, but they had not identified the target – even in daylight – and did not bomb. A second Ramrod, this time directed against the marshalling yards at Abbeville, was ordered for the next day, but when their fighter escort failed to appear the Hampdens returned to base. Abbeville was the target again on 20 September, and on 21 September the Ramrod made for the railway repair shops at Lille, where they caused only minor damage. All six bombers were hit by Flak, but managed to maintain formation and return safely. The next day the power station at Mazingarbe was the objective, but that mission was cancelled after the squadron had been airborne for ninety minutes. Then it was time to repaint the Hampdens: the squadron was to return to night operations.[67]

No 408 was fortunate that its commitment to daytime bombing did not extend beyond the realm of Ramrod operations. Unescorted operations by daylight – mostly the concern of No 2 Group – were far more deadly, leading to a loss rate of 7.1 per cent between July and November 1941, while that for night raids was only 3.5 per cent.[68] Night attacks remained unfruitful, however, and the damage visible in reconnaissance photographs bore no relation to what it should have been if the crews' claims were valid. For one thing, the general purpose bombs then in use – filled with relatively inefficient Amatol and featuring 'too much metal, too little explosive' no matter what their size – were found to be malfunctioning at an alarmingly high rate. Worse, there had been no discernible improvement in bombing accuracy despite the introduction of the fire-raising technique as a rudimentary form of target-marking – in part, it was argued, because the enemy's decoys, set alight in open fields, were so convincing. German records tend to confirm this explanation. In May 1941 over half the bombs dropped by Bomber Command fell in the country, away from villages, towns, and cities.[69]

Suspicions that that might be the case had produced two tactical changes in July. The practice of blind bombing on ETA through heavy cloud was suspended, crews being told to attack instead 'any ... town or built-up area' they could see. The instruction to bomb from 16,000 feet or more, adopted in April but not always followed, was also rescinded once it was realized that, from that height, crews could not 'recognise even the target area.' Pilots were directed to fly lower, in order to pick out their precise aiming points; and if that proved impossible they were to bomb from a height which would allow them to hit 'the particular town in or near which' the aiming point was situated. It was acknowledged that these aiming points might include town squares, churches, or municipal buildings even when, for example, railway marshalling yards or road junctions were the objective of the attack.[70]

This renewed slippage towards area bombing did not go unnoticed. Slessor, for one, warned High Wycombe that it would not 'get away with it'; crews could not be expected to put themselves at risk to hit a specific target when the aiming point was not that target. For his part, Air Vice-Marshal A.T. Harris (Slessor's predecessor at No 5 Group and now DCAS) was concerned not only that embarking on an area campaign directed primarily against German morale was 'a counsel of despair, based on the previous failure of night bombing and the breakdown of the theory of precision attacks,' but also that it 'implied an unbounded optimism ... about what could be achieved at this moment.' With the evidence against Bomber Command's effectiveness mounting, however, the army and navy agreed for the first time in the summer of 1941 that Portal might be right – that the weight of bombs dropped on Germany, not their specific location, was what was going to be important in the long run. 'We must destroy the foundations upon which the [German] war machine rests,' the chiefs of staff declared: 'the economy which feeds it, the morale which sustains it, the supplies which nourish it, and the hopes of victory which inspire it.'[71]

The case for area bombing was confirmed by the findings of D.M. Butt, a civilian member of the War Cabinet staff whose report on Bomber Command's operations, presented in August 1941, became a seminal document in the evolution of bombing strategy. Examining aerial photographs triggered by bomb releases on the hundred-odd raids mounted between 2 June and 25 July, Butt concluded that on average no more than one sortie in five bombed within five miles of the correct target, while over the Ruhr on dark or cloudy nights perhaps only one bomber in ten got within five miles of the objective. Industrial haze – smog – was the major culprit in the Ruhr's especially disheartening statistics. Not yet a true conurbation, the major cities in the valley were nevertheless close to each other and they shared several confusing characteristics. Belching forth smoke and well protected by Flak, all were railway towns bordering rivers or canals. Given any combination of cloud, darkness, fatigue, fear, and navigation error, as well as the understandable inclination of bomber crews to believe they were where they were supposed to be, one city could easily be mistaken for another.[72]

Crews who knew where they were and what to look for should not have been so easily fooled, particularly outside the Ruhr. 'This part of Europe is crisscrossed with some large rivers which are easy to pick out in the moonlight,' one navigator would recall, mentioning the Rhine, Ems, Weser, Elbe, and Spee, and because his bomb-aimer 'was very good at map reading ... he could easily recognize those rivers, their bends and tributaries, and I could rely on an accurate pinpoint from him.' But the moon was not always shining; not everyone was a good map-reader; and until early 1942, when specialist bomb-aimers were added to crews (replacing the second pilot, by then considered a luxury), the observer was over-worked.[*] He had 'more than enough to do ... to get the aircraft within a few miles of the target ... Apart from all the other difficulties ... the work he had done as a navigator left him no time to get his

---

[*] Hampden crews at this time comprised one pilot, an observer, and two wireless operator/air gunners. Wellingtons carried two pilots, an observer, two wireless operator/air gunners, and one air gunner. More highly trained specialist navigators replaced observers in the fall of 1942. There was even greater specialization in Halifax and Lancaster crews, which, along with the required number of gunners, normally comprised a pilot, navigator, wireless operator, air bomber, and flight engineer.

eyes conditioned to the darkness, which he would have to do before trying to spot the aiming point.'[73]

An RCAF observer serving in an RAF squadron provided some answers based on his experience of operations in August. Despite the dangers involved in obtaining the necessary fixes – it took about two minutes of straight and level flight to obtain one good sight, and about five such observations to fix one's position – more observers had to learn to use astro-navigation, something taught in Canadian BCATP schools but not everywhere else. Beyond that, Pilot Officer Allan Fawley had learned that he needed an aiming point he could see clearly and trust, and urged that 'crack' crews be selected as the fire-raising force. Finally, he thought that squadrons and groups should regularly be given particular objectives of their own, so they could learn to memorise the landmarks on the way. When small targets (and the stars) could not be seen, however, Fawley could do no better than to recommend the bombing of large areas based on ETA, in order to cause at least some damage.[74]

Although it had been decided that larger fires must be set, the better to mark the target, the time was not yet ripe for all of Fawley's observations and ideas to be shared and implemented. Instead, the AOC of No 4 Group proposed that High Wycombe insist on more detailed and critical post-raid debriefings to instil determination and discipline among the crews. Otherwise, he argued, 'some of them would take less trouble in finding their particular objectives.' This follow-up would entail increased reliance on bombing photographs as evidence of satisfactory performance; but it also meant that intelligence officers had to be warned against accepting statements they 'would like to accept' and against asking leading questions likely to 'invite an affirmative answer.'[75]

This was one of the first occasions when the dedication of bomber crews to their task was questioned, but given the impossibility of exercising direct operational control over individual crews, Air Vice-Marshal Carr's suggestions seemed reasonable enough. Nevertheless, his memorandum did not address the central problem of night bombing put forward in the Butt report – that crews were having difficulty coming within a five-mile radius of their aiming point whenever flying conditions were less than ideal. And if they did find the target, their average bombing error was about half a mile. No amount of dedication would enable crews to see landmarks or stars through cloud, and greater determination would offset only some of the limitations of bombsights then in use.

The main hope for the future, therefore, lay in technological advance and, in the late summer of 1941, there was room for some optimism in that regard. The Mark XIV bombsight, then undergoing tests, needed only good wind readings to manipulate automatically data relating to air speed, target height above sea level, atmospheric pressure, and the terminal velocity of the main bomb being carried to reduce the average error (on test flights) to as little as sixty yards from a height of 10,000 feet. (Over Germany in 1943, however, errors of two to three hundred yards would be 'the common order' from the same altitude – and more from higher up.) More importantly, on 18 August 1941 the Air Ministry decided that a radio-navigation aid, code-named Gee, was ready for operational use, and a week later instructions were issued to fit it to bomber aircraft on the factory assembly line, beginning no later than December. The Telecommunications Research Establishment responsible for Gee was also intensifying its work on a second navigation aid called Oboe.[76]

The sooner both these navigation aids appeared the better, as little was going to be accomplished from raids like two flown by No 405 Squadron in late August. Sent to Kiel on the 19th/20th, its crews ran into a series of thunderstorms over the North Sea and could only guess they had reached land, close to Sylt, near the Danish-German border, by the heavy Flak they encountered. All but one crew reported they had attacked the target (judging from their time of arrival and what they could discern of the Flak dispositions), but none saw results, not even the crew that dropped down to 4000 feet. The crew that did not attack Kiel 'toured Schleswig-Holstein for half an hour' looking for something on which to drop their bombs, but eventually gave up and returned to base. Kiel reported little damage and no casualties.[77]

Three nights later the target was Mannheim, but the weather was so bad that, with one exception, the crews observed 'no land or water features' near the target. Although all five claimed hits on the city and reported there was 'little doubt that the target area was bombed with success,' their photographs showed 'only cloud' and that 'no fires of importance' had been started. German records indicate that a total of six high-explosive bombs struck the city, badly damaging one house and injuring one air-raid worker.[78]

15

The Offensive at Risk,
Fall 1941–Spring 1942

There was no chance, as the summer of 1941 turned to autumn, that the bombing of Germany would be suspended altogether, but the operations of Bomber Command came under increasingly harsh scrutiny following the revelations of the Butt report. Sir Richard Peirse had to admit that the number of aircraft reaching the target was 'appallingly low,' and as an initial step to improve things he urged his group commanders to 'take a personal grip' to 'kill ... complacency' – the second time in just a few weeks that Bomber Command's disappointing performance was linked to a lack of intensity and dedication on the part of its crews.[1]

Valid as Peirse's criticisms may have been, some – including J.C. Slessor – believed that the recent strictures against bringing bombs back to England, even if the target could not be seen, had contributed to the indifference. These restrictions merely reinforced the impression already held by many crews that it was sufficient to 'pitch hundreds of tons into open country' with little concern for accurate navigation. Bomber Command's senior air staff officer (SASO), Air Vice-Marshal R.H.M. Saundby, sympathized with Slessor, but he knew that Peirse could not be budged from his position. If the primary objective could not be located, the alternates given in their briefings, 'any good-looking built-up area in Germany' or certain approved targets in occupied territory, would be acceptable substitutes.[2]

Interpreting these instructions permissively, crews could easily justify sorties which went nowhere near the main objective. Accordingly, there is little wonder that when RAF scientists extended Butt's research in the fall of 1941 they duplicated his results. Two-thirds of the bomb-release photographs showing ground detail had been taken between four and forty miles from the assigned target, while over the Ruhr, even on bright, clear nights, the best to be hoped for was that 30 per cent of the attacking force would arrive within five miles of the aiming point. When weather conditions were bad, or there was no moon, the figure fell to 15 per cent. In raids against Berlin, where there was less smog and fewer large cities nearby to cause confusion, results were marginally better, while those for targets on the coast were almost twice as good.[3]

Weather conditions were clearly an important variable in these results, but everyone anticipated that the electronic navigation aids then being developed would eventually lead to a substantial rise in the number of aircraft reaching the target. In the meantime, the extremely effective 4-lb incendiary bomb just making its appearance would have to suffice as the only way of enhancing prospects of finding, marking, and damaging the objective. Larger, fiercer fires, started in the right places, would not only attract more of the attacking force to the target area but would also produce more widespread destruction than scattered bursts of high-explosive.[4] Still uncomfortable with the idea of area attacks, however, and wary of German decoys, Peirse ignored instructions to experiment with large-scale incendiary raids and continued to mount operations against transportation targets when good weather was forecast; against industrial areas (but without increasing the proportion of incendiary bombs) when it was not; and on a scale he considered practical – about five sorties a month per aircraft, often in small packets. In addition, to spread the German defences as well as to cause the widest possible alarm, he usually selected two primary objectives on those nights when Bomber Command went out in strength.[5]

Once it returned to night operations during the last week of September 1941, No 408 Squadron was most often employed against transportation targets and specific war industries. But despite favourable weather forecasts, raids on Karlsruhe, Hamburg, Essen, Hüls, and Mannheim were all hindered by cloud, haze, or fog, and consequently failed to live up to expectations. The last two operations in October were probably the most frustrating. On the 29/30th, ten RCAF crews joined thirty-five others for an imaginative attack on Schipol (Amsterdam) airport, where German bombers (recently returned from a raid on England) were parked: but the weather was so bad, with gale-force winds, heavy cloud, snow, and sleet, that the target could not be identified and, since there were no authorized alternates in the area, most crews returned with their bombs still aboard. Again, on Hallowe'en, ten crews made for the Blohm and Voss shipyards in Hamburg, but only three saw the docks through cloud, the rest bombing the city centre or outlying communities.[6]

No 405 Squadron, meanwhile, had sent eight aircraft to Berlin on 7/8 September, and several crews reported seeing their 'actual aiming points.' They may not have been exaggerating, as four factories were damaged and 2800 civilians lost their homes. Turin, in northern Italy, was attacked next, with the intention of exploiting the 'mercurial temperament' of Germany's ally. The Canadians enjoyed a magnificent view of the Alps on their outward flight, but they found the target blanketed by cloud and could only bomb the glow from fires started by earlier arrivals. Raids on Frankfurt, Hamburg, Stettin, and Essen followed over the next three weeks, and then, on 12/13 and 14/15 October, they participated in two large attacks on Nuremburg, ideological home of the Nazi party, an important railway centre, and the site of diesel, electronics, and ball-bearing factories. The first, mounted in good weather, seemed to be a complete success, with 'huge blazes' being reported around the railway yards, but according to German records very little damage had been done. The heaviest bombing had actually occurred at Lauingen, sixty-five miles away, and at Lauffen, ninety-five miles distant and near Stuttgart's decoy fire – two towns which, like Nuremburg, were located on wide rivers and might easily have been mistaken for that city. Thick cloud, snow, and icing dominated the second raid and, as might be expected, results were poorer still, two-thirds of the force (but none from 405 Squadron) deciding to make for alternate targets.[7]

No 408 Squadron, after its return to night operations, lost only one of ninety-five sorties until the end of October, but No 405's losses – three of ninety-three, or 3.2 per cent – placed it on the same curve that now applied to all Bomber Command, showing an increase from 2.2 per cent in early summer to 3.5 per cent by mid-fall. When those aircraft severely damaged and either written off or requiring extensive repair were added to the tally, the trend was even more disturbing. It almost doubled from 3.9 per cent of sorties in May to 7.7 per cent in August. Furthermore, both loss and damaged rates continued to be at their highest during the poor weather favoured for area operations, largely because of the many accidents that occurred when flying conditions were bad. In short, Bomber Command's least effective raids were now also its most costly and, instead of lasting the predicted twenty-three sorties, operational aircraft were averaging only eleven.[8]

Such losses compounded the problems created by shortfalls in aircraft production and shortcomings in the aircrew training system. So long as navigation remained as poor as ever, the only way to increase the amount of explosives falling on the target was to increase the amount carried each night – 15 per cent of 500 tons hitting an objective was better than 15 per cent of 100 tons. Larger aircraft, with bigger payloads, were an obvious remedy, but complications in the Short Stirling, Handley-Page Halifax, and Avro Manchester/Lancaster programs – all heavy bombers with larger bomb-carrying capacities – were delaying their appearance as front-line aircraft.[9]

When, therefore, the government decided in late September 1941 that Bomber Command must grow, in order to increase the tonnage dropped on the Ruhr, the Ministry of Aircraft Production (MAP) again found it convenient to prolong and extend the production of current types rather than to convert factories to the manufacture of the latest designs. Unhappily, however, the need to replace damaged and missing machines continued to eat up the resources intended for expansion, while the British aircraft industry, never as efficient as MAP wanted to believe, continued to lose ground in its effort to meet the projected output of established designs.[10]

Short of its full strength by 316 heavy and medium bombers in mid-August 1941, and with production forecast to be in arrears by another 425 machines at the end of the year, the Air Ministry had to cut back High Wycombe's immediate expansion plans even before submitting those for long-term growth to the Cabinet. Thus the formation of additional medium- and heavy-bomber squadrons, including those promised to the RCAF by the Ralston-Sinclair agreement, would have to be postponed: only forty-eight could be counted on to be operational by the end of the year instead of the seventy-five originally planned. As a result, Air Vice-Marshal L.F. Stevenson, senior RCAF officer overseas, advised Ottawa that, rather than wait for the necessary aircraft to be completed, BCATP graduates intended for these units should be sent to the RAF where they could gain experience – subject to recall to newly formed Canadian squadrons when they were required. In the event, only two RCAF squadrons, Nos 419 and 420, were added to High Wycombe's order of battle before the end of the year, and the Air Ministry's willingness to break up crews in order to exercise that recall provision was never tested.[11]

Slowing down Bomber Command's rate of expansion was, at least in one respect, a blessing. By the fall of 1941 Peirse was running short of experienced aircrew, particularly pilots, not only because of casualties and the transfer of some squadrons to the Middle East and Coastal Command, but also because of changes in the training system. When expansion had seemed likely in the spring, and the flow of crews to Bomber Command needed to be accelerated, the syllabus at operational training units had been curtailed with the aim of producing pilots in as little as six weeks. But the experiment was not a success. Graduates of the abbreviated syllabus were not adequately trained for bad-weather flying and their inexperience was a major factor in the elevated accident rate observed since late summer. In other words, by late 1941 there was a fundamental incongruity between what Peirse was being asked to do and the resources he was given to do it with. As losses outstripped the supply of aircraft and properly prepared crews, the more likely Bomber Command was to fail. Moreover, given the fact that inexperienced crews tended to be killed, injured, or captured at higher rates, the process of self-destruction could only accelerate with each attempt.[12]

Here was a powerful argument for a strategy of conservation. The prime minister had raised just such a possibility in mid-August, when the disheartening conclusions contained in the Butt report were first circulated, but Sir Charles Portal had successfully parried his thrust at that time and then, through the director of bombing operations (DBOps), had argued that the area offensive against selected German cities should actually be intensified.[13] 'It must be realised,' Air Commodore J.W. Baker explained: 'that attack on morale is not a matter of pure killing, although fear of death is unquestionably an important factor. It is rather the general dislocation of industrial and social life arising from damage to industrial plant, dwelling houses, shops, utility and transportation services ... from interference with all that goes to make up the general activity of a community.'

Basing his plan for the destruction of Germany's forty-three largest cities on evidence accumulated from the Luftwaffe's raid on Coventry in November 1940, Baker concluded that all commercial and social activity within any city could be reduced to nil within a six-month period if one ton of bombs was delivered accurately for each 800 inhabitants. Allowing for known navigation and bombing errors, weather and wastage, Baker calculated that Bomber Command would have to carry 75,000 tons of high-explosive to Germany in order to achieve the desired result. That would require a front-line force of 250 squadrons equipped with 4,000 heavy bombers – a seven-fold jump from the thirty-four night-bomber squadrons on the current order of battle – each flying six sorties a month.[14]

Although the prime minister was reconciled to enormous increases in production which came close to meeting these requirements – 11,000 machines were to be manufactured in Britain by July 1943, and another 5500 would come from the United States – Baker's proposal went too far and it momentarily rekindled the doubts Churchill had expressed about bombing just a month before. The prime minister was especially unhappy with the putative mathematical precision of the arguments put forward by Baker and with their underlying premise that 'bombing by itself will be a decisive factor in the present war.' 'On the contrary,' Churchill responded, 'all that we have learnt since the war began shows that its effects, both physical and moral, are greatly exaggerated. There is no doubt that the British people have been stimulated and strengthened by the attack made upon them so far. Secondly, it seems very likely that the ground defences and night fighters will overtake the Air attack. Thirdly, in calculating the number of bombers necessary to achieve hypothetical and indefinite tasks, it should be noted that only a quarter of our bombs hit the target.' Improving this last statistic by a factor of two, he added, would halve the size of the force required, thereby easing pressures on the aircraft industry. 'The most we can see is that [bombing] will be a heavy and, I trust, a seriously increasing annoyance [to the enemy].'[15]

On 7 October, however, for reasons best known to himself, Churchill suddenly acknowledged that not only was bombing 'the most potent method of impairing the enemy's morale we can use at the present time,' but also that Bomber Command deserved to expand 'on the largest possible scale.' The opposition to area (and fire) bombing within the air staff melted away shortly thereafter, a change that may have been prompted by the War Cabinet meeting of 20 October, which revived the early 1941 idea of allocating first priority to the Battle of the Atlantic and attacks on U-boat bases – something against which almost all senior RAF officers could unite. In any case, on 25 October, the same day that the Air Ministry was asked to give special attention to Hamburg, Kiel, Bremen, and Wilhelmshaven, High Wycombe was invited to undertake a massive fire raid (by 1941 standards) involving as many as 60,000 incendiary bombs. If results were 'fully satisfactory,' Peirse was told, 'it may well be that we shall find ourselves able to undertake the systematic destruction of German towns at a much earlier date than we have been able so far to hope for.'[16]

If external support were needed for such an enterprise, it came, conveniently, from the *Sunday Express* which, on 2 November, commented sharply on Bomber Command's recent lack of 'persistence, regularity, and enterprise against targets in Germany. Berlin has been off the RAF visiting list for six weeks ... There is a tendency in official circles to blame the weather for decreased RAF activity over Germany. Yet no one would dare suggest that the ... Halifax and Stirling bombers [then entering squadron service] are fair-weather planes or accuse their crews of less fortitude and resolution than those who manned the Wellingtons and Whitleys a year ago.'

Five days later Berlin was attacked despite a weather forecast so miserable that – at Slessor's insistence – No 5 Group (including No 408 Squadron) was withdrawn from the operation and sent to Cologne instead. Heavy cloud, icing, hail, sleet, and electrical storms plagued the crews who made their way to the German capital, where the enemy defences proved to be alert despite the weather. Twenty-one machines were lost, 12.4 per cent of those dispatched, and only half of the crews who returned claimed to have found even the outskirts of the city. Seven public or commercial buildings were damaged, fourteen houses destroyed, and eleven people killed.[17] No 405 Squadron's experience was typical. Ten crews took off for Berlin, five attacked the general vicinity of the target, and four chose alternates at Kiel and Wilhelmshaven. One aircraft went missing, three were damaged, and one crash-landed on its return to England. All in all, the squadron diarist concluded, the operation was 'practically abortive.'[18]

Flight Lieutenant J.E. Fauquier (of whom we will hear more in this book) had been uneasy about the operation from the first few minutes of his briefing, when the meteorologist had been 'nervous and seemed unable to make up his mind about the wind velocity for the return to base.' Although everything went well on the way out, Fauquier soon found that, because of the overcast, 'we had nothing but dead reckoning and forecast winds to get us to the target.'

Finally, we reached the point where we thought, and hoped, Berlin lay ... dropped our bombs and turned for home. It wasn't long before I realised we were in trouble because the winds had increased greatly in strength and were almost dead ahead. Eventually, I lost height down to a few hundred feet – to avoid icing conditions and to save fuel since the head wind would be less strong.

I have seen the North Sea in many moods but never more ferocious than that night. Huge waves of solid green water were lifted from the surface and carried hundreds of feet by the wind. After what seemed like hours in these appalling conditions I realised we were unlikely to make base. I had little or no fuel left and told the crew to take up ditching positions ... It was then I saw briefly one of those wonderful homing lights and made a bee-line straight for it.

Landing at a non-operational airfield amidst stakes erected to thwart enemy invasion landings, Fauquier and his crew were immediately surrounded by members of the Home Guard quite prepared to lock them up until contact could be made with station Pocklington. 'Utterly fatigued, half frozen and disgusted,' Fauquier, like most of the rest of No 405 Squadron, bitterly resented 'being launched on a major operation against the German Capital in weather totally unfitted to the task.'[19]

No 5 Group suffered no losses over Cologne, but the aiming point was just as difficult to find as it was at Berlin and the bombing was equally erratic. Only eight high-explosive and sixty incendiary bombs fell on the city. At Mannheim, meanwhile, seven of fifty-three Wellingtons from Nos 1 and 3 Groups were lost, while nine of ninety-three aircraft on minor operations went missing. Overall losses for the night totalled thirty-seven, 9.4 per cent of sorties dispatched.[20]

That was enough for the prime minister, who immediately called Peirse to Chequers. Maintaining that the previous night's casualties were unnecessary and could not be justified, particularly in light of the weather over Germany, Churchill berated the AOC-in-C and directed him to conserve his force for the present. He made the same point to Sir Archibald Sinclair and to Portal: 'I have several times in Cabinet deprecated forcing the night bombing of Germany without due regard to weather conditions. There is no particular point at this time in bombing Berlin. The losses sustained last week were most grievous. We cannot afford losses on that scale ... Losses which are acceptable in a battle or for some decisive military objective, ought not to be incurred merely as a matter of routine. There is no need to fight the weather and the enemy at the same time. It is now the duty of both Fighter and Bomber Commands to re-gather their strength for the Spring.'[21]

Despite the pressure they had applied to Peirse, the under-secretary of state and the CAS protested bitterly that they had not 'forced' the operation and that neither of them regarded the bombing of Germany as a matter of mere routine. Industry, transportation, and morale were 'decisive military objectives,' well worth the cost. But the prime minister was adamant and the policy of conservation stood. Although bombing would not be suspended altogether, operations would not take place 'if weather conditions were unfavourable or if our aircraft were likely to be exposed to extreme hazards.'[22]

Portal's gambit – indeed, all of his twisting and turning since August – had failed. Conservation meant that, for the next few months at least, there would be no sustained area offensive against enemy morale. But if the alternative to doing nothing was to strike at specific targets, something had to be done about the lackadaisical approach to navigation that still permeated much of Bomber Command. How else could one explain the performance of one No 5 Group crew, sent to Düsseldorf, which bombed the vicinity of Dunkirk?[23]

It was also important to forge ahead with production of the new families of bombs developed to replace the now-discredited General Purpose series: the relatively thin-skinned, cylindrical (and therefore 'unaimable') High Capacity blast bombs, including the 2000-pounder and 4000-pounder 'cookie,' and the considerably more aerodynamic (and consequently more accurate) Medium Capacity series, with stronger casings and better able to penetrate buildings but which sacrificed only a little in terms of blast effect.[24] Profound improvements in navigation, it was agreed, depended on the electronic aids originally promised for November and December, but the introduction of the Gee radio-navigation aid had to be delayed because of production problems, while Oboe, the subject of research since June, was still under development and would not be ready until late 1942 at the earliest. A third possibility, modification of the downward-looking centimetric Air to Surface Vessel (ASV) radar so it would 'picture' the ground below, was raised in November; but even if the project proved feasible (as it eventually did, producing the device known as H2S), this could only be a long-term solution. In the interim, therefore, more conventional steps would have to be taken.[25]

The net to identify these measures was cast very wide indeed, reaching not only the highest echelons in Whitehall and at High Wycombe, but also every observer in Bomber Command. The evidence accumulated was sobering in the extreme. Along with faulty planning, there seemed to be flaws in the training system so serious that they threatened to prevent any improvement in navigation standards. Observers trained in Britain, for example, still had little experience of night-flying before their posting to operational squadrons; they received next to no instruction in astro-navigation, a deficiency that left them practically helpless when it came to checking their position whenever the ground could not be seen. Observers trained overseas, by comparison – and particularly those who came from Canada – knew astro-navigation but were so poor at map-reading they could not make proper use of landmarks to find the target on moonlit nights.[26]

As Wing Commander S.O. Bufton, the newly appointed deputy director of bomber operations, explained, however, there were no guarantees that the benefits of more rigorous and thorough training would be felt uniformly throughout Bomber Command so long as squadrons (and, indeed, in some cases, individual crews) were independent entities, left to mount operations as they saw fit. It was essential, therefore, that High Wycombe assert its authority and centralize control over the bomber offensive to give it coherent direction. This meant not only 'collecting, sifting, trying and putting into general practice those ideas which emerge in squadrons from time to time' – in short, introducing a coordinated tactical system which would be adhered to by all.[27]

Bufton had solid backing for his criticism, having recently compared operational procedures in Nos 10 and 405 Squadrons. The former, with long experience of night-bombing, used flares in abundance to mark and illuminate the target, and crews who were absolutely certain they had found the aiming point fired red Verey lights to attract others to it. In No 405, in contrast, flares were rarely used, crews preferring to navigate by landmarks until they reached a point from which they could make a timed run to the target – and, since landmarks were frequently misidentified, the run itself became meaningless. The Canadians would do better, it was clear, if they adopted No 10 Squadron's tactics, but Bomber Command's uncoordinated way of doing things neither guaranteed that its procedures would be communicated to other units nor ensured that they would be adopted when they were. Perhaps, Bufton suggested, a specialist target-marking force was required.[28]

All four night-bomber group commanders agreed that more had to be done in the way of marking and illumination, but only Air Vice-Marshals R.D. Oxland (No 1 Group) and C.R. Carr (No 4 Group) were amenable to the creation of a special force. Both Slessor (No 5 Group) and Air Vice-Marshal J.E.A. Baldwin (No 3 Group) feared that morale and overall expertise would suffer if the best personnel were skimmed off into an élite formation. Slessor, Baldwin, and Bufton himself were also increasingly inclined to believe that the root of the problem lay in the debilitating influence of area bombing, which, by its very nature, did not demand high standards of target identification and bomb-aiming and therefore had weakened crews' 'determination to find and hit targets.' This was particularly so when aiming points were selected 'that bore little obvious relation to any military objective.' Finally, the effect of Flak and night-fighters had to be taken into account, as it was clear that when a pilot had to take evasive action his observer was rarely able to chart the changes in course.[29]

The two most obvious ways to protect bombers against Flak and fighters (adding more armour in the first case, and more powerful defensive weapons in the second) were still rejected because they involved too great a sacrifice in payload and in the altitudes at which aircraft could fly. Height was especially important, since Flak was more dangerous at lower altitudes and was not to be sacrificed lightly. Indeed, about all that could be offered when the question of bomber defence was discussed in late summer was a promise to 'comb-out' air gunners whose night vision was deficient.[30] For the foreseeable future, then, Bomber Command's main tactic would continue to be to evade rather than fight.

Finding ways around the German defensive system had been relatively easy early in the year. The main night-fighter zone had been limited to the Dutch coast, leaving open flanks in France, Denmark, and northern Germany, while the seachlight and Flak belts behind it, in the Ruhr and around Mannheim, Frankfurt, and Stuttgart, were not radar-directed. Furthermore, bad weather was still a powerful ally. Lacking both airborne interception (AI) radar and de-icing equipment, the majority of the enemy's night-fighters were severely handicapped in poor visibility and did not fly when icing-up was likely.[31]

A new and disturbing picture of General Josef Kammhuber's organization began to emerge over the summer, however – the result of careful monitoring of German radio and radar transmissions, a regular program of reconnaissance flights, and accurate analysis of the information so gathered. It was apparent, for example, that the open flanks in France and Denmark were being closed as the night-fighter zone was extended to Liège in the west and the German-Danish border in the east, while in some places two crews were being allocated to each air-defence box. Würzburg radar, which plotted height, distance, and course, and was therefore suitable for ground-controlled interception (GCI), was appearing not only in the Flak regiments for which it was originally intended, but also in the fighter zone. At the same time, the formerly safe areas in front of, and behind, the main searchlight belts were being patrolled by Dunkelnachtjagd (non-illuminated, or dark night-fighting) interceptors whose pilots operated on a freelance basis, picking out targets silhouetted against the moon or cloud, or revealed by the flames from their exhausts. Finally, point defences combining Flak, fighters, and searchlights were being provided for those cities attacked most frequently – Berlin, Hamburg, Bremen, Kiel, Cologne, Düsseldorf, Frankfurt, Darmstadt, and Munich.[32]

'A few miles from the coast,' one air gunner recalled, 'Germany seemed a belt of light from north to south,' with searchlights in groups of ten and fifteen or more probing the darkness. 'At first we felt no aircraft could penetrate the barricade of lights, anti-aircraft guns and fighters.' Although he survived the raid on Essen, 'the trip had been four hours and forty minutes on a razor's edge,'

GERMAN NIGHT FIGHTER DEFENCES
AND BOMBER COMMAND

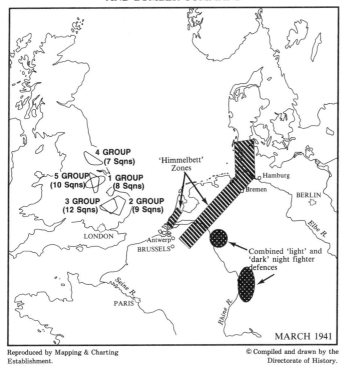

4 GROUP
(7 Sqns)

'Himmelbett'
Zones

Hamburg

5 GROUP
(10 Sqns)

1 GROUP
(8 Sqns)

Bremen

BERLIN

3 GROUP
(12 Sqns)

2 GROUP
(9 Sqns)

Elbe R.

LONDON

Antwerp°
BRUSSELS°

Combined 'light' and
'dark' night fighter
defences

Seine R.

PARIS

Rhine R.

MARCH 1941

Reproduced by Mapping & Charting
Establishment.

© Compiled and drawn by the
Directorate of History.

a description indicative of the constant strain under which bomber crews operated.[33]

Weaknesses were identified as well. Even if the number of fighters assigned to the air-defence boxes was doubled or trebled, controllers still seemed to handle only one at a time and each box appeared to stand alone, neither supporting nor receiving help from its neighbours. In time, the reasons for these shortcomings were also discovered. Beyond the fact that Kammhuber was, himself, wedded to the idea that successful night defence demanded strict control from the ground, his system was influenced by the nature and amount of equipment made available to him. Because there was no IFF (identification friend or foe) link between fighters and Würzburgs, the ground controllers could not determine who was who simply by looking at their cathode-ray screens: and that, more than anything else, accounted for the fact that only one interception, by one fighter, was attempted at any one time; that fighters seldom strayed from their own box; and that freelance interceptors rarely entered the controlled night-fighting zones. By standardizing and systematizing procedures, Kammhuber had ensured a crude mission profile which would help his ground controllers distinguish between friendly and hostile aircraft.[34]

It did not require a complete understanding of why such shortcomings existed to exploit them, however, and the air staff was able to deduce an ap-

GERMAN NIGHT FIGHTER DEFENCES
AND BOMBER COMMAND

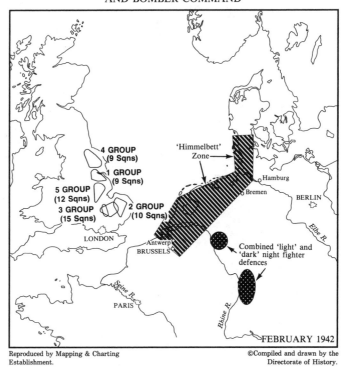

Reproduced by Mapping & Charting
Establishment.

©Compiled and drawn by the
Directorate of History.

propriate response long before all these details were known. If routes and timings were chosen so as to pass a large bomber force through a minimum number of air-defence boxes in the shortest possible time, the enemy could be overwhelmed. But the AOC-in-C was not ready to impose any such solution on Bomber Command as a whole: not only was it contrary to the spirit of decentralized control which dominated Peirse's approach to his job, but it also seemed to ask too much of his crews, especially given the congestion likely on takeoff. The matter of increased concentration was therefore left to each group to decide.[35]

Concentration was also opposed by those at High Wycombe and the Air Ministry who feared that a compact bomber force would be an easy target for the enemy's Dunkelnachtjagd crews, and even more inviting prey for fighters equipped with airborne interception (AI) radar, which was expected to appear at any moment. In fact, these fears were premature, as experiments with the Lichtenstein B/C AI had only just begun. While it temporarily prevented Bomber Command from fully recognizing the benefits of concentration, however, such sensitivity to the potential of electronic warfare was no bad thing in the long run because it hastened British research on possible countermeasures. Work was already underway to develop a tail-mounted device that would give warning of the approach of AI-using fighters. (Under the codename Monica, it would became standard equipment in the summer of 1943.) Alternatively, radars might be jammed by strips of metallic foil dropped by the leading aircraft of an attacking force. For the moment, however, that idea was rejected for fear that the Germans might use it against British radars, too.[36]

Some procedures that were adopted owed little to the laws of physics. Throughout 1941, but particularly over the summer, it was reported that the enemy's searchlights were doused whenever a bomber's IFF was switched on. On 28/29 August, for example, No 405 Squadron recorded 'IFF used a lot, but mixed reports as to its efficacy, though [Wellington No] 137 used IFF with immediate effect vicinity of Rheydt.'[37] There was no scientific basis for this phenomenon and every reason to avoid prolonged IFF transmissions over enemy territory, where fighters could home in on them. Yet, despite having issued firm instructions against unfettered use of IFF once the enemy coast had been crossed, High Wycombe eventually succumbed to the popular belief that something was happening and, on 1 September, allowed that IFF could be switched on briefly whenever 'embarrassment from enemy searchlights and Flak is being experienced.'[38]

Happy that officialdom had confirmed their irrational convictions, many crews did not take seriously the warning to avoid prolonged use. Describing the 10/11 October raid on Essen, for example, the diarist of No 405 Squadron noted 'IFF on and off used by all captains over the target area with some impression of success, but Q, using it continually over Holland on return and flying at 1,000 [feet] enjoyed complete freedom from both searchlights and Flak.' The most likely reason for 'Q's' easy passage was not its crew's use of IFF, however, but rather that Sergeant V.E. Sutherland was flying so low that he passed over searchlight and Flak batteries before they could react or, by the fickle fortune of war, happened to fly between them. Nevertheless it is easy to imagine how, in the mess or the debriefing room, the talk was not about low-flying or lucky misses but the searchlight-dousing properties of IFF; and how, in time, these alleged properties became an article of faith. It should come as no surprise, therefore, that at Emden, ten days later, John Fauquier switched his IFF on and off 'at one second intervals' and reported that not once was he coned by searchlights.[39]

As time went on, more and more crews used it continuously, and by the late spring of 1942 this practice was officially sanctioned in a No 4 Group primer on tactics. Then, in June, the Air Ministry approved a modification of the IFF set – the J-switch – that allowed it to radiate continuously for one half-second in every twelve. So much for the danger that the enemy was homing on to electronic transmissions, but perhaps the strengthening of morale was worth the risk. 'We plunged on, now with both turrets useless,' was how Pilot Officer George Sweanor described his first raid (to Kiel) with No 419 Squadron, 'while Flak and searchlights increased ominously in intensity.' Suddenly a powerful blue beam (the white light appears blue when it locks on to you) caught us, and ten more beams arced over to join it. We were blinded! Pat shut his eyes, and tried to weave by instinct while I remembered the boffin and his new device. I groped my way back to the panel, felt for the [IFF] switch, and began flicking it on and off. We were being flung about the sky by exploding shells ... Then, suddenly, all searchlights arced away. *"My God – it works!"* We shouted in disbelief as our eyes slowly adjusted to the darkness again.' In fact, the IFF had not worked at all. Following some rewiring on the navigator's instrument panel, Sweanor had actually been switching his landing lights on and off – and may, in the process, have persuaded the searchlight crew that his was a German machine.[40]

Concerned at the still-rising casualty rates, Sir Richard Peirse knew that the makeshift use of IFF was not enough and on 22 October he asked Portal to approve a concerted effort to jam all known enemy radars and fighter-control broadcasts. Taking a longer view, the Air Ministry replied that it was too early to begin widespread electronic counter-measures for fear they would be compromised before they were truly effective, and it was suggested instead that High Wycombe take another look at concentration. Peirse was as reluctant as ever and would not issue orders to that effect; but besides directing groups to reduce their time over the target, he did suggest they might experiment if they wanted to. However, the degree of concentration he proposed – no more than a hundred aircraft an hour over the target – was so low that some scoffed it was hardly concentration at all, and certainly not enough to saturate the German defences. Doubling Peirse's figure was, in Wing Commander Bufton's view, closer to what was needed.[41]

Quite unexpectedly, the generally lackadaisical compliance with Peirse's relaxed and permissive proposal unleashed the process of centralization in Bomber Command. Within seven days, having discovered that times over target were not, in fact, being reduced, the AOC-in-C brought his own staff into the coordination of raids to a greater extent than ever before. While each group was still free to develop its own plan of attack, these plans now had to be transmitted to High Wycombe for review and, if necessary, for modification based in part on the latest wind and weather forecasts. Once they were approved, no deviation was permitted.[42]

Circumstances dictated, however, that these new operational procedures would have only a minor impact until a new bombing policy emerged in February 1942. Abysmal weather and Churchill's demand for conservation were combining to limit not only the number of raids but also their size. Operations occurred on just fifty-four nights between 10 November 1941 and 22 February 1942, and more than two hundred aircraft were dispatched on only four occasions, the usual scale being just less than half that number. Few deep penetrations were attempted, and not once was the whole front-line strength of Bomber Command committed to battle. The total night loss rate during this period amounted to 2.5 per cent of sorties flown, a welcome reduction of one full point from the previous summer and early fall, but some raids still produced casualty figures that could only be categorized as alarming. On 30 November/1 December, for example, thirteen of 181 aircraft sent to Hamburg failed to return, 7.2 per cent of those dispatched, while a small raid on Münster on 28/29 January 1942 claimed five of eighty-four bombers, 6 per cent of the total.[43]

More acceptable results came on 28/29 December when eighty-six Wellingtons were sent to Wilhelmshaven and eighty-one Hampdens to Hüls. The main railway station and yards at Wilhelmshaven were extensively damaged and the chemical factories in Hüls hit hard, all for the loss of five aircraft (2.9 per cent), four of them Hampdens.[44] One of the Hampdens, flown by Flight Lieutenant S.B. Brackenbury of 408 Squadron, was shot down in a letter-perfect Helle Nachtjagd interception facilitated by radar-directed searchlights.

The moon was nearly full, and vis[ibility] was very good. About 30 min[ute]s away from the target, Hüls, we could see a large fire directly on track, we identified canal that led up to target, and proceeded to glide in from 14,000'. The flak was right over target, and we did a steady glide at 180 miles an hour. The Nav. released his bombs at 9000' and I started to climb. There was a great fire burning. Having climbed to 14000' again we were over searchlight belt. Stray searchlights picked us up but on turning into them, [I] put them off. Then a bluish searchlight picked us up and I couldn't shake it off. I climbed, dived, and did 90 degrees turns, but to no avail. Then more and more searchlights coned me and it was impossible to look out as it was momentarily blinding. There was no flak [but] I warned the crew to look out for fighters. I flew a straight course to get out of the cone. The W[ireless]/Op[erator] reported an a/c on the st[ar]b[oar]d. quarter high. We were still in the searchlights when the fighter attacked ... I heard the guns at the back give a burst and just then a white tracer went by. I turned sharply into the attack and then straighten[ed] up. I called up the crew but there was no answer, the i[nter]/c[om] was OK. The next attack was made shortly [after] and it was in the same quarter high. As soon as I saw the tracer I again turned into it. I could hear the cannon fire hitting the a/c and then saw port engine burst into flames. I pressed the [extinguishing] button, but nothing happened. I called on the i/c but it was u[n]/s[erviceable]. The fuselage behind me was burning, and I think the fire was caused by the flares, which had not been released, having been hit by the cannon fire. The third attack was from the same place. I had no crew to tell me when to take evasive action, so I turned into the attack when I saw tracer. The fourth attack was from the stern. The tracer was going over and by each side, the fuselage was burning, and the engine. I decided to try a crash-land[ing], but at 5000' I decided I couldn't make it. In case any other crew was alive I pushed the call light button then baled out. I saw the trail of flame hit the ground and little red balls rolling on the ground. I lit [sic] safely in a pine tree.[45]

Brackenbury languished in prisoner-of-war camps for the remainder of the war. The three other members of his crew were killed.

The slow pace of the winter's operations are well illustrated in the diaries of Nos 405 and 408 Squadrons. After reasonably successful raids on Wilhelmshaven and Emden in late December, the former flew only eight operations in all January 1942, involving a total of forty-four sorties. Among them, five crews had mechanical failures and brought their bombs back, two could not find the target and did the same, and two returned early. In February the squadron flew only twenty-eight sorties, of which sixteen either jettisoned their bombs or returned with them. A raid on Mannheim carried out on 14/15 February was typical. With cloud cover varying between 7/10ths and 10/10ths, it was 'impossible for captains to identify sufficient ground features [and] no precise information can be given as regards success of attack.' The diarist added, somewhat optimistically, 'it is thought that most captains were over or near the target.'[46] Mannheim, meanwhile, reported only a light raid in which just two buildings were destroyed, fifteen were damaged, and one civilian was wounded.[47]

No 408 Squadron had an even unhappier time. Uprooted from Syerston because of runway construction there, the squadron's flying elements moved first to Balderton in mid-December and then, when its grass fields were found to be too soft, when wet, to support fully loaded Hampdens, the operational component went to North Luffenham, leaving the training flights at Balderton and the administrative staff at Syerston. After a good effort in the 28/29 December raid on Hüls (for which the squadron was congratulated by the AOC), it was scheduled, along with the rest of the largely Hampden-equipped No 5 Group, to be used in daylight raids, under cloud cover and with fighter escort, against French, Dutch, Belgian, and German port facilities. These were routinely called off, however, whenever the predicted cloud or assigned fighter escort did not appear as scheduled. The squadron had no more luck than any other in Operation Fuller (the 'Channel dash' of the German fleet units, recounted in detail in chapters 6 and 12), but, because it had also been involved in night-time minelaying in the North Sea, it was able to share some of the credit for damaging *Scharnhorst* and *Gneisenau*, which hit air-laid mines in Frisian waters before reaching port.[48]

Those mines (code-named Vegetables) had not been laid with *Scharnhorst*, *Gneisenau*, or *Prinze Eugen* in mind. Rather, the damage done to them was a serendipitous by-product of an on-going campaign of aerial mining against coastal shipping (code-named Gardening) in which Bomber Command had been engaged since mid-April 1940. Pre-war plans had originally given Coastal Command responsibility for all mining, but since its Blackburn Bothas and Bristol Beauforts lacked the range to carry the offensive to the Baltic, in the end Bomber Command – and more specifically No 5 Group – was assigned the role of long-range Gardening.[49] The responsibility for siting minefields rested with the Admiralty, and in the beginning the mines (all of them magnetic at this time, ranging between 1000 and 1500 lbs) were sown in heavily used 'choke' points where the water was deep enough (over thirty feet) to prevent their easy recovery. Although technically they could be laid from any height between 400 and 6000 feet, to ensure accuracy most Gardening operations took place at between 1000 and 2000 feet, at an air speed of 180–90 miles per hour.[50]

The initial campaign lasted only until the Blitzkrieg against Western Europe, when No 5 Group was thrown into the Battle of France, and in that time just over one hundred mines were sown – not very many, but enough to cause casualties and to force the Germans to divert resources to their anti-mining effort. Once France collapsed, the group was ordered to resume Gardening, but although more than one thousand mines were laid by the end of the year, sinking eighty-six ships and damaging another ten (for the loss of only thirty-one aircraft), Gardening was never the group's predominant activity. Mining sorties averaged only about one hundred a month and were usually mounted when cloud conditions militated against bombing missions. Because they required long-distance navigation yet resulted in relatively few engagements with enemy aircraft, it was soon realized that Gardening sorties were a good way to introduce new crews to the rigours of operations and the practice was adopted by all groups.[51]

In mid-December 1941, as part of the delayed Bomber Command expansion scheme, the two orginal RCAF squadrons were joined by a third and fourth, Nos 419 and 420. Allocated Wellington Mark IC's pending the appearance of faster and higher-flying Mark III's, 419 Squadron was assigned to Mildenhall, Suffolk, in the No 3 Group area, a prewar field with concrete runways and permanent messes and quarters which it shared with an RAF Stirling squadron. Its first raid was flown on 11 January, when two machines were sent to Brest. No 420, equipped with Hampdens, began forming at Waddington, Lincolnshire, in late December and was declared ready for operations on 21 January, when five aircraft attacked Emden and a sixth dropped mines near Heligoland.[52]

At the outset it had been agreed that a serious effort would be made to post all available RCAF personnel to the new units. No 3 Group, whose AOC was prepared to transfer predominantly Canadian crews from RAF to RCAF squadrons, kept the Air Ministry's promise so far as No 419 was concerned – on 11 January fully 85 per cent of the aircrew were Canadian.[*] However, despite the fact that RCAF graduates of the BCATP had been arriving in Britain by the thousands over the preceding seven months, this exemplary level of Canadianization was not always maintained. While the non-flying proportion rose steadily, the percentage of RCAF aircrew fell to 80.25 per cent on 26 January and to 67 per cent on 11 February before rising to 90 per cent by March. That was good compared with Nos 405 and 408 Squadrons, where the Canadianization rates on 31 December had been only 37 per cent and 31 per cent, repectively; and it was much better than in No 420 Squadron where, on 31 January, only one of sixty-eight aircrew positions was filled by a Canadian – because, it was said, RCAF graduates had not been sent to Hampden OTUs early enough.[53] Canadians may have been arriving in Britain in quantity, but as Slessor, the AOC of No 5 Group explained, they were not being posted to RCAF squadrons largely on account of oversights made by the Air Ministry and Flying Training Command.

---

[*] The corresponding figure for groundcrew and tradesmen was 6 per cent, but the responsibility for posting RCAF groundcrew to RCAF squadrons lay with Ottawa.

This business of the Article 15 Squadrons is awfully difficult, particularly until we can persuade the Air Ministry to post Dominion crews to the right OTUs serving the proper Dominion Squadrons ... What happens at the moment of course is that we get driblets of crews at odd times and they have to go into anywhere where there is a vacancy; subsequently, it is very difficult to move them because it means breaking up crews and usually they are extremely averse to leaving the squadrons with which they have begun their operations.

Slessor, who later observed that the implications of Article XV were both 'senseless' and 'a pity from the broad point of view of Commonwealth unity,' was averse to breaking up crews, particularly if it meant taking Canadians 'away ... from, say, a Manchester or Lancaster Squadron' and posting them to an RCAF Hampden squadron – in which case 'we should never get the heavy Squadrons operational.'[54]

Overseas Headquarters never pressed hard for the breaking-up of formed crews in order to hasten the process of Canadianization, nor even for the transfer of predominantly Canadian crews to RCAF squadrons, but Air Vice-Marshal H. Edwards, the RCAF's AO-in-C Overseas, was not happy with the Air Ministry's apparent inability to post Canadian components (pilots, observers, etc.) to the right OTUs in the appropriate mix and numbers, so they would have a chance to form themselves into all-Canadian crews. Made aware of his dissatisfaction, Air Vice-Marshal J.E.A. Baldwin, who was temporarily acting AOC-in-C of Bomber Command, directed his OTUs to ensure not only that crews with two or more Canadians were posted to RCAF squadrons but that as many crews as possible were 'one hundred per cent Dominion.' The air member for personnel at the Air Ministry, Air Marshal P. Babington, also noted that a special effort must be made to improve the situation. For the future, he added, the only specific problems anticipated related to the supply of observers and wireless operator/air gunners, of whom there seemed to be a temporary shortage.[55]

Edwards thanked the Air Ministry for 'all that you are doing and have done to assist in bringing this perplexing question to a conclusion which will be satisfactory to everyone.' In fact, the AOC of No 4 Group, a New Zealander in the RAF who had one RCAF squadron under his command, was 'very much against the formation of ... all-Canadian squadrons' and, believing mixed units were happier, he told Edwards so. 'I feel that your Canadians miss a lot by being posted to RCAF Squadrons. In RAF Squadrons they mix and operate with English personnel and personnel from the other Dominions, and all get to train and respect each other. The various personnel gain a great deal from their association and assimilate fresh ideas from many parts of the world which broadens their outlook.'[56]

However, Air Vice-Marshal Carr had already been instructed that the political situation was such 'that we must do everything possible, short of interfering with the operational efficiency of any particular crew,' to ensure their complete Canadianization as soon as possible. Five months later, in July, the Canadianization rate for aircrew in 419 Squadron was as laudable as ever, standing at 88 per cent, but the same could not be said of Carr's group. In

405 Squadron, now flying Halifax IIs, only half the aircrew were Canadian. In No 5 Group, meanwhile, where the shortage of Hampden-qualified crews was to have been corrected, the corresponding figure was 59 per cent for 420 Squadron and 41 per cent in No 408, admittedly a vast improvement since December but nothing like what was being accomplished in No 3 Group by Baldwin.[57]

Although RCAF Headquarters viewed the progress in Canadianization up to February 1942 as 'entirely unsatisfactory,'[58] it accepted that effective leadership required operational experience, a commodity that was still in short supply in the RCAF. Thus, as had been the case in Nos 405 and 408 Squadrons, the first commanding officer of No 419 was a Canadian in the RAF, Wing Commander J. Fulton, DFC, who had completed a tour of operations with No 99 Squadron and a posting to the Armament Defence Flight Experimental Section at Farnborough (for which he was awarded the Air Force Cross). The two flight commanders also came from the RAF: Squadron Leader E.G.B. Reid, a British officer, and Squadron Leader F.W.S. Turner, a veteran of Nos 107 and 110 Squadrons and a Canadian participant in the first bomber mission of the war.

Fulton established his presence early, as did his two flight commanders. Apparently ignoring the instructions issued to the senior officers of Nos 405 and 408 Squadrons to restrict their operational flying – presumably with the intention of conserving experienced leaders – Fulton participated in 419's first two raids (with at least one of the flight commanders going on each of the next three) and subsequently flew many more, at times camouflaging his presence by listing his second pilot on the battle order and then taking the latter's place. Every mistake, no matter how minor, was recorded and commented upon, and the commanding officer was not above criticizing himself. After its first raid, for example, the squadron's operational summary noted that Pilot Officer T.C. Cottier's crew checked to ensure that no bombs remained 'hung up' in the bomb bay (that is, had not dropped but were no longer locked in place), while Fulton's forgot this simple task. This was not just petty carping. On 21 January a British pilot inadvertently returned from Boulogne with six 250-lb bombs on board, having failed to check the bomb bay or to activate the jettison bar. Squadron Leader Turner made the same mistake, again at Boulogne, on 28 January, returning with two bombs; and on 31 January Sergeant J.F. Vezina had one bomb hang up. All these crews were lucky. Although bombs were fitted with arming vanes designed to ensure they did not become 'live' until they had fallen some distance through the air, such safety devices were not infallible. Detonation could occur on impact, and any landing made with bombs aboard and which were not still locked in place involved a degree of risk.[59]

Some failed to press home their attacks or to find worthwhile alternate targets. On 21 January one crew returned from Boulogne with a full load of bombs, claiming it was 'too hazy to see anything definite' despite the fact that another had been able to find and attack searchlight and gun positions near the docks. Ten days later a third crew, seeing nothing of Brest, jettisoned its bombs in the Channel, while a fourth, having flown around for an hour looking for a target, brought its bombs back to base. So far as the squadron diary was concerned, all this added up to 'a bad month.' Fulton was especially worried by 'the amazing lack of keenness among some of the observers,' and an instrument technician on the squadron was also aware of problems. Writing to a friend in a letter intercepted by the censors, he noted that so many 419 Squadron crews had been returning with full bomb loads in the past few weeks that he fully expected the British Broadcasting Corporation to report that 'a strong force of Bomber Command aircraft raided Brest & Emden. All our *bombs* returned safely.' Indeed, he continued, he had heard armourers 'complaining that the bombs have got more flying hours in than some of the aircraft.'[60]

Sharing their risks and working tirelessly to correct such faults, Fulton earned a reputation of caring deeply for his men. One crew that completed a mission despite a serious fuel leak and had to make an emergency landing at Exeter, two hundred and fifty miles from Mildenhall, with almost nothing left in the tanks was astounded when, late the next day, their commanding officer flew in to see what had happened to them and berated the pilot for not turning back.[61] This combination of dedication and concern would lead the squadron into taking Fulton's nickname for its own after his death in action, and eventually getting it officially recognized, so it became No 419 (Moose) Squadron, RCAF – the only Canadian squadron to be named after a person.

When the weather was good and operations seemed likely, crews had little opportunity to relax. While they might lounge around in the morning, waiting for orders, once No 419 was placed on 'stand by,' Pilot Officer Jerrold Morris recalled:

captains would follow Flight Commanders to their offices to find out if they were on the battle order. We had only just enough crews to man all aircraft, so unless there was some special assignment calling for a limited effort, everybody would be on ... Each crew was allotted its own aircraft and whenever possible had exclusive use of it. We air-tested the plane in the afternoon, going over all the equipment to make sure that it would be serviceable at night.

It was then time for the briefing.

When everyone was settled, Moose would take the stand and call for silence while the roll was called; then the briefing began. First he would give us general facts about the raid, such as the number of aircraft detailed and the concentration; then the Intelligence officer would outline the nature of the target and reasons for the attack. The Met man took over to give us an estimate of weather conditions likely to be encountered, and finally Moose would run over tactics to be employed, and give advice generally. He usually ended up by saying, 'Enemy fighters – I don't think you'll have any trouble with them. Good luck!'

Next, specific preparations had to be made.

When I got to the hangar, navigators were working around a large table with their topographical maps and plotting charts. Distances had to be entered on the flight plan with airspeeds and height; then the predicted winds were applied, and groundspeeds and courses to fly worked out. This gave an ETA (estimated time of arrival) for each leg. Navigators made their own calculations, and then compared results with others.

When we had finished we went to the locker room, where the rest of the crew members were wandering in to collect their gear. Dressing up was a long process for the gunners; it was a cold ride in the turrets and they wore as much clothing as they could from woollen underwear to electrically heated suits. On top of this went a Mae West buoyancy jacket and parachute harness.

Outside the hangars we stood around and chatted, waiting for transport. The last rays of the sun spread over the flat landscape and there was a chill in the air. The padre handed out flying rations, and the doctor offered caffeine pills to anyone inclined to be sleepy. We scrambled into vans, packed in tight, the navigators hugging their bags of equipment; at each dispersal a crew dropped off and farewells were shouted.

There was work to be done around the machines in the hour before take-off. Gas cocks to check, photoflashes to fuse and mount, detonators to load in the secret equipment [Gee] for emergency destruction and, more often than not, propaganda leaflets to stow near the flare-chute. The wireless operator and navigator had to arrange their gear and settle everything handy in their compartments. Finally the selector panel and bombsight were checked. When we were through we could lie down under the kite and smoke and chat with the ground crew.[62]

Sometime thereafter, the flying control officer would make his rounds, engines would be started, and it was time to go. Cancellations (usually due to weather) at any time other than the beginning of this procedure obviously took their toll.

You went through all the motions, the briefing room, news of the target, the tension of waiting, even the final 'good luck' could be said, and the operation scrubbed. Everyone would be ready, physically and emotionally and the bubble was pricked. Rarely would such a cancellation release any jubilation; most of us went about our duties with no mention of fears or anxieties, just tried to make as many trips as possible, learning to build a shell against emotion. But inwardly we were bound to think.[63]

A period of good weather and sustained operations would probably have helped the squadron to shake off the problems Fulton had identified, but as we have already seen, the first two weeks of February were marked by cloud, snow, and rain. Raids took place only on the nights of 6/7 and 10/11 February, in complete overcast, and neither could be judged successful. Indeed, Brest was so covered by cloud on the first occasion that three crews returned to base without attacking anything, while another, making more than one serious navigation error, finally jettisoned its bombs from an altitude of 2000 feet only seventeen miles from Nottingham. On 12 February the squadron participated in Operation Fuller. Three aircraft were dispatched, but only Fulton returned;

having seen nothing through thick haze, low cloud, and intermittent rain, he brought his bombs back. The next day, the first Wellington Mark III arrived and conversion training began. The shift to IIIs was not a major one and the squadron was not taken off operations, but because of the training effort only a few sorties were flown each night.[64]

In No 420 Squadron, the first CO, Wing Commander J.D.D. Collier, DFC, the unfortunate Squadron Leader V.T.L. Wood, commander of B flight who was lost on the squadron's first mission, and Wood's successor, Squadron Leader G.L.B. Harris, were not Canadian; the officer commanding A flight, Squadron Leader G.C. Campbell, was, however, having joined the RAF in 1938. Because it was equipped with Hampdens, already obsolescent for most night-bombing operations, No 420 was heavily involved in mining operations, mainly off Heligoland, as well as in attacks on French ports, during its first few weeks of operations. In addition, six aircraft were committed to Operation Fuller, of which two, including that piloted by Squadron Leader Harris, the second flight commander to go missing in just three weeks, failed to return.[65]

Bomber Command's unhappy performance in Operation Fuller was, in many respects, a fitting end to a most unsettling winter campaign that, since 10/11 November, had cost 116 aircraft on night bombing operations,[66] and had done little physical damage to Germany. Altogether, as *The Spectator* had suggested as early as 26 December, it was a complete puzzle to the British public.

The RAF has in the last week been well plastering Brest by night and day. It has visited Ostend. It has looked in at St. Nazaire. Once or twice, rather less recently, it has got as far as Wilhelmshaven, but a raid on Germany seems now the exception rather than the rule. The public is perplexed by this change of tactics, and with some reason. Weather, no doubt, has something to do with it, and no one wants to see brave men and good machines risked recklessly, but the Air Minister has promised repeatedly such intensified and sustained assaults on Germany's productive power and communications as will materially affect the future of the war. That, of course, is what our own interest demands, and Russia at the same time is entitled to expect from us the exertion of every possible effort against Germany. It is virtually on the RAF alone that we must rely for that. Actually, instead of 1941 ending with a crescendo of attack, Germany, except for a few towns in the north-west, has rarely had so long a period of uninterrupted nights. Some authoritative statement of the cause, and, if the facts justify it, a reiteration of Sir Archibald Sinclair's assurances regarding our intentions, would relieve the growing perplexity considerably.

Two days after Fuller, a new directive issued to Bomber Command dramatically altered how (and how frequently) all four Canadian squadrons would be employed. The policy of conservation was abandoned and High Wycombe was told to conduct operations 'without restriction, until further notice' against the industrial centres of western Germany except when weather conditions were 'unfavourable or ... your aircraft are likely to be

TABLE 3
The Changing Shape of Bomber Command, 27 March 1941– 4 February 1943

Aircraft Type	Number of Operational Squadrons and Aircraft			
	27 March 1941	6 March 1942	18 September 1942	4 February 1943
Light Bomber Blenheim, Boston, Ventura, Mitchell Mosquito	9 squadrons (218 aircraft)	6 squadrons (91 aircraft)	4 squadrons (65 aircraft)	6 squadrons (95 aircraft)
Medium Bomber Whitley, Hampden, Wellington	32 squadrons (512) aircraft)	27 squadrons (509 aircraft)	11 squadrons (163 aircraft)	20 squadrons (354 aircraft)
Heavy Bomber Halifax, Stirling, Manchester, Lancaster	5 squadrons (80 aircraft)	11 squadrons (167 aircraft)	20 squadrons (335 aircraft)	33½squadrons (642 aircraft)

exposed to extreme hazards.'[67] The new directive of 14 February 1942 was the handiwork of Air Commodore J.W. Baker, the director of bomber operations. Concluding that German morale was now at its lowest point since the beginning of the war, due largely to the Wehrmacht's failure to defeat the Soviet Union before the onset of winter, he urged that a renewed bombing offensive be opened against the large industrial centres of the Ruhr, adding that the objective should be the complete destruction of their built-up areas, something he now considered possible for the first time. His vision was not based on any startling increase in High Wycombe's strength since March 1941. Having lost just over a thousand crews in the past twelve months (and still seeing trained crews as well as formed units allocated to other theatres and commands), in March 1942 Bomber Command was only marginally larger than it had been a year before. In terms of equipment, moreover, now that the United States was in the war, it was inevitable that much American production originally intended for the RAF would go, instead, to equip the US Army Air Forces.[68] Although these losses would be offset to some extent by the appearance of the four-engined Stirlings, Halifaxes, and Lancasters, with their greater bomb-carrying capacity, the number of heavy bomber squadrons immediately available was not yet sufficient to make an appreciable difference (see table 3).[69]

The destructive potential of the new blast bombs (complemented by torrents of incendiaries) also contributed to Baker's optimism, but the most significant innovation lying behind the new directive was Gee, the radio-navigation aid which had been hovering in the background and now, like a 'magic box of tricks,' was 'expected to produce the answer' to all of Bomber Command's woes. Originally scheduled for delivery in November or December 1941, the first hand-crafted Gee sets had begun to appear in January 1942 and they would be in good supply once mass production began in the spring. Moreover, it was assumed that Gee would serve not only as a navigation aid, able to guide crews to the target area, but also as a blind-bombing device that would enable them to hit 'a selected area in or through 10/10ths cloud,' thereby increasing the number of nights when effective bombing was possible from an average of three a month to twenty.[70] Bad weather for takeoff and/or landing would prevent operations the other ten nights.

Such results were expected because of Gee's simplicity, security, and synchrony. Relatively easy to maintain, robust (the overall serviceability rate was 95 per cent between April 1942 and March 1943), involving no tell-tale emissions to attract fighters, and usable by an unlimited number of bombers, Gee consisted of three widely spaced transmitters in the United Kingdom sending out synchronized pulse signals and an airborne receiver which, after measuring the difference in time of receipt of these transmissions, provided the basis from which the aircraft's distance from each transmitter could be calculated. Transferring this data to specially prepared lattice-grid maps, a Gee operator could then establish his position and pass course corrections to his pilot.[71]

Moreover, the prospect of bombing through thick cloud, when the enemy's night-fighters were usually ineffective and often did not fly, and only radar-directed Flak was a real threat, was promising. Heavy, punishing, bombloads should be deliverable at little or no cost. Indeed, the only drawbacks were that Gee would, in time, be discovered by German radio intelligence and jammed – probably within six months of its introduction, but perhaps not before other navigation devices still in the developmental pipeline could be made operational. All parts of the Ruhr were within its range; cities in the area were large enough that near misses would still count; and they were all apparently susceptible to incendiary attack. But to achieve the greatest impact, Baker's offensive would have to begin soon, before the Wehrmacht recovered in the east and civilian morale improved. When he learned (just a few days after completing his work) that Gee could not be fitted to all aircraft for some time, Baker argued that the campaign should commence as scheduled, with those crews having Gee marking targets for those who did not.[72]

Gradually, the pieces of a new bombing strategy were fitting together. Additional justification came when the Ministry of Economic Warfare (MEW) produced a list of objectives that coincided nicely with Baker's selection and gave it even greater credibility. Nothing was more important than the Ruhr. On 14 February, then, the 'primary object' of Bomber Command's operations became 'the morale of the enemy civil population and in particular, of the industrial workers,' and to that end High Wycombe was given a list of 'selected area targets,' of which Essen, Duisburg, Dusseldorf, and Cologne were the most important. To make sure there was no misunderstanding about what was being called for, the next day Portal told his DCAS to remind High Wycombe that 'the aiming points are to be the built-up areas, *not*, for instance, the dockyards or aircraft factories where these are mentioned.'[73]

The new directive challenged everything Sir Richard Peirse had stood (and fought) for over the previous year, but his opinion no longer counted. He had been relieved of his command on 8 January 1942, victim of the costly raid on Berlin in November and the serious doubt as to whether, because of his convictions, he was the man to lead a sustained 'area bombing' offensive. When reports had begun to surface that the morale and confidence of Bomber Command was plummetting, his fate was sealed.[74]

Arriving at High Wycombe on 22 February 1942, the new AOC-in-C, Air Marshal Arthur Harris, did not rush the implementation of the new directive. First, the German warships missed during Fuller were to be attacked in their home ports. Thus on 22/23 February fifty aircraft were sent to Wilhelmshaven to attack the floating repair dock, and then, on 25/26 and 26/27 February, to Kiel. Although no warship was damaged in the first raid on Kiel, almost 150 workmen were killed – about 3 per cent of the total number of German civilian deaths attributable to bombing in all of 1942 – when the accommodation ship *Monte Samiento* was hit and burnt out. The next night *Gneisenau* was knocked out of the war, with the loss of 116 of its crew; but the Danish town of Vejle, a hundred miles away, was also attacked by bomber crews who had lost their way.[75]

Another raid slightly outside the main scope of the new bombing directive also deserves mention, both as a portent of things to come in terms of the intensity and technique of Bomber Command operations and as an illustration of how, from time to time, political considerations influenced target selection. French factories had, until now, been more or less immune to attack because of the fear of killing civilians, but with the development of new target-marking methods the opportunity to do damage to this virtually undefended class of target (and perhaps bolster French morale) could finally be seized. Churchill actively promoted the project and the Renault factory at Billancourt, just outside Paris, was selected as the target.[76]

On 3/4 March 235 bombers, including crews from all four Canadian squadrons, set out in three waves, the first comprising of the most experienced personnel. The plan, laid down at High Wycombe and marking a new era in centralized direction, depended on strict timings, abundant use of flares, and a high degree of concentration over the target; since there was no Flak, bombing would be conducted from very low level. The raid met most of its goals. The target was easily seen, marking was good, and practically every crew claimed it had hit the factory. Indeed, perhaps the only criticism that could be offered was that made by Wing Commander J.D.D. Collier, leading No 420 Squadron, who noted that the flares were so numerous they were a 'hindrance,' their smoke blocking out details and forcing him to spend 'nearly an hour' looking for an aiming point before he could drop his bombs.[77] Three hundred bombs fell on the complex, knocking out two-fifths of its buildings, disrupting production for a month, and destroying 2300 trucks in an attack lasting just under two hours. Only one bomber was lost, but French casualties were heavy; 367 civilians, mainly factory workers living in the vicinity of the plant, were killed – too many for this type of attack to be repeated on a regular basis.[78]

Five days later, on 8/9 March, came the initial raid launched in conformity with the new bombing directive – in effect, the first attack of the first battle of the Ruhr. Essen was the target, the aiming point was the centre of the old town, and Gee was used to support the new Shaker plan of attack, which involved a first wave of aircraft laying a flare path six miles long upwind of the aiming point to mark the approach, a second wave of fire-raisers, and then the main force, carrying both high-explosives and incendiaries. Many of the 211 aircraft dispatched found the general target area, one pilot from No 420 Squadron reporting he could see the flares over Essen 'when approaching the Dutch coast.' But marking was not as good as anticipated, even with Gee, and much of the main force, partially blinded by smog, went awry.[79]

The failure of the Shaker technique on this occasion was a disappointment, but it could be attributed to the crews' unfamiliarity with the new equipment, since only eleven of the twenty markers had actually used Gee. Navigation could be expected to get better as crews became more comfortable with, and confident in, the device. But this did not happen quickly. Following a second raid on Essen on 9/10 March, there was 'no evidence that any attack was delivered on the primary' while Duisburg and Hamborn were both bombed. The next night solace was taken from the fact that although Essen was covered in cloud, 'one aircraft over Dortmund may ... have achieved useful results.' The outcome was better on 12/13 March, when Kiel was the target and Gee was used as a navigation aid to the limit of its range; and even more encouraging at Cologne, one night later, when 50 per cent of the attacking force bombed the city. The markers, illuminators, and fire-raisers all did a good job, and the main force had no difficulty in finding the objective. However, on both these raids skies were relatively clear and this may have had more to do with improved results than Gee or Shaker.[80]

Weather and the lunar cycle forced a ten-day break in major bombing operations following the Cologne raid, but Gardening continued on a more intensive basis than ever before. Harris had decided that all groups should take part in aerial mining as an alternative to 'wasting' bombs on naval targets and, indeed, on 25 March Bomber Command secured the responsibility for mine-laying in home waters as well, so long as it did not 'prejudice' the 'normal bombing effort.' In No 5 Group, meanwhile, half of all sorties flown during March were to lay mines, and by the end of the month the total number of ships sunk by aerial mines since April 1940 stood at 157 (159,465 tons), with a further twenty-four damaged (99,646 tons).[81]

As the weather and moon conditions improved, Bomber Command returned to Essen and again employed the Shaker technique of marking and fire-raising which, since it had received its Gee sets, now involved No 419 Squadron in the first wave. Despite good visibility on 25/26 March, crews were drawn away from the city by 'large fires burning in the open country to the north,' while the next night there was 'no indication that any useful concentration was achieved over the target or over any other built-up area.'[82] Once again, Gee was something less than the anticipated revolutionary improvement. 'It could take us to the Ruhr,' one senior officer recalled, 'and within sight of the objective, but the precise aiming point, more often than not hidden by smoke and industrial haze, had to be discovered by visual means – an almost impossible task in the deluge of heavy flak bursts and dazzling searchlights.'[83]   Pilot Officer Jerrold Morris would have agreed.

Long before you reached the target area you would see ahead of you a confusing maze of searchlights quartering the sky, some in small groups, others stacked in cones of twenty or more. These often had a victim transfixed, as if pinned to the sky, their apex filled with red bursts of heavy flak. The ground would soon be lit with lines of reconnaissance flares like suspended street lights, here and there illuminating water, perhaps a section of river, that you would frantically try to identify. As the raid developed, sticks of incendiaries criss-crossed the ground sparkling incandescent white, until a red glow would show the start of a fire.

The Germans liberally sprayed the ground with dummy incendiaries and imitation fire blocks in the neighbourhood of important targets, hoping to attract a share of the bombs. Gun flashes, photoflashes, bomb-bursts, streams of tracer of all colours, and everywhere searchlights – it was all very confusing, especially when the air gunners were directing the pilot to avoid flak and searchlights in all directions at the same time.[84]

Operations over Essen and the rest of the Ruhr looked much the same from the German perspective. On 26/27 March Wilhelm Johnen, the pilot of an Me 110 from I/*Nachtjagdgeschwader* 1 based at Venlo in Northern Belgium, was patrolling an area near Duisburg which, so scattered was the bombing, he mistook for the main objective.

A bare twenty minutes later I reached the scheduled height of 17,000 feet and circled above my beacon west of Wesel. The sky towered majestically above me and the stars seemed to be closer, so wonderfully bright was the night ... The earth was far away ... How dark it was below. Here and there I could see the blood red glow of the blast furnaces which, now that the enemy was approaching, would be extinguished. A few searchlights suddenly went on and began their play in the sky ... From south to north in a broad sweep glittered a smooth grey ribbon – the Rhine ... The first flares fell and flooded the landscape with a ghostly light. The British were looking for their target.

Told to attack 'any machine caught in the searchlight beams above 15,000 feet,' the ceiling set for the Flak, he very quickly found a Wellington.

Hesitantly the white beams flitted to and fro like the arms of an octopus until at last they had caught a bomber. The British machine was flying at about 14,500 feet and took no avoiding action. The gunners below made him their target but they were shooting too far ahead. I decided to attack. Risop [Johnen's radio operator] quickly transmitted the code word '*PAUKE, PAUKE*' to the ground station. I dived from my superior altitude and got the bomber in my sights. The air speed indicator needle rose to 330 mph. The bomber grew ever larger in the sights. Now I could clearly see the tall tail unit and the rear gunner's Perspex turret. My machine came into the search-light area and a few well-aimed bursts lashed the bomber's fuselage, tearing off huge pieces of the fabric. The Tommy was on fire and turned over on its back.

Later that night Johnen (who would end the war credited with thirty-four enemy machines destroyed) attacked a Stirling (the first he had ever seen), but his Messerschmitt was riddled by one of the bomber's gunners, set on fire, and then exploded at 9000 feet. Johnen parachuted to safety, but Risop was already dead.[85]

Bomber Command's loss rate over Essen, given the meagre damage done, was cause for concern: thirty-five of 893 sorties (3.9 per cent) overall, but twenty of 369 sorties (5.4 per cent) on the last two raids. Of these, just over half had been shot down by night-fighters,[86] yet to many crews Flak was the main worry.

The most alarming factor of the German defences was undoubtedly the searchlights. They had master beams, radar controlled, during the preliminary search ...once caught, every searchlight in range would fix you and, wriggle and squirm as you might, you couldn't shake them off. Then the guns joined in and filled the apex of the cone with bursts; it was a terrifying thing to watch. All too often the sequel was a small flame, burning bright as the aircraft fell towards the ground, followed by the beams all the way down, as if loath to leave their victim; then darkness, until the beams lifted to begin their search again. Everyone dreaded being coned; if it happened, the only sensible thing to do was to head away from the defended area by the shortest route, but pilots often executed hair-raising manoeuvres, falling into spins or diving almost to ground level: some got away with it.[87]

Harris needed a success. He was undoubtedly aware of the Air Ministry's unhappiness with Bomber Command under Peirse, and the rumblings of discontent had not stopped. Group Captain Bufton (deputy DBOps), for example, worried that High Wycombe was wasting what might be a last, 'fleeting opportunity ... to prove its worth and for the Air Staff to justify its bomber policy,' while Air Commodore Baker (DBOps) still seemed to view Bomber Command as a poorly knit team badly in need of 'imaginative, co-ordinated and positive direction and control.'[88]

So far, Harris and the air staff had been at odds over almost every issue that came before them except targeting. Although the AOC-in-C agreed that the appearance of Gee and other navigation aids required dividing the observer's responsibilites between two specialist aircrew categories – the navigator, who would guide the pilot to the target area, and the bomb-aimer, who would direct him on the run-up to the aiming point – he was not at all happy with the air staff's decision to do away with second pilots on heavy bombers. That proposal, while increasing the number of operational captains available, nevertheless ran afoul of long-standing conventional wisdom regarding the complexities of piloting large aircraft. 'We all moaned like hell and didn't believe it could be done,' Morris recalls. 'We were used to relieving each other every few hours, and thought the fatigue would be excessive on long trips.' But the AOC-in-C's arguments against the policy went unheeded, as did his request to double the commitment of crews to Bomber Command to four tours, two operational and two at OTUs.[89] Moreover, he greatly feared that he would continue to lose squadrons and individual crews to other commands. The 'situation now and the outlook for the future is desperate,' he told his group commanders. 'This is directly due to inexcusable, needless, and fantastic extravagance in posting broadcast throughout the world, for every conceivable job except bombing, vast numbers of OTU trained bomber crews, many of whom have never started, let alone completed, an operational tour ... I am at present engaged in a riot with the personnel side of the Air Ministry, whom I have filled with alarm and despondency on the subject.'[90]

There was also harsh criticism outside the air force. Although Harris bristled at what he felt was uninformed sniping by parliamentarians and the 'gutter' press, his real complaint was over the demands made by the army and navy not only to secure a greater allocation of air resources for themselves, at Bomber Command's expense if necessary, but to have a greater say in the making of air policy as well. That was unlikely so long as Churchill supported the bomber offensive unequivocally. On 13 March, however, after the first three unproductive raids on Essen, the prime minister was inclined to think that while bombing was 'better than doing nothing, and indeed is a formidable method of injuring the enemy,' it was not going to be decisive.[91]

Searching for a dramatic (and inexpensive) illustration of area bombing's potential, and with the Ruhr apparently too tough a nut to crack, Harris settled on the ancient Hanseatic port of Lübeck, included in the February directive as an alternative industrial objective. Situated on the Baltic, relatively easy to find, poorly defended, and, above all, extremely susceptible to fire because of its narrow streets and old, timbered houses, the city was attacked by 234 aircraft on 28/29 March 1942. In clear skies, aided by a nearly full moon which 'facilitated pin-pointing of coastal features despite the presence of ice,' Bomber Command registered an outstanding success. Employing mixed bomb-loads (the total force carried 144 tons of incendiaries and 159 tons of high-explosives, including as many 4000-lb blast bombs as possible), 191 crews claimed to have bombed the city centre, turning it into 'one mass of reddish orange glow,' destroying 1425 buildings and severely damaging another 1976. Over 90 per cent of the total were residental buildings, so it was surprising, perhaps, that only 312 people were killed and 136 seriously wounded; but 15,000 were rendered homeless. Bomber Command's casualties were heavy: twelve aircraft (including one from No 419 Squadron) failed to return, a loss rate of 5 per cent, many falling victim to Dunkelnachtjagd crews.[92]

Losses, and the weather, again persuaded Harris to give his men a week's rest from major raids, but not from Gardening, with its normally manageable casualty rate. On 1/2 April No 419 became the first Wellington squadron to join the mining campaign, and by the end of the month it had laid thirty-one mines without loss. (The RCAF total for the month was ninety-eight.) No 408 Squadron was not so fortunate, however. On 27/28 March, when most of Bomber Command was attempting to support the naval and commando raid on St Nazaire, it committed eight aircraft to lay mines on the north-west German coast, including five freshmen crews sent to the Nectarines minefield skirting the Frisian Islands. These five all returned safely to base, but the three veteran crews, sent to the Yams minefield on the Wilhelmshaven approaches, were never heard from again.[93]

After this brief interlude, Bomber Command returned to the Ruhr, attacking Cologne, Dortmund (twice), Hamburg (twice), and Essen (three times) between 5/6 and 17/18 April. The results were every bit as bad as before. Bombing photographs rarely showed the target, and bomb damage recorded by subsequent photographic reconnaissance flights was negligible. More unsettling still, several of these raids had occurred in the marginal weather that simply had to be overcome (presumably with Gee's help) if the sustained area offensive called for by the 14 February directive was to have any chance of accomplishing its objectives; in that respect it was clear that current methods of target-finding and marking were inadequate. The Dortmund raids of 14/15 and 15/16 April were typical. Despite using Gee, most crews from No 419 Squadron could not identify the target area with any certainty and so could only assume they had dropped their incendiaries in it. When other squadrons arrived, the fires they aimed at may or may not have been in the city. On 14/15 April, when the cloud cover was not particularly heavy, one 420 Squadron pilot claimed no more than that his 'bombs dropped over Germany.'[94]

Whether Gee would ever live up to expectations as a blind-bombing device was becoming increasingly doubtful. An advanced design whose performance startled the Germans when they tested a set recovered from a downed bomber, Gee was nevertheless neither flawless nor capable of pinpoint accuracy. Its systemic error – due entirely to deficiencies inherent in the equipment and having nothing to do with mistakes made by operators – meant that, even with a purportedly accurate fix, a crew could be sure only that it was somewhere within a rough diamond-shaped area three to four miles long by one-half mile at its widest point.[95]

A concrete illustration of Gee's limitations came on 22/23 April, when sixty-nine aircraft were sent to Cologne with instructions to bomb on their Gee-fix only. Although some bombs fell on the city, others hit as far as ten miles away. No 419 Squadron had 'a black night.' Of eleven aircraft detailed for the raid, three suffered Gee failure – one before takeoff (the sortie was scrubbed), one on the way to the target (the pilot bombed Balkenburg), and one on the homeward route. Two other machines returned early with unserviceable rear turrets and, following a 'misunderstanding,' one rear gunner baled out from a perfectly serviceable aircraft over Ipswich.[96]

Perhaps the only redeeming feature of these and other recent raids was that the loss rate fell one full percentage point from the average incurred between 8 and 27 March. But casualties were never distributed equally and on some nights individual squadrons suffered heavily. Of the 13 aircraft missing from 360 sent on the two Dortmund raids already described, No 420 Squadron lost two and No 405 Squadron three (half of its effort for the night of 14/15 April).[97] Flight Lieutenant J.D Pattison, a former fighter pilot and Battle of Britain veteran who had recently joined 419 Squadron, was over the city on

14/15 April, and he described the raid (his first) as a 'strange sight to the novice.'

The target area was brilliantly lit up by flares which were being shot up from the ground to aid the night-fighters by silhouetting the bombers against the low cloud and haze. Off our starboard bow, as we ran in to bomb, there was a huge cone made up of about seventy-five searchlights and reaching up to over 15,000 feet. Into this cone, *Flak* was being pumped by many guns in the area ... The flares, fires, and searchlights made it very uncomfortable around the target as it was lit up like day. One feels so conspicuous in a bomber which has neither darkness nor cloud to hide in ... As we came up to the Dutch coast on the route home, I was just beginning to think the whole thing was fairly easy and the dangers much exaggerated, when things started to happen off our port side. About five miles away a searchlight came on, followed immediately by five or six others, forming a cone at about our height, 12,000 feet, into which they started shooting flak. Almost at once the aircraft in the apex of the cone caught fire and began to glow, as it descended slowly. The searchlights held it all the way down, as it burned like a great golden star, and exploded as it hit the deck. After that incident we got out to sea as quickly as we could. Some poor chap, almost safely over the coast, had been unlucky enough to fly smack over Ostend; that was a good lesson for me; I never again underestimated what we were up against.[98]

There was still reason to experiment with Gee in area attacks, however, and to this end Rostock, another old and inflammable port on the Baltic, was attacked on four successive nights. The first raid, when incendiaries made up two-thirds of the bombload, was a failure, most bombs falling in the suburbs rather than the city centre. The second saw more aircraft over the town, but the Heinkel works, the main industrial target, was not hit. The third attack finally did damage, while the fourth – again employing two-thirds incendiaries – was, in the words of the British official history, a 'masterpiece.'[99] Fifty-two bombing photographs showed the target area, and thirteen revealed the Heinkel factory. The fifty-five bombers from Nos 3 and 5 Groups (including 420 Squadron), directed all four times to make low-level precision attacks on the factory while the rest bombed the city as a whole, eventually did so accurately, No 3 Group bombing from about 6000 feet, No 5 Group from below 2000, and the entire raid was over in less than an hour. All told, the four raids – but mainly the last two – destroyed 70 per cent of the old town, briefly persuading Joseph Goebbels, German propaganda minister, that 'community life ... is practically at an end.' Despite the appearance of cataclysmic damage, however, production at the Heinkel works actually returned to 100 per cent within three days.[100]

With Rostock apparently destroyed, Bomber Command turned to other targets over the next month, generally avoiding the Ruhr when conditions there favoured the defence. Nevertheless, losses could still be heavy on occasion. No 419 Squadron suffered 12 per cent casualties in the month or so following the Rostock raids, and on 28/29 April very nearly lost its commanding officer. Wing Commander Fulton was attacked by a Messerschmitt 110 over Kiel which, his rear gunner recalled, was 'about 100 yards away when I spotted him.' 'I only got in about twelve rounds before he began firing. Cannon shells and machine-gun bullets smashed into our "Wimpey." When the fighter closed in to twenty yards the "wingco" flung the kite over, stuck the nose down, and turned back into the dark, away from the moon.' Damage to the aircraft was extensive. The hydraulics had been hit, so that the undercarriage dropped and the bomb-bay doors fell open, the port airscrew was splintered, there were countless holes in the fuselage, and the rear gunner had to be chopped out of his turret. But Fulton made his way back to Mildenhall, made a successful belly landing in which no one was hurt, and was subsequently awarded a DSO.[101]

During these last raids operational research suggested that Gee was doubling the number of aircraft arriving over the target area, leading one observer to describe it as an 'unqualified success' as a navigation aid. (Even Harris, now, was prepared to admit that as a blind-bombing device it was an abysmal failure, and that its sole contribution was to get bomber crews 'into [the] neighbourhood' of the target.) Yet as much as Gee was helping to solve the problem of closing the last ten or twenty miles to the target area, many crews were still being fooled by decoy fires near the objective.[102] When it happened again at Mannheim on 19/20 May, Harris was livid.

It is apparent from the night photographs and from the reports of crews, that almost the whole effort of the raid was wasted in bombing large fires in the local forests, and possibly decoy fires. Nevertheless, in spite of the now incontrovertible evidence that this is what in fact occurred, the reports of the crews on their return from the raid were most definite in very many cases that they had reached the town and bombed it. Many reports spoke of recognising features of the town and the river, and of fires being definitely located in the town. The cause of this failure is beyond doubt to be found in the easy manner in which crews are misled by decoy fires or by fires in the wrong place. If any fire is distinctive in its nature and comparatively easy to recognise it is a forest fire. The results on this occasion show that few if any of the crews took the trouble, or alternatively came low enough, to make certain of the nature of the fires. AOCs must again personally impress on crews the fearful waste of effort which is occasioned if, after all the labour in providing them with training and with aircraft, their operations are rendered nugatory owing to lack of skill or carelessness in pushing home their attacks to the correct objectives. In particular, somehow or other we must cure this disease, for it is a disease, of wasting bombs wholesale upon decoy fires ... Apart from impressing upon them the necessity to avoid being sold dummies or misled by other peoples' efforts, they must be made to realise that, within the short compass of their operational career, if they do not on every flight make some worthwhile contribution to the aim of destroying valuable objectives then the whole of the effort that has been put into training and mounting them is being thrown away and the conclusion of the war indefinitely postponed.

If such failures continued, Harris added, crews were to be told (as they had been after the first two raids on Rostock) that they would be sent back to

Mannheim again and again until the job was done properly. He also warned his group commanders that if they did not exercise closer supervision, the 'large number of influential people who ... are quite convinced that the Bomber force is not justified ... will have their way in destroying it, and consequently possibly the RAF also as a separate service.'[103]

That, of course, was a wild exaggeration. Despite the general staff's talk about forming a ninety-squadron army air force, and the navy's desire to increase the resources available for maritime war, the RAF's independence was still secure. There was, however, considerable discontent with the government's bombing policy and with the way the bombing offensive was being conducted. Although Lord Cherwell, Churchill's scientific adviser, fully endorsed the concept of area bombing, arguing that 'dehousing' the German labour force was a worthwhile objective in itself and that direct damage to factories was not necessary, both Sir Henry Tizard, scientific adviser to the air staff, and P.M.S. Blackett, head of operational research at Coastal Command, believed that High Wycombe must do significantly more in the fight against the U-boat. In time, their opinions, along with those of the naval and army staffs, led to the creation of a formal inquiry under Mr Justice Singleton to study the most effective use of the bomber force and, in particular, to suggest ways in which it could contribute more to the Battle of the Atlantic. Although the inquiry caused a few anxious moments at High Wycombe, Singleton concluded that, since it was impossible to predict how accurate bombing might become in eighteen months, and since, in the interim, Bomber Command could not bomb accurately enough to damage U-boat factories, there was nothing to be gained from issuing a new bombing directive giving priority to these targets.[104]

Others found different reasons to object to area bombing. Slessor, never an advocate and now, as ACAS (Policy), in a position of some influence, complained that the operations of Bomber Command were 'not co-ordinated with our strategic policy as a whole.' In particular, he was concerned that 'the directive under which Bomber Command are operating contains no reference to the G[erman] A[ir] F[orce], lays down the primary object as the morale of the civil population, and in the list of priority targets only includes three out of twenty-nine that have any direct relation to the German aircraft industry at all.' Acknowledging the difficulty in attacking the latter, Slessor nevertheless believed it necessary to revise the 14 February directive to include such targets 'even if it only means selecting objectives for area bombing which will lower the morale and dislocate the lives of workers in the aircraft or associated industries.' Group Captain Bufton went further, arguing that only daylight raids on aircraft factories (like that against Augsburg conducted, experimentally, on 17 April, which cost seven of the twelve Lancasters involved) could do significant damage. Air Vice-Marshal N.H. Bottomley, ACAS (Ops), agreed that such targets needed attention, and asked that they be included as alternates in the night-bombing campaign.[105]

More threatening still was the powerful evidence that area bombing would not seriously dislocate industrial production, either directly, by the destruction of physical plant, or indirectly, through its impact on workers' morale. Closer

study showed that the examples cited by Lord Cherwell to justify a 'dehousing' campaign against Germany indicated that there was no 'panic resulting
either from a series of raids or from a single raid' in the English cities bombed
during the enemy's night-time Blitz, while the loss of production attributable
to air raids on Hull and Birmingham in 1940 and 1941 had been no more than
5 per cent. At the same time, the officer who analysed the effects of the Luftwaffe's attacks on Bristol, and who had originally concluded that worker
morale was more vulnerable than factory buildings, admitted that he, too, had
been wrong. Morale had actually recovered very quickly, he explained, so 'our
primary aim ought to be the direct destruction of the factory.'[106]

Portal and Harris were not to be swayed, however, and they took comfort
from recent prisoner-of-war interrogations, neutral newspapers, and intelligence
agents suggesting that German morale could be severely strained 'by bringing
home to the maximum number of German civilians the utmost horrors of
war.'[107] To persuade others of this effect, however, and to satisfy them that
anything other than an intense and sustained area offensive was misguided,
would require yet another convincing demonstration by Bomber Command,
involving the largest possible force and the lowest possible casualty rate. Harris
arrived at a characteristic solution, dramatic in its stark simplicity. A thousand
bombers over a single city on a single night had the right, Wagnerian, ring to
it.

16

The Expansion of Bomber Command, Summer 1942

While Bomber Command had been experimenting with night operations, the enemy had been developing his defences. Now, in the spring of 1942, High Wycombe's main concern was with General der Nachtjagd Josef Kammhuber's system of radar-assisted, ground-controlled interception.

Piecing together the changes in the German air-defence puzzle had taken several months. That Freya provided the enemy with early warning of air raids had been acknowledged since at least October 1941. Würzburg had been identified shortly thereafter (and a nearly complete set captured in the commando raid on Bruneval on 27 February 1942), but that it was used to control fighters as well as Flak was not fully understood until installations were discovered around night-fighter bases at St Trond, Belgium, Domberg in the Scheldt Estuary, and later in Denmark. Intelligence officers were then able to deduce how the system worked: the Freya stations gave a generalized warning of impending attack and furnished the Würzburgs with the data on the enemy's course and height they needed to begin their search. These assumptions, tested through aerial reconnaissance and electronic monitoring of the enemy's response to such probes, completed most of the rest of the picture. By May 1942 High Wycombe knew not only that German controllers handled only one interception at a time, but also that fighters rarely strayed beyond the range of their ground control radars – information that had allowed the staff to deduce the size, shape, and boundaries of the night-fighter 'boxes.'[1] Corroborated by casualty statistics showing that the enemy usually did better against dispersed raids, this analysis persuaded Sir Arthur Harris (he was knighted on 11 June) of the value of concentration.

Although Kammhuber had lost the searchlights on which his defensive system had originally relied so heavily – he called their transfer to the major cities to satisfy disgruntled Gauleiters 'a terrible blow' – their absence was more than compensated for by new equipment and better tactics. Almost every night-fighter box now had two Würzburg or the improved, longer-range Würzburg-Riese ground radars, one to track the bomber, the other to direct an interceptor to a position a few hundred yards behind its quarry. The old Freya early warning chain was also being supplemented by longer-range radars, Mammut and Wasserman, with height-finding and identification friend or foe

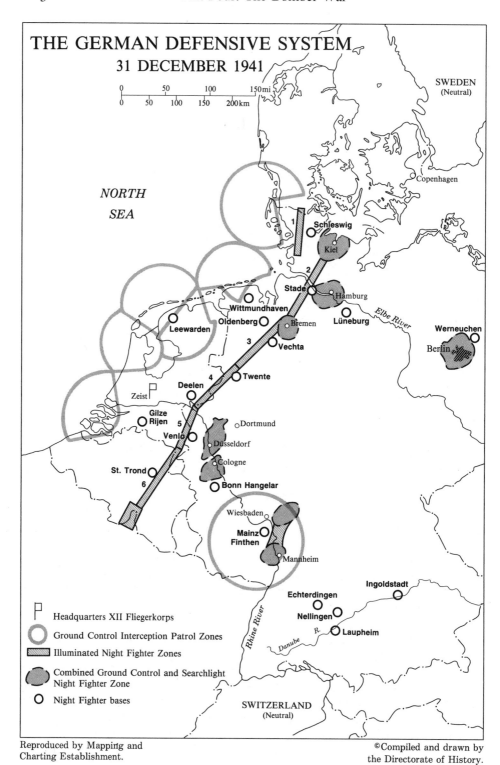

THE GERMAN DEFENSIVE SYSTEM
31 DECEMBER 1941

SWEDEN
(Neutral)

NORTH
SEA

Copenhagen

1

Schleswig

Kiel

2

Stade

Hamburg

Wittmundhaven

Lüneburg

Oldenberg

Bremen

Elbe River

Leewarden

3

Vechta

Werneuchen

Berlin

Twente

4

Deelen

Zeist

Gilze
Rijen   5

Dortmund

Venlo

Düsseldorf

Cologne

St. Trond

6

Bonn Hangelar

Wiesbaden

Mainz
Finthen

Mannheim

Ingoldstadt

Echterdingen

Headquarters XII Fliegerkorps

Nellingen

Ground Control Interception Patrol Zones

R.

Laupheim

Illuminated Night Fighter Zones

Rhine River

Danube

Combined Ground Control and Searchlight
Night Fighter Zone

Night Fighter bases

SWITZERLAND
(Neutral)

Reproduced by Mapping and
Charting Establishment.

©Compiled and drawn by
the Directorate of History.

capabilities (IFF),[*] while General Wolfgang Martini's Horchdienst, the German radio intelligence service, had greatly expanded its surveillance effort. By eavesdropping on the warnings of Bomber Command operations passed to Allied shipping in the English Channel and monitoring the testing of electronic equipment that had to take place prior to a raid, Martini was often able to predict as early as mid-afternoon not only that an attack was planned for that night, but also which squadrons were involved and what routes they would be taking. Unhappily, from Kammhuber's perspective, there was no direct link in the chain of command between his headquarters and Martini, and the informal arrangements to exchange information sometimes broke down; but when the system worked, the night-fighter force was given a considerable head-start in the coming battle.[2]

Night air defence had also been the object of considerable scientific research. Spanner, an infra-red device to detect hot exhaust gases and flames introduced as early as 1941, was known to the British and featured in their assessments of German capabilities until August 1942, but it was too often fooled by ground fires (and sometimes even the moon) to be of much use. Of more immediate importance, the IFF set developed for the Freya and other early warning radars allowed more detailed and specific warnings to be passed to the Würzburg operators, whose equipment still had no IFF. The great breakthrough, however, was the appearance of Lichtenstein B/C airborne interception (AI) radar, finally available in quantity in the late spring and early summer of 1942.[3]

Kammhuber was not responsible for the delay. Although he may not have recognized the importance of radar when first appointed in 1940, he had soon learned precisely what he wanted: a lightweight apparatus with streamlined aerials, giving 360° search and having a range from five hundred yards to ten miles. But he had not enjoyed the support of his superiors, Göring for one declaring that 'a fighter cannot have things [ie, aerials] sprouting from its head.' Then, when the need for airborne radar could no longer be challenged, weaknesses in the German electronics industry, particularly in those sectors designing and producing vacuum tubes, and the non-technical bent of most of the Luftwaffe's senior staff, caused further delays.[4]

With the help of Martini, however, Lichtenstein was ready for testing in the early summer of 1941. The set was not all that Kammhuber had asked for, having only 140° horizontal search, 60° vertical, and a range between two hundred yards and two miles. Design and production problems delayed the project, however – many of the first sets produced were routinely unserviceable – and, apart from six successful interceptions in August and September 1941, when the equipment was being tested, the first AI-assisted victory did not occur until June 1942. By then, Lichtenstein's reputation as an untrustworthy device

---

[*] Fitted in aircraft and consisting of a combined receiver and transmitter, both British and German IFF equipment responded to signals emitted from air-defence radars with distinctive and sometimes coded replies which indicated the nationality (and sometimes the type) of aircraft.

was widespread, as was the knowledge that it robbed fighters of twenty-five miles per hour in speed, leaving some types with only the barest margin of superiority over the bombers they were trying to track. In time, modifications and refinements in design, production, and calibration produced a reliable piece of equipment, but even so Kammhuber had to overcome the prejudices of a group of fighter pilots who, like all their ilk, still preferred to slip anything that tied them to the surly bonds of Earth. Although AI radar theoretically extended their freedom by making freelance operations more practical, used in the way Kammhuber intended it would be just another bothersome link to ground control. Rather than allowing his fighters to stalk their prey all the way into Germany and back, as the British expected, he was determined to strengthen his system of ground-controlled interception in a procedure called Himmelbett.[5]

Himmelbett was the logical successor to, and extension of, all Kammhuber's previous thinking about air defence. As he conceived it, airborne radar would simply replace searchlights as the main tool in 'illuminating' enemy aircraft. Once the early warning radars picked up approaching aircraft, determined they were hostile, and passed on their height and bearing to the ground control stations, the Würzburg operators would swing into action, one – the 'blue' – fixing on the night-fighter circling his beacon, the other – the 'red' – tracking whichever bomber (if there were more than one) offered the best chance of interception. When both Würzburgs had picked up their targets, the data they provided were passed to plotters who translated this information into graphic form by projecting coloured dots representing the bomber and the fighter onto a translucent screen. Now the ground controller took over. Watching the situation unfold before him, he passed courses, speeds, and altitudes to the fighter pilot, vectoring him into a position slightly below and about a mile or so behind the bomber, where the chances of his AI acquiring the target were good. The controller then maintained a watching brief while the fighter's radar operator guided his pilot into visual contact. If an attack could not be made before the fighter ran up against the boundary of its 'box,' however, the pilot was required to return to his beacon and await the next call, leaving the bomber to some other fate. If two fighters were stationed in the 'box,' a second set-piece attack was perhaps already underway against another target.

Simple, orderly, even elegant, Himmelbett was seductive, if inflexible. All that was required to defeat Bomber Command, it seemed, was to expand the system so that no part of Germany or its western and northern approaches was left unboxed. When that had been achieved, enemy bombers could be engaged all the way to the target and back through a succession of ground-controlled interceptions, and there would be no reason ever to resort to the potential chaos of freelance pursuit.* In early May 1942, then, Kammhuber asked for sufficient resources to extend his system throughout the Reich. That would entail

---

* This emphasis on inflexible, centralized control was in sharp contrast to the decentralization and flexibility of German army doctrine as expressed in the mission-oriented orders of Auftragstaktik, with which Kammhuber would have been familiar before his transfer to the Luftwaffe.

production of six hundred additional Würzburgs, the provision of 270 night-fighters and crews (three new Geschwader), an equal number of Lichtenstein B/C sets, and an additional 150,000 ground personnel. He also asked that work begin to develop panoramic radar, which would give 360° coverage, and purpose-built night-fighters that would not be transferred out of his command even in the event of emergencies elsewhere.[6]

Had Bomber Command been causing serious damage to Germany or had the Luftwaffe been free of its massive commitments in the east, Kammhuber's requests might have received a more sympathetic hearing. But in May 1942 the night air war was, for Hitler and his acolytes, still a minor, incidental skirmish, almost a side-show, while the scale and intensity of operations in the Soviet Union were still growing. Kammhuber's demands were therefore denied. The design of specialized night-fighters was put off; most Junkers Ju 88s and Dorner Do 217s continued to be allocated to the Ostfront as bombers; radar development did not receive a higher priority; and, at the political level at least, Flak remained the air-defence weapon of choice.[7]

For the immediate future, then, Kammhuber would have to rely on a force cobbled together from what was available: some two hundred machines – about 60 per cent of establishment – made up of a disparate collection of Me 109s without radar available for point defence over target cities; Do 217s equipped with dive brakes and bomb racks and rightly regarded as 'absolute monsters' in the night-fighter role; and Me 110s and Ju 88s, eventually the mainstay of the force but which, with their Lichtenstein antennae, were only marginally faster than the current Halifax and Lancaster variants. For all these reasons, the Himmelbett system grew more slowly than Kammhuber had hoped for. Expansion took place mainly within the original western belt, extending from the tip of Denmark to Paris, in the Ruhr, and around the Frankfurt, Mannheim, and Stuttgart industrial complex. Parts of Germany, particularly in the south and east, were left without adequate fighter protection, and it was still possible for a bomber force to burst through the outer crust into relatively ill-defended air space. Everything hinged on the results obtained over Holland, the most heavily used bomber route. It was here that the best pilots, controllers, and ground support units were concentrated – and it was here, for the moment, that Bomber Command's losses were highest.[8]

Himmelbett had been designed to meet the needs of night air defence as they had developed over the past year, when Bomber Command crews had gone about their business individually. Unknown to the Luftwaffe, however, the scale and style of the bombing offensive against Germany was about to expand and change dramatically. At the time of his appointment as AOC-in-C, Harris could normally call upon four or five hundred crews on any given night, but he was now contemplating launching a thousand bombers, organized into a compact stream no more than forty miles wide, 'against a single target in a single night.'[9] The material effect of such a blow might be great but the moral effect would surely be greater, both on the enemy and on those in Britain who were incessantly questioning the value of the 'strategic bombing' campaign. To have the desired impact, Harris knew that his 'thousand plan,' or Operation

Millennium, had to be directed against a major industrial centre 'round which the enemy was bound to concentrate effective and heavy defences. So far all that the Lübeck and Rostock attacks had proved was that we could saturate the passive defences of a town by concentration of attack; it remained to be seen whether the active and passive defences of a vital industrial area could be similarly overcome.'[10] It was the requirement to swamp the enemy's defences and to produce 'mass destruction around the aiming point'[11] that demanded the use of a great many aircraft, but there was nothing special about the figure of one thousand other than its public relations value.

To obtain one thousand aircraft, Harris could not rely on Bomber Command's resources alone without using every machine and crew from OTUs and Heavy Conversion Units (HCUs). If Coastal and Army Co-operation Commands joined in, however, the required number would be available, using only the most experienced OTU pupils and their instructors.[12] This was a bold gamble. There was a great deal to be gained if it succeeded.

We should have before us a definite and attainable goal, a measure of what could be achieved as soon as our expansion really began. The result of using an adequate bomber force against Germany would be there for all the world to see, and I should be able to press for the aircraft, crews, and equipment we needed with far more effect than by putting forward theoretical arguments, however convincing, in favour of hitting the enemy where it would hurt him most. Such a demonstration was, in fact, the only argument I could see which was at all likely to prevent our squadrons from being snatched away and our effort diverted to subsidiary targets, or to extract the equipment we so desperately needed, the radar navigational aids and the target indicators, from the torpid departments which withheld them for so long.[13]

There were also risks. If the raid failed to do visible, palpable damage, the future of the strategic bombing campaign might be even more imperilled, while if losses were heavy Bomber Command's front-line strength and its replacement capability would both be severely affected.

Harris quickly received the approval in principle of Portal and Churchill, the latter declaring on 17 May that he was prepared to accept the loss of a hundred aircraft on the proposed operation. (Harris believed he might lose only sixty, so this was something of a bonus.) Not wanting to lose the initiative, within two days he produced a plan for an attack on either Hamburg or Cologne, knowing that the final choice, depending on the weather, would have to be delayed until the last minute.[14]

It remained only to secure the cooperation of the other commands and services. After broaching the subject with the First Sea Lord, who exercised operational control over Coastal Command, the prime minister assured Harris (through the CAS) that there should be no difficulties from that quarter, and on 21 May its AOC-in-C, Air Chief Marshal Sir Philip Joubert de la Ferté, offered 250 machines – the lion's share of the three hundred Harris needed to raise from outside Bomber Command. Flying Training Command added thirty, and the OTUs another 370. Including the Blenheims from No 2 Group and Army

Co-operation Command, and those aircraft from Fighter Command carrying out intruder operations against night-fighter airfields along the route, well over a thousand aircraft would be committed to the proposed raid, now scheduled to take place a few days either side of 30 May because of the advantages accruing from moonlight.[15]

Operation Order No 147 was issued on 23 May. Hamburg, a favourite target but outside Gee range, would be the primary objective and Cologne the alternate on 27/28 May. Two days later, with planning almost complete, the Admiralty suddenly vetoed Joubert's offer and Flying Training Command halved its commitment, leaving only eight hundred bombers available for Millennium. A last-ditch effort had to be made to find the necessary crews and aircraft for the operation, now postponed by bad weather, and it was decreed that all OTU and HCU crews would take part.[16]

The revised operation order was issued on 26 May, prescribing the exact routes to be followed and the timings to be adhered to on the way to and over the target. Crews were told, for example, to turn for home no later than zero plus ninety minutes, 'wherever they may be and whether they have dropped their bombs or not,' to ensure that the raid lasted no longer than the scheduled hour and a half. The height of attack was left for each group AOC to decide, except that the minimum bombing altitude was established at 8000 feet to avoid the worst of the light and medium Flak. Emphasis would be given to fire-raising, with crews carrying 'the maximum load of 4-lb and 30-lb incendiary bombs, made up as necessary with H[igh] E[xplosive] bombs.'[17]

Harris could not keep so large a force on stand-by indefinitely, but weather delayed Millennium until the morning of 30 May 1942, when conditions over the Ruhr/Rhine were predicted to be good enough for an attack that night against Cologne. Once the AOC-in-C had decided upon the alternate target (just after 0900 hrs), High Wycombe and group staffs worked out the final procedures and tactics for the raid. Fuel requirements were calculated, after which it was possible to stipulate the weight of bombs which could be carried and the mix between incendiaries and high-explosives. Concentration points and times were worked out so that crews taking off from all over England would merge smoothly into one large bomber stream, and every squadron was allocated to one of its three waves. For those worried about the risk of collision, given the density of aircraft over the target, the operational research scientists had predicted that only two crews were liable to be lost that way.[18]

The four RCAF squadrons contributed a total of seventy-one aircraft and crews, but only after much work. Taken off operations on 18 April to begin converting to Halifax IIs, No 405 Squadron spent the last few days of May 'working with fury' so as to be ready for Millennium. By 27 May sixteen crews were qualified on the new aircraft, and fourteen machines were fully serviceable. Two more were ready by the 29th, and a seventeenth became available the next day when one Halifax from the squadron's conversion flight was outfitted for operations. Bombing-up was a problem, however, as the groundcrews 'could not get the bombs out of our dump fast enough. Every vehicle was hauling bomb carts ... The logistics of aircraft carrying double the previous loads needed some methods which we had not yet mastered.' No 408 Squadron had also just begun to convert to a new type, but for Millennium would muster nineteen Hampdens and its sole Manchester. Nos 419 and 420 committed eighteen Wellingtons and fifteen Hampdens, respectively.[19]

In No 419 Squadron crews were apprehensive when the target was an-nounced – 'the much dreaded Cologne' – but when the intelligence officer also stated that 'around 1,150 aircraft would be on this target, we all got a terrific boost.'[20] They got an additional boost at takeoff. Double summertime meant there were still glimmers of light in the western sky at 11:30 PM, and, 'when we got to our kite and stood around smoking,' one participant recalled: 'a couple of bombers passed overhead going eastward, then a couple more. The air started to roar with aero engines; we could see bombers everywhere ... Shortly after this we taxied down and took off. When we got settled down we started to see aircraft everywhere. The sky was full of them. There were Stir-lings, Hampdens, Lancasters, etc.; I don't think there was a single type of British bomber in use that we did not see that night.'[21]

No 419's Gee-equipped Wellingtons reached Cologne in the first wave. The weather was fine, with bright moonlight and only a small amount of cirrus cloud, and the aiming point in the city centre was clearly visible. The weather was just as good for the night-fighters, of course, but 419's crews commented on the relative lack of opposition. Fulton, the squadron's commanding officer, noted that the 'ground defences seemed very ineffective,' while Squadron Leader D.L. Wolfe thought that 'the large number of A[ir]C[raft] ... com-pletely upset Flak and searchlight prediction. No fighters seen or evidence of fighters.'[22] Squadron Leader J.D. Pattison, the one-time fighter pilot now well-acquainted with bomber operations, reported the same: 'The moon was full, so we didn't expect much darkness to hide in ... [but] the enemy defences were completely foxed from the outset. There was no serious Flak all the way in. When we first got to the target area, the defences appeared to be trying to pick up the aircraft with searchlights, but by the time we left they had given it up as a bad job.'[23] Only Flight Sergeant A.H. Harris noted seeing 'several fighters ... about 10 miles north-west of Cologne,' too far away to matter. It was, as the squadron diary noted, a 'piece of cake.'[24]

By the time Nos 405, 408, and 420 Squadrons arrived over Cologne with the rest of the last wave, fires were burning fiercely and the city was much easier to find. This was also the most highly concentrated part of the bomber stream, and that which would suffer the fewest casualties. The enemy's de-fences en route had been overwhelmed, while over the target the moderate Flak had diminished significantly. Yet this part of the raid was not entirely without incident. John Fauquier, now commanding No 405, was coned by searchlights as he left the scene, two other crews saw aircraft going down in flames, and a third was 'approached from astern by s[ingle]-e[ngined] enemy aircraft without engaging.' But it was Pilot Officer R.S. Turnbull of 405 Squadron's conversion flight who had the closest encounter with the enemy – possibly with one of the fighters Flight Sergeant Harris had glimpsed ten miles north-west of the target. For at this precise location, the squadron diary reported,

Turnbull (who had completed one tour as a non-commissioned pilot with RAF squadrons, winning a DFM, and who would reach the rank of wing commander by November 1942) was 'approached from below and dead astern by Me 110 which closed to 100 yards and fired 10 second burst then broke away to starboard. Our rear gunner replied with two bursts as E[nemy]/A[ircraft] broke away. Our A/C hit in tailplane, but no casualties.'[25]

No 408 Squadron's lone Manchester was forced to return early, as were two of the Hampdens, but the other seventeen crews reached the target and bombed successfully. No 420 Squadron also had an easy time, although one of its Hampdens crashed into a Lancaster after landing at Waddington and was badly damaged, with two crew members hurt. Indeed, as it turned out, landing was one of the riskier parts of Operation Millennium. Never as tidy a process as takeoff, it took over three hours for all the aircraft returning from Cologne to set down, either at their own base or, for one reason or another, at someone else's. All told forty-one aircraft went missing – giving a loss rate of 3.9 per cent of the 1047 sorties, of which about 870 had actually bombed the target. Three-fifths of all bombing photographs were plotted within three miles of the aiming point.[26]

The crews knew even then that they had witnessed a resounding success. Pattison concluded (with some exuberance and exaggeration) that 'this raid will go down as one of the greatest events of this war. We had very nearly wiped a great city of three-quarters of a million people off the map in ninety minutes.'[27] Another Canadian participant, whose enthusiastic views were noted by the censors, was happy to be punishing Germans in this fashion: 'The Jerries are going to be crying for mercy in the near future, and we'll go on pounding them until they quit. I'll be able to say I took part in the greatest bombing raid in the history of the world. It gives me real pleasure to sit up there and see the German cities burn. We really made up for the blitzing of London and added some.'[28]

Harris was equally elated with the success of his tactical experiment. Although more German fighters than usual had been scrambled, he had saturated the enemy's defences with a bomber stream no more than twenty miles wide, narrow enough that it had passed through only eight night-fighter boxes and been engaged by very few of the enemy crews standing guard. Better still, while the loss rate was actually a little higher than that suffered during previous attacks on Cologne, it was lower than average for raids conducted on moonlit, cloudless nights; and for the last, most concentrated wave, in which three RCAF squadrons flew, casualties were an astonishingly low 1.9 per cent. Moreover, there was considerable evidence that Flak, not fighters, had been the major cause of casualties, a conjecture that was substantiated after the war. Only twenty-five ground-controlled Himmelbett interceptions were carried out, while hundreds of pilots and radar operators remained idle, bypassed by the bomber stream.[29]

More significantly, it was certain that exceptional damage had been done – a fact borne out by photo-reconnaissance flights conducted a week later. 'Damage seen in Cologne resulting from this raid is on a larger scale than anything yet seen in any German city. Damage is heavy and widespread. Not only are large areas of the centre of the city devastated, involving the destruction of public and administrative buildings and business premises, but industrial and residential property in all suburban areas have been seriously affected by fire and H[igh] E[xplosive].'[30] Closer analysis revealed six hundred acres of nearly complete devastation, half in the city centre which bore the brunt of the attack. Some 250 factory buildings or railway workshops had been damaged, and it was believed that 100,000 people had been evacuated. Moreover, there was an uncorroborated report that there had been a complete breakdown of order, with Nazi officials (including members of the SA and the SS) among those fleeing the city. If the morale of Party members broke, it was felt, the resolve of the civilian population as a whole was surely close to collapse.[31]

The German victims were, indeed, impressed. Contrary to British estimates placing the number of civilians killed in the tens of thousands, the death toll was relatively small – about five hundred – but with 3300 buildings destroyed, and more than 2500 separate fires started, there was a manifest sense of doom. One resident recalled that 'when at last that Sunday morning dawned, a tremendous fire-cloud hung over the city.' 'The sun was dimmed and all we could see of it was a purple disc behind the writhing smoke, a circle which at its edges broke up into the colours of the rainbow, then into deepest black. Suffering and death, fire and destruction raged in the streets in the ghostly twilight of a total eclipse. For many hours the glare of the flames was brighter than day-light.'[32] The official German communiqué complained how 'British bombers [had] carried out terrorist raids on the inner city of Cologne.' 'Great damage was done by the effect of explosives and fires, particularly in residential quarters. Several public buildings were hit, among them three churches and two hospitals. In this attack directed exclusively against the civilian population, the RAF suffered severe losses. Night fighters and AA artillery shot down 36 of the attacking aircraft. In addition one bomber was shot down in the coastal area by naval artillery.'[33] The first issue of the *Kölnische Zeitung* to be published after the raid noted: 'Those who survived were fully aware that they had bade farewell to their Cologne, because the damage is enormous and because the integral part of the character, and even the traditions, of the city is gone forever.' Yet within two weeks life in the city had more or less returned to normal. The citizens' moral fibre held and, since the main industrial centres on the outskirts were not seriously damaged, the loss of war production caused by this massive assault was probably no more than one to two months.[34]

The AOC-in-C immediately laid on another 'thousand raid' for Hamburg the very next night, but bad weather forced its postponement. After a twenty-four-hour pause, the second raid was mounted against Essen, on 1/2 June. This time 956 aircraft were involved, all but two from Bomber Command, and twenty Gee-equipped Wellingtons acted as target-finders, dropping flares to mark it for the rest. The four Canadian squadrons committed sixty-three aircraft, losing only two, but a heavy and persistent haze prevented accurate bombing and only one in ten bombing photographs were plotted within three miles of the aiming point. Very few of the crews reaching Essen claimed that their bombs had fallen on, or even near, their objective, reporting instead that the fires they saw were scattered all over the Ruhr. One pilot from No 419 Squadron, who had 'bombed near [an] enormous fire,' was not sure he had identified Essen at all.[35]

The Germans were equally mystified as to Bomber Command's objective. Recording just 106 casualties and only eleven houses destroyed in the city, they never realized that Essen had been the sole target. Nevertheless, Harris remained convinced of the validity of his enterprise. Believing that the first two raids had solidified support both for the concept of an area offensive and for the four thousand-bomber expansion program adopted in October 1941, he launched a third very large attack (involving 1067 aircraft, including 102 from Coastal Command) on 25/26 June. In part because Bremen, another port, was usually easy to find, and in part because of pressure from the navy, High Wycombe added a new tactical wrinkle to this operation. While most of Bomber Command carried out a standard area attack, No 5 Group (including 408 Squadron) and crews from Coastal Command were detailed for precision bombing of the Deutsche Schiffwerke shipyards and the Focke Wulf factory producing the long-range FW 200 Condor aircraft used against Allied convoys.[36]

Despite thin cloud cover, and in contrast to the Essen raid, Gee brought the first bombers right to the target, and they set fires large enough to attract the rest of the stream. Dockyards, railways, and shipworkers' houses were all damaged. Finding a pinpoint target was rather more difficult. No 408 Squadron crews flying as low as 3000 feet could not locate their aiming points through the haze, and simply bombed an area they assumed to be Bremen. Yet someone from No 5 Group managed to flatten one whole assembly shop with a single 4000-lb bomb. The Germans registered 572 houses destroyed, 6108 damaged, and eighty-five civilian deaths, but air-raid officials estimated the size of the raid at only eighty machines.[37]

The 'thousand bomber force' was now dispersed. In retrospect, apart from the initial powerful impact of the attack on Cologne, its operations were by and large a disappointment. The bombing had not been accurate, and altogether 125 crews had been lost, 4 per cent of sorties. Almost a third of these had come from the OTUs,[*] imposing a lien on Bomber Command's future and ensuring that the question of employing training crews or instructors on operations would be looked at very closely if it were ever raised again.

On a broader level, by the end of June 1942 there was reason to doubt whether Harris had, in fact, solved the strategic, operational, and tactical puzzle that was now two years old: Could Bomber Command obtain worthwhile results against important targets often enough, and with acceptable losses? At the same time, the psychological element of the Millennium plan had also backfired. Despite unequivocal statements by the prime minister that such a

---

[*] That the loss rate among OTU crews (5.1 per cent) was considerably higher than the 3.4 per cent suffered by operational groups strengthened the case of those who objected to their further employment and argued that lack of experience was a major cause of casualties.

massive effort could not be routinely repeated, public and private reaction to
the more customary raids involving two or three hundred sorties to which
Harris returned between Essen and Bremen and thereafter was one of frustration and letdown – as if Bomber Command was actually failing in its task
when it could not find one thousand. The navy in particular was dissatisfied.
Less than helpful when he refused to provide Coastal Command aircraft for the
first two 'thousand' raids, the First Sea Lord now asked that Harris's squadrons
play a greater, and more direct, role in the Battle of the Atlantic. Portal rushed
to Bomber Command's defence, noting that the 'echoes of Cologne' were
already spreading around the world, but his intervention could not prevent the
transfer of about a tenth of High Wycombe's front-line strength to Coastal and
Army Co-operation Commands.[38]

Bitterly opposed to what was happening, on 17 June Harris complained
directly to the prime minister, simplistically dismissing Coastal Command's
incessant search 'for the needle in the haystack' – U-boats in the immensity
of North Atlantic waters – as 'an obstacle to victory.' He was even more
virulent in his comments on what he viewed – perhaps more correctly – as the
mad decision to employ bomber aircraft with Army Co-operation Command
to transport parachute troops, with all that that implied.

Involvement in land campaigns, especially Continental campaigns, serves but to reduce
us to the level of the Horde. We are not a Horde. We are a highly industrialised,
under-populated, physically … small nation. Our lead is in science, not spawn; in
brains, not brawn. To enter upon a continental land campaign, other than on a mop-
ping-up police basis, is to play right into Germany's hands; to invite her, without need
or reason, to take best advantage of the one superior asset remaining to her, a vast and
efficient army … Once we get a footing on the Continent our last bomb will have been
dropped on Germany. Thereafter the whole of our Air effort will be required to bolster
up our land struggle in France. It will not be enough … It is imperative, if we hope
to win the War, to abandon the disastrous policy of military intervention in the land
campaigns of Europe, and to concentrate our air power against the enemy's weakest
spots. But, instead, we are displaying a growing inclination to revert to old and archaic
methods of war. Wilfully to reduce ourselves to the level of the Horde by engaging
in Continental gladiatorial combat. Such a decision history will show to have been
grievously wrong.[39]

However, when Harris asked for the immediate return of all bomber squadrons serving elsewhere, Churchill responded in his usual fashion, skilfully
playing to both sides at the same time. Admitting that strategic bombing was
no longer the only way to win the war now that the United States and the
Soviet Union were fully involved, he nevertheless declared that it would be a
mistake not to increase the intensity of the bombing offensive. But despite
expressing his 'sorrow and alarm [at] the woeful shrinkage of our plans for
Bomber Command,' he did not halt the transfer of squadrons to other commands.[40]

Meeting the goals of the October 1941 expansion program had always depended on receiving a healthy share of United States production, but on 21 June 1942 the Arnold-Portal-Towers agreement on aircraft allocation confirmed President Roosevelt's wish that American-built machines should, as a rule, be flown by American crews in American units. With that the Air Ministry's ambitions crumbled, and it was compelled to adopt a revised plan that would limit Bomber Command's maximum strength to about 2500 aircraft and 125 squadrons instead of the 4000 machines set down only a few months before. Furthermore, because everything would henceforth depend on the output of British (and perhaps Canadian) factories alone, it would take longer to reach this revised figure. Instead of sixty-two squadrons by the end of the year, there would be only fifty (of which, it turned out, only forty-one would be operational within Bomber Command). Six were RCAF.[41]

The reduced rate of growth, coupled with significant shortfalls in production (especially of Wellingtons, in arrears by 245 machines at the end of November 1942) immediately called into question promises made regarding the pace at which new RCAF squadrons would come into being. As far back as January 1941 Canada had asked that fifteen bomber squadrons be established overseas as part of the Article XV complement; and in July Air Minister C.G. Power had been assured that the formation of a Canadian bomber group would follow when there were sufficient RCAF squadrons overseas and when aerodrome facilities were complete. This arrangement was reconfirmed and then strengthened at the Ottawa Air Training Conference of May-June 1942, when it was decided that ten new RCAF squadrons would come on strength by the end of 1942, enough for the creation of a Canadian group early in 1943.[42]

Ten additional squadrons would have given the RCAF 30 per cent of Bomber Command's revised total of fifty by the end of 1942, just a shade too many given the numbers of Canadians serving under Harris; but they also represented just under 60 per cent of the total number of new squadrons to be established by the end of the year – a demonstrably disproportionate share. For political reasons, however, and in fairness to the RCAF's enormous contribution to the bomber offensive, the Air Ministry decided it could not renege on commitments made to Canada, and Bomber Command was so informed.

Having received enough bad news in the preceding six weeks, and never happy with the idea of forming dominion squadrons, Harris reacted bitterly. 'Canadians make good crews,' he told the vice chief of the air staff, 'but I, for one, should be most perturbed to see almost the entire expansion going into Canadians for the rest of the year.'

It would be quite unacceptable. We are always being accused, as a nation, of fighting with the bodies of Colonial and dominion personnel in preference to British – so far unjustly. But why lend colour to it.

Furthermore because, for political reasons, the Canadians are insisting on forming their own group, the provision of ten Canadian squadrons in addition to the five now in existence would throw both the number of Canadian squadrons in the Command

and the size of the Canadian group out of all proportion to the remainder. What with Canadians, Poles, Rhodesians and Australians, we shall at this rate ... very soon arrive at the stage where most of the operational squadrons are manned by coloured troops.[43]

Sir Wilfrid Freeman agreed, but, predicting that the politicians would 'give away all we can,' he did not think much could be done to stop them. His instincts were essentially sound. The undersecretary of state for air, Harold Balfour, asked the secretary of state not to abrogate Britain's undertakings to Canada, modifying them only so that the number of RCAF squadrons to be formed by December should be decreased by three to reflect overall reductions. Sir Archibald Sinclair accepted Balfour's advice, and Ottawa was so informed.[44]

Although disappointed by this turn of events, the Canadian government was in no position to contest matters of supply and wisely chose not to do so. Sir Arthur Harris was less obliging, however, and turned on Sinclair. 'Dominion representation is growing out of all proportion. Although I realise that the increase in the Canadian squadrons is a political matter, we shall thereby be jumping out of the frying pan into the fire politically ... I must urgently represent that if we have in fact engaged to form ten more Canadian squadrons by the end of this year, then not more than half of these should be in this command.'[45] In fact, the number (as Harris should have known) had already fallen to seven, which was as far as the Air Ministry was prepared to go given that Canada was providing a quarter of all bomber aircrew.[46]

Harris had made his point and lost, and for the moment he did not pursue the matter further. Nor did he attempt to shift the focus of his opposition to the formation of additional RCAF squadrons by raising the issue of operational efficiency, something he was perfectly free to do as a commander-in-chief. The same could not be said of some Canadians, however, whose views were expressed in a *Globe and Mail* editorial of 16 September 1942: 'Setting up a separate Canadian bombing command is working against the whole trend that has been shown reaching fruition – that of unity of command. The RAF has the experienced operational officers who have gone through three years of the sternest fighting. The RAF men and operational officers have proved their ability time and again ... The RCAF has not the trained men to direct these raids ... Canadians will without doubt rise to their places in the operational command, but to have a separate bombing command simply for nationalistic purposes interferes with the effective fighting of the war in the air.'[47]

The *Globe* misunderstood the structure of Bomber Command, believing erroneously that the formation of a Canadian group would somehow give the Canadian component a degree of independent action similar to that enjoyed by the embryonic US Eighth Air Force. Apparently, some feared that 'Canadianization' would lead to a bureaucratic divorce along these lines and Power eventually had to speak out strongly, when given the opportunity by *Maclean's* magazine in November. Asked whether it meant 'tossing overboard' all the help that the RCAF received from the British, he retorted 'not in the slightest. We have absolutely no intention of setting up a separate operational command in Britain. That might come, perhaps in some other part of the world where Canadians might be doing the greater part of the fighting. But not in Britain today. Right now the United States has its own operational command in Britain, but for Canada it's not necessary or advisable.' Nothing, he added, would be done 'at the expense of fighting efficiency,' even if this meant that RAF officers would command Canadian stations and squadrons until RCAF officers were qualified.[48]

Power was not dissembling. Although the proposed Canadian group would be identified as an RCAF formation, to be manned and administered by Canadians to the maximum extent practicable, it would not act independently, selecting its own targets and planning its own missions outside Bomber Command's control. Rather, like all the other groups, it would remain subordinate to Harris and mount operations according to instructions received from High Wycombe.

With so many RCAF aircrew on their way to (or already in) Britain, it was assumed that Canadianizing the group's squadrons should be a relatively straightforward matter. Problems would arise, however, when it came to providing the experienced technical, administrative, and operational staff officers required at group, base, and station headquarters, whose influence on living and working conditions could be great, but who were simply not to be found in the RCAF Overseas. At the outset, therefore, it was accepted that a number of these specialist and technical billets would also have to be filled by non-Canadians, but this blow to complete Canadianization – if, indeed, it were that – was softened considerably when, during the discussions leading to the decision to form a Canadian group, the RAF readily agreed to post RCAF officers to other headquarters as staff learners, so they would be prepared to take over senior appointments early in the life of their own group.[49]

Canadian acquiescence in British planning and management did not mean that the RCAF had to remain disinterested and passive when it came to such matters as deciding how the group should be formed, where it should be based, what aircraft it would fly, and what RAF group it should be associated with. The problem, for British and Canadian officials alike, was that these were not separate, discrete questions but were inextricably linked together by High Wycombe's policy of homogeneity – the thoroughly sensible view, from the standpoint of rationalizing maintenance and repair as well as aircrew training, that whenever possible bomber groups should operate a single aircraft type, and that groups flying the same types should be neighbours.

Complete homogeneity was impossible so long as Bomber Command was still converting from medium bombers (Wellingtons, Whitleys, and Hampdens) to heavy bombers (Stirlings, Halifaxs, and Lancasters). Until the process was complete, at least two types, the old and the new, would be in service in each group at any one time. Furthermore, there were differences within type: Lancaster IIs and Halifax IIIs shared Bristol Hercules radial engines, while Halifax II/Vs and Lancaster I/IIIs were powered by in-line Merlins, albeit of different marks. The situation was even more muddled in the Canadian case. With No 405 having already switched to Halifax IIs, three different types were in use by RCAF squadrons – Halifax, Hampden, and Wellington – and a fourth would soon be added if No 420 proceeded with its planned re-equipment with Manchesters. Yet because Canada had undertaken to produce Lancaster Xs at Victory Aircraft in Toronto, it also made sense to consider this type for the Canadian bomber group. And, indeed, that was what was decided in May 1942. Although Wellingtons would probably make up the initial equipment of new squadrons, the 'ultimate aim' was to create a Lancaster group flying Canadian-made Mark Xs. (The fact that 405 flew Halifaxes was inconsequential for such long-term planning, while the conversion of 420 to Manchesters was soon halted; it re-equipped with Wellington IIIs beginning in August.)[50]

With this question resolved, other things fell into place. Selecting the Lancaster, generally considered the best of the British bombers, more or less ruled out an association between the Canadian group and No 3 Group (Stirlings) and No 4 Group (Halifaxes). No 5 Group was already converting to Lancasters from Hampdens and had two Canadian squadrons under command, but because of its somewhat special status[*] since the beginning of the war the possibility of linking the Canadians with it seems never to have been considered. That left No 1 Group, sandwiched between Nos 4 and 5 Groups in Lincolnshire and southern Yorkshire, for which an ultimate heavy bomber type had not yet been selected, but which was currently flying Wellingtons and Halifaxes, and thus could readily accommodate most RCAF squadrons. Largely because it was thought likely that it would eventually be equipped with Lancasters, some RCAF officers overseas had suggested that it might be better for Canada to take over No 1 Group (with all its bases and infrastructure) than to create a new group from scratch – a process which would involve extensive construction of runways and buildings and which might very well delay the group's fitting-out with four-engined machines. Convinced that Canadianization would proceed more quickly in a new formation, Ottawa thought otherwise, but links to No 1 Group were nonetheless forged. In late June instructions were prepared to post all Canadian bomber squadrons to bases in its area until No 6 (RCAF) Bomber Group became operational.[51]

From the standpoint of operational flying, somewhere further south would have been preferable. There was less smoke and industrial haze to contend with in, say, East Anglia, and the distances to be flown to the Ruhr and most other German targets were not so great. But much of the south was reserved for the burgeoning US Army Air Forces and Bomber Command's Pathfinder Force (see below, 612–13), while East Anglia was also home to No 3 Group, whose marginally effective Stirlings needed every possible advantage.[52]

As things turned out, however, No 6 Group was not established on Lancasters, and Canadian squadrons were not moved to the No 1 Group area. Instead, the Halifax was chosen as the Canadians' immediate heavy bomber

---

[*]Commanded in turn by Harris, Bottomley, Slessor (the latter two now assistant chiefs of the air staff), and Coryton (a future ACAS) since the beginning of the war, and the first to be equipped with Lancasters, No 5 Group always regarded itself (and was regarded) as something of an élite force.

(with Wellington IIIs and Xs as their interim medium bomber) and, following from that, No 6 Group's territory was carved out of the northern extremity of No 4 Group in the Vale of York. Surrounded by hills that were often shrouded in smog and fog, its dangerously overlapping bases were also the most distant from the majority of German targets. In short, as Sir Arthur Harris admitted much later, the Canadians were 'unfortunately placed geographically.'[53]

The idea of equipping the new group with Halifaxes seems to have occurred to Harris at least as early as 20 June 1942, less than a month after the initial decision to assign Lancasters to it. The move to No 4 Group's area was worked out a month later, and it was only then that the RCAF was made aware of the change.[54] The reasons for the shifts are not entirely clear, and some of the evidence is conflicting, but there is no mistaking Harris's suspicion that 'the Canadians will not produce sufficient Lancasters to equip a Group, or for that matter even to provide OTU backing and equipment for one Squadron' or his contention that, because of Ottawa's decision, the RCAF had a right only to Canadian-built Lancasters.[55]

Sir Arthur's scepticism was not ill-informed. He had been present at the talks held in September 1941 to arrange for the production of Lancasters in Canada and had heard C.D. Howe, Canadian minister of munitions and supply, speak about producing 250 machines in total, at the rate of fifteen a month, beginning 'as soon as possible in 1943' – a schedule which, taking into account wastage and training requirements, would equip only a few squadrons at best. With no British-made Lancasters to spare, except at the expense of RAF squadrons, and the production of the unsatisfactory Stirling being phased out, Harris made what was, for him, the easy decision to equip the Canadians with Halifaxes. Moreover, mid-summer 1942 was a propitious moment for the formation of another Halifax group. Following the transfer of two Whitley squadrons to Coastal Command, No 4 Group's conversion to Halifaxes was nearing completion. In addition, the latter's AOC believed that, because of the experience his crews had gained on the type, the training they could provide would be 'of the highest standard, and ... will enable new Halifax squadrons to become operational in much less time than if these were under other control.'[56] It helped, of course, that there was room for another bomber formation in the north, beside No 4 Group, and that the Canadians were pressing for the earliest possible conversion of their group to four-engined machines.

The British expected the RCAF to object to the Halifax, and perhaps to the Wellington as well. They were right. On 6 August Wing Commander H.L. Campbell, director of air staff at Overseas Headquarters, warned Air Marshal H. Edwards, AOC-in-C of the RCAF Overseas, that there was a 'feeling ... prevalent amongst a number of the Canadian aircrew' in RAF squadrons that they did not want to come to RCAF squadrons flying obsolescent aircraft like the Wellington. Campbell was also concerned that with four Wellington squadrons and, as yet, only one Halifax unit, the Canadian Group might, in fact, become a Wellington group. He therefore suggested that Edwards press the Air Ministry to reverse its decision. 'In view of the large percentage of our squadrons that have operated, and are operating, on obsolescent aircraft I think we are quite justified in holding out very strongly for the equipping of Canadian squadrons with Lancasters, particularly so since the production is good, and they are being built in Canada. Also, in the event that a shortage of aircraft arises when they are in production in Canada, it will be very easy to say that they are of Canadian manufacture, and the allotment of them to Canadian squadrons is only reasonable.'[57]

Air Vice-Marshal L.N. Hollinghurst, director-general of organization at the Air Ministry, was still sensitive, and perhaps even sympathetic, to the Canadian position. Convinced both of the logic and the 'political significance' of giving them the same type that Canadian factories would be turning out, he worried that equipping RCAF squadrons with Halifaxes in the near future because of the temporary shortage of Wellingtons could be seized upon 'as an argument against mounting the Group on Lancasters' later on. Moreover, Hollinghurst was certain that 'we should eventually be forced to give way' and provide Lancasters, and he urged his Air Ministry colleagues not to 'lose both the point and the kudos of having made a graceful gesture' when the time came. Without specifying what type they might fly in the interim, Harris was told simply that 'the Canadian group must, within a reasonable time, re-equip with Lancasters.' Hollinghurst's advice was disregarded, however, as on 26 September the VCAS, Sir Wilfrid Freeman, ruled that the 'Canadians were not to get more Lancasters than they were producing in their own country,' a decision, Portal observed, which met Harris's objections.[58]*

Beset by design problems during development and in its earliest operational marks, underpowered in its later variants, the Halifax never overcame the signal disadvantages of an inadequate operational ceiling and a certain sluggishness in handling which was a handicap in evading night-fighters. No fan of Handley-Page since he had seen his first Hampden, Harris was disgusted by the constant stream of problems the Halifaxes posed, and even as he was asking that No 6 Group fly them he was also insisting that someone 'get to the bottom of Halifax vulnerability.' Better still, he argued, the CAS should find a way to substitute 1300 Lancasters for the 1800 Halifaxes then scheduled to be built. Failing that, he proposed putting all his bad eggs in one basket. The in-line Rolls Royce Merlin XXs used on the Halifax II/V should be transferred to Lancaster production lines, so that factories could build more Lancaster Is and IIIs and abandon the much inferior Lancaster II, powered by Bristol's radial engines. The Hercules thus released could be fitted to Halifaxes as Mark IIIs, which would then be used on easier operations and to meet 'such Naval demands for long range aircraft as may be inflicted upon us.'[59]

That, however, could not be arranged. The Lancaster II and Halifax III remained front-line bombers (both of which were allocated to No 6 Group squadrons), and Harris complained to the Ministry of Aircraft Production (MAP)

---

* In fact, Nos 408 and 432 squadrons were converted to Lancaster IIs in October 1943, and Nos 424, 427, 429, and 433 Squadrons received Lancaster I/IIIs between January and March 1945 once Lancaster Xs had become available.

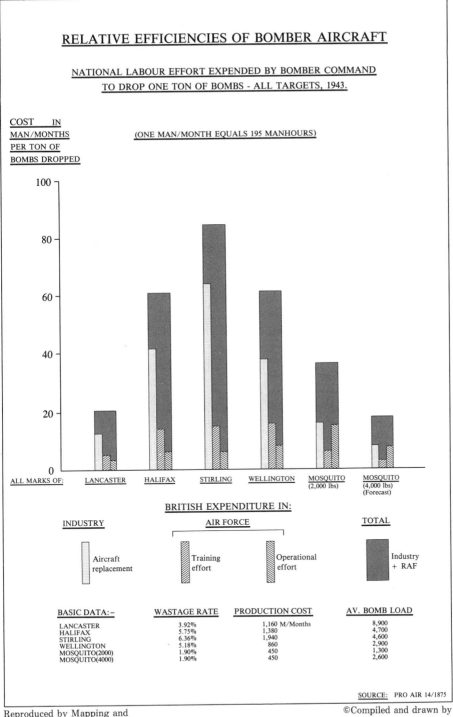

RELATIVE EFFICIENCIES OF BOMBER AIRCRAFT

NATIONAL LABOUR EFFORT EXPENDED BY BOMBER COMMAND
TO DROP ONE TON OF BOMBS - ALL TARGETS, 1943.

COST   IN
MAN/MONTHS   (ONE MAN/MONTH EQUALS 195 MANHOURS)
PER TON OF
BOMBS DROPPED

ALL MARKS OF: LANCASTER   HALIFAX   STIRLING   WELLINGTON   MOSQUITO (2,000 lbs)   MOSQUITO (4,000 lbs) (Forecast)

BRITISH EXPENDITURE IN:

INDUSTRY   AIR FORCE   TOTAL

Aircraft replacement   Training effort   Operational effort   Industry + RAF

BASIC DATA:−	WASTAGE RATE	PRODUCTION COST	AV. BOMB LOAD
LANCASTER	3.92%	1,160 M/Months	8,900
HALIFAX	5.75%	1,380	4,700
STIRLING	6.36%	1,940	4,600
WELLINGTON	5.18%	860	2,900
MOSQUITO(2000)	1.90%	450	1,300
MOSQUITO(4000)	1.90%	450	2,600

SOURCE: PRO AIR 14/1875

Reproduced by Mapping and
Charting Establishment.

©Compiled and drawn by
the Directorate of History.

that he was saddled with a force of Halifaxes that not only 'stinks' but which was also 'cracking' the morale of his crews. Harris may have been exaggerating, but there was no denying the Halifax's startling and unacceptably high loss rate since it had entered squadron service. In raids on Berlin and on north and central Germany (including the Baltic coast), losses were running in the region of 10 per cent, and stood at 5 per cent on operations against the North Sea ports.[60]

Yet at this stage during the summer of 1942, Ottawa's preference for the Lancaster seems to have had very little, if anything, to do with its unmistakable superiority to the Halifax II. Instead, the question boiled down to supply. Not only was it hoped that conversion to an all-heavy-bomber group would occur sooner if the Lancaster was selected, but (thinking the best of Victory Aircraft) once Lancaster Xs began to roll off the line in Toronto there might be greater security of supply than if the Canadian group had to depend on an allocation of British-made machines.[61]

No matter which heavy bomber was selected for No 6 Group, there would be an unavoidable period when most RCAF squadrons (and certainly all those recently formed) would be flying medium bombers. Conversion of the whole of Bomber Command to four-engined machines was not possible all at once and, where practicable, within each group Harris allocated heavy bombers to squadrons more or less by seniority. Accordingly, although Nos 408 and 419 would switch over to the Halifax II and V over the winter of 1942-3, new squadrons would form on Wellington IIIs. That made some sense, as experienced crews usually did a better job of finding and bombing the target and it would have been a waste to give heavy bombers with their larger payloads to units which, from April 1942, were being formed with as few as five experienced crews, the rest coming directly from their training units.[62]

Having made its first flight in 1936, the Vickers Wellington was now an old design, but one that had been extensively up-graded. Its development is well illustrated by the improvements in performance from the Mark I, which cruised at 165 miles per hour and had a service ceiling of 15,000 feet, through the Mark III, with a cruising speed of 180 miles per hour and a ceiling of 19,500 feet, to the Mark X, which could operate at altitudes of 20,000 feet or more and also cruised at 180 miles per hour, but could reach 240 miles per hour for a short period of time, a tremendous asset when trying to throw off a pursuing night-fighter.[63] Like the Halifax, however, Wellingtons were not always comfortable. 'The Wellington III and X were great aircraft to operate,' Flight Lieutenant C. Hughes, a navigator in No 427 Squadron, recalled, 'having a higher operational ceiling than the Halifax.'

I think I'm right in saying that a 'Wimpy' X could reach 21,000 feet, whereas the Halifax V tended to 'stick' at 19,000 feet. The trouble (from my personal point of view) with the Wellingtons was the cold and draught. I normally had to stick the heating pipe into my boot to thaw out my feet, and the face microphones became iced up at altitude and only worked after stopping work to break the ice. Draught was always a problem, especially when our Wellingtons were adapted to carry a 4,000 pound 'Cookie' bomb. For this, on our unit, the bomb doors were removed, leaving the bomb partly outside the bomb bay and successfully deflecting a stream of icy air into the cabin.[64]

Moreover, as we have seen, the loss rate for Wellingtons of all types over north-central Germany and the Rhineland was high enough to cause concern. (About 6.6 per cent overall, but much higher on occasion.) An attack on Nuremburg on 28/29 August, undertaken in bright moonlight, cost 14.5 per cent of all sorties, but a staggering 34 per cent of the Wellingtons involved. The Luftwaffe had obviously recovered its balance after Cologne and, extrapolating from a consistently rising overall loss rate (4.1 per cent in June, 4.4 per cent in July, and 6.6 per cent August), the operational research scientists warned that the figure might soon reach 7 per cent. That was disturbing news, to say the least, but Harris had every reason to believe that concentration and careful routeing were still the keys to success. Indeed, as the location of more and more enemy radars, air-defence boxes, and night-fighter beacons and bases were pinpointed, thanks to electronic intelligence and agents on the ground (particularly a group of Belgians, who managed to steal a map of the air-defence organization in that country), the ability to minimize the bomber stream's proximity to known strongpoints increased and High Wycombe wisely took over responsibility for selecting routes to and from the target.[65]

Yet losses continued to rise despite the greater attention given to concentration and route selection, and by fall operational research scientists in both Bomber Command and the Air Ministry were looking for new options to add to Harris's tactical repertoire. Flying low enough to avoid radar detection would, of course, 'embarrass all known forms of fighter control,' but this was hardly practical when there was Flak to contend with. Similarly, although constant, unpredictable course alterations would make it more difficult for the German controllers to follow individual bombers, it was felt that the risk of collision within the bomber stream would also rise, and an even greater burden would be placed on pilots and navigators who had trouble enough finding their targets without the extra work involved in keeping track of a constantly shifting flight path.[66]

The Germans, too, recognized the growing success of their night-fighting operations and much of the discontent with Himmelbett which had followed immediately after the Cologne raid dissipated. Kammhuber's system was not being swamped every night, and the combination of ground control and AI radar was producing enough 'kills' to quiet even the individualists who favoured uncontrolled night fighting. Kammhuber himself boasted that Himmelbett was 'repeatedly successful' given 'particularly good control officers,'[67] an assertion well illustrated by the following account of the 22 June 1943 raid on Krefeld (but equally applicable to the summer before) when Leutnant Heinz-Wolfgang Schaufer was ordered to Box Meise, about fifteen miles northeast of Brussels, at 1 AM. Schaufer circled his beacon for about twenty minutes until he received instructions to intercept a bomber, apparently far off course, approaching from the west.

On the ground, the men of No. 13/211 Signals Company ... were already tracking Schaufer's Messerschmitt with one Giant *WÜRZBURG* radar: now the other swung around and began sweeping the night sky, looking for the raider. The hand-over from the *FREYA* early-warning system went without a hitch, and by 1:26 a.m. the flight path followed by the unsuspecting British crew was already appearing as a series of co-ordinates on the fighter controller's grid, and as a red spot of light went across the screen of *MEISE*'s *SEEBURG* table ... the fighter control officer ... guided Schaufer over the radio-telephone into position for a 'parallel head-on' interception. This form of attack, designed to bring the fighter into contact with its quarry at the greatest possible range from the ground radar, allowed the maximum room for error ... Schaufer's orders were to fly straight towards the bomber then, just before the two aircraft crossed, turn through a half circle; the night fighter slid round neatly on to the tail of the bomber – a perfect interception. In the rear of the Messerschmitt Second Lieutenant Baro, the radar operator, observed a small hump of light rise up from the flickering base line of his screen: an enemy aircraft, range 2,700 yards. No need for further instructions from the ground, unless things went wrong. Baro passed Schaufer a running commentary on the bomber's position until 1:30 a.m. when, in Schaufer's words: 'I recognised at 500 yards above and to the right a Short Stirling and succeeded in getting in an attack on the violently weaving enemy aircraft. It caught fire in the fuselage and wings, and carried on still blazing. Then it went into a dive, and crashed two miles north-east of Aerschot.' At first light, the fighter-controller drove out to inspect the bomber's wreckage to verify Schaufer's claim. 'There was a crew of seven,' he reported, 'all of whom were lying dead in the wreckage.'[68]

Given Himmelbett operations like that, extending from Denmark to Switzerland and into the interior of Germany, the only thing preventing decisive success, Kammhuber declared after the war, was 'a lack of night fighter planes and trained night fighter crews.'[69]

In fact, the average number of serviceable night-fighters rose from 154 in January 1942 to 362 in December and the number of available crews nearly doubled from 386 to 741, but there were still flaws in Himmelbett that went beyond the availability of men and materiel. Even with the assistance of Lichtenstein B/C, interceptions could take as long as thirty minutes from the moment a fighter first left its beacon until its return, ample time for many other enemy aircraft to pass through the box. Although it was technically possible to add breadth to the system by placing additional fighters in each box, the benefits would have been offset to some extent by the Würzburg's lack of IFF, which made it difficult for controllers to decipher who was who. Moreover, as High Wycombe soon discovered, the Würzburgs could be fooled if the aircraft they were tracking made drastic changes in course – even to the point of causing them to switch coverage, so that the operator assigned to track the night-fighter actually began to plot the progress of its quarry.[70]

Convinced, however, that it was essential to perfect the means by which a single, ground-controlled fighter could shoot down a single enemy bomber, Kammhuber – known by his detractors as the 'Pope of Night Fighting' because he preached the infallibility of his system – brushed these problems aside. He also wanted to make the minimum demands on his crews. Night-flying was risky enough and night-fighting sufficiently demanding in terms of the mental concentration involved – patrols often lasted up to three hours – that he did not want his crews to worry about long-distance navigation and landing at unfamiliar stations under adverse conditions. That rarely happened with Himmelbett, of course, as crews usually flew over familiar territory and almost always landed at their home base.[71]

General der Flieger Adolf Galland was nevertheless right when he complained that the encouraging results obtained by Himmelbett in the summer of 1942 lulled both the Luftwaffe as a whole and Kammhuber in particular into a false sense of security. 'Our command,' he explained, 'allowed the enemy to dictate the necessary defensive measures instead of countering actively with original measures planned with foresight.' In November 1942, for example, when he knew he was short of aircraft and might be even shorter in the future, Kammhuber rejected an offer of a purpose-built, wooden night-fighter based on the de Havilland Mosquito because he feared it would not show up well on the Würzburg radars and would hinder Himmelbett ground control.[72]

There was some innovation, however, as the leading night-fighter crews began to teach their colleagues a new and highly destructive technique first observed by Bomber Command crews in the late spring of 1942. Instead of the standard attack from astern, when fire was opened at between two and four hundred yards, they approached the bomber from behind and below, climbed slowly, almost to the point of stalling, and then raked the underside of the bomber as it passed through their gunsight. Since rear gunners were looking back, not down – where their view was, in any event, obstructed by their guns and the turret floor – they were rarely in a position to give any warning, and many machines, no doubt, were lost without trace.[73]

Once Bomber Command discovered that two-thirds of the machines returning to England with fighter damage had been attacked from below, consideration was given to fitting ventral turrets or free-swinging, individually mounted ventral guns, but because that would involve considerable redesign and also threatened to sacrifice bomb load, the decision was not to be taken hurriedly. Meanwhile, working closely with their pilots, rear gunners were expected to hunch forward over their guns, half-standing, and search the sky below while the pilot conducted a series of alternate banking turns, but the physical demands on the gunner made it impracticable for him to do that for any length of time. Losses continued to rise into the fall, and many surprise attacks were still reported as coming from 'underneath and astern.' No 5 Group, recognizing that 'something is wrong,' asked, 'What is it? Is the method of searching what it should be?' Evidently, it was not. No new tactical manoeuvre was adopted, however, even though the normal evasive tactic preferred by Bomber Command at that time – a simple, diving turn (as opposed to the 'corkscrew' that became the standard in 1943) – played into the hands of a fighter approaching from the rear and below.[74]

Another alternative, long supported by Bomber Command but so far resisted by the Air Ministry for fear of compromising Britain's own security, was to undertake an electronic counter-measures campaign against the enemy's radars and radio communications. The idea, code-named Window, put forward a year earlier of dropping strips of metallic foil cut to a length that would cloud Würzburg screens was still the least complicated solution, but because of its simplicity – it could easily be turned against British radars – it was rejected out of hand. With losses mounting, however, the Air Ministry was finally persuaded that counter-measures had to be introduced, and in October 1942 it gave its blessing to two specific jamming methods: Shiver, which involved modifying the IFF device (already believed, by some, to douse searchlights) so that its transmissions jammed Würzburg; and Mandrel, an airborne and ground-based jammer aimed at Freya.[75]

Shiver went into use almost immediately, and for the first month seemed a great success as the losses of Shiver-equipped aircraft to radar-controlled Flak fell markedly. When it became apparent that this correlation was actually a statistical accident, however – over the longer term there was no appreciable difference in missing rates – and it was also discovered that Shiver was interfering with British radars, the device was abandoned in February 1943. Mandrel was not used until December 1942, when a third technique, Tinsel (the jamming of the fighter control radio band with airborne transmitters) was also introduced. Together they were instant successes as the Germans were forced into the bothersome practice of altering their radio frequencies to avoid jamming. As it turned out, however, it was easier for the enemy to change frequencies than it was to expand Mandrel's coverage or boost its power. Airborne Mandrel was also abandoned for the moment, but not before a number of RCAF squadrons had used it on operations.[76] Tinsel remained in service, and would play a crucial part in the complex tactical manoeuvres attempted later in the war.

Turning back to the summer and to the effectiveness of bombing, the smaller operations mounted after 30 May followed the same general procedures as the 'thousand' raids and demonstrated the same unpredictable patterns and inconsistencies in Gee's effectiveness, both as a navigation aid and as a blind-bombing device. Four raids carried out against Emden between 6 and 23 June showed, for example, that crews using Gee could still be fooled even against a relatively easy-to-find coastal target. On 19/20 June, Osnabrück, sixty miles away, was marked and bombed by almost a quarter of the main force, while, three nights later, decoy fires (clearly identified as such by No 405 Squadron) pulled many crews away from their objective. Only the 6/7 June raid, flown in good weather and featuring extremely good illumination by flares, produced appreciable damage: thirty acres of housing and small businesses were badly burned, fish processing facilities were destroyed, and the railway lines were cut. A 408 Squadron crew reported seeing the fires from sixty miles away.[77]

Four smaller raids on Essen were all failures as crews consistently missed the target area and bombs were dropped all over the Ruhr. On 2/3 June No 405 Squadron received 'no help at all from flares ... except perhaps that they were a general guide to the target area,' and one crew specifically noted them falling well away from the objective. Three nights later crews from No 408 admitted no more than having bombed 'in the Ruhr district,' but they did no worse than the rest of Bomber Command. The attack was widely scattered, and there was very little property damage. On 8/9 June the target was missed again, but this night the German defences played a large part in Bomber Command's failure. Nineteen aircraft of the 170 dispatched were lost (11.2 per cent), and Flak deterred many others from making a disciplined bombing run. Six crews from 405 Squadron reported that, although they managed to reach the target area, 'the terrific opposition, intense S[earch]/L[ight] glare, and ground haze prevented any identification of ground features,' so there was 'very little evidence ... of any weight of attack.'[78]

The worst of these raids was probably the last, when the weather was anything but helpful. Only sixteen of 106 crews found and bombed the target on 16/17 June, while forty-five chose to attack Bonn as an alternative. One of the latter was captained by J.D. Pattison of No 419 Squadron. Running into heavy cloud at 6000 feet and experiencing severe icing on his way across the North Sea, he was able to climb no higher than 12,000 feet before crossing the Dutch coast. With his controls very sluggish because of a layer of ice on the wings, he turned back to base, got within twenty miles of England, and found clear air. The ice immediately began to fly off, the aircraft climbed, and Pattison chose to try again. This time he crossed the coast at 14,000 feet, having kept just above the cloud, but, realizing he would be too late for Essen, he made for Bonn instead.[79]

Losses on this abortive attempt were heavy – just under 8 per cent of the aircraft dispatched – and No 419 Squadron had a particularly miserable time. Two aircraft out of thirteen were lost, one returned early without attacking, one crew bombed short 'owing to intensity of defences and consequent necessary evasive action,' and three others had minor Flak damage. Another, piloted by Flight Sergeant M.L. Swanson, was already on fire after being hit by Flak four times when it was attacked by a German fighter. Soon it had lost its hydraulics, was severely holed, and had its landing gear and bomb-bay doors locked in the open position. Nevertheless, with the help of his wireless operator, Flight Sergeant K.E. Crosby, Swanson maintained control while Flight Sergeant P.S.O. Brichta, the navigator, 'immediately attempted to extinguish the flames ... in spite of the ... possibility that he would fall through the badly burned bottom of the fuselage.' Once the fire was out, Brichta returned to his charts and coolly directed Swanson back to England, where he crash-landed in a wheat field. All three were awarded the Distinguished Flying Medal.[80]

What was especially frustrating in all this was the unmistakable evidence that, despite Gee, Bomber Command still could not destroy targets in the Ruhr, the primary focus of the area offensive to date. When Harris asked the AOC of No 3 Group if he had any suggestions to facilitate operations there, Baldwin admitted he did not. It seemed to him that the enemy's defences would always lead 'the weaker brethren' to release their bombs on the outer perimeter of the target area and thereby reinforce the view, already prevalent among his crews, that they could not achieve useful results in that part of Germany. It was therefore better, he thought, to spread Bomber Command's effort in the hope that this would force further dispersion of the enemy's defences and 'thus open up areas which at the present moment are so strongly defended as to be expensive when attacked.' Failing that, he could only pass on the suggestion made by one of his station commanders that a specialist target-finding force be created – an idea he had opposed six months earlier.[81]

These were not the answers Harris was looking for. The first flew in the face of all that was known about the strengths and weaknesses of Kammhuber's defensive system, while the latter gave credibility to an idea the AOC-in-C had consistently put down because he feared the effect of 'creaming off' the best crews from existing squadrons to form such an elite force. Under pressure from Portal to reconsider his position so that Gee could be exploited to the fullest before it was jammed – still considered inevitable – Harris concocted two new arguments against the concept of target-finders. The main problem, he declared, was not that crews were unable to locate the target but that they could not see it well enough through the smoke and cloud to be sure of where they were and to drop their bombs accurately. In this respect, a target-finding force would be no better off, and he wondered what difference it would make. Beyond that, the formation of such a force was likely to create political problems when it came to working out how dominion crews should be fitted in. Neither argument cut any ice. Portal and Sinclair both observed that integrating these crews into the target-finding force might well offset 'our present policy of segregating Dominion and foreign personnel within their own homogenous units.'[82]

It did not. When the the matter of dominion participation was raised with Canadian authorities, the proposal to integrate crews completely into RAF squadrons was turned down and it was accepted that room would have to be made for distinctly RCAF flights. The administrative problems that might entail were matters of little consequence to Portal and Sinclair, however. The two had been persuaded that the creation of a target-finding force was essential for Bomber Command to realize its potential and, although Portal did not want to force the idea on his subordinate, in the end Sir Arthur caved in. A Pathfinder Force (as Harris demanded it be called) would be formed and ways would be found to accommodate Canadian interests.

Manned by volunteer crews that had already proved their ability to find and hit their targets, but would undergo further extensive training to become even more proficient in all aspects of navigation and bomb-aiming,[*] the Pathfinder Force (PFF) was initially set up within No 3 Group. It nevertheless comprised squadrons from all four night-bombing formations and had its own AOC, Group Captain D.C.T. Bennett, a ruthless perfectionist. Eventually, a

---

[*] The AOC of the Pathfinders went so far as to enlist the help of eye specialists to develop drops to improve the night vision of bomb-aimers and to produce anti-glare glasses to offset the effect of searchlights.

separate, independent No 8 (Pathfinder) Group was established in January 1943, and in April No 405 Squadron was transferred to it as the No 6 Group affiliate.[83]

Almost two months passed between the decision to form a Pathfinder Force and its first operation. The raids mounted in the interim simply confirmed that Bomber Command could not consistently locate its targets or achieve consistent results even against those in the same geographical area. An effective raid on Bremen (2/3 July) was followed, for example, by one on Wilhelmshaven a week later in which most bombs fell in open country.[84] Moreover, these operations were not economical. The Canadian squadrons were all heavily engaged on 26/27 July, clawing their way to Hamburg through cloud and ice, when the overall loss rate was 7.2 per cent. No 420 Squadron lost two of the fifteen Hampdens sent (and had four early returns), while four crews from No 408 found themselves coned by searchlights or intercepted by night-fighters but were fortunate enough to get away. Pilot Officer David Williams was caught by a large number of lights shortly after completing his bombing run at 8000 feet, and in the glow he saw that he was also in the midst of a balloon barrage.

Immediately heavy *Flak* began bursting near and around the aircraft, one of the shells exploding under the port wing causing the aircraft to turn over on its back and one of the engines cutting momentarily. After some evasive action the aircraft was righted, and escape through the balloon barrage was successfully completed. Taking a northerly direction *en route* home, the W[ireless] O[perator]/A[ir] G[unner] advised the pilot that a single engine, one-tail[fin] aircraft (presumed to be a Me 109) was outlined against the moon flying on their port quarter. The pilot took immediate evasive action to evade the enemy's cone of fire, made a right hand turn and dove for cloud cover which was about 500 feet below.[85]

Lacking Lichtenstein, the Messerschmitt could not follow the bomber in cloud and Williams escaped.

Pilot Officer R.N. Rayne from 420 Squadron was less fortunate, falling victim to a fighter over the enemy coast.

Just as the Nav[igator] said he could see coast, W/Op, Sgt. Axford, told me to turn to s[tarboard] quickly as there was a fighter coming up. Immed[iately] banked over and turned. Just as we were in the middle of the turning a stream of tracer came just over my head right in the centre of the a/c so that our turn took us into it & out of it in a moment. I continued the turn for a while. As I straightened, I felt the a/c shudder and go into a spin to s[tarboard]. I corrected this immed. by throttling down outer engine & nearly went into a spin to port, but corrected this in the same way.

After asking his crew if they were hurt, and finding everyone fine, Rayne suddenly found his Hampden engulfed in fire and ordered the crew to bale out.

I have never been able to remember what happened the next moment; the next thing I realised was that a/c was diving to the ground and that there were flames all round me which burnt my unprotected face. I tried to release my harness but could not find the pin nor see anything. I tried to break out of it, & then felt for the pin again. After several unsuccessful attempts I suddenly found myself loose; I stood up & was sucked out of the diving a/c. Then, as I fell through the air, I could not find the ripcord until I looked down and saw the chromium plate gleaming in the moonlight about 6 inches out from my chest ... I pulled it, & the 'chute opened out ... I fell for a few seconds and then heard the sea below me; I was just wondering whether I should land in the sea, when I came down on my back with a big thud on the sand ... The Germans who captured me told me that the fighter that shot me down made two attacks; I was aware of only one.[86]

Rayne was also told that the rest of his crew was dead.

Losses on 28/29 July totalled thirty aircraft, of which twenty-five were from No 3 Group, 15.2 per cent of its contribution. One of them was John Fulton, the inspirational commanding officer of No 419, whose death cast a pall over the squadron for a considerable time. Indeed one sergeant air-gunner, shot down the next night in a raid on Saarbrücken, later reported that the loss of the CO and the fact that the squadron had flown on operations on five of the last eight nights meant that they were 'anything but enthusiastic' about having to do another one. Worse still, Fulton's successor, Wing Commander A.P. Walsh, a Canadian in the RAF, was killed in action within a month of taking over command.[87]

Four raids on Duisburg were just as futile, and none more so than that mounted in moonless conditions (to make things difficult for the enemy's fighters) on 21/22 July. The marking, done entirely on Gee, was wildly erratic although visibility was not bad. No 405 Squadron reported only some industrial haze while crews from No 419 declared they had 'excellent visibility' and could pinpoint the docks and railway marshalling yards as well as the town itself. Still, many bombs fell in open country, across the Rhine from the city centre. Exactly the same thing happened the night of 6/7 August, when the bombing again fell mainly to the west of the city. Photographs taken after the raid, but looking at the results of all four, indicated there were no large areas of devastation in spite of the scale of attack. The Thyssen steel works, to be sure, gave evidence of having suffered some damage, but on the whole there was not much to show for more than a thousand sorties, and the analysts had to reach for something positive to say: 'The proportion of H[igh] E[xplosive] damage in suburban districts is such that probably many more houses than are actually seen to have been destroyed or damaged have in fact been rendered uninhabitable by blast.'[88]

The loss rate at Duisburg was a manageable 3.4 per cent,[89] but it could easily have been higher had it not been for the flying skills of some pilots and the ability of their machines to take punishment and keep flying. Among the latter was the Hampden flown by Sergeant R.G. Bell of No 408 Squadron. On the way to the target on 5/6 August, a night-fighter 'suddenly pounced upon our Hampden from out of cloud cover.'

The attack was so sudden that before the WOP/AGs could notice the enemy aircraft and take necessary action, the enemy fired with all guns at a range of approximately between 50–100 yards ... The first sign of attack was when tracer bullets were fired at the Hampden from dead astern ... The pilot immediately put the Hampden into a deep diving turn to starboard, pulling out at 6,000 ft., and the attacking aircraft was lost from sight and not seen again ... The attack was so fierce that the pilot's impression was that all shells and bullets seemed to hit everywhere.[90]

There were three large holes in the elevators and one in the port fin, a rent where the tail boom and fuselage intersected, and holes in the port aileron and engine nacelle. In addition, the port wing fuel tanks were riddled (fortunately without causing a fire), the upper gunner's turret smashed and his guns put out of action, the hydraulics shot away, and the whole fuselage scored by cannon fire. One shell had struck the main spar just behind the pilot's shoulder. Despite all this, Bell flew on to the target, bombed it, and turned for home. Ten minutes later the port engine gave up and the aircraft fell to 4000 feet. Struggling to keep control, he managed a belly-landing on the sand dunes near RAF Station Lakenheath. He was awarded a Distinguished Flying Medal. The only injuries were those suffered by the mid-upper gunner, Sergeant J.S. Murray, who had pieces of shrapnel, shell splinters, and perspex removed from his head, but who returned to operational duties in January 1943.[91]*

On 9/10 August, at Osnabrück, conditions were very much as they had been at Duisburg on 21/22 July. Visibility was good over this 'vital rail junction' on the Berlin-Holland and Ruhr-Hamburg lines, site of iron foundries and steel rolling mills, and an inland port on the Rhine with links to Bremen and Berlin via the Mittelland canal. Yet although the marking was again scattered – probably because the Germans effectively jammed Gee for the first time – the bombing was reasonably accurate and the damage was severe: 206 houses were destroyed, 4000 buildings were damaged, the docks were hit hard, and sixty-two people were killed.[92]

Unhelpfully, however, the clear skies that made navigation and bomb-aiming easier also served the Germans well. The attack on Düsseldorf on 31 July/1 August, which damaged 15,000 buildings and killed 279, cost twenty-nine aircraft, 4.6 per cent of the attacking force. Similarly, the 28/29 August raid on Saarbrücken, considered an easy target, and where Flak defences had not been built up, claimed 6.2 per cent.[93] For No 408 Squadron in particular the operation was a disaster. Seventeen aircraft were dispatched, and four (23.5 per cent) did not return. Moreover, one of the lost crews included Wing Commander J.D. Twigg, the commanding officer, as well as the squadron's

---

*Murray was shot down over France and captured on his twentieth operation, 14 April 1943. Sergeant Bell and the rest of his crew were accidentally killed in the course of a fighter affiliation exercise on 9 November 1942.

bombing leader, signals officer, and gunnery leader. Leadership by example had its positive aspects, but risking so many key officers in one crew was foolish.[94]

Despite recent losses, the AOC-in-C remained faithful to the principle of concentration, both as a defensive measure and because he believed that one raid by a thousand bombers would accomplish significantly more than ten by one hundred. He also agreed with the AOC of No 4 Group that too many small-to-medium raids in bad weather would cause fatigue to no worthwhile end. Until Bomber Command was much stronger, therefore, he decided on 24 July to restrict its effort to very large raids of seven hundred sorties or more on the three to seven nights a month when there was good weather, and to Gardening and other minor operations when there was not. He anticipated, and would accept, losses averaging about 5 per cent on the larger raids. Appropriately enough, the day before this policy was announced the MAP finally received the absolute priority in allocations of industrial manpower it required to complete the heavy bomber program approved in October 1941 and modified in June.[95]

An overall loss rate of 5 per cent would be approaching the theoretical limit of sustainability later worked out at the Air Ministry but already suspected at the time. 'A strategic bomber force would become relatively ineffective if it suffered operational losses in the region of 7 per cent over a period of three months of intensive operations,' it was calculated, 'and the operational effectiveness may become unacceptably low if losses of 5 per cent were maintained over this period.' With a 7 per cent loss rate, for example, only about one in ten crews could hope to survive an operational tour of thirty missions, while at 5 per cent that proportion would increase to one in five. It was not just the manpower implications of replacing so many dead, wounded, or prisoners of war that had to be taken into account. Bomber crews generally got better with experience, but high casualty rates meant that few would be around long enough to make their experience felt. With 7 per cent losses, crews would stand a 50 per cent chance of surviving only nine trips, while at 5 per cent they would have the same chance of surviving thirteen. In the latter case, on any given day the average experience of Harris's crews would be between thirteen and sixteen missions. If the Gardening and other minor operations the AOC-in-C intended to mount remained low-risk affairs and, when they were taken into account, the overall loss rate stood at 3 per cent, crews would stand a 40 per cent chance of surviving their tour and the average level of experience would rise to as high as twenty trips.[96]

To find seven hundred crews for even as few as three raids a month would require the help of the OTUs, and Harris therefore still ran the risk of mortgaging Bomber Command's future. However, based on evidence provided by Flying Training Command, he was persuaded that any casualties they suffered would be offset by other, perhaps more tangible, benefits. Trainees and instructors who knew they would fly on operations were likely to be keener, he thought, while the experience they gained from major raids would do far more than Gardening to prepare them for their operational tours. In the event, overall losses were higher than anticipated. Indeed, in No 4 Group's Halifax squadrons they averaged just over 6 per cent, a rate that forced the AOC-in-C to withdraw these units for a period of three to four weeks of recuperation and further training,* and by the end of the summer the policy of employing OTUs on operations was again under review.[97]

Although Harris was convinced that the new policy of conducting a few very large raids in good weather should see more bombs falling on the target, the AOCs of Nos 3 and 5 Groups were not persuaded. While it was true that it would be easier to identify ground detail, including aiming points, on clear nights, it did not follow that those navigators already suspected of indifference and relying too much on Gee (and too little on their sextants) would necessarily apply themselves more diligently. Nor was much expected of the many pilots who 'had lost their sense of responsibility toward the navigational effort.'[98] For the moment, however, Harris was inclined to put his faith in technology, and he looked forward to the appearance of three new navigation aids, still in the final stages of testing but scheduled to be ready for issue by the year's end. Linked to the bomber's compass and air-speed indicator, the air position indicator (API) displayed an aircraft's true course, latitude, and longitude at any given instant – provided there was no wind or that the wind and its effect were being measured and computed correctly. Given reasonably competent operators, it was estimated that the API should be accurate to within 4 per cent of the distance flown since the last firm fix – twelve miles over three hundred, for example – not sufficient for pin-point bombing, perhaps, but good enough to keep crews from becoming hopelessly lost.[99]

That was the big advantage of Oboe, theoretically so accurate that it held out great promise as a blind-bombing device as well as a navigation aid. Essentially nothing more than a two-way radio system in which a ground station indicated, by transmitting dots or dashes, how far (and to which side) an individual aircraft had strayed from its course, and then signalled the exact moment of bomb-release, Oboe seemed foolproof so long as it was not jammed and so long as the navigator, to put it simply, did what he was told. As was the case with Gee, however, transmission and response were by 'line of sight,' so that the range of Oboe was limited by the curvature of the Earth and the height at which the aircraft could fly. Furthermore, with just a few ground stations being built, Oboe could be used by a limited number of aircraft at any one time and, as a result, Harris decided early on that it would be fitted to Pathfinder aircraft only, specifically to the high-flying Mosquitoes once they became available. Rather than guiding individual main-force crews to the target, then, Oboe's main contribution would be to improve marking.[100]

H2S, in contrast, was a downward-looking radar totally independent of communication with ground stations which could be used by any number of crews carrying the equipment. Presenting its operator with a bleary, but fundamentally accurate, outline of ground features such as rivers, lakes, coastlines,

---

* Looking ahead, No 6 Group would suffer 7 per cent losses in May and June 1943, and losses close to or above 6 per cent in October and December 1943 and January and February 1944. Its squadrons would not be withdrawn from operations, however.

and built-up areas over which the aircraft was flying, H2S seemed likely to allow navigators to identify isolated population centres from distances of between twelve and eighteen miles, while cities like Essen, part of the Ruhr's urban sprawl, might be distinguished from six miles – reliably enough to provide, at minimum, the data necessary to maintain an accurate API plot. Moreover, it was estimated that 42 per cent of the bombs dropped on a large town using only the H2S image as a guide should fall within a mile of the aiming point – in any and all weather. In short, the equipment could also serve as a blind-bombing device that would be good enough for area raids. Although considerable training would be required of navigators and bomb-aimers (both of whom might be called upon to use it), the potential of H2S was so great that the decision to supply it to all main-force crews was a relatively easy one. Like Oboe, it was expected to be ready for operations in December 1942.[101] Until then, however, improved bombing would depend entirely on the Pathfinder Force.

The first Pathfinder-led raid, against the U-boat factories and other facilities at Flensburg on the Baltic shore of Schleswig-Holstein, took place the night of 18/19 August, just a few hours before a large part of the 2nd Canadian Division touched down on the French coast near Dieppe. As at Dieppe, it was not an auspicious occasion. Although usually easy to find, the lead crews ran into unexpectedly strong head winds that pushed them, and the main force, away from Flensburg into German-occupied Denmark, where most bombing took place. In spite of a bright moon, the Pathfinders again failed to find Frankfurt on 24/25 August because of haze and cloud below, and all that was claimed was that 'at least one aircraft bombed the target.' Sixteen, however, failed to return – 7 per cent of the total sent. The weather was better over Kassel on 27/28 August and some of the Pathfinders managed to lay their flares across the city, but the main force did not find the marking distinctive enough – the Germans had decoys in the vicinity – and the most concentrated bombing took place a mile and a half from the aiming point. However, 10 per cent of the attackers were shot down. Somewhat better results were obtained over the next week, but there was also one abject failure when, on 1/2 September, the Pathfinders missed Saarbrücken entirely, marking Saarlautern instead (and perhaps Saarlouis as well), between ten and thirteen miles away. The main force followed dutifully behind, completely unaware that anything was amiss, No 419 Squadron reporting that there were plenty of good fires to bomb, while crews from No 405 noted that 'no one found any difficulty in finding the target with the aid of markers and PFF incendiaries ... seen at and near the aiming point.'[102]

This less-than-sterling performance of the Pathfinders could be attributed to their specific lack of experience in target-marking, but it is also true that recent modifications made to Gee had not satisfactorily countered the enemy's jamming. Indeed, jamming would interfere with target-finding by Gee throughout the fall, especially in attacks on northern cities, and by January 1943 it could no longer be relied upon except as a homing device for crews returning to England after a raid.[103] Yet if the Pathfinders had momentarily lost the secure navigation aid necessary to supplement their generally superior navigational abilities, they were developing new target-marking techniques (and equipment) to provide the best possible visual display for the main-force crews who came after them.

The 'Red Blob Fire,' a target-indicator (TI) bomb improvised from the standard 250-lb incendiary and designed to burn with a fierce, distinctive brilliance, was introduced in early September.[104] But realizing that he could not rely on a single marker or colour (for fear that the enemy would copy them and set out decoys), Bennett, AOC of the Pathfinder Force, campaigned hard for the development of an array of coloured flares and target indicators. As these began to spill out of the laboratories and pyrotechnic factories, he was able to devise a more sophisticated marking scheme which, with some variations, remained the standard procedure until the end of the war. The Pathfinders were divided into a number of waves, each with specific functions and responsibilities. 'Finders' laid parallel flare paths six to eight miles long leading to the target area; 'illuminators' dropped white flares in close groupings to light up the area over the city; 'primary markers' dropped coloured flares on the aiming point after they had identified it visually; and 'fire raisers' and 'backers-up' dropped their TI 'blobs' on the primary markers to attract the main force.[105]

This procedure promised to be much more reliable than the Shaker technique introduced at Rostock earlier in the year, but it was by no means foolproof. There was still a significant element of judgment required of main force crews.

Air bombers had their aiming points defined for them by a pattern of coloured markers ... [that] ... burned for several minutes ... Unless otherwise instructed main force air bombers were told to aim their bombs at what they judged to be the mean point of impact of these large patches of light, neglecting any markers which were grossly misplaced. This judgement of the mean point of impact (known as visual centreing) was often extremely difficult owing to weather conditions and operational hazards over heavily defended targets as well as the visually distracting effect of burning incendiaries, fires, searchlights, and flares. In addition the indicator pattern was continually changing since to maintain the marking, further target indicators were dropped at intervals ... aimed visually at the estimated centre of the existing pattern.[106]

Nevertheless, the results of bombing continued to be uneven. In major raids against German targets between 16 September and 10 November, for example, the Pathfinders failed to mark the target three times, marked the wrong one once, and enjoyed two unambiguous successes – at Osnabrück on 6/7 October, when No 405 Squadron acknowledged the 'excellent support by PFF flares,' and at Kiel a week later.[107] There were also two partial successes of which one, the Essen raid of 16/17 September, resulted in one of the most productive attacks on this city during the whole war. However, the good results obtained from a very low-level raid (crews bombed from between 1000 and 2000 feet) conducted against Flensburg on 1/2 October were offset by the loss of twelve of twenty-seven Halifaxes – 44 per cent of those involved. No 405 Squadron lost three of eight crews that night, all experienced.[108]

To no one's surprise, weather was still the critical variable. On good nights the Pathfinders usually had no difficulty finding their objectives, but they often erred when the weather was bad or the winds were noticeably different from those predicted. Overall, the correct targets were found and marked, at least 'partially successfully,' about half the time. Yet even this degree of success meant little if the main force did not drop its bombs where indicated. On the basis of bombing photographs, it was estimated that 60 per cent of the main force was not bombing within three miles of the aiming point, although the bombing concentration was better. When the wrong target was marked, a whole mission could go astray without the main force ever being aware that anything was wrong. When No 405 Squadron applauded the Pathfinders for the flares and fires that gave a good view of the streets and buildings below them on 8/9 September, for example, they were actually over Russelsheim, not Frankfurt, while on 5/6 October they bombed Mechelen, not Aachen. On that occasion, however, navigators throughout Bomber Command complained that severe electrical storms had knocked out their Gee.[109]

By the end of 1942 High Wycombe itself was admitting that no more than a quarter of all bombing sorties were 'doing really useful work.' Normal navigation and 'pilotage' problems were mainly responsible, due in part to inadequate training at OTUs, but it was also 'conclusively apparent that a large number of crews, having undergone all the risks of attaining to the neighbour-hood of the objective,' are not sufficiently staunch to press home their attacks with determination.' As a result, it was acknowledged – in the strange statistical tabulations favoured at the time – that of all the acreage the command had attempted to attack since December 1941, less than 3 per cent had been destroyed.[110]

Thus there was reason to call the bombing offensive into question, particularly in light of the Allies' desperate need for more tanks, landing craft, and resources for the anti-submarine campaign. Now, however, that the bomber offensive had become part and parcel of the Allied debate on the overall conduct of the war, necessity forged sometimes unexpected alliances among the British service chiefs and between American and British airmen who were already arguing over how the air war should be prosecuted.[111]

These alliances had begun to form over the summer of 1942, when the British chiefs of staff successfully fended off US Admiral Ernest King's suggestion that heavy bombers should be used primarily in anti-submarine operations – and in the process persuaded senior American commanders that Bomber Command's proper role was to attack 'centres of population' in order to do 'moral damage' to German civilians. Meanwhile, an Air Ministry staff officer was explaining to his director of plans that 'industrial centres' should be inserted in official documents in place of 'centres of population' because the latter was 'contrary to the principles of international law – such as they are – and also contrary to the statement made some time ago by the P[rime] M[inister] that we should not direct our bombing to terrorise the civilian population.' It was therefore 'unnecessary and undesirable' to draw attention to the fact that this was precisely what was happening.[112] Though few of the airmen who were risking their own lives night after night thought about it in that way, killing and injuring civilians as much as the destruction of built-up areas was becoming the principal purpose of Bomber Command.

Questions regarding the priorities to be assigned to the bomber forces arose again in the fall, when the British chiefs of staff were trying to convince their American colleagues not only that there should be no cross-Channel invasion in 1943, but also that this postponement should be exploited by intensifying the bomber offensive to the point where, perhaps, no such assault would be required. Their argument was based primarily on Sir Charles Portal's estimate that a combined Anglo-American bomber force four to six thousand strong should be delivering 50,000 tons of bombs a month by the end of 1943, and 90,000 a year later – an effort, he predicted, that would destroy six million homes, render twenty-five million Germans homeless, kill almost a million, and injure a million more. It would also destroy a third of the enemy's industry and, because the economy was already stretched to the limit, it would force the enemy to choose between the collapse of the war potential or that of the internal economy.[113]

Portal's assessment of the fragility of the German economy was wildly wrong. There was still considerable room for expansion, and in fact by the end of 1942 armament production had actually increased 80 per cent over the previous year. Moreover, as it turned out, the CAS did not have all the support he imagined from the other service chiefs. On 24 November he had to issue a revised memorandum in which bombing was spoken of as a softening-up exercise before the invasion of Europe, and in which the ultimate size of the combined bomber force was left open for further negotiation with both the British and American service chiefs and with Churchill and Roosevelt.[114]

Long before these discussions took place, the bombing offensive had begun to change character. The approach of winter always meant the return of bad weather and a curtailment of Bomber Command's activities. Furthermore, to lend support to the British 8th Army's advance across the Western Desert from El Alamein, and to Operation Torch, the Allied landings in Morocco and Tunisia, Sir Arthur Harris was busy attacking the Italian cities of Turin, Milan, and Genoa, his main targets between 22 October and 12 December. Indeed, only three major raids were undertaken against German cities in those six weeks, and all three failed because of cloud, winds, and icing.[115] Finally, the Essen raid of 16/17 September was the last occasion for some time to come on which OTU crews were employed on operations against Germany. Their losses since 30 May had been 6.4 per cent of sorties, and morale was beginning to suffer. 'For weeks there had been an undercurrent of unrest among staff and students,' one Canadian under training observed, 'because none of us agreed with the policy of sending OTU crews over Germany in antiquated aircraft.'

We knew that our CO endorsed our views and that he had protested with no apparent results. Our losses were out of all proportion to our numbers and our contribution to the war effort. One OTU course had lost ten of fourteen crews. Most of our instructors were dead. Monday, 14 September, our OTU was again ordered to contribute to the raiding force. Tension was at the boiling point at Atherstone where the crews were united in their opposition, and their spokesman advised the CO: '*Sir, we are not cowards, but we refuse to go on any more ops in these old kites.*'

The CO, although sympathetic, warned of the terrible consequences of mutiny; and tried to convince them that they were contributing to the war effort; and, in any event, they had no choice in the matter. The crews stood fast in their refusal, so the Air Officer Commanding (AOC) was advised, and he flew immediately to Atherstone. Fortunately, the weather turned bad, and Bomber Command cancelled the night's show ... Tuesday, we were again ordered to contribute, and Atherstone crews agreed to go on condition that their complaints be aired right at Bomber Command Headquarters ... The target was Essen ... The next night no crews were requested from OTUs. It appeared that the mutiny was having the desired results![116]

Quite possibly reacting to such incidents, but also accepting that he could not keep up the pace, particularly if it meant losing experienced instructors, Harris directed that OTU crews be withdrawn from bombing missions until Bomber Command's normal establishment was large enough for it to saturate the enemy's defences again.[117]

The day after the Essen raid, but before the new policy was announced, Wing Commander H.L. Campbell had complained to Air Marshal Edwards about the high losses suffered by crews still under training. The OTU missing rate had risen to 10 per cent over the last three raids, he noted, and it was 'reasonable to suppose that a number of Canadians were in the crews.' Such concern for the well-being of Canadian pilots, navigators, gunners, and bomb-aimers was the job of Overseas Headquarters at any time, and it was one to which Edwards returned a few weeks later, when the idea of using OTU crews on operations was debated again, and after it was reported that three Canadian sergeants had gone absent without leave rather than fly 'clapped out' training aircraft on operations.[118] In mid-September 1942, however, Overseas Headquarters had other reasons for being concerned with operational losses of Canadians at OTUs. In the next six weeks, six new RCAF bomber squadrons would have to be formed if No 6 Group was to become operational, on schedule, on 1 January 1943. If they were to be as Canadian as possible from the outset, a 10 per cent casualty rate among trainees could not be tolerated, particularly among those destined for the newly formed No 425 (French Canadian) Squadron.

17

The Formation of No 6 (RCAF) Group, Fall 1942–Spring 1943

The prewar RCAF had been a unilingual institution. Operating aircraft of mainly British or American design, its manuals were all in English and, as in the more technical branches of the army, its need was only for bilingual French Canadians who would work mostly in English. The outbreak of war and the subsequent expansion of the RCAF did nothing to alter the fact that English was inevitably the language of work. Moreover, the commitments made under the British Commonwealth Air Training Plan (BCATP) to train airmen from all parts of the Empire-Commonwealth, and the fact that Canadian aircrew sent overseas would serve in RAF commands (and, in most cases, in RAF squadrons), undoubtedly reinforced this fundamental truth.

Air Force Headquarters had recognized, however, that the language problem constituted a major barrier to recruiting in Quebec, and early on it had established a language school to teach basic English to French-speaking airmen, opened a Manning Depot in Quebec City which offered courses in science and mathematics, and (under the aegis of Air Commodore H. Edwards, then air member for personnel, and Group Captain J.L.E.A. de Niverville, director of air force manning) created a special section to publicize the achievements of French Canadians in the RCAF in the hope that this would encourage others to join. In addition, French-speaking administrative officers were posted to all schools where French-Canadian trainees were undergoing training, and age restrictions that might impede enlistments were ignored whenever possible. The intake of French Canadians still fell short of expectations.[1]

To some, including Flight Lieutenant J.P. Desloges, a prewar career officer who had been wounded during the Battle of Britain and subsequently sent on a recruiting tour in Quebec, the only solution was to find French-speaking instructors to staff French-Canadian flying training schools and, eventually, to form a number of French-Canadian squadrons – a recommendation he passed to de Niverville in April 1941.[2] As a means of stimulating enlistment, Desloges's plan might well have worked, but there were practical difficulties in the short term. The infrastructure required to accommodate French-language instruction within the BCATP could not be provided quickly, and it would take even longer to form an operational squadron adequately backed up by replacements. Moreover, the scheme did not address the fact that English would still be the primary language of work, command, and control for any operational unit in the RCAF.

It was for this reason, perhaps, that Air Minister C.G. Power, himself a Quebecker sympathetic to Desloges's point of view, chose not to implement the plan immediately. In late September 1941, with two Quebec by-elections in the offing, however, Power appealed to young French Canadians to join the RCAF with the promise that 'Depuis longtemps, je caresse l'espoir de voir se former outre-mer une escadrille essentiellement candienne-française, et commandée par un chef canadien-français. Dès que nous compterons un nombre suffisant de pilotes, de radio-télégraphistes-mitrailleurs, d'observateurs, de mécaniciens et d'auxilliares de langue française, nous constituerons une telle escadrille ... Dans le ciel agité de la vieille Europe, l'escadrille canadienne-française continuera les traditions de vaillance, de force héroïque et de fierté nationale qui caractérisent votre race.'³ Six weeks later, instructions were sent to Overseas Headquarters to begin the process of creating the new squadron. As many as possible of the 183 French-speaking aircrew who had proceeded to England so far were to be posted to the unit, and the commissioning of French Canadians was to be accelerated.⁴

Serving out his last few days as the overseas air officer-in-chief, Air Vice-Marshal L.F. Stevenson agreed that 'forming squadrons identified with racial or other groups' in order to enlist their support for the war effort could have its advantages. But he was not persuaded that significant benefits would accrue in this instance and, indeed, complained that 'this one golden opportunity to weld French and English Canada closer together is being thrown away.' He also feared that 'if the French Canadian squadron meets with hard luck the repercussions may be far reaching.' As the senior RCAF officer overseas, Stevenson certainly had a right to offer his opinion to the government on matters of policy, and if the Air Ministry was likely to object on operational grounds to the formation of 'racial or other' units, it was his clear duty to pass such information to Ottawa. But with Polish, Czechoslovak, Dutch, Norwegian, and Free French squadrons having been accommodated in the RAF for over a year, there was little reason to anticipate opposition to the bilingual squadron the Canadian government so desperately wanted.⁵

It was also Stevenson's job to pass Ottawa's message to the Air Ministry and then oversee the formation of the new unit. In fact, he disregarded his instructions, apparently aiming to slow down the process, and in so doing surely overreached his authority. Fighter Command was asked only to 'make a survey of its French Canadian resources, to see whether the formation of a French Canadian squadron is feasible or desirable.' More to the point, when Stevenson asked the Air Ministry to 'appreciate the catastrophe' if the project failed and to let him know 'if it indicates [the] possibility of failure,' he was almost inviting a negative reply.⁶ However, he was not there to receive it. On 23 November Stevenson left for Canada, replaced as the senior RCAF officer overseas because of his perceived hostility to Canadianization.

His successor, Air Marshal H. Edwards, was, by contrast, not only a strong

advocate of Canadianization, but he had also backed the idea of forming a
French-Canadian squadron from the beginning and was prepared to bring the
project to fruition quickly, as L.S. Breadner and Power wanted.[7] Aware,
apparently, only of his predecessor's statement that he had passed on the idea
to the British – and not of his negative, semi-official correspondence with
Bentley Priory and the director general of organization at the Air Ministry –
Edwards was shocked by the response that arrived from the latter at Overseas
Headquarters on 13 December. 'Stevenson asked us for our candid comments
on the proposal,' reported Air Vice-Marshal L.N. Hollinghurst, and 'frankly we
are not too keen on it.'

Quite apart from the fact that the more 'penny packets' there are, the more complicated the posting, etc., procedure becomes, there are more cogent objections from the
operational point of view, particularly if the Squadron is to be a fighter squadron. We
understand that French-Canadians are primarily French-speaking individuals and that
their English is often not too good. When they are together, they speak French exclusively and tend to forget their English. If the proposed squadron is a fighter squadron,
the language difficulty in connection with control is likely to arise.

On the other hand, Stevenson was not very keen on the suggestion that it should be
a bomber squadron. He felt that there were psychological objections to this. Also that
as the majority of Canadians now in this country were in fighter squadrons, it would
probably be easier to find French-Canadian fighter pilots than French-Canadian bomber
crews.

We fully appreciate that from the Canadian political point of view, there are advantages in having a French-Canadian squadron. It is a question of evaluating these advantages against the disadvantages. Perhaps you could let me know whether the Canadian
view is that this Squadron should be formed despite the objections – also whether you
have any real objection to it being a bomber squadron.

Incidentally, it would be as well if we could have a definition of a French-Canadian
as we understand that the term is not necessarily restricted to residents in the Province
of Quebec.[8]

Edwards was in a quandary. If the French-Canadian squadron was to be
formed from crews already overseas, the assistance of the RAF's personnel
organization would be crucial, but from Hollinghurst's letter it seemed that
help might be given only reluctantly. Moreover, although Ottawa had assumed
all along that the squadron would serve in Fighter Command, which seemed
quite capable of coping with polyglot crews, the Air Ministry's view that a
bomber squadron would be preferable raised many new questions. Since it was
proving difficult enough to form all-Canadian bomber crews overseas, given
the procedures and resources available to the RAF's personnel branch, was it
even feasible to form French-Canadian crews? Unsure of how much had been
left to him to decide, Edwards passed these concerns on to Power – including
a subtle jab at British English and an unhelpful assessment of Desloges's time
in Fighter Command.

If French Canadian Squadron formed and had misfortune to suffer heavy casualties in one attack severe repercussions might occur, French Canadians in Canada believing their men doing all dirty jobs. The difficulty experienced by English speaking RCAF pilots in understanding R/T instructions is very great. French speaking pilots have more difficulty. Squadron Leader Desloges was lost a number of times owing to misunderstanding instructions sent by radio and he speaks excellent English. Similar cases on record. Severe losses encountered by non-English speaking squadrons due to not understanding radio instructions. Fighter Command even put Polish speaking control personnel into sector offices to help situation but was not found practical. Not sufficient well trained fighter pilots of French Canadian extraction to form squadron. In view of these experiences the Air Ministry are not too keen on squadron, now inquiring if we would object to it being bomber squadron.[9]

There was an additional problem. Just as Canadianization had met (and was meeting) with some resistance from RCAF aircrew who were quite content to remain on their RAF squadrons, so a number of French-Canadian pilots objected to the idea of forming a 'separate squadron,' feeling they would be 'segregated and put on spot.' Edwards had little sympathy with their position, however, and recommended that the project go ahead.[10]

Power was not at all happy with the contents of Edwards's message. Not only was he inclined to link the negative British attitude to the frustratingly slow progress of Canadianization in general, but he also did not accept the somewhat lame excuses offered regarding radio procedures, particularly in light of the postings that had recently taken place. 'Would like information ... as to reason for placing almost all French Canadian pilots in RAF sqdn[s] instead of RCAF squadrons since it is presumed [their] difficulty of understanding cockney English greater than understanding Canadian English.' The air minister offered no objection to a French-Canadian bomber squadron 'if this can be realized within reasonable time' and if its advantages could be clearly demonstrated. Whatever was decided, the formation of a squadron was to proceed 'as soon as possible.'[11]

By now, Edwards had a better idea of what he was up against in terms of identifying where the strongest opposition to the plan actually lay. Although British authorities asked again on Christmas Eve whether the RCAF still wished to form a French-Canadian squadron and what type was preferred, the Air Ministry at Hollinghurst's prodding had already surveyed the operational commands in Britain and produced a list of 224 individuals 'who claim to be French Canadian.' Among them were thirty-six pilots, a potential cadre; however, representation from other trades and specialties did not provide 'much with which to form a squadron.' In fact, this list was incomplete – Ottawa saw at once that seventy wireless operator/air gunners had been missed – but at least a start had been made, and a positive one at that, by a surprisingly helpful Air Ministry.[12]

The same could not be said of the staff at Overseas Headquarters, some of whom Edwards described as 'slough from Canada'; as the former air member for personnel, he was quite willing to shoulder responsibility for their posting to London. They, more than anyone else, appeared to be the source of obstruction. Although 'we are going hard as we can on the formation of a French Canadian squadron,' Edwards informed deputy minister S.L. de Carteret on 6 January 1942, 'I meet opposition everywhere. It is apparent that, up to my arrival here, no one liked the idea and everyone found a thousand reasons why it should not be formed. I have to break down all these opinions before I can really get started. Although the policy sent over here was definite and clear, I feel that it was laughed at. In any event, it was passed over to the Air Ministry with a tongue in the cheek, and a good deal of chatter from top to bottom against it, went on.[13] Nevertheless, after gathering his staff together and laying down the law he was confident they now 'could see the light as I wished them to see it.' Among other things, that meant pressing ahead with the new squadron – and deciding as well that it should be formed in Bomber Command both to 'absorb more aircrew and ground crew' and because it could be more easily 'controlled from operational point of view in as much as radio contact is not continuous during operations.' There would be some delay involved in obtaining enough experienced men; but twelve pilots, ten navigators, and thirteen wireless operator/air gunners were available almost immediately, and on this basis Edwards asked that he be allowed to proceed.[14]

Almost three weeks passed before the AOC-in-C received an answer from the minister, and when it came it was really no answer at all. Power, it seemed, did not care what kind of squadron was formed, but was concerned only that it be done quickly.[15] And on 20 January 1942 a signal arrived from Breadner indicating not only that speed was of the essence, but that the French-Canadian content of the new unit could also be diluted, at least in the beginning.

Ministry has reached conclusion that probably bomber squadron would be most suitable. Only disadvantage is delay in formation. Suggest this might be overcome to some extent by immediate formation of, say, number 425. Let it be known that this will eventually become a French Canadian Squadron. Organize [it] at once under experienced RAF or RCAF English-speaking commander. Attach immediately experienced aircrew referred to in your signal. Comb OTU and holding unit for French Canadians and train as bomber pilots ... Bring up to appropriate strength with experienced RCAF bomber pilots observers and gunners. Squadron need *not* necessarily be designated French Canadian immediately or until majority of aircrew are French Canadian ... Press on Air Ministry commissioning of bomber pilots mentioned above. There should be no difficulty in finding French Canadian ground crew overseas [but] if so could send some from Canada.[16]

The Air Ministry's reaction to Breadner's telegram was once again helpful. The new unit could be designated 'No 425 (French-Canadian) (Bomber) Squadron, RCAF' immediately, Hollinghurst told Edwards, 'so that it will build up its reputation as a French Canadian squadron.' Meanwhile, a search was on within existing RAF and RCAF units for potential members – those who voluntarily identified themselves as French Canadian – and procedures to extract them from their current posting or redirect them, if necessary, through the training system so as to end up on the squadron were being worked out. Similarly, French Canadians arriving at the RCAF reception centre at Bournemouth were being earmarked for No 425. A few may even have been formed into crews there and sent on to the appropriate Wellington OTU.[17]

All this took time (particularly now that the RAF had adopted a one-pilot policy for Bomber Command, creating a momentary surplus that was adjusted for by slowing down the training stream) and it was not until 25 June 1942 that the new squadron was formed at Dishforth as part of No 4 Group. Its first commanding officer was Wing Commander J.M.W. St Pierre, who had commanded No 11 Elementary Flying Training School before his arrival in Britain in February, just as the final arrangements to form the squadron were being made. Because of his experience in the prewar auxiliary and the BCATP, St Pierre was given a free hand to find recruits for the squadron, a task he did not find easy at first. As was proved time and again, crews quickly developed loyalties to their squadrons and resented any suggestion they should leave an established home for something new. A number of men posted to No 425 objected.[18] But as time went on, the censors reported, the job of selling the unit became easier.

Although by no means free of birth-pangs, the formation of 425 Squadron has provoked what appears to be joy unconfined among the French Canadians. Men promised a posting to 425 find the prospect alluring, and letters from men already embodied reveal excellent morale and much enthusiasm. The fact that French Canadians form a special racial group may make it unwise to assume that their experience is a valid reflection of the situation as a whole. There are some adverse comments, one regretting that in a French Canadian Squadron he will forget his English. Many object to posting to 425 merely because they have French names, and some suspect the purpose of the formation of the Squadron to be purely propagandist.[19]

To outside observers, however, there was no doubting the keenness of the crews St Pierre had selected – on his August 1942 visit to the United Kingdom Power concluded that it was 'the most cheerful and keenest Squadron we have met to date' – including the two flight commanders, Squadron Leaders G.A. Roy and J.L. Savard. Sons of prominent Quebec jurists and politicians, both had been instructors in the BCATP and had gained operational experience with No 419 Squadron; both would be awarded the DFC in the summer of 1943; and both would subsequently command their own squadrons.[20]

Flying began in August 1942, and No 425 was declared operational in October. Its first raid was the 5/6 October attack on Aachen, when icing and severe electrical storms played havoc with navigation; its crews suffered along with the rest of Bomber Command. Two returned early and one was involved in a crash at Debden which killed all aboard. The five who reached the target area considered that to be accomplishment enough and made no great claims as to the accuracy of their bombing. The next night Osnabrück was the target, and by the end of the month the squadron had flown six operations, two of them (Krefeld, 23 October, and Emden, 31 October) in daylight. Losses were very light, just one of forty, while the early return rate, expected to be high in new units, was a commendable 12 per cent.[21]

Although the number of operations doubled in November, many were small affairs involving no more than three machines, and sorties for the month totalled only forty-six. Casualties remained light – two crews lost, both on the Hamburg raid of 9/10 November – but the early return rate climbed to fifteen, or 33 per cent. There were two daylight operations, of which the first (when two machines were sent to bomb Wilhelmshaven at 2000 feet on 6 November) was the more difficult. One crew had no trouble whatsoever with the enemy defences but the other, captained by Pilot Officer A.T. Doucette, was pounced on by three fighters as it approached the objective. Despite considerable damage to the aircraft and severe wounds to wireless operator Sergeant G.J.R. Bruyère, Doucette completed his attack before turning for home. Applauded for their 'indomitable courage and unswerving devotion to duty under extremely difficult conditions,' Doucette was awarded the DFC and Bruyere the DFM. From 10 November 1942 to 14 January 1943 Gardening operations accounted for 73 of the squadron's 118 sorties. Losses were still low, but the early return-abort rate rose to 38 per cent. Weather was always an important factor in causing Gardening missions to be abandoned, as crews were told to come back if they could not pinpoint the target area; but the early return rate on bombing raids was almost as high.[22]

Under other circumstances, No 425 Squadron's performance might have been looked at closely to discover if anything was wrong, but over the winter of 1942/3 higher command had other things on its mind, one being the organization and formation of a Canadian bomber group to be known as No 6 (RCAF) Group. Discussions during and after the Ottawa Air Training Conference of May–June 1942 had determined how many RCAF squadrons would be formed by the end of the year, what aircraft they would probably fly, and where, generally, they would be located. It was also agreed that although Canadianization would be a priority, with the Air Ministry attempting to send the right mix of aircrew trades to operational training units in order to facilitate the formation of RCAF crews there, it would not necessarily be the most important priority – apart from the special case of No 425 Squadron. While Nos 405, 408, 420, 424, and 425 Squadrons all had RCAF commanding officers by the fall of 1942, there were still not enough experienced Canadians to command every squadron. There were certainly too few to command every station and base and fill all the staff appointments at No 6 Group Headquarters when it took shape. One way to increase the RCAF's share of these billets, to reduce its dependency on British officers, and to add to its institutional experience would have been to allow and encourage Canadians serving in the RAF to transfer to the RCAF, but this did not happen – in part, it seems, because Air Force Headquarters did not want to offer them permanent RCAF commissions.[23]

Any lingering misunderstanding on these general questions could have been addressed when Power arrived in the United Kingdom for talks with Air Ministry officials in August 1942. But being more concerned with commissioning policy in general and in finding ways to keep Overseas Headquarters informed of where Canadians were serving, Power dealt with the usually thorny topic of Canadianization only briefly; apart from raising again the long-term goal of equipping the bomber group with Lancasters, he scarcely touched on the Canadianization issue. When he journeyed to High Wycombe to meet Sir Arthur Harris – who, he was warned, might prove somewhat 'sticky' on the question of forming an RCAF group – the outcome was a pleasant surprise. Promising full co-operation, the AOC-in-C left Power with the impression that he 'welcomed the formation of No 6 Group and, subject to operational exigencies, would give his full support to the Canadianization of RCAF Squadrons,' even going so far as to suggest that he might withdraw complete RCAF crews from RAF squadrons as a nucleus around which to build new units.

For their part, the Canadians did not press for any precise definition of what Harris thought might constitute such exigencies, nor did they ask that individual Canadians serving in RAF squadrons be transferred to RCAF units when they were formed, something to which he would certainly have objected. The belief that existing crews should not be broken up was a matter of high principle at High Wycombe. Finally, Power did not flinch when he was told, for the first time, that only seven RCAF squadrons could be created by the end of the year, rather than the ten previously agreed upon.[24]

In short, bringing No 6 Group into existence was, by now, primarily an administrative task involving the RAF's personnel branch and the directorates of supply, organization, and movements, with RCAF Overseas Headquarters acting as the overseer of national interests. Yet the job at hand – marrying up the right people and equipment at the right location – was not easy and things did not always work out as anticipated. While some care was taken to find RCAF crews for the new units from OTUs and other squadrons – 427 Squadron received a number of Wellington crews from No 419 when the latter converted to Halifaxes – their initial Canadianization rates were not satisfactory. In January 1943 only 34 per cent of the aircrew in No 429 Squadron were RCAF, for example, while in No 431 the figure was only 17 per cent, largely because it had received crews from No 24 OTU (recently allocated to 6 Group) before the latter could empty itself of its British, New Zealand, and Australian trainees.[25]

It was not just the number of RCAF crews that mattered, however, but also the number of individuals who happened to be in what was officially designated a 'Canadian' crew. In heavy bombers, for example, exclusively Canadian crews were a rarity because of the belated opening in Canada of facilities to train flight engineers – the first group did not graduate until the summer of 1944. Even among those aircrew categories produced by the BCATP there seems to have been continuing difficulty in managing output and postings so that – allowing for training failures, wastage, and other such factors – the right numbers of pilots, navigators, bomb aimers, air gunners, and wireless operators arrived at OTUs backing RCAF squadrons in the right proportions at the right time. In October 1942 it was estimated that although the BCATP's monthly output could be organized into 101 purely Canadian crews, there would also be a surplus of some two hundred navigators and air-bombers, respectively, who, presumably, would have to be posted somewhere other than No 6 Group.[26] Furthermore, the allocation of particular crews (no matter their composition) to squadrons depended, in part, on how well they had done at their OTU. 'The allotment of crews to Squadrons is further complicated by the fact that all crews are not necessarily recommended for heavy bombers and, therefore, any crews below standard from OTUs which are backing heavy [bomber] squadrons must be transferred to Wellington Squadrons. As the majority of Wellington Squadrons are Canadian, it is inevitable that they must receive the majority of crews who are not recommended for heavy aircraft irrespective of whether they are Canadian, Australian, British, or any other nationality.'[27] Not only would the number of non-RCAF aircrew in No 6 Group be inflated, but, then the group's overall level of competence in flying skills, based on crew performance at OTUs, would be somewhat less than that of Bomber Command as a whole.

Originally, it had been intended that No 6 Group would occupy and control fifteen stations but, because of a lack of materials and the labour force for construction, Bomber Command's own slowed expansion, and a degree of overcrowding in Yorkshire, four of the proposed stations were never built; when the group became operational in January 1943, only seven were ready – Croft, Dalton, Dishforth, East Moor, Leeming, Middleton St George, and Topcliffe.[28]

Which squadrons served where, when, and for how long are questions of more than trivial interest. There were appreciable differences between the prewar stations with their well-constructed and comfortable living, dining, and recreational facilities, and those opened during the last three years. The latter featured Nissen huts, built of curved corregated-steel sheets with brick or wood ends, and often, like Dalton, plagued by a 'lack of heating in living quarters … and also absence of running water' as well as unsatisfactory sewage systems. It is impossible to know precisely how the environment of a particular station affected the officers and men posted to it, but one keen observer certainly noticed such things. Flying Officer F.H.C. Reinke (a journalist commissioned into the RCAF and sent overseas to record his impressions of air force life) had no doubt whatsoever that a squadron's morale depended, at least in part, on where it happened to be. Linton-on-Ouse, a prewar station and home at times to Nos 408 and 426 Squadrons, was aesthetically pleasing despite its 'utilitarian … almost grim' camouflaged headquarters buildings. Wherever possible 'lush grass, shrubs, and countless young trees' and rose beds had been planted 'to soften the general effect.' Messes, bars, and dining rooms were all attractively decorated in warm colours, and there were ample recreational facilities – two softball diamonds, along with a lacrosse field and horseshoe pitching sites. In addition, vegetable gardens were being harvested to supplement normal rations. For those who wished to go off station, there were a dozen or so pubs within easy cycling distance, while the city of York was a bus-ride away.[29]

The same could not be said of Skipton-on-Swale, a satellite station which housed (at various times) Nos 420, 432, 433, and 424 Squadrons. It was 'inconvenient and unattractive,' with only 'ordinary fence-line hedges and a few scattered trees' to relieve the barrenness of row upon row of 'black and dingy brown' Nissen huts. At the time Reinke was there, the airmen's showers were a mile from their billets, the officers' mess was bleak, and the YMCA's Canada House, meant to be a refuge, required airmen to pull old socks over their boots to protect the highly polished wooden floor, a regulation that deterred many from going. The kitchens had no steam tables, so the cooks had to prepare several sittings or serve food that was tepid or cold, and recreational facilities were entirely lacking until a sports officer was appointed in May 1944. A number of pubs were reasonably close by, but breweries would not deliver to the station messes because they were so isolated. Perhaps more important, there was no bus service to Skipton, so servicemen returning from leave or a night on the town in York had to make their own way to the base from the railway station at Topcliffe, one-and-a-half miles distant, or that at Thirsk, just over three miles away.[30]

New stations did not have to be dismal, however, as Reinke discovered when he visited Tholthorpe. At Skipton it seemed that no one had cared about the station's amenities since its opening in the fall of 1942 – the officers' mess had refused the offer of a piano, for example – but at Tholthorpe, which opened in August 1940, lawns had been planted around the Nissen huts, the messes were well decorated (the officers' 'inexpensively but with a skilled eye to effect'), and they had become the hub of station life despite there being pubs nearby. The differences, Reinke thought, were probably attributable to the personalities of the base, station, and squadron commanding officers.[31]

Already physically attractive, Linton-on-Ouse also benefited from the personality of at least one of its commanders. A veteran of anti-submarine operations on Canada's Atlantic coast, Group Captain C.L. Annis's gregariousness and easy ability to mix with all ranks set him apart from some of the other RCAF station commanders – enough to be commented on at the time, it might be added – and ensured the loyalty and cooperation of everyone at Linton. He cajoled and encouraged with tolerance, humour, and understanding; his enthusiasm and zest were infectious; and his empathy for his men was especially appreciated by the non-flying personnel.[32] On one occasion, for example, he warned against going absent without leave in a way that was entirely foreign to the usual application of *King's Regulations*. 'There was too much of it going on,' he announced over the station Tannoys:

so he was going to get tough, to throw the book at us, that is, unless we had a good alibi. e.g. This airman's wife lived in London and he had a forty-eight hour pass. She would meet him at King's Cross Station. He went out to catch the bus into York but there were so many ahead that the bus was full. As a result, he had to wait another hour. When he got to York, he had to take a later train to London. His wife, tired of waiting, went home. When he got home she was taking a bath and it took hours and hours for his clothes to dry. You have to make allowances if there is a good excuse.

Well, nearly everybody in our room started laughing but it took me awhile to see what was funny.[33]

Officers from Canada's Home War Establishment were found for two of the new RCAF squadrons formed in the fall of 1942. Wing Commander H.M. Carscallen, a prewar regular and graduate of the Royal Military College of Canada, who went to No 424, had commanded Nos 5 and 10 (BR) Squadrons between November 1940 and July 1942, while Wing Commander S.S. Blanchard, who had joined the RCAF in 1931 and led Nos 8 and 116 (BR) Squadrons, took over No 426. Carscallen remained with No 424 until April 1943, when he was succeeded by another Canadian, and subsequently commanded the stations at Leeming and East Moor.[34] When Blanchard was killed in action on 14 February 1943, however, he was replaced by Wing Commander L. Crooks, a British officer who had already won a DSO and a DFC.[35] RAF officers also initially commanded the new squadrons formed in November 1942 but, reflecting 6 Group's increased experience, they were all subsequently replaced by RCAF officers. Slowly but inexorably, Canadians were gaining the operational and administrative experience and expertise that would fit them to command their own squadrons, stations, and bases.

Still, the posting of Carscallen and Blanchard directly from the Home War Establishment, even more than St Pierre's appointment to No 425 Squadron after his brief apprenticeship in 419, raised an interesting question. Was the wartime RCAF a comprehensive entity, in which officers and men (but primarily senior officers) with service only in Canada were competent to fill operational positions overseas despite their lack of experience there? Or were conditions in Europe so different that North American service was largely irrelevant? When it came to filling the 50 officer and 175 other-rank vacancies at No 6 Group headquarters, curiously enough, it was the CAS in Ottawa who wanted all but a few senior appointments filled by personnel already in Britain, and the AOC-in-C Overseas who asked for officers to be sent from Canada because the pool of experienced staff officers and technicians in England was not large enough to stand the strain. Indeed, when Breadner insisted, somewhat unhelpfully, that Edwards fend for himself, the latter warned his superior indignantly that 'there is no purpose in proceeding with [the] organization [of a] Canadian Group as required personnel not available in this country.'[36]

As a former member of the Air Council responsible for personnel matters, Edwards certainly knew most of the senior officers available in Canada and he must have realized that if operational experience overseas became the main criterion, his friends and colleagues still at home might never get to England. It is possible, therefore, to construe his stand as reflecting a desire to further the careers of these friends, but with only three RCAF officers having commanded bomber squadrons so far he could not have made the group headquarters fully Canadian except at the expense of operational units. Given the enthusiasm with which he pursued his mandate to put the RCAF 'on the map,' it is more likely that he saw the essential illogic and hypocrisy of forming a

'Canadian' bomber group headquarters if, in the absence of help from Canada, he had to turn to the RAF to find the expertise required.

Still convinced that those with the appropriate technical, administrative, and operational backgrounds were available overseas, Breadner was not persuaded and again told Edwards that he should staff group headquarters from his own overseas resources. There the matter stood until the CAS went to England in mid-August, met with Edwards, reiterated his view that overseas personnel should be appointed first, and then conceded he would not stand in the way of the odd posting from Canada. As it turned out, two of the most senior appointments at No 6 Group went to officers posted from Canada, one to an overseas RCAF officer, one to a Can/RAF officer, and one to a British specialist. Group Captain C.R. Slemon, posted in from Ottawa where he had been director of air operations, was an unequivocal success as senior air staff officer (SASO).[*] The senior administrative officer (SAO), Wing Commander C.G. Durham, was a First World War RFC veteran who had been SAO at RCAF Station Digby. The chief training officer, Wing Commander T.C. Weir, was a Canadian in the Royal Air Force, while the chief signals officer, Wing Commander T.W. Hodgson, was British. Slemon's right-hand man as senior operations staff officer (SOSO) was Wing Commander J.E. Fauquier, who had just relinquished command of No 405 Squadron. As Edwards had warned, however, there were not enough RCAF officers available overseas to fill every appointment, and on 1 January 1943 twenty of the forty-seven male officers, and fifty-five of 177 male other ranks, came from the RAF.[37]

There was also one officer from the RCAF (Women's Division). She was the first of several hundred – there were 567 female officers and 372 other ranks at Allerton Park alone on 8 May 1945 – to be employed throughout No 6 Group, initially as clerks, cooks, drivers, telephone operators, and hospital assistants. By April 1943 the regulations had been amended to permit women to serve as wireless operators (ground), parachute riggers, meteorologists, and instrument mechanics and to interpret reconnaissance and bombing photographs. As such, they eventually played a significant and direct role in the operational life of RCAF bases and stations.[38]

One appointment, that of air officer commanding (AOC), had to go to a Canadian and to an officer currently serving at home, since no one overseas had the right combination of operational and administrative experience. Furthermore, in Edwards's view, 'no one with suspected views or otherwise against Canadianization should be sent,' an attempt, perhaps, to ensure that Air Vice-Marshal L.F. Stevenson was not brought back from Western Air Command. Edwards actually had three candidates in mind: Air Vice-Marshal G.E. Brookes, AOC of No 1 Training Command, whom he preferred; Air Commodore C.M. McEwen, currently combatting the German U-boat threat while commanding No 1 Group in Eastern Air Command; and Air Vice-Marshal J.A.

---

[*] Slemon subsequently became deputy air officer commanding-in-chief of the RCAF overseas, a postwar CAS, and eventually, in the Cold War era, deputy commander of the North American Air Defence Command.

Sully, the RCAF's air member for personnel. Brookes, who was British-born but had come to Canada with his family in 1910, was chosen.[39]

Then forty-seven years old, Brookes had seen service overseas with the Royal Flying Corps in the First World War, had joined the RCAF at its birth on 1 April 1924, and was thought to be something of a specialist in flying training, a useful talent as the Canadian group worked towards becoming operational. He also had experience at a major operational headquarters, having been SASO in Eastern Air Command as it expanded in 1939–40. A fatherly type who, it was felt, could care for and nurture his formation and get along well with senior British officers in the process, Brookes looked ideal for the job.[40] The real question was whether he had the talent for, and interest in, the operational responsibilities Harris demanded of his group commanders. 'Owing to the weather and other factors, there was seldom more than a day's notice for laying on any ordinary operation and it would have been impossible for the Command to give all the necessarily detailed orders directly to its stations. The Command issued the orders to the Group Headquarters giving the target and the general plan for co-ordinating the whole attack, and the Groups themselves issued detailed orders to the units ... The Group Commanders were given absolute freedom within the limits set by the necessity of co-ordinating an attack.'[41]

After Brookes arrived in England on 26 July 1942 one of his first tasks was to find a site for his headquarters, the initial choice at Northallerton having been rejected because it could not be fitted out with the communications systems necessary to run an operational group. On 1 September an agreement was reached with the Air Ministry to requisition Allerton Hall, a sprawling, seventy-five room mansion located near Knaresborough, fourteen miles from No 4 Group's headquarters at York. The resentful owner – 'the worst pessimist I have ever met for a man of forty-seven, no patriotism & full of himself & his troubles,' according to Brookes – raised so many questions and complaints about the inevitable alterations (and where he was to live in the meantime), however, that it was not entirely ready when the group became operational on 1 January 1943. Temporary living quarters for the headquarters staff had to be found in the surrounding villages as well as at Dishforth and Linton, and some were still living and eating at Linton and Dishforth as late as May 1943. No 6 Group Headquarters was officially established on 25 October 1942, but until remodelling at Allerton Hall was complete it also worked out of Linton, just under seven miles distant.[42]

Brookes, meanwhile, attended the daily conferences held at No 4 Group Headquarters, getting a feel for the job, and oversaw the progress of the new squadrons in flying training. Space for basic administrative work finally became available in November, but workmen still swarmed over the office areas while an inadequate water supply – the Harrogate Fire Department had to fill the storage tanks on the grounds – meant that the heating and plumbing systems could not be relied upon.[43] Brookes moved into his own office on 4 December, but since there were no electric lights he could not work into the evening. A week later he saw some improvements, yet much remained to be done. 'The Hall is beginning to look a bit cleaner at last, & not so much noise & hammering near my office. My washroom is finished by plumber, & most of the offices on second floor [are] now in use, but [telephone] lines only about 70 per cent completed. Had a good look around the building sites & sewer job, using gum boots, & got in again just before dark. Buildings coming along well, sewer job *very slow*.'[44]

As we have seen, shortages of construction materials and labour threatened the entire airfield construction program that autumn, but it was only in December 1942 that Brookes learned he would definitely lose the proposed bases at Piercebridge, West Tanfield, Easingwold, and Strensall. Some reshuffling of assignments was necessary as a result, and arrangements also had to be made to give some of the satellite fields hard-surfaced runways earlier than had been scheduled, which again required the shifting of squadrons from one station to another as work was begun and completed.[45]

Meanwhile, the AOC continued to read into his new appointment and learn about the conduct and management of bombing operations from observations made in his visits to High Wycombe and to Nos 4 and 5 Groups. Unhappily, the diary Brookes kept of his time overseas was strictly personal. There are few entries of operational concern in its pages, making it impossible to chart his development from a kind of neophyte staff learner in August 1942 to full-fledged group commander five months later. Moreover, what entries there are reflect a singular detachment from the hard realities of the bomber war. He admits to having 'helped in a small way to work out details' for an attack on Nuremburg on 28/29 August 1942, for example, but made only a passing reference to the 34 per cent losses suffered by the Wellington crews involved. 'Our lads had a good crack at them last night,' he wrote, '& also caught a crack themselves.' He would keep that same remote perspective on the operational losses of his own group when the time came, at least in his diary. What Harris thought of the Canadian AOC when he arrived at High Wycombe we do not know, but by early December he was 'alarmed at the prospects' of No 6 Group under Brookes's command.[46]

As the Canadian group was finally declared operational, Brookes nevertheless received a congratulatory telegram from Harris. 'A happy birthday and a prosperous new year to No. 6 RCAF Group. As individuals and as RCAF squadrons you have done fine work already. As the RCAF Group I know that you will maintain and even surpass your own high standards. We are proud to have you with us. Hail Canada! Hail Hitler, with Bombs.'[47] Looking back on the day in the privacy of his own room, the Canadian commander noted simply:

Usual routine, everything ready for tonight. Raised plenty of fuss at our admin. conference re: tardiness in putting in material for the Ops. Record Book & ripped a full blown raspberry for [my personal staff officer] on same subject. Ops. Room in good shape, clean & maps completed, & all ready to go except that G[eneral] P[ost] O[ffice] [telephone technicians] still fiddling here & there. The morning passed quickly with much talking, phoning etc. & got a little reading done ... until 1845 & then collected the gang for dinner. 9 p.m. news & then returned to the office ... round the

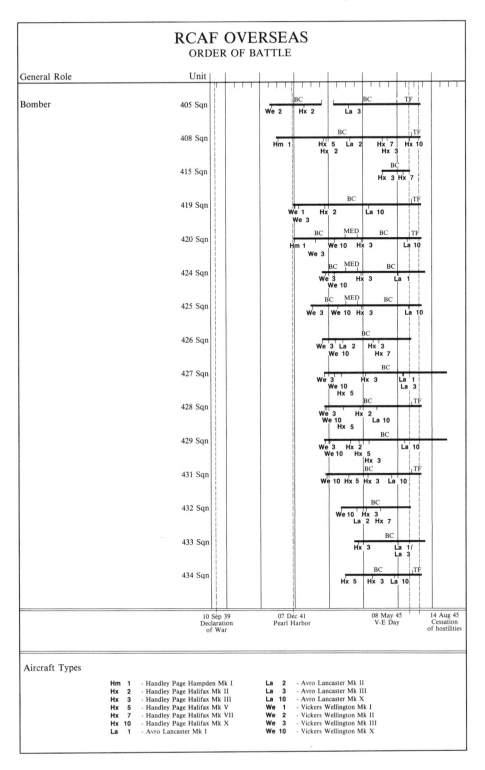

RCAF OVERSEAS
ORDER OF BATTLE

General Role	Unit
Bomber	405 Sqn
	408 Sqn
	415 Sqn
	419 Sqn
	420 Sqn
	424 Sqn
	425 Sqn
	426 Sqn
	427 Sqn
	428 Sqn
	429 Sqn
	431 Sqn
	432 Sqn
	433 Sqn
	434 Sqn

405 Sqn: BC / BC / TF — We 2, Hx 2, La 3

408 Sqn: BC / TF — Hm 1, Hx 5, La 2, Hx 7, Hx 10, Hx 2, Hx 3

415 Sqn: BC — Hx 3, Hx 7

419 Sqn: BC / TF — We 1, We 3, Hx 2, La 10

420 Sqn: BC MED BC TF — Hm 1, We 3, We 10, Hx 3, La 10

424 Sqn: BC MED BC — We 3, We 10, Hx 3, La 1

425 Sqn: BC MED BC — We 3, We 10, Hx 3, La 10

426 Sqn: BC — We 3, La 2, We 10, Hx 3, Hx 7

427 Sqn: BC — We 3, We 10, Hx 5, Hx 3, La 1, La 3

428 Sqn: BC / TF — We 3, We 10, Hx 5, Hx 2, La 10

429 Sqn: BC — We 3, We 10, Hx 2, Hx 5, Hx 3, La 10

431 Sqn: BC / TF — We 10, Hx 5, Hx 3, La 10

432 Sqn: BC — We 10, Hx 3, La 2, Hx 7

433 Sqn: BC — Hx 3, La 1/ La 3

434 Sqn: BC / TF — Hx 5, Hx 3, La 10

10 Sep 39 Declaration of War	07 Dec 41 Pearl Harbor	08 May 45 V-E Day	14 Aug 45 Cessation of hostilities

Aircraft Types

Hm	1	- Handley Page Hampden Mk I	La	2	- Avro Lancaster Mk II
Hx	2	- Handley Page Halifax Mk II	La	3	- Avro Lancaster Mk III
Hx	3	- Handley Page Halifax Mk III	La	10	- Avro Lancaster Mk X
Hx	5	- Handley Page Halifax Mk V	We	1	- Vickers Wellington Mk I
Hx	7	- Handley Page Halifax Mk VII	We	2	- Vickers Wellington Mk II
Hx	10	- Handley Page Halifax Mk X	We	3	- Vickers Wellington Mk III
La	1	- Avro Lancaster Mk I	We	10	- Vickers Wellington Mk X

building & then had a small party in my office to see the New Year in; about a dozen of us.[48]

No 6 Group took over control of Middleton St George and Croft at one minute past midnight on 1 January 1943, Leeming and Skipton-on-Swale the next night, and Topcliffe, Dishforth, and Dalton one night later. Its initiation into operations was almost as quiet as the AOC's New Year's party. Fourteen crews were detailed for Gardening on 1/2 January, but bad weather intervened, and the next night only six aircraft were dispatched to lay mines (with thirty-six others from the rest of Bomber Command) off the Biscay coast. Weather was again a hindrance, however, and three of the RCAF crews returned to base with their ordnance still on board.[49]

All six of these machines came from No 427 Squadron which, having been formed as recently as 7 November, had made remarkably quick progress in becoming operational. Some of the credit had to go to its British commanding officer, Wing Commander D.H. Burnside, DFC, who remained with the unit until his tour expired in September 1943. However, its development was also materially assisted by the influx of experienced personnel from No 419 Squadron. Indeed, if No 427 had not made such good progress, Brookes would have had only two squadrons to call upon on 1 January – Nos 420 and 425. The senior squadron in the group, No 405, was on temporary loan to Coastal Command, where it was flying convoy escort and anti-submarine patrols, while the rest were either converting to heavy bombers or not yet trained to operational standards. Slow progress was not always their fault. No 431 – still part of No 4 Group – did not fly its first mission until March, largely because of serviceability problems with its brand-new Wellington Xs. All of them had to have their airscrews repaired or replaced, and when that was corrected the maintenance staff discovered flaws in the fabric skin and turret installations which again put a stop to flying training. Still, by the end of January, every squadron was declared ready for operations.[50]

The customarily poor flying conditions experienced during the winter meant that Bomber Command's overall effort against German targets was limited even as Brookes's group was added to the order of battle. Lorient, the French port on the Bay of Biscay which served as the Kriegsmarine's main U-boat base, was, however, bombed five times between 14 and 31 January. Sir Arthur Harris had never been enthusiastic about attacking Lorient, calling it a 'childish task of bouncing bombs off impenetrable submarine pens.' But the enemy's success in the Battle of the Atlantic – U-boats had sunk almost five million gross tons of merchant shipping in the North Atlantic in 1942, up three million from the year before – was causing enough concern in London to direct Bomber Command away from its long-term objectives in order to help the Admiralty (and to ignore the risk to French civilians, which had heretofore been a major constraint on its operations over France). From 14 January, therefore, Harris was ordered to undertake 'area bombing against the U-boat operational bases on the west coast of France' – Lorient, St Nazaire, Brest, and La Pallice – with a view to 'effectively devastating the whole area in which are located the submarines, their main-tenance facilities, and the services ... and other resources upon which their operations depend.' In other words, these towns could be flattened. In keep-ing with the Air Ministry's belief that the air offensive against the enemy homelands should continue, however, Harris was also authorized to attack Berlin and other 'important objectives' in Germany and Italy whenever the weather was suitable.[51]

The importance of the German U-boats as a target system was reinforced by the strategic bombing directive issued by the combined American and British chiefs of staff following their January 1943 meetings at Casablanca. Harris and General Carl Spaatz, commanding the US Eighth Air Force, were told: 'Your primary object will be the progressive destruction and dislocation of the Ger-man military, industrial and economic system, and the undermining of the morale of the German people to a point where their capacity for armed resis-tance is fatally weakened.'

Within that general concept, your primary objectives, subject to the exigencies of weather and of tactical feasibility, will for the present be in the following order of priority:
(a) German submarine construction yards
(b) The German aircraft industry
(c) Transportation
(d) Oil plants
(e) Other targets in enemy war industry

The above order of priority may be varied from time to time according to develop-ments in the strategical situation. Moreover, other objectives of great importance either from the political or military point of view must be attacked. Examples of these are:
(i) Submarine operating bases on the Biscay coast ...
(ii) Berlin, which should be attacked when conditions are suitable for the attainment of specially valuable results unfavorable to the morale of the enemy or favorable to that of Russia ...[52]

No 6 Group was in the thick of the renewed anti-submarine campaign from the beginning. Of 316 sorties detailed in January, 195 were against Lorient and ninety-eight were Gardening missions in the Bay of Biscay and the North Sea. The other twenty-three were daylight Moling operations to the Ruhr, which were to be mounted only under protective cloud cover. The latter cost two crews who, it was felt, had 'disobeyed instructions' and proceeded on to the target when the required cloud was not present. Although minelaying was gen-erally less risky (four crews, or 3.7 per cent, failed to return), individual operations could take a heavy toll, as No 6 Group discovered on 21/22 Jan-uary, when forty-two machines were sent to the Nectarines sector, off the Frisian Islands. Good clear weather made for easy pin-pointing of the target area, but it also made things easy for the enemy's gunners, who shot down three Wellingtons.[53]

Well defended by Flak and air fighters, Lorient was an increasingly dangerous target and, by the end of the month, six raids on the town had cost eight
aircraft, 4.1 per cent of those dispatched. The last of these raids, mounted on
29/30 January and involving sixty-nine crews from the Canadian group, was
by far the worst. Weather conditions were terrible, as severe icing, heavy
cloud, rain, and electrical storms made for difficult flying; with no Pathfinders
to mark the target, bombing was scattered. Twenty-three crews decided to
return to base early, while the forty-two that bombed the port reported heavy
Flak. Four were missing, accounting for all of Bomber Command's losses that
night.[54]

February 1943 was a much busier month for Bomber Command and No 6
Group alike. The latter flew 1005 sorties, 312 in four raids on Lorient, another
193 to Wilhelmshaven, and eighty-four on one raid to St Nazaire. Together
these claimed nine crews (1.6 per cent). Gardening occurred on nine nights,
and cost seven of 203 sorties (3.4 per cent). There were also three raids against
German cities – Cologne twice, Hamburg once – on which the loss rate was
3.5 per cent of just under two hundred sorties. The attack on Hamburg was
especially difficult. Only nineteen of the forty-six Canadian crews dispatched
actually made it to the target area, the rest returning early because of ice and
cloud; but while group headquarters acknowledged that the effort was not
'particularly successful,' it nevertheless hoped that 'if the Pathfinder force
dropped flares in the correct position, the attacking aircraft bombed the target
with fair concentration.' In fact, the marking was neither concentrated nor
sustained and the bombing was well scattered. Perhaps because so many crews
had turned back, however, No 6 Group's loss rate was much lower than the 6.1
per cent suffered by Bomber Command as a whole. For once the enemy's
fighters were effective despite the bad weather.[55]

Fighters were also being seen more frequently on Gardening operations and
were thought to be responsible for at least some of the seven crews lost.
Several were encountered on the night of 18/19 February, when clear skies and
bright moonlight were ideal for interception, but only one No 419 Squadron
Halifax went missing while three enemy fighters were reported damaged or
destroyed. The most likely of these claims was that submitted by Sergeant T.V.
Sylvester's crew from No 428 Squadron, who were attacked twice, once on the
way to the target and once on the way back. It was during the latter engagement that a Ju 88 was reported to have fallen into the sea, on fire, after being
hit several times.[56]

But it was Lorient that was again Bomber Command's main preoccupation.
No 6 Group was happiest with its performance on 16/17 February, reporting
excellent results with many fires in the target area and 'all crews returning in
high spirits,' although an analysis of bombing photographs indicated that this
was the poorest raid by far, only 37 per cent of crews bombing within three
miles of the aiming point. (The best operation had come two weeks earlier, on
4/5 February, when the corresponding figure was 80 per cent.) Nevertheless,
by the end of the month the cumulative effect of six weeks of bombing suggested that the campaign against Lorient had been very effective indeed. The

docks and town were almost completely destroyed, and half the suburbs had been razed. Craters were also seen around the submarine pens.[57]

Not for the last time appearances were deceiving. After a series of 1941 attacks the Germans had moved all their essential stores and maintenance and repair facilities into the immensely strong concrete shelters they had built – unhindered, it must be said, by further Bomber Command raids – and removed all non-essential services to surrounding villages, so that although the town of Lorient itself was flattened and a number of French civilians killed, almost nothing was done to the U-boat installations. Lorient was not attacked at all in March – there were two raids on St Nazaire – and in mid-April the emphasis on operations against Brittany by night was suspended. Harassing raids were still to be carried out, largely by 'freshman crews ... with a view to their obtaining operational experience,' but the main weight of bombs would be delivered by the Americans by day.[58]

Harris's stubborn insistence on German cities as the bedrock of the night-bomber offensive, and his disdain for such peripheral issues (to him) as the anti-U-boat campaign, turned Bomber Command to a five-month-long campaign against the Ruhr. By the end of July, when the focus would shift again, he had launched 14,177 sorties against the industrial cities of the Ruhr and the Rhineland, on which he lost 673 crews – 4.7 per cent. No 6 Group had contributed 2095 sorties, but lost 161 crews – 7.6 per cent. Moreover, the group's loss rate, consistently among the highest in Bomber Command, rose almost continually: it stood at 2.8 per cent in March, 5.1 per cent in April, 6.8 per cent in May, 7.1 per cent in June, and 4.3 per cent in July.[59]

Although a number of reasons were eventually advanced to explain this situation, it was clear from the beginning that the relative inexperience of RCAF squadrons was among the more significant factors underlying these figures. The roots of the problem were easy enough to discern. The formation of seven new squadrons in the latter part of 1942 had required a large influx of recent OTU graduates into the group as well as groundcrews who had only just completed their training in Canada, and this simply put too much pressure on the personnel system. During January, for example, forty-five errors made by No 6 Group armaments crews had been identified, of which twenty-eight were considered 'avoidable.' In one case, a squadron had not been able to bomb-up all the aircraft detailed for the night's mission because the squadron armament officer had not been able to find the bombs; in another, an armourer removed the guns from a turret while they were still loaded; and in a third, incendiary bombs were loaded with the jettison bars armed, so that as soon as the electrical circuits were closed the bombs fell on the runway.[60]

February's performance was no better. These administrative and technical blunders were readily verifiable: those that affected operational performance over enemy territory were less distinguishable, since the perpetrators were often the victims. And no amount of posting of veterans from established squadrons to these new units could overcome the diluting effect of expansion on the group's overall level of experience. To compound the problem, No 6 Group had only a brief period in which to settle in before a number of squadrons began to convert to heavy bombers ahead of schedule for the simple reasons that the Canadians were scheduled to receive the next Halifax Heavy Conversion Unit (HCU) to be formed and because they needed a pool of Halifax squadrons to provide trained crews for their Pathfinder unit.[61]

When No 405 Squadron left the group in April 1943 to become the Canadian component of No 8 (Pathfinder) Group, its place at Leeming was taken by No 427, which exchanged its Wellingtons for Halifax Vs in May, thereby permitting the formation 432 Squadron on the medium bombers that No 427 had given up. After a lengthy conversion program, No 419 Squadron had finally become operational on the Halifax in February, and would soon be joined at Middleton St George by No 428, which switched its Wellington IIIs for Xs that same month and then moved on to Halifax Vs in June. No 429 would convert to Halifax IIs in August, while 431 Squadron, operational on Wellington Xs since January, converted to Halifax Vs in July. No 426 Squadron, meanwhile, gave up its Wellingtons in June and became the first RCAF squadron to receive Lancasters (admittedly Hercules-powered Lancaster IIs, which were inferior to the Merlin-powered I and III) – because, Sir Arthur Harris argued, the Canadians 'have been promised & deserve one Lanc. sqdn.' It was joined at Linton-on-Ouse by No 408 when it converted to the same type in late summer, once again because Harris (proving to be better than his word) believed it right to divide Lancaster II squadrons evenly between Nos 3 and 6 Groups despite the latter's designation as a Halifax formation. In doing so, of course, he was also taking advantage of the Canadian squadrons' experience with Hercules radial engines, with which the Mark II Lancaster was provided.[62]

In No 8 (Pathfinder) Group No 405 Squadron began its conversion to Lancaster Is and IIIs in August. That same month, Victory Aircraft in Toronto turned out its first Lancaster X – the *Ruhr Express* – which was immediately flown to England and presented to the squadron at Gransden Lodge in October, but this had been an outright publicity stunt. The machine was far from operationally ready, only thirteen more Lancaster Xs were built before the end of the year, and the first squadron was not equipped with the type until No 419 Squadron received them in March 1944.[63]

All told, then, between April and August 1943 seven RCAF squadrons began flying new types.[64] So much for the bald allegation, made then and now, that under Harris the Canadians – because they were Canadians – invariably did 'not get good aircraft'[65], and that they 'found themselves last in line ... for new aircraft and improved technology,'[66] a charge which even the nationalistic Edwards was moved to describe as 'an absolute lie.'[67] Harris said that seniority was the overriding principle governing the allocation of aircraft to squadrons, but that misrepresents what actually happened as much as the myth that the Canadians were discriminated against because they were Canadians. The desire to maintain commonality of engine type within groups and, where possible, between neighbouring groups played a part, as did the simple matter of availability: a perceived shortage of Merlin engines was responsible for the existence of the Hercules-powered Lancaster II which was given to three No 6 Group squadrons in 1943. In addition, in the case of No 6 Group the Canadian government not only undertook eventually to equip it with Lancaster Xs, but also exerted pressure on the Air Ministry to convert the Canadian formation to four-engined machines as early as possible, without specifying which type. (In Ottawa's view, Halifaxes were more prestigious than Wellingtons.) Overall, it may be said that No 6 Group got better aircraft sooner than some other groups.

As it was, with each conversion squadrons lost their operational currency on type and the whole process entailed considerable shifting of units from one station to another, requiring crews to adjust to new surroundings and landing patterns. Croft, Dalton, and Topcliffe were all shut down as operational bases between 19 April and 16 May to make way for the HCUs that prepared crews to fly the Halifax and Lancaster. Dishforth closed in mid-June to permit runway repair and expansion so that it could handle heavy bombers, while Burn was given back to the RAF. Two new stations, Tholthorpe and Linton-on-Ouse, were opened when they were taken over from No 4 Group. As a result of these openings and closings – as well as the conversion program – and not counting 405 Squadron's move to No 8 Group, between 2 April and 18 June 1943 five RCAF squadrons changed base at least once: 424 moved from Topcliffe to Leeming to Dalton, 426 from Dishforth to Linton, 427 from Croft to Leeming, 428 from Dalton to Middleton St George, and 431 from Burn to Tholthorpe.[68]

With all this happening (or scheduled to happen), and given its initial loss rates, it might have been best if No 6 Group had been left to settle down and establish a degree of continuity and stability. However, on 3 April 1943 the Air Ministry asked Canada to approve the transfer of three experienced Wellington squadrons to North Africa to support Operation Husky, the invasion of Sicily, for about two months.[69]

The suggestion that Canadian bomber squadrons might be sent outside Britain had first been raised in August 1942. Concerned about the growing 'dominionization' of his command and convinced that a number of bomber squadrons would be called upon to support Operation Torch, the Allied landings in French North Africa, the AOC-in-C had insisted that Canadian, Australian, Polish, and other such squadrons should not be free from the obligation to serve outside Britain. He wanted his command to remain at least two-thirds British. When a specific request for bombers was made in October 1942, Harris had proposed that the RCAF provide the two Wellington squadrons required. As things turned out, nothing came of that, largely for security reasons;[*] but when a need to reinforce the North African theatre arose in early December, Canada was asked for – and quickly agreed to send – the two squadrons despite the fact that their detachment would leave behind 'a small and relatively ineffectual Canadian Bomber Group': an indication, Ottawa

---

[*] Knowing that RCAF Overseas Headquarters would require the approval of the Canadian government to make such a commitment, and not trusting the security of trans-atlantic communications, British authorities did not want to risk revealing any information about Operation Torch, in which connection this request was made.

noted, of the government's policy 'not to refuse any reasonable operational request.'[70]

Although nothing happened again, an important precedent had been set. When the April 1943 appeal was made, Air Marshal Edwards pointed out that the move would 'reduce temporarily our Bomber Group which we are now striving to increase,' but he was also persuaded that the detachment of three squadrons would be 'a definite help in the pursuance of successful operations.' His agreement was nevertheless conditional. The three squadrons had to be Canadianized, serve together in the same wing under the command of an RCAF officer, and return to No 6 Group within three months. He also expected that three new Canadian bomber squadrons would be formed to replace them. The Canadian government accepted Edwards's recommendations, and the Air Ministry was so informed on 10 April.[71]

Nos 420, 424, and 425 Squadrons were selected to form No 331 Wing, part of US General Carl Spaatz's Northwest African Air Forces under Sir Arthur Tedder's Mediterranean Air Command. They exchanged their old Wellingtons for new Mark Xs which, since they would be operating from the semi-arid climate of central Tunisia, had to be tropicalized and modified to protect them against the ubiquitous dust and sand. The air- and groundcrews also had to prepare for their new surroundings. They were issued with tropical kit, suffered through the inevitable inoculations and vaccinations, and provided with emergency rations and medical supplies which contained, among other things, anti-mosquito cream and water sterilizing tablets.[72]

Establishments were increased so the squadrons could operate twenty machines instead of the standard sixteen in Bomber Command and, because of their isolation and the increased incidence of disease in Africa, they were authorized to carry five extra air crews. (The augmented groundcrew establishment did not provide for this 'sickness' and 'isolation' component, despite the fact that their life would be every bit as harsh as that of aircrews.) While most of these crews were filled by RCAF personnel, the three squadrons were still not Canadianized to the degree Edwards had anticipated. Although the Air Ministry sympathized with his position, it would not sacrifice experience for national identity. Mixed crews with a minority of Canadians might be declared ineligible for the transfer and replaced by complete RCAF crews from OTUs or other squadrons, it was decided, but no crews could be broken up (or mixed crews with a majority of RCAF personnel posted out) to enhance Canadianization.[73]

After some juggling, the aircrew Canadianization rate in the three squadrons was increased from about 73 per cent at the end of April to 80 per cent in mid-May, just before their departure for North Africa, while that for ground-crew reached 99 per cent. That was also likely to be the maximum. With replacements still required for No 6 Group as well as No 331 Wing, the Air Ministry decreed that only eighteen of the thirty Wellington crews to be sent to North Africa each month would come from RCAF sources. Accordingly, if the three Canadian squadrons suffered heavy casualties early on, before a pool

NO 331 WING OPERATIONS
IN THE MEDITERRANEAN
26 JUNE - 6 OCTOBER 1943

ITALY

YUGOSLAVIA

LIGURIAN
SEA

▲Pisa 1(26)
■Leghorn 1(27)

Bastia 1(31)■

CORSICA

Elba

▲Grosseto 1(20)

▲Viterbo 3 (69)

Civitavecchia 1 (22)■ ▲Cerveteri 1(21)
                        ○ROME
Lido di Roma 1 (3)▲
Cisterna 1 (24)▲
Frosinone 1(30)▲

Oblia 1(18)▲

SARDINIA

■Castelnuovo 1(23)

Formia 6(129)■ ■Foggia 1 (29)
Aversa 1(14)
Gaeta 1 (4)▲
Grazzanise 1(23)▲ ▲Benevento 1(23)
Villa Literno 1 (27)▲ Capodichini 6(145)
                  Naples 4 (112)■
Bagnoli 1(27)■ ■Battipaglia 4 (124)
Torre Annunziate 2 (41)■   ■Taranto 2(41)
Pompei 1 (32)■
Salerno 3 (77)■
Montecorvino 3 (61)■

TYRRHENIAN
SEA

▲Villacidro 1(18)
■Cagliari 3(41)

○ Sapri

IONIAN
SEA

Paola 1 (26)■

NOTE: Bold figures indicate number of
raids. Figures in brackets record
sorties flown. Sorties do not include early returns, leaflet raids
and electronic jamming missions.

Evacuation of Sicily   Pizzo 2 (48)■
Total 6 (137)
                        San Giovanni 2 (43)
Messina 10 (228)■ ■ ■Reggio di Calabria 1 (8)

Trapani 1 (16)■
                Randazzo 1(24)▲
                Enna 1 (25)
Sciacca 1 (15)▲   Catania 2 (14)▲
                ■   Catania 1 (27)
Caltagirone 1 (6)▲
                    ■Syracuse 1(15)
Gerbini 3 (53)

TUNIS○

Pantelleria
(Italy)

TUNISIA

No 331 Wing⚥   MALTA
Kairouan   (Gt. Br.)

○Sousse
○Monastir

Airfields . . . . ▲△
Transportation centres . . ■
German Evacuation
August 11-17 1943 . . . .●

Sfax○

MEDITERRANEAN   SEA

ADRIATIC SEA
Genoa
Bologna ○

of RCAF replacements had been built up, they would inevitably find themselves with a higher proportion of British and other Commonwealth crews.[74]

No 331 Wing formed at West Kirby, in Cheshire, on 7 May 1943, under the command of Group Captain C.R. Dunlap, a prewar regular who had spent three years as director of armaments in Ottawa before taking command at Leeming late in 1942.[*] Wing headquarters consisted of twenty officers, all RCAF, and 122 other ranks, of whom only seven were RAF. After embarkation leave, the groundcrews, wing staff, and some of the additional aircrew sailed from Liverpool on 18 May. Dunlap himself flew out to North Africa on 21 May to select and set about preparing the wing's landing fields. He found that no one in Mediterranean Air Command 'appeared to be assuming any responsibility for the matter' and that the Americans had already taken most of the good locations. (The RAF's No 205 Group, with headquarters at Kairouan and comprising Nos 231 and 236 Wings and including one Spitfire and five Wellington squadrons, was also close at hand.) However, with the assistance of US Army Engineers he eventually found two sites near the town of Kairouan, midway between Tunis and Sfax, about thirty miles inland from Sousse on the Mediterranean coast. Nos 420 and 425 Squadrons, along with 331 Wing Headquarters, would settle in at Zina, a 'great barren plain covered with dry thistles,' while No 424 Squadron would be located at Pavillier, which boasted some 'stunted olive trees' and 'a tall cactus hedge' to provide 'a modicum of shelter in the domestic area.'[75]

All the aircraft took off from England between 1 and 4 June, flying a circuitous route over the Atlantic but, nevertheless, No 420 Squadron was attacked in broad daylight over the Bay of Biscay by 'several Junkers ... in close formation.' Two aircraft went missing and were presumed shot down. One machine from No 425 was also attacked and the crew eventually forced to bail out over Portugal, where they were interned.[76]

Most of the ground parties and equipment reached the Kairouan area by 19 June, and work on building up the two stations began the next day. Tents had to be set up, latrines dug, and roads and servicing areas laid out – in temperatures approaching 128° Fahrenheit (53° Celsius). In the evening of 22 June, however, a tremendous rainstorm began which lasted until late the next day – 'something quite unprecedented in this district during the summer season.' With most vehicles immobilized, all work came to a halt, and a message was sent to hold No 424 Squadron at Telergma, on the Tunisian coast, until the ground hardened. It was not received 'due to the poor signals communication,' however, and crews began to fly in just as the rain stopped. 'Fortunately, none were damaged during the landing in heavy mud.' Although No 331 Wing was declared ready for operations three days later, on 26 June, much work still had to be done. On 12 July twenty-five Arab labourers were hired 'to dig slit trenches and do heavy work in the bomb and petrol dumps' and it was not until 13 July that British engineers completed a 'permament shower bath ...

---

[*] He retired from the RCAF in 1966 having served as chief of the air staff (1962–4) and deputy commander-in-chief of the North American Air Defence Command (1964–6).

utilizing a disused Arab well.' Unhappily, the showers 'only lasted a half hour. The supports holding the tank gave way' and could not be repaired for two days.[77]

The Sicilian campaign to which the three squadrons were assigned was a strategic compromise decided on at the Casablanca conference of January 1943. At that time the Americans would have preferred 'to close immediately with the German enemy in Western Europe or even in Southern France,' but the British feared that a cross-Channel assault launched too soon might well prove disastrous. To them, the logical course was to pursue the initiative in the Mediterranean 'to strike,' as Winston Churchill put it, 'at the under-belly of the Axis in effective strength and in the shortest time.' The Americans reluctantly accepted that the capture of Sicily and the opening of the Mediterranean shipping lanes were useful goals in their own right. However, the Allied commander-in-chief, US General D.D. Eisenhower, reaffirmed that this was not an open-ended commitment. Sicily was a worthwhile objective, he declared, in part because 'its occupation after capture would not absorb unforeseen amounts of Allied strength in the event that the enemy should undertake any large-scale counteraction.' Furthermore, it did not follow that a further advance into Italy was necessary or desirable – one reason why, when the request was made for the three Canadian squadrons, it was felt that they would be needed for only two or three months.[78]

The operations in which the three Canadian squadrons would be involved were quite different from those with which they were familiar in Northwest Europe. For one thing, this was no 'area bombing' campaign. The main targets selected were the enemy's airfields in Sicily and Italy, in order to prevent the enemy from bringing its air power to bear against the landings, and supply routes to the island in order to keep the Germans and Italians from reinforcing and resupplying their garrisons. Summer flying conditions were also much different in the Mediterranean theatre. The weather was generally much better, and crews often found themselves in clear, calm skies, which made visual pinpointing of the target much easier; however, since Gee was not available, long-distance navigation over the Mediterranean required more emphasis on dead-reckoning and astronomical observations. The opposition, however, was of a different order from that encountered over Germany. Although Flak could be heavy at times in some places, particularly along the Straits of Messina, the night-fighter organization was primitive and weak, and on most raids it was reasonable to bomb from well below 10,000 feet.[79]

The first raid by No 331 Wing took place on 26/27 June, when Nos 420 and 425 Squadrons attacked the air base at Sciacca on Sicily's southern coast, about three hundred miles from Tunisia. There was a good deal of Flak and the searchlights cooperated well with the fighters, but the two squadrons suffered only one loss and claimed one Ju 88 destroyed. No 424 Squadron began operations on 27/28 June and had a much more difficult time. One crew lost a 4000-pound bomb on takeoff, but continued on to the target unaware of what had happened. Another machine burst a tire on takeoff and crashed, dropping its bomb as well. Fortunately, neither exploded, and two other crews took off not having noticed the accidents. Four more were not bombed-up in time, however, and had to abort their sorties. That was blamed on the armourers, some of whom had 'arrived in England just a few weeks before the Squadron moved' and had very little experience. Things were worse the next night, when the target was Messina, as the squadron lost two crews to enemy action. By the end of June No 424 was responsible for three of the seven machines missing or severely damaged since the wing began flying operations. Added to the three machines shot down en route from England to Tunisia, this meant that thirty-five aircrew had become casualties in a month.[80]

Whether it was because the initial attacks on enemy airfields had achieved their objective or because the targets selected were more dispersed, losses on operations due to enemy action fell from five (5.3 per cent of sorties) in June to three (0.5 per cent) in July – although there were also six forced landings in the latter month. Missions themselves were also more varied. Between 2 and 8 July, in generally good weather, the wing operated against airfields at Catania, Villacidrio, Olbia, and Gerbini – the enemy's main fighter base on Sicily – and photographs taken on the 9th showed that the Gerbini and its satellites had been rendered 'completely unusable.' They also attacked the railroad yards and barracks at Cagliari, on the island of Sardinia; a seaplane base at Lido di Roma, where the Tiber flows into the Tyrrhenian Sea; and Trapani, on Sicily's far west coast.[81]

No 424 Squadron was nevertheless enduring a period of bad luck during this period, which may have accentuated the sourness expressed in its diary. It lost four of the six No 331 Wing crews killed or missing in the first three weeks of July, one of them on the 6th when a fully fuelled and bombed-up Wellington caught fire in the dispersal area and exploded, killing three crew who had been sitting under the wing and wounding a number of others. 'Fragments from the bursts flew all over the camp setting grass fires,' and a few seconds later a second machine was also on fire. It too blew up. What caused the fire was never discovered, but it was suspected that, as in the case of a No 420 Squadron Wellington that blew up two days before, the intense heat of the day might have had something to do with it.[82]

Dysentery, diarrhoea, malaria, and what was called jaundice were also taking their toll, and there had been tremendous grumbling about food – 'bully beef three times a day' – since the squadron's arrival in Tunisia. Indeed, in late June the grousing had reached the point that the commanding officer (Wing Commander G.A. Roy, formerly a flight commander in No 425) felt compelled to call a muster parade at which he promised to find extra food by fudging the squadron's ration strength. In the meantime, all ranks were encouraged to contribute a portion of their pay to a squadron fund to buy additional foodstuffs on the local economy. Here they made good use of the linguistic talents of the wing's Protestant chaplain, Flight Lieutenant Herbert Ashford, who knew both French and Arabic and who 'brought back to the squadrons many little things to make life easier – straw mats on which to lie, earthenware bottles from which to drink comparatively cool water, as well as chickens and other delicacies to relieve the monotony of issue rations.' However, complaints continued about rations, the unit's water supply, and what some saw as the unfair rating of Mediterranean Air Command sorties as counting only three-quarters of a trip towards completion of the thirty-trip operational tour.[83]

There were also problems simply maintaining the effort on the ground, and attempts to solve these challenges led to one sergeant in No 420 Squadron being recommended for a British Empire Medal.

Sergeant [E.K.] McLeod has been Senior NCO in charge of the Motor Transport Section during his squadron's stay in North West Africa. From the start he has been faced with a shortage of M[otor] T[ransport] Drivers and equipment. On many occasions he has improvised fitting spares obtained from British, American, and enemy vehicles lying derelict in the surrounding country to his own ... At the same time his shortage of MT Drivers has forced him to work his men to the limit throughout the period of the squadron's stay. Despite this, his men have never complained but rather have taken a great pride in their section and have given him their full support. In consequence, motor transport serviceability has remained at a very high standard and no transport facilities have ever gone lacking for the squadron.[84]

However, like many others, this award was not approved; perhaps because there were just too many non-flying personnel working every bit as diligently as McLeod to ensure that aircrew could carry out their operations with as few inconveniences and interruptions as possible.

Sicily was invaded on 10 July, and the three RCAF squadrons were assigned to targets over the whole island, supporting the landings, bombing marshalling yards and troop concentrations at Catania, and attacking the seaplane base and marshalling yards at Syracuse and the aerodrome at Cataglieroni from as low as 4000 feet. Perhaps the most important assignment, however, was that flown by six crews from the three squadrons that, equipped with the Mandrel jamming device, patrolled off the coast, hiding the invasion fleet behind an electronic curtain. With Allied troops (including the 1st Canadian Infantry Division and the 1st Canadian Army Tank Brigade) safely ashore, the squadrons operated every night until 15 July against enemy strongpoints and airfields.[85]

Twice they won praise for their efforts from Spaatz and James H. Doolittle, who led the strategic component in the Northwest African Air Forces. On the first occasion, on 11/12 July (the day American and Canadian forces linked up at Ragusa), No 424 Squadron took advantage of the bright moon and light defences to strafe the airfield at Monte Corvino, near Salerno, after their bombing runs and claimed forty enemy aircraft destroyed – most of them, by now, Italian. The next day Nos 420 and 425 Squadrons pounded German troop concentrations and the roads around Enna, whose capture had become something of a 'friendly rivalry' between the Canadian and American armies. By mid-month the wing had mounted 253 sorties on twelve nights. There were only six early returns, and despite the ever-present dust and sand of Tunisia, which had to be scrupulously removed from vital components like guns, fuel tanks, and the bomb-bay door closing mechanism, maintenance standards in this period of intensive operations were amazingly high. Of the fifty-six or fifty-seven Wellingtons normally on strength in the wing, an average of fifty-two were available for operations each night – 91 per cent.[86] A serviceability rate so good in Northwest Europe would have earned high praise.

On 15 July the Canadians began to attack Italian targets, concentrating on airfields, port facilities, and railway yards in the Naples area, about four hundred miles from Kairouan and two hundred from the Sicilian battlefields. (Poor transportation facilities in southern Italy meant that Naples was a major loading point for the shipment of war materiel to the Axis forces in Sicily.) Flak near major cities like Naples was accurate and sometimes intense, and on 16/17 July Nos 420 and 424 Squadrons reported as many as forty searchlights operating around the Capodichino airfield. Three nights later, when all three squadrons returned to Capodichino, the defences had been strengthened further, and crews estimated there were now up to seventy-five searchlights in the area, with a particularly efficient group of about ten near Mount Vesuvius. A number of night-fighters were seen, but there were no losses. Naples was attacked again on 20/21 July, through heavy Flak and good visibility, but the area was covered in cloud on 21/22 July and the bombing at Capodichino was not well concentrated.[87]

On 25 July Italian dictator Benito Mussolini was brought before his party's Fascist Grand Council to be dismissed and placed under house arrest, giving rise to hopes that Italy might soon withdraw from the war. That same day No 331 Wing was given a brief respite from operations, its first since mid-month. With the scirocco winds blowing off the desert and daytime temperatures rising to 125° Fahrenheit, the opportunity to go swimming at Sousse or the wing's rest camp (set up by the YMCA) at Monastir was more than welcome. Moreover, on 28 July 'Sheikh Amor Bouguerra Sheikh du Sidi Amor Bou Hadjela Caidat Kairouan, head of one of the villages near Monistair [sic], visited Group Captain Dunlap and presented the G/C with 8 live chickens, one live sheep and about 7 dozen eggs' – a most agreeable supplement to an increasingly boring diet.[88]

This late July layoff certainly lifted the spirits of Sergeant L. MacLauchlan, one of No 424's hard-working ground crew. 'Life out here is certainly different, to say the least,' he informed his old BCATP station:

... but we have become accustomed to the sun and sweat, sand and flies ... No wet canteen to go to when work is done, though. We get a half bottle of beer per week sometimes ...

Our '48s' [two-days' leave] are spent at a rest camp on the Mediterranean, where we live the life of Riley. Not quite like Port Stanley [a summer resort on Lake Erie], perhaps, no music or pretty figures but lovely water and cool breezes. And if you care to, you can bargain with the countless Arabs for grapes, melons and almonds, and if you are lucky, a bottle of 'Vino Rouge.' Altogether not a bad life ...

The usual topic of conversation, believe it or not, is not women, but food. Beef steak and ice cream lead the list by a good margin. Also I believe a nice cool ale is a favourite subject.[89]

Losses were not really a problem by late July. Earlier in the month, however, the combination of accidents, sickness, June's battle casualties, and the three crews missing from the flight from England to Tunisia had forced Dunlap 'to accept a fairly large number of RAF crews from the Middle East pool,' 'de-Canadianizing' his command from about 80 per cent to 74 per cent. Although he knew that turning to the British pool for replacements was contrary to Air Marshal Edwards's policy, Dunlap believed that, under the circumstances, his action would meet with the latter's 'full approval' because it allowed the Canadians to fulfil all their operational commitments. He was wrong. Convinced that the RCAF replacement crews sent out in June had somehow been sidetracked and probably posted to RAF units, Edwards was 'greatly distressed'; not about to allow No 331 to become an RCAF formation in name only, he directed that the ceiling on the number of RCAF crews to be sent out each month should be raised beyond the eighteen authorized by the Air Ministry.[90]

Edwards's concern was such, in fact, that the matter was raised while Sir Charles Portal was in Quebec City attending the Quadrant conference of Allied leaders in August, and it was only then that it was realized that Dunlap's problem was a temporary one brought on by the late arrival of the first batch of RCAF replacements. In fact, from 6 July Dunlap was reporting that his Canadian replacements were pouring in, and it was relatively easy, in time, to restore the Canadianization rate to 80 per cent, about the maximum possible given the shortage of Canadian wireless operator/air gunners. The only problem arose with No 425 Squadron. Since its arrival in North Africa it had received no French-Canadian crews. During the first week of July, however, when Canadianization rates were lowest, it was still 70 per cent RCAF, compared with 65 per cent in 420 Squadron and 80 per cent in No 424.[91]

When the wing returned to operations in August, the Allied armies were pinching the enemy into the northeastern corner of Sicily. (The 1st Canadian Division was taken out of the line on 6 August, to prepared for the assault on Italy, and the 1 Canadian Army Tank Brigade four days later.) What mattered now was to prevent any escape to the mainland, and as a result the three Canadian squadrons were busy attacking barges, military transport, and the beaches over which the enemy was trying to flee. Despite over a thousand sorties by Allied aircraft (including 350 by the Canadians) and nightly incursions into the Straits by patrol boats of the Royal Navy, the movement of some 40,000 German and 62,000 Italian troops to the mainland could not be prevented. Moreover, the cost was high. The Germans moved in considerable Flak to protect their withdrawal, and it was said that the intensity of the fire at times rivalled that found over the Ruhr. The Canadians alone lost five machines (and twenty-five airmen) in these attacks.[92] Another was very lucky. On 13 August Pilot Officer A.G. Grout of No 424 Squadron took off to bomb the beaches at Cape Bardi.

At approximately 0210 hours the port oil pressure gauge started to fluctuate between 90 degrees and 60 degrees. The oil and cylinder head temperatures were normal. This fluctuating continued for approximately five to ten minutes, then the gauge dropped to zero ... The target being ten to fifteen minutes away ... we decided to go ahead and bomb.

After bombing the target we set our course out, being in the neighbourhood of 7,500 feet we gradually let our height decrease to 6,000 feet. Reaching this height and approximately ten minutes from the target the port engine began to sputter and cut out immediately ...

... I noticed flame showing from the port engine exhaust pipe. This died down, but soon started again, only it seemed much worse than before. Thinking that the engine had a small fire ... I ... started the prop, so it turned over very slowly. The fire died down and seemed to go completely out. Waiting a few seconds, I then stopped the prop from windmilling. A few minutes after doing this the fire started again, but it seemed to be much fiercer ... We decided to head for the main-land [Sicily] ...

Reaching the mainland the fire seemed to be out of control ... The coast was covered by cloud and we were below the hilltops which protruded above the clouds. Our height was approximately 2,000 feet. The starboard engine was overheating and the aircraft would not hold height. I had ordered the crew to stand by for bailing out. We hit the coast and turned west.

The fire on the port engine by this time was very fierce and protruded underneath the wing. The fabric caught fire and I could see the leading part of the wing blazing. I ordered the crew to bail out ... As the wireless operator left the aircraft a large mountain loomed up, I had to bank very steeply to the left and I opened the starboard engine to its fullest power. As I missed the wall, I dived out of the aircraft ... [which], a few second later, exploded against a ravine wall.

... by 0600 hours I had climbed out of the ravine and I then started to look for the rest of the crew ... At approximately 0830 to 0900 hours I ran across some American Army men who accompanied me in my search for the rest of the crew ... In the meantime the bomb aimer and rear gunner had found each other and together they located the wireless operator, who had either broken or badly sprained his ankle ... Helped by Italians they carried the wireless operator to the coast. On reaching the coast, the Americans took them in a railway station, giving the wireless operator more first aid.

Eventually Grout joined up with these three, and they boarded an American transport aircraft for Tunis. 'We were on course for approximately thirty minutes when the aircraft ran into a [barrage-] balloon cable. The bomb charge on the cable blew approximately two square yards out of the wing of the C-47 [Dakota]. Losing control of the aircraft, the pilot finally picked up the stalled wing and landed at a fighter drome called Lacata. During the bomb charge exploding, shrapnel pierced the fuselage and struck the bomb aimer ... in the arm, behind the ear, and cut the ear itself.'[93] With the bomb-aimer and the wirless operator both in hospital, Grout and his rear gunner finally made it back to Kairouan, where they met up with the navigator who had arrived the day before, having been found by another American soldier in Sicily and flown on to Tunis separately.

The capture of Sicily, it will be recalled, had not been intended as a prelude to the invasion of Italy, but was undertaken as a limited operation to secure the Mediterranean for Allied shipping. At the Washington conference of May 1943 (Trident), however, the pull of Italy proved irresistible, although the decision to carry the war to the mainland involved considerable compromise. In return for supporting an extended campaign in the Mediterranean (against which they had protested so vigorously five months before), the Americans extracted significant concessions from the British, who finally agreed to conduct a major cross-Channel amphibious assault in May or June 1944. The strategic goal in the Italian theatre would be met when the Allies occupied the country as far north as Naples and the airfield complex around Foggia – and perhaps took Rome.[94]

The initial plan called for a landing only at Reggio di Calabria, in the Italian toe, but with Mussolini's fall from power a second assault was added in the Gulf of Salerno so that Naples could be taken more quickly. Operations in Calabria would begin on 3 September, and those around Salerno two days later. The original commitment of No 331 Wing was to have ended on 31 July, but it had now been extended to 15 September so that the three Wellington squadrons could participate in the bombing operations required during the first two weeks of the Italian campaign. That meant another few weeks in Tunisia, where the rainy season was about to begin (not a pleasant prospect for men under canvas) or, as Dunlap learned on 4 September, it might mean a move to Malta 'until such a time as Italy stops fighting.'[95] That was an event that grand strategists thought might occur at any moment.

Initially, the Canadians concentrated on the railway yards around Naples and the airfields at Foggia, but they also attacked the steel works at Bagnoli, Torre Annunziata (near Naples), and the railway yards and roads behind the Salerno beaches in the last few days before the landings. These operations achieved their intended effect. By the time the invasion began, the bombing of a few nodal points had virtually paralysed the elemental southern Italian railroad system and no supplies could be brought through Aversa, Concelo, Benvento, Foggia, Battipaglia, Sapri, Paola, Pizzo, or Catanzaro to any of the Allied landing areas. Then, as the month drew to a close, Taranto and Salerno were the targets. General Doolittle visited the wing on 1 September, and went on a night-bombing operation to the Aversa marshalling yards with Squadron Leader A.J. Lewington's 'illuminator' crew from No 420 Squadron to see first-hand how the Wellington force used flares to mark its objectives.[96]

Once the armies were ashore on the Italian mainland (1st Canadian Division playing a key role in the Reggio assault,) No 331 Wing turned to tactical bombing behind the Salerno beachhead in order to blunt any German counter-attack. 'Enemy communications and supplies were assaulted without respite. The main roads were literally plastered with bombs.' The Germans fought with such ferocity at Salerno, however, that for a time the success of the landing seemed threatened, and a request was made to retain the wing for an indefinite period, until the Allied bridgeheads had been secured and the advance north had begun. Again Edwards agreed, the Canadians being warned that they might actually move to mainland bases in November and spend some time there. Just as they should have been packing up to return to England, the three RCAF squadrons contributed to a mission which, according to Sir Arthur Tedder, 'may have saved the day.'

On the night of 14/15 September, the road from Battipaglia to Eboli [the main axis for a heavy German counterattack spearheaded by strong armoured formations] was buried beneath 237 tons of bombs delivered in one raid by 126 Wellingtons. This was the greatest effort yet made by night bombers in this theatre. It was also the justification for the request we had put to Portal for the retention of the three Canadian Wellington squadrons. I had told him...shortly before the main German counterattack against the centre of our bridgehead was launched, that in my opinion, and in Eisenhower's, we could not afford any reduction in our night bomber effort until the situation was clearer.[97]

The Canadians flew forty-three sorties and dropped eighty-two tons of bombs on the line of march of three German divisions: the 15th and 29th Panzergrenadier and the Hermann Göring Panzerdivision. Attacking from altitudes of 2800 to 10,000 feet, crews reported the whole area covered by a thick pall of smoke. The next night they concentrated on the Torre Annunziata-Pompeii road, where the enemy also threatened to break through to the Salerno beachhead. The main problem, it turned out, was congestion over the target area, and a number of crews made up to four runs before dropping their bombs.[98] 'I have recently seen some account of the exceptionally good work done by the Canadian Wellington Wing in the Mediterranean,' Sir Charles Portal commented to Edwards when he learned of these efforts. 'I am told that the scale of effort in relation to the size of the force has probably been higher than has ever been achieved anywhere in the past and included operations on 78 of 80 successive nights, with a nightly average of 69 sorties ... Tedder has signalled in very warm terms about this outstanding achievement. I have already asked him to convey my appreciation to all concerned but I should like to let you know personally how greatly I am impressed by this splendid record of No 331 Wing. We are all greatly looking forward to the time when, with newer and better equipment, they will resume their operations against Germany.'[99]

That time was not far off. The German counter-attacks failed, bludgeoned by naval gunfire and the bombing, and although air operations subsequently shifted to the north, to Rome and Corsica, which the enemy was now evacuating, by 8 October it was all over for No 331 Wing.[100] The front had stabilized sufficiently for the three squadrons to be withdrawn after a total of 2182 sorties on 82 nights out of 102 spent in the theatre – and after losing only eighteen machines (0.8 per cent) on operations and another eighteen to accidents, mostly involving takeoff and landing. Leaving their aircraft behind, the squadrons travelled by bus to Tunis on 18 October, boarded two 'very dirty' trains to Algiers, where they spent two days, and set sail for England on 27

October. They disembarked at Liverpool, to music by the RCAF Band, in snow and rain on 6/7 November, travelled to their bases at Dalton, Skipton, and Dishforth, rekitted, enjoyed some leave, and then began to re-equip on Halifaxes to take part in the battle of Berlin.

18

No 6 Group Falters,
Spring and Summer 1943

Issued by the combined Anglo-American chiefs of staff under the authority of US president Franklin D. Roosevelt and British prime minister Winston Churchill, the Casablanca directive of 21 January 1943 established the framework of Allied bombing policy for 1943–4. As a prelude to the planned cross-Channel invasion, now postponed until 1944, and allowing for 'exigencies of weather and tactical feasibility,' the Allied air forces were to attack four main sectors of the German war economy: submarine yards on the Baltic coast and U-boat bases on the Biscay coast (the focus of operations for most of January and February), the aircraft industry, transportation, and oil. The assault on these targets would place a premium on accurate and precise bombing. To that end, the US Eighth Air Force based in England (which was only just beginning to mount raids involving more than one hundred machines in March 1943, but would be sending three hundred to German targets by July) was committed to a daylight bombing offensive. By the end of the year American crews would be all too familiar with targets like the oil refineries at Gelsenkirchen, Bochum, and Hüls; the Messerschmitt factory at Regensburg; and the ball-bearing industry at Schweinfurt.[1]

Having spent the better part of thirty months failing to find or significantly damage these types of targets – and the better part of a year (since Sir Arthur Harris became AOC-in-C) arguing that the attempt to destroy them was not worthwhile – Bomber Command was not particularly happy with lists of specific objectives. 'Ever since the beginning of the war,' Harris recalled in his memoirs, High Wycombe had been told repeatedly to attack 'a whole class of objectives which at Bomber Command we always called "panacea" targets. These were targets which were supposed by the economic experts to be such a vital bottleneck ... that when they were destroyed the enemy would have to pack up ... The enthusiasm of the experts was so great that I was actually told that I should be fully justified in accepting such losses to achieve the destruction of Schweinfurt ... as would put the whole of the bomber force out of action for two months. They paid no attention to the fact that Schweinfurt was too small and distant a town for us to be able to find and hit in 1943.'[2]

However, since the Casablanca conference involved compromise at every turn, ways were found for Bomber Command to continue with the night-bombing offensive preferred by Harris and Sir Charles Portal alike. Berlin was included in the list of specific objectives as were 'other targets in [the] enemy war industry,' and together these provided more than enough leeway to keep doing what they were already doing for those wedded, by necessity or inclination, to area attacks. But there was more. The first sentence of the Casablanca directive told the 'bomber barons' that their 'primary objective will be the progressive destruction and dislocation of the German military, industrial and economic system and the undermining of the morale of the German people to a point where their capacity for armed resistance is fatally weakened.'[3]

Portal and Harris could scarcely have found better words to justify Bomber Command's effort to date, although the latter felt it necessary to do so. In a memorandum to the Air Ministry, he misquoted the directive to suggest that the 'progressive destruction and dislocation' of the German military, industrial, and economic system was specifically aimed at 'undermining' morale – further vindicating, in a very small way, his fixation with area bombing.[4]

Just what the CAS and Harris wanted to accomplish had been made clear in October 1942, as part of the autumnal ritual in which Portal laid out his hopes and plans for the coming year to the other chiefs of staff and the War Cabinet – occasions used to squeeze more resources out of the British economy and to protect Bomber Command from what they both considered to be the depredations of the army and navy. Despite the slowing down of expansion, forced by production delays and, to a lesser extent, by the transfer of aircraft, squadrons, and crews to other commands and theatres, Portal's vision for 1943 still looked forward to the creation of an Allied bomber force of four to six thousand machines which, able to deliver fifty thousand tons of bombs a month by the end of the year, would 'shatter the industrial and economic structure of Germany.' Indeed, by that time the CAS estimated that six million dwellings would have been destroyed, rendering twenty-five million people homeless, and that 900,000 Germans would be dead, with another million injured. 'Proportionate destruction,' he added, would occur in industrial sectors.[5]

Given the way most manufacturing centres had developed, however, the areas most susceptible to attack were not the industrial parks on the outskirts but the downtown cores, full of old buildings and narrow streets, where flames could spread easily. This was where the greatest weight of bombs should fall, his DBOps advised, and where the aiming points should be located, using fire as the main instrument of destruction, to cause 'fear of death ... injury and the loss of private property.'[6] With parameters like those, the Ruhr/Rhineland industrial basin, within range of all navigation aids, close enough to sustain operations through the shorter nights of spring and summer, and sufficiently dense that near misses would still count, was a natural choice for an area offensive. Almost a year to the day since the start of the last great attempt to knock it out, the second battle of the Ruhr began on 5/6 March 1943 with an attack on Essen.

Some things had changed, however. This time, Harris has explained: 'In no instance except in Essen [where the sprawling Krupp facilities were practically an area target in themselves] were we aiming at any one factory during the

Battle of the Ruhr; specifically, the destruction of factories ... could be regarded as a bonus. The aiming points were usually right in the centre of the town ... The objective ... was to reduce production ... at least as much by the indirect effect of damage to services, housing, and amenities, as by any direct damage to the factories or railways themselves.'[7] Furthermore, where previous operations had involved an average of two hundred aircraft, of which about thirty were four-engined machines, in 1943 Harris would routinely send six hundred crews to the target, and could call upon three hundred Stirlings, Halifaxes, and Lancasters. Some nights as many as eight hundred sorties were mounted, without all the special administrative arrangements and intercommand negotiations required for the 'thousand' raids launched the previous summer. At minimum, and all other things being equal, the bomb load carried on each attack should, on average, be five times greater than in 1942.[8]

Harris and Portal expected the weight of bombs falling in the target area to increase by much more than a factor of five because of Oboe and H2S, and because of the Pathfinder Force's growing repertoire of flares, target indicators, and marking techniques. (Although it had been modified to use multiple frequencies, Gee was still susceptible to jamming, and its greatest value by 1943 was probably to guide crews back to their bases in Britain.) Better marking, it was hoped, might treble the number of crews bombing within three miles of the aiming point, leading to a fifteen-fold increase in the bomb tonnage dropped in the target area – enough to remove cities like Essen and Duisburg from the economic order of battle.[9]

Technically, Oboe worked as well as anticipated but, requiring two-way communications between a limited number of ground stations and airborne transponders, it would never be available for use by all main-force crews – who, in the event, could not fly high enough to exploit its maximum range. (At the outset, only six Oboe-equipped machines could be dealt with in one hour.) The solution, of course, was for the Pathfinders to use Oboe as their principal navigation and target-marking aid; for this purpose the perfect instrument was the high-flying de Havilland Mosquito, with a ceiling well above 30,000 feet, which was so much faster than the Luftwaffe's night-fighters that it could fly straight and level for the ten minutes required for an accurate bomb-release signal with relative impunity. High Wycombe consequently began an intensive campaign to acquire Mosquitoes for the Pathfinders; when the battle of the Ruhr began, twenty-two were on strength in No 8 Group.[10]

H2S, the downward-looking radar which could be fitted to, and used, by any number of aircraft, was originally intended to be a blind-bombing device for all crews, but its limitations became apparent soon after its introduction on 30/31 January 1943. Although it had been thought that each built-up area would have its own distinctive H2S 'signature,' in areas like the Ruhr ground detail displayed on the cathode-ray screen often appeared as a featureless blob, and any hopes that crews would be able to identify specific aiming points were soon shattered. Indeed, even No 8 Group's more conservative estimate that H2S-assisted marking and bomb-aiming would allow three-quarters of the main force to bomb within two miles of the aiming point (and about one-third within

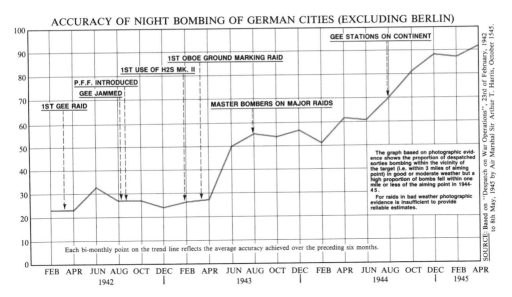

ACCURACY OF NIGHT BOMBING OF GERMAN CITIES (EXCLUDING BERLIN)

GEE STATIONS ON CONTINENT

1ST OBOE GROUND MARKING RAID

1ST USE OF H2S MK. II

P.F.F. INTRODUCED

GEE JAMMED

1ST GEE RAID

MASTER BOMBERS ON MAJOR RAIDS

The graph based on photographic evidence shows the proportion of despatched sorties bombing within the vicinity of the target (i.e. within 3 miles of aiming point) in good or moderate weather but a high proportion of bombs fell within one mile or less of the aiming point in 1944-45.

For raids in bad weather photographic evidence is insufficient to provide reliable estimates.

Each bi-monthly point on the trend line reflects the average accuracy achieved over the preceding six months.

FEB APR JUN AUG OCT DEC FEB APR JUN AUG OCT DEC FEB APR JUN AUG OCT DEC FEB APR
1942   1943   1944   1945

SOURCE: Based on "Despatch on War Operations", 23rd of February, 1942 to 8th May, 1945 by Air Marshal Sir Arthur T. Harris, October 1545.

a mile) was also wildly optimistic. Based on preliminary analysis, it seemed likely that the probable systemic error for blind-bombing with H2S would be somewhere in the order of half the diameter of the target being attacked; when the device was used as a navigation aid it was accepted that crews were liable to be off-track by as much as 10 per cent of the distance flown. Added to disappointing serviceability rates (70 per cent) early in its career, there was reason enough for main-force crews not to forget their other navigation aids: Gee (when it was not jammed), astro, and those landmarks that could be seen.[11]

Once at the target, it was the bomb-aimer's task to hit it. The Mark XIV course-setting bombsight introduced gradually – much too gradually for Harris's liking – beginning in the summer of 1942 allowed a single crew member to enter all the relevant variables of the bomb-aiming equation into the sight's computing device: air and ground speed, wind velocity and direction, altitude, atmospheric pressure, the ballistic characteristics (if any) of the bombs being carried, and their terminal velocity. It was felt, as a result, that the Mark XIV sight should produce 'at any time during the bombing attack the point on the ground [which when] covered by the graticule cross represented the point of impact of a bomb released at that instant.' There was, inevitably, a margin of error, but this was estimated to be no more than 150 yards from 20,000 feet. Perhaps just as important, the new sight afforded pilots some tactical freedom. Sufficiently stabilized that perfectly straight and level flight was not required, the Mark XIV sight meant that moderate evasive manoeuvres over the target would no longer nullify the two- or three-hour flight to get there.[12]

The introduction of these new technologies was complemented by advances in Pathfinding techniques and equipment. Best results continued to come from visual pinpointing of the aiming point followed by ground-marking, a method code-named Newhaven, but the clear skies (and absence of smog) required for this procedure could not be counted on, especially over the Ruhr. Accordingly, when haze or thin cloud obscured the aiming point but ground flares could nevertheless be seen, No 8 Group used Oboe and/or H2S (depending on the target's distance) to determine when to release their ground markers, and then backed up their marking throughout the attack to reduce the 'creep-back' occurring when, eager to avoid the Flak concentrations in the target area, crews tended to bomb short. Known as Paramatta, and Musical Paramatta when Oboe was involved, this method was necessarily less precise than visual marking; and since main-force crews were instructed to bomb what they perceived to be the centre of concentration of the target indicators, there was inevitably a wider spread of bombs.

Following the first few raids when Musical Paramatta was employed, it seemed that 60 per cent of crews would bomb within three miles of the aiming point. Additional experience gained at Essen and elsewhere soon proved that this, too, was in error, and that the estimate should be reduced by about 20 per cent. Although disappointing in terms of anticipated performance, even the revised figure, when it was combined with the five-fold increase in average bombload now being carried, would result in a substantially greater weight of bombs falling around the aiming point. Since cities like Düsseldorf, Dortmund, Duisburg, Frankfurt-am-Main, and Wuppertal could all be fitted into circles three miles in diameter, it was expected they would receive a heavy weight of bombs if only half the crews, on very large raids, achieved the three-mile standard. Whether that would lead to the results Portal and Harris anticipated was another question.

Without doubt, however, the most important innovation from the perspective of its force-multiplying potential was the development of sky-marking assisted by H2S (Wanganui) or Oboe (Musical Wanganui). Until its introduction, the many dark or cloudy nights that offered the best chance of evading the enemy's defences resulted in bombing more or less by guess and by God. The glow of fires far below, diffused by cloud, smog, and smoke, was frequently the sole clue as to the location of the aiming point, and it was then that bombing was most scattered. Common sense dictated that Wanganui could not produce results comparable to Newhaven. Flares and target-indicators dropped by parachute drifted in the wind and often had to be released at some distance from the aiming point to compensate for such drifting, but well-placed sky-markers – and here Oboe's superiority to H2S was overwhelming – provided a focus for bomb-aimers so much better than the reflected glare of ground fires that Harris could almost begin to consider Bomber Command an all-weather force. The great limiting factor that remained (and which was not solved before the end of the war) was that none of his bombers could fly above storms, and thus did not operate when the meteorologists forecast unsafe flying conditions.[13]

Hand in hand with these navigation aids there appeared a whole new range of target indicator bombs and flares with improved ballistic properties for greater accuracy; brilliant pyrotechnics to distinguish them from ground fires; and more intense colours, which not only caught the eye but were also more difficult for the Germans to duplicate. On a given raid, then, the target would be marked and illuminated by a blaze of red, green, and yellow TIs – 'Christmas trees' to the Germans – as well as by the brilliant white of ground-markers, all released in the particular pattern set down for that night.[14]

To further enhance coordination and control, No 8 Group not only used flares to mark the turning points en route to the target but, from 1 January 1943, all groups used the same wind forecasts provided by Bomber Command.[15] Although the adoption of common winds was generally for the best, it may have occasionally worked to No 6 Group's disadvantage. Because of their location, the Canadian squadrons often did not join up with the rest of the main force until just before the Dutch coast, having approached it on a tangent. If the forecast winds were considerably in error they could be well off-track before even reaching their intended rendezvous and so fail to enter the bomber stream as scheduled; like anything else that worked against concentration, this problem played to the strengths of Himmelbett.

As it was, the German air defence organization had been considerably strengthened in the twelve months separating the two battles of the Ruhr. Although Hitler still would not give priority to the production of night-fighters, and the Luftwaffe was allocating most Me 110s, Ju 88s, and Do 217s to the Russian front, the number of machines available to Kammhuber had doubled from about two hundred in March 1942 to four hundred a year later, and many more of them were equipped with AI radar. Furthermore, the training program Kammhuber had put in place in 1941 was finally paying dividends, so there was no shortage of trained crews. The area covered by Himmelbett had also been extended. The creation of Jagddivisionen in France and southern Germany and the provision of both static and mobile Würzburg radars had helped to fill gaps in the defensive line there. In the north the radar-picket and fighter-control ship *Togo* was keeping station in the Baltic, covering the northern flank against both Gardening and bombing operations, and some consideration was being given to employing submarines in the same role.[16]

Coordination of the night air battle had also been improved. The large control rooms at the Jagddivision headquarters (ultimately established at Deelen, Stade, Metz, Döberitz, and Schleissheim) and at the central Luftwaffenbefehlshaber Mitte in Berlin were provided with sufficient communications links and relays to make it easy (and safer) to pass control over an interceptor from one Himmelbett 'box' to another, and so to give each night-fighter crew more time to stalk and shoot down its prey. In some areas, night-fighter boxes were now routinely grouped in sets of three, with up to three machines operating in each box. Slowly, ways were being found to cope with larger, more concentrated raids, so that the defences were not swamped as they had been at Cologne, but the cost was tremendous. In October 1942, for example, when General Friedrich von Paulus's 6 Armee was fighting its way into oblivion at Stalingrad, Kammhuber asked not only for six hundred more ground control radars but for 150,000 additional men as well, a request that infuriated Reichsmarschall Hermann Göring. It would be 'cheaper to at-

GERMAN NIGHT FIGHTER DEFENCES
AND BOMBER COMMAND

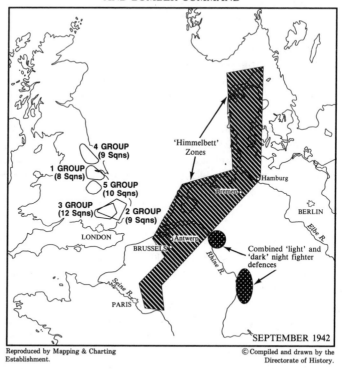

4 GROUP
(9 Sqns)

1 GROUP
(8 Sqns)

5 GROUP
(10 Sqns)

3 GROUP
(12 Sqns)

2 GROUP
(9 Sqns)

'Himmelbett'
Zones

Hamburg

Bremen

BERLIN

Elbe R.

LONDON

BRUSSELS

Antwerp

Combined 'light' and
'dark' night fighter
defences

Rhine R.

Seine R.

PARIS

SEPTEMBER 1942

Reproduced by Mapping & Charting
Establishment.

© Compiled and drawn by the
Directorate of History.

tack the British directly,' he observed, 'than to build up this gigantic organization.'[17]

The heavy investment in men and materiel necessary to create a nationwide Himmelbett network was one reason why, despite the recent improvements, there was dissatisfaction within the Luftwaffe with what Kammhuber had achieved by March 1943. Although the number of bombers shot down by fighters was growing steadily, it had not reached the 10 per cent of sorties which the Germans – looking back on their own experience during the Battle of Britain – believed was the point at which losses became intolerable. Moreover, night-fighter losses had also been climbing in 1942, and would continue to do so in 1943, rising sharply from thirty-one in February to forty-three in March, sixty-four in April, sixty-eight in May and June, and 107 in July. With the supply of new aircraft so limited, at this rate there would be no expansion of the night-fighter force, but, at best, only the replacement of battle casualties.[18]

There was also discontent with Kammhuber's unyielding commitment to ground-controlled interception. Unofficial experiments in pursuit (or route) interception, in which fighters were infiltrated by ground control into the bomber stream and then left to fly with it to the target, shooting down what they could on the way, had taken place in the fall of 1942, without much suc-

GERMAN NIGHT FIGHTER DEFENCES
AND BOMBER COMMAND

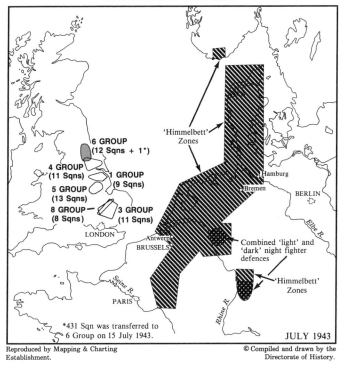

Reproduced by Mapping & Charting
Establishment.

© Compiled and drawn by the
Directorate of History.

cess. But the idea of what would come to be called Zahme Sau (Tame Boar) night-fighting was revived in the spring of the new year by Oberst Viktor von Lossberg, a former bomber pilot. Although he agreed that Zahme Sau was 'tactically correct,' Kammhuber rejected the idea for the moment, both because he did not want to weaken his Himmelbett organization and because he believed that, with the AI radar then available, it would be 'more or less left up to chance' whether crews would find the bomber stream and then individual bombers.[19]

Others, meanwhile, were urging Kammhuber to supplement Himmelbett with day-fighters (flown by former bomber and transport pilots) over the target at night, to take advantage of the illumination provided by searchlights and by the flares and target-markers dropped by Bomber Command. Kammhuber was unalterably opposed to such Wilde Sau tactics, seeing only the potential for chaos, but his reluctance to try new ideas was beginning to tell against him. 'For a year, our night-fighter system has remained at the same level, hasn't made one step forward,' Göring complained in mid-March; 'on the contrary, its successes have in fact become fewer and fewer ... even at those places where the radars are located.' This was an exaggeration, of course, but that mattered little. Aware of Göring's opinion, in April Generaloberst Hubert Weise, commanding Luftwaffenbefehlshaber Mitte, told Major Hajo Herrmann, a former bomber pilot and principal advocate of Wilde Sau, to test his theories just as the battle of the Ruhr was testing Kammhuber's ability to defend Germany's industrial heartland by relying primarily on Himmelbett.[20]

With the promise of reasonably good weather and skies, Bomber Command sent 442 aircraft to Essen on 5/6 March, including seventy-seven from No 6 Group. All told, the main force carried 1014 tons of bombs, five times the average taken to Essen a year earlier, and not much less than was dropped during the thousand-bomber raid on the city in June 1942. The target, even if attacked indirectly, was production from the Krupp complex which, despite all the raids so far, was still turning out tanks, bombs, and the highly effective, dual-purpose 88 millimetre anti-tank and anti-aircraft gun.[21]

The five main-force groups were informed that this was a special operation and they were told to take great care to find the red TIs which, it was predicted, should be 'within 100 yards of the aiming point.' Indeed, those who had not seen any red target indicators up to fifteen minutes after the scheduled start of the attack were to turn left, circle to the east, and begin a second run-in to the target. If all went well, the AOCs were told, 'this most important target will be entirely destroyed.' To emphasise the point, it was laid down that all crews for whom cameras could be made available would take photographs, while each squadron was to designate a senior pilot to report on what he had seen immediately on his return to base.[22]

Harris's insistence on obtaining so much information so quickly from so many sources betrayed his anxiety about Oboe's ability to support a sustained and effective campaign against the Ruhr. When the night was over he had much to be pleased with. To be sure, some things had gone wrong: three Pathfinder Mosquitoes had been forced to turn back because of technical problems; and fifty-six crews from the main force (12.6 per cent) returned early, among them eight from No 6 Group (9.2 per cent).[23] Yet the marking had been very good and the bombing, which took just under an hour, was well concentrated around the aiming point, with more than three-quarters of all photographs taken within three miles of it.[24] Crews, meanwhile, reported seeing a solid ring of fire about two miles in diameter, one describing the city as 'an immense pot boiling over.'[25]

Reconnaissance photographs taken the next day confirmed these assessments. 'Exceptionally severe and widespread' damage was reported, with the heaviest coming in the town centre, where it was estimated that three-quarters of the buildings had been damaged or destroyed. At Krupp, thirteen main buildings had been hit, and another fifty-three shops 'affected' by the attack, the Germans themselves estimating that about one-third of the complex was a 'total loss.'[26] The battle of the Ruhr had got off to a fine start, and the AOC-in-C later concluded that, with Oboe, 'the key to successful night raiding in the Ruhr, which Gee had failed to provide, had at last been found.'[27] Things had gone right even from the standpoint of evading the enemy's defences. Only 3.2 per cent of the total sorties dispatched failed to return, not bad for Essen on a nice spring night.[28]

Harris congratulated his crews in a typically vehement message.

The attack on Essen has now inflicted such vast damage that it will in due course take historical precedence as the greatest victory achieved on any front. You have set a fire in the belly of Germany which will burn the black heart out of Nazidom and wither its grasping limbs at the very roots. Such attacks, which will continue in crescendo, will progressively make it more and more impossible for the enemy to further his aggressions or to hold where he now stands. The great skill and high courage with which you pressed home to your objectives has already impressed the inevitability of disaster on the whole of Germany, and within the next few months the hopelessness of their situation will be borne in upon them in a manner which will destroy their capacity for resistance and break their hearts.[29]

No 6 Group could certainly share in the triumph. It had a lower early return rate than the rest of Bomber Command; forty-one photographs, while showing 'little or no ground detail,' were assessed as being within the main area of concentration; and at least one night-fighter was beaten off. Its loss rate (three crews, or 3.9 per cent) was slightly higher than the overall figure, but the absolute number was low.[30]

The next three raids, relatively deep penetrations to Nuremburg, Munich, and Stuttgart, involved only heavy bombers and so limited No 6 Group's participation to the three Halifax squadrons, Nos 408, 419, and 405 – the latter having returned from Coastal Command and not yet left for No 8 Group. But as all three cities were beyond Oboe range and there was little or no moon, marking had to be done entirely by H2S. The bombing was not accurate, and only Munich suffered more than slight damage. Like the rest of Bomber Command, the Canadian squadrons emerged from the first two raids relatively unscathed, but Stuttgart was a different story. Of thirty-five Canadian sorties, five returned early and another five were lost, four from No 405 Squadron alone. There was also an alarming report from No 419 Squadron that one of its aircraft had been stalked and attacked by a Wellington, a verdict with which Bomber Command initially agreed, accepting the possibility that the Germans had salvaged and repaired a machine lost sometime earlier. Only later was it realized that the enemy aircraft was probably one of the new (and largely unsuccessful) Messerschmitt Me 210s.[31]

Following these three long-distance operations, Bomber Command returned to Essen on 12/13 March in another Oboe raid. No 6 Group dispatched ninety-three crews, of which seventeen returned early – four from No 424 Squadron – and three were lost. The raid was successful, however, with most bombs falling across the Krupp complex on the western side of the city centre. Five hundred houses were also destroyed.[32] After a week's hiatus from operations over Germany because of the full-moon period, and taking advantage of cloud predicted for the target, Harris chose on 26/27 March to attack Duisburg in an operation that went badly awry when five of the nine Oboe sky-marking Mosquitoes had to return early because of technical problems. The main force was left to do the best it could in an entirely unfocused raid, the participants themselves reported that their bombing had been 'scattered over a considerable area of the Ruhr.'[33]

Then, at the behest of the War Cabinet and in line with the Casablanca policy of attacking Berlin 'when conditions are suitable for the attainment of specially valuable results unfavourable to the morale of the enemy or favourable to that of Russia,' there followed two raids on the German capital in order to 'rub in' the effects of Soviet Marshal S.K. Timoshenko's successful offensive at Smolensk. The first occurred on 27/28 March, just a day or so after Sergeant C.E. McDonald – a fighter pilot from 403 Squadron shot down near Lille in August 1941, who had just escaped from his prison camp – incredibly spent a day 'sightseeing' in the German capital as he made his way (successfully) to Gibraltar. He saw 'very little bomb damage' as he toured the city, and might not have seen much after the raid either. Involving a main force of 396 heavy bombers, including thirty-one Halifaxes from Nos 405, 408, and 419 Squadrons, the attack was judged a failure largely because the Pathfinders had marked two separate aiming points, neither accurately. The Germans recorded only ten high-explosive bombs falling on the city, yet perhaps because the bombing was so scattered there were two lucky hits. A troop train full of men on leave from the Russian front was struck, killing eighty and wounding one hundred; and a Luftwaffe stores depot eleven miles southwest of the city was destroyed, along with its radio and radar sets and components. Losses, fortunately, were low: nine overall, and just two from No 6 Group, although six crews returned early.[34]

The next raid on Berlin came two nights later, when 149 Wellingtons, half of them from No 6 Group, were also sent to Bochum. Both attacks failed miserably. Icing, very strong winds that the meteorologists had not predicted, and poor marking led the main force well south of the capital, while Bochum was spared on account of long gaps in the marking and (so far as the Canadians were concerned) because sky-marking had been selected instead of Oboe-assisted ground-marking. 'Comment on the operation,' No 6 Group reported, was 'generally subdued.' Bomber Command lost 6.4 per cent of the force sent to Berlin, and 8 per cent at Bochum. The news for No 6 Group was more depressing still. Just six of the twenty-three crews sent to Berlin had found the target, fifteen returned early, and two were missing. At Bochum, meanwhile, twenty-two returned early, and six were missing, just over 8 per cent of those dispatched. That brought the month's losses against German targets to thirty-three, 4 per cent of those involved – not a critical rate but one which, in light of the forthcoming transfer of No 405 Squadron to 8 Group and the formation of No 331 Wing, represented a considerable drain of experienced crews.[35] St Nazaire and Lorient were also bombed at this time in relatively small raids that turned out to be the last attempts to destroy the submarine pens there until 1944. No 6 Group sent 106 crews to St Nazaire on 28/29 March to flatten what was left of the town, and nineteen to St Nazaire and Lorient on 2/3 April. They reported accurate marking on both occasions, and the port areas of both towns were engulfed in flame. The U-boat facilities were not touched, however, and, as most of the civilian population had already been evacuated, there were few casualties.[36]

A sense of frustration had begun to replace the optimism engendered by the first few raids of the campaign against the Ruhr. Oboe was not doing as much as had been anticipated to increase the numbers bombing within three miles of the aiming point, while H2S was a major disappointment on the deep penetrations carried out so far. At Munich and Stuttgart it appeared that less than a third of the attackers had come within a three-mile zone. Yet, as High Wycombe's radar officer tried to point out, such grumbling about H2S was unreasonable. The equipment had been designed to 'enable bombs to be dropped on a specific built-up area,' he explained, and it was never intended that 'all aircraft using it could drop their bombs on a specific point within a built-up area.' But that was easier said than understood or accepted by Harris and his deputy, Saundby, and despite evidence to the contrary the battle of the Ruhr continued to be predicated on the assumption that H2S was sensitive and reliable enough to allow most crews to do significantly better than they were doing. When they failed to measure up, ineptitude rather than the inherent limitations of their equipment tended to be cited as the reason.[37]

No 6 Group participated in all ten of the major raids undertaken in April. Thick cloud predominated early in the month, forcing the Pathfinders to resort to sky-marking, but better weather later on allowed for reasonably accurate attacks on Mannheim and Stettin in mid-month, and again at Essen on 30 April/1 May. Indeed, at Stettin, a major port far to the east (in what is now Poland), the city's clear H2S response and good visibility combined to produce a concentrated attack in which 81 per cent of bombing photographs were taken within three miles of the aiming point. Immense fires were seen, one hundred acres of the central core were destroyed, and public utilities were knocked out for a week.[38]

Balanced against this success, however, was the egregious failure at Stuttgart, attacked on 14/15 April in 'good visibility with no cloud' and where 'the moonlight made the river and town identifiable.' RCAF crews reported that the 'marker flares were also well placed' and that, by the end of the operation, 'the whole town appeared to be a blazing mass.' But there was significant 'creep back' from the aiming point, and less than a fifth of the bombing photos were plotted within three miles of it. Things were even worse at Pilsen, site of the large Skoda works, two nights later. Despite a full moon, the Pathfinders somehow mistook an asylum at Dôbrany, seven miles away, for their objective, marked it thoroughly, and so produced a heavy raid on an otherwise sleepy Czech village on the Berouka river. The Canadians were fooled every bit as much as everyone else. 'In good weather with small amounts of cloud,' No 6 Group reported, '... the raid on the Skoda works appears to have been most successful. The works themselves were clearly identified and received the great majority of the bombs, although some incendiary bursts and one large fire were seen in the town.' (This may have been the German army barracks hit that night, clearly by accident, killing two hundred.) Even without such mistakes, however, April was a cruel month for No 6 Group. Although the number of crews claiming to have attacked the primary target rose to 83 per cent, that was still the lowest rate in Bomber Command, and 7 per cent off the pace being set by No 4 Group. The early return rate also remained high, about 15 per cent of sorties.[39]

Much more alarming was the fact that the group's loss rate on these major raids had climbed to 8 per cent, while that for Bomber Command as a whole was 5 per cent, troubling enough in itself. Moreover, the most costly raids had come in quick succession. Eight crews were missing at Stuttgart, and another eight failed to return two nights later, four from Mannheim and four from Pilsen, the latter all from No 408 Squadron.[40]

Harris looked carefully at Bomber Command's performance throughout the month and grew increasingly unsatisfied. With bombing concentrated from four to five miles from the aiming point the attack on Stuttgart had been a complete failure, he observed on 16 April; and he was persuaded that his crews were allowing themselves 'to be misled' to the point that they would bomb 'any concentration' of fire or explosions (or decoys) without checking their positions.[41] A week later he complained that the main force was bombing early, even before No 8 Group had begun its marking,[42] and on 5 May he sent yet another rebuke to his AOCs, telling them that they must control their formations with a firmer hand.

There is irrefutable evidence that some of the less skilled or weaker brethren fail to get into the target in circumstances which are inexcusable provided even an approximate ETA was kept and the captain was doing his best.

There is also irrefutable evidence that if and when a determined and skillful effort is made by all members of a force of more than 300 heavy bombers to get into the average target almost complete destruction results.

When, however, such efforts are not made or are not successful repeated visits to the same target have to be made with a resulting far greater incidence of loss affecting particularly the stouter and more skilled crews. This we cannot allow, and I must ask you ... to stiffen up the procedure of cancelling [credit for] sorties [against completion of an operational tour] whenever negligence or lack of determination are suspect.

We cannot allow our best crews to suffer avoidable casualties or the operational effort to be diminished by such negligence or lack of determination.

He was also concerned that too many crews were missing the aiming point because they were taking evasive action which, over 'hotly defended' targets, was 'meaningless.'

The collision risk is seriously increased. It results in no saving of aircraft. Attempts by turning away to avoid *Flak* bursting ahead are just as likely to lead to a hit from other bursts off the original track. Violent evasive action makes it impossible for gunners either to see or to hit attacking fighters. Heavy bombers cannot 'out-manoeuvre' properly handled fighters. Finally, evasive action in the target area makes accurate bombing impossible and necessitates, therefore, repeat attacks; these in turn lead to an overall higher total of casualties in achieving a given object ...

I need hardly point out the vastly improved bombing which would result if in fact we find that evasive action does not pay and that a straight run across the target exposes the aircraft to less risk than the longer run caused by weaving or violent evasion.[43]

Harris soon had reason to be happier. Along with accurate raids on Turin and the Schneider armament works at Le Creusot, 170 miles south of Paris, Bomber Command on 16/17 May pulled off one of the great public-relations coups of the war. Nineteen Lancasters from No 617 Squadron, including twenty-nine RCAF aircrew, struck at the Möhne, Eder, Sorpe, and other dams in the Ruhr, breaching the first two and unleashing a spectacular, if brief, flood that reached as far as Essen. The supply of power to the Ruhr was interrupted and crops were destroyed but, 'measured against the frightful losses which the terror attacks caused in the German cities,' General Kammhuber recalled, '... the dam attacks were less significant,' a fact Harris may have admitted in his memoirs when he acknowledged that Operation Chastise was only 'one incident in the Battle of the Ruhr.' The Eder dam, for example, was not even an industrial or hydroelectric reservoir, while the Sorpe, probably the most important of all, was not given high priority. But nothing like this was said at the time, when it was important to think that Chastise 'must undoubtedly have caused great alarm and despondency in Germany.'[44]

Along with Chastise, and reflecting the continuing expansion of Bomber Command, High Wycombe undertook sixteen major operations averaging six hundred sorties each between 5 May and 24 July, when the battle of the Ruhr came to a close. Record bombloads were carried on 23/24 May, when 826 aircraft (including 662 four-engined machines) were sent to Dortmund; because of the better summer weather, estimates of the numbers bombing within three miles of the aiming point rose to as high as 80 per cent. On 29/30 May, when this figure was reached at Wuppertal because the Pathfinder backers-up (including No 405 Squadron) were able to fill the void left by gaps in the Oboe primary marking, the Barmen district suffered a ferocious attack which severely damaged or destroyed 8000 housing units, and it was felt that no new raids were required on that part of the town. At Duisburg, where Bomber Command had stumbled near the end of March, 77 per cent of 572 main-force crews were within the zone on 12/13 May. Given near-perfect marking, they devastated the city centre, damaging 18,000 houses, knocking out four steel plants, and sinking almost 19,000 tons of shipping.[45]

Josef Goebbels, Hitler's propaganda minister, confided ruefully to his diary that 'one does not need to be a great mathematician to prophesy when a large part of the industry of the Ruhr will be out of commission.'[46] Harris, for his part, was buoyed by the recent results and sent a quite different message to his crews than the one issued only a month before. After congratulating them for their work at Berlin, Stettin, Munich, and Nuremburg, he explained that 'all that and much more has been merely incidental to your main task of destroying the Ruhr.'

In that you have largely succeeded already. Cologne is over half destroyed. Düsseldorf protests a lugubrious claim to be even harder hit. The Duisburg, Ruhrort, Hamborn complex is at least as busy licking its wounds as in war production ... Essen ... is shattered and for all practical purposes a dead city ... and as for Barmen – the night photo plot and what the crews saw together assure us of what will be revealed when the smoke blows away ... You have unhoused untold numbers and probably the majority of the key skilled workers in those areas and you are making conditions intolerable for all of them. The direct damage to war industries ... has had the most profound effect on every enemy warlike activity ... You will now proceed to knock him flat.[47]

Despite confusing marking on the 11th, when one Pathfinder Mosquito released its flares fourteen miles away, 83 per cent of the main force bombed within three miles of the aiming point at Düsseldorf, causing a fire zone of fifteen square miles, destroying sixty factories, killing 1189, and rendering 140,000 homeless. Results at Krefeld ten days later were much the same, with half the town centre (including 6000 houses) burnt out. The Eberfeld half of Wuppertal was hit hard by a very concentrated attack on 24/25 June, when 6000 houses were destroyed and a small firestorm was created over an area of almost three square miles. There were failures, of course, when cloud obscured the target or the Pathfinder marking was inaccurate or thin, but such was the size of the main force now being sent out that considerable damage could still be done even when the bombing was scattered. The most powerful illustration of this kind of serendipitous battering occurred on 28/29 June. Despite 10–10ths cloud and the late arrival of the Pathfinders, a scattered attack on Cologne killed 3400, destroyed 6400 houses, and knocked out forty-three factories – much greater damage than was done four nights later when 80 per cent of an even larger main force were plotted within three miles of the aiming point.[48]

In terms of the number of houses that could be destroyed, factories damaged, or civilians killed – 2900 in April, 7700 in May, 9100 in June, and 45,000 in July[49] – Bomber Command was becoming an increasingly effective bludgeon. But it was an unpredictable bludgeon, and an indiscriminate one as well. Not all factories were of equal value to the German war economy; not all the labourers who lost their houses were involved in crucial war work; and not all streets blocked by debris were important thoroughfares. In addition, although the Ministry of Economic Warfare (MEW) concluded that bombing was having an effect on all branches of the German economy by June 1943, it also noted that much of the damage to industrial premises could be compensated for by the surplus of plant capacity which existed in Germany.[50]

What MEW did not know was that Germany was just beginning to rationalize its war industries, so that some of the damage Harris was so ready to gloat about had been done to non-essential industries. After ten months of bombing, perhaps as little as six weeks' production had been lost in the Ruhr. Moreover, the fall in output was only temporary: production in badly bombed areas often recovered within a month or two. More to the point, the dispersal of important factories, which had begun on a small scale in 1942, accelerated in 1943, so that Bomber Command's attacks on cities would be aimed at increasingly insignificant sectors of the enemy's economy. For these reasons, Albert Speer, Hitler's armaments minister, concluded that area bombing alone was not a major threat to war production. The 'dehousing' effort, by comparison, had more long-lasting and potentially serious effects, since there was no surplus stock of residential accommodation in Germany. People just had to 'double up'; but even though the number of homeless, and presumably miserable, German civilians was growing, postwar analysis of their morale suggests that its decline, while cumulative, began in earnest only in mid-1944, and even then could not be attributed only, or even primarily, to the bombing.[51]

Of more immediate concern, despite avoiding the full-moon periods so helpful to the Luftwaffe, Bomber Command's loss rate on these major raids had climbed steadily until it reached 5.4 per cent in June, while that for all night operations was 4.3 per cent. (For Stirling and Halifax crews, the rate was 6 per cent.) In attacking the Ruhr, Harris had taken on the strongest parts of Germany's air-defence system, and he had not won. [52]

For No 6 Group, May, June, and July 1943 were worse months even than April. Although the early return rate on major raids fell from almost 19 per cent in March to about 11 per cent in July, the percentage bombing the primary target remained the lowest in all of Bomber Command. While the groundcrews were doing better work and had reduced the number of technical failures leading to early returns despite the culling out of veteran technicians for No 331 Wing, a representative from the Royal Aircraft Establishment visiting the Canadians as late as September 1943 heard frequent complaints about 'the lack of adequately trained personnel' which, he observed, 'must result in poor servicing of equipment and an increase in the number of faults.'[53]

There were two distinct periods when No 6 Group's missing rate rose to 11.5 per cent – 11–13 May and 21–25 June – and the worst night of all for the group as a whole came on 12/13 May, when eight of sixty sorties (13.3 per cent) did not return from Duisburg. Night-fighters were out in force, but Flak was also very heavy. It claimed one of two No 426 Squadron crews lost that night, killing the second pilot,[*] but not before the navigator, Flight Lieutenant G. Miller, made a splendid effort to keep the Wellington airborne. 'With the hasty use of linen maps' he managed to mend the severed fuel lines and then 'spliced the elevator controls with aerial wire.' The pilot, as a result, was able to fly his crippled machine as far as the Belgian coast when, too much fuel having been lost, he ordered his crew to bail out.[54]

---

[*] Although bomber aircraft no longer carried two pilots as part of their regular crew, new pilots fresh from OTUs accompanied experienced crews on at least one raid before becoming operational with their own.

Six jumped, and five were captured. The sixth, Flight Sergeant O.W. Forland, the rear gunner, who in civilian life had been a riveter in an aircraft factory – and perhaps should not have been permitted to join the RCAF because of that – evaded capture. Landing in marshlands away from the rest, he quickly took off his flying clothes and began to head south. Suffering from a slight knee injury incurred when he hit the ground, however, he soon decided he could not continue, crawled into a ditch, and slept. Having recovered somewhat, he walked for twelve hours the next day until, seeing three German soldiers, he had to hide quickly.

In my haste to avoid them, I dropped and lost my second compass. That night I slept in the woods. Next morning, 14 May, I crossed the Spa-Stavelot railway line near Hochai. There I saw a working man. I can speak no language but English, but I showed him my [RAF] badges and he managed to confirm my opinion as to the points of the compass. A little later I came to signposts marked Malmedy and Liege. I followed the post marked Liege.

I now cut off the uppers of my flying boots, and bound the rubber soles to my walking shoes with strips torn from my [escape] purse. Though I realized the risk I ran, I decided to walk along the road even though [it was] in broad daylight.

About 1630 hrs I met a man pushing a bicycle. I showed him my map, and said inquiringly 'Liege?' He took me a little off the road, and indicated to me that I was twenty kilometers from Liege. He also was obviously warning me to avoid Spa, as it was full of German troops. He offered me one hundred Belgian francs, and eventually himself took me to an isolated farm nearby. Here I showed the farmer my identity discs, and was given food, and made welcome. Next morning, 15 May, a woman came to see me. She spoke to me in German and then in English, took away my identity discs, and asked me a number of questions about the aircraft, and the names of the other members of my crew. She seemed very doubtful of my identity. Finally I showed her some Canadian cigarettes, which appeared to convince her. Later she told me that had I been a German masquerading as a Canadian, I would not have resisted the temptation to smoke these myself.

She then removed my RAF uniform, and the farmer gave me civilian clothes. I retained my Oxford walking shoes [which were worn under the Canadian pattern flying boots]. I remained here till 1 Jun 1943. During this time I was photographed by the woman, who visited me several times. She told me that one member of my crew had been captured by a German forest guard immediately after landing, and had unfortunately told his captor that the crew comprised six persons instead of the normal complement of five. Since the Germans found one dead body in the aircraft, and later captured three other members of the crew, they continued to conduct a local search for the sixth man, who was myself. For this reason I had to spend a good deal of my time sleeping in the woods rather than in the farmhouse. The farmer told me that German m[otor]c[ycle] police with binoculars constantly patrolled the district during daylight.

On 1 June 1943 my subsequent journey from here was arranged for me.[55]

Forland left Gibraltar on 12 July and was back in England on the 14th, just over two months after bailing out.

Although he has left us no account of how he managed to move through occupied Belgium and France into Spain and thence to Gibraltar, he was not the first to follow this route, nor the last. Set up by a twenty-five-year-old artist, Andrée de Jongh, and her father Frédéric, an escape line under the aegis of British military intelligence (MI9) code-named Comet had existed in Belgium since 1941; Andrée and her father had personally escorted well over a hundred evaders from Belgium through Paris over the western Pyrenees to Spain. It is quite likely that Flight Sergeant Forland was aided by this group. If so, he was lucky on a number of accounts even if he had adhered to the advice MI9 gave to all aircrew: get clear of the landing area, avoid towns, and seek help at isolated farm houses and churches. The fact that he had to lie up the first night may have saved him from the initial German hue and cry. Beyond that, the Germans had begun to penetrate Comet in late 1942, arresting Andrée de Jongh and her sister early in 1943; probably just before Forland passed through Paris, Frédéric was betrayed and caught while in the company of five British airmen and an American. He was taken away and shot; the others were sent to prison camps. However, the de Jonghs had chosen their helpers carefully, and Comet lasted until 1944.[56]

Flak was an ever-present risk about which even veteran airmen could do very little. In most circumstances, a turn to the left or the right, a climb, or a dive could just as easily carry a bomber into the next burst as maintaining a straight course. Encounters with night-fighters were different. Even when using AI radar, the enemy could be eluded if seen in time and if the bomber took appropriate evasive action. Alertness was the key, yet it seems that it could not always be taken for granted over six or seven hours in the air. Pilots have recalled how they annoyed their gunners (but perhaps kept them alive) by frequently asking for situation reports. Help was forthcoming with the introduction of Monica in the spring of 1943. A tail-mounted radar which detected aircraft approaching from the rear and automatically emitted warning bleeps into the intercom, it took some pressure off the gunners. But because Monica did not differentiate between enemy fighters and other bombers in the stream, crews could not be absolutely sure of what was following them and some, at least, became twitchier than ever when, especially in highly concentrated attacks, their earphones chirped away continuously. A more discriminating device was clearly wanted, and, in part because of a brave and successful mission flown by five Canadians and an English wireless operator from the RAF's No 1474 Flight based at Gransden Lodge,[*] such equipment also became available in the spring of 1943.

Air Intelligence had long suspected that the enemy was using AI radar. Indeed, they even surmised that its frequency range was about the same as that of Würzburg – one reason why it was so hard to find – but until they had

[*] This seems an appropriate moment to recall once again that a majority of RCAF aircrew served in British or other Commonwealth squadrons during the course of the war. This history, which is concerned with the RCAF as an operational organization, regrettably does not normally recount their experiences.

obtained hard evidence of its existence and its performance characteristics there was little point in trying to develop appropriate counter-measures. The issue became more pressing in the autumn of 1942, when losses to fighters mounted as the Luftwaffe responded well to the bomber stream tactics introduced following the late May raid on Cologne. It took only a little persuasion to convince High Wycombe that it was worth the risk to send out reconnaissance aircraft as bait and to try to find the German AI through electronic eavesdropping.

At first this was done entirely independently of regular bombing operations, as specially trained and equipped crews flew off on their own over the Kammhuber line. Precisely for that reason, the effort failed. The Germans guessed what these probes were about and refused to be drawn. On the night of 3/4 December 1942, therefore, a different approach was taken. Pilot Officer T. Paulton's Wellington would accompany the bomber stream almost as far as Frankfurt, the main force's target for the night, and then veer north in an attempt to persuade the enemy that it was nothing more than a hapless straggler, ripe for the picking. The ploy worked perfectly. Shortly after the turn the bomber was picked up by a Lichtenstein-equipped Ju 88 whose AI radar was readily identified, and Flight Sergeant William Bigoray, the wireless operator, was able to send out two messages giving full details of the transmissions his crewmates were reading. However, they paid the price. The fighter closed in for the attack and, despite Paulton's best attempts to throw it off with violent evasive manoeuvres, his machine was hit several times before the enemy apparently ran out of ammunition. Four of the crew were wounded, two of them seriously; both turrets were put out of action; the engines raced dangerously at full boost, the throttles having jammed or been shot away; the starboard aileron was blown off; the hydraulics were wrecked; and the navigator could scarcely read his blood-spattered maps. Struggling with the controls, Paulton was nevertheless able to reach England where, having dropped Bigoray by parachute (the wireless operator's shattered legs could not cope with scrambling out of a downed machine), he successfuly ditched in the Channel off Deal on the Kentish coast. Bigoray landed safely and, together with the rest of the crew, who were quickly rescued, was able to confirm the data that he had transmitted while still airborne, north of Frankfurt.[57]*

Lichtenstein's wavelength had been found – it *was* in the same frequency range as Würzburg's – and on the basis of that information it was a relatively easy matter to produce Boozer, a passive receiver/detector tuned to the same frequency. Superior to Monica because it could not give off false alarms – with Boozer there was no doubting whether the targeted radars were being used – the device nevertheless had significant limitations. Responding as it did to both Würzburg and Lichtenstein, Boozer was no better than Monica in providing crews with specific and direct warning of an impending attack on their aircraft;

---

* Pilot Officer Harold Jordan, RAF, who had initially discovered the Lichtenstein transmission and who was blinded during the engagement with the Ju 88, received the DSO; Paulton and Pilot Officer William Barry, the navigator, received the DFC; and Bigoray and Sergeant Everett Vachon, the rear gunner, were awarded DFMs.

and wherever the Flak was radar-directed, Boozer was just as likely as Monica to give off a continuous – and consequently useless – alarm. And, of course, it produced no warning whatsoever of the approach of fighters that were not using their radar, or had none to begin with.[58]

The twin-engined fighters that were the mainstay of Himmelbett made extensive use of radar. On 3/4 July, however, something new was introduced, as single-engined fighters without any radar were encountered in strength within the Kammhuber line.[*] 'Warned by MONICA that an aircraft was closing in,' Warrant Officer G.F. Aitken, rear gunner in a 419 Squadron Halifax, directed his pilot 'to dive, climb and bank to port and starboard so I would have a fighter search.'

I could see nothing. The pips from MONICA became more rapid so I told the pilot to do some violent evasive action. At the same instant a Me 109 came in from port quarter from underneath and fired a medium burst. [I] told the pilot to dive and corkscrew. The front of the aircraft was hit. The fighter broke away to starboard, [and] when he got above [the] horizon I got a glimpse and fired [a] short burst. The pips became rapid again and I told pilot to dive port. The fighter broke away to starboard and climb[ed], when he got above [the] horizon I pressed the tit but all guns refused to fire. I immediately cocked two guns, when the pips became more rapid once more. I told pilot to dive port once more, and the fighter fired medium burst which missed our aircraft. Fighter broke away to starboard and climbed. I got [a] bead on the E[nemy]/F[ighter] but guns would not fire. I told pilot to climb starboard and cocked the other two guns and at same time [a second] E/F came in from below and astern and fired long burst which hit starboard outer [fuel] tank which immediately broke into flame. The guns refused to work on this attack also. All incidents happened approx. [twenty miles] north of Brussels. Guns were tested over sea and worked perfectly.

The pilot ordered his veteran crew to bail out, but he and two others did not get clear. The five who did were captured, and 419 lost eight men whose average experience was over twenty missions.[59]

No 419 had been something of a hard-luck squadron over the past few weeks, losing twelve crews – a little over half its establishment – in just over a month and twenty-two (on attacks on German targets) in four. No 408 lost even more, twenty-eight, over the same period, while Nos 428 and 429 had just under twenty crews each fail to return. The other RCAF squadrons, all of which had either been taken off operations while they converted to new types or had entered the battle late, lost fewer than fourteen.[60] No commanding officers were replaced as a result of these casualties, however, because, quite sensibly, losses were just one of a number of factors including discipline, morale, serviceability, and accident rates, as well as the number of early returns, that were considered when decisions of that sort had to be taken.

---

[*] These single-engined fighters were part of the Wilde Sau experiments being conducted by Major Hajo Herrmann, and Herrmann himself recorded his first victory this night.

However, No 6 Group's loss rate as a whole over Germany since early March – 8.8 per cent – was cause for concern and, as we shall see, it kept operational research scientists at High Wycombe and Allerton Hall busy for a number of months. Focussing completely on Canadian participation in the battle of the Ruhr not only distorts what RCAF squadrons were doing, however, but exaggerates the risks they ran. Of the 911 aerial mining sorties flown by No 6 Group in 1943, 258 came during this period.[61]

By the end of 1942 it was estimated that Gardening had sunk or damaged 340 ships (in fact, the number was 383). Furthermore, minelaying had forced the enemy to divert considerable resources – perhaps as many as 500 ships and 20,000 sailors and technicians – to finding counter-measures, had delayed the sailing of coastal convoys, and had caused them to be routed away from recently mined areas.[62] It had slowed delivery of raw materials to industry in the Ruhr and had interfered with the supply of men and materiel to the Eastern front. At the same time, aerial mining remained a favourite method of easing new crews, squadrons, and even No 6 Group itself into operations. Beyond that, Gardening was a useful foil that allowed Harris and Portal, when asked by the Admiralty to do more for the navy, to reply that Bomber Command was already doing enough. In 1943, therefore, Bomber Command undertook to lay at least 1000 'vegetables' a month.[63]

Although far removed from the heart of Germany's air defences, minelaying was not always easy or entirely free of risk. The most important 'gardens' were located in the main shipping channels where the water was neither too shallow (under thirty feet) nor too deep (over one hundred feet) for the effective employment of mines. But unless the minefield was within Gee range, it was not possible to pinpoint the target area without working from a reference point on land, preferably no more than twenty miles away. When crews could not find their reference point, from which they made a timed run to the 'garden,' they were instructed to bring their mines back or (if that was was not possible) to drop them 'safe' in deep water at least seventy miles from Britain.[64] Since Gardening sorties were often scheduled when the meteorologists' forecasts for inland objectives were unpromising, and weather systems often extended from central Germany to the far north, groundcrews sometimes had considerable unloading to do. On 27/28 April, for example, twelve of thirty No 6 Group sorties returned early, having failed to find their pinpoint; and on 21/22 May, five of seven from No 429 Squadron came back fully loaded.[65]

Until March 1943, mines had to be laid from 4000 feet or below for the sake of accuracy and because of the weapon's arming mechanism. Considering the weight of small-calibre Flak the enemy had positioned in the north, particularly to defend Kiel, Lübeck, Rostock, and Stettin, the narrow channels around the Baltic islands, and the mouth of the Elbe, flying at such altitudes was dangerous. On 15 March, modifications having been made to the inner workings of most mines, the maximum altitude for Gardening was raised to 6000 feet – with the proviso that this should not serve as an excuse for inaccuracy. Whatever additional protection that provided was short-lived, however, as a new type of mine incorporating acoustic and magnetic triggering and firing mechanisms to make minesweeing more difficult was introduced in April, and it had to be planted from between 1000 and 3000 feet.

Coincidentally, at about this time it was realized that flying so low involved risks besides Flak. Accurate altimeter readings depended upon the correct atmospheric pressure being set in the device, but as crews passed through frontal zones, particularly near and over the ocean, atmospheric pressure was found to change enough to throw the altimeter off by as much as four hundred feet. Some crews had crashed because of that. Others, having had close calls and subsequently overcompensating for them, flew higher than they should. Beginning in May, then, everyone was issued with new pyrotechnics – 'Calibrators, Altimeter Flash'- which they were to release whenever they had any doubts about the veracity of their altimeter reading, enabling them to make corrections if there was a discrepancy.[66]

No 6 Group mounted 111 Gardening sorties on six nights in March 1943, and 103 on six nights the next month. Most of these were aimed at U-boats operating from the Biscay and Brittany ports, and they culminated in a large operation (Pruning, 160 sorties) on the 27th/28th. The next night the focus shifted to the Heligoland Bight and the Baltic. In Operation Weeding, Bomber Command flew 226 Gardening sorties, of which thirty-seven were by No 6 Group crews. Meant to complement the sustained offensive on the Ruhr as well as the recent heavy bombing raid on Stettin, Pruning and Weeding were tremendously successful, accounting for twenty-four ships sunk and damaged. There were also reports that all ships on the Elbe–Hook of Holland route subsequently sailed with a 'numbered wreck-buoy attached,' to facilitate quick salvage. Although Pruning occurred almost without incident, Weeding took crews close to intense Flak over Heligoland and around the mouth of the Elbe, claiming most, if not all, of the twenty-two aircraft (10 per cent) lost. In No 6 Group three failed to return (8 per cent), two of them from No 428 Squadron.[67]

Bomber Command (and No 6 Group) could not afford many nights like 28/29 April. Even special Gardening operations like Weeding were meant to ease freshman crews and new squadrons into operations – and to provide useful, but relatively safe, employment for older aircraft unfit to be risked on deep penetrations. They were not supposed to cost over 10 per cent of sorties dispatched. With the coming of summer and its shorter nights (when the risk of interception was greater), and given all the indications that the German defences in the Baltic had been strengthened, the intensity of minelaying fell off; much of it was now restricted to operations against less heavily protected French Biscay and Britanny ports. As a result, only three crews from No 6 Group went missing between May and July, 2 per cent of sorties, bringing the overall Gardening loss rate since February to 3.8 per cent.[68]

The relative success of recent minelaying operatins was about the only good news to arrive at Allerton Hall, for No 6 Group's performance in almost every category was among the worst in Bomber Command. Serviceability hovered

TABLE 4

Bomber Command Loss Rates on Night Operations, by Group, February–July 1943

| Group | Percentage of sorties dispatched | | | | | |
	No 1	No 3	No 4	No 5	No 6	No 8
February	1.4	3.3	1.3	2.7	1.8	1.4
March	2.1	3.2	2.9	2.2	2.8	3.7
April	4.4	5.1	5.4	3.2	5.1	5.2
May	3.4	5.3	5.7	3.8	6.8	3.5
June	4.8	4.9	4.4	3.8	7.1	5.1
July	2.5	3.8	3.4	2.7	4.3	2.7

around 60 per cent; the number of crews lacking in moral fibre and declared to be 'waverers,' although only .45 per cent in June, was the second highest in the command; and the number of Gee sets unserviceable at any given time was about 15 per cent, 6 per cent higher than the next worst group, No 4. Similarly, while the number of crews reporting they had attacked the primary objective on Gardening and bombing operations rose slowly but steadily from April's 83 per cent to 89 per cent in July, all other main-force groups did better.[69] The clearest and most disturbing data, however, related to casualty rates (see table 4).

All this evidence suggested very strongly that something was wrong in the Canadian group. Growing pains had been anticipated, of course, and by no one more than the AOC-in-C himself, who already had his doubts about the competence of senior dominion airmen: 'A serious aspect of the matter is the very poor type of Commanding Officer which the Dominions seem to produce. Mostly hangovers from a prehistoric past. At the best they are completely inexperienced, and at the worst they are awful. I heard a comment the other day that the Canadian fighting crews were venting strong objection to being commanded by officers whose experience was limited to "six months flying training and 28 years political intrigue."'[71] Harris was undoubtedly indulging in exaggeration to make his point, but his concern was not entirely unfounded. With such small pools of prewar regular officers to pick from, dominion air forces, including the RCAF, were hard-pressed to provide individuals whose service backgrounds approached those of their British counterparts. Brookes, unwittingly, may have reinforced his AOC-in-C's suspicions. As late as April 1943, a month after the battle of the Ruhr began, the Canadian AOC observed that while the other group commanders arrived for a conference at High Wycombe 'armed with heaps of charts and graphs,' he took nothing, 'and in listening ... picked up plenty of information.'[72] While Brookes's willingness to learn was admirable, the impression it left with Harris may have been counter-productive.

There are also indications that early in the life of No 6 Group Brookes and his staff, like ambitious schoolboys eager to impress, tried to compensate for their lack of professional standing by doing more than they were asked to do. In January and February 1943, for example, the Canadian AOC boasted to his diary that he had committed more, and sometimes many more, crews to individual operations than High Wycombe had asked for. The same desire to please and impress – and to get results when others could not or chose not to – may explain why, during the same period, operations were cancelled (because of weather) much later in the day by Brookes's headquarters than they were by other groups farther to the south, where flying was almost always less risky in good or bad conditions. The medical officer from No 420 Squadron was certainly aware of this tendency and complained that, by holding squadrons at readiness until the last moment, hoping they might fly despite already bad or deteriorating weather, the AOC was placing the glory of his group first rather than concerning himself with flying safety or the additional strain he was causing his crews on an almost daily basis.[73] It was also possible that No 6 Group headquarters lacked the confidence to decide when the weather was too bad to permit operations.

Whatever the reason, both practices had ceased by April, so they cannot be held accountable for the heavy losses sustained during the later stages of the battle of the Ruhr. By then, however, other problems had come to light. For one thing, the impression that Canadian squadrons would invariably receive 'obsolescent equipment' was so well entrenched that it was seen not only to have an 'adverse effect on ... morale,' but also 'to produce a lack of desire on the part of RCAF personnel to serve in Canadian units.' (There was little truth to this perception, but like many such intuitive beliefs it was difficult, if not impossible, to counter.) At the same time, the group's flying accident rate remained high, even after squadrons had a chance to settle into their new stations where – the point is worth making one more time – 'with the hills at 1,200 to 1,500 feet five miles on our east side, and others at 1,800 to 2,400 feet on the west side only twelve miles distant, descending simply on [radio] contact was a chancy business.'[74]

However, Brookes and his senior staff officer, Air Commodore C.R. Slemon, were persuaded that the root cause of accidents was bad flying discipline. That also seemed to explain No 6 Group's higher losses: ignoring the routes laid down by command, too many pilots were straying from the protective cover afforded by the bomber stream. At the same time, however, one of the OTUs backing the Canadian group was complaining that navigators recently graduated from the BCATP and arriving from Canada were not only slow in chart work, astro-navigation, and map-reading, but that the pilots they teamed up with had little sympathy for navigational burdens - an endemic problem, it seems, since the same criticism had been voiced for some time. Harris's suggestion that, in addition to all this, some Canadian crews had 'unjustifiably failed to press home their attack' was undoubtedly the most damning and worrying comment on No 6 Group's operations. Admitting that squadron and station commanders had doubts about the 'keenness' of some of their crews, the AOC replied they would be more vigilant in identifying those who were failing to pull their weight.[75] Greater attention would also be paid to the tactics of bombing and evading enemy defences, something Brookes agreed had been neglected.[76]

As they cast about to find the reasons for No 6 Group's comparatively lacklustre performance to the end of May, the AOC and his staff quickly recognized the significance and the implications of the absolute (and relative) inexperience of their airmen. If, as was generally acknowledged, crews did not reach their peak efficiency until half-way through their first tour, then the Canadian group had 'a great weakness of operational experience' which was bound to affect performance. More than half had flown fewer than ten operational sorties, Brookes told High Wycombe's air officer for training on 3 June, and three-quarters had yet to reach their fifteenth, in large measure because of the requirement to post experienced RCAF flying personnel to No 331 Wing.[77] Since losses were heaviest among the least experienced crews, he scarcely needed to add, the higher toll would probably continue.

Brookes's statistics could not be gainsaid, and the direct relationship between loss rates and inexperience was well known, but for some reason Harris was not satisfied with the AOC's responses and he asked his operational research section (ORS) to look closely at No 6 Group and to find explanations for everything that seemed unsatisfactory. Quite correctly, the ORS maintained that studies of this sort could not be undertaken in isolation: the Canadian group's northern location and the types of aircraft it flew were obvious variables likely to influence its performance. Accordingly, the ORS decided from the outset to compare No 6 Group's data with that of its closest neighbour, No 4 Group, which also happened to be flying Wellingtons and Halifaxes.

The ORS draft report submitted on 10 July 1943 raised the possibility that there were significant differences between the two groups over which their AOC's had some measure of control and influence. Not only had the Canadians' loss rate increased 'both absolutely and in comparison with that of No 4 Group,' but they were also being attacked more often by night-fighters. Although that could be attributed to the fact that No 6 Group entered the main bomber stream 'very close to the enemy coast' on missions to the Ruhr and so benefited less from its concentration – a situation attributable to the group's northerly location – the ORS speculated that the Canadians were employing 'inferior' tactics.

No 6 Group's early return rate was also cause for concern, particularly the large number caused by problems with oxygen supplies, guns and turrets, and icing. These, it seemed, could be the result of widespread deficiencies in maintenance and training stemming in part from the Canadians' failure to make good their early instruction at the hands of No 4 Group. Echoing Harris's remarks, the ORS suggested that early returns might also reflect 'lowered morale' in the group, but because of the incomplete nature of the evidence the scientists did not want to draw firm conclusions. On one issue, however, they agreed with Brookes. Although there was no obvious reason why Canadian Halifax losses were so high, the sudden jump in Wellington losses from 4.4 per cent in April to 7.1 per cent in May and 9 per cent in June had much to do with the combing out of experienced crews for No 331 Wing in North Africa.[78]

Raising almost as many questions as it answered, the uncompromising language in this speculative report was too tough for Air Vice-Marshal R.H.S.

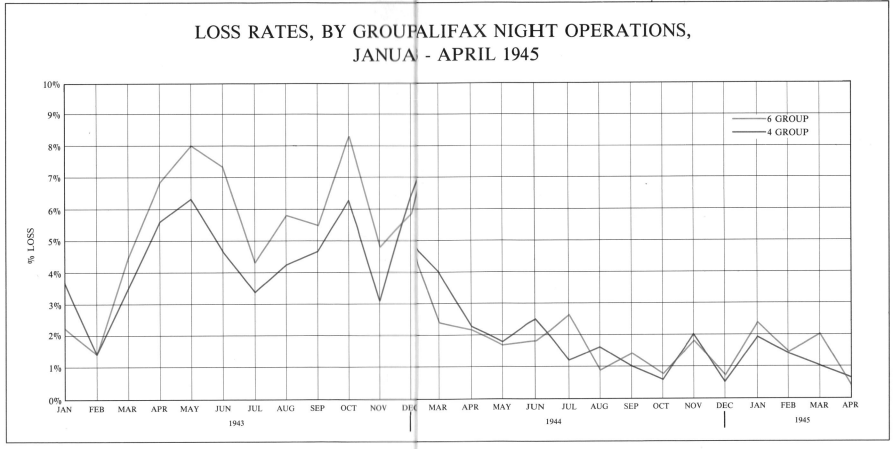

LOSS RATES, BY GROUP, HALIFAX NIGHT OPERATIONS, JANUARY - APRIL 1945

...Quarters, Operational
...e, Losses; heavy bomber
...Bomber Command: HQS.
... DHIST 79/220.

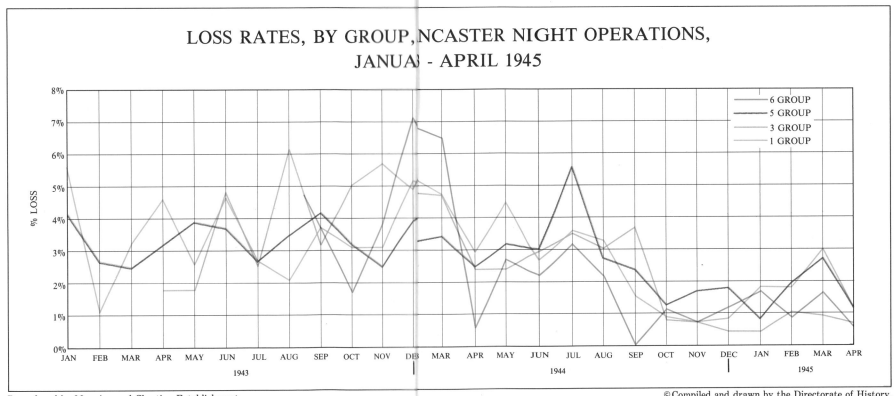

LOSS RATES, BY GROUP, LANCASTER NIGHT OPERATIONS, JANUARY - APRIL 1945

Reproduced by Mapping and Charting Establishment.

©Compiled and drawn by the Directorate of History.

Saundby, Harris's deputy, to send to Allerton Park, and Brookes received a carefully edited and revised version. Although its thrust remained essentially the same, the language of some of the more contentious points was softened considerably. The 'inferior tactical handling' of No 6 Group became 'a difference in their tactical doctrine'; the new draft referred to a 'lowering of the standard in training' rather than generally deficient training; and instead of suggesting that the Canadians had 'failed to make good' their instruction under No 4 Group, it spoke only of a 'lack of training.' Most significantly, however, the unambiguous statement that the transfer of crews to No 331 Wing had hurt the group was altered to allow only that it 'may have caused a drain of experienced crews.' In that respect, Saundby may well have wanted to undercut Brookes's argument that the withdrawal of squadrons to North Africa, the result of a British initiative, had been the primary reason for No 6 Group's problems.[79]

The ORS had not explained what differences there were in the tactical handling of Nos 4 and 6 Groups and, in fact, the researchers had acknowledged that there were similarities in the operational instructions the two headquarters passed on to their squadrons. Both told their crews to strive for height, a natural thing for them to do anyway in order to avoid Flak and hide from fighters among the Lancasters. But once No 4 Group determined that fully loaded Halifaxes had little tactical freedom because they were bound to an 'excessively' narrow height band, it quickly reduced their bombload by as much as a ton. Introduced at a time when No 6 Group losses were soaring, information about this change in procedure seems not to have been passed on to the Canadians by either No 4 Group or High Wycombe. Instead, echoing the old formula about bad flying discipline in the RCAF, the only specific advice given to Brookes was that there was too much 'straying from the main bomber route' in his group and that the 'greatest improvement may well be obtained by giving close attention to this point and thus improving the concentration.'[80]

Canadian authorities did not take the ORS study lightly when they first received it. Air Marshal Edwards, for example, thought that No 6 Group might have to be withdrawn from operations altogether until a logical solution could be found, while Brookes admitted that 'causes under our own control,' including 'weakness in navigation' and in the techniques of evading Flak and fighters, were responsible for at least some losses. After looking at the data more closely, however, the AOC became increasingly convinced that he had been right in the first place and that his group's lack of experience was primarily responsible for most of the problems identified by the ORS. Furthermore, when the waverer rate dropped to .13 per cent in August, the lowest of all the night-bomber groups, Edwards began to think the same, telling Brookes that 'we can pride ourselves on being in a rather happy courageous state.'[81]

Again at Harris's prompting, the ORS conducted a second study which by and large confirmed what Brookes was saying. A third study, completed in October, provided additional proof that Brookes's original assessment had been correct. The conversion of a number of squadrons to Halifaxes had been an unhelpful distraction at best, while 'a large part of the increase in Wellington

losses after the end of April was due to the influx of new crews ... consequent
on sending three squadrons overseas' and to the fact that 'pilots not considered
good enough to operate heavy aircraft may find their way to Wellington squadrons.' As for the Canadians' tactics, the ORS concluded that while 'frequent
straining after maximum height ... appeared to be of rather doubtful merit,'
Brookes's operational plans nevertheless 'appeared to be sound ... to differ
only slightly from those adopted by 4 Group ... [and] on the whole ... there
is no reason to suppose that the tactical planning of the Group is inferior to
that of other groups.'[82]

The formation's brief history might still be a handicap. 'Many of the Group
Air Staff and Specialist Officers are comparatively inexperienced at their
work,' the report concluded,

and although it is not suggested that this has led to bad results, the realisation of the
fact by themselves and in the squadrons may have retarded the development of a real
confidence in the Group tactics and general policy.

What this means in terms of measurable actions is hard to say but there appears
little doubt that a Group under a Commander and Air Staff who have already reputa-
tions for success and containing squadrons with a long period of steady development
must be more successful than a Group which has only had a short history and which
has been perpetually distracted by growing pains ...

Probably the best thing to be done for the Group is to let it alone giving the Commander an assurance that his past difficulties have been due to 'teething troubles' and
that he should now be able to settle down to develop a well-knit efficient Group.[83]

A parallel inquiry conducted by the operational research organization recently established at RCAF Overseas Headquarters agreed in general with these conclusions, but found additional reasons for No 6 Group's tribulations: the
frequent changes of station that accompanied conversion from medium to
heavy bombers; a 'sudden' influx of Canadian groundcrew 'relatively untrained
in handling certain parts of operational aircraft'; and the formation's northerly
location. All but the latter, it concluded, should be resolved with the passage
of time.[84]

That seemed to have happened as early as January 1944. No 6 Group's
Halifax loss rate was now lower than No 4 Group's, and its Lancaster II loss
rate was lower than No 3 Group's. Indeed, the Canadians compared unfavourably with other groups only when operating against targets in the Ruhr and
southern Germany, in which case the fact that their bases were 'at the extreme
north of all the bomber groups' was assumed to have had 'an adverse effect.'
It had taken a number of months, but now at least there were satisfactory
answers for what had happened during 1943's battle of the Ruhr.[85] Of them all,
inexperience had been the most important.

That was all very well, but another issue lay just below the surface of all
these discussions which, in the context of Canadian casualties, no one was eager to raise. Even if No 6 Group's data had been as good as No 4's, Halifax
crews still stood a significantly greater chance of being shot down than Lan-

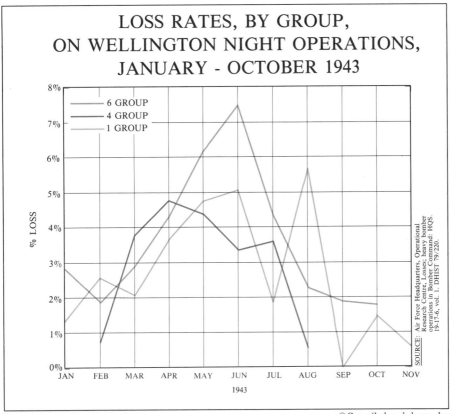

LOSS RATES, BY GROUP, ON WELLINGTON NIGHT OPERATIONS, JANUARY - OCTOBER 1943

SOURCE: Air Force Headquarters, Operational Research Centre, Losses; heavy bomber operations in Bomber Command: HQS. 19.17-6, vol. 1. DHIST 79/220.

Reproduced by Mapping and Charting Establishment.

© Compiled and drawn by the Directorate of History.

caster crews. That was not news to Harris. Aware of the disparities in missing rates between the two types since at least the summer of 1942, he warned the Air Ministry on 30 December of that year that Bomber Command would be 'sunk' unless the Halifax Mark II and V were modified in the immediate future and steps were taken to replace them with Lancasters and Halifax Mark IIIs, a type for which the AOC-in-C still held out some hope. He did not expect much from Sir Frederick Handley-Page, who, he complained, was 'always weeping crocodile tears in my house and office, smarming his unconvincing assurances all over me and leaving me with a mounting certainty that nothing … is being done to make his deplorable product worthy for war or fit to meet those jeopardies which confront our gallant crews. Nothing will be done until H-P and his gang are also kicked out, lock, stock, and barrel. Trivialities are all that they are attempting at present, with the deliberate intent of postponing the main issue until we are irretrievably committed.' Moreover, he did not think that anything could be achieved through 'polite negotiation with these crooks and incompetents. In Russia it would long ago have been arranged with a gun, and to that extent I am a fervid Communist! If I write strongly it is because I feel strongly, as I know you do, for the jeopardy ... my gallant crews [face] and the compromising of our only method of winning this war.'[86]

Three days later, though surely not as a result of this outburst, priority for the allocation of labour within the jurisdiction of the Ministry of Aircraft Production (MAP) was given over to the Lancaster. That pleased the AOC-in-C, but he returned to the attack in early summer, when Halifax losses were soaring, the Mark III program seemed irretrievably bogged down, and no headway was apparently being made on modifications to the flame dampeners and tail assemblies on the Mark II and V – which, in No 6 Group, were in service with Nos 408, 419, 427, 428, and 431 Squadrons. Indeed, the only real improvements to the latter variants, he complained, were those initiated by individual squadrons, and these consisted primarily of cleaning up the nose, usually by replacing the front turret with a Perspex blister. That reduced drag, giving the IIs and Vs slightly better speed and altitude, but it also reduced their defensive firepower.[87]

A few months before, when morale was allegedly 'cracking,' Harris had suggested doing away with the Halifax altogether, concentrating production on the Lancaster, or at least completely redesigning the Halifax wing to make that type more like the Lancaster. Although morale could easily have been worse in May 1943 given recent losses, there was by then no hope of shifting production in that way. For one thing, MAP was boasting that with an uninterrupted run of nine to twelve months the aircraft industry might well exceed its bomber production quota for 1944; after the many battles fought to increase the size of his command, it would have been difficult for Sir Arthur to demand time-consuming modifications that could only bring a decrease in output. For another, Harris had already decided that he would soon have to withdraw his Stirlings from all operations over Germany and that Wellingtons could not make the deep penetrations that would follow once he had finished with the Ruhr; if he also withheld the Halifax IIs and Vs from long-range missions, Bomber Command would be left with an all-purpose main force of about four hundred Lancasters and whatever Halifax IIIs had been produced – scarcely enough to sustain an intensive campaign.[88]

For the moment, then, Harris had to live with the Halifax in all its variants, but he ensured that their weaknesses were neither forgotten nor hidden – and by doing so probably reinforced the view prevalent in OTUs that they were 'a machine to be avoided.' Pilots were warned against taking 'violent' evasive manoeuvres, for example, because of the risk of spins and the possibility that their machines might break up altogether under the strain. At the same time, the AOC-in-C was determined to make the Halifax as air- and battle-worthy as possible, and to this end he was adamant that steps be taken immediately to improve its defensive armament and, in particular, the Fraser Nash FN 20 tail turret – a 4 × .303 mounting which, besides its unsatisfactory fire power, was 'useless' from the standpoint of the air gunner. Nothing could have been worse, he declared, except to have built 'the whole turret solid'; if attempts to give it a better downward view failed, the FN 20 was to be got rid of altogether. In the meantime, however, as a desperate measure to counter the increased number of attacks from below, Harris told his Halifax squadrons to cut holes in the floors of their aircraft, fitting Perspex navigation blisters made surplus by previous modifications, and to jury-rig downward vision ports (something with which Nos 4 and 6 Groups were already experimenting). That the lookouts using them would have to lie flat and, for the best view, stick their heads down into the blister was an unavoidable discomfort and inconvenience.[89]

Such makeshift measures were hardly satisfactory and, impatient with the lack of progress in producing new turrets, in June 1943 Harris demanded a meeting with representatives of the Air Ministry and MAP to reiterate his demands for heavier armament and better downward vision. The request was not universally welcomed in Whitehall, where Sir Arthur's persistent complaining about all manner of things was often a source of frustration and exasperation – especially when one of his recommended turret modifications would have required gunners to 'have their legs amputated' if they had any hope of fitting inside. The conference was called, however, and Harris succeeded in gaining some sympathy for the plight of his crews. He also won approval for his own pet project – a $2 \times .5$-inch rear turret designed by Rose Brothers, a Gainsborough firm he had approached informally and in private; but, with twelve months likely to elapse before mass production could begin, neither the Air Ministry nor MAP could offer much in the interim. The meetings broke up after agreeing only that vision ports cut in the floor were acceptable and, as another temporary measure, that the FN 20 turrets could also be removed and replaced by Perspex blisters fitted with two hand-held guns. Although firepower would be reduced, gunners would at least have a better view below, where, by now, the greatest danger clearly lay.[*90]

Beyond that, with the failure of Airborne Mandrel and Tinsel to interfere decisively with the enemy's early warning radars and radio communications, and given the imperfections in Boozer and Monica, additional measures were needed to overcome Himmelbett if casualties were to be kept at acceptable levels. This was particularly so if most raids were to be mounted on those clear nights when Pathfinder ground-marking techniques could be exploited to the fullest – but night-fighter crews could best see their prey. The alternative was to rely even more on navigation and bombing aids to attack on dark and cloudy nights, but Oboe and Gee each had their limitations, while H2S was simply not precise enough to serve as a reliable blind-bombing instrument.

Facing the facts, and arguing that target selection must reflect what was possible rather than conform to economic theory, Harris declared that while he was willing to concentrate on 'the most valuable target' on clear nights when ground-marking was practical, he did not want to attempt deep penetrations in summer, preferring to use the shorter nights to attack precise targets in France

---

[*] This was a permissive instruction, not an order; and, as with many other modifications to turret installations (a particularly enigmatic topic), it is difficult to know how widely it was applied.

or German objectives east of Emden-Dortmund-Munster. Larger areas would have to suffice when visibility was marginal or winds were high, but because of recent experience over the Ruhr he was convinced that Bomber Command could not return to the same area night after night without risking heavy losses. The focus of attack would be shifted frequently. He was also ready to undertake shuttle raids in which the main force flew past the target to bases in North Africa, Cyprus, or Malta, leaving behind those fighters ready to pounce on the bomber stream as it returned to England.* In the poorest weather, however, he promised the CAS no more than that he would make for the largest possible area where 'even a very scattered raid is likely to do worthwhile damage.' In that regard, instructions were soon issued to main-force crews to use H2S as a navigation aid only in the expectation that it would 'certainly enable one without fail to hit the town somewhere.'[91]

Even then, however, there was reason to doubt whether crews would routinely find the right city. Navigation was becoming more complex, in part because of the increased bad-weather flying and the higher altitudes manageable in the Halifax and Lancaster, which increasingly precluded map-reading, but also because all the new electronic equipment intended to help crews adhere to strict courses and timings had to be monitored. Beginning in June, therefore, Bomber Command asked that changes be made in the composition of main-force crews to ease this burden, either by substituting a second, fully trained navigator for the bomb-aimer or, failing that, by reallocating duties within the existing crew to create a 'navigation team' in which the navigator would be freed as much as possible from monitoring and manipulating equipment and left to do what he was trained for: using a variety of data and his own knowledge and experience to produce an accurate plot.

This was the solution eventually adopted, with bomb-aimers being trained to use H2S as a navigation aid and to do most of the astro-navigation, and wireless operators, already the electronic warfare specialists, doubling on Gee. Beyond that, to guard against the 'stupid mistakes' that were still occurring all too frequently, the final approach to the target would be a timed run on a set speed and course from an unambiguous reference point. It was further laid down that continuous evasive action, which offered no protection against unpredicted Flak and did not fool seasoned Lichtenstein operators, but did much to reduce navigation and bombing accuracy, was to be avoided. Instead, crews were to fly a steady and straight course to, over, and from the target – except when they were 'actually singled out for engagement.'[92]

For its part, the Luftwaffe was making its own adjustments in the summer of 1943. By early July, General Martini's radio-intelligence organization was so efficient that it could monitor upwards of 70 per cent of Bomber Command's

---

* This was tried for the first time in a major way on 20/21 June 1943, when No 5 Group flew on to North Africa after bombing the Würzburg factory at Friedrichshafen, and returned to England via Spezia, near Genoa on the Italian coast, three nights later – without suffering any losses on either raid.

day-time radio traffic, and from that was almost always able to deduce not only the nights for which operations were planned but also how many bombers were likely to take part. Although High Wycombe was aware of this, and issued instructions to limit transmissions during preraid test flights, the element of surprise could no longer be counted upon.[93] Furthermore, while Bomber Command was right in thinking that most of its losses resulted from radar-controlled and -assisted interceptions,[94] Major Herrmann's Wilde Sau experiments with single-engined machines had proved remarkably successful. On clear nights his pilots had had little difficulty in finding, following, and opening accurate fire on enemy machines, particularly those whose positions were given away by their tell-tale exhaust flames. Eager to do more, on 6 July he informed Generalfeldmarschall Erhard Milch, secretary of state for air, that he had assembled 120 pilots experienced in night flying, and asked that permanent Wilde Sau units be created to supplement the regular Himmelbett organization.

In the area of the *Flak* division in the Ruhr, where the illumination conditions are fairly good, you can expect, on the average, that 80 to 140 enemy targets will be captured by the searchlight beams in the course of an air raid, and in fact will be tracked for more than two minutes. The requirement I place on crews is that every target which is tracked longer than two minutes by the searchlights will be shot down. I believe I can say that if the British continue these attacks in this kind of weather, as they've done up to now, they can quite easily lose an additional 80 aircraft during the course of one night, if I get the necessary aircraft to do the job.[95]

Although Kammhuber remained opposed to freelance night-fighting, Herrmann's logic was unassailable. Using single-engined machines belonging to (and still being flown by) day-fighter units, the Wilde Sauen would strengthen the night defences without requiring any more aircraft. They would also be operating directly over the target cities, where there were no Himmelbett boxes, and whatever success they enjoyed was likely to boost the morale of the civilians below. Too good to pass up, Herrmann's request to form three Wilde Sau Geschwader was quickly approved.[96]

Elsewhere in Germany, the electronics industry was well advanced in the development and production of the next generation of AI radar, Lichtenstein SN2. Using a different frequency from the B/C then in service – it was actually hidden within the Freya band – SN2 was more difficult to jam and had a better search pattern over a much improved range. German scientists and technicians had also made significant strides in the design of two homing devices to be fitted to all twin-engined interceptors – Flensburg, useful against Monica from up to sixty miles, and Naxos, which detected H2S emissions from as far away as thirty miles.[97]

Meanwhile, Hauptmann Rudolf Schoenert had already claimed a number of victories using Schräge Musik, a pair of oblique (60°), upward-firing 20-millimetre cannon mounted in the fuselage of his Me 110, and following his success the installation of up to six such guns was authorized for the Dornier 217, the Junkers 88C-6, and the Messerschmitt 110 fighters. Capable of devastating destruction, Schräge Musik was fired from the blind spot of most British bombers, from below and just slightly behind, and so made Harris's concerns about downward vision all the more appropriate. It would also prove to be a great leveller in terms of Bomber Command casualties. Until now, experienced crews generally had a better chance of surviving an operation in part because they had learned how to evade night-fighters once they were discovered. With Schräge Musik, however, the attacker was rarely visible before he opened fire, and that advantage was lost. 'Absolutely nothing had been seen,' the second pilot of a No 426 Squadron Lancaster told intelligence officers after his release from prison camp in 1945, 'when we were hit from underneath.' Knowing nothing about the new weapon at the time of the attack – the RAF confirmed the existence of Schräge Musik only in 1944 – Flying Officer Joseph Heron could only guess that his machine had been destroyed by 'incendiary rockets fired from vertical guns of a fighter' – reasonable enough under the circumstances.[98]

The Luftwaffe high command was nevertheless uneasy by the late summer of 1943. Despite the northward extension of the Kammhuber line and the stationing of the night-fighter control ship *Togo* in the Baltic, bomber streams approaching from the north were sometimes lost after they passed Denmark. More radars and better trained observers might have alleviated this problem to some extent, but the pressure of the war on the Russian front meant that resources were still being siphoned away from the night air defence organization as experienced observers, electronics technicians, and even scientists in good physical condition were ordered into active military service – a blow for the present and the future. Most important, it would still be a few months before Naxos, Flensburg, Lichtenstein SN2, and new Panorama ground control radars would be available in quantity and, until then, the pillars of Himmelbett continued to be Würzburg and Lichtenstein B/C, which operated on virtually the same frequency and could therefore be put out of action by the same jamming device. If the British learned that soon enough – and their superiority in electronics and jamming was widely acknowledged – the whole edifice would crumble.[99]

19

Into the Electronic Age, Hamburg and After, July–October 1943

Sir Arthur Harris was ready for the next stage of the bombing offensive even before he had mounted his last raids against the Ruhr. Persuaded that considerable damage had been done to Germany's main industrial area and fearful of the rising loss rate there, he issued an order on 27 May 1943 for a concentrated campaign against Hamburg. If 10,000 tons of bombs could be dropped on the city, its total destruction might follow; and that, he believed, would serve as a fitting and appropriate prelude to a similarly sustained campaign against Berlin.[1]

Hamburg was considered an ideal target for Bomber Command even on short summer nights. Situated at the head of the Elbe estuary, the city was comparatively easy to find, its H2S signature was distinctive, and it could be approached with minimal exposure to the enemy's air defences. The elimination of its U-boat base and construction yards was also an important objective for the Royal Navy, and an intensive effort against it might placate at least some of the Admiralty critics who complained that Harris was not doing enough against the submarine threat. Moreover, as Europe's largest seaport, Germany's second largest city, and the site of more than one hundred power stations, oil refineries, and factories – including nine plants involved in the manufacture of aero engines and aircraft components – Hamburg met practically every criterion outlined in the Casablanca directive.[2]

Inspired in large measure by the American preference for attacking precise objectives, that directive had singled out four 'strategic' target systems for particular attention in a combined Anglo-US bomber offensive: submarines, oil, transportation, and the aircraft industry. Since then, USAAF planners had extended and refined their analysis of German industry and, in cooperation with the British Ministry of Economic Warfare (MEW) and the staff of the director of bomber operations at the Air Ministry, they had produced a list of seventy-six facilities whose destruction, it was claimed, would severely reduce the enemy's capacity to make war. Five of these were located in Hamburg.[3]

Submitted for the consideration of the Combined Chiefs of Staff at the Trident conference held in Washington in May 1943, the revised proposals approached the proposed Combined Bomber Offensive (CBO) from a decidedly

American perspective. Thinking it 'better to cause a high degree of destruction in a few really essential industries than ... a small degree of destruction in many industries,' Major General Ira C. Eaker, commander of the American heavy bomber force in Europe, urged that the combined effort be directed principally at 'all-out attacks' on targets which would affect 'a limited number of selected objective systems.' He anticipated that these attacks would involve 'precision bombing ... by day and night where tactical conditions permit, and area bombing by night against the cities associated with these targets' when conditions were less favorable.[4]

Having previously met and overridden similar arguments put forward by the Admiralty, MEW, and the RAF's own director of bomber operations, Harris was not overly impressed (or persuaded) by Eaker's intervention. But not wanting to impede the build-up of the United States Army Air Forces in England, Harris did not challenge the American commander directly, observing only that restricting the offensive to seventy-six individual facilities 'may prove somewhat inelastic.'[5] Sir Charles Portal shared the AOC-in-C's concern, but he too went along with Eaker's submission, commenting (in a subtle and inverse fashion) that it was the 'perfect complement of our own night bombing operations' – as if area bombing were the key element in the proposal.[6]

Once at the Trident conference, Portal did what he could to secure the greatest possible operational freedom for Bomber Command within the framework of the CBO. The doctrinal statement regarding the importance of causing 'a high degree of destruction in a few really essential industries' was not included in the Pointblank directive which grew out of the Washington meetings. Similarly, although the Combined Chiefs declared that Bomber Command should complement and complete American operations, they added that it would customarily bomb 'the surrounding industrial area,' not individual plants or factories. 'Fortunately,' they observed, 'the industrial areas which ... Bomber Command has selected for mass destruction' contained most of the seventy-six specific objectives included in Eaker's list. Because the Americans would bomb by daylight, when the enemy's defences were likely to be most effective, they insisted that the German fighter force had to be neutralized before they could take on most other targets. Since Portal agreed that defeating the Luftwaffe was an 'intermediate objective ... second to none in priority,' both to allow the Americans to proceed and to achieve air superiority before the cross-Channel invasion (now tentatively scheduled for 1 May 1944), he could hardly object to the employment of Harris's bombers in efforts to a-chieve it. Nor did he want to. Thus, while reaffirming that Harris's overriding aim would still be 'the general disorganisation of German industry,' Pointblank specifically instructed Bomber Command towards:

(i) the destruction of German air-frame, engine and component factories and the ball-bearing industry on which the strength of the German fighter force depend
(ii) the general disorganisation of those industrial areas associated with the above industries

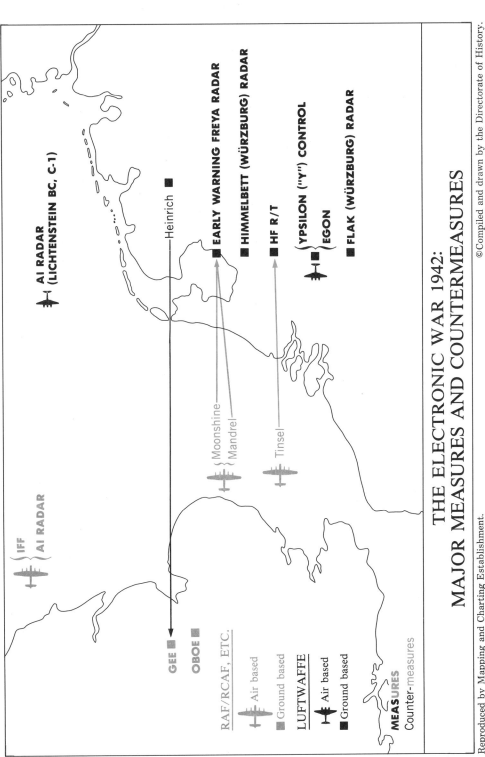

THE ELECTRONIC WAR 1942:
MAJOR MEASURES AND COUNTERMEASURES

IFF

AI RADAR

GEE

OBOE

RAF/RCAF, ETC.
Air based
Ground based

LUFTWAFFE
Air based
Ground based

MEASURES
Counter-measures

Moonshine
Mandrel

Tinsel

Heinrich

AI RADAR
(LICHTENSTEIN BC, C-1)

EARLY WARNING FREYA RADAR

HIMMELBETT (WÜRZBURG) RADAR

HF R/T

YPSILON ("Y") CONTROL

EGON

FLAK (WÜRZBURG) RADAR

©Compiled and drawn by the Directorate of History.

Reproduced by Mapping and Charting Establishment.

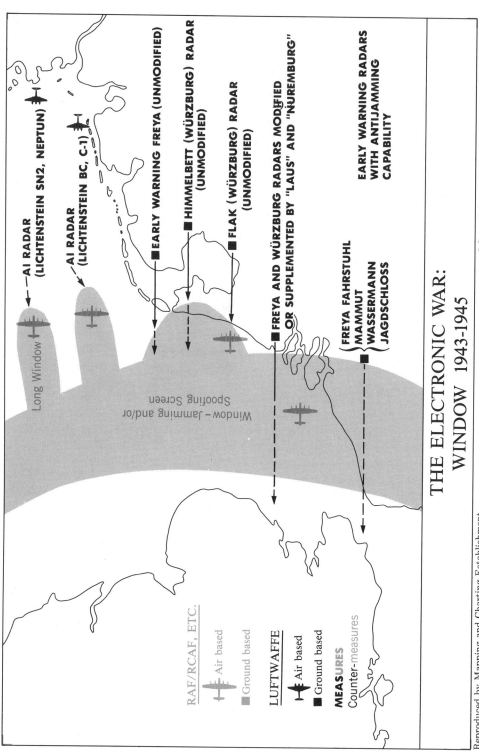

THE ELECTRONIC WAR:
WINDOW 1943-1945

AI RADAR
(LICHTENSTEIN SN2, NEPTUN)

AI RADAR
(LICHTENSTEIN BC, C-1)

EARLY WARNING FREYA (UNMODIFIED)

HIMMELBETT (WÜRZBURG) RADAR
(UNMODIFIED)

FLAK (WÜRZBURG) RADAR
(UNMODIFIED)

FREYA AND WÜRZBURG RADARS MODIFIED
OR SUPPLEMENTED BY "LAUS" AND "NUREMBURG"

EARLY WARNING RADARS
WITH ANTIJAMMING
CAPABILITY

FREYA FAHRSTUHL
MAMMUT
WASSERMANN
JAGDSCHLOSS

Long Window

Window–Jamming and/or
Spoofing Screen

RAF/RCAF, ETC.
Air based
Ground based

LUFTWAFFE
Air based
Ground based

MEASURES
Counter-measures

© Compiled and drawn by the Directorate of History.

Reproduced by Mapping and Charting Establishment.

(iii) the destruction of those aircraft repair depots and storage parks within range, and on which the enemy fighter force is largely dependent

(iv) the destruction of enemy fighters in the air and on the ground.[7]

Although Bomber Command was also feeling the Luftwaffe's sting, Harris had not been persuaded that the aircraft industry was anything other than a panacea target – a seductive one, to be sure, but one whose effective elimination would be difficult and probably very costly. Whether he would willingly restrict his effort to a few cities – many of which were hard to find at night, involved deep penetrations, and were well defended – and whether it was at all reasonable to expect that his crews could destroy small factories in them, remained open questions. Predating Pointblank by ten days, Harris's plan for the obliteration of Hamburg – Operation Gomorrah – revealed his conception of what the CBO was all about.

Although the city was included in both the Casablanca and the Eaker lists, and the Americans, whom Harris had invited to participate, would attempt selective, pinpoint precision bombing of specific manufacturing and military facilities, the battle of Hamburg would be a terror campaign, pure and simple, for High Wycombe. Despite the neat concentration of industrial targets on the Elbe's southern shore, the aiming points and areas of anticipated 'creep-back' were located mainly in the residential districts north of the river. Furthermore, great emphasis would be placed on fire-raising, an indiscriminate form of attack, not because Hamburg was particularly inflammable – a large fire in 1842 had destroyed many of its readily combustible medieval buildings, while the canals and waterways which threaded their way through the city would act as fire-breaks – but rather because incendiary bombs tended to cause 'more serious and lasting ... damage ... [than that] inflicted by similar weights of high explosive bombs' if houses, not factories, were the target. Indeed, the main contribution of high-explosives in the early stages of the attack would be to force firefighters to take cover and to open up buildings so that the flames would spread. Under the circumstances, Gomorrah was an appropriate codename.[8]

The battle of Hamburg would also feature an important and powerful innovation – and a delay in its introduction was one reason for the two-month interval between 27 May, when Harris issued his operation order, and 24/25 July 1943, the first night of the campaign. For well over a year Bomber Command had known that strips of metallized paper or aluminum foil cut to half the wavelength used by Würzburg and dropped in clusters from approaching bombers could jam the enemy's radars by multiplying the echoes registering on their cathode-ray screens. A force of two hundred bombers might thus look like two thousand to confused operators unable to distinguish between the real and the false, while the residual effect of hundreds of thousands of strips drifting slowly to the ground would create interference on radar screens through which almost nothing could be seen.[9]

The havoc that should be created in an air-defence organization predicated on rigid ground control was obvious: but it was for this very reason that the use of Window (as this counter-measure was called by the British) or Chaff (as the Americans would know it) was prohibited throughout 1942 and early 1943 despite forecasts that it could reduce losses by a third. For if the Luftwaffe learned to turn Window against Britain following its introduction over Germany – an argument which assumed that the enemy had not already thought of it themselves – then the RAF would be responsible for placing the air defence of Great Britain at risk. British radars were every bit as susceptible to jamming as German ones, even if Fighter Command's system of ground control was less rigid than Kammhuber's. The equation would change only when there was unmistakable evidence that the Germans had developed the technique on their own, or when a way had been found to shield British radar against it.

No less competent than their British counterparts, German physicists knew all about the jamming and deception properties of Window (which they called Düppel), and indications they were experimenting with it had begun to accumulate in November 1942.[*] Because of that, it was decided that British night-fighters would receive American SCR 700 radar (known in the RAF as Mark X AI) to replace their Mark IX sets. The Mark X was better able to discriminate between Düppel and bombers, but as it would not be available until the late summer of 1943 the use of Window by Bomber Command was postponed until then. In the interim, however, on 9 May a German night-fighter crew defected to Britain in a Lichtenstein B/C-equipped Ju 88 which confirmed beyond all doubt what had been learned the previous December: Window would also affect the only known German AI radar. Opposition to its use weakened, but not wanting to give anything away before Operation Husky, scheduled for 10 July 1943, the Air Ministry now decided to wait until air superiority over Sicily had been firmly established and the beachheads there were secure. Released for operational employment two weeks after the landings, Window was introduced over Hamburg on the night of 24/25 July 1943 – dropped down the flare chute by either the bomb-aimer or the flight engineer in two-pound bundles of 2000 strips at a rate of one bundle per minute.[10]

The results satisfied all expectations. The early warning Freyas, Wassermans, and Mammuts, operating on wavelengths that were only mildly affected by the type of Window employed, detected the bomber stream over the North Sea an hour before the first bombs began to fall. The Würzburgs were then tuned and set for the anticipated approach, the ground control organization came to life, and fighters were dispatched to their Himmelbett boxes. The Pathfinder element was correctly identified, the first plots projected onto control-room screens, but suddenly everything stopped. 'For minutes the illuminations on the screen representing the enemy had stuck in

---

[*] In an instructive example of mirror-imaging, Reichsmarschall Hermann Göring had prohibited its use by the Luftwaffe for exactly the same reasons it was denied to Bomber Command.

the same positions. The signals officer switched into the direct lines to the radar stations and asked what was the matter. He received the same answer from all of them: 'Apparatus put out of action by jamming' ... The screens of the Würzburgs ... became an indecipherable jumble of echo points resembling giant insects, from which nothing could be recognised at all.'[11] Listening intently to the German radio nets, British intelligence intercepted a number of transmissions from ground controllers to fighter crews describing their utter inability to assist them. The night-fighters would have to fend for themselves.[12]

It was no better in the air. One veteran pilot recalled that 'all that could be done now was to go fishing in the murk,'[13] while another remembered that 'my radar operator suddenly had more targets than could have been possible. I know that I got some directions from him to head on but these were impossible to maintain because we couldn't possibly have overtaken the bombers so fast if they had been real targets. I was picking up targets that didn't exist everywhere. We kept jumping up behind a target but there was never the slip-stream of the bomber.'[14] Some Himmelbett controllers gave up in disgust and turned their crews into freelance night-fighters.

When we reached our box, we were immediately told by the fighter control officer that everything was jammed and that we were simply to fly in the direction of Hamburg. This was unusual; I had never heard this order before. I was surprised. We flew towards Hamburg and soon had many contacts on my radar screen. We thought that we were right in the centre of the bomber stream. The first impression was that the bombers were heading straight for us. Therefore, we turned, in order to get in behind one of these but, after the turn, they were still coming too fast. I said 'slow down, slower still, you're too fast.' The pilot said there must be something wrong because he had already let down the flaps and was flying as slowly as possible. We got contact after contact but not one of them was a firm one... This went on for a good hour. We landed at Stade ... My pilot went into the headquarters and had a conversation with *Major* Lent, whom he knew very well. He came back and said something like 'they seem to be all helpless and bewildered.'[15]

That portion of the Flak which depended upon Würzburgs for fire-control data was similarly affected, and many bomber crews remarked that the German gunners had obviously been 'groping blindly.'[16]

With so much of the Himmelbett organization unhinged, the German defensive effort was sporadic. Only twelve bombers failed to return, 1.5 per cent of those dispatched, and most of the victims, it was felt, were shot down because they had gone off track and so were outside the area protected by the mass of Window.[17] All seventy-two Canadian crews returned, three-quarters of them being plotted within five miles of the allotted course to the target.[18] Yet the bombing was not as concentrated as expected. Only half of the photographs taken were within three miles of the aiming point, and the creep-back extended six miles into the relatively open country north of the city. Although large fires were started (firefighting crews being called from as far away as Berlin) and the death toll of 1500 was comparatively high, the city had already begun to recover by mid-day on the 25th.[19]

The same could not be said of the Luftwaffe. Despite its theoretical familiarity with the technique, no work had been done to find a counter-measure to Düppel, and nothing very useful could be improvised over the course of a single day. The Germans were therefore no better prepared to meet the second Window raid, carried out against Essen the next night. Although losses rose to 3.7 per cent, that was largely because of the heavy, but necessarily random, Flak put up over the Ruhr. The results of the attack were probably worth those higher casualties, however, as this was possibly the most effective of all the operations carried out against Essen during the war, and certainly the most damaging to the Krupp works. No 6 Group did slightly better than average, with only two of sixty-six crews (3 per cent) failing to return.[20]

After a pause the next night, when not even Gardening missions were flown, Bomber Command returned to Hamburg on 27/28 July in a raid involving 787 crews, seventy-eight from No 6 Group, that would mark the zenith of its ten-day campaign against the city.[21] A combination of freakish weather and atmospheric conditions (abnormally high temperatures, low humidity, and unusually juxtaposed frontal systems) together with concentrated bombing produced a firestorm which covered as much as five square miles of the city centre. Large and ever-growing fires raised the temperature at the core to several hundred degrees, and this super-heated air rose so rapidly that it sucked in behind it great quantities of cooler, oxygen-rich air at velocities approaching hurricane strength (65 miles per hour). These winds encouraged fires on the periphery, spreading the conflagration further – all while the bombing continued.[22] Firefighting was impossible in such circumstances, and even those flying far above the city were soon aware that something extraordinary was happening. Canadian crews returning from the mission 'were all emphatic that Hamburg was blazing more furiously than on Saturday night ... The smoke from the fires was so thick that it penetrated into the cabins of the bombers, almost choking the crews ... Hamburg was blazing like a paper box.'[23]

More than 40,000 Germans died in this one attack, many in shelters which functioned like ovens and which, once they were cool enough to be opened, revealed next to nothing of their former occupants. 'From a soft stratum of ash,' the city's police president explained, 'the number of persons who lost their lives [in one large shelter] could only be estimated by doctors at 250 to 300.' Elsewhere, there were stories of bodies lying in the 'coagulated black mess of their own molten fat tissue.'[24]

Refugees had to make their way over the dead and dying. The sick and the infirm had to be left behind by rescuers as they themselves were in danger of burning ...

Many of these refugees even then lost their lives through the heat. They fell, suffocated, burnt or ran deeper into the fire ... Many wrapped themselves in wet blankets or soaked their clothes and thus reached safety. In a short time clothes and blankets became hot and dry. Any one going any distance through this hell found that his clothes were in flames or the blanket caught fire and was blown away in the storm ...

Numbers jumped into the canals and waterways and remained swimming or standing up to their necks in water for hours until the heat should die down. Even these suffered burns on their heads. They were obliged to wet their faces constantly or they perished in the heat. The firestorm swept over the water with its heat and its showers of sparks so that even thick wooden posts and bollards burned down to the level of the water ...

The streets were covered with hundreds of corpses. Mothers with their children, youths, old men, burnt, charred, untouched and clothed, naked with a waxen pallor like dummies in a shop window, they lay in every posture, quiet and peaceful or cramped, the death-struggle shown in the expression on their faces. The shelters showed the same picture, even more horrible in its effect, as it showed in many cases the final distracted struggle against a merciless fate. Although in some places shelterers sat quietly, peacefully and untouched as if sleeping in their chairs ... in other shelters the position of remains of bones and skulls showed how the occupants had fought to escape from their buried prison.[25]

Such were the scale of suffering and the length of the casualty lists on this single night that it was known immediately as *Die Katastrophie*, and the psychological impact on all of Germany was enormous.* Feldmarschall Wilhelm Keitel, Chef der Oberkommando der Wehrmacht, told his wife to 'leave Berlin as soon as possible' since Hamburg-like raids could be expected there once 'the nights are long enough. I am afraid of vast conflagrations consuming whole districts, streams of burning oil flowing into the basements and shelters, phosphorous, and the like.'[26]

The industrial damage, too, seemed spectacular. Production at several chemical works, engineering firms, and shipyards was halted altogether; 'the entire tram and Underground system was brought to a standstill'; all the large gas works were put out of action; electrical supplies were interrupted; and some 250,000 of the city's 450,000 flats and apartments had been 'completely destroyed.' Indeed, Albert Speer informed the Führer that raids of similar intensity on six other cities 'would bring Germany's armaments production to a total halt.' Josef Kammhuber was profoundly disturbed by the thought that his crews would have to stand by 'helplessly' and 'watch the great cities of their country go up in flames one after the other' if the results of this raid could be replicated elsewhere.[27]

---

* An official count of 41,800 killed was the final figure, 'but even this was obviously incorrect since in many of the cellars a pile of ashes or charred bones was the only evidence that people had been trapped. Again, after the war, when bulldozers levelled the sites before rebuilding began, they unearthed the legs and arms of people whose bodies had been buried under the piles of rubble and had not been found.' More than 10 per cent of the dead were children, and half were women. In addition to the dead, the police president of Hamburg estimated that 900,000 were homeless (out of a population of 1.7 million) and that many had left the city. German raids on Britain during the whole war killed about 50,000.

But they could not. As Harris later admitted, 'even with all the luck in the world, we could not have hoped to destroy in a brief space of time, six more great cities.' The product of rare and peculiar circumstances, firestorms could not be created at will, night after night; and, in fact, there may have been only two more before the end of the war in Europe, one at Kassel in October 1943, and the other at Dresden in February 1945. Moreover, the effect on Hamburg's war production was not as devastating as first imagined. Although a good part of the city had been burnt out, residential areas had suffered most, and commercial and industrial damage in the main affected businesses that were only marginally connected to the war effort. In fact, from one perspective the raid was actually beneficial to the German war economy. Workers displaced from non-essential tasks were soon doing more important things, a fact that helps to explain why Hamburg lost only about two months' worth of war production as a result of these raids and why, within five months, total output had recovered to about 80 per cent of pre-raid levels.[28]

After one more experience with Window, the Luftwaffe also began to recover. On the night of the firestorm, the British had listened with considerable interest to radio broadcasts by ground controllers which gave 'something of a running commentary' to fighter crews, directing them either into the vicinity of the bomber stream as it made its way to the target or, more frequently, to Hamburg itself. From them, it was correctly deduced that the enemy was turning away from Himmelbett and allowing even twin-engined fighters to engage in freelance operations. It was also apparent that especially skilled Würzburg operators could distinguish, at least to some extent, between genuine echoes and false Window ones.[29]

Meanwhile, Erhard Milch had decreed that in addition to releasing Me 110 and Ju 88 crews for point defence once Bomber Command had passed through their Himmelbett boxes, a crash program to develop radars able to resist jamming would be pursued. He also advocated a strengthening of the fighter arm, even if it meant curtailing bomber production. Göring would not go so far, but he did agree that the single-engined Wilde Sauen should be increased to three Geschwader and that intruder operations in the vicinity of Bomber Command's home bases should be resumed. Slowly, but inexorably, flexibility was being added to the German air-defence system. Although the enemy was still working out a response to Window, by 3 August – the last day of the battle of Hamburg – the missing rate on major raids against German targets since 24/25 July was just over 3 per cent, double that of the first Window operation. Yet Harris had been right in his overall assessment of its potential. While the enemy tactic of mass target interception had enjoyed 'a considerable degree of success,' Window had reduced casualties by a third or more and it seemed that it was particularly effective in protecting the most heavily concentrated waves of the main force.[30]

No 6 Group's loss rate (2.9 per cent) was actually lower than the Bomber Command average during the battle of Hamburg, but High Wycombe was still inclined to think that not everything was right with the Canadian formation. Although icing and storms had affected all the participants on 2/3 August, giving rise to an overall 42 per cent early return rate, the corresponding figure in No 6 Group, which benefited from the route selected that night and had a shorter distance to fly, was 59 per cent. Worse still, of the forty-three RCAF crews that returned early from Hamburg, only two had made any attempt to find and bomb an alternative target. 'It is possible,' an ORS investigator hypothesized, 'that too much emphasis had been placed on the danger of attempting to fly through the cloud bank.' Though unwilling to extend this tentative conclusion to comment generally about the tenacity of No 6 Group, the ORS nevertheless wondered whether RCAF crews were guilty of making 'a less determined attempt to get over enemy territory than some of the other Groups.'[31]

Having delivered almost 10,000 tons of bombs to Hamburg, and believing for the moment that it had, indeed, been knocked out, Harris suspended the campaign against the city following the raid of 2/3 August. He would have preferred to concentrate on other German targets, but for the rest of the month Bomber Command was ordered to conduct a number of operations against targets in Italy, in an effort to persuade the government of Maresciallo Pietro Badoglio (which had superseded that of Mussolini in July) to surrender to the Allies. No 6 Group participated in one of these raids, when it sent forty-seven crews to Milan on 11/12 August, losing one, on a wonderfully clear night over the Alps.[32] But Badoglio clung to the Axis connection until 3 September, the day of the Allied landings in southern Italy.

Along with extensive Gardening operations, which accounted for most Canadian sorties in early August, some attention was still paid to German cities. Mannheim was attacked through cloud on 9/10 August, and Nuremburg was bombed the next night, also through cloud. As might be expected, the effect was scattered on both occasions, but the combination of Window and weather had handcuffed the German defenders. Only twenty-five crews were missing, about 2 per cent of those dispatched, and once again No 6 Group was fortunate, losing just one of eighty. Then, on 17/18 August, again on Air Ministry orders, Bomber Command set out to destroy the German rocket development complex at Peenemünde, located on a small peninsula on the Baltic coast due north of Berlin.[33]

Operation Hydra was noteworthy for a number of reasons. Aimed at a specific facility, which had been identified only after painstaking intelligence work, it was an obvious anomaly in Harris's area offensive. Peenemünde's destruction also demanded precision bombing, and thus the attacking force was directed to operate between 6000 and 10,000 feet – unusually low altitudes for the main force of Bomber Command – and 'a new and much-improved marker bomb,' readily identifiable and difficult to simulate, was to be used.[34] Closely allied with it, and perhaps the most interesting innovation that night, was the employment of a senior Pathfinder officer, Group Captain J.H. Searby, RAF, as a 'master bomber' or on-scene commander, who would circle the target and, broadcasting over a reserved VHF frequency, 'provide the bomber force with minute to minute information regarding the progress of a raid ... issue warnings of misplaced markers, give the position of dummies and generally to assist the bomber force in successfully attacking the correct aiming point. It is further hoped that such commentaries will serve to strengthen the determination of less experienced crews, thereby reducing wastage of effort from this cause.'[35]

This technique had been pioneered in the breaching of the Möhne and Eder dams, and Searby had rehearsed his role over Turin on 7/8 August. At Peene- münde, one of his deputies was Wing Commander John Fauquier,[*] now com- manding No 405 Squadron, Canada's Pathfinder unit – which itself contributed twelve crews to the operation.[36] Both the master bombers and the Pathfinders anticipated that H2S would be of great value on the raid. 'We believed at the time that Peenemünde was the ideal target in terms of radar echoes,' Searby recalled; 'not only is the peninsula itself quite distinctive, providing good con- trast between land and water, but the small islet of Ruden [where the timed run was to begin] lay almost due north of the ... targets ... The radar experts assured us somewhat gleefully that this pimple set in the sea would stand out well on the screen.'[37]

Window would be used, of course, but two additional tactical wrinkles were included in the operational plan to assist the main force in deceiving, and thereby evading, the enemy. Having noted how the Germans were now sending the bulk of their fighters to the likely target, and suspecting that they would always react to a threat to Berlin, Harris dispatched eight Mosquitos to the German capital about an hour before the start of the Peenemünde attack. Meanwhile, the route chosen for the main force not only skirted known strong- points, but also reinforced the deception that Berlin was the objective for as long as possible.

Hydra began well enough in bright moonlight and patches of thin cloud, with the initial markers falling accurately on the main aiming point. But a number of Pathfinders went awry because, contrary to the confident predictions of the 'experts,' H2S was of less help than anticipated. 'The return echoes were weak and some crews failed altogether to pick up the datum on their sets.' The marking error was soon corrected by the master bomber, however, proving his value, and by the end of the raid he was convinced that it was one of the 'most accurate' ever achieved, an opinion that was shared by the entire Path- finder Force. Although more harm might have been inflicted, extensive damage had been done – enough to set back the V-2 rocket program by two months and to reduce its overall scale.[38]

---

[*] Fauquier, who was awarded two bars to the Distinguished Service Order along with the DFC in the course of his career, had commanded the squadron from February to August 1942, when he finished his initial operational tour and was posted first to RCAF Overseas Head- quarters and then to No 6 Group Headquarters. He returned to the squadron as commanding officer when it was transferred to No 8 (Pathfinder) Group, receiving his promotion to group captain in September, and remained with it until January 1944, when he completed a second tour. He was again posted to No 6 Group Headquarters, was subsequently promoted to air commodore, but voluntarily stepped down to group captain when he volunteered (and was selected) to command the RAF's No 617 Squadron - famous as the 'Dambusters' - in Decem- ber 1944.

The tactical and technical deceptions had also worked well. Although Kammhuber and Generaloberst Hubert Weise, at the Luftwaffe air-defence command centre in Berlin, had both received their customary early warning of an impending attack, neither was able to respond effectively. Window had worked so well that not one ground-controlled interception was recorded as the main force made its way over the North Sea, Denmark, and the Baltic coast. Then, transfixed by the threat to Berlin, both commanders sent all available fighters there in time to meet the Mosquito diversion, which was mistaken for No 8 Group Pathfinders, and to patrol the sky above the capital against the anticipated arrival of the main force. Indications that there was activity over Peenemünde were discounted until very late, so that when the fighters were finally sent north only thirty-five were available, the rest having landed to refuel.

Although short on numbers, those thirty-five fighters nevertheless took a terrible toll of the bombers still at Peenemünde and accounted for most of the forty crews lost that night – almost 7 per cent of the total dispatched. No 6 Group, assigned to the last wave of attackers, suffered the heaviest casualties, with twelve of sixty-two sorties failing to return, a missing rate of almost 20 per cent. (Nos 419, 428, and 434 Squadrons lost three machines each, No 426 Squadron two, and No 427 one). Among the missing were the commanding officer of No 426 and five other veteran crews. 'I had never seen such a night before,' recalled Pilot Officer R.W. Charman, navigator in a No 427 Squadron Halifax: 'All over the sky, RAF planes were going down.'[39]

The clearness of the night, which reduced the fighters' dependence on radar and so made Window less of a factor, was the major reason for the Luftwaffe's success. 'It was so easy,' Oberleutnant Friedrich-Karl Müller, an FW 190 Wilde Sau pilot, remembered.

I could see fifty bombers ... I chose a Lancaster. The tail gunner fired back, of course ... [but] it was a quick combat. He didn't take any evasive action. I tried to hit the tanks between the engines in the right wing, and I think I must have hit both engines on that side because I saw the propellers windmilling and he kept swinging to the right... he couldn't maintain altitude. I didn't see any parachutes and I watched him make a forced landing among the breakers a few yards off the shore. There was a great cloud of spray.

I flew back to the target area and found another Lancaster, easily visible against the smoke. I attacked again ... The right wing caught fire and, then, about a minute later, the wing fell off and he spiralled down ... I never saw a raid at such low level and in such clear visibility.[40]

Walter Barte, an Me 110 pilot who made his way to Peenemünde from St Trond, Belgium, 'did not need to do any radar work; it was so light that the operator was helping me with visual sightings.'[41] He shot down two machines, one a Halifax, before running low on fuel. Another crew from St Trond, new to the business of night-fighting, had a busier night still.

We picked up the first one by radar but the rest were all spotted visually ... We got [it] in the fuel tanks between the engines. One burst was enough ...

We saw the second one while the first was still going down, fifty metres below us and to the right ... We slowed down and one burst of fire caused the bomber to explode.

We climbed again and could see the target burning seven or eight kilometers away. We saw the third bomber below us. This one needed two or three bursts before it burned... Only a minute or two later, we made another attack; I believe this one went down but we didn't see it crash.[42]

Despite its successes in the latter stages of the Peenemünde raid (and earlier the same day against the Americans at Schweinfurt and Regensburg, where the USAAF lost sixty of 376 machines, 16 per cent of sorties dispatched), the Luftwaffe was nevertheless reeling from the pressure of the Allied attacks mounted in July and August. Not only had significant damage been done to important targets, but losses, most of them due to flying accidents, were also heavy, amounting to 145 night-fighters (about 30 per cent of Kammhuber's front-line strength) and over 500 day-fighters, all in less than sixty days. This 'disastrous rate of attrition' – it would reach 141 per cent in the last three months of 1943 – cut deeply into the pool of experienced fighter crews and forced less-well-trained pilots into operations earlier than was good for them.[43]

Depressed by Germany's manifest inability to thwart the ever-growing air offensive, knowing he had been partially to blame for the Luftwaffe's neglect of air defence, and hammered continually by Göring – 'A note lay by the dead man: "I can no longer work together with the *Reichsmarschall*"' – General-oberst Hans Jeschonnek, the forty-four-year-old chief of Hitler's air staff, shot himself the morning after Peenemünde. More productively, Göring called a conference of his remaining senior commanders to try to find a solution. Repeating the message he had delivered just two weeks before, State Secretary Milch declared it was now time for the Luftwaffe to go over to the defensive, to concentrate on building up the fighter arm, sacrificing quality for quantity, and to put all its effort into defeating the enemy's bomber offensive by day and night. 'If we fail,' he warned, 'and the percentage of enemy aircraft shot down remains at the same level as up to the first half of July, we shall be crushed.'[44]

This time everyone agreed and, emboldened by the unity of purpose he saw around him, Göring went immediately to Hitler, seeking his approval to change production schedules in favour of the manufacture of fighters. The Reichsmarschall returned a short time later, staring straight ahead, talking to no one. After a few minutes an aide explained what had happened. 'During the course of a heated discussion,' Adolf Galland was told, Hitler had rejected 'all our suggestions [and] Göring had completely broken down ... The *Führer* had ... announced that the *Luftwaffe* had disappointed him too often, and a changeover from offensive to defensive in the air [war] against the West was out of the question.' Germany would fight terror with terror, Hitler insisted, and launch another Blitz on England. Instead of the 1600 additional night-fighters that

Kammhuber had asked for in May, scheduled production would barely keep up with losses over the last half of 1943.[45]

Josef Kammhuber did not preside much longer over the night-fighter arm. Although he had shown some flexibility after the attacks on Hamburg, admitting that Wilde Sau, 'as it is now being carried out, is the only way we'll actually achieve success in [combatting] an attack on Berlin,' what most concerned his critics was his intense loyalty to the rigidities of Himmelbett and his incessant and hopelessly unrealistic demands for more and new equipment. Göring still regarded him as something of a megalomaniac, and could not forgive the way in which he had initially belittled Herrmann's Wilde Sauen, calling them a rabble 'shooting madly all over the place' and observing that 'the name "Wild Pig" was certainly aptly applied.' 'The entire night fighter system [has] degenerated into a state of stagnation,' the Reichsmarschall complained on 27 August, and it was only because of 'suggestions submitted by younger officers ... which had in fact all been rejected by their immediate superiors, that this state of stagnation has been overcome.' Three weeks later Kammhuber was removed from his command, and in December he was dispatched to Luftflotte 5 in Norway, where he remained until early 1945.[46]

Generalleutnant Josef Schmid, Kammhuber's successor at XII Fliegerkorps (soon to be reorganized as I Jagdkorps) was no admirer of Himmelbett. Its 'gigantic' infrastructure and 'oversized, overstaffed, overequipped' Jagddivision control rooms – 'battle opera houses' or 'Richard Wagner theatres' as they were widely and disparagingly known – were an 'excrescence' in Schmid's eyes precisely because they aimed at nothing more than leading a single night-fighter to engage a solitary bomber. But beyond freeing his crews from strict ground control and its susceptibility to jamming, Schmid was under no illusions about what he could do. Labour was in short supply, and adequately trained technicians to man, repair, and perhaps modify his radars were scarcer still; research and development of detection equipment capable of withstanding jamming seemed to be slowing rather than accelerating; and the mainstays of his Nachtjagdgeschwader were getting old. The Ju 88C-6, having 'lost much of its combat value on account of its weak engine,' was 'too slow,' while the Dornier Do 217 'scarcely ... rated' as a combat aircraft. To make matters worse, not only was fighter production falling, but with fierce battles raging on the Ostfront, the fall of Naples on 2 October, the growing threat of invasion in the West, and Allied success in protecting the North Atlantic convoys, night air defence was hardly the most pressing problem facing the Oberkommando der Wehrmacht as it sought to allocate resources.[47]

There was some reason for optimism, however. Large-scale production of SN2 radar which, besides having improved range and a wider search angle, was immune to Window, was just beginning. Although only five sets had been supplied to operational units by mid-September, it was expected to be ready for most of the night-fighter force by late autumn and, believing it would take the British some time to discover its existence and produce the appropriate antidote, the Germans hoped to get good use out of SN2 while they tried to develop other counter-counter-measures. They were also experimenting with

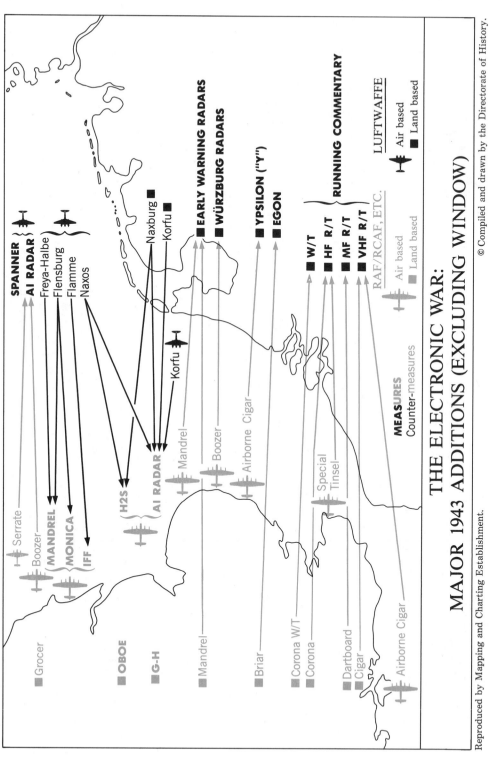

THE ELECTRONIC WAR:
MAJOR 1943 ADDITIONS (EXCLUDING WINDOW)

© Compiled and drawn by the Directorate of History.

Reproduced by Mapping and Charting Establishment.

Neptun, a small and compact radar which could be fitted to single-seat fighters; Naxos, a portable variant of Naxburg able to detect H2S emissions from a distance of about thirty miles; and Ypsilon (Benito to the Allies) and Egon, two forms of Morse radio transmission significantly more difficult to jam than radio telephony and which promised much more sophisticated command and control. With Ypsilon, for example, ground controllers could vector as many as two hundred fighters into the bomber stream at one time. Egon, in contrast, employed an airborne transmitter that enabled loose combinations of fighters to be brought into the bomber stream by a scouting crew that had already linked up with it.[48]

Once this equipment, and SN2 in particular, was available in quantity, Schmid intended to cease point-defence night-fighting, which was so vulnerable to deception, and to begin pursuit operations, the 'most elegant form' of air defence, on a grand scale. Fighters – preferably long-range He 219s* with their six 20-millimetre cannon and an IFF compatible with Würzburg – would be infiltrated into the bomber stream all along its path. For the moment, however, target-oriented night-fighting would continue to hold sway, by both the twin-engined Nachtjagdgeschwader and the single-engined Wilde Sauen, although Schmid did not expect much of the latter. Losses among Herrmann's original experienced and well-trained pilots had been heavy enough, but they were even higher among the less experienced replacements who, one cynic remarked, had more parachute jumps than victories to their credit as a result of losing their way and running out of fuel.[49]

Schmid's problems and concerns would have come as welcome news at High Wycombe, where initial enthusiasm over the success of Window was beginning to sour. Although the Berlin feint mounted on the night Peenemünde was attacked had demonstrated that enemy fighters could be drawn away from the main force, the damage done by the thirty-five fighters that eventually arrived at the real target illustrated that Window was still an imperfect solution to the *tactical* problem of evasion: once night-fighters saw their prey, they did not need radar – and no amount of deception or jamming would help. Furthermore, the Luftwaffe's success against the final wave over Peenemünde had rekindled long-standing fears about the potential threat posed by freelance fighters exploiting the concentration of bombers in the stream to make several interceptions in short order. Those fears were heightened by the recognition that Window could actually help the enemy once it had switched over to pursuit

---

* Fast, manoeuvrable, and heavily armed, the Heinkel 219 was the only piston-engined night-fighter capable of meeting the Mosquito on equal terms, but it was never made available in sufficient numbers to have a significant effect on the course of the air war over Germany. For one thing, an air raid on Rostock in March 1943 destroyed over three-quarters of the almost completed blueprints of the He 219 operational prototype, slowing its development considerably. For another, Erhard Milch was increasingly unhappy with Dr Ernst Heinkel's apparently dogged pursuit of profit and would not approve the retooling required to increase production of the 219.

operations. Confirming the general whereabouts of the main force, the Window cloud would – and did – act as a magnet for fighters ordered in from all over Germany.[50] Three raids mounted in quick succession against Berlin illustrated the extent to which the Luftwaffe, under favourable circumstances, was anything but impotent even in the early stages of its recovery from the chaos experienced over Hamburg. A total of 727 aircraft took off for the German capital on 23/24 August, and fifty-six were lost – 7.9 per cent, and the highest total suffered so far in a single operation. The low-flying Stirling squadrons were worst hit, losing 13.2 per cent, while Halifax losses were 8.5 per cent. No 6 Group sent sixty-eight crews and lost five (7.3 per cent), but eleven (16 per cent) returned early. Six of these were from No 434 Squadron, which had only recently become operational, yet had already lost four crews.[51]

Berlin's Flak defences had always been formidable enough, but post-raid analysis indicated that despite heavy Windowing, it was the two hundred fighters called to the scene that did the damage. Provided with a running commentary from the time that the main force passed over Amsterdam, they were ordered to the capital forty minutes before the Pathfinders arrived there. The German controllers had guessed right, and in clear but moonless conditions electronic counter-measures were scarcely a factor. Enemy pilots and observers singled out their victims visually by the light of ground fires, searchlights, and Pathfinder flares.[52] Hajo Herrmann, in his Me 109, found that flaming bombers 'were my pathfinders, so to speak.'

As I approached the bombers' route, I saw some of the 'torches' going down, bombers crashing ... On the frequency of my own unit, I heard Müller reporting that he had found a bomber about one hundred kilometers west of Berlin and another of my pilots reported the course was still due east. I heard the ground control order them not to attack but to fly with the bombers and plot the exact course of the bomber stream. We kept being told that the *Spitze* – the vanguard of the stream – had reached a certain point. Then, suddenly, I felt the turbulence of the bombers' slipstream and I knew that I had arrived.

They seemed to turn at Potsdam and go straight into Berlin from the south-west. I think I arrived a bit later than the others. I did not need the glare from the target; it was searchlight fighting that night. It was clear, no moon, and the searchlights were doing a good job. I tried for one bomber, but I was too fast and went past him without firing ...

I came up to the next one more slowly, level, from the rear, but before I could open fire another chap coming down from above me attacked the bomber and set it on fire ...

I circled back over the target and had no difficulty finding a third bomber. Normally, if a fighter wanted to attack a bomber in the searchlights, we should have fired a flare, so that the *Flak* would cease fire, but we Wild Boar men rarely bothered to do this. We usually waited until the bomber weaved or dived out of the searchlights and then attacked it. I shot that third bomber down.[53]

The radar operator of an experienced Himmelbett crew who was participating, somewhat uneasily, in his first 'free-for-all' target-defence mission,
confirmed how easy it was to pick out the enemy aircraft.

Radar had nothing to do with our success that night, only the Wild Boar method in
the Berlin area. Our crews was somewhat reluctant to try this new method; a new
crew, not so set in their ways, would probably have been more willing. I do not know
who saw our first bomber; it was not me, I was looking out of the back. The pilot
or the flight engineer saw the Stirling below, against the light of the raid. We were
directly over Berlin. I turned round and saw it for myself, a silhouette about a thousand metres below. Frank throttled back and reduced speed. We lost height and
attacked it – not in our normal method, *von unten hinten* [from behind and below],
but in a dive from above, just like a day fighter, the first time we had ever attacked
in this way.
The crew of the bomber must have seen us because it tried to evade us – but too
late. When we were sure that its petrol tanks were well on fire, we left it; we knew
it would go down and we did not want to follow it down into the *Flak*.
We caught the second one, a Halifax, at the same height and we attacked it from
the right rear. Our fire opened ahead of the bomber and it flew right through it. The
right wing caught fire and down it went …
The situation over Berlin was hectic by then. We saw about twenty bombers in a
short time; we could have shot down a whole squadron. We fired on three of them but
we were being shot at by the gunners from some of the other bombers and we were
not able to make careful attacks. We got out of it after a bit, pulling away to find a
quiet corner for a while to check our oil and petrol. We went back again to the centre
but it was about all over by then.

Yet despite their success, this crew was not altogether happy about the new
way of doing things.

We did not have enough fuel to go back to our base so we landed at Brandenburg. We
had no trouble getting down; it was well organized. We immediately asked for something to eat and where we could sleep. It was early the next day that we talked to the
other crews about their experiences. There were also a lot of questions from senior
officers about that first Wild Boar night. My own crew agreed that it had been a
success, but we were really *Einzelkämpfer* – lone operators – and we still did not like
being mixed up with this mass of other aircraft.[54]

The aiming point was in the northwest part of Berlin and, with a southern
approach, the anticipated creep-back was expected to cover the city centre.
Things did not go as planned, however. Unable to determine where they were
by H2S alone, despite the network of waterways that lay along the western
edge of the city and the River Spree which ran through its centre from east to
west, the Pathfinders marked an area considerably to the south and west;
despite the best efforts of the master bomber for the night, John Fauquier, to

bring the bombing back on target, only five of the 468 bombing photographs plotted were within three miles of the aiming point. Still, there was considerable destruction on the ground. Thirteen industrial works and 2115 houses were totally destroyed, as were the barracks of the Leibstandarte Adolf Hitler (the German dictator's SS bodyguard), the officers' school at Köpenick, and buildings at Tempelhof airfield.[55] In the Steiglitz, Friedenau, Lichterfelde, and Marienfelde districts of the city, one survivor noted:

We came upon places through which it was impossible to pass by car. Craters filled with water, heaps of rubble, fire-hoses ... firemen and convoys of lorries blocked the streets, where thousands of those rendered homeless were searching the ruins, trying to rescue some of their possessions, or were squatting on the pavements and being fed from field-kitchens. Although eighteen hours had passed since the attack, fires were still burning everywhere.

The tramway lines had been destroyed. Burnt-out buses jammed the streets. Hundreds of trees had been shattered or bereft of their branches and foliage. Of one block of single-family houses all that remained was one solitary chimney ... In the pale, dust-laden sky, the red fiery ball of the evening sun glowed like the harbinger of the Day of Judgment ... The attack had been plunged into the heart of Berlin, like a knife in a cake, and had sliced out a great triangle ...

The question on everybody's mind is – was Monday's attack the beginning of the end, or was it merely a warning shot, designed to bring home to the Berliners the might of the Royal Air Force?[56]

Another observer, this one Swiss, whose report made its way to London, confirmed the underlying tension brought about by these raids.

At the Alexanderplatz station women fought for places, because their children were already in the train and it was on the point of leaving. The urgent desire to get away from Berlin is enormous. Many people start off without knowing where they are going. Many workers have fled from their work and dare not return for fear of expected punishment. In some cases there have been death sentences. Schools are closed and it was planned that children and teachers would be evacuated together ... In many places there is a passive attitude, which is, however, countered with the greatest severity. Overtired office workers often fall asleep. Berliners hold very sober views about the end of the war. They do not, however, dare to think about what will come afterwards.[57]

This was precisely the kind of reaction Harris was after. And it was one that frightened Goebbels, who (with Albert Speer) noted that the physical damage done to factories 'can be more easily repaired than is the case with the disorganization caused in the cities and especially in residential sections.' It did not help that, just as these raids began, the first severe cuts to rations had been made, and that much of the elasticity had recently been removed from the consumer sector of the economy as the Allied stranglehold on Germany began to tighten. Goods and services, including public utilities, whose availability at near prewar levels had been taken for granted even at the beginning of 1943, now were increasingly unobtainable.[58]

But Harris, Goebbels, and Speer had wildly overestimated the non-physical effects of bombing to date. It was only one factor in the general deterioration of civilian morale that took place in the latter half of 1943 – the loss of Sicily; confusion about Mussolini's ouster in Italy; the relinquishment of Orel, Kharkov, and other Russian cities; and the failure of the great Kursk counter-attack being others. However, if Germans were becoming war weary by early autumn 1943, their attitude by and large was not yet affecting their behaviour in any profound or prolonged way. If absenteeism rose with the intensity of the bombing and workers left the most heavily bombed cities altogether, these were generally only passing reactions to momentary crises and disruptions; there was no mass neurosis or hysteria sufficient to threaten an internal collapse. Indeed, when order was restored in Hamburg, Schweinfurt, and other cities, most of the workers who had left returned home and resumed work. Only in 1945, as a 'result of several momentous and coinciding ... catastrophes' involving primarily the advance of the Red Army into Prussia and the Anglo-American thrust into the Ruhr, would morale break in the way Harris wanted and Goebbels feared.[59]

Another raid on Berlin, involving 622 aircraft, came eight nights later, and once again the Luftwaffe reacted strongly, interceptions being recorded from the Dutch coast all the way to the target. Stragglers outside the protective confusion of Window again suffered the most. Over the target, meanwhile, the enemy employed a new tactic. Bomber crews now found themselves illuminated by brilliant white parachute flares released by enemy machines flying above them that made them easier targets for the fighters not equipped with AI radar. 'The psychological effect of this action cannot be described,' one No 405 Squadron pilot recalled.[60]

Although the Germans estimated that 10,000 incendiary, 500 phosphorous, and 135 high-explosive bombs fell in the vicinity of Berlin, damage on this occasion was only slight. One factory was destroyed, and the death toll was fifty-eight, with a further nineteen killed in the surrounding countryside.[61] The Pathfinders had begun marking too far south, and this pull away from the aiming point was reinforced when German night-fighters 'by chance shot down a Pathfinder which fell 20 km farther south, along with his whole cascade of marker bombs, and continued burning on the ground.'[62]

Forty-seven aircraft did not return, 7.6 per cent of those dispatched, but seventeen of them were Stirlings (16 per cent of the number taking off) – further evidence that the type had outlived its usefulness on operations involving deep penetrations. No 6 Group contributed fifty-eight sorties and lost seven, at 12 per cent substantially higher than the average. More telling, the overall early return rate for the raid was 14 per cent, an indication, perhaps – given the good weather – that crews were not eager to take on Berlin again.[63]

The corresponding figure for No 6 Group was just below average, but it included five of the eleven Lancaster IIs dispatched by No 426 Squadron: two because of intercom failure between pilot and rear gunner, two because of en-

TABLE 5
Anticipated Number of Squadrons, June–December 1943[64]

Type	June	September	December
Halifax II/V	23	24	18
Halifax III	0	0	13
Lancaster I/III	20	23	29
Lancaster II	2	4	4
Lancaster X (RCAF)	0	0	1
Stirling I	13	13	17
Wellington X	12	12	13
Total	70	76	95

gine trouble, and one because its compass was unserviceable. Something was wrong – perhaps because Lancaster IIs were still relatively new to the unit – and following further instances of unserviceability and the testing of those that had returned early 'to iron out the kinks which had caused the turnbacks,' on 4 September 'an operational stand-down was ordered and the efforts of all maintenance personnel were directed towards getting all A/C into a serviceable condition.' Undoubtedly because of its recent heavy losses, No 434 Squadron sent only four crews to Berlin on 31 August: all four bombed the target and returned safely.[65]

The third and last raid of the series occurred on 3/4 September and, reflecting what had happened to the Stirling and (to a lesser extent) the Halifax squadrons in the first two missions, was limited to 316 Lancasters and four Mosquitoes. It caused more damage than the previous attack and the loss rate fell to 6.3 per cent, but that was still too high for a sustained campaign; Harris, despite his preference for striking 'just when everybody in Berlin ... had been thrown into a state of panic ... after the destruction of Hamburg,' drew back from what may have been the start of his yearned-for offensive against the German capital.[66] He would wait, now, until the fall and winter, when the nights were longer and when more heavy bombers, particularly Lancaster IIIs, would be available (see table 5).

Within this framework, it had been intended that the three RCAF squadrons returning from the Middle East should receive Lancaster Is or IIIs; but with too few Lancaster-trained crews emerging from No 6 Group's Heavy Conversion Units, it was agreed that Nos 420, 424, and 425 would receive Halifax IIIs, pending their ultimate conversion to Lancaster Xs. Although Harris warned the Air Ministry planners that 'we must see to it that sufficient Canadian Lanc sqdns are kept up to absorb Canadian Lanc production as forecast, otherwise we shall get in wrong with Canada,' he approved this allocation because Canadian output of the Lancaster was currently 'infinitesimal' and therefore, 'for the present,' the RCAF should not take umbrage. Since the production of as many as fifteen Lancaster Xs a month was not expected to begin until October 1943 (and did not, in fact, begin until June 1944), the Canadians would be in an awkward position for a considerable time to come. Despite the

TABLE 6
Mark II H2S Responses from Selected German Cities[67]

City	Range and Quality of H2S Response
Berlin	Too large for the 10/10 scan, and the 30/30 scan must be used for bombing. The city gives a strong response visible for 20 miles. Lakes in and around the city are not dependable [and] the outline of the town cannot be used as a reference point ... because the apparent shape changes with the gain [scan] setting ...
Düsseldorf	Stands out well from other Ruhr towns ...
Hanover	... is visible at 23 miles range ... and gives a strong response ... however it breaks up under 5 miles range and accurate bombing is difficult ...
Kassel	Gives a strong signal visible up to 18 miles, but at short range is inclined to break up ...
Stettin	Is a good clear target with the lakes and edges of the town clearly defined ...
Stuttgart	Is a difficult H2S target surrounded by hills ... thus giving very short range – about 10 miles – and a broken response ...
Wuppertal	Gives a strong echo and is clearly defined ...

reneging on Lancasters, the prospect of receiving Halifax IIIs was welcomed by the RCAF Overseas. As recently as August, Air Marshal Brookes, having complained about the decision to form No 433 Squadron on obsolescent Halifax IIs 'cast off from other squadrons,' had been told to expect only a 'trickle' of Lancasters and Halifax IIIs for the foreseeable future. The new arrangement therefore represented progress.[68] 'From the morale point of view it has always been the object of this Group Headquarters to avoid having Halifax IIs or Vs on the same station or even in the same base with Lancasters [and Halifax IIIs.] The difference in performance ... is so obvious ... that [at Heavy Conversion Units] it is impossible to prevent an unhealthy regard for the Halifax II and V aircraft among the crews destined to operate these aircraft.'[69]

There was another reason for Harris to wait for winter before attacking Berlin again. As we have seen, although the various aids and devices developed so far had improved both navigation and bombing accuracy, they had not been particularly successful against sprawling urban targets like Berlin. Even 10-cm Mark II H2S, with which main force crews in No 6 and the other Groups were now being equipped, was sometimes of only marginal value.[70]

However, a new Mark III H2S was about to become available which promised to give a substantially clearer picture of large cities, especially where highlighting reference points such as lakes or shorelines was concerned, because of its shorter 3-centimetre wavelength and substantially narrower beam. With estimates suggesting that it would double, and perhaps triple, the number of Bomber Command's outstanding successes, there was good reason to await its appearance, even if, in the first instance, it could only be issued to Pathfinder squadrons. However, all crews were slated to be equipped with the

Ground Position Indicator (GPI), an attachment to the Air Position Indicator (API) which automatically took the navigator's latest wind readings into account and thus allowed him to plot more precisely where he was. The GPI nevertheless depended upon accurate wind readings; and at this stage fewer than half the operational navigators could assess wind velocities accurately enough to be within ten miles of the course set down.[71]

Finally, and most promising, was G-H. Essentially Oboe in reverse, an operator in the bomber transmitted a signal to two ground stations in the United Kingdom and then plotted his position according to their response. Theoretically accurate to within two to four hundred yards, G-H could be used by up to eighty aircraft for each pair of ground stations, and was to be fitted to all Lancaster IIs (including those of Nos 408 and 426 Squadrons) which could not be fitted with H2S because of their large bomb-bay doors, designed to accommodate 8000-lb bombs. However, G-H had two serious drawbacks. Its transmissions could be homed on by the enemy and, like Oboe, it was dependent on line-of-sight communications, which also limited its range.[72] For that reason, G-H would be withdrawn from No 6 Group's Lancaster squadrons when they were committed to the battle of Berlin and allocated instead to medium bombers assigned to attack targets requiring only shallow penetrations.[73]

That may have been a strategic error of considerable consequence. Perhaps heavy bombers equipped with G-H should have been directed against German aircraft factories within its range in the fall of 1943. For although they understood the significance of electronic counter-measures in evading night-fighters, a number of officials at the Air Ministry argued that such devices were nevertheless an unsatisfactory method of dealing with Bomber Command's main opponent. If enemy fighter strength grew, cautioned Air Vice-Marshal N.H. Bottomley, Harris would be 'unable to maintain the night offensive' no matter what jamming took place; and the DCAS therefore called for a sustained effort against aircraft manufacturing and assembly plants in Brunswick, Stuttgart, Hanover, Kassel, and Leverkusen, for example.[74]

The director of bomber operations, now Air Commodore S. Bufton, *vice* Baker, concurred. Although he had not objected to the three operations against the German capital, hoping that Bomber Command could mount a successful repetition of the Hamburg raid 'on any industrial area, Berlin or anywhere else,' it was still essential that Harris 'start towards the specific targets [of Pointblank] eventually.' For if Bomber Command and the Americans did not between them destroy the Luftwaffe's capability to resist, he cautioned ominously, postwar analysts would regard the bombing offensive as a failure in the strategic employment of air power. Observing that it might be time to hold a conference with Harris and Eaker, Portal seemed to agree.[75]

Harris himself was as unimpressed as ever with the targeting philosophy put forward by Bottomley, Bufton, or anyone else who thought that the destruction of a single sector of the German economy would produce decisive results – and who, though no more than staff officers, acted as if they were 'commanders in the field.' 'Panacea-mongers,' he called them, with considerable distaste.[76] But given such external pressure (and since Harris did not want to attack Berlin for the moment anyway), over the next ten weeks Bomber Command conducted area raids against the cities the DCAS had mentioned.

Although it was unlikely that any of them would be defended as heavily as Berlin, the Luftwaffe still could not be ignored. However, the threat posed by both roving and point-oriented night-fighters could be countered, at least to some extent, in a number of ways. Diversions might be made more convincing; several targets could be attacked each night; or the main force could be broken down into smaller streams, each using a different route to the same target. It was also possible to attack the enemy directly, either by bombing and strafing bases and intercepting fighters as they took off, landed, or circled their beacons – Intruder operations – or by sending out fighters with the bomber stream to shoot down enemy machines en route to and from the target – 'offensive' night-fighting.

Intruder squadrons had initially been employed against the German bomber force as part of the air defence of Great Britain and were not turned loose on Flower missions against Luftwaffe night-fighter bases until the Cologne raid of 30/31 May 1942. One RCAF squadron, No 418, had been a participant from the beginning. Flying American-built Douglas Boston IIIs, its crews had maintained standing patrols over specified airfield for as long as possible (up to forty-five minutes) and had then dropped their bombloads on the main runways before making for home.[77]

Though probably a source of irritation to the enemy, Flower patrols in 1942 achieved little in terms of the number of enemy aircraft destroyed, or even seriously inconvenienced. Blacked-out airfields were hard to find, the bombsights on the Bostons were not precise enough to ensure accurate results, and, without AI, they were ill-equipped for aerial hunting. In addition, they lacked the range to operate against many airfields in Germany. Better things usually happened when other kinds of targets were attacked and, thus, like all other Intruder squadrons, No 418 was soon spending at least half its time machine-gunning railway traffic in France and the Low Countries. By the end of September 1942 it had claimed at least twenty locomotives destroyed or damaged.[78]

Interest in sustaining a night-fighter offensive against the Luftwaffe was rekindled in the spring of 1943 – in part because of rising losses during the battle of the Ruhr, but also because a night-fighter variant of the de Havilland Mosquito had begun to be made available. Armed with four machine guns and four 20-millimetre cannon, and able to carry four 500-lb bombs, it was faster than any German night-fighter except the He 219. Moreover, when equipped with auxiliary fuel tanks it had an operational range of more than 1000 miles, and so could escort the main force to Berlin and back or stand long watches over less-distant night-fighter fields. In addition, those supplied to the escort squadrons were equipped with AI radar and other electronic homing and warning devices. No 418 Squadron was understandably elated when it received its first dual instructional Mosquito in February 1943, but it was not until July that all its Bostons were retired from operations. By then, the squadron was heavily engaged in the latter stages of the battle of the Ruhr, patrolling and bombing bases in France, Belgium, Holland, and western Germany. During the battle of Hamburg, the Canadians extended their operations far to the east, reaching as far as Stendal, Parchim, and Griefenwald in the final week of August in support of the initial raids on Berlin.[79]

Despite the introduction of the Mosquito, the Air Ministry did not expect that Intruder squadrons would shoot down many enemy aircraft. Enemy fighters already in pursuit of the bomber stream would not be concentrated around their bases or at assembly beacons, and, given the presence of Mosquitoes over their home fields, they would presumably land elsewhere. Bomb-damage to runways, however, might prevent some pilots from taking off at a critical moment, and it was hoped that at least some disorganization would be caused as controllers tracked, identified, and passed on warnings about the Intruders. 'Jerry couldn't help but know that we were up there,' one crew from No 418 Squadron recalled, 'and that's exactly what we wanted.'

None of their aircraft were likely to take off or land while we were there. As it turned out, none did. Some must have thought about making an attempt to land, because on four different occasions on our 45-minute patrol the German ground controllers shot up a series of Very cartridges to give their aircraft the old *Achtung* sign – 'enemy aircraft in the vicinity.' If they [are] receiving the same reception at every drome they come home to, there must have been now several new members of the German Cater-pillar Club* as well as bags of Jerry aircraft still grounded on the runway.[80]

In September 1943 No 418 achieved some spectacular results. On the night of 5/6 September Squadron Leader R.J. Bennell and Flying Officer F. Shield were ordered to Worms/Biblis, where they found the airfield lit 'and at least twelve aircraft ... landing.' They attacked one, 'which exploded in mid-air and crashed in flames' and then moved on to Mainz-Ober-Olm, where they shot down a Do 217 'from dead astern.'[81] Three weeks after that, Flight Lieutenant M.W. Beveridge and Sergeant B.O. Bays 'sighted several aircraft about to land at an aerodrome south-west of Stuttgart.' They attacked three and claimed two destroyed, the same results that had been achieved by Flight Lieutenant H.S. Lisson and Flying Officer A.E. Franklin over Hanover two nights earlier. By the end of the month No 418 had eight enemy aircraft to its credit.[82]

But September's pace could not be maintained. Although Harris needed help (claiming that having played 'the best of our counter measure cards,' Bomber Command now risked 'prohibitive losses') and although the Intruder squadrons were willing to assist, they were at the mercy of the deteriorating autumn weather. Many sorties had to be abandoned or cancelled altogether, in part because there were no bombsights on Mark II and VI Mosquitoes but also because navigation was difficult, particularly beyond the range of Gee, the only

---

* The recognition given by the Royal Air Force to those who had made a successful jump by parachute from a fatally stricken aircraft.

electronic navigation aid these night-fighters carried. And since Intruder squadrons like No 418 did not have AI radars, they could not take full advantage of October's major intelligence coup, when information provided by a Belgian agent revealed the location of all the Luftwaffe night-fighter beacons in Western Europe. The number of enemy aircraft claimed by all intruder squadrons fell from twenty in September to just six over the next three months.[83]

Weather had less impact on the offensive night-fighters which, equipped with AI, Monica, and Serrate – an electronic device which detected and provided a bearing to German AI radar transmissions to a range of one hundred miles – did not have to depend on clear skies to find the enemy. In time, Serrate-equipped crews flying in the bomber stream as part of the distinct No 100 (Bomber Support) Group formed in November 1943, and other Monica- and AI-equipped squadrons undertaking Mahmoud patrols around the enemy night-fighter beacons, would give the Germans a self-admitted case of Mosquitophobia from which they never totally recovered. But not in the latter months of 1943. With just five squadrons (including, very briefly, No 410) involved at various times, there were very few combats and only one confirmed enemy aircraft destroyed.[84] Evasion and tactical and electronic countermeasures, not fighter support, remained the keys to bomber survival.

Some, indeed, looked on evasion as their only hope. Not entirely convinced that there was safety in numbers, they chose to fly higher or lower (but usually higher) than their briefing called for, thinking they might avoid the main concentration of enemy fighters if they put some distance between themselves and the main bomber stream. A few were lucky, but others, having abandoned the protective Window screen, were not. Still others, while staying in the stream and remembering how many times they had been told that their task was 'to bomb and not to fight,' sought to make themselves as inconspicuous as possible by withholding fire when they saw enemy aircraft.[85]

Harris had already issued warnings about the dangers of leaving the stream. Now he cautioned that, with the Luftwaffe well supplied with radar, the practice of withholding fire was 'timorous and deluding.' Enemy fighters were unlikely to attack a bomber that had demonstrated its 'alertness,' he explained, particularly if they found themselves in an 'unfavourable position.' The deterrent effect of defensive fire was not something that could be demonstrated in a convincing fashion, however, and eventually the AOC of No 5 Group, for one (Air Vice-Marshal, the Hon. R.A. Cochrane, *vice* Coryton), felt it necessary to instruct his crews to open fire on all enemy aircraft whether or not they showed signs of attacking. The Canadian group did not go so far, but there, too, an attempt was made to increase the aggressive spirit of bomber crews. While confirming that evasive manoeuvres were the proper course of action on being approached by an enemy, Allerton Hall announced that the purpose of evasion was not to '*lose* the fighter,' but to present it with a 'difficult target' while providing the bomber's own gunners with a good field of fire.[86]

There was every reason for those in authority to worry about crews leaving the bomber stream. Besides putting themselves at risk, the whole effort at achieving concentrated bombing would be undermined if the practice became too widespread. Whether crews within the stream were well served by frequent use of their guns was another matter. Test interceptions conducted between a Halifax and the Lichtenstein-equipped Ju 88 which had landed in England in July 1943 indicated that a diving turn followed by a rapid climb of 1500 to 2000 feet not only presented the fighter with an extremely difficult deflection shot, but often enough ensured that it lost visual and AI contact as well, allowing the bomber to escape.[87] Furthermore, No 4 Group was soon complaining that 'there is quite obviously a considerable amount of indiscriminate firing taking place. Reports of Halifaxes being fired at by other Halifaxes and Lancasters are becoming much too frequent. While the safety of aircraft dictates that necessity of treating all approaching aircraft with suspicion, it is reasonable to treat a four-engined aircraft as friendly unless and until its behaviour becomes definitely threatening.'[88]

In the light of this evidence, and following an analysis of recent aerial combats, High Wycombe acknowledged on 2 October that the 'timorous' crews might have been right after all, declaring that the use of guns 'must take second place' when enemy aircraft were seen. Subsequent investigations confirmed the wisdom of this instruction. Having looked closely at No 5 Group's experience during the period when its crews were ordered to open fire on all enemy aircraft, the operational research scientists concluded that the practice increased not only the likelihood of attack but also the chances of hitting friendly aircraft. Seen in this light, the ORS concluded (somewhat impishly) that Air Vice-Marshal Cochrane's 'aggressive' policy was something from which 'the Group as a Group has not benefitted.'[89]

Gunnery was clearly not the answer – at least not so long as the .303 machine gun remained the only defensive armament carried, and so long as air gunners (many of whom were previously failed pilots, navigators, and bomb-aimers) were as poorly motivated and trained as recent evidence had suggested.[90] Until there were more Mosquitoes available to fly escort and Intruder missions, Bomber Command would have to rely on spoofs, diversions, and misdirection – much of it electronic – in order to maintain the offensive: and from late September 1943 such measures began to feature more prominently in its operations.

Because he still needed to mass his main force to ensure that a sufficient weight of bombs fell on the target, Harris chose first to mount relatively simple decoy raids in which a few Mosquitoes and heavy bombers used Window, flares, target indicators, and whatever ordnance they carried to simulate the approach of a major raid while the main force made a very concentrated attack elsewhere. This was one step beyond the Mosquito-only diversion attempted over Berlin when Peenemünde was attacked, and the first true decoy operation took place on 22/23 September when eight Mosquitoes and twenty-one Lancasters feinted over Oldenburg while the main force, over seven hundred strong, bombed Hanover, about eighty miles away. From the standpoint of results, the raid was a 'record flop' so far as Harris was concerned. Most crews had failed to make 'the slightest attempt' to approach the target on the course set down, and at one point, as No 6 Group confirmed, 'aircraft were bombing from all points of the compass.' 'Unless AOC's take a firm grip now & put this deplorably state of affairs right,' Sir Arthur cautioned, 'we are faced by the prospect of wasted effort, futile casualties, & consequent failures which cannot be.'[91]

Not everything about the attack had been negative, however. 'Some confusion was caused before the target was identified' by the enemy controllers, and the loss rate was under 4 per cent. More cautious, now, High Wycombe was loath to attribute the lower casualty rate solely to the Oldenburg effort. Still sensitive to the threat to Berlin, the enemy might well have withheld some fighters to defend the capital – something that could not be counted on every night. Moreover, the decoy had not worked indefinitely. Fighters had appeared over Hanover in strength before the last waves of the main force had departed, and they 'were apparently responsible' for most of bombers shot down.[92]

Why the Oldenburg feint did not fix the enemy's night-fighters there for the whole night cannot be explained with absolute certainty but it seems likely that, with only eighty miles between them, target and decoy were simply too close together. Seeing an attack developing off to the southwest and freed from the old Himmelbett restrictions on taking the initiative, many night-fighter crews had simply moved to Hanover on their own. That was certainly what happened the next night, when the target (Mannheim) and decoy (Darmstadt) were only twenty-five miles apart – five to seven minutes flying time – and the loss rate was 5.1 per cent. Four nights later, when thirty miles separated Hanover and Brunswick, casualties rose to 5.6 per cent.[93] Perhaps having chosen to minimize the significance of Oldenburg in the first place, the staff at High Wycombe could not now draw the appropriate conclusion from follow-on raids. Unfettered by Kammhuber's dogma, night-fighters only a few minutes from the target were not going to remain as passive as they had near Cologne fifteen months earlier.

It probably did not help matters that the best example of what High Wycombe was trying (and so far failing) to achieve occurred on a night when there was no decoy operation at all. On 29/30 September the main force attacked Bochum while eleven Mosquitoes bombed oil facilities at Gelsenkirchen and fourteen Lancasters were Gardening in the Baltic. Yet the German controllers were completely baffled. The bomber stream followed a course which led the Luftwaffe to identify Bremen as the likely target, Window worked well enough to hide the turn towards Bochum, and all fighters were sent to the North Sea port. At that point the original error turned to self-deception. The Flak at Bremen began firing, responding, no doubt, to the presence of the night-fighters; flares dropped by the latter were mistaken for Pathfinder target indicators; and the main controller at 2 Jagddivision, whose headquarters at Stade was only forty miles from Bremen, announced that bombs were falling along the Weser when, in fact, the main force was over the Ruhr, 120 miles to the southwest.

The controller at 1 Jagddivision in Belgium tried desperately to correct his colleague's instructions, but with limited success because he was, in turn, countermanded by Stade. As a result, Bomber Command lost only 2.6 per cent

THEORETICAL AND ACTUAL DISTRIBUTION OF LOSSES IN BOMBER COMMAND SQUADRONS RESULTING FROM RAIDS ON GERMAN TARGETS MAY – SEPTEMBER 1943

Each squadron is placed in a column above its corresponding value of 'q' – 'q' being a measure of how each squadron's losses differed from the average overall loss for all squadrons. ('q' has been standardized so that squadrons flying different types of aircraft are comparable.) Based on the assumption that all squadrons are similar, the shaded area within the Gaussian (or bell) curve illustrates the theoretical distribution of 'q' values.

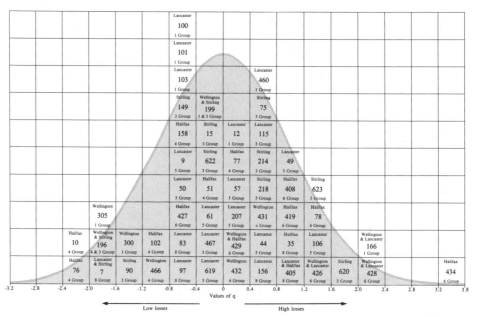

Values of q

Low losses　　　High losses

Source: PRO Air 14/1801

Late in 1943, the Operational Research Section of Bomber Command compiled this chart in an effort 'to discover whether the idiosyncracies of particular squadrons are an important influence on losses,' arranging squadrons 'in an "order of merit" … to detect any non-random influences that may be at work.' As might be expected, the actual distribution of losses deviated somewhat from the distribution forecast by the laws of probability.

Losses in No 6 – the newest and therefore least experienced formation – placed all but one of its squadrons on the high side of the predicted range. No 428 Squadron showed indications of 'a slight non-random tendency to high losses' (as did No 1 Group's 166 Squadron), but 434 Squadron – operational only since August, with loss rates half again as high as those incurred by any other squadron in Bomber Command – suffered casualties which were 'very seriously above the limits of chance fluctuations.'

No one determined scientifically what 'non-random influences' were responsible for these misfortunes, but continuing high losses would earn No 434 an unenviable reputation as the RCAF's 'chop' squadron.

of the 352 bombers sent to the target. No 6 Group did not do nearly so well, losing three of thirty-nine crews, 7.6 per cent; and two of those came from No 434 – continuing a run of misfortune that, in October, momentarily led Air Vice-Marshal Brookes to consider replacing its commanding officer, a Canadian in the RAF unsympathetic to Canadianization. But despite the squadron's increasingly unenviable reputation, no operational fault could be attributed to Wing Commander C.E. Harris, who retained command until his tour expired in February 1944.[94]

Aware from radio intercepts of the confusion caused in the enemy camp, the Air Ministry looked very closely at the Luftwaffe's response in attempts to divine what weaknesses in German air-defence organization unearthed that night could be exploited further. To R.V. Jones, who had pioneered the RAF's electronic intelligence gathering, the evidence suggested overwhelmingly that the enemy's defences were 'unstable,' and there were clear indications where they were most vulnerable. 'Once the controller has formed a picture of the situation it becomes increasingly easy for him to convince himself he is right. Having made his guess ... he sends his fighters to a convenient beacon. These fighters are then reported by sound observations [listening posts on the ground] and ... may be easily misidentified. The controller then interprets the observations as referring to British aircraft, and is thus confirmed in his initial misjudgment.'[95]

The brilliance of Jones's deduction was that he avoided the obvious. What was critical in explaining the low loss rate suffered at Bochum was not that the enemy had been misled or had fooled himself, Jones observed, or even that his reaction depended so much on his initial guess, but rather that, by the time the German controllers had recovered, there were few British aircraft left over the target. And this had happened not because the deception, self-imposed or otherwise, had lasted longer than usual, but because the main force involved was small and had finished its work in less than thirty minutes. The advice he tendered to Portal flowed logically from that conclusion. Instead of wasting time and effort trying to lay on perfect diversions – which were probably impossible anyway – Harris should consider mounting smaller raids that took less time to carry out.[96] Perhaps, then, if the main force attacking Hanover on 22/23 September had not been so large and had done its business more quickly, there would have been no one left there for the fighters from Oldenburg to intercept.

Analysis of a number of operations mounted in early October suggested that Jones was, indeed, right. Raids featuring smaller, all-Lancaster main forces and taking a short time to complete usually suffered relatively low casualties: 0.8 per cent at Hagen on 1/2 October, 2.7 per cent at Munich on 2/3 October, and 1.2 per cent at Stuttgart on 7/8 October. But when Bomber Command went out in strength – five hundred aircraft or more – to one target, the loss rate averaged about 5 per cent.[97]

Jones's hypothesis was not the only one which provided an adequate explanation for what was happening, however, and some of the others were naturally more appealing to Harris because they were in harmony with – or at least did not openly contradict – his determination to deliver the greatest weight of bombs possible to every target. Weather was still a factor in determining loss rates, as was the depth of penetration into Germany, irrespective of the size of the main force. Leipzig, bombed by 358 Lancasters on 20/21 October, involved a longer approach over enemy territory than Berlin, and that gave the Luftwaffe ample opportunity to react. Sixteen machines were shot down, 4.5 per cent of the total.[98]

One crew from No 426 Squadron was attacked no fewer than seven times before it reached (and bombed) the target.

The first ... was delivered at 1940 hours ... The enemy aircraft was first sighted by the rear gunner on the starboard quarter when he opened fire at 300 yards. The rear gunner ordered combat manoeuvre 'diving turn starboard' and opened fire. During this attack the enemy aircraft, which was identified as an Me 109, scored hits on the tail plane, fuselage, [and] wings, rendered the mid-upper turret unserviceable and wounded the mid-upper gunner ... The second attack was delivered on the port quarter down at 500 yards. Evasive action was taken and the rear gunner opened fire. The enemy aircraft closed in to 200 yards and broke away [on the] starboard beam. The third attack came from astern and again evasive action was taken, the rear gunner opening fire at 400 yards. The enemy aircraft closed in to 200 yards and broke away starboard beam. The fourth attack came from astern, ten degrees to port at 500 yards. Evasive action was again taken and the rear gunner opened fire simultaneously with the enemy aircraft. The attack was pressed to 200 yards and the enemy aircraft broke away and was not seen again. Shortly after the aircraft had set course it was again attacked by an enemy night fighter, identified as a Ju 88. The enemy aircraft was first sighted on the starboard quarter by the rear gunner at 700 yards. Our aircraft took evasive action and opened fire at 500 yards. The enemy aircraft fired a short burst and broke away at 400 yards on the port beam. The next attack came from astern at 500 yards. Evasive action was again taken and the rear gunner opened fire. The enemy aircraft fired a short burst and broke away at 300 yards. The seventh and final attack was delivered from astern and slightly to port. Successful evasive action was again taken and the attack was not completed as our aircraft entered cloud.

The mid-upper turret and pilot's windscreen had been shattered, the hydraulics and trailing aerial shot away, and the Gee, wireless receiver, starboard inner fuel tank, and starboard fuselage and wings all holed. Flight Sergeant F.J. Stuart nevertheless brought his machine back to Linton-on-Ouse and, although a higher award might have been more appropriate, received the Conspicuous Gallantry Medal.[99] He was killed over Frankfurt, six weeks later.

However, the most powerful argument against Jones's suggestion, and one which would support the continuation of large raids, was the fact that the evidence could be arranged and manipulated to show that deceptions had worked. For, in Harris's view, the principal lesson to be derived from the raid that had taught Jones so much was not that the operation was shorter than usual but that German pilots would 'take instructions [from] the controller giving the most convincing narrative.' The man at 2 Jagddivision who declared so emphatically that bombs were falling on Bremen, and had tangible evidence

in the form of flares and Flak to back him up, was substantially more persuasive than his counterpart at Deelen, who knew only that Bremen was not the
target but had no dramatic alternative evidence to proffer. It seemed, therefore,
that it was not essential to fool the entire German air-defence system but only
one element of it, no matter how large the main force or how long it took to
bomb.[100] Several of October's raids could be made to fit that model, at least
superficially. On 3/4 October, when the target was Kassel and diversions were
mounted over Hanover and Cologne, controllers in the west initially decided
that Magdeburg, further east, was the real objective and, try as he might,
General Weise in Berlin could not override them and divert to Kassel the twin-
engined units assigned to cover northern Germany until many were low on
fuel. There was similar confusion five nights later – the last time Wellingtons
were sent to Germany – when Hanover and Bremen (just sixty miles apart)
were bombed. Fooled by the complex route High Wycombe had laid down, the
German controllers left their fighters to-ing and fro-ing between the outskirts
of the two cities without actually contacting the raiders until relatively late in
the night.[101]

In both these cases, however, the loss rate had to be ignored in order to
make the perfect fit Harris thought he saw. Twenty-four bombers had been
shot down on 3/4 October, 4.4 per cent of those dispatched, and when the
enemy fighters finally did make contact on 8/9 October they shot down most
of the twenty-seven Halifaxes and Lancasters that were lost. Here was additional evidence that time over the target was the critical variable – the main
force had lingered at Hanover and Bremen so long that the controllers had
finally been able to get a correct grip on the situation.

What clinched the matter, however, in determining whether Jones's advice
would be taken was Harris's understandable desire to knock out his targets in
as few raids as possible and thereby reduce the risk to his crews. When navigation and bomb-aiming left so much room for improvement, and when there
were too few Pathfinders available for multiple, simultaneous operations, that
meant launching a few very heavy blows to produce significant damage. It was
purely a matter of scale. Better that half the bombs from eight hundred aircraft
should fall on Berlin one night and Magdeburg the next than half from four
hundred on each city over two successive nights, when the enemy might be
laying in wait. For the foreseeable future, then, Bomber Comand would continue to rely on one main penetration supported by one or more small diversions. Nevertheless, since the enemy could not be expected to err every night
– controllers were bound to deduce the right target from time to time, even if
for the wrong reasons – and since High Wycombe was also likely to get its
diversions, spoofing, and main-force route wrong at least some of the time, it
was absolutely essential to move ahead with plans to confound the enemy
controllers' running commentaries.[102]

As we have seen, the assault on the Luftwaffe's command, control, and communications systems had actually begun in December 1942, when Tinsel was
used to disrupt Himmelbett ground-to-air transmissions by broadcasting engine

noise on the fighter-control frequency, and Mandrel attempted to jam the early warning Freya radars with only partial success. However, the transmitter power available in Tinsel aircraft was so limited that the interference it caused was easily countered by increasing the strength of the ground control signal, and Tinsel's range was too limited to jam the running commentaries broadcast by stations all over Germany once the Luftwaffe adopted that procedure. Cigar, a ground-based jammer introduced in July 1942, also targeted the enemy's VHF broadcasts, but with a maximum range of 140 miles it, too, was ineffective against most of the Jagddivision commentaries. Grocer, meanwhile, was designed to jam Lichtenstein B/C. Airborne variants of Cigar and Grocer were eventually introduced, but for the moment it was Corona, introduced on the 22/23 October raid on Kassel, that was the most imaginative and, for the time being, the most promising of all Allied radio counter-measures.[103]

Conceived originally as a simple, high-powered jammer, it was soon discovered that, by superimposing a German-language commentary over that provided by the Jagddivision controllers, Corona could be used to deliver false information and fake instructions that might, at best, draw night-fighters away from the target and reinforce any diversion that was taking place and, at worst, introduce an element of uncertainty into the night-fighter phalanx. The bomber stream would not only be protected, it was felt, but the trust between the pilots and the ground-controllers that was so essential to night-fighter operations might also be broken down. The key to making Corona effective went far beyond providing a voice speaking idiomatic German, however; it required accurate renderings of Luftwaffe code-words and procedures while displaying a genuine controller's complete and intimate understanding of his own air-defence organization. The knowledge to accomplish this had been built up, painstakingly and piece by piece over the previous three years, by radio and electronic eavesdropping until, as we have seen, the last crucial gap was filled in October 1943.[104]

The initial impact of Corona seemed impressive enough, throwing the main I Jagdkorps controller 'into an exceedingly bad temper ... At one stage [he] broke into vigorous cursing, whereupon the Corona voice remarked that "The Englishman is now swearing." To this the German retorted that "It is not the Englishman who is swearing, it is me."' But the deception, which aimed at identifying Frankfurt as the target and the Mosquitoes sent there as the main force, did not last. Having followed the bomber stream's progress across Western Europe with fighters employed in a shadowing role – whose AI, because they were travelling in the same direction as the bombers, was less affected by jamming – employing Würzburgs modified to resist the worst effects of Window, and with Naxos detecting (and measuring the volume of) H2S transmissions, the Germans identified Kassel as the objective the moment bombs began to fall there. They were soon giving accurate and unequivocal reports on the progress of the raid. So compelling were these reports that, by the end of the night, 193 fighters had been directed to Kassel, and forty-three bombers (7.6 per cent of the 569 aircraft dispatched) shot down. The loss rate in No 6 Group squadrons was higher still. Twelve of 107 crews failed to return

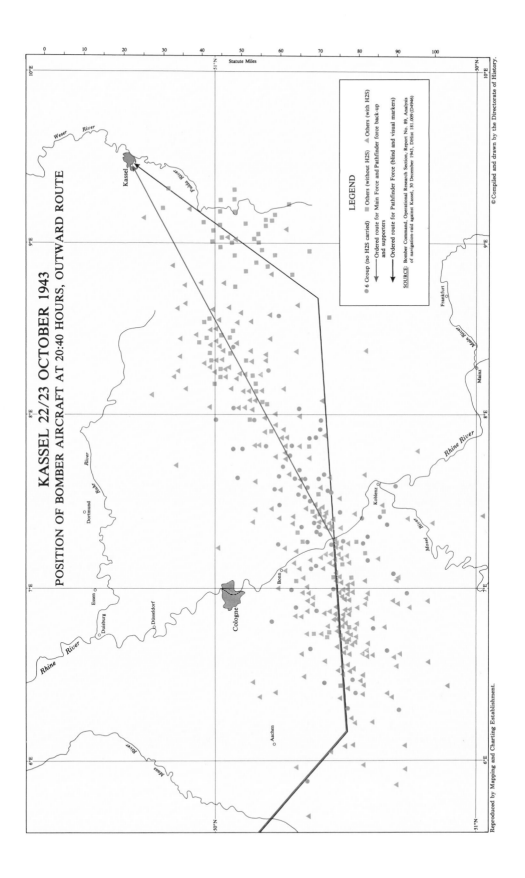

KASSEL 22/23 OCTOBER 1943
POSITION OF BOMBER AIRCRAFT AT 20:40 HOURS, OUTWARD ROUTE

LEGEND

● 6 Group (no H2S carried)   ■ Others (without H2S)   ◄ Others (with H2S)

→ Ordered route for Main Force and Pathfinder force back-up
   and supporters

→ Ordered route for Pathfinder Force (blind and visual markers)

SOURCE: Bomber Command, Operational Research Section, Report No. 89, Analysis
of navigation-raid against Kassel, 30 December 1943, DHist 181.009 (D4946)

© Compiled and drawn by the Directorate of History.

Reproduced by Mapping and Charting Establishment.

(11.2 per cent), and of these four came from No 434 Squadron – whose crews
were on time and on track – and three from No 427.[105]

Although most interceptions took place in the vicinity of the target, the
Germans also had considerable success against bomber crews who, because
of icing and thick cloud and haze en route, had gone off track and were not
protected by Window. In that respect, having to battle the weather longer and
not yet fully equipped with H2S, No 6 Group crews had more difficulty than
some of their colleagues in maintaining their course, and that may well
explain why their losses were so much higher than the Bomber Command
average.[106]

Harris had reason to be satisfied despite the losses, however. Although the
weather en route to Kassel had been difficult, the skies cleared over the
target and the markers there were both accurate and well concentrated. The
incendiaries took hold in the city centre, a small firestorm was created, and
at night's end Bomber Command had produced the most destructive raid
since Hamburg.

The bulk of this attack was concentrated in the highly built-up central part of the city,
and ... the entire area was practically destroyed. It is estimated that 65 per cent of the
weight of bombs over the target fell in an area of seventeen square miles in and
around the centre of the town ... [and] that 50 per cent of the buildings in the zone
of bombfall caught fire immediately and fired the adjoining buildings. The H[igh]
E[xplosive] bombs loosened roof tiles and opened up windows so that buildings which
were not hit were easily ignited by flying sparks and radiant heat ...

Communications and essential services were disrupted, as fires were of such proportions that no firefighting agency could cope with them. The firemen devoted themselves to saving lives and trying to check the fires at the perimeter. It was impossible
to do any fire-fighting in the centre of the fire zone ...[107]

Almost half of Kassel's houses and apartment blocks were damaged or
destroyed, leaving upwards of 100,000 homeless; as many as 8500 were killed.
The railway network around the city was heavily hit, and 155 industrial buildings, including the three Henschel locomotive, tank, and gun plants, were
smashed or badly damaged.[108]

The interpretation of these results quickly became the source of bitter controversy. Since September the Air Ministry's public relations branch had been
increasingly emphasizing the industrial damage done by Bomber Command as
an integral part of the CBO. The stories released about the Kassel raid were no
exception. 'A great force of RAF and RCAF heavy bombers fought their way
through many Nazi fighters last night,' the Associated Press reported, 'to deliver a concentrated attack on the German war industrial centre of Kassel in the
ninth – and costliest – major British raid of the month.'

The heavy bombers again added their terrific punches at German industry to the night
and day attacks that lighter RAF and American planes have been conducting against
Nazi communications and fighter fields ...

Kassel, which is one hundred miles northeast of Cologne, is one of Germany's key aircraft towns and also site of the Henschel Locomotive Works, largest of its kind in Europe. The city has a big assembly works for Messerschmitt 109s.[109]

To Harris, who knew what the aiming points in Kassel had been, such an account was a gross distortion and misrepresentation, and he said so. What was important about the raid, he told the undersecretary of state for air, was not that 'the Henschel locomotive works and various other ... factory premises' had been hit, but that 'Kassel contained over 200,000 Germans, many of whom are now dead and most of the remainder homeless and destitute.' Besides giving the wrong impression to the British people, who might be led to think that Bomber Command was primarily concerned with 'the bombing of specific factory premises' when its real goal was 'the obliteration of German cities and their inhabitants,' these stories also threatened morale within his squadrons. 'Our crews know what the real aim of the attack is. When they read what the public are told about it, they are bound to think (and do think) that the authorities are ashamed of area bombing. It is not to be expected that men will go on risking their lives to effect a purpose which their own Government appears to consider at least as too disreputable to be mentioned in public.' Moreover there was a risk that, by misconstruing what strategic bombing was actually achieving, others would 'steal credit' when the war was over. 'The fact that bombing has won the war and forced the German armies to give in to the Russians will never be accepted in quarters where it is important that it should.'

For a number of reasons, then, the AOC-in-C asked that the purpose of the bombing offensive, 'and the part which Bomber Command is required by agreed British–US strategy to play in it, should be unambiguously stated.'

That aim is the destruction of German cities, the killing of German workers and the disruption of civilised community life throughout Germany.

It should be emphasised that the destruction of houses, public utilities, transport and lives; the creation of a refugee problem on an unprecedented scale; and the breakdown of morale both at home and at the battle fronts by fear of extended and intensified bombing, are [the] accepted and intended aims of our bombing policy. They are not by-products of attempts to hit factories.

The successes gained should publicly be assessed in terms of the extent to which they realise this policy. It should be made clear that the destruction of factory installations is only a part and by no means the most important part of the plan. Acreages of housing devastation are infinitely more important.[110]

Harris – no mincer of words – was asking his government to confirm one of two things: either indiscriminate attacks were all that Bomber Command could manage for the moment; or, capabilities aside, they were what the British bombing offensive was really all about.

This posed something of a public relations problem for a government that, while acknowledging that 'heavy casualties to the civil population' were unavoidable, nevertheless desired, in the words of Sir Arthur Street, permanent undersecretary of state for air, 'to present the bomber offensive in such a light as to provoke the minimum of public controversy and so far as possible to avoid conflict with religious and humanitarian opinion.' In fact, it had been a problem, to some extent or other, since the spring of 1941 when the bishop of Chichester had demanded to know (in the correspondence columns of *The Times*) how 'the bombing of towns by night and the terrorizing of non-combatants' could be excused; Dr Cosmo Lang, archbishop of Canterbury, had observed that although it was a 'very natural and human' reaction for Britons to want to repay the enemy in kind for 'the ... ruthless treatment' inflicted on London and Coventry, 'that view ought not to be allowed to prevail. It was one thing to bomb military objectives and to cripple war industries, and in so doing it may be impossible to avoid inflicting losses and suffering on many civilians; but it is a very different thing to adopt the inflicting of such losses and suffering as deliberate policy.' However, looking on the bright side, he did not believe that 'the great majority of British folk, even in the bombed areas, really want such a policy, and it is to be hoped that the Government, some of whose members have been using disquieting language, will resist any pressure [and instead] strive so as to be patriots as not to forget that we are Christians.'[111]

Dr Lang thought too well of his fellow man, public and private. One member of parliament had asserted in May 1942 that he was 'all for the bombing of working-class areas in German cities. I am Cromwellian – I believe in "slaying in the name of the Lord," because I do not believe you will ever bring home to the civil population of Germany the horrors of war until they have become tasted in this way'; and the secretary of state for air, Sir Archibald Sinclair, had replied he was 'delighted to find that you and I are in complete agreement about ... bombing policy generally.'[112]

Moreover, although the goverment would never admit openly that civilian casualties were anything but an unfortunate by-product of attacks on industrial areas, there is little reason to believe that the general public would have complained had it been told otherwise.[113] The press accounts of the fire raids on Rostock and Lübeck of March and April 1942 left little doubt not only that these were not precision raids, but also that the widespread damage caused was to be welcomed. A.C. Cummings, a Southam News journalist, had reported that 'Rostock is an empty shell of gutted buildings,' and added that he had been assured by 'the best-informed source here in London'

... that such bombings will be spread over a 2,000-mile front in western Europe and deep into Germany itself, where every city in any way helping Hitler to victory will be left in ruins.

'The Nazis will get it back,' I was told, 'with a greater weight of bombs, with greater accuracy, with greater force, until troops at the front in Russia and the people at home wonder what the end of it for them will be.[114]

Such sentiments were not limited to those intimately involved with the bombing offensive. In far-off Ottawa, Mackenzie King noted in his diary that 'it was Hitler who started total war and [the] killing of women and children,' and he therefore had no sympathy for those suffering under the recent British attacks. Nor did most Canadians. A Gallup Poll taken at the turn of 1942 revealed that 57 per cent of them approved of 'bombing Germany's civilian population,' while only 38 per cent disapproved. 'Thus,' announced the Canadian Institute of Public Opinion, 'the ordinary citizens of Canada, who have never yet been called blood-thirsty, even by their bitterest enemies, give a majority approval of bombing civilians in Axis countries.'[*] Interestingly enough, there was the usual split along language lines, however. While 60 per cent of anglophones approved – nearly 70 per cent in British Columbia – only 47 per cent of francophones agreed with them.[115]

Unlike many, B.K. Sandwell, editor of *Saturday Night* and 'the ears and voice of Canadian liberalism,'[116] was worried about what men thought as they planned and undertook the business of mass killing. 'Should we go about that task in a spirit of vengeance, or of cruelty, or of vainglory and lust for power,' he cautioned, 'we shall be lowering ourselves to the level of the enemy and losing the right to regard ourselves as the agents of a more than mortal justice.' But in the end, like most of his contemporaries, liberal or otherwise, he had to side with killing. 'The defeat of Germany can only be brought about by killing Germans,' and if 'the object of these raids [is] to kill Germans ... it is a perfectly proper object ... The blood of such innocent persons as these is not upon us... The whole German people brought upon themselves whatever calamities may issue for them out of this war, when they put themselves under the kind of government which was bound to make such a war ultimately inevitable. It is our unavoidable task to make Germany suffer.'[117]

The politicians' tone changed somewhat as the tempo of bombing accelerated in 1943. When asked in the British House of Commons on 6 May whether the offensive against the Ruhr marked the end of attempts at precision bombing, Sir Archibald Sinclair (who had privately been 'delighted' with the idea of 'slaying in the name of the Lord' only a year earlier) flatly denied the allegation, observing that although 'it is impossible to distinguish in night bombing between the factories and the dwellings which surround them ... No instruction has been given to destroy dwelling houses rather than armament factories.'[118] This impression was reinforced three weeks later when, asked the same question, Labour MP and deputy prime minister Clement Attlee replied emphatically that 'there is no indiscriminate bombing ... The bombing is of those targets which are most effective from the military point of view.'[119]

The Canadian press seems not to have been concerned with such niceties. In its editorial of 31 May 1943, the *Toronto Telegram* declared that, while bombing undoubtedly meant 'misery and death for the people of the Axis nations ... it is better that they should be blotted out entirely than that the world should be subjected to the rulers they have tolerated so long, and there are many who hold that they must be made to know in full the horrors of war

---

[*] Fifty-one per cent approved of bombing Italian civilians and 62 per cent approved of bombing the Japanese.

if a new war is to be avoided.' The *Winnipeg Free Press*, meanwhile, had already belittled the few who demanded limitations on bombing because they were asking 'air crews still more to endanger their own lives so that they may perhaps save the lives of workers in industrial war facilities or living in the immediate neighborhood of those targets.'[120]

The aiming points that were selected for the battle of Hamburg belied Attlee's claim but, even though these were not public knowledge, the sheer scale of destruction achieved and bragged about was an open indication that bombing policy had changed, whether it was admitted or not. So was an Association Press report on 7 August which contentedly described the devastation inflicted on Düsseldorf. Making it clear that civilian casualties were heavy, the writer went on to explain that 'official ... totals can be multiplied three or four times without inaccuracy since only victims recognized during the most urgent salvage work are listed officially as dead. The stench in the streets is proof that many are never found and never listed.'[121]

However, it was one thing to 'de-house,' maim, and kill German civilians, and quite another, as Sinclair protested, to say publicly that 'the principal measure of our success' was defined in terms of the number of civilians killed and houses burnt and, moreover, that these were the premeditated and willful objectives of area bombing.[122] Even 'acreage destroyed' – Portal's compromise suggestion as the way to measure Bomber Command's effort without upsetting public opinion – went too far for Sinclair, who maintained that the government must continue to 'lay the emphasis – rightly in my opinion – on the fact that our prime objective is German war industry and transport ... and that damage to the built-up areas, though inevitable and huge, is incidental.'[123] Perhaps the best that could be hoped for, in explaining what were (or were not) the collateral effects of bombing, was expressed by Air Marshal Sir Richard Peck when he suggested that all would be well once the British public had been educated to the point where everyone agreed with Harris that 'an industrial city is in itself a military objective.'[124] In that case, of course, the bothersome distinctions between civilian and military casualties and between intended and incidental damage would be blurred – sufficiently, he hoped, so as to become altogether meaningless.

20

On to Berlin,
November–December 1943

In the four weeks following the 22/23 October raid on Kassel, Bomber Command attempted only one large operation, when 577 Lancasters and Halifaxes were sent to Düsseldorf on 3/4 November 1943. Although not included in the Casablanca or Pointblank lists,* Düsseldorf was home to several aircraft components plants and, in the view of MEW, was 'as important as Essen and Duisburg ... so far as the production of armaments and general engineering is concerned.' A raid on the city could, therefore, be justified and defended as meeting the spirit, if not the letter, of the two most recent Allied bombing directives.[1]

Target indicators were easily seen through the ground haze, and No 6 Group crews left the target area convinced that the raid had been a success. 'During the early stages ... fires appear to have been somewhat scattered but as the attack progressed a large concentration was observed around the markers and smoke could be seen rising up to 8/10,000 ft. Several large explosions are reported notably at 1947 hrs, 1950 hrs, 1955 hrs, 2003 hrs. Flames were observed rising to 8/900 ft from this last explosion and the glow of fires could be seen for a considerable distance on the return journey.'[2] Photographic reconnaissance missions mounted after the operation confirmed their opinion, as considerable damage was caused to both industrial and residential areas. Equally encouraging, while some German fighters intervened energetically, the overall 3.1 per cent and No 6 Group's 3.47 per cent loss rates were low for operations over this part of Germany, and were attributed to the successful feint attack mounted over Cologne.[3]

The most interesting feature of the night's operation, however, was the precision attack mounted concurrently with the larger area raid. Thirty-eight Lancasters, including twenty-five from Nos 408 and 426 Squadrons, were directed to bomb the Mannesmann-Rohrewerke tubular steel plant on the northern fringes of Düsseldorf, using G-H as their sole navigation aid and

* The twenty-two cities included in the Pointblank directive were Augsburg, Berlin, Bernburg, Bremen, Brunswick, Dessau, Eisenach, Frankfurt, Friedrichshafen, Gotha, Hamburg, Hanover, Kassel, Leipzig, Munich, Oschersleben, Paris, Regensburg, Schweinfurt, Stuttgart, Warnemünde, and Wiener-Neustadt, all of which had either aircraft components and assembly plants or were centres of ball-bearing production.

blind-bombing device. Although the failure rate of the new equipment was high (almost one-third of the G-H sets becoming unserviceable), all photographs taken by crews whose equipment was working were plotted within one mile of the aiming point. That was much better than the results commonly achieved with H2S or Oboe sky-marking, and the ORS at High Wycombe predicted that, with practice, the bombing accuracy achievable with G-H would eventually surpass Oboe ground-marking as well.[4]

The impact of the bombing on Mannesmann-Rohreworke's output was negligible. Although it had been accurate enough, damage to the plant's vital machine tools was estimated at less than 1 per cent, due largely to 'the loftiness of the buildings which caused the bombs to explode in mid air.' Moreover, despite the destruction of their houses, 'there was no lack of initiative in the workers … food was good and this was a very important stiffener to morale,' but these details were not known in London, and both the area raid and the precision attack were marked down as notable accomplishments which would bear repeating.[5]

Because of moon and weather conditions, the main force undertook only three bombing missions in the next three weeks and all three involved relatively small raids against precision targets, with mixed results. However, these precision raids were not a prelude of things to come so far as Bomber Command's principal effort was concerned. With the return of winter's long nights, made to order for deep penetrations, and the bad weather which was known to inhibit the Luftwaffe's night-fighter effort, Sir Arthur Harris had once again set his sights on launching an area offensive against Berlin. The force of Lancasters and Halifaxes available on a daily basis had climbed above seven hundred machines; H2S was being introduced into main-force squadrons at a steady rate (twenty-three would have Mark II H2S in April); and the impending formation of No 100 (Bomber Support) Group, with its Serrate-equipped night-fighters and specialized electronic warfare capabilities, promised (along with improved Monica, Fishpond, and Boozer warning devices as well as Corona and other forms of jamming) to keep casualties to about 5 per cent, even in a sustained offensive.[6]

In other words, or so Harris thought, Bomber Command had arrived at the point where it could make a decisive contribution to the war effort and, in a campaign lasting about five months – he expected to be finished by 1 April 1944 – it could add the German capital to the list of nineteen cities considered already to have been 'virtually destroyed.'[*] 'If the USAAF will come in on it,' he told Winston Churchill on 3 November, 'We can wreck Berlin from end to end. It will cost between us 400–500 aircraft. It will cost Germany the war.' Implicit in his claim was the idea that a cross-Channel invasion scheduled for May or June 1944 might yet be unnecessary.[7]

---

[*] Hamburg, Cologne, Essen, Dortmund, Düsseldorf, Hanover, Mannheim, Bochum, Mülheim, Köln Deutz, Barmen, Elberfeld, München-Gladbach/Rheydt, Krefeld, Aachen, Rostock, Remscheid, Kassel, and Emden. 'Seriously damaged' were Frankfurt, Stuttgart, Duisburg, Bremen, Hagen, Munich, Nuremberg, Stettin, Kiel, Karlsruhe, Mainz, Wilhelmshaven, Lübeck, Saarbrücken, Osnabrück, Münster, Rüsselsheim, Oberhausen, and Berlin.

The morale of Berliners was the primary objective of the proposed campaign, but the German capital was also an economic target of considerable significance. It accounted for almost 8 per cent of Germany's total industrial output, and, although not all of Berlin's production was vital to the Wehrmacht, there were twelve aircraft and aero-engine manufacturing and assembly plants as well as twenty-five major engineering and armaments facilities. The city was also home to 40 per cent of the German electronics industry and deserved its place in the Pointblank list for that reason alone.[8]

The trouble, however, was that the factories in and around Berlin were not the easiest to find or destroy. A number of important establishments, particularly those associated with the electronics industry, were housed in relatively small, unremarkable facilities that did not stand out as did, for example, the Krupp complex in Essen; because they were of reasonably modern construction, these buildings were not as susceptible to fire as the timbered structures found in cities such as Rostock and Lübeck. Indeed, Berlin in general was less vulnerable to fire and the threat of firestorms because of its many broad avenues and parks, and following the disastrous raids on Hamburg attempts had been made to fire-proof the capital's more vulnerable old buildings.[9]

No matter what the goal, since Berlin lay far beyond best Gee, Oboe, and G-H range, Harris had no choice but to rely on H2S as his principal navigation and bombing aid; and because he needed the protection afforded by cloud and moonless nights, most bombing would be done blind, by H2S alone or on skymarkers which were themselves dropped according to what was displayed on the Pathfinders' H2S screens. That was asking a lot not only of the equipment, in terms of both its serviceability and its effectiveness in highlighting aiming and other reference points, but also of its operators, who had to fiddle constantly with their sets to obtain and hold a useful image. 'The operation of the H2S was an art,' one navigator has recalled. 'When the operator put on too much power, the screen was all white.' Even when tuned properly, 'it was necessary to remember which blob was which city. This required almost continuous monitoring,' and, once lost, crews did not gain much help from H2S because the 'blobs had no real shape or form' and looked alike.[10]

The idea of savaging Berlin had been close to Churchill's heart since August 1940. The same could not be said of the secretary of state for air or, indeed, most members of the air staff. For them, it was a matter of inconsequential results at far too great a cost, especially when, as the DCAS observed, the Luftwaffe fighter force had not yet been neutralized and Berlin was the best defended of all German cities. Sir Charles Portal needed no tutoring on that issue. He had already agreed that the defeat of the Luftwaffe in the west was a cardinal objective in Allied strategy, and at Teheran in late November he would agree to commit 'the whole of the available air power in the United Kingdom, tactical and strategic ... to create the conditions essential' to launching Operation Overlord. A long offensive against Berlin which drew Bomber Command away from other targets would be of little use unless it achieved everything Harris expected of it.[11]

Furthermore, as he knew, the attempt to knock out the Luftwaffe and its industrial base was not going well. Harris had done very little so far, while the Americans had been losing heavily in recent weeks, the disastrous mission to Schweinfurt on 14 October having, in fact, reduced both the number and weight of their attacks against German targets. More disquieting still, on 4 November (the day after Harris addressed Churchill), the CAS received new intelligence estimates of enemy fighter production and strength that were, to put it simply, altogether staggering. Where Pointblank aimed at reducing the number of machines available in the west to less than seven hundred, it now appeared that the Luftwaffe would have 1500 in operational units there in December and as many as 1700 at the end of April 1944, just before Overlord was scheduled to take place.[12]

Despite the weight of opinion against opening a campaign against Berlin – Harris was supported only by Air Vice-Marshal F.F. Inglis, his chief of intelligence, who seems to have been a prisoner of his hopes and what some of his sources were telling him about the state of German morale – Portal chose not to heed the warnings proffered by his staff. Having sided with Churchill and Harris before on the question of Berlin, he did so again, but his endorsement was not open-ended. High Wycombe was told firmly that operations against the German capital would be stopped if they began to involve heavy casualties – and when it was time for Harris to turn his attention more directly to Overlord some time in the spring. For the moment, however, losses would be the determining factor.[13]

When, in his effort to support Harris, Inglis had observed that a prolonged and tightly focused offensive against Berlin was a good way for Bomber Command to outwit the enemy and avoid the casualties which worried his colleagues, he was uttering nonsense bordering on lunacy. True, there was evidence that the Germans had not fully recovered from all the effects of Window, although Harris was fully aware that the 'relief' it provided was 'very incomplete,' especially for those crews flying in the upper echelons of the bomber stream. It was known that the enemy had done very little to improve the all-weather capability of its night-fighter force, a welcome oversight on the eve of a winter campaign. And electronic jamming continued to pay off. If Corona was not preventing the German controllers from passing on information, it was clearly annoying and frustrating them, buying time in the process, while Airborne Cigar seemed to be working well enough against VHF radio broadcasts. Dartboard, a new jammer, would soon be introduced against the MF band. Finally, knowing nothing about SN2 radar, Inglis still believed that skilled crews using Monica and Boozer stood a good chance of avoiding interception.[14]

What he did not seem to understand, however, was that there were limits to what the current electronic warfare campaign could achieve. By late March 1944 the Germans were using nine speech and two Morse channels for their running commentary, and to blot out all eleven at the same time proved impossible.[15] He also failed to see that diversions were less effective – and

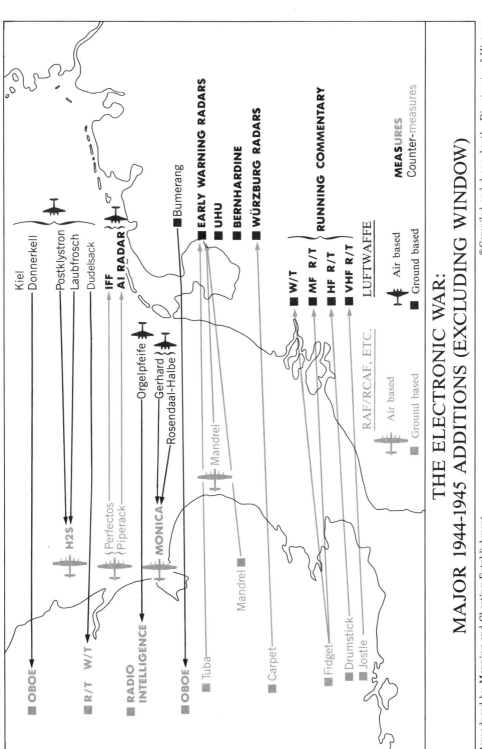

THE ELECTRONIC WAR:
MAJOR 1944-1945 ADDITIONS (EXCLUDING WINDOW)

Reproduced by Mapping and Charting Establishment.

©Compiled and drawn by the Directorate of History.

losses rose two-fold, on average – whenever the bombing lasted more than half an hour, something that was all too likely on raids to distant targets like Berlin unless time- and track-keeping were near perfect. Nevertheless, the greatest intelligence failure was the degree to which the air staff and Bomber Command underestimated German progress in finding tactical and technological counter-measures to British initiatives in the radio and radar war.

Generalleutnant Schmid had already strengthened the reconnaissance elements within his Jagddivisionen – both shadowers and route-markers – to help ease some of the confusion caused by diversions and jamming, while Laus equipment based on the Doppler principle was being added to fighter and Flak-control Würzburgs to penetrate Window. Beyond that, Bernhardine and Uhu – direct data-link systems employing, respectively, a coded ticker-tape and visual display on the AI screen to give the position of the bomber stream – were past the experimental stage and, when brought forward, promised to neutralize Corona altogether. Tinsel, the jammer aimed at the enemy's high- frequency commentary, had been neutralized by the simple introduction of more powerful radio transmitters, and that could be done across the entire radio band. These were in addition to Bumerang, Flamme, Flensburg, Naxos, Naxburg, Rosendaal, and Korfu equipment – which began to appear during the winter of 1943–4 and enabled the Luftwaffe signals intelligence and air-defence organizations to detect, plot, and in some instances home on to Bomber Command's Oboe, IFF, Monica, and H2S emissions, thereby decreasing the effectiveness of Window and the diversions and deception associated with it. Because of sheer volume, the electronic signature of a large main force using all its equipment could not be concealed. By the same token, the volume of H2S and other such emissions from only twenty or thirty would never approach that of a large main force. Little wonder, therefore, that as he probed his enemy's weaknesses, Schmid was consistently amazed by the way in which Bomber Command allowed its crews to switch on their electronic equipment for prolonged periods – oblivious, it seemed, to the fact that every minute's use increased the vulnerability of the bomber stream as a whole.[16]

In addition, no one at senior levels in the Air Ministry or at High Wycombe suspected the existence of Schräge Musik, the lethal upward-firing cannon that was now 'universally common in the night-fighter formations.' And while the expanding Flak defences were carefully recorded (the number of heavy guns in the west increased from 5500 in December 1942 to 8000 a year later), High Wycombe seized upon reports that the enemy was firing so-called Scarecrow flares to simulate aircraft blowing up, 'for deterrent effect,' rather than concede the possibility that German anti-aircraft artillery might have become more effective.* That was a terrifying prospect now that

---

* Crews were warned constantly not to 'play into the enemy's hands by allowing either a Scarecrow or an actual aircraft in trouble to affect their determination to carry out their task.' In fact, the Germans never used pyrotechnic devices for this purpose, and all alleged Scarecrows were genuine mid-air explosions: aircraft blowing up after being attacked by fighters equipped with Schräge Musik, bombs going off prematurely because of faulty or improperly set fuses, or bombs colliding in mid-air. (In December 1944 it was discovered that some 500-

Bomber Command was about to take on the most heavily defended city in Germany.[17]

So much for Inglis's bizarre expectation that the enemy could be outwitted, tactically or technologically, in a sustained effort against its capital.[18] Indeed, convinced since October that Bomber Command would soon focus its attention 'especially on Berlin,' Luftwaffe commanders had made its defence their 'point of main effort. [Air defence] would only be a problem if [Bomber Command] attacks small targets, as has been the case recently, and practises deception. If he does that, we can get very badly burned, as we have seen. As opposed to that, we're not going to let ourselves be fooled in his attacks on Berlin' There, Kammhuber had concluded (before his departure for Norway), apart from the weather, 'we have no great worries.'[19]

The battle of Berlin began on 18/19 November, and the plan of attack adopted at High Wycombe reflected much that had been learned (or surmised) about the enemy's defences over the past two months. Along with whatever electronic interference could be generated, spoofs and diversions would be mounted to draw enemy fighters as far away as possible from the target, and, whenever possible, depending on wind and weather, the route would be selected to avoid the beacons around which fighters gathered, waiting for the target to be identified and broadcast to them. In addition, as evidenced by the first night of the battle, Harris hoped to catch the Germans off guard from time to time by sending out two main forces of roughly the same size to attack two different targets. The larger, made up of 440 Lancasters (including twenty-nine from Nos 408 and 426 Squadrons) and assisted by four Mosquitoes, would attack Berlin, while the other, comprising 395 Lancasters, Halifaxes, and Stirlings, would make for Ludwigshafen, three hundred miles away to the south-west. Both streams were to cross the enemy coast at the same time, and they were to be concentrated as never before, the raid on Berlin being scheduled to last only sixteen minutes. To add to the confusion, the southern force was to fly north and east of its target, towards Frankfurt (where Mosquitos would conduct a feint attack), before doubling back to Ludwigshaven.[20]

The enemy controllers saw and reacted to both incursions, and split their defence in two. At Berlin, where the weather was bad and many fighters were ordered to land, only nine bombers were lost, 2 per cent of those dispatched, and the two Canadian squadrons emerged unscathed. The weather was better over Ludwigshafen, however, and twenty-three failed to return, 5.8 per cent of those sent. Seven of those lost were from No 6 Group, 7.4 per cent of its effort, and an eighth ditched in the Channel. The early return rate was uniform-

---

lb bombs released from the rear centre section of the Lancaster bomb bay had hit 2000- and 4000-lb bombs dropped from further forward and had exploded on impact.) However, it is not difficult to understand why the existence of Scarecrows was given credence at all levels within Bomber Command. It was convenient, even comforting, for everyone from Sir Arthur Harris down to have such a congenial and non-threatening explanation for otherwise terrifying and demoralizing occurrences.

ly high, largely because of the heavy cloud, fog, and icing encountered en route, and for some crews the intense cold was also a problem. The RCAF base at Middleton St George reported three men suffering frostbite as a result of temperatures as low as −40° Celsius: one was a rear gunner who had cut out a clear-vision panel in his turret, while the other two were navigators whose photo-flash camera hatches were exceedingly draughty. The Germans recorded only seventy-five high-explosive bombs falling on Berlin, of which eleven were duds or delayed-action, and no industrial buildings were destroyed. At Ludwigshafen, the bombing was 'widely scattered,' and, in No 6 Group's view, the raid was a failure.[21]

The chemical plants at Leverkusen were attacked the next night by 266 aircraft. The weather was still bad, grounding most of the target night-fighters, but Himmelbett missions were flown in Holland. Although the overall casualty rate was just under 2 per cent, No 434 Squadron continued its run of misfortune. It had lost two crews at Ludwigshafen, and two more (of the nine dispatched) failed to return from Leverkusen. The attack itself was a flop. The Pathfinders suffered a number of Oboe failures, the marking was not concentrated, and only one high-explosive bomb was reported as having fallen within the town. The return flight was also difficult, the weather having deteriorated, and by the time the bomber stream arrived over England fog had blanketed a number of airfields, forcing crews to find and land at alternate bases. Three machines crashed, including one from No 428 Squadron, but − after months of effort − a way had been found to reduce the dangers associated with landing in poor visibility. FIDO (Fog Investigation Dispersal Operation), which used pots of burning oil as a dispersant, was tried out at Gravely, and following its success was installed at other bases shortly thereafter.[22]

After a three-day break because of weather, more than 750 aircraft were dispatched to Berlin on 22/23 November, the largest number yet directed to the capital and, in terms of the tonnage of bombs dropped, the second heaviest attack so far − the heaviest being the Hanover raid of 22/23 September. No 6 Group contributed 110 crews. No diversions or feints were attempted, it being anticipated that the persistent fog and low cloud over northern Germany would continue to keep most fighters on the ground, and High Wycombe selected a direct route in order to facilitate an even greater degree of concentration than on the first raid. Bombing was to last just twenty-two minutes. In the event that fighters could get off the ground, Mosquitoes would be dropping decoy fighter flares to draw them away.[23]

The Germans were not fooled at all. Through electronic eavesdropping the bomber stream was picked up in good time, the controllers deduced that Berlin would be the target, and their appreciation was good enough to identify the five separate waves into which Harris had divided the main force. But the night-fighters were helpless because of the weather, and it was Flak that accounted for most of the twenty-six bombers shot down. No 434 Squadron had another bad night, losing two more crews − its tenth and eleventh in exactly one month − but there appears to have been no good or logical reason for the squadron's heavy casualties. It had been assigned to different waves in each of the raids mounted so far in November; it was never among the first over the target; and it had been in the last wave only over Ludwigshafen. Yet that was not a particularly dangerous place to be on 18/19 November, as No 428 and 429 Squadrons, also in the last wave, lost only one crew between them. Similarly, No 434 Squadron's 'wave-mates' at Leverkusen, again Nos 428 and 429, had lost only one crew. At Berlin, all the Halifax squadrons were in the same, middle wave, sandwiched between the Lancasters.[24]

The bombing was concentrated and accurate despite the cloud and fog. The Pathfinders had found the aiming point with H2S and their sky-markers were concentrated, well-placed, and visible. No 6 Group reported as well that a few had managed 'to see and bomb on the green ground markers cascading in the gaps' through the clouds they found over the capital. Over 1750 civilians were killed (including five hundred in one large shelter that received a direct hit), nearly 7000 injured, and 180,000 made homeless. With Telefunken, Blaupunkt, Siemens, and Daimler-Benz factories all severely damaged, Josef Goebbels was appalled by what he saw the next morning: 'Blazing fires everywhere ... Transportation conditions are ... quite hopeless ... Devastation is ... appalling in the government sector as well as in the Western and northern suburbs ... Hell itself seems to have broken loose over us.' Just as important, it was annoying, he observed, that 'the English fly in bad weather ... all the way to Berlin; but the German pursuit planes can't rise from the ground in Berlin because weather prevents!'[25]

Hans-Georg von Studnitz, who worked in the Foreign Ministry, was equally shattered.

We have lived through an indescribable experience and survived what seems like the end of the world ... The road leading to [the subway station in Rosenthalerplatz] consisted of nothing but a row of smouldering shops and offices ... Hundreds of people had taken refuge on the subterranean platforms, with such of their possessions as they had been able to salvage. Wounded, bandaged and their faces smothered in dust they hunched apathetically on their bedding or whatever else they had been able to bring with them ... All around the destroyed station in the Alexanderplatz the great warehouses were burning fiercely ... The *Zeughaus*, the university, the *Hedwigskirche* and the National Library had all been reduced to ashes ... In the Pariser Platz the headquarters of IG Farben was burning ... On the other side of the [Brandenburg] Gate the Tiergarten looked like some forest battle-scene from the First World War. Between whole battalions of fallen trees stood ... jagged stumps of oak and beech ... bereft of the crowning glory of their foliage ... Of the thirty-three houses in [our] street only three had survived the night. In the dim light of the dawning day we found, at the corner of the Tiergarten, some linen and a few clothes which our cook, Klara, had been able to rescue ... Everything else was irretrievably lost – our supplies of food, which we had built up over the years, three hundred bottles of wine, our furniture, everything.[26]

Similar accounts appeared in the neutral press, the Swiss *Gazette de Lausanne* commenting that Berliners were 'completely stunned by the catastrophe' and everywhere were saying that their city 'will become a second Hamburg.'[27] Stockholm's *Svenska Dag-bladet* meanwhile confirmed that the government districts had been hard hit. 'Hitler's residence near the Reich Chancellery received a direct hit and burnt fiercely, and so did the Foreign Office. The French Embassy received a direct hit and was set on fire. It was useless to try to extinguish it. The [former] British Embassy was hit and a fire broke out ... The Armament Ministry ... was burned down to the first storey. The whole of the Tiergartenstrasse looked like a curtain of fire even several hours after the raid.'[28]

Bomber Command conducted a smaller raid the next night, yet despite heavy jamming, the dropping of decoy fighter flares, and the imaginative use of Corona to order the night-fighters to land (by a German-speaking woman who had been standing by in case the enemy employed a female voice to give the running commentary), the loss rate was higher than before. Twenty of the 382 sorties dispatched were lost, 5.2 per cent. No 6 Group committed only nineteen, from Nos 408 and 426 Squadrons, of which one failed to return, but No 405 Squadron also lost one crew whose pilot had quite clearly exercised bad judgment. 'We were experimenting with Fishpond [fitted to H2S to warn of approaching fighters],' recalled Flight Lieutenant C.W. Cole, a navigator with forty-three operations to his credit, when the wireless operator 'reported that he thought there was an A/C approaching from [the] rear.' Since the gunners saw nothing, however, the pilot decided against taking evasive action. Several minutes later there were 'loud crumps' which the pilot took to be Flak, but as the bomber was near Groningen, away from all known anti-aircraft batteries, Cole protested this could not be. Still the pilot did not listen, left the automatic pilot switched on, and shortly thereafter a night-fighter attacked from the rear, causing an explosion that killed everyone except Cole, who became a prisoner of war.[29]

The damage to Berlin was considerable, adding to the sense of chaos in the German capital. The Felsch aero-engine works and the Siemens and BMW plants in Charlottenburg were destroyed; another 1315 civilians were killed, 6383 injured, and an additional 300,000 left homeless.[30] As the zoo had also been hit, 'fantastic rumours' were soon circulating. 'Crocodiles and giant snakes are supposed to be lurking in the hedgerows of the Landwehr canal. An escaped tiger made its way into the ruins of the Café Josty, gobbled up a piece of ... pastry it found there – and promptly died. Some wag, who drew uncomplimentary conclusions regarding the quality of Josty's cake-making, was sued for libel ... The Court ordered a post-mortem of the dead animal which found, much to the satisfaction of the confectioner, that the tiger's death had been caused by glass splinters found in its stomach.'[31]

Forty-eight hours later, on the morning of 26 November, there were signs that Berlin was beginning to recover. 'The Wilhelmplatz has already undergone quite a change,' Goebbels noted. 'The fires are out, the atmosphere is clear, smoke has disappeared. There is no blaze left to extinguish. In short, although one sees the bare ruins of buildings ... the most serious catastrophe has already been overcome. It is remarkable how fast everything goes. I thought it would

take weeks; in reality, only two days were needed to get back to some sem-
blance of order.'[32]

The city might still have been burning if a raid scheduled for 25/26 November had not been cancelled at the last moment because of weather. The supporting diversion to Frankfurt, however, proceeded as planned. It was not a
good effort. Heavy cloud covered both the route and the objective, obscuring
not only the target but also the Pathfinder flares and markers, and damage to
the city was slight. There were also strong winds, which may have pushed a
few off course, but on the whole they probably worked to Bomber Command's
advantage by delaying the arrival of some fighters and persuading others to
land in accordance with Corona instructions. Twelve bombers were lost (4.6
per cent), but for once No 434 Squadron had no concerns on that score. 'It was
really something,' the unit's diarist exclaimed, 'to have all our a/c and crews
return safely from a trip after the bad luck of the past few weeks.' Instead it
was the turn of Nos 429 and 431 to suffer. Both had experienced very few
casualties over the previous three months, but this night the former lost three,
and the latter two, of the six No 6 Group crews missing from the eighty-eight
sent.[33]

A new tactical wrinkle was introduced the next night. Two main forces were
involved, one making for Stuttgart (regarded as second in importance only to
Schweinfurt as a centre of German ball-bearing production)[34] and the other for
Berlin. Instead of being widely separated, however, they were to fly the same
route until just northwest of Frankfurt, where they would make their respective
turns to the south and north. That, the planners hoped, would initially persuade
the Germans that Frankfurt was again the target and lead them to concentrate
their fighters there; but if the ruse failed, it was hoped that one or the other of
the two bomber streams might yet escape notice altogether as it turned on to
the last leg of its route.

The manoeuvre worked wonderfully well and the bombers sent to Stuttgart
met very little opposition. Only six of 178 went missing, and all these losses
occurred in the vicinity of Frankfurt, before the two streams went their separate
ways. The bombing was considered to be 'highly successful,' with fires well
established on both sides of the Neckar River, although the actual damage to
the city was less than that caused by the 7/8 October raid and the only industrial plant knocked out was a Daimler-Benz factory which produced speed-
boats. Moreover, Hermann Göring happened to be in Generaloberst Weise's
command centre as the night's drama unfolded and, taking charge, the Reichsmarschall ordered all available fighters to Frankfurt. By the time the real situation became clear – even to Göring – it was too late to send many of the target
interceptors to Berlin, although there were some night-fighters over the capital.
About twenty SN2-equipped machines had been infiltrated into the bomber
stream long before it reached Frankfurt by Himmelbett crews under Ypsilon
(Benito) control in Holland, and these Zahme Sauen stayed with the bombers
all the way, accounting for most of the twenty-eight Lancasters missing from
the force committed to the capital. That represented a 6.3 per cent loss rate,
much too high for a night when Bomber Command's deception plan had

worked better than anticipated. (No 6 Group lost only two of thirty-nine sorties, although four returned early, including three from No 426 Squadron.) The operation nevertheless appeared to have been a success, RCAF crews reporting a 'fierce conflagration burning in a solid mass around the markers over a large area in the centre of the target' and 'another large fire' to the south-west. They were probably right. Officials in Berlin recorded 981 houses destroyed, 25,000 homeless civilians, and about fifty industry facilities severely damaged or destroyed.[35]

For many, the greatest danger experienced this night came on their return to England. Fog and mist blanketed almost all the airfields in the south, and as many as thirty bombers crashed or were crash-landed as pilots tried desperately to land. For once, No 6 Group's location in the northern part of Yorkshire was to its advantage, most of its stations enjoying relatively clear skies, and only one crew crashed on landing because of the weather. Another did so because of battle damage. Lancaster G of No 408 Squadron, piloted by Flight Sergeant R. Lloyd, temporarily lost one engine just before reaching Berlin, was hit by Flak, and then attacked by a Ju 88 which knocked out a second engine – this one permanently – and the mid-upper turret. Lloyd made it back to England, but another engine failed, the aircraft went into a spiral dive, and he eventually crash-landed in a sewage disposal site near Lincoln. The navigator, shattered by the experience, suffered a nervous breakdown and had to be invalided home to Canada.[36]

There were no major raids for the next four nights. The need to regroup after so many had landed away from their home stations caused one night's delay, and bad weather over England added three more. It was a welcome break, particularly for the Lancaster squadrons who had carried the main burden against Berlin so far (and would continue to do so for the rest of the campaign). Indeed, when operations resumed on 2/3 December Harris again dispatched a predominantly Lancaster main force to the German capital, supported by a Mosquito diversion to Bochum. High winds drove the stream north, scattering it en route, and the attack broke down almost from the beginning. The overall early return rate was 9 per cent, about normal for the kind of weather encountered, but No 6 Group's 22 per cent was very high. No 426 Squadron led the way again, with four crews coming back early, but No 432's three were not far behind.[37]

The Luftwaffe had no trouble handling this raid. Bomber Command had selected a direct route to Berlin, and the city was identified as the probable target nineteen minutes before the bombing began. The feint at Bochum, meanwhile, failed miserably. The Mosquitoes there were seen for what they were, while the shadow aircraft Schmid had inserted into the main bomber stream confirmed that it had flown past the Ruhr.[38] Altogether, forty bombers were shot down, 8.7 per cent of those dispatched. No 6 Group again fared better than average, losing just two of thirty-five machines, perhaps in part because the Canadians were gaining in experience. One crew from No 426 Squadron, for example, was singled out for the exemplary cooperation between pilot and mid-upper gunner in warding off multiple fighter attacks. 'While flying over the target, aircraft was coned by 50-70 searchlights … during which time they were attacked five times by enemy aircraft and damaged by *Flak*.'

The M[id-]U[pper] G[unner] first sighted a Ju 88 on the port quarter down at 400 yards … and gave combat manoeuvre corkscrew port and the fighter immediately broke off his attack. No exchange of fire … The second attack developed from starboard quarter down and the MUG … gave combat manoeuvre corkscrew starboard and again fighter immediately discontinued his attack and broke off … No exchange of fire. The third attack came from the port quarter down. Again MUG gave combat manoeuvre … and enemy aircraft broke off … Fourth attack developed from starboard quarter down … and MUG once again gave combat manoeuvre … and again fighter immediately discontinued his attack … The fifth and last attack developed from port quarter down … Enemy aircraft came in to 60 yards range and broke away to port beam above giving MUG sitting target … sparks and tracer were seen to ricochet off fighter and enemy aircraft dived steeply … The rear gunner was completely blinded throughout these five attacks by the blue master … and other searchlights.[39]

The next night the Halifax squadrons were committed in strength after nearly a week's layoff. Although nine Mosquitoes carried out a feint attack on Berlin, the main deception was once more included in the tactical plan developed for the main force. It drove straight for the capital and then turned south just fifty miles short of it – just as the Mosquitoes reached their objective. With their attention fixed firmly on Berlin, the German controllers did not notice the change of course at first, and realized that Leipzig was the actual target only when the city's Flak detachments reported bombs falling there. Weather also hindered the Luftwaffe's effort. High-altitude fog and dangerous icing conditions limited its response to about seventy sorties, all by experienced crews, and mostly confined to Himmelbett operations over Holland. Still, twenty-four bombers were lost, 4.5 per cent of those dispatched, of which twelve seem to have fallen to Flak over Frankfurt, where many had strayed on the way home. The same icing that thwarted the Germans also led to some early returns, but No 6 Group's 19 per cent rate was once more higher than average. No 432 Squadron had five crews return early, making eight in two nights, while No 429 recorded four.[40]

As Leipzig registered well on H2S, the cloud sitting over the city had little effect on No 8 Group's marking. The town centre, filled with crowded tenements, was also extremely vulnerable to fire, and suffered heavy damage as a result. An actor interviewed by the Swiss *Tribune de Genève* reported that 'the arrival of waves of bombers over Leipzig was so unexpected and rapid that the AA batteries did not go into action until a quarter of an hour after the first wave had passed over. Hundreds of houses were burning. The Opera House, the Dresdener Bank, the Reichsbank, the University, the central Post Office and the Exhibition Hall were all in flames and were later completely destroyed. All the principal hotels … and all the fashionable coffee houses in the centre of the city were also destroyed. It could be said without exaggeration that the whole of Leipzig had ceased to exist … On 5th December at midday it was still dark … The whole city was covered by black smoke which stung and made it impossible to breathe. A London fog was nothing compared with it.' Almost 200,000 people were left homeless. More important, however, a seventeen-building assembly plant used for the construction of Ju 88s was destroyed.[41]

This was the last large raid for twelve nights. All else being equal, and allowing for the weather, bomber operations ebbed and flowed with the lunar cycle, and Harris decided to stand his command down almost entirely during the December moon period. Apart from a large Gardening effort to the Frisians in which No 6 Group was not involved, until 16/17 December only Mosquitoes from No 8 (Pathfinder) Group and Whitleys and Wellingtons dropping leaflets and conducting radio counter-measures training were on operations over the continent.[42]

As it happened, the mid-December stand-down coincided with the week or two it usually took for High Wycombe and the six bomber groups to prepare and circulate their customary month-end reviews of operations, and those produced at this time gave the various staffs their first opportunity to make formal assessments of the progress of the battle of Berlin to date. The ORS at High Wycombe was unequivocally optimistic. Although no photographic reconnaissance flights had yet been made over the city, it seemed even from the 'usual sensational stories from neutral sources' that Berlin was being hit hard, sometimes very hard, and perhaps hard enough to cause morale to deteriorate. H2S, especially the Mark III variant, had proved satisfactory enough for area raids, and a solution had been found to the main cause of its 23 per cent failure rate in November – freezing in the scanner motor. Moreover, although navigators' wind-finding still left much to be desired, help would soon be available when specially selected and experienced crews from each group would begin to broadcast corrections to the predicted wind velocity and direction given to crews at their briefing.[43]

Just as important, losses over Berlin were holding at about 5 per cent, precisely as Harris had foreseen, and although they had risen above that figure on the last two raids there was no reason to suspect that this marked the beginning of an unwelcome trend. It was even assumed that some of the German successes could be written off as accidents, pure and simple. Twice, in fact, Schmid's controllers had guessed wrong about the target, but their error led them quite by accident to direct fighters to the bomber stream's turning point. Although the play of fortune obviously could not be predicted, High Wycombe felt reasonably confident that jamming, Intruders, and the escorts of No 100 Group would eventually gain ascendency over both Himmelbett and freelance fighters. In particular, Serrate, which homed on to Lichtenstein B/C radar, was now in quantity production, and it had taken only five weeks to develop Dartboard to jam the 100-kilowatt radio station in Stuttgart which was first used for night-fighter control in early November. When, however, the Germans began incorporating a musical code into shows broadcast over their domestic radio network – playing waltzes to signify raids on Berlin and accordion music to denote attacks on Leipzig, for example – 'legal objections were raised against the jamming of this kind of programme' for fear that the enemy would retaliate by jamming the domestic service of the BBC. Accordingly, the Germans were left free to use their code 'with little or no interference from the middle of December 1943 until it was superseded in the middle of February.'[44]

Although SN2 remained a mystery, hidden in the witches' brew of radio waves that now flowed freely over northern Europe, British intelligence had done reasonably well in figuring out how to attack the enemy's command and control organization and in identifying other 'active' systems. That the Germans would also use passive homing and eavesdropping equipment seems not to have been taken as seriously as it should have been, however, and at this stage the fact that H2S could be homed on to had not raised concern. Even when there was evidence that the Germans were reading IFF transmissions, Harris initially did nothing to limit its use, knowing that his crews took comfort from its alleged jamming properties. Eventually persuaded that it was costing him twenty crews a month, the AOC-in-C issued the appropriate warning in February 1944, but not everyone listened and IFF transmissions emanating from deep inside Germany could still be monitored in Britain well into 1944. However, Harris's phlegmatic reaction to the first warnings about the vulnerability of IFF so angered the assistant director of intelligence (science) that he was persuaded to use very strong words to condemn the AOC-in-C. High Wycombe, R.V. Jones charged, was guilty of an 'immoral practice' for the way in which it encouraged 'brave men to clutch at false straws in their hour of greatest danger.'[45] But perhaps false straws were important from time to time, so long as the overall cost was not counter-productive.

No 6 Group was reasonably pleased with November's statistics. Its overall loss rate was only marginally higher than Bomber Command's as a whole, a welcome change from just a few months before. As a result of better course- and time-keeping, the number of Canadian crews credited with bombing the primary target was now higher on average than in Nos 3 and 4 Groups. Only the early return rate was not altogether satisfactory. Too many times equipment that had purportedly malfunctioned in the air en route to the target was found to be 'OK on test' after a crew returned early, effectively absolving the ground-crew of any responsibility for the alleged fault; and there were too many borderline cases that stretched the permissible or reasonable limits for returning early. Some crews, for example, had aborted missions because their bombsight had failed, scarcely a fundamental concern in an area offensive conducted exclusively at night, often in thick cloud, with less than perfectly concentrated marking, and in which only half the bombs dropped blindly on H2S fell within a four-mile diameter circle.[46]

In Air Vice-Marshal Brookes's view, either his crews did not know how to use all their equipment or they were exhibiting a 'lack of offensive spirit.' When there was no medical cause for this lack of spirit and disciplinary measures were taken, the worst cases were deemed to lack moral fibre and declared to be 'Waverers.' Determined to deal 'more vigorously and rigorously

NO 6 GROUP RAIDS - WINTER 1943-1944
NORTH-EASTERN GERMANY

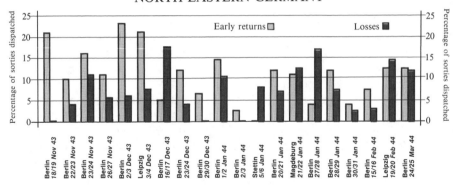

The Battle of Berlin, which lasted from 18/19 November 1943 to 30/31 March 1944, was undoubtedly Bomber Command's greatest test of the war. Although targets other than Berlin were attacked, never before had Sir Arthur Harris's crews flown so many long, fatiguing operations in such strength, in the worst weather of the year, to what was, arguably, the most heavily defended city in Germany. Harris predicted that the battle would cost him 500 machines, but boasted that Germany would lose the war as a direct result. In fact, 1117 aircraft were lost on all night operations during the period. Against Berlin itself, 472 of 8145 sorties dispatched failed to return or crashed in England upon their return, 5.79 per cent of the total. No 6 Group sent 1292 sorties to the German capital, losing eighty-three, 6.42 per cent of the total.

The early return rate was also high. There were, of course, always legitimate reasons for crews to break off their missions, some of which were laid down in Bomber Command's procdecures.

The two charts on this page, using figures extracted from No 6 Group's operational record book, show the shifting relationships between loss and early return rates, which (in the northeast, where the battle was generally more intense) were at their closest in January 1944. The early return figures are raw data, and no attempt has been made to determine which were legitimate and which may have reflected crews' manufacturing a reason not to complete a particular operation.

Both charts suggest that early return rates rose and fell in a predictable pattern. When loss rates rose, within a relatively short time early return rates rose too. Even against the less well-defended targets of southern Germany, the overall trend of early returns generally reflected the loss rate – as if it were a reaction it.

NO 6 GROUP RAIDS - WINTER 1943-1944
SOUTHERN GERMANY

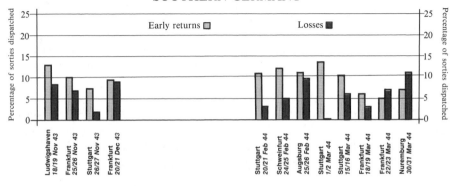

with certain types of early returns,' the AOC laid down the law. Henceforth, in by far the majority of cases, early returns would be sanctioned only if the weather or mechanical and technical malfunctions put a crew at risk. Even then, however, the legitimacy of a crew's decision to turn back would be determined largely by how far it had got into enemy territory, Brookes contending that it was usually safer to go on once the enemy's defences had been penetrated than to return alone. Similarly, although intercom failure between the rear gunner and the pilot was almost always reason to turn back because it impeded the latter's ability to take effective evasive action, a simple turret or gun failure generally was not. 'Shooting down an enemy aircraft is more a luxury,' the AOC observed, than 'a necessity.'[47]

Brookes was so exercised by the problem he saw before him that he wanted to penalize crews found to have returned early without due cause by compelling them to fly additional sorties beyond the current regulation thirty-trip tour – a suggestion High Wycombe turned down cold, on the very reasonable grounds that operations should never be made to look like punishment. Since a penalty of a kind was already built into unjustified early returns – the sortie in question did not count towards the completion of a tour – this was a sensible response, but one which offered nothing new to solve a problem that would shortly get worse throughout Bomber Command.[48]

Despite the blemishes in the record, in mid-December 1943 it was possible to construe the battle of Berlin, and therefore Harris's strategy, as on the way to achieving its objectives. 'This is the Twilight of the Gods,' a foreign diplomat was reported to have said after the second November raid; and since then, Bomber Command's intelligence staff added, playing with the metaphor, 'the twilight has deepened into darkness … mark[ing] the beginning of the end … of the reign, "nasty, brutish, and short," of the false gods worshipped by Hitler's Germany.' The enemy capital could apparently be attacked without disruptively heavy losses, and although it was clear that the city would not be crippled in a matter of days, the AOC-in-C had never promised quick results. It would take twenty to twenty-five raids, he had forecast in August, and about 40,000 tons of bombs. But after just five, if the neutral press and diplomatic corps could be believed, large sectors of Berlin's downtown core no longer existed. In addition, significant damage had been done of which no one in Britain was aware. The electronics industry in Berlin had been so severely disrupted (tube and condenser production having already fallen by 20 per cent and the manufacture of AI radars significantly delayed) that plans were being considered to disperse production, notwithstanding the additional inconvenience that such a major strategem would entail.[49]

Harris hoped that the steady accumulation and skilful presentation of evidence about what Bomber Command was accomplishing would give his Berlin offensive sufficient momentum to quiet any lingering opposition to it.[50] His critics had not yet been silenced, however, and the AOC-in-C was challenged strongly during the December bombing pause. The issue was ball-bearings. Identified by many as the most vulnerable point in the German war economy, the ball-bearing industry had become a *cause célèbre* among the 'panacea merchants' on the air staff whom Harris loved to deride. This was especially so since the Americans had suffered such horrendous losses at Schweinfurt in October – heavy enough to ensure they would not be returning there in the near future – and even more so as a result of Sweden's decision in early November to cut back its exports of ball-bearings to Germany. One or two raids, it was felt, might put Schweinfurt out of action for good. As a result, on 30 November the Air Ministry declared the city to be 'the outstanding priority target in Germany' and proposed that Bomber Command take it on.[51]

Confident that the Germans had taken the elementary precaution of stockpiling such essential items, Harris had never believed that ball-bearings were a critically important objective and had only reluctantly accepted the task of bombing the plant at Stuttgart in late November. Even less did he want to attack Schweinfurt. It was too small, he said, and too hard to find. Moreover, the whole program of area bombing (including the battle for Berlin) might be at risk if he succumbed to the blandishments of the director of bomber operations and his allies, and he said as much when he answered a second memorandum from the deputy chief of the air staff, sent on 17 December, urging him once again to attack Schweinfurt. Not only was such a raid not a 'reasonable operation of war,' but it was surely clear that 'the destruction of about one-third of Berlin, including large numbers of high priority factories, is of incomparably more value in preparing for OVERLORD than the destruction of the town of Schweinfurt would be.'[52] As it was, the campaign against the German capital had resumed the night before. It would take considerably more pressure before Harris, against his better judgment, committed his crews to an attack on Schweinfurt.

The two-week layoff during which this debate took place was welcomed by the Luftwaffe. Although there was no decline in the confidence displayed by its senior commanders as the battle of Berlin began, night-fighting in winter was a risky and fatiguing business, especially in the absence of the advanced electronic flying aids and navigational equipment enjoyed by the RAF and RCAF. Of the 127 night-fighters destroyed or missing in November and December 1943, only about one in three could be attributed to the direct result of enemy action, the rest being lost in the general course of operations (crashing while trying to land, for example) or on training and maintenance flights. Similarly, of the sixty-nine machines damaged over this period, just fifteen were due to enemy action. Bomber Command was waging an unintended but surprisingly effective war of attrition against the German night-fighter force which would see the latter's overall casualty rate rise to an average of 15 per cent of sorties between January and March 1944.[53]

Some of the non-operational losses noted above were undoubtedly due to fatigue. In the Luftwaffe there was no such thing as being 'screened' following the completion of an operational tour, so that apart from occasional periods of leave and (for a fortunate few) postings to administrative or other jobs on the ground, aircrew simply kept on flying until they were killed or incapacitated. Major Heinrich Prinz zu Sayn-Wittgenstein, holder of the Knight's Cross with

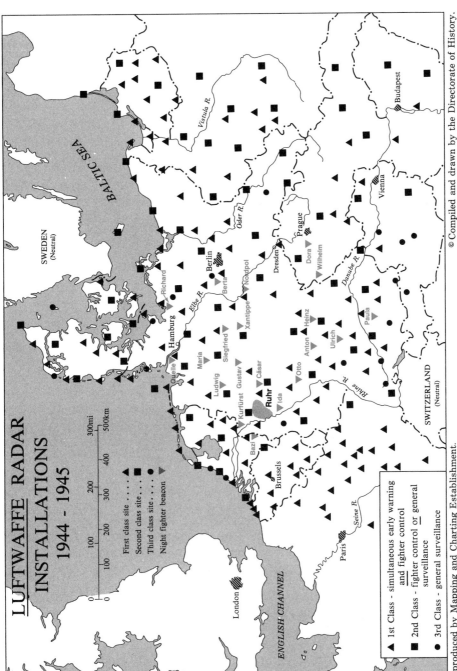

LUFTWAFFE RADAR INSTALLATIONS 1944 - 1945

	1st Class - simultaneous early warning and fighter control
	2nd Class - fighter control or general surveillance
	3rd Class - general surveillance

First class site . . . . ◢

Second class site . . . . ■

Third class site . . . . ●

Night fighter beacon ◢

SWEDEN (Neutral)

BALTIC SEA

SWITZERLAND (Neutral)

ENGLISH CHANNEL

London

Paris

Seine R.

Brussels

Hamburg

Berlin

Prague

Vienna

Budapest

Dresden

Ruhr

Quelle

Richard

Maria

Ludwig

Siegfried

Gustav

Kurfürst

Baz

Ida

Cäsar

Otto

Berta

Xantippe

Nordpol

Anton

Heinz

Ulrich

Paula

Dora

Wilhelm

Vistula R.

Oder R.

Elbe R.

Rhine R.

Danube R.

300mi

500km

© Compiled and drawn by the Directorate of History.

Reproduced by Mapping and Charting Establishment.

Oak Leaves and Swords and credited with eighty-three victories before his death on 21/22 January 1944, was a twenty-seven-year-old veteran of twenty-eight months as a night-fighter pilot when he met Georg von Studnitz at the Adlon Hotel in Berlin on 6 December 1943. Von Studnitz found him 'pale and haggard, and, like most young pilots, suffering from nervous strain.' So much so, in fact, that 'he has to take strong sleeping pills to get any sleep at all, and even then he wakes up every half hour.'[54] All German pilots were being drained, physically and emotionally, and, as the pressure increased and veteran pilots were used up, the need to replace casualties meant not only that there would be no rest for the remaining crews, but also that the amount of basic flying training given to new pilots was steadily cut back. The burden of providing effective defence consequently fell on those who, through weariness and fatigue, were able to give less all the time.[55]

The situation was not yet critical in early December 1943, however, and the Luftwaffe remained convinced that Bomber Command could be beaten. The single, most glaring weakness in Germany's air-defence organization, 1 Jagdkorps noted,[*] was the utter lack of offensive action over the United Kingdom, because bombers taking off, fully loaded, or trying to land with nearly empty tanks or battle damage, were in no position to take evasive action and were not protected by Window. Generalleutnant Schmid therefore proposed that intruder operations on a large scale should begin against Bomber Command using Ju 88s and He 219s equipped with the latest electronic equipment, but Steinflug (as this operation was called) was turned down by Hitler because, it was said, he preferred bombers to be shot down over Germany, where they could be seen by civilians.[56][†]

Meanwhile, the increased availability of SN2 radar persuaded Schmid that it was also time to begin pursuit (or route) night fighting on a grand scale. Although Himmelbett would continue in the west, and both Wilde Sauen and some of the twin-engined interceptors would still be sent to the target, henceforth his controllers would endeavour to insert as many fighters as possible into the bomber stream as far forward as possible. The enemy would then be under attack continuously from the North Sea all the way to the target and back – depending on weather and fuel. The choice as to which new equipment should be given priority flowed naturally from this decision: SN3 radar, which could be fitted with Erstling IFF and enjoyed twice the range of SN2; an improved and more discriminating Spanner infra-red detector to help the Wilde Sauen pick up exhausts from four-engined heavy bombers; and Uhu.[57]

---

* After Kammhuber's dismissal, Fliegerkorps XII was broken up into three separate commands: 1 Jagdkorps, which covered central and northern Germany and the Low Countries, moved its headquarters from Zeist to Dreibergen, and comprised three Jagddivisionen headquartered at Döberitz, Stade, and Deelen; II Jagdkorps, at Chantilly, part of Luftflotte 3 in France; and 7 Jagddivision, located at Schleissheim in southern Germany with a subordinate Jagdführer in Austria. 1 Jagdkorps and 7 Jagddivision were subordinate to the central command in Berlin, initially to Generaloberst Weise in Luftwaffenbefehlshaber Mitte, and subsequently to Generaloberst Stumpff in the renamed Luftflotte Reich.
† Something like Steinflug would be attempted only in February 1945, under the code Gisela, when it was far too late.

Schmid seems to have tried his hand at large-scale route night-fighting when Bomber Command returned to Berlin on 16/17 December.[58] Having carefully tracked the bomber stream across the North Sea, 1 Jagdkorps directed its crews to Bremen, where they would begin their pursuit. But heavy fog eventually grounded all but the most experienced, and the total effort for the night ultimately amounted to fewer than one hundred sorties, equally divided among Himmelbett, route fighting, and point defence. These were all tormented by very heavy jamming, from England as well as by the fledgling No 100 Group flexing its electronic muscles, and on many fighter control frequencies little could be heard except a bizarre collage of Hitler's speeches and readings of the poetry of Johann Wolfgang Goethe. Nevertheless, twenty-five Lancasters went missing, 5.1 per cent of the 483 dispatched, of which four (10 per cent) were from No 6 Group. The Naxos H2S homing device was immune to all of Bomber Command's electronic countermeasures and the jamming, though intense, was not all-pervasive; frequencies within five kilocycles of Bomber Command's group-control channels were left open to ensure that important signals could get through, and all jamming was suspended every half hour to allow the newly instituted wind-finders to transmit their readings to High Wycombe and for Bomber Command headquarters, in turn, to use these more up-to-date wind values to correct those given at the pre-raid briefing. As the Germans soon discovered, there was always at least one free channel for their fighter commentary, and several more during the winds broadcasts.

Although the attack was scheduled to last only fourteen minutes, in the hope of preventing outlying fighter units from responding in time, that degree of concentration was not achieved. Bombers were over Berlin for ninety minutes, and while more than one hundred large fires were started and 545 civilians were killed, only a handful of industrial facilities were destroyed.[59] Twenty-five bombers were lost to enemy action, but worse was to come. Low cloud covered all of Britain except Scotland and the West Country, and thirty-four crews, including three from No 405 Squadron, crashed their aircraft as they tried to land. That brought the night's total to fifty-nine machines, 12 per cent of those dispatched.

The weather finally cleared after this raid, making possible the first photographic reconnaissance of Berlin since the battle had begun, and the results added considerably to Harris's credibility.

Damage is widespread and severe. The area in which the greatest havoc is seen, due almost entirely to fire, stretches from the East side of the central district of Berlin to Charlottenburg in the Northwest and Wilmersdorf in the southwest and covers an area of nearly eight square miles. There is also severe damage in the important industrial districts of Reinckendorf and Spandau.

   In the Tiergarten district, which has been most heavily hit, whole island blocks can be seen completely gutted. The diplomatic and ministerial quarter adjoining the Tiergarten has suffered severely ... The great War Office building has been damaged, the part used as the secret service headquarters of the three armed services being gutted.

A large building West of the Zoological Gardens, probably the main Income Tax Offices, has been seriously damaged in one wing.

In Mitte, the central area, very important damage is seen along Wilhelmstrasse ... Here part of Hitler's Chancellery has been burned out, but repairs are already in progress. Other damaged buildings include the British Embassy, the old Air Ministry building, the Ministry of Food and Agriculture, the Ministry of Justice, the Foreign Office, the Treasury, the Ministry of Transport with adjoining State Railways Directorate, the old President's Chancellery and buildings known to be the headquarters of the *Gestapo* and official residence of Himmler ... Dr Goebbel's house in Hermann Goering Strasse has had its top floor burned out but roofing repairs are well in hand ...

In Charlottenburg the eighteenth century Palace of Frederick the Great and three large buildings in the Fair and Exhibition Grounds, now probably used as military stores, have all been seriously damaged. There is roof damage to the short-wave broadcasting studios ... Also in this district a number of technical colleges and institutes connected with the University have suffered as a result of fire.

Most important of the industrial works damaged are those situated in Tegel ... Here the great armaments factory of the Rheinmetall Borsig A.G (priority 1+) producing guns, torpedoes, mines, bombs, fuses, tanks, and armoured fighting vehicles has had many of its buildings severely damaged by fire and high explosive. The Alkett motor transport assembly works is one-third gutted and four large engineering works, manufacturing small arms and other weapons and together covering 129 acres, have had no less than 25 buildings destroyed or damaged. The great Siemens electrical engineering works (priority 1 plus) in West Spandau, severely hit in the August and September raids, shows damage to six more departments, while the Siemens cable works (priority 1 plus) has also been affected, but less seriously. The iron foundry and turbine assembly works of A.E.G. (priority 1) and the radio valve works of Osram G.m.b.H. (priority 2) both previously damaged, show further extensive damage. Fire has destroyed buildings in the important chemical works of Schering A.G. (priority 1) at Wedding, also part of a block shared by Pallas Apparate G.m.b.H. and A.E.G. (priority 1) producing aero-engine carburetors, motors and calibrating machines.

A considerable number of factories engaged in manufacturing aero-engines and aircraft components have been damaged, some severely. Included amongst these must be mentioned B.M.W., Argus, Dornier and Heinkel, priority firms, all of which have important works in Berlin. Of the damaged factories producing electrical and wireless equipment, Bergmann Electricitäats Werke A.G. (priority 1) and Dr. Cassirer A.G. (priority 3) are probably the most vital.

In addition to the priority firms some eighty identified and numerous unidentified or small works, laboratories, storage and repair depots have been damaged, a few being almost completely destroyed. These industries cover a wide range and their products include vehicles of all types, engines, engine components, armaments, machine tools, electrical equipment, precision tools, various metals, chemicals, dyes, plastics, ceramics, fabrics and foodstuffs. Commercial premises listed in the damage summary number over forty but many more have been omitted as being of small importance ...

Four gas works (all priority 2) and two gas storage depots have been damaged, two gas holders ... being burned out. The gas works at Tegel is the largest in the city and here the coal and coke storage depot, a retort house, and two screening houses have been damaged. Other damaged public utilities, where services must have been considerably affected as a result of the raids, include seven water works and pumping stations, five tramway depots and the main postal depots in the central area. Damage to military property includes, besides the War Ministry buildings, five or six barracks and several military stores and motor transport depots ...

An examination of the statistical analysis of damage shows that over 1250 net acres of business and residential property has been affected in the fully built-up and 50 per cent to 70 per cent built-up areas covered by these sorties and that over 60 per cent of the buildings in the Tiergarten district alone have been destroyed. Very substantial figures are also given for Charlottenburg, Mitte, Schöneberg, Wedding, Wilmersdorf and Reinckendorf.

All told, it was concluded, Berlin had suffered a 'deadly wound' from which it would not recover, and morale there was collapsing. However, as had been found in London, the suffering and hardships endured by Berliners were actually drawing them closer together and may even have strengthened their morale.[60]

The capital was spared further attacks while this photographic reconnaissance program was under way, and on 20/21 December Harris sent a large main force to Frankfurt supported by a small diversion to Mannheim. Forty-one crews were lost from the former, 6.3 per cent of those sent, among which were ten (8.6 per cent) of the 116 sent by No 6 Group. The Mannheim raiders, in contrast, all returned safely. Trying to explain the discrepancy, High Wycombe drew the obvious conclusion that the diversion had failed and, in one sense, it was right – although not for the obvious reason. Bomber Command's flying discipline was so poor that the two formations were identified as belonging to one badly scattered main force making for Frankfurt, and the enemy had simply sent his fighters where the concentration of bombers was heaviest. I Jagdkorps had also made another attempt at pursuit night-fighting, and in mainly clear skies the technique worked wonderfully well. Returning bomber crews reported combats all along the route to the target, and some described lanes of fighter flares at least a hundred miles long.[61]

Bomber Command returned to Berlin twice before the end of the year. Because of poor weather in northern Yorkshire, the only RCAF squadron involved in the 23/24 December raid was the Pathfinder Force's No 405 which, along with the rest of No 8 Group, had a difficult time trying to find the aiming point through heavy cloud. The bombing was therefore scattered, but even so some worthwhile damage was done, including the Erkner Vereinigten Kugellager ball-bearing works at Niederbarnim, outside the city limits in Mark Brandenburg.[62] Four nights later, however, the Canadians were out in strength, contributing 143 sorties to a 712-strong main force. This was the second largest raid on Berlin to date, and the largest single effort by No 6 Group. Losses were light, just twenty overall (2.8 per cent) and five (3.5 per cent) among the Canadian crews. Always eager to ascribe that kind of result to its own efforts, High Wycombe was inclined to credit the imaginative routing scheme adopted for the raid for the unusually low casualties. Supported by small groups of Mosquitoes, the main force conducted feints against both Magdeburg and Leipzig before turning northwest, and this, it was felt, had confused the enemy. In fact, it was the weather which kept the Luftwaffe at bay.[63]

Four Canadian crews who returned safely had been attacked by fighters. In three cases Monica provided little or no warning of the fighter's approach, illustrating its limitations, and only the vigilance of rear and mid-upper gunners enabled their pilots to take evasive manoeuvres in time. In the other, Monica did provide ample warning, but it was the mid-under gunner who first saw the fighter 'silhouetted against cloud, below, passing from Starboard to Port.'[64]

This 'mid-under' position was a recent modification adopted by No 419 and other non-H2S squadrons to address the threat of fighters approaching from below. It also reflected the fact that despite Harris's persistent and powerful pleading, little had been done to improve bomber armaments since 1939. Bomber crews consequently remained prisoners of decisions taken, reversed, and sometimes reversed again as High Wycombe constantly re-evaluated what constituted the greatest threat and how it might be countered. Indeed, in June 1943 Harris himself had gone so far as to suggest that his bombers should be stripped of all their armament in order to increase their speed and altitude, but shortly afterwards he was asking the turret designers and aircraft manufacturers to meet his essentially conflicting demands for more guns, heavier guns, and better vision, all without adding significantly to the aircraft's gross weight or altering its centre of gravity.[65]

In fact, by the autumn of 1943 there were as many as seven designs under active consideration for an improved rear turret as well as two proposals for belly mountings. Each had the support of one or another agency within the RAF and MAP, and each in its own way was something of a disappointment. The .5-inch under-mounting for non-H2S aircraft, for example, could not be produced on schedule because components from the United States failed to arrive.[66] At about the same time, a two-gun tail blister designed for the Lancaster and giving a good view behind and below was found to be 'crude and, with its almost complete lack of protection for the tail gunner ... quite unacceptable,' while the Frazer Nash FN82, once championed by Harris for its heavier .5-inch armament and because it would take the radar-assisted gun-laying device (AGLT, code-named Village Inn) then under development by the Telecommunications Research Establishment (TRE), would not be available until 1945. But that no longer concerned the AOC-in-C, who had recently decided that the FN82 did not offer his gunners a good enough view below.[67]

Chaotic would not be an unfair way to describe the situation, and to help sort things out a conference was called for 3 November, the very day that Harris had submitted his Berlin memorandum to the prime minister. However, there were no quick fixes to be had. Work would continue on the Rose turret, Harris's preferred choice because of its tremendous downward view, but these would still be individually handcrafted, and therefore in short supply, until

1945. Overriding the AOC-in-C's objections, the conference also decided to push on with the FN82 and a new .5-inch ventral (or belly) gun, but both projects were already well behind schedule and it was not clear that the gap could ever be closed. In the meantime, it was left to individual squadrons (like No 419) or groups to do what they could to help their gunners.[68]

As things turned out, much of this talk was academic, for as early in 1944 the whole program to improve bomber defences began to unravel. For one thing, the interest of key Air Ministry staff had started to turn to the Pacific war and to the development of the Lancaster IV, with its six .5-inch and two .303-inch guns, so that the RAF could participate in 'full-scale daylight bombing as undertaken by the Americans.' More important, almost none of the projects approved on 3 November 1943 actually worked. The AGLT prototype had so many defects that operational testing had to be put back until August 1944, and after that the supply to Bomber Command was not expected to exceed a miserly six sets a week. Then, quite unexpectedly, the project foundered altogether. Although the technology required for the AGLT was eventually successful, which was in itself an admirable achievement, the weapon system depended on a perfectly discriminating IFF – if it were only 99 per cent accurate it was estimated that gunners using Village Inn would shoot down four times as many bombers as night-fighters – and that proved to be beyond TRE's capabilities.[69]

The Rose turret, meanwhile, vibrated so badly when the gunners opened fire that they could not take accurate aim unless the rate of fire of their guns was reduced from 750 to 400 rounds a minute. Work on the FN82 was simply falling further behind schedule, leading one staff officer to lament that the Americans could 'develop, produce, and operate more progressive defence armament in six months than we can do in two years.' Even the relatively simple task of coming up with a .5-inch belly gun for the Halifax had proved difficult. The design tested in No 4 Group over the winter of 1943/4 not only detracted seriously from the aircraft's performance and offered a disappointingly narrow angle of fire, but with temperatures of -21° Celsius being registered around the fitting, the gunners – not surprisingly – complained constantly of the cold.[70]

There was nothing very new about gunners complaining about the cold, however. While efforts were made to improve the delivery of engine heat to the rear turret in Merlin-engined bombers (the goal being to maintain a temperature of 0° Celsius at 25,000 feet), little progress was achieved. The situation was much worse in the Halifax III, which had air-cooled engines. Fitting turrets with space heaters seemed an obvious solution, but the gravity-fed Gallay of British design would not work during evasive manoeuvres while orders for the American-designed Selas had to be abandoned because of production problems in the United States. Experiments with American-designed Flak jackets conducted over the winter of 1943/4 left a number of gunners more uncomfortable still. British turrets were generally too small and cramped for the cumbersome garments, and since it was predicted they would save only one casualty in a thousand, 'the weight of the jacket, its interference with movement, the additional fatigue induced and the consequent reduction in efficiency' were not considered to be worth the meagre additional protection.[71]

As the armament program foundered, Harris became increasingly bitter at the quality and quantity of aircraft supplied to him by an industry which, because of the looming manpower crisis, was scheduled to release half a million workers to the armed forces in 1944–5. As usual, the Halifax bore the brunt of his criticism, particularly the much-vaunted Mark III, which was supposed to correct most of the flaws associated with earlier models, and with which many RCAF squadrons would be supplied beginning in early 1944. Following their first operational flights on the type, however, many crews had complained that their maximum ceiling of 18,000 feet was little better than the Stirling's, and almost all had suffered from the cold, some navigators recording temperatures as low as -27° Celsius around their compartment.[72] Moreover, its efficiency as a bomb-carrier seemed likely always to be considerably lower than the Lancaster's. Based on recent operations, Harris told MAP on 2 December, 'one Lancaster is to be preferred to four Halifaxes, [which were] an embarrassment now and will be useless for the bomber offensive within 6 months if not before. ... [A]ll attempts to boost up the Halifax to the Lancaster class will fail – if only because the Lancaster will by then be boosted beyond the class at which the Halifax has long aimed and always fallen far short of. I issued the same warning about the Stirling. It is now useless and flooding the market. I cannot too strongly warn you yet again that a continuance on Halifaxes leads us straight and soon for disaster.'[73]

The Air Ministry and Sir Wilfrid Freeman had heard this all before, but in the past they had usually been able to point to the imminent appearance of yet another new Halifax variant to mitigate the AOC-in-C's concern. During the winter of 1943/4, however, it was difficult to avoid the conclusion that the Halifax was, at best, a mediocrity when compared to the Lancaster. Indeed, when production costs and training time were considered along with payload and loss rates, it could be shown that the Halifax required more than eleven thousand man-hours of labour to deliver one ton of bombs while the Lancaster needed only about four thousand. Or, put another way, while Lancaster squadrons were dropping about 107 tons of bombs per missing aircraft, their Halifax colleagues could do no better than forty-eight.[74]

Sir Archibald Sinclair seems, finally, to have been persuaded that the Halifax was not living up to the claims once made for it, and he indicated his willingness 'to pay a heavy price in Halifaxes ... to see a greater production of Lancasters.' So did the Cabinet War Committee on Supply, which decreed (on 3 January 1944) that while all heavy bomber production remained a top priority, whenever possible preference in the allocation of labour and material resources would go to the Lancaster. Evidence against the Halifax III meanwhile continued to mount. Notwithstanding its improved flame dampeners, thought to have solved one of the main defects of the Mark II and V, at one point the Mark III's loss rates actually exceeded those of its predecessors. As a result, the director of bomber operations argued – and the Cabinet Defence Committee (Supply) agreed – that once Bomber Command was operating in support

TABLE 7
Crew Position and Survivability in Bomber Command Aircraft, January–June 1943[75]

Crew Position	Lancaster	Halifax	Wellington
		per cent	
Pilot	9.6	20.8	14.6
Navigator	13.8	36.2	21.0
Wireless operator	11.9	32.5	18.5
Flight engineer	12.4	34.0	—
Bomber-aimer	13.2	31.4	18.5
Mid-upper gunner	8.5	27.3	—
Rear gunner	8.0	23.4	14.6
Overall	10.9	29.0	17.5

of the army, after the invasion, Halifaxes should be used exclusively 'in conditions of shallow penetrations and [against] lightly defended targets.' Strategic work, in other words, would be reserved for the Lancasters.[76]

In the event, it did not take long for at least some Halifaxes (the Marks II and V) to be withdrawn from operations over Germany. After the disastrous raid on Leipzig on 19/20 February, when their loss rate approached 15 per cent, Harris felt compelled to reassign the seven squadrons (including Nos 419, 428, 431, and 434) equipped with those variants to Gardening or to bombing transportation targets in France.[77] Damning as the Halifax's loss rate was, however, individual Halifax crew members had a much better chance of escaping from a stricken aircraft than their Lancaster colleagues. The Avro design featured not only a less roomy interior and smaller escape hatches, but it also tended to catch fire and break apart in mid-air more readily than the Handley-Page. Thus, while 29 per cent of Halifax crew members survived being shot down, the corresponding figure for the Lancaster was just 10.9 per cent. Pilots, who usually stayed at the controls while the rest of their crew tried to bale out, generally had the worst survival rate of all (see table 7).[78]

Although it is exceedingly unlikely that air crews in England knew anything at all about these differences in survival rates, they were certainly aware of the higher loss rates on Halifax squadrons. Such unofficial comparisons were discouraged, of course, on the grounds that it served no useful purpose to suggest, let alone confirm, that Halifax crews faced greater risks. The official line, as Flying Officer Reinke discovered in informal briefings during his visit to No 6 Group, was that there was little to choose between the two principal bomber types, although at night, in the pubs, it was clear that 'the boys know the score ... tho' only in a general way' when they declared their 'dislike and fear of the Halifax.' Indeed, Sir Arthur Harris had realized in February 1944 that there would be 'trouble' when it came time to re-equip Canadian Lancaster II squadrons with the Halifax III, such was the feeling against the latter, but he had had no choice in the matter, now that the Lancaster II was obsolescent and Lancaster IIIs were not available in the required quantities.[79]

RELATION BETWEEN LOSS RATE
AND PERCENTAGE OF CREWS
SURVIVING 10, 20 AND 30 OPERATIONS

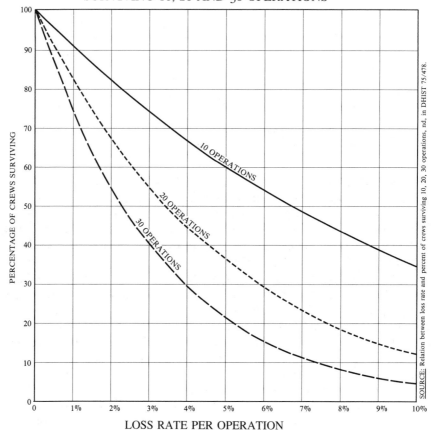

LOSS RATE PER OPERATION

This graph depicts air crews' chances of survival given a constant loss rate
(which never happened) or the average loss rate for the period in which they
flew. No. 6 Group's loss rate of 5.5 per cent from March–June 1943, which suggested that only 18 per cent of crews would survive thirty operations, was cause
for considerable concern at Bomber Command Headquarters and in Ottawa.

The Germans, too, had learned essentially the same thing. A downed airman from No 426 Squadron told them that there had been considerable resistance (and some refusals to fly) when his unit had converted from Lancaster
IIs to Halifax IIIs in April 1944.[80] The squadron diary makes no mention of
anyone's refusing to fly on operations in April or May 1944, but it does not
hide the fact that the conversion 'is not looked forward to with very much
enthusiasm by our experienced crews who would like to complete their tour
of operations on Lancaster II a[ir]c[raft.]' To make matters worse, 'It was
strongly suspected that the Squadrons turning over their [Halifax IIIs] to this
unit had passed on the ones which had given the most trouble from a serviceability standpoint.'[81]

No 432 Squadron made the same conversion in February and March 1944, and one pilot recalled that as he looked over the unfamiliar type it seemed he was switching to a machine that had been 'thrown together rather than designed.'[82] The squadron diarist acknowledged that there was a serviceability 'snag' arising from the change of aircraft in February, but by March things seemed to have sorted themselves out; and, by the end of May, No 426 Squadron's commanding officer was observing that while 'the older crews still tend to heave a sigh for the Lancasters, now that experience is being gained with the Halifaxes everyone seems to be quite happy about the whole thing.'[83] That was probably not far from the truth. As squadrons received new crews who had no experience with Lancasters, there would be fewer who had anything with which to compare the Halifax. There is also considerable and persuasive anecdotal evidence that, for their own peace of mind as much as anything else, many aircrew were only too happy and ready to be persuaded that the bomber type they flew was a sturdy and reliable machine as they took seven hours or more to make the return trip to heavily defended targets, listened to the casualty figures broadcast the next day over the BBC, saw the empty chairs in their mess, and then took another trip that night.

As we have seen, No 6 Group was due to become a Lancaster formation once Lancaster Xs began to arrive in England from Victory Aircraft in Toronto. With the Halifax selected as the Canadians' intermediary heavy bomber, the ratio of Lancaster to Halifax squadrons in the group was thus determined largely by the rate of Canadian production – and on that score there was only disappointment.[*] After the *Ruhr Express* bombed Berlin with No 405 Squadron on 27/28 November 1943, its first operational sortie, no other Lancaster Xs saw active service until No 419 Squadron began converting to the type in March and April 1944. Even though output from Victory Aircraft rose to between twenty and thirty machines a month through the summer, in May 1945 only three additional squadrons, Nos 428, 431, and 434, were flying Xs on operations. Once Lancaster Xs began to be supplied, however (following the logic of the ultimate plan for No 6 Group) Lancaster I/IIIs were made available, and by the end of the war four squadrons were equipped with that type.

Management and labour problems in Toronto were one reason for the delay in the Lancaster X program, but there were others. The Bendix radio equipment originally ordered for Canadian Lancasters proved unpopular in No 6 Group, and by December 1944 it was being replaced by British-designed Marconi equipment.[84] In addition, Canadian-built Lancasters required over a thousand man-hours of work to bring them up to operational standard after they were

---

[*] The Bristol Hercules-powered Lancaster IIs produced in limited numbers as a hedge against a collapse of Rolls Royce Merlin engine production and supplied to Nos 408, 426, and 436 squadrons were stopgaps, and all three would convert to Halifax IIIs in 1944. The Lancaster IIs were nevertheless allocated to No 6 Group, an erstwhile Halifax formation, at a time when the Halifax II/V, the obvious alternative, was becoming increasingly suspect after Sir Arthur Harris acknowledged that the Canadians had been promised – and deserved – at least one squadron of Lancasters even before the Lancaster X was operational.

delivered to England because of modifications developed in the United Kingdom and which could not be incorporated quickly into the production lines at Victory Aircraft.[85] There were also changes in Canadian specifications, including, among other things, 'the substitution of larger skin panels on the fuselage, substitution of self-tapping screws for plug rivets in the skin attachment to spar booms, substituting a metal fin leading edge for the original wooden one, introducing a metal door in place of wood, introducing Acme threads in all trim-tab jacks instead of square threads ... In cases where a modification affected more than one component and/or system, a trial installation was sometimes made before putting it into the production line.'[86]

By far the most important change came with frame KB 783, which was fitted with an American-designed Martin mid-upper turret armed with two .5-inch Browning machine guns. This modification had been cancelled by Avro in Britain because of engineering problems, but went ahead in Canada, where Victory Aircraft had already begun retooling.[87] At first, the handling characteristics of KB 783 did not seem up to standard because of the new, heavier turret, and it had to be tested at Boscombe Down before the modificiation could be approved. It passed its flying test, and the Martin turret continued to be fitted, but upon further examination it was found that the Canadian-supplied ailerons were not exactly the same as their British counterparts because of confusion in the supply of drawings, and resolving that problem caused further delays in the provision of Lancaster Xs to RCAF squadrons overseas.[88] By January 1945, however, there were few causes for complaint except the slow rate of production.[89]

Concerns about tardy delivery of Lancaster Xs were probably put on hold, however, as 1943 turned to 1944 and No 6 Group celebrated both the New Year and its first birthday. In twelve months it had grown from eight squadrons to thirteen, mounted 7355 sorties, and dropped 13,630 tons of bombs. Twice in the past month it had sent more than a hundred crews to Berlin. Although the Canadian loss rate was still higher than most, the gap between it and the Bomber Command average was narrowing. The serviceability rate had climbed from 64 per cent in January 1943 to 78 per cent in December, while the flying accident rate had been almost halved.[90]

Whatever anniversary celebrations were in order were enhanced when a heavy raid scheduled for Frankfurt was cancelled late on the afternoon of New Year's Eve. Happily, New Year's Day was also a holiday for the Halifax squadrons, but there was no rest for many of those flying Lancasters. With a reasonable weather forecast over England – 'Variable strato-cumulus in well-broken layers, base 1,500 feet, tops 6,000 feet ... good to moderate visibility' -and cloudy conditions over Germany, High Wycombe decided to attack Berlin again, with a diversion on Hamburg. The original route was to have passed over Denmark, away from the Dutch Himmelbett sites, but a delay occasioned by changes in the weather forecast forced a more direct approach across the Netherlands. Route-markers would be dropped near Bremen and Brandenburg; Window would be used 'at the rate of one bundle every minute to a point forty miles from the target; two bundles every minute from that point to the target, and back; and one bundle every minute for the rest of the route home, until the supply was exhausted.' Zero hour was scheduled for 0300, British time. Four hundred and seventy-four aircraft, including thirty-seven Lancasters from No 6 Group, would be equally divided among three waves scheduled to bomb four minutes apart in an operation designed to take no more than twenty minutes over the target. The bombload was set at one 4000-lb high-explosive bomb and clusters of 4-lb incendiaries, and crews were instructed 'if possible to aim ... at the centre of the TI green; if, however, cloud conditions prevent TIs being seen, main force aircraft should aim their bombs at the centre of all [red] flares with green stars whilst holding an exact heading of 093 degrees.'[91]

After making its calculations of the amount of fuel to be carried and deciding upon the altitudes at which crews would operate, No 6 Group Headquarters sent its instructions to the bases and stations concerned at 1:30 P.M. That gave some time for ground crews and the fitters, riggers, and mechanics of the maintenance sections to swing into action.

Many of the ground trades really worked hard and had a hell of a life on a bomber station. The fitters and riggers repaired aircraft and engines night and day in all kinds of weather. They worked out in the open or under a bit of canvas shelter. The armourers hauled and loaded bombs, changed bomb loads, fused and defused bombs, rain or shine, at all hours of the day ... [When a raid was laid on the] armourers would manhandle the [bomb] trolleys under the plane and raise the bombs into the bomb bay. They had a hydraulic powered winch most of the time but on occasion it was powered by hand. The fuel trucks ... loaded the specified amount of fuel to get the plane to the target and back. There was never very much to spare ... Another truck would deliver the type and amount of Window ... While all this was going on members of the ground crew who looked after an aircraft had to check it thoroughly. Engines would be run up and tested; radio men, radar men and instrument men would call at each aircraft and check the various pieces of equipment and instruments. The camera would be checked and loaded with film. Ammunition would be put in the turrets. The many thousands of rounds for the tail turret were carried in canisters near the bomb bay and ammo tracks ... ran along the fuselage to the tail turret.[92]

Those who had complained of problems on their last operation would almost certainly make a pre-operational test flight of their machine to ensure that the necessary repairs or adjustments had been made. Depending upon how long this test flight took and when the operational order was received at their station, aircrew might have three or four hours to themselves before beginning their pre-operational routine. They drew their flying clothes and made a last inspection of their machine about five hours before takeoff, and then ate supper. Afterwards it was time for the main briefing, when the target and route were identified, the 'met' officer gave his weather and wind forecasts, the intelligence officer provided what was known about enemy defences en route and decoys in the target area, and the navigation and bombing leaders outlined the Pathfinder procedures (and colours) for the night. Separate, more detailed, and complex briefings were subsequently given to the pilots, navigators, bomb-aimers, and radio operators and then, about an hour or so before takeoff, crews began to head out to their machines again. The raid having been delayed somewhat, on 'New Year's Day' most got off the ground just after midnight on 2 January.[93]

Berlin, Mining, and Preparations for Overlord, January–April 1944

On the night of 1/2 January 1944 the ninth of what Bomber Command liked to call 'the great winter raids' eventually involved 421 Lancasters, some squadrons (as often happened) finding it impossible to make ready the number of machines Sir Arthur Harris had called for. Berlin was again covered by cloud rising to 18,000 feet, but it was largely because the Pathfinder backers-up failed to exploit 'the good concentration of flares ... achieved by the primary markers' that 'the attack soon became scattered' and bombs fell all over greater Berlin. The main force also did a poor job of time-keeping, only 7 per cent of crews bombing within the four-minute span allocated to them, and the raid consequently lasted an hour instead of the scheduled twenty minutes. That added to No 8 Group's woes, as the markers had to try to keep the target properly illuminated much longer than had been anticipated.

The next day German radio spoke only of 'damage in residential areas.' That was a convenient way of saying nothing likely to benefit the enemy while reiterating the main point of Joseph Goebbels's propaganda campaign, which charged Bomber Command with engaging in a premeditated program of unadulterated terror bombing. In some respects at least these broadcasts were not far off the mark. Surveying the effects of the raid, German officials wrote off only one industrial structure and listed two more as damaged, along with two military installations. So far as the 'damage to residential areas' was concerned, however, on this occasion only twenty-one houses had been destroyed.

The one positive feature of the operation from High Wycombe's perspective was that the enemy's fighters had not been a factor over Berlin. Despite the cloud, however, it was a different story en route to and from the target as twenty-eight bomber crews failed to return, 6.7 per cent of those committed. The Luftwaffe lost fifteen fighters, 9 per cent of those scrambled, most of them due to flying accidents caused by the poor visibility.[1]

All thirty-one of No 6 Group's aircraft returned from this raid, but their good fortune did not last. Not counting the Pathfinders of No 405 Squadron, who lost ten crews in January 1944, the RCAF mounted a further 586 heavy-bomber sorties against area targets over the course of the month and forty-eight of them (8.2 per cent) went missing, a figure 1.6 per cent higher than the

Bomber Command average. No 434 Squadron led the way, losing eight crews in just three nights' work, while No 427 Squadron, in the process of converting from Halifax Vs to IIIs, had the highest loss rate, 14 per cent of sorties. Among the Canadian Lancaster squadrons (who flew every raid to Berlin) the missing rate was 5.4 per cent, about half that of the Halifax squadrons who were exempted altogether from five of these missions.[2]

A number of factors contributed to January's higher overall toll. For one thing, the element of strategic surprise was lacking from Bomber Command's effort as fully half of all sorties were directed against Berlin. Moreover, two of the other targets, Leipzig and Magdeburg, involved equally deep penetrations which relied on H2S for both navigation and target-marking – a situation tailor-made for pursuit night-fighters equipped with SN2 radar and the Naxos H2S homing device – and, indeed, losses among aircraft equipped with H2S were 'unusually high,' illustrating both its vulnerability to detection and the extent to which the Germans relied on its emissions to find the bomber stream. Convinced, however, that the threat from Himmelbett was 'too great, even with WINDOW,' to permit dispersion, Harris demanded still greater concentration, further enriching the night-fighter crews' already abundant hunting grounds. With a running commentary now being broadcast over all the bands commonly available to radio, their chances of success had increased many-fold since the autumn.[3]

For all that, the details of each month's raids were unique. On 2/3 January, for example, a sharp turn to the north, near Bremen, fooled some controllers as well as the fighters already assembled over the Hanover beacon and there was little route interception past that point. Since Berlin was identified as the target forty minutes before bombs began to fall, however, most of the Hanover force arrived over the capital before the last TIs had burnt out. Twenty-seven Lancasters were shot down, including ten Pathfinders from No 8 Group (of which two were from No 405 Squadron). The Luftwaffe lost ten fighters, accidents again being the main culprit.[4]

On 5/6 January, when Stettin was the objective, the operational plan called for the bomber stream to make directly for Berlin and then to turn north, towards the target, at a point seventy miles short of the capital. When the raid was over and only sixteen crews (4.5 per cent, and none from No 6 Group) were missing, Bomber Command happily assumed that the Germans had indeed been 'completely deceived': the fighters' 'aerial flarepath' was 'laid on to Berlin ... in the early stages of the attack,' just as had been anticipated, and it was not until much later that they appeared in the target area.[5]

In fact, the low casualty rate could not be attributed exclusively to Bomber Command's tactics. Radars north and west of the capital had broken down, with the result that the turn to Stettin was not seen on the ground. Additionally, and compounding the failure, fighters already in the bomber stream neglected to report their own change of course northward. The Wilde Sauen, meanwhile, remained over Berlin, where they tried to engage the small Mosquito diversion sent to the capital. Although none of this was known at High Wycombe, there was no reason for celebration when a less than sterling performance by the enemy – for whatever reason – still resulted in the loss of sixteen bombers.[6]

After a nine-day moon and weather pause, and following a surprisingly costly (7.6 per cent) raid on Brunswick, Bomber Command returned to Berlin on 20/21 January. Assisted by multiple diversions to Düsseldorf, Kiel, and Hanover, and flying a new route far to the north, the large main force of 759 Halifaxes and Lancasters was nevertheless intercepted over the North Sea, where it had been picked up by the radar picket-ship *Togo* as well as by land-based stations. Although bad weather limited the number of fighters scrambled, thirty-five bombers were shot down, 4.6 per cent of those sent. For its part, No 6 Group lost nine crews, or 6.25 per cent. Three of these came from No 434 Squadron, which should have been safely wrapped up in the middle of the bomber stream, in the third of five waves.[7]

In Berlin, 243 Germans were killed, 465 injured, and another 10,000 rendered homeless; five industrial plants were destroyed and another ten severely damaged.[8] While the Air Ministry announced, simply, that there had been another heavy and concentrated attack on the German capital, Toronto's *Globe and Mail* was well satisfied. 'Berlin has been blasted again. Nine RCAF squadrons helped carry the 2,300 tons of bombs which smashed the German capital Thursday night. So, Berlin will be destroyed, beaten into the dust, a thing despised. The thrill, the sheer delight, which news of the Canadians' contribution to these raids sends through the nation each time it is repeated comes not from the satisfaction of destroying. It resides in the pride which all the people have in the courage and stern idealism of the young men of the RCAF.'[9]

The object of a number of feints and diversions in recent weeks, and home to important steel, synthetic oil, and aero-engine plants, Magdeburg was the target for 645 crews on 20/21 January, this time in clear weather – the precise conditions the pilots of 1 Jagdkorps had been waiting for. They made the most of them. Altogether 169 fighters were scrambled, many making contact before the bomber stream crossed the Dutch coast, and twenty-two Lancasters were shot down, 5.2 per cent of those taking off. That was bad enough, but the Halifax squadrons lost thirty-five crews, a staggering 15.6 per cent of those dispatched. Perhaps the most chilling news, however, came when a damaged Lancaster from an RAF Squadron struggled back to base and provided the first concrete evidence that the Germans had equipped their fighters with upward-firing guns.[10] The Lancaster in question had been 'homebound from Magdeburg at 23,000 feet when fighter flares were seen and an attack developed. Warning was given by ... MONICA and a Ju 88 was sighted directly below the rear turret at 500 yards. Our rear gunner opened fire and the Lancaster corkscrewed. The enemy aircraft followed for about 45 min[utes], positioning itself below the rear turret so that neither gunner could bring his guns to bear. On several occasions the enemy aircraft opened fire causing damage which was later examined and found to have been caused by 20mm H[igh] E[xplosive] and A[rmour] P[iercing shells] from a direction almost vertically below.'[11] Yet this crew had been more than a little lucky. In the forty-five minutes during which they were stalked and attacked, the fighter could not finish the job while, in the same span of time, the veteran Prinz zu Sayn Wittgenstein accounted for five enemy aircraft before he himself was shot down and killed.

Warrant Officer I.V. Hopkins, pilot of a No 419 Squadron Halifax, also seems to have been subject to Schräge Musik in the course of a singularly harrowing mission, but word of his experience had to await the end of the war and his repatriation from a prisoner-of-war camp.

After trying to climb for 50 min[utes], we were at 5,000 feet. A loud bang shook a/c so I had [the] Eng[ineer] check everything but all was O.K. Upon looking out the wheels could be seen so I dropped them & then I put [them] up again but [they were] still visible. We crossed enemy coast at 13,000 feet and couldn't get higher, so had [the] B[omb] A[imer] jettison some incendiaries [and] the aircraft went to 20,000 feet very nicely. We bombed target and trying to get required speed had to put nose down. Just after turning near Leipzig a fighter cut in front from p[ort] to s[tarboard]. I told R[ear]/G[unner] to watch for him but immed[iately] got [instruction to] dive s[tarboard]. The enemy did not fire but stbd. outer [engine] burst into flame as soon as evasive actions started ... engine was feathered & fire put out. Couldn't hold above 10,000 feet and had just got back on course when attacked from below, getting us from stem to stern down stbd. alley-way, mid-under hit. R/G saw enemy go thru' his cone of fire. Put a/c in dive stbd, but were hit before it reacted. Levelled out and had another attack, three of guns u[n]/s[erviceable], Eng. had reported the stbd. inner heating up and again upon starting evasive action the stbd. inner burst into flame, cannon-shell hit selection box and shrapnel hit me in leg & shoulder, also wiping out some instruments, not noticeable because I was too busy feathering one engine. A fire was in bomb-bay and somewhere in fuselage back of Eng[ineer.] The a/c was very difficult to hold, Eng. then reported port petrol tanks leaking. I had throttled through the gate, but couldn't maintain height or slow descent and port engines were heating so I ordered crew to bale out at approx. 5,000 feet. I stayed to make sure all got safely out and then made my very difficult exit ... It immed[iately] rolled over and dove onto deck.

All seven crew members jumped safely and were captured, but in a tragic mistake the navigator, Flight Sergeant W.E. Mackenzie, was killed on 19 April 1945 when Typhoons attacked the POW column in which he was being herded east from Stalag 357 at Fallingbostel, near Hanover.[12]

Bomber Command now took a five-day break from area bombing because of poor weather over England which also prevented most practice flying. Ground-crews, who were rarely idle, took advantage of the layoff to give their machines a thorough check.[13] By 1944 maintenance had been largely centralized at station rather than squadron level in order to increase efficiency, although the new policy was not entirely welcome: aircrew generally believed that squadron loyalties would ensure more careful servicing than that provided by a maintenance pool under base control, and the servicing echelons were encouraged to maintain close affiliation with their parent squadrons.[14] It was, perhaps, an academic argument. 'Whereas Canadian aircrew are as good [as] but not better than other Empire aircrew,' John Fauquier informed Air Marshal L.S. Breadner, AOC-in-C at Overseas Headquarters since 1 January 1944, 'Canadian groundcrew have been showing themselves to be unquestionably the best in the world.'[15]

Some, like Flight Sergeant S.A. McKenzie, No 408 Squadron, were rewarded for their efforts – in his case, with the British Empire Medal. 'This non-commissioned officer,' commented the chief technical officer at Linton-on-Ouse, 'has built A flight up into the best organized and smoothly functioning section on the station. Their record of serviceability and operational failures are second to none.'

A very hard working and conscientious man with a thorough knowledge of his trade, he above all has a vast amount of initiative which he does not hesitate to display... While other flights have complained loudly, and called for help ... whenever they had more than eight aircraft to look after, Flight Sergeant McKenzie has cheerfully prepared as many as twelve for operations quickly and efficiently without a murmur of complaint. This was not an isolated case either, but occurred daily throughout the period that 'B' Flight was converting to Halifax aircraft and 'A' Flight was looking after all the Lancasters.[16]

Some lost their lives, and others took extreme risks in trying to save doomed comrades.

Corporal [P.W.] Butler [No 433 Squadron], on the morning of December 19th, 1943, was running the engines of aircraft 'Q' Queenie in conjunction with Leading Aircraftman O'Connor and Leading Aircraftman McEvoy when aircraft 'C' Charlie crashed while taking off and landed on top of the aircraft in which Corporal Butler was working. Both aircraft immediately burst into flame. [LAC] O'Connor was rendered unconscious by the crash and Corporal Butler, despite the intense flames, attempted to remove him through the pilot's escape hatch, but was unable to do so. In his attempt to remove his comrade, he stayed in the cockpit of the aircraft despite intense flames and smoke until almost overcome. It was only then that he thought of self-preservation and ... crawled out of the pilot's escape hatch and jumped from the nose of the aircraft into a pile of flaming debris, thereby breaking both his heels. He proceeded to crawl on his hands and knees through the flaming mass. Corporal Butler showed outstanding courage and determination in his effort to save his fellow worker.

He was Mentioned in Despatches.[17]

Controversy, meanwhile, was swirling around High Wycombe and the Air Ministry. Following a late December meeting with Sir Arthur Harris and senior American commanders to determine how Pointblank (and more particularly the offensive against the German aircraft industry, code-named Argument) should proceed in order to support the forthcoming cross-Channel invasion, on 3 January the CAS had issued a genial reminder to Harris. Bomber Command not only had a definite, direct, and significant role to play in Overlord, but 'the

criterion by which bombing [operations] are judged' would soon 'be the extent
to which they assist OVERLORD and not as present the extent to which they
weaken Germany's ... power to make war.'[18]

Harris, however, seemed quite prepared to ignore or challenge Portal's
message.* Stettin, attacked two days later, was not even on the Pointblank list,
while on 13 January Harris not only misrepresented Allied strategic planning
in responding to Portal, but also questioned whether switching Bomber Command's role would serve any worthwhile purpose. If Overlord 'must now
presumably be regarded as an inescapable commitment,' he observed with ill-
concealed disdain, 'the best, indeed the only effective support which Bomber
Command can give ... is the intensification of attacks on suitable industrial
areas in German as and when the opportunity offers. If we attempt to substitute
for this process attacks on gun emplacements, beach defences, communications
or dumps in occupied territory we shall commit the irremediable error of
diverting our best weapon from the military function for which it has been
equipped and trained ... as an independent strategic weapon.'[19]

By now, however, his remonstrations that he be allowed to maintain the
purity of strategic bombing as practised by Bomber Command were becoming
increasingly unpersuasive. As the deputy chief of the air staff pointed out,
Harris's definition of 'suitable industrial areas' was so loose that he could
probably wriggle out of taking on the enemy's aircraft factories and ball-
bearing industry if he wished. And although it was partly true – as Harris had
observed, time and again – that technical limitations prevented Bomber Command from isolating precise objectives within the built-up area of cites like
Schweinfurt, Sir Norman Bottomley was convinced that it should still be able
to ·'destroy the town ... and at the same time the ball-bearing factories,' and
the AOC-in-C must be told as much.[20] Needing little persuasion on this score,
on 14 January the CAS instructed Harris more forcefully to 'adhere to the
spirit' of the Pointblank directive.[21]

Brunswick, a legitimate Pointblank target, was attacked that night with
heavy (7.6 per cent) losses. But as we have seen, on 20/21 January Harris
returned to Berlin and then made for Magdeburg the next night – a city which,
like Stettin, was not on the Pointblank list and was chosen for attack only to
facilitate future deceptions and spoofs when Berlin was again the target. As
such the raid may have made good operational sense, but coming so soon after
Portal had asked Harris to adhere to the 'spirit' of Pointblank, it moved the
CAS to issue even firmer directives. On 27 January the AOC-in-C was told that
Schweinfurt, Leipzig, Brunswick, Regensburg, Augsburg, and Gotha were to
be Bomber Command's next objectives, and they were to be attacked in that
order.[22]

Protesting that the weather in the south was not right and, besides, that it
took more time than the air staff realized to work out an appropriate plan to
bomb small towns, Harris ignored the instruction to take on Schweinfurt.

* 'At certain levels of responsibility,' the French general Maurice Gamelin once observed, 'it
is no longer a matter of giving orders but of persuading.'

Rather than waiting until the weather had improved (conserving his strength in the process) or mounting a raid against other cities directly associated with the ball-bearing or aircraft industries, he sent his main force to Berlin three times between 27 January and the end of the month. These operations involved a total of 1710 heavy-bomber sorties (219 from No 6 Group), of which 112 failed to return, an overall loss rate of 6.5 per cent, and 8.2 per cent among the RCAF squadrons. Tactically, those operations mounted on 27/28 and 28/29 January followed the same pattern. Large Gardening efforts and diversions were sent to Heligoland and other areas in the north up to three hours before the main force took off, and they succeeded in provoking a premature reaction from at least some of the German controllers. On the third raid, however, Harris decided not to employ any diversions, choosing instead to send the main force on a route designed to suggest that it was the pre-raid Gardening operation and that the real bomber stream would follow some hours later. This tactic also worked, momentarily at least, as the German controllers held their forces back. No fighters were sent out over the North Sea, and only a handful of Lancasters were seen to have been shot down on the way to the target, but there was nothing in Bomber Command's repertoire of tactics and tricks to impede 1 Jagdkorps' effort on the return route, and thirty-three sorties failed to return.[23]

Together, these three raids killed about 450, left 200,000 homeless, and damaged (but did not destroy) some plants and facilities owned by Siemens, Askania, Telefunken, Agfa, Kodak, Zeiss-Ikon, Daimler-Benz, and Rhein-metall-Borsig, among others.[24] Since photographic reconnaissance flights over Berlin were not possible because of cloud cover, High Wycombe had no idea what had actually been accomplished – and nothing to deduce from the bombing photographs plotted at Stettin and Magdeburg: while two-thirds of crews were estimated to have been within three miles of the aiming point at the former, only one in ten at the latter managed to do as well.[25] Stories in the Swedish press which were picked up and quoted extensively by *The Times,* however, suggested that the blows against Berlin had been quite hard.

There is no longer any block of buildings in Berlin that has escaped damage, says the Berlin correspondent of *Dagens Nyhter* ... after three days virtual suspension of communications ...

Fires so large and numerous that it takes several days to put them out, and many persons are buried in cellars; but life still goes on, although in a very primitive form ...

Describing his walk home [the Berlin correspondent of *Allehandra*] says he spent a full hour wandering past blocks where the fires were still burning and through streets where the pavements were encumbered with mountains of furniture and household goods ... Even for those who lived through the catastrophic Berlin days around November 23rd, the impressions of the bomb-storm then pale before what we have experienced in these days.[26]

BOMBING ACCURACY IN NIGHT OPERATIONS, 1942–44

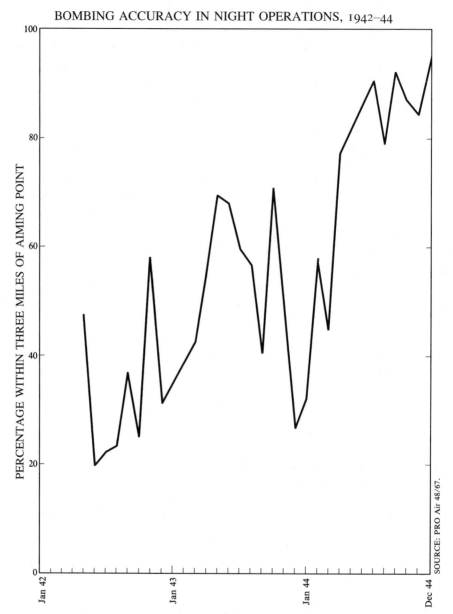

Percentage of sorties against primary targets bombing within three miles of the aiming point on raids for which photographic evidence was obtainable – excluding precision attacks against marshalling yards and coast defences in France.

Although this graph is correct in showing a general improvement in bombing accuracy from 1942 to 1944, it probably exaggerates Bomber Command's overall performance. the bombing on raids for which no photographic evidence was available (usually those conducted in the worst weather), and which are therefore not plotted here, tended to be less accurate.

Perfect for public consumption, such reports were certainly welcome ammunition in Harris's struggle with the panacea mongers. Aware, perhaps, that the time for decisions concerning the use of air power and the inauguration of a Second Front were approaching, and that it was necessary to build up the positive features of his offensive against Berlin, his own intelligence staff soon proclaimed that 'the morale of Berliners has sunk even further into the "Slough of Despond."' At the same time, however, they had to admit that, since German citizens had no real freedom to oppose their government, whatever despondency Bomber Command might be causing was unlikely to produce direct action helpful to the Allied cause. Moreover, when photographic reconnaissance flights over Berlin were at last possible, they revealed much less damage than had been anticipated; but, reflecting the primacy of hope over experience so prevalent at High Wycombe, everyone was cautioned against 'taking too gloomy a view' of the disappointing results.[27] The enemy had at least been bloodied, if not bowed, and if left alone Bomber Command might yet compel Germany to submit. Berlin, in short, was worth the effort.

If Sir Arthur Harris was able to take comfort from ambivalent results, his main opponent did not. Generalleutnant Josef Schmid estimated that his night-fighters were shooting down about 5 per cent of Harris's bombers – a remarkably accurate guess – and he saw no reason for this figure to fall. The British had not adopted significantly new tactics or electronic counter-measures in recent months, and their H2S transmissions were still being read clearly.[28] But Schmid was also aware that despite their success, his night-fighters were powerless to break up attacks before they reached the target area, much less force Harris to call off his offensive altogether. Accordingly, unless the night-fighter arm was strengthened, Berlin (and other cities) would continue to be bombed, sometimes heavily. In mid-January, therefore, he had asked for substantially increased production of SN2 radar, Naxos, and other homing devices, only to be told that except for SN2, supplies of electronic equipment for air defence had low priority.[29]

The same was true of aircraft. Fighter production in general fell from July to December 1943; and while the switch to pursuit night-fighting had paid obvious dividends, its success ultimately depended on having interceptors fast enough to overtake the bomber stream from behind or from the flanks. The early models of the Ju 88 had enjoyed such an advantage until they were laden down with all the external paraphernalia required to wage electronic warfare: but by early 1944 only the G-1 and G-6 series were entirely satisfactory and their production at times took second place to that of the Ju 88 bomber variants destined for the Russian front. Of the other fighters in service or soon to be so, the He 219 remained the clear favourite despite its requirement for long runways. Capable of taking on Mosquitoes as well as heavy bombers, it was also a dedicated night-fighter design unlikely to be stolen away by other branches of the Luftwaffe. However, no one could be found who would call a halt to the manufacture of obsolete machines like the Me 110 and Do 217, or such obvious disappointments (for night-fighting purposes) as the Me 210 and 410, which continued to roll off the assembly lines instead of the far more useful He 219.[30]

Finally, wastage among fighter crews, mostly because of accidents and fatigue, was becoming a significant factor. In December, 1 Jagdkorps lost twenty-four crews, 3 per cent of sorties, but that figure increased to fifty-nine in January (4.2 per cent), fifty-three in February, and then jumped to eighty-seven (6.7 per cent) in March. The Wilde Sauen suffered even heavier losses over this period – about 45 per cent – although many came on daylight sorties Herrmann's pilots were now flying against the Americans. These casualties were offset to some extent by the output from the training system – 1943 was a good year for the production of night-fighter pilots, seeing a surplus of 268 over the number of aircraft built – but that was unlikely to continue. Indeed, forecasts for 1944 called for a deficit in the supply of pilots in terms of the number of new aircraft received – not good news when, as we have seen, night-fighter losses were rising. Even more important, a large number of experienced and very skilled hands – zu Sayn-Wittgenstein, with eighty-three victories, Hauptmann Manfred Meurer (sixty-five), Oberfeldwebel Heinz Vinke (fifty-four), Major Egmont Prinz zur Lippe-Weissenfeld (fifty-one), and Major Alois Leuchner (forty-five) – were killed between 21 January and 14 March, and they could not be easily replaced. Night-fighting was a highly specialized endeavour in which this relatively small group of *Experten* had accounted for a hugely disproportionate share of enemy aircraft destroyed. Little wonder, therefore, that Schmid was not optimistic.[31]

At the Air Ministry the air staff's distress, dismay, and anger with Harris's fixation on Berlin and his insolent failure to do what he was told, had mounted considerably with the resumption of attacks on the capital in mid-February.* Even Air Vice-Marshal F.F. Inglis, ACAS (Intelligence), in the beginning the one senior staff officer to have fully supported Harris's Berlin campaign, was finally being forced to admit that Bomber Command's assault on morale would produce results only through a 'slow process of attrition' and even so would not, by itself, 'exercise a decisive influence on the outcome of the war.' More to the point, when Harris returned to Berlin in mid-February, D-Day was less than four months away. Yet largely because of weather, the Argument portion of Pointblank, calling for a devastating and concentrated Allied offensive against the German aircraft industry, had not yet begun despite general agreement that it had to be completed by 1 March in order to free the Anglo-American heavy bombers for other operations in support of Overlord. 'At long last,' however, 'on 19 February 1944, the weather over the German fighter factories began to open up,' and 'Big Week,' as Argument came to be known, began

---

* Like Sir Bernard Montgomery after Alamein, Sir Arthur Harris had been raised to almost mythic proportions by a media desperate to find and exhibit British success stories during a war in which successes had, as yet, been all too infrequent. Moreover, the AOC-in-C appeared to enjoy the complete confidence of an even greater mythic hero, Winston Churchill, so that it was exceedingly difficulty for Sir Charles Portal to discipline him. Indeed, had he tried and failed, the CAS's own position might have become untenable.

the next day when the heavy bombers of the US Eighth and Fifteenth Air Forces, escorted by long-range P-51 Mustangs, attacked the Messerschmitt, Junkers, and Focke Wulf plants in the Brunswick-Leipzig area.[32]

Having long ago agreed that Bomber Command would participate in Argument and that its night area attacks would 'coincide with the [American] daylight missions both in time and place,' Portal had spent the last six weeks failing miserably to persuade his AOC-in-C to take advantage of Bomber Command's bad-weather capabilities and begin the assault even without American support. But his directive regarding the inception of Argument was an unambiguous order and Harris chose to obey it.[33] Bomber Command's target for 19/20 February 1944 was Leipzig and 823 aircraft were dispatched on a raid that featured a very complex tactical plan. Bombing was not scheduled to begin until four in the morning, much later than usual, and it would be preceded by all sorts and conditions of spoofs and diversions. Led by four Pathfinders using H2S, forty-five Stirlings dropped mines in Kiel Bay; fifteen Mosquitos bombed Berlin; sixteen more, using Oboe, attacked night-fighter bases in Holland; and Window fell everywhere. All for nought. Although the German controllers scrambled their first interceptors just after midnight, in response to the aerial minelaying underway north of Kiel, the Mosquito effort over Holland persuaded a number of them to abandon that mission and to hold their fighters over Hamburg instead, in case the enemy's main effort came further south. It was from that point that they were inserted into the bomber stream.

This time there were no radar failures and no careless errors of omission. The fighters maintained communications with ground controllers throughout, and so negated High Wycombe's imaginative plan of attack, which saw the main force double back to Leipzig after feigning an approach on Berlin. All told, seventy-eight bombers were shot down (9.5 per cent), of which thirty-four were Halifaxes, just over 13 per cent of those dispatched. Understandably, Nos 4 and 6 Groups suffered the most, the former losing 12 per cent, and the latter 14 per cent, with another fifteen RCAF crews (almost 12 per cent) returning early. Heaviest hit once again was No 434 Squadron, in the fourth wave, with a third of its nine crews missing, but No 408 (in the first wave) and No 429 (in the fifth) were not far behind, losing four (of eighteen) and three (of sixteen), respectively.[34] Because of their extraordinary and unsupportable losses over the past few weeks, that was the last occasion when Harris would send Halifax IIs and Vs (then in service with Nos 419, 428, 429, 431, and 434 Squadrons) on deep penetrations into Germany.

Within Bomber Command it was increasingly evident that the enemy's switch from target to route interception had nullified most of the electronic and tactical counter-measures introduced since July 1943. To some it even seemed that the balance of the night air war had been tilted in the Luftwaffe's favour. Greater efforts would therefore have to be made, not only to mask the location and identity of the bomber stream better, but also to mitigate the effectiveness of those fighters which were successfully inserted into it. Although Harris would soon order his crews to fire 'upon every identified night-fighter,' this did not reflect any change of heart or policy on his part. He would still have preferred them to evade rather than fight, but thought that Bomber Command had to become more aggressive now, so as not to lose 'the spirit of offensiveness so necessary ... for successful operations.'[35]

Hoping to make operations more difficult for the enemy, two possibilities were raised besides restricting bomber operations to those nights when bad weather grounded a large part of the night-fighter force. First, reducing the length of the main stream by dispersing it more vertically, a move which should make it more difficult to find; and, second, dividing the main force into two streams taking different routes to the same target. (Harris still argued, however, that there were too few Pathfinders to mark two or more targets simultaneously.) So far as diversions were concerned, it was finally understood that if they were to have any effect at all, they would have to be mounted in greater strength and early enough to get the enemy airborne and committed before the main force was picked up on radar. That was possible, given the squadrons of otherwise redundant Halifax IIs and Vs that had become available for such operations. Moreover, a number of these aircraft were fitted with H2S, so even though the enemy's dependence on exploiting H2S transmissions was still not fully recognized, by happenstance the volume of their transmissions as an integral part of diversions would soon increase and cause the Germans considerable difficulty.[36]

One of the new tactical measures was implemented the very next night after Leipzig, when 156 crews were sent on a Bullseye navigation training exercise over the North Sea in advance of the raid on Stuttgart, another Pointblank target – and it worked. The German fighters were drawn far to the north, and only nine crews were lost from the main force, 1.5 per cent of those dispatched. The next night, after all his prevarications, Harris selected Schweinfurt as the target. In addition to 289 Bullseye and Gardening sorties to distract the enemy, numerous offensive (Serrate) patrols by British night-fighters, and a strong Intruder effort against the German fighter bases in Holland, the attack was planned in two parts. One wave of bombers was scheduled to arrive over the target just after 2300 hours and the second two hours later, No 6 Group squadrons being a part of both attacks. Neither was to last more than fifteen minutes. Once again, the enemy reacted strongly to the Gardening and Bullseye forces, but the gap between their appearance over the North Sea and the start of bombing was not long enough. When the main force was discovered and reported 'far to the west' at about 2100 hours, the fighters were immediately rerouted and, following the stream, many arrived in the Schweinfurt area before the first wave had departed. Worse, the time between the two bombing waves was probably too long, as many of these same fighter crews had the time to land and refuel before the second wave appeared. Altogether, thirty-three bombers were lost (4.5 per cent), two-thirds of them in the first wave. No 6 Group lost five of seventy crews, about the average, and had twelve early returns.[37]

Even so, these were not bad results in light of Harris's long-standing contention that attacking Schweinfurt was too risky for Bomber Command. He was also wrong when he forecast that the Pathfinders would not be able to find the aiming point in such a relatively small town. But there was trouble marking it. 'Excellent visibility in the target area with nil cloud,' Wing Commander R.J. Lane, commanding No 405 Squadron reported.

Target was identified visually. Many details of town and adjacent country positively identified. Load released at 2303 from 17,000 feet on the aiming-point. Ran up river from southwest. Six cans of flares white (first can 2259 hours) and T[arget] I[ndicator] green over woods two to three miles south of target. Target not sufficiently illuminated. Aiming-point not seen until over it. Circled to starboard and made second run from southeast along railway. Found one visual marker T.I. red on aiming-point, another on east end of marshalling yard, and another in the new town. Own T.I. red undershot 6 to 700 yards to southeast. Saw one large bomb burst on island immediately south of aiming-point. By 2310 hours, whole town area well covered with incendiaries with three very good fires, but many incendiaries and several red T.I.'s were spreading up to five miles west of town. Route-marking good.[38]

Squadron Leader J.B. Millward, also a visual marker from No 405, faced similar problems.

Visibility was clear in target area. Aiming-point was identified visually. Load was released at 2301 hours from 16,800 feet on aiming-point, cluster of buildings north of bridge at northeast end of island in river. Saw first white flares going down at 2259 hours and green T.I. burst about half a mile northeast of aiming-point. At 2259 hours, visually identified river and island in river and picked out aiming-point. Pressed bomb tit but graticule light failed. Made another run and released high explosive only. By this time the raid was spreading back with one T.I. red cascading over A.-P. And others spreading back to open fields approximately five to six miles from A.-P. Another concentration of red T.I.'s were in fields to east of A.-P. and a lot of bomb bursts seen in open fields. On leaving target, it was evident that the attack was exceedingly scattered with a tendency to undershoot. Saw the glow of fires from factory west of town which was probably the result of the daylight attack [by the Americans.] Smoke from flares concealed most of the built-up area on our second run.[39]

'Big Week' ended later that day when, with the return of bad weather, the Americans were prevented from operating with anything like the intensity that had marked the preceding five days. Raids on other targets associated with Overlord and Pointblank – oil refineries, V-1 sites in France, and the railway lines linking Germany and the Channel coast – now had to be considered, but the campaign against the Luftwaffe and the German aircraft industry did not cease altogether. Between 25 February and 1 April 1944 the Americans pounded Brunswick, Frankfurt, Ludwigshafen, Düsseldorf, Augsburg, and Schweinfurt, among other places, and by the end of March they had knocked a sizeable, if temporary, hole in the enemy's aircraft production. The number of new single-seater fighters delivered to the German air force fell from 1162 machines in January 1944 to 794 in February, rising slightly to 934 in March,

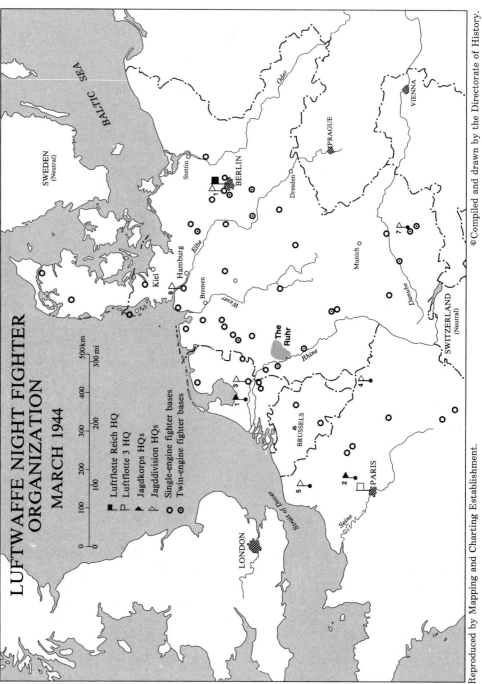

LUFTWAFFE NIGHT FIGHTER ORGANIZATION MARCH 1944

BALTIC SEA

SWEDEN
(Neutral)

Stettin

BERLIN

Oder

PRAGUE

VIENNA

Dresden

Elbe

Hamburg

Kiel

Bremen

Weser

Munich

Danube

The Ruhr

Rhine

SWITZERLAND
(Neutral)

BRUSSELS

PARIS

Seine

Strait of Dover

LONDON

	Luftflotte Reich HQ
	Luftflotte 3 HQ
▲	Jagdkorps HQs
△	Jagddivision HQs
○	Single-engine fighter bases
◉	Twin-engine fighter bases

0   100   200   300   400   500 km
0   100   200   300 mi

©Compiled and drawn by the Directorate of History.

Reproduced by Mapping and Charting Establishment.

and the total lost production between 20 February and 1 April may have been as high as 1000 aircraft.* Now, however, that the Americans' long-range P-51 Mustang escorts had been freed to range far and wide in enormous numbers while protecting the bomber formations, they were hammering the Luftwaffe in aerial combat. It has been estimated that the Germans lost one-third of their day-fighter strength in the west during the Big Week fighting, and half of what was left in the month that followed. New production, no matter how well organized, could not keep up with attrition like that; nor could the training system keep up with pilot wastage on such a scale.[40]

Bomber Command also continued to attack cities associated with aircraft production after 25 February, and sometimes the results were startlingly effective. In clear skies, with the city standing out against a covering of new-fallen snow, Harris's crews destroyed the heart of Augsburg on 25/26 February in a raid which saw 90 per cent of bombing photographs taken within three miles of the aiming point. Nearly three thousand houses were damaged beyond repair, 85,000 civilians (almost half the population) were rendered homeless, and thirty-seven factories were hit – among them a diesel engine plant and an aero-engine factory, both top priority targets. The enemy had been decidedly – and inexplicably – thrown off balance. Although both waves of the main force were identified as such and a few night-fighters were infiltrated into them as far forward as Metz, almost all of 1 Jagddivision's interceptors were held back against the possibility of an attack further north, and so intervened only on the bombers' return route.[41]

Flight Sergeant P.E. Fillion of No 408 Squadron, on his third sortie, did not reach Augsburg. He had been forced to abort his first trip, to Leipzig, because of engine trouble on 19/20 February, though he completed the raid on Schweinfurt with no trouble five days later. Now he found his oil temperature high and the pressure dangerously low, so he again chose to jettison his bombs early and return home. Some fifteen or twenty minutes later he saw a night-fighter take off far below and begin to climb towards him in large circles with navigation lights on. These were switched off when the fighter reached about 7000 feet, but another light allowed Fillion to follow its progress clearly. Eventually the Canadian opened fire and the enemy 'burst into flames ... and went down.' The victim was undoubtedly a Himmelbett crew held back to pick off stragglers. Fillion, meanwhile, flew on into France where, with the oil temperature much too high and the pressure falling, all four engines seized up and he crashed near Abbeville.[42] Two of his crew evaded capture and, making their way through France with the help of the Resistance, returned to London in late March 1944. Like some 2700 other Canadian airmen, however, Fillion and the others were taken prisoner, Fillion himself near Arras.

Every man's experience as a POW was different, 'some brooding in silent despair to the point of madness or even suicide,' most evincing 'a common

---

* After that, fighter output soared, standing at 1875 single-engine machines as early as July 1944. The focus of Allied bombing changed to pre-invasion targets and the Germans, given Hitler's long-awaited authorization to allocate the highest priority to fighter production, and now directed by Albert Speer, completely reorganized and rationalized their aircraft industry.

determination to make the best of it all, a refusal to be downcast.'[43] Some tried to escape, but fewer than is commonly believed. 'People are apt to imagine,' observed an official study commissioned by the RAF immediately after the war, 'that when captured a man automatically longs to get away and that it is only the physical difficulties which prevent him. This is not true. Only a small percentage of prisoners of war ever make persistent attempts to escape; sooner or later the majority accept captivity and try to endure it with as much cheerfulness as possible.'[44] That reflected neither cowardice nor dereliction of duty, but rather a strong assertion of the instinct for survival as well as 'the force of inertia.' Once a prisoner reached 'the seclusion of the barbed wire' his 'first sensation was one of relief. At least he ceased to be "on show."'

Having been stared at, pointed at, segregated from those around him by special guards, perhaps interrogated for long hours, he was among his own people. The sound of his own language raised his spirit and he could laugh once more without a guilty feeling that he was fraternising with the enemy; within the limits of the camp he could move how and where he pleased.

When these first sensations had worn off, others took their place. The mere fact of being a prisoner offered endless possibilities. A man might dream of reading Shakespeare, of learning languages, of playing the piano, of doing some of the things he had often longed to do but for which he had never found time.[45]

There were men for whom the barbed wire was a symbol of security. As a prisoner of war, they reasoned, there were no responsibilities. You neither looked for your food nor paid for it. You could read, paint, act, or play the trombone, sleep for long hours and eat when you felt like it. You did not have to go anywhere or get dressed for Sunday. You were never alone … Laws and regulations were not multifarious and complex, but rigid and easy to understand.[46]

For many, learning to cope within this environment was a better way of spending their days than thinking of escape which, at best, had a slender chance of success: of the ten thousand Commonwealth airmen imprisoned in permanent camps in Germany, Italy, and present-day Poland and Lithuania, fewer than thirty ever reached Britain or neutral territory following an escape.[47]

For RAF and RCAF POWs (officers especially – one reason the Canadian government eventually insisted upon a very liberal commissioning policy) life was at least bearable until very late in the war. Food, while not available in quantity or variety, met minimum standards, and Red Cross parcels, with their cigarettes, chocolate, and other luxuries, came in comparatively freely at this stage of the war. A Red Cross report on conditions at Stalag Luft I, at Barth on the Baltic coast near Stettin (which housed 1,959 prisoners on 9 March 1944, thirty-nine of them Canadian), noted, 'each camp has an adequate kitchen.'

Rations are regulation ones, checked by the officers in charge of the kitchen. Foodstuffs issued by the German Authorities are always entirely used up without satisfying

IRI...

Upas Tree
34/46

Sultanas
19/44

Jellyfish
194/307/3

Brest

186/806/1

Pte du Toulinguet
6/8

L

Artichokes
98/182

BAY

OF

BISCAY

Reproduced by Mappin

the appetites of the prisoners. Their principal nourishment, therefore, consists of the contents of Red Cross Food Parcels.

Condition of clothing of prisoners who have been in camp for several months is satisfactory. The reserve stocks in hand, however, are insufficient to cater for new arrivals ... A large increase has been asked for in regard to reserve supplies of food in view of the increasing strength of the camp.

The Senior [Allied] Officers have complete control of food and clothing parcels, and have unrestricted liberty in administering them. Store room for food and clothing is large enough to house all the articles asked for ... Hygiene satisfactory ...

The Medical Section has lately been directed by a German doctor who is permanently resident at the camp. The prisoners seem to like him ...

In conclusion, it is difficult to precisely judge the quality of this Camp as it is in full tide of alteration. The officers in charge are encountering great difficulties in organizing the intellectual life and leisure occupations of their comrades while their numbers continually vary. Housing accommodation and living conditions are, however, satisfactory.[48]

The largest camp for Commonwealth and American aircrew was Stalag Luft III and it was here that Flying Officer Fillion – he was promoted effective the date he went missing – was first sent.[*] A rectangle of some three square miles cut out of the deep pine forests near Sagan in Lower Silesia (present-day Polish Zagan), Stalag Luft III was seventy-five miles northeast of Dresden. Opened in April 1942, it was 'a model of what a prisoner of war camp should be – from the captor's point of view.'

Between the double wire of the perimeter fence loose coils of barbed wire lay thick on the ground so that it was impossible to walk across the intervening space. Exactly above the fence, at intervals of about a hundred yards, stood watch towers on each of which was a machine gun covering the interior of the camp ... Immediately inside the wire was an area of dead ground six to fifteen yards wide, bounded by a low guard rail; if any prisoner crossed it, he could be shot without warning. At night boundary lights lit the perimeter ... and from each guard tower searchlights swept the compounds.[49]

A few climbed over the wire in heavy blizzards and thick fog; some climbed it at night, rather more cut their way out, and a number were killed in the attempt. But tunnelling through the sandy earth offered the best chance, and it was from Sagan, on 24 March 1944, that 'the Great Escape' took place, when seventy-six POWs including six RCAF and four Canadians in the RAF successfully exited Harry, one of three tunnels upon which work had begun almost a year before.[50]

---

[*] In July he was transferred to Stalag 357, a combined army–air force camp located at Oerbke, near Fallingbostel, thirty miles north of Hanover. Here 'living conditions were bad because of dilapidated barracks, leaking roofs, and insufficient heating and lighting, and with the passage of time these conditions were worsened by over-crowding as further batches of Army prisoners arrived from other camps further east.'

The RCAF officer in charge of security for the escape plan was Flying Officer G.R. Harsh, an American who had been convicted of armed robbery and murder in the late 1920s and who, after being pardoned,[*] enlisted in the RCAF in May 1941 and was shot down over Cologne in October 1942.[51] The chief engineer was also from the RCAF. Pilot Officer C.W. Floody, a native of Chatham, Ontario, who had flown Spitfires with No 401 Squadron before being shot down in October 1941, consciously traded upon his brief experience working in the gold mines of Kirkland Lake, Ontario, to become involved in the project. 'I knew the idiosyncracies of every member of the team. We were an international shift composed of men from England, Ireland, Scotland, Wales, France, Denmark, Norway, South Africa, Canada, Australia, New Zealand and the Argentine ... Even when feeling ill or hungry they had turned up for work day after day with nothing worse than a crack at me for always picking on them when there was dirty work to do. Oddly enough it was with a feeling of sorrow that we went below to complete the final stages.'[52]

Harsh and Floody were moved out of the main compound to a subcamp at Belaria, a few kilometers down the road, before the mass escape took place, and that may well have saved their lives. Of the seventy-six airmen who exited the tunnel before the Germans discovered what was happening, just three – two Norwegians and a Dutchman – made home runs, reaching Britain in fairly short order. Fifteen were captured in the immediate vicinity of the camp and were returned to it straight away. Of the rest, eight would be caught and sent to other camps (including the concentration camp at Sachsenhausen), but an unfortunate fifty, including six Canadians, who had been turned over to the Gestapo after being apprehended were summarily executed.

Two raids on Stuttgart were almost as successful as that on Augsburg, damaging the Bosch and Daimler-Benz works with relatively little loss to the attacking force. On 1/2 March, for example, when cloud from the Channel to the target grounded both 1 and 2 Jagddivisionen and the Wilde Sauen and limited 3 Jagddivision's response to fifty-three sorties, the main force lost only four aircraft, 0.7 per cent. However, two weeks later, on 15/16 March, when the weather was somewhat better, 4.3 per cent of the 836 aircraft involved were lost even though the Germans were so confused that at one point Augsburg, almost one hundred miles to the south-east, was identified as the target. Much the same happened at Frankfurt, where two raids involving more than eight hundred heavy bombers each knocked out public utilities and facilities belonging to I.G. Farben, again with manageable losses. On 18/19 March just twenty-two bombers went missing, 2.6 per cent, while four days later thirty-three (4 per cent) failed to return.[53]

Three of the raids on Stuttgart and Frankfurt had been supported by large Gardening and other diversionary operations in the north and west, and all four

---

[*] He spent twelve years in jail, many of them working on a chain gang and some as a hospital orderly, and had been pardoned only after he performed a successful emergency appendectomy on a fellow inmate 'by the flickering light of candles and kerosene lanterns, assisted only by another convict and a stiff tot of medicinal alcohol and ginger ale.'

involved complex and imaginative routes. That, among other things, suggested to some of the operational research scientists at High Wycombe that the tactical stalemate existing since early winter could be broken if bomber crews curtailed their use of IFF over enemy territory.* At the same time, they cautioned, the gaps in the enemy's southern defences that had helped keep losses low at Schweinfurt, Augsburg, and now Stuttgart would soon be filled, and operations there would then involve the same risks as in the north. They were right. Beginning in late March, radar and fighter units were transferred to southern Germany and to France, astride the route to southern targets.[54]

The ORS was also keeping a close watch on No 6 Group in the early months of 1944, but by March the Canadian casualty statistics were 'reassuring,' as Harris himself observed. They were no longer the worst in Bomber Command and, although still too high for comfort, some of the losses could be accounted for by the large number of Halifax IIs and Vs used on bombing operations until mid-February. Better still, when losses were compared by aircraft type, it was found that the experienced Canadian Halifax squadrons had fared better than the No 4 Group average, and that the Lancaster squadrons were doing better than their counterparts in No 3 Group despite the longer distance they had to fly to most targets and the often worse weather besetting the bases in the Vale of York. Apparently having found its feet, No 6 Group had passed through its worst period, and its tactical refinements, as decided upon by Air Vice-Marshal Brookes and his operations staff, were now giving it an edge. In particular, the Canadians were well served by their practice of maintaining altitude after bombing rather than converting height into speed by diving away from the target, the standard procedure in No 4 Group.[55]

As it happened, Brookes was no longer AOC of the group when Harris communicated his sense of satisfaction with its performance to Overseas Headquarters. Having supervised the original organization, and having nurtured it through some very difficult times, Brookes was exhausted and the strain had begun to show. Called to London on the morning of 17 February 1944, he was informed by Air Marshal Breadner of his pending 'return posting home' (he would retire from the RCAF altogether in November), and his diary expresses neither surprise nor disgruntlement at the unexpected turn of events. He drove that afternoon to High Wycombe and spoke for just under an hour with Harris, whom he found 'in good form,' and then returned to London, spending the next day with Breadner and the AOC-designate, Air Vice-Marshal C.M. Mc-Ewen, station commander at Linton-on-Ouse.[56]

Like Brookes, McEwen was a veteran of the First World War who had joined the RCAF when it was formed. He had attended the RAF Staff College in 1930 and had been judged a good organizer and an excellent trainer of men. Following a tour as AOC of No 1 Group (St John's) in the RCAF's Home War Establishment, he had been posted overseas, first to command the Canadian

---

* That H2S was being routinely plotted and its volume measured by the Germans was still lost on the ORS, who, mistakenly and tragically, continued to assert that intercepted IFF transmissions were 'the only accurate means left to the enemy to plot and engage the bomber stream.'

training base at Topcliffe and subsequently the operational base at Linton in June 1943. There he was considered to be a stickler for discipline and correct dress, attitudes he took with him to Allerton Hall. He also took a burning commitment to the principle of training and yet more training, even for established operational crews. Improving their standard of navigation was clearly important, but so, too, was giving them more practice in defensive tactics through fighter affiliation exercises.

McEwen felt that training was the area where his predecessor had been weakest – although in Brookes's defence it must be said that throughout most of 1943 the Air Ministry had allocated only three Spitfires per group to practise defensive tactics, a number he, Carr of No 4 Group, and High Wycombe considered inadequate and which was subsequently increased. In the event, McEwen soon imposed a rigorous new regimen on his squadrons, insisting that all crews do regular cross-country navigation and fighter affiliation exercises to hone their skills. He boasted later that that was the major reason why the group's losses soon came down, and it undoubtedly was a factor, although the conversion from the Halifax II/V to Halifax III also played a part. On the five raids flown between 25 February and 23 March – just after McEwen took over but before he could have had any appreciable impact – the loss rate of 5.6 per cent seemed explicable entirely in terms of poor flying discipline and, in particular, because of poor time- and track-keeping, faults the extra training he instituted was designed to correct.[57]

The well-documented and well-understood link between navigation and losses was demonstrated again when Bomber Command returned to Berlin on 24/25 March and seventy-two crews, 9 per cent of the 793 dispatched, did not return. Surprised by unbelievably strong north winds of 100 miles per hour, many navigators simply could not believe their findings as they checked their positions en route to the target and so did not make the appropriate corrections to their course. The bomber stream was pushed well to the south, losing cohesion in the process, as individual crews, trying to come to grips with the discrepancy between their wind forecast and what they were experiencing, decided on their own what measures to take. Eventually many navigators appear to have gained confidence in their observations, but by then the stream was well spread out in time and space. At zero hour about half the force was still more than twenty miles off track and two-thirds at least ten miles away from where they were supposed to be. The night-fighters had been up early and in strength – about two hundred of them from 1 Jagdkorps alone – and they had a relatively easy job picking off isolated prey. Others, following a new tactic introduced by Schmid as a hedge against diversions, were held back for insertion into the stream on its return route, and they too had considerable success.[58]

Switching gears, Bomber Command made for Essen two nights later. Harris's selection of a target in the Ruhr surprised the enemy controllers who, anticipating a second and deeper penetration, initially withheld their fighters. Then, when finally convinced that Essen was the only objective, the risk of icing limited the number of interceptors they could put up. Just eight bombers were shot down, at a cost of twenty of the 105 fighters scrambled in 1 Jagd-korps. After four years of experiment and effort, when it came to keeping losses down, bad weather remained Bomber Command's greatest ally and the Germans' biggest foe.[59]

The next operation, to Nuremburg on 30/31 March 1944, brought the battle of Berlin to a formal and prearranged close. For those involved, this raid was a shattering experience. Ninety-five of the 786 heavy bombers dispatched were lost, 12 per cent, and a further twenty-six were heavily damaged – the highest absolute total recorded during the war. Furthermore, in terms of the damage done to the target, the raid was an abysmal failure. Strong winds pushed some crews over Schweinfurt – not altogether a waste, given the importance of its ball-bearing plants – but over Nuremburg, where there was cloud, the Pathfinders missed their aiming point. That, and the fact that many crews were well aware of the carnage around them and wanted nothing more than to get home safely, led to extensive creep-back in the northern suburbs, and there was only slight damage to the city centre. Of the industrial facilities hit, a steel rolling mill and a margarine works suffered most, but neither was a significant objective.[60]

Because of the horrendous casualties, the Nuremburg raid has since been the subject of microscopic scrutiny.* Like many military disasters where obvious rules appear to have been broken, a body of mythology has grown up around it. But the central element of the Nuremburg myth – that the enemy had specific foreknowledge both of the raid and the target, and that German fighter crews were lying in wait for the bomber stream – can be dispensed with easily, particularly when the Luftwaffe's strong and early response is cited as the main evidence for the alleged forewarning.[61]

As we have already seen many times, the Luftwaffe's radio intelligence and electronic-tracking capabilities were more than good enough to explain its deft riposte. Moreover, there is compelling evidence that, although the Germans knew that the weather in the north did not favour operations there, Harris's selection of a distant southern target during the moon period and on such a clear night came as a complete surprise. The enemy had anticipated raids further west, if any were mounted at all, a predisposition that was sub-sequently strengthened by the route laid down for the main force and by the early diversionary flights over Cologne. Under these circumstances, when it became obvious that Bomber Command would be operating, 1 Jagdkorps simply assembled the bulk of its fighters at the IDA and OTTO beacons, near Frankfurt and Cologne, and waited, ready to defend the Ruhr and the Rhine industrial basin and poised on the flank of a possible approach to Berlin. As it happened, because of high winds, much of the bomber stream passed direct-ly over IDA, leaving the enemy interceptors well placed for insertion into the bomber stream without their having any special knowledge of where it was going.

---

* The process began in early April, with Bomber Command's own 'Report on casualties in night operations, 30/31st March 1944: Nuremburg,' PRO Air 19/169.

Indeed, once it was clear that the enemy did not intend to double back to the Ruhr or Rhineland, first Frankfurt and then Berlin were announced as Bomber Command's likely objectives, and in the end all Wilde Sauen within range were sent to the capital. Nuremburg itself was never identified as the target, no fighters were directed there, and even after the bombing began one Staffel based in the vicinity of the town remained on the ground. From the perspective of concealing the identity of the target and thereby illustrating High Wycombe's mastery over the Luftwaffe's efforts at point defence, the Nuremburg operation was a magnificent success.[62]

As an illustration of the power, even triumph, of pursuit night-fighting, however, Nuremburg tells a different, perhaps not altogether surprising, story – and one which should not have shocked Bomber Command's research staffs. The ORS had already observed that the enemy's defences in the south were likely to improve, and as recently as 21 March it had warned against dropping route-markers (because of their value to the enemy) and against passing the main force too close to the 'natural' routes between night-fighter beacons. Route markers were not a factor on 30/31 March, but as we have seen the bomber stream not only strayed into one of those natural routes because of unpredicted winds, but actually passed right over one of the beacons, so that upwards of fifty Halifaxes and Lancasters were lost before they reached the last turning-point at Fulda.[63]

Even with the issue of German foreknowledge laid to rest, it has still been possible for bitter survivors to wonder, given the ORS warnings, why Nuremburg was selected as the target in the bright moonlight prevailing on 30/31 March. Meteorological flights mounted in the late morning and early afternoon of 30 March found that the cloud cover anticipated en route was not likely to materialize – although there would be cloud at the target – and it was at this point, Harris's deputy Sir Robert Saundby recalls, that 'everyone, including myself, expected the C-in-C to cancel the raid.'[64] But he did not, and beginning at 9:30 in the evening the crews from No 6 Group, who had the farthest to fly, began to taxi to their dispersal points and then takeoff. By the time they reached Belgium they realized that, flying in brilliant, cloudless moonlight, and with their condensation trails visible for miles, they were in for a difficult night. 'Just how difficult,' Flying Officer F.F. Hamilton of No 424 Squadron recalled, 'became apparent with a beautiful clear night and lots of fighter activity.'

[It was] easy to see the tracer, then the ball of fire and scratch one of Bomber Command. I began to think that what I saw could not be bombers going down but some German scare technique but I soon realized that it was the real thing and that Bomber Command was taking some terrible punishment.

The fact that I was hit head-on gives some indication of the visibility; all I saw was white tracer getting near, then Bang! It all happened in one or two seconds. The aircraft was on fire and I knew we probably had ten seconds to get out [but we] were hit again from above and behind and the flames were shot right out [extinguished] by this second burst ... and no one jumped. We were hit a third time ... jettisoned the incendiaries and continued on our happy way with the main stream across Nuremburg.[65]

The Germans, in contrast, had an extraordinarily easy time. 'We were flying from Laon,' Unteroffizier Erich Handle of III/NJG I remembered, 'and had been told by the running commentary that the bombers were about five minutes away. I hadn't even switched on the SN2 set when the gunner poked me in the back and pointed. "There he is up there, the first one!" As we came round we saw another straight away, about 200 metres directly above. I switched on my SN2 but we had dropped 2,000 metres behind in the turn and had lost them. When the set warmed up I saw three targets on it at once. I headed for the nearest ... Weather was marvelous – clear sky, half-moon, little cloud and no mist – it was simply ideal, almost too bright.'[66]

Although losses were heavy, they were not equally divided among all groups or squadrons. While Bomber Command lost 12 per cent overall, No 4 Group, with all its crews flying Halifaxes, lost 16.5 per cent, and No 6 Group, with one-third Lancasters, all from Linton, only 11 per cent. At Leeming, where squadrons had been assigned to the highest (and usually the safest) height band, five of twenty-nine crews failed to return. The Tholthorpe units, placed in the lowest band, lost only one of twenty-six machines.[67] For some (and for once) the key to survival may have been to arrive late, which two-thirds of the Canadians did.[68] 'We were some twenty minutes late to the target, but ... being off track and behind time worked to our advantage, for when we arrived in the vicinity of Nuremburg there was no enemy activity whatsoever. The last of the markers had died ... so we released our load at the approximate point where the glow of the red target indicators faded. Heaven only knows where our bombs went.'[69]

Keeping in mind that the loss of ninety-five aircraft meant the loss of almost seven hundred aircrew – about the strength of an entire infantry battalion, or the ship's company of a large cruiser – the Nuremburg raid was in its own way an apposite conclusion to the battle of Berlin. In early November, it will be recalled, Harris had predicted that a combined Anglo-US offensive against the enemy capital was likely to cost five hundred bombers and lose Germany the war – a forecast he did not change even when the Americans chose not to participate. The first half of his prediction was accurate. On raids against Berlin from November 1943 to March 1944 five hundred machines (including 187 from No 6 Group) were lost out of 8983 sorties – 5.56 per cent – and another fifty-nine crashed in England. Just over 3000 aircrew were killed and another 750 were captured – of which 1300 came from the RCAF. However, the AOC-in-C was not even close on his second prediction. Germany did not sue for peace because of the battle, nor did Berliners' morale crack, despite their 10,000 dead, several hundred thousand injured and homeless, or the additional '2,180 gross acres of devastation' Sir Arthur felt it necessary to emphasize in his *Despatch on Operations*.[70]

Moreover, despite the unanticipated disruption caused to that part of the electronics industry situated in Berlin, it cannot be said that the German war

TONNAGE OF BOMBS DROPPED BY BOMBER COMMAND, (INCLUDING 6 GROUP) AND EIGHTH US AIR FORCE

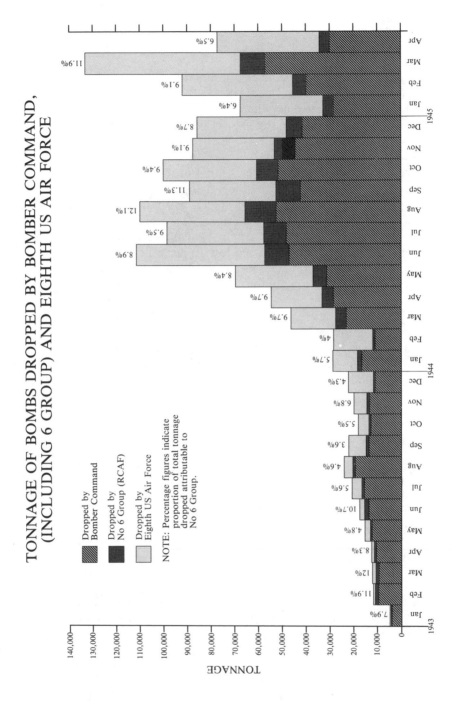

Dropped by
Bomber Command

Dropped by
No 6 Group (RCAF)

Dropped by
Eighth US Air Force

NOTE: Percentage figures indicate
proportion of total tonnage
dropped attributable to
No 6 Group.

TONNAGE

economy suffered long-lasting, much less permanent and irreparable, harm because of the sixteen raids on the capital mounted between November 1943 and March 1944. Much of what was destroyed was simply not essential for waging war and, as elsewhere in Germany, there was enough elasticity in the industrial system to take up the slack and to allow labour and materials to be shifted from one sector to another. To be sure, the need to disperse production because of bombing created temporary shortages and the campaign against Berlin, taken in conjunction with the burgeoning American bombing effort, undoubtedly contributed to the German decision to give higher priority to air defence and so withdraw resources and personnel from other branches of the Wehrmacht. However, it would be wrong to ascribe too much to the offensive against Berlin in this regard. As even the postwar British bombing survey admitted, 'area attacks,' including those on Berlin, 'could not have been responsible for more than a very small part of the fall which ... actually occurred in German production.'[71]

Area attacks, the survey added, were also 'a very costly way of achieving the results which they did achieve.' Few were more so than the campaign against Berlin, and when it was over High Wycombe was forced to concede not only that the loss rate had become unsustainable, but also that Bomber Command's store of tactical innovations was now 'practically exhausted.' 'We did not fail for lack of trying,' a Pathfinder group captain recalled, 'but there was nothing left in the kitty' to allow for the destruction of Berlin at acceptable cost. 'The battering we received over the North German Plain cost us more than a thousand aircraft and between seven and eight thousand lives. Berlin wasn't worth it.'[72]

Indeed, Harris was now finally convinced that to achieve his purpose he could no longer simply hide from the enemy, but must instead seek it out and beat it in battle with a much strengthened offensive night-fighter force. However, Mosquitoes in the numbers he wanted were simply not available. What saved things, then, in terms of the casualty rate, was the gradual shift in target systems (to assist Overlord) that began on 1 April, the day after Nuremburg.

This shift in objectives was also a tonic for Bomber Command's morale. During the Battle of Berlin, with its disheartening return runs to the same target area and its high losses, Bomber Command most noticeably 'balked at the jump.' Reports of 'fringe merchants' – those who aimed at quickly getting into, and away from, the crude target area, caring little about the aiming point or the Pathfinders' markers – and of those who dropped their heaviest bombs over the North Sea in order to gain height, proliferated. And perhaps because of the strain (but the effect of flying in cloud and bad weather must always be taken into account), the early return rate remained consistently around 10 per cent, higher than the norm of comparatively quiet periods.[73]

'Fear,' one RAF veteran observed, was the 'eighth passenger' in all heavy bombers, and in some aircrew it produced sufficient physiological or neuro-psychiatric distress that they had to be taken off operations. Others simply tried to avoid flying. That it was 'difficult to draw a line on one side of which a man was condemned as a coward and on the other absolved as being a victim of circumstances beyond his control' was always acknowledged. But when no recognized medical or psychological explanation could be found and they lost the confidence of their commanding officers, these men could be classified as lacking in moral fibre and, as 'waverers' be removed from their base, stripped of their rank and flying badges, and employed in the lowest rank on the ground until they were either sent to the army or to the coal mines.[74]

That was British practice. It was consciously designed to dissuade. It worked. And because of that, at times, it was harsh, as Murray Peden, a Canadian pilot in No 100 Group, observed first hand.

One crew flew three nights in a row ... They found themselves on the battle order the fourth day. This sort of thing rarely happened because the weather was seldom favourable that long. This time it did happen, and the crew were extremely tired. It is entirely possible that if they had gone to see Doc Vyse before they went to briefing, he would have ordered them, on medical grounds, taken off the battle order for one night. Instead, they discussed it amongst themselves, and took the indefensible but understandable position: '... If it's a short trip, we'll go; if it's a long trip, to hell with it.'

... The target was Berlin ... The pilot told the Flight Commander that they were not going. He in turn told the Wing Commander. The Wing Commander came over.

'Look,' he said, not unkindly, 'I'll pretend that this has not happened. You know you can't come to briefing and then decide you are not going to do the operation. Now get your gear together and be ready to go to the aircraft with the other crews.'

The pilot and two other members of the crew realized immediately that they had put themselves in an untenable position by going to briefing before telling anyone that they felt incapable of flying a long operation. These three indicated at once that they would fly the duty as detailed. The other four members refused to go ... insisting that all they wanted was one night's rest.

The recalcitrant crew members were immediately placed under close arrest ... were posted to Uxbridge, where they were reduced to the ranks, given LMF endorsements on their records, and sentenced to 180 days detention

I knew the pilot, an Australian, and saw a good deal of him in the weeks after this unhappy event. I did not know the crew members who had persisted in their refusal to fly, but I always felt that they had been their own worst enemies. It was harsh treatment to label them LMF, bearing in mind the service they had rendered and the ordeals they had already endured, but they had tied the Wing Commander's hands by the procedure that they had adopted.

Indeed, Peden elaborated, 'the harsh treatment was necessary simply because the strain was so great. If there had been an easy and graceful way to abandon operational flying, many crews would have found the temptation hard to resist.'[75]

In the RCAF from 1943 on, however, largely at the insistence of Air Minister C.G. Power, suspected LMF cases were returned to Canada for a thorough physical and mental-health examination before a final decision was taken. Greater emphasis was placed on medical and psychological assessments in

Canada, and there was a much greater inclination to find 'genuine' cases of 'flying stress'(particularly among those reaching the latter stages of their operational tour) who, for that reason, would not have to be treated as waverers. It was left to the minister to make the final disposition. Despite the more understanding policy in vogue in the RCAF, many Canadian aircrew nevertheless abhorred the idea of LMF and all that accompanied its use.[76]

Although there are hints of waverers in the Canadian squadron records before November 1943, it was not until late February 1944, at the height of the battle and just before he left No 6 Group, that Air Vice-Marshal Brookes had to deal with his first 'disposal' case. It involved a twenty-six-year-old pilot (and former aerobatics instructor at the Central Flying School in Canada) who had been posted to England just five days after the birth of his son. He had begun to exhibit some symptoms of 'neuro-psychiatric hysteria' when he realized not only that he would not be able to travel home to see his wife, who had suffered post-natal complications, but also that he would be given an operational posting in Bomber Command. He considered himself better suited to instructional duties. OTU and HCU courses kept him occupied for a few months, but he was eventually posted to a bomber squadron where, on his fourth operation, he returned to base within an hour of setting out because he believed he did not have enough fuel to reach the target. There was unimpeachable evidence that he had purposely mishandled his aircraft to ensure he would use an abnormal amount of fuel, and he was labelled 'LMF.' Having lost the confidence of his commanding officer, he was interviewed by Brookes, who concluded he should be removed from flying duties and returned to Canada as a possible waverer. Once in Ottawa he was brought before the special board established to review such cases. While agreeing that he had 'failed in gaining his crew's confidence, lacked the ability to gain proper crew co-operation, [and was] a poor leader' and that 'his claim of inexperience was ... a feeble excuse for his inefficiency,' the board nevertheless concluded that wavering 'could not, with the evidence, be proved.' With the concurrence of the air member for personnel, the chief of the air staff, and the minister, he was retired as 'inefficient' but permitted to keep his rank and flying badge.[77]

Although the fact (and the issue) of wavering is a part of the RCAF and Bomber Command story, it would nevertheless be altogether misleading to put too much emphasis on it. During the whole war, in all commands in all theatres, fewer than 3000 Commonwealth aircrew were categorized as lacking moral fibre – less than 0.2 per cent of those who served. More to the point, in Bomber Command between July 1943 and June 1944 – when hopes that Window and other counter-measures would permanently befuddle the enemy's defences were raised and dashed in just a few months, and casualties were frequently high – less than 0.4 per cent of its aircrew strength were identified as being even possible LMF cases.[78]

The battle of Berlin was arguably the central event in Bomber Command's war, and the Nuremburg raid of 30/31 March 1944 was demonstrably the single most dramatic episode within that battle. But while 786 bomber crews made for southern Germany that night, another forty-nine, including thirty from Nos 419, 428, and 434 Squadrons, were operating far to the north, dropping mines on the shipping lanes around Heligoland.[79]

Besides having a genuine military value, Gardening was often used to introduce novice crews to operations because of the relatively low casualty rates involved. The comparative ease and safety of mining was not obvious in late July and August 1943, when Window momentarily confused the enemy's defences and bomber losses fell, but it became startlingly so again during the battle of Berlin. While 1081 crews failed to return from 24,754 night bombing sorties (4.36 per cent), mining cost just twenty-one of 2078 sorties (1.01 per cent). No 6 Group contributed 395 of the latter, losing four crews, or exactly the overall percentage rate.[80] Because of statistics like these, minelaying came to be regarded as a good means of employing obsolescent aircraft as well as introducing new crews to operations.

Wellingtons bore the brunt of the Gardening effort in the summer and early autumn of 1943, Stirlings were added in November, after their withdrawal from operations over Germany, and in early 1944 it was the turn of the Halifax IIs and Vs, following the disastrous mid-February strike on Leipzig. Like area bombing, Gardening had its own rhythms based on weather and season. Since accuracy was crucial (it was essential not to lay mines where British ships or submarines might operate, or to let them fall on land or in shallow water where the enemy could recover them and devise counter-measures), crews were invariably instructed to bring their mines back if they could not find the aiming point or a designated safe dropping zone in deep water. Given the vagaries of European weather, a sustained effort against any single area was therefore often impossible.

The focus of operations also shifted seasonally. Because of the risk of interception, northern Gardens were rarely sown during the short summer nights, and the weight of mining was moved to the approaches to French ports and the coastal sea-lanes inside the Frisian Islands. These regions had the advantage of lying within Gee range, which promised greater accuracy, but the pickings were not so good as in the Baltic, where there was considerable traffic to Norway, Sweden, and the Eastern Front. Indeed, success outside the Baltic was sometimes measured by the sinking of a single ship. Such was the case in September 1943 when Nos 4 and 6 Groups, and particularly Nos 429 and 432 Squadrons (the last of the Canadian formation's Wellington units and regarded, by then, as minelaying specialists), were credited with the beaching of the *Strasbourg*, a 17,000-ton liner commandeered from its Dutch owners, before it could make a run for the Baltic to replace the troopship *Gneisenau* (not to be confused with the battle-cruiser of the same name), which had also been sunk by mines while ferrying reinforcements to the Russian front.[81]

The greatest threat to Gardening crews, whether they were off the French coast, over the Frisians, or in the Baltic, was anti-aircraft artillery fire. The earlier aerial mines had to be sown from 6000 feet or below, well within the range of ground-based or shipborne light Flak. There was good reason, there-fore, for Bomber Command to ask that experiments be conducted and refinements made in mine design to permit operations from heights up to 15,000 feet, using both timed runs from visible landmarks and H2S as navigation aids. This was done; and, allowing for inexperienced crews and mistakes in wind-finding of up to fifteen miles per hour, it was found that the average dropping error should be between 1000 and 2000 yards. That was good enough, in all but the narrowest channels.[82]

High-level minelaying using H2S required a commitment of heavy bombers to Gardening, something which, in the autumn of 1943, even the Royal Navy did not expect Sir Arthur Harris to do immediately or regularly. Indeed, if the deputy director of operations (mining) at the Admiralty is to be believed, the sailors were actually quite content to know that Harris was 'fully alive' to the importance of obstructing enemy shipping, especially in the Baltic – actual sinkings were always a secondary consideration – and that he hoped 'to get going in this area at an early date,' once he had sufficient stocks of suitable mines.[83]

Largely because of the relegation of No 3 Group's Stirlings to minelaying and the conversion of the remaining RCAF Wellington squadrons to Halifaxes, No 6 Group did very little Gardening in November and December 1943.[84] But when new mines became available in January 1944, just as Canadian Halifax squadrons began to receive H2S on a regular basis, that unforeseen and happy coincidence led to Allerton Hall's being asked to continue No 3 Group's high-altitude trials. These occurred on 4/5 January, when Nos 419 and 428 Squadrons mined the waters outside Brest, and then again two nights later at Brest and St Nazaire. Both missions were successful – photographs confirmed that all mines had been laid within 2100 yards of the aiming point – and that meant that a number of inner German harbours, heretofore too risky to approach at 6000 feet or below, could now be attacked.[85]

Besides permitting an expansion of Gardening activities, the development of effective high-altitude mining techniques also had an impact on the planning and conduct of the area offensive against German cities. Gardening forces approaching the enemy coast at low altitude and without using H2S were not normally identified by the enemy as the main bomber stream, and so they played no role in deceiving controllers as to the latter's whereabouts. But a mining mission flown at 15,000 feet could deceive the enemy, particularly after the 106 Halifax IIs and Vs of Nos 4 and 6 Groups, which had been withdrawn from operations over Germany in mid-February, were added to the eighty-odd Stirlings of No 3 Group already committed to the task. Together, and using Window and H2S, they made an impressive display on radar screens and at the enemy's electronic listening posts. Indeed, as early as 24/25 February 1944, just six days after Leipzig, large minelaying forces were dispatched to Kiel before the bombing raid on Schweinfurt, and again the next night in advance of the attack on Augsburg.[86]

Of course, Gardening through cloud required that the target area be marked for those crews that did not have H2S. But when High Wycombe decided it could not routinely spare any of No 8 Group's Pathfinders for the task, target indicators were cobbled together for the most experienced H2S crews in Nos

4 and 6 Groups, and on 24/25 February 419 Squadron found itself marking for No 3 Group in Kiel Bay and the Kattegat. No 428 joined 419 over Kiel Bay the next night and, although some non-H2S crews had difficulty finding the marker flares (three crews from 434 Squadron returning early for this reason), Harris was persuaded that the experiment had been a success and that this make-shift pathfinding force was adequate to the task. On 9 March, therefore, he issued instructions to supply them regularly with all the necessary pyrotechnics for the job.[87]

By then, the intensified, high-altitude mining campaign begun in mid-February 1944 was already paying dividends. A Dutch fisherman 'liberated' by the Royal Navy reported that German minesweeping crews were suffering severe psychological distress.[88] More to the point, the number of ships damaged and sunk had increased dramatically, from seven sunk (919 tons) and two damaged (1,377 tons) in November 1943 to nineteen sunk (19,496 tons) and four damaged (4929 tons) in March 1944.[89] However, beginning in March, the RCAF's Halifax II/V squadrons would find themselves increasingly busy over France, where they were carrying bombs, not mines.

That the Allied heavy-bomber forces would be used in direct support of Operation Overlord was a foregone conclusion following the May 1943 Trident conference held in Washington. But what they would be asked to do, once Luftwaffe fighter strength in the west had been dealt with, was not determined in any specific way. Rather, the architects of Pointblank and the initial Overlord planners simply assumed that the resources of Bomber Command and the American strategic air forces would be employed against the Wehrmacht in Normandy as required, without preordained restraints or limits – a presumption shared by General Eisenhower after his appointment as supreme allied commander in December 1943.[90]

As we have seen, Sir Arthur Harris thought differently, arguing on 13 January 1944 that the results would be better (and the needs of Overlord better served) if he were left to continue and even expand the night-bombing effort against 'suitable industrial areas' in Germany. For his part, while preferring precision daylight bombing, General Carl Spaatz, now commanding the US Strategic Air Forces in Europe, was no more eager than Sir Arthur to surrender strategic control of his heavy bombers to the requirements of a ground campaign. Believing, like Harris, that it was only from the 'pure' application of air power against strategic targets that something decisive would be achieved, he did not want to see them withdrawn from operations against the Luftwaffe or, when the goals of Argument had been realized, the German oil and rubber industries, whose destruction would render the Germans immobile on *all* fronts, not just in Normandy. But when the Wehrmacht had been pushed out of the Caucasus and denied access to Russian crude, and Romanian supplies were threatened, it was the attack on oil in particular, Spaatz would observe on 5 March, that held out 'great promise for hastening German defeat.'[91]

As supreme allied commander in Europe (SACEUR), Eisenhower was likely to win any power struggle with the 'bomber barons' over the future employment of the forces under their command. But when, in January 1944, Harris and Spaatz began to prepare their ground, the newly appointed SACEUR had not made any firm decisions about how the heavy bombers would be used to support Overlord. It was obvious that some action would have to be taken against German U-boats, surface warships, coastal batteries, and radar sites in France and the Low Countries. Experience in the Mediterranean theatre, from which he had just arrived, suggested that it was also feasible to cut off enemy forces in the invasion area from their sources of supply and reinforcement by attacking railways in France and western Germany. But whether the railways could be dealt with best by a relatively brief program of interdiction ('line-cutting, strafing, bridge-breaking, and the destruction of a few ... focal points') immediately before the invasion, or whether it would require a longer-term effort that included the destruction of locomotives, rolling stock, repair shops, roundhouses, stations, signal boxes, and the entire infrastructure of the railway system all over Western Europe, was at issue until the last week of January at least. It was then that SACEUR's deputy, Air Chief Marshal Sir Arthur Tedder, and his overall air commander, Air Chief Marshal Sir Trafford Leigh-Mallory, convinced by civilian specialists in the Air Ministry, plumped for the latter.[92]

The 'Transportation Plan,' as the proposed campaign of attrition came to be called, was never expected to bring all rail traffic to a halt – there were simply too many railway lines in France for that to be possible – but it was hoped that most major centres could be put out of action by the time Overlord took place. Attacks would have to commence in early March to ensure that everything had been completed before the inevitable last-minute panic calls for bomber support elsewhere. Accordingly, on 4 March, while the US Eighth Air Force was bombing Berlin and the day before General Spaatz submitted his formal counter-proposal to give oil priority, the CAS directed High Wycombe to attack the French railway marshalling yards at Trappes, Aulnoye, Le Mans, Amiens, Courtrai, and Laon to 'obtain experience of the effects of night attacks' on such targets before the main pre-Overlord air assault began. It was, in essence, to be a test of the transportation plan and of Harris's assessment that his bombers would not be able to contribute to it effectively.[93]

This time the AOC-in-C responded promptly to Portal's directive, perhaps because those aircraft which could no longer be used against German targets might well be used for this plan. (Indeed, because No 6 Group had so many Halifax IIs and Vs in service, fully half of the crews taking part in these experimental attacks would come from RCAF squadrons.) The first such raid took place just two nights later, on 6/7 March, when 267 Halifaxes of Nos 4 and 6 Groups and six Mosquitoes from No 8 (Pathfinder) Group attacked the yards at Trappes, a few miles southwest of Paris.[94] Enjoying the full benefits of No 8 Group's Oboe ground-marking on this shallow penetration (the preferred method for the rest of the March series) and facing relatively light opposition, the main force was able to bomb from 13,000 feet with no casualties. Indeed, the most dangerous aspect of the raid was not enemy fighters or Flak but the 'great congestion of a/c over the target,' which led at least one crew from No

431 Squadron to drop down to 8000 feet to avoid the possibility of collision despite the not insignificant risk of being hit by bombs dropped by other aircraft. Many were able to identify the target visually, and 263 crews reported that they had hit the aiming point. Photographs backed up their claims – the average bombing error, not counting the few wildly inaccurate efforts, was less than three hundred yards – and confirmed that 'enormous damage' had been inflicted on the railway tracks, rolling stock, and installations around Trappes. Bad weather over England forced a number of crews to land at alternate bases, but for some hours it was 'almost assumed' that one crew from No 431 Squadron had gone missing. Nothing was heard from them until the next morning, when it was learned they had put down at Chipping Warden in Northamptonshire, far to the south of the Vale of York. Although Chipping Warden was home to No 12 OTU in No 92 Group, and so was part of Bomber Command, the station orderly officer, acting on the orders of his commanding officer, refused to give the crew beds. They could sleep on the floor instead.[95]

The next night 304 crews from Nos 3, 4, 6, and 8 Groups made for Le Mans, where the main lines from Paris branched off to Brittany and the Biscay ports. Heavy cloud with a base of 5000 feet and the late arrival of the Pathfinders combined to create a great deal of congestion as crews orbited the target area searching, often in vain, for markers on which to drop their bombs. Because this was France, they were forbidden from releasing their bombs unless they could see the target indicators clearly; by the same token, however, because this was France and there was less Flak to worry about, circling the target area to find markers was not as risky a business as it was over Germany.[96] All told, about a third of the crews eventually gave up on the attempt, including forty-four of the 140 sent by No 6 Group, but they had not done so easily. One crew from No 424 Squadron, for example, took twenty-two minutes to make two complete circuits of the target area before turning for home. Others were more patient, however, and their persistence paid off. A crew from No 433 Squadron 'arrived over target at 2115 hours, PFF very late, orbited for 26 minutes, saw second lot of TI and made successful bombing run.' After circling for thirteen minutes, another from 419 Squadron had already turned for home when they finally saw markers going down. They returned to the target area and 'bombed the centre of red TI seen in cloud.' Although the effort seemed unimpressive to those involved, three hundred bombs were recorded as falling in the railway yards; six locomotives, one turntable, and 250 freight cars were hit and many lines were cut.[97]

For the next two nights only No 5 Group was active over France, conducting its patented low-level moonlight raids on precision targets like the Michelin works at Clermont-Ferrand. On 13/14 March, however, Nos 4, 6, and 8 Groups returned to Le Mans and, in clear weather, and following timely and accurate marking, the main force caused considerably more damage than in the initial attack mounted a week before. Eight hundred freight cars and fifteen locomotives were claimed and many more lines were cut.[98]

Although Bomber Command would continue its experiment, Eisenhower had already been convinced that the transportation plan would work. It was nevertheless important that the location of these raids not give the enemy a clue as to where, exactly, the invasion would take place and for that reason, as part of Operation Fortitude (the overall deception plan for Overlord), many attacks were mounted against targets less directly related to the proposed landing area. On 15/16 March, for example, 863 crews made for Stuttgart and twenty-two Lancasters from No 5 Group were sent to bomb the aero-engine factory at Woippy, near Metz, while 140 machines from Nos 3, 4, and 6 Groups raided the marshalling yards at Amiens, due north of Paris and east of Dieppe. With the target area soon obscured by thick smoke, many crews concluded that the attack at Amiens 'was not particularly successful,' although High Wycombe later claimed that much damage had been done to the yards. For the fourth successive raid No 6 Group suffered no casualties as a result of enemy action, but two machines were lost in flying accidents on the way home.[99]

Amiens was the target again the next night, when 130 Halifaxes, Stirlings, and Mosquitos did considerable damage with no losses. But such easy operations could not be taken for granted. The sixth raid of the series, mounted against Laon, southeast of Amiens and northeast of Paris, on 23/24 March, went poorly (the average bombing error at one of the aiming points was over a mile) and the four Canadian squadrons involved did not hesitate to express their frustration and disappointment both with the failure of the raid itself, and with what was in their judgment, the cause of the failure – the unsatisfactory performance of the Pathfinders despite clear skies and easily visible ground detail. No 431 Squadron's diarist recorded that Pathfinder flares were 'non-existent, and after much circling and vain waiting, our aircraft returned … The English Channel took a terrific weight of bombs. Other more daring crews brought their bombs back to base.' His commanding officer, while admitting that 'two out of eight markers is not a very good show' and not happy about the four orbits he had done around the target area trying to find something to bomb on, was nevertheless willing to accept that 'there may have been extenuating circumstances.' A report from Laon, meanwhile, observed that half the bombs dropped hit the railway yards, but the remainder were scattered up to three kilometres from the target. Two aircraft were lost on this raid – nightfighters were stationed at Laon – but all No 6 Group's aircraft returned safely.[100]

Two nights later, on 25/26 March, every Canadian squadron except No 433 contributed to an attack on Aulnoye, midway between Amiens and Liège, close to the Belgian border. After the strain of venturing deep into Germany, those squadrons flying Lancasters and Halifax IIIs viewed this mission almost as light relief. No 426 Squadron, for example, offered 'five sprog [totally inexperienced] crews, the target being an easy one in France … All five took off, bombed the target and returned without incident.' Bombing from an average height of only 7000 feet and in good visibility – a welcome change from raids over Germany, where pilots strained for altitude and often battled heavy cloud – most could see the ground clearly and, keeping the well-concentrated target indicators in their sights as they released their bombs, they concluded that Aulnoye 'had been well pranged for the size of the raid.' That was also the view of Air Vice-Marshal McEwen, who had flown as second pilot with a crew from No 431 Squadron.[101]

On 26/27 March, when the selection of Essen as the Lancasters' and Halifax IIIs' main target caught the Germans by surprise, 102 Stirlings and Halifax IIs and Vs made for the railway yards at Courtrai, 150 miles away in Belgium, which they attacked without loss. In keeping with the precedent set by the AOC the night before, Air Commodore C.R. Slemon, No 6 Group's senior air staff officer, flew as the second pilot with Wing Commander W.F.M. Newsom of No 431 Squadron and was happy to report that the raid had been a success. He was probably optimistic. A number of crews with more operational experience noted that the markers had been 'slightly scattered,' and one pilot from No 419 Squadron reported that of the '3 TIs seen, only one ... appeared to be at [the] A[iming]/P[oint].' Similarly, a crew from 428 Squadron estimated that two of the three target indicators it saw were northeast of the aiming point 'in a line about a mile apart.' If these assessments were correct, neither the markers nor the bombing could have been concentrated on the marshalling yards, and that, in fact, was the case. Damage spread into the town, where 313 buildings were destroyed, including the jail and the school, and 252 civilians were killed. But there was a positive side – several prisoners were able to escape from the damaged jail, including a butcher who had been caught aiding downed airmen.[102]

After the raid on Courtrai, Bomber Command had attacked all six of the French railway targets included in Portal's directive, and two, Le Mans and Amiens, had been bombed twice. Before the month was over, however, Harris ordered one additional raid, and on 29/30 March seventy-six Halifaxes and eight Mosquitos attacked the railway yards at Vaires, near Paris, in bright moonlight. The bombing was accurate and, by chance, caught two ammunition trains in the yards. They blew up, killing some 1200 German troops. The Canadian group contributed fifty of the machines sent to Vaires and, although annoyed once again that the late arrival of the Pathfinders had forced them to orbit the target, most were satisfied they had hit the aiming point on their second run. Despite weak opposition, one crew failed to return from the raid, the first from No 6 Group to be lost on these early transportation operations, and it is sadly appropriate that it should have come from No 434 Squadron, still the RCAF's hard-luck unit or 'chop' squadron.[103]

The next night, of course, Bomber Command would suffer terribly on the way to and over Nuremburg. From 1 April on, however, although area raids would continue to be mounted, High Wycombe's effort would increasingly be in support of Operation Overlord. In this respect there could be little doubt that, with bombing errors generally running less than seven hundred yards, the nine March raids on French railway targets had been outstandingly successful – demonstrating, at times, 'an accuracy and concentration ... far exceeding that ... achieved by the American heavies by day.'[*][104]

---

[*] After the war, the United States Strategic Bombing Survey estimated that, bombing visually by day in clear weather, the Eighth Air Force was able to get half its bombs within one-third of a mile of the aiming point; bombing non-visually by day, in heavy cloud, it got only one-half its bombs within 3.9 miles of the aiming point.

Indeed, four objectives (Trappes, Vaires, Le Mans, and Amiens) were considered by Eisenhower's staff to have been sufficiently damaged as to require no further attention in the immediate future. While still able to function, the remaining three (Laon, Aulnoye, and Courtrai) had nevertheless sustained significant damage, and it was felt they could be put out of action relatively easily during April and May. Moreover, Bomber Command had achieved these results while inflicting far fewer casualties on the French civilian population – and at far lower cost to itself – than had been anticipated. The death toll in France was probably under four hundred, and only seven crews had been lost through enemy action. Harris's prediction that Bomber Command would not be able to cut rail lines 'could not,' the air staff concluded, 'have been further from the truth.' Indeed, in his memoirs Sir Arthur recalled the surprise with which he learned of his crews' successes: 'I myself did not anticipate that we should be able to bomb the French railways with anything like the precision that was achieved.' From 25 March 1944, by which time Eisenhower's staff had seen the results from these early raids, there was no turning back. 'Everything he had read,' the supreme allied commander announced, 'convinced him that apart from the attack on the G[erman] A[ir[F[orce], the transportation plan was the only one which offered a reasonable chance of the air forces' making an important contribution to the land battle during the first vital weeks of Overlord.'[105]

Two days later the Allied chiefs of staff made their decision and as a result, all of No 6 Group would soon be attacking railway targets all over Western Europe.[106]

Working for SHAEF,
April–September 1944

Although Sir Arthur Harris was far from enamoured of the new chain of command, the first bombing directive issued by General Eisenhower's headquarters gave him considerable (and unexpected) leeway in determining how Bomber Command would conduct its operations. To be sure, the AOC-in-C was reminded that 'all possible support must ... be afforded to the Allied Armies ... to assist them in establishing themselves in the lodgement area' in France. But, the directive continued, 'in view of the tactical difficulties of destroying precise targets by night,' his crews would 'continue to be employed in accordance with their main aim of disorganizing German industry ... [except that] where tactical conditions allow ... targets will be selected so as to give the maximum assistance in the aims of reducing the strength of the German Air Force, and destroying and disrupting enemy rail communications.'[1]

Whenever Harris had seen such permissive language before – as in the Pointblank directive, for instance – he had usually hastened to make the most of it. Confident that Bomber Command could do great damage to Berlin within reasonable margins of safety and survivability, he had made the German capital, and not the enemy's factories and refineries, the focal point of attack over the winter of 1943–4. Then, flaunting hopeful damage assessments and lurid newspaper reports in front of the nay-sayers, he had for the most part successfully stood up to his critics. Schweinfurt, it will be recalled, was not bombed until 24/25 February 1944, months after it had been singled out as a priority target because of its ball-bearing production.

Now, however, although still convinced that German civilian morale would not 'stand many more heavy night attacks,' the AOC-in-C was not nearly so sanguine about what might be achieved through routine area raids. In recent weeks bombing accuracy had fallen off, while the casualty curve suggested that the night offensive 'could not in the long run be sustained' unless wastage rates could somehow be reduced. In fact, future prospects were probably bleaker than that. With the approach of summer's shorter, brighter nights, the likelihood that the Luftwaffe would inflict 'very severe losses' had to be taken into account. Weather permitting, rather than risk a running fight like that on the approach to Nuremburg when fighters had been called in from all over

Europe to engage a single bomber stream, henceforth each night's effort would involve multiple routes to several objectives.[2]

It had taken some considerable time, but High Wycombe had at last recognized that, with Himmelbett eclipsed by other forms of night-fighting, dispersion no longer played so directly into the enemy's hands. Rather, as they struggled to organize pursuit operations based on electronic eavesdropping, the German controllers were likely to be hard-pressed by the simultaneous appearance (aided and abetted by all sorts of spoofs and diversions) of several widely dispersed bomber streams, increasing the odds that some attackers might slip through unmolested. Not everyone would be so lucky, however, and that was what worried Harris. Complaining that the three squadrons of Mosquitoes then on strength with No 100 Group lacked even 'nuisance value,' he repeated his request that the number of night-fighters assigned to bomber support be increased. Initially rebuffed for security reasons,[*] the AOC-in-C was eventually allocated another five squadrons, but none were operational before D-Day.[3]

The Germans were also making adjustments to correct a number of the problems and deficiencies that had come to light in the later stages of the battle of Berlin. Besides closing the radar gap in the south with both fixed and mobile installations, they moved a number of freelance fighters to the Rhine to permit their earlier insertion into the bomber stream, and a few were stationed in France – but only a few, it having been decided that the Paris-based Luftflotte 3, still an independent command, would not be reinforced until after the invasion, which OKW anticipated would come later that spring or summer. Indeed, so as not to confuse Luftflotte 3's controllers, fighters based in the Reich were ordered not to fly into France.[4]

Within Germany, meanwhile, there was a general consolidation of the air-defence organization when, on 1 April, 1 Jagdkorps, the Wilde Sauen, all day-fighter units and Flak batteries, and the air raid reporting service were brought together under a single headquarters, Luftflotte Reich, located in Berlin, creating for the first time an integrated air-defence command at the strategic level. Taking advantage of the as-yet-unjammed Ypsilon (Benito) and Egon communications systems, however, control of the night battle at the operational level was increasingly left to subordinate formations, both to make it more difficult for Bomber Command to fool the entire night-fighter organization on any given night and to improve the response against the kind of dispersed attacks Harris was now contemplating.[5]

Somewhat uncharacteristically, but perhaps with recent loss rates in mind, High Wycombe did not take full advantage of Eisenhower's offer to continue with the area offensive while remaining 'on call' for other things in the spring of 1944. Between 17 April and 6 June there were only thirteen main-force raids into Germany as against almost one hundred on railroads, coast-defence instal-

---

[*] Not wanting the new Mark X AI radar to fall into enemy hands, the Air Ministry initially restricted its use to the air defence of Britain despite the limited threat of attack on the United Kingdom.

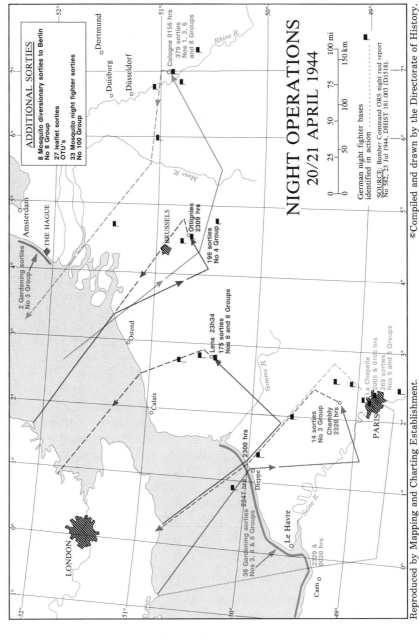

ADDITIONAL SORTIES

8 Mosquito diversionary sorties to Berlin
No 8 Group

27 leaflet sorties
OTU's

33 Mosquito night fighter sorties
No 100 Group

Dortmund

Duisburg
Düsseldorf

Rhine R.

Cologne 0156 hrs
379 sorties
Nos 1, 3, 6
and 8 Groups

Amsterdam
THE HAGUE

2 Gardening sorties
No 3 Group

Maas R.

BRUSSELS
Ottignies
2309 hrs
196 sorties
No 4 Group

Ostend

Lens 23h34
175 sorties
Nos 6 and 8 Groups

Calais

Somme R.

2300 hrs

14 sorties
No 3 Group
Chambly
2320 hrs

La Chapelle
0005 & 0106 hrs
PARIS   269 sorties
Nos 5 and 8 Groups

Dieppe

36 Gardening sorties 2247 hrs
Nos 3, 4 & 6 Groups

Le Havre

Seine R.

2329 &
0020 hrs

LONDON

Caen

NIGHT OPERATIONS
20/21 APRIL 1944

0   25   50   75   100 mi

0   50   100   150 km

German night fighter bases
identified in action ....

SOURCE: Bomber Command ORS night raid report
No 582, 23 Jul 1944, DHIST 181.003 (D1518).

©Compiled and drawn by the Directorate of History.

Reproduced by Mapping and Charting Establishment.

lations, and airfields in France and the Low Countries.[6] As had been anticipated, the number of casualties fell, far enough for Harris to ask that sorties
to France, Belgium, and Holland should not count as a full 'trip' towards completion of the normal thirty-mission operational tour. Otherwise, he warned,
'some aircrews must inevitably finish their operational tour having experienced
far less risk and strain than others, which is obviously undesirable.' Once the
Air Ministry agreed, each formation was left to do its own pro-rating, and in
No 6 Group a point system was eventually adopted that differentiated between
easy and difficult targets. The result was that the average operational tour now
required about thirty-five sorties and remained at that number until March 1945
when, because of a surplus of crews, it fell again to thirty.[7]

With all Halifax IIs and Vs withdrawn from operations over Germany, No
6 Group participated in just eight of the thirteen raids over the Reich, losing
twenty-three of 560 sorties, or 4 per cent. Fourteen of its losses came in the
space of three days. Eight crews (including three from No 433 Squadron)
failed to return from Düsseldorf (22/23 April), while six were lost at Karlsruhe
on 24/25 April. The casualty rate at Düsseldorf was in line with that suffered
by the rest of Bomber Command, but why Canadian losses should have been
so high at Karlsruhe (4.3 per cent) compared with the rest of Bomber Command (2.6 per cent), when RCAF crews reported night-fighter activity to have
been 'on the whole negligible,' is difficult to explain unless it is attributed to
simple bad luck.[8]

The Luftwaffe's continuing lack of navigation aids, de-icing equipment, and
a reliable IFF device for its Würzburgs went a long way in determining the
extent of its success or failure at this time. On 20/21 April, for example, the
air-defence organization had timely radio and radar warning of the Cologne
raid; but because a small formation of German bombers was returning from
attacks on Hull, Bristol, and Portsmouth along approximately the same track
as that on which Bomber Command forces were approaching the Continent
(and could not be reliably distinguished from the latter because there was no
IFF), most of the fighters scrambled were not committed to battle. At Düsseldorf (22/23 April) and Friedrichshafen (27/28 April), in contrast, the German
effort was effective. The radio intelligence service identified the bomber stream
while it was still over England, and route interception began early – a pattern
that was repeated in May, when the five raids on German targets cost Bomber
Command ninety-seven of 1700 sorties (5.7 per cent) and No 6 Group eight
of 118 sorties (6.7 per cent). Less than a month before D-Day, despite all the
jamming and other counter-measures available to Bomber Command (and
despite heavy daytime attacks by American forces against the German aircraft
industry), the enemy's ability to defend its his own air space at night, at least
when the weather was good, had been eroded scarcely at all.[9]

Indeed, the potential of Luftflotte Reich to do damage at night was growing
in May.[10] Almost one thousand SN2 airborne interception radars (still undiscov-
ered by High Wycombe and now being modified to operate on more than one
wavelength) had been delivered by the end of the month, while Neptun, also
unjammed, was being fitted to the Wilde Sauen's FW 190s. Nachtjagd-

geschwader 6's experiments with Ypsilon and Egon control to guide groups of fighters into the bomber stream had proved so successful that they were being copied by other formations, and German signals intelligence was beginning to read centimetric Mark II Oboe. (It had been jamming Mark I since November.) That not only gave additional early warning of attack but, on occasion, could also be exploited to identify Bomber Command's specific target – a fact that was recognized by the air staff with understandable horror in July.[11]

These improvements were not extended to the skies over France. Since Berlin had limited the Luftwaffe's night-fighter strength there, for most of the spring Bomber Command faced only elements of III/NJG I at Laon, the inexperienced crews of NJG 4 working under equally inexperienced controllers at Luftflotte 3 in Paris and the Me 410s of Kampfgruppe 51, a bomber-intruder unit based at Calais whose crews also flew Wilde Sauen operations. To some considerable extent, that was the payoff for earlier decisions to limit night-fighter production. At the same time, the strict separation between Luftflotte Reich and Luftflotte 3 was frustrating to the German-based Gruppen which, having to scramble every time the alarm sounded but prohibited from flying into France, were suffering casualties for that reason alone. But when I Jagd-korps asked permission to station some of its units on forward bases in France and allow the rest access to French air space, Oberkommando der Luftwaffe denied Josef Schmid's request.[12]

The first April raid by No 6 Group against a transportation target came on Easter Sunday, when 160 crews were sent to the marshalling yards at Lille and Villeneuve St George. None was lost to enemy action (although two collided on the way to the target) and the damage was spectacular. At Villeneuve the repair shops were especially hard hit, while at Lille 'an ammunition train blew up in the reception siding.' Civilians died in both cities: ninety-six at Ville-neuve and 456 at Lille, where almost 5000 houses were destroyed. The railway yards at Tours, Tergenier, Ghent, Aulnoye, and Laon, as well as the airfield at St Cyr, were targets the next night, and there were civilian casualties at all six places. No 6 Group dispatched eleven squadrons to Ghent, where, with good marking, the Merelbeke sheds were heavily damaged, but so was the residential area southwest of the aiming point, and four hundred Belgians were killed.[13] Winston Churchill's concerns about friendly casualties were not unfounded.

Tergenier, Rouen, Juvisy, and Noisy-le-Sec (Paris) were the objectives on 18/19 April, No 6 Group concentrating on the latter, where 'the locomotive sheds, repair shops, trans-shipment sheds, reception sidings, sorting sidings, road bridge, passenger station, and goods depot were all seriously affected. Many tracks were cut and much rolling stock was destroyed.' In addition, some two hundred delayed-action bombs continued to explode in the weeks following the raid, obstructing repair work and distracting those doing it. Nearly a thousand houses were knocked down and 464 civilians killed. Of the four RCAF crews who failed to return only one was credited to a fighter, while two 'probably collided' near the target and the fourth fell to Flak.[14]

As two dozen Lancasters from Nos 408 and 426 Squadrons joined the raid on Cologne the next night, and the other groups attacked the marshalling yards at La Chapelle, Chambly, and Ottignies, 158 RCAF crews made up the entire main force sent to Lens. It was a successful night for the Canadians. Cologne and Lens were both heavily hit and only one crew went missing, but two of fourteen crews detailed by No 428 Squadron crashed on their return to England, killing three crew members and injuring four.[15]

Laon, attacked on 22/23 April by Halifax squadrons while the Lancasters were busy at Düsseldorf and Brunswick, cost High Wycombe nine of the 181 aircraft dispatched; probably because they were in the first wave, No 6 Group lost only one of forty.[16] Five days later at Montzen, where the overall loss rate was 11.36 per cent, the Canadians lost ten crews from fifty-five sorties (18.2 per cent). No 431 Squadron suffered most heavily, losing four of eleven, while No 434 (which had been doing better recently) lost two of sixteen. Both squadrons had been assigned to the later waves, which were attacked as soon as they crossed the Dutch and Belgian coasts and then again from St Trond to halfway across the Channel on the return route, by some of the three hundred fighters scrambled.[17]

One pilot of No 431 Squadron (who had not been to Nuremburg) was shaken by the ferocity of the enemy response. 'More aircraft seen shot down than on any other trip,' he reported after the raid, 'too many to log by Navigator.' His commanding officer, Wing Commander W.F.M. Newson, who would take over No 405 Squadron in November and lead it until April 1945, was equally dismayed by the heavy casualties but was also unhappy with the way in which the raid had been planned. 'It is felt that this attack was technically unsound,' he observed in the impersonal passive voice common to official reports,

due to these three factors: (1) The number of aircraft employed were spread over a long period of time, consequently concentration in time and space was not achieved, thus enabling controlled fighters to be vectored on to each individual aircraft throughout the whole route. (2) It is considered that the zero hour should have been one hour later, due to the height and brilliance of the moon. (3) It is considered that P[ath] F[inder]F[orce] should not have opened attack so early before zero hour. In so doing, this enabled fighter concentration in this area to be vectored into the stream, there being too long a period for the number of bombers in the attack.[18]

No 405 Squadron lost a single Lancaster at Montzen from which Squadron Leader E.M. Blenkinsop, deputy master bomber for the operation, was the sole survivor. Succoured by the Belgian 'underground' Resistance, Blenkinsop elected to continue the fight with them rather than attempt a return to England. He was finally captured by the Gestapo in December 1944 while participating in an attempt to blow up a house used by the Germans. Never identified as a downed airman, he was eventually sent to Neuengamme concentration camp where he died of heart failure on 23 January 1945, perhaps, it has been suggested, as the result of a lethal injection.[19]

Because Blenkinsop had worked with the Resistance and was engaged in sabotage while wearing civilian clothes, he had forfeited whatever rights he may have had as a captured airman and no 'war crime' was committed against him. The treatment accorded another crew member from 405 Squadron, shot down over Belgium on 27/28 April, was more difficult to judge. Of the eight men aboard the Lancaster, six were killed outright, one escaped, and the last, Flight Lieutenant G.J. Smith, who was bleeding steadily from the nose, mouth, and ears, was taken to the German hospital at Diest, where he died. After the war Allied investigators were told that 'the German doctor in charge ... is known to have given strict orders that Smith not be touched in any way and that the door to his room be at all times locked' – a clear case, it seemed, of criminal neglect. When it was learned, however, that 'there is ... local Continental medical opinion that patients with serious head injuries ... should be given "complete rest," which precludes even the taking of X-Rays,' the initial assessment was called into question. When the Canadian director of medical services subsequently reviewed the case he concluded that the doctor had, in fact, been guilty of 'gross negligence' and charges were filed with the United Nations War Crimes Commission. By then, however, it was too late to follow up stale leads.[20]

Sometimes there were fewer doubts. It was almost certain, for example, that Flying Officer W.S. Sewell of No 434 Squadron shot down over Kassel on 22/23 October 1943 'had been ... hanged by the civilians in Kassel, on landing.' And it was even clearer that Flying Officers H.W. Birnie and D.S. Jamieson of No 426 Squadron, who would be shot down over France on 28/29 June 1944 and would try to return to allied lines in civilian clothes, had been executed by the Gestapo.[21]

Any mistreatment of bona fide prisoners of war by service personnel, the police, or civilians is, like the murder of the fifty who escaped from Stalag Luft III in March 1944, to be despised and condemned. But these incidents, deplorable as they otherwise might have been, need to be placed in context. The RCAF had just over 2400 aircrew taken prisoner (and Bomber Command some 11,000), yet the number believed to have died in unacceptable circumstances is very low – perhaps about a dozen in the RCAF's case including those who took part in the 'Great Escape.' Given the horrific conditions that existed in German cities after the heavier and more successful raids, that is a remarkable statistic.

With 1 Jagdkorps still barred from French air space, the Luftwaffe could not manufacture many nights like Montzen. Indeed, Bomber Command's loss rate over France and the Low Countries in April 1944 was negligible compared with that sustained over Germany and well below the figure likely to cause concern at High Wycombe or the Air Ministry. But April's missing rate over occupied territory was also more than double that experienced in March; and if nothing else it said something about the enemy's defensive capabilities when Flak and a small number of fighters, stationed well forward (where their reaction time was short) and under the guidance of inexperienced controllers, could achieve so much. One wonders what might have happened had 1 Jagdkorps been allowed to participate (see tables 8 and 9).[22]

TABLE 8
Losses on Bomber Command Operations, March–May 1944[23]

	March	April	May
Sorties to German targets	6,038	4188	2453
Losses against German targets	270 (4.5%)	121 (2.9%)	102 (4.15)
Sorties to non-German targets	2,837	5014	7906
Losses against non-German targets	18 (0.6%)	76 (0.5%)	165 (2.1%)
Minelaying sorties	518	854	826
Minelaying losses	2 (0.4%)	19 (2.2%)	9 (1.15)

TABLE 9
Bomber Command Loss Rates by Group, March–May 1944

Group[a]	March	April	May
No 1 Group	4.7	2.9	4.5
No 3 Group	2.8	2.2	2.4
No 4 Group	3.9	2.3	1.8
No 5 Group	3.4	2.4	3.1
No 6 Group	2.8	2.1	1.8
No 8 Group	1.8	1.2	1.2

[a] No 2 Group had been assigned to 2nd Tactical Air Force.

The focus of Bomber Command's attack shifted even more dramatically over the next month. Between 1 May and 5 June about three thousand sorties were flown against German targets (with losses slightly above 5 per cent), while there were nearly 9000 (including Gardening missions) over occupied Europe. Just over two hundred crews failed to return from the latter, a missing rate of 2.3 per cent – higher than April's figure but still acceptable. No 6 Group contributed 2826 of these sorties, two-fifths of the total, but lost only twenty-four, 0.85 per cent, considerably less than the average.[24] The RCAF's worst night came on 8/9 May at Haine St Pierre, when six of seventy-five crews – 8 per cent – failed to return. The skies had been clear, which helped the enemy, and it was thought that the Canadians had taken insufficient care to discharge Window at the prescribed rate; but they had also been sent to the one objective out of five which, for no discernible reason, the Luftwaffe had singled out for attention. Fighters pounced on the bomber stream long before it reached the target and pursued it forty miles over the English Channel on the return route.[25]

Although the AOC of No 5 Group, Air Vice-Marshal R.A. Cochrane, always maintained that his group's low-level target-marking produced significantly better bombing results than those of other groups, the scientists who studied the photographs from April's and May's transportation raids discovered that No 6 Group's data were almost as good – just under half its crews appeared to have bombed within five hundred yards of the aiming point, and three-fifths within seven hundred – and much better than those turned in by Nos 1 and 3

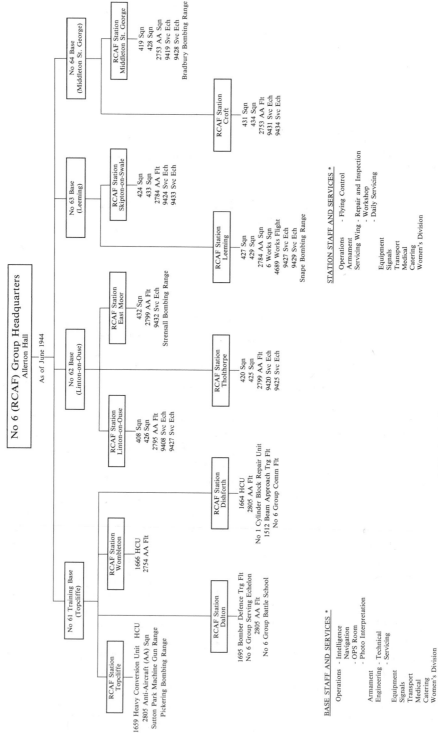

No 6 (RCAF) Group Headquarters
Allerton Hall
As of June 1944

No 61 Training Base (Topcliffe)

RCAF Station Topcliffe
1659 Heavy Conversion Unit HCU
2805 Anti-Aircraft (AA) Sqn
Sutton Park Machine Gun Range
Pickering Bombing Range

RCAF Station Wombleton
1666 HCU
2754 AA Flt

RCAF Station Dalton
1695 Bomber Defence Trg Flt
No 6 Group Serving Echelon
2805 AA Flt
No 6 Group Battle School

RCAF Station Dishforth
1664 HCU
2805 AA Flt
No 1 Cylinder Block Repair Unit
1512 Beam Approach Trg Flt
No 6 Group Comm Flt

No 62 Base (Linton-on-Ouse)

RCAF Station Linton-on-Ouse
408 Sqn
426 Sqn
2795 AA Flt
9408 Svc Ech
9427 Svc Ech

RCAF Station East Moor
432 Sqn
2799 AA Flt
9432 Svc Ech
Strensall Bombing Range

RCAF Station Tholthorpe
420 Sqn
425 Sqn
2799 AA Flt
9420 Svc Ech
9425 Svc Ech

No 63 Base (Leeming)

RCAF Station Skipton-on-Swale
424 Sqn
433 Sqn
2784 AA Flt
9424 Svc Ech
9433 Svc Ech

RCAF Station Leeming
427 Sqn
429 Sqn
2784 AA Sqn
6 Works Flight
4689 Works Flight
9427 Svc Ech
9429 Svc Ech
Snape Bombing Range

No 64 Base (Middleton St. George)

RCAF Station Middleton St. George
419 Sqn
428 Sqn
2753 AA Sqn
9419 Svc Ech
9428 Svc Ech
Bradbury Bombing Range

RCAF Station Croft
431 Sqn
434 Sqn
2753 AA Flt
9431 Svc Ech
9434 Svc Ech

BASE STAFF AND SERVICES *

Operations - Intelligence
            Navigation
            - OPS Room
            - Photo Interpretation
Armament
Engineering - Technical
            - Servicing
Equipment
Signals
Transport
Medical
Catering
Women's Division

STATION STAFF AND SERVICES *

Operations - Flying Control
Armament
Servicing Wing - Repair and Inspection
            - Workshop
            - Daily Servicing
Equipment
Signals
Transport
Medical
Catering
Women's Division

* Major elements only.

SOURCE: Compiled from organization charts and narratives in DHIST files 181.009(D4206), 72/360, and 72/383.

Groups. The reason, they explained, was that Canadian navigators, like those in No 4 Group, were using the revised wind values broadcast by Bomber Command to check their own readings, while Nos 1 and 3 Groups left wind-finding entirely up to individual crews, who often got it wrong. When this trend continued in June and July, High Wycombe finally had to act. Although reluctant to interfere with the prerogatives of AOCs, all groups were directed to follow the Nos 4 and 6 Group procedure.

Despite its superior performance, neither Air Vice-Marshal McEwen nor his senior air staff officer, Air Commodore Slemon, were entirely satisfied with No 6 Group's effort and they continued to look carefully at what was going wrong on those occasions when results were significantly worse than the norm. They found that Bomber Command's winds were sometimes wrong, but there was also powerful evidence that veterans of the battle of Berlin in particular, but also those of area bombing in general, had become afflicted with a 'general carelessness' about operations that had everything to do with their previous experience, when accurate bombing hardly mattered at all. The Ghent raid of 10/11 April, when just 7 per cent of bombs fell in the target area, four hundred Belgians were killed, and almost 1600 buildings were damaged and destroyed, was a case in point. 'Many aircraft ... in complete disregard of the orders issued ... bombed when no ground markers were burning,' unmistakable evidence of 'bad discipline.' Senior squadron officers were also responsible because of their 'failure to stress sufficiently at briefings the absolute necessity for crews adhering to the bombing heights, headings, and airspeeds laid down.'[26]

Mistakes like that were out of the ordinary, however, and by 5 June 1944 Bomber Command had done practically everything asked of it by General Eisenhower. Of the thirty-seven railway targets assigned to Harris, twenty-two were 'sufficiently damaged to require no more attention until further notice,' fifteen were 'severely damaged' and, as the Germans themselves admitted, the whole transportation system linking France and the Reich had been 'most seriously crippled.' Only around Paris was the rail network still functioning because, for political reasons, targets close to the centre of the French capital were not subjected to intense attack. In addition, heavy cratering was seen on seven of the twelve enemy airfields assigned to Harris, and a number of radar and radar stations had also been knocked out. Mount Couple, a site housing almost sixty transmitters but measuring just 300 by 150 yards, was obliterated by Nos 6 and 8 Groups on 31 May, while a slightly smaller installation at Au Fèvre was damaged. Ammunition dumps (and 21st Panzer Division) had been hit in early May by Nos 1 and 5 Groups, while thirty coastal batteries were attacked over the whole month. Finally, 2198 minelaying sorties, 854 by No 6 Group, had been launched as part of the prelude to Overlord in March, April, and May, with special emphasis (as D-Day drew nearer) on protecting the flanks of the invasion corridor. Harris, who had never believed that his command was capable of such precison, was amazed, and he was not the only one. 'The U.S. air forces, who specialise in precision visual attacks by day, are in particular astonished at the results,' he informed his crews; 'You have in fact wiped their eye for them at their own game.'[27]

After a nerve-wracking day's delay (which gave five Canadian squadrons the chance to bomb Calais again without loss, contributing nicely to Fortitude, the overall D-Day deception scheme), Operation Neptune, the assault phase of Overlord, began the night of 5/6 June. Bomber Command sent 1135 crews to attack ten artillery batteries covering the invasion beaches, No 6 Group (which provided about one-fifth of the total) making for Merville, Franceville, Houlgate, and Longues for the loss of only one crew. Most reported that they had bombed their primary targets using Oboe and H2S blind-marking, but because of cloud the results of their attack were not immediately known. As it turned out, they did not measure up to the claims that were made. While the garrison at Merville was apparently shaken, it was not too dazed to resist when British paratroopers attacked the battery at dawn. One of the guns at Longues was put out of action, but the other three, and the battery at Houlgate, continued to fire on the British and Canadian beaches until suppressed by naval gunfire.[28]

No 100 (Bomber Support) Group, formed originally to deceive the German night-fighter force, came into its own as part of the immediate D-Day cover and deception plan. 'Five Fortresses of 214 Squadron,' Canadian pilot Murray Peden recalled,

together with a force of about three times as many Lancasters, were to establish a strong patrol line some 80 or 90 miles north-east of the beaches, protecting the left flank of the great assault from aerial interference. We would be dropping WINDOW continuously, to maintain the threat of other heavy bomber forces thrusting inland, and blanketing with a continuous and impenetrable curtain of jamming every channel of communication used by the German night fighters ...

We steered for our appointed patrol line, situated just north and east of Dieppe, and began our run inland almost perpendicular to the coastline. We were flying well above the Lancasters at 27,000 feet, and our orders called for us to Window and carry the jamming barrier inland some 80 or 90 miles.

Our orders were to patrol our lengthy beat eight times (counting the inbound and outbound legs separately); so, for seven hours we plied black and forth in the darkness, WINDOWING and jamming for all we were worth ... On the last leg we began to descend towards the coast ... We left the French coast behind, continuing our descent, and headed back towards England. It was not yet daylight, but the darkness had begun to soften. Suddenly we saw a sight that brought a lump into my throat.

Sometime earlier that night, schoolboy John Keegan had heard hundreds of aircraft flying low over his house (see chapter 9). Now Murray Peden saw them. 'A tremendous, awesome aerial armada was passing us in extended formation a mile or two on our left side. They were going in. We were coming out. For a minute I watched them sailing silently onward to their date with destiny. I thought of the men squatting nervously inside and felt like a slacker. After five or six hours in the air we were on our way home, heading back to a good breakfast and a clean bed. They were only a quarter of an hour away from going in by parachute or glider – to face what? We flew in silence for some time.'[29]

Along with Window and Airborne Cigar, No 100 Group was also employing Mandrel, a counter-measure originally introduced in 1943 for use against early-warning radars but quickly withdrawn when the enemy greatly expanded the number of Freya frequencies. Subsequently (and substantially) modified to increase its power and range as well as the spectrum of frequencies that could be blotted out, the 1944 Mandrel variant required as many as forty transmitters to be carried and operated by the crew of a single aircraft, and its reintroduction was delayed until the invasion to maximize its effect during the most critical military operations yet undertaken by the Western allies. On the night of 5/6 June, then, just twenty aircraft from Nos 199 and 803 Squadrons were able to produce an electronic screen 'behind which aircraft could operate unseen.' After the beachhead was secure and the Royal Navy had withdrawn its objections to the routine use of Mandrel over the English Channel (for fear that it would inadvertently cover the approach of German forces), the equipment would be employed in support of almost all bombing operations. Besides reducing the effective range of the German early warning radar chains, it also greatly facilitated the carrying out of spoofs and diversions.[30]

When the target to be bombed lay in southern Germany, for example, the plot might shape up like this. Just before dusk, a dozen or fourteen MANDREL aircraft would fly out and take up their stations off the enemy coast, strung out in pairs in a great line so as to shield our bases completely from observation. At the appointed moment, the operator in each aircraft would switch on MANDREL, blanketing all of the FREYA's screens with snow. The central German fighter controller would thus have no early information on which to base his preliminary concentrations ... After some considerable time, however, an attacking British force would suddenly come thrusting through the northern portion of the MANDREL screen and begin to be discernible to the FREYA ... But as the controller well knew, at least after the first time Bomber Command did it ... the powerful bomber stream reported to be heading for the Frisians ... might only be a handful of Fortresses dropping WINDOW ... while at the same time, Main Force, which had gone into France at low level ... suddenly appeared on the German radar screens far to the south.[31]

But Mandrel was not the be-all and end-all of electronic counter-measures. Provided the Window anti-jamming kits developed for their large Würzburg Riesen were working, the Germans could still identify the bomber stream while it was fifty miles out to sea, which offered at least some early warning, while undisciplined use or testing of H2S was always a dead give-away of the stream's location. And, since the Germans were able to monitor both Mark I and Mark II Oboe, it was possible for them to penetrate the jamming even when Mandrel was present – although whether they would always react correctly was a different question. Accordingly, No 100 Group undertook to exploit the enemy's understandable anxiety to see through the jamming – and its equally understandable propensity to believe that whatever appeared on its radar screens when electronic counter-measures were not present had to be genuine. They began to 'simulate the breakdown of the Mandrel screen,' giving German controllers a tantalizing glimpse of what seemed to be an approaching bomber stream but was actually a sham. After two or three spoofs based on this pattern, by which time the enemy was probably conditioned to accept these bogus penetrations as Bomber Command's latest deception gimmick, High Wycombe would allow the genuine main force to be revealed behind the Mandrel screen in the hope that the Luftwaffe would ignore it.[32]

Sometimes the technique worked perfectly. On 18/19 July No 6 Group lost only one of 154 crews in a low-level approach (2500 feet) to the synthetic oil plant at Wesseling, a little south of Cologne, an area that was usually heavily defended. The Canadians were ignored, however, because they were identified as spoofers when they emerged from the Mandrel screen.[33]

After D-Day Bomber Command continued to attack targets selected by Eisenhower's headquarters. Indeed, although the US Eighth Air Force was to have been equally involved in the assault on the French railways, the fact that American crews had little blind-bombing experience meant that its operations were often cancelled because of low cloud and inclement weather. Bomber Command, however, simply continued with its well-tried Pathfinder marking techniques using Gee, Oboe, and H2S. The first post-invasion raids on rail centres in the Paris area took place on 7/8 June. With crews flying well below 10,000 feet, heavy Flak accounted for most of the twenty-eight sorties lost (8.3 per cent of the 337 dispatched), but all targets were hit heavily and accurately. For its part, No 6 Group contributed one hundred crews, of whom six returned early, four were lost, and one crashed on landing. (One of those returning early did so with only three men on board, the other four having baled out without their captain's knowledge after their aircraft had been damaged by anti-aircraft fire.)[34]

Flak would remain the main threat to the bomber stream by day, when the German gunners did not have to rely upon radar to see what they were shooting at. At the same time, however, now that the invasion had taken place, the Luftwaffe moved a number of fighter units into France and western Germany – although not so many as had been called for in April's plan. There was also further decentralization of command to improve the response against multiple shallow penetrations. More importantly, the old line of demarcation between Luftflotte 3 and Luftflotte Reich was erased completely, and the Germans were soon mounting a strong and resolute defence over France, Belgium, and Holland. On 12/13 June fighters, not Flak, accounted for most of the twenty-three aircraft lost (3.4 per cent) in Bomber Command's operations against transportation targets, and most again of the fifteen (8.2 per cent of those dispatached and including three each from Nos 408, 419, 427, and 434 Squadrons) lost by No 6 Group over Arras and Cambrai. Similarly, three weeks later night-fighters took advantage of clear skies and a 'virtually full moon' to shoot down nine of the 102 crews (8.8 per cent) No 6 Group sent to Villeneuve St George.[35]

While the scale was decidedly different, the similarities with the Nuremburg raid of 31 March 1944 are striking.

It was on the night of 12/13 June that the only Victoria Cross awarded to a No 6 Group airman was earned. Pilot Officer Andrew Mynarski was the mid-upper gunner of a No 419 Squadron Lancaster X which was 'attacked from below and astern by an enemy fighter.'

As an immediate result of the attack, both port engines failed. Fire broke out between the mid-upper turret and the rear turret, as well as in the port wing. The flames soon became fierce and the captain ordered the crew to abandon the aircraft.

Pilot Officer Mynarski left his turret and went towards the escape hatch. He then saw that the rear gunner was still in his turret and apparently unable to leave it. The turret was, in fact, immovable, since the hydraulic gear had been put out of action when the port engines failed, and the manual gear had been broken by the gunner in his attempts to escape.

Without hesitation, Pilot Officer Mynarski made his way through the flames in an endeavour to reach the rear turret and release the gunner. Whilst so doing, his parachute and his clothing, up to the waist, were set on fire. All his efforts to move the turret and free the gunner were in vain. Eventually the rear gunner clearly indicated to him that there was nothing more he could do and that he should try to save his own life. Pilot Officer Mynarski reluctantly went back through the flames to the escape hatch. There, as a last gesture to the trapped gunner, he turned towards him, stood at attention in his flaming clothing and saluted, before he jumped out of the aircraft. Pilot Officer Mynarski's descent was seen by French people on the ground. Both his parachute and his clothing were on fire. He was found eventually by the French, but he was so severely burnt that he died from his injuries.

Thrown clear when the Lancaster hit the ground, Flying Officer G.P. Brophy, the rear gunner whom Mynarski had been trying to save, had a miraculous escape. Delivered to the Resistance by French civilians, he was back in Britain by September to tell his, and Mynarski's, story.[36] Although there would be seventeen more attacks on railway targets before the end of the month, after which the volume of all French rail traffic had been reduced to 20 per cent of January's levels, the real damage had been done by the end of the second week of June. 'All main lines' had been broken, authorities in Berlin observed; 'the coastal defences have been cut off from supply bases in the interior [and] large-scale strategic movement of German troops by rail is practically impossible.' In London, meanwhile, the air staff drew some satisfaction from the fact that Harris's pessimistic prediction that he could best support the invasion by intensifying his attacks on German cities had proved to be 'very far ... from the truth' – and even more parochial glee from the evidence that Bomber Command's 'accuracy and concentration on small targets [exceeded] that ... achieved by the American heavies by day.'[37]

Once the railways had been cut – No 6 Group had provided about a third of all transportation plan sorties – and with Allied intelligence estimating that the Wehrmacht's total fuel reserve had dwindled to about two months' supply, it was only to be expected that petroleum refining would now re-emerge as a priority target system. Portal and Sir Norman Bottomley, the deputy chief of air staff, were both convinced of its importance, while Harris, who had once regarded oil as the 'panacea of panaceas,' had arrived at an informal agreement with Air Chief Marshal Sir Arthur Tedder, Eisenhower's deputy, to take on the enemy's synthetic petroleum industry whenever the tactical situation in Normandy permitted.[38]

Since these synthetics were used primarily to produce aviation fuel for the Luftwaffe, the bomber forces would be helping their own cause – and to an extent they might not have considered possible just a few months before. 'Precision bombing on markers dropped by Oboe in average weather proved far more effective than we had any right to expect,' Harris observed after the fact, and the Americans became increasingly proficient with H2X (their version of H2S). As a result of the combined assault, monthly output of synthetic oil was reduced from 436,000 to 152,000 tonnes between May and September, while production of aviation fuel fell from 156,000 to 10,000 tonnes a month over the same period (and to 1000 tonnes in February 1945) at a time when the Luftwaffe required about 320,000 tonnes a month. The strategic reserve fell from 314,000 tonnes to a paltry 30,000 tonnes over the same period (although the decline was at least partially attributable to the amount of fuel set aside for the forthcoming German offensive in the Ardennes).[39]

On 16/17 June, when the refinery at Sterkrade was the target, the Luftwaffe was disappointed with its effort as weather grounded many of its crews. Yet, despite the full functioning of the Mandrel screen, No 6 Group crews reported that fighter activity had been 'rather intense.' All told, thirty-two aircraft failed to return (10 per cent), including twelve of the one hundred from No 6 Group (among them four each from Nos 431 and 434 Squadrons, the latter again having a spell of heavier-than-normal casualties). As had happened before, and for reasons that are no longer discernible, the bomber stream had passed very close to one of the beacons around which a large number of night-fighters were orbiting. Beyond that, however, now that the Germans were using as many as nine voice and two Morse channels simultaneously to broadcast their running commentaries, and changing frequencies every half hour, even Bomber Command's extensive and sophisticated repertoire of electronic counter-measures could not frustrate all the German controllers. 'The effort was concentrated on those channels which were considered to be most dangerous,' signals intelligence reported, but even so one of them 'remained readable' in England.[40]

Although Harris would later remark that his time under Eisenhower's command was a period of consistency and continuity in terms of the objectives he was given, the post-invasion bombing of France entailed considerably more than attacks on railways and oil refineries. A formal but sporadic campaign against the V-weapons launch sites (Operation Crossbow) had begun in December 1943, mostly by light bombers and fighter-bombers (as recounted in the Fighter War section of this book). When the first flying bomb (V-1) fell on the United Kingdom on 12/13 June, however, the attack on the launch sites was intensified and High Wycombe was told to bomb storage and supply facilities as well. Although not entirely happy with these orders, Harris sent 405 crews to attack four V-weapon supply depots on 16/17 June, and followed that up with sixty-three separate raids before the end of August.* Operating by night as well as by day, when crews were instructed to fly in 'broad and reasonably short' columns to allow fighter escorts to cover them, Bomber Command dropped 24,292 tons of bombs on Crossbow targets in July (two-fifths of its total effort for the month) and continued on at almost the same pace in the first two weeks of August. One such operation, against the V-1 storage site at St-Leu-D'Esserent on 5 August, saw No 6 Group deliver 1193 tons of bombs, the most it dropped on any one raid during the whole war.[41] Results were nevertheless 'disappointing' despite the intense effort – in part because Crossbow sites were difficult to find, but also because it had been decided to deplete the large stocks of obsolete GP [General Purpose] bombs against them rather than employ the more modern and efficient 'middle capacity' bombs used against other precision targets, particularly oil refineries and synthetic plants.[42]

Allied planners had anticipated that the Germans would make a concerted effort with their French-based destroyers, E-boats, and other light surface vessels against Allied ships sailing between England and Normandy. To that end, it was important to maximize damage to port facilities on each side of the Baie de la Seine and any naval vessels which might be using them. The Channel ports north of the River Orne were assigned to Bomber Command, and Harris, taking advantage of Allied air superiority, chose to attack Le Havre and Boulogne at twilight so as to limit collateral damage and casualties. No 6 Group joined the attack on 15 June, providing 162 of 297 crews sent to Boulogne. While there was some disagreement among the Canadians as to the placement of the markers, the bombing seemed to have been accurate and there would be less interference with cross-Channel shipping by E-boats sailing from that port. (Destroyers and E-boats were, however, active from Le Havre.) Although Harris undertook all these missions dutifully enough and boasted about their successes in his memoirs, at the time he was still inclined to regard them as a serious misapplication of strategic air power. 'I do not believe,' he told Tedder, 'that apart from the damage to the rocket firing sites and to supply dumps, any of this bombing has had a worthwhile effect ... while it has had the deplorable effect ... of taking virtually the whole of Bomber Command and much of the American effort off targets in Germany for 3-1/2 months.'[43]

What worried him most, however, because General Eisenhower had never concealed his intention to use both the Eighth Air Force and Bomber Command as a kind of heavy artillery, was the likelihood that he would be called upon to support ground operations as a matter of course. And, indeed, the first such mission took place on 7/8 June, when elements of Nos 1, 5, and 8 Groups

---

* With General Spaatz objecting even more strenuously to any diversion of the American bombing effort, Bomber Command in fact took on most Crossbow targets. The US Eighth Air Force became involved only when 'it could not operate against German industry' and, in July and August, it contributed just over a quarter of all Crossbow sorties.

(with No 405 Squadron providing twelve Lancasters) were assigned the task of attacking a six-way road junction near the First US Army front. Unhappily, a stray marker which fell six miles from the aiming point attracted most of the 795 tons of bombs dropped. The next such attack, an attempt to cover the withdrawal of British armour from Villers-Bocage on 14/15 June, did not prevent the Germans from attacking on the 16th; but a similar raid against 9 SS Panzer Division in the same area on 30 June, for which No 405 Squadron provided ten target-markers, proved 'most effective' because 'it delayed their attempt to take Cheux.'[44]

Although Bomber Command carried out several more interdiction attacks – bombing enemy troop concentrations and supply lines behind the battlefront – by daylight, it was not until 7 July 1944, when General Montgomery asked for an aerial bombardment to assist in taking the city of Caen, that High Wycombe (and Allerton Hall) became involved in close support of ground operations. The attack on Caen was launched shortly before last light on the 7th, when 467 machines from Nos 1,4,6 and 8 Groups dropped more than 2500 tons of bombs in less than an hour on some two-and-a-half square miles of the northern half of the city. Eighty-seven crews from No 6 Group 'were enthusiastic over the success of this raid,'[45] but Wing Commander J.E. Johnson, the top-scoring British fighter ace who was now leading No 144 (RCAF) Wing of Spitfire escorts, had his doubts.

It was quite apparent that a number of bombs had fallen well outside the target area.

As I watched the terrible destruction wrought on the French city, I could not help but wonder whether we were using a sledge-hammer to crack a nut. We were well aware of the military necessity to break the enemy at Caen so that our ground troops could eventually deploy into open country. But we were not so sure that this object could only be achieved by the wholesale destruction of Caen and the death of a great number of its inhabitants.

Some of the bombs were timed to explode up to six hours after the attack, so that there would not be too large a time lag before the ground force went in the next morning. Flying low on the fringe of the attack, I distinctly saw a German tank thrown into the air, like a child's toy, and turning over and over before it fell to the ground.[46]

The Canadian infantrymen, who had just succeeded in capturing part of Carpiquet airfield on the western edge of the city in two days of costly fighting, found the 'smoke and flame wonderful,' reporting that it had 'improved their morale 500 per cent.' No doubt it did much the same for the British troops on their left, half encircling the city. The enemy, however, found the bombing ineffectual. The senior staff officer of the 12th SS (Hitler Jugend) Panzer Division recorded that his formation 'suffered only negligible casualties ... Some tanks and armoured personnel carriers were toppled over or buried under debris from houses, but after a short while nearly all of them were again ready for action.' Of course, the bulk of his troops, like the other defenders of Caen, were solidly dug in along an arc of villages and hamlets north of the city, where they escaped this intense bombardment; in order to limit the dangers of friendly fire, 'it had previously been decided that pending further experience the bombline should be 6,000 yards ahead of the nearest [Anglo-Canadian] troops.'[47]

Indeed, there was little that was 'close' about this operation in terms of either time or space. For reasons probably connected with 21st Army Group's reluctance to assault by night, as well as Bomber Command's preference for visual identification of aiming points when undertaking such a precise attack, the bombardment was carried out at last light on the 7th, while the troops did not begin to move until first light on the 8th – an interval of some six hours during which those Germans who had been subjected to the bombing could, and did, largely recover their poise. In the end, it took a day-and-a-half of heavy fighting (that included naval fire support from the 16-inch guns of HMS *Rodney,* out in the English Channel) to take Caen at a cost of 3500 casualties – more than a thousand of them Canadian.[48]

Although the cratering and rubble created by the bombing had made it difficult for those fighting through the city, there was still much enthusiasm on the part of most soliders for this new kind of fire support. The mere sight of a massive bomber attack quickened the spirit of troops who were, by now, coming to rely upon overwhelming firepower for any success at all and who realized, as postwar studies would confirm, that heavy bombers produced a barrage 'out of all comparison with that attainable by any artillery concentration that can at present be contemplated.' Montgomery asked for 'the whole weight of air power' to fall on the defended areas and strongpoints flanking his proposed thrust as he planned Operation Goodwood – the second attempt to unhinge the German defences south of Caen and open the way to Falaise. What he got, on 18 July, was (in the words of Leigh-Mallory, penned the following November) 'the heaviest and most concentrated air attack in support of ground forces ever attempted.'[49] This time Bomber Command, including almost two hundred crews from No 6 Group, came in broad daylight, shortly after dawn.

Again the troops forming up for the ground attack were properly impressed. A soldier waiting to advance with the British armoured division that would spearhead the ground assault watched the approaching air armada with awe.

High in the sky and away to our left a faint and steady hum caught our attention and, as we watched, it grew into an insistent throbbing roar and the first aeroplanes appeared high up in the pale sky. Then the whole northern sky was filled with them as far as one could see – wave upon wave, stepped up one above another and spreading out east and west until it seemed there was no room for any more ... The bombers flew in majesticaly and with a dreadful, unalterable dignity, unloaded and made for home; the sun, just coming over the horizon, caught their wings as they wheeled. Now hundreds of little black clouds were puffing round the bombers as they droned inexorably to their targets and occasionally one of them would heel over and plunge smoothly into the huge pall of smoke and dust that was steadily growing in the south ... Then the guns took up in a steadily increasing crescendo the work which the bombers had begun.[50]

The airmen delivered over three thousand tons of bombs in forty-five minutes, and at some points the bombline was no more than nine hundred yards in front of the foremost British troops. The attack was directed against five fortified villages, two on each flank of the army's line of advance and one – Cagny – directly in its path. Allocated to two of the five targets, those Canadians who bombed the one reported it 'well plastered' and those assigned to the other thought their bombing 'well concentrated in the target area; they had, in fact, caused substantial damage and temporarily demoralized many of the enemy. But the army did not begin its advance until 0745 hours, ninety minutes after the heavy bombers had finished their work and time enough for the Germans to recover sufficiently to offer significant resistance. Despite having pierced the enemy's defensive crust and advanced up to four miles, Montgomery's armoured spearheads (and the 3rd Canadian Infantry Division on the right) ground to a halt, the roads behind them so congested that it was impossible to reinforce success.[51]

While the question of bomblines could be (as we shall see) an extraordinarily tricky one, it is hard to comprehend why the matter of timing could not have been coordinated more closely from the beginning, with the air attack concluding at the same prearranged moment that the soldiers began to move forward. Even so, Generalfeldmarschall Hans von Kluge (who had been appointed to command Army Group B after Rommel had been injured in a fighter-bomber attack on 17 August) found this new kind of heavy bombardment disturbing. 'The psychological effect on the fighting forces, especially the infantry, of such a mass of bombs raining down upon them with all the force of elemental nature, is a factor which must be given serious consideration,' he told Hitler.[52]

Montgomery's next attempt to open the road to Falaise was planned and executed by Lieutenant-General Guy Simonds's II Canadian Corps, with the British 51st (Highland) and Polish Armoured Divisions under command. A night operation, Totalize called for close support by heavy bombers despite Harris's doubts about the ability of his crews to bomb accurately enough in the dark; and, indeed, although 1100 aircraft were dispatched, only 660 of them actually attacked, the others being called off by the master bomber as the target areas became obscured by smoke and dust. Altogether, 133 of 235 crews from No 6 Group squadrons were permitted to bomb, those who did reporting 'very concentrated bombing' in what they assessed as a 'good attack.'[53]

Because the bombing ended early, the ground attack (which had been scheduled to begin half an hour *before* the last bombs fell on the most distant targets) actually began half an hour *after* the bombardment had concluded. Dust and smoke from the bombing, combined with darkness (and sadly inadequate map- and compass-reading) led many of the attackers to lose direction, but, even so, by dawn they had again created a distinct breach in the German defences. General Simonds intended to launch his two armoured divisions – the Polish and 4th Canadian – through that breach, sped on their way by more close support bombing, to be delivered in daylight by the US Eighth Air Force. Of 678 machines dispatched, 492 actually attacked, dropping nearly 1500 tons of bombs. Unfortunately, twenty-four of them bombed wrongly, killing and wounding more than three hundred officers and men of the Polish armoured divison and the 3rd Canadian Infantry Division, including the latter's commander, Major General R.F. Keller, among the wounded. The second phase of Totalize petered out.[54]

Away to the southwest, meanwhile, the Americans were now lunging forward in a gigantic right hook that showed every prospect of trapping a vast German army in the so-called 'Falaise pocket' if only Montgomery's armies could push southeast, past Falaise, and join up with the Americans at Argentan. To that end another Canadian assault was mounted on 14 August, under the code-name Tractable, in which just over eight hundred aircraft from Nos 1, 4, 6, and 8 Groups hit at enemy concentrations and strongpoints about a mile in front of the start-line. No 6 Group provided 227 crews for the operation, of which 105 made for aiming point 23, on the northern fringe of the battlefield near Bons Tassilly, and the rest for aiming point 28, slightly to the south, at Aisy/Potigy.[55] 'The area in which these aiming points lie,' crews were informed,

is high ground infested with guns, tanks and defended localities and forms the main stumbling block between the Canadian Army and FALAISE. The intention of this attack is to remove this stumbling block by disorganising, neutralizing, and destroying everything in the area surrounding the Aiming Point and by using blast to force the survivors to keep their heads down while the Canadians attack to capture the key town of FALAISE. In this attack Bomber Command are adding their massive weight to the team that is steadily pulling tight the neck of the bag round the nearly trapped enemy divisions and their contribution, if successfully carried out, may well be the decisive factor in the completion of the first major victory over the German armies on French soil in this war.[56]

The Bons Tassilly force, comprising crews from Nos 408, 415,[*] 420, 425, 426, 432, and 433 Squadrons, was by and large able to 'map-read [its] way to the aiming point' despite only 'fair ... horizontal visibility'; most crews reported that they had 'bombed on concentration of T[arget] I[ndicator]s or centre

___

[*] No 415 Squadron, as we have seen earlier, was transferred to Bomber Command on 12 July 1944 at Ottawa's request because the Canadian government was not satisfied with the role it had been given in Coastal Command. In terms of personnel, only the groundcrew and headquarters staff went to No 6 Group, the Wellington and Albacore aircrews moving to other RAF squadrons. No 415 flew its first bomber mission on 28/29 July, when it bombed Hamburg. For the first month or so, however, perhaps because there were so many new aircrew, one pilot found No 415 to be 'a sloppy squadron with a morale problem,' something not helped when, in mid-August, a mid-air collision during practice flying killed the commanding officer and most of the other senior officers as the former attempted too tight a formation. Wing Commander J.H.L. Lecomte, the popular and successful CO of No 425 Squadron, was transferred to No 415 and immediately set his stamp on it by stepping up training and, letting the adjutant handle his paper work, flying as many operations as possible. When he was promoted to group captain and took over the station at Tholthorpe in November, No 415 Squadron had fully recovered.

of smoke and dust covering the target area, with 1 second overshoot' as instructed by the master bomber. Even so, a few bombs fell short, fortunately into open country.[57]

The group that attacked Aisy had rather more difficulty. Although there was 'no cloud over the target ... vertical visibility [was] poor due to dust and smoke from earlier attacks.' Moreover, some could not make out the master bomber's broadcast clearly. In the end, because of the debris in the air, he apparently called off the attack on 'TIs Y[ellow],' asking them instead to aim (like those to the north) for the 'centre of smoke and dust ... with a one second overshoot.'[58] On the whole, results were good. All seven targets were struck hard and the Canadian troops were able to advance with light casualties past enemy positions that had previously held them up.[59]

A few bombs did not fall in the proper area, however, and the master bomber 'was heard to stop some crews from bombing a quarry short of the target, and there were a number of undershoots, 3 or more miles short of the aiming point.' In fact, 126 crews, including forty-four from No 6 Group, had bombed the quarry in question, which was being used as a staging area by the 12th Field Regiment, Royal Canadian Artillery. All told, sixty-five soldiers were killed, 241 wounded, and ninety-one were missing. In addition, according to Major-General George Kitching, the commander of the 4th Canadian Armoured Division, 'the radios in the tanks and on the jeeps were badly affected at the most critical time.'[60]

The army's curious request that, notwithstanding unfavourable winds, the bombing should take place from north to south, perpendicular (rather than parallel) to the front, 'in order to conform to the ground movement,' was in part responsible for the accident.[*] Such subordination of Bomber Command's effort to army requirements had bothered Harris when he first saw the plan for Totalize, but Sir Arthur had also been nervous because, persuaded that they would not show up in daylight, the army had chosen not to fire coloured marker shells to identify the target. Accordingly, elaborate precautions had been taken to reduce risks. There would be both visual and Oboe marking; each of the seven targets would have its own master bomber and a deputy; crews were to make timed runs from the Channel coast to the target; and navigators and bomb-aimers were to map-read carefully.[61]

Some airmen actually blamed these precautions for the subsequent target-finding error. 'Perhaps too many different safeguards were devised,' recalled Flight Lieutenant J.A. Morris from No 429 Squadron, 'which confused the bomb-aimers and navigators.'

We were to do a timed run from the coast to a check point inland, and from there use stop watches to calculate the number of seconds required to reach the target. In

---

[*] Following the abortive attempt to begin Operation Cobra on 24 July 1944, US General Omar Bradley had been shocked and astonished to discover that the Eighth Air Force had made a perpendicular bomb run in support of the American First Army, charging the airmen with 'a serious breach of good faith in planning.'

addition to this, we were using GEE, and Pathfinders would mark the aiming points. Map-reading was also stressed, but the artillery marking by star shells, that had been so successful[*] in the first raid, had been abandoned.

There were three separate targets to be covered, all close together, and ours was timed to be the last. When we reached the area, there was a great deal of smoke around from the first attacks, and it was not clear which was the last target. At this moment of uncertainty some aircraft dropped his bombs short, others followed, and the damage was done. The bomb-aimers were probably concentrating on their stop-watches instead of map-reading, and when they saw bombs falling ahead, either lost count, or mistrusted their calculations. Anyway, some forty planes bombed two minutes early, and hit concentrations of our armour waiting for zero hour. The Master Bomber, instead of using the code-word to stop the attack, called on R.T. 'Don't bomb the quarry; your target is ahead.' The bombs continued to fall.

I had no idea at the time that anything was wrong, and was horrified when [Wing Commander A.F.] Avant called me aside after interrogation and told me of the short bombing. Cameras were sealed and the films sent to Group, with the navigators' and bomb aimers' logs. I felt quite confident that we were not involved because Brownie [Flight Lieutenant J. Brown, Morris's navigator] reported that we bombed at the correct time. However, the next day it was disclosed that practically the whole squadron was involved; photographs showed that a quarry being used as an assembly point ... had been straddled. Our own picture showed bombs falling beside the main road leading to Falaise, far short of the target; fortunately there was nothing on the road. We all felt very badly about the mishap. It was a serious business, and was bound to have consequences; the worst could be that the army might lose confidence, and not request any further assistance from us.[62]

Despite his later claim that he had 'no idea ... that anything was wrong,' Morris was so unsure of himself at the time that he brought one 500-lb bomb back to base. Others in his squadron were equally flummoxed when they could not see the yellow target markers that were supposed to mark the aiming point and were instructed (somewhat vaguely it must be said) to bomb the middle of the smoke instead, while still observing all the safeguards built into the mission. While Flying Officer J.C. Lakeman's stop-watch timing was 'right on' when he released his bombs, others were nearly a minute early when they followed the master bomber's instructions. For some, it proved altogether impossible to follow the prescribed procedures. 'Timed run from Caen ... was not used,' Flying Officer P.J. Cormier reported. 'Had to weave to avoid other aircraft.'[63]

It was not just No 429 Squadron that had difficulty, and upon their return to base many crews indicated they were uneasy about whether they had bombed the correct target, an alarming state of affairs given its proximity to friendly troops. 'M[aster] B[omber] called for bombing yellow TIs, some con-

---

[*] Morris exaggerates. The star shells were not brilliant enough to show through dust and debris, and the master bomber, it will be recalled, had to call off the attack early.

fusion over which A[iming]/P[oint] was ours,' announced one; 'approaching column of smoke which we took to be our target 50 secs. early on E[stimated] T[ime] of A[rrival],' reported another. Several said they had witnessed 'under-shooting,' and some, like Flying Officer W. Edmondsen of No 428 Squadron, freely admitted dropping his bombs '1 min early in error.' The formal investigation which ensued asserted, unforgivingly, that the bombing of the quarry at Hautmesnil 'was started by two aircraft of No 428 (RCAF) Squadron who bombed almost simultaneously,' was continued by crews from an Australian squadron, and completed by crews from No 1 Group.[64]

Soldiers subjected to the bombing found the experience not nearly as stimulating as watching the enemy being bombed. 'The second wave hit at the factory buildings south of Quesnay Woods,' Captain T.J. Bell of the 12th Field Regiment recalled:

and as this bombing was very close to us everyone had a grandstand seat for the show. It really looked impressive and one wondered how the Jerries could live through it. Soon we were to know ... The next wave bombed behind us. Great pillars of smoke arose and at our gun position we thought perhaps the *Luftwaffe* was bombing from above our heavies. It wasn't so, however, as the next wave dropped their bombs directly on us. The giant planes came over at less than a thousand feet and as they approached we could see the bomb doors open and the bombs come tumbling out ... In a steady, stately procession the heavies came over, wave after wave, unendingly. The first bombs dropped on us at 1430 hours and at 1540 hours we had our last.

During that time there were frantic efforts by officers and men to set out our identification markers and ignite our yellow smoke canisters. The attempts were dismal failures as they only seemed to rivet the attention of the bombers on us, as a target, more thoroughly. They not only bombed us but they machine-gunned us as well. No Germans ever presented a finer tactical target than we did on that day with all our guns pointing unmistakably south and all our vehicles with their clearly visible white stars. The bombers were so low we could clearly see the figures of the pilot and co-pilot and surely they could see us as well.[65]

Knowing, as we do, that the Pathfinders were dropping yellow target indicators, it is easy to understand why, as the gunners fired their yellow smoke, they felt they were becoming even more of a target for the bomber stream. And when, a little later, an army-controlled and piloted Auster observation aircraft had taken off and fired red Verey lights in a further attempt to halt the bombing, these too were mistaken for target indicators.

The Canadians, in fact, had been following Eisenhower's (and First Canadian Army's) standing orders when they fired yellow smoke to mark their forward positions and warn friendly aircraft away – orders of which High Wycombe was unarguably aware. Apoplectic at the way in which the press was holding his command entirely responsible for the mishap, however, and even more incensed that the Auster crew was credited with preventing a still greater tragedy, Harris lamely tried to spread the blame by maintaining that during the planning for Tractable the soldiers had made no specific mention of their intention to fire yellow smoke as a warning – a bizarre way, indeed, to interpret and treat 'standing' orders. The AOC-in-C was also more than a little aggrieved that, having made manifest his misgivings about the Tractable bombing plan, Bomber Command was now said to be at fault when things happened as he had cautioned they might.[66]

Sir Arthur attached no blame to the master bombers. So far as he was concerned, they had done a difficult job well, as evidenced by the fact that the majority of main-force crews had bombed where they were supposed to. Furthermore, he did not fault the one master bomber who had tried to stop the bombing at the quarry but did not use the recognized code that would have called off the entire attack. Rather, the misadventure had resulted from incomplete planning, and particularly from the failure to generate a simple, standardized procedure to call off a few crews bombing inaccurately while the rest were where they should have been. Even so, although only No 6 Group had issued stop-watches to all crews and taken particular care to ensure that they understood the importance of the timed run, it had been RCAF crews 'who were the most in error' despite these precautions, and they had to shoulder some of the responsibility as well.[67]

The AOC-in-C's conclusions by and large reflected those reached by the groups involved. No 6 Group's report of findings, for example, heavily criticized those who had bombed before their timed runs had expired – despite the mitigating circumstances that could be adduced in their favour.

The attack on A[iming] P[oint] 23 was preceded by attacks on 3 aiming points in the same area and consequently it was anticipated that the resulting dust and smoke would probably make definite identification ... difficult. Therefore, in order to avoid the very mistake which was subsequently made, all the aircrews ... were briefed to make a timed run from the enemy coast to Caen and from Caen to the release point.

It now transpires that one of the chief contributing factors was that those crews which bombed short had their navigators take the time check, and thus intercommunication between the navigator and the bomb aimer was essential to ensure against dropping before the ETA at the target. Unfortunately, the Master Bomber's comments received over the intercommunications system seriously interfered with the time checking conversation.

Nonetheless, the report concluded, 'the blame for this inaccurate bombing appears to lie with the bombing teams in that they neglected to check their E[stimated] T[imes of] A[rrival] carefully ... thus disobeying the carefully prepared instructions.'[68]

Under these circumstances, crews who had bombed short were left with very little excuse for their part in the incident. 'No matter what misleading conditions and indicators existed,' Harris observed, 'any adequate effort to maintain the check on a timed run from the coast line to the target areas could and would have prevented ... errors.' Accordingly, squadron and flight commanders personally implicated lost their appointments and their acting rank, and most were posted away to other units. (The Pathfinders who had gone wrong

– none of whom were from No 405 Squadron, it should be said – left No 8 Group and returned to normal flying duties.) A list was also compiled of all crews who had bombed in the vicinity of the quarry so they would not again be 'employed within thirty miles forward of the bomb line until reassessed by the AOsC after further experience on targets outside the operational area of our own troops.' That, Harris thought, should lessen the chance of a similar occurrence in the future.[69]

No 429 Squadron's Jerrold Morris was one pilot who lost command of his flight. 'I was called to Six Group for an interview with a high ranking officer,' he explained. 'He told me that he was very sorry to have been deputed to carry out the orders of the Command … All officers involved were to be deprived of acting rank, and all crews were to undertake bombing details on the ranges, to produce results up to specified standards, before being allowed to take part in further army co-operation raids. He said that he realized that the accident was not due to carelessness, as much as to fortuitous circumstances. I felt quite sorry for the man.'[70]

High Wycombe also took a number of steps to strengthen the 'essential safeguards' built into its army support operations after Tractable. Wind direction and smoke drift would henceforth be 'overriding considerations' in planning such missions; timed runs were to be adhered to by all crews; a master switch was to be installed on the navigator's panel 'with which he can prevent bombs being released by the bomb-aimer before the expiry of the timed run'; extra master bombers with 'cancellation pyrotechnics' were to be employed; and the troops on the ground were to be given orders 'to use no pyrotechnics likely to be confused as target markers.'[71] General H.D.G. Crerar, commanding the First Canadian Army, was satisfied. 'I remain a very strong advocate of the use of Heavy Bombers in closely integrated support of the Army,' he told Harris, '... by day as well as by night.'[72]

In his memoirs, Sir Arthur Harris argued that 'without the intervention of Bomber Command the invasion of Europe would have gone down as the bloodiest campaign in history unless, indeed, it had failed outright – as it would undoubtedly have done.' Overstatement was still the AOC-in-C's forte, and whatever he may have said after the fact about the pride and pleasure he took from Bomber Command's contribution to the battle for Normandy, he sent his crews back to the cities of Germany as soon and as often as he could: five times in July, not counting raids on synthetic oil plants, twelve times in August, and five again in the first two weeks of September, before the strategic bomber forces were released from Eisenhower's control. The target lists were all too familiar – Kiel, Stuttgart, Hamburg, and Brunswick, among others – and so, at times, were the casualty lists as well. It should be noted, at the same time, that in terms of weight of attack the air war was entering a new phase. Of all the bombs that were dropped on Germany during the Second World War, '72 per cent fell after 1 July 1944.'[73]

The first of these 'extra-curricular' raids, against Kiel on 23/24 July, involved 629 crews (but only forty-two from No 6 Group). Having lost sight of the low-flying main force at Rostock, where it had appeared for an instant through the Mandrel screen and was dismissed as a Gardening effort, the German air-defence system gave only a few minutes' early warning. Only four bombers failed to return. Stuttgart was attacked the next night by 614 crews, forty of them from No 6 Group. Despite haphazard navigation – some aircraft (including a number from No 6 Group) 'violated Swiss territory on return from Stuttgart,' upsetting the Swiss and forcing Bomber Command to concoct suitably soothing replies – damage was heavy, with both the Bosch and Zeiss lens factories hit. But so were Bomber Command's casualties. Twenty-three crews, 4.6 per cent, failed to return, including one from No 419 Squadron.[74]

Stuttgart was also the target on the next two raids into Germany. On 25/26 July, with 85 per cent of crews bombing within three miles of the aiming point, damage was very heavy, but the low casualty rate of 2.2 per cent mystified the analysts at High Wycombe. From intercepted radio traffic it was clear that the target had been identified by the enemy in good time; fighters were scrambled at nearby beacons from bases in Germany, Belgium, and France; there were no diversions; and yet there was 'nothing … to account for the comparative lack of success which the enemy … achieved … Their tactical moves were timely and their general dispositions organised to put a large force of fighters into the bomber stream well before the target was reached.' There being little else to go on, the chief signals officer at Bomber Command deduced that weather had been the bomber stream's greatest ally, and that 'on a night when visibility was poor and considerable reliance was placed on the use of AI, our … WINDOW … prevented a large numbers of fighters from completing an interception.'[75]

Wing Commander J.K.F. Macdonald, a veteran of the 1942 Aleutian campaign against the Japanese who had recently taken over command of No 432 Squadron, chose to fly this operation because 'we had had a series of relatively short-distance trips down into the Brittany Coast, and I didn't feel like sending the squadron off to Stuttgart, which was a ten hour trip, unless I was prepared to go myself.' As his own crew had been screened, Macdonald 'cast around … to find out who I had who could come with me.'

Unfortunately … the only people available were the navigator leader, gunnery leader, and engineering leader … We never got to Stuttgart. We went down somewhere east of Chateaudun, France. In the crew I had picked up, the radio man didn't know how to operate FISHPOND … I didn't know that he didn't know … The first we knew that we were under attack was when we were hit with 20 [mm] cannon on the starboard inner engine … We were on fire … I ordered them to abandon the aircraft … Apart from [the rear gunner, who had cut his jugular vein while parachuting] we all got out reasonably safely … I hid under a cornstalk … The farmer that picked me up was not part of the underground, but he had contact with somebody who was.

After obtaining civilian clothes and an identification card showing him to be 'a French labourer, deaf and dumb,' Macdonald was moved through the Resistance network back to Chateaudun, where he waited until the Americans arrived in late August. Returning to England, Macdonald refused the normal evaders' leave and asked for re-assignment to his old squadron, only to be told by Air Vice-Marshal McEwen that 'there was no way ... I would get it ... I should be court martialed for losing all those leaders.' Promising never to take his senior staff on operations again, Macdonald repeated his request, McEwen relented, and on 27 September he resumed command of No 432 Squadron.[76]

Two nights later, this time in good weather, Bomber Command levelled Stuttgart's city centre (but scored 'no hit ... on armaments firms where only superficial damage was inflicted'). There was heavy Windowing, and a 'clever' plan made full use of all available counter-measures – Mandrel, Drumstick, Airborne Cigar, Tinsel, Jostle, and Fidget – all for nought. Taking full advantage of the clear skies, 'the enemy's dispositions ... were good ... fighters were so placed that they could intercept in strength,' and thirty-nine Lancasters, 7.9 per cent of the attacking force, were shot down. All 235 of No 6 Group's crews were sent to Hamburg that night – it was the first anniversary of the firestorm raid – and although the skies were not quite so clear there as at Stuttgart they, too, suffered heavily, especially on their homeward flight. Twenty-two crews (7.2 per cent, but 9.6 per cent of the Halifaxes) failed to return, with No 431 Squadron losing five of seventeen.[77]

With results like that to ponder, by the end of July the operational researchers had arrived at a disheartening conclusion. 'The enemy night fighter organization has got ahead of our tactical counter-measures,' they cautioned, and 'unless there is a radical change in the tactical picture we would be likely to incur prohibitive casualties in strategical operations by night against Germany in the coming winter.' Sir Charles Portal thought the same, submitting on 31 July his own, equally pessimistic, predictions about the future of bombing to the prime minister. Recent losses, he asserted, were 'another pointer to the increasing efficiency' of the Luftwaffe and illustrated how the enemy was 'surmounting the difficulties presented by our radio countermeasures,' especially in good weather. If such loss rates continued, he added, Bomber Command would have to alter its tactics, provide better defensive equipment for its aircraft, use long-range escort fighters at night, or switch over to day bombing.[78]

For his part, Harris told the undersecretary of state for air that 'it is an acknowledged fact that the only branch of the German Air Force which has survived and maintained a high degree of efficiency and morale is the Night Fighter force, and it is logical to suppose that the rate of loss which will follow the renewal of strategic bombing with the deeper penetration involved, will not fall below that previously experienced and may well prove considerably more severe.'[79]

Because of the tactical situation in Normandy – and the continuing need to take on V-weapon sites – there were no further operations to German cities until mid-August. By then, Bomber Command was the beneficiary of an extraordinary bit of good luck. On the night of 13 July the crew of a Ju 88 night-fighter, having lost their way while chasing a small Gardening force, landed by mistake in Suffolk. From it, the British learned the secrets of SN2 radar (hidden up to now because it used a frequency that was also employed by part of the Freya chain) as well as Flensburg and Naxos. High Wycombe recognized at once the vulnerability of H2S, Monica, and IFF, and from this date forward periods of radar and radio silence were included in all its operational plans. Counters to SN2 were also quickly developed – first type MB ('Long') Window, then the Piperack jammer.[80]

However, the Ju 88 revealed more than just electronic secrets, for when the airframe itself was examined Bomber Command discovered the extent to which the Germans had fitted armour to their night-fighters. The ten-millimetre plate in the nose was 'virtually invulnerable' to .303 ammunition, and that led Harris once again to ask that production of turrets capable of taking .5-inch guns be hastened. The Air Ministry, annoyed by Harris's inconsistent and infelicitous demands (first for better vision, then for more firepower) as much as by the ease with which he brushed aside difficult design and production problems, did not relish entering into another prolonged argument with him on the issue of bomber defence, but it was agreed that work on the Frazer Nash 82 turret would be accelerated. But only a few were produced by the end of the war, while work on turrets mounting 20-millimetre cannon never advanced beyond the prototype stage.[81]

Moreover, although the radar-assisted automatic gun-laying turret (AGLT, or Village Inn) was ready for operational testing in the summer of 1944, the somewhat tardy recognition of how advanced the enemy were in exploiting Bomber Command's radio and radar transmissions as clues to finding the bomber stream led to fears that it, too, might become a homing device for the Luftwaffe. Not only were there radar emissions for night-fighters to intercept and track, but the infra-red IFF signal that had been designed for it could be detected from the ground as well as in the air. Harris, however, was only too eager to provide his crews with a radar that searched out to 1330 yards in a 30° cone that could be increased, by traversing the turret, to 100° left/right and 60° up/down. Even with its .303-inch guns, he exclaimed, Village Inn was 'a formidable weapon against the night-fighter,' and he urged that production forge ahead. To bring the sad story of AGLT to a close, however, only four squadrons had been equipped by May 1945, and although their loss rate was cut by two-thirds they did not utilize it fully. The equipment proved to be too sophisticated for some air gunners, while others, who understood intuitively that they were more likely to shoot down bombers than night-fighters unless AGLT's IFF component worked perfectly, relied on Village Inn as a warning device only. Because its radar was a marked improvement over other varieties, they were at least able to take evasive action earlier – hence their lower casualties – but blind-firing occurred in only four sorties per thousand.[82] To all intents and purposes, then, Bomber Command ended the war with the same defensive armament it began with five years earlier.

That was all in the future. For the present, losses suffered on the experimental 12/13 August 1944 H2S blind-bombing raid to Brunswick – 'a complete failure' with fewer than 10 per cent of crews hitting the target – and an
accompanying mission to Rüsselsheim, merely confirmed Portal's and Harris's
suspicions that the enemy was more capable of thwarting attacks than ever.
The German controllers had not responded to the initial incursions appearing
on their screens, and the fighters sent to intercept the two genuine main forces
arrived in plenty of time. Losses were heavy: 7.1 per cent of the force sent to
Brunswick (slightly higher in the last wave, to which Nos 4 and 6 Groups were
assigned), and 6.7 per cent of those who went to Rüsselsheim.[83] Once it was
realized that careless use of H2S was not altogether to blame, but that the
enemy tracking and radio-intercept services were cleverly using all their
resources and all kinds of clues[*] including Oboe 'to identify the target and
often to recognise diversions as such,' it seemed to some that the only recourse
was 'to stop all transmissions from our aircraft.' That was not going to happen;
if nothing else, night-bombing required electronic aids to navigation to remain
at all practicable.

At the same time, Air Ministry scientists were warning Harris that the time
had come to cease relying exclusively on evasion and electronic jamming to
protect the bomber stream; instead, they explained, 'nearly all the emphasis
needs to be put on destroying enemy fighters' – a daunting task given Bomber
Command's meagre armament.[84] The solution, it was clear, was to take the
offensive, and on 15 August Harris dispatched a thousand aircraft to join
nearly seven hundred American bombers – all supported by a thousand fighters
– in a massive daylight assault on nine fighter bases in Holland and Belgium.
'There is one section of the G[erman] A[ir] F[orce] which is not merely intact,'
briefing notes pointed out, 'but is actually gaining in strength.'

This operation in which American and RAF Bomber Command will be working
together is aimed primarily at the airfields used by the GAF Night Fighters during the
short summer nights. These fighters operate from forward aerodromes fairly near the
coast and while they are thus sticking their necks out it is a good opportunity to take
a crack at them and to reduce them to the same level of impotence as the enemy's day
fighters. The airfields allotted to Bomber Command are in the heart of the night fighter
area and carry an average of 20 to 30 night fighters each; many of them operate
whenever night attacks are made on the continent which they will not be able to do
if the airfields and runways are pitted with craters. The intention of these combined
and simultaneous attacks is to produce an immediate reduction in the fighting efficiency of the GAF by direct attack – in other words to deliver a smashing punch on the

---

[*] Besides the Naxos and Flensburg devices with which we are familiar, the German Y Service employed a number of direction-finding devices against the broad range of British radio
and radar transmissions. Laubfrosch looked for H2S, at a distance of 500 kilometers; Gerhard
looked for Monica at a similar distance; Flamme and Sägebock were used against Bomber
Commands IFF; Lux and Grille looked for the AI used by Mosquito night-fighters; Donnerkell
was aimed at Oboe; and Dudelsack looked for the British R/T and W/T jammers.

nose which, if it does not knock the [opponent] completely out of the ring, will anyway keep him on the floor at this critical moment.[85]

Favoured by good weather and meeting scarcely any opposition, Bomber Command did considerable damage to six of the airfields. No 405 Squadron provided Pathfinders for the attack on the Brussels/Melsboek facility.

At 1156:12 hours, Master Bomber dropped TI red 50 yards N.E. of Aiming Point 'A' on the runway and told Main Force to bomb 50 yards to starboard of them. Backers-Up dropped TIs between Aiming Point and S[outh] dispersal area and also 500 to 1,000 yards NE of Master Bomber's reds on runway. Meanwhile, Main Force, which was two minutes late, had thoroughly bombed the S[outh] dispersal area and the E[ast] and S[outh] runways, so Master Bomber later told them to undershoot reds on runway by 100 yards. After he repeated this several times, the bombing moved back to the N[orth] dispersal area. Bombing was good. Only two or three sticks seen outside the airfield ... By the end of the raid, the airfield was covered in smoke and dust.[86]

For the next two weeks, loss rates on all raids, including those to Germany, dropped significantly, but the Luftwaffe soon bounced back. The six damaged sites were repaired, aircraft replaced, and as August turned to September – and Anglo-Canadian ground forces overran the flying-bomb sites, thus eliminating them from High Wycombe's targeting calculations – losses began to rise again. While a raid on Stettin early in August had suffered very few casualties, another on 29/30 August cost 5.7 per cent of crews, while operations against Königsberg the same day brought losses of 7.9 per cent.[87]

In response, and also in anticipation of the Market Garden operation of 6 September, 670 crews (including 105 from No 6 Group), escorted by more than two hundred fighters, attacked German fighter fields at Deelen, Soesterberg, Venlo, Volkel, Eindhoven, and Gilze Reijen, in the late afternoon of 3 September, knocking out all six. Like almost all the daylight missions to France, Holland, and Belgium at the time, this attack produced very few casualties. Just two crews failed to return. Indeed, as we shall see, American P51 Mustangs had so diminished the Luftwaffe's day-fighter strength that daylight raids to Germany were only marginally more costly.[88]

With operations taking place by both night and day to support Operation Overlord and subsequent army operations in France, Bomber Command's (and No 6 Group's) sortie and tonnage-dropped statistics had climbed significantly while they were under General Eisenhower's control. So had the number of consecutive nights (and days) when operational flying took place. Nevertheless, under McEwen's direction the number of flying training hours was also increased. That may have accounted for the very high number of crews attacking the primary target – indeed, from January to August 1944 the Canadian average was the best in Bomber Command – and it probably contributed to the declining early return and flying accident rates as well (see table 10).

At the same time, the quickening tempo of operations put a tremendous strain on groundcrew, who were almost entirely Canadian by this time. Not

TABLE 10
No 6 Group Operations, January–August 1944[89]

	January	February	March	April
Sorties	651	678	1,665	1,646
Operational flying hours	7,020	9,179	13,147	11,525
Training flying hours	3,165	3,718	5,213	5,104
Flying accidents/1000 hours	26	27	27	18
Loss rate: per cent of sorties	7.4	5.4	7.8	2.1
Early return rate: per cent	8.6	9.0	4.8	2.6

	May	June	July	August
Sorties	1,719	2,929	2,742	3,704
Operational flying hours	12,097	16,573	16,798	21,969
Training flying hours	5,535	4,350	6,415	7,257
Flying accidents/1000 hours	19	15	13	14
Loss rate: per cent of sorties	1.8	1.5	1.6	0.6
Early return rate: per cent	2.3	1.4	1.4	1.9

only were they loading many more aircraft much more often – it took about five hours to bomb-up the machines on a two-squadron station with up to two hundred tons of bombs – but, with the variety of operations undertaken, particularly those involving army support, they often had to do so on extremely short notice. Although fewer aircraft were being lost over France, there was nevertheless considerable battle damage to repair: 3 per cent of all sorties in June, 3.2 per cent in July, 4.6 per cent in August, and 11.1 per cent in September, most due to daytime Flak. However, serviceability rose to near 90 per cent in June and July (and the number of non-starters fell), and even the falloff to 83 per cent in August caused only passing comment. McEwen was satisfied with serviceability of about 85 per cent, and noted that the group's performance over the summer of 1944 was a marked improvement over the 1943 average of 64.7 per cent. In the Luftwaffe, at this time, the serviceability rate was about 65 per cent.[90]

The September 1944 submission recommending the award of an MBE to Flight Lieutenant W.S. Hall – he was eventually Mentioned in Despatches – for his work at Tholthorpe illustrates the calibre of the groundcrews' effort:

Non-starters have been kept to an absolute minimum by this officer's constant and vigilant supervision of the Daily Servicing Line. During the past six months, out of a total of 2,000 aircraft detailed for operations, there have been only nine non-starters. From the 21st April 1944 to the 7th July 1944, thirty-five operations were carried out from this station without one non-starter. On June 6th 1944, when this station was asked for a maximum effort from both squadrons, 36 aircraft were detailed, 36 aircraft took off, and 36 aircraft returned. One of these aircraft had been received on this station on the afternoon of June 5th, and upon inspection was found to have unserviceable turret generators. The Servicing Squadron immediately set to and by almost superhuman efforts were able to get this aircraft on line and carry out a successful sortie on June 6th.[91]

Groundcrews were also in some danger – fuelling and bombing up aircraft could be a perilous business – and the summer of 1944 saw a number of ground personnel recognized for their courage. The most memorable incident probably took place at Tholthorpe, on 27/28 June. Although the attack on a V-1 site at Ardouval had proceeded without any losses, a crew from No 425 Squadron landing on three engines collided with another machine on the ground 'which was parked in the dispersal area and fully loaded with bombs.'

The former aircraft had broken into three parts and was burning furiously. [The base commander], Air Commodore Ross, was at the airfield to attend the return of aircraft from operations and the interrogation of aircrews. Flight Sergeant St Germain, a bomb aimer, had just returned from an operational sortie and Corporal Marquet was in charge of the night ground crew, whilst Leading Aircraftmen Mackenzie and Wolfe were members of the crew of the crash tender. Air Commodore Ross, with the assistance of Corporal Marquet, extricated the pilot who had sustained severe injuries. At that moment ten 500-pound bombs in the second aircraft, about 80 yards away, exploded, and this officer and airman were hurled to the ground. When the hail of debris had subsided, cries were heard from the rear turret of the crashed aircraft. Despite further explosions from bombs and petrol tanks which might have occurred, Air Commodore Ross and Corporal Marquet returned to the blazing wreckage and endeavoured in vain to swing the turret to release the rear gunner. Although the port tail plane was blazing furiously, Air Commodore Ross hacked at the perspex with an axe and then handed the axe through the turret to the rear gunner who enlarged the aperture. Taking the axe again the Air Commodore, assisted now by Flight Sergeant St Germain as well as by Corporal Marquet, finally broke the perspex steel frame supports and extricated the rear gunner. Another 500-pound bomb exploded which threw the three rescuers to the ground. Flight Sergeant St Germain quickly rose and threw himself upon a victim to shield him from flying debris. Air Commodore Ross' arm was practically severed between the wrist and elbow by the second explosion. He calmly walked to the ambulance and an emergency amputation was performed on arrival at station sick quarters. Meanwhile, Corporal Marquet had inspected the surroundings and, seeing petrol running down towards two nearby aircraft, directed their removal from the vicinity by tractor. Leading Aircraftmen McKenzie and Wolfe rendered valuable assistance in trying to bring the fire under control and they also helped to extricate the trapped rear gunner, both being seriously injured by flying debris.

Ross was awarded the George Cross, Flight Sergeant St German and Corporal Marquet the George Medal, and LACs Mackenzie and Wolfe the British Empire Medal. LAC E.T.L. Foidart was Mentioned in Despatches for driving an ambulance to the immediate vicinity and 'unhesitatingly' giving assistance, and LAC F.W. Jardine and Squadron Leader K.H. Running, the medical officer, were similarly recognized. Jardine, it was reported, 'drove a Fire Crash Tender into the vicinity of the fire and unhesitatingly carried out his duty until he was rendered unconscious by an explosion,' while Dr Running 'entered the burning aircraft and with assistance removed the pilot who was seriously injured. Squadron Leader Running continued the rescue and as the last occupant was being removed [he] and his staff were thrown to the ground by the explosion of ten 5-cwt bombs from the aircraft in dispersal. Despite this, Squadron Leader Running continued with his rescue and first aid, being subjected to a further explosion a few minutes later. When all personnel were safely removed, the Squadron Leader proceeded to Station Sick Quarters and carried out an emergency amputation on one of the injured [Air Commodore Ross].'[92] Usually unsung, and often taken for granted (in this history as well as in their work), the ground staff were the glue which held No 6 Group together.

Armageddon over Germany,
September 1944–May 1945

Although it had taken longer than anticipated for the Allies to break out of Normandy, victory seemed to be in sight by mid-September 1944. In the west, most of France had been liberated, British and Canadian forces were deep inside Belgium, and the Americans had arrived on the German frontier near Aachen. In Italy, Anglo-American armies (including a Canadian corps) had broken through the Gothic Line and were approaching Ravenna. On the Eastern front, the Red Army had taken Romania in the south and was poised to debouch onto the Hungarian plain; further north, having reached an armistice with Finland, the Soviets were preparing to clear their Baltic flank and push through Poland into East Prussia.

Bomber Command was already benefiting from the advance across France and Belgium – something of an ironic twist, given Sir Arthur Harris's early opposition to Operation Overlord and his initial reluctance to provide bombing support for the Allied armies as they fought their way inland. However, their success on the ground had forced the Luftwaffe to pull most of its fighter units back to Germany, abandoning many of its early warning radar sites in the process. With less time left for 'anticipatory deployment' and 'Schwerpunktbildung' – concentration at the vital point – 1 Jagdkorps and Luftflotte Reich had far fewer opportunities to organize and undertake the kind of route interception that had proved so costly to Bomber Command during the Battle of Berlin.[1]

At the same time, Luftwaffe bases in western and central Germany were beginning to come within operational range of the Allied tactical air forces established on the Continent and closing up behind the advancing armies, and night-fighter losses on the ground, incurred during the day, began to exceed those sustained in the air. Already on the rise, the latter would increase dramatically from 2.5 per cent of sorties flown in September to 6.2 per cent in October and 11.6 per cent in December. Although slightly over half did not involve any Allied action – overworked night-fighter crews were suffering from fatigue, and the flying accident rate was climbing sharply – 'Mosquitophobia' was becoming a very real phenomenon. Indeed, despite the fact that many Mosquito sorties involved bombing and target-marking rather than Intruding, some Nachtjagdgeschwader appear to have ordered their crews to land whenever Mosquitoes were reported in the vicinity.[2]

Luftflotte Reich's combat effectiveness was being further eroded by the shortage of fuel and lubricants felt throughout the Wehrmacht after the Russian capture of the Ploesti oilfields and Allied bombing attacks on the synthetic plants in western Germany over the spring and summer of 1944. With production of aviation fuel having fallen by about three-quarters since June, and with reserve stocks dwindling, consumption now had to be strictly controlled. Thus, while the operational strength of the night-fighter force was actually rising, from 792 machines in September to 982 in December 1944, because of the fuel shortage the number of combat sorties would fall from 1300 in September to nine hundred in October, climbing only slightly to 955 in November and 980 in December. Training, too, had to be curtailed.[3]

Yet, from a Luftwaffe perspective, the situation was not entirely hopeless. Most nights at least one radio channel was open for the running commentary. Similarly, although Allied jamming of AI was often very effective, so that fighter crews knew they were in the bomber stream 'only ... from the air disturbance caused by the slipstreams of the bombers'[4] – the same clue that had helped the pioneers of German night-fighting three years before – Naxos and Flensburg enabled them to track and intercept bombers through their H2S and Monica emissions. In fact, 'hair-raising' accounts about the efficiency of Naxos would soon produce 'great disquiet' at High Wycombe, especially when linked to the 'unpleasant potentialities' of Schräge Musik's upward-firing guns.* Even after tactical countermeasures had been devised and instructions laid down to restrict the use of H2S until the bomber stream was well inside Germany, the morale problem in Bomber Command was 'not ... readily redeemable.' Many crews remained convinced that, for all its value as a navigation aid, H2S was also a potential danger even when used judiciously, and they conveniently forgot to turn it on.[5]

It was difficult, then, to say that the tide of war had necessarily or inevitably turned in Bomber Command's favour. Indeed, persuaded there were few holes left to exploit in the enemy's air-defence system, and beginning to see the electronic war as something of a stalemate, Sir Arthur Harris feared that his crews might again suffer 'prohibitive losses.' 'Like the U-boat,' he told Winston Churchill on 30 September, 'the heavy bomber ... will meet its counter in the end,' and it was therefore essential to 'get going while the going is good.'[6]

In fact, the going would remain better than Harris anticipated for quite some time. Although senior Luftwaffe officers spoke wistfully about new radars able to withstand jamming and the commitment of jet-powered aircraft in large numbers to the night-fighter role, it was expecting too much of an economy under siege to produce such technologically advanced and sophisticated equipment quickly and in quantity. As for active defence, Adolf Hitler still insisted that Flak should have first priority, and until November 1944 he

---

* The director of air tactics had produced a reasonably accurate analysis of Schräge Musik in August 1944. His estimates were confirmed in December 1944 when a Do 117 equipped with upward-firing guns landed at Zürich, Switzerland. Before destroying the aircraft (in exchange for ten Me 109 fighters), the Swiss made a thorough investigation of the equipment, and their findings found their way to the Air Ministry.

was determined that the jet-engined Me 262 should not be employed defensively.[7]

While German aircraft production had finally begun to drop, between them the US Eighth and Fifteenth air forces could now call upon an average of just over 3000 heavy bombers and perhaps a thousand fighters every day. The sixty-seven main-force squadrons of Bomber Command (forty-two Lancaster, twenty-five Halifax) added another 1300–1400 to the total. (No 6 Group's fourteen squadrons – eleven Halifax, three Lancaster – accounted for just under three hundred.) In Bomber Command alone, the monthly average number of sorties had risen from 5400 in 1943 to 14,000 in 1944, while average payload per sortie had nearly doubled.* Beyond that, there were about 1000 medium bombers in the Allied tactical air forces, along with another 3100 fighters and fighter-bombers – most of them now the equal of or better than their German counterparts and their pilots far better trained.[8]

At the beginning of September 1944, all this striking power was still at the direct disposal of Eisenhower and no date had been set for the return of the heavy bombers to air force control. Although initially reluctant to serve under SACEUR, Harris had come to welcome the operational freedom he enjoyed over the summer and was relieved not to have been 'harassed by confused and conflicting directives' emanating from the Air Ministry. For a number of reasons, however, the air staff was not content to leave Bomber Command under Eisenhower until victory had been won. Air Commodore S.O. Bufton, for one – an original champion of 'panacea' targets – had now been persuaded that it might be useful to mount at least one massive operation (Thunderclap) against the centre of Berlin in the hope that 'total devastation' of the German capital would not only provide 'a spectacular and final object lesson to the German people on the consequences of ... aggression' but also offer 'incontrovertible proof to all people of the power [and] the effectiveness of Anglo-American air power.' But if one purpose of the lesson would be to reinforce the air force's operational independence, it would be illogical to do so while its main striking power was under the control of a soldier; and it was partly in that context that the director of bomber operations recommended Bomber Command's return to Air Ministry jurisdiction. Bufton also agreed with Sir Charles Portal, an original architect of area bombing who was increasingly receptive to the strategic importance of oil, that Bomber Command must revert to Air Ministry control to ensure that Harris would bomb the enemy's synthetic plants as often as possible.[9]

The Americans, by comparison, had little interest in tampering with the existing chain of command. However, at the Octagon conference, held in

---

* Striking power depended on payload as well as numbers. The range of an American Boeing B-17 – the workhorse of the US Eighth Air Force – carrying 4000 lbs of bombs was about 2000 miles. The Avro Lancaster could carry an internal bomb load of 18,000 pounds without modification to the standard bomb bay, while specially modified machines could carry the 22,000-lb 'Grand Slam' over a range of 1500 miles. Even the maligned Halifax III could carry an 8000-lb 'Blockbuster' to Berlin.

Quebec City from 10 to 17 September, Portal and Churchill convinced their American allies that a change would be beneficial. As a result, on 25 September overall control of the Combined Bomber Offensive was passed back to Portal, as CAS, and to General H.H. Arnold, commanding general of the US Army Air Forces. A new bombing directive issued the same day reflected their joint strategic vision. Oil was the first priority; tank and motor-vehicle production came second; while direct support of land operations should be furnished 'promptly' upon request from Eisenhower. The area offensive had not been put aside, however, and attacks on important industrial cities 'using blind bombing techniques as necessary' would still be permitted 'when tactical conditions are unsuitable for operations against specific primary objectives.'[10]

Indeed, area bombing of a sort received important new support just four days after that directive was issued. With the palpable failure of Field Marshal Montgomery's Operation Market Garden to force a crossing of the Rhine at Arnhem, the Allied air commanders agreed to mount a massive assault on the Ruhr (Operation Hurricane) to 'demonstrate ... the overwhelming superiority of the Allied Air Forces [and] bring home to the enemy a realisation ... of the futility of continued resistance.' Oil, transportation, *and* civilian morale would be the principal targets, with High Wycombe directed to take on 'the undamaged parts of the major industrial cities [with] the maximum tonnage ... in order to achieve a virtual destruction of the areas attacked.' The Americans, meanwhile, were to attack more specific objectives.[11]

Bomber Command's third battle of the Ruhr, which would eventually involve 14,000 sorties delivering 61,000 tons of bombs, began the night of 6/7 October 1944, when 523 crews were detailed to bomb Dortmund. Boasting six railway marshalling yards and the southern terminus of the Ems Canal, the city was a transportation and communications target of considerable significance and also had a munitions industry. Underscoring the nature of the campaign, however, the main force was directed to attack the undamaged section of the town around the aiming point rather than any of these specific objectives. Operation Sprat involved three hundred RCAF crews: seven Pathfinders from No 405 Squadron, and 293 main force from No 6 Group. Since it was the largest single enterprise ever attempted by Canada's bomber force, the raid of 6/7 October deserves more than a passing mention.[12]

With a satisfactory weather forecast in hand, Harris chose Dortmund as the target at mid-morning. The hours of daylight had decreased with the coming of autumn and bombing would begin relatively early in the evening, the main force attacking in four waves over a fourteen-minute span between 2025 and 2039 hours. The specialist briefings began shortly after lunch. That was when the navigators learned what routes and altitudes would be used to and from the target, which Flak batteries and night-fighter beacons were likely to be encountered en route, where route-markers (if any) would be dropped, where spoof and secondary raids would take place – in this instance at Berlin and Ludwigshafen/Mannheim, while No 5 Group attacked Bremen – and which emergency airfields would be available on their return.

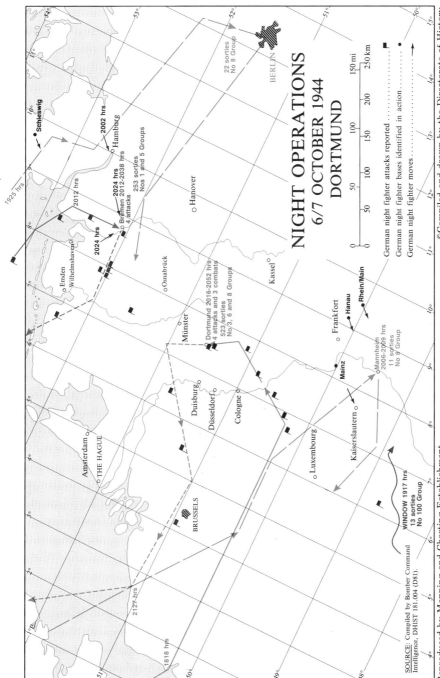

NIGHT OPERATIONS
6/7 OCTOBER 1944
DORTMUND

Schleswig

1925 hrs

2002 hrs
Hamburg

2024 hrs
Bremen 2012-2038 hrs
4 attacks
253 sorties
Nos 1 and 5 Groups

22 sorties
No 8 Group

BERLIN

2012 hrs

2024 hrs

Emden
Wilhelmshaven

Osnabrück

Hanover

Münster

Dortmund 2016-2052 hrs
4 attacks and 3 combats
523/sorties
No/3, 6 and 8 Groups

Kassel

Amsterdam

THE HAGUE

2127 hrs

1818 hrs

Duisburg
Düsseldorf
Cologne

Frankfort
Hanau
Rhein/Main

Mainz

Mannheim
2006-2009 hrs
11 sorties
No 8 Group

Kaiserslautern

Luxembourg

BRUSSELS

WINDOW 1917 hrs
13 sorties
No 100 Group

German night fighter attacks reported ....
German night fighter bases identified in action ....
German night fighter moves ....

| 0 | 50 | 100 | 150 | 200 | 250 km |

| 0 | 50 | 100 | 150 mi |

SOURCE: Compiled by Bomber Command
Intelligence, DHIST 181.004 (D81).

©Compiled and drawn by the Directorate of History.

Reproduced by Mapping and Charting Establishment.

The bomb-aimers, meanwhile, learned what payload they would carry, how they should set their sights for the correct bombing altitude, and which pyrotechnics would be employed by the Pathfinder Force that night – red, with green backers-up. Using master stations now established in France, the Pathfinders would employ Oboe ground-marking with visual backing-up and correction by the master bomber. Although fog was expected over the coast as the main force returned to England (and many crews, including the majority from No 424 Squadron, would have to divert to other landing fields), the skies over Europe were forecast to be clear, with a few patchy clouds.

Following the specialist briefings, which lasted about forty-five minutes, crews gathered for the main briefing, when the intelligence officer explained the significance of the target, repeated what the navigation leader had said about enemy defences, gave the location of reference points and decoy fires on the ground, and (this night) warned against any jettisoning of bombs near '52.14°N 05.57°E where there is a Red Cross POW Camp.' At Leeming, he concluded with a warning: 'Remember to empty your pockets. If you have the bad luck to become a POW, remember security and give name, rank, and number only. Do not emulate the [non-Canadian] Beaufighter crew who gave the Hun a complete history of the Squadron's activities ... also special equipment of which [the enemy] had no knowledge.'[13] After that it was time for the preflight meal and then to dress. Once in their flying gear, crews boarded the trucks that took them to the dispersal point where, following further preflight inspections and other arcane rituals,[*] they climbed aboard, taxied to the runway, and awaited the green flare that heralded their takeoff.

While twenty-two Mosquitoes mounted a diversionary operation to Berlin, No 5 Group flew to Bremen at low altitude, hoping to avoid detection; but that was not feasible for the main force heading inland to Dortmund. There was heavy Flak to contend with on the approaches to the city and everyone had been told to strive for height as they crossed France on a track for Frankfurt. When they finally turned north to the target, near Coblenz, the secondary stream continued on to Ludwigshafen/Mannheim, taking most of the nightfighters with it. Only nine fighter attacks were recorded between Coblenz and Dortmund and just five machines went missing. That represented a loss rate of less than 1 per cent, and on a clear night over the Ruhr results like that were unacceptable to Luftflotte Reich. In a subsequent radio message intercepted by the British Y Service, Generalleutnant Schmid expressed his astonishment that 'in spite of pains and admonitions, and orders throughout the whole year, I have not succeeded in bringing the Jagddivisionen at least to the point of being able to distinguish in what strength and in what direction the enemy is approaching. In my view there is no excuse whatever for this failure.'[14]

The two Canadian crews who failed to return both fell to Flak. One, from No 426 Squadron, lost both port engines and caught fire shortly after leaving the target, forcing the crew to bail out. The other was hit before it reached

---

[*] Many crews habitually urinated on the tail wheel, either in a group or in a pre-established pecking order, before climbing into the aircraft.

Dortmund, but the pilot pressed on and bombed the target before crash-landing at Duisburg. In a bizarre twist of fate, the four crew members who had taken up their crash positions perished while those who had not, though badly injured, survived.[15]

The bombing proved to be heavy, accurate, and concentrated, and crews in the last wave over the city saw numerous fires taking hold.[16] Reconnaissance flights the next day revealed 'extremely severe and widespread damage.'

All the through-running tracks of the main passenger station were cut, and the carriage sidings were 80 per cent unserviceable ... All the approaches to the marshalling yards were severed ... The *Stahlwerke* [and] *Elektrizitätswerke* and ... municipal power station ... were badly damaged ... Business/residential property was largely devastated, 70 per cent of the fully built-up area being quite destroyed.[17]

Half the city was without gas, water, and electricity, and the largest steel works was shut down for three weeks.[18]

Because of commitments to the British and Canadian armies clearing the Scheldt estuary, Harris was able to take on only two German industrial targets over the next week. Both were largely Canadian operations since, as we shall see, No 6 Group was not called upon to help their fellow countrymen secure the approaches to Antwerp. On 9/10 October the RCAF provided just under half the 435 crews who attacked Bochum in a raid that, because of dense cloud, did only scattered damage. This was followed by a daylight attack on the oil plant at Wanne-Eickel on the 12th, for which No 6 Group provided the entire main force of 111 Halifaxes and Lancasters. Although the refinery was not knocked out, a large chemical factory producing synthetic ammonia was destroyed.[19]

Bomber Command resumed Operation Hurricane two days later, when Duisburg was attacked twice within the space of fourteen hours by a total of 2013 sorties. No 6 Group contributed 258 of the 1013 crews taking part in the morning raid, covered by a heavy fighter escort that included twelve Mark IX B Spitfires of No 441 Squadron (fitted with jettisonable fuel tanks to achieve the necessary range) which had just been transferred back from Second TAF to No 11 Group of Fighter Command.[*] As explained in the briefing given at Leeming, No 1 Group's task was to 'destroy steel works. The purpose of all other attacks including ours is to destroy dispersed intact areas of the town.' 'This time we went after the city,' a gunner from No 429 Squadron recalled, 'aiming the bombs at any built-up area, no matter what it was,' and most crews selected the built-up area that lay between the Rhine and the marshalling yards. A few scattered fires were seen as the attack petered out, but these must have taken hold later because, when crews returned that night, 'they found the target clear of cloud and burning fiercely.' Only one fighter was observed during the first raid – it was apparently shot down – and all fourteen bombers lost (1.4 per cent) fell to Flak.[20]

When the Canadians returned to their bases, at about noon, the groundcrews

---

[*] The Air Defence of Great Britain was renamed Fighter Command on 15 October 1944.

NO 6 GROUP NOTABLE STATISTICS
Figure 23.1

MOST SORTIES TO A SINGLE TARGET, 1943-1945

Duisburg	1,312
Hamburg	1,298
Cologne	1,138
Essen	1,117
*Berlin	1,070

GREATEST TONNAGE DROPPED ON A SINGLE TARGET, 1939-1945

Duisburg	4,903
Hamburg	4,666
Cologne	4,248
Essen	3,594
*Dortmund	3,141

GREATEST TONNAGE DROPPED IN A SINGLE RAID

** St. Leu d'Esserent	1,194	5 Aug 1944
*Duisburg	1,179	14 May 1943
Essen	1,107	23/24 Oct 1944
Oberhausen	995	1/2 Nov 1944
Cologne	978	30/31 Oct 1944

MOST SORTIES DESPATCHED ON A SINGLE RAID

Dortmund	293	6/7 Oct 1944
Essen	261	23/24 Oct 1944
Duisburg	250	14 Oct 1943
Oberhausen	244	1/2 Nov 1944
** St. Leu d'Esserent	240	5 Aug 1944

MOST SORTIES LOST ON A SINGLE RAID

Magdeburg	24	21/22 Jan 1944
Hamburg	22	28/29 Jul 1944
Leipzig	18	19/20 Feb 1944
Berlin	15	28/29 Jan 1944
Nuremburg	15	30/31 Mar 1944

* Raids to distant targets like Berlin sacrificed bomb load for fuel.

** V-1 storage site in France.

SOURCE: PRO Air 48/67.

began at once to repair, refuel, and rearm them for the night raid. For the second time that day they had to load hundreds of thousands of gallons of fuel, oil, and coolant, several million litres of oxygen, and millions of rounds of ammunition. This time Duisburg was to be attacked in two waves, two hours apart, in the hope of catching fighters on the ground refuelling and rearming when the second wave arrived, and there would also be several smaller operations and spoofs to complicate the task of Luftflotte Reich. Sixteen Mosquitoes were to bomb Berlin, twenty would attack Hamburg, and eight the marshalling yards at Mannheim. Another thirty-seven from No 100 Group would fly Intruder sorties over night-fighter fields and beacons, while forty-seven equipped with Serrate (which homed on to German AI radar) were to accompany the bomber stream, seeking out the night-fighters en route. In addition, forty-five crews from No 100 Group would conduct Window, Mandrel, Jostle, and other jamming; No 5 Group was to send 250 sorties to Brunswick; and 141 Halifaxes, Wellingtons, Lancasters, and Stirlings from Heavy Conversion and Operational Training Units would make a diversionary raid on Heligoland. Including the thousand-odd machines sent to Duisburg, Harris had committed 1575 aircraft to the night's operation and, in the process, mounted the 'most ambitious deception scheme yet attempted.'[21]

The largest of the main-force groups, No 6 Group contributed more crews than any other to each of the two Duisburg missions. Moreover, although the Canadians and No 1 Group were the only formations to have conducted large-scale operations in the two days prior to the double raid, the former met 98 per cent of their commitment in the morning and 96 per cent that night, with an early return rate only two-thirds of No 1 Group's. That was testimony not only to the generally low casualties suffered on the first attack – No 6 Group lost three sorties (1.16 per cent) – but also to the Canadians' steadily improving maintenance and repair organizations.[22]

The combination of depleted fuel stocks, limited early warning, jamming, spoofs, and multiple incursions humiliated the German night-fighter organization again. None of the bomber streams was plotted accurately. Reacting like 'a badly battered boxer swinging desperately in the hope of scoring a lucky hit,' Luftflotte Reich mounted only eighty-nine sorties and only seven machines were shot down (some of them by Flak and only one from No 6 Group), about 0.7 per cent.[23]

The only Canadian crew lost was commanded by Flight Lieutenant J. Galipeau, on his twentieth mission with No 425 Squadron, who 'received a direct hit in the starboard wing by *Flak*, the shell going through without exploding' just after releasing his bombs.

Then the mid-upper gunner spotted a fire in the wing and told me so. The engineer told me one tank was draining fast. After that I tried to feather the propellers without success. We could not put out the fire. I told the crew we might have to bale out. The only other thing which I could do was to take a chance and dive the aircraft a bit in hopes of blowing out the flames ... but the effort was not successful.

I expected the aircraft to blow up at any time so reduced the speed to about 160 mph and told the crew to do an emergency bale-out ... After I saw the bomb aimer leave I checked the intercom to see that everybody was out. Having no answer I started to get out of my seat. I looked back and there was quite a bit of smoke in the aircraft. I could not see anyone so I baled out. I saw the aircraft go in a spiral and enter a thin layer of cloud. I went through the clouds after which I saw two or three other chutes. When I got down fairly close to the ground the Germans opened fire on me ... I spilled air out of my chute and luckily enough I reached the ground without being hit. I was captured immediately on reaching the ground.

Three other crew members also survived.[24]

Wilhelmshaven was attacked next, in part to 'further disrupt [Germany's] internal supply situation' but also to destroy the factories producing the Schnorkel-equipped U-boats which were proving so elusive at sea.[25] Then, so far as large raids were concerned, it was the turn, in order, of Bonn, Stuttgart, and Nuremburg – at a cost of only sixteen crews out of 1402 sorties, 1.14 per cent.[26]

Interspersed among army support and specialist attacks by both Nos 3 and 5 Groups, Bomber Command returned to the Ruhr in strength on 23/24 October. Essen was the target, and the 1055 aircraft dispatched represented the largest number yet sent to a single objective. (Unlike the 'thousand' raids of 1942, this total was achieved without the participation of No 5 Group, and no training units had to be called upon.) Carrying mainly high-explosive bombs – there was little left to burn – the attackers caused extensive damage, which was added to by a large daylight raid involving 771 crews thirty-six hours later. The aiming point in both cases was 'the centre of Krupp's large clutch of factory buildings which is west of the central city area but still roughly in the centre of Essen proper.' Because of cloud, crews had to bomb on sky-markers and that inevitably spread the attack out, but the effect on Krupp's facilities was 'severe to very severe in most departments.' About 1500 buildings were destroyed in the rest of the city and some 1400 people were killed, while bomber losses were negligible: twelve crews, three from No 6 Group, failed to return, 0.65 per cent of those sent. That same day Lancasters from Nos 6 and 8 Groups also attacked the Meerbeck oil refinery at Homberg, near Duisburg, without loss, but the weather system that concealed Essen also hid Meerbeck – a much smaller target – and spoiled their effort.[27]

The assault on the Ruhr-Rhine area continued with three quick strikes against Cologne involving 2031 sorties, one to Düsseldorf (992 sorties), and another to Bochum (749 sorties). There was almost no opposition at Cologne and the loss rate at Düsseldorf was under 2 per cent, but at Bochum, on 4/5 November, twenty-eight crews were shot down, 3.7 per cent, including five from No 6 Group. The attackers were discovered by the Horchdienst while still assembling over the English coast and, because of heavy cloud over France, they had approached their objective via the old North Sea route, which compelled them to fly a considerable distance over German territory. Interceptors scrambled in good time and order were easily inserted into the bomber stream, and pursuit night- fighting worthy of the previous winter took place all the way to the target. Battered, reeling, even punch-drunk, the Nachtjagdgeschwader may have been, but like many an old boxer they were still capable of landing hard blows.[28]

With the Allied armies closing up on the German border, however, the chances of evading capture were much better, even for aircrew who parachuted into the Reich. His Halifax hit by Flak and ordered to bale out, Flying Officer O. Cook, a navigator with No 426 Squadron, hit his head on the hatch as he jumped and lost consciousness. Approximately an hour later he awoke 'in a field.' Seeing no one, but hearing voices 'which seemed to be getting louder ... I vaguely remember walking in a westerly direction, using my escape compass and the stars as a guide.'

... I estimated that I had touched down near [Mönchen]-Gladbach. I was considerably dazed at the time and I cannot remember how I disposed of my parachute, harness, etc.

At dawn the next day I repaired my trousers which had been slit up the sides and removed my Canada flashes and navigator's brevet from my tunic. I continued walking west through the woods and fields, and apart from two German convoys which I saw moving along a nearby highway I encountered no-one. I heard gun fire to the west and assumed it to be coming from the front line so I continued in that direction. At this point I must have again lost consciousness, as I do not remember anything of my further movements or what happened to me until I awoke the following morning and found that I was in a tent in a US Army field hospital. I have no idea how I got there and I was not told by the hospital staff.

On arrival at the field hospital I was wearing a German airman's jacket and was wounded in my neck. The bullet had entered the left side of my neck and passed out below my left shoulder, but strangely enough there was not any bullet mark in the German jacket. I had also lost my identity bracelet, a wrist watch, some money, and a chamois leather jacket. I am unable to explain how I was wounded, where I got the German jacket, or what had become of my belongings which were missing.

Kept under guard until he was returned to England and questioned by puzzled intelligence officers, Cook's story was finally accepted at face value.[29]

The casualties sustained during the Bochum raid were entirely at odds with High Wycombe's most recent assessments of Luftflotte Reich's capabilities. Noting particularly the 'complete failure of the ground control organization' during recent operations, the research teams at Bomber Command Headquarters believed that the German air-defence organization had 'deteriorated into hopeless confusion and impotence,' and they would soon speak confidently and optimistically about the 'eclipse' of the enemy's night-fighters.[*] Bochum, in short, could be dismissed as a lucky hit. These days, of course, an occasional

---

[*] The Germans themselves were scarcely more sanguine, Josef Schmid going so far as to argue that useful results would be obtained only by going over to the offensive – in a massive intruder effort aimed at catching Bomber Command as it returned to base. But Operation Gisela, as Schmid's plan was called, would not be approved and attempted until February 1945.

lucky hit was not likely to disconcert, much less deter, Sir Arthur Harris. Unlike the battle of Berlin, when he had been risking almost his entire front-line strength in a few very large attacks, now the raids against the Ruhr were only one part of Bomber Command's multiple attacks. Yet there were those who had been arguing for many months that the best way for High Wycombe to deal with the possibility of a night-fighter revival was to avoid it altogether by taking up daytime operations. Such had been the Americans' success in winning the battle for air superiority, they said, that even over Germany proper the risks of daylight bombing had been dramatically attenuated. And, indeed, pressure on Harris to recast his thinking mounted steadily as his crews proved time and again during the battle for Normandy that they could do what he had always maintained they could not.[30]

The AOC-in-C nevertheless had legitimate reasons to be sceptical about taking up daylight bombing full time. Partly it was a matter of scale. Relying on No 11 Group's Spitfires and Hawker Tempests to escort small to medium-sized forays into France – and even as far as the Rhine – over the summer of 1944 had been practicable, but No 11 Group had too few first-line fighters to accompany major raids deep into Germany on a regular basis. The Americans might be able to help out from time to time, but High Wycombe certainly could not count on their assistance as a matter of course. The main thing, however, was that there was no room for error. As everyone knew, or should have known by now, inadequately protected Halifax and Lancaster crews operating by day would be helpless if the Germans decided to attack.[31]

There were also complex questions of tactics and training. The Americans flew in tight formations, in order to concentrate their heavier (.5-inch versus .303-inch) defensive fire against the 20- or 30-millimetre cannon of their opponents, and they had found that, done properly, formation bombing carried out in unison reduced the overall bombing error. Since it did not employ formations at night, Bomber Command had never wasted valuable hours of its training syllabus preparing pilots for something they would not be expected to do; and so far as High Wycombe was concerned any attempt to bring them up to American standards would have been prohibitively time-consuming.[32] At the same time, knowing full well that some daylight missions would be necessary if only to support the Allied armies, as early as 9 July 1944 attempts had been made to introduce a degree of order to the daytime bomber stream in order to make the escorts' job easier. Although each group was free to experiment further, Harris decreed that, at minimum, crews would fly in a more cohesive column of pairs.[33]

Air Vice-Marshal McEwen, for one, had taken up the invitation with con-siderable enthusiasm, and for a time in August the Canadians had experimented with the American 'twelve-ship stagger' or squadron wedge, an intricate forma-tion which proved too difficult (even in practice) for most of his crews to master and was soon dispensed with. Instead, the group tried to arrange squad-rons in Vics of three but that, too, was less than satisfactory and in October experiments began with yet another rudimentary formation. Squadrons from each station would 'form up in Vics of 3 aircraft, spaced at 100 ft intervals …

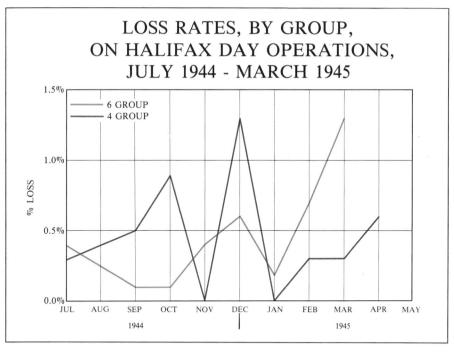

LOSS RATES, BY GROUP,
ON HALIFAX DAY OPERATIONS,
JULY 1944 - MARCH 1945

SOURCE: Air Force Headquarters, Operational
Research Centre, Losses; heavy bomber
operations in Bomber Command: HQS.
19-17-6, vol. 1. DHIST 79/220.

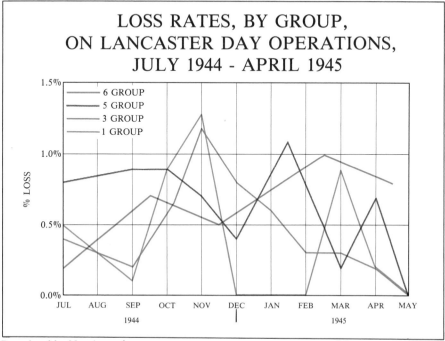

LOSS RATES, BY GROUP,
ON LANCASTER DAY OPERATIONS,
JULY 1944 - APRIL 1945

Reproduced by Mapping and
Charting Establishment.

©Compiled and drawn by
the Directorate of History.

in line astern stepped down with 100 yards between each Vic ... according to their take-off order, and not necessarily as squadrons.' That too proved cumbersome, so that from late November most daylight raids were mounted in 'gaggles.' Considerably less rigid than American-style formations yet also more compact than the traditional bomber stream, a gaggle theoretically comprised a number of ten-aircraft groupings flying in reasonably close proximity to each other. In the event, however, individual crews made enough minor errors in height and time-keeping that most gaggles came to resemble nothing so much as a shortish 'stream.' And, at least once, gaggles from two different bases, sent to two different targets, got mixed up with each other.[34]

It was not just the enemy's day-fighters that worried High Wycombe, however. Although jamming remained effective, electronic counter-measures were less significant during the day when Flak gunners often did not need radar to see their prey; and when Bomber Command's Halifaxes and Lancasters flew below 18,000 feet (as they had to when instructed to identify the aiming point visually), they were well within range of both heavy and medium guns. Aware that the incidence of Flak damage had already risen significantly over France – it had damaged 2.5 per cent of night sorties, but 36.7 per cent of daytime sorties – High Wycombe feared that the toll over Germany would be greater still. Furthermore, although operations over France had shown that the Pathfinder's target-marking techniques worked by day, there were also limits to how well they worked. In particular, the standard pyrotechnics did not show up well by daylight in the smoke and dust kicked up by exploding bombs, so the average aiming error by day was often greater than the corresponding night-time error.[35]

A return to Germany by day nevertheless could not be avoided, and Bomber Command's first such raid since the experimental (and costly) attack on Augsburg by twelve Lancasters in April 1942 took place on 27 August 1944, when Nos 4 and 8 Groups made for the oil refineries at Homberg.[36] No 6 Group joined in ten days later, when 139 crews bombed Emden, trying to knock out both its submarine yards and the surrounding urban area. Escorted by Spitfires from No 11 Group and USAAF Mustangs, all 139 machines bombed and returned to base, although one in six suffered some kind of Flak damage.[37] The first crews to reach the target saw the initial markers clearly and, when a few fell short, the corrections made by the backers-up were also readily distinguished. The city was soon 'a mass of flames, with thick black oily smoke rising up to 10,000 feet'; but that created grave problems for those who arrived later and could not see any target indicators through the smoke. Switching the plan of attack, the master bomber directed them to use the column of smoke as their main reference point – a technique which, under the codename of Pickwick, would become a standard procedure by the end of the month.[38]

The raid was a complete success. 'Quay buildings in the *Alter Binnenhafen* are for the most part destroyed,' and heavy damage was also observed in the city's business and residential areas. However, several RCAF crews 'got no satisfaction out of their Emden attack despite or because of the fact that they could see what was happening down below. They couldn't help thinking about the people down there. The centre of the town was the aiming point.' This was not the first occasion when 'the centre of the town' had served as Bomber Command's aiming point, nor was it the first time that crews had left their target 'a mass of flames.' But at night, in the dark, there was greater psychological as well as physical distance between them and what lay below; although in the aftermath of war a civilian bombing analyst would contend that the fact crews 'at long last [saw] where their bombs exploded' was, for the majority, a 'morale-raising experience.'[39]

There was certainly less moral ambiguity involved in bombing oil plants, but demonstrably more physical difficulty in hitting them. Thus Castrop Rauxel, Dortmund, Wanne Eickel, Bottrup, and Sterkrade became No 6 Group's objectives in a campaign which, by early winter, must surely have frustrated the exponents of daytime 'precision' bombing. Despite 'clear weather with good visibility' and reports of 'a highly concentrated attack,' the plant at Castrop Rauxell was only slightly damaged on 11 September; and, while raids on Dortmund and Wanne Eickel the next day were reportedly more successful, there was 'some evidence of indiscriminate bombing' to the south of the latter. In addition, fifty RCAF crews sent to Wanne Eickel – half those committed – actually dropped their bombs on the fringes of Scholven, No 4 Group's aiming point, about six miles away. Contributing to the damage at Scholven as it did, theirs was not an entirely wasted effort. Nevertheless, because of certain superficial similarities between this raid and that at Falaise in August, which had resulted in the bombing of Canadian troops (and led to the adoption of much more rigorous standards to avoid repetition of the mistakes made then), Allerton Hall launched a far-reaching inquiry in which each crew found to have bombed at the wrong target was called to account for its error. Although there were many more mavericks at Scholven than at Falaise, since no Allied troops had been killed the repercussions that followed were far less severe. Rather, the confusion caused by practically coincidental attacks in the same general area (of which No 6 Group crews were ill-informed) seems to have been accepted as a reasonable excuse for what went wrong.[40]

Bad weather near the end of the month was an additional handicap. While cloud at Bottrup and Sterkrade blinded the Flak (which had damaged about half the sorties returning from Castrop), it also produced some very scattered bombing.[41] Not, however, by Flight Lieutenant J.A. Anderson, a pilot on No 419 Squadron who was recommended for the Victoria Cross for his efforts at Bottrup. Anderson was no stranger to adversity. On 28 July, returning from Hamburg on three engines, his crew had beaten off five attacks by an enemy fighter before shooting it down, and he had survived heavy Flak damage five times in August and September (and would do so three more times in October), pressing on to the target in each case and, on one occasion, again thwarting five fighter attacks. But Anderson's most 'outstanding feat,' in the opinion of his commanding officer, 'was performed during a daylight attack on the oil refinery at Bottrup.'

On arriving at the target, it was found that this was obscured by 9/10th cloud cover. The target was sighted through a gap in the clouds too late to afford an accurate bombing run. Anti-aircraft fire was very heavy but, without any hesitation, F/L Anderson decided to do an orbit to ensure an accurate bombing run was made. At the beginning of the orbit, the aircraft was repeatedly hit by shell fragments and both port outer and inner engines were put out of action. The port outer engine was also set on fire, the hydraulic system was rendered unserviceable and the controls were damaged to such an extent that he had to call on the assistance of two members of his crew to pull manually on the rudder controls. With complete disregard of the heavy opposition, and the difficulty in controlling his crippled aircraft, F/L Anderson completed the orbit and made a steady bombing run, enabling his Air Bomber to attack the target very accurately.

Shortly after leaving the target, it was found that the starboard inner engine had also been badly damaged and was giving less than half power. Through superb planning, crew co-operation and flying skill, F/L Anderson successfully flew his crippled aircraft back to this country, with only full power from the starboard outer, half power on the starboard inner engine, and made a masterly landing without causing further damage to his aircraft or crew.[42]

There would be no Victoria Cross; but on 21 December Anderson was awarded the DSO, often – when awarded an officer of his rank – described as 'the poor man's VC.'[43]

Another DSO went to Flying Officer C.M. Hay, a navigator on No 432 Squadron, for his performance on the same raid.

While over the target the pilot was severely wounded and lost control of the aircraft which went into a dive. Displaying great presence of mind, F/O Hay took over the controls and succeeded in levelling out. Although inexperienced as a pilot and despite the fact that some of the instruments were unserviceable, he flew the aircraft back to an airfield and landed. On touching down the undercarriage collapsed and the aircraft caught fire but the crew got clear uninjured.[44]

Missions to the same target undertaken on 30 September and 6 November in even heavier cloud produced even worse results; while at Homberg on 25 October one participant thought that 'for all the good we could do ... we should have stayed at home, for the target was totally obscured by cloud.' No 6 Group's senior air staff officer, now Air Commodore J.E. Fauquier, DSO, DFC, a former master bomber himself, was distressed by the poor results in the late summer and early fall of 1944. Overall bombing accuracy had 'deteriorated considerably,' he observed, 'in part due to the gross errors incurred by a minority of crews who, through bad navigation, inefficiency, and poor captaincy negligently wasted their bombs.' Fauquier's scorn embraced more than the most negligent few. Not only were H2S operators in particular making far too many mistakes, but the H2S serviceability rates left much to be desired. It was also clear that (as in all other groups, it must be added) many crews were loath to make the prescribed bombing run through heavy Flak. In

November, therefore, he decreed that squadron bombing leaders were to test and rate all their crews on a weekly basis, so that those with training errors greater than 280 yards or operational errors more than one thousand yards could be taken off the order of battle temporarily and given further training.[*][45]

While No 6 Group was fulfilling the mandate of Operation Hurricane, by day and by night, the rest of Bomber Command had been heavily engaged in support of the army. On 7 October Nos 1, 3, 4, and 8 Groups attacked the Rhenish towns of Cleve and Emmerich in order to protect the right flank of Field Marshal Montgomery's 21st Army Group, left dangerously exposed because of the failure of Operation Market Garden. Soon, however, High Wycombe was asked to participate in a land campaign which, before it ended, caused even those airmen who were most sympathetic to the army to wonder whether the soldiers had become so 'drugged with bombs' that they would not put a foot forward without heavy bomber support.[46]

Although the Belgian port of Antwerp, at the head of the Scheldt estuary, had been liberated in early September, its approaches had not yet been cleared; and with Boulogne, Calais, Dunkirk, and Le Havre still in German hands (they would hold Dunkirk until the war ended), Allied supply lines stretched all the way back to Normandy and the Atlantic ports. First Canadian Army, on the left of the allied line, was given the task of clearing the Scheldt and, in accordance with the 25 September bombing directive, High Wycombe committed over two thousand sorties to the task – not, by any means, its full support and, strangely (given the Canadian commitment on the ground) none from No 6 Group. Attempts to knock out bunkers and gun emplacements from the air had not been very successful in Normandy and were no more successful here, but the capture of Walcheren, a low-lying island on the north side of the estuary, was greatly facilitated by the breaching of the perimeter dyke by Harris's heavy bombers.[47]

There was only one call to support Allied ground forces in November, a request from the US Ninth Army, preparing for its advance on Cologne. While American heavy bombers dropped fragmentation bombs on forward German positions, on 16 November Bomber Command obliterated the three fortified towns of Düren, Jülich, and Heinsburg lying just behind the enemy front. No 6 Group contributed 204 crews to the attack on Jülich and, in bright daylight with good visibility, they saw both their target indicators and 'a line of smoke pots indicating the front line position of our front line troops.' While twenty-three machines were holed by Flak, there were 'no ... fighters, no combats, no claims' and no losses. But, as had been the case when Caen had been bombed,

---

[*] Fauquier's language and actions were tough: although the record is not complete, one crew that missed Wanne Eickel on 12 October seems to have lost credit for the sortie towards its operational tour. On 28 December 1944, however, believing that No 6 Group was now in good shape and having volunteered for the job, he reverted in rank to group captain to take over command of No 617 Squadron RAF – the Dambusters – whose precision bombing of specific objectives undoubtedly gave him more satisfaction.

the soldiers could not take full advantage of the bombing because their start
line was too far back.[48]

In the meantime, on 1 November yet another revised bombing directive had
been sent to Sir Arthur Harris and General Spaatz which effectively called a
halt to Operation Hurricane. Although 'the maximum possible disorganization
of the enemy's transportation system ... particularly in the Ruhr,' remained an
objective, it was clearly subordinated to the oil campaign. While direct support
of land operations remained a 'continuing commitment,' tank production, the
Luftwaffe, and the German aircraft industry were abandoned altogether as
target systems, partly because of the results of previous attacks and partly
because of the changed military situation; the war in Europe was winding
down, and since no one expected to be fighting great air or tank battles in a
year's time, there was no need to worry about the future output of aeroplanes
or armoured fighting vehicles.[49]

Perhaps the most significant change so far as Bomber Command was concerned, however, was that relating to the conduct of area raids. Still authorized
whenever weather or the tactical situation precluded precise attacks, they were
now to be 'directed so as to contribute to the maximum destruction of the
petroleum industry' or the dislocation of other specific objectives.[50] Shades of
Casablanca and Pointblank, which had also attempted, without much success,
to wean High Wycombe away from mere city-busting.

Harris's reaction to the new directive and other unsolicited advice was
immediate. On 26 October Sir Arthur Tedder, Eisenhower's deputy and the
senior airman at Supreme Headquarters, Allied Expeditionary Force (SHAEF),
had circulated his proposals for the future conduct of the bomber offensive,
emphasizing the significance of the transporation plan, and on 1 November Sir
Charles Portal had questioned Sir Arthur closely about the selection of Cologne
as the objective the previous night when more important transportation targets
had been ignored. 'Here we go round the Mulberry bush,'[51] Harris observed
to his deputy, Sir Robert Saundby, firing off a lengthy critique to the CAS.
Since, by his calculations and standards, Bomber Command had already
'virtually destroyed 45 out of the leading 60 German cities,' was adding
another two or three to the tally each month, and had never let the army down
when it asked for support – and so long as area bombing was doing more to
underwrite victory than any offensive directed against 'panacea' targets – it
only seemed reasonable to persevere with a campaign begun, at Portal's behest,
on 14 February 1942. 'The destruction of Magdeburg, Halle, Leipzig, Dresden,
Chemnitz, Breslau, Nuremburg, Munich, Coblenz, Karlsruhe, and the completion of Berlin and Hanover are required to finish the plan. That it can be completed without depriving the Army of the support it requires is obvious from
our experience since June, and its completion will do more towards accelerating the defeat of Germany than anything the armies have yet done – or will
do.'[52]

As for oil plants, he continued on 6 November, many of them had already
been attacked and he was keeping a close watch for any 'signs of manufactur-

ing activity.' Where there were none, it was his view that the facility need not be bombed again until it 'showed signs of coming to life.' If, however, the intention was to go on 'flogging' such 'temporarily dead horses until they are utterly destroyed,' he was profoundly concerned about the 'vista of additional losses and loss of effort in every other direction.'[53]

Bombast beyond doubt, but also a passionate defence of area bombing (and a commander's need for operational freedom) in typical Harris style that had rarely failed to move the CAS in the past. Times had changed, however. In a prolonged exchange of demi-official letters, Sir Charles Portal announced his conversion to the oil campaign 'at the risk of your dubbing me "another panacea merchant,"' and despite the danger that losses might rise when Bomber Command concentrated on just a few targets: for oil was now the 'knife edge' on which 'the whole war situation is poised.' The usefulness of area bombing had come to an end. If 'complete victory' could be anticipated 'in the next few months,' a campaign of attrition aimed at achieving results over the long haul was obviously irrelevant, and because of that he would no longer accept at face value Harris's excuses for attacking targets falling outside the terms of the new directive.[54]

So bitter and deep was the break between them, in fact, that on 18 January 1945 Sir Arthur raised the possibility of his resigning – something Portal would not accept for military or political reasons. Eventually the CAS more or less broke off the exchange with the observation that the two 'must now agree to differ' and let history judge who had been right. Since he would not flatly order the AOC-in-C to attack particular objectives,[*] regretted that Sir Arthur did 'not believe' in oil, and yet understood that it was 'no use my craving for what is evidently unattainable,' Portal accepted Harris's assurances 'that you will continue to do your utmost to ensure the successful execution of the [authorized] policy.'[55]

It would be an exaggeration to say that the AOC-in-C ever did his utmost to knock out the German oil industry. Operations in November and December featured an eclectic mix of objectives in which the proportion of sorties given over to the destruction of the enemy's synthetic oil plants was less than one in four. Pure area raids – against Munich, Münster, Neus, Duisburg, Hagen, Essen, Ludwigshaven, Witten, and Ulm – totalled about 40 per cent, and attacks on transportation targets accounted for most of the rest. Even so, Bomber Command's greatest successes during this period came against the oil plants of western Germany – Gelsenkirchen, Wanne-Eickel, Castrop-Rauxell, Harburg, Dortmund, Homberg, Bottrup, Sterkrade, and Osterfeld – and they came as much by night as by day. Indeed, by late November the western refineries had been so heavily damaged that High Wycombe was asked to take on plants in central Germany, particularly those at Leuna and Pölitz, which had originally been assigned to the Americans but where they had not enjoyed much

---

[*] 'The Chief of the Air Staff has no personal or individual right to issue instructions to Commands,' it had been ruled in 1935; rather, 'when the CAS issues instructions he does so on behalf of the Air Council.' PRO Air 8/258

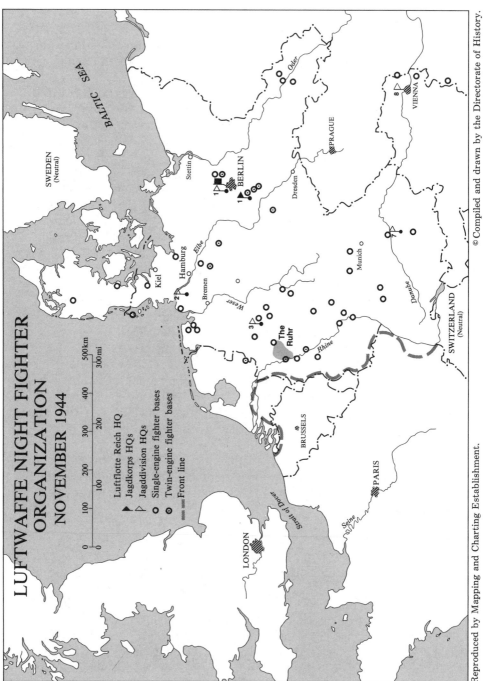

LUFTWAFFE NIGHT FIGHTER ORGANIZATION NOVEMBER 1944

Luftflotte Reich HQ ▲

Jagdkorps HQs △

Jagddivision HQs ○

Single-engine fighter bases ○

Twin-engine fighter bases ◉

Front line

0 100 200 300 400 500km
0 100 200 300mi

BALTIC SEA

SWEDEN
(Neutral)

Stettin

BERLIN

Elbe

Kiel

Hamburg

Bremen

Weser

Oder

PRAGUE

Dresden

Munich

Danube

VIENNA

8

The Ruhr

Rhine

SWITZERLAND
(Neutral)

BRUSSELS

Strait of Dover

LONDON

PARIS

Seine

2

3

1

1

© Compiled and drawn by the Directorate of History.

Reproduced by Mapping and Charting Establishment.

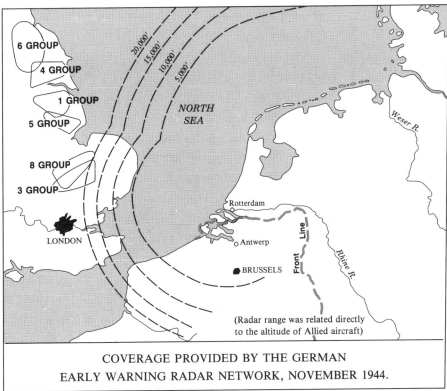

6 GROUP

4 GROUP

1 GROUP

5 GROUP

8 GROUP

3 GROUP

20,000'
15,000'
10,000'
5,000'

NORTH
SEA

Weser R.

Rotterdam

LONDON

Antwerp

BRUSSELS

Front Line

Rhine R.

(Radar range was related directly
to the altitude of Allied aircraft)

**COVERAGE PROVIDED BY THE GERMAN
EARLY WARNING RADAR NETWORK, NOVEMBER 1944.**

Reproduced by Mapping and Charting Establishment.   © Compiled and drawn by the Directorate of History.

success. Their bombs, as Albert Speer, the German minister of war production, subsequently explained, had less effect than the larger and heavier ordnance carried by Bomber Command. Harris complained, fearing heavy losses, but by the end of December he was complying with the request – and again very effectively. Production from the five major synthetic plants fell from 46,750 tons in January 1945 to 11,260 in March and 730 in April.[56]

Overall losses remained low in November and December despite mounting so many attacks against targets the Germans wanted desperately to defend. At High Wycombe the enemy's performance suggested it was suffering from 'muddled thinking' exacerbated, from time to time, by a touch of panic.[57] There were, nevertheless, a few disturbing signs. At Osnabrück on 6/7 December, three crews from No 426 Squadron reported being attacked by, and shooting down, 'a bright ball of light' – one of the new Messerschmitt 163 rocket fighters.[58] Furthermore, there had already been many reports of jet-engined Me 262s operating at night. John McQuiston, a pilot in No 415 Squadron, had seen his first at Düsseldorf in November. 'It travelled at terrific speed,' he recalled, 'and I caught a brief impression of bulbous, underslung engines.' Not knowing about jets, he 'wondered if my eyes or nerves were playing tricks. Nothing flew that fast.'[59]

No 6 Group was involved against all the target systems attacked in November and December. Of its 3300 sorties, just under two-thirds were mounted against area targets, oil and transportation accounting for about 450 each and army support for another 250. Sixty-nine involved Gardening, and 150 were sent to attack the German airfield at Düsseldorf on Christmas Eve. The overall loss rate of 1.8 per cent was marginally higher than Bomber Command's, but Canadian casualties were also concentrated in early November. Flak was mainly a daytime concern. Of the 154 aircraft damaged in November, 137 by Flak, seventy-one had been hit in 620 daylight sorties, and sixty-six in 1384 night sorties.[60]

Attacks on oil targets like Castrop-Rauxell were meant to immobilize the Wehrmacht, but in mid-December, having husbanded his resources carefully, Hitler gambled on one last great throw of the dice – his counter-attack into the Ardennes code-named Wacht am Rhein and subsequently known to the allies as the 'Battle of the Bulge.' Weather was the great equalizer, and surprise enabled it to attain a brief momentum. For well over a week, leaden, drizzly skies kept the Allied air forces away from the battlefield proper, and it was only on 19 December that the G-H-equipped Lancasters of No 3 Group were called upon to bomb railway marshalling yards behind the German front line. Two nights later, Nos 4, 6, and 8 Groups attacked similar objectives around Cologne, causing 'severe damage' to the facilities at Nippes. Cologne and Trier were attacked again over the next few nights, while the Americans continued to attack bridges and marshalling yards behind the front. Despite his on-going quarrel with Sir Charles Portal, Harris did the same without any special pleading by the CAS. Once the weather had cleared, Bomber Command, together with the Eighth Air Force and the Allied tactical air forces, did much to help seal off von Rundstedt's spearheads. Most of his troops and equipment had to detrain on the east bank of the Rhine, very little transport of any kind could move by day, and before the end of the year Wacht am Rhein simply petered out.[61]

Still, the oil offensive had clearly not rendered the Wehrmacht completely immobile, a fact Sir Arthur Harris did not fail to emphasize.[62] 'You will recall the last meeting at 21 Army Group headquarters prior to D-Day,' he reminded Portal on 28 December.

I warned them then that if we laid off bombing German war industry for five months she would recover all that was necessary to her war production. We did not lay off, entirely, for five months. But the aggregate of our diversions, on the railway plan, on helping the Armies, and now on oil, very far exceeds the five months' estimate.

We need look no further for the cause of what has happened in the last fortnight.

With a vista opening in front of us of bombing nothing but tactical and oil targets – which means a final stopper on bombing Germany, in the way that had given her her "worst headache" – we are finally discarding the substance for the shadow. And an M[inistry of] E[conomic] W[arfare] shadow at that.[63]

Of course, Harris's half-empty cup was also half full. While he was un-doubtedly correct in thinking it was impossible to knock out all the roads, rail

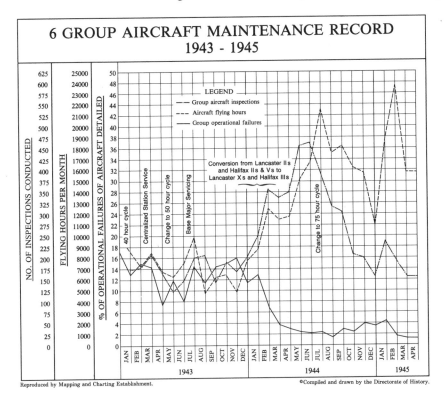

6 GROUP AIRCRAFT MAINTENANCE RECORD 1943 - 1945

LEGEND
—·— Group aircraft inspections
- - - Aircraft flying hours
——— Group operational failures

Conversion from Lancaster II s and Halifax II s & V s to Lancaster X s and Halifax III s

Reproduced by Mapping and Charting Establishment.   ©Compiled and drawn by the Directorate of History.

ways, bridges, and canals over which the Germans had moved to the Ardennes, or to deny them all their fuel, once they had used up the limited resources hoarded to support the offensive their oil cupboard was essentially bare. Nor is his contention that area attacks would have done more to thwart the enemy easily supported by the evidence.[64]

A year earlier, on 1 January 1944, when No 6 Group had celebrated its first birthday in the midst of the battle of Berlin, it will be recalled that it had just been getting over its growing pains: loss and early return rates had been high while serviceability was low, and both navigation and bomb-aiming left much to be desired. Two squadrons, Nos 420 and 434, were commanded by RAF officers, and there were still as many as 20 per cent non-Canadian groundcrew on some squadrons. Probably most disturbing, however, were the indications that, given a choice, RCAF bomber crews graduating from OTUs would have preferred to be posted somewhere else. Much had changed over the past twelve months. Canadianization was, by and large, an accomplished fact, and serviceability and casualty rates had improved to the point where they were among the best in Bomber Command. Even so, the Canadians were not completely satisfied, and at Eastmoor, which enjoyed 'an enviable record for non-starters,' additional steps were being taken to deal with the 'snags, boggings, and other hitches' that led crews to abort their missions. Among these were the detailing of 'trouble-shooters' to patrol dispersal areas before each operation, providing a caravan of specialists from each trade to do last-minute repairs, and ground staff to signal whether bomb doors, flaps, and rear entrance hatches were in the correct position for takeoff.[65]

Perhaps because of measures like that, No 6 Group's image and reputation had changed – so much, in fact, that OTU graduates were now eager to be posted to it.[66] Yet Fauquier's successor as SASO, Air Commodore R.E. McBurney, remained concerned about the frequency of bombing and navigation errors and he was even more upset by the number of so-called manipulation errors – failures to use electronic aids correctly – which, together with the 'lack of offensive spirit' exhibited by a minority of crews, were causing an unacceptably high early return rate. He recommended that repeat offenders be dealt with quickly and firmly, adding that disciplinary action might be necessary. Although the idea of punishing crews by refusing to credit them with completion of an operational sortie when they were far off track did not win widespread approval among the squadron commanding officers, there was rarely any disagreement with the kind of treatment meted out to one navigator who, having knowingly bombed Hamburg fifteen minutes early on 31 March 1945, was removed from operations and sent to the retraining centre at Sheffield for three weeks.[67]

There were cycles in No 6 Group's history that were beyond anyone's control, however, and one of these – a marked falling off in the number of experienced crews available – was bothering Allerton Hall late in 1944. Once again, the loss rate was responsible, but in exactly the opposite way to 1943. With the tremendous decline in casualties after June 1944 and the sharp increase in the number of sorties flown, significantly more crews were completing their operational tours in substantially less time. Veterans were usually replaced by novices fresh from their Heavy Conversion Unit and, when such screenings came in bunches, as happened in late 1944, the overall level of expertise was bound to fall. It was not only that navigation and bomb-aiming suffered as a result – reason enough for Air Vice-Marshal McEwen's concern – but also, as we have seen, that artlessness in dealing with enemy fighters cost lives. Accordingly, there would be no let-up in the strict training regimen he had introduced nine months before.[68]

The cycle was about to turn in another way as well. Over the fall and winter of 1944 No 6 Group lost five or more crews on a single night just three times. Indeed, the low casualty rates had led General der Flieger Adolf Galland (about to be dismissed from his appointment as inspector of fighter forces) to complain on 5 January 1945 that 'today the night fighter achieves nothing.'[69] In the last four months of the war, however, when the Nachtjagdgeschwader were desperate for fuel, losing experienced crews, and facing still more powerful jamming, Bomber Command's loss rate at night actually rose a little. No 6 Group, for example, lost five or more crews in a single night six times.[70]

Largely because of the weather – the repetition, while tedious, is necessary – major night operations in January were clustered into short periods of intense

NIGHT OPERATIONS - 5/6 JANUARY 1945 - HANNOVER

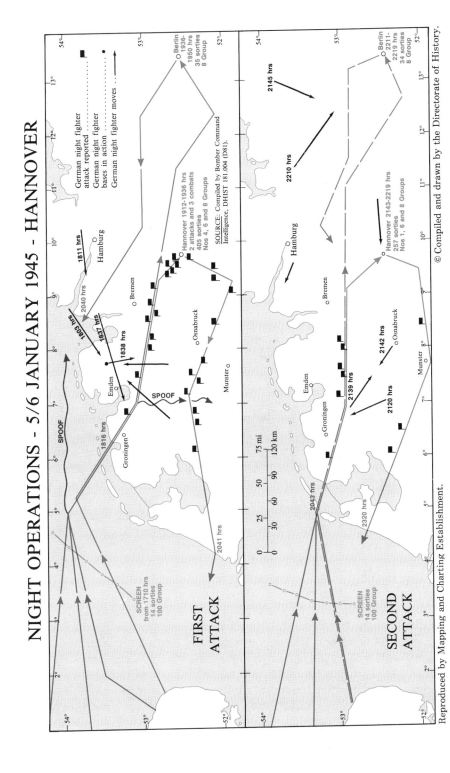

German night fighter attack reported .... ■

German night fighter bases in action .... •

German night fighter moves .... →

FIRST ATTACK

SCREEN from 1710 hrs 14 sorties 100 Group

Hannover 1912-1936 hrs 2 attacks and 3 combats 405 sorties Nos 4, 6 and 8 Groups

Berlin 1936-1950 hrs 35 sorties 8 Group

SPOOF

1811 hrs
2040 hrs
1803 hrs
1637 hrs
1838 hrs
1816 hrs
2041 hrs

Hamburg
Bremen
Osnabruck
Munster
Emden
Groningen

SOURCE: Compiled by Bomber Command Intelligence, DHIST 181.004 (D81).

SECOND ATTACK

SCREEN 14 sorties 100 Group

Hannover 2143-2219 hrs 257 sorties Nos 1, 6 and 8 Groups

Berlin 2211-2219 hrs 34 sorties 8 Group

2145 hrs
2210 hrs
2142 hrs
2139 hrs
2120 hrs
2320 hrs
2043 hrs

Hamburg
Bremen
Osnabruck
Munster
Emden
Groningen

0   30   60   90   120 km
0   25   50   75 mi

© Compiled and drawn by the Directorate of History.

Reproduced by Mapping and Charting Establishment.

activity during the first and third weeks. Total losses were quite manageable, about 1.7 per cent of sorties, but a few old-style area raids provoked old-style responses. Thirty-one crews failed to return from Hanover on 5/6 January, 4.7 per cent of the total, of which ten were from No 6 Group and three from No 425 Squadron, flying Halifax IIIs. At least one of the latter fell to Schräge Musik, to which there was still no effective counter if the enemy's approach was made correctly. 'The whole trip went very smoothly,' Sergeant E.J. Faulkner, a flight engineer on No 425 Squadron, recalled. 'We were in sight of the target and preparing for the bombing run. Suddenly we were perforated with cannon shells from below.' With their machine out of control and on fire, the crew bailed out. Five were taken prisoner, but two of the gunners were killed. Eleven nights later, seventeen Halifax crews were lost at Magdeburg and a further ten Halifaxes at Zeitz, both deep penetrations. No 6 Group was fortunate at Zeitz, as only one crew failed to return, but seven of the 136 sent to Magdeburg (5.1 per cent) did not come back, including four from No 420 Squadron.[71]

The enemy had ample warning of the Hanover operation. Since cloud prevented the low-level approach originally planned (and some bomber crews flew past the outer fringes of the Mandrel screen), ground radars picked up the stream in good time. Fighters, including a number of jets, were scrambled 'in unusual strength.' Luftflotte Reich had good warning of the Magdeburg raid as well, and 'fighters ... were active from the coastline through the target to the Dutch coast.' Luck played some part in the Germans' success, as the Gruppen detailed to defend Zeitz crossed the path of those bombers bound for Magdeburg and, having found the enemy, stayed put; but fortune often cuts both ways and a second group of fighters, originally directed to Magdeburg but subsequently diverted to Zeitz, arrived there too late to intervene in strength.[72]

Although the Luftwaffe and the German aircraft industry had been removed from November's directive, the Americans had become increasingly worried about the frequent appearance of jet aircraft and on 19 January jet fighter production, training, and operational establishments again became a 'primary objective for attack.' 'Certain objectives in the enemy's U-boat organisation' were also included in the new directive, although it was anticipated that these could be dealt with by a 'marginal effort ... incidental to other operations.' Area targets could still be considered, and although a list of these (almost entirely in the Ruhr) 'calculated to make the best contribution to our strategic aims' had been drawn up, the directive did not preclude Harris from selecting other cities when the towns on the preferred list could not be attacked.[73]

Yet even as this latest instruction was being drafted the idea of launching a series of punishment and demonstration raids, similar to Operation Hurricane, against a variety of targets was being resurrected. These included Clarion, the American plan to disrupt communications and morale by widespread bombing and fighter attacks; Thunderclap, the British plan to deliver a catastrophic blow on Berlin, first adumbrated by Harris in June 1944 and subsequently put forward by Portal and Bufton in August 1944; and Bugle, a continuation of the concentrated offensive against the Ruhr meant to prepare the way for the

British, Canadian, and American crossings of the Rhine. With an eye to assisting the Russian winter offensive just under way, Bufton was inclined to substitute Breslau and Munich for the German capital in Thunderclap. For his part, Harris, who had already compiled his own list of cities needing to be finished off, added Chemnitz, Dresden, and Leipzig, as they would 'equally share with Berlin the task of housing German evacuees from the East.' Like Bufton, Portal now questioned whether decisive results would result from attacking Berlin, but neither he nor the Air Staff had any qualms about Thunderclap's purpose. Since it was to have 'primarily ... morale and psychological effect' it must not be dissipated by concurrent attempts to knock out 'tank production ... jet engine factories etc.' The prime minister was thinking along roughly the same lines, asking 'whether Berlin, and no doubt other large cities in East Germany should not now be considered especially attractive targets?'[74]

The next day Harris was given the task of bombing these centres, subject only to the 'overriding claims of oil, U-boats, and rocket and jet engines.' In due course, Halle, Plauen, Dessau, Potsdam, Erfurt, and Magdeburg were also added to the Thunderclap list. Thus was set in motion the chain of events that would produce Bomber Command's most controversial operation of the war, the attack on Dresden of 13/14 February 1945. It had the wholehearted support of everyone who mattered in the chain of command and, as we have seen, the city had been singled out for attack by Harris and others long before there was any consultation with the Red Army. Indeed, when (during the Yalta conference) the Soviets were asked whether the bombing of east German cities would assist them, only Berlin and Leipzig fitted the bill. Dresden, Vienna, and Zagreb were mentioned only as reference points along a general bombline east of which the Western Allies should not bomb.[75]

Until the weather in the east was right, a few oil and transportation targets of 'overriding priority' were attacked, along with one city that did not fall comfortably into either category. Wiesbaden, a community of some 160,000 people known primarily for its spas and having no war industry of significant magnitude, had seen only a few light raids up until this point in the war.[76] On 2/3 February, however, 495 sorties were dispatched on an operation which, from the briefings given to those involved, could only be described as a kind of general – even visceral – punishment. 'From the Ruhr to the Swiss frontier,' crews were told, 'there is no sizeable town ... which has not suffered serious damage at the hands of the Allied air forces with the single exception of Wiesbaden. In view of the acute shortage of accommodation in Germany, the value to the enemy of the expensive barracks and ... hotels ... of the pre-war spa ... is considerable and it is also a well situated centre for front line troops to rest and refit. It is proposed to let Wiesbaden share the state of most other German towns and by destroying it to eliminate one of the last few remaining places where the German army can be assured of sound shelter from the rigors of winter.'[77]

Despite cloud cover the town was hit hard, with some five hundred killed and thirty thousand left homeless. Still, it was not an entirely satisfactory operation from High Wycombe's point of view. Failing to compensate for the lighter-than-forecast tail winds, Nos 1 and 3 Groups bombed late. Nos 5 and 6, by comparison, went so far as to alter their routes while the attack was in progress, and both arrived over the target on time. Indeed, so seriously were the Canadians taking the problems of navigation and timing errors that one crew faced the possibility of disciplinary action for bombing six minutes late, until they convinced the authorities that the fault lay in their aircraft, not themselves.[78]

Oil and transportation targets were attacked again over the next two nights and then, on 7/8 February, Bomber Command set out to prepare the way for First Canadian Army's campaign to take the Rhineland. 'The bomber role is to destroy the two small towns of Cleve and Goch, killing troops stationed there, hamper movements and deny ... enemy reinforcements entry into the battle area.' The army was prepared to accept some cratering as an inevitable by-product of heavy-bomber support, but there was more of it than bargained for at Cleve. At Goch, meanwhile, smoke and dust – not weather – forced a premature conclusion to the bombing, so that only forty-eight of the two hundred RCAF crews taking part actually dropped their ordnance. The damage was less than anticipated, particularly where the enemy's bunkers and pill-boxes – the prime objects of the attack – were concerned. 'The RAF had not succeeded in smashing these fortifications,' one soldier has recalled. 'Only the shops, houses, church spires, and factory chimneys had been reduced to rubble – providing additional protection to the defender.[79]

Refineries in Pölitz, Wanne Eickel, and Krefeld were attacked next, crews being informed that 'the battle for oil is reaching a climax.' Then, after a four-day break because of weather (that forced cancellation of operations to Bremen and Dortmund), on 13/14 February 796 crews (including ten from No 405 Squadron and sixty-seven Lancasters from No 6 Group) took off for Dresden; another 368 (including 115 from No 6 Group, all Halifaxes) were sent to the synthetic oil plant at Böhlen, near Leipzig, both to continue the oil offensive and to confuse and divert the defenders of Dresden.[80]

'That the bombing of Dresden was a great tragedy none can deny,' Harris's deputy admitted after the war. 'That it was really a military necessity ... few will believe. It was one of those terrible things that sometimes happen in war-time, brought about by an unfortunate combination of circumstances.' There were, as we have seen, no industrial objectives of immediate importance in Dresden – an abrasives plant and Zeiss lens factories were probably the most significant – but the aiming point, a large sports stadium, was chosen because it could be seen easily, not in order to lead the bomber stream to either of those installations. Similarly the railway yards, given as the objective to some squadrons and also easily seen, did not serve as an aiming point until the last few waves flew over the city.[81]

The possibility of raising a firestorm had been incorporated in the operational plan from the beginning; carrying a bombload largely made up of incendiaries, the main force (guided by the flames from No 5 Group's preparatory attack) was able to do just that. The glow was perfectly visible to those returning from Böhlen, over a hundred miles to the northwest. The old city centre was 'almost completely wiped out,' and at least 25,000 were killed and an additional 35,000 missing.[82] As at Hamburg, German eye-witnesses had lurid tales to tell.

In 1948 Margret Freyer, a twenty-four-year-old with an undoubted will to live at the time, recalled her experience on the edge of the fire storm.

I stumbled on towards where it was dark. Suddenly, I saw people again, right in front of me. They scream and gesticulate with their hands, and then – to my utter horror and amazement – I see how one after the other they simply seem to let themselves drop to the ground. I had a feeling they were being shot, but my mind could not understand what was happening. Today I know that these unfortunate people were the victims of lack of oxygen. They fainted and then burnt to cinders. I fall then, stumbling over a fallen woman, and as I lie right next to her I see how her clothes are burning away. Insane fear grips me and from then on I repeat one simple sentence to myself continuously: 'I don't want to burn to death – no, no burning – I don't want to burn!' ...

I try once more to get on my feet, but I can only manage to crawl forward on all fours. I can still feel my body, I know I'm still alive. Suddenly, I'm standing up, but there's something wrong, everything seems so far away and I can't hear or see properly any more. As I found out later, like all the others, I was suffering from lack of oxygen. I must have stumbled forward roughly ten paces when I all at once inhaled fresh air. There's a breeze! I take another breath, inhale deeply, and my senses clear. In front of me is a broken tree. As I rush towards it, I know that I have been saved but am unaware that the park is the Bürgerwiese.

Twenty-four hours later, I asked for a mirror and did not recognise myself any more. My face was a mass of blisters and so were my hands. My eyes were narrow slits and puffed up, my whole body was covered in little black, pitted marks ... Possibly the fire-sparks ate their way through my clothing.[83]

Mounting only twenty-nine sorties, the Luftwaffe was scarcely to be seen, and only six bombers were lost to enemy action, less than 1 per cent of those dispatched.

In a continuation of Thunderclap, Bomber Command made for Chemnitz, about thirty-five miles to the southeast, the following night. 'The centre of Germany's hosiery and underwear manufacture,' the city also contained some automobile, motor cycle, and machine tool factories, and while 'not on one of the main ... through routes,' it was 'an important centre for the railway system of ... Saxony.' The Americans had bombed the town four times – twice in 1944 and twice (as part of Thunderclap) in February 1945 – including that very afternoon when, concentrating on the southern suburbs, they had damaged a number of industrial plants. Bomber Command's night attack was less successful. Bombing through cloud, the 688 crews (including 64 Halifaxes and 51 Lancasters from No 6 Group) struggled to hit the railway yards whose destruction, they had been told, would be 'of great assistance to good old Stalin and his marshal Zhukov, who are only a hundred miles away.' Despite the scatter, some damage was done. 'The firm of Auger and Sohn, manufacturing ammunition boxes, was completely destroyed ... the bandage manufacturers Max Arnold suffered medium to heavy damage [and] drinking water was cut off.' The Luftwaffe's response was better than at Dresden despite extensive jamming and spoofing, and thirteen machines were lost, 2.6 per cent, of which three were from No 6 Group.[84]

For the next few weeks the Canadians were operating all over Germany, taking on oil, railway, and Thunderclap targets as well as returning to the Ruhr, in the process of being sealed off by the American armies. Perhaps the most successful area raid in the region occurred on 23/24 February at Pforzheim, a jewellery and clock-making town on the Karlsruhe-Stuttgart main line.[85] The marking, done from about 8000 feet, was accurate, and the 258 crews from No 1 Group and fifty from No 6 produced 'destruction on a scale [and] as complete as at any target ever attacked. There was hardly a single building left intact throughout the whole area, and apart from the tremendous gutting by fires many ... buildings were levelled to the ground. Damage to railway facilities was also heavy, the goods yard was completely burnt out, rolling stock destroyed, two of the river bridges had collapsed and the road over the rail bridge ... was ... hit and rendered unserviceable.'[86] Seven thousand were reported killed, and 45,000 left homeless.[87] Although supported by Mandrel, Window, and raids on Darmstadt, Würms, Berlin, Frankfurt, Essen, and Oslo, the attackers nevertheless lost twelve crews, eleven from No 1 Group.[88]

That was one of the features of operations in February and March 1945, as each bomber group tended to suffer higher than average casualties in turn. No 5 lost fourteen crews in bright moon light at Karlsruhe on 2/3 February (5.6 per cent) and thirteen (7.9 per cent) near Gravenhorst three weeks later. Nos 1 and 8 Groups, meanwhile, had eight crews fail to return from an attack on Bottrop on 3/4 February.[89] For No 6 Group there were four bad raids. On 21/22 February (a night when the German night-fighter ace Major Heinz-Wolfgang Schnaufer recorded nine kills) the Canadians lost six of 111 sorties sent to Würms (three of them from No 432 Squadron) because the enemy received 'unusually early warning by some means unknown' to High Wycombe at the time. Even single-engined fighters were in action over Holland.[90] Much the same thing happened on 7/8 March, when five of 182 Canadian crews went missing at Dessau and Hemmingstedt.

Eight more were lost before noon at Hamburg on 31 March, when thirty Me 262s ripped into the Canadian gaggle. 'I felt as if we were standing still,' recalled Flying Officer D. Saunders; 'the gaggle closed in and were wing tip to wing tip ... creating the closest formation of bombers I have ever seen.'[91] But the worst night, by far, was 5/6 March, when 185 machines from No 6 Group formed about a quarter of the bomber stream sent to Chemnitz to finish the job begun three weeks before. 'The take-off took place in full daylight,' Flight Lieutenant J. McQuiston remembered, and '... our crew had about thirty minutes to kill before it would be time to set course.'

The sky was covered with broken cloud, about 4/10th. I decided to use my spare time to fly around seeking clear patches to climb through, as we ascended to our briefed altitude of five thousand feet. No point in risking a mid-air collision in a cloud, if a little patience could void the possibility ...

As I circled the general base area, I observed an explosion off to my left. I informed Gerry of the location and gave my opinion that it was an aircraft exploding on the ground. He booked it in the flight log.

'There's another one,' Steve exlaimed, ... 'farther south and later' ...

'There's another one,' Jimmy chimed in ...

By this time we had reached our intended altitude and were above all cloud cover. As I looked over my left shoulder, I saw a Lancaster wallow through the cloud and then plunge back in. Moments later the flash of an explosion was clearly seen through the cloud ...

'Keep a sharp watch for intruders,' I ordered.

... Before we had even set course, we saw no less than seven explosions that looked, for all the world, like aircraft exploding as they hit the ground.[92]

McQuiston's crew carried on to the target, but because of bad weather on their return they had to divert to Tangmere, a fighter base, and so did not discover the cause of these explosions until the next day. They had had good reason to worry about intruders as, two nights earlier, the Luftwaffe had finally mounted Operation Gisela, sending 142 Ju 88s over England to pick off aircraft of Nos 4 and 5 Groups as they returned from Kamen and the Dortumund-Ems canal. The night-fighters had attacked forty-three bombers, shooting down twenty-two and damaging eight more. Many crews had been taken completely by surprise and, with their landing lights on, were easy pickings.[93] On 5/6 March, however, the cause of the crashes on No 6 Group's airfields was not enemy fighters. Rather, 'in the final analysis, icing was determined to be the cause. A small unexpected triangle of icing cloud had crossed our base at take-off, and we had borne the brunt, losing six of the seven. All the losses were from Linton and Tholthorpe, and Eastmoor was spared, for the moment. The defenses over Chemnitz had been scattered, but on the first leg home, fighters were active. In all we lost ten per cent of our attacking force – an unusually high rate, and twelve of the losses were from our base.'[94] The final tally: nine machines had crashed on takeoff, killing forty-five; another six were missing over the target, which meant forty-two officers and men failed to return; and a further three crashed on landing, leaving seventeen dead.[95]

With the growing chaos and breaking down of order and restraint, this was a particularly unhealthy time to parachute into Germany. Between 1 February and 30 April 1945 as many as seven RCAF airmen may have been murdered, including Flying Officer T.D. Scott of No 432 Squadron, shot down after the 15/16 March raid on Hagen and executed by the Gestapo the next day. Two more were shot after baling out near Opladen on 30 March.[96] However, there were still numbers of evaders and escapers loose in both Germany and those parts of Holland and Denmark occupied by the Wehrmacht – among them Sergeant J.L.N. Warren from No 434 Squadron, whose odyssey was dramatic enough to deserve a Hollywood treatment.

Shot down over Cologne in November 1943, Warren had given himself up at that time because of the wounds and bruises suffered when his machine crashed, and he was subsequently imprisoned at Stalag IVB at Mühlberg. He made his first escape attempt on 17 March, 'joining a party of French prisoners going out for supplies.'

When the party reached the stores he broke away and went to a cemetery where, by pre-arrangement, he was to have met a Canadian airman who had previously escaped. On arrival, Sergeant Warren learnt that the other airman had been recaptured and the guards had been reinforced [and as] he had neither food nor maps, Sergeant Warren decided to return to the camp and await a more favourable opportunity. He regained the camp undetected.

On 1st May, 1944, Sergeant Warren made a further attempt using the same method as before. He met an RAF officer and both successfully evaded the search parties and guards for five days. Four other escapers soon joined them and all managed to get a train carrying rolls of paper to Holland. On arrival ... the party split up, and Sergeant Warren and one companion travelled north until they made contact with the Dutch underground movement at Borne. They stayed for five weeks and then moved on to Nijverdal, owing to the activities of the Germans.

Warren moved about Holland until November, spending six weeks 'hiding in a cave under a pigsty in company with two Poles and a Dutchman,' but they were eventually taken when the Germans made a surprise search of the Gorssel area. Despite showing his captors his identity discs, Warren was 'treated as a "terrorist" and severely manhandled during his interrogation, after which he was put in a cell measuring 12ft x 6ft with thirteen others ... Later he was taken to an empty house for interrogation and further brutal treatment was carried out,' no doubt as the Germans tried to learn more about his escape route. Then, on 1 February 1945, Warren and ninety-three others were put into two box-cars and sent to Germany.

During the journey, some of the party pried open a window... and made an attempt to escape but the guards saw them and opened fire. Sergeant Warren succeeded in getting away and evading capture by walking all night through water waist-high. The next evening he made contact with an underground organization, and was taken to Lobith [on the Dutch/German frontier.] The next night an attempt to cross the Rhine was made but those who tried had to return ... owing to strong enemy opposition. The party was then taken to a farm by a Dutch nurse and given shelter. On the 22nd February 1945 the Germans ordered all farms to be evacuated, so Sgt Warren and some others posed as members of the farmer's family and moved with them. Later he posed as a Dutch policeman in order to prevent being taken again. He continued to evade capture until liberated by British Forces in April 1945.[97]

His reward for completing this amazing odyssey was a British Empire Medal.

High Wycombe, meanwhile, was taken aback by the apparent resurgence of the enemy's air-defence organization in February and March 1945. Despite sophisticated jamming, and intricate diversions and spoofs, Luftflotte Reich was obtaining early warning of many raids, plotting main forces accurately enough, and, by reading Gee, Oboe, G–H, and H2S, among other things (too many crews were still failing to maintain H2S silence en route), the German controllers were often identifying targets before the bombs began to fall.[98] When the supply of fuel and weather permitted the night-fighters to fly, moreover, Benito, Uhu, Bernhardine, and their use of multiple radio frequencies gave them generally reliable communications with the ground, while in Wasserman, Elefant, Neptun, Berlin, Flensburg, Naxos, and modified Freyas and SN2 they had radars, homing devices, and sensors which penetrated and negated many of Bomber Command's electronic counter-measures. In No 6 Group, for example, the number of aircraft found to be damaged by enemy action upon their return to base rose from 3.2 per cent in January to 5.9 per cent in March, with Flak and fighters both enjoying increased success.[99]

The extent to which the electronic war was reaching equilibrium only became clear after the war, however, when Operation Post Mortem tested a portion of the enemy's raid reporting and control system that had been captured intact in Denmark and northern Germany. Using cooperative Luftwaffe prisoners of war, and involving a series of increasingly complex combinations of jamming and spoofs, Post Mortem demonstrated that much of No 100 Group's effort in the last months of the war had had only marginal impact.

Mandrel was probably the greatest disappointment. Relied on as the foundation on which other jamming tactics were based, not only was its screening effect imperfect, but (as had happened with Window) the Germans had eventually developed a knack for using the size and shape of the Mandrel screen to help give them a fix on the location of the bomber stream. Moreover, the Post Mortem experiments may have underestimated German capabilities. Although they had not taken Mosquito operations into account – which were intimidating, even to veterans like Heinz-Wolfgang Schnaufer, much to the surprise of the Mosquito crews themselves – neither had they included the intelligence-gathering of the Horchdienst. Furthermore, although the captured controllers were willing enough, having spent the last few months of the war in a relative backwater, they were not the most experienced operators in Luftflotte Reich and probably not the most effective. But German search and destroy capability was hardly crucial when the Nachtjagdgeschwader had no fuel – and no aviation gas at all was produced in March.[100]

On 16 April a final directive to Harris and Spaatz was drafted which reflected the imminence of victory. Because of the 'extent to which the destruction and dislocation of the enemy's industrial and economic systems had already been achieved,' the priority now was to 'give direct assistance to the land campaign.' Strategic operations would in general be limited to attacks on oil supplies, such as they were, and to lines of communications, although 'policing attacks' against the Luftwaffe would be made as necessary, as would the previously approved 'marginal effort' against U-boats.[101]

An escape clause existed which could have allowed for the continuation of area raids, but such raids were fast becoming a political problem. On 17 February 1945 a war correspondent at Eisenhower's headquarters had put out a story explaining that the 'Allied air chiefs' had finally decided 'to adopt deliberate terror bombing of German population centres as a ruthless expedient to hastening Hitler's doom.' Given the purpose of Thunderclap, this was basically honest reporting, but it caused considerable difficulty in both London and Washington.[102] Privately, on 28 March, Winston Churchill used similar language to decry Thunderclap, of which he had recently and wholeheartedly approved. 'It seems to me,' he told his chiefs of staff, 'that the moment has come when the question of bombing of German cities simply for the sake of increasing the terror, although under other pretexts, should be reviewed.'

Otherwise, we shall come into control of an utterly ruined land ... The destruction of Dresden remains a serious query against the conduct of Allied bombing. I am of the opinion that military objectives must henceforward be more strictly studied in our own interests rather than that of the enemy.

The Foreign Secretary has spoken to me on this subject, and I feel the need for more precise concentration upon military objectives, such as oil and communications behind the immediate battle-zone, rather than on mere acts of terror and wanton destruction, however impressive.[103]

That comment came just six days after a daylight raid that perfectly illustrated his new-found anxiety. 'Our target today is Hildesheim,' Nos 427 and 429 Squadrons had been told. 'The town centre is largely built of half timbered houses and has preserved its mediaeval character. This should make a good fire.' Although there were rail lines in the vicinity, along with a farm implement factory and sugar refinery, the aiming point was 'in the centre of the built-up area.' Including the Pathfinders from No 405, just over one hundred crews from RCAF squadrons took part, and the master bomber for the raid, also from No 405 Squadron, reported that their bombing formed [a] nice horseshoe around a[iming] p[oint],' with only '5 lots of bombs seen, wild.' 'About half the town area was destroyed,' according to German police records, including the town hall and the cathedral; 1600 were killed, and 40,000 left homeless.[104]

Nevertheless, neither Portal nor Harris reacted well to Churchill's minute, and the prime minister was persuaded to withdraw the original and replace it with a less abrasive substitute on 1 April.

It seems to me that the moment has come when the question of the so called 'area bombing' of German cities should be reviewed from the point of view of our own interests. If we come into control of an entirely ruined land, there will be a great shortage of accommodation for ourselves and our Allies: and we shall be unable to get housing materials out of Germany for our own needs because some temporary provision would have to be made for the Germans themselves. We must see to it that our attacks do not do more harm to ourselves in the long run than they do to the enemy's immediate war effort. Pray let me have your views.[105]

The CAS took up some of these arguments but carefully defended the principle, as well as the continued practice, of area bombing. 'In spite of recent advances in our ability to make precise attacks at night, the operational considerations which have in the past necessitated area attacks still exist. Nevertheless, it is recognised that at this advanced stage of the war no great or immediate additional advantage can be expected from the attack of the remaining industrial centres of Germany, because it is improbable that the full effects of further area attacks upon the enemy's war industries will have time to mature before hostilities cease. Moreover, the number of targets suitable for area bombing is now much reduced.'[106]

No 6 Group's last offensive operation came on 25 April against coastal batteries on Wangerooge, in the Frisian Islands. At this late date it should have been easy, but seven of the 482 crews dispatched were lost, five of them Canadian, the latter all through a chain-reaction of collisions caused when one Lancaster, catching the slipstream of another, rammed into a third. Forty-one airmen died, twenty-eight of them Canadian.[107]

After that came better things, however. The Dutch people had suffered terribly during the war, but never more so than over the winter of 1944–5 when their food ran out. Working in great secrecy, Allied authorities entered into discussions with Arthur Seyss-Inquart, the German governor of the Netherlands, which opened the way for the supply of food by air to the three million inhabitants of that part of western Holland which had not yet been cleared of German troops. Operation Manna, assigned to Nos 1, 3, and 8 Groups, began on 29 April 1945 and in ten days over 7000 tons of food were delivered. No 405 Squadron marked the drop zones at The Hague from 30 April to 5 May, and then at Rotterdam on 7 May.[108]

On 8 May, the day the war in Europe ended, all of Bomber Command including No 6 Group began flying liberated prisoners of war back to England (Operation Exodus), the Canadians accounting for 4329 of the nearly 75,000 airlifted home.[109] With Exodus over, No 6 Group began to disappear. Eight RCAF squadrons – Nos 405, 408, 419, 420, 425, 428, 431, and 434 – had been selected to participate in the war against Japan as part of Tiger Force, and on 31 May they began to fly their Canadian-built Lancaster Xs back to Canada. The others were disbanded in England between 15 May 1945 and June 1946.

On 8 May 1945 Canadians knew a good deal about what Bomber Command had been doing to Germany for the past five years. Along with stories filed by journalists who accompanied the Allied armies into western Germany, there were photographs and newsreel films that bore witness to almost unbelievable devastation. From what could be seen, they seemed to prove every claim Sir Arthur Harris had ever made for the bombing offensive. 'City after city has been systematically shattered,' General Eisenhower had declared earlier that spring, and the German war economy had all but ceased to function.[110]

Taking its cue from Eisenhower's remarks, Toronto's *Globe and Mail* rendered its verdict on the strategic air offensive on 23 March 1945. Not doubting for one moment that bombing had ruined the German economy, the *Globe* nevertheless did not view 'the real victory of Allied air power' in that light. Rather its 'great achievement' was likely 'a thing of the mind – a lesson so terrible as never to be forgotten.' 'This time,' the *Globe* observed, comparing the situation in Europe to that which existed at the end of the First World War, 'Germany is being conquered and occupied, rubble-heap by rubble-heap. But this time the German people will not need the presence of Allied armies to persuade them that they lost this war. The storm which is sweeping them from the air ... is convincing them that they have suffered the most terrible defeat ever inflicted on a people in all history.' Perhaps, the editorial continued, the Germans would learn from their defeat, and discover a new way of life which would allow them to exist 'constructively and compatibly alongside the neighbors they have made [into] enemies.'[111]

If that were the case, then the long casualty lists the *Globe* had published over the last five years would have some meaning. Bomber Command had mounted 364,514 operational sorties during the course of the war, of which 8,325, 2.3 per cent, failed to return. Well over a thousand more were lost in crashes. No 6 Group flew 40,822 of these sorties, of which 814, 1.9 per cent, failed to return, while more than a hundred crashed in England.[112] In his memoirs (but not his official report), Sir Arthur Harris stated that 125,000 aircrew flew at least one operational or training sortie in Bomber Command.[113] How and where he obtained this figure has never been explained – what kind of Second World War personnel records system would be geared to extracting that sort of information? – but so far as can be determined there is no alternative to his estimate and it will therefore have to serve as our best guess – however erroneous – as to the total cumulative aircrew strength of Bomber Command.

Casualties, of course, are easier to account for – systems *are* geared to record that kind of information – and 47,268 were killed in action or died as prisoners of war, and 8195 in flying or ground accidents. A further 9838 became prisoners of war; 4200 were wounded on operations but returned to base; and 4203 were injured in flying or ground accidents. If Harris was right, then 44 per cent of those who flew with Bomber Command died on operations or during training, while total casualties (including prisoners) amounted to 58.9 per cent. Total RCAF fatal battle casualties during the Second World War numbered 13,498, of which 9919, almost three-quarters, came in Bomber Command. No 6 Group lost 4272 dead – the vast majority, but not all of them, being Canadian – almost a third of the Canadian total.[114]

Given Germany's unconditional surrender, and what seemed to be the part played by strategic bombing in achieving it, the effort put forward by Harris's crews appeared to have been an unqualified success. But the cracks in Bomber Command's success story began to appear within a month of VE Day. 'There is no question that Berlin is a ruin and that many other German cities have been reduced to rubble,' journalist J.V. McAree reported on 6 June.

... but German war industry has in general survived. That is one of the surprising discoveries made by correspondents since they have been free to roam about the country ...

... by far the greater part of German industry remains untouched by the war ... Alfred Krupp von Bohlen und Halbach [scion of the great munitions conglomerate at the heart of Germany's war production], who, we are sorry to see, is at large and capable of issuing statements, issued one to the effect that the vast German industrial plant is ready to resume production of locomotives, rail track, bridges, girders and steel almost immediately. The only thing lacking is water, for without water to be turned into steam, coal itself is valueless as power ...

... While the war raged we heard about the destructive bombing of Germany, but we heard little about Germany's amazing ability to restore what was bombed. For example, the Leuna oil plant had to be destroyed three times ...

The Schweinfurt ball-bearing industry seemed to have been destroyed, but it was only dispersed and was turning out its vital product almost normally when the war ended. Dispersal also saved the German *Luftwaffe* so that when the war ended Germany had more completed planes than before the invasion ... it is plain that the Germans could make them faster than the Allies could destroy them ...[115]

Krupp was exaggerating, but the doubts he raised about the bomber offensive's impact on the economy were not far off the mark, as both the American and British postwar bombing surveys discovered when they carried out more thorough investigations in the months that followed. Incomprehensible as it seemed to those who had seen the rubble in the Ruhr, the Rhineland, Hamburg, and Berlin, production in the Third Reich had actually increased significantly between 1942 and the summer of 1944; and although the flow of raw materials to factories had ebbed in the last two months of 1944, because of stockpiling it was only in February and March 1945 that the output of tanks, ships, aircraft, and ammunition showed signs of collapse. By then, however, the Russians were advancing on Berlin, the Western Allies were closing the ring around the Ruhr, and the Third Reich's defeat was already certain. The German economy, it turned out, had been far more elastic than any of the Allies had realized in September 1939, both in terms of the size of the workforce and what it was being employed to produce.[116]

Indeed, despite the imperfect nature of the evidence, both survey teams arrived at remarkably similar conclusions about the effectiveness of Allied bombing, and particularly of area bombing. While not denying the acres of devastation (Sir Arthur Harris's favourite measure of success) in the cities shattered by air attack, the British report explained that area raids 'could not have been responsible for more than a very small part of the fall which ... actually occurred in German production by the spring of 1945 and ... in terms of bombing effort, they were actually a very costly way of achieving the results they did achieve.' The Americans meanwhile noted that 'attacks against city areas ... did not have a decisive effect upon the ability of the German nation to produce war material ... due primarily to the fact that the direct loss imposed was of a kind which could be absorbed by sectors of the German economy not essential to war production.'[117]

The resilience of the German people was another surprise. Perhaps 600,000 – mostly older men, women, and children – had died as a direct result of bombing; many more were mutilated and wounded; and as many as seven million may have been left homeless. No one denied that morale had been affected by the frequent air raids or that they had caused temporary bouts of depression and pessimism, but it was clear that bombing was less important than other military developments in producing any sense of defeatism among the population at large. That was true even in the thirty-seven towns and cities which had had more than half their built-up area destroyed by bombing. Hamburg, never a Nazi hotbed in the first place, may have been hit hard in July 1943, but the spirit of its people was not destroyed. Nor, as Albert Speer testified, had their 'will to work' been broken.[118] Berlin, too, had survived the twenty-week battle fought over the winter of 1943–4.

It was not just area bombing that proved to be something of a disappointment, however. Attacks on most of the panacea targets, about which Sir Arthur Harris had complained so vigorously, by and large failed to produce decisive results. The campaign against the ball-bearing industry, for example, had proved unavailing because (as Harris had predicted) the Germans not only had access to Swedish output in the early years of the war, but also had built up their own large stocks and plant was difficult to destroy. The predominantly American attack on the German aircraft industry that began in February 1944 was unquestionably productive, largely because the Luftwaffe was forced to do battle with the former's Mustang escort fighters, but output nevertheless rose consistently until September, and even in December 1944 more machines were produced than the previous January.[119]

While a significant number of submarines were destroyed in German shipyards, assaults on U-boat pens were less successful, as these facilities were too well hardened to be damaged by anything other than very heavy bombs like the British 22,000-pounder, only available from early 1945. Gardening, another naval priority, paid better dividends, accounting for 717 ships sunk and 565 damaged while seriously impeding the training of submarine crews in the Baltic. It is worth remembering that in late 1943 and then again during the first months of 1944, RCAF Wellington and Halifax II/V squadrons came to be regarded as Gardening specialists and that No 6 Group pioneered the techniques of high-altitude aerial minelaying.[120]

In the final analysis, oil (and its related rubber, chemical, and explosives industries) was probably the most important of all target systems, and once the Russians had captured the Romanian oilfields Germany's synthetic refineries were the most profitable of the 'panacea' targets singled out for attention. Eventually, German tanks and aircraft sat idle for lack of fuel. Still, the oil campaign began too late to immobilize the Wehrmacht in 1944.

Although the Combined Bomber Offensive against Germany did not begin to meet its objectives – the progressive, if not sudden, decline in enemy war production and, later, civilian morale – until the last months of 1944, four full years after it began in earnest, it is also true that, bit by bit, bombing at least played some part in slowing the rate of expansion in the German war economy and so contributed to the Allies' already significant materiel superiority. Precisely by how much, however, is difficult to determine.

Of much greater significance, particularly as the concluding topic in this section, was the extent to which the bomber offensive against Germany constituted a 'Second Front' long before the Allied invasion of Northwest Europe, and even when only Bomber Command was heavily involved in it. In terms of manpower alone, the Germans used between 500,000 to 800,000 workers to repair bomb damage and organize the dispersal of vital industries, labourers who could otherwise have been involved in the direct production of war materiel, while the Flak arm required some 900,000 men in 1943 and was still 656,000 strong in April 1945 – many of whom might otherwise have played a significant part in the ground war.[121]

The enemy was also forced to allocate considerable equipment to air defence. In March 1942, as the German army was fighting critical battles in Russia and Bomber Command had not yet launched its first 'thousand' raid or its initial battle of the Ruhr, there were already 3970 heavy Flak guns deployed around German cities which could have been made into mobile artillery or bolstered anti-tank defences in the east. By September 1944 that number had grown to 10,225. Indeed, according to Albert Speer, of the 19,713 88-millimetre and 128-milimetre dual-purpose Flak/anti-tank artillery pieces produced between 1942 and 1944, only 3172 could be allocated to the army for use in the anti-armour role because of the pressure of air attack. Similarly, the threat posed by Bomber Command's night raids meant that the German night-fighter force accounted for a consistently increasing percentage of Luftwaffe front-line strength – more than 20 per cent of the total by December 1944. Several hundred of those on strength in late 1943 and 1944 were machines which could have been used to great advantage in other roles ón other fronts.[122]

PART FIVE

Air Transport

A Douglas Dakota of No 435 Squadron returns from the squadron's first operational sortie, a supply-dropping mission to Pinlebu, Burma, on 20 December 1944. (PL 60123)

Canadian Dakotas unload their cargoes at a forward landing field in Burma. (PL 60109)

Troops from one of the two African divisions that fought in Burma board an RCAF Dakota in January 1945. (PL 60111)

Guarded by a solitary Hurricane fighter (top, centre), parachutes and supplies lie on the drop zone after a successful resupply mission. (PL 27008)

RCAF aircrew snatch a hurried meal of K-rations before taking off on another trip in early 1945. (PL 60258)

Living under canvas in the Burmese jungle, 1945. (PL 60257)

Dakotas of the airborne portion of the Allied crossing of the Rhine, which included aircraft of No 437 Squadron, over Caulille, Belgium, in March 1945. (PMR 74-324)

Belgian prisoners of war board a Dakota of No 437 Squadron for repatriation in May 1945. (PL 44178)

'Kickers' heave cargo out of a Dakota over Tiddim, Burma, in May 1945. (PL 60727)

Canadian aircrew unload squadron rations from a No 437 Squadron Dakota soon after that unit's arrival at its new base in Nivelles, Belguim, on 7 May 1945. (PL 44171)

Introduction

The Royal Canadian Air Force regularly carried men, materiel, and mail as it fulfilled its responsibilities connected with civil government air operations between the two world wars. As in most other air forces at the time, however – including the RAF – Canada's 'bush pilots in uniform' rarely thought about the potential of tactical air lift or using air transport to supply armies in the field, and no transport squadrons were mobilized in September 1939. Indeed, as late as 1 January 1943 there were only two true Royal Air Force transport squadrons based in England, and seven in the Middle East. When a separate Transport Command was established two months later it was regarded primarily as a successor to Ferry Command, and its main task was to deliver North American-built aircraft from the factory to active theatres of war.

The planners for Operation Overlord recognized the requirement for a sizeable air transport organization both to tow gliders and carry parachute troops to Normandy and to secure the flanks in the early hours of D-Day. Subsequently, air freighters would be needed to fill urgent requests for weapons, food, fuel, and medical supplies as well as to evacuate the seriously wounded. There might also be – and, in the event, was – a need to provide air transport for further airborne operations.

In Southeast Asia, meanwhile, once the Japanese offensive in northern Burma and eastern India had been stopped at Kohima and Imphal in March and April 1944, Lieutenant General William Slim's Fourteenth Army would have to rely on air supply if it had any hope of retaking Rangoon by an overland advance before the onset of the 1945 monsoon: the forbidding terrain and lack of good roads precluded logistical support on any other basis.

With Transport Command growing and (because of the casualty rates) Ottawa being unwilling to form any more bomber squadrons in order to complete Canada's Article XV allocation of thirty-five squadrons overseas, the RCAF offered to create three transport squadrons in June 1944 – one in England and two in Southeast Asia – an offer the Air Ministry readily accepted. All three would be equipped with American-built Douglas C-47 Dakotas, a design well suited to the task.

Formed at Blakehill Farm in September 1944, No 437 Squadron's first task was to tow British airborne troops in Horsa gliders to Arnhem where, in

Operation Market Garden, they were to capture and hold bridges over the Rhine. Despite heroic – and generally successful – efforts by Transport Command (including No 437 Squadron) to reinforce and resupply the airborne army, Market Garden failed.

No 437 Squadron was then engaged in routine carriage of freight between England and the Continent until mid-December 1944, when the Germans launched their offensive in the Ardennes. Transport Command was called upon to undertake emergency airlifts, and when the weather permitted No 437 transported part of an American division to the front. In March 1945 the squadron helped to lift British airborne forces across the Rhine as part of Operation Varsity. Once the war was over, it carried liberated prisoners of war from small landing fields in Germany to the larger airports where bombers were waiting to carry them back to England; and, between June 1945 and its disbanding in July 1946, the squadron carried men and freight all over Europe, from Oslo in the north to Naples in the south and Vienna in the east.

Although air transport was never critical to the success of the Allied armies in Europe, in Burma it alone made possible General Slim's advance from Imphal to Mandalay, and then to Rangoon in early May 1945. Nos 436 and 437 Squadrons were formed in India in September 1944 and mounted their first operation two months later, adding substantially to the air-lift resources available to Slim. They flew over the most difficult country and through the worst weather encountered by any airmen during the war – through mountain valleys and monsoon rains, often to poorly marked landing- and drop-zones under enemy fire – with few of the ground facilities available to their colleagues in Europe. Despite moving forward by stages into Assam and to islands off the Burmese coast, they were so far from their drop zones (and the need for their help was so great) that month after month they operated well beyond the maximum flying hours suggested for their machines.

Nos 435 and 436 Squadrons remained in Burma until September 1945. They then moved to England where they, too, flew transport missions to the Continent until they were disbanded in the late spring of 1946.

24

Airlift in Europe and Southeast Asia, 1944–5

Just after one o'clock on the morning of 6 June 1944 a café proprietor in the small Normandy town of Bénouville, two miles inland from the English Channel, was awakened by his wife, who had heard the sound of 'wood breaking.' Looking out the window towards the nearby bridge over the Caen canal, Georges Grondée observed a German sentry standing, apparently transfixed, by what he saw: '*Parachutistes!*'[1]

Reasonably enough, Grondée thought that a crew from one of the bombers in action that night had been forced to bale out and was about to be captured, but the sound of spreading small-arms fire soon dispelled that notion. What his wife had heard was the sound of Horsa gliders touching down near the bridge, and the parachutists were, in fact, soldiers of the British 6th Airborne Division sent to take and hold 'Pegasus Bridge' and thus protect the left flank of the D-Day landings. Four miles to the east, the 1st Canadian Parachute Battalion would soon be completing its task, the destruction of the bridges over the River Dives at Varaville and Robehomme. Fifty miles to the west, at the base of the Cherbourg peninsula, the American 82nd and 101st Airborne Divisions were dropping near St Mère Eglise and Carentan. In the largest airborne operation to date, three divisions of Allied glider and parachute troops had been carried to France by an aerial armada of about one thousand aircraft to cover the flanks of the amphibious assault phase of Operation Overlord.[2]

Five British, American, and Canadian divisions would land on the Normandy coast later that morning. At least five times that number were to be ashore within three months, and more than half as many again in the fall, by which time Allied planners hoped that the decisive battle for Germany proper would have begun. To secure these objectives – and avoid being hurled back into the sea – it was essential that the Allies build up the strength of their armies on the Continent faster than the Wehrmacht could reinforce its formations in France.

That would be accomplished, in part, through an intensive bombing campaign – the Transportation Plan – designed to deny the enemy the use of the lines of communication running between France and Germany (see chapter 22). The larger problem, however, was to ensure a steady build-up of supplies and follow-on forces in France. Clearly, as General Dwight Eisenhower's armies grew from five to over forty divisions, most of the men and materiel required to sustain his operations on the Continent would have to be shipped to France (and, later, Belgium) by sea, and then trucked to the front. However, the Overlord logistical plan also recognized that urgent requests for weapons, ammunition, food, fuel, and medical supplies (especially blood and blood by-products), as well as the requirement to evacuate the seriously wounded to England, would be better met by air.

Air supply had its beginnings in the First World War, mainly on the periphery and almost entirely on an ad hoc basis. In mid-April 1916 in Meso-potamia, for example, a composite force built around No 30 Squadron, Royal Flying Corps, but also including seaplanes of the Royal Naval Air Service, had been called upon to drop food and ammunition to the 14,000 men who had been cut off by the Turkish army at Kut-el-Amara, a town on the Euphrates halfway between Baghdad and Basra. The beleaguered garrison needed a min-imum of five thousand pounds of supplies a day, but despite removing the machine-guns and bomb racks from their machines to increase payload (until German fighters put in an appearance) and strapping bags of food to the fuselage, wings, and chassis struts of their aircraft, the airmen were rarely able to deliver more than three thousand. Facing starvation, the garrison capitulated before the month was out. Two years later, and also on the periphery, No 14 Squadron acted as a 'rudimentary transport squadron carrying personnel and supplies forward' as the campaign in Palestine drew to a close. While secure land links were easier to maintain in France and Flanders, a number of Royal Air Force squadrons were employed there to drop food and ammunition by parachute as the fighting became more mobile during the summer of 1918.[3]

Although military air transport was a common enough activity between the wars, and the Soviets, in particular, had tested the concepts of airborne oper-ations on a large scale, the idea of supplying ground forces by air while they were in contact with (or near) the enemy seems to have attracted less attention. This was true even in British India, where scattered army units trying to keep the peace in the mountainous terrain of the northwest frontier could usefully have been supplied by air. But when, in the early 1930s, a junior officer on the Indian Army staff, Captain W.J. Slim – the future field marshal who would revolutionize the Burma campaign of 1944–5 by the way in which he supplied his army by air – asked the RAF to consider how air supply could 'free ... a [ground] force from the need to move along valley bottoms, tied to its supply train,' his proposal for joint service discussions was angrily declined.[4]

Whether such anger abated after the Second World War began is a moot question. Because of the need to give priority to bomber and fighter produc-tion, no new transport aircraft were provided to the Royal Air Force between 1938 and early 1943,[*] and of the two true transport squadrons based in Eng-

---

[*] Indeed, in October 1940 the British government decided to rely on US production, the Americans initially offering between 7 and 11 per cent of their output of air freighters. Once the United States was in the war, however, the Ministry of Aircraft Production realized that the American forces would have first call and introduced a small transport program of its own.

land on 1 January 1943 (there were seven in the Middle East) one, No 271, had to rely on obsolescent Handley-Page Harrows for routine carriage of freight and personnel. (It was still equipped with a few Harrows in 1945, a number of which were destroyed during the Luftwaffe's New Year's Day attack on Allied air fields in Belgium.) The other, No 511, was flying converted Consolidated Liberator bombers and Armstrong-Whitworth Albermarles in mid-1943. Under the circumstances, the RAF had little to offer the army in the way of tactical airlift and supply, and that did not change when a separate Transport Command was established in March 1943. The new organization was regarded primarily as a successor to Ferry Command, and its principal responsibility was the delivery of North American-built aircraft from the factory to active theatres of war.[5]

It became clear that more needed to be done as soon as the planning for Overlord began, and to that end six new transport squadrons were established in Britain between April 1943 and June 1944, equipped mainly with the American-designed and -built Douglas DC-3 Dakota but with some Avro Yorks and Vickers Warwicks as well. New airfields had to be built to accommodate them, and since the squadrons' initial task would be to deliver glider and parachute battalions on D-Day, they were located in southwestern England, close to the Allied airborne armies.[6]

Although three of the thirty-five Article XV squadrons agreed upon at the Ottawa Air Training conference of May 1942 still remained to be formed, the RCAF did not contribute to this expansion of Transport Command. When, however, in May 1944 the Air Ministry urged Canada to complete its Article XV program through the creation of three more bomber squadrons for No 6 Group – and air minister C.G. Power agreed – the air officer commanding-in-chief of the RCAF Overseas quickly advised Ottawa to reverse its decision. 'Casualties are highest in bombing operations,' Air Marshal L.S. Breadner explained; and although Canada had waged a long and difficult political campaign to secure the formation of No 6 Group, he now thought that fifteen heavy-bomber squadrons were enough. Instead, he recommended the formation of one light-bomber and two transport squadrons. Power deferred to the AOC-in-C, and arrangements were begun to form these units.[7]

As it turned out, however, the RAF's light-bomber program was already complete and Breadner therefore asked that another transport unit be substituted. This was quickly approved in Ottawa and, following discussions with the Air Ministry, it was decided that two of the new squadrons would be formed in India (where there was a desperate need for air lift) and the third in England, as part of No 46 Group in Transport Command. Nine weeks later, on 14 September 1944, advance parties from No 437 Squadron moved to Blakehill Farm, a Nissen-hutted station completed in March 1944 and located near Swindon, about 120 miles due west of London. Because of a recent reorganization within Transport Command which had reduced squadron establishments, thirteen RCAF crews already serving in No 46 Group were available for posting. Without raising the thorny issue of breaking up existing crews, anathema throughout the RAF, all were sent to No 437, where they seem to have maintained their separate national identity. Although sharing Blakehill Farm with an RAF squadron, one observer noted in March 1945, the Canadians kept to themselves. 'There was the usual cleavage between the RAF and RCAF common to most stations where the S[tation] H[ead]Q[uarters] and one squadron were RAF and [the other] RCAF. There was little mingling in the mess, almost none between the SHQ and the squadron, apparently to their mutual satisfaction.'[8]

The squadron's first commanding officer was also a Canadian, albeit one of the legion of Canadians who had joined the RAF before the war, but he had already applied to transfer to the RCAF. Certainly, no one could question his experience. Wing Commander J.A. Sproule had completed a tour with Bomber Command, served as a navigation instructor with the BCATP in Canada, and then returned to England to join No 24 (Transport) Squadron, which operated 'anywhere between Iceland and China.'[9] Promoted to command No 48 Squadron (one of 437's sister units in No 46 Group), he had towed gliders to the D-Day beachheads and then, in early August, dropped ammunition to the hard-pressed Polish troops holding the mouth of the Falaise 'pocket.'

KG 421, flown by Wing Commander Sproule, left Down Ampney at 0530 and met very bad weather conditions. With cloud base at 300 ft, Sproule flew low finding his D[rop] Z[one] lit by fires. Enemy gunners found the slow Dakota an easy target and had soon damaged its wings and engines. More enemy fire poured through the windows, hitting the navigator in the shoulder and cutting the second pilot's face. The captain had splinter wounds. First aid was given to the navigator by the wireless operator as the course was set for B14 [Amblie, France]. With the rudder useless the crew tried to maintain course with engine power as the despatcher threw out disposable items ... Then another burst of *Flak* hit the batteries. The oil temperature fell, the controls were heating and, although the engines were at maximum revs, the A[ir] S[peed] I[ndicator] showed only 110 mph. Then, the inevitable. The aircraft smashed into the top of a tree. Wing Commander Sproule ordered crash stations before managing a skilful landing on a hilltop west of Jurques.[10]

Awarded the DFC, Sproule had to be hospitalized because of the wounds to his leg, and it was after his release that he took over 437 Squadron.[11]

His new command was also equipped with Dakotas. Compared with the bombers of all types that had heretofore been pressed into service to tow gliders and transport men and equipment, the DC-3s were versatile, efficient, and economical; and despite a few disadvantages (such as a side door too high for easy loading and unloading), they were more than merely adequate for their role. 'A gentler aircraft ... has never been made. It is as reliable as a steamship, responds to the slightest pressure on the control column, and even without using the automatic pilot it can be trimmed to such steadiness you can relax almost to sleep.' Dakotas were extremely strong, and, because of their exceptional stability, well suited to airdropping since cargo could easily be shifted and off-loaded in flight.[12]

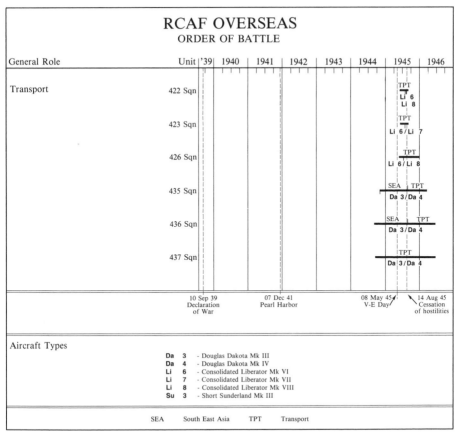

RCAF OVERSEAS
ORDER OF BATTLE

General Role	Unit	'39	1940	1941	1942	1943	1944	1945	1946
Transport	422 Sqn							TPT / Li 6 / Li 8	
	423 Sqn							TPT / Li 6 / Li 7	
	426 Sqn							TPT / Li 6 / Li 8	
	435 Sqn							SEA / TPT / Da 3 / Da 4	
	436 Sqn							SEA / TPT / Da 3 / Da 4	
	437 Sqn							TPT / Da 3 / Da 4	

10 Sep 39
Declaration
of War

07 Dec 41
Pearl Harbor

08 May 45
V-E Day

14 Aug 45
Cessation
of hostilities

Aircraft Types

Da	3	- Douglas Dakota Mk III
Da	4	- Douglas Dakota Mk IV
Li	6	- Consolidated Liberator Mk VI
Li	7	- Consolidated Liberator Mk VII
Li	8	- Consolidated Liberator Mk VIII
Su	3	- Short Sunderland Mk III

SEA	South East Asia	TPT	Transport

Of course, as workhorses rather than thoroughbreds, the unarmed and un-armoured Dakotas were slow, and this left them highly vulnerable to both Flak and fighters. Their normal cruising speed of about 160 miles per hour was reduced by one-third when they were towing gliders; and as the glider that No 437 Squadron pilots usually towed – the Horsa – stalled at about ninety miles per hour in level flight, there was little margin for error or mishap. 'The work was as hazardous as any in the air during operations since the Daks tugging their gliders were like sitting ducks for ack-ack batteries, travelling at 110 miles an hour in a straight line from which they could not deviate.' The Horsa itself was 'a biggish aircraft' (in fact, it was approximately the same size as the Dakota and, when fully loaded, not much lighter) and it was 'not an easy aircraft to fly.' On takeoff the glider 'had to be airborne before the tugging plane, a point which required experienced co-operation between the [two] pilots ... This was effected via the intercom, the wires of which ran through the silk or nylon towrope.'[13]

The first nine crews to join Sproule at Blakehill Farm arrived just in time to participate in Operation Market Garden, Field Marshal Sir Bernard Montgomery's attempt to secure an early crossing of the Rhine in order to allow the British Second Army to 'penetrate the Ruhr and the northern plains to Berlin.'

It was planned in two parts. In the first, Market, airborne forces were to seize the bridges over the Maas, Waal, and Rhine rivers at Grave, Nijmegen, and Arnhem to prepare the way for Second Army, and it was this action in which No 437 Squadron took part on the morning of 17 September. Wing Commander Sproule and his nine crews, plus two others seconded to him, towed twelve Horsa III gliders containing 146 soldiers of the 1st British Airborne Division together with sixteen bicycles, ten motorcycles, five jeeps, four 'blitz' buggies (jeeps mounting a .50 calibre machine-gun), six trailers, two hand carts, and three wireless sets to the Arnhem area. Happily, they caught the enemy by surprise. 'Our force went in practically unopposed. The Luftwaffe put up no interceptors and except for a few bursts of L[ight] F[lak] from the vicinity of L[anding] Z[one] and at the Dutch coast there was no deterrent offered by the enemy.' All twelve crews released their gliders over the landing zone, which was, unfortunately, too far from the division's prime objective – the Arnhem bridge over the Rhine. The British 'had selected drop and landing zones six to eight miles to the west of Arnhem bridge,' apparently because 'the RAF was reluctant to fly close to the heavy ack-ack near the bridge; thus they would not make a drop there. Furthermore, they wanted to avoid flying over Deelen Airfield several miles north of Arnhem, which was also surrounded by heavy ack-ack.'[14]

There was no longer any prospect of surprise the next day, and opposition stiffened. Although enemy fighter forces again failed to appear, Flak was heavy along the route to the landing zone and the machine flown by Flying Officer J.A. Delahunt 'sustained many perforations due to small arms and L/F fire. One shell burst in a/c just behind long-range tanks,' but all the gliders were released satisfactorily and were seen landing in the allotted zone, and no aircraft were lost.[15]

The Germans were stronger than anticipated on the ground, however, and for the next few days practically all of Transport Command was hauling gliders and supplies to airborne troops fighting to survive until the arrival of XXX (British) Corps which, on 21 September, was still ten miles away. That was the day the Luftwaffe finally became active in the battle area and, having no escorts to protect them, a number of Dakotas fell to Messerschmitts and Focke Wulfs before reaching the drop zone. Those who had run that gauntlet successfully faced devastating fire from the enemy's light Flak as they crossed the drop zone at less than a thousand feet. One young soldier who saw 'another fleet of supply planes [come] over to drop urgently needed ammo and food,' recorded his impressions of what transpired:

The cold-blooded pluck and heroism of the pilots was quite incredible. They came in in their lumbering ... machines at fifteen hundred feet searching for our position ... The German gunners were firing at point-blank range, and the supply planes were more or less sitting targets ... How those pilots could have gone into it with their eyes open is beyond my imagination ... They came along in their unarmed, slow twin-engined Dakotas as regular as clockwork. The greatest tragedy of all, I think, is that hardly any of these supplies reached us.[16]

Five of ten crews sent by No 437 Squadron failed to return, among them that let by Flying Officer G.P. Hagerman, who had tried valiantly to ensure that his supply panniers did land in the right place, making two runs over the drop zone 'despite intense and concentrated *Flak*.' After leaving the target area, however, 'his Dakota was attacked by six enemy aircraft, receiving such extensive damage that the crew had to bail out. Hagerman coolly and courageously remained at the controls until, sure that his companions had left, he jumped,' landing safely behind Allied lines. He was awarded the DFC.[17]

In a bizarre blend of operations and administration, the flights to Arnhem coincided with the formal handover of quarters and offices to the Canadians at Blakehill Farm, and when they were not being shot at by enemy Flak or fighters the aircrew had to take up their share of the domestic chores involved in settling in. On 19 September, for example, those who were not flying 'were busy laying Lino[leum] in the Flight offices.' However, the battle for the Rhine crossing was never far away. Sixteen crews were called upon on 23 September, and the fourteen who made it to the objective (one aborted before takeoff, while another was shot down) delivered 195 panniers despite the inexperience of their dispatchers, 'many of whom were on the job for the first time.'[18]

The dispatchers – or loadmasters – were army engineers whose job it was to ensure secure storage of the supplies and then to push them out over the target on a signal from the pilot. A normal lift consisted of sixteen panniers – heavy wicker baskets carrying an average load of 350 pounds – which 'might consist of almost anything under combat conditions.'

The panniers were pushed to the door of the aircraft on roller conveyors, the release cord of their parachutes being fastened to a sliding ring on a wire running the length of the cargo compartment. When the aircraft was over the target area (usually 1,000 yards square, with a fifteen-foot white wooden X in the middle) at about 750 feet, the captain turned on the red light over the rear door as a signal to the army despatchers to get ready to discharge the load. A green light flashed on when they were to let the load go. This could be accomplished in as little as twelve seconds. The discharging of airborne cargo could be considerably speeded up if the pilot lifted the nose of the aircraft, thus helping the panniers [to] slide to the rear door, so long as he did not raise it enough to slide them past the door and up the slope to the rear bulkhead![19]

Such precision was not always possible, however, as at least two crews discovered on the 23rd despite the unambiguous marking of the drop zone. A shell exploded under the tail of one Dakota, causing it to dive steeply after only two panniers had been dropped and upsetting the rest of the load so much that the dispatcher was forced to jettison six panniers 'well within our lines' so that he could rearrange the remainder. Another pilot was compelled to take violent evasive action to avoid being hit by the load dropped from an aircraft directly ahead. This caused nine panniers to slip off their rollers, and these had to be brought back to base.[20]

The last bridge to Arnhem proved to be a bridge too far for XXX Corps, and the link-up between ground and airborne forces never took place. Most of the soldiers were killed or taken prisoner. Those few who could do so evaded the enemy by night and slipped away across the Rhine, back to Allied lines. But that was not the end of No 437 Squadron's operations in the area. On the 27th it ferried personnel and equipment of three Hawker Tempest squadrons to the Continent; the next day it evacuated some of the airborne troops who had evaded capture; and on the 29th it carried 330 reinforcements for the Guards Armoured Division.[21]

Having to pause, now, in order to tidy up the rear areas and subsequently rocked by a German counter-offensive in the Ardennes, the Allies were in no position to mount another airborne assault until Operation Varsity in March 1945, when Montgomery's armies finally crossed the Rhine. In the interim, No 437 Squadron – by now four-fifths Canadian in air- and groundcrew – was given rather more routine and less hazardous transport missions hauling freight to, and casualties from, the Continent. The list of crews working on a given day would be posted in the late afternoon of the preceding day. Takeoffs were usually scheduled for early morning, typically 0700 hours, with briefings an hour before in the operations room. There, a huge map of Northwest Europe covered one wall, while blackboards displayed information on the current state of each aircraft, its captain, the load it was assigned, its destination, and schedule. Transport briefings did not usually take long, since crews soon became familiar with most of the destinations and routes they were likely to be assigned. If they were going to a new airfield they would ask about its surface. If it was close to German lines they would want to know about Flak positions. They would listen especially carefully to the meteorologist's forecast, as the weather was always unpredictable.

English winter mornings were often foggy and, if they were unable to take off immediately after the briefing, crews would pass the time playing cards, reading, writing letters, or playing table tennis until the weather cleared sufficiently for them to be on their way. Their Dakotas could safely carry a load of 5000 pounds. They rarely went to the Continent with less, and they always departed fully topped up with fuel so as not to deplete the limited continental stocks. They would usually fly at an altitude of between 1500 and 2000 feet. Landing at their destinations called for caution and vigilance, for wartime airfields had little resemblance to those of today, and crews could rarely be certain how well runways had been repaired, or how badly they had deteriorated, since their last visit. In any event, landings were almost certain to be rough, especially if 'PSP' – pierced steel planking – had been used to lay the runway. Such surfaces were usually uneven and often warped, with the result that 'even the most careful captain sometimes found [that] his aircraft bounced twenty-five feet on the touchdown forcing a go-around for a smoother landing.'[22]

Every effort was made to avoid flying back empty. Often it would be necessary to go to another airfield to pick up the return load, and then deliver it to another base in England before returning to Blakehill Farm; sometimes that load would consist of casualties – the Dakotas could accommodate a nurse and eighteen stretcher cases, stacked three deep. The cargo they carried was, more often than not, described as 'mixed' or 'various.' In October, for example, besides blood and plasma, they carried 'newspapers, mail, documents, maps, money, rocket projectors, ammunition, phosphorous bombs, clothing, wireless and photographic equipment, machinery, tank tracks, wheels, tractor treads, drop tanks for aircraft, casualties, German prisoners of war, captured enemy bombs and equipment, and even bedsteads!'[23]

On occasion, however, there was an element of 'cloak and dagger' in their work. The entry in the Squadron's Operations Record Book for 1 October 1944 is cryptic but intriguing: 'the load back [from Brussels] consisted of "Special Fluid" which was brought back under armed guard. The fluid was river water, which, it was believed could give the Allies some insight into the progress the Germans were making into atomic research. If they were using the Rhine river or any of its tributaries to cool an atomic reactor, an analysis of water samples might show traces of radioactivity.'[24] There was, of course, no such trace.

Although 'routine,' these operations were often conducted at a hectic pace and involved considerable stress.

Crews flew long hours and ground personnel performed servicing miracles. In the month of September 1944, they flew 58,153 ton/miles and carried 392 casualties together with 783 other passengers for a total of 337,386 passenger/miles.

During October, their first full calendar month of operations, despite constantly changing groundcrew, serviceability was maintained at eighty-one percent, 171,232 ton/miles were flown, 2,316 passengers were carried on 500,690 passenger miles, and 645 casualties were returned to the UK. Serviceability in November went up to eighty-three percent, 52.1 tons of freight, 1,946 passengers and 577 casualties being transported for totals of 166,575 ton/miles and 707,340 passenger/miles.[25]

The routine ferrying of supplies to France and Belgium was upset in mid-December 1944 when the Germans launched their desperate counter-offensive in the Ardennes – later known as the Battle of the Bulge – slicing through the thinly held American front line, hoping to split the allied Armies and drive through to re-take Antwerp. Transport Command was called upon to join American squadrons in flying emergency missions delivering reinforcements, fuel, ammunition, and other supplies to the front. One of No 437 Squadron's tasks was to assist in moving an American division to the Continent as quickly as possible, but the heavy fog that descended on Blakehill Farm prevented their leaving until 26 December, when seven crews were able to deliver 137 American soldiers to Denain Prouvy in France.[26]

Other crews, meanwhile, continued to haul any and all loads allocated to them. On 24 December, for example, three machines carried 15,104 pounds of Christmas pudding to Antwerp – perhaps not as frivolous as it sounds given the importance of maintaining morale among front-line troops during the battle – while two more delivered 5040 pounds of pudding and a number of musical instruments to Melsbroek. Then, as the German attack petered out, it was back to routine – but not always uneventful – duty. On New Year's Eve, Flying Officer V.J. Dale was 'shot up by enemy aircraft' while delivering 4800 pounds of 'army freight' to Antwerp. There were no casualties, although the aircraft sustained some damage.[27]

In early February the squadron carried troops to the Continent – 218 on the 9th, 211 the next day, 199 the day after that, and 445 on the 13th – after which steel matting for forward airfields became its stock in trade.[28] Subsequently, on 21 March twenty-six crews flew to Birch, in Essex, to prepare for Operation Varsity, and three days later twenty-four of them towed Horsas to Wesel.

Their total load consisted of 230 personnel of 1st Ulster Rifles, 13 jeeps and trailers, 2 jeep trailers, 6 jeeps and six pounder guns. 2 handcarts and ammunition, 4 bicycles and two motor-cycles. All aircraft reached the L[anding] Z[one]…and through very thick haze all made successful releases of gliders. Crews on return reported moderate medium and heavy flak over the LZ and Deersfordter-Wald but it was mostly inaccurate. Four aircraft were very slightly damaged. No aircraft were lost … and all crews returned safe with no casualties.

The weather over the whole route was excellent except for dust and smoke at the LZ … Operation Varsity took place in the area across the Rhine north of Wesel.[29]

On completion of the lift, the Canadians landed at Nivelles, in Belgium, and stood by for possible resupply flights in support of the units they had helped carry to battle. But the combined ground and air attack had been so successful that further air transport was not required, and on 26 March the crews returned to Blakehill Farm.[30]

The largest single air transport operation of the war took place between 29 April and 7 May – not by Transport Command, however, but rather by elements of the United States and British strategic bombing forces. The objective of Operation Manna was to provide food for the near-starving population of a large part of western Holland still occupied by the Germans and which the Allies, seeking to end the war quickly by moving directly into Germany, intended to bypass. Their own meagre resources ravaged by departing Germans before the enclave was sealed off, the three-million inhabitants were paying a harsh price for Allied successes all around them, although it was probably going too far to suggest – as the International Red Cross did – that the Germans, and 'especially Field Marshal von Rundstedt himself,' were 'planning to starve the Dutch people to death.'[31]

Even prior to the crossing of the Rhine, General Eisenhower had recommended to the Combined Chiefs of Staff that air transport would be the best way to deliver food, at least in the early stages of the relief operation. At first it was envisaged that transport aircraft would play a major role, but the air staff at Supreme Headquarters Allied Expeditionary Force (SHAEF) subsequently concluded that, because transport aircraft were in such demand (and, as the European war wound down, there was less for the heavy bombers to do), the supply drops would be carried out exclusively by RAF Bomber Command and the US Eighth Air Force.

In late April a truce was arranged between the Allies and the German occupation forces, who, with the end of the war in sight, no doubt found it expedient to cooperate. The formal agreement regarding food delivery, which designated ten drop zones and provided for truck convoys to be admitted into German-occupied territory for further distribution, was not signed until 2 May, but by then relief missions had already begun.[32] The first drops were made on 29 April, at the village of Waardenburg on the river Waal, three miles behind the German front line. 'The riverbank bristled with German anti-aircraft guns and the village was occupied by a detachment of paratroopers,' one of its inhabitants recalled. 'The day was sunny and clear.'

Around ten o'clock in the morning there was a steady drone of many approaching bombers. When we looked up to the sky, we observed squadron after squadron of Lancasters and Liberators. They flew so low that the pilots were clearly visible. It was a unique moment. For five years, Allied planes had been watched with both hope and fear. This time they carried no bombs. But perhaps the most remarkable fact was that the German guns, which used to greet even single fighter or observation planes with their shells, remained silent. The gunners stood at their usual positions, but their orders were not to fire. Most of them were pale and nervous, and one of them raised his fist to the sky and shouted: 'Those damned things up there.'[33]

No 6 Group played no part. The Canadian contribution to Manna was limited to the marking carried out by the Lancasters of No 405 Squadron, serving with No 8 (Pathfinder) Group on 30 April and on 1, 2, 4, and 5 May at The Hague, and on the 7th at Rotterdam.

Although there was no enemy opposition – indeed, the extent of German cooperation must have seemed strange to bomber crews fresh from recent raids on Berchtesgaden and Wangerrooge – the marking was on occasion inexplicably bad. On 30 April, for example, one No 405 Squadron crew reported: 'Dropped TIs at 1650.2 hrs. Rain and snow squalls. Visibility very bad at times. Marking was scattered, approximately 400 yards overshoot.' The next day the markers also fell 400 to 500 yards beyond the white cross laid out on a race-course as their target, with one aircraft reporting a 'load of groceries dropped on markers.' And on the 4th, of three aircraft detailed, one dropped its markers 'near the Gas Works, approximately five miles south of the Dropping Zone, after the 'bomb doors were opened due to possible electric failure; another brought its markers back to base after they had hung up; and the third dropped its markers from 350 feet into a small wood, overshooting the white cross by approximately 450 yards. Several bundles of supplies were seen falling onto the race-track. On the 5th, three Canadian crews dropped their markers 450 yards past the target and observed other target indicators burning a thousand yards east of it and still others half a mile to the north. Indeed, it was only on the 7th, at Rotterdam, that things went exactly according to plan. In good weather and clear visibility, eight crews dropped their indicators from 350 feet 'just overshooting the White Cross ... Early supplies seen dropping were well placed in the field around the White Cross.' That marked the end of Manna.[34]

By then British and American heavy bombers were engaged in another task very different from the one they had been designed and produced to perform. By late April, hundreds of prisoners of war (POWs) freed by the Allied advance had arrived at Brussels and a plan for their evacuation by air, prepared by SHAEF in March, was put into effect. This time the Dakotas of Transport Command, including those of No 437 Squadron, would also be heavily involved. However, air evacuation of POWs was just one of a number of 'non-operational' tasks to be carried out by Transport Command during Operation Eclipse, the 'military continuation of OVERLORD from the moment of ... surrender until control in Germany is taken over from the Supreme Commander by the Tripartite Government or by separate United States and British Commanders.' Others included moving scientists and intelligence officers and their equipment to those places in Germany where their particular skills were needed; supplying scheduled and emergency requirements to ground and air forces advancing into Germany; providing an air courier service; delivering emergency supplies of food and medicine to POWs; and 'any other Air Lift' tasks not previously envisaged and arising out of Eclipse conditions.[35]

To carry out these various missions, SHAEF planners intended to employ as many heavy bomber and transport aircraft as could be provided by the US Strategic Air Forces, RAF Bomber Command, and the Combined Air Transport Operations Room at SHAEF, which coordinated transport operations. In round figures they anticipated that, subject to operational requirements, there could be as many as 1800 B-17 and B-24 aircraft, 1000 Lancasters and Halifaxes, and 1400 transport aircraft available.[36] Because of all these commitments, SHAEF intended that air evacuation 'should supplement rather than supplant other methods of moving POWs out of GERMANY.' Even so, it was an enormous undertaking. There were over a million former prisoners of war to be repatriated from POW camps that were scattered throughout the Reich, often in thinly populated areas many miles from the nearest airfield. Moreover, with the recent Russian advances, large numbers of POWs were being moved westward by the Germans along with even larger numbers of foreign workers, displaced persons, and refugees making their own way to the west.

All this suggested the need for a heavy commitment of transport aircraft. In the early stages of Eclipse, however, there would be limited fuel stocks at forward airfields, and until they could be built up SHAEF planned to employ heavy bombers for the task because they could fly from England deep into Germany and return with a load of POWs without refuelling. But heavy bombers required hard runways of not less than 5000 feet for takeoffs and landings, and most of the airfields in Germany that were receiving POWs simply did not meet this requirement. As a result, Dakotas were required to transport the former prisoners from the smaller airfields to the larger ones from which the heavy bombers could operate.[37]

Bomber Command flew its first POWs back to England on 26 April, when forty-four Lancasters were dispatched for that purpose. The evacuation of POWs then became a regular commitment until 1 June, by which time the Lancasters and Halifaxes of Bomber Command (including No 6 (RCAF) Group) had carried some 75,000 men back to England.[38] In the meantime, the equally sterling efforts of Transport Command's Dakota crews had gone relatively unnoticed. Yet, they, too, had been transporting POWs to England, or from one European airfield to another, in impressive numbers, demonstrating in the process the great versatility of the Dakota. On 13 May, for example, four crews from No 437 Squadron delivered 20,000 pounds of fuel to the German town of Rheine and then returned to England with a total of forty-seven ex-POWs picked up on the way back at Limbourg, Aachen, and Brussels.[39]

In the middle of the month eighteen of [No 437's] Daks set an amazing record. In two days (April 17th and 18th) these aircraft transported 205,000 pounds of petrol and M.T [Motor Transport] fuel, 80,000 pounds of ammunition, 681 liberated prisoners of war, seventy-six casualties and two passengers in the most incredible flying time of 310 hours and twenty-five minutes. This was accomplished between 0900 hours one day and slightly after midnight the following day. One crew...in thirty seven hours and thirty minutes elapsed time spent exactly twenty-one hours in the air on twelve shifts.[40]

On 7 May 1945 No 437 Squadron moved from Blakehill Farm to Nivelles in Belgium. Although its arrival there coincided with the end of the war in Europe, the squadron's work was not over. 'From dawn to near midnight became a common schedule, doing two lifts a day between Brussels and up near Hamburg, with long pauses at each stop. The urgent task at hand was hauling out ex-POWs and taking in supplies of all kinds, from twenty-five pounder ammo, to petrol and blood plasma. The strain was wearing, especially on one crew which did 163 hours flying in one month ... only to read in the London papers how "RAF Lancasters" had flown home so many thousands of ex-POWs. That, they proclaimed loudly, was too much!'[41] By the middle of June, the Squadron (now flying out of Melsbroek) had transported nearly 20,000 Allied POWs, either from Europe to England or, more often, from one location in Europe to another, as well as substantial numbers of displaced Allied civilians. They had also carried high-ranking enemy officers and prominent German scientists to Britain. During July the squadron helped to prepare for the 'Big Three' conference in Berlin by ferrying stores to Germany and then carrying a considerable number of VIPs, including British foreign secretary Anthony Eden and General Sir Miles Dempsey, until recently the commander of Second British Army and soon to be the commander of Allied Land Forces in Southeast Asia.[42]

On 17 July No 437 Squadron extended its reach to Oslo, Norway, where a small detachment maintained a regular schedule between that city, Stavanger, and Bardufoss for several months. On 1 August another detachment was established at Odiham, in Hampshire, to operate between that place and Athens, Rome, Naples, Vienna, Marseilles, Oslo, Copenhagen, and Paris. In

September Wing Commander Sproule was replaced by Wing Commander A.R. Holmes and the main body of the squadron moved from Melsbroek to nearby Evère, where it stayed until the middle of November. It then returned to England – to Odiham – whence it continued to operate until the spring of 1946. Operations ceased at the end of May. Two weeks later fifteen of the squadron's Dakotas left Odiham to fly back to Canada where, in July 1946, the unit was disbanded.[43]

Apart, perhaps, from its involvement in the airborne operations conducted on D-Day, the contribution of Transport Command was never critical in determining the outcome of the campaign in Northwest Europe: Market Garden failed because XXX Corps could not advance quickly enough from Nijmegen to Arnhem; the German offensive in the Ardennes was pinched out primarily by American ground forces; and Varsity, the February 1945 Rhine crossing, went so smoothly that its airborne component was almost incidental to its success. For the most part, moreover, overland logistical support to the Allied formations at the front was never an unsurmountable problem.

That was not the case in Southeast Asia where, after their brilliant early victories, the Japanese outreached themselves logistically despite their spartan requirements – which were impossibly meagre by European standards. Advancing over the uncompromisingly tough terrain of central and northern Burma (where all-weather roads and railways were inadequate, or did not exist at all) in order to cut Allied supply lines to southern China, the Japanese Fifteenth Army by June 1944 was disintegrating from hunger and disease following its repulses in battle at Kohima and Imphal.

The Anglo-Indian Fourteenth Army of Lieutenant General William Slim could now take the offensive, but what the Japanese had tried and failed to do, the Allied chiefs of staff were reluctant to attempt. 'The problem of maintenance along an ever lengthening and tenuous line of communications render a campaign based on [an] overland advance unrealistic,' the joint staff planners had cautioned in October 1943, while 'logistical considerations alone preclude the possibility of advancing very far into central Burma' from Bengal. If Slim was to seize the moment and drive his weakened opponent back on Rangoon, he could only do so with air supply on a massive scale – particularly if the fighting continued into the 1945 monsoon season, which would begin in May.[44]

Fourteenth Army, however, could not count on all the Allied transport aircraft in the India-Burma theatre. Although Prime Minister Churchill desperately wanted a victory there to restore imperial prestige (and to ensure that British possessions in Asia were liberated by British troops), the Americans were involved in Burma primarily to reopen the supply road to Chiang Kai-shek's Kuomintang armies in China. The proposed campaign to liberate southern Burma, while not to be denied, was of only subsidiary interest to them. Take all of Burma at the earliest possible date, the combined chiefs of staff directed Lord Louis Mountbatten, the Allied supreme commander in Southeast Asia, but not to the point of prejudicing the security of existing air supply routes to China including the all-important air staging post at Myitkyina, just under two hundred miles north and east of Imphal.* Most of the 700 transport aircraft in the theatre, then, were employed exclusively in supplying the Chinese, flying over the Himalayan 'hump.'[45]

Indeed, Slim could not even count on all 252 transport aircraft made available to him for the defence of Kohima and Imphal in the spring of 1944. Of these, fully ninety (from one RAF and six USAAF squadrons) had been provided on loan from the Middle East and were withdrawn in early June, so that by mid-month, despite the arrival of three new American combat cargo groups and one US transport squadron, only 191 remained on call to Fourteenth Army – a number that would fall to 166 in August. Accordingly, Air Marshal Breadner's offer to form two RCAF transport squadrons in Southeast Asia Command (SEAC) was understandably welcome – so much so that in August the air commander, Sir Richard Peirse, observed that 'operations this coming winter [would] depend entirely on prompt arrival of 435 and 436 RCAF squadrons and their being operationally ready during October and December respectively.'[46]

In fact, British hopes had almost been dashed earlier in the summer when a Canadian air liaison mission to India, headed by Air Vice-Marshal L.F. Stevenson, had argued that because of climatic conditions and the difficulty of dealing with the Indian government, the RCAF should reconsider its intention to commit squadrons to Southeast Asia. For his part, air minister Power was insisting that if the two squadrons were dispatched, they should operate as a Canadian wing, perhaps at an RCAF station.[47]

A compromise was soon arrived at, however, which resolved both these problems. When the Air Ministry indicated that the Canadian squadrons could be withdrawn from the theatre when the war in Europe ended, even if the war against Japan continued (thereby obviating Stevenson's concerns about a long-term commitment), the Canadian minister agreed that it would be impractical to establish a separate RCAF command structure on such a short-term and temporary basis. At the same time, Power insisted that Canadians fill vacancies on the Transport Command staffs in Southeast Asia. 'Unless we obtain experience in this manner,' he argued, 'the Air Ministry may raise objection to the operation of RCAF group later.' By May 1945 twenty-three Canadian officers were serving in No 229 (Transport) Group headquarters.[48]

Because of the urgent need, the formation of 435 and 436 Squadrons proceeded more rapidly than that of No 437. Seventy-six complete crews (out of a total establishment of eighty) were shipped from Canada to Chaklala, near Rawalpindi, in northwest India, by the end of September, to begin their transport conversion there. The groundcrews, numbering almost six hundred, sailed to Britain from Canada on 30 August and were then flown to India in late September and early October. Once training was complete, it was hoped that both squadrons would be operational at RAF station Gujrat, near Lahore, by 1 November. The commanding officers both had considerable experience. Wing Commander T.P. Harnett had left the non-permanent RCAF to join the RAF in

---

* The combined chiefs reiterated this message at the Octagon Conference, held at Quebec City in September 1944, and again at Argonaut, held at Malta in February 1945.

November 1938 and had served with the night-fighters of No 219 Squadron during the Battle of Britain before a posting to Coastal Command. He transferred to the RCAF in November 1944. Wing Commander R.A. Gordon was a veteran of convoy escort, anti-submarine, and anti-shipping operations in the Home War Establishment.[49]

It took longer than anticipated for the two units to work themselves into shape. Part of the problem was purely administrative. For some reason No 233 Group, responsible for administration at Gujrat, was not told of its pending arrival there until 20 September, and no provision had been made for it at the unoccupied and sadly neglected station. The buildings, largely brick and mud and only two years old, had suffered greatly during the previous monsoon and were teeming with white ants and scorpions. Not surprisingly, disease (including malaria, hepatitis, dysentery, and sandfly fever) was also a problem, especially among men unaccustomed to the Indian climate (and water), yet the medical facilities and stores were so deficient that members of the Canadian air liaison mission left their own supplies behind when they departed after a visit on 25 October.[50]

In addition, the Dakotas assigned to the two squadrons required substantial modification, including the installation of non-skid floors and American-pattern parachute racks. But the slow arrival of conversion kits and US tools – virtually none of the facilities or equipment for aircraft maintenance were available in the first few weeks – the late arrival of the required technical officers, and the fact that Gujrat, built as a fighter base, did not have the appropriate hangars and dispersal points, hampered efforts to put things right. Even so, using the British station at Lahore as its fuel and servicing base, No 435 Squadron managed to carry out its first formation flying before the end of October. Not, it must be added, without risk. 'At Gujrat,' the squadron diary observed, 'our flying control consists of the adjutant sitting hopefully in a 3 ton truck with a 15 cwt [light truck] used as a mock-up crash tender. But, alas, we have no crash equipment or fire equipment to put on it.'[51]

Anxious to 'enhance [the RCAF's] reputation' in Southeast Asia, Wing Commander D.C.S. MacDonald, DFC, the RCAF liaison officer* at No 229 Group who was also acting station commander at Gujrat, brought 'heavy pressure to bear' to have the two squadrons declared operational at the earliest possible date, and in the first two weeks of November they completed 1500 hours of flying training. Previously, during their three-week conversion course at Chaklala, they had concentrated on supply dropping and on training their wireless operator/air gunners as jumpmasters and dispatchers. Now, during squadron training at Gujrat, they emphasized formation flying, cross-country

---

* RCAF liaison officers served on the staffs of most RAF home commands and of some overseas groups and wings. Their job was to strengthen the Canadian (and RCAF) presence in the administrative echelons in these theatres and to ensure, so far as possible, that RCAF policies regarding postings, promotions, and pay were adhered to in the case of the many RCAF personnel serving in RAF units. They also took care of 'good and welfare' problems such as the delivery of mail. There were, in addition, RCAF District Headquarters at seven locations in Britain as well as in the Middle East and Southeast Asia.

navigation, glider-towing, and troop and supply dropping; and on 17 November seven aircraft of No 436 Squadron, flying in a formation led by Wing Commander Gordon, para-dropped full loads of twenty soldiers and their equipment, as well as six 300-pound containers which had been slung under the belly of the aircraft.[52]

That was a considerable achievement for a group of aircrew who, in contravention of normal practice, had not been employed on 'airline and ferry work for a period of climatization and experience in local conditions before reporting to a front-line Transport Squadron.' Before the end of the month, the two units had accomplished even more. Initially through 'scrounging,' but then as spares began to arrive, they were able to complete the modifications and maintenance required on their machines and put all they had into the air at once: twenty for No 435 and fifteen for No 436. This despite the fact that there were no hangars or any form of maintenance shelters at Gujrat.[53]

Thirty-five Dakotas represented a considerable increase in airlift capacity for Southeast Asia Command where, on 23 November, excluding its two Canadian units, there were still only one Hudson/Warwick and five other Dakota squadrons from Commonwealth air forces. Each Dakota could carry a 7000-pound cabin payload, and in Southeast Asia these ranged from mules to howitzers, jeeps to medical stores or fuel, bagged rice to boxed ammunition. Carrying gasoline was particularly hazardous over the mountains of India and Burma, as the vapour in the 55-gallon drums expanded at altitude and occasionally cracked them, resulting in a scramble to find the leaking container and heave it out the cargo door. Meanwhile, the Dakota's exceptional stability, which allowed crews to shift and off-load cargo while in flight without upsetting its balance, was a particularly valuable characteristic in Burma, where most dropping was done at low speeds and altitudes.[54]

Early in December 1944, having driven the battered enemy from Imphal, the capital of the Indian province of Manipur, Fourteenth Army crossed the Chindwin and prepared to move on Mandalay. Sir William Slim (he was knighted on 15 December 1944) and Lord Louis Mountbatten were determined to take Rangoon, the Burmese capital which lay some 350 miles to the southeast, before the monsoon began because they doubted whether the army could be kept adequately supplied by land or air from northern Burma once the rains began. But when three American transport squadrons were diverted to China to meet a Japanese offensive there, Slim began to despair that his overland approach would not succeed in time: 'a firm allotment of air lift,' one of the foundations 'on which all our plans had been made, was swept away.' Partly for this reason, Mountbatten continued pressing for approval of an amphibious assault against Rangoon.[55]

It was at this vital juncture that Nos 435 and 436 Squadrons became operational, initially helping to move the groundcrew and equipment of RAF fighter squadrons forward to Imphal. Then, on 15 December, No 435 Squadron was ordered to Tulihal, in the Imphal valley (with No 436 assisting in its move) to support Slim's advance on Shwebo, a railway junction twenty miles north of Mandalay. The Canadians arrived at Tulihal on 19 December to find that once again virtually no preparations had been made for them. While reporting to a joint Anglo-American Combat Cargo Task Force for operations, for administrative and logistical support they came under three widely scattered RAF groups – No 229 at Delhi, No 221 at Imphal, and No 224 at Chitagong – and that, naturally enough, produced chaos. Although the situation gradually improved, the tangle was undone only in April 1945, with the formation of No 232 Group at Comilla, which took over responsibility for all such support.[56]

At Tulahil, in late December, the squadron was eating hard rations and living and sleeping in the open. 'The mechanics had to use flashlights and coins to remove cowlings and with make-shift tools accomplished the impossible.'[57] There were no first-aid or jungle survival kits and, since there were no refuelling trucks, all gasoline had to be pumped by hand. Nevertheless, on 19 December, the day he arrived, Wing Commander Harnett was informed that a maximum effort would be required the next day. Borrowing the necessary equipment (the neighbouring USAAF squadrons were particularly helpful), on 20 December nine aircraft were able to mount fifteen sorties in support of the Fourteenth Army.[58] Five days later, fifteen crews flew thirty-one sorties.[59] The Dakotas had an economical range of 250 miles. (Greater ranges reduced both the payload and the number of sorties that they could carry out in one day.)

The administrative arrangements for No 436 Squadron's arrival in the Imphal valley, at Kangla on 6 January 1945, were scarcely better than they had been for No 435's at Tulihal. A water shortage was partly solved by flying in a 200-gallon tank from 435 Squadron's thin resources, but there was insufficient permanent accommodation and there were not enough tents. The squadron motor transport had to be collected at Comilla, north of Chittagong in India, and driven in – a punishing two-week task for drivers and vehicles. Although the bulk of the squadron only arrived on the 14th, it began operations the next day, when seven aircraft flew seventeen sorties landing, para- and free-dropping supplies at Shwebo.[60]

The arrival of the Canadian squadrons at Imphal (together with the unexpectedly quick return from China of two of the American squadrons in February) meant that Slim would have 'sufficient carrying capacity to meet all requirements' – providing that the aircraft could operate within their economical range of 250 miles – to start his overland advance on Rangoon. Nevertheless, it was soon found that the sustained flying rate for each machine had to be raised from 100 hours a month to 125 hours, and the intensive rate to 185 hours. In the event, most squadrons flew at or over the intensive rates for months at a time despite the obvious risks and the additional burden on the maintenance staff in ensuring that the overworked Dakotas remained safe to fly.[61]

The crews, too, were under stress. For one thing, rumours were rife in No 435 Squadron that Breadner now thought that the formation of the two transport squadrons in India had been a mistake; and his unexplained failure to visit the unit on 8 January 1945 during his tour of India simply aggravated the situation. The stories were not entirely unfounded, as on 27 January the government would again attempt to withdraw the squadrons from Burma. It only reluctant-

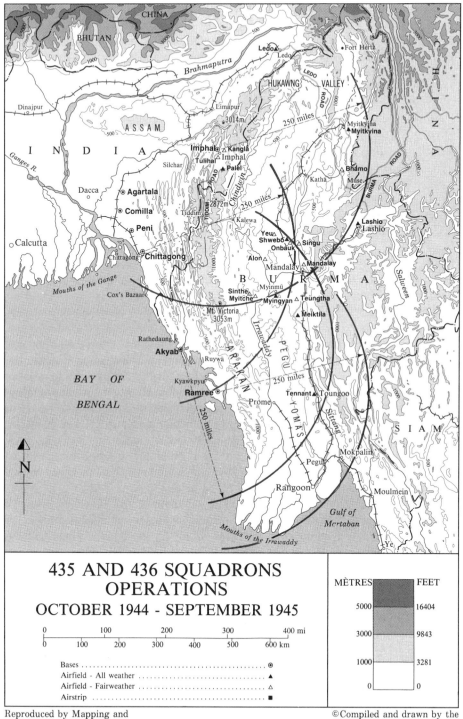

CHINA

BHUTAN

Brahmaputra

Ledo • Fort Hertz

LEDO ROAD

HUKAWNG VALLEY

Dinajpur

Imaphur
3014m

250 miles

Myitkyina
▲ Myitkyina

ASSAM

I N D I A

Ganges R.

Imphal ◉ △ Kangla
Tulihal △ Imphal
Silchar ▲ Palel

Bhamo ▲
Muse

BURMA ROAD

Dacca
◉ Agartala

Katha

◉ Comilla
Tiddim
2872m

Kalewa

● Peni

Yeu △
Shwebo ▲
Onbauk ● Singu

Lashio ▲
Lashio

○ Calcutta

Chittagong ● Chittagong

Alon △

Mandalay ▲ Mandalay

Salween

B   U   R   M   A

Mouths of the Gange

Cox's Bazaar

Myinmu
Sinthe △
Myitche ● Myingyan △ Teungtha

Mt. Victoria
3053m

Irrawaddy

▲ Meiktila

Rathedaung

A R A K A N

P E G U

Akyab ●

Ruywa

BAY   OF

Kyawkpyu

250 miles

BENGAL

Ramree ◉

Prome ○

Tennant ▲ Toungoo

Y O M A S

Sittang

250 miles

S I A M

Mokpalin

N

Pegu ○

Rangoon ○

Moulmein

Gulf of
Mertaban

Mouths of the Irrawaddy

Ye

435 AND 436 SQUADRONS
OPERATIONS
OCTOBER 1944 – SEPTEMBER 1945

0	100	200	300	400 mi
0	100	200	300	400	500	600 km

Bases . . . . ◉
Airfield - All weather . . . . ▲
Airfield - Fairweather . . . . △
Airstrip . . . . ■

MÈTRES		FEET
5000		16404
3000		9843
1000		3281
0		0

Reproduced by Mapping and
Charting Establishment.

©Compiled and drawn by the
Directorate of History.

ly accepted the advice of the CAS in Ottawa, Air Marshal Robert Leckie, and
the Air Ministry that, given the uncertainty of American commitments, such
a move would be a mistake – receiving, in return, a reaffirmation of the
promise that the two units would be withdrawn when the war in Europe had
ended. (Breadner, nevertheless, promised No 436 Squadron, which he did visit,
repatriation after three years of overseas service.)[62]

Another reason – and this applied to both squadrons – was that operations
from Imphal were not easy. Lying in a deep valley, and with two steep, jungle-
cloaked ridges between it and the Chindwin River and the plains of central
Burma, the Imphal area was no place to have an accident – always a threat
given the sudden changes in cloud cover and rapid development of storm
fronts. The Canadians had to adjust the flying techniques learned so laboriously
over the plains and in the relatively quiet skies of northwestern India. Instead
of flying in formation, which had taken up so much practice time in India,
operations in Burma were usually undertaken by single aircraft or small flights,
since neither the airfields, drop zones, or loading and unloading facilities could
handle many aircraft at a time. Moreover, the closely timed troop-dropping
exercises, which had formed a major part of the squadron's training, were not
used until the capture of Rangoon because Slim did not wish to expend air
resources in such operations. Air supply of his ground forces was considerably
more important.[63]

The preferred method of delivering cargo was the conventional and obvious
one of landing at one of the forward landing strips and unloading it there; but
this method was not always the easiest or safest for the crews, who invariably
found these strips small and rough, and often with restricted approaches.
Landing with heavy loads frequently resulted in burst tires, and the need for
steep approaches and takeoffs subjected both pilots and aircraft to severe stress.
Many of the airfields had been hastily built by the advancing army for only
temporary use and they usually lacked even rudimentary air traffic control, so
that the crew of the first machine to land was often required to serve in that
capacity for the benefit of those who followed.[64]

Although flying weather was generally excellent outside the monsoon
season, dust clouds rising to 300 feet were a severe problem at a number of
the airfields; and the degree of hazard was simply increased when they became
congested with aircraft circling, landing, unloading, and taking off again,
always in sweltering heat and sometimes under threat of Japanese air and
ground attack. Since crews could not count on much assistance from people
on the ground, in the end they determined the speed of turn-around themselves.
The Canadian squadrons reported usual turn-around times of ten minutes,
although off-loading four-gallon jerricans of fuel took up to thirty minutes.[65]

When landing was impracticable, loads were free- or para-dropped. However, because of the lead time required and the army's speed of advance, the
location of drop-zones was usually predicted rather than fixed and, as they
were often poorly marked or obscured, they were not easy to find. Once over
the drop zone, pilots normally circled it eight to ten times (and sometimes
more) as over six thousand pounds of cargo had to be moved to the door and

pushed out by three or four men in carefully timed bursts of ten to fifteen seconds. When the drop zones were close to the front line, as they often had to be, the Dakotas, circling at minimum speed no more than six hundred feet above the ground (and often much lower as free drops were carried out at the lowest possible altitude), were exceptionally vulnerable to enemy ground fire. Furthermore, nearby hills or adjacent drop zones, with their circuiting aircraft, often hampered delivery as the pilot had to find space for a straight run over his drop zone and still have room to circle. To prevent cargo being lost to the enemy or to the exuberant jungle, accuracy was vital, particularly in the case of free drops where crew inexperience could easily cut the recovery rate in half.[66]

Despite its many sterling qualities, the Dakota was not entirely suited to these operations. The main shortcoming was that, when fully loaded, it could not successfully complete a takeoff or landing if one engine failed. The extreme heat in India and Burma further reduced single-engine capability and, under some conditions, even a machine already in flight could not maintain altitude on one engine unless its load was lightened by jettisoning the cargo very quickly. There were compensations, however. The aircraft could take a lot of punishment from ground fire and, if it crashed, its rugged construction added considerably to the crew's chances of survival.[67]

Groundcrew worked in trying conditions of heat and humidity, servicing machines without adequate heavy equipment but maintaining a high rate of serviceability on aircraft which were consistently flown at, or over, the recommended intensive rate – and in very rough service. When, as was inevitable, an aircraft was grounded by mechanical problems at a forward strip, groundcrew were flown in and, if necessary, remained with the aircraft overnight to effect repairs. Groundcrew also played an important role in the actual conduct of air operations. In both squadrons they volunteered to act as 'kickers' in ejecting the cargo over the drop zones. This was hard, uncomfortable, and sometimes dangerous work. Many accumulated hundreds of hours of flying time and some were killed in action.[68]

Air transport relied heavily on a substantial degree of air superiority, particularly over the forward areas where the transports were concentrated and most vulnerable. Although it was provided with 'knock-out' rifle holes in the windows, the Dakota was virtually defenceless against fighter attack, and a crew's only hope of survival lay in evasion. The basic tactic was to get the slow, ponderous machine as low as possible as quickly as possible, thereby limiting the surfaces exposed to enemy fire and forcing an attacker to pull out of his dive early. As the attacker approached effective range – 500 to 1000 yards – a steep turn towards it would, with luck, cause the much faster fighter to overshoot, with few effective rounds fired. But a Dakota stood little chance against a determined or numerically superior enemy; and despite the overall air superiority enjoyed by the Allies during 1945 – in December 1944 they had 650 fighters in Southeast Asia, while the Japanese 5th Air Division in Burma, now being left to wither on the vine, had sixty-six, a figure that fell to fifty by April – the enemy was still capable of some offensive action, particularly if it concentrated on the air transports. In spite of this threat, however, the nearly four hundred Allied transport aircraft operating all over Burma (five hundred by May) usually flew unescorted because there were simply too few fighters available to escort them; ground support for the army and attacks on the enemy's airfields had priority.[69]

The Japanese preferred to use their diminishing air power in direct support of their own land forces rather than to interdict Allied air supply. On 11 January, however, No 435 Squadron was told that a number of enemy fighters had been moved up to the forward area, and the next day five of its Dakotas flying over Shwebo were attacked by an uncertain* number of 'Oscars' (Nakajima Ki 43s). This attack lasted only ten minutes but left two Dakotas destroyed and one damaged, and killed six aircrew. Indeed, the losses might have been higher except that the Japanese had been attacking ground targets and engaged the Canadian aircraft only after completing their primary mission and expending most of their ammunition.[70]

Flight Lieutenant H. Coons, in command of a flight which was circuiting at four hundred feet over a drop zone, first spotted the Japanese aircraft and broadcast a warning as he dived for the tree tops. His aircraft was attacked five times, and on the fifth pass it lost four feet of wing tip when it hit a tree during the evasion turn. A groundcrew 'kicker,' Corporal A.M. White, was injured, but the aircraft returned safely to base. Another Dakota was shot down on its first pass, with only one survivor who was thrown clear of the aircraft on impact. Flight Lieutenant R.P. Simpson (the only RAF aircraft captain in the squadron) was shot down with a full load of ammunition, but despite fire in the cargo he was able to crash-land and evacuate his crew – although one of them later died of cannon-shell wounds. A fourth machine was able to avoid the enemy by violent corkscrewing, while a fifth, alerted by Coons's warning, landed at a nearby strip. Its crew assisted the rescue party which went to the scene of Simpson's crash. For their skill and courage, Coons received a Bar to his DFC and Simpson the DFC.[71]

The Canadians modified their tactics following this episode, ordering pilots to fly at tree-top level and, in the case of No 435 Squadron, to set back the flying day so that it started at noon and ended fifteen hours later in order to take advantage of the darkness. Soon, however, the Japanese air forces were less of a concern. Concluding that their forward air bases had become untenable because of Allied pressure, and needing to strengthen their forces in the Pacific, where the Americans had already liberated much of the Philippines and were preparing to take Iwo Jima, they ordered most of their fighter units from Burma, and by the end of January No 435 Squadron was again flying by day.[72]

Meanwhile, on 14–15 January 1945, Slim's troops had established the first bridgeheads across the Irrawaddy River, forty miles north of Mandalay and

---

* Estimates of the number of fighters attacking the transports ranged from a low of five to a high of twelve; thirty had attacked the airfield at Shwebo and twelve at Onbauk, where they destroyed four Dakotas on the ground.

fifteen miles east of Shwebo. The enemy fought bitterly to pinch these out, and No 435 Squadron was called upon to drop supplies to hard-pressed Gurkhas holding forward positions near Kyaukmyaung. The first Canadian aircraft to cross the Irrawaddy in support of ground forces was flown by Warrant Officer F.M. Smith on 23 January. Because of the drop zone's location, Smith was required to circle in part over Japanese lines subject to light but effective ground fire. A groundcrew 'kicker,' Sergeant N. Jarjour, was hit on the third circuit and, after two more circuits, Smith flew him to a field hospital at Shwebo. He then returned and dropped the remainder of his load on the river bank, farther from the front line. The pilots on these missions endeavoured to make their dropping runs from south to north, so that if their aircraft was hit by ground fire – some were – and an engine put out of commission, they could glide back over the river to British territory. Strangely, however, although both Canadian squadrons were flying in the same general vicinity, crews from No 436 did not come under enemy fire at this time, from either the ground or the air.[73]

The requirement to support forward units as well as to build up reserves at Shwebo meant that all transport units were extremely busy in January. The average round trip from the Imphal valley to the front took between two and three hours and, if there were no delays in loading and unloading, crews could put in three sorties each day. On 20 January No 436 Squadron reported that it had topped all RAF transport squadrons with a lift of 145 tons – a figure the squadron exceeded in the final days of the month – and over one two-week period it lifted 2500 tons of cargo and 735 passengers in 2087 tactical hours. No 435 was only marginally less busy. This hectic pace continued into early February, when the latter was primarily engaged in flying the 'milk run' from Imphal to Shwebo. On one occasion, crews counted fifty transport aircraft on the ground at Shwebo, with another ten in the landing circuit. It is testimony both to the Dakota's reliability and to the hard work and improvisation of the groundcrews that, despite parts and tool shortages, serviceability was still being maintained near 90 per cent in both squadrons. Slim was amazed, commenting that 'the heroes of this time were the men who kept the wheels turning and the wings flying.'[74]

Among the latter he should, perhaps, have included the navigators as well. Radio beacons in Burma were often unreliable and it was relatively easy to get lost, particularly at night or in heavy cloud. On 7 February 1945, for example, Squadron Leader R.L. Denison of No 436 Squadron spent two hours trying to contact his base, receiving 'nothing encouraging' until his port engine began to fail. Deciding, with his navigator, that they must be somewhere near Imphal, Denison let down through a hole in the clouds only to find himself 'surrounded by a black void, [with] only one brush fire visible.' With no other reference points to go by, and as their radar screen was now a blank, Denison decided that his crew would have to bail out, and he therefore climbed to a safe height to give them a chance. Once they had jumped, he 'trimmed the aircraft for one engine, left the controls and after considerable difficulty managed to capture the chest pack but could not get hold of my jungle kit as the aircraft had commenced a deep spiral dive. I managed to crawl out the door about a minute to a minute and a half after the others had left.' Fortunately, they had been over British territory and the villagers where most of the crew landed were friendly. Denison himself, however, came down in the Chindwin and had to swim to shore. After spending a night on the river bank, he too was found by a friendly Burmese and eventually reunited with his crew.[75]

In part because of air supply, the bridgeheads across the Irrawaddy held and the Allied forces in the north began their move down to Mandalay. 'We rumbled down the cattle tracks in the heavy dust,' Major John Masters, a British Gurkha officer, recalled, past stands of jungle where the crackle of small-arms fire showed that we had caught some Japanese.'

The tank treads clanked through villages blazing in huge yellow and scarlet conflagrations, palm and bamboo exploding like artillery, gray-green tanks squatting in the paddy round the back ... We passed the twenty-five-pounder gun-how[itzer]s ... bounding and roaring in a score of clearings, hurling their shells far ahead into yet another village. Tanks again, the troops that had cleared the village back there, rumbling on, twenty Gurkhas clinging to the superstructures. Infantry, trudging along the sides of the road, plastered with dust and sweat ... the mules of the mountain artillery ... Japanese sprawled in the road ... their chests blown in, some by tank shells, some by suicide ... The light hung sullen and dark over all, smoke rose in vast writhing pillars from a dozen burning villages, and spread and joined to make a gloomy roof above us. Every village held some Japanese, every Japanese fought to the death, but they were becoming less and less organized.[76]

Additional crossings of the Irrawaddy were made farther to the south in early February, with the road and rail centres of Meiktila and Thazi as their objectives. When these had been secured, the way to Rangoon would be open. But the farther his 300,000 men marched from Imphal, the more Slim doubted whether the air forces could continue to provide them with the nine-tenths of their supplies upon which they relied and on which further advances depended. He had already been putting heavy demands on the fourteen transport squadrons now assigned to his army – eight American, four RAF (with 225 Canadian air crew), and two RCAF – and he realized that 'the administrative side of the battle began to look more like a gamble' than he relished. It was a question, essentially, of economical range – too much fuel had to be carried for the Dakotas' round trips between Imphal and the south – and of wear and tear: squadrons were averaging over two hundred flying hours every month on each machine as they strove to make three lifts a day.[77]

In mid-February No 435 Squadron began landing at Myitche, a dirt strip 1900 yards long by 35 wide (with only an Aldis Lamp for flying control) located west of Meiktila. No 436 Squadron, in turn, began landing at Meiktila on 6 March, just three days after its capture by IV (British) Corps. But the surrounding countryside had not yet been cleared of the enemy and Meiktila itself soon came under heavy counter-attack, so that the Canadian crews were often flying low over Japanese-held territory. The risks in pushing them so far forward so fast were obvious, but the longer distances to be flown if they were not cut very close to the essential margin of supplies. 'Time and again,' Slim recalled, 'and just in time, the bare essentials for their operations reached those who so critically needed them.'[78]

What the transport squadrons clearly required were bases which would put southern Burma within economical range while still enjoying good communications with India. These could be found only on the Arakan coast, where small amphibious operations had secured the Akyab and Ramree Islands in December 1944 and January 1945. On 10 March, then, No 436 Squadron (along with No 194) started its move to Mawnubyn, on Akyab Island. They were ready for operations ten days later. Meanwhile, heavy fighting continued around both Myitche and Meiktila and, despite the fact that the move to Akyab had reduced the flying time to the latter by about forty-five minutes, 436 Squadron's total daily sorties did not increase significantly. Aircraft were frequently diverted from one objective to another as drop zones changed hands, with the result that a single sortie might last as long as four hours. Indeed, possession of Meiktila was still contested by the rival ground forces, and for some time the pilots were told whether they could use the airstrip there only when they were well en route. The strip itself was recaptured and held by the Japanese between 22 and 31 March, but was taken again on 1 April and thereafter remained in Allied hands.[79]

Further south, ground forces had meanwhile entered Mandalay on 8 March, and were soon engaged in a prolonged struggle for possession of Mandalay Hill. Flying out of Imphal with Meiktila as its main destination, No 435 Squadron supplied Allied forces near Mandalay until that city was firmly in Allied hands on 20 March. No 436 began landing supplies there four days later. Depending on the availability of air transport, taking Rangoon by an overland approach before the monsoon arrived was now a possibility, but only just, even against a disorganized enemy.[80]

That meant calling upon the Imphal-based squadrons, even if they were out of economical range. In mid-April, for example, No 435 flew from Imphal to Tennant, an airfield near Toungoo on the railway less than a hundred miles from Rangoon. The flight took over six hours and required a refuelling stop at Meiktila, using fuel which itself had to be flown in. That could be justified upon occasion, but not as a regular occurrence, and for that reason No 435 spent most of its time flying to Meiktila and Myitche, where stockpiles were still being built up.[81]

The squadron had been located in the Imphal Valley long enough now to have established many of the rudiments of what might be called station life. Like No 436, it operated an all-ranks mess in order to reduce labour requirements and avoid hiring native helpers, who were considered to be unsanitary in their habits and unsuited to the preparation of North American food. The rations were monotonous, reflecting transportation, storage, and availability problems, and relied heavily on tinned corned beef and fish. This situation was common to most messes in Southeast Asia (although units in Ceylon were considered to be much better off), and the Canadian Air Liaison Mission had declared that 'the standard of messing ... is ... far inferior in every respect to that enjoyed by the RCAF in Canada.'[82]

Japanese resistance north of Rangoon began to melt away in April, and Slim's forces made quick progress.[83] John Masters looked on in silence as General Slim, '4 Corps Commander ... and three divisional commanders watched the leading division crash past the start point.'

The dust thickened under the trees lining the road until the column was motoring into a thunderous yellow tunnel, first the tanks, infantry all over them, then trucks filled with men, then more tanks, going fast, nose to tail, guns, more trucks, more guns – British, Sikhs, Gurkhas, Madrassis, Pathans ...

This was the old Indian Army going down to the attack, for the last time in history, exactly two hundred and fifty years after the Honourable East India Company had enlisted its first ten sepoys on the Coromandel Coast.[84]

But the monsoon season was now very close at hand and, as a hedge against its slowing Slim's advance, Mountbatten decided to proceed with Operation Dracula, the seaborne assault on Rangoon.

The approaching change of season was already noticeable to the airmen. Thunderstorms were becoming more frequent, and the almost daily early morning rains rendered the largely soft-surfaced forward air strips unusable until late afternoon, when they had dried out. The unstable air was especially evident over the mountains, where the always dangerous up- and down-drafts increased in intensity. Flying in from Akyab Island, No 436 Squadron crews in particular began to see the first of the towering cumulo-nimbus clouds that marked the coming of the monsoon, at first welcomed as useful aids to navigation but subsequently recognized for the hazard they were. Early in April, crews were involved primarily with the 'milk run' to Myitche and Meiktila, but by mid-month they were following Fourteenth Army on its march south, dropping provisions to front-line units. On 27 April, in fact, their drop zone was just sixty-five miles north of Rangoon, well over four hours from base; yet one crew, led by Squadron Leader F. Smith (who would later undertake dangerous weather reconnaissance flights during monsoon season), managed three lifts in a day, working without rest from seven o'clock in the morning to nine at night. By the end of the month the squadron had carried 3907 tons of supplies and 1300 passengers (including thirty former prisoners of war who had become separated from their guards while being evacuated from Rangoon and who simply walked north until they reached the Allied front). To accomplish that had required an average of 230 flying hours for each serviceable aircraft, an effort that could not be maintained indefinitely.[85]

No 435 Squadron, meanwhile, continued flying supplies to the bases in the north in April. Meiktila, Myingyan, Taungtha, and Sinthe were the principal destinations for its widely varied cargoes, although it was also beginning to carry staple foods and supplies to the native population in smaller centres.

Sharing the Imphal valley with only one American transport squadron, they too were extremely busy, flying 3809 hours to move 3390 tons of supplies and 2562 passengers.[86]

The focus of operations, however, was now at Rangoon, where Operation Dracula was ready to proceed after ten days of hectic planning. 'Shortly after 7 o'clock in the morning of 2 May, seasick, drenched to the skin, stiff from six hours of crouching in the bellies of their little assault boats, men of the 9th Jats, 13th Frontier Force rifles, 8th Gurkhas, Lincolns, 1st Punjab, and Garwhalis with their British gunners, tanks, and other supporting arms, ran up the soggy beaches on both sides of the ... river – ten miles below Rangoon.'[87] The enemy had already pulled back, and 'the only casualty of the actual landing was one man, gored by a bull, although in the latter stages casualties occurred to sea mines and during the round-up of small parties of Japanese die-hards.' The next day, the landing force re-embarked in their craft and sailed easily into the city. All in all it was an anti-climax, even if a joyful one.[88]

Both Canadian squadrons had been called upon for Dracula, although somewhat indirectly. Worried about the coastal battery at Elephant Point, where the Rangoon River emptied into the Bay of Bengal, Mountbatten's planners had laid on an airborne assault to silence the guns, and the two RCAF units were ordered to supply jump-masters. Accordingly, twenty wireless operator/air gunners from each joined two USAAF troop-carrier squadrons and, after ten days of intensive training in formation flying and dropping, they, their American crews, and a battalion of Gurkhas assembled at Akyab on 29 April. The small force left at 0300 hours on 1 May and, three hours later, with no enemy opposition, dropped the Gurkhas exactly on target.[89]

Rangoon was captured on 3 May, just twelve days before the monsoon arrived in full force. By the end of the month it had reached Mandalay and Akyab as well. Characterized by heavy rain, high winds, and frequent severe thunderstorms, the monsoon made life on the ground miserable as rivers and creeks flooded and ground turned to deep mud. Groundcrews struggled manfully despite the lack of proper shelter – a situation which made electrical repairs particularly difficult.[90] From a flyer's point of view, the main problems were poor visibility, severe turbulence, unpredictable weather, particularly over mountains and near the coast, and the large, exceptionally dangerous cumulonimbus clouds which had to be avoided at all cost. 'After crossing the Irrawaddy River and starting over the Arakan Zone the clouds started to build up higher,' Flight Lieutenant R.W. Cornell of No 436 Squadron reported, 'but conditions were very good and I was brushing through the tops of the clouds, alternating between clear and momentary instrument flying.'

I had entered what appeared to be a small layer of cloud when it began to rain. After flying instruments for about a minute three sudden bursts of extremely heavy rain, possibly hail, hit the aircraft ... I immediately put the aircraft into a turn to starboard ... but had only completed half of it when the force of the C[umulo]N[imbus] hit the aircraft.

My recollection of what happened at that instant is rather hazy. Both gyro horizons toppled ... The next thing I knew we were in a terrific dive. The control column was absolutely frozen so that I had to rely entirely on elevator trim to try and pull out. The airspeed indicator was reading in the vicinity of 300 miles per hour, the vertical speed was at 6,000 feet per minute down and the altimeter was unwinding at a frightening rate. I cannot say how much altitude I lost, as my one idea was to pull out of the dive before the aircraft went right into the ground. It finally did pull out and in a fraction of a second the vertical speed read 6,000 feet per minute up. I frantically applied more down trim and forward pressure on the control column, but could not do it fast enough and the next thing I knew the aircraft was on its back and I was hanging on to my safety belt. I applied full aileron and kicked full rudder and ... the aircraft must have half rolled and ended up in another dive. This time I was able to level out, and suddenly came into a clearing between the clouds. From there I was able to pick my way through the cloud till we reached clear conditions over the water.[91]

Despite the problems it posed, the monsoon did not appreciably alter the pattern of operations. But although aircraft still set off for their destinations singly or in small sections, the onus was now on the pilot to turn back at his discretion or to pick his way through as best he could. This was often a difficult decision to make – most pilots were extremely reluctant to 'abort' their missions and flew whenever possible. Sometimes, however, having fought their way through to the landing zone, they found it completely 'socked in' and could not land.

Although the capture of Rangoon was the symbolic culmination of Fourteenth Army's advance, it did not end the fighting in Burma. Slim's forces, many of them inaccessible to land transport, were now widening the railway corridor down which they had thrust and were attempting to destroy the Japanese forces making their way east out of Burma. Native guerrilla groups led by British officers were also active in rear areas, and they, too, had to be supplied by air. 'As a navigator I served for about a year on 436 Squadron,' Alvin Hamilton (later minister of agriculture in the government of John Diefenbaker) recalled; 'on several occasions I flew missions which I did not fully understand, but understood that I was not to talk about [them.]' Indeed, he admitted, he was 'confused many times as to what I was doing in those special operations,' flying to remote drop zones in the Pegu Yomas and Chin Hills and along the Sittang River, where there was always the possibility of enemy fire.[92]

Some of the pressure was relieved when the port of Rangoon was opened in mid-June, but the withdrawal of all American transport units from the area, agreed to much earlier, left only seven RAF and RCAF squadrons to support Slim – and they would be flying in much worse weather. Except for No 435 – still at Imphal – all of them were committed to the continuing fight in the south, and No 436 Squadron moved from Akyab to Kyaukpyu, on Ramree Island, where it could operate economically to destinations between Meiktila and Rangoon.

A separate problem was posed by the civilian population, particularly that in the north. Their normal means of livelihood, indeed of survival, had largely been destroyed during the fighting, and in the less fertile, hilly, jungle-clad north the food situation was especially serious. Mountbatten had directed that the local population be supplied to the level 'necessary to prevent disease and unrest and to secure the maximum assistance for the war effort.'[*] Many of the villages in north and central Burma were inaccessible to vehicles and, in any case, land transport resources were heavily committed to moving supplies south. Once again, air supply was the only possibility and No 435 Squadron was directed 'to succour the most distressed areas.'[93]

Its crews began devoting most of their efforts to that commitment early in June. The main cargo was bagged rice and most of it was dropped at Lashio, Bhamo, Myitkyina, and Muse and a wide range of drop zones in mountainous, northern Burma and across the Chinese border. When weather permitted, operations were intense. During one four-hour sortie on 30 May 1945 one crew dropped a total of 6200 pounds of rice and mail to four separate drop zones and then, only one hour after their return to base, carried 6200 pounds of fuel to Myingyan - a trip of three-and-a-half hours.[94] Another flew ten hours on 1 June 1945, to move a total of 10,500 pounds of freight from port areas to the interior, moving from Tulihal to Jessore, India, to Toungoo in southern Burma, to Ramree, and finally to Myingyan and then home to Imphal. This was the longest flying day undertaken by any 435 Squadron crew, although days of seven and eight flying hours were not uncommon.[95]

Nothing like that was possible during the monsoon season, however, as many of the outlying landing zones could not even be approached safely. Crews tried in vain to find Fort Hertz (far to the northeast, in the upper reaches of Assam, 280 miles from Imphal) for two days through the cloud-covered mountains, and when they finally located it on the third day they discovered the airfield to be water-logged, overgrown, and only a thousand yards long – in other words, unfit for operations. At Htawgaw, meanwhile, where a guerrilla and special-operations base camp was located on one side of a hill between peaks 8000 feet high, approaches in good weather were risky enough, and only one crew managed a drop there despite several attempts. During the worst storms – some were reported measuring sixty miles wide and rising to 25,000 feet – long detours were necessary; but since there were no alternate airfields in the vicinity there was no way to avoid landing at Imphal even if the weather there had changed for the worse over the course of the day. Nevertheless, June's cargo total of 3062 tons exceeded the squadron's commitments (although it required an average of 187 flying hours for each serviceable aircraft.) In July it managed to lift 2951 tons of cargo and 1204 passengers – good enough to rank second – but required 231 flying hours per serviceable aircraft. Rain and cloud from 300 to 10,000 feet stopped all flying on 31 July, but two crews that took off before the grounding was announced 'managed to fight their way through to Meiktila and Lashio, but came back convinced that they'd be safer on the ground.'[96]

[*] He was also, of course, concerned with ensuring minimum resistance to the re-establishment of British rule, which he referred to as the 'long-term British interest.'

To the south, meanwhile, No 436 Squadron was still engaged in tactical support missions for XV Corps in the Arakan and IV Corps along the Sittang River railway corridor, where 17,000 soldiers from the Japanese Fifteenth Army were trying to make their way to Thailand. (Only four thousand succeeded.) It was also serving the supply depots at Meiktila, Toungoo, and Myingyan. To reach the drop zones they often had to fly over territory still occupied by Japanese forces, and on at least one occasion a drop was lost to enemy troops who had gained temporary possession of the zone. Weather was a factor there, too. Flying was severely restricted on fourteen days in June, but in July No 436 surpassed No 435's totals, delivering 3585 tons of cargo and 1170 passengers – at an astonishing 305 flying hours for each serviceable aircraft.[97]

No 436 Squadron's base at Ramree was probably more unpleasant than Imphal, and on several days more than five inches of rain were recorded. Morale was nevertheless high, although the reaction to the news of victory in Europe was somewhat subdued: 'There is a surprising lack of enthusiasm ... All have been eagerly awaiting this moment, and now ... the dull realization that we are still at war in this theatre seems to overshadow the good news. Unfortunately, too, our beer ration is not available, and the airmen have nothing with which to celebrate the occasion.'[98]

Perhaps they were thinking about their own future. Although informed in March that they would be withdrawn from Burma once Germany had been defeated, no word of that move was forthcoming. Indeed, although the Canadian government was under the impression that the agreement had been firm, the British were less definitive, observing that the availability of replacements had always been regarded as the ultimate determinant of when the Canadians would be able to leave. Ottawa was not impressed and, making its position very clear, in mid-June warned the Air Ministry to expect 'in the very near future that there will be greater insistence on their return to this country.' Five months earlier, Air Command South East Asia had asked for an increase of seventeen medium-range transport squadrons to carry the war to Japan itself – and allow the Canadians to leave – but now that that request was proving difficult to meet the question of the Canadians' departure was complicated further. 'I have all along had in mind our undertaking to withdraw these squadrons from India as soon as practicable after VE Day,' the British vice chief of the air staff, Air Marshal Sir Douglas Evill explained, 'and that is what we are seeking to do under the circumstances which are, in fact, more unfavourable even than I had pictured.'[99]

Ottawa remained unsympathetic, however, and the chief of the air staff, Air Marshal Robert Leckie, told Air Marshal G.O. Johnson, the senior RCAF officer overseas, that 'this is just another instance of the difficulty we find in making plans on Air Ministry promises which, however sincerely made, cannot apparently be kept. The result must inevitably make us very unwilling to enter into agreements – the implementation of which cannot be relied on.' Choosing to weather the Canadian protests, the Air Ministry waited until 10 July 1945 to nominate two RAF squadrons to replace the Canadians. Moreover, as the normal overseas posting procedures would take several weeks and the Air Ministry wanted these replacements fully acclimatized before committing them to operations, South East Asia Command was informed that the withdrawal of Nos 435 and 436 Squadrons might have to be postponed until October or November.[100]

The Canadian units therefore kept flying, and not just on routine missions. In the first three weeks of August, for example, each was asked to provide a small detachment to support guerrilla groups in the Shan Hills, east and south of Mandalay, who were engaged with Japanese forces trying to make their way out of Burma. No 436 sent two crews, led by Flight Lieutenant H.W. Pearson and Warrant Officer D.G. Parker, and in eighteen days they flew forty-eight sorties out of Toungoo, 'an airstrip with the worst general weather conditions in the whole area.' Located in valleys or on cloud-obscured hills, the drop zones on these sorties were not easy to locate, and the two crews often spent hours of tricky flying trying to approach them while having to worry about the continuous threat from enemy ground fire. After 'valley crawling from Sittang,' they arrived 'rather shakily into the DZ. This we practically dive-bombed as our circuit was partly in cloud and almost solid with rain. Windshield wipers packed up and it was no fun groping about in there.' Pearson and Parker each received the DFC for their work. Four crews from 435 Squadron arrived in the area on 21 August, and over the next five days flew thirty-five sorties from Toungoo, breaking 'all previous records' in the volume of supplies delivered. Furthermore, as the British commander of the guerrillas reported, they had made extremely accurate drops.[101]

By then, of course, the war in the Pacific was over. Following the atomic bombing of Hiroshima and Nagasaki on 6 and 8 August, the Japanese surrendered on the 15th; but word of the capitulation did not immediately reach all of the scattered enemy forces deep inside Burma. According to the letter and the spirit of the January 1945 agreement, the defeat of Japan should have been justification enough for the early withdrawal of Nos 435 and 436 squadrons from Southeast Asia; but with the British eager to reoccupy the rest of Burma and Malaya as quickly as possible, the RCAF staff officer at Air Command South East Asia, Group Captain D.S. Patterson, had to refuse a British request to extend the aircrews' operational tour, which would have facilitated such efforts. Succumbing to the inevitable, and recognizing that many RCAF personnel were approaching the end of their tour, South East Asia Command backed down and decided it would not be necessary, after all, for the Canadians to 'double-bank' with their British replacements. In other words, they could leave.[102]

This they did in early September, in the aircraft their replacements had flown out, moving to Down Ampney and, subsequently, in the case of No 436 Squadron, to Odiham in England. Those crews due for repatriation returned to Canada, but the squadrons continued to fly transport operations in Europe – not, it must be said, without incident. On 13 February a Dakota from No 435 Squadron 'crashed into the side of a hill' on farmland near Croydon, killing the pilot and co-pilot and six of twenty British servicemen being brought back from Buckeburg, Germany. When the ambulances arrived, the rescuers found 'residents of nearby cottages attempting to pull the injured from the wreckage. An eye-witness said the plane was a "complete wreck" and lay only a few yards from a main road.' The crash, according to Canadian Press, 'occurred in what airmen call "the valley of death," so named because of difficult climatic conditions which prevail in the vicinity.' It could hardly have matched some of the squadron's Burmese drop zones.[103]

Less serious, the way things turned out, was the six-day work stoppage conducted by airmen from No 437 Squadron (Odiham) and the two Burma squadrons at Down Ampney between 5 and 11 February. 'Odiham went on strike today,' No 436 Squadron's diarist reported, 'as a protest against false repatriation reports in the Canadian press, and the lack of any definite information on the dates of repatriation. The question has been raised by numerous personnel as to how long they can be held for service in the RCAF in view of the fact that hostilities ceased on 14th August, 1945.' The protest moved to Down Ampney two days later: 'At an unauthorized meeting at 1000 hrs. at Canada House, airmen decided to go on strike in sympathy with Odiham strikers as from 1200 hrs today. Principal demands of strikers are: (i) replacement of all non-volunteers for occupational duties; (ii) public announcement ... that four/fifths of occupational force are volunteers; (iii) better standard of food.' Officers and NCOs immediately took over responsibility for cooking and other administrative and custodial functions, and the flying schedule of the squadrons did not suffer. As the RCAF was still on active service, the airmen could 'legally be held in uniform at the pleasure of the Government,' a fact explained to them (not entirely to their satisfaction) by representatives from Overseas Headquarters. However, the work stoppage ended on the 11th, No 436 Squadron's diarist predicting, correctly, that 'it is doubtful that any action will be taken against the strikers. A great deal of publicity has been given the "demonstrations" in the Canadian press, and it has doubtlessly served to let the Canadian people know that ... the majority of personnel serving overseas are anxious to get home to their families.'

He was right. On 14 February it was announced that although No 435 Squadron would disband in April, and Nos 436 and 437 Squadrons in June, there would be a 'general reshuffle of crews between Squadrons ... in order to repatriate all non-volunteer aircrew and allow some who may now wish to return to Canada to be released from 436 and 437 Squadrons, and at the same time make room for No 435 Squadron personnel who wish to stay on' to transfer to Nos 436 or 437 until they too returned to Canada.[104]

All told, during its time in Southeast Asia, No 435 Squadron had flown 29,873 operational hours and delivered 27,095 tons of cargo and about 15,000 passengers and casualties, while No 436 had flown 31,719 operational hours to deliver 28,950 tons of cargo and 12,725 passengers and casualties. Both had averaged well over the established intensive flying rate despite some of the worst flying weather in the world and exceptionally inadequate facilities.[105] As

General Slim concluded, 'by trial and error' they had contributed 'towards a new kind of warfare.'

We were the first to maintain large formations in action by air supply and to move standard divisions long distances about the fighting front by air … The decisive stroke at Meiktila and the advance on Rangoon were examples of a new technique that combined mechanized and air-transported brigades in the same divisions. To us, all this was as normal as moving or maintaining troops by railway or road, and that attitude of mind was, I suppose, one of our main reformations. We had come a long way since 1928 when, as a junior staff officer, I had been concerned with other Indian Army officers in a struggle … to introduce operational air transport and supply on the North-West Frontier.

Although we moved great tonnages and many thousands of troops by air, the largest number of transport aircraft we ever had was much less than would elsewhere have been considered the minimum required. It was quite easy theoretically to demonstrate that what we were doing was impossible to continue over any length of time. Yet the skill, courage and devotion of the airmen … both in the air and on the ground, combined with the hard work and organizing ability of the soldiers, not only did it, but kept on doing it month after month. As in so many other things, we learnt to revise accepted theories and, when worth it, to risk cutting our margins.[106]

Appendices

APPENDIX A

RCAF Casualties Overseas by Years of War

Date	Flying Battle				Flying Accidents				All Causes				
	Killed	Missing	POW	Wounded or Injured	Killed	Missing	POW	Wounded or Injured	Killed	Missing	POW	Died Natural Causes	Wounded or Injured
Aircrew													
3.9.40–2.9.41	169	8	48	41	133	—	7	76	303	8	55	1	123
3.9.41–2.9.42	1,428	96	303	228	594	10	2	337	2,046	115	307	5	582
3.9.42–2.9.43	2,875	274	641	307	750	20	1	455	3,645	297	646	11	786
3.9.43–2.9.44	3,918	740	937	436	1,029	17	3	404	4,970	759	940	6	866
3.9.44–8.5.45	1,941	610	327	245	415	19	—	166	2,367	632	327	6	447
9.5.45–14.8.45	29	42	1	8	40	2	—	15	77	44	1	4	34
Total	10,360	1,770	2,257	1,265	2,961	68	13	1,453	13,408	1,855	2,276	33	2,838
Groundcrew													
3.9.40–2.9.41	—	—	—	—	—	1	—	2	1	1	—	1	2
3.9.41–2.9.42	1	3	—	—	3	—	—	3	5	5	2	6	9
3.9.42–2.9.43	7	6	2	—	21	1	—	6	46	11	8	5	30
3.9.43–2.9.44	2	2	—	1	9	—	2	10	39	12	2	8	57
3.9.44–8.5.45	23	1	—	4	17	—	—	5	74	4	2	10	101
9.5.45–14.8.45	—	1	—	—	2	—	—	2	16	1	—	5	17
Total	33	13	2	5	52	2	2	28	181	34	14	35	216
Grand Total	10,393	1,783	2,259	1,270	3,013	70	15	1,481	13,589	1,889	2,290	68	3,054

Source: 'Gross Royal Canadian Air Force Casualties by Years of War,' nd, PRO, Air 22/312

Senior RCAF Appointments, Second World War[*]

CANADA

Minister responsible for the RCAF
Hon. Ian A. Mackenzie   23 Oct. 1935–18 Sept. 1939
Hon. Norman McL. Rogers   19 Sept. 1939–22 May 1940
Hon. C.G. Power, MC   23 May 1940–26 Nov. 1944
Hon. Angus L. MacDonald   27 Nov. 1944–10 Jan. 1945
Col. the Hon. C.W.G. Gibson, MC, VD   11 Jan. 1945–12 Dec. 1946

Deputy minister responsible for the RCAF
Maj.-Gen. L.R. LaFlèche, DSO   3 Nov. 1932–7 Sep. 1939
Lt-Col. K.S. Maclachlan   8 Sep. 1939–10 April 1940
J.S. Duncan   11 April 1940–2 Feb. 1941
S.L. DeCarteret, CMG   3 Feb. 1941–21 April 1944[†]
H.F. Gordon, CMG   15 Jan. 1944–12 March 1947[†]

Chief of the Air Staff
Air Vice-Marshal G.M. Croil, AFC   15 Dec. 1938–28 May 1940
Air Marshal L.S. Breadner, CB, DSC   29 May 1940–31 Dec. 1943
Air Marshal R. Leckie, DSO, DSC, DFC   1 Jan. 1944–31 Aug. 1947

RCAF OVERSEAS

SENIOR OFFICER, RCAF OVERSEAS

RCAF Liaison Officer
Wing Commander F.V. Heakes   15 Jul. 1937–31 Dec. 1939

Officer Commanding, RCAF in Great Britain
Wing Commander F.V. Heakes   1 Jan. 1940–6 March 1940
Group Captain G.V. Walsh   7 March 1940–3 June 1940

---

[*] Highest rank and decorations while serving in this appointment
[†] Shared appointment

Air Officer Commanding, RCAF in Great Britain
Air Commodore G.V. Walsh   4 June 1940–15 Oct. 1940
Air Vice-Marshal L.F. Stevenson   16 Oct. 1940–6 Nov. 1941

Air Officer in Chief, RCAF Overseas
Air Vice-Marshal L.F. Stevenson   6 Nov. 1941–24 Nov. 1941
Air Marshal H. Edwards   25 Nov. 1941–15 Jul. 1942

Air Officer Commanding-in-Chief, RCAF Overseas
Air Marshal H. Edwards, CB   16 July 1943–31 Dec. 1943
Air Marshal L.S. Breadner, CB, DSC   1 Jan. 1944–31 March 1945
Air Marshal G.O. Johnson, CB, MC   1 April 1945–22 July 1946

SENIOR STAFF, OVERSEAS HEADQUARTERS

Senior Air Staff Officer
Squadron Leader W.I. Clements   6 Aug. 1940–25 Aug. 1940
Group Captain A.P. Campbell   26 Aug. 1940–25 May 1941
Group Captain E.L. MacLeod   26 May 1941–21 Nov. 1941

Deputy Air Officer-in-Chief
Air Vice-Marshal W.A Curtis, DSC   22 Nov. 1941–15 July 1942

Deputy Air Officer Commanding-in-Chief
Air Vice-Marshal W.A. Curtis, CBE, DSC   16 July 1942–15 Jan. 1944
Air Vice-Marshal N.R. Anderson, CB   16 Jan. 1944–22 March 1945
Air Vice-Marshal C.R. Slemon, CBE‡   23 March 1945–7 July 1945
Air Commodore H.B. Godwin, OBE   8 July 1945–2 Jan. 1946

Director of Air Staff
Wing Commander G.R. McGregor, DFC   1 Sept. 1941–15 April 1942
Squadron Leader V.B. Corbett, DFC   16 April 1942–21 July 1942
Group Captain H.L. Campbell   22 July 1942–20 Sept. 1943
Group Captain G.G. Truscott   21 Sept. 1943–25 Sept. 1944
Group Captain M. Costello   26 Sept. 1944–6 April 1945
Group Captain H.B. Godwin   7–27 April 1945
Group Captain H.H.C. Rutledge   28 April 1945–12 Nov. 1945

‡ Between September 1944, when he left No 6 Group Headquarters as SASO, and March 1945, when he assumed the position of deputy AOC-in-C of the RCAF Overseas, Air Vice-Marshal Slemon was posted to Bomber Command Headquarters, to understudy the appointment of deputy SASO at High Wycombe; he served as acting AOC-in-C of No 6 Group when Air Marshal McEwen was in Canada; and he replaced Air Vice-Marshal Anderson as deputy AOC-in-C at Overseas Headquarters while the latter was ill.

Senior Personnel Staff Officer
Wing Commander A.P. Campbell   21 July 1939–25 Aug. 1940
Wing Commander R.H. Foss   26 Aug. 1940–9 July 1941
Wing Commander J.L. Jackson, MC   10 July 1941–1 Sept. 1941

Director of Personnel
Wing Commander J.L. Jackson, MC   2 Sept. 1941–23 Aug. 1942
Air Commodore F.G. Wait   24 Aug. 1942–10 Oct. 1943
Air Commodore E.E. Middleton, CBE   11 Oct. 1943–20 May 1945
Group Captain C.C.P. Graham   21 May 1945–16 Sept. 1945

Director of Administration
Air Commodore F.G. Wait   11 Oct. 1943–8 May 1944
Group Captain G.E. Scott   May 1944–3 Sept. 1945

SENIOR RCAF COMMANDERS AND STAFF, NO 6 GROUP, BOMBER COMMAND

Air Officer Commanding
Air Vice-Marshal G.E. Brookes, CB, OBE   25 Oct. 1942–28 Feb. 1944
Air Vice-Marshal C.M. McEwen, CB, MC, DFC   29 Feb. 1944–13 July
    1945

Air Officer Commanding, No 6 Group Main Headquarters, Halifax, NS
Air Commodore J.G. Kerr, AFC   14 July 1945–1 Sept. 1945

Air Officer Commanding, No 6 Group Rear Headquarters, Allerton Park
Air Commodore J.L. Hurley   14 July 1945–1 Sept.1945

Senior Air Staff Officer
Air Commodore C.R. Slemon, CBE   March 1943–15 Sept. 1944
Air Commodore J.E. Fauquier, DSO and 2 Bars, DFC   16 Sept. 1944–27
    Dec. 1944
Air Commodore R.E. McBurney, CBE   28 Dec. 1944–15 Sept. 1945

No 61 Base (Topcliffe) No 76 (RCAF) Base (Topcliffe) No 7 Group
Air Commodore C.M. McEwen, MC, DFC   5 April 1943–25 June 1943
Air Commodore B.F. Johnson   26 June 1943–16 Feb. 1944
Air Commodore R.E. McBurney, AFC   17 Feb. 1944–15 May 1944
Air Commodore F.G. Wait   16 May 1944–7 Aug. 1944
Air Commodore J.L. Hurley   1–18 Sept. 1944
Air Commodore F.R. Miller   19 Sept. 1944–12 Jan. 1945
Air Commodore J.G. Kerr, AFC   13 Jan. 1945–30 May 1945
Air Commodore N.W. Timmerman, DSO, DFC   1 Aug. 1945–1 Sept.
    1945

No 62 Base (Linton-on-Ouse)
Air Commodore C.M. McEwen, MC, DFC   18 June 1943–28 Feb. 1944
Air Commodore A.D. Ross, GC   29 Feb. 1944–27 June 1944
Air Commodore J.E. Fauquier, DSO and 2 Bars, DFC   28 June 1944–18
    Sept. 1944
Air Commodore J.L. Hurley   19 Sept. 1944–30 May 1945
Air Commodore J.G. Kerr   31 May 1945–15 July 1945

No 63 Base (Leeming)
Air Commodore J.G. Bryans   1 May 1944–12 Jan. 1945
Air Commodore F.R. Miller   13 Jan. 1945–25 May 1945
Air Commodore J.L. Hurley   30 May 1945–13 July 1945

No 64 Base (Middleton St George)
Air Commodore R.E. McBurney   1 May 1944–28 Dec. 1944
Air Commodore C.R. Dunlap, CBE   22 Jan. 1945–24 April 1945
Air Commodore H.B. Godwin   25 April 1945–29 May 1945
Air Commodore H.T. Miles   30 May 1945–15 June 1945

No 331 Wing (Mediterranean Air Command)
Group Captain C.R. Dunlap   1 May 1943–16 Nov. 1943

SENIOR COMMANDERS, RCAF FIGHTER, FIGHTER-BOMBER, AND
RECONNAISSANCE WINGS

Digby Wing (Fighter Command/Air Defence of Great Britain)
Wing Commander G.R. McGregor, DFC   14 April 1941–31 Aug. 1941
Wing Commander H.P. Blatchford DFC (Can/RAF)   8 Sept. 1941–30
    April 1942
Wing organization not used on operations, May 1942–March 1943
Wing Commander L.S. Ford, DFC and Bar   19 April 1943–4 June 1943
Wing Commander L.V. Chadburn, DSO and Bar, DFC   5 June 1943–30
    Dec. 1943
Wing Commander N.H. Bretz, DFC   31 Dec. 1943–30 April 1944

Kenley Wing (Fighter Command)
Wing Commander J.C. Fee, DFC   25 Nov. 1942–17 Jan. 1943
Wing Commander K.L.B. Hodson, DFC   22 Jan. 1943–28 Feb. 1943
Wing Commander J.E. Johnson, DSO and Bar, DFC and Bar (RAF)
    21 March 1943–4 July 1943

*No 39 Wing (Army Co-Operation Command/Fighter Command/Second
Tactical Air Force)*
Group Captain D.M. Smith   12 Sept. 1942–9 Feb. 1944
Group Captain E.H.G. Moncrieff, AFC   10 Feb. 1944–8 Feb. 1945
Group Captain G.H. Sellers, AFC   9 Feb. 1945–15 May 1945
Group Captain R.C.A. Waddell, DSO, DFC   16 May 1945–7 Aug. 1945

No 17 Sector (Second Tactical Air Force)
Group Captain W.R. MacBrien   4 July 1943–13 July 1944

No 22 Sector (Second Tactical Air Force)
Group Captain P.Y. Davoud, DSO, DFC   9 July 1944–13 July 1944

No 126 Wing (Second Tactical Air Force)
Wing Commander J.E. Walker, DFC and 2 Bars   9 July 1943–26 Aug.
  1943
Wing Commander K.L.B. Hodson, DFC and Bar   27 Aug. 1943–19 July
  1944
Group Captain G.R. McGregor, OBE, DFC   20 July 1944–27 Sept. 1945

No 127 Wing (Second Tactical Air Force)
Wing Commander M. Brown   11 July 1943–18 July 1944
Group Captain W.R. MacBrien, OBE   19 July 1944–11 Jan. 1945
Group Captain P.S. Turner, DSO, DFC and Bar (Can/RAF)   12 Jan.
  1945–7 July 1945

No 128 Wing (Second Tactical Air Force)
Squadron Leader J.D. Hall, DFC   20 July 1943–3 Aug. 1943
Wing Commander J.M. Godfrey   4 Aug. 1943–2 July 1944

No 129 Wing (Second Tactical Air Force)
Wing Commander E.H.G. Moncrieff, AFC   4 July 1943–10 Feb. 1944
Wing Commander D.C.S. MacDonald, DFC   27 Feb. 1944–13 July 1944

No 143 Wing (Air Defence of Great Britain/Second Tactical Air Force)
Wing Commander F.W. Hillock   12 Jan. 1944–14 July 1944
Group Captain P.Y. Davoud, DSO, DFC   15 July 1944–31 Dec. 1944
Group Captain A.D. Nesbitt, DFC   1 Jan. 1945–7 Sept. 1945

No 144 Wing (Air Defence of Great Britain/Second Tactical Air Force)
Wing Commander J.E. Walker, DFC and 2 Bars   4 March 1944–25 April
  1944
Wing Commander A.D. Nesbitt, DFC   1 May 1944–13 July 1944

TIGER FORCE (RCAF PACIFIC FORCE)

Air Officer Commanding
Air Vice-Marshal C.R. Slemon, CBE   14 July 1945–1 Sept. 1945

No 661 Wing
Wing Commander F.R. Sharp, DFC   15 July 1945–5 Sept. 1945

No 662 Wing
Group Captain J.R. MacDonald, DFC   4 Aug. 1945–5 Sept. 1945

No 663 Wing
Group Captain J.H.L. Lecomte, DFC   4 Aug. 1945–5 Sept. 1945

No 664 Wing
Group Captain W.A.G. McLeish, DFC   6 Aug. 1945–1 Sept. 1945

Notes

Full references to books and articles are given the first time they are mentioned in each part. Short references are used thereafter.

CHAPTER 1: THE RE-CREATION OF A COLONIAL AIR FORCE

1 Department of National Defence, *Report ... for the Fiscal Year Ending 31 March 1940* (Ottawa 1940), 89, and *Defence Forces List 1939* (Ottawa 1940), 576ff; W.A.B. Douglas, *The Creation of a National Air Force* (Toronto 1986), 92; RCAF General List, Aug. 1939; C.R. Slemon biog. file, DHist
2 RCAF General List, Aug. 1939; biog. files, DHist; Douglas, *The Creation of a National Air Force,* app. A
3 'Our First CAS,' *Roundel,* June 1959, G.M. Croil biog. file, DHist
4 Chiefs of Staff Committee memorandum, 'Canada's national effort (armed forces) in the early stages of a major war,' 29 Aug. 1939, HQS 5199-S, vol. I, PARC 395072
5 Defence Committee of the Cabinet minutes, 5 Sept. 1939, DHist 83/345; Chiefs of Staff Committee memorandum, 'Canada's national effort (armed forces) in the early stages of a major war,' 5 Sept. 1939, DHist 83/345
6 'Notes for CAS,' 12 Sept. 1939, DHist 77/543; Emergency Council (Committee on General Policy) of the Cabinet minutes, 15 Sept. 1939, DHist 83/345
7 Campbell to Skelton, with enclosure, 6 Sept. 1939, HQS 5199-S, PARC 395072
8 Heakes to CAS, 5 Sept. 1939, and Croil to minister, 10 Sept. 1939, HQS 5199-S, PARC 395072; King to Campbell, 12 Sept. 1939, quoted in C.P. Stacey, *Arms, Men and Governments: The War Policies of Canada, 1939–1945* (Ottawa 1970), 18
9 Croil to minister, 15 Sept. 1939, HQS 5199-S, PARC 395072
10 Croil to minister, 15 (three memoranda) and 17 Sept. 1939, HQS 5199-S, PARC 395072; Emergency Council (Committee on General Policy) of the Cabinet, minutes, 15 Sept. 1939, DHist 83/345
11 APSO to ASO, 23 Sept. 1939, HQS 5199-S, PARC 395072
12 'Policy Respecting the Distribution, War Establishments and Duties of RCAF Squadrons,' 25 Sept. 1939, DHist 77/543

13 Canliaison Air Ministry to RCAF HQ Ottawa, 26 Sept. 1939, and Croil to minister, 27 Sept. 1939, and secretary of state for the Dominions Office to secretary of state for external affairs, 26 Sept. 1939, HQS 5199-S, PARC 395072

14 Douglas, *The Creation of a National Air Force,* 344; secretary of state for external affairs to secretary of state for the Dominions Office, 28 Sept. 1939, and Croil to deputy minister, 4 Oct. 1939, HQS 5199-S, PARC 395072

15 S.F. Wise, *Canadian Airmen and the First World War* (Toronto 1980), 76–120; 'Dominion Air Training Scheme, Report of the Riverdale Mission to Canada,' Dec. 1939, 24–5, PRO Air 2/3160; Douglas, *The Creation of a National Air Force,* 207; King diary, 17 Oct. 1939, National Archives of Canada (NA), MG 26 J13; J.W. Pickersgill, *The Mackenzie King Record,* I: 1939–1944 (Toronto 1960), 42–3; Riverdale to Kingsley Wood, 6 Nov. 1939, PRO Air 20/338

16 Croil to minister, 23 Nov. 1939, DHist 80/408, pt 2

17 Stacey, *Arms, Men and Governments,* 20–6, and 'British Commonwealth Air Training Plan Agreement, 17 Dec 1939,' app. D; Croil to minister, 23 Nov. 1939, DHist 80/408, pt 2

18 'Item from the Conclusions of a Meeting of the War Cabinet held on Wednesday 13th December 1939,' nd, PRO Air 2/3159

19 Ibid. and 'Memorandum by the Chancellor of the Exchequer,' 12 Dec. 1939, PRO Air 2/3159

20 'Notes of a meeting held at the Department of National Defence at 2pm on 14th December 1939' [14 Dec. 1939], DHist 80/408, pt 2

21 'Extract from the 118th Conclusions of the War Cabinet Meeting held on December 18th, 1939,' nd, PRO Air 2/3159

22 Douglas, *The Creation of a National Air Force,* 219

23 'Extract from the 118th Conclusions of the War Cabinet Meeting held on December 18th, 1939,' nd, PRO Air 2/3159

24 Ibid.

25 Brooke-Popham to Sir Arthur Street, 23 Dec. 1939, Street to Sir Eric Machtig, 14 Jan. 1940, PRO Air 2/3170

26 Air Ministry to United Kingdom high commissioner in Canada (UKHC), No 101, 23 Jan. 1940, and UKHC, to Dominions Office, 7–8 March 1940, No 485, pts I and II, Dominions Office to UKHC, 12 April 1940, No 624, 13 April 1940, No 625, all PRO Air 2/3170; Dominions secretary to secretary of state for external affairs, 24 Feb. 1940, and secretary of state for external affairs to Dominions secretary, 5 March 1940, *Documents on Canadian External Relations* [DCER], VII, 676–8; Croil to Maclachlan, 4 March 1940, DHist 80/408

27 Gilbert to Rowlands, 27 March 1940; EATS Committee, 'Notes of the 5th Meeting Held on Wednesday 20th March, 1940'; 'Extract from Draft Minutes of 197th Progress Meeting, 26th March, 1940'; 'Empire Air Training Scheme; Interpretation of Article 15 of the Riverdale Agreement,' 21 March 1940; Telegrams 624, 625, 626 to UKHC, 12 and 13 April 1940; telegrams from UKHC, 15 April 1940, Nos 770 and 778; Hollinghurst to PAS, 29 April 1940; and Liesching to Campbell, 23 May 1940, all PRO Air 2/3170

28 Norman Ward, ed., *A Party Politician: The Memoirs of Chubby Power* (Toronto 1966), 206–7

29 Ibid., 207; Wise, *Canadian Airmen and the First World War*, 42, 144–5; L.S. Breadner biog. file, DHist

30 L.S. Breadner personnel file, National Personnel Records Centre

31 Officer in charge, RCAF Overseas Records, to officer commanding, RCAF in Great Britain, 29 March 1940, HQ RCAF Ottawa to Canliaison Air Ministry, X.744, 19 April 1940, DHist 181.009 (D865); Hollinghurst minute, 26 Oct. 1940, DHist 181.009 (D863); Massey to Eden, 22 April 1940, PRO Air 2/5066

32 Stacey, *Arms, Men and Governments*, 211–13, 255; Memorandum on the the Visiting Forces (British Commonwealth) Act, 1933, 16 Jan. 1942, DHist 181.006 (D601); 23–24 George V, ch. 21

33 Massey to Eden, 22 April 1940, PRO Air 2/5066

34 Air Ministry minute, 3 May 1940, PRO Air 2/5066

35 Stacey, *Arms, Men and Governments*, 210; L.B. Pearson, *Mike: The Memoirs of the Rt-Hon. Lester B. Pearson*, I, (Toronto 1972), 149

36 Caldecott to Massey, 19 May 1940, Overseas Headquarters ORB, May 1940, app. B, and AOC, RCAF in Great Britain, to No 1 Squadron, 16 Aug. 1940, Overseas Headquarters ORB, Aug. 1940, app. F, DHist; Handley to Walsh, 19 June 1940, with enclosures, and Walsh to Air Ministry, 29 June 1940, PRO Air 2/5066

37 Ward, ed., *A Party Politician*, 206

38 Cabinet War Committee minutes, 9 Oct. 1940, DHist 83/345; Heeney to Power, 12 Oct. 1940, Queen's University Archives, C.G. Power Papers, box 53, folder D1001

39 CAS to Roycanairf, 31 Aug. 1940, DHist 181.009 (D769)

40 Campbell to high commissioner for Canada, 5 Sept. 1940, DHist 181.009 (D769)

41 CAS to Overseas Headquarters, 7 Sept. 1940, DHist 181.009 (D769)

42 Stevenson interview, 21 Oct. 1974, L.F. Stevenson biog. file, DHist; Air Council minutes, 26 Sept. 1940, S.840-108, pt 1, PARC long-term loan to DHist

43 Cabinet War Committee minutes, 9 Oct. 1940, DHist 83/345

44 Ibid.

45 King Diary, 9 Oct. 1940, DHist 83/530; Cabinet War Committee minutes, 9 Oct. 1940, DHist 83/345

46 Heeney to Power, 12 Oct. 1940, Power Papers, box 53, file D1001

47 Breadner to minister, 12 Oct. 1940, ibid.

48 Roycanairf to CAS, 26 Sept. 1940, DHist 181.009 (D769); Overseas Headquarters ORB, 11 Sept. 1940, DHist; Campbell to AOC Eastern Air Command, 3 Feb. 1943, A.P. Campbell biog. file, DHist

49 Hollinghurst to Stevenson, 18 Oct. 1940, DHist 80/481, vol. 1

50 Ibid.

51 Roycanairf to CAS, 22 Oct. 1940, DHist 80/481, vol. 1

52 Ibid., 24 Oct. 1940, A.892, DHist 181.009 (D769)

53 CAS to Roycanairf, 25 Oct. 1940, X.79 C.96, and CAS to Roycanairf, 31 Oct. 1940, X.198, A.219, both DHist 181.009 (D769)

54 Roycanairf to CAS, 14 Nov. 1940, DHist 181.009 (D769)

55 Campbell to Cranborne, 17 Oct. 1940, PRO Air 2/3170

56 EATS Committee minutes, 1 Nov. 1940, PRO Air 20/1379; Dominions Office to UKHC, 9 Nov. 1940, No 2289, PRO Air 2/3170

57 UKHC, telegram, 17 Nov. 1940, No 2299, PRO Air 19/219

58 Ibid.

59 EATS Committee minutes, 29 Nov. 1940, PRO Air 20/1379; Empire Air Training Scheme, 'Note for the Secretary of State for Air on Article 15 of the main Riverdale Agreement,' nd, PRO Air 19/219

60 Cabinet War Committee minutes, 5 Nov. 1940, DHist 83/345; UKHC telegram, 17 Nov. 1940, No 2299, PRO Air 19/219

61 R.S. Malone, *A Portrait of War 1939–1943* (Toronto 1983), 18, 30; Campbell to Machtig, 17 Nov. 1940, No 2300, and Cranborne to Sinclair, 5 Dec. 1940, PRO Air 19/219; King diary, 24 Jan. 1941, DHist 83/530

62 'Diary of the Hon. J.L. Ralston,' 28 Nov. 1940, National Archives of Canada (NA), MG 27 III, B11, vol. 1

63 'Aide Memoire on Article 15, Air Training Agreement,' nd, DHist 80/481, vol 1; 'Diary of the Hon. J.L. Ralston,' 4 Dec. 1940, NA, MG 27 III, B11, vol. 1

64 'Aide Memoire on Article 15, Air Training Agreement,' nd, DHist 80/481, vol. 1

65 Ibid. and 'Memorandum Relating to RCAF Squadron Representation Overseas,' nd, DHist 80/481, vol. 1; Empire Air Training Scheme, 'Note for the Secretary of State on Article 15 of the main Riverdale Agreement,' nd, PRO Air 19/219

66 'Aide Memoire on Article 15, Air Training Agreement,' nd, DHist 80/481, vol. 1; 'Diary of the Hon. J.L. Ralston,' 9 Dec. 1940, NA, MG 27 III, B11, vol. 1

67 'Note of Discussion with Mr. Ralston at the Air Ministry on Friday, 13th December, 1940, on Article 15 of the Main Riverdale Agreement,' nd, PRO Air 19/219

68 Ibid.

69 Roycanairf to CAS, from Ralston for prime minister and Power, 14 Dec. 1940, and CAS to Roycanairf, Power for Ralston, 15 Dec. 1940, DHist 80/481, vol 1; King Diary, 14 Dec. 1940, 9 Jan. 1941, DHist 83/530

70 'Article 15 of the Main Riverdale Agreement, Note of a Meeting held at Whitehall on 16th December, 1940 at 11 am,' nd, PRO Air 2/3160

71 Stevenson, 'Memoranda for Colonel Ralston regarding Matters being discussed with Air Ministry Authorities,' 16 Dec. 1940, DHist 80/481, vol. 1

72 'Note of a discussion held at the Air Ministry on 16/12/40,' 18 Dec. 1940, PRO Air 2/3160

73 Ibid., Howard to Abraham, 18 Dec. 1940, PRO Air 2/3160

74 Massey to External [Affairs], from Ralston to prime minister and Power, 24 Dec. 1940, Sinclair to Ralston, 6 Jan. 1941, DHist 80/481, vol. 1

75 Ibid.

76 Stacey, *Arms, Men and Governments*, 262

77 R.S. Sayers, *Financial Policy 1939–45* (London 1956), 335; Roycanairf to CAS, from Ralston to prime minister and Power, 14 Dec. 1940, DHist 80/481, vol. 1

78 Riverdale, 'Empire Air Training Scheme, Article No 15,' 12 March 1940, PRO Air 2/3170

79 C.P. Stacey, *Canada and the Age of Conflict*, vol. 2: *1921–1948, The Mackenzie King Era* (Toronto 1981), 356–60

80 External to Dominions Office, 29 Jan. 1941, DHist 80/481, vol. 1; Stacey, *Arms, Men and Governments*, 261; King Diary, 14 Dec. 1940, DHist 83/530

81 'Aide Memoire on Article 15, Air Training Agreement,' nd, DHist 80/481, vol. 1

82 Stevenson to Breadner, 20 Jan. 1941, Overseas Headquarters ORB, Jan. 1941, app. E, DHist

83 Air Council minutes, 21 Feb. 1941, S.840-108, pt 2, PARC long-term loan

84 Stevenson to RAAF air liaison officer, 9 April 1941, DHist 181.009 (D767)

85 Stevenson to high commissioner for Canada, 3 April 1941, DHist 181.009 (D767)

86 Campbell to Stevenson, 8 April 1941, DHist 181.009 (D767)

87 Stevenson to high commissioner for Canada, 3 April 1941, Campbell to Stevenson, 8 April 1941, and Roycanairf to CAS, 4 April 1941, DHist 181.009 (D767)

88 Air Council minutes, 16 April and 14 May 1941, S.840-108, pt 2, PARC long-term loan

89 'Re Air Commodore Stevenson's memorandum on "Administration of RCAF Units Overseas"' [18 April 1941], DHist 181.009 (D767)

90 Pearson to Stevenson, 18 April 1941, and Johnson to AMSO, 1 May 1941, DHist 181.009 (D767); EATS Committee minutes, 23 May 1941, PRO Air 20/1379

91 Quoted in Stacey, *Arms, Men and Governments*, 263

92 Cabinet War Committee minutes, 24 June 1941, DHist 83/345; Stacey, *Arms, Men and Governments*, 263–4

93 BCATP Supervisory Board minutes, 14 July 1941, app. I, Report of CAS, 9, DHist 73/1558, vol. 4; AMP, Progress Report, 6 Oct. 1941, DHist 73/1174, vol. 2

94 Kent to Campbell, 30 Sept. 1941, L.F. Stevenson personnel file, National Personnel Records Centre; Overseas Headquarters ORB, 19 May 1941, app. C, DHist

CHAPTER 2: THE FOUNDATIONS OF CANADIANIZATION

1 Power to King, 23 June 1941, Power Papers, box 58, folder D1028

2 Ibid.

3 King Diary, 10 June 1941, DHist 83/345; Robert Bothwell, Ian Drummond, and John English, *Canada 1900–1945* (Toronto 1987), 298

4 King Diary, 24 June 1941, DHist 83/345; Overseas Headquarters ORB, 30 June and 1 July 1941, DHist; Edwards to Breadner, 5 June 1941, H. Edwards personnel file, National Personnel Records Centre; Breadner minute, 18 June 1941, on Edwards to Breadner, 5 June 1941, H. Edwards personnel file, National Personnel Records Centre

5 'Note of a meeting held at the Air Ministry, London, on 8th July, 1941, between representatives of the Governments of the United Kingdom and Canada on various matters connected with the Commonwealth Air Training Scheme and the employment of RCAF personnel and formations with the Royal Air Force,' nd, DHist 80/525

6 Ibid.

7 Ibid.

8 Ibid.

9 'Report on Proposed Movement of RCAF Overseas Records Office to Gloucester and Assuming Control of JATP Canada Records,' nd; Stevenson to MacPherson, 20 Sept. 1941; MacPherson to officer in charge of records, Ruislip, 7 May 1942; and Squadron Leader H.M. Sinclair minute, 13 July 1943, all DHist 181.009 (D1186)

10 Director of intelligence (security) to Stevenson, 19 July 1941, 'RCAF Personnel in Britain, General Summary,' nd, DHist 181.009 (D293), vol. 2

11 Stevenson to AFHQ, 20 May 1941, DHist 181.009 (D283)

12 Squadron Leaders J.D. Parks and G. Vlastos, Morale Survey [Dec 1942], DHist 181.003 (D3456)

13 RAF Station Digby to No 12 Gp, 24 July 1941, DHist 181.009 (D767)

14 Quoted in John Sbrega, 'Anglo-American Relations and the Selection of Mountbatten as Supreme Allied Commander, South East Asia,' *Military Affairs*, 46, 3 (Oct. 1982): 142

15 Stevenson to Breadner, 1 Oct. 1941, DHist 181.009 (D724)

16 Ibid.

17 OSHQ ORB, 24 Oct. 1941, DHist; Breadner to Stevenson, 21 Oct. 1941, L.F. Stevenson personnel file, National Personnel Records Centre

18 *Ottawa Citizen*, 10 Dec. 1941, 14

19 Cabinet War Committee minutes, 19 Dec. 1941, DHist 83/345

20 Curtis interview, July 1975, W.A. Curtis biog. file, DHist; Edwards evaluation report, 26 Jan. 1940, H. Edwards personnel file, National Personel Records Centre

21 W.A. Curtis biog. file, DHist; Stacey, *Arms, Men and Governments*, 272

22 Edwards to de Carteret, 6 Jan. 1942, and Edwards to Breadner, 21 Feb. 1942, Power Papers, box 64, folder D1084; Curtis interview, July 1975, W.A. Curtis biog. file, DHist; Office of the High Commissioner for the United Kingdom to secretary of state for external affairs, 12 Sept. 1941, Power Papers, box 53, folder D1001

23 J. Halley, *The Squadrons of the Royal Air Force and Commonwealth, 1918–1988* (Tonbridge, Kent 1988), passim; RCAF squadron ORBs, 30 June 1942, DHist; AMP, Progress Report, 6 Oct. 1941, 30 June 1942, DHist 73/1174; see also PRO Air 22/312.

24 CAS to Roycanairf, 17 Oct. 1941, Roycanairf to CAS, 17 Oct. 1941, and CAS to Roycanairf, 22 Oct. 1941, DHist 181.009 (D774)

25 Edwards to de Carteret, 6 Jan. 1942, Power Papers, box 64, file D1084; Overseas Headquarters ORB, 22 and 25 Nov. 1941, DHist

26 Curtis to director of postings, Air Ministry, 19 Dec. 1941, DHist 181.009

(D774); Overseas Headquarters ORB, Nov.–Dec. 1941, DHist; Curtis interview, July 1975, W.A. Curtis biog. file, DHist

27 RCAF Squadron ORBs, 31 Dec. 1941, DHist; Squadron Progress Reports for period ending 26 Dec. 1941, DHist 181.003 (D68); Edwards to de Carteret, 6 Jan. 1942, Power Papers, box 64, file D1084

28 Breadner to Edwards, 21 Jan. 1942, Edwards to Breadner, 21 Jan. 1942, Breadner to Edwards, 23 Jan. 1942, Breadner to Power, 29 Jan. 1942, Power Papers, box 64, file D1081; Breadner to Power, 2, 5, 8, 12, 19, 23, 26, and 27 Jan. 1942, DHist 181.003 (D68); Roycanairf to CAS, Jan. 1942, 181.003 (D50); RCAF Squadron ORBs, 31 Jan. 1942, DHist

29 Power to Breadner, 30 Jan. 1942, Power Papers, box 64, file D1081; Breadner to Edwards, 3 Feb. 1942, DHist 181.009 (D774)

30 Edwards to Breadner, 5 Feb. 1942, DHist 181.009 (D774)

31 Power to Edwards, 18 Feb. 1942, and Edwards to Babington, 5 Feb. 1942, DHist 181.009 (D774)

32 Babington to Edwards, 8 Feb. 1942, Babington to Edwards, 12 Feb. 1942, Edwards to Breadner, 16 Feb. 1942, Edwards to Babington, 19 Feb. 1942, DHist 181.009 (D774)

33 Babington to Edwards, 12 Feb. 1942, DHist 181.009 (D774)

34 Babington to Joubert, 10 Feb. 1942, PRO Air 15/52

35 'A statistical return on Canadianization,' nd, DHist 181.003 (D3596); Nos 404, 407, 413, and 415 Squadron ORBs, 31 Jan. and 30 June 1942, DHist

36 Baldwin to MacNeece-Foster, 25 Jan. 1942, PRO Air 14/1942

37 MacNeece-Foster to Bomber Command, 13 Feb. 1942, PRO Air 14/1942

38 W.A. Curtis interview, July 1975, W.A. Curtis biog. file, DHist

39 J.C. Slessor, *The Central Blue* (London 1956), 334–5

40 Slessor to Edwards, 1 Feb. 1942, DHist 181.009 (D774)

41 Ibid.

42 RCAF Squadron ORBs, Jan.–June 1942, DHist; 'Statistical return on Canadianization,' nd, DHist 181.009 (D3596); S. Kostenuk and J. Griffin, *RCAF Squadron Histories and Aircraft, 1924–1968* (Toronto 1977), 89, 94, 112, 113

43 Quoted in Babington to Edwards, 14 Feb. 1942, DHist 181.009 (D774)

44 MacGregor to AO-in-C, 18 Feb. 1942, DHist 181.009 (D774)

45 Edwards to Breadner, 21 Feb. 1942, Power Papers, box 64, file D1084

46 Curtis interview, July 1975, W.A. Curtis biog. file, DHist

47 Edwards to Power, 20 Feb. 1942, and Babington to Edwards, 23 Feb. 1942, DHist 181.009 (D774)

48 Squadron ORBs, 31 Dec. 1941, 31 March 1942, DHist; 'Statistical return on Canadianization,' nd, DHist 181.009 (D3596); Kostenuk and Griffin, *RCAF Squadrons and Aircraft*, 107

49 Edwards to Power, 27 March 1942, Power Papers, box 64, file D1090

50 Edwards to Breadner, 21 Feb. 1942, ibid., file D1084

51 Edwards to de Carteret, 6 Jan. 1942, ibid.

52 Cranborne to Sinclair, 3 Feb. 1942, and Street to Liesching, 22 Feb. 1942, PRO Air 2/5394

53 Meeting in Power's office, 17 March 1942, Power Papers, box 64, file D1084
54 Edwards to Breadner, 30 March 1942, ibid.
55 Edwards to Breadner, 21 Feb. 1942, ibid.
56 Edwards to Breadner, 30 March 1942, ibid.
57 Edwards to Breadner, 21 Feb. 1942, ibid.
58 Ibid.
59 H.L. Campbell personnel file, National Defence Records Centre
60 Edwards to Breadner, 21 Feb. 1942, Power Papers, box 64, file D1084
61 'Minutes of Squadron Commanding Officers' Conference,' 6 March 1942, DHist 181.003 (D4761); Edwards to Breadner, 30 March 1942, Power Papers, box 64, file D1084
62 'Minutes of Squadron Commanding Officers' Conference,' 6 March 1942, DHist 181.003 (D4761)
63 Director of personnel to AOsC-in-C, March 1942, DHist 181.009 (D774)
64 SASO, No 5 Group to station commanders, 22 April 1942, DHist 181.009 (D774)
65 'Minutes of Squadron Commanding Officers' Conference,' 6 March 1942, DHist 181.003 (D4761)
66 Ibid.
67 Ibid.
68 Carr to Edwards, 21 Feb. 1942, DHist 181.009 (D774)
69 No 405 Squadron ORB, Feb.–July 1942, DHist
70 Babington to Edwards, 16 March 1942, DHist 181.009 (D774)
71 Babington to Edwards, 23 Feb. 1942, ibid.
72 Overseas Headquarters to Babington, 2 March 1942, and Curtis to Babington, 30 May 1942, DHist 181.009 (D774)
73 Babington to Curtis, 17 June 1942, DHist 181.009 (D774)
74 OSHQ ORB, 7 and 15 April 1942, DHist
75 Dominions Office to United Kingdom high commissioner in Canada (UKHC), 27 April 1942, PRO Air 19/339
76 Edwards to Breadner, 1 May 1942, A.P. Campbell personnel file, National Personnel Records Centre
77 Edwards to CAS, 7 Aug. 1942, A.P. Campbell personnel file, National Personnel Records Centre; Campbell to AOC, EAC, 3 Feb. 1943, A.P. Campbell biog. file, DHist
78 Edwards to Breadner, 30 March 1942, Power Papers, box 64, file D1084
79 Edwards to CAS, 7 May 1942, DHist 181.009 (D774)
80 Cowley to Breadner, 28 April 1942, Power Papers, box 64, file D1081
81 UKHC to Dominions Office, 7 May 1942, PRO Air 19/339
82 UKHC to Dominions Office, 19 May 1942, ibid.
83 Cabinet War Committee minutes, 22 May 1942, DHist 83/345
84 King Diary, 27 May 1942, DHist 83/530
85 UKHC to Dominions Office, 23 May 1942, and Balfour to Sinclair, 26 May 1942, PRO Air 19/339
86 Ibid.
87 UKHC to Dominions Office, 23 May 1942, ibid.

88 UKHC to Dominions Office, 23 May 1942, Dominions Office to UKHC, 26 May 1942, ibid.
89 UKHC to Dominions Office, 25 May 1942, ibid.
90 Balfour to Sinclair, 26 May 1942, PRO Air 19/339
91 'Memorandum of Agreement,' June 1942, app. III, DHist 80/255
92 'Minutes of the Second Meeting of the Chairmen's Committee,' 24 May 1942, DHist 80/255
93 UKHC to Dominions Office, 26 May 1942, PRO Air 19/339
94 Ibid.
95 Balfour to Sinclair, 26 May 1942, PRO Air 19/339
96 UKHC to Dominions Office, 26 and 29 May 1942, PRO Air 19/33; Group Captain D. Massey, 'Report on Canadianization,' 24 Nov. 1943, 66, DHist 181.003 (D1228); 'Memorandum of Agreement,' June 1942, DHist 80/255
97 UKHC to Dominions Office, 26 May 1942, UKHC to Dominions Office, 29 May 1942, Dominions Office to UKHC, 31 May 1942, PRO Air 19/339; 'Memorandum of Agreement,' June 1942, DHist 80/255
98 UKHC to Dominions Office, 26 May 1942, Dominions Office to UKHC, 27 May 1942, PRO Air 19/339; Balfour to Power, 28 May 1942, Power Papers, box 64, file D1081
99 UKHC to Dominions Office, 28 May 1942, PRO Air 19/339
100 Cabinet War Committee minutes, 28 May 1942, DHist
101 UKHC to Dominions Office, 28 May 1942, PRO Air 19/339
102 UKHC Dominions Office, 29 May 1942, ibid.
103 Dominions Office to UKHC, 31 May 1942, ibid.
104 UKHC to Dominions Office, 3 June 1942, ibid.
105 'Analysis of Post Graduate Aircrew Personnel at RAF Posting Disposal on 1st December, 1943,' July 1946, PRO Air 22/312; 'Canadianization Overseas Squadrons,' nd, DHist 181.003 (D3596)
106 'Memorandum of Agreement,' June 1942, DHist 80/255
107 Ibid.

CHAPTER 3: STRUGGLE AND DISSENT

1 Overseas Headquarters ORB, 29 June, 2 and 17 July 1942, DHist
2 'Canadian Bomber Group – Progress Meeting,' 3 July 1942, DHist 181.009 (D612)
3 'Diary, Mission to United Kingdom – 1942,' 3 and 19 Aug. 1942, Power Papers, box 64, file D2011
4 Harris to Freeman, 29 July 1942, PRO Air 20/2978; Harris to Portal, 12 Aug. 1942, Portal Papers, DHist 87/89, box C, folder 2; A.T. Harris, *Bomber Offensive* (New York 1947), 64
5 'Canadianization,' 4 Feb. 1943, Power Papers, box 64, file D1081
6 'Diary, Mission to the United Kingdom – 1942,' 19 Aug. 1942, ibid., file D2011
7 'Canadianization,' 4 Feb. 1943, ibid., file D1081; Power to King, 9 Sept. 1942, DHist 181.009 (D6155)

8 Overseas Headquarters ORB, 30 June 1942, DHist

9 Quoted in Stacey, *Arms, Men and Governments*, 283; Tinker to Brodribb, 27 Aug. 1942, Edwards to Sinclair, 31 Aug. 1942, Street to Edwards, and Aide Memoire, 24 Sept. 1942, Ault to AOC-in-C, nd, all DHist 181.009 (D774); Brian Loring Villa, *Unauthorized Action* (Toronto 1989), passim

10 Edwards to AMP, 26 Sept. 1942, DHist 181.009 (D720)

11 Sutton to Edwards, 9 Oct. 1942, DHist 181.009 (D720); 'Memorandum of Agreement,' June 1942, DHist 80/255; Personnel Reception Centre, 'Minutes of a Meeting held ... 2.7.42,' DHist 181.009 (D800)

12 Overseas Headquarters ORB, 31 Oct. 1942, DHist; Curtis to AFHQ, 18 Nov. 1942, Wait to Edwards, 'Report on Station Bournemouth,' 18 Jan. 1943, and Flying Training Command to Edwards, 2 March 1943, all DHist 181.009 (D800); Edwards to Flying Training Command, 3 May 1943, and Babington to Edwards, 10 May 1943, DHist 181.009 (D720)

13 Breadner to Power, 2 Oct. 1942, Power Papers, box 64, file D1081, and Edwards to Breadner, 30 Jan. 1943, ibid., file D1084; Overseas Headquarters ORB, 14 and 25 Sept. 1942, DHist; 'Information Regarding RCAF District Headquarters, India and South East Asia,' 18 Sept. 1945, DHist 181.009 (D762)

14 Edwards to Breadner, 11 Aug. 1942, Power Papers, box 64, file D1084; 'Minutes, Conference held at RCAF OSHQ,' 13 Aug. 1942, 'Note of a Special Meeting Held in the Air Council Room,' 18 Aug. 1942, and 'Extract of Minutes of Conference No 2,' 18 Aug. 1942, all DHist 181.009 (D6155); Stacey, *Arms, Men and Governments*, 283

15 Edwards to Breadner, 30 Oct. 1942, Curtis to Breadner, 1 Dec. 1942, Power Papers, box 64, file D1084; Overseas Headquarters ORB, Sept. 1942, app. III, DHist

16 Overseas Headquarters ORB, 9 Sept. 1942, DHist

17 Edwards to Power, 9 Sept. 1942, and 'Extract from *The Economist*,' 14 Sept. 1942, DHist 181.009 (D771); Overseas Headquarters ORB, 5 Sept. 1942, DHist

18 'Edwards Flays Belief Step is Blow to Bond of Empire,' *Hamilton Spectator*, 5 Sept. 1942

19 Shapiro to Bassett, 15 Oct. 1942, DHist 181.009 (D771)

20 Breadner to Edwards, 9 Sept. 1942, DHist 181.009 (D771)

21 Quoted in Breadner to Edwards, 11 Sept. 1942, DHist 181.009 (D771)

22 Toronto *Globe and Mail*, 10 Sept. 1942

23 Breadner to Edwards, 12 Sept. 1942, DHist 181.009 (D771)

24 Edwards to Breadner, 14 Sept. 1942, ibid.

25 Canadian Institute of Public Opinion, 'Gallup Poll Releases, 1941–1942,' 27 June 1942

26 *Toronto Telegram*, 26 Sept. 1942; *Kitchener Daily Record*, 18 Sept. 1942; *Winnipeg Free Press*, 12 May 1943

27 *Vancouver Daily Province*, 15 Sept. 1942; *Toronto Star*, 12 Sept. 1942; *Kitchener Daily Record*, 18 Sept. 1942; *Edmonton Journal*, 10 Sept. 1942; *L'Action Catholique*, 12 Sept. 1942; Clark to Edwards, 14 Sept. 1942, DHist 181.009 (D771)

28 Parks and Vlastos, 'Morale Survey,' nd, DHist 181.003 (D3456)
29 Ibid.
30 Ibid.
31 Ibid.
32 Sutton to Edwards, 16 Oct. 1942, DHist 181.009 (D774)
33 D. Massey, 'Report on Canadianization,' nd, app. 6, DHist 181.003 (D1228)
34 Edwards to Breadner, 21 Oct. 1942, DHist 181.009 (D774)
35 Edwards to Breadner, 30 Oct. 1942, Power Papers, box 64, file D1084
36 'Visit of Air Marshal Edwards, Middle East, India and Ceylon,' nd, Overseas Headquarters ORB, DHist; Nos 424, 426, 427, 428, 429, and 431 Sqn ORBs, 31 Dec. 1942, DHist; 'Statistical Return on Canadianization,' nd, DHist 181.003 (D3596)
37 'Statistical Return on Canadianization,' nd, DHist 181.003 (D3596)
38 No 3 PRC to Overseas Headquarters, 16 July 1942, DHist 181.009 (D800); Massey, 'Report on Canadianization,' nd, app. 6, DHist 181.003 (D1228)
39 Squadron ORBs, 30 June and 31 Dec. 1942, DHist; AMP, Progress Report, 7 Jan. and 30 June 1942, DHist 73/1174; Massey, 'Report on Canadianization,' nd, app. 6, DHist 181.003 (D1228)
40 Breadner to Edwards, 9 Jan. 1943, DHist 181.009 (D774)
41 Breadner to Edwards, 20 Jan. 1943, ibid.
42 Edwards to Breadner, 22 Jan. 1943, ibid.
43 Curtis interview, July 1975, W.A. Curtis biog. file, DHist
44 Edwards to Air Ministry, 22 Jan. 1942, PRO Air 8/742
45 'Note on Dominionization of Article XV Squadrons,' 24 Jan. 1943, PRO Air 8/742
46 Empire Air Training Scheme Committee minutes, 25 Jan. 1943, PRO Air 8/742
47 Edwards to Breadner, 27 Jan. 1943, Power Papers, box 64, file D1090
48 Breadner to Edwards, 27 Jan. 1943, ibid.
49 Edwards to Breadner, 29 Jan 1943, ibid.
50 Breadner to Edwards, 28 Jan 1943, ibid.
51 Edwards to Breadner, 30 Jan 1943, ibid.
52 Stacey, *Arms, Men and Governments*, 286n
53 'Diary, Mission to United Kingdom – 1942,' 19 Aug. 1942, Power Papers, box 64, file D1090
54 UKHC to Dominions Office, 4 Feb. 1943, PRO Air 8/742
55 Vincent Massey, *What's Past Is Prologue* (Toronto 1963), 326–7
56 Breadner to Power, 3 Feb. 1943, Power Papers, box 64, file D1090
57 'Note of a Meeting held in DG of P's Room, Air Ministry,' 4 Feb. 1943, DHist 181.009 (D774)
58 Sutton to all AOsC-in-C and AOsC, 19 Feb. 1943, DHist 181.009 (D769)
59 Stacey, *Arms, Men and Governments*, 287
60 'A Statistical Return on Canadianization,' nd, DHist 181.003 (D3596); AMP, Weekly Progress Reports, Jan. and Dec. 1943, DHist 73/1174
61 Edwards to Breadner, 27 Jan. 1943, Power Papers, box 64, file D1090; Stacey, *Arms, Men and Governments*, 287–8
62 Wait to Edwards, 12 March 1943, DHist 181.009 (D769)

63 Power to Edwards, 13 April 1943, Power Papers, box 59, file D1033

64 Curtis interview, July 1975, W.A. Curtis biog. file, DHist; see also Campbell to Edwards, 13 April 1943, DHist 181.009 (D774)

65 Sully to Sutton, 13 Nov. 1942, Power Papers, box 66, file D1106; 'Trained Strength of RAF,' nd, PRO Air 22/312

66 Air Ministry letter, 24 March 1943, attached to Edwards to Breadner, 21 April 1943, Power Papers, box 64, file D1084

67 Edwards to Breadner, 30 Jan. 1943, Power Papers, box 64, file D1084

68 EATS Committee minutes, 24 Nov. 1942, 15 Jan. 1943, PRO Air 20/1379; *Vancouver Daily Province*, 15 Oct. 1942, 13 Jan., 9 Feb. 1943; *Toronto Daily Star*, 14 Sept. 1942; *Winnipeg Free Press*, 12 May 1943; *Edmonton Journal*, 4 June 1943; Minutes of Meeting held in Power's office, 2 Jan 1943, Power Papers, box 66, file D1106

69 EATS Committee minutes, 12 Feb. 1943, PRO Air 20/1379

70 Ibid., 16 April and 14 May 1943, PRO Air 20/1379

71 Sully to Sutton, 13 Nov. 1942, Power Papers, box 66, file D1106; 'Trained Strength of RAF,' nd, PRO Air 22/312; AMP, Progress Report, 31 Aug. 1943, 6 Oct. 1944, DHist 73/1174

72 Curtis interview, July 1975, W.A. Curtis biog. file, DHist; Curtis to minister, 17 June 1944, 17-1-4, pt 2, NA, RG 24, vol. 5210

73 Stacey, *Arms, Men and Governments*, 268; H.L. Campbell biog. file, DHist; Douglas, *The Creation of a National Air Force*, 585

74 Massey, 'Report of Canadianization,' 24 Nov. 1943, app. 6, DHist 181.003 (D1228)

75 'Note of Meeting held in DG of Ps Room,' 4 Feb. 1943, DHist 181.009 (D774); 'Monthly Strength Return of RCAF Squadrons,' 26 Jan. 1943, DHist 181.005 (D2101); EATS Committee minutes, 15 July 1943, PRO Air 20/1379; CAS, 'Progress Report No. 46,' 18 Oct. 1943, DHist 73/1558; AMP, Weekly Progress Reports, Feb.–Aug. 1944, DHist 73/1174; Daily Strength Returns, No 3 PRC, Jan.–July 1944, DHist 181.003 (D1440-1)

76 'Monthly Strength Return of RCAF Squadrons,' 26 Jan. 1943, DHist 181.005 (D2101); AMP, Weekly Progress Report, 29 Dec. 1942, DHist 73/1174; Sutton to Edwards, 16 Oct. 1942, Sully to Air Ministry, 14 Nov. 1942, DHist 181.009 (D774)

77 Edwards to Breadner, 30 Jan. 1943, Power Papers, box 64, file D1084

78 Massey, 'Report of Canadianization,' 24 Nov. 1943, 10, app. 1, app. 38, DHist 181.003 (D1228); Roycanairf to CAS, 12 Jan. 1944, D/DPC minute, 2 Feb. 1944, DHist 181.009 (D4160); Edwards to Sutton, 30 Aug. 1943, Sutton to Edwards, 13 Sept. 1943, DHist 181.009 (D769)

79 'Monthly Strength Return of RCAF Squadrons,' 26 July 1943, DHist 181.005 (D2102); 'Statistical Return on Canadianization,' nd, DHist 181.003 (D3569); Massey, 'Report on Canadianization,' 24 Nov. 1943, app. 1, 5, 6, 25, DHist 181.003 (D1228)

80 Sutton to Edwards, 13 Sept. 1943, DHist 181.009 (D769); Massey, 'Report of Canadianization,' 24 Nov. 1943, 58, DHist 181.003 (D1228)

81 Edwards to Sutton, 30 Aug. 1943, DHist 181.009 (D769)

82 Sutton to Edwards, 13 Sept. 1943, DHist 181.009 (D769)

83 Massey, 'Report of Canadianization,' 24 Nov. 1943, app. 9, app. 25, DHist
    181.003 (D1228); 'Statistical Return on Canadianization,' nd, DHist 181.003
    (D3596)

84 Massey, 'Report of Canadianization,' 24 Nov. 1943, v, DHist 181.003 (D1228);
    Edwards to Breadner, 25 Sept. 1943, Power Papers, box 64, file D1084

85 Power to Edwards, 16 Oct. 1943, H. Edwards personnel file, National
    Personnel Records Centre; Stevenson interview, 21 Oct. 1974, L.F. Stevenson
    biog. file, DHist; Breadner to Croil, 7 and 14 Sept. 1939, L.S. Breadner
    personnel file, National Personnel Records Centre; Curtis interview, July 1975,
    W.A. Curtis biog. file, DHist; Overseas Headquarters ORB, 27 Oct. 1943,
    DHist; Breadner to minister, 9 Nov. 1943, Edwards to Breadner, nd, Power
    Papers, box 64, file D1090

86 Breadner to Power, 5 Feb. 1944, DHist 181.0-09 (D769); Campbell to Overseas
    Headquarters staff, 19 Aug. 1943, Curtis to AFHQ, 8 Dec. 1943, and enclosure,
    Power to Breadner, 12 Feb. 1943, Breadner to Power, 16 Feb. 1943, DHist
    181.009 (D5162); Overseas Headquarters ORB, 24 Jan. 1944, DHist

87 UKHC to Dominions Office, 8 Feb. 1944, PRO Air 20/4983

88 Ibid.

89 Ibid.; Stacey, *Arms, Men and Governments*, 300, app. L

90 Cabinet War Committee minutes, 9 Feb. 1944, and aide memoire, DHist
    83/345

91 EATS Committee minutes, 12 Feb. 1944, PRO Air 20/1379

92 Street circular, 14 April 1944, DHist 181.009 (D769)

93 EATS Committee minutes, 3 March and 21 April 1944, PRO Air 20/1379

94 Stacey, *Arms, Men and Governments*, app. L; Edwards to Breadner, 25 Sept.
    1943, Power Papers, box 64, file D1084; Overseas Headquarters ORB, 17 Aug.
    1943, DHist; Young to AMP, 4 Feb. 1944, Middleton to AOC-in-C, 8 Feb. 1944,
    DHist 181.009 (D867); Breadner to Power, 9 Feb. 1944, DHist 181.009 (D766)

95 Pirie to Edmunds, 28 Aug. 1943, DHist 181.009 (D766)

96 Power to Breadner, 12 Feb. 1944, Power to Breadner, 17 Feb. 1944, Power to
    Breadner, 4 March 1944, DHist 181.009 (D766); Power to Breadner, 21 Feb.
    1944, and handwritten minute, nd, 181.009 (D878); Pirie to Edwards, 28 Aug.
    1943, DHist 181.009 (D766); EATS Committee minutes, 17 March and 21 April
    1944, PRO Air 20/1379; Power to Balfour, 25 April 1944, DHist 181.003
    (D4910)

97 EATS Committee minutes, 17 March and 21 April 1944, PRO Air 20/1379;
    Power to Breadner, 21 Feb. 1944, and enclosure, DHist 181.009 (D878);
    Power to Balfour, 25 April 1944, DHist 181.003 (D4910); Balfour to Power,
    2 June 1944, Power to Balfour, 14 June 1944, 17-1-4, pt 2, NA, RG 24, vol.
    5210

98 Bendickson to Overseas Headquarters, 24 Aug. 1944, DHist 181.003 (D1522)

99 'Strength Return by Units,' 31 March 1945, DHist 181.005 (D850)

100 Air Council minutes, 18 April, 3 and 23 May 1944, PRO Air 6/75; Dominions
    Office to UKHC, 10 May 1944, Power to Breadner, 13 May 1944, Power to
    MacDonald, 19 May 1944, MacDonald to Power, 22 May 1944, Power to

Balfour, 14 June 1944, Balfour to Power, 28 June 1944, Power to MacDonald, 29 June 1944, NA, RG 24, vol. 5210; Power to Breadner, 17 and 26 June 1944, DHist 181.009 (D774)

101 Overseas Headquarters ORB, 9 Oct. and Dec. 1944, DHist

102 'Minutes of Meeting on Bomber Command Operational Tour,' 14 March 1945, PRO Air 14/1018; W.S. Carter, 'An Acid Test of Sovereignty: Bomber Command and the Operational Tour, 1945,' CHA Conference Paper, May 1992

103 Harris to Sutton, 12 March 1945, PRO Air 14/1018; Air Council minutes, 13 March 1945, PRO Air 6/75

104 'Minutes of Meeting on Bomber Command Operational Tour,' 14 March 1945, PRO Air 14/1018; Carter, 'An Acid Test of Sovereignty'

105 Kostenuk and Griffin, *RCAF Squadron Histories and Aircraft,* 78, 207

CHAPTER 4: CUTTING OUT A PAPER TIGER

1 Stacey, *Arms, Men and Governments*, 54–62; King Diary, 20 Sept. 1944, NA, MG 26, J13; Cabinet War Committee minutes, 5 Oct. 1944, NA, MG 26, J4, vol. 425; Ivan Ciuciura, 'Policy and Planning for Participation in the War against Japan,' MA research paper, Royal Military College, 1974, 12–13

2 John Ehrman, *Grand Strategy,* VI (London 1956), 237–9; King Diary, 21 Oct. and 16 Nov. 1943, 9 Feb. 1944, NA, MG 26, J13; T.W. Melnyk, 'RCAF Planning for Tiger Force,' May 1978, 6–7, unpublished DHist narrative

3 King Diary, 5 and 7 Jan. 1944, NA, MG 26, J13; C.G. Power, *A Party Politician* (Toronto 1966), 242

4 Power, *A Party Politician*, 240–4; Melnyk, 'RCAF Planning for Tiger Force,' 9

5 UKHC to Dominions Office, 8 Feb. 1944, PRO, Air 20/4983; 'Factors Affecting the Employment of the RCAF in the War against Japan,' nd [but late 1943], DHist 181.009 (D3696)

6 'Aide Memoire by the Canadian Government' [10 Feb. 1944], PRO, Air 8/194; Cabinet minutes, 9 Feb. 1944, NA, MG 26, J4, vol. 425; King Diary, 10 Feb. 1944, NA, MG 26, J13; Stacey, *Arms, Men and Governments*, 300

7 'Aide Memoire by the Canadian Government' [10 Feb. 1944], PRO, Air 8/194; Cabinet minutes, 9 Feb. 1944, NA, MG 26, J4, vol. 425; King Diary, 10 Feb. 1944, NA, MG 26, J13; Stacey, *Arms, Men and Governments*, 300

8 Empire Air Training Scheme Committee minutes, 12 Feb. 1944, PRO, Air 20/1379

9 Ibid.; Sutton to VCAS, 21 March 1944, DG (Plans) to AMSO, 15 Feb. 1944, Evill to ACAS(P), 18 Feb. 1944, PRO, Air 20/4983; Sinclair to Churchill, 26 Feb. 1944, MacDonald to Dominions Office, 11 Feb. 1944, PRO, Air 8/794

10 Heeney to Power, 19 Feb. 1944, Power Papers, box 55, file D1020; Cabinet minutes, 22 Feb. 1944, NA, MG 26, J4, vol. 425; Power, *A Party Politician*, 246

11 King to MacDonald, 25 Feb. 1944, Power Papers, box 55, file D1020; Cabinet minutes, 22 March 1944, NA, MG 26, J4, vol. 425

12 Breadner to Power, 20 Feb., 2 and 11 March, and 5 April 1944, Power Papers, box 58, file D1029; King Diary, 10 March 1944, NA, MG 26, J13; Melnyk,

'RCAF Planning for Tiger Force,' 15–16; AMP to Evill, 21 March 1944, Dominions Office to MacDonald, 31 March 1944, Air Ministry document, 14 April 1944, PRO, Air 20/4983

13 Dominions Office to MacDonald, 31 March 1944, PRO, Air 20/4983; Pickersgill, *The Mackenzie King Record*, I, ch. 23; King Diary, 15 May 1944, NA, MG 26, J13

14 Evill, 'Canadian Contribution to the Japanese War,' 12 May 1944, PRO, Air 8/794; Melnyk, 'RCAF Planning for Tiger Force,' 16–17, 19–20; Curtis to Leckie, 17 April 1944, 'Canadian Participation in the War against Japan after Cessation of Hostilities against Germany,' 19 April 1944, S 15-26-10, NA, RG 24, vol. 5425

15 'Note Summarizing Discussions between RCAF O/S Headquarters and the Air Staff Air Ministry regarding the Possible RCAF Target Force for the Japanese War Phase,' 19 May 1944, DHist 181.009 (D3696)

16 CSC minutes, S 85-1-2, NA, RG 24, vol. 5425; 'Memorandum to the Cabinet War Committee re Canadian Participation in the War against Japan,' 14 June 1944, NA, RG 2 7c, vol. 15; Cabinet minutes, 24 May, 14 June 1944, NA, MG 26, J4, vol. 425

17 Power to Balfour, 14 June 1944, DHist 181.009 (D3696); Power to Breadner, 17 June 1944, DHist 181.009 (D1044); King to Churchill, 27 June 1944, PRO, Air 8/794

18 Air Ministry note, 19 July 1944, PRO, Air 20/4984; Breadner to Power, 7 July 1944, DHist 181.009 (D3696)

19 Curtis to Leckie, 19 July 1944, DHist 181.002 (D258); Power to Breadner, 25 July 1944, DHist 181.009 (D3696)

20 Power to Breadner, 25 July 1944, Breadner to Power, 7 July 1944, DHist 181.009 (D3696); Breadner to Power, 3 Aug. 1944, Leckie minute, 14 Aug. 1944, S 85-7-4, NA, RG 24, vol. 5427

21 Air Ministry to Balfour, 9 Aug. 1944, Balfour to Evill, 16 Aug. 1944, PRO, Air 8/794; Power to Breadner, 23 Aug. 1944, DHist 181.009 (D3696); MacDonald to Dominions Office, 21 Aug. 1944, Evill to Balfour, 19 Aug. 1944, PRO, Air 20/4984

22 Air Ministry to Balfour, 9 Aug. 1944, Balfour to Evill, 16 Aug. 1944, PRO, Air 8/794; Power to Breadner, 23 Aug. 1944, DHist 181.009 (D3696); Evill to Breadner, 8 Aug. 1944, ACAS(P) item 4, chiefs of staff meeting, 30 Aug. 1944, MacDonald to Dominions Office, 21 Aug. 1944, Evill to Balfour, 19 Aug. 1944, PRO, Air 20/4984; Leckie minute, 13 Sept. 1944, PRO, Air 8/1284

23 'Aide Memoire on the employment of Canadian Forces After the Defeat of Germany,' 24 July 1944, Power to Breadner, 18 Aug. 1944, PRO, Air 20/4984; King Diary, 31 Aug., 13 Sept. 1944, NA, MG 26, J13; Power to King, nd, NA, MG 26, J1, vol. 369; Cabinet minutes, 31 Aug. 1944, NA, MG 26, J4, vol. 425

24 'Canadian Participation in the Pacific War and in Europe after the Defeat of Germany,' 6 Sept. 1944, S 85-1-2, NA, RG 24, vol. 5425; King Diary, 6 Sept. 1944, NA, MG 26, J13; Power, *A Party Politician*, 247

25 King Diary, 13 Sept. 1944, NA, MG 26, J13

26 Ibid.; C.P. Stacey, *Mackenzie King and the Atlantic Triangle* (Toronto 1976), 52–3; Stacey, *Arms, Men and Governments*, 182–4

27 King Diary, 14 Sept. 1944, NA, MG 26, J13

28 Ibid.

29 Ehrman, *Grand Strategy*, VI, 203, 220, 233

30 Cabinet minutes, 14 Sept. 1944, PRO, Cab 66/55; Leckie to Power, 18 Sept. 1944, DHist 181.009 (D3696); Curtis to Leckie, 18 Sept. 1944, Leckie minute, nd, S 85-1-2, NA, RG 24, vol. 5425

31 Leckie to Power, 18 Sept. 1944, DHist 181.009 (D3696)

32 'Aide Memoire: RCAF Participation in the War against Japan,' 12 Oct. 1944, DHist 181.002 (D258)

33 Leckie to Power, 18 Sept. 1944, DHist 181.009 (D3696)

34 King Diary, 20 and 28 Sept. 1944, NA, MG 26, J13; Cabinet minutes, 20 Sept. 1944, NA, MG 26, J4, vol. 425

35 Breadner to Power, 31 Oct. 1944, DHist 181.009 (D3696); Cabinet minutes, 11 Dec. 1944, NA, MG 26, J4, vol. 425

36 Leckie to AMP, 5 Jan. 1945, DHist 181.002 (D258); Stacey, *Arms, Men and Governments*, 53; UKHC to Dominions Office, 11 July 1945, PRO, Air 8/1288

37 Sully to acting minister, 27 Jan. 1945, DHist 181.002 (D258)

38 Evill to Breadner, 6 Oct. 1944, DHist 181.009 (D3693)

39 Breadner to Evill, 22 Dec. 1944, Evill to Anderson, 26 Oct. 1944, DHist 181.009 (D3696)

40 Melnyk, 'RCAF Planning for Tiger Force,' 46; Ireland to Leckie, 16 Dec. 1944, Roycanairf to acting minister, 16 Dec. 1944, DHist 181.009 (D3696)

41 'Operation MOULD: Outline Administrative Plan,' 23 Nov. 1944, DHist 181.003 (D5092); Ehrman, *Grand Strategy*, VI, 233–4; D (Plans) to DAMAS, 5 Jan. 1945, DHist 181.009 (D258)

42 Portal minute, 27 Jan. 1945, PRO, Air 8/1284

43 Ehrman, *Grand Strategy*, VI, 234

44 Melnyk, 'RCAF Planning for Tiger Force,' 53–5; King Diary, 29 March 1945, NA, MG 26, J13; Canada, House of Commons, *Debates*, 4 April 1945

45 Melnyk, 'RCAF Planning for Tiger Force,' 46–7; Leckie to Breadner, 22 Dec. 1944, DAS to Breadner, 20 Jan. 1945, DHist 181.009 (D3696); Breadner to Leckie, 23 Dec. 1944, S 85-2-4, NA, RG 24, vol. 5426; House of Commons, *Debates*, 4 April 1945

46 AMSO to Leckie, 20 Jan. 1945, and reply, 23 Jan. 1945, DHist 181.009 (D3696); Ehrman, *Grand Strategy*, VI, 234

47 Sully to acting minister, 27 Jan. 1945, Middleton to Breadner, 16 Feb. 1945, DHist 181.002 (D258); minutes of meeting of Redeployment Sub-Committee on VLR Pacific Force, 16 Feb. 1945, DHist 181.003 (D5089)

48 Argonaut to AMSFHQ, 7 Feb. 1945, and reply, 8 Feb. 1945, PRO, Air 8/1284; first meeting of Overseas Headquarters and AFHQ staffs to discuss Phase II, 26 Feb. 1945, DHist 181.002 (D264); Cabinet minutes, 28 Feb. 1945, NA, MG 26, J4, vol. 425

49 Report of Lloyd on visit to Washington and Ottawa, 9 March 1945, PRO, Air 8/1284; Ehrman, *Grand Strategy*, VI, 234

50 Curtis to Leckie, 1 March 1945, minutes of meeting of Joint Planning Committee, 15 March 1945, DHist 181.002 (D258); minutes of meeting of chiefs of staff, 20 March 1945, S 85-1-2, NA, RG 24, vol. 5425

51 Portal note, 17 March 1945, PRO, Air 8/1284; Churchill to King, 20 March 1945, PRO, Air 8/1288

52 King to Churchill, 27 March 1945, PRO, Air 8/1288

53 Melnyk, 'RCAF Planning for Tiger Force,' 58–9; Hollis to Portal, 31 March 1945, chiefs of staff to Churchill, 6 April 1945, PRO, Air 8/1284; Breadner to Leckie, 28 March 1945, DHist 181.002 (D258); DAS (Plans) to D/AOC-in-C, 19 April 1945, DHist 181.009 (D6223)

54 RCAF memorandum for Cabinet, 17 April 1945, DHist 181.002 (D264); Cabinet minutes, 19 April 1945, NA, MG 26, J4, vol. 425

55 Johnson to Leckie, 14 April 1945, DHist 181.009 (D6223); Melnyk, 'RCAF Planning for Tiger Force,' 60; House of Commons, *Debates*, 4 April 1945; Curtis to Johnson, 20 April 1945, DHist 181.002 (D264)

56 Report of Lloyd on second trip to Washington, 21 April 1945, PRO, Air 8/1284; Ehrman, *Grand Strategy*, VI, 235

57 Roycanairf to AFHQ, 28 April 1945, Johnson to Leckie, 14 May 1945, DHist 181.009 (D6223); extract from chiefs of staff meeting, 19 April 1945, PRO, Air 8/1284

58 Melnyk, 'RCAF Planning for Tiger Force,' 66–71

59 Ehrman, *Grand Strategy*, VI, 235; report of Lloyd on third trip to Washington, 2 June 1945, extract from chiefs of staff meeting, 14 June 1945, PRO, Air 8/1286

60 Churchill to King, 16 June 1945, DHist 181.009 (D6779); Johnson to Leckie, 12 June 1945, DHist 181.002 (D260); Heeney to Leckie, 15 June 1945, S 85-1-2, NA, RG 24, vol. 5426

61 Meeting of Combined Staffs, 18 June 1945, DHist 181.002 (D264); King to Churchill, 19 June 1945, DHist 181.009 (D6779); Melnyk, 'RCAF Planning for Tiger Force,' 74–5

62 Meeting of chiefs of staff, 22 June 1945, Portal to Leckie, 23 June 1945, and reply, 25 June 1945, PRO, Air 8/1288

63 'RCAF Participation in the War against Japan,' nd, DHist 181.009 (D5757); Melnyk, 'RCAF Planning for Tiger Force,' 79, 81; King Diary, 28 June 1945, NA, MG 26, J13

64 Melnyk, 'RCAF Planning for Tiger Force,' 80, 82–4; minutes of meeting with Lloyd, 21 July 1945, DHist 181.009 (D5757); 'Matters Arising out of Air Marshal Lloyd's Visit to Pacific,' 27 July 1945, DHist 181.003 (D5089); Tiger Force administrative plan, 30 July 1945, DHist 181.009 (D3366)

65 Report of Lloyd to Chiefs of Staff Committee, 6 Aug. 1945, PRO, Air 8/1286; Ehrman, *Grand Strategy*, VI, 310–13

CHAPTER 5: ESTABLISHING A PRESENCE

1 Guilio Douhet, *Il Dominio Dell' Aria* (1921), translated as *The Command of the Air* (Washington 1983); J.F.C. Fuller, *The Reformation of War* (London

1923); B.H. Liddell Hart, *Paris, or the Future of War* (London 1925); Basil Collier, *The Defence of the United Kingdom* (London 1957), 13–15

2 Sir John Slessor, *The Central Blue* (London 1956), chart opposite 184

3 N.H. Gibbs, *Grand Strategy* (London 1976), I, 596

4 Collier, *Defence of the United Kingdom*, 38; Meeting of 23 July 1937, PRO Cab 16/181; 'Quarterly Report for Period 1-8-37 to 1-1-38,' DHist 75/360

5 John Terraine, *The Right of the Line: The Royal Air Force in the European War* (London 1985), 18

6 'Fighter Command Attacks – 1938,' 10–14, PRO Air 16/51

7 M. Spick, *Fighter Pilot Tactics: The Techniques of Daylight Air Combat* (Cambridge 1983)

8 Douglas to Slessor, 23 March 1938, PRO Air 2/2948

9 Canada, House of Commons, *Debates*, 1939, III, 3237–63

10 C.P. Stacey, *The Military Problems of Canada* (Toronto 1940), 6; *Debates*, 1939, III, 3248; No 1 Squadron Permanent Reference File (PRF), DHist; No 1 Squadron ORB, Feb. 1939, DHist

11 *Debates*, 1939, III, 3247; SAO to minister, 2 Dec. 1938, McGill Papers, DHist 74/628, file A4

12 *Debates*, 1939, III, 3260; DND, *Militia Reports*, 1938 and 1939; 'Record of Cds in RAF-Offrs & ORS,' DHist 181.005 (D270)

13 Collier, *Defence of the United Kingdom*, 72

14 Prime minister to UK high commissioner, 12 Sept. 1939, *Documents on Canadian External Relations (DCER)* (Ottawa 1975), VII, pt 1, 855

15 Dominions Office to UK high commissioner, 17 Sept. 1939, PRO Air 2/3157; Skelton to Campbell, 29 Sept. 1939, *DCER*, VII, pt 1, 857–8

16 Undersecretary of state for external affairs to UK high commissioner, 14 Oct. 1939, *DCER*, VII, pt 1, 860–1; UK high commissioner to Air Council, 16 Oct. 1939, PRO Air 2/3157

17 Campbell to Skelton, 29 Sept. 1939, *DCER*, VII, pt 1, 859; undersecretary of state for external affairs to UK high commissioner, 14 Oct. 1939, *DCER*, VII, pt 1, 860–1; Air Council to UK high commissioner, 27 Oct. 1939, PRO Air 2/3157

18 Hugh Halliday, *242 Squadron, the Canadian Years* (Belleville 1981)

19 Brian Bond, *British Military Policy between the Two World Wars* (Oxford 1980); Malcolm Smith, *British Air Strategy between the Wars* (Oxford 1984); Lee Kennet, *The First Air War, 1914–1918* (New York 1991), 221

20 'Army Co-operaton: Meetings and Memoranda (1939–1940),' PRO Air 9/137; Air Policy: Co-operation between the Army and the RAF (Dec. 1939–June 1940),' PRO WO 106/1596. We are grateful to David I. Hall for these references.

21 'Notes for CAS,' 12 Sept. 1939, DHist 77/743

22 'Liaison Notes,' 24 Nov. 1939, DHist 181.009 (D580). This incomplete unsigned paper appears to be a draft of stenographic notes of the meeting.

23 W.D. Van Vliet personnel file, National Personnel Record Centre, National Archives of Canada (NPRC)

24 McNaughton to Walsh, 8 May 1940, DHist 181.009 (D4791)

25 W.A.B. Douglas, *The Creation of a National Air Force* (Toronto 1986), 207–19; 'Meeting on Air Questions ... on May 6th, 1940,' DHist 181.009 (D4791)

26 C. Carling-Kelly, 'Never a Shot in Anger,' 27, DHist 73/1417

27 Ibid., 44, passim

28 Ibid., 45, 49

29 RCAF Overseas HQ diary, 7 Sept. 1940, DHist

30 Caldecote to Massey, 19 May 1940, RCAF Overseas daily diary, DHist

31 External to dominion, 21 May 1940, RCAF Overseas HQ daily diary, app. C, DHist; No 402 Squadron ORB, June 1940–March 1941, DHist

32 J.R.M. Butler, *Grand Strategy,* II: *September 1939–June 1940* (London 1957), 290; DO(40) 39th Meeting, 31 Oct. 1940, PRO CAB 69/1, quoted in F.H. Hinsley et al., *British Intelligence in the Second World War,* I (New York 1979), 190; Martin Gilbert, *Finest Hour: Winston S. Churchill, 1939–1941* (London 1983), 878; C.P. Stacey, *Six Years of War* (Ottawa 1955), 86, 294–7

33 M.M. Postan, *British War Production* (London 1952), 116; D. Wood and D. Dempster, *The Narrow Margin* (London 1961), 461, 470

34 'Hitler's Reichstag speech of July 19, 1940,' quoted in H.A. Jacobsen and A.L. Smith, *World War II Policy and Strategy* (Santa Barbara nd), 84–5

35 Karl Klee, 'The Battle of Britain,' H.A. Jacobsen and J. Rohwer, eds., *Decisive Battles of World War II: The German View* (London 1965), 80

36 H. Probert and S. Cox, eds., *The Battle Re-thought: A Symposium on the Battle of Britain* (Shrewsbury 1991), 24

37 No 11 Group, 'Operations over France, May–June, 1940,' 6, PRO Air 16/352

38 Tactical Memorandum No 8, PRO Air 16/334; Hugh Dundas, *Flying Start: A Fighter Pilot's War Years* (New York 1989), 63

39 Wood and Dempster, *The Narrow Margin*, 209; E.B. Morgan and E. Shacklady, *Spitfire: The History* (Stamford 1987), 54, 56; R. Hough and D. Richards, *The Battle of Britain: The Jubilee History* (London 1989), 387

40 Air Ministry, Air Historical Branch (AHB), *The Rise and Fall of the German Air Force* (London 1983), 80

41 Gottfried Leske, *I Was a Nazi Flier,* ed. Curt Reiss (New York 1941), 149–52

42 Cajus Becker, *The Luftwaffe War Diaries,* trans. Frank Ziegler (New York 1968), 147; Wood and Dempster, *The Narrow Margin*, 285

43 Becker, *The Luftwaffe War Diaries*, 154–5; Wood and Dempster, *The Narrow Margin*, 298-303; Collier, *Defence of the United Kingdom*, 200n

44 Winston Ramsey, ed., *The Battle of Britain Then and Now* (London 1982), 571–5, 581–90; AHB, *The Rise and Fall of the German Air Force, 1933–1945*, 81; Collier, *Defence of the United Kingdom*, 453–9, 472–4; No 1 Squadron ORB, 17 Aug. 1940, DHist

45 Massey to Eden, 11 May 1940, PRO Air 2/3157; Canadian high commissioner to secretary of state for external affairs, 19 May 1940, *DCER*, VII, pt 1, 872–3

46 Secretary of state for external affairs to Canadian high commissioner, 21 May 1940, *DCER*, VII, pt 1, 874; No 1 Squadron ORB, 22 May and 8 June 1940, DHist

47 McGregor biog. file, DHist
48 S.F. Wise, *Canadian Airmen and the First World War* (Ottawa 1980); No 1 Squadron ORB, 25 June 1940, DHist
49 'Flying Training Syllabus,' DHist 181.009 (D1933)
50 Walsh to AOC-in-C Fighter Command, 13 July 1940, DHist 181.009 (D1933)
51 Park to Walsh, 15 July 1940, DHist 181.009 (D1933)
52 Walsh to Park, 19 July 1940, DHist 181.009 (D1933)
53 AOC-in-C No 11 Group to AOC RCAF in Great Britain, 22 July 1940, DHist 181.009 (D1933)
54 S/Ldr R.H. Foss to SASO, RCAF Overseas Headquarters, 24 July 1940, DHist 181.009 (D1933); AOC-in-C RCAF Overseas to AOC-in-C Fighter Command, 25 July 1940, and AOC 11 Group to AOC-in-C RCAF Overseas, 3 Aug. 1940, DHist 181.009 (D 1933)
55 Foss to SASO, OSHQ, 9 Aug. 1940, OSHQ ORB, Aug. 1940, app. B, DHist
56 No 1 Squadron ORB, 11 and 15 Aug. 1940, DHist
57 Leske, *I Was a Nazi Flier*, 131–4
58 Richard Collier, *Eagle Day: The Battle of Britain* (London 1981), 128
59 No 1 Squadron ORB, 24 Aug. 1940, DHist
60 Ibid., 26 and 27 Aug. 1940
61 Ibid., 30 Aug. 1940
62 Ibid., Sept. 1940
63 No 1 Squadron ORB, 3 Sept. 1940, DHist
64 *Nottingham Evening Post*, 12 Sept. 1940, DHist 181.009 (D509)
65 Intelligence Report, No 401 Squadron ORB, 4 Sept. 1940, DHist
66 Wood and Dempster, *The Narrow Margin*, 332–3; Williamson Murray, *Luftwaffe* (Baltimore 1985), 53
67 Minute, Heakes to P/DDO, 9 July 1940, DHist 181.009 (D768), 23; Account of interview with A/C G.V. Walsh, 23 April 1959, No 401 Squadron PRF, DHist
68 Account of interview with A/C G.V. Walsh, 23 April 1959
69 Ibid.; Walsh to secretary DND, 3 Aug. 1940, DHist 181.009 (D4791); CAS RCAF to Roycanairf, 17 Aug. 1940; No 1 Squadron ORB, 30 Aug. 1940, DHist; DHist 181.009 (D1933)
70 Murray, *Luftwaffe*, 54–7; Telford Taylor, *The Breaking Wave* (London 1967), 152–3
71 Matthew Cooper, *The German Air Force, 1933–1945* (London 1981); Albert Kesselring, *The Memoirs of Field-Marshal Kesselring,* (trans. Lynton Hudson) (London 1953), 76
72 Becker, *The Luftwaffe War Diaries*, 172
73 Ibid., 171–2; Murray, *Luftwaffe*, 54; Kesselring, *Memoirs*, 76
74 No 1 Squadron ORB, 7 Sept. 1940, DHist; RCAF Overseas headquarters diary, 7 Sept. 1940, DHist
75 No 1 Squadron ORB, 7 Sept. 1940, DHist; McNab combat report, 7 Sept. 1940, DHist 181.003 (D4711)
76 Wood and Dempster, *The Narrow Margin*, 336
77 Johannes Steinhoff, *Messerschmitts over Sicily* (Baltimore 1987), 88–9

78 Intelligence report, No 1 Squadron ORB, 9 Sept. 1940, DHist
79 Adolf Galland, *The First and the Last* (London 1955), 73
80 Leske, *I Was a Nazi Flier*, 218–19
81 No 1 Squadron ORB, 11 Sept. 1940, DHist
82 AHB, *The Rise and Fall of the German Air Force*, 85; Intelligence report, No 1 Squadron ORB, 15 Sept. 1940, DHist
83 Ramsey, ed., *The Battle of Britain Then and Now*, 707
84 No 1 Squadron ORB, 15 Sept. 1940, DHist; Collier, *Eagle Day*, 205–6
85 *Rockcliffe Air Review*, May 1941
86 Intelligence report, No 1 Squadron ORB, 18 Sept. 1940, DHist
87 Ibid.
88 Sholto Douglas, *Years of Command* (London 1966), 85–6
89 Ibid.
90 No 1 Squadron ORB, 21 Sept. 1940, DHist
91 Quoted in J.E. Johnson, *The Story of Air Fighting* (London 1985), 111
92 Alfred Price, *World War II Fighter Conflict* (London 1975), 139
93 Operation of Fighter Forces by Day, PRO Air 16/933
94 Tactical Memorandum No. 9, PRO Air 16/334
95 No 1 Squadron ORB, 27 Sept. 1940, DHist
96 Intelligence report, No 1 Squadron ORB, 27 Sept. 1940, DHist
97 No 1 Squadron ORB, 28 Sept., 1 and 2 Oct. 1940, DHist
98 Ibid., 2–5 Oct. 1940
99 Nodwell to PMO, OSHQ, 7 Oct. 1940, No 1 Squadron ORB, DHist
100 No 1 Squadron ORB, 8–10 Oct. 1940, DHist; ibid., 8 Oct.–2 Nov. 1940
101 Ibid., 9 Dec. 1940
102 Ibid., Jan.-Feb. 1941
103 Ibid., March-April 1941

CHAPTER 6: TURNING TO THE OFFENSIVE

1 J.E. Johnson, *Wing Leader* (Toronto 1956), 80
2 AHB, 'The Air Defence of Great Britain,' V, 90–1, DHist 88/49
3 Ibid., IV, 115, PRO Air 14/18
4 'Report, Air Officer Commanding-in-Chief Fighter Command, November 1940–December 1941,' 21 [hereafter 'Report, AOC-in-C'], PRO Air 16/846; Peirse to Portal, 12-13 Feb. 1941, Portal Papers, DHist 87/89, folder 9 (1941)
5 SASO to AOC-in-C, 27 April 1941, PRO Air 16/903
6 Dundas, *Flying Start*, 63
7 Ibid., 63–6; 'Report, AOC-in-C,' 32, PRO Air 16/486
8 Morgan and Shacklady, *Spitfire*, 144
9 No 402 Squadron ORB, 15 April 1941, DHist
10 SASO to AOC-in-C, 27 April 1941, PRO Air 16/903
11 Wing Cdr (Tactics) to AOC-in-C, SASO and G/C Ops, 7 March 1941, PRO Air 16/373
12 'Report, AOC-in-C Fighter Command,' 22, PRO Air 16/846

13 Hinsley et al., *British Intelligence in the Second World War*, I, 473; 'Report, AOC-in-C,' 22, PRO Air 16/846

14 'Report, AOC-in-C, Fighter Command,' PRO Air 16/846

15 Owen Thetford, *Aircraft of the Royal Air Force since 1918* (New York 1968), 92

16 Martin Middlebrook and Lewis Everett, *The Bomber Command War Diaries: An Operational Reference Book, 1939–1945* (New York 1985), 191

17 'Report, AOC-in-C,' PRO Air 16/846

18 McGregor biog. file, DHist

19 No 401 Squadron ORB, 3 July 1941, DHist; No 401 Squadron ORB, 5 July 1941, DHist; H.C. Godefroy, *Lucky Thirteen* (Stittsville 1983), 71

20 SASO to AOC-in-C, 27 July 1941, PRO Air 16/369

21 J.A. Kent, *One of the Few* (London 1971), 165–6

22 Douglas to VCAS, 29 Aug. 1941, PRO Air 16/373

23 'Canadianization of RCAF Sqns O/S ...' DHist 181.003 (D3596)

24 No 411 Squadron ORB, June–Sept. 1941, DHist

25 Ibid., 11 and 14 Sept. 1941, DHist

26 McNair biog. file, DHist

27 No 411 Sqn ORB, 16 June–7 Nov. 1941, DHist; No 411 Squadron Narrative History, DHist 74/316, 5; No 411 Squadron ORB, 12 Dec. 1941, DHist

28 No 411 Squadron ORB, 16 Dec. 1941, DHist

29 No 412 Squadron ORB, 30 June–5 Oct. 1941, DHist

30 Douglas to undersecretary of state [for Air], 17 July 1942, PRO Air 19/286

31 H.A. Halliday, 'Canadians in the Battle of Britain,' *CAHS Journal* (winter 1973): 114; J.D. Morrison personnel record, NPRC; J.D. Morrison biog. file, DHist

32 Quoted in Alfred Price, *The Spitfire Story* (London 1982) 143

33 Intelligence Report, Biggin Hill Wing, 27 Oct. 1941, DHist 181.003 (D4711); No 401 Squadron ORB, 27 Oct., 8 and 22 Nov. 1941, DHist

34 'Report, AOC-in-C,' PRO Air 16/846

35 'Report, AOC-in-C,' app. K, PRO Air 16/846; Collier, *The Defence of the United Kingdom*, 294

36 Combat reports, DHist 73/847; Casualty lists, DHist 90/19

37 'Report, AOC-in-C,' PRO Air 16/846; Wise, *Canadian Airmen and the First World War*, chs. 13 and 14

38 'Report, AOC-in-C,' PRO Air 16/846; Terraine, *The Right of the Line*, 285; 'Memorandum by AOC 11 Group on the Results of "Circus" Operations ...' PRO Air 16/745

39 See Douglas, *The Creation of a National Air Force*, ch. 11, for an account; Lord Tedder, *With Prejudice* (London 1966), 238

40 A/V/M Hollinghurst to director of plans, Air Ministry, 11 Feb. 1942, PRO Air 2/5354; Internal Air Ministry memorandum, 4 July 1941, PRO Air 20/2978; SASO Fighter Command to Air Ministry, 21 Nov. 1941, PRO Air 2/5354; 'Minutes of the War Committee of the Cabinet,' 26 March 1942, DHist 83/345

41 Malfroy to HQs 10 and 14 groups, 14 March 1942, DHist 181.005 (D1564); No 417 Squadron ORB, 13 April 1942, DHist

42 John Deane Potter, *Fiasco: The Breakout of the German Battleships* (New York 1970), 113–22; 'The Channel Breakthrough, 1942,' Adolph Galland's lecture at the Canadian War Museum, 1975, DHist 75/301

43 'No 11 Group report on the Gneisenau and Sharnhorst operation, 14/2/42' [hereafter '11 Group report'], app. B, PRO Air 16/738; No 411 Squadron ORB, 12 Feb. 1942

44 Potter, *Fiasco*, 109, 112; '11 Group report,' app. B, PRO Air 16/738; No 401 Squadron ORB, 12 Feb. 1942, DHist

45 '11 Group report,' app. B, PRO Air 16/738

46 No 403 Squadron ORB, 12 Feb. 1942, DHist; No 403 Squadron Narrative, DHist 74/303; '11 Group Report,' 7 and app. B, PRO Air 16/738; Report of the Board of Enquiry, 14, PRO Air 16/403; 'The Channel Breakthrough, 1942,' Adolf Galland's lecture, DHist 75/301; Potter, *Fiasco*, ch. 13

47 'Extract from Conclusion of Chiefs of Staff Meeting,' PRO Air 16/548, 4A; Fighter Command, 'Appreciation on Methods of Causing by Air Action the Greatest Possible Wastage of the German Air Force in the West' (hereafter Fighter Command, 'GAF Wastage'), 18 April 1942, PRO Air 16/548

48 Murray, *Luftwaffe*, 137; AHB, 'The Air Defence of Great Britain,' vol. V, 102–4, DHist 88/49; Fighter Command, 'GAF Wastage,' 18 April 1942, PRO Air 16/548

49 *Jane's All the World's Aircraft* (1943), 55c, 93c, 107c; Fighter Command, 'GAF Wastage,' 18 April 1942, PRO Air 16/548

50 Ibid.

51 Fighter Command, '"Super Circus" Operations,' 24 April 1942, PRO Air 16/548, 38B; quoted in Martin Gilbert, *Road to Victory* (Toronto 1986), 71; Peter Wykeham, *Fighter Command* (London 1960), 224–5; Fighter Command, 'Large Scale Offensive Operations March to April 1942,' PRO Air 16/548; AHB, 'The Air Defence of Great Britain,' V, 109 and 114, DHist 88/49; Casualty lists, DHist 90/19; Combat reports, DHist 73/847

52 Alan C. Deere, *Nine Lives* (London 1969), 216–18; No 403 Squadron ORB, 2 June 1942, DHist

53 Deere, *Nine Lives*, 222; No 403 Squadron ORB, 2 June 1942, DHist; No 403 Squadron Narrative History, DHist 74/303

54 ACAS (Ops) to AOC-in-C, 13 June 1942, PRO Air 16/538

55 Ibid.; AOC-in-C to Nos 10, 11, and 12 groups, 17 June 1942, PRO Air 16/538

56 Director of Intelligence (O), 'GAF Fighter Reserves,' 6 July 1942, PRO Air 16/538, 90B; we are grateful to Professor John Campbell of McMaster University for establishing this connection for us; AHB, 'The Air Defence of Great Britain,' V, app. 10, DHist 88/49; AOC-in-C to Leigh-Mallory, 10 July 1942, PRO Air 16/538

57 C.F. Rawnsley and Robert Wright, *Night Fighter* (London 1957), 61; 'Night Interceptions,' 5 Feb. 1941 and 19 June 1941, PRO Air 16/524; C.H. Barnes, *Bristol Aircraft since 1910* (London 1964), 290–307; J.R. Smith and A.L. Ray, *German Aircraft of the Second World War* (London 1972), 418; M.M Postan, D. Hay, and J.D. Scott, *Design and Development of Weapons* (London 1964),

387–8; K.E.B. Jay and J.D. Scott, 'History of the Development of Radio and Radar,' 173–4, part II, PRO Cab 102/641

58 No 401 Squadron ORB, May and June 1941; Samuel Kostenuk and John Griffin, *RCAF Squadron Histories and Aircraft 1924–1968* (Toronto 1977), 91–2, 95–7; C.P. Stacey, *Arms, Men and Governments* (Ottawa 1970), 269–70; 'A Statistical Return on Canadianization of RCAF Sqns,' DHist 181.003 (D3596)

59 Combat Reports, DHist 73/847

60 No 406 Squadron ORB, 20 Oct. 1941, DHist; No 409 Squadron ORB, 1/2 Nov. 1941, DHist; No 410 Squadron ORB, 1/2 Nov. 1941, DHist

61 The fatal accidents took place on 8 July and 30 August (410 Squadron ORB), 2 Sept., 11 Oct. 1941, 19 Jan., 28 Feb., and 27 March 1942 (409 Squadron ORB), and 14 Sept. 1941 and 8 Jan. 1942 (406 Squadron ORB); P.Y. Davoud biog. file, DHist

62 Exeter had neither a balloon barrage nor anti-aircraft defences. Collier, *The Defence of the United Kingdom*, 305, 306; AHB, 'The Air Defence of Great Britain,' V, 49, DHist 88/49; No 406 Squadron ORB, 28–29 April 1942, app. V, DHist

63 AHB, 'The Air Defence of Great Britain,' V, 53, DHist 88/49

64 'Provision of an Army Cooperation Squadron for Canadian Armoured Divison,' 21 May 1941, DHist 181.009 (D4790)

65 P.M. Bowers, *Curtiss Aircraft 1907–1947* (Annapolis 1979), 474

66 DHist 181.009 (D283), vol. 1

67 S/L Foss to AOC, 1 July 1941, DHist 181.009 (D4791)

68 Supplement to Report No. C 13, 'RCAF Personnel in Britain: No 400 Squadron, Odiham,' DHist 181.009 (D283), vol. 4

69 Supplement to Report No. C 13, 'RCAF Personnel in Britain: No 400 Squadron, Odiham,' DHist 181.009 (D283), vol. 3, 70; No 400 Squadron ORB, 19 Oct. 1941, DHist

70 Supplement to Report No. C 13, 'RCAF Personnel in Britain: No 400 Squadron, Odiham,' DHist 181.009 (D283), vol. 4

71 Ibid.

72 Charles Carrington, *Soldier at Bomber Command* (London 1987), 82; DMC Air Ministry to Air Vice-Marshal Edwards, 13 May 1942, DHist 181.003 (D1171); 'Co-operation between the Army and Royal Air Force,' nd, McNaughton Papers, file 1-3-7, NA, MG 30, E 133

73 Brian Bond, ed., *Chief of Staff* (London 1974), II, 19–20

74 Carrington, *Soldier at Bomber Command,* 83

75 A/GOC Canadian Corps to AOC RCAF in Great Britain, 21 Nov. 1941, DHist 181.009 (D4791); No 400 Squadron ORB, 13 Dec. 1941, DHist; General McNaughton to Colonel Ralston, 5 May 1942, DHist 181.003 (D1155); A/C Stevenson to C-in-C, Army Cooperation Command, 17 Nov. 1941, DHist 181.009 (D4791)

76 John Swettenham, *McNaughton,* II: *1939–1943* (Toronto 1969), 201–11

77 McNaughton to Portal, 10 May 1942, Nye to McNaughton, 8 May 1942, 'Loose Minute,' DMC to PS to CAS, 12 Aug. 1942, PRO Air 8/664; 'A Meeting held at RCAF HQ, London, at 2100 hrs, 22 June 1942, to discuss … the

formation of the Cdn Air Component Overseas,' 25 June 1942, DHist 181.003 (D1155); Price, *World War II Fighter Conflict*, 108–9

78 Fighter Command Tactical Memorandum No 29, 16 March 1943, PRO Air 14/206

79 Hollinghurst to Edwards, 16 Feb. 1942, DHist 181.002 (D266)

80 No. 402 Squadron, General Report, Roadstead II, 16 Feb. 1942, DHist 74/623

81 It appears that the pilot declined to press his attack, dropping his bombs from 1500 feet but not using his machine guns. He was posted a short time later. No 402 Squadron Progress Report, 27 Feb. to 11 March 1942, DHist 77/229; German Naval Staff Operations War Diary, 17 Feb. 1942, DHist SGR II 261

82 Hollinghurst to Edwards, 16 Feb. 1942, DHist 181.002 (D266); Director of Organization, 'Replacement and Re-Equipment of Squadrons in Fighter Command,' nd, DHist 181.002 (D266); Squadron Leader E. Morrow to Edwards, 3 March 1941 [sic], DHist 181.002 (D266)

83 Barratt to Carr, Headquarters, Eastern Command, 13 March 1942, PRO Air 39/129; G.1 (L), 'A Summary of Recent Exercises within Fighter Command, Aug 1942,' PRO Air 16/776

84 AOC-in-C Fighter Command to groups, 24 Jan. 1942, PRO Air 16/776

85 Ibid.

86 'GHQ Directive on Training in Co-operation with the RAF,' 30 April 1942, PRO Air 16/552

87 'A Summary of Recent Exercises ... Fighter Command,' Aug. 1942, PRO Air 16/776; Carrington, *Soldier at Bomber Command*, 105. In the middle of Dryshod its director, General Montgomery, left to assume command of 8th Army in North Africa.

CHAPTER 7: THE TURN OF THE TIDE

1 Gilbert, *Road to Victory*, 73

2 'CoS Committee meeting No 112, 9 Apr 1942,' PRO Cab 79/56; J.R.M. Butler, *Grand Strategy* (London 1964), III, Pt II, esp. ch. 24

3 Stacey, *Six Years Of War*, chs 10–12; B.L. Villa, *Unauthorized Action* (Toronto 1989). See also Ronald Atkin, *Dieppe 1942: The Jubilee Disaster* (London 1980).

4 Kriegstagbuch, 1 Skl, Teil A, 1 Aug. 1942, US National Archives, T 1022/1674

5 Kriegstagbuch, 1 Skl, Teil A, 4 Sept. 1942, US National Archives, T 1022/1674. (We are indebted to Professor John Campbell of McMaster University for these two references.)

6 'The Dieppe Raid (Combined Report),' 30, DHist 72/502; 'Rutter – Notes for CAS,' 2 July 1942, PRO Air 8/895

7 Price, *The Spitfire Story*, 153

8 'Dieppe Raid (Combined Report),' 149, DHist 72/502

9 'Detailed Chronological Air Narrative – Operation Jubilee,' PRO Air 25/204; RCAF Decorations file, DHist; 'Report of German Commander-in-Chief West,'

4, DHist 594.019 (D8); 302nd Inf Div Report, Pt II (D) and 81st Corps Combat Report, Pt III, DHist

10 'Dieppe Raid (Combined Report),' 22–3, DHist 72/502; 'Combined Operation against Dieppe, Record of Events,' 3A, PRO Air 16/765; DDMC, 'Army Air Support and Tactical Reconnaissance during Operation "Jubilee"', 24 Oct. 1942, PRO Air 39/19

11 'Dieppe Raid (Combined Report),' annex 10, DHist 72/502

12 Carrington, *Soldier at Bomber Command*, 104

13 No 403 Squadron Narrative History, 37, DHist 74/303; 'Short Report on Air Operations Connected with "Jubilee"', PRO Air 8/883; 'Report by the Air Force Commander on the Combined Operation against Dieppe – August 19th, 1942,' PRO Air 37/199

14 No 411 Squadron ORB, 19 Aug. 1942, DHist

15 'Report by J.M. Godfrey,' 20 Aug. 1942, Godfrey biog. file, DHist

16 Ibid.

17 Ibid.

18 Ibid.

19 Ibid.

20 No 412 Squadron ORB, 19 Aug. 1942, DHist

21 Chadburn biog. file, DHist

22 No 416 Squadron ORB, 20 Aug. 1942, DHist

23 'Dieppe Raid (Combined Report),' DHist 72/502; DDMC, 'Army Air Support and Tactical Reconnaissance during Operation "Jubilee"', 24 Oct. 1942, PRO Air 39/19; DDMC, 'Army Air Support and Tactical Reconnaissance during Operation "Jubilee"', 24 Oct. 1942, PRO Air 39/19

24 No 414 Squadron to No 35 Wing RAF, 22 Aug. 1942, PRO Air 37/351

25 No 414 Squadron ORB, 19 Aug. 1942, DHist; Wallace Reyburn, *Rehearsal for Invasion* (London 1942), 115

26 Carrington, *Soldier at Bomber Command*, 104–5

27 Ibid., 105

28 Ibid., 104–5

29 F/L Kidd, 'Combined Operations against Dieppe, Record of Events, 18th August 1942 to 20th August 1942,' PRO Air 16/765

30 Report of the German C-in-C West ... 3 Sept. 1942, DHist 592.011 (D3)

31 'Dieppe Raid (Combined Report),' DHist 72/502; 'Operation Jubilee, Questionnaire for Air Force Commander,' and 'Answers to Questionnaire,' 12 Sept. 1942, PRO Air 16/765

32 'Operation Jubilee, Questionnaire for Air Force Commander,' and 'Answers to Questionnaire,' 12 Sept. 1942, PRO Air 16/765

33 'Short Report on Air Operations Connected with "Jubilee,"' 20 Aug. 1942, PRO Air 20/5186; N.R.L. Franks, *The Greatest Air Battle* (London 1979), 190–3. Franks gives slightly different RAF/RCAF losses from those listed in PRO Air 20/5186 as cited above.

34 Nos 400, 401, 402, 403, 411, 412, 414, and 416 Sqn ORBs, 19 Aug. 1942, DHist

35 'Short Report on Air Operations Connected with "Jubilee,"' PRO Air 20/5186; AHB, 'The Air Defence of Great Britain,' VI, 124, DHist 88/49

36 Murray, *Luftwaffe*, table 22, 104

37 'HQ Fighter Command to HQ 10, 11, and 12 Groups,' 17 March 1942, PRO Air 16/538

38 HQ Fighter Command to 10, 11, 83, and 84 Groups, 1 Aug. 1943, PRO Air 16/705

39 Quoted in Tedder, *With Prejudice*, 360

40 Swettenham, *McNaughton*, II, 94

41 Edwards to undersecretary of state, Air Ministry (DMC), 22 Aug. 1942, DHist 181.003 (D1171); Edwards, 'Order of Detail No. 29,' 5 Sept. 1942, DHist 181.003 (D1155); Van Vliet for CAS, 'Secret Organization Order No. 97,' 14 Sept. 1942, DHist 181.003 (D1155)

42 HQ First Cdn Army, 'Employment of Canadian AC Squadrons,' 11 Nov. 1942, DHist 181.009 (D94); 'Memorandum of Conversation between Lieutenant-General A.G.L. McNaughton, AVM M. Henderson and AVM H.W.L. Saunders,' 18 Nov. 1942, DHist 181.009 (D4919); Order of Battle No 11, 12 Nov. 1942, War Diaries, First Canadian Army, NA, RG 24, vol. 13; C.R. Stein, BGS, 'Employment of Canadian AC Squadrons,' 29 Nov. 1942, DHist 181.003 (D1184)

43 Smith to HQ RCAF OS, 6 Oct. 1942, DHist 181.003 (D1183); Overseas Headquarters, ORB, 1 Jan. 1943, DHist

44 'Report by Minister of National Defence for Air: Visit to United Kingdom,' 10 Aug. 1942–4 September 1942, DHist 79/429

45 Denis Richards and Hilary St George Saunders, *Royal Air Force 1939–1945* (London 1954), II, 145

46 Johnson, *Wing Leader*, 137–8

47 Wesley Frank Craven and James Lea Cate, *The Army Air Forces in World War II* (Chicago 1949), II, 217–19

48 Secret Narrative, Day Fighters, Sept. 1942–Feb. 1943, DHist 73/829

49 Ibid.

50 Ian V. Hogg, *Anti-Aircraft* (London 1978), app. 5; AHB, *The Rise and Fall of the German Air Force* 204; Harold Faber, ed., *Luftwaffe* (London 1979), 148

51 Secret Narrative, Day Fighters, Sept. 1942–Feb. 1943, DHist 73/829

52 J.C. Fee biog. file, DHist

53 'Air Aspect of G.H.Q. Exercise Spartan,' DHist 181.002 (D73); Secret Narrative, Army Cooperation, March–May 1943, DHist 73/832

54 Secret Narrative, Day Fighters, March 1943, DHist 73/829; No 83 Group ORB, 1 April to 4 July 1943, PRO Air 25/698

55 Leigh-Mallory to 9, 10, 11, 12, 13, 14, and 83 groups, 21 April 1943, PRO Air 16/538

56 'Offensive Operations by Home Based Fighters,' Nov. 1942, 'Offensive Operations by Home Based Fighters,' 14 May 1943, PRO Air 16/933

57 No 417 Squadron ORB, 3 July 1943, DHist

58 Pitcher to Greenhous, 7 Dec. 1987, Pitcher biog. file, DHist

59 Massey to Attlee, 8 Dec. 1942, PRO Air 2/5354; External Affairs to Massey, telegram 2242, 4 Dec. 1942, *DCER*, IX, 367–8

60 Portal to Tedder, 28 Dec. 1942, Tedder to Portal, 30 and 31 Dec. 1942, PRO Air 20/2978

61 No 417 Squadron ORB, 13 Sept. 1942, DHist; quoted in Christopher Shores and Hans Ring, *Fighters over the Desert* (New York 1969), 229

62 No 417 Squadron ORB, 26 Sept. and 16 Nov. 1942, DHist

63 Ibid., 1 and 13 Jan. 1943, DHist

64 Ibid., March 1943, and app., 22 March 1943, DHist

65 Ibid., 11, 19 April 1943, DHist

66 Ibid., appendix, 19 April 1943, DHist

67 Ibid., 6 May 1943, DHist

68 Foster to Patterson, 17 March 1943, DHist 181.009 (D1386)

69 P.L.I. Archer biog. file, DHist

70 Foster to RAF HQ Middle East, 30 and 31 March 1943, DHist 181.009 (D1386); No 417 Squadron ORB, 11, 25 June 1943, DHist

71 Patterson to Edwards, 16 July 1943, DHist 181.009 (D1386); ROYCANAIRF to Patterson, received 19 June 1943, DHist 181.009 (D1386); P.S. Turner biog. file, DHist.

72 Street to Distribution List, 16 May 1943, PRO Air 37/226; Secret Narrative, Army Co-operation, June 1943, DHist 73/832

73 WO (D.Air) to Air Ministry (DMC), 29 Dec. 42, PRO Air 2/7412

74 R.P. Pakenham-Walsh, *History of the Corps of Royal Engineers* (Chatham 1958), IX, 373–4

75 Sir Arthur S. Barratt, 'The Creation of an Air Expeditionary Force,' PRO Air 37/226

76 NATO Military Agency for Standardization, 'Air Superiority,' *NATO Glossary of Terms and Definitions* (1986)

77 Edwards to secretary of state for air, 13 Feb. 1943, DHist 181.009 (D719); 'Memorandum of a Conversation Lt-Gen McNaughton–G/C Smith,' 18 March 1943, NA, War Diary, March 1943, app. L, McNaughton Papers, MG 30, E133, vol. 249

78 D Policy to ACAS (P), 3 May 1943, PRO Air 20/4579

79 ACAS (P) to AMSO, 5 May 1943, PRO Air 20/4579

80 VCAS to AMSO, 13 May 1943, PRO Air 20/4579; AMSO to VCAS, 20 May 1943, PRO Air 20/4579

81 'Memorandum of a Conversation General McNaughton–General Paget,' 19 May 43, 'Minutes of Discussion between General A.G.L. McNaughton and AVM W.A. Curtis,' 26 May 1943, PA 1-3-8, McNaughton Papers, vol. 133

82 Howe to Heeney, 10 April 1943, PCO War Committee Memoranda, March–May 1943, NA, Mackenzie King Papers, MG 26, J4, vol. 426; Edwards to Yool, 4 May 1943, DHist 181.009 (D719)

83 Overseas Headquarters ORB, 19 May 43, DHist; 'Memorandum of a

Conference Held at HQ First Cdn Army,' 1 June 1943, PA 1-3-7, McNaughton
Papers, vol. 133

84 VCAS to AMSO, 5 June 1943, PRO Air 20/4579; Breadner to minister, 16 June
1943, PCO War Committee Memoranda, Mackenzie King Papers, vol. 426;
'PCO War Committee Minutes, 18 June 1943,' ibid., vol. 425

85 'Memorandum of Telephone Conversation General McNaughton–AM Edwards,'
19 June 43, PA 1-3-7, McNaughton Papers, vol. 133

86 Ibid.; 'Memorandum on Discussion Regarding Deception Exercises,' 24 June
43, ibid.

87 Secret Narrative, Day-Fighters, July 1943, DHist 73/829; No 430 Squadron
Narrative History, 11, DHist 74/431; Hammond, memorandum, 30 July 1943,
DHist 181.009 (D718); BGS First Canadian Army, 8 July 43, 'Memorandum on
Discussion Regarding Deception Exercises,' 24 June 43, PA 1-3-7,
McNaughton Papers, vol. 133

88 List giving moves of day-fighters within RAF Fighter Command, Sept. 1939 to
mid-1943, DHist 181.005 (D119); Secret Narrative, Day-Fighters, April 1943,
DHist 73/829

89 No 421 Squadron ORB, 28 July 43, DHist

90 'Victories Credited to G/C R.W. McNair, DSO, DFC,' 'Royal Canadian
Air Force Release No 7725, 31 August 1950,' W.R. McNair biog file,
DHist

91 Secret Narrative, Day-Fighters, Aug. 1943, DHist 73/829; numbers derived
from Secret Narrative, Day-Fighters, July 1943, DHist 73/832, and Secret
Narrative, Day-Fighters, Aug. 1943, DHist 73/829; No 411 Squadron Narrative
History, 38, DHist 74/316

92 Murray, *Luftwaffe*, 144, 176–7

93 Johannes Steinhoff, *The Straits of Messina* (London 1971)

94 Ibid., 77

95 No 417 Squadron ORB, 9 July 1943, DHist

96 G.W.L. Nicholson, *The Canadians in Italy* (Ottawa 1956), 75; Steinhoff,
Straits of Messina, 85–90

97 Hedley Everard, *A Mouse in My Pocket* (Picton 1988), 267

98 No 417 Squadron ORB, 16–25 July 1943, DHist

99 Ibid., 24, 26 July 1943

100 Ibid., 11 Aug. 1943

101 Ibid., 13 Aug. 1943; A.U. Houle, unpublished manuscript in the possession of
the author, 213; Carlo D'Este, *Bitter Victory* (London 1988), 499–500

102 D'Este, *Bitter Victory*, 514

103 Thetford, *Aircraft of the Royal Air Force since 1918*, 450–4. The first unit to
receive the Mark VIII's was 145 Squadron, another 244 Wing unit; *Jane's All
the World's Aircraft 1945–46*, 71c; J.R. Smith and Antony Kay, *German
Aircraft of the Second World War* (Norwich 1972), 192–6

104 No 417 Squadron ORB, 21 Aug. 1943, DHist

105 C.P. Stacey, *The Victory Campaign* (Ottawa 1960), 11, 15

106 Carrington, *Soldier at Bomber Command*, 119

107 Sir Frederick Morgan, *Overture to Overlord* (London 1950), 108
108 'Report by the Air Force Commander on Operation "Starkey" 16th August–9th
    Sept.tember 1943,' DHist 73/829

CHAPTER 8: PREPARING FOR D-DAY

 1 L.F. Ellis, *Victory in the West* (London 1962), I, 28
 2 Wykeham, *Fighter Command*, 242
 3 Cooper, *The German Air Force 1933–1945*, 296, 332; Stephen L. McFarland
    and Wesley Phillips Newton, *To Command the Sky* (Washington 1991), 137
 4 Galland, *The First and the Last*, 168
 5 Alfred Price, *Luftwaffe Handbook 1939–1945* (London 1977), 63–4; Douglas,
    The Creation of a National Air Force, 243, 245, 291
 6 W.B. Callaway (SASO) to illegible, 7 Oct. 1943, PRO Air 16/528
 7 Ibid.
 8 AFHQ, Secret Narrative, Fighter Reconnaissance (AFHQ Fighter-Recce
    narrative), Nov. 1943, 7–8, DHist 73/832
 9 Operational Research Section (ORS) Report No 476, PRO Air 37/182
10 Combat Reports, DHist 73/847
11 Quoted in Brian Nolan, *Hero: The Buzz Beurling Story* (Toronto 1981),
    98–9
12 Combat Reports, DHist 73/847; A.R. Mackenzie biog. file, DHist
13 Christopher F. Shores, *2nd Tactical Air Force* (Reading 1970), 3; AFHQ, Day-
    Fighter narrative, Nov. 1943, 3, DHist 73/829
14 Stacey, *Arms, Men, and Governments*, 295–6
15 Portal to Breadner, 25 Aug. 1943, HQC 17-1-4, pt. 2, NA, RG 24, vol.
    5210
16 Douglas, *The Creation of a National Air Force*, 376, 395, 422, 424
17 Fighter Command to D of O, 30 Oct. 1943, PRO Air 37/786; G.G. Truscott
    (DAS), 18 Oct. 1943, DHist 181.009 (D718); 'Decisions Given at a Con-
    ference,' 11 Nov. 1943, PRO Air 37/91; Leigh-Mallory to AMSO, 15 Nov. 1943;
    'Notes of a Meeting,' 24 Nov. 1943, PRO Air 37/91
18 Morris to D of O, 18 Dec. 1943, PRO Air 37/79; Truscott, 4 Jan. 1944, DHist
    181.009 (D718)
19 Truscott to D of O, 15 Jan. 1944, PRO Air 37/79
20 'Memorandum of a Conversation between General McNaughton and General
    Paget, 17 June 1943,' 18 June 1943, PA 1-0-4, McNaughton Papers, vol. 131,
    'Conversation – Lt Gen AGL McNaughton – Lt Gen Sir Archibald Nye, 2
    Sept. 1943,' War Diary, Sept. 1943, app. A, ibid., vol. 250
21 'Memorandum of Discussions with Col Ralston and Lt Gen Stuart,' 10 Nov.
    1943, PA 5-0-3-2, pt. 1, ibid., vol. 167; 'Memorandum of Meeting with CIGS, 1
    November 1943,' War Diary, Nov. 1943, appx B, ibid., vol. 250; Swettenham,
    McNaughton, II, 345; Nigel Hamilton, *Monty, Master of the Battlefield,
    1942–1944* (London 1983), 497–8
22 Truscott, 'Report on Canadian Participation in 83 Group,' DHist 181.003
    (D4738)

23 Ibid.

24 AFHQ, Day-Fighter narrative, Feb. 1944, 2–3, DHist 73/829; AFHQ, Fighter-Recce narrative, Dec. 1943, 1–2, DHist 73/832; Kostenuk and Griffin, *RCAF Squadrons and Aircraft*, 81, 104, 127

25 Coningham to Edmonds, 4 Feb. 1944, PRO Air 37/106

26 ACAS (Ops), to AC-in-C AEAF, 26 Nov. 1943, PRO Air 37/613

27 SASO 2 TAF to 2, 83, and 84 groups, 30 Nov. 1943, PRO Air 37/613; SASO 83 Group to 483 Group Control Centre, 2 Dec. 1943, PRO Air 37/613

28 Norman Longmate, *The Doodlebugs* (London 1981), 51–6

29 D of Ops (AD), 'Report of Panel Appointed by DCAS to Consider Counter-Measures to Enemy Pilotless Aircraft,' 2 Dec. 1943, PRO Air 16/483

30 *German Evaluation of Allied Air Interdiction in World War II* (Fairfax 1969), IV, 8; Hogg, *Anti-Aircraft*, app. 5; AFHQ, Fighter-Recce narrative, Feb. 1944, DHist 73/832

31 J.F Lambert personnel file, NPRC

32 Andrea Schlecht, 'Some Kardex Documents Providing Statistical Information on Canadianization of the RCAF,' DHist 91/116

33 J.F. Lambert, personnel file, NPRC

34 Ibid.

35 No 403 Squadron ORB, unofficial Squadron Diary, 3 Dec. 1943, DHist

36 Conrad biog. file, DHist

37 AFHQ, Fighter-Recce narrative, Nov. 1943, 1, Dec. 1943, 4, DHist 73/832; No 400 Squadron, ORB, Dec. 1943 to Feb. 1944, DHist

38 No 430 Squadron ORB, 5 Feb. 1944, DHist

39 No 430 Squadron narrative history, 26, DHist 74/341

40 Ibid., 24–5

41 No 416 Squadron narrative history, 61, DHist 74/326; Combat Reports, DHist 73/847

42 Healey to D/SASO, 30 Nov. 1943, Leigh-Mallory to ACAS (TR), 17 Dec. 1943, PRO Air 37/798

43 AFHQ, Day-Fighter narrative, March 1944, 3, DHist 73/829; Shores, *2nd Tactical Air Force*, 47

44 AFHQ, Day-Fighter narrative, March 1944, 21–2, DHist 73/829; Christopher Shores and Clive Williams, *Aces High* (London 1966), 193

45 AFHQ, Day-Fighter narrative, March 1944, 22–3, DHist 73/829

46 Ibid., appendix Main HQ to groups, 20 March 1944, DHist 73/829

47 Godefroy, *Lucky Thirteen*, 237

48 OC No 402 Squadron to CO, RCAF Digby, 24 April 1944, DHist 181.009 (D5319); No 402 Squadron ORB, 14 March 1944, DHist; ADGB Training Staff Instruction No 2/44, app. A, 27 March 1944, DHist 181.009 (D5319)

49 AFHQ, Day-Fighter narrative, April 1944, 26–7, DHist 73/829

50 Ibid., 32, DHist 73/829; 'AEAF ORS Report No 16, 10 June 1944,' PRO Air 16/498

51 Cooper, *The German Air Force 1933–1945*, 332; AHB, *The Rise and Fall of the German Air Force*, 316; Heinz Knoke, *I Flew for the Fuhrer* (London 1953), 153

52 Cooper, *The German Air Force 1933–1945*, 332–3; Hajo Herrmann, *Eagle's Wings* (Shrewsbury 1991), 222
53 No 410 Squadron ORB, 15 Aug. 1943, DHist
54 Ibid., 10 Dec 1943
55 Ibid., 13 Feb., 31 May, 6 June 1944
56 Collier, *The Defence of the United Kingdom*, 317–18
57 Ibid., 327; Murray, *Luftwaffe*, 238
58 No 406 Squadron ORB, 19/20 March 1944, DHist; Combat Reports, DHist 73/847; No 406 Squadron ORB, 27/28 March 1944, DHist
59 No 410 Squadron ORB, Combat Report, 3 Feb. 1944, DHist; Combat Reports, DHist 73/847
60 No 410 Squadron ORB, 21 Jan.–19 April 1944, DHist
61 Shores, *2nd Tactical Air Force*, 219
62 Quoted in AFHQ, Day-Fighter narrative, April 1944, 9, DHist 73/829
63 Arthur Bryant, *Triumph in the West*, (London 1959), 178
64 AFHQ, Day-Fighter narrative, April 1944, 23–5, DHist 73/829
65 Ibid., and May 1944, 6, 85–6
66 Stacey, *The Victory Campaign*, 36; AFHQ, Day-Fighter narrative, May 1944, 27–8 and app. E, DHist 73/829
67 AHB, *Air Support* (Air Ministry 1955), 144; numbers derived from ORBs; AFHQ, Secret Narrative, Fighter-Reconnaissance, May 1944, 9, DHist 73/832; Dwight D. Eisenhower, *Crusade in Europe* (New York 1948), 237–8
68 'Extract from Air C-in-C's 15th Conference, nd,' PRO Air 37/636; AFHQ, Secret Narrative, Fighter-Reconnaissance, May 1944, 1–2, DHist 73/832; No 400 Squadron ORB, May 1944, DHist
69 Nicholson, *The Canadians in Italy*, 202–6; C.J.C. Molony, *The Mediterranean and Middle East* (London 1973), V, 239, 242
70 No 417 Squadron ORB, appendix, 2–19 Sept. 1943, DHist
71 Albert Houle, unpublished manuscript, DHist
72 Ibid.
73 No 417 Squadron narrative history, 42, DHist 74/327
74 Molony, *The Mediterranean and Middle East,* V, 473–509; Nicholson, *The Canadians in Italy*, ch. 11
75 No 417 Squadron ORB, 30 Nov. 1943, DHist
76 Ibid., appendix, 3 and 8 Dec. 1943, Jan. 1944; Houle, unpublished manuscript, 241, DHist
77 Winston Churchill, *Closing the Ring* (Boston 1951), 488
78 No 417 Squadron ORB, Jan.–March 1944, DHist
79 Ibid.
80 Ibid., 11, 12, and 28 April 1944
81 Ibid., 7–8, 23 April 1944; Owen Thetford, *Aircraft of the Royal Air Force since 1918* (New York 1968), 454; No 417 Squadron narrative history, 64, DHist 74/327
82 No 417 Squadron ORB, 19, 23–24 April, 19 May 1944, DHist
83 Ibid., appendix, 14 May 1944

84 C.J.C. Molony, *The Mediterranean and Middle East* (London 1984), VI, part 1, 228–9, 232, 251, 274–5

85 George Brown and Michel Lavigne, *Canadian Wing Commanders of Fighter Command in World War II* (Langley 1984), 103–9

86 No 438 Squadron ORB, 8 May 1944, DHist

87 Ibid., appendix, 8 May 1944; Brown and Lavigne, *Canadian Wing Commanders*, 109–11

88 AFHQ, Day-Fighter narrative, May 1944, 85–6, DHist 73/829; No 416 Squadron narrative history, 65, DHist 74/326; No 416 Squadron ORB, 22 May 44, DHist

89 Combat Reports, DHist 73/847

90 Ibid.

91 Price, *World War II Fighter Conflict*, 92–3; Godefroy, *Lucky Thirteen*, 204–41

92 Scott to AOC-in-C RCAF Overseas HQ, 15 May 1944, DHist 181.009 (D718)

93 AFHQ, Day-Fighter narrative, May 1944, 52–3, DHist 73/829

94 Ibid., 58–9, 102–5

95 Ibid., June 1944, 3–4; AFHQ, Secret Narrative, Fighter-Reconnaissance, June 1944, 2, 6, 12, DHist 73/832

96 McFarland and Newton, *To Command the Sky*, 94

97 Robert W. Gruenhagen, *Mustang* (New York 1969), 181–90

98 McFarland and Newton, *To Command the Sky*, 157, 160

99 Galland, *The First and the Last*, 206

100 Murray, *Luftwaffe*, 263; Ellis, *Victory in the West*, I, 567, 28; Galland, *The First and the Last*, 211

101 Hogg, *Anti-Aircraft*, app. 5, 169; Hilary St George Saunders, *Royal Air Force 1939–1945* (London 1954), III, 83

CHAPTER 9: THE NORMANDY CAMPAIGN

1 John Keegan, *Six Armies in Normandy* (London 1982), 14–15

2 AFHQ, Day-Fighter narrative, June 1944, 11, DHist 73/829; No 418 Squadron ORB, 5–6 June 1944, DHist

3 Galland, *The First and the Last*, 213–14; Ellis, *Victory in the West*, I, 72

4 AFHQ, Day-Fighter narrative, June 1944, 12–13, DHist 73/829

5 Ibid., 14; Galland, *The First and the Last*, 213

6 AVM S.C. Strafford, 'A Review of Air Operations Preparatory to and in Support of Operation Neptune,' PRO Air 37/576; No 443 Squadron, Progress Reports, DHist 78/65; AFHQ, Day-Fighter narrative, June 1944, 17, DHist 73/829; 'ADBG Provisional Air Defence Plan for Operation Overlord,' 7 Feb. 1944, PRO Air 16/897; No 441 Squadron narrative history, 38, DHist 74/348

7 No 438 Squadron ORB, 6 June 1944, DHist; No 439 Squadron ORB, 6 June 1944, DHist; No 440 Squadron ORB, 6 June 1944, DHist

8 AFHQ, Day-Fighter narrative, June 1944, 14, DHist 73/829; Shores, *2nd Tactical Air Force*, 55; No 430 Squadron ORB, appendix, 6 June 1944, DHist

9 'Report by Air Marshal Sir Arthur Coningham ... Concerning Operations

Carried Out by Second Tactical Air Force between 6th June 1944 and 9th May 1945,' PRO Air 37/876

10 Cited in Gilbert, *Road to Victory*, 795–6; Ellis, *Victory in the West*, I, 222–3

11 Walter Warlimont, *Inside Hitler's Headquarters, 1939–1945* (New York 1964), 424, 426

12 AFHQ, Day-Fighter narrative, June 1944, 17, DHist 73/829; Combat Reports, DHist 73/847

13 No 414 Squadron narrative history, 64, DHist 74/325; No 5 MFP ORB, July 1944 to May 1945, DHist; No 6 MFP ORB, July 1944 to May 1945, DHist

14 No 414 Squadron narrative history, 59, DHist 74/325

15 AFHQ, Fighter-Recce narrative, June 1944, 6, 12, 73/832; No 414 Squadron narrative history, 60, 71, DHist 74/325; No 430 Squadron narrative history, 38, DHist 74/341

16 Tactical Paper No 4, Sept. 1947, PRO Air 20/6857; AFHQ, Day-Fighter narrative, June 1944, 19, DHist 73/829

17 AFHQ, Day-Fighter narrative, June 1944, 23, DHist 73/829

18 No 441 Squadron narrative history, 31, DHist 74/348; No 414 Squadron narrative history, 62–3, DHist 74/325; No 443 Squadron narrative history, 27, DHist 74/349; AFHQ, Day-Fighter narrative, June 1944, 90–1, DHist 73/829

19 'The Effects of Air Power,' DHist SGR II 264, folder 24

20 'Review of the Night Fighter Force, 4 August 1944,' PRO Air 16/664; No 410 Squadron ORB, June 1944, DHist; No 409 Squadron ORB, June 1944, 26 July 1944, DHist; Naval Staff Historical Section, *Operation 'Neptune' Landings in Normandy, June 1944: Appendices* (1947), 122–3; S.W. Roskill, *The War at Sea 1939–1945* (London 1961), III, part II, 59

21 No 406 Squadron ORB, 14–15 June 1944, DHist

22 Ibid., 15–16 June 1944

23 'Night Fighters,' nd, DHist 75/203

24 Ibid.

25 No 406 Squadron ORB, 21–22 July 1944, DHist

26 Steele to Air Ministry Office, 6 July 1944, Fumerton pers file, NPRC; No 406 Squadron ORB, 25–26 July 1944, DHist

27 'Report by Air Marshal Sir Arthur Coningham,' PRO Air 37/876; Shores, *2nd Tactical Air Force*, 13

28 Strafford, 'A Review of Air Operations Preparatory to and in Support of Operation Neptune,' PRO Air 37/576

29 AFHQ, Day-Fighter narrative, June 1944, 100, DHist 73/829

30 No 441 Squadron narrative history, 30, DHist 74/348; No 403 Squadron narrative history, 73, DHist 74/303

31 AHB, *The Rise and Fall of the German Air Force*, 330; 'Fortnightly Review of GAF Activities on the Western Front,' 16 June 44, PRO Air 16/507

32 No 438 Squadron ORB, 20 June 1944, DHist

33 Extract from RAF Narrative, 'The Breakout and the Advance to the Lower Rhine, 12 June to 30 September 1944,' 7, DHist 83/474; AFHQ, Day-Fighter narrative, June 1944, 53, DHist 73/829

34 Collier, *The Defence of the United Kingdom*, 373; 'Review of the Night Fighter Force,' 4 Aug. 1944, PRO Air 16/664

35 David McIntosh, *Terror in the Starboard Seat* (Don Mills 1980), 64–5

36 *Jane's All the World's Aircraft* (1945–6), 71c; No 402 Squadron ORB, 10, 14, 19 Aug. 1944, DHist; Kostenuk and Griffin, *RCAF*, 85

37 AFHQ, Day-Fighter narrative, June 1944, 37, 41, DHist 73/829; Tactical Paper No 4, Sept. 1947, PRO Air 20/6857; No 412 Squadron ORB, 14 June 1944, DHist; No 416 Squadron ORB, 14 June 1944, DHist; No 421 Squadron ORB, 14 June 1944, DHist; Middlebrook and Everitt, *The Bomber Command War Diaries*, 528

38 Tactical Paper No 1, Feb. 1947, PRO Air 20/6857; AFHQ, Day-Fighter narrative, June 1944, 46, DHist 73/829

39 Johnson, *Wing Leader*, 214

40 No 443 Squadron narrative history, 25, DHist 74/349; AFHQ, Day Fighter narrative, June 1944, 59, DHist 73/829

41 AFHQ, Day-Fighter narrative, June 1944, 66, 77, DHist 73/829; 2nd Gordon Highlanders, War Diary, 26 June 1944, PRO, WO 171/5197; 46 (H) Infantry Brigade, War Diary, PRO, WO 171/648; No 439 Squadron narrative history, 40, DHist 74/347

42 'Daily Reflections on the Course of the Battle by Air Chief Marshal Sir Trafford Leigh-Mallory,' 24 June 1944, PRO Air 37/784

43 No 411 Squadron narrative history, 63, DHist 74/316; AFHQ, Day-Fighter narrative, June 1944, 77, 89, 91, DHist 73/829

44 AFHQ, Day-Fighter narrative, June 1944, 89, 91, App. B, table 1, DHist 73/829; AHB, *The Rise and Fall of the German Air Force*, 330; Max Hastings, *Das Reich* (London 1981), 215–16

45 Hastings, *Das Reich*, 210–11

46 'Air Ministry Weekly Intelligence Summary, No 260,' 26 Aug. 1944, DHist 85/291

47 Ibid.

48 'Air Ministry Weekly Intelligence Summary, No 302,' 16 June 1945, DHist 85/291

49 Ops 7, Air Effort Operation Neptune, PRO Air 37/575; 'Fortnightly Review of GAF Activities on the Western Front – 1 to 16 June 1944,' 14, PRO Air 16/507

50 'Report by Air Marshal Sir Arthur Coningham,' nd, PRO Air 37/876

51 Arthur Tedder, *With Prejudice* (London 1966), 554; Carlo D'Este, *Decision in Normandy* (London 1984), 222–3

52 No 443 Squadron, ORB, 9 July 1944, DHist

53 No 438 Squadron ORB, 9 July 1944, DHist; No 439 Squadron ORB, appendix, 9 July 1944, DHist

54 No 439 Squadron ORB, appendix, 9, 18 July 1944, DHist; 15th Div Recce Regt, War Diary, 7 July 1944, PRO WO 171/474

55 No 402 Squadron ORB, July 1944, DHist

56 No 401 Squadron ORB, 2 July 1944, DHist

57 No 441 Squadron ORB, 13 July 1944, DHist; No 416 Squadron ORB, appendix, 14 July 1944, DHist

58 AHB, *The Rise and Fall of the German Air Force*, 334

59 No 439 Squadron ORB, 14 July 1944, DHist

60 'Report by CSO 83 Group on the Operation of Signals during 1944,' Feb. 1945, PRO Air 37/333; No 441 Squadron ORB, 14 July 1944, DHist

61 No 417 Squadron ORB, June 1944, DHist

62 Ibid., 16 June, 3, 4, 8 July 1944

63 Units named include the 10 Field Battery and 1st Canadian Army Brigade Workshops; No 417 Squadron ORB, 11 July 1944, appendix, Medical Officers Report, July and Aug. 1944, DHist

64 No 417 Squadron ORB, 26 Aug. 1944, DHist

65 CHMQ Report No 187, 12, DHist; Nicholson, *The Canadians in Italy*, 493; figures from W. Jackson et al., *The Mediterranean and Middle East* (London 1987), VI, part II, 106–7, 116–18

66 AHB, *Air Support*, 115

67 Report by CSO 83 Group on the Operation of Signals during 1944, Feb. 45, PRO Air 37/333

68 G (Air), Main HQ 21 Army Group, Notes on Air Support, June–Oct. 1944, 4–5, PRO WO 205/556

69 D'Este, *Decision in Normandy*, 370, 383

70 Ibid.; 'GOODWOOD' Visit – Serial 1, Discussion with A.V.M. Broadhurst, AOC 83 Group at His Headquarters, 26 July 1944, PRO Air 37/762

71 DSASO, 'Examination of Operation Goodwood,' PRO Air 37/762; Discussion with AVM Broadhurst, AOC 83 Group at His Headquarters, 25 July 1944, PRO Air 37/762

72 For more detailed discussions of such problems, see John A. English, *The Canadian Army and the Normandy Campaign* (New York 1991), and d'Este, *Decision in Normandy*.

73 Discussion with AVM Broadhurst, AOC 83 Group at his Headquarters, 25 July 1944, PRO Air 37/762; Discussion with Second Lieutenant P.M. Roberts, nd, PRO Air 37/762

74 Max Hastings, *Overlord* (London 1984), 276; G (Air), Main HQ 21 Army Group, 'Notes on Air Support, June–October 1944,' 5, PRO WO 205/556; 'Report by CSO 83 Group on the Operation of Signals during 1944,' Feb. 45, PRO Air 37/333

75 'Support to First Canadian Army,' 24 July 1944, 1-3-3, NA, Crerar Papers, MG 30, E157, vol. 3

76 Stacey, *The Victory Campaign*, 194

77 No 439 Squadron ORB, 1 Aug. 1944, DHist

78 'Report by Air Marshal Sir Arthur Coningham,' 9, PRO Air 37/876; Hans Speidel, *Invasion 1944: Rommell and the Normandy Campaign* (Chicago 1950), 141; No 438 Squadron ORB, 4 Aug. 1944, DHist

79 No 439 Squadron ORB, 6 Aug. 1944, DHist

80 'Report by Air Marshal Sir Arthur Coningham,' 10, PRO Air 37/876

81 No 442 Squadron ORB, 27 July 1944, DHist; No 401 Squadron ORB, 27 July 1944, DHist

82 Minutes of a Meeting held in the Air Council Room, 28 July 1944, PRO Air

37/636; AFHQ, Fighter-Recce narrative, July 1944, 5, DHist 73/832; Johnstone, 'Re-equipment of Squadrons,' 7 Aug. 1944, PRO Air 37/636; Morgan and Shacklady, *Spitfire*, 398, 458

83 AFHQ, Fighter-Recce narrative, July 1944, 16–17, DHist 73/832

84 Ibid., Aug. 1944, 10

85 Stacey, *The Victory Campaign*, 208

86 'Request for Air Support,' 4 Aug. 1944, PRO Air 25/704

87 Ibid.

88 Stacey, *The Victory Campaign*, 220–1, 250; telegram, HQ AEAF to 2 TAF and 9th AF, 8 Aug. 1944, PRO Air 37/741

89 No 439 Squadron ORB, 9 Aug. 1944, DHist

90 Stacey, *The Victory Campaign*, 231

91 No 438 Squadron ORB, 11 Aug. 1944, DHist; No 439 Squadron ORB, 11 Aug. 1944, DHist

92 Stacey, *The Victory Campaign*, 250; No 416 Squadron narrative history, 80, DHist 74/326; No 403 Squadron narrative history, 81, DHist 74/303

93 No 442 Squadron ORB, 13, 14 Aug. 1944, DHist; No 441 Squadron ORB, 13 Aug. 1944, DHist; No 438 Squadron ORB, 15 Aug. 1944, DHist; Johnson, *Wing Leader*, 236

94 No 414 Squadron ORB, 15 Aug. 1944, DHist; 'Report by Air Marshal Sir Arthur Coningham,' nd, 11, PRO Air 37/876

95 No 441 Squadron ORB, 18 Aug. 1944, DHist; No 442 Squadron ORB, 18 Aug. 1944, DHist; No 411 Squadron ORB, 18 Aug. 1944, DHist; No 401 Squadron ORB, 18 Aug. 1944, DHist

96 No 127 Wing ORB, 18 Aug. 1944, DHist

97 Ibid.

98 No 438 Squadron ORB, 18 Aug. 1944, DHist; No 440 Squadron ORB, 18 Aug. 1944, DHist

99 'Report by Air Marshal Sir Arthur Coningham,' nd, 11, PRO Air 37/876; Ellis, *Victory in the West*, I, 448; Stacey, *The Victory Campaign*, 261; No 83 Group Intelligence Summary No 69 up to 0001 hours, 22 Aug., PRO Air 25/704

100 D'Este, *Decision in Normandy*, 430–1; 'Report by Air Marshal Sir Arthur Coningham,' nd, 11–12, PRO Air 37/876

101 Eisenhower, *Crusade in Europe*, 279

102 2nd Argyll and Sutherland Highlanders, War Diary, 25 Aug. 1944, PRO WO 171/1262

103 James Lucas and James Barker, *The Killing Ground* (London 1978), 158

104 'Account of Escape of F/Lt A.F. Halcrow,' DHist 79/507, vol. 5

105 No 409 Squadron ORB, 7 Sept. 1944, DHist

106 No 410 Squadron ORB, 10 Sept. 1944, DHist

107 No 430 Squadron ORB, 22 Aug. 1944, DHist; No 414 Squadron ORB, Aug. and Sept. 1944, DHist; 'Air Support and Air Reconnaissance Aspects of Combined Operations in Europe, June 1944–May 1945,' chap. 8, app. K, 4, PRO Air 37/881

108 Combat Reports, DHist 73/847; numbers derived from ORBs

109 Numbers derived from Secret Narratives and ORBs

110 G (Air), Main HQ 21 Army Group, 'Notes on Air Support, June-October 1944,' I, PRO WO 205/556; 'The Effects of Air Power,' DHist SGR II 264, folder 24

111 G (Air), Main HQ 21 Army Group, 'Notes on Air Support, June–October 1944,' 3, PRO WO 205/556

CHAPTER 10: FINAL BATTLES

1 Everard, *A Mouse in My Pocket*, 365–6

2 No 401 Squadron ORB, 3 Sept. 1944, DHist

3 Report by Air Marshal Sir Arthur Coningham, 78, PRO Air 37/876

4 'Air Support – 1st Cdn Army. Report on Air Support in 2nd Brit Army and 1st Cdn Army by Lt-Col T.C. Braithwaite, OBE, and Lt-Col W.B.G. Reynolds,' nd, para 11, file 215C1.093 (D3), NA, RG 24, vol. 10, 671

5 Ibid., para 31

6 'Air Support NWE – Lecture by Maj-Gen C.C. Mann to Staff Course at RMC, 25 July 46,' nd, file 215C1.091, ibid.

7 Vincent Orange, *Coningham* (London 1990), 218

8 Ibid.

9 Craven and Cate, *The Army Air Forces in World War II*, III, 608; No 402 Squadron ORB, 17–30 Sept. 1944, DHist

10 No 83 Group ORB, 15 Sept. 1944, PRO Air 25/698; Ellis, *Victory in the West*, II, 44; No 441 Squadron ORB, 25 Sept. 1944, DHist; Combat Reports, DHist 73/847; No 416 Squadron ORB, 25 Sept. 1944, DHist; Combat Reports, DHist 83/847; Casualty Lists, DHist 90/19

11 AHB, *Rise and Fall of the German Air Force*, 336, 340; Squadron Leader D.R. Morgan, 'A Short Historical Account of No 83 Group during the Period 1st April, 1943, to the End of the War in Europe,' 14, PRO Air 37/985; No 412 Squadron ORB, 27 Sept. 1944, DHist

12 No 438 Squadron ORB, 27 Sept. 1944, DHist

13 No 83 Group ORB, 30 Sept. 1944, PRO Air 25/698; Shores, *2nd Tactical Air Force*, 68

14 No 411 Squadron ORB, 15 Oct. 1944, DHist; André Lord biog. file, DHist; 'An Analysis of Fighter Bombing Accuracy,' 9 Aug. 1945, PRO Air 16/498; No 443 Squadron ORB, 31 Oct. 1944, DHist

15 No 402 Squadron Progress Reports, 15 Sept. 1944, DHist 77/229; AHB, *Air Support*, 180–1; No 438 Squadron ORB, 16 and 26 Sept. 1944, DHist; Tactical Paper No 4, PRO Air 20/6857

16 'Strafing Lecture,' André Lord biog. file, DHist

17 AFHQ, Secret Narrative, Fighter-Reconnaissance, Sept. 1944, app. B, 10, Oct. 1944, 4, DHist 73/832; No 400 Squadron ORB, 4 Sept. 1944, DHist

18 No 400 Squadron ORB, 5 Oct. 1944, DHist

19 No 439 Squadron ORB, 13 Sept. 1944, DHist; 'Bits and Pieces,' André Lord biog. file, DHist

20 No 439 Squadron ORB, 5 Dec. 1944, DHist

21 No 401 Squadron ORB, 1 Oct. 1944, DHist; No 411 Squadron ORB, 16 Dec. 1944, DHist; No 440 Squadron ORB, 23 Nov., 30 Dec. 1944, DHist

22 No 402 Squadron ORB, 6 Nov. 1944, DHist

23 No 411 Squadron ORB, 30 Sept. 1944, DHist

24 Bill Olmsted, *Blue Skies* (Toronto 1987), 245–7

25 No 421 Squadron ORB, 10 Oct. 1944, DHist

26 No 406 ASP ORB, 7 Dec. 1944, DHist

27 No 416 Squadron ORB, 10 Sept. 1944, DHist; No 443 Squadron ORB, 28 Nov. 1944, DHist

28 No 421 Squadron ORB, 12 April 1945, DHist

29 Ibid., 10 Mar 1945

30 No 438 Squadron ORB, 10 Jan. 1945, DHist

31 No 441 Squadron ORB, 1 Oct. 1944, DHist; No 402 Squadron ORB, Oct. 1944, Summary for Oct. 1944, DHist; No 402 Squadron Progress Reports, 15 Oct. 1944, DHist 77/229

32 No 440 Squadron ORB, 1 Oct. 1944, DHist; No 403 Squadron ORB, 20 Sept. 1944, 6 March 1945, DHist

33 Winston Churchill, *Triumph and Tragedy* (Cambridge 1955), 52

34 Report by Air Marshal Sir Arthur Coningham, 33, PRO Air 37/876

35 No 400 Squadron ORB, 28 Sept., 2 Oct. 1944, DHist; No 412 Squadron ORB, 2 Oct. 1944, DHist; No 402 Squadron ORB, 17 Oct. 1944, DHist; Collier, *The Defence of the United Kingdom*, 407–8

36 Review by the Directorate of Staff Duties of the Report by Air Staff, SHAEF, on the Allied Air Operations in Europe from October 1st 1944 to May 9th, 1945, 7, PRO Air 37/1067

37 No 438 Squadron ORB, 2 Oct. 1944, DHist

38 Ibid., 2, 29 Oct. 1944; 'Tactics Employed by Fighter Bombers Operating against Special Targets,' 3, PRO Air 37/672; No 83 Group ORB, 29 Oct. 1944, PRO Air 25/698

39 No 412 Squadron ORB, 28 Sept., 18 Oct. 1944, DHist; No 442 Squadron ORB, 28 Sept., 15, 19 Oct. 1944, DHist; 83 Group RAF, 1-3-3, Crerar Papers, vol. 3

40 No 83 Group ORB, 1 Oct. 1944, PRO Air 25/698; No 441 Squadron ORB, 30 Sept. 1944, DHist; No 442 Squadron ORB, 2, 4 Oct. 1944, DHist; No 401 Squadron ORB, 5 Oct 1944, DHist

41 Everard, *A Mouse in My Pocket*, 375–6

42 No 416 Squadron ORB, 2 Oct. 1944, DHist; No 421 Squadron ORB, 6, 12 Oct. 1944, DHist

43 No 440 Squadron ORB, 8 Oct. 1944, DHist; No 400 Squadron ORB, 8 Oct. 1944, DHist

44 No 439 Squadron ORB, 9 Oct. 1944, DHist

45 2 TAF, RCAF Log and Statistics, October 1st, 1944 to February 28th, 1945, Guidance No 48, DHist 75/202; 2nd TAF, RCAF Log and Statistics, October 1st, 1944 to February 28th, 1945, Survey of RCAF Participation in Rail Interdiction Programme of Second Tactical Air Force, DHist 75/202

46 ORS Report No 28, DHist 79/705; No 438 Squadron ORB, 30 Nov. 1944, DHist

47 Numbers derived from Kostenuk and Griffin, *RCAF*.

48 Tactical Paper No 3, Sept. 1947, PRO Air 20/6856

49 See exchange of letters between Air Marshal Roderic Hill and Air Vice-Marshal N.R. Anderson dated 26 Sept. 1944 and 1 Oct. 1944, DHist 181.009 (D4128); Report on visit to No 406 (RCAF) Squadron, 1 Nov. 1944, DHist 181.009 (D4128); AHB, *Rise and Fall of the German Air Force*, 367; Casualty Lists, DHist 90/19

50 Price, *The Spitfire Story*, 171; No 417 Squadron ORB, 23 Nov. 1944, DHist; There was no flying on the following dates: 7, 8, 9, 21–23, 29 Sept., 2, 3, 6, 8–10, 17–19, 22, 23, 26–30 Oct., 1–4, 11, 14, 15, 27–30 Nov., 1, 3 Dec.; W/O2 L.S. Baxter was killed on 12 Sept.tember 1944. P/O B.J. Hayden was shot down on 24 October, P/O R.A. Shannon on 17 November, and F/O J. Waslyk on 4 December.

51 No 417 Squadron ORB, Dec. 1944–Jan. 1945, DHist

52 Ibid., 23 Jan. 1945

53 2 TAF, RCAF Log and Statistics, October 1st, 1944 to February 28th, 1945, Guidance No 76, DHist 75/202

54 Morgan, *A Short Historical Account of No 83 Group*, PRO Air 37/985; No 439 Squadron ORB, 24 Dec. 1944, DHist; No 83 Group ORB, 23 Dec. 1944, PRO Air 25/698; No 83 Group Intelligence Summary, 25 Dec. 1944, PRO Air 25/706

55 Combat Reports, DHist 73/847

56 No 442 Squadron ORB, 25 Dec. 1944, DHist; Jack Boyle biog. file, DHist; No 411 Squadron ORB, 25 Dec. 1944, DHist

57 2 TAF, RCAF Log and Statistics, October 1st, 1944 to February 28th, 1945, Guidance No 82A, DHist 75/202; No 83 Group Intelligence Summary, 29 Dec. 1944, PRO Air 16 1029; No 439 Squadron ORB, 30 Dec. 1944, DHist; No 442 Squadron ORB, 29 Dec. 1944, DHist; Combat Reports, DHist 73/847

58 Combat Reports, DHist 73/847

59 Hugh Halliday, *The Tumbling Sky* (Stittsville 1978), 26–8

60 Everard, *A Mouse in My Pocket*, 13–14

61 Ibid., 31

62 Report by Air Marshal Sir Arthur Coningham, 43, PRO Air 34/876; Werner Girbig, *Six Months to Oblivion*, trans. Richard Simpkin (London 1975), 73–4

63 No 438 Squadron ORB, 1 Jan. 1945, DHist; No 440 Squadron ORB, 1 Jan. 1945, DHist; No 143 Wing ORB, 1 Jan. 1945, DHist

64 Combat Reports, DHist 73/847

65 Ibid.; Norman Franks, *The Battle of the Airfields* (London 1982), app. J, 209–10

66 No 401 Squadron ORB, 1 Jan. 1945, DHist; No 126 Wing ORB, 1 Jan. 1945, DHist

67 Johnson, *Wing Leader*, 272; No 127 Wing ORB, 1 Jan. 1945, DHist

68 No 83 Group ORB, 1 Jan. 1945, PRO Air 25/698; ibid.; Craven and Cate, *The Army Air Forces in World War II*, III, 665; Werner Girbig, *Six Months to Oblivion* (London 1975), 112

69 No 83 Group ORB, 1 Jan. 1945, PRO Air 25/698; No 83 Group Intelligence Summary, 4 Jan. 1945, PRO Air 16/1029

70 Report by Air Marshal Sir Arthur Coningham, 45, PRO Air 37/876; Ellis, *Victory in the West*, II, 250

71 Operation Veritable, Conference at HQ 84 Group, RAF on 27 Jan. 1945, PRO Air 14/1419; Morgan, *A Short Historical Account of No 83 Group*, PRO Air 37/985

72 No 442 Squadron ORB, 8 Feb. 1945, DHist

73 No 439 Squadron ORB, 8 Feb. 1945, DHist

74 Ellis, *Victory in the West*, II, 266; Morgan, *A Short Historical Account of No 83 Group*, PRO Air 37/985; No 83 Group Intelligence Summary, 14 Feb. 1945, PRO Air 16/1029; No 442 Squadron ORB, 14 Feb. 1945, DHist; No 440 Squadron ORB, 14 Feb. 1945, DHist; 2 TAF, RCAF Log and Statistics, October 1st, 1944 to February 28th, 1945, Guidance No 152, DHist 75/202

75 No 442 Squadron ORB, 6 Dec. 1944, DHist

76 No 439 Squadron ORB, 19 Oct. 1944, DHist; No 411 Squadron ORB, 2 May 1945, DHist; No 438 Squadron ORB, 22 Feb. 1945, DHist

77 AHB, *Air Support*, 173; No 439 Squadron ORB, 22 Feb. 1945, DHist; No 442 Squadron ORB, 22 Feb. 1945, DHist

78 Jowsey biog. file, DHist

79 2 TAF/ORS Report No 14: The Accuracy of Ground Strafing, Assessment of Combat Films – December 1944–March 1945, nd, PRO Air 20/4122

80 Fighter Command Target Policy Memorandum No 1/1945, 7 March 1945, PRO Air 16 572; Everard, *A Mouse in My Pocket*, 380

81 No 438 Squadron ORB, 4 March 1945, DHist

82 No 83 Group Intelligence Summary, 28 Feb, 1–2, 12–15, 19 March 1945, PRO Air 16/1029; 2 TAF, RCAF Log and Statistics, March 1st to May 5th, 1945, Guidance No 202, 203, and 204, DHist 75/202

83 Review by the Directorate of Staff Duties of the Report by Air Staff, SHAEF, on the Allied Air Operations in Europe from October 1st, 1944 to May 9th, 1945, PRO Air 37/1067; AHB, *The Rise and Fall of the German Air Force 1933–1945*, 389

84 Report by Air Marshal Sir Arthur Coningham, 27–28, 49, PRO Air 37/876; Lt-Col J.G. Wordsworth, Organization for and Methods of Obtaining Close Air Support in the Tactical Battle, PRO Air 20/3197; No 401 Squadron ORB, 23 March 1945, DHist

85 No 83 Group ORB, 23 March 1945, PRO Air 25/698

86 Report by Air Marshal Sir Arthur Coningham, 52–3, PRO Air 37/876

87 Ibid., 53; 2 ORS Joint Report No 4, DHist 79/705

88 No 83 Group Intelligence Summary, 24 March 1945, PRO Air 16 1029

89 No 400 Squadron ORB, 3 April 1945, DHist

90 No 417 Squadron ORB, 31 March 1945, DHist

91 Ibid., 8 to 30 April 1945

92 Ibid., 3 May 1945

93 No 414 Squadron ORB, 30 March 1945, DHist; No 439 Squadron ORB, 30–31 March 1945, DHist; No 406 ASP ORB, 23 Feb. 1945, DHist

94 Ellis, *Victory in the West*, II, 312; No 421 Squadron ORB, 21 April 1945, DHist; Sheford Bidwell and Dominick Graham, *Fire-power* (London 1982), 263; No 664 Squadron ORB, Dec. 1944, DHist

95 No 664 Squadron ORB, 29 March 45, DHist; Kostenuk and Griffin, *RCAF*, 143

96 No 403 Squadron ORB, 16 April 1945, DHist; No 411 Squadron ORB, 17 April 1945, DHist

97 2 TAF, RCAF Log and Statistics, March 1st to May 5th, 1945, Guidance No 241, DHist 75/202

98 No 402 Squadron Progress Reports, 30 April 1945, DHist 77/229

99 No 83 Group Intelligence Summary, 29–30 April 1945, PRO Air 16/1029; No 83 Group ORB, PRO 29 April 1945, Air 25/698; No 403 Squadron ORB, 30 April 1945, DHist; No 402 Squadron ORB, 30 April 1945, DHist; No 443 Squadron ORB, 30 April 1945, DHist

100 No 412 Squadron ORB, 30 April 1945, DHist

101 No 52 MFH ORB, April 1945, DHist

102 Morgan, 'A Short Historical Account of No 83 Group,' nd, PRO Air 37/985; No 416 Squadron ORB, 1 May 1945, DHist; No 414 Squadron ORB, 1 May 1945, DHist; No 400 Squadron ORB, 2 May 1945, DHist

103 No 438 Squadron ORB, 2 May 1944, DHist

104 No 439 Squadron ORB, 2 May 1944, DHist

105 No 417 Squadron ORB, 8 May 1945, DHist; No 439 Squadron ORB, 4 May 1945, DHist; No 403 Squadron ORB, 4 May 1945, DHist; No 412 Squadron ORB, 5 May 1945, DHist

106 No 442 Squadron ORB, 7 May 1945, DHist; No 441 Squadron ORB, 8 May 1945, DHist

107 Numbers derived from casualty lists, DHist 90/19; No 439 Squadron ORB, 28 April 1945, DHist; Shores, *2nd Tactical Air Force*, 39

108 No 438 Squadron ORB, 7 May 1945, DHist

CHAPTER 11: THE ANTI-SUBMARINE WAR

1 S.F. Wise, *Canadian Airmen and the First World War* (Toronto 1980), 194–228

2 W.A.B. Douglas, *The Creation of a National Air Force* (Toronto 1986), 473–4; Air Ministry, Air Historical Branch (AHB), 'The RAF in Maritime War, II: The Atlantic and Home Waters, The Defensive Phase, September 1939–June 1941' (hereafter Coastal Command narrative), nd, app. IV, DHist 79/599

3 Great Britain, Admiralty, Historical Section, *Defeat of the Enemy Attack on Shipping, 1939–1945* (BR 1736(51)(1), Naval Staff History Second World War; np [1957], 1A, 17–19; ibid., 1B, plans 54–5

4 Douglas, *Creation of a National Air Force*, 469

5 C.B.A. Behrens, *Merchant Shipping and the Demands of War* (London 1978), 108–11; Admiralty, *Defeat of the Enemy Attack on Shipping*, 1B, table 13

6 AHB, Coastal Command narrative, II, app. I, DHist 79/599

7 I.T. Lloyd to Joubert, 28 July 1941, app. C, PRO, Air 15/213; Douglas, *The*

Creation of a National Air Force, 478, 522; Consolidated Catalina/Canso permanent reference file, DHist

8 Douglas, *The Creation of a National Air Force*, 472; AHB, Coastal Command narrative, II, 302–4, DHist 79/599

9 AHB, Coastal Command narrative, II, 304, app. XIX, and III, app. II, DHist 79/599; Alfred Price, *Aircraft versus Submarine* (London 1973), 71–2; AHB, Coastal Command narrative, II, 279, app. I, DHist 79/599; D of O to RCAF GB, 25 June 1941, S.2-3-413, DHist 181.006 (D314)

10 Stevenson to secretary of Department of National Defence for Air, 28 June 1941, and CAS to Roycanairf, 2 July 1941, DHist 181.006 (D314)

11 Douglas, *The Creation of a National Air Force*, 476; CAS to Roycanairf, 2 July 1941, and Stevenson to AMP, 7 July 1941, DHist 181.006 (D314)

12 D of P to Stevenson, 12 July 1941, DHist 181.006 (D314)

13 RCAF Overseas HQ to Air Ministry, 17 July 1941, and Stevenson to D of P, 25 July 1941, DHist 181.006 (D314); R.G. Briese personnel file, National Personnel Records Centre; No 413 Squadron progress report, 28 Sept. 1941, DHist 181.003 (D3851); No 413 Squadron operations record book (ORB), 18 Aug. 1941, DHist

14 Briese to AOC-in-C overseas, 29 Sept. 1941, DHist 181.006 (D314)

15 L.H. Randall to director of history, 19 Oct. 1974, L.H. Randall biog. file, DHist; No 413 Squadron progress report for period ending 11 Oct. 1941, DHist 181.003 (D3851)

16 L.H. Randall to W.A.B. Douglas, 19 Oct. 1974, L.H. Randall biog. file, DHist; No 413 Squadron ORB, 22 Oct. 1941, DHist

17 No 413 Squadron progress reports Nos 7 and 8 and Sullom Voe to 18 Gp, 13 Nov. 1941, DHist 181.003 (D3851); L.H. Randall to W.A.B. Douglas, 19 Oct. 1974, L.H. Randall biog. file, DHist

18 Twigg to AOC-in-C RCAF Overseas, 19 March 1942, J.D. Twigg personnel file, National Personnel Records Centre

19 AHB, Coastal Command narrative, III, 11, DHist 79/599

20 No 18 Group to Air Ministry, 3 March 1942, Twigg to AOC, RCAF Overseas, 19 March 1942, Curtis to CAS, 13 May 1942, and Walker to Edwards, 24 July 1942, J.D. Twigg personnel file, National Personnel Records Centre

21 L.H. Randall to W.A.B. Douglas, 19 Oct. 1974, L.H. Randall biog. file, DHist; J.L. Plant personnel file, National Personnel Records Centre

22 AFHQ to RCAF Overseas HQ, 21 March 1942, DHist 181.009 (D6142); No 413 Squadron ORB, 31 Jan. and March 1942, DHist; No 413 Squadron, ORB daily diary, March 1942, DHist; J.L. Plant biog. file, DHist; T.W. Melnyk, *Canadian Flying Operations in South East Asia 1941–1945* (Ottawa 1976), 26–7

23 J.R.M. Butler, *Grand Strategy* (London 1964), III, pt 2, 483–4

24 S.W. Roskill, *The War at Sea, 1939–1945* (London 1956), II, 25–6

25 Birchall to Douglas, 10 Oct. 1974, DHist 74/686

26 Readers Digest, *The Canadians at War 1939/45*, 2d ed. (Montreal 1986), 102

27 Melnyk, *Canadian Flying Operations in South East Asia*, 29–31; Roskill, *The War at Sea*, II, 26–30

28 Melnyk, *Canadian Flying Operations in South East Asia*, 32–3

29 Randall to Douglas, 19 Oct. 1974, L.H. Randall biog. file, DHist

30 No 413 Squadron ORB, 3 Aug. 1942, DHist

31 Ibid., 5 Aug. 1942, DHist; No 413 Squadron progress reports, June–Aug. 1942, DHist 181.003 (D3851); Randall to Douglas, 19 Oct. 1974, Randall biog. file, DHist.

32 Melnyk, *Canadian Flying Operations in South East Asia*, 39–41, 46, 48–51

33 Ibid., 39–41, 46, 48–51

34 AHB, Coastal Command narrative, III, 14, app. I, DHist 79/599; L.W. Skey biog. file, DHist; No 422 Squadron ORB, 31 July 1942, DHist

35 AHB, Coastal Command narrative, 8, DHist 79/599; No 422 Squadron ORB Aug.–Nov. 1942, DHist

36 Edwards to Air Ministry, 6 Oct. 1942, DGO to Edwards, 31 Oct. 1942, DHist 181.006 (D302); F.H. Hitchens, 'No. 422 Squadron: A Narrative History,' Sept. 1953, DHist 74/333

37 No 423 Squadron ORB, Aug. 1944, DHist

38 No 423 Squadron progress reports, Aug.–Oct. 1942, DHist 181.003 (D2880); No 423 Squadron ORB, 2–3 Nov. 1942, DHist; No 423 Squadron history, 1–6, DHist 74/334

39 Wait to Air Ministry, 17 Sept. 1942, DHist 181.006 (D302); Overseas Headquarters to Air Ministry, 28 Oct. and 23 Nov. 1942, and director of postings to RCAF Overseas, 16 Nov. 1942, DHist 181.006 (D303)

40 No 423 Squadron progress reports, Aug.–Dec. 1942, DHist 181.003 (D2880); No 422 Squadron progress reports, Aug.–Dec. 1942, DHist 181.003 (D3128); Breadner to Edwards, 9 Jan. 1943, and Edwards to Air Ministry, 22 Jan. 1943, DHist 181.009 (D774)

41 Joubert to Air Ministry, 19 Feb. 1942, PRO Air 15/213; Portal to Churchill, 29 March 1942, Portal papers, DHist 87/89 folder 3

42 AHB, Coastal Command narrative, III, 473, 520–1, app. IV, DHist 79/599

43 Joubert to Portal, 2 Sept. 1942, Portal to Joubert, 4 Sept. 1942, Joubert to Portal, 9 Nov. 1942, Portal to Joubert, 10 Nov. 1942, Joubert to Portal, 15 Nov. 1942, Portal to Pound, 17 Nov. 1942, Portal Papers, file 8 (1942), DHist 87/89

44 Portal to Joubert, 17 Nov. 1942, Portal Papers, file 8 (1942), DHist 87/89

45 Joubert to Portal, 28 Nov. 1942, Portal Papers, file 8 (1942), DHist 87/89

46 John Keegan, ed., *Who Was Who in World War II* (New York 1978), 120; Portal to Joubert, 17 Nov. 1942, Portal Papers, file 8 (1942), and Mountbatten to Portal, 13 Oct. 1943, Portal Papers, box C, file 7, DHist 87/89; Philip Ziegler, ed., *Personal Diary of Admiral The Lord Louis Mountbatten, 1943–1946* (London 1988), 226

47 Douglas, *The Creation of a National Air Force*, 548, 551; F.H. Hinsley et al., *British Intelligence in the Second World War*, II (New York 1981), 750

48 Sir John Slessor, *The Central Blue* (London 1956), 523–6

49 AHB, Coastal Command narrative, IV, 28, DHist 79/599

50 AHB, Coastal Command narrative, II, app. X, DHist 79/599

51 AHB, Coastal Command narrative, III, 11, 83–7, 469–514, 520–1, 525–6, and IV, app. I, DHist 79/599; Air Ministry to Britman Washington, 26 Nov. 1942,

and DGO to DONC, 27 Nov. 1942, PRO Air 20/3094; Joubert to Air Ministry, 19 Feb. 1942, PRO Air 15/213; Portal to Churchill, 29 March 1942, Portal Papers, folder 3, DHist 87/89

52 No 405 Squadron ORB, June–Oct. 1942, DHist

53 Larry Milberry and Hugh Halliday, *The Royal Canadian Air Force at War 1939–1945* (Toronto 1990), 281

54 AHB, Coastal Command narrative, III, 83–7, 487–9, and IV, 83–5, DHist 79/599; No 405 Squadron ORB, 27 Nov. 1942 ad 12 Jan.–27 Feb. 1943, DHist; Price, *Aircraft versus Submarine*, 92–3; Douglas, *The Creation of a National Air Force*, 582

55 F.H. Hitchens, 'No 407 Squadron: A Narrative History,' Oct. 1953, 77–82, DHist 74/308

56 Breadner to Curtis, 23 Nov. 1942, DHist 181.009 (D5629); DAS to Edwards, 13 Jan. 1943, DHist 181.006 (D286); 'Report on a Meeting between the AOC-in-C, RCAF Overseas, and the AMSO, RAF, on January 14th, 1943,' DHist 181.009 (D5629); Chris Ashworth, *Action Stations, V: Military Airfields of the South-West* (Cambridge 1982), 58; No 407 Squadron semi-monthly progress report, 5 and 13 March, 7 and 15 April 1943, DHist 181.003 (D4835)

57 No 407 Squadron ORB, 22 and 28 April 1943, DHist; *Befehlshaber der Unterseeboote* (BdU) war diary, 26–29 April 1943, translation in DHist 79/446; F.H. Hitchens, 'No. 407 Squadron,' 93–5, DHist 74/308; AHB, Coastal Command narrative, IV, 96, DHist 79/599

58 BdU war diary, 28 April 1943, DHist 79/446; AHB, Coastal Command narrative, IV, 97, DHist 79/599

59 BdU war diary, 24 May 1943, DHist 79/446; No 407 Squadron ORB, 14–31 May 1943, DHist; AHB, Coastal Command narrative, IV, 98–9, DHist 79/599

60 BdU war diary, 29 May 1943, DHist 79/446; AHB, Coastal Command narrative, IV, 100–34, DHist 79/599

61 Nos 407, 415, 422, and 423 Squadron ORBs, June–Aug. 1943, DHist

62 AHB, Coastal Command narrative, IV, 98–9, 126, app. VI, DHist 79/599

63 BdU war diary, 14 June 1943, DHist 79/446; AHB, Coastal Command narrative, IV, 109, DHist 79/599

64 No 422 Squadron ORB, 17 June 1943, DHist; No 423 Squadron ORB, 3 July 1943, DHist

65 S.W. Roskill, *The War at Sea* (London 1961), III, app. D; AHB, Coastal Command narrative, IV, 126, DHist 79/59

66 Roskill, *The War at Sea, 1939–1945*, III, app. D; AHB, Coastal Command narrative, IV, 126, DHist 79/59

67 No 415 Squadron ORB, 2 Aug. 1943, DHist

68 Admiralty, reports on interrogation of German prisoners of war, U-706, Sept. 1943, DHist 80/582, item 41

69 Douglas, *The Creation of a National Air Force*, 583; No 407 Squadron ORB, 2 Aug. 1943, DHist

70 BdU war diary, 2 and 5 Aug. 1943, DHist 79/446; F.H. Hinsley, *British Intelligence in the Second World War* (London 1984), III, pt 1, 217–20; Ministry of Defence (Navy), *The U-Boat War in the Atlantic, 1939–1945*

(London 1989), III, 14; AHB, Coastal Command narrative, IV, 133–8, DHist 79/599; No 415 Squadron ORB, Aug. 1943, DHist; Nos 422 and 423 Squadron ORBs, Sept. 1943, DHist

71 No 407 Squadron ORB, 6–7 Sept. 1943, DHist; Hitchens, 'No. 407 Squadron,' Oct 1953, 101–2, DHist 74/308; AHB, Coastal Command narrative, IV, 213, DHist 79/599

72 C. Reinke, 'Castle Archdale,' [Oct. 1944], Castle Archdale PR file, DHist; Hitchens, 'No. 407 Squadron,' Oct. 1953, 99, 104–5, 107, DHist 74/308; No 407 Squadron ORB, 27 Sept. 1943, DHist

73 No 407 Squadron ORB, 19–20 Oct. 1943, DHist

74 Hitchens, 'No. 407 Squadron,' Oct. 1953, 99, DHist 74/308; No 407 Squadron ORB, 5 Aug. 1943, DHist; AHB, Coastal Command narrative, III, 17–18, DHist 79/599

75 C. Reinke, 'Castle Archdale,' [Oct. 1944], 7, Castle Archdale PRF, DHist

76 No 407 Squadron ORB, 31 Aug., 30 Sept., 31 Oct. 1943, DHist; 'Canadianization – Overseas Squadrons,' nd, 407 Squadron, DHist 181.003 (D3596)

77 No 407 Squadron ORB, 30 Sept. 1943, DHist

78 Ibid., Sept. 1943–Jan. 1944, DHist; AHB, Coastal Command narratieve, IV, 221, DHist 79/599 ; Hitchens, 'No 407 Squadron,' Oct. 1953, 105, DHist 74/308; R.A. Ashman biog. file, DHist

79 Ashworth, *Action Stations*, 60; No 407 Squadron ORB, 30 Nov. and 31 Dec. 1943, 29 Feb. and 30 April 1944, DHist; Hitchens, 'No 407 Squadron,' Oct. 1953, 105, DHist 74/308

80 Edwards to Air Ministry, 30 June 1943, and Edwards to Pirie, 6 Sept. 1943, DHist 181.003 (D1192)

81 Pirie to Edwards, 15 July 1943, DHist 181.003 (D1192)

82 Inspector General, 'Report No 295,' 29 June 1943, PRO, Air 33/5

83 Ibid.

84 Slessor to Portal, 1 June 1943, Portal Papers, file 8 (1943), DHist 87/89; Douglas, *The Creation of a National Air Force*, 585

85 Nos 422 and 423 Squadron ORBs, 31 Oct. 1943, DHist; F.H. Hitchens, 'No 422 Squadron: A Narrative History,' Sept. 1953, 32, DHist 74/333

86 No 423 Squadron ORB, 12 May 1943, DHist; Douglas, *The Creation of a National Air Force*, 584; Norman Franks, *Search and Kill: Coastal Command's U-boat Successes* (Bourne End, Bucks. 1990), 22

87 AHB, Coastal Command narrative, IV, 147, DHist 79/599; Chaz Bowyer, *Men of Coastal Command* (London 1985), 65; C.H. Barnes, *Shorts Aircraft since 1900* (London 1964), 355

88 'Personal Story Written by F/O A.A. Bishop, DFC, 423 Squadron,' nd, No 423 Squadron ORB, DHist

89 Ibid.

90 Carl Reinke, 'Castle Archdale,' [Oct 1944], 12–14, Castle Archdale PRF, DHist

91 Ibid., 16; C.H. Waddington, *O.R. in World War 2* (London 1973), 113–15

92 AHB, Coastal Command narrative, IV, 230, DHist 79/599

93 No 423 Squadron ORB, 8 Oct. 1943, DHist; Douglas, *The Creation of a National Air Force*, 584

94 No 422 Squadron ORB, Oct. 1943, app. E, DHist

95 Ibid.; AHB, Coastal Command narratieve, IV, 187, DHist

96 AHB, Coastal Command narrative, IV, 454, 465, DHist 79/599; No 407 Squadron ORB, 10/11 Feb. 1944, DHist; Douglas, *The Creation of a National Air Force*, 592

97 No 422 Squadron ORB, 10 March 1944, DHist; Hitchins, 'No 422 Squadron,' Sept. 1953, 43, DHist 74/333; Douglas, *The Creation of a National Air Force*, 592; BdU war diary, 10–12 March 1944, DHist 79/446

98 'Aircraft for the War at Sea,' 19 Jan. 1944, PRO, Air 2/8428; AHB, Coastal Command narrative, IV, 568–9, DHist 79/599

99 CAS to ACAS(P), 21 Jan. 1944, PRO, Air 2/8428

100 D of Ops(M) to VCAS, 6 March 1944, 'The War at Sea in Relation to Overlord,' 17 March 1944, PRO, Air 2/8428; AHB, Coastal Command narrative, IV, 572–4, DHist 79/599

101 'Minutes of a Meeting Held in the Air Council Room … on the 22nd March, 1944, to Discuss the War at Sea in Relation to "Overlord,"' PRO, Air 15/357; AHB, Coastal Command narrative, IV, 576–7, DHist 79/599

102 'Directive on the role of Coastal Command in Overlord,' 18 April 1944, PRO, Air 15/293; AHB, Coastal Command narrative, IV, 580–1, DHist 79/599

103 No 407 Squadron ORB, 2 and 31 May 1944, DHist

104 Ibid., 4 May 1944, DHist; AHB, Coastal Command narrative, IV, 479, DHist 79/599

105 Nos 422 and 423 Squadron ORBs, 18 May–6 June 1944, DHist; AHB, Coastal Command narrative, IV, 484–5, DHist 79/599; Coastal Command ORB, 24 May 1944, app. E, DHist 181.003 (D886)

106 No 423 Squadron ORB, 24 May 1944, DHist

107 *BdU* war diary, 27 May 1944, DHist 79/446; Nos 422 and 423 Squadron ORBs, 24 May 1944, DHist; U-921 log, 24 May 1944, DHist 83/665, vol. 89; AHB, Coastal Command narrative, IV, 485, DHist 79/599

108 AHB, Coastal Command narrative, IV, 240–1, DHist 79/599; Hinsley, *British Intelligence in the Second World War*, III, pt 1, 49

109 Hinsley, *British Intelligence in the Second World War*, III, pt 2, 156; Ministry of Defence (Navy), *The U-Boat War in the Atlantic*, 68

110 AHB, Coastal Command narrative, V, 4–11, DHist 79/599; Ministry of Defence (Navy), *The U-Boat War in the Atlantic*, 69

111 Nos 422 and 423 Squadron, ORB daily diaries, June 1944, DHist; AHB, Coastal Command narrative, V, 9, DHist 79/599

112 No 407 Squadron ORB, 20/21 June 1944, DHist; AHB, Coastal Command narratieve, V, 17–21, DHist 79/599; 'Report on interrogation of survivors from U-971 …' NSS 1487-49, U-971 1650, and HMCS *Haida* 8000, DHist

113 AHB, Coastal Command narrative, V, 58, 81–3, 88, 109, DHist 79/599

114 Ibid., 12–13, 21–2, 32–6; Roskill, *The War at Sea, 1939–1945*, III, app. Y; Nos 422 and 423 Squadron ORBs, July 1944, DHist; 'No 423 Squadron,' nd, 81, DHist 74/334

115 Nos 407, 422, and 423 Squadron ORBs, Aug. 1944, DHist

116 No 423 Squadron ORB, Aug. 1944, app. 'An A/S Sweep by Sunderland "C,"' DHist

117 AHB, Coastal Command narrative, V, 81–3, DHist 79/599; Nos 407, 422, and 423 Squadron ORBs, Aug.–Sept. 1944, DHist; Ministry of Defence (Navy), *The U-boat War in the Atlantic*, 68–80

118 AHB, Coastal Command narrative, V, 82, 88–9, 108–9, DHist 79/599; Marc Milner, 'The Dawn of Modern Anti-Submarine Warfare: Allied Responses to the U-boats, 1944–45,' *RUSI Journal*, spring 1989, 64; No 423 Squadron ORB, 3 Sept. 1944, DHist

119 C. Reinke, 'Castle Archdale,' [Oct 1944], 17–18, Castle Archdale PRF, DHist

120 Ibid., 18–19, 24

121 BdU war diary, 29–30 Oct. 1944, DHist 79/446; 'Report on U/Boat Sighting and Attack by Aircraft,' 4 and 30 Oct. 1944, DHist 181.003 (D4417); Douglas, *The Creation of a National Air Force*, 600; AHB, Coastal Command narrative, V, 96, DHist 79/59

122 *Coastal Command Review*, III, Dec. 1944, 8, plate 1, DHist 181.003 (D963); AHB, Coastal Command narrative, V, 93, 97, DHist 79/599

123 No 423 Squadron ORB, 11 Sept. 1944, DHist; AHB, Coastal Command narrative, V, 84, 98, app. VI, DHist 79/599; Roskill, *The War at Sea*, III, pt II, app. Y

124 RCAF Overseas Headquarters ORB, Oct.–Nov. 1944, DHist; No 422 Squadron ORB, 26 Oct. 1944, DHist

125 Douglas, *The Creation of a National Air Force*, 601; AHB, Coastal Command narrative, V, 102–3, DHist 79/599

126 No 407 Squadron ORB, 20 Dec. 1944, DHist

127 DG Org. to Coastal Command, 26 Jan. 1944, PRO, Air 15/575; Douglas, *The Creation of a National Air Force*, 586; Nos 422 and 423 Squadron ORBs, 31 Dec. 1943, May 1944–April 1945, DHist

128 Power to Breadner, 28 June 1944, and Breadner to Power, 30 June 1944, DHist 181.006 (D314); 'Canadianization – Overseas Squadrons,' DHist 181.003 (D3596); Melnyk, *Canadian Flying Operations in South East Asia*, 69–70

129 'Draft, A Forecast of the "U" Boat Campaign during 1945, Note by the First Sea Lord,' nd, PRO, Air 20/1237; Nos 407, 422, and 423 Squadron ORBs, Jan.–May 1945, DHist; AHB, Coastal Command narrative, V, 209, 217, 230, 232, 246, DHist 79/599; Roskill, *The War at Sea* III, pt 2, app. Y

CHAPTER 12: IN SEARCH OF A STRIKE FORCE

1 AHB, Coastal Command narrative, I, 209, 243–4, DHist 79/599; S.W. Roskill, *The War at Sea, 1939–1945* (London 1954), I, 144; Air Ministry to Commands, 26 Aug. 1939, PRO, Air 14/142

2 AHB, Coastal Command narrative, II, 171–2, DHist 79/599; Roskill, *The War at Sea*, I, 124

3 AHB, Coastal Command narrative, II, 171ff, DHist 79/599

4 Ibid., 177–82; Roskill, *The War at Sea*, I, 338

5 AHB, Coastal Command narrative, II, 185, apps. XIII and XV, DHist 79/599

6 W.N. Medlicott, *The Economic Blockade* (London 1952), I, 30–1; Alan S.
   Milward, *War, Economy and Society, 1939–1945* (Berkeley, Ca. 1979), 308,
   311–12; Alan S. Milward, 'Could Sweden Have Stopped the Second World
   War?' *Scandinavian Economic History Review* 15 (1967): 127–38

7 'Enemy Shipping,' nd, PRO Air 15/629

8 AHB, Coastal Command narrative, II, 179–80, DHist 79/599; Roy Conyers
   Nesbit, *The Strike Wings* (London 1984), 17–19; T.K. Derry, *The Campaign in
   Norway* (London 1952), 10–11; Milward, *War, Economy and Society*, 309

9 AHB, Coastal Command narrative, II, 185–8, DHist 79/599; 'Attacks by Coastal
   Command on Enemy Shipping at Sea,' nd, app. B, PRO, Air 15/270

10 Personal communication with J.K. Abbott, 8 March 1989; AHB, Coastal
    Command narrative, II, apps. XIV and XV, DHist 79/599; S.W. Roskill, *The
    War at Sea* (London 1961), III, app. XX

11 Roskill, *The War at Sea*, I, 124–5, 335–6, 509–10, table 10; AHB, Coastal
    Command narrative, II, app. XIII, DHist 79/599

12 Roskill, *The War at Sea*, I, app. R

13 ROYCANAIRF to CAS, 16 April 1941, D of O to Circulation List, 12 April 1941,
    DHist 181.009 (D774)

14 Ibid.; P.H. Woodruff biog. file, DHist; No 404 Squadron ORB, May–June 1941,
    DHist; Stevenson to AMP, 9 May 1941, DHist 181.006 (D283); CAS to Power,
    31 Oct. 1941, DHist 181.003 (D68); ROYCANAIRF to CAS, 21 May 1941, DHist
    181.009 (D768)

15 Bowhill to Air Ministry, 12 June 1941, PRO Air 15/213; C.M. Sharp and
    M.J.F. Bowyer, *Mosquito* (London 1967), 118

16 AHB, Coastal Command narrative, II, 289, DHist 79/599; Owen Thetford,
    Aircraft of the Royal Air Force since 1918 (New York 1968), 118–19; D of O
    to Circulation List, 12 April 1941, DHist 181.009 (D774); No 404 Squadron
    ORB, 1 May 1941, DHist

17 Kim Abbott, *Gathering of Demons* (Perth, Ont. 1986), 7, 11–12; H.M. Styles
    biog. file, DHist; D of O to Circulation List, 1 May 1941, DHist 181.009
    (D774); CAS to Power, 30 June 1941, DHist 181.003 (D68); Stevenson to AMP,
    7 July 1941, DHist 181.006 (D286); F.H. Hitchens, 'No. 407 Squadron, A
    Narrative History,' Oct. 1953, 4, DHist 74/308; No 407 Squadron ORB, 17 and
    26 July, 5–6 Aug. 1941, DHist; No 407 Squadron progress reports, 16 Sept.
    1941, 13 March 1942, DHist 181.003 (D4835)

18 D of O to Circulation List, 1 May 1941, DHist 181.009 (D774); Air Ministry to
    air officer in charge of records, 13 June 1941, DHist 181.009 (D2540); No 407
    Squadron ORB, 31 May 1941, DHist; 'Air Action against Enemy Surface
    Vessels' [Jan. 1941], PRO, Air 15/629; Thetford, *Aircraft of the Royal Air
    Force*, 360–3

19 Bowhill minute to Lloyd, 29 May 1941, PRO Air 15/213; AHB, Coastal
    Command narrative, II, pt 2, app. XIV, DHist 79/599

20 Director of operations (naval co-operation) to Joubert, 3 July 1941, and Joubert
    to Air Ministry, 14 Sept. 1941, PRO Air 15/213; No 16 Group to Coastal
    Command, 20 Aug. 1941, PRO Air 15/632

21 Portal to Joubert, 1 Dec. 1941, PRO Air 15/213

22 AHB, Coastal Command narrative, II, 185, DHist 75/599; Bowhill to Air Ministry, 12 June 1941, PRO Air 15/213

23 E.L. Wurtele biog. file, DHist; No 415 Squadron progress reports, 11 Sept. 1941–12 Feb. 1942, DHist 181.003 (D5212)

24 No 404 Squadron ORB, Sept. 1941, DHist; AHB, Coastal Command narrative, III, 97–9, 113, 119, 125–8, DHist 75/599

25 AHB, Coastal Command narrative, III, 2, 286–7, DHist 79/599; Hitchens, 'No. 407 Squadron,' Oct. 1953, 61, DHist 74/308

26 AHB, Coastal Command narrative, III, 127, DHist 79/599

27 Abbott, *Gathering of Demons*, 55–7

28 Hinsley, *British Intelligence in the Second World War*, II, 195–6; Personal communication with J.K. Abbott, 1 March 1989

29 Hitchens, 'No. 407 Squadron,' Oct. 1953, 8, DHist 74/308; AHB, Coastal Command narrative, III, 127, DHist 79/599

30 Abbott, *Gathering of Demons*, 70

31 No 407 Squadron ORB, Sept. 1941, DHist; AHB, Coastal Command narratieve, III, 129–30, DHist 79/599; Hitchens, 'No. 407 Squadron,' Oct. 1953, 9, DHist 74/308; Abbott, *Gathering of Demons*, 63, 68–9

32 AHB, Coastal Command narrative, III, 129–30, 132–3, 143, DHist 79/599; Hitchens, 'No. 407 Squadron,' Oct. 1953, 17, 22, DHist 74/308; Coastal Command Headquarters (Intelligence), 'Attacks on Enemy Shipping by Coastal Command Aircraft, October to December 1941,' 12 Feb. 1942, PRO Air 15/270

33 AHB, Coastal Command narrative, III, 132, DHist 79/599

34 No 407 Squadron semi-monthly progress report, 17 Nov. 1941, DHist 181.003 (D4835); No 407 Squadron ORB, 1 Nov. 1941, DHist; Abbott, *Gathering of Demons*, 83–5; Hitchens, 'No 407 Squadron,' Oct. 1953, 4, DHist 74/308

35 AHB, Coastal Command narrative, III, 132, copy in DHist 79/599

36 Abbott, *Gathering of Demons*, 80, 82; AHB, *Armament*, I (London 1952), 129–30; Coastal Command Headquarters, 'Coastal Command Tactical Instruction No 24,' 17 April 1942, PRO Air 15/305; Hitchens, 'No 407 Squadron,' Oct. 1953, 41, DHist 74/308

37 Memo to SIO Coastal Command, 21 Sept. 1942, PRO Air 15/298

38 'Paper of Attacks on Enemy Merchant Shipping in the North Sea,' 19 Sept. 1942, PRO, Air 15/271; AHB, Coastal Command narrative, III, 286–7, DHist 79/599

39 No 407 Squadron ORB, Sept.–Nov. 1941, DHist; Hitchens, 'No 407 Squadron,' Oct. 1953, 55, DHist 74/308

40 Abbott, *Gathering of Demons*, 96–7

41 Hitchens, 'No 407 Squadron,' Oct. 1953, 17, 22, DHist 74/308; No 407 Squadron ORB, Dec. 1941, DHist

42 'Report on flying accident or forced landing not attributable to enemy action,' 15 Dec. 1941, DHist 181.003 (D3468)

43 Ibid., 7, 24, and 26 Jan., 14 Feb., and 3 March 1942; F/Sgt Goulding accident file, 17 Feb. 1942, DHist 181.006 (D130); Hitchens, 'No 407 Squadron,' Oct. 953, 29, DHist 74/308

44 Censorship report No 33, 25–27 Jan 1942, DHist 181.009 (D4159); No 407 Squadron ORB, Dec. 1941–Jan. 1942, DHist

45 Abbott, *Gathering of Demons*, 93

46 No 407 Squadron ORB, 28 Dec. 1941, DHist

47 Abbott, *Gathering of Demons*, 94–5

48 Censorship report No 33, 25–27 Jan. 1942, DHist 181.009 (D4159)

49 No 407 Squadron ORB, 31 Jan., 8 and 12 Feb. 1942, DHist

50 AHB, Coastal Command narrative, III, 224–42

51 Abbott, *Gathering of Demons*, 118–9, 128–9; No 407 Squadron ORB, 12 Feb. 1942, DHist; AHB, Coastal Command narrative, III, 239, DHist 79/599

52 No 407 Squadron ORB, 12 Feb. 1942, DHist; Hitchens, 'No 407 Squadron,' Oct. 1953, 26–7, DHist 74/308; Abbott, *Gathering of Demons*, 128–31; AHB, Coastal Command narrative, III, 239–40, DHist 79/599

53 AHB, Coastal Command narrative, III, 224, 237–42, DHist 79/599

54 Quoted in J.D. Potter, *Fiasco: The Break-out of the German Battleships* (New York 1970), 212

55 Quoted ibid., 196

56 Joubert to Bottomley, 14 March 1942, PRO Air 15/386; AHB, Coastal Command narrative, III, 134, 255–7, DHist 79/599

57 No 407 Squadron semi-monthly progress report, 28 Feb. 1942, DHist 181.003 (D4835); Coastal Command to No 16 Group, 7 April 1942, PRO Air 15/271; AHB, Coastal Command narrative, III, 258, 262–3, DHist 79/599

58 Coastal Command to No 407 Squadron, 15 Dec. 1941, DHist 181.006 (D286)

59 No 407 Squadron ORB, 9 and 15 Feb. 1942, DHist; Hitchens, 'No 407 Squadron,' Oct. 1953, 30, DHist 74/308; A.C. Brown biog. file, DHist; No 407 Squadron semi-monthly progress report, 15 Jan., 13 April 1942, DHist 181.003 (D4835); Babington to Edwards, 10 Feb. 1942, DHist 181.009 (D774); Babington to Joubert, 10 Feb. 1942, PRO Air 15/52

60 Joubert to Babington, 14 Feb. 1942, and Air Ministry to Coastal Command, 7 March 1942, PRO Air 15/52

61 Babington to Edwards, 10 Feb. 1942, DHist 181.009 (D774)

62 AHB, Coastal Command narrative, III, 149, DHist 79/599

63 Ibid., 150; No 404 Squadron ORB, 5 Nov. 1941, DHist; S. Kostenuk and J. Griffin, *RCAF Squadron Histories and Aircraft 1924–1968* (Toronto 1977), 88; Hitchens, 'No 407 Squadron,' Oct 1953, app. H, DHist 74/308

64 Gron Edwards, *Norwegian Patrol* (Shrewsbury, Eng. 1985), 96

65 No 404 Squadron scrapbook, 19 Oct. 1941, 50, DHist 86/128, vol. 1

66 No 404 Squadron progress report, 27 Jan. and 12 Feb. 1942, DHist 181.003 (D1034); No 404 Squadron ORB, 18–27 Dec. 1941, 15 Jan., and 7 and 9 Feb. 1942, DHist; No 404 Squadron scrapbook, 18 Dec. 1941, DHist 86/128, vol. 1; AHB, Coastal Command narrative, III, 170, DHist 79/599; H. St G. Saunders, *Green Beret* (London 1949), 63

67 Woodruff to Curtiss, 21 April 1942, DHist 181.006 (D283)

68 Ibid.

69 Corbett to Curtiss, 4 May 1942, and Curtiss to Woodruff, 28 May 1942, DHist 181.006 (D283); No 404 Squadron, 10 Sept. 1941, DHist

70 Curtiss to Woodruff, 28 May 1942, DHist 181.006 (D283); 'A Statistical Return on Canadianization of RCAF Sqns O/S,' nd, DHist 181.003 (D3596)

71 No 407 Squadron ORB, April 1942, DHist

72 Hitchens, 'No. 407 Squadron,' Oct. 1953, 34, DHist 74/308; No 407 Squadron ORB, 6 and 7 April, 5 May 1942, DHist; No 407 Squadron progress report, 12 May 1942, DHist 181.003 (D4835); AHB, Coastal Command narrative, III, 262–3, DHist 79/599

73 Abbott, *Gathering of Demons*, 177

74 No 407 Squadron ORB, 18 and 29 April and 1–7 May 1942, DHist; Joubert to No 16 Group, 7 April 1942, PRO Air 15/271; Hitchens, 'No 407 Squadron,' Oct. 1953, 35–6, DHist 74/308; AHB, Coastal Command narrative, III, 262, 265–6, DHist 79/599; Abbott, *Gathering of Demons*, 220–3

75 No 407 Squadron ORB, 15 May 1942, DHist; Hitchens, 'No 407 Squadron,' Oct. 1953, 38–41, DHist 74/308; AHB, Coastal Command narrative, III, 281–3, DHist 79/599; *London Gazette*, 16 June 1942

76 Hitchens, 'No 407 Squadron,' Oct. 1953, 41–3, DHist 74/308; No 407 Squadron ORB, 28–29 May 1942, DHist; Abbott, *Gathering of Demons*, 223

77 No 407 Squadron ORB, 31 May 1942, DHist

78 'Meeting convened to Consider Policy of Attacks on Enemy Shipping in the North Sea. HQCC 21 May, 1942,' nd, PRO Air 15/298; AHB, Coastal Command narrative, III, 281–6, DHist 79/599; 'Minutes of Air Officer Commanding-in-Chief's Fourth Meeting with Group Commanders,' 1 July 1942, PRO Air 15/178

79 AHB, Coastal Command narrative, III, 395–8, DHist 79/599

80 Ibid., 251, 254–5, John Rawlings, *Coastal, Support and Special Squadrons of the RAF and Their Aircraft* (London 1982), 209, 224–5

81 Inspector General, 'Visit to Thorney Island on 7.4.42,' 9 April 1942, PRO Air 33/5

82 AHB, Coastal Command narrative, III, 410–12, DHist 79/599; No 415 Squadron ORB, May–June 1942, DHist

83 No 415 Squadron progress report, 2 July 1942, DHist 181.003 (D5212); No 415 Squadron ORB, 19 June 1942, DHist

84 No 415 Squadron ORB daily, 1 July 1942, DHist

85 No 415 Squadron ORB, July 1942, DHist; AHB, Coastal Command narrative, III, 411, app. XXXIII, DHist 79/599

86 Hitchens, 'No 407 Squadron,' Oct. 1953, 63–4, DHist 74/308

87 No 407 Squadron ORB, 30 July 1942, DHist

88 AHB, Coastal Command narrative, III, app. XXXIII, DHist 79/599

89 Joubert to No 18 Group, 27 July 1942, PRO Air 15/486; No 415 Squadron ORB, 1 Sept. 1942, DHist

90 Hitchens, 'No 407 Squadron,' Oct. 1953, 72, DHist 74/308; 'Minutes of the Air Officer Commanding-in-Chief's Third Meeting with Group Commanders,' 26 March 1942, PRO Air 15/178; AHB, Coastal Command narrative, III, 14–17, 401, DHist 79/599; Barnes, *Bristol Aircraft since 1910*, 283–307; Nesbit, *The Strike Wings*, 22; Joubert to Pound, 9 Aug. 1942, PRO Air 15/214; Rawlings, *Coastal, Support and Special Squadrons,* 179

CHAPTER 13: A FORCE TO BE RECKONED WITH

1 AHB, Coastal Command narrative, III, 402, DHist 79/599; No 16 Group to Coastal Command, 1 Dec. 1942, PRO Air 15/379; Nesbit, *The Strike Wings*, 31–9

2 AHB, Coastal Command narrative, III, 402, DHist 79/599; No 16 Group to Coastal Command, 1 Dec. 1942, PRO Air 15/379

3 Coastal Command to Air Ministry, 17 Feb. 1943, PRO Air 15/214; Barnes, *Bristol Aircraft since 1910*, 292–4, 307; AHB, Coastal Command narrative, III, 484–5, and IV, 100–1, DHist 79/599

4 Truscott to Coastal Command, Coastal Command combat report, 25 March 1943, DHist 181.003 (D4002)

5 Ibid.; AHB, Coastal Command narrative, IV, 101, DHist 79/599

6 No 415 Squadron ORB, Nov. 1942–May 1943, DHist

7 Ibid., 22 Dec. 1942, DHist

8 No 415 Squadron progress reports, Oct. 1942–Aug. 1943, DHist 181.003 (D5212); AHB, Coastal Command narrative, IV, 251–2, DHist 79/599

9 Coastal Command to No 16 Group, draft, nd [Jan 1943], Coastal Command to Air Ministry, 7 Feb. 1943, Coastal Command to No 16 Group and Nos 236, 254, and 143 Squadrons, 7 Feb. 1943, D of Ops (Torpedoes) to DAT, 11 Feb. 1943, 'Minutes of a Conference held ... on the 22nd February, 1943, to discuss the operation of 16 Group Beaufighter Striking Wing and Co-operation with this Wing by Aircraft of Fighter Command,' nd, PRO Air 15/379

10 AHB, Coastal Command narrative, IV, 247–8, DHist 79/599; 'Cooperation between Coastal, Bomber, VIIIth American Bomber and Fighter Commands in Attack on Enemy Shipping in Home Waters within the Range of Shore Based Aircraft,' 7 April 1943, PRO Air 15/298

11 Hinsley, *British Intelligence in the Second World War*, II, 195–6, and III, pt 1, 28off

12 AHB, Coastal Command narrative, IV, 249–50, DHist 79/599; No 414 Squadron ORB, 18 April 1943, DHist; Nesbit, *The Strike Wings*, 43–51

13 'Appreciation of the Situation of Enemy Activity on the Dutch Coast by AOC 16 Group' [Aug. 1943], PRO Air 15/630; AHB, Coastal Command narrative, IV, 250–2, 265–6, DHist 79/599

14 Slessor to Air Ministry, 8 Aug. 1943, PRO Air 15/630

15 AHB, Coastal Command narrative, IV, 269, DHist 79/599; minutes of conference, 20 Aug. 1943, PRO Air 41/48; Roskill, *The War at Sea*, III, pt 1, 92; Hinsley, *British Intelligence*, III, pt 1, 28off

16 AHB, Coastal Command narrative, IV, 269, DHist 79/599; minutes of conference, 20 Aug. 1943, PRO Air 41/48; Roskill, *The War at Sea*, III, pt 1, 92; Hinsley, *British Intelligence*, III, pt 1, 28off

17 No 415 Squadron ORB, 24 Sept. 1942, DHist; Edwards to Air Ministry, 2 Oct. 1942, Hollinghurst to Edwards, 31 Oct. 1942, DHist 181.006 (D295)

18 No 415 Squadron progress reports, 29 Aug. and 14 Sept. 1942, DHist 181.003 (D5212); Edwards to AMP, 29 Sept. 1942, No 17 Group to Coastal Command, 11 Oct. 1942, and director of postings to Edwards, 4 Nov. 1942, DHist

181.006 (D295); 'A statistical return on Canadianization,' DHist 181.003 (D3596)

19 Slessor to Air Ministry, 2 March 1943, Edwards to director of postings, 17 March 1943, DHist 181.006 (D295)

20 Edwards to Air Ministry, 2 July 1943, director-general of organization to Edwards, 16 July 1943, both DHist 181.006 (D295)

21 DAS to AOC-in-C, minute 2, 24 Aug. 1943, Edwards to Air Ministry, draft, 20 Aug. 1943, DHist 181.006 (D295)

22 Slessor to Edwards, 28 Aug. 1943, DHist 181.006 (D295)

23 Edwards to Slessor, 13 Sept. 1943 (draft not sent), DHist 181.006 (D295)

24 Edwards to AMSO, 16 Sept. 1943, DHist 181.006 (D295)

25 AHB, Coastal Command narrative, IV, 254–6, 343–7, app. I, DHist 79/599; No 404 Squadron ORB, 27 April 1943

26 AHB, Coastal Command narrative, IV, 351–2, DHist 79/599; Fighter Command, 'Disposition of GAF Fighters on the Western Front,' June–Sept. 1943, DHist 181.009 (D93)

27 AHB, Coastal Command narrative, IV, 255–7, DHist 79/599

28 No 404 Squadron progress reports, Sept. 1942–July 1943, DHist 181.003 (D1034)

29 G.G. Truscott biography, C.A. Willis biog. file, DHist; No 8 Squadron, PR file, DHist

30 No 404 Squadron ORB, 4 July 1943, DHist

31 Ibid., 1, 2, 4, and 17 July 1943, DHist; AHB, Coastal Command narrative, IV, 275–7, DHist 79/599

32 No 404 Squadron ORB, 28 July 1943, DHist

33 Ibid., 28 July 1943, 30 March and 28 June 1944, DHist; Nesbit, *The Strike Wings*, 78–85; Douglas, *The Creation of a National Air Force*, 584; No 404 Squadron Scrapbook, 28 July 1943, 290–3, DHist 86/128; E.J. Keefe biog. file, DHist; *London Gazette*, 7 July 1944

34 No 404 Squadron ORB, Aug. 1943, 22 Aug. 1944, DHist; AHB, Coastal Command narrative, III, 284–5, DHist 79/599

35 No 18 Group to Coastal Command, 6 March 1944, PRO Air 15/481

36 J.M.N. Pike to No 18 Group, 4 Aug. 1943, Ministry of Aircraft Production, 'A Brief Summary of the Characteristics of the Aircraft Rockets Weapon,' 23 April 1943, PRO Air 15/210; AHB, Coastal Command narrative, IV, app. III, DHist 79/599

37 AHB, Coastal Command narrative, IV, 278, 282, 285, 289, DHist 79/599; Admiralty, 'Cancellation of German Transit Traffic through Sweden,' 10 Aug. 1943, PRO Air 15/481

38 AHB, Coastal Command narrative, IV, 277, 289–91, DHist 79/599; No 404 Squadron ORB, Nov.–Dec. 1943, DHist

39 AHB, Coastal Command narrative, 289, 290, 503–4, DHist 79/599

40 No 404 Squadron ORB, 14 Jan. 1944, DHist

41 Ibid., 14 and 20 Jan. 1944, DHist; AHB, Coastal Command narrative, 503–4, DHist 79/599

42 No 404 Squadron ORB, 16 Jan. 1944, DHist

43 Ibid., 26 Jan. 1944

44 Ibid., 1 Feb. 1944

45 AHB, Coastal Command narrative, IV, 504–7, 519, DHist 79/599; C.A. Willis biog file, DHist

46 No 404 Squadron ORB, 19 April 1944, DHist; AHB, Coastal Command narrative, IV, 519, DHist 79/599

47 Hinsley, *British Intelligence in the Second World War*, III, pt 1, 282ff; Roskill, *The War at Sea*, II, 394, III, pt 1, 96, 289, pt 2, app. YY; AHB, Coastal Command narrative, III, app. XXIX, and IV, 248, 254, 295–6, 414–51, 523

48 Hinsley, *British Intelligence in the Second World War*, III, pt 1, 283–5

49 AHB, Coastal Command narrative, IV, 523–6, 529ff, DHist 79/599

50 No 415 Squadron ORB, Nov. 1943–Feb. 1944, DHist

51 'Control of FAA Aircraft in Area of VA Commanding, Dover,' 15 July 1943, PRO Air 15/487; AHB, Coastal Command narrative, IV, 531–3, 542–4, DHist 79/599; No 415 Squadron ORB, 1 Nov. 1943, DHist; Tinker to AOC-in-C, 6 Nov. 1943, DHist 181.006 (D295)

52 No 415 Squadron ORB, Nov. 1943–Jan. 1944, DHist; Courtney to Curtis, 30 Nov. 1943, Truscott to Breadner, 21 Feb. 1944, DHist 181.006 (D295)

53 Slessor to Edwards, 28 Aug. 1943, DHist 181.006 (D295); No 415 Squadron ORB, 23–28 Sept. and 24 Nov. 1943, DHist; No 415 Squadron progress report, 12 Nov. 1943, DHist 181.003 (D5212)

54 Truscott to Breadner, 21 Feb. 1944, DHist 181.006 (D295)

55 *Swordfish: The Story of 415 Squadron* (np 1983), 20

56 Breadner to Power, 14 Feb. 1944, DHist 181.006 (D295)

57 Power to Breadner, 17 Feb. 1944, Breadner, 'Notes on Meeting Held at Headquarters, Coastal Command, on February 22nd, 1944,' DHist 181.006 (D295)

58 Breadner, 'Notes on Meeting Held at Headquarters, Coastal Command, on February 22nd, 1944,' DHist 181.006 (D295); Douglas to Air Ministry, 6 March 1944, PRO Air 15/487

59 Truscott to AOC-in-C, RCAF Overseas, 13 March 1944, DHist 181.006 (D295)

60 Breadner to Power, 30 March 1944, Power to Breadner, 3 April 1944, Ruttan to Overseas Headquarters, 19 April 1944, and Overseas Headquarters to Ruttan, 26 April 1944, DHist 181.006 (D295)

61 No 415 Squadron ORB, Feb–May 1944, DHist; AHB, Coastal Command narrative, IV, 502, 516–19, DHist 79/599

62 No 415 Squadron ORB, 30, 31 March 1944, DHist

63 Ibid., March–May 1944, DHist; AHB, Coastal Command narrative, IV, 511, DHist 79/599; M.J. Whitley, *German Destroyers of World War II* (Anapolis 1991), 158; Erich Gröner, *German Warships 1815–1945: Major Surface Vessels* (Anapolis 1990), 191ff

64 No 415 Squadron ORB, Feb–June 1944, DHist; AHB, *The Rise and Fall of the German Air Force, 1933–1945* (London 1983), 324–5

65 'Minutes of a Meeting held in the Air Council Room ... on the 22nd March, 1944, to discuss the War at Sea in Relation to "Overlord,"' nd, PRO Air

15/357; 'Directive on the Role of Coastal Command in "Overlord,"' 18 April 1944, app. A, PRO Air 15/293

66 'Directive on the Role of Coastal Command in OVERLORD,' 18 April 1944, app. B, PRO Air 15/293; AHB, Coastal Command narrative, IV, 515–16, DHist 79/599

67 AHB, Coastal Command narrative, IV, 520, and V, 4, DHist 79/599; Hinsley, *British Intelligence in the Second World War*, III, pt 2, 161ff; No 404 Squadron progress reports, 17 May, 3 and 16 June 1944, DHist 181.003 (D3007); 404 Squadron ORB, May–June 1944, DHist

68 No 404 Squadron ORB, 6 June 1944, DHist

69 *Kriegstagebuch, 8. Zerstoerer Flotille*, 7–8 June 1944, United States National Archives, micro series T 1022, reel 3287, PG 74146

70 Nesbit, *The Strike Wings*, 123–5; AHB, Coastal Command narrative, V, 7–9, 43, DHist 79/599; Joseph Schull, *The Far Distant Ships* (Ottawa 1952), 286–95

71 No 404 Squadron progress reports, 16 June and 4 July 1944, DHist 181.003 (D3007); AHB, Coastal Command narrative, V, 16, DHist 79/599

72 No 415 Squadron ORB, June and July 1944, DHist; AHB, Coastal Command narrative, V, 13–16, 24–5, DHist 79/599

73 No 415 Squadron ORB, July 1944, DHist; RCAF Record Book of Coastal Command Operations, July 1944, app. C, DHist 181.003 (D886)

74 Coastal Command to Air Ministry, 1 Sept. 1944, PRO Air 15/293; AHB, Coastal Command narrative, V, 24, DHist 79/599

75 No 404 Squadron ORB, July 1944, DHist; No 404 Squadron progress reports, 17 July, 1 Aug. 1944, DHist 181.003 (D3007); AHB, Coastal Command narrative, V, 26–7, DHist 79/599; Nesbit, *The Strike Wings*, 133–4

76 No 404 Squadron ORB, July 1944, DHist; No 404 Squadron progress reports, 17 July, 1 Aug. 1944, DHist 181.003 (D3007); AHB, Coastal Command narrative, V, 26–7, DHist 79/599; Nesbit, *The Strike Wings*, 133–4

77 Coastal Command to Air Ministry, 1 Sept. 1944, PRO Air 15/293; No 404 Squadron ORB, 5, 6, and 8 Aug. 1944, DHist; AHB, Coastal Command narrative, V, 41–4, DHist 79/599

78 P.M.A. Green, 'Enemy Shipping on the Norwegian Coast: Its Probable Enhanced Importance,' 13 June 1944, PRO Air 15/532

79 AHB, Coastal Command narrative, V, 111, 120, 136–7, DHist 79/599

80 No 404 Squadron ORB, 10 May 1941, 23 Aug. 1944, DHist; E.W. Pierce biog. information, DHist 88/45; No 404 Squadron progress report, 1 Sept. 1944, DHist 181.003 (D3007)

81 AHB, Coastal Command narrative, V, 117, app. VIII, DHist 79/599

82 Coastal Command, 'Notes on the Employment of Coastal Command Anti-Shipping Forces during the Winter 1944–45,' 16 Oct. 1944, PRO Air 15/391

83 AHB, Coastal Command narrative, V, 114, DHist 79/599

84 No 404 Squadron ORB, 9 Oct. 1944, DHist; AHB, Coastal Command narrative, V, 118–19, DHist 79/599

85 No 404 Squadron progress reports, 17 Oct. and 3 Nov. 1944, DHist 181.003 (D3007); AHB, Coastal Command narrative, V, app. VIII, DHist 79/599

86 No 404 Squadron ORB, 21 Oct. 1944, DHist

87 Nesbit, *The Strike Wings*, app. III

88 No 404 Squadron progress reports, 21 Nov. and 4 Dec. 1944, DHist 181.003 (D3007); AHB, Coastal Command narrative, V, 120, DHist 79/599

89 'Coastal Command Operational Instruction No. 7/44,' 14 Nov. 1944, PRO Air 15/481

90 No 404 Squadron ORB, 7 Dec. 1944, DHist

91 Ibid., 9 Dec. 1944, DHist; AHB, Coastal Command narrative, V, app. VIII, DHist 79/599

92 AHB, Coastal Command narrative, V, 131, 134–5, 140, 167, app. VIII, app. XII, DHist 79/599

93 Ibid., 167, app. VIII, app. XV, app. XVII

94 Roskill, *The War at Sea*, III, pt 2, app. YY; Green to SASO, 7 Jan. 1945, PRO Air 15/481; AHB, Coastal Command narrative, V, 275–6, DHist 79/599; Nesbit, *The Strike Wings*, 219–24

95 No 404 Squadron ORB, 9 Feb. 1945, DHist

96 AHB, Coastal Command narrative, V, 276, DHist 79/599; Nesbit, *The Strike Wings*, 224, 227–8; No 404 Squadron ORB, 9 Feb. 1945, DHist; No 404 Squadron scrapbook, 14 May 1945, DHist 86/128, vol. 2; M.J. Whitley, *Destroyer! German Destroyers in World War II* (Annapolis, Md. 1983), 172

97 Douglas to Hill, 27 March 1945, PRO Air 15/391

98 No 404 Squadron ORB, March 1945, DHist; AHB, Coastal Command narrative, V, 274–9, DHist 79/599

99 Green to SASO, 7 Jan. 1945, PRO Air 15/481

100 No 404 Squadron ORB, 12 March 1945, DHist

101 Ibid.; AHB, Coastal Command narrative, V, 277–80, DHist 79/599

102 No 404 Squadron ORB, April–May 1945, DHist; AHB, Coastal Command narrative, V, 280–4, DHist 79/599

103 No 404 Squadron progress report, 17 May 1945, DHist 181.003 (D3007); AHB, Coastal Command narrative, V, 285–6, app. VIII, DHist 79/599

104 Roskill, *The War at Sea*, III, pt 2, app. YY; Nesbit, *The Strike Wings*, app. III; Sir Charles Webster and Noble Frankland, *The Strategic Air Offensive against Germany, 1939–1945*, IV (London 1961), 421; AHB, Coastal Command narrative, V, app. I, DHist 79/599

CHAPTER 14: THE GENESIS OF A BOMBING OFFENSIVE

1 Keith Middlemas and John Barnes, *Baldwin* (London 1969), 735; Eugene M. Emme, ed., *The Impact of Air Power* (Princeton, NJ 1959), 51–2

2 H.R. Allen, *The Legacy of Lord Trenchard* (London 1972), 54–9; Sir Charles Webster and Noble Frankland, *The Strategic Air Offensive against Germany, 1939–1945* (London 1961), I, 87–9, and IV, 448ff (hereafter *SAO*). See also Neville Jones, *The Beginnings of Strategic Air Power* (London 1987); H. Montgomery Hyde, *British Air Policy between the Wars, 1918–1939* (London 1976); John Terraine, *A Time for Courage* (New York 1985); Malcolm Smith, *British Air Strategy between the Wars* (Oxford 1984); N.H. Gibbs, *Grand Strategy* (London 1976), I; Peter Lewis, *The British Bomber since 1914*

(London 1967), 266–99; and Sir John Slessor, *The Central Blue* (London 1956)

3 Air Ministry War Room Statistical Section, 'Manual of Bomber Command Operations 1939–1945,' DHist 181.003 (D3992); Air Ministry, Air Historical Branch (AHB), 'The RAF in the Bombing Offensive against Germany,' II, 6–10, DHist 86/286, (hereafter Bomber Command narrative); Webster and Frankland, *SAO*, I, 67, 108, and IV, 400–3; Slessor, *The Central Blue*, 156ff, 178

4 Slessor, *The Central Blue*, 234–5; Martin Middlebrook and Chris Everitt, *The Bomber Command War Diaries* (London 1985), 77 (hereafter *BCWD*)

5 Wilhelm Diest et al., *Germany and the Second World War*, I (Oxford 1990), especially part IV, 594ff, 639ff, 704ff; Hyde, *British Air Policy*, 391–2

6 Gibbs, *Grand Strategy*, I, 283–4, 288; Smith, *British Air Strategy*, 193; Hyde, *British Air Policy*, 408–13, 391–2; Slessor, *The Central Blue*, 164–5; Webster and Frankland, *SAO*, I, 90; Dudley Saward, *'Bomber' Harris* (London 1984), 52–3; Abraham to AOC-in-C, Bomber Command, 15 Sept. 1938, PRO Air 9/90; Ian Colvin, *The Chamberlain Cabinet* (London 1971), 52, 76–83

7 Webster and Frankland, *SAO*, I, 80–3; Bennett to Goddard, 30 Nov. 1938, PRO Air 40/2108

8 Middlebrook and Everitt, *BCWD*, 21–2

9 Sir Basil Embry, *Mission Accomplished* (London 1957), 89; Webster and Frankland, *SAO*, I, 112 n

10 Terraine, *A Time for Courage*, 82–4

11 R.V. Jones, *Most Secret War* (London 1978), 45–6

12 AHB, Bomber Command narrative, I, 167, DHist 86/286; Ronald Clark, *Tizard* (London 1965), 190; ACAS to commands, 9 June 1938, PRO Air 14/69

13 AHB, *Armament* (London 1952) I, ch. 19; Frankland and Webster, *SAO*, IV, 31–9; Cawood to OR 2(a), 8 June 1943, PRO Avia 15/124; 'Notes on bomb sight policy,' 7 March 1941, PRO Avia 15/122; Royal Aircraft Establishment, departmental note no 611, Dec. 1941, PRO Avia 6/12538

14 Air Ministry to commands, 22 May 1939, PRO Air 14/69

15 AHB, *Armament*, II, chs. 1 and 12, and particularly 15–34, 95–6; G.F. Wallace, *Guns of the R.A.F. 1919–1939* (London 1972), ch. 15; Bomber Command, 'Considerations affecting the design of the ideal bomber aircraft ...' Jan. 1938, with comments by R.S. Capon, 10 Feb. 1938, and D.R. Pye, 16 Feb. 1938, PRO Avia 10/15; Lewis, *The British Bomber*, 311–13

16 AHB, Bomber Command narrative, II, 43–5, 56–7, DHist 86/286; Middlebrook and Everitt, *BCWD*, 21–2

17 AHB, Bomber Command narrative, II, 47, DHist 86/286

18 Ibid., 43–5; Middlebrook and Everitt, *BCWD*, 30

19 AHB, Bomber Command narrative, II, 43–5, DHist 86/286; No 77 Squadron history, DHist 80/164

20 Noble Frankland, 'The planning of the bombing offensive and its contribution to German collapse,' April 1945, PRO Air 41/57, 36; AHB, Bomber Command narrative, II, appendix A.1 and A.2, DHist 86/286

21 Ian Hogg, *Anti-Aircraft* (London 1978), 105; Matthew Cooper, *The German Air Force, 1933–1945* (London 1981), 56–7, 181; Generalmajor Walter

Grabmann, 'German air defense, 1933–1945,' June 1957, USAF Historical Study No 164, DHist 86/451, frames 138–42, 259, 271ff, 286ff, 391ff; Gebhard Aders, *History of the German Night Fighter Force, 1917–1954* (London 1976), 14; Diest et al., *Germany and the Second World War*, I, 504n

22 Air Ministry to No 1 and No 2 Mission, 16 Oct. 1939, PRO Air 9/131; Director of Plans memorandum, 27 Sept. 1939, and aide memoire, 13 Oct. 1939, PRO Air 9/191; AHB, Bomber Command narrative, II, 59–60, DHist 86/286; Middlebrook and Everitt, *BCWD*, 25–6

23 AHB, Bomber Command narrative, II, 60–1, DHist 86/286; Middlebrook and Everitt, *BCWD*, 26–30; Max Hastings, *Bomber Command* (London 1979), 26–8; *London Gazette*, 20 Feb. 1940, No 34795, 1055

24 Webster and Frankland, *SAO*, I, 206ff

25 'The attack of German war potential by night,' 13 Jan. 1940, PRO Air 9/102; 'The attack of Germany by night, Plan WA8,' Jan. 1940, PRO Air 9/422

26 Ibid.

27 Webster and Frankland, *SAO*, I, 139–41, 208; Ludlow-Hewitt to secretary of state for air, 25 March 1940, PRO Air 9/102

28 Webster and Frankland, *SAO*, I, 211

29 Ragg to Sigs 1(Ops), minute 6, 15 March 1940, PRO Air 14/520

30 DD Plans (Ops) to director of plans, 10 April 1940, PRO Air 9/131 ; 'Extracts, 67th meeting, chiefs of staff, 7 Apr 1940,' 9 April 1940, PRO Air 2/3161

31 DCAS to CAS, 12 May 1940, PRO Air 9/131; AHB, Bomber Command narrative, II, 39, DHist 86/286; quoted in Martin Gilbert, *Finest Hour* (Don Mills 1983), 333–5

32 Middlebrook and Everitt, *BCWD*, 43

33 William Shirer, *Berlin Diary* (New York 1943) 279–80; Middlebrook and Everitt, *BCWD*, 44

34 AHB, Bomber Command narrative, II, 83, 91, DHist 86/286; Gilbert, *Finest Hour*, 349ff; Terraine, *A Time for Courage*, 149; Denis Richards, *Portal of Hungerford* (London 1977), 153

35 DCAS to Bomber Command, 4 June 1940, PRO Air 9/131; Terraine, *A Time for Courage*, 275; Richards, *Portal*, 154–6; director of plans to Bomber Command, 20 June 1940, PRO Air 9/99; AHB, Bomber Command narrative, II, 105–7, DHist 86/286; Slessor, *The Central Blue*, 296; Middlebrook and Everitt, *BCWD*, 194; and Denis Richards, *Royal Air Force, 1939–1945*, I, (London 1953), 124

36 Gilbert, *Finest Hour*, 408–9, 603

37 Webster and Frankland, *SAO*, I, 147ff; AHB, Bomber Command narrative, II, 118ff, DHist 86/286

38 AHB, Bomber Command narrative, II, 114–17, DHist 86/286

39 Terraine, *A Time for Courage*, 262; Middlebrook and Everitt, *BCWD*, 77; Gilbert, *Finest Hour*, 757

40 Richards, *Portal*, 165; AHB, Bomber Command narrative, II, 118–19, DHist 86/286; Gilbert, *Finest Hour*, 772

41 Gilbert, *Finest Hour*, 795; Air Staff, 'Bombing Policy,' 20 Sept. 1940, PRO Air 9/131; Inglis to D of I, 24 Sept. 1940, PRO Air 9/443; AHB, Bomber Command

narrative, II, 119–20, DHist 86/286; Middlebrook and Everitt, *BCWD*, 85; AOC-in-C, 'Review of bombing policy,' 30 Sept. 1940, PRO Air 9/443; Richards, *Portal*, 300; Webster and Frankland, *SAO*, I, 154; Hastings, *Bomber Command*, 112–13

42 Stevenson to PS to CAS, 21 July 1940, PRO Air 9/132; Richards, *Portal*, 161

43 Douglas to Peirse, 25 Oct. 1940, PRO Air 2/4475; Richards, *Portal*, 167, 218–19; 'Minutes of meeting held 23 Oct 1940 to discuss bombing policy,' PRO Air 9/443; Webster and Frankland, *SAO*, I, 154–7; AHB, Bomber Command narrative, II, 142–5, DHist 86/286

44 Gilbert, *Finest Hour*, 881–2; Peirse to Portal, 13 Nov. 1940, Portal Papers, DHist 87/89, folder 9A (1940)

45 AHB, Bomber Command narrative, II, 144–5, DHist 86/286; Terraine, *A Time for Courage*, 268–9; Middlebrook and Everitt, *BCWD*, 111–12

46 Webster and Frankland, *SAO*, I, 158–62, 169; Churchill to Portal, 17 Nov. 1940, PRO Air 8/407; Peirse to secretary of state, 27 Nov. 1940, Portal Papers, DHist 87/89, folder 9A (1940); Harris to VCAS, minute 56, 27 Nov. 1940, PRO Air 2/4475; Portal to Peirse, 30 Nov. 1940, Portal Papers, DHist 87/89, folder 9A (1940); Bomber Command, 'Review of work of Intelligence 1 Section (Target Intelligence & Damage Assessment), 1939–1945,' I, 18 Aug. 1945, 43, DHist 181.003 (D195); Terraine, *A Time for Courage*, 269; Robert Goralski and Russell W. Freeburg, *Oil & War* (New York 1987), 240; Wolfgang Birkenfeld, *Der Synthetische Treibstoff 1933–1945* (Göttingen 1964), 143–6, translated in DHist SGR II 151

47 Terraine, *A Time for Courage*, 275; Webster and Frankland, *SAO*, I, 158–62; Richards, *Portal*, 301; Portal to Peirse, 15 Jan. 1941, Portal Papers, DHist 87/89, folder 9B (1941); AHB, Bomber Command narrative, II, 145–7, DHist 86/286

48 AHB, Bomber Command narrative, II, 144–6 DHist 86/286; Webster and Frankland, *SAO*, I, 163–5; Middlebrook and Everitt, *BCWD*, 124–9; Portal to Peirse, 29 Feb. 41, and 'Notes by chief of the air staff,' 3 March 1941, Peirse to Portal, 5 March 1941, Portal Papers, DHist 87/89, folder 9B (1941); Richards, *Portal*, 302; Slessor, *The Central Blue*, 371 (emphasis in the original)

49 Webster and Frankland, *SAO*, I, 165; Middlebrook and Everitt, *BCWD*, 131–3; AHB, Bomber Command narrative, II, 134, DHist 86/286; G/C Ops to SASO, 3 Jan. 1941, PRO Air 14/396; and Dudley Saward, *The Bomber's Eye* (London 1959), 44–5, 52–3

50 Bennett, 'Comments on Air Fighting Committee Paper 82,' 15 March 1940, PRO Air 20/4724

51 Air Ministry, Air Scientific Intelligence (ASI), report No 1, 29 Dec. 1942, PRO Air 20/1663; United States Air Forces in Europe (USAFE), 'German air defenses: tactical employment of night fighters in the GAF,' 3 March 1946, DHist 73/1506, microfilm reel 1, frames 462ff; Alfred Price, *Instruments of Darkness* (London 1977), 61–7; Jones, *Most Secret War*, 189–223; Aders, *German Night Fighter Force*, 20–7

52 'Bomber Command analysis of losses, 9/10 Apr 1941 to 17/18 Apr 1941,' 20 April 1941, Portal Papers, DHist 87/89, folder 9B (1941); Bomber Command to Groups, 3 July 1941, PRO Air 14/232

53 Sinclair to Churchill, 2 April 1941, PRO Air 8/405; AHB, Bomber Command narrative, II, 8–10, app. E, and II, 8–10 and app. C, DHist 86/286; Webster and Frankland, *SAO*, IV, 135–40

54 'Note on Dominionization of Article XV Squadrons,' 24 Jan. 1943, PRO Air 8/742; RCAF Overseas Headquarters progress report to AFHQ, 2 May 1941, DHist 181.003 (D34)

55 AOC RCAF Overseas to CAS, 16 April 1941, and CAS to minister of national defence, 18 June, 6 Sept., 4 Nov., and 22 Dec. 1941, all DHist 181.003 (D68), vol. 1; No 408 Squadron PRF file, DHist; Samuel Kostenuk and John Griffin, *RCAF Squadron Histories and Aircraft, 1924–1968* (Toronto 1978), 89–90; Owen Thetford, *Aircraft of the Royal Air Force since 1918* (New York 1968), 484; Hammond to McLeod, 12 June 1941, DHist 181.006 (D284)

56 No 405 Squadron Operations Record Book (ORB), May–June 1941, and No 408 Squadron ORB, 10 July 1941, DHist

57 *408 Squadron History* (Belleville 1984), 10

58 B. Halpenny, *Action Stations No. 4: Military Airfields of Yorkshire* (Cambridge 1982), 64–7, 118–20, 153–4; John Searby, *The Bomber Battle for Berlin* (Shrewsbury 1991), 35; B. Halpenny, *Action Stations No. 2: Military Airfields of Lincolnshire and the East Midlands* (Cambridge 1981), 185–7

59 *408 Squadron History*, 10; Timmerman biog. file, DHist

60 Webster and Frankland, *SAO*, I, 173; Foreign Office and Ministry of Economic Warfare, Enemy Branch, 'The Bomber's Baedeker,' part II, DHist 181.003 (D3993); No 405 Squadron ORB, 13 June 1941, DHist; Middlebrook and Everitt, *BCWD*, 161; RAF Station Driffield to No 4 Group, 13 June 1941, DHist 181.003 (D3876)

61 No 405 Squadron ORB, 17 June 1941, DHist; Middlebrook and Everitt, *BCWD*, 163

62 No 405 Squadron ORB, 18, 19, 23 June, and 4 July 1941, DHist; Middlebrook and Everitt, *BCWD*, 166, 171

63 No 405 Squadron ORB, 24 July 1941, DHist

64 Middlebrook and Everitt, *BCWD*, 161; No 405 Squadron ORB, 24 July 1941, DHist

65 No 405 Squadron ORB, 30–1 July 1941, DHist; Molson, 'Report on German searchlights,' PRO Air 14/1938; AHB, *Armament*, II, 113

66 No 408 Squadron ORB, 11–13 Aug. 1941, DHist; Hastings, *Bomber Command*, 103–4

67 No 408 Squadron ORB, 31 Aug., 17, 18, 21, and 22 Sept. 1941, DHist; Middlebrook and Everitt, *BCWD*, 204

68 Middlebrook and Everitt, *BCWD*, 219

69 OR2 to Ops 2, 6 Jan. 1941, PRO Air 9/132; John A. MacBean and Arthur S. Hogben, *Bombs Gone* (Wellingborough 1991), 45–7; SASO to AOC-in-C, minute

99, 4 May 1941, PRO Air 14/232; AHB, Bomber Command narrative, II, app. W, DHist 86/286

70 SASO Bomber Command to groups, 3 July 1941, PRO Air 14/232

71 Saundby to groups, 18 July 1941, Slessor to Saundby, 21 July 1941, and Saundby to Slessor 26 July 1941, PRO Air 14/232; David Divine, *Broken Wing* (London 1966), 253; Sir Arthur Harris, *Bomber Offensive* (London 1947), 76; Webster and Frankland, *SAO*, I, 180–1

72 AHB Bomber Command narrative, III, 41–6, DHist 86/286; Richards, *Portal*, 303

73 *No 405 Squadron History* (Winnipeg 1991), 19; Harris, *Bomber Offensive*, 96–7

74 Fawley interview, 18 Aug. 1974, Fawley biog. file, DHist; see also his abstract, 'Night bombing over Germany,' Jan. 1942, DHist 74/655, and Henderson to No 1 Air Navigation School, Rivers, Manitoba, nd, PRO Air 14/505; 'Minutes of discussion held at Headquarters, Bomber Command,' 5 Sept. 1942, PRO Air 14/69

75 Bomber Command to groups, 2 Aug. 1941, PRO Air 14/232; No 4 Group to Bomber Command, 22 Aug. 1941, PRO Air 14/1243

76 'Minutes of meeting held at Ministry of Aircraft Production,' 23 July 1941, PRO Avia 15/123; AHB, *Armament*, I, 279; 'Memorandum on the introduction of T.R. 1335 (GEE) into Bomber Command,' Feb. 1944, DHist 181.002 (D112); AHB, Bomber Command narrative, IV, 75–7, DHist 86/286

77 No 405 Squadron ORB, 20 Aug. 1941, DHist; No 405 Squadron to No 4 Group, 20 Aug. 1941, form YA29, DHist 181.003 (D3876); Middlebrook and Everitt, *BCWD*, 194

78 No 405 Squadron ORB, 23 Aug. 1941, DHist; Middlebrook and Everitt, *BCWD*, 195

CHAPTER 15: THE OFFENSIVE AT RISK

1 Bomber Command to groups, 13 Sept. 1941, PRO Air 14/1956

2 Slessor to Saundby, 1 Sept. 1941, and Saundby to Slessor, 15 Sept. 1941, PRO Air 14/232

3 AHB, Bomber Command narrative, IV, 41–2, DHist 86/286

4 Dickens to Saundby, minute 14, 24 Dec. 1941, and Saundby to Harris, minute 15, 27 Dec. 1941, PRO Air 14/1755; MacBean and Hogben, *Bombs Gone*, 68

5 Baker to DCAS, 10 Sept. 1941, minute 16, and CAS to DCAS, 17 Sept. 1941, minute 19, PRO Air 2/7556; DCAS to VCAS, 27 Sept. 1941, minute 113, PRO Air 2/4475

6 No 408 Squadron ORB, 30 Oct. 1941, DHist; Middlebrook and Everitt, *BCWD*, 207–15

7 No 405 Squadron ORB, 8 Sept.–15 Oct. 1941, DHist; Middlebrook and Everitt, *BCWD*, 200, 209–15; AHB, Bomber Command narrative, III, 94–105, DHist 86/286; 'The Bomber's Baedeker,' DHist 181.003 (D3993)

8 AHB, Bomber Command narrative, III, 10 B, 28–33, DHist 86/286; Middlebrook

and Everitt, *BCWD*, 219; No 405 and 408 Squadron ORBs, Sept.–Oct. 1941, DHist

9 Air Staff, 'The heavy bomber – operational requirements ...' 12 Aug. 1941, DHist 181.009 (D196); Lewis, *The British Bomber*, 311–13

10 M.M. Postan et al., *Design and Development of Weapons*, (London 1964), 8–14, 19, 27–8, 92–4, 142–6, 149–52; Corelli Barnett, *The Audit of War* (London 1986), 130–1, 145–55; J.D. Scott and R. Hughes, *The Administration of War Production* (London 1955), 297ff, 343–6

11 AHB, Bomber Command narrative, III, 9–10C, 13ff, DHist 86/286; AOC RCAF Overseas to secretary, Department of National Defence for Air, 10 Sept. 1941, DHist 181.009 (D774)

12 AHB, Bomber Command narrative, III, 10b, 14–15, 24–7, DHist 86/286

13 Ibid., 28–32; Middlebrook and Everitt, *BCWD*, 187, 191

14 DBOps, 'Development and employment of the heavy bomber force,' 22 Sept. 1941, PRO Air 19/186; Webster and Frankland, *SAO*, I, 181–2; AHB, Bomber Command narrative, II, app. C.3, DHist 86/286

15 Sinclair to Churchill, 3 Sept. 1941, PRO Air 19/282; Bomber Command narrative, III, 28–32, DHist 86/286; Churchill to Portal, 27 Sept. 1941, quoted in Webster and Frankland, *SAO*, I, 182–3; Gilbert, *Finest Hour*, 1205

16 Churchill to CAS, 7 Oct. 1941, PRO Air 19/186; Webster and Frankland, *SAO*, I, 185–7; AHB, Bomber Command narrative, III, 137–9, DHist 86/286; Portal to Churchill, 13 Oct. 1941, quoted in Webster and Frankland, *SAO*, I, 185; Bottomley to Peirse, 25 Oct. 1941, PRO Air 14/763

17 Bomber Command narrative, III, DHist 86/286, 34–7; Middlebrook and Everitt, *BCWD*, 217–18; Terraine, *A Time for Courage*, 459–60; Slessor, *The Central Blue*, 378

18 No 405 Squadron ORB, 8 Nov. 1941, DHist

19 Searby, *The Bomber Battle for Berlin*, 40–1, 59

20 Middlebrook and Everitt, *BCWD*, 218; No 408 Squadron ORB, 8 Nov. 1941, DHist

21 Prime minister's personal minute to secretary of state for air and CAS, M.1038/1, 11 Nov. 1941, PRO Air 19/186; AHB, Bomber Command narrative, III, 34–7, DHist 86/286; Webster and Frankland, *SAO*, I, 255–7

22 Sinclair to Churchill, 14 Nov. 1941, PRO Air 19/186; see also DCAS to AOCs-in-C Bomber and Fighter commands, 13 Nov. 1941, PRO Air 19/186

23 '5 Group monthly summary of Group activities, December 1941,' 10 Jan. 1942, PRO Air 14/450

24 MacBean and Hogben, *Bombs Gone*, 43–6, 74–6, 85ff

25 Peirse to undersecretary of state for air, 6 Nov. 1941, PRO Air 14/785; 'Bomber Command Navigation Bulletin,' Nov. 1941, PRO Air 14/503; AHB, Bomber Command narrative, IV, 75–7, DHist 86/286; 'Minutes of meeting on navigation research ... 10 Nov. 1941,' PRO Air 14/69; W/C Nav, Bomber Command, to SASO, 'Summary of Groups' replies,' [Dec. 1941] PRO Air 14/516

26 'Bomber Command Navigation Bulletin,' Nov. 1941, PRO Air 14/503; Peirse to undersecretary of state for air, 2 Dec. 1941, PRO Air 20/909

27 Bufton to DBOps, two letters, 20 Nov. 1941, PRO Air 2/3031

28 Bufton, 'Suggestion for increasing efficiency of night attack,' 5 Nov. 1941, PRO Air 2/3031

29 See, for example, Baldwin, 'Location of targets by night,' 10 Nov. 1941, PRO Air 14/516, and 'Facing the facts,' 7 Dec. 1941, PRO Air 14/1939; 'Minutes, 5 Group station and squadron commanders' conference, 22 Oct. 1941,' PRO Air 14/450; Slessor, 'Location of targets at night,' 6 Nov. 1941, Bufton to Williams, 29 Nov. 1941, and W/C Nav, Bomber Command, to SASO, 'Summary of the Groups' replies,' [Dec. 1941] PRO Air 14/516; Bufton's recommendations in PRO Air 2/3031

30 'Minutes, 22nd Meeting of the Air Fighting Committee, 28 Aug 1941,' PRO Air 20/4724

31 'Summary of Bomber Command reports on raids on Germany since 1st March,' 14 July 1942, PRO Air 8/688; Middlebrook and Everitt, *BCWD*, 254–9; Aders, *German Night Fighter Force*, 46–8; Werner Held and Holger Nauroth, *The Defence of the Reich* (London 1982), 71

32 RAF Wireless Intelligence Service, report No 4, 20 May 1941, PRO Air 16/740; Air Ministry, ADI (K) report No 334/1945, DHist 82/1050; Grabmann, 'German air defense, 1933–1945,' June 57, USAF Historical Study No 164, DHist 86/451, microfilm frames 473–607; General der Flieger Josef Kammhuber, 'Problems in the conduct of a day and night defensive war,' 1 Oct. 1953, USAF Historical Study No 179, DHist 81/947, 58ff, 93; Aders, *German Night Fighter Force*, 25ff; Cooper, *The German Air Force*, 188–90

33 Guy A. Rainville, 'The Airmen,' 38, DHist 90/534

34 RAF Wireless Intelligence Service, report No 4, 20 May 1941, PRO Air 16/740; Air Ministry, ADI (K) report No 334/1945, DHist 82/1050; Aders, *German Night Fighter Force*, 25; Cooper, *The German Air Force*, 180–90

35 RAF Wireless Intelligence Service, report No 4, 20 May 1941, PRO Air 16/740; Air Ministry, ADI (K) report No 334/1945, DHist 82/1050; No 4 Group to Bomber Command, 29 Aug. 1941, PRO Air 14/232; W/C Ops, Bomber Command, to SASO, minutes 117 and 119, 4 and 14 Sept. 1941, and Saundby to No 4 Group, 18 Sept. 1941, PRO Air 14/232

36 'Minutes, 22nd Meeting, Air Fighting Committee, 28 Aug. 1941,' PRO Air 20/4724; Bomber Command, ORS memorandum No 4, 14 Oct. 1941, Portal Papers, copy in DHist 87/89, folder 9B (1941); see also the comments by F/L V.C. Varcoe in 'Minutes of the 3rd Meeting of representatives from operations commands for the purpose of exchanging tactical information in night operations,' 2 Dec. 1941, PRO Air 2/7612; Aders, *German Night Fighter Force*, 39–40, 77; Charles Messenger, *Cologne* (London 1982), 25–6; Martin Streetly, *Confound and Destroy*, (London 1978), 25ff; Webster and Frankland, *SAO*, I, 400–1

37 RAF Station Pocklington to No 4 Group, 29 Aug. 1941, including No 405 Squadron, form YA 31, 28/29 Aug. 1941, DHist 181.003 (D3876)

38 SASO to groups, 1 Sept. 1941, PRO Air 14/477

39 No 405 Squadron to No 4 Group, form YA 49, 11 Oct. 1941, DHist 181.003 (D3876); No 405 Squadron ORB, 21 Oct. 1941, DHist

40 [No 4 Group], 'Tactics,' nd, PRO Air 14/623; AHB, Bomber Command narrative, IV, 88, DHist 86/286; George Sweanor, *It's All Pensionable Time* (Colorado Springs 1981), 63–6

41 AHB, Bomber Command narrative, IV, 87, DHist 86/286; Peirse to Portal, 22 Oct. 1941, Portal Papers, copy in DHist 87/89 folder 9B (1941); DDBOps to DBOps, 10 Nov. 1941, PRO Air 2/3031

42 AHB, Bomber Command narrative, IV, 87, DHist 86/286; DCAS to AOC-in-C, 3 Nov. 1941, Bomber Command to undersecretary of state, 23 Nov. 1941, and Bomber Command to Groups, 30 Nov. 1941, PRO Air 14/396

43 Middlebrook and Everitt, *BCWD*, 223–4, 233, 237; AHB, Bomber Command narrative, III, 39–41, DHist 86/286

44 Middlebrook and Everitt, *BCWD*, 228–9

45 F/L S.B. Brackenbury, Questionnaire for returned aircrew, loss of bomber aircraft, 16 May 1945, DHist 181.001 (D24), folder 3

46 No 405 Squadron ORB, Dec. 1941–Feb. 1942, DHist; No 405 Squadron form YA 94, Mannheim 14/15 Feb. 1942, DHist 181.003 (D3876)

47 Middlebrook and Everitt, *BCWD*, 236

48 Air Force Headquarters, Air Historical Section, 'Historical narrative of the RCAF Overseas (to 31 Aug. 1942),' 100, DHist 79/445; No 408 Squadron ORB, Dec. 1941–Feb. 1942, DHist; see also *408 Squadron History.*

49 AHB, Bomber Command narrative, II, 73, DHist 86/286

50 AHB, 'The RAF in Maritime War,' IV, 409ff, DHist 79/599

51 Harris to Bomber Command, 29 April 1940, PRO Air 14/700; Ministry of Defence, Naval Staff History, *British Mining Operations 1939–1945* (London 1973) (hereafter cited as *British Mining Operations*), I, 461, 500; AHB, 'The RAF in Maritime War, Sept. 1939–June 1941,' II, 334, 407, 410, DHist 79/599; AHB, Bomber Command narrative, III, 179, DHist 86/286

52 SOA, No 3 Group to RAF Mildenhall, 15 Dec. 1941, DHist 181.002 (D76); No 419 Squadron ORB, Jan. 1942, DHist; No 420 Squadron ORB, 21 Jan. 1942, DHist

53 Baldwin memorandum, 1 Feb. 1942, PRO Air 14/1955; SOA, No 3 Group to RAF Mildenhall, 15 Dec. 1941, DHist 181.002 (D76); No 419 Squadron ORB, Jan. 1942, DHist, quoting ROYCANAIRF X6896, 16 Jan. 1942; No 419 Squadron ORB, Jan. and Feb. 1942, DHist, quoting ROYCANAIRF X6738, 3 Feb. 1942, and X6469, 19 Feb. 1942; CAS, 'Progress reports, RCAF squadrons overseas,' Dec. 1941, DHist 181.003 (D68); No 420 Squadron ORB, Jan. 1942, DHist; and AMP (Air Ministry) to Edwards, 10 Feb. 1942, DHist 181.009 (D774)

54 Slessor to Edwards, 1 Feb. 1942, DHist 181.009 (D774); Slessor to DGO, 5 Jan. 1943, PRO Air 20/3096; Slessor, *The Central Blue*, 334–5

55 Edwards to Breadner, 5 Feb. 1942, and Babington to Edwards, 8, 10, and 12 Feb. 1942, DHist 181.009 (D774); Baldwin to MacNeece Foster, 12 Feb. 1942, PRO Air 14/1942

56 Edwards to Hollinghurst, 14 and 24 Feb. 1942, DHist 181.009 (D774); Carr to Baldwin, 9 Feb. 1942, PRO Air 14/1940; Carr to Edwards, 21 Feb. 1942, DHist 181.009 (D774)

57 Baldwin to Carr, 12 Feb. 1942, PRO Air 14/1940; data from DHist 181.003 (D3596)

58 Breadner to Edwards, 4 Feb. 1942, message C118, DHist 181.009 (D774)

59 Clayton to Tait, 10 March 1980, copy in Clayton biog. file, DHist; Jerold Morris, *Canadian Artists and Airmen, 1940–45* (Toronto nd), 73; AHB, *Armament*, I, 225–8

60 Morris, *Canadian Artists and Airmen*, 85–7

61 No 419 Squadron operations summary in ORB, Jan. 1942, DHist; Extract from censored letter, 11 Feb. 1942, DHist 181.009 (D4159); Morris, *Canadian Artists and Airmen*, 85–7

62 Morris, *Canadian Artists and Airmen*, 59–63, 73

63 Rainville, 'The Airmen,' 38–9, DHist 90/534

64 No 419 Squadron ORB, 6/7 and 12–17 Feb. 1942, DHist

65 No 420 Squadron ORB, 12 Feb. 1942, DHist

66 Middlebrook and Everitt, *BCWD*, 220–37

67 Bottomley to Baldwin, 14 Feb. 1942, quoted in Webster and Frankland, *SAO*, IV, app. 8, 143–5

68 Baker to Bufton, 1 Jan. 1942, quoted in AHB, Bomber Command narrative, IV, 129–30, DHist 86/286; ibid., IV, 35–7, and app. IV, DHist 86/286; Street to Bomber Command, 17 April 1942, PRO Air 14/1001; Freeman to private secretary to secretary of state for air, 24 Dec. 1941, PRO Air 19/186

69 AHB, Bomber Command narrative, vol. II, app. C.4, vol. IV, app. 1–3, DHist 86/286

70 'An appreciation of night bombing navigation,' anonymous, Jan. 1942, PRO Air 14/498, but clearly by a specialist navigation officer; DBOps memorandum, 16 Jan. 1942, quoted in Air Chief Marshal Sir Arthur Harris, *Despatch on War Operations, 23rd February, 1942, to 8th May, 1945, Oct 1945*, 9; AHB, Bomber Command narrative, IV, 49–53, DHist 86/286

71 Bomber Command to groups, 5 April 1943, DHist 181.003 (D3889); Saward, *The Bomber's Eye*, 39–40, and *Victory Denied* (London 1985), 232–3; Bomber Command, 'Memorandum on the introduction of T.R. 1335 (GEE) ...' [Feb. 1944] DHist 181.002 (D112); AHB, Bomber Command narrative, IV, 49–51, DHist 86/286

72 Baker to Bufton, 1 Jan. 1942, quoted in AHB, Bomber Command narrative, IV, 51–3, 129–30, DHist 86/286

73 AHB, Bomber Command narrative, IV, 130, DHist 86/286; Bottomley to Baldwin, 14 Feb. 1942, quoted in Webster and Frankland, *SAO*, IV, app. 8, 143–5; Portal to Bottomley, 15 Feb. 1942, quoted in Webster and Frankland, *SAO*, I, 324

74 Webster and Frankland, *SAO*, I, 255–7

75 Middlebrook and Everitt, *BCWD*, 242–4; Larry J. Bidinian, *The Combined Allied Bombing Offensive against the German Civilian, 1942–1945* (Lawrence, Ka. 1976), 39, quoting United States Strategic Bombing Survey, 'The effects of bombing on medical and health care,' 11–12

76 AHB, Bomber Command narrative, IV, 214–28, DHist 86/286

77 Nos 405, 408, 419, and 420 Squadron ORBs, March 1942, DHist; AHB, Bomber Command narrative, IV, 216–18, DHist 86/286; and Middlebrook and Everitt, *BCWD*, 245

78 Middlebrook and Everitt, *BCWD*, 243–5; see also PRO Air 14/1761.

79 No 420 Squadron ORB, 9 March 1942, DHist; Middlebrook and Everitt, *BCWD*, 246

80 AHB, Bomber Command narrative, IV, 54–5, 136–7, DHist 86/286; Bomber Command, 'Introduction of T.R. 1335 (GEE) ...' [Feb 1944] DHist 181.002 (D112); 'Summary of Bomber Command reports ... since 1st March, 1942,' 14 June 1942, PRO Air 8/688; Middlebrook and Everitt, *BCWD*, 246–8; Webster and Frankland, *SAO*, I, 390

81 Harris to Pound, 7 March 1942, Harris Papers, copy in DHist 87/51, folder H101; and Bomber Command to No 3 Group, 9 March 1942, Bomber Command to No 1 Group, 24 March 1942, Saundby to Balfour, 20 March 1942, and Bottomley to Harris, 25 March 1942, all PRO Air 14/703; Nos 408 and 420 Squadron ORBs, March 1942, DHist; AHB, 'The RAF in Maritime War,' III, app. XXIX, DHist 79/599

82 'Summary of Bomber Command reports ... since 1st March 1942,' 14 March 1942, PRO Air 8/688

83 Air Commodore J. Searby, *The Great Raids*, II (Chippenham, Wilts. 1978), 8

84 Morris, *Canadian Artists and Airmen*, 65–7

85 Wilhelm Johnen, *Battling the Bombers* (New York 1958), 35–41; Aders, *German Night Fighter Force*, 235

86 Middlebrook and Everitt, *BCWD*, 246–50; Aders, *German Night Fighter Force*, 242–3

87 *Morris, Canadian Artists and Airmen*, 65–7

88 Bufton to Baker, 27 Feb. 1942, and Baker to Bottomley, 27 Feb. 1942, PRO Air 20/788

89 Morris, *Canadian Artists and Airmen*, 77; AHB, Bomber Command narrative, IV, 35–8, DHist 86/286; Bomber Command to Groups, 20 March 1942, PRO Air 14/937; and Street to Bomber Command, 17 April 1942, PRO Air 14/1001

90 Harris to AOCs, 23 March 1942, PRO Air 14/3547; Harris to undersecretary of state, 21 March 1942, PRO Air 14/1001

91 Harris to Portal, 5 March 1942, PRO Air 8/625; Churchill to Sinclair and Portal, 13 March 1942, PRO Air 19/187

92 No 405 Squadron form YA 105, raid on Lübeck, 28/29 March 1942, DHist 181.003 (D3876); 'Summary of Bomber Command reports on raids on Germany since 1st March,' 14 June 1942, PRO Air 8/688; Middlebrook and Everitt, *BCWD*, 251–2; AHB, Bomber Command narrative, IV, 142, DHist 86/286; No 419 Squadron ORB, 29 March 1942, DHist

93 No 419 Squadron ORB, 2 April 1942, DHist; Air Force Headquarters, Air Historical Section, 'Historical narrative of the RCAF Overseas (to 31 Aug. 1942),' 123, DHist 79/445; No 408 Squadron ORB, 28 March 1942, DHist

94 No 419 Squadron ORB, 15–16 April 1942, DHist; Middlebrook and Everitt, *BCWD*, 254–8; No 420 Squadron ORB, 15 April 1942, DHist

95 Minutes of 21 July 1942 meeting, Milch Papers, reel 15, frames 1555–61, translation in DHist SGR II 217; Bomber Command, 'Memorandum on the introduction of T.R. 1335 (GEE) into Bomber Command,' [Feb 1944] DHist 181.002 (D112); AHB, Bomber Command narrative, IV, 49–51, DHist 86/286

96 Middlebrook and Everitt, BCWD, 259; No 419 Squadron ORB and Operational Summary, 23 April 1942, DHist

97 Nos 405 and 420 Squadron ORBs, 15–16 April 1942, DHist

98 Quoted in 'Moosemen': 419 Squadron History (nd, np), 3–4

99 Webster and Frankland, SAO, I, 394

100 Ibid., 393–4; 'Summary of Bomber Command reports ... since 1st March l942,' 14 June 1942, PRO Air 6/688; Middlebrook and Everitt, BCWD, 260–1; AHB, Bomber Command narrative, IV, 146, DHist 86/286; Terraine, A Time for Courage, 479–80

101 No 419 Squadron ORB, April–May 1942; 'Moosemen,' 4; The Moose Squadron, 1941–1945 (Winnipeg 1977), 22

102 Bomber Command, ORS report No S154, 5 July 1942, DHist 181.003 (D1485); see also reference to ORS report 47 in AHB, Bomber Command narrative, IV, 56–7, DHist 86/286; Harris, Bomber Offensive, 95; Middlebrook and Everitt, BCWD, 261–7

103 Harris to groups, 22 May 1942, PRO Air 14/3548

104 Solly Zuckerman, From Apes to Warlords (London 1978), 142–3; Blackett, 'Note on the use of the bomber force,' April 1942, PRO Air 9/183; AHB, Bomber Command narrative, IV, 232–40, DHist 86/286

105 Slessor to Bottomley, 1 May 1942, and Bufton to Bottomley, 2 May 1942, PRO Air 20/8145; Bottomley to Harris, 5 May 1942, PRO Air 19/187

106 Zuckerman, From Apes to Warlords, 142-4, app. 2; Dewdney to Scott, 22 May 1942, PRO Air 9/99

107 Inter-Services Research Bureau, 'Morale Bombing,' April 1942, quoted in AHB, Bomber Command narrative, IV, 121, DHist 86/286

CHAPTER 16: THE EXPANSION OF BOMBER COMMAND

1 F.H. Hinsley, British Intelligence in the Second World War, I (London 1981), 244ff; Jones, Most Secret War, 193, 227ff, 294-5; Price, Instruments of Darkness, 78–9, 85–90; Streetly, Confound and Destroy, 15–18

2 USAFE, 'Tactical employment of night fighting in the GAF,' 6 March 1946, DHist 73/1506, microfilm reel 1, frames 464–6; Kammhuber, 'Problems in the conduct of a day and night defensive war,' 1 Oct. 1953, USAF Historical Study No 179, 61, DHist 81/947; Price, Instruments of Darkness, 69–70; USAFE, 'GAF signals in Defence,' 6 March 1946, DHist 73/1516, microfilm reel 1, frames 345–51; Air Ministry/USAFE, Intelligence report No 42, 'The German meteorological service in war,' DHist 181.009 (D402); Air Ministry, ADI (K) report No 416/1945, 8 Dec. 1945, 23, DHist 82/1048; Aileen Clayton, The Enemy Is Listening (London 1980), passim

3 USAFE, 'Tactical employment of night fighting in the GAF,' 6 March 1946,

DHist 73/1506, microfilm reel 1, frame 387; Air Ministry, DDI A3b, 'GAF nightfighters,' 3 Aug. 1942, PRO Air 40/1783; Aders, *German Night Fighter Force*, 39, 247

4 USAFE, 'Tactical employment of night fighting in the GAF,' 6 March 1946, DHist 73/1506, reel 1, frame 389; Aders, *German Night Fighter Force*, 39, 77; Horst Boog, 'Higher Command and Leadership in the German *Luftwaffe*, 1939–1945,' in Alfred H. Hurley and Robert C. Ehrhart, eds., *Air Power and Warfare* (Washington 1979), 134–5

5 Aders, *German Night Fighter Force*, 40–1, 247; Streetly, *Confound and Destroy*, 179; Messenger, *Cologne*, 24–6; Air Ministry, ADI (K) report no. 334/1945, 21 June 1945, 7, DHist 82/1050; USAFE, 'Tactical employment of night fighting in the GAF,' 6 March 1946, DHist 73/1506, microfilm reel 1, frames 390–480; Kammhuber, 'Problems in the conduct of a day and night defensive war,' 1 Oct. 1953, 65ff, DHist 81/947; Grabmann, 'German air defense, 1933–1945,' June 1957, 584ff, DHist 86/451

6 Aders, *German Night Fighter Force*, 59, 69

7 Horst Boog, 'The Policy, Command and Direction of the *Luftwaffe* in World War II,' *Proceedings* of the Royal Air Force Historical Society, IV (September 1988): 60–1; Cooper, *The German Air Force*, 186, 194; Harold Faber, *Luftwaffe* (London 1979), 39; Aders, *German Night Fighter Force*, 69–71, 93; Air Ministry, *The Rise and Fall of the German Air Force (1933 to 1945)*, 314

8 Grabmann, 'German air defenses, 1933–1945,' 713–15, DHist 86/451; Aders, *German Night Fighter Force*, 44, 65, 69, 242–3; Cooper, *German Air Force*, 264; USAAF, AI 12, Intelligence report No 37, 'Strength and serviceability of GAF flying units, Sep 1939–Mar 1944,' 27 Aug. 1945, DHist 181.009 (D635); Josef Schmid, quoted in USAFE, 'Tactical employment of night fighting in the GAF,' 6 March 1946, DHist 73/1506, microfilm reel 1, frame 577

9 Webster and Frankland, *SAO*, I, 400–2; Aders, *German Night Fighter Force*, 256; Harris, *Bomber Offensive*, 108

10 Harris, *Bomber Offensive*, 108

11 Harris, *Despatch*, 13

12 Webster and Frankland, *SAO*, I, 339–40, 403ff; AHB, Bomber Command narrative, IV, ch. 17, DHist 86/286; Messenger, *Cologne*, 27ff; and Saward, *Victory Denied*, 261ff

13 Harris, *Bomber Offensive*, 109

14 AHB, Bomber Command narrative, IV, ch. 17, DHist 86/286; Saward, *Victory Denied*, 266–7; Messenger, *Cologne*, 27ff

15 Portal to Harris, 19 May 1942, Joubert to Harris, 21 May 1942, PRO Air 14/276; Harris to AOs-C-in-C and AOsC groups, 20 May 1942, PRO Air 14/2024; appendix A to Bomber Command Operation Order No 148, 26 May 1942, Bomber Command to Nos 2 and 11 groups and Headquarters Fighter and Army Cooperation commands, 25 May 1942, PRO Air 14/276

16 AHB, Bomber Command narrative, IV, 165, DHist 86/286; Messenger, *Cologne*, 31

17 Bomber Command Operation Order No 148, 26 May 1942, PRO Air 14/276

18 Harris, *Bomber Offensive*, 110; Messenger, *Cologne*, 40ff

19 No 405 Squadron ORB, 18 April, 25, 27, 29, and 30 May 1942, DHist; quoted in *No 405 Squadron History*, 27; No 408 Squadron ORB, 30 May 1942, DHist; Nos 419 and 420 Squadron ORBs, 30 May 1942, DHist

20 J.D. Pattison, 'Happy Valley,' DHist 181.001 (D5)

21 Quoted in '*Moosemen*,' 4

22 No 419 Squadron ORB, 30/31 May 1942, DHist

23 Pattison, 'Happy Valley,' DHist 181.001 (D5)

24 No 419 Squadron ORB, 30/31 May 1942, DHist

25 No 405 Squadron ORB, 30/31 May 1942, DHist

26 No 408 Squadron ORB, 30/31 May 1942, DHist; No 420 Squadron ORB, 30/31 May 1942, DHist; AHB, Bomber Command narrative, IV, app. 8, DHist 86/286; Middlebrook and Everitt, *BCWD*, 271–3

27 Pattison, 'Happy Valley,' DHist 181.001 (D5)

28 Air Ministry, AIS (8), 'Extracts of letters, RAF and RCAF reaction to Cologne and Essen raids,' DHist 181.002 (D163)

29 Aders, *German Night Fighter Force*, 56; Webster and Frankland, *SAO*, I, 402–9; Hajo Herrmann, *Eagle's Wings* (London 1991), 169

30 RAF Medmenham Interpretation Report No K 1333 Cologne, 7 June 1942, DHist181.003 (D2437)

31 AHB, Bomber Command narrative, IV, 171–4, DHist 86/286; RAF Medmenham, Interpretation report No K1333, Cologne, 7 June 1942, DHist 181.003 (D2437); 'War Room Manual of Bomber Command Operations, 1942,' 14 Jan. 1943, 17ff, DHist 181.003 (D3991); Earl R. Beck, *Under the Bombs* (Lexington, Ky 1986), 1–9

32 Quoted in Ralph Barker, *The Thousand Plan* (London 1965), 229

33 Quoted in Messenger, *Cologne*, 56

34 Quoted in Barker, *The Thousand Plan*, 232; Webster and Frankland, *SAO*, I, 485–6

35 Nos 405, 408, 419, and 420 Squadron ORBs, 1/2 June 1943, DHist; AHB, Bomber Command narrative, II, app. 8, DHist 86/286; Middlebrook and Everitt, *BCWD*, 274; Messenger, *Cologne*, 59

36 Webster and Frankland, *SAO*, I, 415, 486; AHB, Bomber Command narrative, IV, 174–7, DHist 86/286; Middlebrook and Everitt, *BCWD*, 274, 280–1; No 405 Squadron, Form YA123, Essen, 1/2 June 1942, DHist 181.003 (D3876); Saward, *Victory Denied*, 147

37 No 408 Squadron ORB, 25/26 June 1942; AHB, Bomber Command narrative, IV, 181–4, DHist 86/286; 'War Room Manual of Bomber Command Operations, 1942,' 14 Jan. 1943, 8, DHist 181.003 (D3991); Middlebrook and Everitt, *BCWD*, 280–1

38 Middlebrook and Everitt, *BCWD*, 272, 274, 281; AHB, Bomber Command narrative, IV, 186, DHist 86/286; 'The Bombing of Germany: Note by the First Sea Lord on the Report by Mr Justice Singleton,' 16 June 1942, and Portal's comments, PRO Air 8/258

39 Harris to Churchill, 17 June 1942, PRO Air 14/3507

40 AHB, Bomber Command narrative, IV, 245–6, DHist 86/286

41 Ibid., 3, 15; 'Reorganisation of Bomber Command,' 20 July 1942, PRO Air 14/1050

42 Stevenson to secretary, Department of National Defence for Air, 29 Jan. 1941, DHist 181.009 (D774); AHB, Bomber Command narrative, IV, 16, DHist 86/286; 'Note of a meeting held at the Air Ministry, 8 July 1941,' DHist 181.009 (D897); 'Ottawa Air Training Conference minutes and proceedings, May–Jun 1942,' app. F2, DHist 80/255; United Kingdom High Commissioner in Canada to Dominions Office, for Air Ministry, No. 1032, 23 May 1942, and Balfour to Sinclair, 4 July 1942, PRO Air 20/2978

43 Harris to Freeman, 29 July 1942, PRO Air 20/2978

44 Freeman to CAS, 3 Aug. 1942, and Balfour to Sinclair, 14 Aug. 1942, PRO Air 20/2978; see also Hollinghurst (DGO) to Freeman, 5 Aug. 1942, and Dominions Office to United Kingdom High Commissioner in Canada, 12 Aug. 1942, No 1769, PRO Air 20/3798

45 Harris to Sinclair, 13 Aug. 1942, PRO Air 14/3512

46 Sinclair to Harris, 2 Sept. 1942, PRO Air 20/3798; Hollinghurst to Freeman, 5 Aug. 1942, PRO Air 20/3798

47 Toronto *Globe and Mail*, 16 Sept. 1942

48 'Why Canadianise the Air Force: An interview with the Hon. C.G. Power,' *Maclean's Magazine*, 15 Nov. 1942, 11

49 Canadian bomber group progress meeting, 3 July 1942, DHist 181.009 (D612)

50 Freeman to Courtney, 25 May 1942, PRO Air 20/920; No 420 Squadron ORB, Aug. 1942, DHist

51 Graham to Admin Plans, 20 June 1942, PRO Air 14/1140; Hollinghurst to Edwards, 3 July 1942, DHist 74/727; 'Minutes of progress meeting, Canadian bomber group,' 3 July 1942, DHist 181.009 (D612); Campbell to Edwards, 27 July 1942, DHist 181.009 (D4831)

52 Bufton to Bottomley, 14 May 1943, PRO Air 20/920; Harris to No 6 Group, 26 June 1944, PRO Air 14/1144; Hollinghurst to Edwards, 23 July 1942, DHist 74/727

53 Hollinghurst to Edwards, 23 July 1942, DHist 74/727; S/L L.A. Justason memorandum, 1 June 1945, DHist 181.003 (D5070); Harris to No 6 Group, 26 June 1944, PRO Air 14/1144

54 Graham to Admin Plans, 20 June 1942, PRO Air 14/1140; but see also 'Reorganization of Bomber Command,' 20 July 1942, PRO Air 14/1050; Harris to Hollinghurst, 22 July 1942, PRO Air 14/1140; Hollinghurst to Edwards, 23 July 1942, DHist 74/727.

55 Harris to Portal, 24 Sept. 1942, Portal Papers, copy in DHist 87/89, folder 9 (1942)

56 Self to Craven, 21 Sept. 1941, PRO Avia 15/1569; Saundby to Harris, 27 April 1942, and Carr to Harris, 9 July 1942, PRO Air 14/1140

57 Campbell to Edwards, 6 Aug. 1942, DHist 181.009 (D4831)

58 Graham to Hollinghurst, 19 Sept. 1942, Hollinghurst to Slessor, 23 Sept. 1942, and Hollinghurst to Graham, 24 Sept. 1942, PRO Air 20/1817; see also Lowe to Bomber Command, 23 Sept. 1942, PRO Air 14/1141; Freeman memorandum, 25 Sept. 1942, with draft reply for Portal's signature, PRO Air 20/2978

59 K.A. Merrick, *Halifax* (London 1980), 11, 13, 21, 35, 37; 'Halifax: over-balance of rudder,' undated, unattributed paper in DHist 181.009 (D2184); Bomber Command ORS report No 48, 30 July 1942, PRO Air 14/1794; Portal to Churchill, 12 Aug. 1942, PRO Air 19/169; 'Summary of recommendations accepted at meeting of representatives from Bomber Command, Air Ministry, and Ministry of Aircraft Production,' 12 Sept. 1942, PRO Air 8/330; Saward, *'Bomber' Harris*, 70–1; Harris to Portal, 14 Aug. 1942, Harris Papers, copy in DHist 87/51, folder H81; 'Notes of 2nd meeting on coordination for the bomber offensive,' 2 Sept. 1942, and 'Coordination for the bomber Offensive: Lancaster II and Halifax III,' note by commander-in-chief, both PRO Air 19/354; Harris to Portal, 12 Nov. 1942, Harris Papers, copy in DHist 87/51, folder H81; and 'Notes of 3rd meeting on coordination of the bomber offensive,' 8 Dec. 1942, PRO Air 19/354

60 Harris to Linnell, 16 Oct. 1942, Harris Papers, copy in DHist 87/51, folder H91; Bomber Command ORS report No 66, 'Review of sorties, losses, and interceptions of Bomber Command aircraft in night operations during the period 1st Aug 1941–31st October 1942,' PRO AIR 14/364

61 See, for example, Campbell to Edwards, 6 Aug. 1942, DHist 181.009 (D4831).

62 'Draft conclusions of meeting of Air Council, Meeting 7(42),' 14 April 1942, PRO Air 6/73; Nos 408 and 419 Squadron ORBs, DHist

63 See C.F. Andrews, *Vickers Aircraft since 1918* (New York 1969), 309–63; Webster and Frankland, *SAO*, IV, 448

64 Quoted in Chaz Bowyer, *The Wellington Bomber* (London 1986), 256

65 Middlebrook and Everitt, *BCWD*, 304; Air Force Headquarters (AFHQ), Air Historical Section, 'Narrative of the RCAF Overseas,' 118, DHist 79/445; AHB, Bomber Command narrative, IV, app. 21, 12, DHist 86/286; Air Ministry, DDI A3b, 'GAF nightfighters,' 3 Aug. 1942, PRO Air 40/1783; Aders, *German Night Fighter Force*, 243; Hinsley, *British Intelligence*, 254 ff; Price, *Instruments of Darkness*, 90–1; Jones, *Most Secret War*, 264–74

66 Air Ministry, ORC, TC report No 22, June 1942, PRO Air 14/206; Air Ministry, ORC, TC report No 29, Nov. 1942, DHist 181.009 (D1716); Air Ministry, ASI report No 1, 29 Dec. 1942, PRO Air 20/1663

67 Kammhuber, 'Problems in the conduct of a day and night defensive war,' 1 Oct. 1953, DHist 81/947, frames 82, 96

68 Price, *Instruments of Darkness*, 144–5

69 Kammhuber, 'Problems in the conduct of a day and night defensive war,' 1 Oct. 1953, DHist 81/947, frame 80

70 USSAF Intelligence report No 37, 'Strength and Serviceability of GAF flying units, Sep 1939–Mar 1944,' 27 Aug. 1945, DHist 181.009 (D635); Kammhuber, 'Problems in the conduct of a day and night defensive war,' 1 Oct. 1953, DHist 81/947; Bomber Command, ORC, 'Tactical countermeasures to counter enemy night fighters and anti-aircraft, searchlight, and gun defences,' Aug. 1943, DHist 181.009 (D2591). See also instructions issued to 202 Signal Company by Leutnant W. Jansen, quoted in USAFE, 'German Air Defenses,' 6 March 1946, vol. XIV, app. XII, DHist 73/1507, frames 3071ff

71 Herrmann, *Eagle's Wings*, 198; Kammhuber, 'Problems in the conduct of a day and night defensive war,' 1 Oct. 1953, DHist 81/947, frames 89ff; USAFE, 'Tactical employment of night fighting in the GAF,' 6 March 1946, DHist 73/1506, microfilm reel 1, frames 498 and 577

72 Adolf Galland, *The First and the Last* (London 1955), 197–8; Minutes of meeting, 24 Nov. 1942, Milch papers, DHist SGR II 217, reel 21, frames 3361–6

73 AOC No 4 Group to Bomber Command Headquarters, 25 June 1942, DHist 181.009 (D2802); *Bomber Command Quarterly Review* (April–June 1942): 20–1

74 Bomber Command circular, 10 Dec. 1942, DHist 181.009 (D2800); SASO No 5 Group to GGO, 22 Dec. 1942, minute 15, and Group Gunnery Officer No 5 Group, circular, 28 Dec. 1942, PRO Air 14/457; Bomber Command, ORS report No 66, 13 Jan. 1943, DHist 181.003 (D3474); Minutes of meeting, 27 April 1942, Milch Papers, DHist SGR II 217, reel 13, frames 251–9; AOC No 4 Group to Bomber Command Headquarters, 25 June 1942, DHist 181.009 (D2802)

75 AHB, Bomber Command narrative, IV, 87–90, DHist 86/286; Bomber Command, Signals Branch, 'War in the Ether,' Oct. 1945, 7–11; Price, *Instruments of Darkness*, 114–27

76 Bomber Command, Signals Branch, 'War in the Ether,' 7, 11, 12; AHB, Bomber Command narrative IV, 89, DHist 86/286

77 Bomber Command, Signals Branch, 'War in the Ether,' 15; Middlebrook and Everitt, *BCWD*, 278–9; War Room Manual of Bomber Command Operations, 1942, 14 Jan. 1943, 33, DHist 181.003 (D3991); Nos 405, 408, and 420 Squadron ORBs, 6/7 June and 23 June 1942, DHist

78 Middlebrook and Everitt, *BCWD*, 274, 276–7; No 405 Squadron ORB, 2/3 and 9 June 1942, DHist; No 408 Squadron ORB, 5/6 June 1942, DHist

79 Pattison, 'Happy Valley,' DHist 181.001 (D5), 22; Pattison biog. file, DHist; Middlebrook and Everitt, *BCWD*, 277

80 No 419 Squadron ORB, 9 June 1942, DHist; Air Force Routine Orders (AFRO) 1097/42 and 1653/42, extracts at DHist; Middlebrook and Everitt, *BCWD*, 277; DHist awards file

81 Baldwin to Harris, 9 June 1942, PRO Air 14/3544

82 'Minutes of conference held at Headquarters, Bomber Command, 16 Apr 1942,' PRO Air 14/508; Harris to Portal, 12 June 1942, PRO Air 8/688; AHB, Bomber Command narrative, IV, 65ff, DHist 86/286; Portal to Harris, 14 June 1942, and 'Minutes of meeting to discuss Pathfinder Force,' 8 July 1942, PRO Air 8/688

83 D.C.T. Bennett, *Pathfinder* (London 1983), 164ff; Alan Bramson, *Master Airman* (Shrewsbury 1985), 72ff; Gordon Musgrove, *Pathfinder Force* (London 1976), 12–13; AHB, Bomber Command narrative, IV, 66–9, DHist 86/286; Charles Messenger, *'Bomber' Harris and the Strategic Bombing Offensive, 1939-1945* (London 1984), 84ff

84 Middlebrook and Everitt, *BCWD*, 283–4

85 No 408 Squadron ORB, 27 July 1942, DHist; No 420 Squadron ORB,

Operational Statistics Summary, 27 July 1942, DHist; Middlebrook and Everitt, *BCWD*, 290

86 Questionnaire for returned air crew, loss of bomber aircraft, 26/27 July 1942, Pilot Officer R.N. Rayne, No 420 Squadron, 27 May 1945, DHist 181.001 (D23), folder 8

87 No 419 Squadron ORB, 29 July 1942, DHist; Middlebrook and Everitt, *BCWD*, 290–1; Air Ministry, ADI (K) report No E109/1942, 19 Sept. 1942, PRO Air 14/2380

88 Middlebrook and Everitt, *BCWD*, 288–93; Nos 405 and 419 Squadron ORBs, 22 July 1942, DHist; 'War Room Manual of Bomber Command Operations, 1942,' 14 Jan. 1943, 25, DHist 181.003 (D3991)

89 Middlebrook and Everitt, *BCWD*, 286–9, 292–3

90 No 408 Squadron ORB, 5/6 Aug. 1942, DHist

91 Ibid.

92 'The Bomber's Baedeker, DHist 181.003 (D3993); Middlebrook and Everitt, *BCWD*, 294; Webster and Frankland, *SAO*, I, 432

93 Middlebrook and Everitt, *BCWD*, 291–2; 'War Room Manual of Bomber Command Operations, 1942,' 14 Jan. 1943, 84–5, DHist 181.003 (D3991); 'The Bomber's Baedeker,' DHist 181.003 (D3993)

94 Middlebrook and Everitt, *BCWD*, 304; No 408 Squadron ORB, 29 Aug. 1942, DHist

95 Bomber Command, 'Note on methods of operating bombers,' 23 July 1942, DHist 181.009 (D1905); No 4 Group to Harris, 5 July 1942, PRO Air 14/3545; AHB, Bomber Command narrative, IV, 97–102, DHist 86/286; H.M.D. Parker, *Manpower* (London 1957), 167–8, 206–11, 239

96 Webster and Frankland, *SAO*, IV, App. 42

97 'Minutes of meeting held in CAS room, 30 June 1942,' PRO Air 14/1814; AHB, Bomber Command narrative, IV, 95–6, 186, DHist 86/286; Webster and Frankland, *SAO*, IV, app. 42; No 6 Group, 'Operational losses: per cent missing,' DHist 72/383

98 'Minutes of 3 Group conference of navigation officers,' 9 Aug. 1942, 'Minutes, 5 Group conference of navigation officers, 24 July 1942, PRO Air 14/485; CNO Bomber Command memorandum, 21 May 1943, PRO Air 14/69

99 CNO Bomber Command to SASO, minutes 50 and 78, 30 May and 16 Aug. 1942, PRO Air 14/1603; Musgrove, *Pathfinder Force*, 245

100 Harris to ACAS (Ops), 10 Aug. 1942, PRO Air 2/7922; RDF.1 to CNO Bomber Command, minute 21, 5 May 1942, CNO to SASO, minute 24, 8 May 1942, CSO Bomber Command to SASO, minute 25, 9 May 1942, PRO Air 14/1293

101 'Notes on H2S,' 1 July 1942, PRO Air 14/1293; BDU report No 12, 25 March 1943, PRO Air 20/2121; Harris, *Despatch*, app. A, 68; AHB, Bomber Command narrative, IV, 75–7, DHist 86/286; Saward, *The Bomber's Eye*, 110–13

102 Musgrove, *Pathfinder Force*, 14–16; Middlebrook and Everitt, *BCWD*, 299–306; AHB, Bomber Command narrative, IV, 196, DHist 86/286; Bomber Command

ORS, 'Notes on the Effectiveness of Pathfinder Force Operations to 21/22 November,' app A, PRO Air 14/1804; AHB, Bomber Command narrative, IV, 198–201, DHist 86/286; Nos 419 and 405 Squadron ORBs, 2 Sept. 1942, DHist

103 AHB, Bomber Command narrative, IV, 58–9, DHist 86/286

104 Musgrove, *Pathfinder Force*, 13, 16

105 AHB, Bomber Command narrative, IV, 69, DHist 86/286; Musgrove, *Pathfinder Force*, 17; Bramson, *Master Airman*, 62ff

106 Air Ministry, FPRC, report No 423, July 1945, DHist 181.003 (D3867)

107 AHB, Bomber Command narrative, IV, 207–11, DHist 86/286; No 405 Squadron ORB, 7 Oct. 1942, DHist; Middlebrook and Everitt, *BCWD*, 309–23

108 Bomber Command ORS, 'Notes on the Effectiveness of Pathfinder Force Operations to 21/22 November,' and app. A, PRO Air 14/1804; AHB, Bomber Command narrative, IV, 206, DHist 86/286; Middlebrook and Everitt, *BCWD*, 309, 313; No 405 Squadron ORB, 17 Sept. and 1/2 Oct. 1942, DHist

109 Bomber Command ORS, 'Notes on the Effectiveness of Pathfinder Force Operations to 21/22 November,' and app. A, PRO Air 14/1804; No 405 Squadron ORB, 8/9 Sept. and 6 Oct. 1942, DHist

110 Harris to Groups, 31 Dec. 1942, PRO Air 14/3548; see also Saundby to Harris, 27 Oct. 1942, PRO, Air 14/485; 'Progress of RAF bomber offensive against Germany,' 30 Nov. 1943, included in 'Bomber Command review of work of Intelligence Section (target intelligence and damage assessment) 1939–1945,' vol. 2, 18 Aug. 1945, DHist 181.003 (D195)

111 Webster and Frankland, *SAO*, I, 353–70

112 AHB, Bomber Command narrative, IV, 236ff, DHist 86/286; SO to director of plans to director of plans, 17 Aug. 1942, PRO Air 9/424

113 AHB, Bomber Command narrative, IV, 247–53, DHist 86/286; Webster and Frankland, *SAO*, I, 369ff

114 Webster and Frankland, *SAO*, I, 370–5; Noble Frankland, 'The planning of the bombing offensive and its contribution to German collapse,' 98ff, PRO Air 41/57; AHB, Bomber Command narrative, IV, 247–53, DHist 86/286

115 Middlebrook and Everitt, *BCWD*, 318–33

116 Sweanor, *It's All Pensionable Time*, 53–4; AHB, Bomber Command narrative, IV, 96–7, DHist 86/286

117 AHB, Bomber Command narrative, IV, 96–7, DHist 86/286

118 Campbell to Edwards, 17 Sept. 1942, DHist 181.009 (D4925); Balfour to VCAS, 2 Oct. 1942, Harris Papers, copy in DHist 87/51, folder H16; Edwards to Balfour, 19 Oct. 1942, DHist 181.003 (D5130)

CHAPTER 17: THE FORMATION OF NO 6 GROUP

1 See 'Notes re: meeting in the office of the minister for air,' 27 Aug. 1941, C.G. Power Papers, copy in DHist 79/721, folder 27; Edwards to DCAS, 4 June

1941, and de Niverville to AMP, 22 May 1941, HQC 45-10-7, NA, RG 24, vol. 5368.

2 Desloges to DAFM, 18 April 1941, C.G. Power Papers, copy in DHist 79/721, folder 27

3 Montreal *La Presse*, 1 Oct. 1941, 3

4 CAS to ROYCANAIRF, 12 and 14 Nov. 1941, HQC 17-1-4, vol. 1, NA, RG 24, vol. 5210

5 Stevenson to CAS, 17 Nov. 1941, DHist 181.009 (D725)

6 Stevenson to DGO (Air Ministry) and Stevenson to Hollinghurst, two letters dated 17 Nov. 1941, DHist 181.009 (D725)

7 CAS to ROYCAINAIRF London, 22 Nov. 1941, DHist 181.009 (D725), and ROYCAINAIRF to CAS, 17 Dec. 1941, HQC 17-1-4, vol. 1, NA, RG 24, vol. 5210

8 Hollinghurst to Curtis, 13 Dec. 1941, DHist 181.009 (D725)

9 Edwards to CAS, 17 Dec. 1941, HQC 17-1-4, vol. 1, NA, RG 24, vol. 5210, and DHist 181.009 (D725)

10 Ibid.

11 Power to Edwards, 23 Dec. 1941, and CAS to ROYCANAIRF, 22 Dec. 1941, DHist 181.009 (D725)

12 Hollinghurst to Curtis, 24 Dec. 1941, DHist 181.009 (D725)

13 Edwards to de Carteret, 6 Jan. 1942, Power Papers, copy in DHist 79/721, folder 14

14 Curtis to CAS, 29 Dec. 1941, DHist 181.009 (D725)

15 CAS to ROYCANAIRF, 15 Jan. 1942, DHist 181.009 (D725)

16 Ibid., 20 Jan. 1942

17 DGO to AOC-in-C RCAF Overseas, 26 Jan. 1942, DHist 181.009 (D725); St Pierre to AOC-in-C, 7 May 1942, DHist 181.009 (D4441)

18 Curtis to CAS, 5 Feb. 1942, to DGO, 15 April 1942, and to CAS, 25 April 1942, DHist 181.009 (D725); DP to AOC-in-C, 3 March 1944, copy in J.M.W. St Pierre biog. file, DHist

19 AIS (8) Report, 14 Dec. 1942, HQS 17-1-30, NA, RG 24, vol. 5210

20 C.G. Power, Diary, Mission to United Kingdom – 1942, 15 Aug. 1942, Power Papers, copy in DHist 79/721, folder 18; Crozier to DAS, 27 July 1942, and Edwards to CAS, 29 July 1942, DHist 181.009 (D725); G.A. Roy and J.L. Savard biog files, DHist

21 No 425 Squadron ORB, Oct. 1942, DHist; No 425 Squadron history, 2–4, DHist 74/336; Middlebrook and Everitt, *BCWD*, 313–14

22 No 425 Squadron history, 5–9, DHist 74/336; DHist decorations and awards file

23 Campbell to AOC-in-C, 31 Aug. 1942, DHist 181.009 (D4831)

24 Diary, Mission to United Kingdom, 13–19 Aug. 1942, Power Papers, copy in DHist 79/721, folder 18; 'Record of discussions, Bomber Command,' 19 Aug. 1942, AFHQ 19-10-19, NA, RG 24, vol. 5229; 'Minutes of Conference held at RCAF Overseas Headquarters, 13 and 18 Aug. 1942,' DHist 181.009 (D6155); Harris to Freeman, 29 July 1942, PRO Air 20/2978; and Dominions Office to United Kingdom high commissioner in Canada, 12 Aug. 1942, PRO Air 20/3798

25 Nos 419 and 427 Squadron ORBs, Nov.–Dec. 1942, DHist; Capel to No 4 Group, 2 Jan. 1943, DHist 181.009 (D4236); Edwards to Breadner, report no.

11, 12 Jan. 1943, Power Papers, copy in DHist 79/721, folder 14; CAS to ROYCANAIRF, 20 Jan. 1943, and Edwards to Sutton, 22 Jan. 1943, PRO Air 8/742; Sutton to Edwards, 13 Sept. 1943, DHist 181.009 (D1084)

26 W.A.B. Douglas, *The Creation of a National Air Force* (Toronto 1986), 266; DP (Air Ministry) to Edwards, 16 Oct. 1942, DHist 181.009 (D774)

27 Capel to No 4 Group, 21 Jan. 1943, DHist 181.009 (D4236)

28 AHB, Bomber Command narrative, IV, 29–33, DHist 86/286; on overcrowding, see No 5 Group to Bomber Command, 6 Feb. 1942, PRO Air 14/2198, quoted in Leslie Nuttall, 'Canadianization and the No. 6 Bomber Group R.C.A.F.' (PhD thesis, University of Calgary 1990), 61. See also Halpenny, *Action Stations* No. 4, passim.

29 No 428 Squadron ORB, 11–14 Nov. 1942, DHist; F.H.C. Reinke personal diary, DHist 87/241; Linton-on-Ouse PRF file, DHist

30 Skipton-on-Swale PRF file, DHist

31 Reinke personal diary, DHist 87/241; Tholthorpe PRF file, DHist

32 Reinke personal diary, DHist 87/241; Linton-on-Ouse PRF file, DHist

33 Irvin C. Hundeby, *Only an Erk with the Thunderbirds* (Saskatoon 1985), 74

34 Carscallen biog. file, DHist

35 Blanchard biog. file, DHist, and No 426 Squadron ORB, Feb. 1943, DHist

36 CAS to ROYCANAIRF, 24 July 1942, and Edwards to CAS, 29 July 1942, DHist 181.009 (D612)

37 CAS to ROYCANAIRF, 1 Aug. 1942, Wait to undersecretary of state, Air Ministry, 28 Sept. 1942, and director of postings to Overseas Headquarters, 13 Oct. 1942, DHist 181.009 (D612); 'Extracts of minutes of conference No 3, RCAF Overseas Headquarters,' 26 Aug. 1942, AFHQ 19-10-19, NA, RG 24, vol. 5229; Slemon and Durham biog. files, DHist; No 6 Group ORB, 1 Jan. 1943, DHist

38 RCAF personnel branch history, DHist 74/7; Library of Parliament, History of the RCAF Women's Division, 1941–1971, DHist 78/517

39 Edwards to Breadner, 6 July 1942, and ROYCANAIRF to CAS, 15 July 1942, AFHQ 19-10-10, NA, RG 24, vol. 5229

40 Brookes biog. file, DHist; Newsom interview, 21 Sept. 1982, 2–3, DHist 82/1103; Slemon interview, 20 Oct. 1978, 2–3, DHist 79/128; Edwards to Breadner, 25 Sept. 1943, Power Papers, copy in DHist 79/721, folder 13

41 Harris, *Bomber Offensive*, 33–4

42 'Reorganization of Bomber Command,' 20 July 1942, PRO Air 14/1050, cited in William Carter, 'Anglo-Canadian Wartime Relations, 1939–1945: RAF Bomber Command and No 6 Canadian Group' (PhD thesis, McMaster University 1989), 59; Brookes diary, 27 July–13 Aug., 31 Aug–3 Sept., 21–24 Sept., and 10–19 Oct. 1942, Brookes biog file, DHist; 'Minutes of No 6 Group progress committee,' 30 Sept. and 30 Oct. 1942, DHist 74/727; Campbell to AOC-in-C, 21 Sept. 1942, and Brookes to AOC-in-C, 28 Sept. 1942, DHist 181.009 (D612); No 6 Group ORB, 25–31 Oct. and Dec. 1942, DHist; F/L K.B. Andras, 'History of organization of No 6 (RCAF) Group from Oct 25th 1942 to Nov 1st 1943, and responsibilities of organization branch,' 10 Nov. 1943, DHist 72/383

43 No 6 Group ORB, 1–30 Nov. 1942, DHist; Brookes diary, 6 Nov. 1942, Brookes biog. file, DHist

44 Brookes diary, 11 Dec. 1942, Brookes biog. file, DHist

45 Andras, 'History of Organization of No 6 (RCAF) Group,' 10 Nov. 1943, DHist 72/383

46 Brookes diary, 28–29 Aug. 1942, Brookes biog. file, DHist; Middlebrook and Everitt, BCWD, 301–4; Harris to Portal, 1 Dec. 1942, Harris Papers, copy in DHist 87/51, folder H51

47 Harris to AOC No 6 Group, 31 Dec. 1942, Harris Papers, copy in DHist 87/51, folder H103

48 Brookes diary, 31 Dec. 1942, Brookes biog. file, DHist

49 No 6 Group ORB, 1-3 Jan. 1943, DHist; Middlebrook and Everitt, BCWD, 341

50 Nos 419 and 427 Squadron ORBs, Nov.–Dec. 1942, DHist; No 431 Squadron ORB, 31 Jan.–28 Feb. 1943, DHist

51 Middlebrook and Everitt, BCWD, 340–50; No 6 Group ORB, Jan. 1943, DHist; Harris, 'The strategic control of our anti-submarine campaign,' 19 Dec. 1942, Harris Papers, copy in DHist 87/51, folder H13; AHB, Bomber Command narrative, IV, 270ff, DHist 86/286; Naval Staff, 'Monthly Anti-submarine Report, December 1941,' Jan. 1942, and 'Monthly Anti-submarine Report, December 1942,' 15 Jan. 1943; Bottomley to Harris, 14 Jan. 1943, quoted in Webster and Frankland, SAO, IV, 152–3

52 Combined Chiefs of Staff [Casablanca directive], approved 21 Jan. 1943, copy in DHist 181.006 (D159)

53 No 6 Group tactical report No 1, 4 Feb. 1943, DHist 181.003 (D4472); Nos 420, 427, 429 Squadron ORBs, 21/22 Jan. 1943, DHist; Air Force Headquarters, Air Historical Section, 'Secret narrative, Bomber Command,' Jan. 1943, DHist 79/444, hereafter cited as AFHQ, Secret bomber narrative; No 6 Group ORB, Jan. 1943, DHist

54 No 6 Group, ORB, 29/30 Jan. 1943, DHist; AFHQ, Secret bomber narrative, Jan. 1943, DHist 79/444; Middlebrook and Everitt, BCWD, 349

55 AFHQ, Secret bomber narrative, Feb. 1943, DHist 79/444; No 6 Group War Room, 'Six group activities, Hamburg – night 3/4 February [1943],' 4 Feb. 1943, DHist 181.003 (D1031); Middlebrook and Everitt, BCWD, 351

56 Nos 419 and 428 Squadron ORBs, 18/19 Feb. 1943, DHist

57 No 6 Group War Room, 'Six Group activities – night Feb 16/17, 1943; target – Lorient,' 17 Feb. 1943, DHist 181.003 (D1031); Bomber Command ORS to DD Science, 3 March 1945, PRO Air 14/1756; AFHQ, Secret bomber narrative, Feb. 1943, DHist 79/444

58 Middlebrook and Everitt, BCWD, 337–8; Webster and Frankland, SAO, IV, 155

59 Middlebrook and Everitt, BCWD, 362–409; AFHQ, Secret bomber narrative, March–July 1943, DHist 79/444

60 Nuttall, 'Canadianization,' 205–6, citing Air 14/552, Jan. 1943

61 See minutes by Saundby and Harris, 27 April 1943, PRO Air 14/1142.

62 Harris minute, 27 April 1943, and Sanders and Harris minutes, 24 and 28 June 1943, PRO Air 14/1142; Fred J. Hatch, 'Lancaster IIs of the RCAF in the Battle of Berlin,' Aircraft Illustrated 6 (Jan. 1973): 10–13

63 K.M. Molson and H.A. Taylor, *Canadian Aircraft since 1909* (Stittsville, Ont. 1982), 65–73; Kostenuk and Griffin, *RCAF Squadron Histories*, 112, 139; Francis K. Mason, *The Avro Lancaster* (Bourne End, Bucks. 1989), 307ff

64 See Squadron ORBs, DHist, and Kostenuk and Griffin, *RCAF Squadron Histories*, passim.

65 Edwards to Courtney, 10 March 1943, and Courtney to Edwards, 13 March 1943, DHist 181.009 (D774)

66 Desmond Morton, *A Military History of Canada* (Edmonton 1985), 206

67 Edwards to Courtney, 10 and 13 March 1943, DHist 181.009 (D774)

68 See Squadron ORBs, DHist, and Kostenuk and Griffin, *RCAF Squadron Histories*, passim.

69 DAS to AOC-in-C RCAF Overseas, 3 April 1943, DHist 181.009 (D2692)

70 Harris to Portal, 20 Aug. 1942, Harris Papers, copy in DHist 87/51, folder 81; Harris to Sinclair, 19 Jan. 1943, PRO Air 14/3513; Harris to Slessor, 28 Oct. 1942, PRO Air 14/3516; Street to Harris, 14 Dec. 1942, and Massey to Atlee, 8 Dec. 1942, PRO Air 2/5354

71 ROYCANAIRF to CAS, 7 and 8 April 1943, and Edwards to Street, 10 April 1943, DHist 181.009 (D2692)

72 Bomber Command to Topcliffe, Middleton St George, and Dishforth, 14 April 1943, and Bomber Command to No 6 Group, 22 April 1943, DHist 181.009 (D53)

73 Bomber Command to Topcliffe et al., 14 April 1943; Air Ministry, 'Dispatch of Nos 420, 424, and 425 Squadrons and formation and dispatch of No 331 Medium Bomber Wing to Mediterranean Air Command,' 19 April 1942, all DHist 181.009 (D53)

74 Nos 420, 424, and 425 Squadron ORBs, April–May 1943, DHist; Bomber Command to Topcliffe et al., 14 April 1943; Air Ministry, 'Dispatch of Nos 420, 424, and 425 Squadrons and formation and dispatch of No 331 Medium Bomber Wing to Mediterranean Air Command,' 19 April 1942, all DHist 181.009 (D53)

75 No 331 Wing ORB, 1 Aug. 1943, DHist; No 331 Wing Diary, 3–4, in ORB, DHist; No 420 Squadron ORB, 16 May 1943, DHist; Dunlap to Edwards, 15 July 1943, DHist 181.009 (D2692); AFHQ, 'Secret narrative, Northwest African Air Force, May–November 1943,' DHist 74/452, 4, May–June 1943 (hereafter cited as AFHQ, NAAF secret narrative)

76 Nos 420 and 425 Squadron ORBs, June 1943, DHist; AFHQ, NAAF secret narrative, 4–5, DHist 74/452

77 No 331 Wing Diary, 6–7, DHist; Dunlap to Edwards, 15 July 1943, DHist 181.009 (D2692); No 331 Wing ORB, 8–15 July 1943, DHist

78 Marshall and Eisenhower quoted in G.W.L. Nicholson, *The Canadians in Italy, 1943–1945* (Ottawa 1966), 5–7; 'Note by minister of defence,' 25 Nov. 1942, in Winston Churchill, *The Hinge of Fate* (Boston 1950), 654

79 Zuckerman, *From Apes to Warlords*, 196–8, 210; Lord Tedder, *With Prejudice* (London 1966), 445ff; Aders, *German Night Fighter Force*, 89–90

80 Nos 420 and 425 Squadron ORBs, 26/27 June 1943, DHist and No 425

Squadron History, 31, DHist 74/336; No 424 Squadron ORB, 27–29 June 1943, DHist

81 No 420, 424, and 425 Squadron ORBs, 2–9 July 1943, DHist; AFHQ, NAAF secret narrative, 5–11, DHist 74/452

82 AFHQ, NAAF secret narrative, July 1943, 4–16, DHist 74/452; Dunlap to Edwards, 15 July 1943, DHist 181.009 (D2692), No 331 Wing diary, 4–6 July 1943, DHist, and No 424 Squadron ORB, 6 July 1943, DHist

83 No 424 Squadron ORB, 27–29 June and 22, 23, and 26 July 1943, and Ault to AOC-in-C, RCAF Overseas Headquarters, 26 Sept. 1943, attached to No 424 Squadron ORB, July 1943, DHist; Minton C. Johnston, *Sky Pilots in Blue* (np, nd), 99

84 Recommendations for honours and awards submitted by W/C D.M. McIntosh, No 420 Squadron, 3 Feb. 1944, NA, RG 24, vol. 20, 600

85 Nos 420, 424, and 425 ORBs, 9/10 July 1943, DHist

86 Nos 420, 424, and 425 Squadron ORBs, 9–21 July 1943, DHist; Doolittle to No 205 Group, 14 July 1942, including message from Spaatz, No 331 Wing Diary, 85, and DHist 181.009 (D2692); AFHQ, NAAF secret narrative, 7, 13, July 1943, DHist 74/452; Nicholson, *The Canadians in Italy*, 103; Metzler to No 331 Wing, 15 Oct. 1943, DHist 181.006 (D66); Dunlap to Edwards, 15 July 1943, DHist 181.009 (D2692)

87 Nos 420, 424, and 425 Squadron ORBs, 14–22 July 1943, DHist; see also H.H. Coulson, 'An RCAF bomber wing in North Africa,' 8–9, DHist 74/451; AFHQ, NAAF secret narrative, 8, July 1943, DHist 74/452

88 No 331 Wing ORB, 24–28 July 1943, DHist

89 Quoted in Nora Bottomley, *424 Squadron History* (Belleville 1985), 46

90 Dunlap to Edwards, 15 July 1943, Edwards to DP, 27 July 1943, Edwards to Colyer, 14 Aug. 1943, DAS to DP, 14 Aug. 1943, Breadner to Edwards, 15 Aug. 1943, DP to NASAF, 24 Aug. 1943, DP to EA to AOC-in-C, with enclosures, 8 Sept. 1943, all DHist 181.009 (D2692); A Flight, No 424 Squadron, report to No 331 Wing, 14 Oct. 1943, DHist 181.006 (D66)

91 Minutes of meeting held in room 3403, Château Frontenac, Quebec City, 11 Aug. 1943, Air Ministry to Quadrant, 12, 13, 19 Aug. 1943, all PRO Air 8/783; Dunlap to Edwards, 18 Aug. 1943, Breadner to Edwards, 23 Aug. 1943, Edwards to Breadner, 16 Sept. 1943, all DHist 181.009 (D2692)

92 See Nos 420, 424, and 425 Squadron and No 331 Wing ORBs, 3–18 Aug. 1943, DHist; Nicholson, *The Canadians in Italy*, 168–74; RAF Mediterranean Review No 4, 'The Conquest of Sicily,' quoted in Nicholson, *The Canadians in Italy*, 172.

93 Bottomley, *424 Squadron History*, 43–4

94 Nicholson, *The Canadians in Italy*, 180–5

95 Ibid., 185–7; No 331 Wing ORB, 4 Sept. 1943, DHist

96 Nos 420, 424, and 425 Squadron ORBs, 18 Aug.–5 Sept. 1943, DHist; Tedder, *With Prejudice*, 465; AHB, 'The Italian Campaign 1939–1945,' I, 83, DHist 86/284; No 331 Wing ORB, 1 Sept. 1943, DHist

97 Tedder, *With Prejudice*, 465; AHB, 'The Italian Campaign,' I, 150–6, DHist 86/284; Tedder to Portal, 11 Sept. 1943, and Portal to Tedder, 13 Sept. 1943,

PRO Air 8/782; AFHQ, NAAF secret narrative, Sept. 1943, I, DHist 74/452; AHB, 'The Italian Campaign,' I, 150–6, DHist 86/284

98 No 331 Wing ORB, 15 Sept. 1943, DHist; AFHQ, NAAF secret narrative, Sept. 1943, 37–8, DHist 74/452; No 331 Wing diary, summary of September operations, DHist

99 Portal to Edwards, 27 Sept. 1943, PRO Air 8/782

100 AHB, 'The Italian campaign,' I, 159, DHist 86/284; No 425 Squadron ORB, 16–18 Sept. 1943, DHist

CHAPTER 18: NO 6 GROUP FALTERS

1 Combined Chiefs of Staff [Casablanca directive], 21 Jan. 1943, copy in DHist 181.006 (D159); W.F. Craven and J.L. Cate, eds., *The Army Air Forces in World War II*, II (Chicago 1949), chs. 7 and 9

2 Harris, *Bomber Offensive*, 220–1

3 Casablanca directive, 21 Jan. 1943, DHist 181.006 (D159)

4 Webster and Frankland, *SAO*, II, 14

5 Ibid., 364ff, and 'Note by the chief of the air staff for the chiefs of staff on an estimate of the effects of an Anglo-American bomber offensive against Germany,' 3 Nov. 1942, quoted in *SAO*, IV, 258–65

6 DBOps memorandum, 4 Jan. 1943, DHist 181.003 (D4694)

7 Harris, *Bomber Offensive*, 147

8 AHB, Bomber Command narrative, V, app. 18, DHist 86/286; Middlebrook and Everitt, *BCWD*, 246–56, 365–409

9 AHB, Bomber Command narrative, V, 224, DHist 86/286

10 Bomber Command ORS report No S102, 31 Aug. 1943, DHist 181.009 (D2390); AHB, Bomber Command narrative, V, 182, DHist 86/286; Musgrove, *The Pathfinder Force*, app. I, app. X, and 25ff

11 Minutes of meeting in the Air Council Room, 8 Dec. 1942, PRO Air 8/727; Bufton to ACAS (Ops), 4 Feb. 1943, PRO Air 2/7922; Minutes of meeting at Bomber Command Headquarters, 16 Feb. 1943, PRO Air 14/491; BDU report No 12, 25 March 1943, PRO Air 20/2121; Bomber Command ORS report No S99, 25 Aug. 1943, DHist 181.003 (D2167); Bomber Command ORS memorandum No 73, 16 June 1943, DHist 181.003 (D2166); AHB, Bomber Command narrative, IV, 78–84, DHist 86/286

12 'The history of armament in Bomber Command, Feb 1942–May 1945,' DHist 181.009 (D6119); 'Historical review of No 6 (RCAF) Heavy Bomber Group ... 1943–1945,' June 1945, DHist 181.003 (D5269); ORS 1(c) Bomber Command to ORS, 12 April 1944, PRO Air 14/3935; AHB, *Armament*, I, 283–8

13 Bomber Command ORS report No S133, 21 April 1943, PRO Air 14/1804; Bomber Command, 'The Pathfinder Force ...,' 22 Dec. 1942; 'Methods of target marking: notes for the guidance of operational crews,' nd, and 'Pathfinder Force instructions,' 23 Dec. 1943, all PRO Air 14/2058; Bomber Command ORS report No S102, 31 Aug. 1943, DHist 181.009 (D2390); AHB, Bomber Command narrative, IV, 77–8; Musgrove, *Pathfinder Force*, 38–9 and app. VI

14 Musgrove, *Pathfinder Force*, 248ff

15 Jukes to Dickens, 21 Dec. 1942, and conference of group commanders, 6 Jan. 1943, PRO Air 14/1751

16 Grabmann, 'German air defense, 1933–1945,' June 1957, USAF Historical Study No 164, DHist 86/451, frames 596, 707–14; USSAF AI 12, intelligence report No 37, 'Strength and Serviceability of GAF Flying Units, Sep 1939–Mar 1944,' 27 Aug. 1945, DHist 181.009 (D635); AHB, *The Rise and Fall of the German Air Force (1933 to 1945)*, 314; Aders, *German Night Fighter Force*, 16, 41; Air Ministry/USAFE intelligence report No 67, 21 Dec. 1945, DHist 181.009 (D414)

17 Grabmann, 'German air defense, 1933–1945,' June 1957, DHist 86/451, frames 596, 707–14, 731, 816, 882; USSAF AI 12, intelligence report No 37, 'Strength and serviceability of GAF Flying Units, Sep 1939–Mar 1944,' 27 Aug. 1945, DHist 181.009 (D635); ADI (K) report No 416/1945, 8 Dec. 1945, 3-8, DHist 82/1048; Kammhuber, 'Problems in the conduct of a day and night defensive air war,' 1 Oct. 1953, 70–105, USAF Historical Study No 179, DHist 81/947; Schmid, 'German night fighting from 15 June 1943 to end of war,' 1 Oct. 1945, app. 1 to USAFE, 'Tactical employment of night-fighting in the GAF,' 6 March 1946, DHist 73/1506, microfilm reel 2, frames 570ff; Aders, *German Night Fighter Force*, 16, 41

18 Grabmann, 'German air defenses,' DHist 86/451, frames 715–718; data on night fighter losses from 8th Abteilung Oberkommando der Luftwaffe records, copies in DHist SGR II 265, folder 24

19 Minutes of meeting of 6 Oct. 1942, Milch Papers, DHist SGR II 217, reel 16, frames 2550–73; ASI report No 21, 'Bomber losses and German claims, Dec 1942 to May 1943' [Feb. 1944], PRO Air 14/365; Grabmann, 'German air defenses,' DHist 86/451, frames 734–8

20 Minutes of conferences, 18 March 1943, Milch Papers, DHist SGR II 217, reel 62, frames 5462–71, 5546ff, and 6 July 1943, DHist SGR II 217, reel 21, frames 5566–77, 5581–3; Aders, *German Night Fighter Force*, 61ff; Herrmann, *Eagle's Wings*, 162–9

21 No 6 Group analysis of results, DHist 74/250; Middlebrook and Everitt, *BCWD*, 365–6; AHB, Bomber Command narrative, V, app. 10, 7, DHist 86/286; J.H. Searby, *The Great Raids*, II: *Essen* (Chippingham, Wilts., 1978), 15–16

22 No 6 Group operation order, quoted in Searby, *Essen*, 23–4; AFHQ, Secret bomber narrative, 6 March 1943, DHist 79/444

23 Middlebrook and Everitt, *BCWD*, 365; No 6 Group analysis of results, DHist 74/250

24 ORS to DD Science, 3 March 1945, PRO Air 14/1756; AHB, 'Reports of physical damage resulting from Allied air attacks on Germany, 1943,' compiled and translated from German sources, Oct. 1956, 44, DHist SGR II, folder 79

25 No 6 Group analysis of results, DHist 74/250

26 No 78 Squadron, Interpretation report No K 1497, and Bomber Command night raid report No 284, qoted in Searby, *Essen*, 42–65; AHB, 'Reports of physcial damage resulting from Allied air attacks on Germany, 1943,' Oct. 1956, 44, DHist SGR II 264, folder 79

27 Harris, *Despatch*, app. B, 85 DHist
28 Middlebrook and Everitt, *BCWD*, 365–6
29 Quoted in John Searby, *The Everlasting Arms* (London 1988), 95–6
30 No 6 Group analysis of results, DHist 74/250; Middlebrook and Everitt, *BCWD*, 365–6; AFHQ, Secret bomber narrative, 6–8 (March 1943), DHist 79/444; Bomber Command Night raid report No 284, quoted in Searby, *Essen*, 42–55
31 AHB, Bomber Command narrative, V, 55–6, 356, DHist 86/286; AFHQ, Secret bomber narrative, 10–12 (March 1943), DHist 79/444; Middlebrook and Everitt, *BCWD*, 366–8; No 6 Group analysis of results, DHist 74/250; Nos 405 and 419 Squadron ORBs, 11/12 March 1943, DHist
32 No 6 Group analysis of results, DHist 74/250; No 424 Squadron ORB, 12/13 March 1943, DHist; Middlebrook and Everitt, *BCWD*, 368
33 No 6 Group analysis of results, DHist 74/250; Middlebrook and Everitt, *BCWD*, 370; AFHQ, Secret bomber narrative, 13–14 (March 1943), DHist 79/444
34 Interrogation report, account of escape of Sgt C.E. McDonald, DHist 79/507, vol. 5; AHB, Bomber Command narrative, V, 55–6; No 6 Group analysis of results, DHist 74/250; AFHQ, Secret bomber narrative, 5–6 (March 1943), DHist 79/444; AHB, 'Reports of physical damage resulting from Allied air attacks on Germany 1943,' Oct. 1956, 2, DHist SGR II 264, folder 78; Middlebrook and Everitt, *BCWD*, 371–2
35 No 6 Group analysis of results, DHist 74/250; Middlebrook and Everitt, *BCWD*, 372; AFHQ, Secret bomber narrative, DHist 79/444; AHB, Bomber Command narrative, V, 40, DHist 86/286
36 No 6 Group analysis of results, DHist 74/250; Middlebrook and Everitt, *BCWD*, 370–3
37 ORS to DD Sci, 3 March 1945, PRO Air 14/1756; Saward to CSO, loose minute, 8 April 1943, PRO Air 14/1858
38 AFHQ, Secret bomber narrative, 11–12 (April 1943), DHist 79/444; ORS to DD Sci, 3 Mar 1945, PRO Air 14/1756
39 No 6 Group analysis of results, DHist 74/250; AHB, Bomber Command narrative, V, 57, DHist 86/286; ORS to DD Sci, 3 March 1945, PRO Air 14/1756; Middlebrook and Everitt, *BCWD*, 378–9; No 6 Group analysis of operations, 12 May 43, DHist 181.003 (D4714)
40 No 6 Group analysis of results, DHist 74/250; AFHQ, Secret bomber narrative, 9–11 (April 1943), DHist 79/444
41 AOC-in-C to AOCs, 16 April 1943, DHist 181.009 (D2879)
42 'Minutes of meeting held at Headquarters, Bomber Command, 23 April 1943 to discuss tactical aspects arising from recent operations,' PRO Air 14/1222
43 Harris to Brookes, 5 May 1943, DHist 181.009 (D1925), folio 18A
44 John Sweetman, *Operation CHASTISE* (London 1982), 191 and chs. 10 and 11; Harris, *Bomber Offensive*, 157–9; Webster and Frankland, *SAO*, II, 176–8, 288–92; Noble Frankland, 'The Dams Raid,' *Journal of the Royal United Services Institute*, 109, (May 1964): 127–30
45 Middlebrook and Everitt, *BCWD*, 383–409; AHB, Bomber Command narrative, V, 42–3, app. 18, DHist 86/286; ORS to DD Sci, 3 March 1945, PRO Air

14/1756; Musgrove, *Pathfinder Force*, 44–6; ORS to DD Sci, 3 March 1945, PRO Air 14/1756

46 Quoted by Noble Frankland, 'The planning of the bombing offensive and its contribution to German collapse,' April 1951, PRO Air 41/57, 124–5

47 Quoted in AFHQ, Secret bomber narrative, 21 (May 1943), DHist 79/444

48 ORS to DD Sci, 3 March 1945, PRO Air 14/1756; AHB, Bomber Command narrative, V, 42–3, app. 18, DHist 86/286; Middlebrook and Everitt, *BCWD*, 396–404; AHB, 'Reports of physical damage resulting from Allied air attacks on Germany 1943,' Oct. 1956, 34, DHist SGR II 264, folder 79; Musgrove, *Pathfinder Force*, 52–3

49 AHB, Bomber Command narrative, V, app. 19, DHist86/286

50 Ibid., 158

51 Ibid., 168–72; Bidinian, *The Combined Allied Bombing Offensive*, 65ff, 132–4; Webster and Frankland, *SAO*, II, 260

52 Date from AHB, Bomber Command narrative, V, app. 18, DHist 86/286, and Middlebrook and Everitt, *BCWD*, 362–409

53 No 6 Group analysis of operations, Jan.–July 1943, DHist 181.003 (D4714); No 6 Group analysis of results, DHist 74/250; A.L. Harris report of visit No 2 to No 6 Group, 14–25 Sept. 1943, DHist 181.009 (D5747)

54 Data from No 6 Group analysis of results, DHist 74/250; F/L G Miller's DFC citation; Ray Jacobsen, *426 Squadron History* (np, nd), 15

55 Forland interrogation report, 14–15 July 1943, DHist 79/507, vol. 3

56 M.R.D. Foot and J.M. Langley, *MI9* (London 1979), 79-82, 142ff, 207–11, 221, 306–7

57 George Pollock, 'Flyers Who Spike Germany's Secret Weapon,' *Reader's Digest* (UK edition), Sept. 1987, 59–63; Jones, *Most Secret War*, 280–6

58 Price, *Instruments of Darkness*, 139–40

59 No 419 Squadron ORB, 3/4 July 1943; 'Questionnaire for returned aircrew, loss of bomber aircraft,' DHist 181.001 (D24); see also Herrmann, *Eagle's Wings*, 166–7.

60 No 6 Group analysis of results, DHist 74/250

61 No 6 Group NSO, 'Report of 6 Group mining effort since Jan 1943,' DHist 181.003 (D4718); No 6 Group analysis of results, DHist 74/250

62 L.G.N. Rushbrooke, 'Effect of our offensive minelaying,' 30 March 1943, DHist 181.003 (D5096); AHB, 'The RAF in Maritime War,' IV, part B, app. XIX, DHist 79/599

63 'Gardening operations since May 1942,' DHist 181.009 (D2483); AHB, 'The RAF in Maritime War,' IV, 413, DHist 79/599

64 'Bomber Command instructions on GARDENING,' 25 May 1943, DHist 181.009 (D2482); AHB, 'The RAF in Maritime War,' IV, 413, DHist 79/599; DOps and DTASMW, 'Planning of aircraft minelaying operations' [1946], annex I, PRO Air 20/5837

65 No 6 Group analysis of results, DHist 74/250

66 No 6 Group circular, 15 March 1943, DHist 181.009 (D2482); No 4 Group NSO to No 6 Group, 7 April 1943, DHist 181.009 (D2481); AHB, 'The RAF in

Maritime War,' IV, part B, 411, DHist 79/599; No 6 Group Circular, 15 May 1943, DHist 181.009 (D5599)

67 No 6 Group analysis of results, DHist 74/250; No 6 Group circulars, 19 May and 6 June 1943, DHist 181.009 (D2482); AHB, 'The RAF in Maritime War,' IV, part B, 411, DHist 79/599; Middlebrook and Everitt, BCWD, 382

68 No 6 Group NSO to NSO Bomber Command, 2 Aug. 1943, DHist 181.003 (D3088); Middlebrook and Everitt, BCWD, 362–409; No 6 Group analysis of results, DHist 74/250

69 No 6 Group EO to IO, 5 Sept. 1944, and No 6 Group analyses of operations, DHist 181.003 (D4714); Edwards to Brookes, 16 Sept. 1943, DHist 181.009 (D1925); Bomber Command, 'Report on serviceability of GEE, 28 May–30 June 1943,' 8 July 1943, DHist 181.003 (D3889)

70 Bomber Command monthly reports on casualties, PRO Air 14/364, and No 6 Group analyses of operations, DHist 181.003 (D4714)

71 Harris to CAS, 10 Jan. 1943, Portal Papers, copy in DHist 87/89, folder 10 (1943), and Harris to Balfour, 19 Jan. 1943, PRO Air 20/3798

72 Brookes diary, 23 April 1943, Brookes biog. file, DHist

73 Ibid., 15 Feb. 1943; S/L P.T. Green, 'Service history,' DHist 181.009 (D4254)

74 Extract from staff conference, 10 March 1943, and Wait to AOC-in-C, 12 March 43, DHist 181.009 (D769); T. Sawyer, *Only Owls and Bloody Fools Fly at Night* (London 1982), 68

75 Slemon to bases and stations, 1 Feb. 1943, Brookes to same, 1 March 1943, and Slemon to same, 19 March 1943, all DHist 181.003 (D230); No 6 Group monthly summaries of operations and training activities, DHist 181.003 (D296); No 26 OTU to No 92 Group, 1 March 1943, PRO Air 14/485; Harris to Brookes, 3 May 1943, and Brookes to Harris, 21 May 1943, replying to Harris to Brookes, 21 May 1943, DHist 181.009 (D1925)

76 No 6 Group tactical report No 6, June Operations, 4 July 1943, DHist 181.003 (D4472)

77 Brookes to Capel, 3 June 1943, DHist 181.009 (D1920)

78 Bomber Command ORS draft report No B147, sent to AOC-in-C, 10 July 1943, PRO Air 14/1800

79 Bomber Command report No B147, 15 July 1943, DHist 181.009 (D1925)

80 S.C. Britton, 'Halifax losses; the position at 4 Group, June 1943,' and Dickens to Saundby, minute 13, 30 June 1943, PRO Air 14/1794; Saundby to AOC No 6 Group, 17 July 1943, DHist 181.009 (D1925)

81 Edwards to Power, report No 15, 19 July 1943, Power Papers, copy in DHist 79/721, folder 14; Brookes to Saundby, 21 July 1943, PRO Air 14/1800; Brookes to Saundby, 3 Aug. 1943, and Edwards to Brookes, 16 Sept. 1943, DHist 181.009 (D1925)

82 S.C. Britton, 'The effects of operational experience in No 6 Group,' 15 Aug. 1943, DHist 181.003 (D4840); Bomber Command ORS, 'A further comment on 6 Group losses,' 7 Oct. 1943, PRO Air 14/1794

83 Bomber Command ORS, 'A further comment on 6 Group losses,' 7 Oct. 1943, PRO Air 14/1794

84 [RCAF Overseas Headquarters ORS], 'A review of bomber losses on night operations with special reference to No 6 (RCAF) Group (January 1st, 1943 to September 30th, 1943),' DHist 181.003 (D4223)

85 Bomber Command ORS, Report No B198, 'A note on comparative losses in No 4 and No 6 Groups' [Feb. 1944], PRO Air 14/1794; RCAF Overseas Headquarters ORS, 'Addendum No 1 to review of bomber losses on night operations with special reference to No 6 (RCAF) Group,' 13 Jan. 1944, DHist 181.003 (D4223); Harris to Breadner, 3 March 1944, PRO Air 14/1794; No 6 Group to Breadner, 27 Jan. 1944, DHist 181.005 (D503)

86 Harris to Sinclair, 30 Dec. 1942, PRO Air 14/3512; see also note by C-in-C, 'Lancaster II and Halifax III,' PRO Air 19/354.

87 Chapman to regional controllers (except Northern Ireland), 2 Jan. 1943, PRO Avia 10/269; Harris to Sinclair, 13 May 1943, PRO Air 14/3513

88 Harris to Linnell, 16 Oct. 1942, Harris Papers, copy in DHist 87/51, folder H91; DDG Stats, 'The supply of labour and the future of the aircraft programme,' 19 May 1943, PRO Avia 10/269

89 S.C. Britten, 'Halifax losses: the position of 4 Group, June 1943,' PRO Air 14/1794; Bomber Command to groups, 'Notes to pilots on the handling of controls of heavy bombers in evasive manoeuvres,' [June 1943?] DHist 181.009 (D7652); Harris to Freeman, 30 June 1943, Harris Papers, copy in DHist 87/51, folder H-85; Harris to Portal, 4 Feb 1943, Portal Papers, copy in DHist 87/89, folder 10A (1943); Bomber Command Operations Record Book, June 1944, Armaments section, 978ff, DHist; AHB, Armament, II, 98–9; Harris to Brookes, 3 Feb. 1943, and No 6 Group to Bomber Command, 9 Feb. 1943, DHist 181.009 (D1568); BDU report No 13, 1 May 1943, PRO Air 14/2588

90 Corball to DBOps, 23 June 1943, and 'Bomber defence policy; minutes of meeting held 24 June 1943,' PRO Air 20/4796; AHB, Armament, II, 99–100

91 Harris to Portal, 16 June 1943, Portal Papers, copy in DHist 87/89, folder 10A (1943); Bomber Command to groups, 9 Aug. 1943, DHist 181.009 (D4956); Price, Instruments of Darkness, 128–30, 139–40; Bomber Command, Signals Branch, 'War in the Ether,' Oct. 1945, 10–16; AHB, Bomber Command narrative, V, 76, 226, DHist 86/286; Middlebrook and Everitt, BCWD, 399–401

92 Bomber Command, Ops 1(e) memorandum, 18 June 1943, PRO Air 14/3947; 'Minutes of 5th and 6th meetings on radio and navigation policy,' 15 June and 3 Aug. 1943, DHist 181.009 (D5306); No 6 Group to bases, stations, and squadrons, 9 July 1943, DHist 181.009 (D3004); Bomber Command to Groups, 9 Aug. 1943, DHist 181.009 (D4956); Bottomley to Harris, 30 July 1943, and Bomber Command to ACAS Ops, 15 Aug. 1943, PRO Air 14/69; 'Minutes of a conference held at Air Ministry, 18/19 Aug 1943,' PRO Air 2/4468

93 6 Group to bases and stations, 2 July 1943, DHist 181.009 (D5078)

94 Bomber Command, 'Concentration en route,' 13 July 1943, DHist 181.009 (D1905)

95 Extracts of conference under chairmanship of Generalfeldmarschall Milch, 6 July 1943, Milch Papers, translation in DHist SGR II 217, reel 21

96 Ibid., Price, *Instruments of Darkness*, 146; Herrmann, *Eagle's Wings*, 168ff

97 Aders, *German Night Fighter Force*, 85, 126; David Pritchard, *The Radar War* (Wellingborough 1989), 155

98 Oberst a.D. Mirr, 'Development of German aircraft armament to war's end,' USAF Historical Study No 193, DHist 81/960, 90ff; '*Schräge Musik*,' *Jägerblatt*, XVI, July–Aug. 1967, 16–18; Aders, *German Night Fighter Force*, 66–7; Heron's interrogation report, 'Questionnaire for returned aircrew – loss of bomber aircraft,' in DHist 181.001 (D24)

99 Grabmann, 'German air defense, 1933–1945,' June 1957, USAF Historical Study No 164, DHist 86/451, frames 910ff and 1071ff; Galland's comments at the conference chaired by Milch, 5 Jan. 1943, in Milch Papers, DHist SGR II 217, reel 18, frames 3990–9; minutes of the conference chaired by Göring and Milch, 18 March 1943, Milch Papers, copy in DHist SGR II 217, reel 62, frames 5462–500, 5546–9

CHAPTER 19: INTO THE ELECTGRONIC AGE, HAMBURG AND AFTER

1 Bomber Command operations order No 173, 27 May 1943, DHist 181.009 (D6792); Martin Middlebrook, *The Battle of Hamburg* (London 1980), 93–117; Martin Middlebrook, *The Berlin Raids* (London 1988), 8ff; Gordon Musgrove, *Operation Gomorrah*, (London 1981), 1–13

2 Webster and Frankland, *SAO*, IV, 153–4; 'The Bomber's Baedeker,' DHist 181.003 (D3993)

3 Craven and Cate, *Army Air Forces*, II, 349, 356–66; 'The Bomber's Baedeker,' DHist 181.003 (D3993)

4 Webster and Frankland, *SAO*, II, 18

5 Harris to Eaker, 15 April 1943, quoted in Webster and Frankland, *SAO*, II, 18

6 Portal to Arnold, 15 April 1943, quoted in Webster and Frankland, *SAO*, II, 19; AHB, Bomber Command narrative, V, 73, DHist 86/286

7 Combined bombing offensive plan as approved by the Combined Chiefs of Staff, 14 May 1943, quoted in Webster and Frankland, *SAO*, II, 23–4 and IV, 158–60; Craven and Cate, *Army Air Forces*, II, 366–74; AHB, Bomber Command narrative, V, 70–1, DHist 86/286; Pointblank directive, 10 June 1943, quoted in Webster and Frankland, *SAO*, IV, 158–60

8 Bomber Command to groups, 19 Jan. 42, PRO Air 14/763, but see also Portal to Churchill, 15 Oct. 1943, PRO Air 19/189; Bomber Command operations order No 173, 27 May 1943, DHist 181.009 (D6792); Middlebrook, *The Battle of Hamburg*, 93–117, 239–72; Middlebrook and Everitt, *BCWD*, 413–14; Musgrove, *Operation Gomorrah*, 1–13.

9 Bomber Command ORS report No S98, 19 Aug. 1943, PRO Air 14/1800

10 USAFE, 'German air defenses: Tactical employment of night-fighting in the German Air Force,' 6 March 1946, DHist 73/1506, reel 2, frame 535, and Grabmann, 'German air defense, 1933–1945,' June 1952, USAF Historical Study no 164, DHist 86/451, frames 903–4; Bomber Command, Signals Branch, 'War in the Ether,' Oct. 1945, 33–7; Price, *Instruments of Darkness*, 124–49

11 Cajus Bekker [Hans Dieter Berenbrooke] *The Luftwaffe War Diaries* (New York 1966), 457–8

12 Bomber Command ORS report No S95, 31 July 1943, DHist 181.009 (D2824), and report No S98, 19 Aug. 1943, PRO Air 14/1800

13 Horst Diener, Those days in Leeuwarden, translation of 'Damals in Leeuwarden,' *Jägerblatt für Angehörige Ehemaliger Jagdfliegereinheiten*, Nost 1–5 (1956), DHist SGR II 308, 17

14 Quoted in Middlebrook, *The Battle of Hamburg*, 128

15 Quoted ibid., *The Battle of Hamburg*, 128–9; see also Musgrove, *Operation Gomorrah*, 28ff.

16 Bomber Command ORS report No S95, 31 July 1943, DHist 181.009 (D2824)

17 Middlebrook and Everitt, *BCWD*, 411–12; Middlebrook, *The Battle of Hamburg*, 133

18 No 6 Group analysis of results, Jan. 1943–Dec. 1943, DHist 74/250; No 6 Group plot of Hamburg raid, 24/25 July 1943, DHist 181.004 (D101)

19 Middlebrook and Everitt, *BCWD*, 412; Bomber Command ORS to DD Science, 3 March 1945, PRO Air 14/1756; Beck, *Under the Bombs*, 67–8

20 Minutes of meeting, 5 Jan. 1943, Milch Papers, DHist SGR II 217, reel 18, frames 3990–9; Price, *Instruments of Darkness*, 148; Middlebrook and Everitt, *BCWD*, 412–13; No 6 Group analysis of results, DHist 74/250

21 Hans Brunswig, *Feuersturm über Hamburg* (Stuttgart 1979), 190ff

22 Middlebrook, *The Battle of Hamburg*, 260–3; Musgrove, *Operation Gomorrah*, ch. 6

23 AFHQ, Secret bomber narrative, July 1943, DHist 79/444

24 Extract from the report by the police president of Hamburg on the raids on Hamburg in July and August 1943, dated 1 Dec. 1943, quoted in Webster and Frankland, *SAO*, IV, 310–15; Beck, *Under the Bombs*, 69–70

25 Extract from the report by the police president of Hamburg on the raids on Hamburg in July and August 1943, dated 1 Dec 1943, quoted in Webster and Frankland, *SAO*, IV, 310–15

26 Poster issued by the Gauleiter of Hamburg on 31 July 1943, quoted in Brunswig, *Feuersturm*, 259; Wilhelm Keitel to Frau Lisa Keitel, 3 Aug. 1943, extracted in Walter Görlitz, ed., *In the Service of the Reich* (New York 1979), 187; Musgrove, *Operation Gomorrah*, 167; extracts from the report by the police president of Hamburg, 10 Sept. 1943, DHist SGR II 264, folder 79

27 AHB, 'Reports of physical damage resulting from Allied air attacks on Germany, 1943,' app A, excerpts from the report by the Hamburg police president of Hamburg, DHist SGR II 264, folder 79; Albert Speer, *Inside the Third Reich* (New York 1970), 284; Kammhuber, 'Problems in the conduct of a day and night defensive war,' 1 Oct. 1953, USAF Historical Study No 179, DHist 81/947, 74

28 Harris, *Bomber Offensive*, 180; United States Strategic Bombing Survey (USSBS), *Area Studies Division Report* (Washington 1947), 6–8; Bidinian, *The Combined Allied Bombing Offensive*, 117–18, 150; AHB, Bomber Command narrative, V, 90, DHist 86/286; Middlebrook, *The Battle of Hamburg*, 332; Beck, *Under the Bombs*, 110

29 ORS Bomber Command report No S97, 9 Aug. 1943, DHist 181.009 (D2824); Bomber Command interception/tactics report No 153/43, 4 Aug. 1943, DHist 181.003 (D1429)

30 Air Ministry, ADI(K) report 416/1945, 8 Dec. 1945, 9–13, DHist 82/1048; orders issued by Göring, 30 July 1943, and Weise, 1 Aug. 1943, Milch Papers, copy at DHist SGR II 217, reel 56; Williamson Murray, *Luftwaffe* (Baltimore 1985), 171–4; Aders, *German Night Fighter Force*, 101–2; Middlebrook and Everitt, *BCWD*, 411–16; ORS Bomber Command report No S98, 19 Aug. 1943, PRO Air 14/1800; see also report No 78, 29 Sept. 1943, DHist 181.003 (D3474)

31 No 6 Group analysis of results, Jan. 1943–Dec. 1943, DHist 74/250; S.C. Britten, 'Operations against Hamburg of August 2nd/3rd,' 5 Aug. 1943, DHist 181.003 (D4840)

32 No 6 Group analysis of results, DHist 74/250

33 Middlebrook and Everitt, *BCWD*, 420; No 6 Group analysis of results, Jan. 1943–Dec. 1943, DHist 74/250; Martin Middlebrook, *The Peenemünde Raid* (New York 1982)

34 Webster and Frankland, *SAO*, II, 159

35 SASO No 6 Group to bases and stations, 3 Aug. 1943, DHist 181.005 (D70)

36 SASO No 6 Group to stations, 3 Aug. 1943, DHist 181.005 (D70); AHB, Bomber Command narrative, V, 101–4, DHist 86/286

37 J.H. Searby, *The Great Raids*, I: *Peenemünde* (Chippenham, Wilts., 1978), 19–20

38 'Pathfinder narrative of operations No 74, night 17th/18th August 1943, Peenemünde,' quoted in Searby, *Peenemünde*, 55; ibid., 19–20; AHB, Bomber Command narrative, V, 101–4, DHist 86/286

39 Middlebrook and Everitt, *BCWD*, 422; No 6 Group analysis of results, DHist 74/250; Middlebrook, *Peenemünde*, 166, 247–8; No 6 Group ORB, 17/18 Aug. 1943, DHist

40 Quoted in Middlebrook, *Peenemünde*, 160

41 Ibid.

42 Quoted ibid., 161–2

43 Craven and Cate, *Army Air Forces*, II, 848; German casualty statistics compiled by 8 Abteilung, Oberkommando der Luftwaffe, found in DHist SGR II 265, folder 24; Cooper, *The German Air Force*, 318–19; and Murray, *Luftwaffe*, 175ff, 217

44 L. Karsten quoted in Richard Suchenwirth, *Command and Leadership in the German Air Force*, USAF Historical Study No 174, 288; extracts of conference, 25 Aug. 1943, DHist SGR II 264, folder 62; see also Webster and Frankland, *SAO*, IV, 306.

45 Galland, *The First and the Last*, 223–5

46 Extract of meeting of 8 Oct. 1943, Milch Papers, copy in DHist SGR II 217, reel 62; Schmid, 'German night fighting from 15 July 1943 to end of war, with remarks on the air defense of the *Reich*,' 1 Oct. 1945, app. I to USAFE, 'German Air Defenses,' DHist 73/1506, microfilm reel 2, frames 570–9; Kammhuber, 'Problems in the conduct of a day and night defensive war,' 1 Oct. 1953, USAF Historical Study No 179, DHist 81/947, frames 112–13;

Grabmann, 'German air defense, 1933–1945,' June 1952, USAF Historical Study No 164, DHist 86/451, frame 1104; Aders, *German Night Fighter Force*, 107ff; AHB, *The Rise and Fall of the German Air Force (1933 to 1945)*, 189

47 Schmid, 'German night fighting from 15 July 1943 to end of war, with remarks on the air defense of the *Reich*,' 1 Oct. 1945, app. 1 to USAFE, 'German Air Defenses,' DHist 73/1506, microfilm reel 2, frames 570–9; Air Ministry, ADI(K) report No 416/1945, 8 Dec. 1945, 7–10, 18–19, DHist 82/1048; Josef Schmid and Walter Grabmann, 'The German Air Force against the Allies in the West,' 1954, USAF Historical Studies Nos 158 and 159, DHist 81/930, frames 80–1; 'Operations report and lessons learned by *Generalkommando* XII *Fliegerkorps* for the period 1–31 August 1943,' SGR II 320, folder 68, 19–24. See also extracts of meeting of 3 Aug. 1943, Milch Papers, copy at DHist SGR II 217, reel 23; Streetley, *Confound and Destroy*, 179–80, 262; Aders, *German Night Fighter Force*, 248, 263; and Webster and Frankland, *SAO*, IV, 448–9.

48 Extracts of minutes of meeting of 17 Sept. 1943, Milch Papers, copy at DHist SGR II 217, reel 43; Streetley, *Confound and Destroy*, 180; Air Ministry ASI report No 33, 20 April 1945, PRO, Air 20/1650; Bomber Command ORS report No S98, 19 Aug. 1943, PRO Air 14/1800; ORS report No 80, 11 Sept. 1943, Bomber Command to groups, 18 Sept. and 4 Nov. 1943, all DHist 181.009 (D1716); *Oberst* Paul Günther, 'A methodology and organization for wide-ranging pursuit night fighter operations,' 6 Aug. 1943, Milch Papers, copy at DHist SGR II 217, reel 56; Air Ministry, ADI(K) report No 334/1945, 21 June 1945, DHist 82/1050; Bomber Command ORS report No 88, 16 Dec. 1943, PRO Air 14/1801; Aders, *German Night Fighter Force*, 95–6, 247–50, 252

49 'Operations report and lessons learned by *Generalkommando* XII *Fliegerkorps* for the period 1–31 Aug 1943,' 12 Sept. 1943, copy in DHist SGR II 320, folder 63; Kammhuber, 'Problems in the conduct ...' D Hist 81/947; Schmid, 'German night fighting ...' 1 Oct. 1945, app. 1 to USAFE, Post-Hostilities Investigation, 'German Air Defenses,' DHist 73/1506, microfilm reel 2, frames 570–9; Air Ministry, ADI(K) report No 416/1945, 8 Dec. 1945, 7–10, DHist 82/1048; Schmid and Grabmann, 'The German Air Force against the Allies in the West,' DHist 81/930, frames 80–1; Grabmann, 'German air defense, 1933–1945,' June 1957, DHist 86/451, frames 1083ff; extracts of minutes of meeting 17 Sept. 1943, Milch Papers, copy in DHist SGR II 217, reel 43, translation; J.R. Smith and Anthony Kay, *German Aircraft of the Second World War* (London 1972), 299; David Irving, *The Rise and Fall of the Luftwaffe* (Toronto 1973), 144, 172–3, 225

50 Bomber Command ORS report No 80, 11 Sept. 1943, PRO Air 14/457; Air Ministry ASI report No 33, 20 April 1945, PRO, Air 20/1650; Bomber Command ORS report No S98, 19 Aug. 1943, PRO Air 14/1800; Bomber Command to Groups, 18 Sept. and 4 Nov. 1943, DHist 181.009 (D1716); Oberst von Lossberg, 'Proposal for new night fighter tactics,' 29 July 1943, Milch Papers, copy in DHist SGR II 217, reel 56, translation; 'Fragebogen zur Reichsluftverteidigung (Nachtjagd),' translated as Questionnaire on Reich Air Defence

(Night Fighter Operations), copy in DHist SGR II 320, folder 58. Respondent is likely Grabmann, who commanded 3 Jagddivision under Schmid's I Jagdkorps.

51 Middlebrook, *The Berlin Raids*, 23; No 6 Group analysis of results, Jan. 1943 to Dec. 1943, DHist 74/250

52 Bomber Command ORS report No B163, 26 Aug. 1943, PRO Air 14/1872; SASO No 6 Group to bases and stations, 10 Sept. 1943, DHist 181.009 (D1607); 'No 6 Group monthly summary of operational and training activities, Aug 1943,' 10 Sept. 1943, DHist 181.003 (D296); Bomber Command ORS report No 80, 11 Sept. 1943, PRO Air 14/1801

53 Quoted in Middlebrook, *The Berlin Raids*, 47–8

54 Quoted ibid., 49–51

55 Ibid., 65–6; AHB, 'Reports of Physical Damage Resulting from Allied Air Attacks on Germany, 1943,' Oct. 1956, DHist SGR II 264, folder 79

56 Hans-Georg von Studnitz, *While Berlin Burns, 1933–1945* (Englewood Cliffs, NJ, 1963), 102

57 AFHQ, Secret narrative, Sept. 1943, 8, DHist 79/444

58 L.P. Lochner, ed., *The Goebbels Diary* (New York 1948), 525; USSBS, *The Effects of Strategic Bombing on German Morale* (Washington 1947), I, 9–11; Beck, *Under the Bombs*, 99–100; Bidinian, *Combined Allied Bombing Offensive*, 97–120

59 USSBS, *Morale*, I, 7, 47–65; USSBS, *Area Studies Division Report*, 6–8; Hugh Trevor-Roper, ed., *Final Entries 1945: The Diaries of Joseph Goebbels* (New York 1978), passim

60 Quoted in Middlebrook, *The Berlin Raids*, 80; see also appreciation by No 6 Group duty intelligence officer, DHist 181.003 (D3479) and Musgrove, *Pathfinder Force*, 66–7

61 AHB, 'Reports of physical damage resulting from Allied air attacks on Germany, 1943,' Oct. 1956, DHist SGR II 264, folder 79

62 Extracts of meeting of 9 Oct. 1943, Milch Papers, copy in DHist SGR II 217, reel 63, 8

63 Middlebrook and Everitt, *BCWD*, 427; No 6 Group analysis of results, DHist 74/250

64 Air Ministry to Bomber Command, 28 March 1943, PRO Air 14/1141

65 No 426 Squadron Operations Record Book (ORB), Aug.–4 Sept. 1943, DHist; Middlebrook and Everitt, *BCWD*, 427–8; No 6 Group analysis of results, DHist 74/250; AFHQ, Secret narrative, DHist 79/444; No 434 Squadron ORB, 31 Aug. 1943, DHist

66 Harris, *Bomber Offensive*, 186; AHB, 'Reports of physical damage resulting from Allied air attacks on Germany, 1943,' Oct. 1956, DHist SGR II 264, folder 79; Middlebrook, *The Berlin Raids*, 8, 84; Middlebrook and Everitt, *BCWD*, 417

67 Bomber Command to groups, 'H2S notes on Targets – October,' 26 Oct. 1943, DHist 181.009 (D4956)

68 Admin. Plans to AOA, 22 Sept. 1943, AOA to deputy C-in-C, 23 Sept. 1943, AOT to deputy C-in-C, 23 Sept. 1943, and Harris note, 29 Sept. 1943, PRO Air

14/1143; Department of Munitions and Supply, Aircraft Production Branch, 'Schedule of Airframe – Engine-Propeller Deliveries,' 1 Oct. 1942, 5-9-17, NA, C.D. Howe Papers, MG 27 III, B20, vol. 40; Brookes to Sanders, 15 Aug. 1943, and Sanders to Brookes, 18 Aug. 1943, DHist 181.009 (D1925)

69 AOC No 6 Group to Bomber Command, 3 Nov. 1943, PRO Air 14/1143

70 'Historical review of No 6 (RCAF) Heavy Bomber Group,' app. 232 to No 6 Group ORB, June 1945, 8, DHist 181.003 (D5269); Bomber Command to groups, 26 Oct. 1943, DHist 181.009 (D4956); Bomber Command to ACAS (Ops), 29 Oct. 1943, PRO Air 2/7922

71 Bomber Command to ACAS (Ops), 29 Oct. 1943, Harris to Portal, 2 Nov. 1943, PRO Air 14/1295; 'Minutes of 8th meeting on radio and navigation policy,' 2 Oct. 1943, DHist 181.009 (D5306); Bomber Command ORS report No S189, 13 Aug. 1944, DHist 181.003 (D2167); Harris, *Despatch*, app. A; Saward, *Victory Denied*, 320–1; Musgrove, *Pathfinder Force*, 235ff, 245; Webster and Frankland, *SAO*, IV, 11ff; Bomber Command Navigation Bulletin, Oct. 1943, DHist 181.003 (D147); Donaldson to SASO enclosing 'Determination of wind values for use by main force aircraft,' 12 Nov. 1943, PRO Air 14/516

72 Bomber Command to Nos 3 and 6 groups, 21 Nov. 1943, and to No 6 Group, 25 Jan. 1944, DHist 181.009 (D2292); AHB, Bomber Command narrative, V, 110, 224, DHist 86/286; Webster and Frankland, *SAO*, IV, 15ff; Saward, *Victory Denied*, 265, 295

73 Bomber Command to Nos 3 and 6 groups, 21 Nov. 1943 and 25 Jan 1944, DHist 181.009 (D2292)

74 Quoted in Webster and Frankland, *SAO*, II, 34–5

75 Quoted in Middlebrook, *The Berlin Raids*, 8–9; DCAS to CAS, 25 Sept. 1943, minute 3, CAS to DCAS, 27 Sept. 1943, minute 5, PRO Air 2/8410; see also AHB, Bomber Command narrative, V, 78ff, 159, DHist 86/286, and Webster and Frankland, *SAO*, II, 34

76 Harris, *Bomber Offensive*, 49–50, 220–4

77 Arnold P. Vaughan, *418 (City of Edmonton) Squadron History* (Belleville, Ont., 1984), 13–14

78 No 418 Squadron ORB, June 1942–May 1943, DHist

79 C. Martin Sharp and Michael J.F. Bowyer, *Mosquito* (London 1967), 29–42, 287–301, 338–353, 393–5, 401–3; Alexander McKee, *The Mosquito Log* (London 1988), 67–74, 104–18; B. Gunston, *Night Fighters* (New York 1976), 169; No 418 Squadron ORB, 19–20 Feb. and May–Aug. 1943, DHist; AHB, 'Air Defence of Great Britain,' V, 312, DHist 88/49

80 Douglas Alcorn and Raymond Sousyer, *From Hell to Breakfast* (Toronto 1980), 96; AHB, 'The Air Defence of Great Britain,' V, 313, DHist 88/49

81 No 418 Squadron ORB, 5/6 Sept. 1943, DHist

82 Ibid., 23/24 and 27/28 Sept. 1943, and Feb. 1944, DHist

83 ACAS (Ops) to DCAS, 6 Sept. 1943, minute 5, PRO Air 2/7309; Harris to DG of S, Air Ministry, 7 Sept. 1943, PRO Air 20/8070; AHB, 'Air Defence of Great Britain,' V, 306ff, and app. 24, DHist 88/49; Bomber Command Int 3, 'Note on enemy night air defences,' 1 Dec. 1944, PRO Air 14/2914; Hinsley, *British Intelligence*, III, 555; Clayton, *The Enemy Is Listening*, passim; Jones, *Most*

Secret War, 383–4; Bomber Command, Amendment List No 1 to TC 37 of August 1943, issued 1 Oct. 1943, DHist 181.009 (D2591)

84 Streetley, *Confound and Destroy*, 26–31

85 Bomber Command, 'Tactical note on bomber self-defence at night,' 1 Aug. 1943, DHist 181.009 (D6752)

86 Ibid.; No 6 Group tac. officer to AI, minute 4, 7 Sept. 1943, DHist 181.009 (D2800)

87 Bomber Command to groups, 1 Sept. 1943, DHist 181.009 (D2800)

88 No 4 Group tactical report No 17, 9 Sept. 1943, DHist 181.003 (D4469)

89 Bomber Command to groups, 1 Sept. and 2 Oct. 1943, DHist 181.009 (D2800); Bomber Command ORS report No S113, 12 Nov 1943, DHist 181.009 (D6752)

90 Edwards to secretary, Department of National Defence for Air, 24 Sept. 1943, DHist 181.009 (D4413)

91 Bomber Command Interceptions/tactics report No 197/43, 29 Sept. 1943, DHist 181.003 (D1429); No 6 Group monthly summary of operational and training activities, 9 Oct. 1943, DHist 181.003 (D296); Bomber Command ORS report No 88, 6 Dec. 1943, DHist 181.003 (D3474); No 6 Group to 61 and 62 bases, 26 Sept. 1943, DHist 181.003 (D5148); Bomber Command to groups, 24 Sept. 1943, DHist 181.009 (D1905)

92 Bomber Command Interception/tactics report No 197/43, 29 Sept. 1943, DHist 181.003 (D1429); Middlebrook and Everitt, *BCWD*, 432

93 Middlebrook and Everitt, *BCWD*, 432–4; Bomber Command ORS report No 83, 1 Oct. 1943, DHist 181.003 (D3474)

94 Bomber Command ORS report No 83, 31 Oct. 1943, DHist 181.003 (D3474); Schmid and Grabmann, 'The German Air Force against the Allies in the West,' DHist 81/930, frame 32; memorandum by R.V. Jones, 4 Oct. 1943, quoted in Jones, *Most Secret War*, 381–2; Middlebrook and Everitt, *BCWD*, 434; No 6 Group analysis of results, DHist 74/250; Brookes diary, 27 Oct. 1943, Brookes biog. file, DHist; No 434 Squadron ORB, Jan.–Feb. 1944, DHist

95 Memorandum by R.V. Jones, 4 Oct. 1943, quoted in Jones, *Most Secret War*, 381–2

96 Jones, *Most Secret War*, 381–2

97 Middlebrook and Everitt, *BCWD*, 434–40

98 Ibid., 439

99 AFHQ, Secret bomber narrative, Oct. 1943, 42–3, DHist 79/444; DHist awards files

100 Bomber Command ORS, app. A to Amendment List No 1 of TC 37, issued Oct. 1943, DHist 181.009 (D2591)

101 Appreciation by No 6 Group duty intelligence officer, DHist 181.003 (D3479); Schmid and Grabmann, 'The German Air Force against the Allies in the West,' DHist 81/930, frames 90ff; Aders, *German Night Fighter Force*, 108–9; AFHQ, Secret bomber narrative (Oct. 1943), 12, DHist 79/444; Bomber Command ORS report No 88, 16 Dec. 1943, DHist 181.009 (D4905); Middlebrook and Everitt, *BCWD*, 437–8

102 See, for example, Harris to DG of S, 7 Sept. 1943, PRO Air 20/8070

103 Webster and Frankland, *SAO*, IV, 21–3; 'War in the Ether, Europe 1939-1945,' Oct. 1945, 11–24; Price, *Instruments of Darkness*, 181ff; Streetley, *Confound and Destroy*, 156ff

104 Bomber Command Int. 3, 'Note on enemy night air defences,' 1 Dec. 1944, PRO Air 14/2914

105 Webster and Frankland, *SAO*, IV, 23; Minutes of meeting of 9 Oct. 1943, '*ROTTERDAM* equipment,' Milch Papers, translation in DHist SGR II 217, reel 63, frames 6297–306; Aders, *German Night Fighter Force*, 147; Bomber Command ORS report No S206, 6 March 1945, DHist 181.003 (D315); 'Report no 101 on Department Head conference on 14 Dec 1943,' 7 Jan. 1944, Milch Papers, translation in DHist SGR II 217, reel 60; Leo Brandt, 'German centimetric wave technology at the end of World War II,' 1953, DHist SGR II 264, folder 81; Schmid and Grabmann, 'The German Air Force against the Allies in the West,' DHist 81/930, frame 112; Middlebrook and Everitt, *BCWD*, 440; Bomber Command Interception/tactics report No 218/43, 1 Nov. 1943, DHist 181.003 (D600); No 6 Group map, Kassel, 22/23 October 1943, DHist 181.004 (D101); No 6 Group analysis of results, DHist 74/250

106 No 6 Group analysis of results, DHist 74/250; SASO No 6 Group to bases and stations, 6 Nov. 1943, DHist 181.009 (D1607)

107 USSBS report No PDD61, 'Fire raids on German cities,' quoted in AHB, Bomber Command narrative, V, 116, DHist 86/286

108 Bomber Command ORS report No S242, 21 Oct. 1945, DHist 181.009 (D3629); Middlebrook and Everitt, *BCWD*, 440; No 6 Group analysis of results, DHist 74/250

109 Hamilton *Spectator*, 23 Oct. 1943; Y. Bennet, 'The British pacifist and quasi-pacifist opposition to the strategic bombing policy of the Allies during the Second World War'; Donald M. Schurmann, 'Some thoughts on mass bombing: moral and practical,' DHist

110 Harris to undersecretary of state, Air Ministry, 25 Oct. 1943, PRO Air 14/843

111 Street to Harris, 15 Dec. 1943, PRO Air 14/483; The *Times*, 17 April and 28 May 1941

112 Quoted in Webster and Frankland, *SAO*, III, 115

113 Geoffrey Best, *Humanity in Warfare* (New York 1980), 280–2

114 'Germany howls with rage as mighty RAF attacks spread over great front,' Hamilton *Spectator*, 30 April 1942

115 King Diary, 2 June 1942, NA, King Papers, MG 26, J 13; CIPO news release, 16 Jan. 1943, in Canadian Institute of Public Opinion, Toronto, 'Gallup Poll Releases, 1943'

116 Douglas Fetherling, 'Bernard Keble Sandwell,' *The Canadian Encyclopedia*, 2d ed., III (Edmonton 1988), 1929

117 *Saturday Night*, editorial, 13 June 1942, 13

118 Great Britain, House of Commons, *Debates*, 6 May 1942

119 Ibid., 27 May 1943

120 *Toronto Telegram*, 31 May 1943, 'Few will object to continuance of Allied raids'; *Winnipeg Free Press*, 27 April 1943, 'Bombing Civilians'

121 'Smell of death rank in bombed Nazi cities,' *Globe and Mail*, 7 Aug. 1943

122 Sinclair to Portal, 26 and 28 Oct. 1943, and Portal to Sinclair, 28 Oct. 1943, minute 2, PRO Air 2/7852; Sinclair memorandum, 28 Oct. 1943, PRO Air 19/189

123 Sinclair to Portal, 26 and 28 Oct. 1943, and Portal to Sinclair, 28 Oct. 1943, minute 2, PRO Air 2/7852; Sinclair memorandum, 28 Oct. 1943, PRO Air 19/189

124 ACAS (G) to DCAS, 3 Nov. 1943, minute 8, PRO Air 2/7852

CHAPTER 20: ON TO BERLIN

1 'The Bomber's Baedeker,' 179, DHist 181.003 (D3993); Middlebrook and Everitt, *BCWD*, 441–2; AHB, Bomber Command narrative, V, app. 6, DHist 86/286

2 No 6 Group analysis of results, DHist 74/250

3 No 6 Group ORB, 3/4 Nov. 1943, DHist; AHB, 'Reports of physical damage resulting from Allied air attacks on Germany, 1943,' Oct. 1956, DHist SGR II 264, folder 79; No 6 Group analysis of results,' DHist 74/250; 'Summary of encounters with enemy aircraft,' report No 8, 20 Dec. 1943, DHist 181.003 (D5099); Middlebrook and Everitt, *BCWD*, 441

4 Bomber Command ORS report No S110, 7 Nov. 1943, DHist 181.009 (D2291)

5 Bomber Command ORS report No S239, 27 Sept. 1945, app. ORS/404, No 6 Group ORB, DHist 181.009 (D3629); ORS report No S110, 7 Nov. 1943, DHist 181.009 (D2291); No 6 Group duty intelligence officer immediate appreciation, 4 Nov. 1943, DHist 181.003 (D3479); Middlebrook and Everitt, *BCWD*, 441–2; AHB, Bomber Command narrative, V, app. 10, DHist 86/286

6 Middlebrook and Everitt, *BCWD*, 443–5; Webster and Frankland, *SAO*, II, 190ff; Middlebrook, *The Berlin Raids*; Grabmann, 'German air defense, 1933–1945,' USAF Historical Study No 164, June 1957, 1152, DHist, 86/451; on the Germans' lack of de-icing equipment, see DHist 181.009 (D4398); Eaton to SASO, 1 Nov. 1943, DHist 181.009 (D5306); 'Minutes, 9th Meeting on radar and navigation policy held at Headquarters, Bomber Command, 23 Oct 1943,' 4 Nov. 1943, DHist 181.009 (D5306); AHB, Bomber Command narrative, V, 2, 3, 228, DHist 86/286; Streetly, *Confound and Destroy*, app. 1; R.L. Sykes, 'Policy in regard to future use of H2S; notes for meeting,' 18 April 1944, PRO Air 8/727

7 Webster and Frankland, *SAO*, II, 46ff, 190–8

8 'Bomber's Baedeker,' DHist 181.003 (D3993); USSBS, *German Electrical Equipment Industry Report*, 2d edition, 1947, I, and *Area Studies Division Report*, Jan. 1947, 17–18

9 AHB, Bomber Command narrative, V, 123ff, DHist 86/286; see also Middlebrook, *The Berlin Raids*, chs 1 and 2, and Alan W. Cooper, *Bombers over Berlin* (London 1985), 12–13

10 Ron Cassels, *Ghost Squadron* (np 1991), 38

11 ACAS (Ops) to CAS, 5 Nov. 1943, Sinclair memorandum, 8 Nov. 1943, and DCAS to CAS, 12 Nov. 1943, all PRO Air 19/189; Combined Chiefs of Staff

directive No CCS/398, 18 Nov. 1943, quoted in AHB, Bomber Command narrative, VI, 4, DHist 86/286

12 Webster and Frankland, *SAO*, II, 45–6; AHB, Bomber Command narrative, V, 160; Middlebrook, *The Berlin Raids*, 174

13 ACAS (I) to CAS, 5 Nov. 1943, PRO Air 19/189; D of I (O), 'Allied air attacks and German morale,' 8 Nov. 1943, DHist 181.003 (D4573); Webster and Frankland, *SAO*, II, 31; AHB, Bomber Command narrative, V, 121ff, DHist 86/286

14 ACAS (I) to CAS, 5 Nov. 1943, PRO Air 19/189; BSDU report No 22, 11 Jan. 1945, DHist 181.003 (D4587)

15 Martin Middlebrook, *The Nuremburg Raid* (London 1973), 169

16 Air Ministry, ADI(K) report No 416/1945, 8 Dec. 1945, DHist 82/1048; data compiled by 8th Abteilung, Oberkommando der Luftwaffe, and quoted in USSAF, AI 12, report No 37, 'Strength and serviceability of GAF flying units, September 1939–March 1944,' 27 Aug. 1945, DHist 181.009 (D635); Grabmann, 'German air defense,' 1116ff, 1152ff, 1196–7, DHist 86/451; Schmid and Grabmann, 'The German Air Force against the Allies in the West,' 1954, USAF Historical Studies Nos 158 and 159, DHist 81/930, frames 26, 41, 90; Aders, *German Night Fighter Force*, 112–13, 122–6, 246–52; Bomber Command ORS report No 88, 16 Dec. 1943, PRO Air 14/1801; ORS/ORC Sub-Committee on Tactical Counter-Measures to Enemy Night Fighter and AA Defences, 'Minutes of Meeting,' 10 Aug. 1943, PRO Air 14/1764; Harris to DG of S, 7 Sept. 1943, PRO Air 20/8070; 'German night fighting (from 15 June 1943 to end of war) with remarks on the air defense of the Reich by *Generalleutnant* Josef Schmid,' app. 1 to USAFE, 'German Air Defenses,' 6 March 1945, DHist 73/1506, microfilm reel 2, frames 589-92; USAFE, 'Tactical employment of night fighting in the GAF,' 6 March 1946, DHist 73/1506, microfilm reel 1, frames 489ff, 590ff, 2902–3; Streetly, *Confound and Destroy*, 168–79; Jones, *Most Secret War*, 389–93, 466–70; Hinsley, *British Intelligence in the Second World War*, III, pt 1, app. 21, 560ff; and Air Ministry, ADI(K) report No 334/1945, DHist 82/1050; Leo Brandt, 'German centimetric wave technology at the end of World War II,' 1953, DHist SGR II 264, folder 81

17 Adolf Kaiser letter to editor, *Jägerblatt*, XVI July/Aug. 1967, 17–18, DHist translation; Bomber Command ORS report No B227, 1 Oct. 1944, DHist 181.009 (D841); War Office, MI 14 Tactical Bulletin No 12, 'Phenomena encountered over enemy territory,' Jan. 1943, DHist 181.009 (D4963); 'No 1 Group tactical summary,' April 1943, DHist 181.003 (D3104); Saundby to ORS, minute 1, 13 March 1944, and Bomber Command to groups, 25 March 1944, both PRO Air 14/1801; USAFE Intelligence Report No 113, 14 Feb. 1946, DHist 181.009 (D675); No 6 Group, 'Operational Aspects of Armament, 1943–1945,' 1 June 1945, DHist 181.009 (D1799); Bomber Command ORS report No S165, 14 July 1944, DHist 181.003 (D3474); War Office, 'Deployment of GAF *Flak* guns, searchlights, and balloons, 1939-1944,' 12 Nov. 1944, DHist 181.009 (D2815)

18 Bomber Command ORS report No 88, 16 Dec. 1943, PRO Air 14/1801

19 Minutes of meeting, 8 Oct. 1943, Milch Papers, copy at DHist SGR II 217, reel 62

20 Bomber Command ORS report No 88, 16 Jan. 1944, DHist 181.003 (D3474); Bomber Command ORB, 18/19 Nov. 1943, DHist; Middlebrook, *The Berlin Raids*, 104ff

21 Bomber Command ORB, 18/19 Nov. 1943, DHist; Middlebrook and Everitt, *BCWD*, 452; Schmid and Grabmann, 'The German Air Force against the Allies in the West,' DHist 81/930, frames 138–40, 154–7; No 6 Group analysis of results, DHist 74/250; AFHQ, Secret bomber narrative, Nov. 1943, DHist 79/444; No 6 Group Duty Intelligence Officer appreciation, 18/19 Nov. 1943, DHist 181.003 (D3479); AHB, 'Reports of physical damage resulting from Allied air attacks on Germany, 1943,' Oct. 1956, DHist SGR II 264, folder 79

22 No 6 Group analysis of results, DHist 74/250; Bomber Command ORB, 19/20 Nov. 1943, DHist; Middlebrook and Everitt, *BCWD*, 452–3

23 Bomber Command ORB, 22/23 Nov. 1943, DHist; Middlebrook, *The Berlin Raids*, 112–13

24 Schmid and Grabmann, 'The German Air Force against the Allies in the West,' DHist 81/930, frames 158–9; No 6 Group analysis of results, DHist 74/250; Bomber Command ORB, 22/23 Nov. 1943, DHist; Middlebrook and Everitt, *BCWD*, 453; appendices to No 6 Group ORB, Nov. 1943, DHist 181.003 (D4885)

25 No 6 Group analysis of results, DHist 74/250; B, 'Reports of physical damage resulting from Allied air attacks on Germany, 1943,' Oct. 1956, DHist SGR II 264, folder 79; Middlebrook and Everitt, *BCWD*, 453; Lockner, ed., *The Goebbels Diaries*, 590–3

26 Von Studnitz, *While Berlin Burns*, 137–42

27 Quoted in AFHQ, Secret bomber narrative, Nov. 1943, 49, DHist 79/444

28 Ibid.

29 Bomber Command ORB, 23/24 Nov. 1943, DHist; Middlebrook and Everitt, *BCWD*, 454; Schmid and Grabmann, 'The German Air Force against the Allies in the West,' DHist 81/930, frames 158–63; No 6 Group analysis of results, DHist 74/250; Cole's returned aircrew prisoner-of-war interrogation report, DHist 181.001 (D24), folder 4

30 Lochner, ed., *The Goebbels Diaries*, 597, 599; AHB, 'Reports of physical damage resulting from Allied air attacks on Germany, 1943,' Oct. 1956, DHist SGR II 264, folder 79

31 Von Studnitz, *While Berlin Burns*, 140ff

32 Lochner, ed., *Goebbels Diaries*, 599–600

33 No 434 Squadron ORB, 25/26 Nov. 1943, DHist; No 6 Group analysis of results, DHist 74/250

34 AHB, Bomber Command narrative, V, 141–3, DHist 86/286

35 Bomber Command ORB, 26/27 Nov. 1943; Schmid and Grabmann, 'The German Air Force against the Allies in the West,' DHist 81/930, frames 166–74; No 6 Group analysis of results, DHist 74/250; AFHQ, Secret bomber narrative, Nov.–Dec. 1943, DHist 79/444; AHB, 'Reports of physical damage resulting from Allied air attacks on German, 1943,' Oct. 1956, DHist SGR II

264, folder 79; Aders, *German Night Fighter Force*, 149–50; Middlebrook and Everitt, *BCWD*, 454–5; Air Ministry ADI(K) report No 416/1945, 8 Dec. 1945, 166, DHist 82/1048; Bomber Command ORB, 26/27 Nov. 1943, DHist; Middlebrook, *The Berlin Raids*, 123–32

36 'No 6 Group analysis of results,' DHist 74/250; AFHQ, Secret bomber narrative, Dec. 1943, DHist 79/444; Middlebrook and Everitt, *BCWD*, 454–5; Middlebrook, *The Berlin Raids*, 123–32

37 Bomber Command ORB, 2/3 Dec. 1943, DHist; No 6 Group analysis of results, DHist 74/250; AHB, Bomber Command narrative, V, 131–2, DHist 86/286; AFHQ, Secret bomber narrative, Dec. 1943, DHist 79/444; Middlebrook and Everitt, *BCWD*, 456–7; Cooper, *Bombers over Berlin*, 95; Middlebrook, *The Berlin Raids*, 132–7

38 Schmid and Grabmann, 'The German Air Force against the Allies in the West,' DHist 81/930, frames 206–10

39 No 426 Squadron ORB, 2/3 Dec. 1943, 6 Jan. 1944, DHist; AFHQ, Secret bomber narrative, Dec. 1943, 13–14, DHist 79/444; DHist decorations file; Middlebrook and Everitt, *BCWD*, 456–7; No 6 Group analysis of results, DHist 74/250

40 No 6 Group analysis of results, DHist 74/250; AFHQ, Secret bomber narrative, Dec. 1943, DHist 79/444; Bomber Command ORB, 3/4 Dec. 1943, DHist; Schmid and Grabmann, 'The German Air Force against the Allies in the West,' DHist 81/930, frames 206–12; Middlebrook and Everitt, *BCWD*, 457

41 AFHQ, Air Historical Branch, Secret narrative, Dec. 1943, DHist 79/444; Bomber Command, 'H2S landmarks,' 15 Dec. 1943, DHist 181.009 (D4956); RAF Medmenham interpretation report No K1826, 13 Jan. 1944, DHist 181.003 (D148); AHB, Bomber Command narrative, V, 132–3, DHist 86/286; AHB, 'Reports of physical damage resulting from Allied air attacks on Germany, 1943,' Oct. 1956, DHist SGR II 264, folder 79

42 Bomber Command ORB, 4–16 Dec. 1943, DHist

43 Bomber Command ASI, 'Berlin: Immediate Assessment of Results (Collation of Information received up to 28.2.44),' DHist 181.003 (D1694); Bomber Command ORS reports No S115, 4 Dec. 1943, and No S111, 16 Dec. 1943, DHist 181.003 (D2167); see also the monthly H2S reports in 181.009 (D2167) and Bomber Command to groups, 11 Dec. 1943, DHist 181.009 (D4956); 'Notes on discussion on the supply of winds for Bomber Command operations,' 18 Dec. 1943, PRO Air 14/508.

44 Harris to DG of S, 7 Sept. 1943, PRO Air 20/8070; Bomber Command ORS report No 90, 27 Dec. 1943, DHist 181.003 (D3474); Streetly, *Confound and Destroy*, 35ff, 47ff; Hinsley, *British Intelligence*, III, pt 1, 555; Bomber Command Signals Branch, 'War in the Ether,' Oct. 1945, 28ff

45 K. Mackesy, *Military Errors of World War 2* (London 1987), 169; Harris to McEwen, 28 April 1944, DHist 181.009 (D4218); Jones, *Most Secret War*, 389; Pritchard, *The Radar War*, 106–8

46 No 6 Group monthly analysis of operations, Nov. 1943, DHist 181.003 (D4714); No 6 Group monthly summary of operational and training activities,' 11 Dec. 1943, DHist 181.003 (D2716); AFHQ, Secret bomber narrative, Nov.

1943, DHist 79/444; Brookes to Sanders, 13 Dec. 1943, and Sanders to Brookes, 20 Dec. 1943, DHist 181.009 (D1925); Brookes to bases, stations, 13 Dec. 1943, DHist 181.009 (D6496); Harris to Portal, 2 Nov. 1943, PRO Air 14/1295; Bomber Command ORS report No S189, 13 Aug. 1944, DHist 181.003 (2167)

47 Brookes to Sanders, 13 Dec. 1943, and Sanders to Brookes, 20 Dec. 1943, DHist 181.009 (D1925); Brookes to bases, stations, 13 Dec. 1943, DHist 181.009 (D6496)

48 Brookes to Sanders, 13 Dec. 1943, and Sanders to Brookes, 20 Dec. 1943, DHist 181.009 (D1925)

49 Bomber Command ASI, 'Battle of Berlin: Immediate Assessment of Results (Collation of information received up to 29.12.43),' DHist 181.003 (D1696); Middlebrook, *The Berlin Raids*, 8; Minutes of department heads conference, 14 Dec. 1943, Milch Papers, DHist, SGR II 217, reel 60, frames 4936–46, DHist translation; minutes of meeting, 18 Jan. 1944, DHist SGR II 217, reel 27, DHist translation

50 See, for example, AHB, Bomber Command narrative, V, 155, DHist 86/286

51 Ibid., 141ff

52 Ibid., 145, 156

53 Statistics compiled by Luftwaffeführungsstab Ic in DHist SGR II 265, folder 24; Murray, *Luftwaffe*, 211

54 Von Studnitz, 145; Johnen, *Battling the Bombers*, 64; Aders, *German Night Fighter Force*, apps 2 and 3; Ernst Obermaier, *Der Ritterkreuzträger der Luftwaffe: Jagdflieger 1939–1945* (Mainz 1966), 42

55 AHB, *The Rise and Fall of the German Air Force (1933 to 1945)*, 314ff

56 USAFE, 'Tactical employment of Night Fighting in the GAF,' 6 March 1946, DHist 73/1506, microfilm reel 1, frame 396; ADI(K) report No 416/1945, 8 Dec. 1945, 29–30, DHist 82/1048; Schmid and Grabmann, 'The German Air Force against the Allies in the West,' DHist 81/930, frame 174

57 Minutes of meeting, 13 Dec. 1943, DHist SGR II 217, reel 43, DHist translation; minutes of I Jagdkorps conference, 14 Dec. 1943, DHist SGR II 217, reel 27, DHist translation; Aders, *German Night Fighter Force*, 246

58 Schmid and Grabmann, 'The German Air Force against the Allies in the West,' DHist 81/930, frames 214–17; AFHQ, Secret bomber narrative, Dec. 1943, DHist 79/444; No 6 Group analysis of results, DHist 74/250; Bomber Command ASI Interceptions/tactics report No 256/43,' 24 Dec. 1943, DHist 181.009 (D149); SASO, Bomber Command signals instruction No 26, 30 March 1945, DHist 181.009 (D4201); AHB, Bomber Command narrative, V, 133, DHist 86/286; Bomber Command ORB, 16/17 Dec. 1943, DHist; Middlebrook and Everitt, *BCWD*, 458–60; Cooper, *Bombers over Berlin*, 103ff; Middlebrook, *The Berlin Raids*, 176ff; Price, *Instruments of Darkness*, 183–9; Hinsley, *British Intelligence*, III, pt 2, 555–6

59 Quoted in AFHQ, Secret bomber narrative, Dec. 1943, 17–21, DHist 79/444; see also AHB, 'Reports of physical damage resulting from Allied air attacks on Germany, 1943,' Oct. 1956, DHist SGR II 264, folder 79; Middlebrook, *The Berlin Raids*, 176–96

60 AFHQ, Secret bomber narrative, Dec. 1943, 47–9, DHist 79/444; Bomber Command, ASI, 'Battle of Berlin, immediate assessment of results,' Jan. 1944, DHist 181.003 (D154); *The Berlin Diaries 1940–1945 of Marie 'Missie' Vassiltchikov* (London 1987), 127

61 Bomber Command ORB, 20/21 Dec. 1943, DHist; AFHQ, Secret bomber narrative, Dec. 1943, 56ff, DHist 79/444; No 6 Group analysis of results, DHist 74/250; No 6 Group Intelligence Officer appreciation, 22 Dec. 1943, DHist 181.003 (D3474); Schmid and Grabmann, 'The German Air Force against the Allies in the West,' DHist 81/930, frames 218–19; Middlebrook and Everitt, *BCWD*, 460–1

62 AHB, 'Reports of physical damage resulting from Allied air attacks on Germany, 1943,' Oct. 1956, DHist SGR II 264, folder 79; AFHQ, Secret bomber narrative, Dec. 1943, DHist 79/444; Middlebrook and Everitt, *BCWD*, 461

63 Schmid and Grabmann, 'The German Air Force against the Allies in the West,' DHist 81/930, frames 223–4; Bomber Command ORB, Dec. 1943, DHist; No 6 Group analysis of results, DHist 74/250; AFHQ, Secret bomber narrative, Dec. 1943, DHist 79/444; Middlebrook and Everitt, *BCWD*, 462; Middlebrook, *The Berlin Raids*, 196ff

64 See No 6 Group combat reports, 29/30 Dec. 1943, DHist 181.003 (D53).

65 Brookes to Bomber Command, 22 Nov., 5 Dec., and 6 Dec. 1943, DHist 181.009 (D1925) and (D1564); No 419 Squadron ORB, Oct.–Dec. 1943, DHist; 'Bomber defence policy; minutes of meeting held 24 June 1943,' PRO Air 20/4796; Jones to ACAS (TR), 1 Oct. 1943, PRO Avia 15/1157

66 AHB, *Armament*, II, 97–105, 113–27, 135–9, 146–50, 153–5; DBOps to DOR, 15 Oct. 1943, and DOR to DBOps, 2 Nov. 1943, PRO Air 20/4796

67 Bomber Command ORB, May–June 1944, Armaments section, DHist; DBOps to ACAS (TR), 23 Oct. 1943, PRO Air 20/4796; DOR, 'Measures to improve defences of heavy bombers,' Oct. 1943, PRO Air 20/974

68 'Bomber defence policy; minutes of meeting held at Air Ministry, 3 Nov 1943,' PRO Air 20/4796

69 DBOps, 'Daylight armament for the Lancaster IV,' 25 Jan. 1944, DBOps to ACAS (Ops), 28 March 1944, and DBOps to DOR, 23 May 1944, PRO Air 20/4796; Freeman Dyson, *Weapons and Hope* (New York 1984), 57–9

70 BOps 2(b) to DBOps, 8 April 1944, PRO Air 20/4796; Bomber Command to DArmR, 22 April 1944, DHist 181.009 (D5825); Portal to Harris, 27 April 1944, Harris Papers, DHist 87/51, folder H83; No 4 Group to Bomber Command, 'Report on .5-inch under defence mounting for Halifax aircraft,' 26 March 1944, PRO Air 14/1645

71 Bomber Command ORB, Feb. 1944, April 1944, Armament and ORS sections, DHist; 'Heavy bomber rearmament; minutes of meeting … 22 Nov 1944,' PRO Air 20/4796; No 6 Group to Bomber Command, 3 Feb. 1944, DHist 181.009 (D1084)

72 Parker, *Manpower*, 206–11, 239; Harris to Sinclair, 27 Oct. 1943, PRO Air 19/352; Harris to Sorley, 28 Oct. 1943, Harris Papers, DHist, 87/51 folder H91; AA&EE report No 760, 17th and 35th parts, Feb. and June 1944, PRO Avia 18/708

73 Harris to Freeman, 2 Dec. 1943, PRO Air 8/836

74 Bomber Command ORS, 'Relative efficiencies of bomber aircraft,' PRO Air 14/1875; Bomber Command ORS report No S124, 13 March 1944, PRO Air 14/1795; ORO to DAS, 7 and 16 Oct. 1944, DHist 181.003 (D3693); DDGPS, 'Labour absorption estimates,' 20 May 1944, PRO Avia 10/269; Whitworth to private secretary to secretary of state, 28 Jan. 1944, PRO Air 19/352

75 Bomber Command Headquarters, 'An examination of the emergency escape arrangements from Bomber Command operational aircraft,' 19 May 1945, DHist 181.003 (D4598)

76 Extract of minutes of Defence Committee (Supply), 3 Jan. 1944, Whitworth to personal secretary to secretary of state, 24 Jan. 1944, DBOps, 'Note on operational value of the Halifax,' 27 Jan. 1944, 'Extract from minutes of the Defence Committee (Supply) 27 Jan. 1944,' PRO Air 19/352

77 See Nos 419, 428, 431, and 434 Squadron ORBs, DHist.

78 Bomber Command Headquarters, 'An examination of the emergency escape arrangements from Bomber Command operational aircraft,' 19 May 1945, DHist 181.003 (D4598); Bomber Command ORB, ORS entry, March 1944, DHist; Harris to Freeman, 28 March 1944, PRO Air 14/1795; Harris to Portal, 28 March 1944, PRO Air 2/778; 'Bomber Command ORS report No S163, 28 June 1944,' DHist 181.003 (D422); No 6 Group, 'Damage sustained by bomber aircraft in No 6 Group due to enemy action,' PRO Air 14/3310

79 Reinke diary, 21 July 1944, DHist 87/241; Harris to Saundby, minute 4, 8 Feb. 1944, PRO Air 14/1143

80 Translation of report by Oberkommando des Fremden Heeres West, 11 Dec. 1944, annex 1, DHist RL 211/509 (25)

81 No 426 Squadron ORB, April–May 1944, DHist

82 'Pilot: How would you like to drive 8,000 horses?' in Mike Garbett and Brian Goulding, *Lancaster at War* (London 1979), II, 58ff

83 No 426 Squadron ORB, April–May 1944, DHist

84 Acceptance conference on Lancaster X, Serial No KB 855, 8 Dec. 1944, NA, RG 24, vol. 4974, file 620-38EA, vol. 4. See also Smye to McGill, 15 Feb. 1945, RG 24, vol. 5032, HQ 938EA-1-15.

85 SEO to DAS, 11 April 1944, DHist 181.009 (D986)

86 K.M. Molson and H.A. Taylor, *Canadian Aircraft since 1909* (Stittsville 1982), 67

87 Ibid., 68–9

88 Ibid., 69; Aircraft and Armament Experimental Establishment, 'Lancaster X KB 783, Brief handling trials, October–November 1944,' PRO Avia 18/715

89 Excerpt from report of Fred T. Smye, assistant general manager of Federal Aircraft Ltd, on his trip to England, 8–31 Jan. 1945, attached to Smye to McGill, 15 Feb. 1945, HQ 938EA-1-15, NA, RG 24, vol. 5032

90 No 6 Group Historical Review, DHist 181.003 (D4720)

91 Bomber Command night raid report No 500, 24 March 1944, DHist 181.003 (D715); No 6 Group ORB appendices, Jan. 1944, DHist 181.009 (D4885)

92 Cassels, *Ghost Squadron*, 45–63

93 See, for example, Air 1 to AOC No 6 Group, 16 Oct. 1943, DHist 181.009 (D6784).

CHAPTER 21: BERLIN, MINING, AND PREPARATIONS FOR OVERLORD

1 Bomber Command night raid report No 500, 1/2 Jan. 1944, DHist 181.003 (D715); AHB, 'Reports of physical damage resulting from Allied air attacks on Germany, 1944,' DHist SGR II 264, folder 82; Bomber Command ORB, 1/2 Jan. 1944, DHist; No 6 Group analysis of results, DHist 74/250; AFHQ, Secret bomber narrative, Jan. 1944, DHist 79/444; Schmid and Grabmann, 'The German Air Force against the Allies in the West,' USAF Historical Studies Nos 158 and 159, June 1957, DHist 81/930, frames 272–4

2 AFHQ, Secret bomber narrative, Jan. 1944, DHist 79/444; No 6 Group analysis of results, DHist 74/250; see statistics in DHist 181.005 (D1928); Middlebrook and Everitt, BCWD, 462–9.

3 Bomber Command report on H2S performance for January 1944, DHist 181.009 (D4956); Bomber Command ORS report No B197, 17 Feb. 1944, PRO Air 14/1801; Bomber Command ORS report No 92, 4 March 1944, DHist 181.003 (D3474); No 6 Group tactics notes (interim), 27 Jan. 1944, DHist 181.009 (D1293); RAF Signals Intelligence Service, 'GAF night fighter defensive activity on the Western Front, Jan 1st to Feb 10th 1944,' 181.009 (D1719); Grabmann, 'German air defense,' June 1957, USAF Historical Study No 164, DHist 86/451, frames 1117ff, 1156ff; Schmid and Grabmann, 'The German Air Force against the Allies in the West,' DHist 81/930, frames 198ff; Air Ministry, ADI(K) report No 416/1945, 8 Dec. 1945, DHist 82/1048, 16ff

4 Aders, German Night Fighter Force, 152–3; Schmid and Grabmann, 'The German Air Force against the Allies in the West,' DHist 81/930, frames 275–6; Middlebrook, The Berlin Raids, 210ff; Middlebrook and Everitt, BCWD, 463

5 No 6 Group intelligence officer immediate interpretation, 6 Jan. 1944, DHist 181.003 (D3479)

6 Ibid.; Middlebrook and Everitt, BCWD, 464; Aders, German Night Fighter Force, 152–3; Schmid and Grabmann, 'The German Air Force against the Allies in the west,' DHist 81/930, frames 279–80

7 Schmid and Grabmann, 'The German Air Force against the Allies in the West,' DHist 81/930, frames 289–91; Middlebrook and Everitt, BCWD, 465–6; Aders, German Night Fighter Force, 153; AFHQ, Secret bomber narrative, Jan. 1944, DHist 79/444; No 6 Group analysis of results, DHist 74/250; Bomber Command operations order 20/21 Jan. 1944, DHist 181.003 (D4885)

8 AHB, 'Reports of physical damage resulting from Allied air attacks on Germany, 1944,' Feb. 1957, DHist SGR II 264, folder 82

9 Globe and Mail, 22 Jan. 1944

10 'The Bomber's Baedeker,' 455–6, DHist 181.003 (D3993); Middlebrook and Everitt, BCWD, 466; Bomber Command ORB, DHist; Schmid and Grabmann, 'The German Air Force against the Allies in the West,' DHist 81/930, frames

291–3; No 6 Group analysis of results, DHist 74/250; Bomber Command intelligence report No 13/44, 29 Jan. 1944, DHist 181.003 (D773); AFHQ, Secret bomber narrative, Jan. 1944, DHist 79/444; see the correspondence on 'Schräge Musik' in *Jägerblatt* XVI (July/Aug. 1967): 16–18.

11 Bomber Command ORS report No B227, 1 Oct. 1944, DHist 181.009 (D841)

12 WOI I.V. Hopkins, Questionnaire for returned aircrew, 17 May 1945, DHist 181.001 (D24), folder 9; No 419 Squadron ORB, Jan. 1944, DHist; DHist fatality cards; Aidan Crawley, *Escape from Germany* (London 1985), 301–7

13 No 434 Squadron ORB, 15/16 Jan. 1944, DHist

14 Air Ministry to RCAF Overseas Headquarters, 'Servicing Wing Organization and Servicing Planning,' 23 Sept. 1943, Roach to Brearly, 16 Nov. 1943, DHist 181.009 (D1966)

15 Breadner to Power, 7 July 1944, Power Papers, Queen's University, box 64, file 1083

16 *London Gazette*, 1 Jan. 1945; recommendation by S/L R.P. Vaughan, 7 Sept. 1044, NA, RG 24, vol. 20605

17 *London Gazette*, 8 June 1944; recommendation signed by Wg Cdr C.B. Stinton, NA, RG 24, vol. 20601

18 Portal to Harris, 3 Jan. 1944, Portal Papers, DHist 87/89, folder 10B (1944); AHB, 'The RAF in the bombing offensive against Germany,' V, 134ff, DHist 86/286 (hereafter Bomber Command narrative)

19 Harris to Portal, 13 Jan. 1944, Portal Papers, DHist 87/89, folder 10B (1944)

20 DCAS to CAS, 12 Jan. 1944, minute 67, PRO Air 2/4477

21 Portal to Harris, 14 Jan. 1944, PRO Air 2/4477

22 Portal to Harris, 14, 27, and 28 Jan. 1944, PRO Air 2/4477; AHB, Bomber Command narrative, V, 134ff, DHist 86/286

23 AHB, Bomber Command narrative, V, 147, DHist 86/286; Middlebrook and Everitt, *BCWD*, 467–9; No 6 Group analysis of results, DHist 74/250; AFHQ, Secret bomber narrative, Jan. 1944, DHist 79/444; Schmid and Grabmann, 'The German Air Force against the Allies in the west,' DHist 81/930, frames 299–309; Middlebrook, *The Berlin Raids*, 237–8; Sigs 1 to AOC-in-C, 28, 30, and 31 Jan. 1944, DHist 181.003 (D4774); Bomber Command intelligence/tactics report No 16/44, 3 Feb. 1944, DHist 181.003 (D773); No 6 Group appreciation, 27/28 Jan. 1944, DHist 181.003 (D3479); Bomber Command night raid report No 516, 3 May 1944, DHist 181.003 (D715); Bomber Command ORB, 27–31 Jan. 1944, DHist

24 AHB, 'Reports of physical damage resulting from Allied air attacks on Germany, 1944,' with addenda, Feb.–May 1957, DHist SGR II 264, folder 82

25 ORS to DD Sci Air Ministry, 3 March 1945, PRO Air 14/1756

26 AFHQ, Secret bomber narrative, Jan. 1944, 5, DHist 79/444

27 Bomber Command ASI, 'Progress of RAF bomber offensive against German industry, 1st March 1943 to 31st December 1943,' 19 Feb. 1944, PRO Air 14/1228; Bomber Command ASI, 'Berlin: immediate assessment of results (collation of information received up to 28 February 1944),' DHist 181.003 (D1694); Bomber Command ASI, 'Industrial effects of the RAF bomber offensive,' 22 March 1944, DHist 181.009 (D3296)

28 Schmid and Grabmann, 'The German Air Force against the Allies in the West,' DHist 81/830, frames 267–8

29 Schmid and Grabmann, 'The German Air Force against the Allies in the West,' DHist 81/930, frames 267–8; Air Ministry, ADI(K) report No 416/1945, 8 Dec. 1945, 16, DHist 82/1048; Grabmann, 'German air defense,' DHist 86/451, frames 1154–9; Aders, *German Night Fighter Force*, 124–7

30 Stephen L. McFarland and Wesley Phillips Newton, *To Command the Sky* (Washington 1991), 171; Cooper, *The German Air Force*, 320–5; 'Fragebogen zur Reichsluftverteidigung (Nachtjagd),' RL 2 VI/56 (Questionnaire on air defence of the Reich – Night-fighters), translation in DHist, SGR II 320, folder 58; Grabmann, 'German air defense,' DHist 86/451, frames 1143, 1167–8, 1216–21, 1258

31 Schmid and Grabmann, 'The German Air Force against the Allies in the West,' DHist 81/930, frames 201, 270, 354–60, 446, 914ff; Grabmann, 'German air defense,' DHist 86/451, frames 1152–1221, 1486ff, 1876; ADI(K) report no 416/1945, 8 Dec. 1945, DHist 82/1048, 23; AHB, *The Rise and Fall of the German Air Force (1933 to 1945)*, 280; Kreipe and Koester, 'Technical training in the *Luftwaffe*,' USAF Historical Study No 169, DHist 81/937, frame 780; Aders, *German Night Fighter Force*, app. 4

32 ACAS (I), 'Allied air attacks and German morale,' 11 March 1944, PRO Air 14/843; Craven and Cate, *The Army Air Forces*, III, 30–3

33 Craven and Cate, *The Army Air Forces*, III, 30; Webster and Frankland, *SAO*, II, 84ff; AHB, Bomber Command narrative, V, 138

34 No 6 Group analysis of results, DHist 74/250; AFHQ, Secret bomber narrative, Feb. 1944, DHist 79/444; Middlebrook and Everitt, *BCWD*, 473–4; Schmid and Grabmann, 'The German Air Force against the Allies in the West,' DHist 81/930, frames 376–80; Bomber Command ORS, Night raid report No 531, 25 April 1944, DHist 181.003 (D4775); Bomber Command, Interceptions/Tactics report No 34/44, 2 March 1944, DHist 181.003 (D597); No 6 Group plot of Leipzig raid, 1 March 1944, DHist 181.003 (D3873)

35 Bomber Command to groups, 29 Feb. 1944, DHist 181.009 (D2804)

36 'Minutes of conference held at Headquarters Bomber Command to discuss new tactics to be employed to confuse the enemy,' 20 Feb. 1944, DHist 181.006 (D325), and PRO Air 14/1453. See also Saundby to Harris, minute 92, and Harris to Saundby, minute 93, 22 Feb. 1944, PRO Air 14/233; Saward to Saundby, 17 Feb. 1944, PRO Air 14/1295; and Harris to Brookes, 18 Feb. 1944, DHist 181.009 (D1925)

37 Middlebrook and Everitt, *BCWD*, 474–7; Sigs I to C-in-C, 21 Feb. 1944, DHist 181.003 (D4775); AFHQ, Secret bomber narrative, Feb. 1944, DHist 79/444; Schmid and Grabmann, 'The German Air Force against the Allies in the West,' DHist 81/930, frames 387–91; No 6 Group analysis of results, DHist 74/250

38 No 405 Squadron ORB, DHist; see also AFHQ, Secret bomber narrative, Feb. 1944, DHist 79/544

39 No 405 Squadron ORB, DHist; see also AFHQ, Secret bomber narrative, Feb. 1944, DHist 79/544

40 Craven and Cate, *The Army Air Forces,* III, ch. 2; Murray, *Luftwaffe,* 219ff; David Irving, *The Rise and Fall of the Luftwaffe* (Boston 1973), 271ff; extracts of Milch conference, 23 Feb. 1944, DHist SGR II 264, folder 62, 17ff; AHB, *The Rise and Fall of the German Air Force,* 296ff; McFarland and Newton, *To Command the Sky,* chs 5 and 6

41 Middlebrook and Everitt, *BCWD,* 476; Bomber's Baedeker, DHist 181.003 (D3993); AHB, 'Reports of physical damage resulting from Allied air attacks on Germany, 1944,' Feb. 1957, DHist SGR II 264, folder 82; Bomber Command ORS to DDSci, 3 March 1945, PRO Air 14/1756; Schmid and Grabmann, 'The German Air Force against the Allies in the West,' DHist 81/930, frames 392–5

42 Fillion's returned POW interrogation report is in DHist 181.001 (D24), folder 7.

43 General Sir John Hackett, 'Introduction' to Carlton Younger, *No Flight from the Cage* (London 1981), 5–6

44 Crawley, *Escape from Germany,* 9

45 Ibid., 5

46 Younger, *No Flight from the Cage,* 89

47 Crawley, *Escape from Germany,* 5

48 '*Luft* I, visited by the I.R.C.C. on 9th March 1944,' DHist 181.009 (D2977)

49 Crawley, *Escape from Germany,* 12

50 See Paul Brickhill, *The Great Escape* (London 1950), and Arthur A. Durand, *Stalag Luft,* III (Baton Rouge 1988).

51 Brereton Greenhous, 'You can't hang a million dollars: The Life and Times of George Rutherford Harsh,' *Canadian Defence Quarterly/Revue canadienne de défense* 19, 6 (June/juin 1990): 56–60

52 Quoted in Crawley, *Escape from Germany,* 245–6

53 Schmid and Grabmann, 'The German Air Force against the Allies in the West,' DHist 81/930, frames 448–9, 459–61, 464–72; Aders, *German Night Fighter Force,* 155; Bomber Command ORB, DHist; Middlebrook and Everitt, *BCWD,* 477–83; AHB, 'Reports of physical damage resulting from Allied air attacks on Germany, 1944,' Feb. 1957, DHist SGR II 264, folder 82

54 Aders, *German Night Fighter Force,* 155; Schmid and Grabmann, 'The German Air Force against the Allies in the West,' DHist 81/930, frames 354–9, 387–91, 464–6, 914ff; Grabmann, 'German air defense,' DHist 86/451, frames 1876; Hinsley, *British Intelligence in the Second World War,* II, part 1, 556–7; Air Ministry, ADI(K) report No 416/1945, 8 Dec. 1945, DHist 82/1048, 23; Bomber Command ORS, Night raid report No 537, 15 April 1944, DHist 181.003 (D1518); Bomber Command to groups, 10 March 1944, DHist 181.009 (D4218)

55 Bomber Command ORS report No B198 [Feb. 1944], Harris to Breadner, 2 March 1944, and Dickens to Harris, 26 Feb. 1944, all PRO Air 14/1794; No 6 Group to Breadner, 27 Jan. 1944, DHist 181.005 (D503); No 6 Group statistics in DHist 181.003 (D3993) and (D3998)

56 Brookes diary, Brookes biog. file, DHist

57 Dickens to Saundby, 30 June 1943, and Saundby to SASO, 3 July 1943, PRO Air 14/1794; McEwen biog. file, DHist; McEwen to No 426 Squadron, 1 Sept. 1944, DHist 181.009 (D3067); Middlebrook and Everitt, *BCWD,* 476–83; No 6

Group analysis of results, DHist 74/250; Bomber Command night raid report No 537, 15 May 1944, DHist 181.003 (D715); No 6 Group monthly summary of operational and training activities, 12 April 1944, DHist 181.003 (D2716)

58 See DHist 181.003 (D295) for wireless intelligence intercepts. No 6 Group plot, 31 March 1944, DHist 181.003 (D3873); Bomber Command night raid report No 562, 19 June 1944, DHist 181.003 (D715); Bomber Command ORS report No S139, 7 April 1944, DHist 181.003 (D2167); Bomber Command interception/tactics report No 66/44, 7 April 1944, DHist 181.009 (D1429); Schmid and Grabmann, 'The German Air Force against the Allies in the west,' DHist 81/930, frames 476–8; AHB, Bomber Command narrative VI, 32–3, DHist 86/286.

59 Middlebrook and Everitt, *BCWD*, 488; Schmid and Grabmann, 'The German Air Force against the Allies in the West,' DHist 81/930, frames 478–80; Bomber Command interception/tactics report No 68/44, 9 April 1944, DHist 181.003 (D1429); Aders, *German Night Fighter Force*, 158

60 Middlebrook, *The Nuremburg Raid*, passim; Bombers' Baedeker, DHist 181.003 (D3993); Bomber Command ORB, 30/31 March 1944, DHist

61 Middlebrook, *The Nuremburg Raid*, 294ff

62 Schmid and Grabmann, 'The German Air Force against the Allies in the West,' DHist 81/930, frames 482–7; Grabmann, 'German air defense,' DHist 86/451, frames 131ff; Bomber Command to Hughes, 28 April 1944, PRO Air 19/169; Bomber Command interception/tactics report No 71/44, 12 April 1944, DHist 181.009 (D1429); Bomber Command night raid report No 567, 4 July 1944, DHist 181.003 (D715)

63 Bomber Command ORS Report No S129, 21 March 1944, DHist 181.003 (D2167)

64 Middlebrook, *The Nuremburg Raid*, 102

65 Quoted ibid., 152–3

66 Quoted ibid., 154–55

67 No 6 Group analysis of results, DHist 74/250; Middlebrook, *The Nuremburg Raid*

68 No 6 Group plot, DHist 181.003 (D3873)

69 E.B. Bush, 'Room with a View: A Bomb Aimer's War,' *High Flight* 3 (summer 1983): 70

70 Webster and Frankland, *SAO*, II, 90; Harris, *Despatch*, 21

71 Bidinian, *The Combined Allied Bombing Offensive against the German Civilian*, 110; J.K. Galbraith, *The Affluent Society* (London 1958), 127, 133–8, 162; USSBS, *German Electronics Equipment Industry Report*, 5, 40; Speer, *Inside the Third Reich*, 278–86, 346–50, 406–7; USSBS, *The Effects of Strategic Bombing on the German War Economy*, 31 Oct 1945, 1–28; Webster and Frankland, *SAO*, IV, section V, particularly app. 37, 371–97

72 Bidinian, *The Combined Allied Bombing Offensive against the German Civilian*, 110; Webster and Frankland, *SAO*, III, 147; Searby, *The Bomber Battle for Berlin*, 11

73 Bennett, *Pathfinder*, 211–12; Webster and Frankland, *SAO*, II, 195ff, and III,

310; Roger Denley, '"Coffins or Crackers": An Examination of the Psychological Well-being of Canadian Aircrew in Bomber Command,' 16 March 1982, D Hist 82/447; Bomber Command ORB, DHist; No 6 Group Analysis of Results, DHist 74/250

74 Miles Tripp, *The Eighth Passenger* (London 1969); S.C. Rexford-Welch, *The Royal Air Force Medical Services*, II (London 1955), 136; John McCarthy, 'Aircrew and "Lack of Moral Fibre" in the Second World War,' *War and Society* (Sept. 1984): 87–101; D. Stafford-Clark, 'Morale and Flying Experience: Results of a Wartime Study,' *Journal of Mental Science* 95 (Jan. 1949): 10–50; Terraine, *A Time for Courage*, 520–37; Air Ministry memorandum, 1 June 1943, DHist 181.009 (D3354); Roger Denley, ' "Coffins or Crackers": An Examination of the Psychological Well-being of Canadian Aircrew in Bomber Command,' 16 March 1982, DHist 82/447

75 Murray Peden, *A Thousand Shall Fall* (Stittsville, Ont., 1979), 415–16

76 Air Council minutes, 3 Dec. 1942, file HQS 840-108, vol. 5, NA, PARC box 829985; and Denley, ' "Coffins or Crackers," ' 10ff: D. Parks and G. Vlastos, 'Morale survey for RCAF Personnel in UK, September–December 1942,' DHist 181.003 (D3456)

77 RCAF personnel files

78 Terraine, *Time for Courage*, 534–5; Probert to Douglas, 2 June 1986, DHist 86/364

79 Bomber Command ORB, March–April 1944, DHist; No 6 Group analysis of results, DHist 74/250

80 Harris, *Despatch*, 45, 48; No 6 Group analysis of results, DHist 74/250; Bomber Command ORB, Nov. 1943

81 'Historical review No 6 (RCAF) Heavy Bomber Group, European Theatre, 1943–1945,' DHist 181.003 (D559) (hereafter No 6 Group historical review); see also No 6 Group's reports of operations for August and September 1943, DHist 181.003 (D3088); NSO No 6 Group to NSO Bomber Command, 31 Aug. and 30 Sept. 1943, DHist 181.009 (D4334); 'Report on 6 Group mining effort since January 1943,' DHist 181.003 (D4718).

82 AHB, 'The RAF in Maritime War,' IV, part B, 427, DHist 79/599; No 6 Group historical review, DHist 181.003 (D559)

83 DDOM, 'Offensive minelaying – review,' 29 Dec. 1943, PRO ADM 1/15466

84 No 6 Group summaries of Gardening operations, Nov. and Dec. 1943, DHist 181.003 (D3088); No 6 Group historical review, DHist 181.003 (D559)

85 No 6 Group historical review, DHist 181.003 (D559); 'Report on initial H.L. mining operation, 4/5 Jan 1944,' PRO Air 14/3337; Nos 419 and 428 Squadron ORBs, DHist; AHB, 'The RAF in Maritime War,' IV, 423ff, DHist 79/599; AFHQ, Secret bomber narrative, Jan. 1944, DHist 79/444; No 3 Group to Bomber Command, 24 Nov. 1943, DHist 181.009 (D4956)

86 See Bomber Command ORB, Feb. 1944, DHist; AHB, 'The RAF in Maritime War,' IV, 432ff, DHist 79/599; see also No 6 Group to stations, 30 May 1944, DHist 181.005 (D70), and DAT (Air Ministry), TC 48, 'High-level minelaying by H2S,' Jan. 1945, PRO Air 14/207.

87 No 419 Squadron ORB, Feb. 1944, DHist; No 428 Squadron ORB, Feb. 1944, DHist; AFHQ, Secret bomber narrative, Feb. 1944, 76ff, DHist 79/444; AHB, 'The RAF in Maritime War,' IV, 433ff

88 No 6 Group to bases, stations, 27 March 1944, DHist 181.009 (D4334)

89 AHB, 'The RAF in Maritime War,' IV, 426, 435, DHist 79/599

90 Haywood S. Hansell, Jr, *The Air Plan That Defeated Hitler* (Atlanta 1972), 151–2; Sir Frederick Morgan, *Overture to Overlord* (London 1950), 67

91 Harris to Portal, 13 Jan. 1944, Portal Papers, DHist 87/89, folder 10B (1944); Craven and Cate, *Army Air Forces*, III, 73ff; see also AHB, Bomber Command narrative, VI, 10–11, DHist 86/286; USSTAF Plan 5, March 1944, quoted in W.W. Rostow, *Pre-Invasion Bombing Strategy* (Austin, Texas, 1981), 34; USAFE, AI 12, 'Consumption of aircraft fuel compared with available supplies, statement by Dr Nocker,' 17 Oct. 1945, DHist 181.009 (D6670)

92 Craven and Cate, *Army Air Forces*, III, 73ff; Zuckerman, *From Apes to Warlords*, 221–3; R. Kingston McCloughery, 'The transportation plan,' Kingston McCloughery Papers, DHist 74/619, folder C, file 7(a); AHB, Bomber Command narrative, VI, 7, DHist 86/286

93 AHB, Bomber Command narrative, VI, 8–11, 27, DHist 86/286; Zuckerman, *From Apes to Warlords*, 255–6; Webster and Frankland, *SAO*, III, 27; ACAS (Ops) to Bomber Command, 4 March 1944, DHist 181.006 (D152)

94 Bomber Command ORB, 6/7 March 1944, DHist

95 No 6 Group and Nos 428 and 431 Squadron ORBs, 6/7 March 1944, DHist; ORS Bomber Command, report No S167, 16 May 1944, PRO Air 14/3936; Bomber Command Narrative, VI, 39, DHist, 86/286; Middlebrook, *BCWD*, 479

96 Bomber Command ORB, 7/8 March 1944, DHist; No 6 Group ORB, 7/8 March 1944, DHist; No 408 Squadron ORB, 7/8 March 1944, DHist; AHB, Bomber Command Narrative, VI, 39, DHist, 86/286

97 No 6 Group and Nos 424, 433, and 419 Squadron ORBs, 7/8 March 1944, DHist; Middlebrook and Everitt, *BCWD*, 479

98 Bomber Command ORB, 13/14 March 1944, DHist; No 427 Squadron ORB, 13/14 March 1944, DHist; Middlebrook and Everitt, *BCWD*, 480

99 AHB, Bomber Command narrative, VI, 11, DHist 86/286; Bomber Command and Nos 419, 425, and 431 Squadron ORBs, 15/16 March 1944, DHist; Middlebrook and Everitt, *BCWD*, 481

100 Bomber Command and No 419 and 431 Squadron ORBs, 16/17 and 23/24 March 1944, DHist; Bomber Command ORS report No S167, 16 May 1944, PRO Air 14/3936; Middlebrook and Everitt, *BCWD*, 484

101 Nos 426, 427, 431 Squadron ORBs, 25/26 March 1944, DHist

102 Nos 419, 428, and 431 Squadron ORBs, 26/27 March 1944, DHist; Middlebrook and Everitt, *BCWD*, 486

103 Nos 419 and 434 Squadron ORBs, 29/30 March 1944, DHist; Middlebrook and Everitt, *BCWD*, 486

104 App. 4, Zuckerman, *From Apes to Warlords*, Bomber Command ORS report No S167, 16 May 1944, DHist 181.003 (D2167), and No 6 Group ORS, 'Attacks on

"precision targets" by No 6 (RCAF) Group: estimation of bombing accuracy,'
29 May 1944, DHist 181.009 (D4035)

105 Webster and Frankland, *SAO*, III, 152; Bomber Command Narrative, VI, 14–18,
40, DHist, 86/286; Zuckerman, *From Apes to Warlords*, passim, and app. 4;
Harris, *Bomber Offensive*, 266; R. Kingston McCloughery, 'The transportation
plan,' Kingston McCloughery Papers, DHist 74/619, folder C, file 7(a)

106 AHB, Bomber Command narrative, VI, 19–22, DHist DHist 86/286

CHAPTER 22: WORKING FOR SHAEF

1 'Directive by Supreme Commander ... for support of 'OVERLORD' during the
preparatory period,' 17 April 1944, DHist 181.006 (D144)

2 Minutes, Bomber Command Tactical Planning Committee, 9 April 1944, PRO
Air 14/509

3 Harris memorandum, 7 April 1944, DHist 181.009 (D5825); Webster and
Frankland, *SAO*, III, 147; AHB, Bomber Command narrative, VI, 30–1, DHist
86/286; Schmid and Grabmann, 'The German Air Force against the Allies in
the West,' USAF Historical Studies Nos 158 and 159, 1954, DHist 81/930,
frames 444ff

4 Schmid and Grabmann, 'The German Air Force against the Allies in the
West,' DHist 81/930, frames 720–3

5 Grabmann, 'German air defense, 1933–1945,' USAF Historical Study No 164,
June 1957, DHist 86/451, 1191, 1496; S/L V.C. Varcoe, 'Summary of BMP
report No 660,' 11 April 1944, DHist 181.003 (D1945); AHB, Bomber
Command narrative, VI, 36–7, DHist 86/286; Major Josef Scholls, 'Night
Fighter Tactics,' app. III of USAFE, 'German Air Defenses: Tactical
Employment of Night Fighting in GAF,' 6 March 1946, DHist 73/1506,
microfilm reel 2, frames 652ff; Aders, *German Night Fighter Force*, 159–62;
Schmid and Grabmann, 'The German Air Force against the Allies in the
West,' DHist 81/930, frames 720–3

6 Bomber Command Operations Record Book (ORB), 1 April–6 June 1944,
DHist

7 Harris to undersecretary of state for air, 8 March 1944, PRO Air 2/8039;
Bomber Command circular, 9 March 1944, PRO Air 14/1016; ACAS (Ops) to
director general of personnel, 29 March 1944, and Monk-Jones to Harris, 19
April 1944, PRO Air 2/8039; No 425 Squadron to Station Tholthorpe, 12 May
1944, and No 6 Group circular letter, 19 May 1944, DHist 181.003 (D4796)

8 No 6 Group analysis of results, DHist 74/250; Bomber Command ORB, DHist

9 Schmid and Grabmann, 'The German Air Force against the Allies in the
West,' DHist 81/930, frames 610–17, 624–5, 641–7; Bomber Command ORB,
May 1944, DHist; No 6 Group analysis of results, DHist 74/250

10 Robert Morrison Johnson, 'Strategic Endeavor: 8th Air Force Efffectiveness
over Europe 1942–1945' (PhD dissertation, Georgia State University 1984),
178; Minutes of Jägerstab conference, 17 and 18 April 1944, DHist, SGR II
264, folder 59; Webster and Frankland, *SAO*, IV, app. 496; Cooper, *German Air
Force*, 344; Aders, *German Night Fighter Force*, 128, 131; Air Ministry,

ADI(K) report No 374/1945, app. iv, 13 Aug. 1945, DHist 82/1053; Galland's notes of his conversations with Göring, 15–16 May 1944, DHist SGR II 264, folder 32

11 ADI (Science), Scientific Intelligence Report No 73, 13 July 1944, PRO Air 20/1652; Major Joseph Scholls, 'Night fighter tactics,' app. III, USAFE, 'German air defenses: tactical employment of night fighting in the GAF,' 6 March 1946, DHist 73/1506, microfilm reel no 2, frames 652ff; Aders, *German Night Fighter Force*, 123–30, 159–62; Schmid and Grabman, 'The German Air Force against the Allies in the West,' DHist 81/930, frames 710–13, 720–3; AHB, Bomber Command narrative, V, 225, DHist 86/286; Grabmann, 'German air defense,' DHist 86/451, 1496ff; 'Generalnachtrichtenführer, Anlage A3 zum KTB Nr 2 (3.Abt),' [Annex A3 to War Diary No 2 (3rd Section) of the Chief of Communications] Rl 2 V/30, DHist SGR II 320, folder 38

12 Grabmann, 'German air defense,' DHist 86/451, frame 1197; Streetly, *Confound and Destroy*, app. 3, 221–8; Aders, *German Night Fighter Force*, 114; Schmid and Grabmann, 'The German Air Force against the Allies in the West,' DHist 81/930, 522–4, 582–6, 720–3, 736–46

13 Bomber Command and No 6 Group ORB, 9–11 April 1944, DHist; No 6 Group Analysis of Results, DHist 74/250; Bomber Command ORS, Night Raid Report No 575, 7 July 1944, DHist 181.003 (D1518); Middlebrook and Everitt, *BCWD*, 493; Bomber Command ORS night raid report No 576, 12 July 1944, DHist 181.003 (D1518); AHB, Bomber Command narrative, VI, 34, DHist 86/286

14 Bomber Command ORS night raid report No 581, 15 July 1944, DHist 181.003 (D1518); Bomber Command and No 6 Group ORBs, 18/19 April 1944, DHist; No 6 Group Analysis of Results, DHist 74/250; Middlebrook and Everitt, *BCWD*, 495

15 Bomber Command ORS night raid report No 582, 23 July 1944, DHist 181.003 (D1518); Bomber Command, No 6 Group, and No 428 Squadron ORBs, 20/21 April 1944, DHist; No 6 Group Analysis of Results, DHist 74/250; Middlebrook and Everitt, *BCWD*, 496–7

16 Bomber Command ORS night raid report No 584, 24 July 1944, DHist 181.003 (D1518)

17 Bomber Command and No 6 Group ORBs, 27/28 April 1944, DHist; No 6 Group Analysis of Results, DHist 74/250; Bomber Command ORS night raid report No 589, 4 Aug. 1944, DHist 181.003 (D1518); Middlebrook and Everitt, *BCWD*, 501; Schmid and Grabmann, 'The German Air Force against the Allies in the West,' DHist 81/930, frames 587, 641–7

18 No 431 Squadron ORB, 27/28 April 1944, DHist

19 E.M. Blenkinsop biog. file, DHist

20 Report of No 1 Canadian War Crimes Investigation Unit on Miscellaneous War Crimes against Members of the Canadian Armed Forces in the European Theatre of Operations, 9 Sept. 1939 to 8 May 1945, part II, case 67/Diest/1, DHist 159.95.023 (D1)

21 Ibid., cases 67/Kassel/1 and 67/Bourg Achard/1, DHist 159.95.023 (D1)

22 Bomber Command ORB, April 1944, DHist; No 6 Group Analysis of Results,

DHist 74/250; Schmid and Grabmann, 'The German Air Force against the Allies in the West,' DHist 81/930, frames 587, 641–7

23 Bomber Command monthly reports on casualties and claims, March–May 1944, DHist 181.003 (D4714)

24 Bomber Command ORS report No 104, 14 July 1944, DHist 181.003 (D3474); Webster and Frankland, *SAO*, III, 137

25 Bomber Command ORS report on night operations, No 600, 21 Aug. 1944, DHist 181.003 (D1518); Minutes of Bomber Command Tactical Planning Committee, 7 May 1944, PRO Air 14/509; Middlebrook and Everitt, *BCWD*, 502–20; No 6 Group Analysis of Results, DHist 74/250; No 6 Group Intelligence Officer appreciation, DHist 181.003 (D3474); Bomber Command and No 6 Group ORBs, 8/9 May 1944, DHist

26 No 62 Base to stations, squadrons, 14 April 1944, DHist 181.009 (D56); Bomber Command ORS to SASO, 9 June 1944, ORS I(c) to ORS, 10 Aug. 1944, and report No S185, PRO Air 14/3936; No 6 Group to Bomber Command, 13 May 1944, DHist 181.009 (D2358); Report by Flight Lieutenant Rolfe, DHist 181.003 (D3819), folio 284; Bomber Command ORS report No S167, 16 May 1944, DHist 181.003 (D2167); No 6 Group ORS, 'Attacks on "precision targets" by No 6 (RCAF) Group,' 29 May 1944, DHist 181.009 (D4035); SASO No 6 Group to bases, stations, 3 June 1944, DHist 181.005 (D67) and 181.003 (D4791); Middlebrook and Everitt, *BCWD*, 509–12; No 6 Group review of navigation, No 13, June 1944, DHist 181.003 (D4020); No 6 Group to bases, stations, 24 July 1944, DHist 181.009 (D2358)

27 AHB, Bomber Command narrative, VI, 40ff, DHist 86/286; Luftwaffe operations staff, 'Air Operations against the German rail transport system, during March, April, and May 1944,' 3 June 1944, DHist SGR II 264, folder 49; No 6 Group Analysis of Results, DHist 74/250; Harris to groups, 5 May 1944, Canadian War Museum, McEwen Papers, 58A1, folder 94.1, 41A

28 Bomber Command ORB, 5/6 June 1944, DHist; No 6 Group Analysis of Results, DHist 74/250; Bomber Command report on night operations, report No 625, 24 Sept. 1944, DHist 181.003 (D1518); Charles Carrington, *Soldier at Bomber Command* (London 1987), 149; Middlebrook and Everitt, *BCWD*, 522–4

29 Peden, *A Thousand Shall Fall*, 383

30 Signals Section, Bomber Command ORB, June 1944, DHist; Bomber Command, Enemy raid reaction and radio counter-measures report No 12, DHist 181.003 (D2950); Bomber Command report on night operations, report No 632, 7 Oct. 1944, DHist 181.003 (D1518); RAF Signals Intelligence Section, 'G.A.F. night defensive activity on the Western Front,' periodical surveys 6 June to 10 July 1944, DHist 181.009 (D2805); Bomber Command, Signals Branch, *War in the Ether*, Oct. 1945, 11, 47–50, 64, app. E; Streetly, *Confound and Destroy*, 60, 106ff

31 Peden, *A Thousand Shall Fall*, 416ff

32 Bomber Command ORS report No S172, 12 Aug. 1944, DHist 181.003 (D2167); Air Ministry, Scientific intelligence report No 73, 13 July 1944, PRO Air 20/1652; Peden, *A Thousand Shall Fall*, 413ff

33 Bomber Command report on night operations, report No 665, 12 Nov. 1944, DHist 181.003 (D1518); S/L V.C. Varcoe, 'Summary of BMP reports,' 25 July 1944, DHist 181l.003 (D1945); Bomber Command interception/tactics report No 172/44, 25 July 1944, DHist 181.003 (D3814); No 6 Group Analysis of Results, DHist 74/250; Bomber Command ORB, 18/19 July 1944, DHist

34 Craven and Cate, *Army Air Forces*, III, 14–18, 190, 285ff; AHB, Bomber Command narrative, VI, 81, DHist 86/286; Bomber Command report on night operations, report No 627, 28 Sept. 1944, DHist 181.003 (D1518); Bomber Command ORB, 7/8 June 1944, DHist; No 6 Group Analysis of Results, DHist 74/250; No 426 Squadron ORB, 7/8 Jun 1944, DHist; Middlebrook and Everitt, *BCWD*, 524

35 Schmid and Grabmann, 'The German Air Force against the Allies in the West,' DHist 81/930, frames 881ff; Aders, *German Night Fighter Force*, 169; Grabmann, 'German Air Defense,' DHist 86/451, frame 681; Bomber Command Signals Intelligence Service, 'G.A.F. night defensive activity on the Western Front, June 6th to June 13th 1944', 16 June 1944, and 'G.A.F. night defensive activity on the Western Front, July 1–July 11th 1944,' 13 July 1944, DHist 181.009 (D2805); Bomber Command report of night operations, report No 651, 30 Oct. 1944, DHist 181.003 (D1518); No 6 Group analysis of results, DHist 74/250; Bomber Command interception/tactics report No 157/44, 9 Jul 1944, DHist 181.003 (D3814)

36 Mynarski biog. file, DHist; *The Moose Squadron*, 202–3, DHist 74/331; DHist citation file

37 AHB, Bomber Command narrative, VI, 82–3, 257, DHist 86/286; Zuckerman, *From Apes to Warlords*, 287–304

38 Webster and Frankland, *SAO*, III, 47

39 USSBS, *The Effects of Strategic Bombing on the German War Economy*, 31 Oct. 1945, 79–80; USSBS, *Over-all Report (European War)*, 30 Sept. 1945, 44; Harris, *Bomber Offensive*, 229; Webster and Frankland, *SAO*, IV, 516–17; Rostow, *Pre-Invasion Bombing Strategy*, 68; AHB, Bomber Command narrative, VI, 51–2, 55ff, DHist 86/286; Air Ministry, ADI(K) report No 374/1945, 13 Aug. 1945, DHist 82/1053, 4; Air Ministry, ADI(K) report No 416/1945, 8 Dec. 1945, 30; Beck, *Under the Bombs*, 130ff; Craven and Cate, *Army Air Forces*, III, 280ff

40 Bomber Command RCM quick report No 14, 17 June 1944, DHist 181.003 (D3847); Bomber Command enemy raid reaction and radio counter-measures report No 13, DHist 181.003 (D2950); ORS Bomber Command, Report No S172, 'First operation of the MANDREL Screen and Special WINDOW force,' 12 Aug. 1944, DHist 181.003 (D2167); Bomber Command ORB, 16/17 June 1944, DHist; No 6 Group analysis of results, DHist 74/250; Middlebrook and Everitt, *BCWD*, 530; AHB, Bomber Command narrative, VI, 55–8, 94, DHist 86/286; Schmid and Grabman, 'The German Air Force against the Allies in the West,' DHist 81/930, frames 871–2; Bomber Command report of night operations, No 646, 26 Oct. 1944, DHist 181.003 (D1518)

41 Craven and Cate, *Army Air Forces*, III, 289, 533; No 6 Group ORB, 9 July 1944, DHist

42 Bomber Command to groups, 10 Aug. 1944, DHist 181.003 (D4839); see also AHB, Bomber Command narrative, VI, 90–1, DHIst 86/286, and MacBean and Hogben, *Bombs Gone*, 47–8; Webster and Frankland, *SAO*, III, 176

43 No 6 Group analysis of results, DHist 74/250; Bomber Command ORB, 14 and 15 June 1944, DHist; Middlebrook and Everitt, *BCWD*, 529; Harris, *Bomber Offensive*, ch. 9; Harris to Tedder, 18 July 1944, quoted in Saward, *'Bomber' Harris*, 255–7

44 Bomber Command ORB, 7/8 and 14 June 1944, DHist; AHB, Bomber Command narrative, VI, 85–6, DHist 86/286; L.F. Ellis, *Victory in the West* (London 1962), I, 255ff; J.R.C. de Normann, 'The Use of the Strategic Bomber Forces over Normandy: Success or Failure,' *British Army Review* (Aug. 1990): 16; McKee, *Caen*, 179–80; Ian Gooderson, 'Heavy and Medium Bombers: How Successful Were They in the Tactical Close Air Support War during World War II?' *Journal of Strategic Studies* 15 (Sept. 1992): 367–99

45 No 6 Group analysis of results, DHist 74/250

46 J.E. Johnson, *Wing Leader* (Toronto 1956), 247

47 C.P. Stacey, *The Victory Campaign* (Ottawa 1960), 158ff; No 6 Group, 'Operations July 1944,' DHist 181.003 (D4714), folio 37A; B.L. Montgomery, *Normandy to the Baltic* (London 1946), 73; Bomber Command ORB, 7 July 1944, DHist; AHB, Bomber Command narrative, VI, 86, DHist 86/286; Harris, *Bomber Offensive*, 211; Ellis, *Victory in the West*, I, 311

48 Stacey, *The Victory Campaign*, 212

49 Gooderson, 'Heavy and Medium Bombers,' 369; Stacey, *The Victory Campaign*, 169

50 Ellis, *Victory in the West*, I, 338–9

51 Stacey, *The Victory Campaign*, 169; Gooderson, 'Heavy and Medium Bombers,' 382ff; No 6 Group analysis of results, DHist 74/250

52 Ellis, *Victory in the West*, I, 338–50; Stacey, *The Victory Campaign*, 169–79; Gooderson, 'Heavy and Medium Bombers,' 384–5

53 Stacey, *The Victory Campaign*, 212; No 6 Group analysis of results, DHist 74/250

54 Stacey, *The Victory Campaign*, 212

55 Bomber Command and No 6 Group ORBs, 14 Aug. 1944, DHist

56 DHist 181.009 (D1563)

57 No 6 Group analysis of results, DHist 74/250

58 Ibid.

59 Crerar to Harris, 29 Aug. 1944, Canadian War Museum, McEwen Papers, 58A1, folder 94.1; Stacey, *The Victory Campaign*, 203, 243

60 'Operation TRACTABLE: Bombing error in close support operation of 14 August,' DHist 79/442; Stacey, *The Victory Campaign*, 243; George Kitching, *Mud and Green Fields* (Langley, BC, 1986), 216

61 Harris, 'Report on the bombing of our own troops during Operation TRACTABLE,' 25 Aug. 1944, Harris Papers, copy in DHist 87/51, folder 55; 'Operation TRACTABLE: Bombing error in close support operation of 14 August,' DHist 79/442; Martin Blumenson, *Breakout and Pursuit* (Washington 1966), 231

62 Morris, *Canadian Artists and Airmen*, (Toronto 1974), 175–6

63 No 429 Squadron ORB, 13/14 Aug. 1944, DHist

64 No 6 Group and Nos 419, 427, 428, and 429 Squadron ORBs, 13/14 Aug. 1944, DHist; Harris, 'Report on the bombing of our own troops,' 25 Aug. 1944, 6, Harris Papers, DHist 87/51, folder 55; 'Operation TRACTABLE: Bombing error in close support operation of 14 August,' DHist 79/442

65 T.J. Bell, *Into Action with the 12th Field* (np, nd), 73–4

66 Saundby to Harris, note of action, 31 Aug. 1944, folio 12A, PRO Air 14/860

67 AHB, Bomber Command narrative, VI, 88, DHist 86/286

68 No 6 Group to Bomber Command, 15 Aug. 1944, Harris Papers, DHist, 87/51, folder H103

69 See Harris's covering letter to his 'Report on the bombing of our own troops,' 25 Aug. 1944, Harris Papers, DHist 87/51, folder 55.

70 Morris, *Canadian Artists and Airmen*, 179–80

71 Harris, 'Report on the bombing of our own troops,' 25 Aug. 1944, Harris Papers, DHist, 87/51, folder 55

72 Crerar to Harris, 29 Aug. 1944, Canadian War Museum, McEwen Papers, 58A1, folder 94.1

73 Harris, *Bomber Offensive*, 269; Craven and Cate, *Army Air Forces*, III, 787

74 No 6 Group analysis of results, DHist 74/250; Bomber Command ORB, 23–25 July 1944, DHist; Middlebrook and Everitt, *BCWD*, 548–9; AHB, 'Reports of physical damage resulting from Allied air attacks on Germany, 1944,' Feb. 1957, DHist SGR II 264, folder 82; SASO No 6 Group to bases, 1 Sept. 1944, DHist 181.009 (D1570); report by No 6 Group Navigation Officer to SASO, 8 Aug. 1944, DHist 181.009 (D4168 and 4163)

75 No 6 Group analysis of results, DHist 74/250; Bomber Command ORB, 25/26 July 1944, DHist; Middlebrook and Everitt, *BCWD*, 550; AHB, 'Reports of physical damage resulting from Allied air attacks on Germany, 1944,' Feb. 1957, DHist SGR II 264, folder 82; Bomber Command enemy raid reaction and RCM report night 25/26th July 1944, 27 July 1944, DHist 181.009 (D1946); Squadron Leader V.C. Varcoe, 'Summary of BMP reports 773–783,' 5 Aug. 1944, DHist 181.009 (D1945); Bomber Command ASI interception/tactics report No 178/44, 2 Aug. 1944, DHist 181.003 (D3814)

76 Interview, 7 Feb. 1980, J.K.F. Macdonald biog. file, DHist; No 432 Squadron ORB, July 1944, DHist

77 Bomber Command ORB, 28/29 July 1944, DHist; Middlebrook and Everitt, *BCWD*, 552; Bomber Command ORS report No 109, 11 Sept. 1944, DHist 181.003 (D3474); AHB, 'Reports of physical damage resulting from Allied air attacks on Germany, 1944,' Feb. 1957, DHist SGR II 264, folder 82; Bomber Command enemy raid reaction and RCM report No 19, 30 July 1944, DHist 181.003 (D1946); No 6 Group analysis of results, DHist 74/250; Bomber Command ASI, Interception/tactics report No 181/44, 5 Aug. 1944, DHist 181.003 (D3814)

78 Report of the Operational Research Committee Sub-Committee on Tactical Countermeasures to Enemy Night Fighters and Anti-Aircraft Defences, 31 July

1944, PRO Air 14/1764; Portal to Churchill, 31 July 1944, quoted in Webster and Frankland, *SAO*, III, 138

79 Harris to undersecretary of state for air, 9 Aug. 1944, PRO Air 14/1018

80 BSDU report No 22, 11 Jan. 1945, and BSDU report No 41, April 1945, both DHist 181.003 (D4587); Aders, *German Night Fighter Force*, 167

81 Bomber Command ORB July 1944, Armament section, 1127ff, DHist; ACAS(TR) to CAS, 23 July 1944, PRO Air 2/7839

82 ACAS(TR) to CRD, 10 Aug. 1944, PRO Air 2/7838; Bomber Command memorandum, 27 Aug. 1944, DHist 181.002 (D194); Bombing Development Unit report No 28, 'Identification devices for use with AGL(T),' part II, 1 Aug. 1944, DHist 181.003 (D4588); Bomber Command ORS report No B226, 'The possible exploitation of AGLT transmissions for plotting and homing,' 10 Oct. 1944, DHist 181.009 (D842)

83 Saundby to ACAS Ops, 13 Aug. 1944, DHist 181.006 (D131); AHB, Bomber Command narrative, VI, 96–7, DHist 86/286; Bomber Command ORB, 12/13 Aug. 1944, DHist; Middlebrook and Everitt, *BCWD*, 560–1; Bomber Command, enemy raid reaction and radio countermeasures report No 20, 14 Aug. 1944, DHist 181.003 (D1946); Hopkins to McEwen, 14 Aug. 1944, DHist 181.003 (D3428)

84 Air Ministry, ADI (Science) report No 73, 13 July 1944, PRO Air 20/1652 and report No 83, 26 March 1945, PRO Air 20/1654; S/L V.C. Varcoe, 'Summary of BMP reports Nos 784–796,' 18 Aug. 1944, DHist 181.009 (D1945); Bomber Command enemy raid reaction and RCM report No 20, night 12/13 Aug. 1944, 14 Aug. 1944, DHist, 181.009 (D1946); Air Ministry–USAFE Intelligence Report No 67, 'The GAF Signals Intelligence Service (Y-Service),' 21 Dec. 1945, DHist 181.009 (D414); Bomber Command ORS, 'Aids to bomber offensive during the winter of 1944–5,' 23 June 1944, PRO Air 14/1764; DDSci minute, 31 July 1944, and report of the Sub-Committee on tactical countermeasures to enemy night-fighters and anti-aircraft defences, 31 July 1944, PRO Air 14/1764

85 No 6 Group briefing notes, DHist 181.009 (D1563)

86 Quoted in *No 405 Squadron History*, 56

87 Bomber Command enemy raid reaction and RCM report No 21, 18 Aug. 1944, DHist 181.003 (D1946); Bomber Command ORS report No 111, 11 Oct. 1944, DHist 181.003 (D3474); Air Ministry, ADI(K) report No 599/1944, 2 Nov. 1944, DHist 181.009 (D4398); AHB, Bomber Command narrative, VI, 101, DHist 86/286; Bomber Command ORB, 29/30 Aug. 1944, DHist; Middlebrook and Everitt, *BCWD*, 575

88 AHB, Bomber Command narrative, VI, 101, DHist 86/286; Bomber Command ORB, Sept. 1944, DHist

89 Historical Review, No 6 (RCAF) Heavy Bomber Group, European Theatre, 1943–5, DHist 181.003 (D4720); No 6 Group monthly summaries, DHist 181.005 (D2001)

90 MacBean and Hogben, *Bombs Gone*, 135; No 6 Group, 'Operations, August,' DHist 181.003 (D4714), folio 47A; R.J. Overy, *The Air War* (London 1980), 140–1

91 File 181.009 (D1730), NA, RG 24, vol. 20607
92 Ibid. (D1725)

CHAPTER 23: ARMAGEDDON OVER GERMANY

1 'Oberkommando der Luftwaffe' [Air defence of the *Reich*], Sept. 1944, DHist, SGR II 317
2 Grabmann, 'German air defense,' USAF Historical Study No 164, June 1957, DHist 86/451, 166ff, 1467, 1636ff, 1673ff, 2283; Aders, *German Night Fighter Force*, 171, 203–5, 213; Bomber Command ADI(K) report No 599/1944, 2 Nov. 1944, DHist 181.009 (D4398); statistics compiled by Oberkommando der Luftwaffe 8th Abteilung in DHist SGR II 264, folders 56, 60, 61, 64, 65; Webster and Frankland, *SAO*, III, 14; Streetly, *Confound and Destroy*, 65–73, 95–6, 100–4
3 USAFE, AI 12, 'Consumption of aircraft fuel compared with available supplies; 'Statement by ministerial *Dirigent*, Dr Nocker,' 17 Oct. 1945, DHist 181.009 (D6670); Tedder, *Air Power in War*, 49; Birkenfeld, *Der Synthetische Treibstoff, 1933–1945*, translation in DHist SGR II 151
4 Bomber Command ADI(K) report No 599/1944, 2 Nov. 1944, DHist 181.009 (D4398)
5 See minutes of 5th meeting Bomber Command Tactical Planning Committee, 30 Sept. 1944, PRO Air 14/1453; McBurney (No 64 Base) to stations, squadrons, 13 Oct. 1944, DHist 181.009 (D2365); Bomber Command, 'Report on the use of *NAXOS* by GAF night fighters to home on to H2S aircraft,' 25 Oct. 1944, DHist 181.009 (D1606); TRE to Bomber Command, 9 Jan. 1945, PRO Air 14/1297; SASO No 6 Group to bases, stations, 13 Nov. 1944, DHist 181.009 (D5050); SASO No 6 Group to station radar officers, 6 Dec. 1944, DHist 181.009 (D1606); Bomber Command, ADI(K) report No 599/1944, 2 Nov. 1944, DHist 181.009 (D4398); DGMS to DAT, 23 Dec. 1944, PRO Air 2/5648; BDU report No 61, part III, 'Defence of bombers against upward-firing guns in enemy fighters,' 31 March 1945, PRO Air 14/1798
6 TRE, 'Aids to the bomber offensive during the winter of 1944–1945,' 23 June 1944, PRO Air 14/1764; Harris to Churchill, 30 Sept. 1944, PRO Air 14/3507; Jones, *Most Secret War*, 469
7 'Generalnachtrichtenführer Kriegstagebuch Nr 2, 1944, 3 Abteilung' [War diary No 2, 3rd Section, Chief of Communications], 26 Aug. and 8 Dec. 1944, DHist SGR II 320, folder 38; Grabmann, 'German air defense,' DHist 86/451, frames 1685–97; USAFE, AI 12, 'Interrogation of Director of GAF Signals, Martini, on radar and aircraft reporting service,' 9 Nov. 1945, DHist 181.009 (D292); Webster and Frankland, *SAO*, III, 272
8 Craven and Cate, *Army Air Forces*, III, 596; AHB, Bomber Command narrative, VI, 127, 273, DHist 86/286
9 Harris, *Bomber Offensive*, 214; AHB, Bomber Command narrative, VI, 51–2, 111–15, DHist 86/286; Olaf Groehler, 'Intentions, illusions and irreversible effects related to the background and controversy over the strategic bombardment of Germany in winter/spring 1944–1945'; Norman Longmate,

The Bombers (London 1983), 322–4, 331; Webster and Frankland, *SAO*, III, 50–7; Saward, *'Bomber' Harris*, 261

10 Portal to chiefs of staff, 9 Sept. 1944, and Bottomley to Harris, 25 Sept. 1944, quoted in Webster and Frankland, *SAO*, III, 58–9, 172–3; AHB, Bomber Command narrative, VI, 109, DHist 86/286; Craven and Cate, *Army Air Forces*, III, 319ff

11 Bottomley to Harris, 13 Oct. 1944, quoted in Webster and Frankland, *SAO*, IV, 174–5; Middlebrook and Everitt, *BCWD*, 601

12 Webster and Frankland, *SAO*, III, 184; Bomber Command ORB, Oct. 1944; No 6 Group bombing directive, DHist 181.005 (D2039); Bomber Command ORS report on night operations No 734, 15 Feb. 1945, DHist 181.003 (D1518); AHB, Bomber Command narrative, VI, 131ff, DHist 86/286; Middlebrook and Everitt, *BCWD*, 595–6; William S. Carter, *Anglo-Canadian Wartime Relations, 1939-1945* (New York 1991), 1–17; and Spencer Dunmore and William Carter, *Reap the Whirlwind* (Toronto 1991), 324ff

13 RCAF Station Leeming briefing notes, DHist 181.003 (D3267)

14 AHB, Bomber Command narrative, VI, 132, DHist 86/286; No 408 Squadron ORB, 6/7 Oct. 1944, DHist; Jones, *Most Secret War*, 468

15 Flying Officer A.F. Livingstone, Questionnaire for returned aircrew, 18 May 1945, and Flying Officer V.G.B. Valentine, Questionnaire for returned aircrew, 8 May 1945, DHist 181.001 (D23)

16 No 6 Group intelligence officer appreciation, DHist 181.003 (D3484)

17 Bomber Command ORS report of night operations No 734, 15 Feb. 1945, DHist 181.003 (D1518)

18 Bomber Command ORS report No S238, 28 Aug. 1945, DHist 181.009 (D3629); AHB, 'Reports of physical damage resulting from Allied air attacks on Germany, 1944,' Feb. 1957, DHist SGR II 264, folder 82

19 Bomber Command ORB, 6/7 and 14 Oct. 1944, DHist; Middlebrook and Everitt, *BCWD*, 598–9; 'The Bomber's Baedeker,' DHist 181.003 (D3993)

20 RCAF Station Leeming briefing notes, DHist 181.003 (D3267); Sgt K.E. Kelly diary, DHist 74/340; Bomber Command ORS report of night operations No 741, 16 Feb. 1945, DHist 181.003 (D1518); Bomber Command ORB, 14 Oct. 1944, DHist; No 6 Group analysis of results, DHist 74/250

21 *Bomber Command Quarterly Review*, Jan.–March 1944, 15–16, DHist 181.003 (D1430); Bomber Command ORB, 14/15 Oct. 1944, DHist; Bomber Command, CSO, 'Raid reporting and RCM report, night 14/15 Oct. 1944,' 16 Oct. 1944, DHist 181.003 (D1946)

22 Bomber Command ORB, 14 Oct. 1944, DHist; No 6 Group analysis of results, DHist 74/250

23 Bomber Command, CSO, 'Raid reporting and RCM report, night 14/15 Oct. 1944,' 16 Oct. 1944, DHist 181.003 (D1946); Aders, *German Night Fighter Force*, 167; Middlebrook and Everitt, *BCWD*, 602; AHB, Bomber Command narrative, VI, 132–3, DHist 86/286

24 Chaz Bowyer, *Tales from the Bombers* (London 1985), 208–9

25 RCAF Station Leeming briefing notes, DHist 181.003 (D3267)

26 Bomber Command ORB, Oct. 1944, DHist; No 6 Group analysis of results,

DHist 74/250; Middlebrook and Everitt, *BCWD*, 605; AHB, 'Reports of physical damage resulting from Allied air attacks on Germany, 1944,' Feb. 1957, DHist SGR II 264, folder 82. For a fuller discussion of G–H see Webster and Frankland, *SAO*, IV, 15ff.

27 Bomber Command ORB, 23–25 Oct. 1944, DHist; RCAF Station Leeming briefing notes, DHist 181.003 (D3267); No 6 Group analysis of results, DHist 74/250; AHB, 'Reports of physical damage resulting from Allied air attacks on Germany, 1944,' Feb. 1957, DHist SGR II 264, folder 82; Middlebrook and Everitt, *BCWD*, 607

28 'The Bombers' Baedekker,' DHist 181.003 (D3993); AHB, 'Reports of physical damage resulting from Allied air attacks on Germany, 1944,' Feb. 1957, DHist SGR II 264, folder 82; Bomber Command ORB, 28 Oct.–5 Nov. 1944, DHist; Middlebrook and Everitt, *BCWD*, 613–15; No 6 Group analysis of results, DHist 74/250; Bomber Command ORS report No 116, 27 Dec. 1944, DHist 181.003 (D3474); 'Oberkommando der Luftwaffe, 8th Abteilung,' [The problems of German air defence in 1944], AHB translation, DHist SGR II 264, folder 12

29 MI9/S/PG-2936, April 1945, DHist 79/507

30 Bomber Command ORS report No 115, 25 Nov. 1944, DHIst 181.003 (D3474); Air Ministry, ASI report No 79, 'The present eclipse of the German Night Fighters'; Harris to Portal, 24 Nov. 1944, Harris Papers, DHist 87/51, folder H83; USAFE, 'German air defense: tactical employment of night fighting in the German Air Force,' 6 March 1946, DHist 73/1506, frames 5427ff

31 Saundby to ACAS(TR), 4 Oct. 1944, PRO Air 2/5655; AHB, Bomber Command narrative, VI, 76–7, DHist 86/286

32 Minutes, 5th meeting Bomber Command tactical planning committee, 24 June 1944, PRO Air 14/1453

33 AHB, Bomber Command narrative, VI, 75, DHist 86/286; see also USSBS, 'Description of Royal Air Force bombing,' 3 Nov. 1945, PRO Air 48/67.

34 No 6 Group to bases, stations, 7 Aug., 15 Sept., and 11 Oct. 1944, and 5 April 1945, and Bomber Command to groups, 28 Sept. 1944, DHist 181.009 (D6752); Bomber Command tactical conference, 13 Nov. 1944, DHist 181.009 (D4214); No 6 Group bombing leader to SASO, 13 April 1945, DHist 181.003 (D3443); SASO No 6 Group memorandum, 15 April 1945, DHist 181.009 (D1603)

35 Webster and Frankland, *SAO*, III, 139; Bomber Command ORS, reports No S181, 19 Sept. 1944, and S185, 29 Sept. 1944, DHist 181.003 (D2167); J.W. Hopkins (ORS No 6 Group) to H.L. Beard, 30 July 1944, DHist 181.003 (D3428); Hopkins to R. Ross, 9 Oct. 1944, DHist 181.009 (D4036); DD Science, 'Visual daylight attacks by Bomber Command,' 4 Nov. 1944, DHist 181.009 (D1705)

36 Bomber Command ORB, 27 Aug. 1944, DHist

37 Bomber Command and No 419 Squadron ORBs, 6 Sept. 1944, DHist; Bomber Command ORS report No 112, 4 Nov. 1944, PRO Air 14/3651

38 No 6 Group analysis of results, DHist 74/250; No 6 Group to bases, 25 Sept. 1944, DHist 181.009 (D1603); AHB, Bomber Command narrative, VI, 99, DHist 86/286

39 Bomber Command immediate interpretation report No K3115, 7 Sept. 1944, DHist 181.003 (D3908); Flight Lieutenant F.H.C. Reineke diary of overseas tour, 23 May 1944 to 11 Oct. 1945, DHist 87/241, vol. 1; H.L. Beard minute, Oct. 1945, PRO Air 14/1752

40 Bomber Command ORB, 11–12 Sept. 1944, DHist; Bomber Command immediate interpretation report, No K3162, 13 Sept. 1944, DHist 181.003 (D1758); No 6 Group analysis of results, DHist 74/250; No 426 Squadron to SNO Bomber Command, 18 Sept. 1944, DHist 181.003 (D3819)

41 Bomber Command ORS, report No 112, 4 Nov. 1944, PRO Air 14/365; Bomber Command and No 6 Group ORBs, 27 Sept. 1944, DHist; No 6 Group analysis of results, DHist 74/250

42 Wing Commander D.C. Hagerman, Recommendation for honours and awards, immediate, 23 Oct. 1944, J.A. Anderson biog. file, DHist

43 Harris to Anderson, 21 Dec. 1944, Anderson biog. file, DHist

44 DHist awards file

45 Bomber Command ORB, 30 Sept. and 6 Nov. 1944, DHist; No 6 Group analysis of results, DHist 74/250; Bomber Command immediate interpretation report, No K4458, 7 Nov. 1944, DHist 181.003 (D1559); E.F. Bush, 'Room with a View: A Bomb Aimer's War,' *High Flight* III (summer 1983): 72; No 6 Group review of navigation, Oct., Nov., and Dec. 1944, DHist 181.9003 (D4020); Navigation officer, RCAF Station Leeming, to station commander, 23 Dec. 1944, DHist 181.003 (D3819); SASO, No 6 Group, to station radar and navigation officers, 6 Dec. 1944, and Bomber Command file, 'Operational use of H2S, Nov 1944,' 18 Dec. 1944, both DHist 181.009 (D1606); SASO, No 6 Group, to bases, stations, 10 Oct. 1944, DHist 181.003 (D4674); No 62 Base to RCAF Linton, 4 Nov. 1944, and No 6 Group to bases, stations, 10 Jan. 1945, DHist 181.009 (D3067); Bomber Command ORS report No S209, 4 March 1945, DHist 181.003 (D2167); SASO, No 6 Group, to bases, stations, 26 Nov. 1944, DHist 181.009 (D3254)

46 Bomber Command ORB, 7 Oct. 1944, DHist; Tedder to Portal, 25 Oct. 1944, quoted in Webster and Frankland, *SAO*, III, 68–9

47 Stacey, *The Victory Campaign*, ch. 14, but especially 421; Terry Copp and Robert Vogel, *Maple Leaf Route: Antwerp* (Alma, Ont. 1984), 92–123; AHB, Bomber Command narrative, VI, 89ff, 138–40, DHist 86/286

48 Bomber Command ORB, 15–16 Nov. 1944, DHist; No 6 Group analysis of results, DHist 74/250; AHB, Bomber Command narrative, VI, 182, DHist 86/286

49 Craven and Cate, *Army Air Forces,* III, 649

50 Bottomley to Harris, 1 Nov. 1944, quoted in Webster and Frankland, *SAO*, IV, 177–9

51 Quoted Webster and Frankland, *SAO*, IV, 177

52 Harris to Portal, 1 Nov. 1944, Harris Papers, DHist, 87/51, folder H83

53 Harris to Portal, 6 Nov. 1944, Harris papers, DHist 87/51, folder H83

54 Portal to Harris, 5 and 12 Nov., 6 and 22 Dec. 1944, and 8, 20, and 25 Jan. 1945, Harris Papers, DHist 87/51, folders H83 and H84

55 PRO Air 8/258; Harris to Portal, 18 Jan. 1945, and Portal to Harris, 20 Jan.

1945, Harris Papers, DHist, 87/51, folder H84; Webster and Frankland, *SAO*, III, 75–9

56 Bomber Command ORB, Nov. and Dec. 1944, DHist; Middlebrook and Everitt, *BCWD*, 614ff; Speer to Hitler, 19 Jan. 1945, quoted in Webster and Frankland, *SAO*, III, 234–5; Craven and Cate, *Army Air Forces,* III, 640–6; DCAS to DCMG, 13 Nov. 1944, DHist 181.006 (D243); DBOps to DCAS, 22 Dec. 1944, PRO Air 20/8058; AHB, Bomber Command narrative, VI, 146–56, 168–9, 186, and 211, DHist 86/286

57 Bomber Command ASI, Interception/tactics reports No 298/44, 5 Dec. 1944, and No 301/1944, 9 Dec. 1944, DHist 181.003 (D433); Bomber Command ORB, Nov. and Dec. 1944, DHist; Middlebrook and Everitt, *BCWD*, 614ff; Bomber Command, CSO, Signals intelligence and RCM report No 15, DHist 181.003 (D449); Bomber Command ORS, Monthly report of losses to Bomber Command aircraft, No 119, 18 Jan. 1945, DHist 181.003 (D3474); S/L V.C. Varcoe, 'Summary of BMP pamphlets,' 11 Dec. 1944, DHist 181.003 (D1945); Bomber Command, Int 3, 'Note on enemy night air defences,' 1 Dec. 1944, DHist 181.009 (D4398); Harris to Portal, 24 Nov. 1944, Harris Papers, DHist 87/51, folder H83

58 Dunmore and Carter, *Reap the Whirlwind*, 340; No 6 Group analysis of results, DHist 74/250

59 John H. McQuiston, *Tannoy Calling: A Story of Canadian Airmen Flying against Nazi Germany* (New York 1990), 91

60 Report by No 6 Group battle damage inspector, Nov. 1944, DHist 181.003 (D2975)

61 AHB, Reports of physical damage resulting from Allied air attacks on Germany, 1944, DHist SGR II 264 folder 82; Bomber Command ORB, 16–22 Dec. 1944, DHist; Kit C. Carter and Robert Mueller, *The Army Air Forces in World War II* (Washington 1973), 531ff; AHB, Bomber Command narrative, VI, 184–7, DHist 86/286

62 Webster and Frankland, *SAO*, III, 242; Craven and Cate, *Army Air Forces,* III, 653ff

63 Harris to Portal, 28 Dec. 1944, Harris Papers, DHist 87/51, folder H83

64 Alfred C. Mierzejewski, 'Intelligence and the Strategic Bombing of Germany: The Combined Strategic Targets Committee,' *Intelligence and Counter-intelligence* 3 (summer 1990): 89ff; Speer to Hitler, 19 Jan. 1945, quoted in Webster and Frankland, *SAO*, IV, 337–40

65 Base commander, Eastmoor, to squadrons, 6 Feb. 1945, DHist 181.009 (D3961)

66 Draft notes for No 6 Group summary of operations, 1 Jan. 1943–15 Dec. 1944, DHist 181.003 (D4714); DHist 181.003 (D3819) (folio 218 A/B)

67 SASO to No 62 Base, 11 Jan. 1945, DHist 181.009 (D6341); minutes of squadron commanders conference, 25 Jan. 1945, DHist 181.009 (D5254); draft notes for No 6 Group summary of operations, 1 Jan. 1943–15 Dec. 1944, DHist 181.003 (D4714); DHist 181.003 (D3819) (folio 218 A/B)

68 McQuiston, *Tanny Calling*, 16–17, 71, 85; draft notes for No 6 Group summary of operations, 1 Jan. 1943–15 Dec. 1944, DHist 181.003 (D4714)

69 Quoted in Price, *Instruments of Darkness*, 226

70 Bomber Command ORB, Oct. 1944–May 1945; Middlebrook and Everitt, *BCWD*, 641, 704

71 Bomber Command ORB, Jan. 1945, DHist; No 6 Group analysis of results, DHist 74/250; Questionnaire for returned aircrew, DHist 181.001 (D24), folder 7

72 Bomber Command ORS, Night raid report Nos 810 and 817, April 1945, DHist 181.003 (D1518); Bomber Command ASI, Interception/tactics report No 5/45, 10 Jan. 1945, and No 14/45, 22 Jan. 1945, DHist 181.009 (D1429); No 6 Group analysis of results, DHist 74/250

73 Bottomley to Portal, 13 Jan. 1945, PRO Air 20/3361; Craven and Cate, *Army Air Forces*, III, 716–21; Bottomley to Harris, 19 Jan. 1945, including revised bombing directive, 15 Jan. 1945, quoted in Webster and Frankland, *SAO, IV*, 179–83

74 Webster and Frankland, *SAO*, III, 97–104, 111, 255; Richard G. Davis, 'Operation THUNDERCLAP: The US Army Air Forces and the bombing of Berlin,' *Journal of Strategic Studies* 14, 1 (1990): 90–111; Bottomley to Portal, 26 Jan. 1945, Portal to Bottomley, 26 Jan. 1945, and Air Staff, 'Strategic bombing in relation to the present Russian offensive,' 26 Jan. 1945, PRO Air 20/3361

75 Bottomley to ACAS and to Harris, 27 Jan. 1945, PRO Air 20/3361; AHB, Bomber Command narrative, VI, 196–202, DHist 86/286; Webster and Frankland, *SAO*, III, 106–8

76 'The Bomber's Baedeker,' DHist 181.003 (D3993)

77 RCAF Station Linton-on-Ouse briefing notes, DHist 181.009 (D1563)

78 AHB, 'Reports of physical damage from Allied air attacks on Germany, 1945,' May 1957, DHist SGR II 264 folder 84; report by Bomber Command navigation officer, Group Captain J.H. Searby, 15 Feb. 1945, PRO Air 14/836; DHist 181.003 (D3819), folio 186A; minutes of No 6 Group navigation officers conference, 7 Feb. 1945, DHist 181.009 (D4986)

79 RCAF Station Linton-on-Ouse briefing notes, DHist 181.009 (D1563); Denis and Shelagh Whitaker, *Rhineland* (Toronto 1989), 125

80 RCAF Station Leeming briefing notes, DHist 181.009 (D1563); Bomber Command ORB, 13/14 Feb. 1945, DHist; No 6 Group analysis of results, DHist 74/250

81 Sir Robert Saundby's foreward to David Irving, *The Destruction of Dresden* (London 1963), 5

82 Irving, *The Destruction of Dresden*, especially 96–146; Terraine, *A Time for Courage*, 678; Dunsmore and Carter, *Reap the Whirlwind*, 347ff

83 Alexander McKee, *Dresden 1945* (London and Toronto 1982), 173–5

84 'The Bomber's Baedeker,' DHist 181.003 (D3993); AHB, 'Reports of physical damage resulting from Allied air attacks on Germany, 1945,' May 1957, DHist SGR II 264, folder 84; Carter and Mueller, *The Army Air Forces in World War II*, 747; Bomber Command ORB, 14/15 Feb. 1945, DHist; Nos 427 and 429 Squadron briefing notes, DHist 181.003 (D3267); No 6 Group analysis of results, DHist 74/250

85 'The Bomber's Baedeker,' DHist 181.003 (D3993)
86 Bomber Command ORS, Night raid report No 846, 25 March 1945, DHist 181.003 (D1518)
87 AHB, 'Reports of physical damage resulting from Allied air attacks on Germany, 1945,' May 1957, DHist 181.003 (D3993)
88 Bomber Command ORB, Feb. 1945, DHist
89 Ibid., Feb. and March 1945
90 Aders, *German Night Fighter Force*, 211; No 6 Group analysis of results, DHist 74/250; Bomber Command ORS report No 123, 22 March 1945, DHist 181.003 (D3474)
91 No 6 Group analysis of results, DHist 74/250; Dunsmore and Carter, *Reap the Whirlwind*, 355; No 6 Group summary of encounters with the enemy, March 1945, DHist 181.005 (D2091); No 6 Group monthly summary of operations for March 1945,' DHist 181.003 (D5271); No 11 Group to Bomber Command 'Concerning the raid of 31 Mar 1945,' DHist 181.009 (D6752); Alfred Price, *The Last Year of the Luftwaffe* (Osceola, Wisc., 1991), 138; E.F. Bush, 'Room with a View: A Bomb-Aimer's War,' pt 2, *High Flight* (summer 1983): 76
92 McQuiston, *Tannoy Calling*, 197–8
93 Bomber Command ORS report No S217, 3 May 1945, DHist 181.009 (D4704); Simon W. Parry, *Intruders over Britain* (London 1987) part III; Price, *The Last Year of the Luftwaffe*, 140; Middlebrook and Everitt, *BCWD*, 674
94 McQuiston, *Tannoy Calling*, 197–8
95 Bomber Command ORB, 5/6 March 1945, DHist
96 Report of No 1 Canadian War Crimes Investigation Unit on Miscellaneous War Crimes against Members of the Canadian Armed Forces in the European Theatre of Operations, pt II, 30 March 1946, cases 67/Hagen/1 and 67/Opladen/1, DHist 159.023 (D1)
97 DHist awards file
98 No 6 Group to bases, 25 March 1945, DHist 181.009 (D4283)
99 See No 6 Group damage reports, DHist 181.003 (D3062).
100 Bomber Command ORS report No 123, 22 March 1945, report No 125, 24 April 1945, report No 135, 25 April 1945, DHist 181.003 (D3474); Bomber Command ORB, April 1945, DHist; SASO No 100 Group to stations, 13 June 1945, DHist 181.009; report on Exercise Post Mortem, PRO Air 20/4464; CSO Bomber Command to deputy commander-in-chief, 20 March 1945, PRO Air 14/1300; Bomber Command interception and tactics reports, DHist 181.003 (D179); Webster and Frankland, *SAO*, III, 236
101 Bottomley to Harris, 5 May 1945, including directive of 16 April, quoted in Webster and Frankland, *SAO*, IV, 183–4
102 Webster and Frankland, *SAO*, III, 112
103 Churchill to Ismay, 28 March 1945, PRO Air 20/4069
104 Nos 427 and 429 Squadron briefing notes, DHist 181.003 (D3267); No 405 Squadron ORB, 22 March 1945, DHist; AHB, 'Reports of physical damage resulting from allied air attacks on Germany, 1945,' May 1957, DHist SGR II 264, folder 84; Middlebrook and Everitt, *BCWD*, 685

105 Churchill to Ismay, 1 April 1945, quoted in Webster and Frankland, *SAO*, III, 117

106 Quoted in Saward, *Victory Denied*, 357–8

107 Bomber Command ORB, 25 April 1945, DHist; Dunsmore and Carter, *Reap the Whirlwind*, 361ff

108 No 405 Squadron ORB, 29 April–7 May 1945, DHist

109 Walter B. Maass, *The Netherlands at War: 1940–1945* (London 1970), 233ff; Bomber Command ORB, April and May 1945, DHist; Historical Review No 6 (RCAF) Heavy Bomber Group, 1943–1945, DHist 181.003 (D4720), (hereafter No 6 Group historical review); AHB, Bomber Command narrative, VI, 244, DHist 86/286

110 *Globe and Mail*, 23 March 1945

111 Ibid.

112 Webster and Frankland, *SAO*, IV, 439; Middlebrook and Everitt, *BCWD*, 782ff; No 6 Group historical review, DHist 181.003 (D4720)

113 Harris, *Bomber Offensive*, 247

114 Ibid., 267; Middlebrook and Everitt, *BCWD*, 708–11; No 6 Group historical review, DHist 181.003 (D4720)

115 *Globe and Mail*, 6 June 1945

116 This discussion is based on the multi-volume report by the United States Strategic Bombing Survey, Webster and Frankland, *SAO*, III, chs 14 and 15, and IV, section V; Craven and Cate, *Army Air Forces*, III, especially 787ff; Birken-feld, *Der Synthetische Treibstoff 1933–1945*, translation in DHist SGR II 151; Bidinian, *The Combined Allied Bombing Offensive against the German Civilian*; Galbraith, *The Affluent Society*, 127–38, 162; R.J. Overy, *The Air War 1939–1945* (New York 1981), 122ff.

117 Webster and Frankland, *SAO*, IV, 49, 482; Zuckerman, *From Apes to Warlords*, app. 6; AHB, Bomber Command narrative, VI, 253, DHist 86/286; USSBS, *Area Studies Division Report*, Jan. 1947, 23

118 USSBS, *The Effects of Strategic Bombing on German Morale*, 2 vols, Dec. 1946–May 1947, I and passim; interrogation of Albert Speer, 18 July 1945, quoted in Webster and Frankland, *SAO*, IV, 382–3

119 USSBS, *The German Anti-Friction Bearings Industry*, Jan. 1947, especially ch. 3; interrogation of Albert Speer, 18 July 1945, quoted Webster and Frankland, *SAO*, IV, 389, and ibid., 495; USSBS, *Aircraft Division Industry Report*, Jan. 1947, especially ch. 5

120 MacBean and Hogben, *Bombs Gone*; S.W. Roskill, *The War at Sea, 1939-1945* (London 1961), vol. III, part II, 140ff, and app. Y; USSBS, *Overall Report (European War)*, 30 Sept. 1945, 68; No 6 Group Historical Review, 14ff, DHist 181.003 (D4720)

121 AHB, Bomber Command narrative, VI, 253, DHist 86/286; Air Ministry, *The Rise and Fall of the German Air Force*, 274, 395

122 MI 15, 'Deployment of GAF *Flak* guns, searchlights, and balloons, 1939–1944,' 12 Nov. 1945, DHist 181.009 (D2815); Saward, *Victory Denied*, 318–19; Webster and Frankland, *SAO*, IV, 501–3, citing records of the 6 Abteilung, Oberkommando der Luftwaffe Generalquartiermeister staff

CHAPTER 24: AIRLIFT IN EUROPE AND SOUTHEAST ASIA

1 *By Air to Battle* (London 1945), 5–6
2 Ibid.; C.P. Stacey, *The Victory Campaign* (Ottawa 1960), 92–3; Major-General David Belchem, *Victory in Normandy* (London 1981), 68
3 H.A. Jones, *The War in the Air*, V (London 1935), 278ff; John D.R. Rawlings, *Coastal, Support and Special Squadrons of the RAF and Their Aircraft* (Guildford 1982), 33–4, 47
4 Ronald Lewin, *Slim* (London 1976) 54
5 M.M. Postan, *British War Production* (London 1952), 484–5; *The Second World War: A Guide to Documents in the Public Record Office* (London 1972), 36; Raymond Callahan, *Burma 1942–1945* (London 1978), 128–9; Owen Thetford, *Aircraft of the Royal Air Force since 1918* (New York 1968), 62
6 Air Vice-Marshal Neil Cameron, '46 Group,' *Royal Air Forces Quarterly* (autumn 1972), 165–73; *RAF Confidential List*, April 1943–June 1944; C.G. Jefford, *RAF Squadrons* (Shrewsbury 1988)
7 Power to Breadner, 13 May 1944, Breadner to Power, 3 June 1944, and Power to Breadner, 9 June 1944, NA, RG 24, vol. 5210
8 Breadner to Power, 7 July 1944, NA, RG 24, vol. 5210; Air Ministry to Transport Command, 24 Aug. 1944, DHist 181.009 (D803); Flight Lieutenant F.H.C. Reinke, 'Dakota Transport: 437 Squadron,' March 1945, DHist 74/346
9 Transport Command to AOC-in-C, RCAF Overseas, 20 July 1944, DHist 181.009 (D803); *437 Squadron History* (Belleville 1985), 10; Flight Lieutenant F.H.C. Reinke, 'Dakota Transport,' March 1945, DHist 74/346
10 Michael J.F. Bower, *Action Stations* (Cambridge 1983), VI, 129
11 No 437 Squadron ORB, 4 Sept. 1944, DHist
12 Terence O'Brien, *The Moonlight War* (London 1987), 28; A. Pearcey, *The Dakota, RAF and RCAF* (London 1972), 25–7
13 Flight Lieutenant F.H.C. Reinke, 'Dakota Transport,' March 1945, DHist 74/346; *437 Squadron History*, 27, 33; A. Pearcy, *The Dakota at War* (London 1982)
14 John Ehrman, *Grand Strategy*, V (London 1956), 526; No 437 Squadron ORB, 17 Sept. 1944, DHist; James M. Gavin, *On to Berlin* (New York 1978), 150
15 No 437 Squadron ORB, 18 Sept. 1944, DHist; *437 Squadron History*, 27; Flight Lieutenant F.H.C. Reinke, 'Dakota Transport,' March 1945, DHist 74/346
16 Anonymous, *Arnhem Lift* (London 1945), 62–3
17 Flight Lieutenant F.H.C. Reinke, 'Dakota Transport,' March 1945, DHist 74/346; 437 Squadron History, 11–12; DHist decorations file
18 No 437 Squadron ORB, 19 and 23 Sept. 1944, DHist
19 F/L F.H.C. Reinke, 'Dakota Transport: 437 Squadron,' March 1945, DHist 74/346
20 No 437 Squadron ORB, 23 Sept. 1944, DHist
21 Ibid., Dec. 1944

22 Ibid., 30 Sept. and 25, 27, and 30 Oct. 1944; Flight Lieutenant F.H.C. Reinke, 'Dakota Transport,' March 1945, DHist 74/346; *437 Squadron History*, 32

23 Flight Lieutenant F.H.C. Reinke, 'Dakota Transport,' March 1945, DHist 74/346; *437 Squadron History*, 14

24 No 437 Squadron ORB, 1 Oct. 1944, DHist; *437 Squadron History*, 14

25 *437 Squadron History*, 14–15

26 No 437 Squadron ORB, 19–27 Dec. 1944, DHist

27 Ibid., 26–31 Dec. 1944

28 Ibid., Feb.–March 1944

29 Ibid., 24 March 1944

30 *437 Squadron History*, 18

31 PRO WO/220/77

32 Air Ministry, Air Historical Branch, 'The RAF in the bombing offensive against Germany,' V, 246–9, DHist 86/2865 (hereafter AHB, Bomber Command narrative)

33 Walter B. Maas, *The Netherlands at War* (London 1970), 239

34 No 405 Squadron ORB, 30 April and 1, 2, 4, 5 and 7 May 1945, DHist

35 SHAEF Air Staff, A3 Division (Plans), 'ECLIPSE Memorandum No 4 – Air Lift Plan, 23 March 1945, PRO, Air 14/1685

36 Ibid.

37 Appendix 'F' to 'ECLIPSE Memorandum No 4 – Air Lift Plan,' 23 March 1945, PRO Air 14/1685

38 AHB, Bomber Command Narrative, V, 250–1, DHist 86/286

39 No 437 Squadron ORB, 8–14 April 1945, DHist

40 *437 Squadron History*, 19

41 Ibid., 32–3

42 No 437 Squadron ORB, Summary of Operations for July 1945, DHist; *437 Squadron History*, 19–20

43 *437 Squadron History*, 23

44 Callahan, *Burma 1942–1945*, 108

45 Ibid., 108, 123–4, 128–9, 134, 143–4; S. Woodburn Kirby, *The War against Japan*, IV (London 1965), 1–13

46 S. Woodburn Kirby, *The War against Japan*, III (London 1961), 515–16, and IV, 20, 34; W.F. Craven and J.L. Cate, *The Army Air Forces in World War II*, IV: *The Pacific: Guadacanal to Saigon August 1942 to July 1944* (Chicago 1950), 508–9; Charles F. Romanus and Riley Sunderland, *Stilwell's Command Problems* (Washington 1956), 191–203; ACSEA to Air Ministry, 5 Aug. 1944, DHist 181.003 (D1035)

47 For a more detailed account of the political background to the formation of Nos 435 and 436 Squadrons, see T.W. Melnyk, *Canadian Flying Operations in South East Asia 1945–1946* (Ottawa 1976), 106–10.

48 Power to Anderson, 11 Aug. 1944, NA, RG 24, vol. 5247; RCAF Base Records Office progress report, 29 May 1945, DHist 181.003 (D3064)

49 No 435 and 436 Squadron ORBs, Sept. and Oct. 1944, DHist; T.P. Harnett and R.A. Gordon biog. files, DHist

50 No 435 and 436 Squadron ORBs, Oct. 1944, DHist

51 Ibid., Nov. 1944; No 435 Squadron Substitute Form 540, 1 Oct. 1944, DHist 181.003 (D4922); No 436 Squadron Substitute Form 540, 28 Oct. 1944, DHist 181.003 (D5038)

52 Breadner to Power, 16 Nov. 1944, DHist 181.009 (D804); No 436 Squadron ORB, 16–17 Nov. 1944, DHist

53 Anderson, 'Formation of Three Medium Range Transport Squadrons (Article XV),' 28 June 1944, DHist 181.009 (D774); No 435 and 436 Squadron ORBs, Oct.–Nov. 1944, DHist

54 C.F. Romanus and R. Sutherland, *Stilwell's Command Problems* (Washington 1953–9), 99–100

55 Field Marshal Sir William Slim, *Defeat into Victory* (London 1956), 329

56 No 435 and 436 Squadron ORBs, Dec. 1944, DHist; Melnyk, *Canadian Flying Operations*, 116; Air Vice Marshal J.V.R. Hardman, 'A Review of RAF Transport Support Operations in the Burma Campaign, December 1944–August 1945,' 53, DHist 181.003 (D1002); Slim, *Defeat Into Victory*, 450

57 Harnett to Melnyk, 5 Oct. 1975, DHist R S7 435

58 No 435 Squadron ORB, 20 Dec. 1944, DHist

59 Ibid., Dec. 1944

60 No 436 Squadron ORB, 1–15 Jan. 1945, DHist

61 Kirby, *The War against Japan*, IV, 410–11; J.G. Taylor, *Air Supply in the Burma Campaign* (Washington 1957), 42

62 Melnyk, *Canadian Flying Operations*, 117–18; Air Ministry to ACSEA, 30 Jan. 1945, PRO Air 20/920

63 No 435 Squadron ORB, 18 March 1945, DHist; Slim, *Defeat into Victory*, 313, 319

64 Hardman, 'RAF Transport Support Operations,' 35, DHist 181.003 (D1002)

65 Ibid.

66 Hardman, 'A Review of Air Transport Operations,' 3, DHist 181.009 (D554); No 1 Indian ORS, 'Principal Factors Affecting the Success of Supply Dropping' [Oct 1945], PRO Air 23/2844; Taylor, *Air Supply in the Burma Campaign*, 95

67 H.L. Buller, 'The C-46 and C-47 in CBI Operations,' *Aerospace Historian* 22 (June 1975): 81

68 Ibid.

69 D. Martin, 'Determined to Deliver: The Wartime Story of No 435 (Chinthe) Squadron,' *The Roundel* 5 (Feb. 1953): 4; Eastern Air Command Weekly Summary, 9 May 1945, DHist 181.009 (D1010); Kirby, *The War against Japan*, IV, 401ff and app. 4; W.F. Craven and J.L. Cate, *The Army Air Forces in World War II*, V (Chicago 1953), 244

70 Kirby, *The War against Japan*, IV, 179

71 Martin, 'Determined to deliver,' 4–7; No 435 Squadron ORB, 12 Jan. 1945, DHist

72 No 436 Squadron ORB, 16 Jan. 1945; No 435 Squadron ORB, 15 Jan. and March 1945, DHist

73 P.N. Khera and S.N. Prasas, *The Reconquest of Burma*, II (New Delhi 1959),

249; No 435 Squadron ORB, 28 Jan. and 3 Feb. 1945, DHist; No 436 Squadron ORB, Jan.–Feb. 1945, DHist

74 No 435 Squadron ORB, 21 Jan., 10 Feb., and 11 June 1945, DHist; No 436 Squadron ORB, 31 Jan. 1945; Slim, *Defeat into Victory*, 343

75 No 436 Squadron ORB, Report by S/L Denison, Feb. 1945, DHist

76 John Masters, *The Road Past Mandalay* (New York 1961), 295–6

77 Slim, *Defeat into Victory*, 367; ORS Memorandum No 35, 9 Nov. 1945, PRO Air 23/2844

78 No 435 Squadron ORB, Feb. 1945, DHist; No 436 Squadron ORB, March 1945, DHist; Slim, *Defeat into Victory*, 364

79 No 436 Squadron ORB, March 1945, DHist

80 Ibid.; Kirby, *The War against Japan*, IV, 313; Craven and Cate, *The Army Air Forces in World War II*, V, 249

81 No 435 Squadron ORB, April 1945

82 Cork, 'Medical Liaison Officer's Report on Tour,' 28 March 1945, DHist 181.003 (D1482); 'Report of RCAF Mission to South East Asia July–October 1944,' 319–24, DHist 181.003 (D1035)

83 George Forty, *XIV Army at War* (London 1982), 123–4

84 Masters, *The Road Past Mandalay*, 306–7

85 A.P. Heathcote, 'The Flying Elephants,' *The Roundel* 14 (April 1962): 20; No 436 Squadron ORB, April 1945, DHist

86 No 435 Squadron ORB, 31 April 1945, DHist

87 Forty, *XIV Army*, 134

88 Ibid.

89 No 436 Squadron ORB, 28 May 1945, DHist; Taylor, *Air Supply in the Burma Campaign*, 120

90 ORS memorandum No 35, 9 Nov. 1945, PRO Air 23/2844

91 No 229 Group, 'Monsoon flying,' 18 June 1945, 7, DHist 181.009 (D1695)

92 Alvin Hamilton to W.A.B. Douglas, 4 Feb. 1988, on inside cover of DHist library copy of Terence O'Brien, *The Moonlight War* (London 1987)

93 Admiral Louis Mountbatten, *Report to the Combined Chiefs of Staff by the Supreme Allied Commander South East Asia 1943–45* (London 1951), 196; Slim, *Defeat into Victory*, 423

94 No 435 Squadron ORB, 30 May 1945, DHist

95 Ibid., 1 June 1945

96 Ibid., July–Aug. 1945; No 435 Squadron Medical Officer to Senior Medical Officer 345 Wing, 3 June 1945, DHist 181.009 (D881)

97 John Bowen, *Undercover in the Jungle* (London 1978), 191–2; No 436 Squadron ORB, July 1945, DHist

98 No 436 Squadron ORB, 7 May 1945, DHist

99 ACSEA to Air Ministry, 11 Jan. 1945, and Air Ministry to ACSEA, 30 Jan. 1945, DHist; PRO Air 20/920; ACSEA to Air Ministry, 8 Aug. 1945, DHist 181.009 (D3828); Johnson to Evill, 8 June 1945, NA, RG 24, vol. 5427; Evill to Johnson, 12 June 1945, DHist 181.009 (D6223); Johnson to undersecretary of state for air, 4 June 1945, DHist 181.009 (D804)

100 Leckie to Johnson, 18 June 1945, NA, RG 24, vol. 5427; Air Ministry to ACSEA, 14 July 1945, DHist 181.009 (D3828)

101 F.R. Coyle, ed., *Canucks Unlimited* (Toronto nd), 83; No 436 Squadron ORB, Aug. 1945, DHist; No 435 Squadron ORB, 30 Aug. 1945

102 Patterson to RCAF staff officer 229 Group, 13 Aug. 1945, and ACSEA to Transport Command, 30 July 1945, DHist 181.009 (D3828)

103 No 435 Squadron ORB, Feb. 1946, DHist

104 No 435, 436, and 436 Squadron ORBs, 5–15 Feb. 1946, DHist; see also *The RCAF Overseas: The Sixth Year* (Ottawa 1949), 430.

105 Cochrane to Johnson, 6 Oct. 1945, DHist 181.003 (D4922)

106 Slim, *Defeat into Victory*, 443

Index

All bases and stations are indexed under the heading 'air bases and stations.' Operations with codenames are indexed under the headings 'operations, Allied,' and 'operations, German.' Army and naval units and formations are indexed under national service headings – British Army, German Army. National air forces are indexed under their name – Royal Canadian Air Force, Luftwaffe. Allied air force units, formations, and commands are indexed under such designations as commands, wings, groups, squadrons, and schools. Civilian casualties are indexed under the heading 'casualties'; military casualties are indexed under the command, formation, or unit involved. Operational entries are indexed by the main functional types: for example, fighter opertions, bomber operations, anti-shipping operations, and anti-submarine operations.

air bombers, *see* bomb aimers
Air Defence of Great Britain, *see* commands
Air Fighting Development Unit 185, 233
Air Force Cross: awarded to W/C R.M.
Fenwick-Wilson 548; to W/C J. Fulton 571
air forces (Operational)
– Allied Expeditionary Air Forces: formed
268; commends No 143 Wing 304; other
refs 279, 284, 294, 302–3, 406, 407
– Desert Air Force and development of
ground support doctrine 164, 244; No 417
Squadron serves in 165, 252, 254, 287;
and dominance over the Luftwaffe 310;
other refs 95, 249–51, 345
– Second Tactical Air Force (TAF):
formation and organization 244, 254, 265,
268–71, 272–5, 329; RCAF component
259, 271, 273; role and responsibilities
278–9, 324–5, 327, 343, 346; preparations
for Operation Overlord 282–3, 289; losses
to Luftwaffe on 1 January 1945 343; No 2

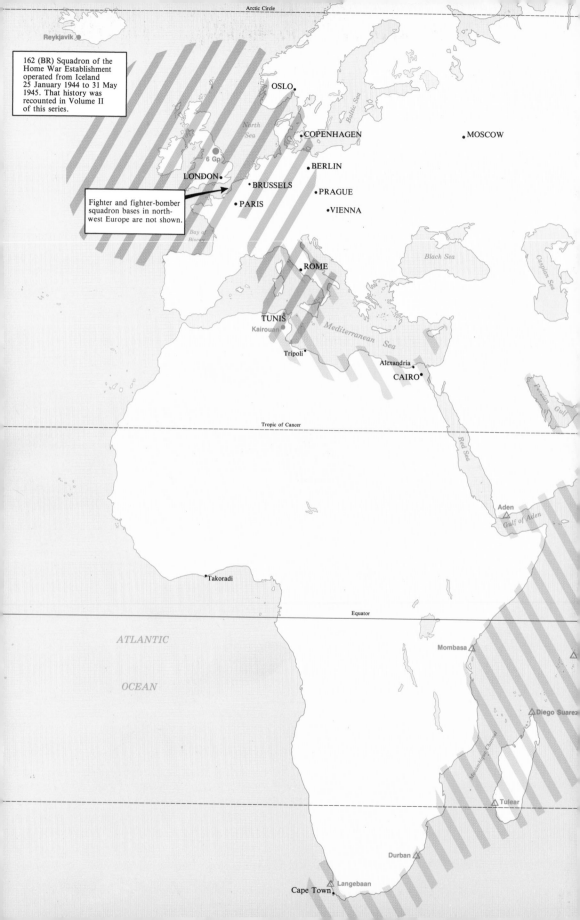

162 (BR) Squadron of the
Home War Establishment
operated from Iceland
25 January 1944 to 31 May
1945. That history was
recounted in Volume II
of this series.

Fighter and fighter-bomber
squadron bases in north-
west Europe are not shown.

Reykjavik

OSLO

COPENHAGEN

MOSCOW

6 Gp

North
Sea

Baltic Sea

LONDON

BERLIN

BRUSSELS

PRAGUE

PARIS

VIENNA

Bay of
Biscay

Black Sea

Caspian Sea

ROME

TUNIS

Kairouan

Mediterranean Sea

Tripoli

Alexandria

CAIRO

Persian Gulf

Tropic of Cancer

Red Sea

Aden

Gulf of Aden

Takoradi

Equator

Mombasa

ATLANTIC

Diego Suarez

OCEAN

Mozambique Channel

Tulear

Durban

Langebaan

Cape Town

Arctic Circle